FEDERAL AGENCY PROFILES *for Students*

FEDERAL AGENCY PROFILES *for Students*

Kelle S. Sisung, Senior Editor

DETROIT • LONDON

Federal Agency Profiles for Students

The Gale Group Staff

Editorial: Kelle S. Sisung, *Project Manager/Series Editor*; Gerda Ann Raffaelle, *Associate Project Editor*; Stephanie Samulski, *Associate Editor*; Bernard Grunow, *Assistant Editor*; John F. McCoy, *Assistant Editor*

Data Entry: Janine Whitney, *Data Entry Coordinator*; Ellie Allison, *Data Entry Manager*; Nikkita Bankston, Shanita Watkins, Frances Monroe, *Data Entry Associates*

Graphic Services: Barbara J. Yarrow, *Graphic Services Manager*; Randy Bassett, *Image Database Supervisor*; Robert Duncan, Mike Logusz, *Imaging Specialists*; Pamela A. Reed, *Imaging Coordinator*

Permissions: Maria Franklin, *Permissions Manager*; Margaret Chamberlain, *Permissions Manager*

Product Design: Cynthia Baldwin, *Product Design Manager*; Pamela A. E. Galbreath, *Senior Art Director*

Production: Mary Beth Trimper, *Production Director*; Evi Seoud, *Assistant Production Manager*; Cindy Range, *Production Assistant*

Graphics Creator: Eric E. Wisniewski

Copyright Notice

Library of Congress Cataloging-in-Publication Data

Federal agency profiles for student / Kelle S. Sisung, editor.
p. cm.
Includes bibliographic references and index.
ISBN 0-7876-2795-X
1. Administrative agencies—United States. 2. Executive departments—United States. 3. Administrative agencies—United States—Directories. 4. Executive departments—United States—Directories. I. Sisung, Kelle.
JK421.F42 1999
351.73'025 dc21 98-42255
CIP

ISBN 0-7876-2795-X
Printed in the United States of America
10 9 8 7 6 5 4 3 2

Table of Contents

O

P

R

S

T

U

W

Table of Contents by Government Organization

Legislative Branch

Judicial Branch

Executive Branch

DEPARTMENTS

INDEPENDENT AGENCIES

Advisors and Contributors

Advisory Board

A nine-member advisory board consisting of teachers, media specialists, and other experts on U.S. government was consulted to help determine the scope and content of *Federal Agency Profiles for Students.*

Howard Ball: Professor of Political Science, University of Vermont

Marion J. Cannon: Library Media Specialist, Winter Park High School, Winter Park, Florida

Catherine Chauvette: Library Media Specialist, Fairfax County Public Library, Alexandria, Virgina

Fran Cohen: Library Media Specialist (retired), Conestoga High School, Berwyn, Pennsylvania

Michael D. Leahy, Ph.D.: Library Media Specialist (retired), Eastern High School, Bristol, Connecticut

Frank J. Orfei: History Department, Pelham Memorial High School, Pelham, New York

Harriet B. Sawyer: Social Studies Department Chair, Franklin High School, Livonia, Michigan

Jay A. Sigler, Ph.D.: Professor of Public Policy and Administration, Rutgers University

Lavonna Brown Williams: Educator, Minot Public School District, Minot, North Dakota; Bonneville Joint School District, Bonneville, Idaho

Contributors

Many writers contributed to the text of *Federal Agency Profiles for Students.* An asterisk (*) indicates an author who was a primary contributor.

Sheree L. Beaudry*

Susan L. Beaudry

Carol Brennan

Gerald E. Brennan*

R. Craig Collins*

Gloria Cooksey*

Pete Hendley

Janelle Powell

Joseph Sheltraw

Janet P. Stamatel*

James D. Wiljanen

Preface

Federal Agency Profiles for Students (*FAPS*) is the first volume in the U.S. Government for Students series, to be followed by *Special Interest Group Profiles for Students* (release date, June 1999) and *Presidential Administration Profiles for Students* (release date, July 1999). The purpose of the series is to provide an overall view of the workings of the United States government geared specifically to meet the curriculum needs of high school students, undergraduate college students, and their teachers. Each profile in a U.S. Government for Students volume will cover not only the basic facts found in directories such as the *United States Government Manual,* but will include the historical and political context, or the how and why. Furthermore, the series focuses on the relevancy and immediacy of government, explaining how an agency, a special interest group, or a presidential administration can impact the life of an average citizen and, in some cases, how a citizen can become actively involved in the federal government. While the series was designed to reflect curriculum standards, the general reader and researcher will also be able to find answers to their questions about the U.S. government.

FAPS includes profiles of over 175 government agencies. The term "agency" is used generically here to describe any government body and is not always included in a group's official name. Therefore, *FAPS* includes profiles of:

- *Departments,* which are agencies of cabinet rank. There are 14 cabinet-level departments including the Department of Education and the Department of Health and Human Services.
- *Government Corporations* and *Authorities,* including agencies like the Federal Labor Relations Authority, which are headed by a board and a manager and are involved in activities that are business related.
- *Administrations,* such as the Farm Credit Administration, which is headed by a single administrator.
- *Commissions,* which are agencies that regulate business activities. An example is the Securities and Exchange Commission. Commissions may also be an investigative, advisory, or reporting entity such as the Federal Election Commission. All commissions are headed by a group of high-level officers called commissioners.

Some agencies are affiliated with a specific branch of government and act in a supportive or advisory capacity. For instance, during the Clinton administration there were 11 agencies that comprised the Executive Office of the President (EOP). Each president reorganizes the EOP to reflect the issues and needs of the current administration. EOP agencies include the Office of National Drug Control Policy and the Council on Environmental Quality. Other support agencies include the Administrative Office of the United States Courts, which is part of the judicial branch and has the purpose of assisting the federal court system.

Many agencies function as a bureau, branch, office, or division of one of the 14 departments. The scope of some of them merit a separate profile from the parent organization. An agency such as the the National Institutes of Health is part of the larger parent Department of Health and Human Services, but has developed over time into a substantial body with its own vast network of subagencies. There are also more than 200 independent agencies that exist outside department boundaries.

Selection Criteria

Not surprisingly, selecting which government agencies to profile in FAPS was a daunting task. Gale editors began by surveying high school civics and government sources including top-rated textbooks and the *National Standards for Civics and Government.* We also relied on course curriculu supplied by our advisors that represented various school districts across the United States. A core list soon emerged that included the 14 departments and approximately 50 agencies. We were then faced with a myriad of independent agencies, quasi-subagencies, bureaus, and offices. Our advisory board, consisting of high school teachers, media specialists, and subject experts, helped sort through and pare down the list based on their knowledge of common classroom assignments.

We were also faced with the quandary of whether or not to include agencies that no longer exist because they had become defunct or perhaps been subsumed by a larger agency. The list suddenly began to expand again as we attempted to untangle the ever surging web of government reorganization. Through discussions with our advisors, it became apparent that *FAPS* should encourage a dynamic look at the immediacy of the U.S. government during the current administration. Our advisors also suggested that *FAPS* include profiles of the Senate, the House of Representatives, and the Supreme Court. While they are not agencies, these bodies serve as the core of the United States government around which the satellite bodies revolve. After taking this advice under consideration, we arrived at the current list.

How Each Profile is Organized

Profiles are arranged in alphabetical order, according to the official name of the agency as presented in the *United States Government Manual.* Each profile heading also includes the agency's acronym or other variant names. For additional access, readers should also refer to the index for alternative name representations and the two tables of content: one is in book order, the second is based on government organization. The following elements may be contained in each profile:

- **Parent Organization:** Indicates the government body to which the agency reports or identifies that the agency is considered "independent." If an agency is part of a subagency under a larger parent parent, deference was made to the largest parent. This information was also used to organize FAPS's second table of contents.
- **Established:** Generally refers to the date that the organization as we know it today was established. Many of the agencies went through multiple incarnations. For instance, the original predecessor of the Coast Guard was the Revenue-Cutter Service established in 1790. The profile's "History" section outlines the agency's progression over the ensuing 200 years, but this field includes the date it became officially known as the Coast Guard.
- **Employees:** Includes the number of employees retained by the agency based on 1998 figures. If figures are based on non-1998 information, the date is included in parentheses. The number of employees is an approximate figure as the structure of an agency can often be quite complicated. For example, the structure of the Foreign Service is complex with officers serving in a multitude of countries.
- **Contact Information:** General mailing address, telephone number, toll free telephone number, TDD number, fax number, E-mail, and URL.
- **Agency Heads:** Limited to the inclusion of the agency's top officials. These individuals shift positions frequently, especially with each presidential administration.
- **What is Its Mission?:** The mission usually contains a quote directly from the agency being profiled, which encapsulates the agency's primary motivation. Information was taken directly from published statements released by the agency administrator or from annual federal reports. In some instances authors attempted to further define the mission if the statement required clarification.
- **How is it Structured?:** Outlines the general structure of each agency. The section begins by placing the agency within the larger construct of the federal government and continues by outlining the internal administrative organization at the national level progressing all the way down to the regional and local branches.
- **Primary Functions:** This is the action center of the profile that offers a broad brush look at what an agency or department does. What are its primary responsibilities as a whole? Does it enforce guidelines, create legislation, conduct research? How does it interact with other agencies, branches of government, or special interest groups? Authors made a particular effort to stress the connection between agencies and branches to underscore that the federal government is truly a collaborative enterprise.
- **Programs:** Offers a general overview of the number and type of programs the agency administers. The section also profiles one or two of the agency's most notable or newsworthy. For instance, the Medicare program is highlighted in the entry on the Health Care Financing Administration.
- **Budget Information:** Budget information is primarily based on 1998 actual or 1999 estimated figures. The section details where the agency's funding comes from and how resources are allocated. When possible, the section will also include what percentage of the federal budget is targeted for the agency. Figures are based on information supplied by the agency and reported in the annual federal bud-

get. An agency's budget does not usually change drastically from year to year; the greatest difference usually occurs between administrations. The Office of Management and Budget site on the Internet at http://www.access.gpo.gov/su_docs/budget includes a comprehensive breakdown of each agency of the federal government, along with a *Citizen's Guide to the Federal Budget,* and Economic Reports from the president, both past and present. Readers may also obtain the budget for the current fiscal year (and other years) from the Government Printing Office or any U.S. government bookstore.

- A budget graphic accompanies most profiles, which illustrates the agency's outlay of funds. It is sometimes quite dramatic to see how very much, or very little, of an agency's dollars are spent on a particular initiative.
- **History:** This section details the history of the agency, including key events, administrations, people, and legislation. The narrative usually includes history that pre-dates the organization's formation explaining why it was necessary for this department or agency to be established.
- **Political Issue:** The political issue section serves as the nerve center of the profile. It begins with a brief introduction that outlines the agency's current concerns and the controversies surrounding them. A case study is then highlighted to illuminate a particular issue. Authors were careful to include all sides of the story by relating how the agency is involved with the issue, how the public was impacted by the event, how the public feels about the agency, and how other government agencies, special interest groups, or other countries responded.
- **Successes and Failures:** A variety of indicators determine a success or a failure. A success is apparent when an agency establishes a benchmark for success, such as timeliness in delivering work results. For example, the General Accounting Office reported that completion of an average task from start to finish decreased from 9.5 months to 5.4 months in 1998 and considered this a mark of success. Other successes and failures are much less tangible and tend toward the subjective. If a piece of legislation is pushed forward by the Forest Service that allows for logging to occur within an environmentally protected area, an activist group like the Sierra Club may not necessarily consider it a success. Authors were careful to include events that would invite analysis by *FAPS* readers.
- **Future Directions:** Where is the agency headed? What challenges does it faces? What are the agency's projected goals for the future? Information for this section was gleaned from reports submitted by agency administrators.
- **Agency Resources:** Resources refers to agency hot lines, information clearinghouses, dockets, information centers, libraries, databases, document repositories, and archives. The section includes how to access the information whether via mail, E-mail, telephone, or Internet.
- **Agency Publications:** The section provides information about the number and type of publications the agency makes available. Representative pamphlets, newsletters, and other publications are included along with contact information on how an interested party can access them.
- **Bibliography:** An alphabetical list of sources, including books and current periodicals quoted in the profile, with full bibliographic information. Also lists other critical sources that may prove helpful for the student and researcher.

In addition, a *FAPS* profile may contain one or more of the following supplementary sidebars:

- **Get Involved:** A key sidebar that includes suggestions as to how an individual can become involved with an agency. Key, because the primary reason for producing *FAPS* is to have students understand that government issues are "living" and that students and the general public can be active participants. All activities include full contact information. A "Get Involved" may also incorporate examples of how local groups got involved in the workings of a larger government initiative.
- **Fast Facts:** At-a-glance facts that are current and reflect how the agency impacts the daily lives of all citizens. Facts may reflect the workings of the agency being profiled or might illustrate the issues that have been discussed throughout the essay. Each fact is fully cited.
- **Biography:** An individual who was pivotal to an agency's history is profiled in a biography sidebar that includes birth and death dates, identifier, a brief sketch, and a thumbnail photo.

Additional Features

In an attempt to create a comprehensive, one-stop reference tool for the study of the U.S. federal government, *FAPS* also includes:

- Illustrations that depict historic events, notable individuals, and current issues along with graphics and maps.
- A chronology of over 750 key events in U.S. history that allows students to place each agency in an historical context.
- A glossary containing over 400 political terms used throughout the profiles.
- A subject index for easy access to agencies, people, places, and events.
- Diagram appendices that depict graphically the organization of the federal government, the system of

checks and balances, breakdown of the federal budget, and how a bill becomes a law.

Acknowledgments

It is important for Gale to acknowledge the bounty of materials available to us and all researchers through the United States government. Specifically, the *United States Government Manual* was a much-thumbed, constant source of information that helped untangle the vast web known as the federal government. It is a valuable first-stop directory that is held by most libraries and is available for purchase at U.S. government bookstores. It is also available on-line at http://www.access.gpo.gov/nara/nara001.html. The Government Printing Office (GPO) is the United States's preeminent publisher that offers a plethora of information resources on every facet of government. Catalogs may be requested by writing to 732 N. Capitol St. NW, Washington, DC 20401 or visit the GPO Web site at http://www.access.gpo.gov/#info.

We must also recognize the contribution made by each of the agencies profiled. Agency Web sites made good launching pads for beginning research. To further guarantee accuracy of information our industrious researchers and authors went further and made many persistent requests by telephone, fax, and e-mail. They were often rewarded for their efforts thanks to agency representatives.

Special thanks must be extended to our advisory board who continue to serve as the backbone of the U.S. Government for Students series. Their input was invaluable from the genesis of the series and remains constant through each volume. In addition, we must mention our various contributors, many of whom are former teachers. Their classroom experience led to the creation of well-researched, thoughtful, and enjoyable profiles that hopefully will stimulate students' interest in U.S. government.

We Welcome Your Suggestions

The editor of *Federal Agency Profiles for Students* welcomes your comments and suggestions. Please direct all correspondence to:

Editor, *Federal Agency Profiles for Students*
The Gale Group
72500 Drake Rd.
Farmington Hills, MI 48331-3535

Chronology

1492: Columbus discovers the Americas.

1565: St. Augustine, Florida, is founded by the Spanish.

1607: Over 140 men and boys form a settlement at Jamestown, Virginia; approximately one-half die before the end of the year. Jamestown becomes the second oldest town in North America, after St. Augustine, and the first permanent British settlement.

1614: Dutch found the colony of New Amsterdam.

1619: Martial law in Virginia is replaced by a general assembly of twenty-two burgesses, the first representative assembly in America.

1620: Off of present-day Cape Cod, Massachusetts, 41 male passengers on the *Mayflower* sign the Mayflower compact, establishing a preliminary civil body politic and the authority to legislate laws as necessary. The people who debark are known as the Pilgrims.

1629: The Massachusetts Bay Company is formed by English Puritans allowing the company to have governmental autonomy once on the American mainland.

1630: English Puritans, sponsored by the Massachusetts Bay Company, found Boston and ten other settlements in Massachusetts.

1643: Massachusetts, Connecticut, New Haven, and Plymouth form a confederation called the United Colonies of New England.

1647: Rhode Island adopts its first constitution which declares separation of church and state and freedom of religious expression.

1660: Parliament passes the first of the Navigation Acts, which restricts the trade of New England merchants to England and the British West Indies by imposing taxes and duties on goods traded with other countries.

1675: King Philip's War begins and pits the New England Confederation against Indian tribes led by Chief Philip of the Wampanoags. The two-year conflict results in great loss and destruction for both sides. Twelve New England towns are leveled, and for every 16 white men of fighting age, one loses his life.

1682: William Penn establishes his Frame of Government which allows for the creation of an assembly, council, and governor's office in Pennsylvania.

1685: The Dominion of New England is formed, and the following year Sir Edmund Andros is appointed governor.

1696: William III commissions the Board of Trade to oversee commercial (trade and fishing) and political (powers of appointment and legislative review) concerns in the American colonies.

1702: As part of the War of the Spanish Succession (1702–1713), known as Queen Anne's War in America, James Moore, the English governor of South Carolina, attacks Saint Augustine, burning outposts and missions in Apalachee, or northern Florida.

1754–1763: The French and Indian War results in the British and Indian allies capturing Quebec and defeating the French.

August 17, 1754: The Albany Plan, formulated by Benjamin Franklin, is rejected. It would have joined the colonies in a defense against the French and would have established an intercolonial council to handle relations with the Indians.

1763: The Treaty of Paris is signed, concluding the French and Indian War; Britain is given Canada and all French territory east of the Mississippi River and Florida.

1763: The Proclamation of 1763 prohibits colonists from settling west of the Appalachian mountains beyond the reach of British authorities. It is also issued to pacify the American Indians.

April 5, 1764: Parliament passes the Sugar Act, reducing the tariff on molasses imported into North America. However, it also sends custom agents and collectors to the colonies to strictly enforce the remaining laws in effect.

1765: Britain imposes the Stamp Act.

October 7–25, 1765: Nine colonies represented at the Stamp Act Congress in New York protest Parliament's taxation of the colonies.

March 17, 1766: Parliament rescinds the stamp tax but insists it has the power to tax the colonies.

1767: Townshend Acts are passed by British Parliament, imposing import tax on American colonies and contributing to revolt against British rule.

May 16, 1769: After Virginia's House of Burgesses rejects Parliament's right to tax the colonies, the governor dissolves the assembly, which continues to meet privately, agreeing not to import British goods.

January 19–20, 1770: The Battle of Golden Hill, New York, results in one death as the Sons of Liberty skirmish with British soldiers trying to remove liberty poles from Golden Hill, Manhattan.

April 12, 1770: Parliament repeals all the Townshend duties except the one on tea.

November 2, 1772: The Boston town meeting creates a 21-member committee of correspondence to communicate with other towns in the colony and to defend the rights of colonists "as Men, as Christians, and as Subjects."

December 16, 1773: In the act that came to be known as the Boston Tea Party, a mob dumps a cargo of tea into Boston Harbor to protest Great Britain's tea tax.

March 31, 1774: Parliament enacts the Boston Port Bill, closing the port of Boston in retaliation for the Tea Party.

May 20, 1774: The Massachusetts Government Act suspends the colony's charter.

May 27, 1774: A call for a Continental Congress goes out to consolidate action and support economic pressure to force Great Britain to rescind the Massachusetts Government Act.

September 5–October 16, 1774: The First Continental Congress meets in Philadelphia to work out constitutional issues; each state has one vote in this body.

October 18, 1774: The Continental Congress adopts the Continental Association, pledging to cease imports from England after December 1, 1774.

1775–1783: The American Revolution.

February 9, 1775: The king declares Massachusetts to be in rebellion.

May 5, 1775: The Second Continental Congress convenes for the purpose of uniting the colonies for military action.

June 14, 1775: The Department of the Army is founded as the Continental Army by the Second Continental Congress; George Washington is appointed as its first commander in chief.

October 13, 1775: The Department of the Navy is founded; it is commissioned by the Continental Congress and plays a decisive role in the British decision to abandon the American colonies.

November 10, 1775: The U.S. Marine Corps is founded when two battalions of "marines" are authorized by the Continental Congress to serve in the Revolutionary War against Great Britain.

July 2, 1776: The Continental Congress votes unanimously that "these thirteen colonies are, and of right, ought to be, free and independent states."

July 4, 1776: The Declaration of Independence is adopted.

November 15, 1777: The Continental Congress adopts the Articles of Confederation and Perpetual Union; it requires the endorsement of all the state legislatures to take effect.

July 9, 1778: Delegates from 8 of the 10 states that have ratified the Articles of Confederation sign them.

May 18, 1779: The U.S. Army Corps of Engineers is founded to provide engineering, management, and technical support to the United States in peace and war.

September 13, 1779: John Jay, president of the Continental Congress, asks the states to collect taxes in order to pay requisitions to the federal treasury.

January 10, 1781: The Continental Congress creates a ministry for foreign affairs.

May 26, 1781: The Pennsylvania legislature charters the Bank of North America.

April 18, 1783: The Continental Congress proposes a revenue system as a way of paying the national debt.

September 3, 1783: The Treaty of Paris, which recognizes American independence, is signed by British and American negotiators.

December 23, 1783: George Washington resigns his commission as commander in chief of the Continental Army.

January 14, 1784: The Continental Congress ratifies the Treaty of Paris.

January 11, 1785: The Continental Congress moves from Philadelphia to New York City.

May 20, 1785: The Continental Congress passes the Land Ordinance of 1785, revamping the system for settling western areas and setting aside land and revenue to support public education.

May 25–September 17, 1787: The Constitutional Convention meets in Philadelphia with delegates from all states except Rhode Island present. Power is divided among three branches of the federal government and between the federal and state governments.

May 29, 1787: Edmund Randolph submits the Virginia Plan to the Constitutional Convention, proposing a bicameral legislature based on proportional representation, a national executive and judiciary, and a congressional veto of state laws.

May 31, 1787: The Constitutional Convention votes that the people should directly elect members to what will be the House of Representatives.

June 15, 1787: William Paterson presents the New Jersey Plan to the Convention, proposing to retain the unicameral national legislature (with each state having an equal vote) and to expand congressional control over trade and revenue.

July 11, 1787: The Constitutional Convention votes to count three-fifths of the slave population for taxation and representation purposes.

July 13, 1787: The Continental Congress passes the Northwest Ordinance, establishing the Northwest Territory (present-day Illinois, Indiana, Ohio, Michigan, Wisconsin, and parts of Minnesota). The Ordinance defines the steps for the creation and admission of new states and bars slavery in the area.

July 16, 1787: The Constitutional Convention approves the "Great Compromise," granting proportional representation in the House of Representatives and equal state representation in the Senate.

August 29, 1787: The Convention gives the Continental Congress power to pass navigation acts, approves a fugitive slave clause, and forbids Congress from regulating the slave trade before 1808.

December 7, 1787: Delaware is the first of the original 13 states to ratify the Constitution.

December 12, 1787: Pennsylvania is the second of the original 13 states to ratify the Constitution.

December 18, 1787: New Jersey is the third of the original 13 states to ratify the Constitution.

January 2, 1788: Georgia is the fourth of the original 13 states to ratify the Constitution.

January 9, 1788: Connecticut is the fifth of the 13 original states to ratify the Constitution.

February 6, 1788: Massachusetts is the sixth of the original 13 states to ratify the Constitution.

April 28, 1788: Maryland is the seventh of the original 13 states to ratify the Constitution.

May 23, 1788: South Carolina is the eighth of the original 13 states to ratify the Constitution.

June 21, 1788: New Hampshire is the ninth of the original 13 states to ratify the Constitution.

June 25, 1788: Virginia is the tenth of the original 13 states to ratify the Constitution.

July 26, 1788: New York is the eleventh of the original 13 states to ratify the Constitution.

March 4, 1789: The first Congress to meet under the Constitution convenes in New York City.

April 30, 1789: George Washington and John Adams are inaugurated as the first president and vice president of the United States.

May 11, 1789: The Office of the Vice President is founded; the two mandates of the vice presidency under the original Constitution are to preside over the Senate and to succeed to the presidency in time of emergency.

July 4, 1789: Congress, led by James Madison, passes the Tariff Act of 1789, creating a source of revenue for the federal government.

July 27, 1789: The Department of State is founded with the appointment of Thomas Jefferson as the first secretary of state; its highest concern is the protection of American interests at home and abroad.

July 31, 1789: The U.S. Customs Service is founded to collect the taxes on imported and exported goods, to document data relating to cargo and passenger ships, and to fine people or companies that defy the newly instituted laws.

September, 1789: The Office of Attorney General is established.

September 2, 1789: The Department of the Treasury is founded to not only manage the nation's finances but also to provide leadership in setting its fiscal policy in order to plan the country's financial future.

September 11, 1789: Alexander Hamilton is appointed the first secretary of the Treasury.

September 24, 1789: Congress passes the Judiciary Act of 1789, creating a federal court system and giving the Supreme Court the right to review the constitutionality of state laws.

September 25, 1789: Congress, led by James Madison, submits the first ten constitutional amendments (later known as the Bill of Rights) to the states.

September 26, 1789: John Jay is appointed the first chief justice of the United States.

November 10, 1789: The U.S. Marshals Service is created by Congress by the Judiciary Act of 1789.

November 21, 1789: North Carolina is the twelfth of the original 13 states to ratify the Constitution.

November 26, 1789: President George Washington consults department heads on foreign and military affairs, establishing the practice of regular cabinet meetings.

February 2, 1790: The Supreme Court of the United States convenes for the first time with the responsibility of applying the Constitution and laws in deciding cases.

May 29, 1790: Rhode Island is the thirteenth of the original 13 states to ratify the Constitution.

July 1, 1790: Congress approves a site on the Potomac River as the future capital of the United States (Washington, D.C.).

July 26, 1790: Congress passes Secretary of the Treasury Alexander Hamilton's program for assuming the states' debts; his program for funding the national debt by issuing interest-bearing securities is passed on August 4.

February 25, 1791: President George Washington signs a bill creating the First Bank of the United States after receiving conflicting opinions regarding the bank's constitutionality from Secretary of the Treasury Alexander Hamilton and Secretary of State Thomas Jefferson.

March 3, 1791: Congress passes an excise, or internal, tax on whiskey.

March 4, 1791: Vermont becomes the 14th state.

December 12, 1791: The First Bank of the United States opens in Philadelphia with branches in other cities.

December 15, 1791: The Bill of Rights becomes part of the Constitution. These ten amendments include protection of freedom of religion, speech, and the press.

March 1, 1792: Congress passes the Presidential Succession Act. In case of the death or disability of the president and vice president, power will pass to the president pro tempore of the Senate followed by the Speaker of the House.

April 2, 1792: The U.S. Mint is founded by the Mint Act of 1792, which among other duties determines the materials, denominations, and inscriptions to be used in making U.S. coins.

June 1, 1792: Kentucky becomes the 15th state.

October 13, 1792: The cornerstone of the new executive mansion is laid in Washington, D.C.

February 12, 1793: Congress passes the first Fugitive Slave Law, enforcing part of Article IV, Section 2, of the Constitution.

February 13, 1793: In *Chisholm v. Georgia* the Supreme Court rules that states can be sued in federal court by citizens of other states.

March 4, 1793: President George Washington and Vice President John Adams are inaugurated for a second term.

April 22, 1793: Determined to keep the United States out of the war between France and Great Britain, President Washington issues the Proclamation of Neutrality.

September 18, 1793: President Washington lays the cornerstone for the Capitol building in Washington, D.C.

July–November, 1794: Farmers in Pennsylvania resist officials trying to collect the whiskey tax. President Washington and Secretary of the Treasury Hamilton lead a militia to enforce the law, but what became known as the Whiskey Rebellion is over by the time they arrive.

November 19, 1794: Jay's Treaty is signed in London, England. Terms include Great Britain's evacuation of posts in the Northwest Territory by 1796 and limited U.S. trade in the West Indies.

August 3, 1795: The United States and 12 Indian tribes in the Northwest sign the Treaty of Greenville, opening much of present-day Ohio to white settlement.

October 27, 1795: The United States and Spain sign the Pinckney Treaty, recognizing the 31st parallel as the southern boundary of the United States and granting Americans free navigation of the Mississippi River.

March 7, 1796: In *Ware v. Hylton* the U.S. Supreme Court declares a state law unconstitutional for the first time.

March 8, 1796: In *Hylton v. United States* the Supreme Court upholds the constitutionality of an act of Congress for the first time.

June 1, 1796: Tennessee becomes the 16th state.

March 4, 1797: President John Adams and Vice President Thomas Jefferson are inaugurated.

May 16, 1797: President Adams recommends that Congress approve a three-man diplomatic mission to France, arm merchant vessels, create a navy, fortify harbors, and enlarge the army.

1798: The United States and France begin the "Quasi-War," an undeclared naval conflict in the Caribbean.

January 8, 1798: The Eleventh Amendment is ratified. It declares that states cannot be sued by citizens of another state or foreign country in federal court.

May–July, 1798: Congress revokes all treaties with France and approves an enlarged army, a new Navy Department, harbor defenses, and the seizure of all French vessels interfering with American shipping.

June 18, 1798: Congress passes the Naturalization Act, the first of four Alien and Sedition Acts, limiting freedom of speech and the press and the rights of foreigners. The act also increases the residency period required for citizenship to 14 years.

July 9, 1798: Congress passes a direct tax on land, houses, and slaves to pay for the Quasi-War with France.

July 14, 1798: Congress passes the Act for the Punishment of Certain Crimes (the Sedition Act) by a vote of 44–41. The act imposes heavy fines and imprisonment on anyone convicted of writing, publishing, or speaking anything of "a false scandalous and malicious nature" against the government and its officers.

November 16, 1798: The Kentucky Resolutions, drafted by Thomas Jefferson and passed by the Kentucky state legislature, declare that states can judge the constitutionality of federal laws, and that the Alien and Sedition Acts are unconstitutional and thus "void and of no force."

November 22, 1799: The Kentucky state legislature passes resolutions reaffirming nullification as a proper constitutional solution.

1800: The Virginia state legislature passes a resolution proposing that freed slaves be resettled in Africa.

January 2, 1800: Free African Americans petition Congress in opposition to slavery and the slave trade. By a vote of 85–1, Congress refuses to accept the petition.

April 24, 1800: The Library of Congress is established by the "Act to Make Provision for the Removal and Accommodation of the Government of the U.S." While originally only members of Congress and other government officials are allowed to use the facilities, it later opens its doors to the public.

September 30, 1800: The United States and France sign an agreement ending the Quasi-War.

November 17, 1800: Congress convenes in Washington, D.C., for the first time. John Adams becomes the first president to live in the new Executive Mansion.

January 20, 1801: John Marshall is appointed chief justice of the United States, serving until his death in 1835.

February 13, 1801: Congress passes the Judiciary Act of 1801, reducing the number of Supreme Court justices from six to five, establishing sixteen circuit courts, and increasing the number of judicial officers.

March 4, 1801: Thomas Jefferson is the first president to be inaugurated in Washington, D.C. His vice president is Aaron Burr.

March 8, 1802: Congress repeals the Judiciary Act of 1801.

April 6, 1802: Congress abolishes all internal taxes, including the unpopular whiskey tax.

April 29, 1802: Congress passes a new Judiciary Act, authorizing six Supreme Court justices, one session a year for the Supreme Court, and six circuit courts, each presided over by a Supreme Court justice.

August 1, 1802: The U.S. Military Academy is founded to serve as a training facility for military engineers.

August 25, 1802: The Patent and Trademark Office is founded with the mission of administering laws relating to patents and trademarks and advising the government on patent, trademark, and copyright protection.

February 24, 1803: In *Marbury v. Madison* the Supreme Court declares an act of Congress (the Judiciary Act of 1789) unconstitutional for the first time and expands its power of judicial review.

March 1, 1803: Ohio becomes the 17th state in the Union and the first to outlaw slavery from the beginning of statehood.

April 30, 1803: The United States purchases the Louisiana Territory from France for $15 million.

February 25, 1804: In the first congressional caucus Democratic-Republicans unanimously nominate President Thomas Jefferson for a second term and nominate George Clinton for vice president.

March 26, 1804: In the Louisiana Territory Act, the federal government declares for the first time that its intention is to move Indians living east of the Mississippi River to the West.

September 25, 1804: The Twelfth Amendment to the Constitution is ratified, providing separate ballots for president and vice president.

March 4, 1805: President Thomas Jefferson is inaugurated for a second term. His vice president is George Clinton.

March 29, 1806: Congress authorizes the construction of the National Road, connecting Cumberland, Maryland, with Wheeling, Virginia.

April 18, 1806: Congress passes a Non-Importation Act, prohibiting the importation of British goods in protest against the British seizure of American ships and sailors.

March 2, 1807: Congress decides to prohibit the African slave trade and importation of slaves into the United States as of January 1, 1808.

March 4, 1809: President James Madison is inaugurated with George Clinton as vice president.

July 2, 1809: The Shawnee tribal leader Tecumseh begins forming a confederacy of Native American tribes.

September 30, 1809: William Henry Harrison, governor of Indiana Territory, signs a treaty at Fort Wayne by which Indian tribes cede three tracts of land along the Wabash River.

March 4, 1811: After the Senate votes against rechartering the Bank of the United States, its charter expires.

November 7, 1811: Native Americans under Tecumseh's brother, the Prophet, attack Governor Harrison's army in the Battle of Tippecanoe; they are repulsed and Prophet's Town is burned. As a result

Tecumseh and his followers cross into Canada, later joining British forces in the War of 1812.

November 20, 1811: Construction begins on the National Road, increasing the flow of settlers to the West after the War of 1812.

December 24, 1811: Congress authorizes the completion of enlistments in the regular army, the enlistment of 25,000 additional regulars for five years' service and 50,000 volunteers for one year's service, and the call-up of one hundred thousand militia for six months' service at the president's request, and approves additional funds for the navy.

April 30, 1812: Louisiana becomes the 18th state in the Union.

June 18, 1812: After sending a war message to Congress, President James Madison signs the declaration of war with Great Britain, citing impressment, violations of American trade, and the incitement of Indian warfare as the causes for hostilities with England.

March 4, 1813: President Madison is inaugurated for a second term.

September 13, 1814: As he watches the British attack on Fort McHenry at Baltimore, Francis Scott Key composes the "Star Spangled Banner."

December 24, 1814: The United States and Great Britain sign a peace treaty at Ghent. There are no territorial changes, and all other issues are unresolved or postponed.

January 5, 1815: The Hartford Convention, a forum for delegates to discuss ways and means of sectional defense and to take steps to revise the Constitution, ends with hints of secession. The delegates uphold a state's right to nullify federal law and propose constitutional amendments to limit the power of the federal government. After the signing of the Treaty of Ghent they have come to be regarded as treasonous for opposing the war.

December 5, 1815: President James Madison urges Congress to approve a national bank, protective tariffs, and a program of national funding for transportation and education.

1816: The first postwar Congress charters the Second Bank of the United States and passes an internal improvements bill and the Tariff of 1816.

December 11, 1816: Indiana is admitted to the Union as the 19th state.

March 4, 1817: James Monroe is inaugurated as president with Daniel D. Tompkins as vice president.

November 20, 1817: Settlers attack Native Americans in Florida, igniting the First Seminole War. Spain is believed to support the Seminoles during the yearlong conflict.

December 10, 1817: Mississippi is admitted as the 20th state of the Union.

1818: The Convention of 1818 between the United States and Great Britain sets the border between the United States and Canada at the forty-ninth parallel and establishes joint occupation of Oregon.

December 3, 1818: Illinois is the 21st state admitted to the Union.

1819: Under the Adams-Onis Treaty, Spain cedes Florida to the United States.

December 14, 1819: Alabama is admitted to the Union as the 22nd state.

March 2, 1820: As part of the Missouri Compromise, Congress prohibits slavery in the Louisiana Purchase north of 36°30', but admits Missouri, the 24th state, as a slave state.

March 15, 1820: Maine is admitted as the 23rd state of the Union.

March 4, 1821: James Monroe begins his second term as president.

August 10, 1821: Missouri becomes the 24th state of the Union.

December 2, 1823: President James Monroe delivers a message to Congress, warning European countries not to colonize or interfere with the Western Hemisphere. This policy comes to be known as the Monroe Doctrine.

March 30, 1824: Speaker of the U.S. House of Representatives Henry Clay defines his "American System" in a speech supporting a protective tariff that would generate revenue to fund internal improvements that would in turn expand the American economy.

August 29, 1824: The Bureau of Indian Affairs is founded with the primary functions of acquiring Indian lands and containing the Indian people and their culture.

November, 1824: John Quincy Adams, Andrew Jackson, Henry Clay, and William Crawford run for the presidency. Jackson wins the popular and electoral votes but fails to secure an electoral majority, requiring the House of Representatives to determine the winner.

1825: President James Monroe calls for the voluntary removal of Americans Indians from the East to lands west of the Mississippi River.

March 4, 1825: After the House selects John Quincy Adams as president, he is inaugurated with John Caldwell Calhoun as his vice president.

May 19, 1828: President John Quincy Adams signs the "Tariff of Abominations," a law that provides extremely high rates on imports of raw materials and manufactured goods. Southerners call it a "hateful law."

March 4, 1829: Andrew Jackson is inaugurated as president. His vice president is John Caldwell Calhoun.

April 13, 1830: At the annual Jefferson Day Dinner, in John C. Calhoun's presence, Andrew Jackson clearly warns against nullification of the 1828 Tariff of Abominations with his toast, "Our Federal Union, it must be preserved."

May 28, 1830: Jackson signs the Indian Removal Act to provide money to purchase land from the Creeks, Seminoles, Cherokees, Chickasaws, and Choctaws and to relocate them in present-day Oklahoma and Arkansas.

May 31, 1831: Congress adjourns before President Andrew Jackson acts on several improvement bills. Jackson thus institutes the concept of "pocket veto" by refusing to sign legislation before the end of the congressional session.

July 10, 1832: Jackson vetoes the charter for the Second Bank of the United States, claiming the bank is a "monster" because of its exclusive power.

November, 1832: South Carolina nullifies the tariffs of 1828 and 1832 with the *Ordinance of Nullification*. Subsequently, a more moderate tariff is passed but it does not offer much relief for the southern agricultural economy.

December, 1832: At President Jackson's request Congress passes the Force Bill to compel South Carolina to abide by federal tariffs.

March 1, 1833: The Compromise Tariff of 1833 and Force Bill are signed into law.

March 4, 1833: Andrew Jackson is inaugurated for a second term. His vice president is Martin Van Buren.

November, 1835–1842: The Second Seminole War is fought in Florida when some Seminole Indians, led by Osceola, refuse to leave their land in defiance of an 1832 treaty.

June 15, 1836: Arkansas is admitted to the Union as the 25th state.

January 26, 1837: Michigan is admitted as the 26th state of the Union.

March 4, 1837: Martin Van Buren is inaugurated as president with Richard Johnson as vice president.

March 4, 1841: William Henry Harrison is inaugurated as president with John Tyler as vice president.

April 4, 1841: President William Henry Harrison dies of pneumonia, and John Tyler assumes the presidency.

1842: The Webster-Ashburton Treaty settles the border between the United States and Canada in the Northeast.

March 3, 1845: Florida is admitted to the Union as the 27th state.

March 4, 1845: James Polk is inaugurated as president with Henry Clay as vice president.

October 10, 1845: The U.S. Naval Academy is founded to replace the U.S. Navy's former practice of relying on at-sea apprenticeships for midshipmen.

December 29, 1845: Texas is admitted as the 28th state of the Union.

May 13, 1846: The United States declares war on Mexico. The Senate votes 40–2 and the House votes 174–14 in favor of war.

June 15, 1846: The Senate ratifies a treaty with Britain fixing the Oregon Territory border at the forty-ninth parallel.

August 10, 1846: The Smithsonian Institution is established with funds bequeathed to the United States by English scientist and inventor James Smithson for "the increase and diffusion of knowledge."

February 2, 1848: American diplomat Nicholas Trist signs the Treaty of Guadalupe Hidalgo with Mexico. The United States receives California, New Mexico (including modern Arizona and Nevada), and Texas to the Rio Grande for $15 million.

March 10, 1848: The Senate ratifies the peace treaty with Mexico, 38–14.

May 29, 1848: Wisconsin is admitted to the Union as the 30th state.

March 3, 1849: The Department of the Interior is founded to manage the sale and lease of federal lands; its focus later shifts to the conservation and protection of U.S. natural resources.

March 4, 1849: Zachary Taylor is inaugurated as president. His vice president is Millard Fillmore.

January 29, 1850: The Compromise of 1850 is introduced by Senator Henry Clay, admitting California as a free state, allowing the territorial legislatures of New Mexico and Utah to settle the slavery issue on their own, exacting a stronger fugitive slave law, outlawing the slave trade in the District of Columbia, and giving Texas $10 million to abandon its claims to territory in New Mexico.

July 9, 1850: President Zachary Taylor, an opponent of Henry Clay's compromise to end the conflict over slavery in the territory won from Mexico, dies. Vice President Millard Fillmore, who favors the compromise, becomes president.

September 9, 1850: California is the 31st state admitted to the union.

December 24, 1851: A fire at the Library of Congress in Washington, D.C., destroys two-thirds of its collection.

March 4, 1853: Franklin Pierce is inaugurated. William Rufus De Vane King is vice president.

March 31, 1854: Commodore Matthew C. Perry signs the Treaty of Kanagawa, opening Japanese ports to American trade.

May 30, 1854: The Kansas-Nebraska bill is signed into law by President Franklin Pierce.

January 15, 1856: A free state governor and legislature are elected in Kansas, which now has two governments.

March 4, 1857: James Buchanan is inaugurated as president with John C. Breckinridge as vice president.

May 11, 1858: Minnesota is the 32nd state admitted to the union.

June 16, 1858: Abraham Lincoln, nominated for the Senate by Illinois Republicans, delivers his "House Divided" speech.

February 14, 1859: Oregon becomes the 33rd state.

June 23, 1860: The Government Printing Office is founded by Joint Resolution 25 to provide printing services to the U.S. government that are efficient, reliable, and not vulnerable to corruption.

December 20, 1860: South Carolina secedes from the Union. Florida, Alabama, Georgia, Mississippi, Louisiana, and Texas soon follow.

1861–1865: American Civil War.

January 29, 1861: Kansas is admitted to the Union as the 34th state.

February 9, 1861: Jefferson Davis is elected president of the Confederate States of America.

March 4, 1861: Abraham Lincoln is inaugurated as president of the United States. Hannibal Hamlin is vice president.

April 17–May 20, 1861: Virginia, Arkansas, Tennessee, and North Carolina secede from the Union.

May 15, 1862: The Department of Agriculture is founded to enhance the quality of life for Americans by supporting the production of agriculture.

July 1, 1862: The Internal Revenue Service is founded; initially named the Bureau of Internal Revenue, it is created in response to the need for increased revenue to fund the War Department during the American Civil War.

August 29, 1862: The Bureau of Engraving and Printing is founded to produce paper currency as part of the U.S. Department of Treasury's plan to finance the American Civil War; it later becomes the sole manufacturer of the nation's paper currency and postage stamps.

January 1, 1863: The Emancipation Proclamation is declared in effect.

February 25, 1863: Congress creates a national banking system.

March 3, 1863: Congress passes the Conscription Act.

June 20, 1863: West Virginia is admitted as the 35th state.

November 19, 1863: Lincoln delivers the Gettysburg Address.

October 31, 1864: Nevada becomes the 36th state.

1865: The Thirteenth Amendment abolishing slavery is ratified.

March 4, 1865: Abraham Lincoln is inaugurated for a second term with Andrew Johnson as vice president.

April 9, 1865: Robert E. Lee surrenders the Confederate Army at Appomattox Courthouse, Virginia.

April 15, 1865: Lincoln is assassinated at Ford's Theater by John Wilkes Booth; Andrew Johnson becomes president.

July 5, 1865: The U.S. Secret Service is founded with the mission of protecting U.S. leaders, visiting world leaders, and the integrity of U.S. financial systems.

April 9, 1866: A civil rights act is passed over President Johnson's veto.

June 13, 1866: Congress approves the Fourteenth Amendment to the Constitution which gives African Americans citizenship and guarantees all persons due process of law.

March 1, 1867: Nebraska becomes the 37th state.

February 24, 1868: The House of Representatives impeaches President Johnson.

May 16, 1868: President Johnson is acquitted of violating the Tenure of Office Act.

November 6, 1868: Red Cloud and other Lakota tribal leaders sign a treaty with U.S. government officials at Fort Laramie, Wyoming, establishing a reservation in nearly all of present South Dakota west of the Missouri River. This area includes the sacred Black Hills.

March 4, 1869: Ulysses S. Grant is inaugurated as the 18th president with Schuyler Colfax as vice president.

September 24, 1869: Black Friday on Wall Street occurs when financiers drive up the price of gold.

March 30, 1870: The Fifteenth Amendment, stating a right to vote regardless of race, color, or previous status of servitude, is declared to be in effect.

May 31, 1870: Congress passes the Enforcement Act to protect African American voters.

June 22, 1870: The Department of Justice is founded during the administration of Ulysses S. Grant and is officially charged with the supervision of all federal law officers and attorneys, the control of immigration, and the investigation of federal crimes.

March 4, 1873: Ulysses S. Grant begins his second term as president. Henry Wilson is vice president.

September 18, 1873: Beginning of the financial panic of 1873.

March 1, 1875: Congress passes the Civil Rights Act; key provisions are held unconstitutional in the *Civil Rights* cases of 1883.

August 1, 1876: Colorado is admitted as the 38th state.

March 4, 1877: Rutherford B. Hayes is inaugurated as president with William A. Wheeler as vice president.

March 3, 1879: The U.S. Geological Survey is founded with a combination of responsibilities, including "classification of the public lands, and examination of geological structure, mineral resources, and products of the national domain."

November 17, 1880: The United States and China sign a treaty that allows the United States to "regulate, limit, and suspend" Chinese immigration but not to ban it outright.

March 4, 1881: James Garfield is inaugurated as president. Chester A. Arthur is vice president.

May 6, 1882: Congress passes the Chinese Exclusion Act, suspending Chinese immigration to the United States for 10 years.

September 19, 1882: President James Garfield dies of complications from the wounds he sustained in July from political rival Charles Guiteau and is succeeded by Vice President Arthur the next day.

January 16, 1883: Congress passes the Pendleton Civil Service Reform Act, an attempt to depoliticize appointments of federal employees engaged in governmental operations. Signed into law by President Arthur, the act establishes a Civil Service Commission and specifies rules for a merit system based on competitive exams.

March 4, 1885: Grover Cleveland is inaugurated as president. Thomas A. Hendricks is vice president.

January 19, 1886: Congress passes a Presidential Succession Act; if both the president and vice president are unable to serve, they are succeeded by members of the cabinet in the order that their departments were created.

October 25, 1886: In *Wabash, St. Louis & Pacific Railway v. Illinois*, the Supreme Court rules that only the federal government, not the individual states, may regulate interstate railway rates.

November, 1886: Samuel Gompers establishes the American Federation of Labor which emphasizes "bread and butter" unionism.

February 4, 1887: Congress passes the Interstate Commerce Act establishing the Interstate Commerce Commission, the first national regulatory commission, in an attempt to curb price fixing and other abuses by interstate railroads.

February 8, 1887: Congress passes the Dawes Act, which provides for the division of tribal lands among individual American Indians and the sale of "surplus" land to non-Indians.

March 4, 1889: Benjamin Harrison is inaugurated as president. Levi P. Morton is vice president.

November 2, 1889: North Dakota and South Dakota become states, followed by Montana on November 8 and Washington on November 11, becoming the 39th through 42nd states of the Union, respectively.

April 14, 1890: At a conference that began in Washington, D.C., on October 2, 1889, Western Hemisphere nations form the Pan-American Union.

July 3, 1890: Idaho becomes the 43rd state.

July 10, 1890: Wyoming becomes the 44th state.

March 3, 1891: The Immigration and Naturalization Service is created by the Immigration Act of 1891; originally called the Bureau of Immigration, it is the first federal agency in charge of enforcing immigration laws and standards.

March 4, 1893: Grover Cleveland is inaugurated to a second term as president. Adlai E. Stevenson is vice president.

May 5, 1893: Stock prices on Wall Street drop. More than 600 banks close their doors in June as the United States enters a financial depression that lasts four years.

October 3, 1893: Following a meeting of the National League for Good Roads, a lobbying group dedicated to the passage of national road legislation, the Federal Highway Administration is founded as the Office of Road Inquiry, an agency in the Department of Agriculture.

June 26–August 3, 1894: Supporting the Pullman strikers, the American Railway Union, led by Eugene V. Debs, strikes against most railroads. President Cleveland sends in federal troops to break up the strike, based on a court injunction prohibiting workers from interfering with the delivery of mail.

May 20, 1895: The Supreme Court in *Pollock v. Farmers' Loan and Trust Company* rules that the federal income tax provision of the Wilson-Gorman Tariff Act is unconstitutional.

January 4, 1896: Utah becomes the 45th state.

March 4, 1897: William McKinley is inaugurated as president with Garret A. Hobart as vice president.

April 24, 1898: Spain declares war on the United States.

July 7, 1898: Recognizing the strategic military value of its base at Pearl Harbor, Congress approves the annexation of Hawaii by joint resolution.

1899: The expansion of the federal government makes it one of the leading U.S. employers, reaching close to 250,000 by 1899.

1899: Secretary of State John Hay convinces Great Britain, France, Russia, Germany, Italy, and Japan to agree to an "Open Door" policy to assure all nations equal trading rights with China.

January 9, 1899: Congress ratifies the treaty with Spain, which is signed by President McKinley on February 10. The United States acquires Puerto Rico and Guam, and Spain grants independence to Cuba.

The United States buys Spanish holdings in the Philippines, gaining virtual control over the islands.

April 13, 1900: For the fourth time in eight years the House of Representatives adopts a resolution favoring a constitutional amendment for the election of U.S. senators by direct vote of the people instead of by state legislatures. The Senate finally concurs in 1911.

September 18, 1900: The first direct primary in the United States is held in Hennepin County, Minnesota.

March 3, 1901: The National Institute of Standards and Technology is founded to provide better measurements and more uniformity, precision, and control in laboratory and factory activities.

March 4, 1901: William McKinley is inaugurated for a second term as president; Theodore Roosevelt is sworn in as vice president.

September 14, 1901: After being shot by an anarchist seven days earlier, President McKinley dies. Theodore Roosevelt becomes president.

November, 1901: Alabama adopts a new constitution that effectively disenfranchises African Americans (and some poor whites) by including literacy and property tests, as well as a measure known as the "grandfather" clause, which states that a person cannot vote if his grandfather was ineligible. It also denies suffrage to individuals convicted of certain "criminal" acts.

December 3, 1901: In his first State of the Union message to Congress, President Roosevelt calls for the regulation of business trusts "within reasonable limits" and becomes the first president to advocate the conservation of natural resources on public land.

March 6, 1902: The Bureau of the Census is founded, responsible for collecting information regarding the U.S. population and its economic and social institutions.

March 10, 1902: At President Roosevelt's instigation, Attorney General Philander C. Knox files to dissolve the Northern Securities Company under the Sherman Antitrust Act.

July 8, 1902: The Bureau of Reclamation is founded to study, locate, and construct large-scale irrigation projects in the West.

April 27, 1903: The Supreme Court upholds the clause in the Alabama constitution denying African Americans the right to vote.

November 18, 1903: The United States and Panama sign the Hay-Bunau-Varilla Treaty giving the United States permanent rights to a ten-mile-wide canal zone in return for $10 million and an annual payment of $250,000 after nine years.

March 14, 1904: The Supreme Court upholds the Sherman Anti-Trust Act in *Northern Securities Company v. United States*.

January 20, 1905: President Roosevelt invokes the Roosevelt Corollary (asserting the right of the United States to intervene in Latin American internal affairs) for the first time, as the United States begins to supervise the payment of national and international debts owed by the Dominican Republic.

February 1, 1905: The Department of Forestry, created in 1881, is renamed the Forest Service; it is charged with studying forest conditions, disseminating forest information, and protecting and managing the national forests.

March 4, 1905: Theodore Roosevelt is inaugurated as president for a second term. He is the youngest elected president to date. His vice president is Charles Warren Fairbanks.

June 29, 1906: Congress passes the Hepburn Act, which puts teeth in the Interstate Commerce Act by permitting regulation of rates charged by railroads, pipelines, and terminals. President Roosevelt has strongly endorsed the act and helped guide it through Congress.

June 30, 1906: The Federal Food and Drug Act is passed.

September 29, 1906: The United States invokes the Platt Amendment (an amendment to Cuba's constitution allowing the United States to intervene to maintain order) and assumes military control of Cuba. The United States continues to govern Cuba until January 1909.

October 1, 1907: A downturn in the stock market touches off the Panic of 1907. At the request of the federal government J. Pierpont Morgan and fellow bankers bring $100 million in gold from Europe to restore confidence in the economy and end the currency panic that has caused runs on banks.

November 16, 1907: Oklahoma becomes the 46th state.

June 8, 1908: At the urging of Gifford Pinchot, head of the U.S. Forest Service, President Roosevelt appoints a 57-member National Commission for the Conservation of Natural Resources, naming Pinchot as chairman. The commission's job is to compile the first list of all American natural resources.

July 26, 1908: The Federal Bureau of Investigation is created by Attorney General Charles J. Bonaparte as a corps of special agents to serve as the investigative arm of the Department of Justice.

March 4, 1909: William Howard Taft is inaugurated as the twenty-seventh president of the United States. James S. Sherman is vice president.

July 12, 1909: Congress proposes the Sixteenth Amendment, which authorizes a federal income tax. It is ratified by the states in 1913.

March 17, 1910: Congressman George W. Norris (R-Neb.) introduces a resolution to limit the power of speaker of the house during Joseph G. Cannon's dictatorial speakership. The measure passes, indicating the growing strength of progressive Republicans.

June 18, 1910: Congress passes the Mann-Elkins Act, which extends jurisdiction of the Interstate Commerce Commission (ICC) to include telephone, telegraph, cable, and wireless companies. It also augments ICC regulation of railroads, and it establishes a Commerce Court (which is abolished in 1913).

June 25, 1910: Congress passes the Publicity Act, which requires members of Congress to report campaign contributions.

January 21, 1911: The National Progressive Republican League, founded by Sen. Robert M. La Follette of Wisconsin and other insurgent Republicans, issues its platform, which calls for direct election of U.S. senators, the initiative, the referendum, the recall, and other reforms.

July 24, 1911: The United States renews its commercial treaty with Japan. Among its provisions, the treaty reaffirms the "Gentlemen's Agreement" of 1907, in which President Theodore Roosevelt pledged to see that Japanese residents of the United States were well treated if Japan voluntarily prevented Japanese laborers from immigrating to the United States.

January 6, 1912: New Mexico becomes the 47th state.

February 14, 1912: Arizona is admitted as the 48th state.

August 2, 1912: Sen. Henry Cabot Lodge (R-Mass.) introduces a resolution—subsequently known as the Lodge Corollary—extending the Monroe Doctrine to pertain to foreign companies and non-European nations.

March 4, 1913: Woodrow Wilson takes the oath of office and becomes the twenty-eighth president of the United States with Thomas R. Marshall as vice president.

March 4, 1913: The Department of Labor becomes a separate department from the Department of Commerce "to foster, promote, and develop the welfare of working people, to improve their working conditions, and to enhance their opportunities for profitable employment."

March 4, 1913: The Bureau of Labor Statistics is founded as part of the Department of Labor with the goal of protecting workers and improving their working conditions by providing accurate statistics.

May 31, 1913: The Seventeenth Amendment to the Constitution, providing for the direct election of U.S. senators, is officially adopted following ratification by thirty-six states. Previously senators were selected by state legislatures.

December 23, 1913: The Federal Reserve System is established by the Federal Reserve Act of 1913 to counter financial disruptions by coordinating the Federal Reserve banks and by controlling the "discount rate," or interest rate at which banks could lend each other money.

August, 1914: World War I begins.

August 3, 1914: The Panama Canal opens.

September 1, 1914: The Federal Trade Commission is created and granted an unprecedented authority by the Federal Trade Commission Act of 1914 to investigate, publicize, and prohibit all unfair methods of business competition.

April 28, 1915: The U.S. Coast Guard is founded; over the years it becomes responsible for, among other things, patrolling U.S. shores for icebergs, performing lifesaving operations, and enforcing Prohibition laws and drug control policies.

May 7, 1915: The *Lusitania,* a British passenger liner, is sunk off the Irish coast by a German submarine. The dead include 128 Americans.

June 3, 1916: Congress passes the National Defense Act, which provides for the expansion of the regular army to 220,000, authorizes a National Guard of 450,000 men, establishes the Reserve Officers Training Corps (ROTC) at colleges and universities, and makes provisions for industrial preparedness.

August 25, 1916: The National Park Service is founded to promote and regulate the use of national parks and monuments.

September 7, 1916: Congress passes the Shipping Act, which authorizes the creation of the U.S. Shipping Board to oversee the requisition of ships through the Emergency Fleet Corporation.

September 7, 1916: Congress passes the Workmen's Compensation Act, which offers coverage to half a million federal employees.

September 8, 1916: The U.S. International Trade Commission is founded as the United State Tariff Commission and is charged with the duty of providing Congress with trade information and statistics that would help members of Congress make rational decisions regarding tariff revisions.

1917: Jeannette Rankin is elected to the House of Representatives. She is the first woman elected to Congress.

March 5, 1917: President Wilson is inaugurated for his second term in office.

April 4, 1917: The United States declares war on Germany.

July 24, 1917: Congress appropriates $640 million to develop an army air force. The goal is to build forty-five hundred planes by the spring of 1918.

November 6, 1917: An amendment to the New York State constitution gives women the right to vote in state elections.

January 8, 1918: In an address before Congress President Wilson puts forward his proposal for peace (the Fourteen Points).

March 19, 1918: To conserve energy during the war, Congress passes legislation that puts daylight saving time into effect.

1919: The Eighteenth Amendment, known as the Prohibition amendment, is ratified.

February 14, 1919: President Wilson delivers his proposal for a League of Nations to the Paris Peace Conference.

June 28, 1919: The Treaty of Versailles is signed, officially ending World War I.

September 25, 1919: After making his fortieth speech in support of the League of Nations, President Wilson collapses in Pueblo, Colorado, and is forced to return to the White House, where he suffers an incapacitating stroke from which he never fully recovers.

October, 1919: The Volstead Act is passed to provide for the enforcement of the Eighteenth Amendment (the Prohibition Amendment).

1920: The Nineteenth Amendment, which grants women the right to vote, passes.

March 19, 1920: In a victory for opponents of the Treaty of Versailles, the Senate rejects U.S. membership in the League of Nations.

March 4, 1921: Warren G. Harding is inaugurated as twenty-ninth president of the United States. Calvin Coolidge is vice president.

May 19, 1921: Harding signs the Emergency Immigration Act, restricting immigration to the United States from any European country to 3 percent of the individuals of that nationality in the United States at the time of the 1910 census. The act also creates an annual ceiling of 355,000 immigrants.

September 1, 1921: The General Accounting Office is founded and given the authority to interpret any laws concerning government payments, to investigate receipt and use of public funds, to recommend to Congress ways of making government expenditures more economical and efficient, and to standardize accounting systems, forms, and procedures among all government agencies.

October 3, 1922: Rebecca Felton, age eighty-seven, of Georgia becomes the first female U.S. senator. Her term, to which the governor of Georgia appointed her following the death of Sen. Thomas Watson, lasts only one day.

April 9, 1923: The U.S. Supreme Court rules the minimum-wage law for women and children in Washington, D.C., to be unconstitutional in *Adkins v. Children's Hospital.*

August 2, 1923: President Harding dies in San Francisco on a goodwill tour of the country that took him all the way to Alaska.

August 3, 1923: Calvin Coolidge is sworn in as the thirtieth president of the United States.

May 17, 1924: Congress overrides President Coolidge's veto of the Veterans' Bonus Bill, which allocates $2 billion for veterans of World War I.

May 24, 1924: The United States decides that it must become more involved in international affairs after the tremendous loss of life in Word War I (1914–18); the Foreign Service is thus created by the Rogers Act of 1924 to better represent the country's political and economic interests abroad.

March 4, 1925: Calvin Coolidge is inaugurated and begins his first elected term as president. Charles G. Dawes is vice president.

March 4, 1929: Herbert Hoover is inaugurated as the thirty-first president of the United States. Charles Curtis is his vice president.

June 18, 1929: President Hoover signs the reapportionment bill, which gives the president the authority to reapportion Congress after each decennial census if Congress fails to act. Hoover finds this legislation necessary because Congress has so far refused to reapportion congressional districts on the basis of the 1920 census.

October 29, 1929: Prices on the New York Stock Exchange collapse and the United State enters the Great Depression which will last into World War II (1939–45).

May 14, 1930: The Bureau of Prisons is founded under an act of Congress to consolidate the operations of all federal prisons.

May 26, 1930: The National Institutes of Health is founded; it is originally a federal laboratory dedicated to the research of diseases, navigable stream pollution, and information dissemination.

July 21, 1930: President Hoover signs into law an act establishing the Veterans Administration.

July 26, 1930: The Food and Drug Administration is founded to enforce the regulations set out in the Food and Drug Act of 1906 and the Meat Inspection Act, establishing federal food standards and prohibiting the misbranding and adulteration of food and drugs.

September–October, 1931: Hoarding of gold increases as the economic depression worsens; banks are failing in great numbers (522 close during October alone), and their depositors, uninsured by the government, lose most of their savings.

February 2, 1932: On the recommendation of President Hoover, Congress establishes the Reconstruction Finance Corporation, giving it wide-ranging power to extend credit to private banks and businesses.

February 27, 1932: Congress passes the Glass-Steagall Credit Expansion Act, making $750 million of the government gold reserve available for industrial and business needs.

February 6, 1933: The Twentieth Amendment to the U.S. Constitution, the "lame duck" amendment, is ratified. It moves the date of the presidential inauguration from March 4 to January 20 and sets the beginning of terms for senators and congressmen as January 3, which is also established as the first day of the new session.

March 4, 1933: Franklin D. Roosevelt is inaugurated president of the United States. John N. Garner is vice president.

March 5–13, 1933: Because bank runs and closings continue to sweep the country, President Roosevelt declares a "bank holiday," suspending regular bank business to provide a cooling-off period.

March 9–June 16, 1933: Congress convenes to deal with the banking crisis, beginning the "First Hundred Days" of the "First New Deal." Many emergency bills are passed, such as the National Industrial Recovery Act, the Emergency Banking Relief Act, the Agricultural Administration Act, and the Farm Credit Act.

May 18, 1933: The Tennessee Valley Authority is founded; originally established to provide flood control, navigation, and electric power to the people in the Tennessee Valley area, it grows to become the United States's largest electric power producing company.

June 12– July 27, 1933: At the London Economic Conference, European nations and the United States are unable to develop a plan for international cooperation in ending the wide fluctuation of exchange rates and reducing trade barriers.

July 26, 1933: The Farm Credit Administration is founded.

November 16, 1933: The United States formally recognizes the Soviet Union, sixteen years after the Bolshevik Revolution of 1917.

December 5, 1933: The Twenty-first Amendment repealing Prohibition is ratified.

1934: Democrat Arthur L. Mitchell of Chicago becomes the first African American elected to Congress.

1934: Congress passes the National Housing Act, which establishes the Federal Housing Administration (FHA).

January 1, 1934: The Federal Deposit Insurance Corporation (FDIC) is established to help restore the country's confidence in its banking system as a result of the bank failures of the Great Depression.

February 2, 1934: The Export-Import Bank of the United States is founded; it is inspired by the economic conditions of the 1930s when exports are seen as a desperately needed stimulus for the economy of the Great Depression.

June 21, 1934: The National Mediation Board is founded to handle disputes that often arise between labor and management.

July 2, 1934: The Securities and Exchange Commission is founded to administer federal securities laws that curb fraudulent stock and investment practices.

July 26, 1934: The Federal Communications Commission (FCC) is founded to combine the functions of the Federal Radio Commission (regulating airwave use and radio licenses) with the telephone and telegraph policies previously regulated by the Interstate Commerce Commission and the Postmaster General.

January 4, 1935: The "Second New Deal" begins as President Roosevelt outlines a program for social reform that will benefit laborers and small farmers.

July 5, 1935: The National Labor Relations Board is founded by the Wagner Act, a response to an appeal by President Roosevelt for a greater degree of "industrial peace" so that economic recovery from the Great Depression could be achieved.

August 14, 1935: The Social Security Administration is founded to promote the security of the U.S. economy by managing the nation's social security programs.

January 1, 1936: The Rural Utilities Service is founded to provide assistance to rural areas of the United States in establishing electricity, water, and telecommunications.

January 20, 1937: President Roosevelt begins his second term, declaring, "I see one-third of a nation ill-housed, ill-clad, ill-nourished." John N. Garner is his vice president.

February 5, 1937: President Roosevelt requests that Congress pass legislation to increase the number of justices on the U.S. Supreme Court to as many as fifteen. His proposal is decried as "court packing" and fails.

August 5, 1937: The National Cancer Institute is founded by legislation providing for federal involvement in the prevention and control of cancer.

September 2, 1937: President Roosevelt signs the National Housing Act, creating the U.S. Housing Authority.

December 12, 1937: Japanese planes bomb and sink the U.S. gunboat *Panay* on the Yangtze River in China; two American sailors are killed. Two days later Japan formally apologizes for the incident, but relations between Japan and the United States are further strained.

February 16, 1938: President Roosevelt signs the second Agricultural Administration Act, replacing the first AAA, which had been declared unconstitutional in 1936.

February 27, 1939: The U.S. Supreme Court rules wildcat strikes (strikes in violation of a contract) to be illegal.

May 16, 1939: The U.S. Department of Agriculture introduces food stamps, which needy people can redeem for surplus agricultural goods.

July 1, 1939: The Office of Management and Budget is founded with the responsibility of assisting the president in overseeing the preparation of the federal budget and supervising its administration in executive branch agencies.

August 7, 1939: The Administrative Office of the U.S. Courts is founded to handle all administrative duties for the federal courts and to continually study, research, and make recommendations for running the court system.

September 3, 1939: Responding to the German invasion of Poland on September 1, Great Britain and France declare war on Germany. On the same day 30 Americans are killed when Germany sinks a British passenger ship; President Roosevelt restates U.S. neutrality.

September 8, 1939: The White House Office is founded; early staff positions involve mostly clerical duties, although by the twentieth century, the office grows to include more advisory and political positions.

October 11, 1939: The NAACP Legal Defense and Education Fund is organized and pledges an all-out fight against discrimination.

January 26, 1940: The 1911 U.S.-Japan Treaty of Commerce expires, and Secretary of State Cordell Hull informs the Japanese government that trade will continue only on a day-to-day basis.

May 25, 1940: President Roosevelt establishes the Office of Emergency Management.

June 30, 1940: The Bureau of the Public Debt is founded to borrow money needed to operate the government by issuing Treasury bills, notes, and bonds, guaranteeing repayment of the value plus interest to the owner.

September 1, 1940: The U.S. Fish and Wildlife Service is founded to study the abundance, distribution, and habits of fish and wildlife and to manage national wildlife refuge sites.

September 27, 1940: The Tripartite Pact, a ten-year military and economic alliance among Germany, Italy, and Japan, is formalized. The three Axis powers pledge mutual assistance to one another in case of attack by any nation not already at war with another member. Observers see this pact as a clear warning to the United States.

October 29, 1940: Secretary of War Henry Stimson draws the first number in the Selective Service lottery, initiating the first peacetime draft in American history.

January 6, 1941: In his State of the Union Address President Roosevelt asks Congress to support the Lend-Lease program by lending or leasing war supplies to Great Britain. He also outlines the "four essential freedoms" for which the Allies are fighting: freedom of speech, freedom of worship, freedom from want, and freedom from fear.

January 20, 1941: Roosevelt and Henry A. Wallace are inaugurated as president and vice-president. Roosevelt becomes the first three-term president.

February 3, 1941: The U.S. Supreme Court rules in *United States v. Darby Lumber Co.* that the Fair Labor Standards Act of 1938 is constitutional.

June 28, 1941: The Office of Scientific Research and Development (OSRD) is set up by executive order, with Dr. Vannevar Bush as chairman. The OSRD will coordinate the development of radar, sonar, and the first stages of the atomic bomb.

August 14, 1941: President Roosevelt and British prime minister Winston Churchill meet to discuss the Atlantic Charter, which becomes the blueprint for the United Nations.

November 17, 1941: In Washington, D.C., Japanese ambassador Nomura Kichisaburo and special envoy Kurusu Saburo suggest that war could result if the United States does not remove its economic embargo and refrain from interfering with Japanese activities in China and the Pacific.

December 7, 1941: Japan attacks Pearl Harbor, Hawaii, as well as U.S. bases in Thailand, Malaya, Singapore, the Philippines, Guam, Wake Island, and Hong Kong.

December 8, 1941: Calling the Japanese attack "a date which will live in infamy," President Roosevelt asks Congress for a declaration of war against Japan. Only one member fails to vote for the declaration: Rep. Jeannette Rankin of Montana, a committed pacifist who was against American involvement in World War I.

December 11, 1941: Germany declares war on the United States, with Italy following suit.

January 12, 1942: The National War Labor Board is established to settle labor disputes.

June 13, 1942: The Office of Strategic Services (OSS), the forerunner of the Central Intelligence Agency, is established with Maj. Gen. William "Wild Bill" Donovan as director.

November 8, 1942: Operation Torch begins with four hundred thousand Allied troops landing in Algeria and Morocco in northern Africa under the command of General Eisenhower

January 14, 1943: The Casablanca Conference begins. President Roosevelt and Prime Minister Winston Churchill decide to demand unconditional surrender from the Axis powers of Germany, Italy, and Japan.

May 1, 1943: In the name of "national security," President Roosevelt seizes all bituminous-coal mines in the eastern United States in response to wildcat strikes that threaten war production.

June 10, 1943: The Current Tax Payment Act takes effect, requiring the withholding of federal income taxes from individual paychecks on a regular basis. This act revolutionizes the collecting of taxes and gives government more power to spend than before.

December 17, 1943: Congress repeals all Chinese Exclusion Acts enacted throughout the century.

January 22, 1944: President Roosevelt creates the War Refugee Board to help resettle millions of refugees after the war.

March 29, 1944: Congress authorizes $1.35 billion to seed the United Nations Relief and Rehabilitation Fund, initiating a massive program to aid Europe's displaced millions.

April 3, 1944: In *Smith v. Allwright* the U.S. Supreme Court rules that African Americans cannot be denied the right to vote in the Texas Democratic primary.

June 6, 1944: The long-planned "Operation Overlord," the invasion of Nazi-occupied France, begins on D-Day on the beaches of Normandy in northern France. By day's end 150,000 troops successfully land, catching the Germans off guard. Within a week more than 350,000 troops are moving toward Germany.

June 20, 1944: The Battle of the Philippine Sea ends with the decisive defeat of Japanese forces.

July 22, 1944: The Bretton Woods Conference in New Hampshire, begun July 1, ends. Representatives of 44 nations, not including the Soviet Union, establish the International Monetary Fund (IMF) and the International Bank for Reconstruction and Development (the World Bank).

August–October, 1944: The Dumbarton Oaks conference is convened by President Roosevelt, with delegates from Great Britain, China, and Russia in attendance, to work out proposals that will serve as a basis for the United Nations charter.

January 20, 1945: Roosevelt is inaugurated for an unprecedented fourth term as president, with Harry S. Truman as vice president.

February 11, 1945: The Yalta Conference ends with Roosevelt, Winston Churchill of Great Britain, and Joseph Stalin of Russia agreeing on the postwar division of Europe and Asia, on the treatment of war criminals, and on holding the first meeting of the United Nations to discuss further issues.

March 27, 1945: The National Technical Information Service is founded as a result of the government's attempts to deal with the release of thousands of war-related documents to U.S. industry following World War II.

April 12, 1945: President Roosevelt dies of a cerebral hemorrhage. Truman is sworn in as president.

May 8, 1945: Germany surrenders, ending the European war. Victory in Europe (V-E) Day is declared in the United States as massive celebrations erupt.

August 6, 1945: The United States drops an atomic bomb on Hiroshima, Japan. The resulting devastation amazes even the scientists who created it. More than fifty thousand people perish in seconds, and four square miles of the city are reduced to rubble.

August 9, 1945: An atomic bomb is dropped on Nagasaki in southern Japan, killing forty thousand Japanese civilians immediately. Tokyo announces its intention to surrender.

August 27, 1945: The Allies begin to divide Korea, with the Soviets occupying territory north of the 38th parallel, the Americans the southern half of the peninsula.

September 2, 1945: Japan signs a formal surrender onboard the *U.S.S. Missouri* in Tokyo Bay.

September 6, 1945: President Truman announces his economic recovery plan to Congress. Later known as the "Fair Deal," the program promises full employment, a substantial raise in the minimum wage, the extension of Social Security, national health insurance, federal aid to education, and government-sponsored housing for the poor.

December 14, 1945: General Marshall is named special ambassador to China to make peace between the Communist forces of Mao Tse-tung and the Nationalist forces of Chiang Kai-shek.

December 31, 1945: President Truman dismantles the War Labor Board, replacing it with the Wage Stabilization Board in an effort to slow the pace of rapidly growing labor unrest.

January 10, 1946: The first General Assembly of the United Nations meets in London. Heading the American delegation are Secretary of State James F. Byrnes and former first lady Eleanor Roosevelt.

January 21, 1946: The United Steelworkers close down the nation's steel plants over wage contracts.

February 20, 1946: The Employment Act of 1946 is passed by Congress, establishing the Council of Economic Advisers to help the nation's economy change from a high-production wartime economy to a civilian economy without a loss in stability or employment.

April 29, 1946: The U.S. Department of Agriculture reports that farm prices, and hence the cost of food, are at record highs, underscoring the need for higher wages among workers.

June 3, 1946: The U.S. Supreme Court rules in *Morgan v. Commonwealth of Virginia* that segregated seating on interstate buses is unconstitutional.

July 1, 1946: The Centers for Disease Control and Prevention is founded to eradicate communicable diseases; it later expands its activities beyond the bounds of infectious disease to include areas such as nutrition, chronic disease, and occupational and environmental health.

July 4, 1946: The United States grants political independence to the Philippines, but maintains the right to station ships and planes on Philippine territory at Subic Bay and Clark Air Base.

July 16, 1946: The Bureau of Land Management is founded with the responsibility for managing public land use by focusing on the extraction of livestock forage, timber, and energy and mineral commodities.

August 1, 1946: Under the McMahon Act, the U.S. Atomic Energy Commission (AEC) is established to provide civilian control over military and nonmilitary atomic-energy development.

August 2, 1946: Congress passes the Legislative Reorganization Act, which requires registration of political lobbyists and the reporting of expenses.

November 9, 1946: Responding to pressures from business and conservatives, President Truman lifts price controls on most consumer goods even though recently enacted legislation is supposed to safeguard against this for six more months.

December 5, 1946: Despite conservative opposition, especially in the South, President Truman issues Executive Order 9809, creating the Committee on Civil Rights to investigate the treatment of African Americans in the United States—the first time in American history that a president focuses on civil liberties for racial minorities.

January 1, 1947: The Federal Mediation and Conciliation Service is founded to minimize interruptions of business that grow out of labor disputes and to settle labor and management disputes through conciliation and mediation.

March 12, 1947: Announcing his "containment policy," President Truman declares that the United States will provide $400 million to Greece and Turkey to fight communism. The Truman Doctrine will commit the United States to becoming a global anticommunist policeman.

June 23, 1947: Over President Truman's veto, Congress passes the Taft-Hartley Act (Labor Management Relations Act), which bans the closed shop by which only union members may be hired and which permits employers to sue unions for damages incurred in strikes. The act also allows the government to enforce an eighty-day cooling-off period, forbids political contributions by unions, and requires union leaders to swear they are not Communists.

July 18, 1947: The Presidential Succession Act is passed, making the Speaker of the House of Representatives next in line for the presidency after the vice president. Following the Speaker is the president pro tempore of the Senate and cabinet members according to rank.

July 26, 1947: The National Security Council is founded "to advise the president with respect to the integration of domestic, foreign, and military policies relating to the national security."

September 2, 1947: President Truman flies to Brazil to sign the Inter-American Treaty of Reciprocal Assistance (Rio Pact), in which nineteen American nations commit themselves to "collective defense against aggression."

September 8, 1947: The Joint Chiefs of Staff is founded as a collaboration of operations among the nation's military branches.

September 18, 1947: The Central Intelligence Agency is founded to gather and analyze intelligence information and to document the activities of foreign governments in order to better protect national security interests.

September 18, 1947: The Department of the Air Force is founded as its own agency, replacing the Army Air Force.

October 18, 1947: The House Un-American Activities Committee (HUAC) launches an extensive investigation into Communist activities in the movie industry.

March 8, 1948: The U.S. Supreme Court rules in *McCollum v. Board of Education* that religious training in public schools is unconstitutional.

April 30, 1948: The International Conference of American States, with twenty-one members in attendance at Bogotá, Colombia, establishes the Organization of American States (OAS).

May 14, 1948: Israel declares its independence from Britain as a sovereign state. The United States becomes the first nation to recognize the new country.

June 11, 1948: The Vandenberg Resolution passes in the Senate, allowing the United States to enter into collective security alliances outside the Western Hemisphere.

June 26, 1948: In response to the Soviet shutdown of all traffic from the West into Berlin on June 24, the United States initiates the Berlin airlift. For the next year nearly 275,000 flights will provide Berliners with 2.3 million tons of food and fuel.

August 3, 1948: Former Communist Whittaker Chambers accuses Alger Hiss, a high-ranking State Department diplomat, of membership in the Communist Party, lending credence to right-wing charges that subversives have infiltrated the government.

November 1, 1948: The National Institute of Allergy and Infectious Diseases is founded as a division of the National Institutes of Health to establish federal research in the areas of allergy and infectious diseases.

January 20, 1949: President Truman is inaugurated for his second term with Alben W. Barkley as vice president. In his speech Truman emphasizes foreign aid.

March 2, 1949: To prove that the United States possesses intercontinental air-strike capabilities, the U.S. Air Force's B-50 bomber circumnavigates the globe.

April 15, 1949: The National Institute of Mental Health is created to address the critical lack of knowledge about mental illness and a lack of mental health professionals.

July 1, 1949: The General Services Administration is founded with the responsibility for all of the federal government's purchases; it is later redefined in the 1990s when it opens itself up to competition from the private sector.

July 21, 1949: The Senate ratifies the North Atlantic treaty creating the North Atlantic Treaty Organization (NATO). The United States has never before concluded an alliance treaty with any European power during peacetime.

August 10, 1949: The Department of Defense is founded to create a command and interservice cooperation of land, sea, and air forces, both at home and in foreign countries where U.S. armed forces are stationed.

August 10, 1949: President Truman signs an amendment to the National Security Act of 1947, placing military secretaries under the authority of the Department of Defense.

October 1, 1949: Mao Tse-tung announces the creation of the People's Republic of China. The United States does not recognize the new government.

October 26, 1949: The Fair Labor Standards Act is amended to raise the minimum wage from forty cents to seventy-five cents an hour.

May 10, 1950: The National Science Foundation is founded, establishing the U.S. government's role in promoting and sponsoring scientific discoveries and projects.

May 24, 1950: The Maritime Administration is founded to regulate the maritime industry, determine subsidies, and oversee federal Merchant Marine programs associated with the Department of Commerce.

June 1950–July, 1953: The Korean War is fought.

1951: The Twenty-second Amendment, limiting the president's service to two terms, is ratified.

October 24, 1952: The National Security Agency is founded with the responsibility for the signals intelligence and communications security activities of the U.S. government.

January 20, 1953: Dwight David Eisenhower is inaugurated president and Richard Nixon as vice president.

July 27, 1953: An armistice is concluded in Korea that leaves that country divided. The United States guarantees economic aid and military security.

August 1, 1953: The U.S. Information Agency is founded to consolidate all the United States's overseas information and cultural programs into one centralized agency to make them more efficient.

August 2, 1953: The Foreign Agricultural Service is founded to increase exports, to administer import quotas on foreign agricultural goods, and to provide the government with information for trade negotiations.

October 1, 1953: The Small Business Administration is founded to provide financial, technical, and management assistance to small business owners.

May 17, 1954: In *Brown v. Board of Education* the Supreme Court rules that racial segregation in public schools is unconstitutional.

May 18, 1954: The U.S. Air Force Academy is legislated by Congress and signed into law by President Eisenhower; its construction near Colorado Springs, Colorado, is completed in 1958.

1955: The United States opposes the entry of additional Communist nations, especially "Red" China, into the United Nations.

1955: The eighty-fourth Congress has a record eighteen women (sixteen in the House, one in the Senate, and one nonvoting delegate from Hawaii).

September 1, 1955: The Indian Health Service is founded, creating the staff, facilities, and programs necessary to provide treatment and preventative care for American Indians.

January 20, 1957: Dwight David Eisenhower is inaugurated for his second term as president with Richard Nixon as vice president.

May 18, 1957: The United States Commission on Civil Rights is founded with a mission of reporting to the president and Congress about all forms of discrimination throughout the United States.

September 24, 1957: President Eisenhower orders U.S. Army paratroopers to prevent interference with racial integration at Central High School in Little Rock, Arkansas.

April 1, 1958: The National Aeronautics and Space Administration is founded; it becomes the principal operating agency for manned space flight, space science, and launch-vehicle development, as well as a significant research-and-development source for space-flight technology and aeronautics.

August 2, 1958: The Federal Aviation Administration is founded with roots in the Air Commerce Act of

1926 which provides for the regulation of pilots and aircraft, for setting up a system of airways and navigational aids, and for fostering air commerce in general.

January 3, 1959: Alaska becomes the 49th state.

August 21, 1959: Hawaii becomes the 50th state.

November 16, 1959: The Justice Department initiates a lawsuit in U.S. District Court to end "white primaries" in Tennessee, where blacks had been prohibited from voting.

December 31, 1959: The Bureau of International Labor Affairs is created to focus on international economic and labor issues and to exchange information with other countries about labor issues.

May 5, 1960: The Soviet Union shoots down an American U-2 spy plane and captures the pilot, Francis Gary Powers. Consequently a conference between President Dwight D. Eisenhower and Soviet premier Nikita Khrushchev is canceled.

June 10, 1960: The National Center for Atmospheric Research is founded to support meteorological research at universities and to support the education and training required to carry on an expanded program of atmospheric research.

1961: The Twenty-third Amendment grants voting rights in presidential elections to citizens who reside in Washington, D.C.

January 1, 1961: The Federal Maritime Commission is established to ensure that U.S. goods shipped overseas receive fair treatment and that foreign goods shipped to the United States are fairly tariffed.

January 20, 1961: John F. Kennedy is inaugurated president with Lyndon B. Johnson as vice president.

March 1, 1961: Kennedy establishes the Peace Corps by executive order.

March 15, 1961: The U.S. Arms Control and Disarmament Agency is founded to deal with arms control and the threat of nuclear proliferation.

April 17, 1961: Cuban exiles backed by the CIA invade Fidel Castro's Cuba at the Bay of Pigs. Cuba defeats the invaders by April 20, and the surviving members of the force are captured and imprisoned.

May 4, 1961: The Freedom Riders begin their bus travels to various southern cities, seeking to eliminate segregation in interstate transportation.

May 5, 1961: Slightly more than three weeks after Soviet cosmonaut Yuri Gagarin became the first human to fly in space, American astronaut Alan B. Shepard is launched in the *Freedom 7* spacecraft into space.

May 18, 1961: The Agency for International Development is founded to provide foreign assistance and humanitarian aid to advance the political and economic interests of the United States.

August 13, 1961: East Germany closes its borders with West Berlin and begins construction of the Berlin Wall.

November 3, 1961: Gen. Maxwell Taylor and State Department official Walt Rostow return from a fact-finding trip to South Vietnam and recommend quick military action.

February 19, 1962: John Glenn, a lieutenant colonel in the U.S. Marine Corps and pilot of the *Friendship 7* spacecraft, who later becomes a senator from Ohio, is the first American to orbit Earth. He orbits the Earth three times.

October 14, 1962: The United States discovers Soviet missiles in Cuba and issues an ultimatum demanding their removal. Cuba is placed under a U.S. naval blockade. After several days of tense confrontation, the Soviets agree to remove their missiles from Cuba on October 28.

October 17, 1962: The National Institute of Child Health and Human Development is founded by Public Law 87-838, which allows for the establishment of an institute committed to maternal health, child health, and human development.

January 15, 1963: The Office of the U.S. Trade Representative is created and given responsibility and authority to negotiate all international trade agreement programs that had been authorized under the Tariff Act of 1930 and the Trade Expansion Act of 1962.

August 28, 1963: Civil rights supporters march on Washington and listen to Dr. Martin Luther King, Jr.'s now-famous "I have a dream" speech.

November 22, 1963: President Kennedy is assassinated while riding in a motorcade in Dallas, Texas. Lee Harvey Oswald is later charged with the murder. Subsequently, Lyndon B. Johnson is sworn in as president of the United States on board Air Force One en route from Dallas to Washington, D.C.

1964: The Twenty-fourth Amendment passes. It bans the poll tax, which is used to prevent many African Americans from voting.

June 10, 1964: The Senate invokes the cloture rule, ending a southern filibuster designed to prevent a vote on a civil rights bill—the first time cloture has successfully been invoked on civil rights legislation.

July 2, 1964: President Johnson signs the Civil Rights Act of 1964, the most extensive and far-reaching civil rights act since the Reconstruction.

August 3, 1964: U.S. ships are attacked in the Gulf of Tonkin by North Vietnamese patrol boats, prompting a retaliation by the United States and passage of the Tonkin Gulf Resolution, giving Johnson congressional approval for all future actions he takes regarding the war.

August 20, 1964: Johnson signs the War on Poverty Bill.

January 20, 1965: Lyndon B. Johnson is inaugurated for a second term. Hubert H. Humphrey is vice president.

March 2, 1965: U.S. aircraft begin bombing North Vietnam.

March 8, 1965: The first U.S. combat troops are sent to Vietnam; earlier forces had consisted primarily of military advisers and support personnel.

April 28, 1965: The United States invades the Dominican Republic, ostensibly to prevent a Communist takeover.

July 2, 1965: The Equal Employment Opportunity Commission is established under Title VII of the Civil Rights Act of 1964 to investigate and conciliate all claims of discrimination in the workplace on the basis of race, color, national origin, sex, and religion.

August 6, 1965: President Johnson signs the Voting Rights Act of 1965.

August 7, 1965: The Administration on Aging is founded to carry out the provisions of the Older Americans Act, the first comprehensive plan for social services for aging citizens.

August 10, 1965: The Economic Development Administration is founded under the terms of the Public Works and Economic Development Act to target federal resources to economically distressed areas and to help develop local economies in the United States.

September 25, 1965: The National Endowment for the Humanities is founded after advocates of the humanities in the United States see the large investments being made for improvements in the sciences and argue that improving the disciplines of the humanities is equally important to the country's interests.

September 29, 1965: The National Endowment for the Arts is founded; since its creation, it has sponsored thousands of individual and organizational arts projects, supported the establishment of arts councils in every state, and worked to make the arts in America excellent and accessible.

November 9, 1965: The Department of Housing and Urban Development is founded to form an integrated approach to addressing housing and community development needs, taking into consideration the social, physical, and economic conditions that help communities thrive.

September 9, 1966: President Johnson signs a bill authorizing the establishment of federal automobile safety standards.

October 15, 1966: The Department of Transportation is founded as a cabinet-level agency responsible for creating and regulating policy for the entire transportation industry in the United States.

October 15, 1966: The Federal Railroad Administration is founded to enforce laws concerning railroad safety issues, such as hours of service, accident reporting, signals, and locomotive inspections, that were previously enforced by the Interstate Commerce Commission.

November 1, 1966: The National Institute of Environmental Health Sciences is founded as a division of the National Institutes of Health as a national center dedicated to environmental health problems.

1967: The Twenty-fifth Amendment is ratified, whereby the vice president assumes the presidency, if the president dies or becomes disabled.

April 1, 1967: The National Transportation Safety Board is founded to investigate transportation accidents and to recommend ways of preventing future accidents.

April 14, 1967: The Federal Judicial Center is founded to study and analyze the methods and procedures used in the court systems and to educate court members in their duties.

March 31, 1968: President Johnson announces to a national television audience that he is halting the bombing of North Vietnam; he invites North Vietnam to begin peace negotiations and announces he will not run for reelection.

April 4, 1968: Civil rights leader Martin Luther King, Jr., is murdered in Memphis, Tennessee. Riots occur in many U.S. cities.

April 11, 1968: The Civil Rights Act of 1968 is directed at reducing racial discrimination practices in housing and is signed by President Johnson.

June 5, 1968: New York senator Robert F. Kennedy, brother of slain president John Kennedy, is shot and killed hours after winning the California Democratic presidential primary.

July 1, 1968: The Federal Transit Administration is established by the Urban Mass Transportation Act of 1964 (now known as the Federal Transit Act) to provide programs for matching grants, technical assistance, and research on mass transit to be funded by the federal government.

July 1, 1968: The Nuclear Non-Proliferation Treaty is signed by the United States, the Soviet Union, and many other nations.

January 20, 1969: Richard M. Nixon is inaugurated president with Spiro Agnew as vice president.

March 5, 1969: The Minority Business Development Agency is founded to "stimulate those enterprises that can give members of minority groups confidence that avenues of opportunity are neither closed nor limited."

July 20, 1969: Neil Armstrong and Edwin Aldrin,

American astronauts, are the first people to walk on the moon.

August 8, 1969: The Food and Nutrition Service is founded to oversee the U.S. Department of Agriculture's (USDA) food assistance programs, ensuring that every American family has sufficient and nutritious food.

September 1, 1969: The Inter-American Foundation is founded to provide for a mutually beneficial alliance between the Americas.

November 15, 1969: Over 250,000 march in Washington, D.C., to protest the Vietnam War. American opinion is deeply divided over the war effort; "Hawks" call for increased military action while "Doves" want to reduce military activity.

January 1, 1970: The Council on Environmental Quality is founded as part of the National Environmental Policy Act of 1969 to provide for systematic reorganization of environmental control activities.

January 1, 1970: The Occupational Safety and Health Administration is founded with the goal of preventing injuries and deaths in the workplace and protecting the health of U.S. workers.

March 19, 1970: The National Highway Traffic Safety Administration is founded by the National Traffic and Motor Vehicles Act of 1966 that made auto design and manufacturing subject to federal regulation.

May 14, 1970: The Congressional Research Service is founded to provide a full range of research and information services to Congress and its committee members.

June 15, 1970: In *Welsh v. United States* the Supreme Court rules that the claim of conscientious-objector status can be argued on the basis of moral objection to war, rather than long-standing religious belief alone.

August 1, 1970: The Postal Rate Commission is founded by the Postal Reorganization Act of 1970 to review postal rate and mail classification changes requested by the U.S. Postal Service.

August 5, 1970: The National Credit Union Administration is founded with responsibility for administrating the National Credit Union Insurance Fund (NCUIF) and regulating U.S. credit unions.

August 12, 1970: The U.S. Postal Service is founded with the mandate to provide prompt, reliable, and efficient postal services to the people of the United States.

September 22, 1970: President Nixon signs a bill authorizing a nonvoting congressional representative to the House of Representatives for the District of Columbia, the first since 1875.

October 3, 1970: The National Oceanic and Atmospheric Administration is founded as a response to what President Richard Nixon described as an urgent need for better protection of life and property from natural hazards, as well as a need for exploration and development leading to the intelligent use of marine resources.

December 2, 1970: The Environmental Protection Agency is founded as a coordinated and inclusive effort to control pollution in all its forms.

December 31, 1970: The National Institute on Alcohol Abuse and Alcoholism is founded to develop health, education, training, research, and planning programs for alcohol-related problems.

1971: The Twenty-sixth amendment lowers the voting age to 18.

February 11, 1971: The United States, the Soviet Union, and sixty-one other nations sign the Seabed Arms Control Treaty, banning nuclear weapons from the ocean floor.

April 7, 1971: The Supreme Court upholds court-ordered busing to achieve racial balance.

October 25, 1971: With the support of the United States, members of the United Nations vote to admit the People's Republic of China and expel Nationalist China (Taiwan).

January 1, 1972: The Bureau of Economic Analysis is founded to gather information about the nation's economy in order to predict and avoid further national financial disasters; its predecessor, the Bureau of Foreign and Domestic Commerce, was created during the 1940s to measure the effect of World War II on the U.S. economy.

January 22, 1972: In *Roe v. Wade* the Supreme Court decides that states cannot prevent a woman from obtaining an abortion during the first trimester of pregnancy.

February 14, 1972: President Nixon announces that he will take steps to limit the scope of court-ordered busing.

March 22, 1972: The Twenty-seventh Amendment to the Constitution, prohibiting discrimination on the basis of gender, is passed by Congress and sent to the states for ratification. By the end of 1972, twenty-two of the necessary 38 states have ratified the amendment, also known as the Equal Rights Amendment.

April 7, 1972: The Federal Election Campaign Act goes into effect. The law sets limits and requires disclosures on personal contributions to political candidates.

May 22–30, 1972: President Nixon becomes the first American president to visit Moscow. While in the Soviet Union he signs treaties on antiballistic missiles and other strategic weapons.

July 1, 1972: The Bureau of Alcohol, Tobacco, and Firearms is founded as a distinct division of the Department of the Treasury for the regulation of alcohol, tobacco, and firearms.

September 12, 1972: The Senate approves President Nixon's $33.5-billion revenue-sharing plan that will disburse federal funds to state and local governments over a five-year period.

November 27–30, 1972: Following a full collapse in the Paris peace talks, Nixon orders massive bombing raids against Hanoi and Haiphong. The campaign continues for eleven days, pausing only for Christmas.

December 2, 1972: The Employment Standards Administration is founded as one of the major divisions of the Department of Labor (DOL), sharing the DOL's primary mission to improve and monitor the U.S. workplace.

January 20, 1973: Nixon begins a second term as president.

January 30, 1973: Former Nixon campaign members James W. McCord and G. Gordon Liddy are convicted of breaking into and illegally wiretapping the Democratic party headquarters at the Watergate office complex.

February 27–May 8, 1973: Members of the American Indian Movement (AIM) exchange gunfire with federal agents in Wounded Knee, South Dakota. They seize a church and post office and hold them for 73 days to call attention to grievances they have against the federal government and tribal management.

April 30, 1973: In the wake of the Watergate scandal, H. R. Haldeman, White House chief of staff; John Ehrlichman, domestic policy assistant; John Dean, presidential counsel; and Richard Kleindienst, attorney general, all resign their offices. In a televised address President Nixon denies any involvement in the Watergate break-in or cover-up.

May 14, 1973: The Consumer Product Safety Commission is created under the Consumer Product Safety Act and is charged with regulating consumer products, enforcing compliance with manufacturing safety standards, and developing a widespread consumer information system.

July 1, 1973: The Drug Enforcement Administration is founded to fight illegal drug use and trafficking.

July 31, 1973: Rep. Robert F. Drinan (D-Massachusetts) introduces a resolution calling for Nixon's impeachment on four grounds: the bombing of Cambodia; the unauthorized taping of conversations; the refusal to spend impounded funds; and the establishment of a "supersecret security force within the White House."

October 10, 1973: Agnew resigns the vice presidency and pleads nolo contendere (no contest) to income-tax evasion in return for the dropping of other criminal charges. He receives a three-year suspended sentence and a ten-thousand-dollar fine. Gerald Ford is sworn in as vice president on December 6.

November 7, 1973: Over Nixon's veto Congress passes the War Powers Act, requiring congressional approval for any commitment of U.S. forces abroad over sixty days.

January 1, 1974: The Commodity Futures Trading Commission is founded to organize forward markets, allowing farmers to space deliveries throughout the year without worrying about seasonal price fluctuations and guaranteeing buyers a solid price, thus reducing financial risk for both parties.

January 2, 1974: President Nixon signs into law a bill that requires states to lower speed limits to 55 MPH in order to receive federal highway funds. The bill is designed to help conserve energy.

April 24, 1974: The Legal Services Corporation is founded by Congress under the Nixon administration as a bipartisan nonprofit federal corporation to ensure equal access to legal services under the law for all Americans.

May 31, 1974: The National Institute on Aging is founded after the federal government recognizes the need for a separate institute on aging at the 1971 White House Conference on Aging.

July 24, 1974: The Supreme Court rules, in *United States v. Richard M. Nixon,* that the White House has no claim to "executive privilege" in withholding the Watergate tapes from Special Prosecutor Jaworski. President Nixon turns over the tapes on July 30 and August 5.

August 8, 1974: In a televised address Richard Nixon announces his resignation from the presidency, effective at noon on August 9. He becomes the first president in American history to resign.

August 9, 1974: Gerald R. Ford is inaugurated as the thirty-eighth president of the United States.

August 20, 1974: President Ford nominates former New York governor Nelson A. Rockefeller for vice president. He is confirmed in December.

August 25, 1974: The Pension Benefit Guaranty Corporation is founded to ensure pension benefit payments to private sector employees who are in a defined pension program.

September 8, 1974: President Ford grants Nixon "a full, free, and absolute pardon" for any crimes he might have committed while in office. In opinion polls Ford's popularity drops from 71 percent to 49 percent.

October 10, 1974: Congress passes legislation providing for public funding of presidential primaries and elections.

October 17, 1974: The National Institute on Drug Abuse is established in response to the growing national concern over the rapid rise of casual drug use and the abuse of some prescription medications.

November 21, 1974: Over President Ford's veto Congress passes the Freedom of Information Act, increasing public access to government files.

January 19, 1975: The Nuclear Regulatory Commission is founded; its predecessor, the Atomic Energy Commission, was established in 1946 and charged with the responsibility of promoting the potential of nuclear power as an energy source and regulating its use.

February 24, 1975: The Congressional Budget Office is founded to give Congress more control over the nation's finances and to counter growing presidential power in budgeting.

April 14, 1975: The Federal Election Commission is founded, charged with enforcing the Federal Election Campaign Act of 1971, which had provisions requiring full reporting of campaign contributions and expenditures, limiting advertising in the media, and allowing corporations and labor unions to form Political Action Committees (PACs) through which they could solicit contributions.

May 2, 1975: The Labor Department announces an unemployment rate of 8.9 percent in April, the highest since 1941.

November 15, 1975: The Manpower Administration is renamed the Employment and Training Administration; its mandate is to help administer unemployment payments and to provide workers with the access and training to available jobs.

1976: *Viking I* and *Viking II* space probes land on Mars and send detailed information back to Earth about that planet's surface.

January 30, 1976: The Supreme Court upholds the provisions of the 1974 Campaign Financing Reform Act. It also requires that members of the Federal Election Commission be appointed by the president, not Congress.

May 11, 1976: The Office of Science and Technology Policy is founded to provide support and counsel to the president in matters of science and technology.

July 2, 1976: The Supreme Court upholds the death penalty laws of Georgia, Florida, and Texas. It strikes down death penalties in North Carolina and Louisiana.

January 19, 1977: The Mine Safety and Health Administration is founded; recognizing the need for setting and maintaining safety standards in mining operations, it is charged with inspecting and enforcing standards in all mines and establishing financial and criminal penalties for violation.

January 20, 1977: Jimmy Carter is inaugurated president of the United States. Walter Mondale takes the oath of office as vice president.

March 9, 1977: The Health Care Financing Administration is founded to more effectively coordinate Medicare and Medicaid and to address the issues created by escalating health care costs and the growing number of beneficiaries.

August 3, 1977: The Office of Surface Mining Reclamation and Enforcement is founded to encourage environmentally sound methods of surface coal mining and to ensure that when mined land is abandoned it is reclaimed.

October 1, 1977: The Department of Energy is founded to bring energy-related activities and programs and incorporate nuclear technology as a key component to providing an alternative energy source within the United States.

October 1, 1977: The Federal Energy Regulatory Commission is created by the Department of Energy Organization Act of 1977 to establish and oversee U.S energy policy.

March 27, 1978: The National Telecommunications and Information Administration is founded as part of the Department of Commerce as the government's adviser on domestic and international telecommunications and information technology issues.

April 18, 1978: The Senate ratifies a Panama Canal treaty that will turn control of the waterway over to Panama in 1999.

June 10, 1978: The National Council on Disability is founded as an advisory board within the Department of Education to address educational issues affecting the disabled.

June 28, 1978: The Supreme Court hands down the Bakke decision; it upholds a reverse discrimination ruling made after Allen Bakke was rejected twice for admission to California Medical School at Davis because a special-admissions minority program reduced the number of positions available for whites.

October 6, 1978: The Senate votes to extend the deadline for ratification of the Equal Rights Amendment to June 30, 1982. Thirty-five states have approved the amendment, three short of the necessary thirty-eight.

January 1, 1979: The Federal Labor Relations Authority is created under Title VII of the Civil Service Reform Act, to oversee the certification of federal employees' bargaining units and to handle labor management issues.

January 1, 1979: The Office of Special Counsel is founded; its responsibilities focus specifically on the investigation and prosecution of Prohibited Personnel Practices (PPPs) and violations of the Hatch Act which poses restrictions on the ability of certain government employees to participate in political activities.

January 1, 1979: The United States recognizes the People's Republic of China and terminates its mutua defense treaty with Taiwan.

March 26, 1979: Egyptian president Anwar Sadat and Israeli prime minister Menachem Begin sign a formal peace treaty between their two nations in a ceremony held at the White House. The peace treaty, ending thirty-one years of warfare, was based upon negotiations mediated by U.S. president Jimmy Carter at Camp David in 1978.

March 31, 1979: The Federal Emergency Management Agency is founded with the primary mission to help the country recover in the event of a nuclear attack; helping people recover from disasters is its secondary function. By the 1990s, however, the agency is transformed from a primarily national defense-oriented agency to one that proactively assists people experiencing disasters.

June 18, 1979: In Vienna the SALT II Accord, limiting production of nuclear weapons, is signed by President Carter and Soviet president Brezhnev.

June 27, 1979: The Supreme Court upholds the affirmative action program by ruling that an employer can establish voluntary programs to eliminate racial imbalance.

November 4, 1979: In Tehran several hundred Iranian militants storm the U.S. embassy and seize the diplomatic personnel. The militants announce they will release the hostages when the United States returns the shah, who is recovering from medical treatments in a New York hospital, to Iran to stand trial. President Carter declares he will not extradite the shah.

January 1, 1980: The International Trade Administration is founded with the task of promoting and developing commerce and industry in the United States.

January 4, 1980: President Jimmy Carter reacts to the Soviet invasion of Afghanistan on December 29, 1979 by withdrawing the SALT II arms-control treaty from consideration by the U.S. Senate. He also places an embargo on the sale of grain and some types of electronic equipment to the Soviet Union.

February 2, 1980: The news media report the results of a two-year sting operation (code name: Abscam) in which an FBI agent posing as a wealthy Arab offered bribes to elected officials. Among those arrested and eventually convicted on bribery or related charges are Sen. Harrison Williams Jr. (D-N.J.) and Representatives John W. Jenrette, Jr. (D-S.C.), Richard Kelly (R-Fla.), Raymond Lederer (D-Pa.), John M. Murphy (D-N.Y.), Michael Myers (D-Pa.), and Frank Thompson, Jr. (D-N.J.).

April 18, 1980: The African Development Foundation is founded to raise the standard of living in developing African countries through a unique program of grants and aid.

May 4, 1980: The Department of Education is founded; its predecessor was created by Congress in 1867 to collect information on schools and teaching that would help the states establish more effective school systems.

May 4, 1980: The Department of Health and Human Services is founded; its roots go back to the earliest days of the nation when the first marine hospital was established in 1798 to care for sailors.

June 14, 1980: The Agency for Toxic Substances and Disease Registry is founded by Congress to implement the health-related sections of the Comprehensive Environmental Response, Compensation, and Liability Act (CERCLA) that protect the public from hazardous wastes and environmental spills of hazardous substances.

July 1, 1980: The Trade and Development Agency is founded as an operating unit within the U.S. Agency for International Development to promote economic growth in developing countries while broadening the market for U.S. firms.

August 20, 1980: The Defense Department announces the development of the Stealth aircraft, which can elude detection by radar.

October 3, 1980: The U.S. Holocaust Memorial Museum is founded as a memorial for victims of the Holocaust of World War II.

January 20, 1981: The Iran hostages are freed on the same day that Reagan is inaugurated as president and George Bush is inaugurated as vice president.

March, 1981: President Reagan directs the CIA to assist "Contra" guerrilla forces opposed to the Marxist Sandinista government of Nicaragua.

April 11, 1981: President Reagan returns to the White House and a restricted work schedule after surgery and eleven days of hospitalization resulting from a March 30 assassination attempt.

June 17, 1981: The Food Safety and Inspection Service is founded to focus attention on the problem of quality and purity of food products sold to the public.

September 29, 1981: President Reagan orders the U.S. Coast Guard to turn back boatloads of Haitian refugees fleeing their country without proper immigration papers.

1982: Because three-fourths of the states have failed to ratify the Twenty-seventh (Equal Rights) Amendment, even after an extension, it dies.

January 19, 1982: The Minerals Management Service is founded to support the leasing of mineral rights to the energy industry while overseeing the industry's accountability for its financial and environmental activities.

September 1, 1982: The Health Resources and Services Administration is founded when two previous agencies of the Public Health Service—the Health Resources Administration and the Health Services Administration—are merged with the goal of meeting the health needs of minority and low-income Americans.

October 1, 1982: The House of Representatives votes down a proposed constitutional amendment requiring a balanced federal budget.

December 8, 1982: Congressman Edward Boland (D-Mass.) successfully sponsors legislation making it illegal to use U.S. funds to overthrow the Sandinista government of Nicaragua. Congress renews the amendment in 1983, 1984, and 1985, extending it through the 1986 fiscal year.

March 23, 1983: President Reagan proposes the development of a defense shield—at least partly based in space—to intercept incoming missiles. Formally called the Strategic Defense Initiative (SDI), this proposal is popularly known as "Star Wars."

April, 1983: The American public learns that the CIA assisted a Contra attack on Nicaraguan oil terminals.

October 25, 1983: U.S. troops invade Grenada after the assassination of Grenadan prime minister Maurice Bishop during a coup led by militant leftist Gen. Hudson Austin.

April 9, 1984: Nicaragua asks the International Court of Justice to rule that U.S. aid to the Contra rebels and its role in mining Nicaraguan harbors is illegal. On May 10 the court orders the United States to pay reparations to Nicaragua and to refrain from further involvement with the Contras. The United States contends that the court has no jurisdiction on the matter.

July 17, 1984: Congress passes a bill that will cut federal highway funding for states that fail to raise their minimum drinking age to twenty-one.

August 1, 1984: The U.S. Institute of Peace is founded; its first president, Richard Solomon, describes the new agency as "a complement to the military academies, which train for war fighting. We were set up to wrestle with ways to manage conflict with peaceful means."

September 26, 1984: Congress passes a law requiring tougher health warnings on cigarette packages.

October 1, 1984: The Office of Justice Programs is founded to help the nation's justice system become more effective in preventing and controlling crime by dispensing federal aid and providing assistance to law enforcement agencies.

November 26, 1984: The United States and Iraq resume diplomatic ties, severed since 1967.

1985: Israeli intelligence tells the United States that Shiite Muslims will exchange western hostages for arms for Iran.

January 20, 1985: President Reagan takes the oath of office marking the beginning of his second term; George Bush becomes vice president. Because of the bitter cold, public ceremonies are postponed until January 21.

March 12, 1985: The United States and the Soviet Union reopen formal arms-control talks in Geneva.

April 1, 1985: The National Archives and Records Administration is founded to preserve U.S. history by overseeing the management of federal records.

October 10, 1985: The U.S. Sentencing Commission is founded as a permanent independent agency for formulating national sentencing guidelines that strictly define judges' actions.

1986: The national debt soars to over $2 trillion. The trade deficit worsens as does the budget deficit.

January 1, 1986: The Pension and Welfare Benefits Administration is founded to prevent abuse and mismanagement of funds collected from employees in the private sector as part of pension and benefit plans.

January 7, 1986: President Reagan declares a state of emergency between the United States and Libya, ordering U.S. oil companies out of Libya and ending trade and transportation between the two nations.

January 28, 1986: All seven astronauts aboard the U.S. space shuttle *Challenger* perish when their craft explodes. It is the worst accident in the history of the U.S. space program.

February 25, 1986: The United States recognizes the Philippine government of Corazon Aquino after the Reagan administration at first refused to acknowledge that outgoing president Ferdinand Marcos had attempted to prevent her election victory through vote fraud.

June 25, 1986: The House approves $100 million in humanitarian and economic aid to the Contras.

July 7, 1986: The Supreme Court declares unconstitutional a key provision of the Gramm-Rudman Act that would allow the comptroller general to decide precise spending cuts in each federal department.

September 27, 1986: Congress passes the most sweeping tax-reform bill since the 1940s.

October 2, 1986: Congress overrides President Reagan's veto of the Comprehensive Anti-Apartheid Act, which condemns racial separation in South Africa, institutes an embargo on most South African imports, and bans most American investment in that nation.

November 13, 1986: President Reagan says the United States has sent Iran a few defensive weapons and spare parts, but he denies any attempt to exchange weapons for hostages.

February 4, 1987: Congress overrides President Reagan's veto of a $20 billion Clean Water Act. It is identical to an act he vetoed successfully in 1986.

February 26, 1987: The Tower Commission report places chief blame for the Iran-Contra affair on National Security Council director Robert McFarlane, Lt. Col. Oliver North, Adm. John Poindexter, and former CIA director William Casey. It also criticizes the president for remaining too remote from the planning process.

April 2, 1987: Congress overrides President Reagan's veto of an $87.5 billion highway and transit bill that also allows states to raise speed limits to 65 MPH on interstate highways in sparsely populated areas.

October 1, 1987: The Bureau of Export Administration is founded to curtail exports to enemy nations who might become powerful through trade in materials that would benefit their strategic effort.

October 19, 1987: Black Monday. The stock market plunges a record 508 points during one session.

November 18, 1987: In its final report on the Iran-Contra hearings Congress criticizes those involved in the operation for "secrecy, deception and disdain for the law."

December 8–10, 1987: During a summit meeting in Washington, D.C., President Reagan and Premier Gorbachev sign the Intermediate Nuclear Forces (INF) Treaty, agreeing to eliminate intermediate-range weapons from their nuclear arsenals.

March 22, 1988: Congress overrides President Reagan's veto of the Civil Rights Restoration Act, which extends federal antibias laws to an entire school or other organization if any of its programs receive federal funding.

May 11, 1988: The Office of Technology Policy is founded to develop policies that maximize technology's contribution to U.S. economic growth, the creation of high-wage jobs, and improvements in quality of life.

September 13, 1988: President Reagan signs a bill extending the Fair Housing Act of 1968 to protect the disabled and families with children.

September 29, 1988: The Defense Nuclear Facilities Safety Board is founded to serve as an independent oversight organization within the executive branch and is charged with advising the secretary of energy on nuclear safety issues.

October 22, 1988: Congress passes a Taxpayer's Bill of Rights.

1989: The Communist party in Poland loses power in the national elections. New governments replace the Communist regimes in Romania, Bulgaria, and Czechoslavakia.

January 20, 1989: George Bush is inaugurated president with Dan Quayle as vice president.

January 23, 1989: The Supreme Court invalidates a Richmond, Virginia, affirmative action program calling it reverse discrimination.

January 29, 1989: The Office of National Drug Control Policy is founded to establish policies for the nation's drug control program with the goal of reducing drug abuse, manufacturing, and trafficking; drug-related crime and violence; and drug-related health consequences.

October 1, 1989: The Office of Government Ethics is founded to ensure that employees of the executive branch of government perform their public duties in an ethical manner.

June 11, 1990: A constitutional amendment proposing to make the desecration of the American flag a crime is overturned by the House of Representatives.

July 26, 1990: The Americans with Disabilities Act is signed into law prohibiting discrimination on the basis of disability in employment, programs, or services provided by the government.

August 2, 1990: Iraqi forces, on the order of dictator Saddam Hussein, invade Kuwait; in response, President George Bush dispatches American military forces to the Persian Gulf.

October 22, 1990: President George Bush vetoes the Civil Rights Act of 1990 on the basis that the act would create "quotas" in the workplace.

November 15, 1990: The Clean Air Act is signed by President Bush, setting restrictions on automobile and utility emissions and the use of chlorofluorocarbons.

November 21, 1990: The Cold War is formally brought to an end with the signing of the Charter of Paris by the leaders of 34 North American and European nations.

1991: Forces from 34 nations, including the United States, overwhelm troops in Iraq and occupied Kuwait in Operation Desert Storm. On February 27, President Bush's popularity soars to 89 percent when he declares to Congress, "Kuwait is liberated."

April 18, 1991: The Administration for Children and Families is founded as part of a reorganization effort that merges former Department of Health and Human Services (HHS) agencies to deliver more comprehensive and cost-efficient services to families and to address increasing concerns over children's issues.

July 31, 1991: The Strategic Arms Reduction Treaty is signed between the United States and the Soviet Union to reduce and limit strategic offensive weaponry.

October 23, 1991: After televised Senate Judiciary Committee hearings into charges of sexual harassment made against Clarence Thomas, a federal appeals court judge, by former colleague Anita F. Hill, Thomas is sworn as Court Justice of the Supreme Court of the United States.

November 1, 1991: The National Institute for Literacy

is founded as part of the National Literacy Act with the goal of ensuring 100 percent literacy for all adults in the United States by the year 2000.

December 21, 1991: Following continued economic and political deterioration, Soviet republics with the exception of Georgia sign a pact establishing the Commonwealth of Independent States. President Gorbachev resigns on December 25, heralding the official end of the Union of Soviet Socialist Republics (U.S.S.R.).

1992: Navy Secretary H. Lawrence Grant III is forced to resign after scandal erupts from the 1991 Tailhook Association convention in Las Vegas, Nevada, where women were assaulted by members of the navy. Three navy admirals are disciplined as a result of the incident.

May 7, 1992: The Twenty-seventh Amendment to the Constitution is ratified barring pay raises for members of Congress between terms.

October 1, 1992: The Substance Abuse and Mental Health Services Administration is founded to provide federal research and service activities in the areas of substance abuse and mental health.

December 9, 1992: Twenty-eight thousand U.S. troops are sent to Somalia in Operation Restore Hope, an effort to stem widespread famine and restore order among warring clans.

December 17, 1992: The North American Free Trade Agreement (NAFTA) is signed by the leaders of the United States, Canada, and Mexico to abolish most restrictions on trade between the countries.

January 20, 1993: Bill Clinton is inaugurated president with Al Gore as vice president.

January 25, 1993: The National Economic Council is founded by President Bill Clinton as an advisory council to help formulate and coordinate economic policy throughout the government in both domestic and international arenas.

February 5, 1993: The Family and Medical Leave Act is enacted, entitling eligible employees to take up to 12 weeks of unpaid, job-protected leave for specific family or medical reasons.

March 3, 1993: The National Partnership for Reinventing Government is founded when President Bill Clinton appoints Vice President Al Gore head of the National Performance Review; Gore is given six months to study the problems associated with the federal government and then report recommendations for improvement.

March 12, 1993: Janet Reno is sworn in as the first woman attorney general of the United States.

September 21, 1993: The Corporation for National and Community Service is founded as a fulfillment of a campaign promise by President Bill Clinton to institute and revitalize America's long-standing commitment to community service.

November 30, 1993: President Clinton signs the Brady Bill, which requires a five-day waiting period for hand gun purchases. The bill is named after President Ronald Reagan's press secretary who was wounded while protecting the president in an assassination attempt.

May 6, 1994: A unprecedented sexual-harassment suit is filed against President Bill Clinton by a former Arkansas state employee, Paula Jones.

July 26–August 5, 1994: Congressional hearings take place concerning the Whitewater affair, questionable financial dealings that took place in the 1980s linked to President Bill Clinton and First Lady Hillary Rodham Clinton.

July 30, 1994: In *Madsen v. Women's Health Center, Inc.* the Supreme Court rules to inhibit pro-life activists from blocking public access of abortion clinics and from physically abusing persons entering or leaving the clinic.

August 28, 1994: U.S. Forces occupy Haiti and force General Cédras to step down, restoring President Jean-Bertand Aristide to power.

October 15, 1994: The Farm Service Agency is created by the secretary of agriculture to centralize the government's farm programs, assuming functions of the Agricultural Stabilization and Conservation Service, the Farmers Home Administration, and the Federal Crop Insurance Corporation.

December 7, 1994: The National Resources Conservation Service is founded to study and treat the growing problem of resource erosion and depletion.

June 5, 1995: The White House Office for Women's Initiatives and Outreach is founded to serve as a liaison between the White House and women's groups around the country and to ensure that the concerns of women are heard by the administration.

November, 1995: Serbs, Muslims, and Croats of Bosnia sign a U.N.-brokered peace accord after the United States conducts limited air raids on the country, which led the warring parties to the negotiation table.

December 31, 1995: The Agency for Health Care Policy and Research is founded to establish new research initiatives in all areas of health care, including technology and information dissemination, serving not only policymakers but also consumers, health care providers, researchers, and health plan purchasers.

February 8, 1996: The Telecommunications Act is signed by President Bill Clinton; its objectives include allowing all Americans access to the Information Superhighway and developing technology that will allow parents to have more control over the type of television programming watched by their children.

April 9, 1996: President Bill Clinton signs a bill permitting line item veto, or the veto of specific spending or taxing provisions of legislation, modifying past stipulations that allowed a president to veto an entire bill only.

May 20, 1996: In *Romer v. Evans* the Supreme Court rules to overturn an amendment to the Colorado constitution that prohibits extending legal protection from discrimination to homosexuals, stating it violates the Fourteenth Amendment's equal protection clause.

June 13, 1996: The Supreme Court rules in *Shaw v. Hunt* that a redistricting plan in North Carolina assigning voters to a district based mainly on their race is unconstitutional, violating the Fourteenth Amendment.

June 26, 1996: The case of *United States v. Virginia* is decided by the Supreme Court, finding the male-only admission policy of the Virginia Military Institute (a public institute of higher learning) to be unconstitutional.

August 22, 1996: President Bill Clinton signs into law the Personal Responsibility and Work Opportunity Reconciliation Act, replacing previous welfare programs with one requiring work in exchange for monetary assistance.

1997: Congress passes a bill reducing funds for Medicare by $115 billion over five years.

January 20, 1997: Bill Clinton begins a second term in office.

May 27, 1997: Denying an attempt by President Bill Clinton to delay a sexual harassment lawsuit initiated by former employee Paula Jones, the Supreme Court decides in *Clinton v. Jones* that a serving president is not entitled to immunity for actions previous to or outside of office responsibilities.

June 26, 1997: Two Supreme Court cases challenging the ban against physician-assisted suicide are overturned. In *Vacco v. Quill* and *Washington v. Glucksberg*, the court rules that states may continue denying terminally-ill patients the right to a doctor's assistance in ending their lives.

June 26, 1997: The Supreme Court rules in *Reno v. American Civil Liberties Union* that a 1996 law prohibiting "indecent" material from being displayed on the Internet is unconstitutional, violating the First Amendment right of free speech.

June 27, 1997: In *Printz v. United States* the Supreme Court overturns a provision of gun control legislation (Brady Bill) requiring local law enforcement officers to perform background checks on potential handgun purchasers.

August 5, 1997: President Bill Clinton signs a federal budget bill promising to balance the budget by 2002.

January 21, 1998: Reports of an alleged sexual relationship between President Bill Clinton and former White House intern Monica S. Lewinsky surface. President Clinton denies the allegations.

March 4, 1998: The Supreme Court rules that sexual discrimination in the workplace extends to include same-sex sexual harassment in *Oncale v. Sundowner Offshore Services, Inc.*

May 22, 1998: Federal judge Norma Holloway Johnson rules against White House attempts to protect aides from testifying in accusations against the president by citing executive privilege by ruling that the Secret Service must testify before the grand jury.

June 25, 1998: The Supreme Court rules in *Bragdon v. Abbott* that individuals with HIV, even if they are not suffering from symptoms of AIDS, are protected from discrimination under the Americans with Disabilities Act.

June 25, 1998: In *Clinton v. New York City* the Supreme Court strikes down the line-item veto law, stating that giving the president power to veto specific items in spending bills is unconstitutional and disrupts the balance of power.

September 9, 1998: Independent Counsel Kenneth Starr submits to Congress a 445-page report documenting evidence collected during an investigation of President Clinton, triggering the first impeachment review against a president since Watergate.

October 29, 1998: Seventy-seven year old John Glenn and six fellow astronauts take off aboard the space shuttle *Discovery.* Glenn was the first American to orbit the earth in 1962. The launch, the 123rd in the U.S. space program, makes Glenn the oldest person to go into space. NASA plans extensive medical studies on Glenn to determine how space travel effects older people.

November, 1998: The House Judiciary Committee begins hearings on whether or not to recommend impeachment of President Clinton to the House of Representatives.

Administration for Children and Families (ACF)

PARENT ORGANIZATION: Department of Health and Human Services
ESTABLISHED: April 18, 1991
EMPLOYEES: 1,800

Contact Information:

ADDRESS: 370 L'Enfant Promenade SW
Washington, DC 20447
PHONE: (202) 401-9200
URL: http://www.acf.dhhs.gov
ASSISTANT SECRETARY: Olivia Golden

WHAT IS ITS MISSION?

The mission of the Administration for Children and Families (ACF) is to promote the economic self-sufficiency of families and the well-being of children. Since the ACF was created in 1991 by merging the Family Support Administration and the Office of Human Development, its mission has been focused on moving families from financial support programs to financial independence.

HOW IS IT STRUCTURED?

The Administration for Children and Families (ACF) is part of the U.S. Department of Health and Human Services (HHS), which is a cabinet-level department of the executive branch of the federal government. The ACF is overseen by an assistant secretary who is nominated by the president and confirmed by the Senate. ACF administrative offices include the Office of Public Affairs, which produces public information, publications, and educational materials, and the Office of State Systems, which assists states in administering ACF programs.

The seven divisions headquartered in Washington, D.C., that administer ACF programs are the Administration on Children, Youth, and Families, the Administration on Developmental Disabilities, the Administration for Native Americans, the Office of Child Support Enforcement, the Office of Community Services, the Office of Refugee Resettlement, and the Office of Family Assistance. The ACF also operates ten regional

offices throughout the United States, which oversee and provide technical support to ACF programs administered in their regions.

BUDGET:

Administration for Children and Families

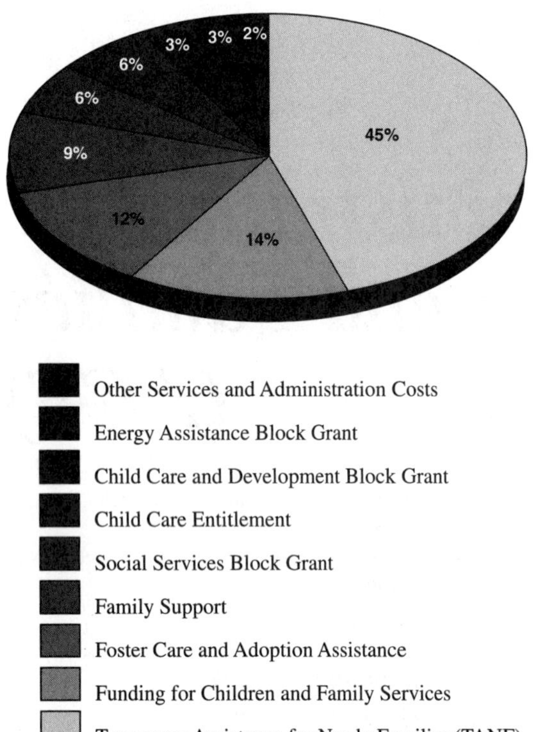

PRIMARY FUNCTIONS

The Administration for Children and Families (ACF) is responsible for programs that address the needs of American children and families. The ACF provides financial and employment assistance, child care and child protective services, and it makes grants to states and communities for social services for families. Child protective services include child abuse prevention and treatment programs and foster care and adoption programs that provide stable homes for abused or hard-to-place children. Social service grants fund a variety of programs including day care, preschool, after school care, tutoring, counseling, and recreational services. The ACF works closely with other HHS divisions and government agencies by researching the needs of children and families and cooperating in interagency program partnerships.

PROGRAMS

The ACF administers more than sixty programs for children and families. The Social Services Block Grants program provides almost $3 billion to states to fund a wide range of social services. State and local governments must determine community needs and present action plans to apply for these funds. Grants have funded child and adult abuse prevention and treatment programs, employment and job training services, services for children with disabilities, and child care programs.

The Child Support Enforcement program ensures children are financially supported by both parents. Enforcement programs are usually run by state or local agencies that provide services free-of-charge to families receiving federal financial assistance and at a low or state-paid rate for families that are not receiving government financial assistance. The program helps families obtain child support payments by locating absent parents, establishing paternity, establishing legal child support obligations, and enforcing child support orders. The agency processes about four million requests to locate absent parents annually, about eighty percent of which an address is found for. In 1995 about $10 billion in child support payments was collected through the CSE, and paternity was established for more than 590,000 children, clearing the way for child support orders.

The ACF also administers the Low Income Home Energy Assistance Program, which provides grants to states, territories, and tribal organizations to help low-income households with heating and cooling costs and energy-saving repairs. In 1995 the program provided more than $3 million to almost seven million households for heating, cooling, weatherization, and energy crisis assistance. And the Refugee Assistance Program has been successful in helping more than 125,000 refugees each year achieve economic self-sufficiency and social adjustment. This program offers cash and medical assistance, social services, preventative health services, a matching grant program, and a targeted assistance program.

BUDGET INFORMATION

The 1998 budget of the ACF was approximately $37.2 billion and was appropriated by Congress. The largest amount of the budget, $16.7 billion (45 percent), went to the Temporary Assistance for Needy Families (TANF) program. Second to the TANF was funding for children and family services, consuming approximately 14 percent of the ACF budget; the Head Start program accounted for most of this money (12 percent of the total ACF budget). The rest of the budget was divided as follows: payments to states for foster care and adoption assistance, 12 percent; payments to states for family support, 9 percent; social services block grant, 6 percent; child care entitlement, 6 percent; childcare and development block grant, 3 percent; and energy assistance block grant (LIHEAP), 3 percent. About 2 percent of the ACF budget went to other services and included administration costs.

HISTORY

The Administration for Children and Families (ACF) was created on April 18, 1991, as part of a reorganization effort that merged two former Department of Health and Human Services (HHS) agencies, the Office of Human Development and the Family Support Administration. Before they were combined into the ACF, the Office of Human Development oversaw mental health and child welfare programs for families, and the Family Support Administration handled financial assistance and employment programs. These agencies were combined to deliver more comprehensive and cost-efficient services. The ACF brought together several long-standing programs, including the Children's Bureau, which was established in 1912 to address increasing concern over children's issues such as child labor, child abuse, and education. Also transferred to the ACF were programs from other HHS divisions such as the Head Start program, which was created under the Office of Economic Opportunity in 1965. New ACF programs were also created with the establishment of the Temporary Assistance for Needy Families program in 1994.

CURRENT POLITICAL ISSUES

After much debate, on August 22, 1996, President Bill Clinton signed into law the Personal Responsibility and Work Opportunity Act (PRWOA), a comprehensive, bipartisan welfare reform plan. The PRWOA replaced guaranteed financial assistance programs with the Temporary Assistance for Needy Families program, which requires families to work in order to be eligible for assistance. It also limits the amount of time assistance may be received to five years.

Opponents of the PRWOA argued the plan would be disastrous for children living in poverty whose parents could not or would not seek work or comply with the plan's other requirements. Many also believed the PRWOA did not make adequate provisions for child-care assistance and that children would receive substandard care if their parents could not earn enough money or were terminated from assistance. The PRWOA also made no allowances for families facing extreme hardships or emergencies that would necessitate assistance beyond the five-year eligibility limit.

Supporters of the plan argued that previous assistance programs allowed recipients to depend on the federal government for support indefinitely and that it provided no motivation for parents to seek work to improve their family's standard of living. They also argued that reducing the number of families receiving assistance and the amount of assistance received would free up limited federal dollars for programs that would help families through job training, child care support, and job subsidies. To counter objections, the federal government also pledged to strengthen programs that would assist families making the transition from welfare to work, such as Head Start, the earned income tax credit, and child support enforcement.

Case Study: Child Support Enforcement

Studies showed in 1994 that 11.5 million families with children had a parent living elsewhere. Of these, 54 percent had awards or agreements for child support. But of the $17.7 billion owed for child support $5.8 billion went unpaid. Also, among those due support payments, about one-half received the full amount, about one-quarter received partial payment, and about one-quarter received no payment.

Upon passage of the PRWOA, the federal government promised to continue strengthening the ACF's Child Support Enforcement program to provide the additional income to families in order to make assistance unnecessary or to ease the transition from welfare to work. The PRWOA instituted enforcement measures that were projected to increase child support collections by $24 billion and reduce federal welfare costs by $4 billion by 2006. Specifically, the new federal law requires each state to operate a child support enforcement program, and it requires new hires to register with

FAST FACTS

As a result of the Personal Responsibility and Work Opportunity Reconciliation Act (1996), 1.7 million former welfare recipients gained employment, and welfare case loads decreased by 27 percent, as of March 1997.

(Source: Administration for Children and Families. "Press Release," August 4, 1998.)

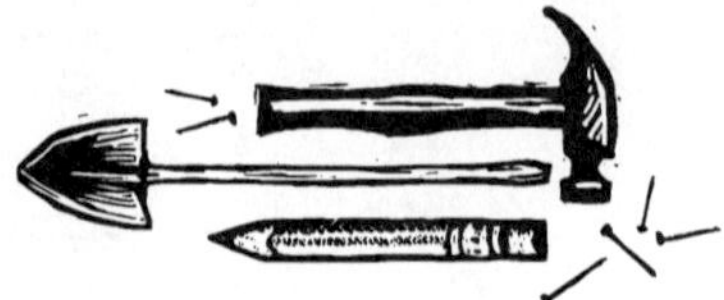

GET INVOLVED:

Each bureau in the ACF's Administration for Children, Youth, and Families division employs student interns. Internship programs are offered throughout the school year; some summer positions are available. Many interns are social work students or individuals interested in pursuing social work as a career, but all are welcome to apply. There is no formal process for selecting interns. A resume and writing sample are usually requested, and interviews are conducted to determine proper placement. To pursue an internship contact the Department of Health and Human Services at DHHS/ACF, 330 C St. SW, Washington, DC 20201.

a national directory so that those who owe child support may be found.

The PRWOA also calls for tougher penalties and streamlined paternity establishment. Penalties for non-payment of child support may include the docking of income tax refunds, docking military or government benefits, or criminal prosecution. Paternity is to be established at birth and recorded on original birth certificates. Establishing paternity for older children will require fewer legal proceedings and, once established, paternity will be nationally recognized, eliminating the need for determining paternity in each state a child may reside in. The ACF is expected to play a major role in developing new guidelines for child support enforcement programs, in overseeing the administration of state programs, and in providing funding.

SUCCESSES AND FAILURES

Since its creation in 1991 the Administration for Children and Families (ACF) has weathered many program changes, restructuring, and the implementation of new initiatives. The Child Care Development Fund, established in 1996, has been particularly successful. This fund has made more than $3 billion available to low-income families and those making the transition off welfare. Moneys are put toward child care so that parents can work or attend training or education programs. Parents in the program select a legally-operating child care provider and receive subsidies through certificates or contracted programs. A minimum of four percent of Child Care Development Fund moneys must be used to improve the quality of child-care and offer additional services to parents, such as resource and referral counseling regarding the selection of appropriate child care providers.

FUTURE DIRECTIONS

The ACF will face challenges in carrying out its mission in the face of changes made to welfare programs in 1996. Programs such as Aid to Families with Dependent Children and Job Opportunities and Basic Skills Training are expected to be phased out. The Temporary Assistance for Needy Families program on the other hand, is expected to be put into long-term action as welfare case loads decrease.

Crafters of the Adoption 2002 initiative hope to double the number of children adopted each year by 2002. The ACF will assist in developing strategies to move children more quickly from foster care to permanent homes. Adoption 2002 establishes federal goals for a child welfare system: safety, well-being, and permanency. States will be encouraged to achieve Adoption 2002 goals by means of increased technical assistance and per-child financial bonuses. Federal regulations regarding adoption will also be streamlined.

AGENCY RESOURCES

The ACF's National Center on Child Abuse and Neglect operates a clearinghouse of research materials, studies, reports, and other information on the prevention, identification, and treatment of child abuse and neglect. The center's catalogs can be viewed on-line at http://www.calib.com/nccanch or may be ordered by calling (202) 205-8646. Also, the Child Care Bureau operates the National Child Care Information Center, which provides child care information to states, providers, parents, and the general public. This center may be contacted by phone at 1-800-616-2242, by fax at 1-800-716-2242, or on-line at http://ercicps.ed.uiuc.edu/nccic.

AGENCY PUBLICATIONS

The Office of Child Support Enforcement publishes reports and handbooks, including the *Child Support Enforcement Guide.* Materials can be viewed on-line at http://www.acf.dhhs.gov/programs/cse. The National Clearinghouse on Families and Youth produces booklets such as *Supporting Your Adolescent: Tips for Parents, Reconnecting Youth and Community,* and *Surviving Adolescence.* For information on these and other publications, call (301) 608-8098, fax (301) 608-8721, or access them on-line at http://www.acf.dhhs.gov/programs/fysb.

BIBLIOGRAPHY

Brookman, Amber. "A Winning Formula for Welfare Reform." *USA Today,* 29 January 1997.

DeWan, George. "Student Briefing Page on the News." *Newsday,* 29 March 1995.

Fuentes, Frank, Virginia D. Cantu and Robert Stechuk. "Migrant Head-Start: What Does It Mean to Involve Parents in Program Services?" *Children Today,* 22 June 1996.

Geier, Thom. "Young and Abused." *U.S. News and World Report,* 30 September 1996.

Lewis, Anne C. "Trends in the Well-Being of America's Children and Youth." *Education Digest,* December 1996.

Moran, Julio. "LACA Turns the Corner After 2 Years of Turmoil." *Los Angeles Times,* 1 January 1995.

Rowe, Pat. "ACF Supports Efforts to Serve Teen Parents." *Children Today,* winter–spring 1994.

Shanahan, Eileen. "Creating the Deadbeat Clearinghouse." *Governing,* January 1997.

Thibodeau, Patrick. "Welfare Agencies Off Schedule." *Computerworld,* 3 March 1997.

Administration on Aging (AoA)

PARENT ORGANIZATION: Department of Health and Human Services
ESTABLISHED: 1965
EMPLOYEES: 175

Contact Information:

ADDRESS: 330 Independence Ave. SW
Washington, DC 20201
PHONE: (202) 401-4541
TOLL FREE: (800) 677-1116
TDD (HEARING IMPAIRED): (202) 401-7575
FAX: (202) 260-1012
E-MAIL: esec@ban-gate.aoa.dhhs.gov
URL: http://www.aoa.dhhs.gov
ASSISTANT SECRETARY FOR AGING: Jeanette C. Takamura

WHAT IS ITS MISSION?

The mission of the Administration on Aging (AoA) is "to enable the Department [of Health and Human Services] to respond to the diverse needs of our aging population." The agency focuses on fulfilling the goals of the Older Americans Act, which details the services that are to be provided to senior Americans. The AoA leads the nation in promoting the vision that aging is a process, not a stage of life.

HOW IS IT STRUCTURED?

The Administration on Aging (AoA) is an independent entity within the Department of Health and Human Services (HHS), a cabinet-level department in the executive branch of the federal government. The AoA is headquartered in Washington, D.C., and it operates ten regional offices throughout the country. The agency works closely with state and local area agencies on aging in planning, coordinating, and delivering services funded by it to meet the unique needs of seniors. The AoA is headed by the assistant secretary for aging, who is appointed by the president and confirmed by the Senate.

PRIMARY FUNCTIONS

The Administration on Aging (AoA) provides funding for a range of programs that offer services and opportunities for older Americans, especially economically-disadvantaged and low-income minority seniors,

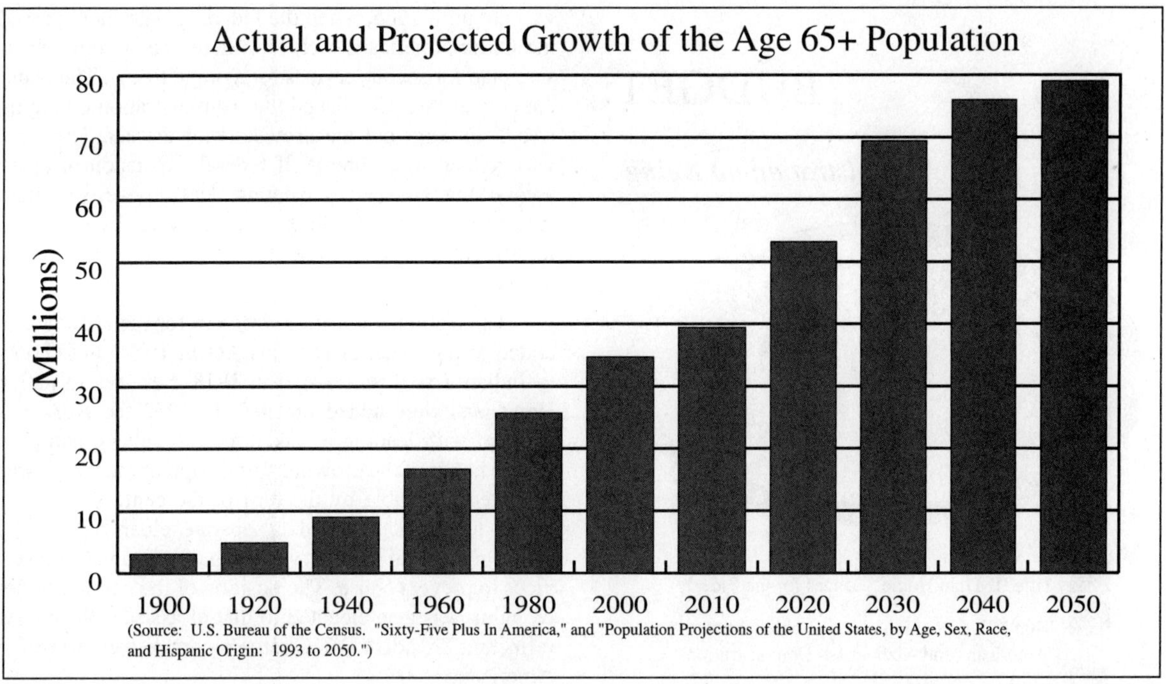

(Source: U.S. Bureau of the Census. "Sixty-Five Plus In America," and "Population Projections of the United States, by Age, Sex, Race, and Hispanic Origin: 1993 to 2050.")

according to the provisions of the Older Americans Act. The agency builds the nation's knowledge and understanding of aging through research, project demonstrations, training, and technical assistance, which are provided to community organizations. As the lead government agency relating to aging, the AoA also advises the Department of Health and Human Services and other agencies on the needs and characteristics of older Americans.

PROGRAMS

Title III of the Older Americans Act directs the Administration on Aging (AoA) to fund programs designed to assist both active older persons and those at risk of losing their independence. Title III funds pay for state and local supportive services, nutrition services, and senior centers. One of the most widespread programs funded by the AoA is the Elderly Nutrition Program. Begun in 1972, the program provides nourishing meals and companionship to more than three million older people each year. Because of this program, older persons who might otherwise be isolated or lonely, or those who cannot grocery shop or prepare meals, have the opportunity to obtain low- or no-cost nutritious meals at senior centers that also provide social activities. The nutrition program also delivers meals to home bound seniors, and volunteer deliverers often spend additional time visiting with recipients and assisting them with other needs. The meals provide forty to fifty percent of suggested daily nutrients, and participants have more social contact than they otherwise might.

The AoA also funds programs for seniors in nursing homes and other long-term care facilities. One of the most important programs for older Americans is the Ombudsman Program, for which state and local ombudsmen speak and act on behalf of the 2.5 million residents of care facilities. Complaints are made and investigated through this program, and anyone may register a complaint. These include complaints regarding accidents, menus, personal hygiene care, staff attitudes, unanswered calls for assistance, or any other issue that is detrimental to a resident's well being. After an investigation an ombudsman works with the necessary agencies and officials to resolve problems. The program also operates at the state and federal levels to resolve major issues affecting large numbers of residents. The Ombudsman Program assisted more than 100,000 people in 1996 and served many more through input on regulations governing care facilities.

BUDGET INFORMATION

The budget for AOA was approximately $871 million in 1998. All funds for the AOA are appropriated by Congress and correspond to the services or service areas specified in the title sections of the Older Americans Act. Thirty-four percent of the budget is allocated to Title III-B, ombudsmen, elder abuse, and supportive services. Nutrition services, under Title III-C, receive 56 percent of the total budget for congregate meals (43 percent) and home-delivered meals (13 percent). Two percent of the AOA budget pays for administrative

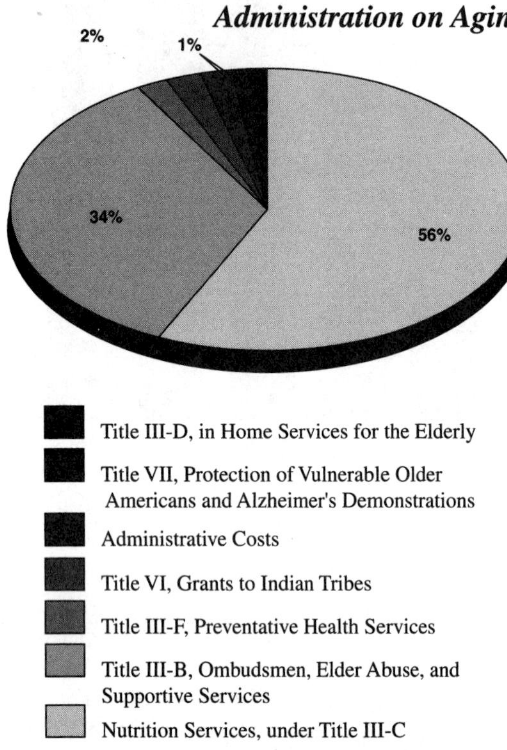

costs. The remaining funds pay for Title III-D, in-home services for the frail and elderly (1 percent); Title III-F, preventative health services (2 percent); Title IV, research and training demonstrations (1 percent); Title VI, grants to Indian tribes (2 percent); and Title VII, protection of vulnerable older Americans (1 percent); and Alzheimer's disease demonstrations (1 percent). State Agencies on Aging receive Title III funds based on the number of older persons in the state and then allocate funds to local Area Agencies on Aging (AAOA) based on older persons in the service areas. AAOAs provide direct services or contract with other organizations to provide services.

HISTORY

The U.S. government has traditionally provided limited financial assistance for older Americans, from pensions for widows of soldiers of the American Revolution (1775–83) to Social Security, which was established in the 1930s to provide old-age benefits to workers. But it was not until 1965, when the federal government passed the Older Americans Act, that there was a comprehensive plan for social services for aging citizens. The Older Americans Act established the Administration on Aging (AoA) to carry out the provisions of the act. The AoA was created in a climate of federal expansion in many areas of human services to counteract the poverty of older Americans. By the 1960s people were living much longer, so there were more older Americans with diverse needs.

The National Nutrition Program for the Elderly was added to the Older Americans Act in 1972, and Grants to Indian Tribes was added in 1978. Services to native Hawaiians were added in 1987. In 1992 the AoA was charged with leading a task force to evaluate and plan for the needs of the growing aging population, which was expected to double by the turn of the century. Amendments to the act created a separate elder rights title, including ombudsman services, legal assistance, and services to prevent abuse. The position of the commissioner on aging was also elevated to that of assistant secretary, reflecting President Bill Clinton's commitment to senior Americans.

CURRENT POLITICAL ISSUES

In the mid-1990s Republicans in Congress attempted to reduce the federal programs they believed should be run by states and localities. Because programs funded by the Administration on Aging (AoA) were coordinated and administered by states and localities, the agency became a target for elimination. Those favoring termination of the AoA said the federal government was not intended to meet all needs of all segments of the population. They argued that the federal budget should be brought into balance and that federal funds should support programs affecting all citizens or those concerned with the national interest. They proposed that each state have the right to decide its own funding levels for services to the aging and prioritize which services should be provided, without federal guidance or oversight.

Supporters of the AoA, including the administration of President Bill Clinton and senior citizens' organizations, defended the AoA and the need for continued federal involvement in issues and services related to aging. They said the AoA, through the Older Americans Act, provides a minimum level of service to a population heavily made up of low-income and ill people. AoA services must be guaranteed to all seniors by federal law, they argued. These groups also pointed out that longer life expectancy and the growing numbers of aging persons have necessitated comprehensive national planning, as seniors impact economies, health care systems, tax bases, and legal issues.

Opponents of the AoA could not gather enough votes in Congress to eliminate the agency. The AoA continues to operate, but issues related to its role are revisited during congressional budget debates.

SUCCESSES AND FAILURES

In the 1990s the Administration on Aging (AoA) expanded its programs to meet the needs of aging persons who were still active. The AoA's Older Americans Act Eldercare Volunteer Corps uses the talents of more than half a million senior volunteers who assist with programs supported by the act. The corps also supports volunteer programs that place senior volunteers in preschool, school, and after-school programs as tutors, mentors, role models, and surrogate grandparents. Senior volunteers also work with Head Start program children and their parents. They act as counselors to troubled youth and as providers of respite care for handicapped children. More than three million Americans have benefited from the services of senior volunteers and many millions of dollars have been reallocated because of savings made possible by senior volunteer services.

The AoA has also implemented an effective Disaster Preparedness and Response program to assist older persons in their homes and local communities within 48 hours of presidentially-declared disasters. Through this program states target special assistance at older persons, including case management, temporary relocation assistance, identification of losses, filing of claims, and facilitation of chore services, meals, repairs, and transportation. The AoA released $500,000 in April 1997 to assist older persons affected by flooding in the Ohio River Valley. These funds payed for individual assistance to seniors and made it possible for services such as meal delivery to continue.

FUTURE DIRECTIONS

The Administration on Aging's future challenges lie in maintaining service levels while planning for a growing aging population. To this end the agency has established an initiative on redefining retirement, which laid the foundation for changing behaviors, attitudes, and choices in planning for aging. The initiative seeks to educate and motivate baby boomers so that they will make better choices now to protect their futures. The initiative will bring together public- and private-sector leaders to begin a process of setting national planning objectives for an aging society. Partnerships will also be established with other federal agencies and with state governments to explore the impact of an aging population on economies and policy making. A National Academy on Aging will serve as a resource for information on policy issues associated with the Older Americans Act, Medicare, Medicaid, and Social Security.

FAST FACTS

A child born in 1997 can expect to live 75.5 years, about 28 years longer than a child born in 1900.

(Source: Fernando Torres-Gil. "Challenging Times for the Aging Network." *Aging,* March 1, 1996.)

AGENCY RESOURCES

The Elder Care Locator is a public service of the Administration on Aging (AoA) that provides a national directory of local support services for aging Americans. It provides names and telephone numbers of organizations within a specific location in the United States. Information is available for a variety of services including meal programs, home care, transportation, home repair, recreational and social activities, volunteer programs, and legal services. Search the Elder Care Locator on-line at http://www2.ageinfo.org/naicweb/elderloc or call 1-800-677-1116.

The National Aging Information Center, operated by the Administration on Aging, is a central source for a wide range of policy and program materials and demographic and statistical data on the health, economic, and social status of older Americans. Staff provides responses to user inquiries, or the center's bibliographical databases can be searched on-line at http://www.ageinfo.org/bibinfo.html. Call the center at (202) 619-7501, fax (202) 401-7620, or E-mail naic@ban-gate.aoa.dhhs.gov.

To assist seniors in accessing the wealth of on-line information regarding services for seniors, the Department of Health and Human Services (HHS), acting through the Health Care Financing Administration, provided senior centers with computers in 1997. In doing so the HHS made it easier to access up-to-date information of interest to seniors, particularly the AoA Web site at http://www.aoa.dhhs.gov.

AGENCY PUBLICATIONS

The National Aging Information Center collects and makes available Title IV projects, AoA reports, statistical data, newsletters, training materials, and books on aging and aging issues. A complete list of available materials can be viewed on-line at http://www.aoa.dhhs.gov/naic, and materials may be ordered by calling (202) 619-7501 or by faxing (202) 401-7620.

BIBLIOGRAPHY

"Conference on Older Women Leads to New AoA Initiative." *Aging,* Fall 1994.

LaRock, Seymour. "Helping the Boomers Plan for Retirement." *Employee Benefit Plan Review,* August 1996.

Mixsom, Paula M. "How Adult Protective Services Evolved, and Obstacles to Ethical Casework." *Aging,* 1 March 1996.

Muha, Laura. "The Essence of Caregiving: A Guide to Making Decisions and Finding Help When a Loved One's Health Is Failing." *Newsday,* 22 April 1995.

"National Resources on Elder Abuse." *Aging,* 1 March 1996.

Parsons, Robert-Bruce Higley. "Assessing the Needs of Our Elders." *Public Management,* 1 February 1995.

Torres-Gil, Fernando. "Challenging Times for the Aging Network." *Aging,* 1 March 1996.

Wilcox, Melynda Dovel. "New Help with Your Pension Problems." *Kiplinger's Personal Finance Magazine,* December 1994.

Administrative Office of the United States Courts (AO)

ESTABLISHED: August 7, 1939
EMPLOYEES: 1,200

Contact Information:

ADDRESS: One Columbus Circle NE
Washington, DC 20544
PHONE: (202) 273-1120
URL: http://www.uscourts.gov
DIRECTOR: L. Ralph Mecham

WHAT IS ITS MISSION?

The mission of the Administrative Office of the United States Courts (AO) is to provide a variety of support functions to the United States federal judiciary. The AO prepares and submits the budget for the courts to the Judicial Conference for approval by Congress. It analyzes legislation from Congress that will affect the courts' operations or personnel, and it interprets and applies the new laws. It also provides administrative help to members of the courts in the form of clerks, pretrial officers, court reporters, and public defenders.

HOW IS IT STRUCTURED?

The Administrative Office of the United States Courts (AO) is part of the judicial branch of the U.S. government. Its director is appointed by the Chief Justice of the Supreme Court in consultation with the Judicial Conference of the United States, the body that sets the national and legislative policy of the federal judiciary. The Judicial Conference is composed of the chief judges from each judicial and geographic circuit and the chief judge of the Court of International Trade; it directs and supervises the AO.

The AO operates through an Associate Director for Management and Operations, an Associate Director, and a General Counsel. It also works through various offices in the federal judiciary including the Office of Congressional, External, and Public Affairs; the Office of Judicial Conference Executive Secretariat; the Office of Court Programs; the Office of Facilities, Security, and

FAST FACTS

Prisoners on death row wait an average of ten years before they are executed because of the lengthy legal reviews and appeals that usually take place.

(Source: Ted Gest. "A House Without a Blueprint: After 20 Years, the Death Penalty is Still Being Meted Out Unevenly." *U.S. News and World Report,* July 8, 1996.)

Administrative Services; the Office of Finance and Budget; the Office of Human Resources and Statistics; the Office of Information Technology; and the Office of Judges Programs. Each of these offices is responsible for its own specific area such as staffing, the functioning of specific courts, budget analysis, employee training, and technology support and training.

PRIMARY FUNCTIONS

The Administrative Office of the United States Courts (AO) manages spending, compiles and publishes statistics on the courts, and presents studies and recommendations on making the court system more efficient. Recommendations are made in regard to staffing, salaries, the number of judges needed, and the budgeting of public defenders. These responsibilities fall ultimately on the director. Under its legislative mandate the AO also supervises bankruptcy courts, federal magistrate judges, and federal defenders.

The AO works closely with people and institutions concerned with the operations of the court system such as the general public, congressional committees, government agencies, and state courts. The AO provides secretarial, legal, and statistical services for the Judicial Conference, and it is responsible for any new or changing duties requested by the Judicial Conference or the U.S. Supreme Court. The AO also audits offices of the judiciary.

PROGRAMS

The programs of the Administrative Office of the United States Courts (AO) are as varied as its functions. Programs aim at maximizing the effectiveness of the federal court system. For example, the Methods Analysis Program identifies the most efficient methods of administration, and in 1996 the National Academy of Public Administration completed a study of the most effective alternative court structures and practices.

Many programs deal with the use of new technologies, such as the launching of a new data communications network in the judiciary and an automated bankruptcy noticing system. In a bankruptcy case, the courts must inform the creditors involved that the business that owes them money has filed for bankruptcy protection. The new notification system will allow the courts to notify these creditors electronically en masse instead of individually through the mail. If one-quarter of all notices are sent electronically, the AO estimates the judiciary will save almost $4 million annually.

The Court Personnel System manages staffing and facilitates the decentralization of the agency. By allowing court managers to determine how to best budget their own funds, within limits set by the AO, courts can better address their own needs. The result is a more expedient and thrifty judicial system that consumes a decreasing percentage of the overall federal judiciary budget each year.

BUDGET INFORMATION

The overall budget appropriated by the US. Congress for the AO in 1998 was an estimated $54 million. This represents an increase of about 23 percent since 1991. Faced, however, with the federal government's goal to economize, the agency has practiced a hiring freeze in recent years and as a result, has reduced staffing from previous levels.

HISTORY

The court system in the United States began in the 1800s with few cases. It was a small, simple operation with no legal guidelines for its management. But as the population and the number of states grew, more and more court cases arose, causing the judicial system to expand and complexify. With this growing complexity came the need for increased efficiency, which requires that specific attention and organization be given to improving court operations.

For nearly one hundred years the Department of Justice handled these managerial responsibilities. Finally, however, the work load became so burdensome that in 1939 Congress created the Administrative Office of the United States Courts (AO) to handle administrative duties for federal courts. The AO was also assigned to continually study, research, and make recommendations on the running of the court system.

With the ever increasing work load of the federal judicial system, the duties of the AO have grown accordingly, and it is considered a cornerstone of the federal judicial system. Faced with a reduced federal budget, the AO has been charged with maximizing its effectiveness within budgetary limitations. In the 1980s the AO began to reorganize, delegating to the courts themselves many of the administrative responsibilities that Congress had originally granted to the AO, thus decentralizing its responsibilities and streamlining its own operation.

CURRENT POLITICAL ISSUES

In an effort to address concerns about crime, Congress passed legislation in the 1990s that turned many state offenses into federal crimes, whose penalties are stricter and often carry mandatory sentencing guidelines. For example, carjacking that results in death is punishable in federal court with a life sentence without parole. Formerly the crime would have been handled according to a weaker state law. Congress proposes to reclassify thousands of other crimes as federal offenses including domestic violence, child pornography, and defacement of religious property.

But tougher federal laws have caused problems in the federal court system. More criminals have been removed from the streets, but more judges, personnel, and prisons are needed for them. Whether this system is appropriate has been called into question. From 1980 to 1990, for example, the number of federal prosecutors doubled, but the number of drug cases tried in federal courts jumped from 3,100 to 16,400, more than five hundred percent. The number of federal district judges available to try these cases increased only 11 percent, from 516 to 575. In addition, new mandatory sentencing guidelines for third-time offenders mean that more people are spending more time in prison, causing a need for more incarceration facilities.

SUCCESSES AND FAILURES

Implementation of new technology like the Public Access to Court Electronic Records (PACER) system has proved hugely successful for the Administrative Office of the United States Courts (AO). This electronic bulletin board provides specific information on court cases; in 1996 it handled more than 3 million requests for information. Similarly, the U.S. Supreme Court clerk's Automated Response System (CARS) allows people to call to learn the status of cases being considered by the Court.

One of the AO's growing problems, however, is the rise of illegal common-law courts. Militia groups in states such as Montana, Missouri, and Idaho have begun a campaign to harass the federal court system by flooding it with phony liens on judges' properties. These liens have no legal effect on the judges but can be difficult to rescind.

FUTURE DIRECTIONS

The Administrative Office of the United States Courts (AO) is determined to continue to decentralize its operations by delegating more responsibilities to the courts themselves. This emphasis, the AO believes, will allow the courts to run more efficiently because they understand their own needs better than the AO. As a result the AO hopes to develop more programs that in some way analyze and study management systems used in the judicial branch. It also hopes to implement new technologies as they become available.

AGENCY RESOURCES

Information is available from the public information officer at the Administrative Office of the United States Courts (AO). Call (202) 273-1120 or look at the home page of the U.S. federal judiciary on the Internet at http://www.uscourts.gov or at http://www.uncle-sam.com/unclesam/uscourts.html.

AGENCY PUBLICATIONS

Publications dealing with the various offices under the administration of the Administrative Office of the United States Courts (AO) are available from the Federal Judicial Center. Single copies of most publications are available free-of-charge including *The Federal Courts and What They Do,* and *Welcome to the Federal Courts.* Call (202) 273-4153 or fax (202) 273-4025. More than 46 publications are available via the Internet at http://www.fjc.gov. These include the *Reference Manual on Scientific Evidence,* the *Manual for Complex Litigation,* and the *Survey on the Federal Rules of Bankruptcy Procedure.*

BIBLIOGRAPHY

Barnes, Patricia G. "Collecting Fines and Criticism." *ABA Journal,* November 1996.

Charles, Joel. "Replies to Negative Questions in the Courtroom." *American Speech,* Spring 1996.

Corbett, Richard. "Governance and Institutional Developments." *Journal of Common Market Studies,* August 1996.

de Figueiredo, John M. "Congressional Control of the Courts: A Theoretical and Empirical Analysis of Expansion of the Federal Judiciary." *Journal of Law & Economics,* October 1996.

"Editors, Judges Hold Conference." *American Editor,* July 1996.

Ellement, John. "Judge: Selection Process Is a Sham." *National Law Journal,* 23 September 1996.

France, Mike. "Order in the Business Court." *Business Week,* 9 December 1996.

Gest, Ted. "A House Without a Blueprint: After 20 Years, the Death Penalty is Still Being Meted Out Unevenly." *U.S. News and World Report,* 8 July 1996.

Hansen, Mark. "Federal Trial Judges Surveyed." *ABA Journal,* November 1996.

African Development Foundation (ADF)

WHAT IS ITS MISSION?

According to its 1998 report to Congress, the mission of the African Development Foundation (ADF) is to "serve as the principal U.S. foreign assistance agency for empowering sustainable community development in Africa."

HOW IS IT STRUCTURED?

The African Development Foundation (ADF) is both a public corporation and an independent government agency managed by a seven-member board of directors that is appointed by the president with the advice and consent of the Senate. The president designates one member of the board to serve as chairman of the board and one to serve as vice chairman. Five members of the board are appointed from the private sector, and two come from among officers and employees of government agencies concerned with African affairs. No more than four members may belong to the same political party.

All members of the board are appointed on the basis of their understanding of and sensitivity to community-level development processes. Thirty employees assist the board, and native Africans serve as country liaison officers. They work with ADF staff to ensure funds, supplies, and training reach the appropriate African countries in a timely manner. The ADF works closely with the World Bank and the State Department's USAID program in developing nontraditional paths to economic stability.

PARENT ORGANIZATION: Independent
ESTABLISHED: 1980
EMPLOYEES: 30

Contact Information:

ADDRESS: 1400 I St. NW
Washington, DC 20005
PHONE: (202) 673-3916
FAX: (202) 673-3810
E-MAIL: info@adf.gov
URL: http://www.adf.gov
CHAIRMAN: Ernest Green
VICE CHAIRMAN: Willie Grace Campbell

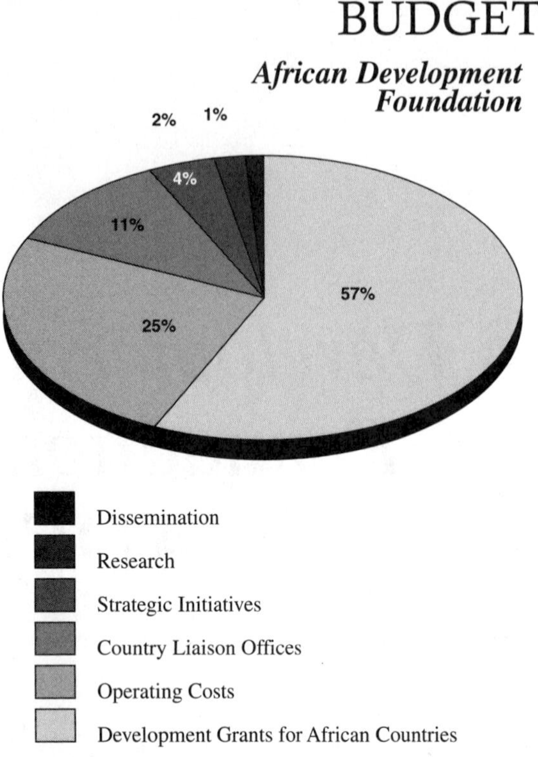

PRIMARY FUNCTIONS

The purpose of the African Development Foundation (ADF) is to strengthen the bonds of friendship and understanding between Africa and the United States by supporting local activities that promote community development in Africa. This stimulates African participation in its own development, and it encourages institutions that foster development. To carry out its purposes, the foundation offers grants, loans, and loan guarantees to private groups, associations, or other African entities engaged in peaceful community development.

The ADF has three goals: to strengthen U.S. relations with Africa, to empower the poor through support of African-led initiatives, and to increase the use of participatory development methodologies by other donors and by African governments. To achieve these goals the ADF develops small enterprises that generate sustainable income and employment, improve community-based natural resource management, strengthen civil society, and develop repeatable models for expanding grassroots participation.

PROGRAMS

The African Development Foundation (ADF) focuses on grassroots organizations, the primary recipients of its grant money. Small grants are provided directly to community groups; no grant money is channeled through governments. All activities supported by the grants are locally conceived and implemented, not imposed by outside interests. Technical assistance is provided at low cost through indigenous specialists and local institutions rather than foreign operatives. Grants are based on community self-reliance in building the capacity of nongovernmental intermediary organizations. Countries that are eligible for grants are Benin, Mali, Botswana, Namibia, Cameroon, Niger, Cape Verde, Senegal, Ghana, Tanzania, Guinea, Uganda, Lesotho, and Zimbabwe. These countries are considered to be on the path to democracy and are also among the poorest countries in the world.

BUDGET INFORMATION

The estimated 1998 budget for the ADF as appropriated by Congress was $14 million. The largest portion of this total, $7.95 million (57 percent), was spent on development grants for African countries, most notably Zimbabwe ($800,000), Benin ($725,000) and Tanzania ($700,000). The remaining funds went to operating costs (25 percent), country liaison offices (11 percent), strategic initiatives (4 percent), research (2 percent), and dissemination (1 percent).

HISTORY

Since it was established by Congress in 1980 and began operations in 1984, the African Development Foundation (ADF) has raised the standard of living in developing African countries through a unique program of grants and aid that focuses on grassroots organizations. Congress mandated that the ADF support "grassroots development in Africa . . . thus enabling the poor to participate in the process of development, to solve their development problems, develop their potential, fulfill their aspirations, and enjoy better, more productive lives."

The ADF was founded in a spirit of fostering cooperation between the peoples of Africa and the U.S. government. During its early years the agency set up country liaison offices in 35 countries and has promoted self-reliance and sustainable development, alleviating poverty and other seemingly insurmountable problems confronting sub-Saharan Africa in the process. In 1985 the ADF agreed to help Zimbabwe study ways to alleviate poverty at the grassroots level. This cooperative program included loan grants to women in agricultural areas to help them operate their own businesses. Instead of the patronizing attitude prevalent in earlier aid programs, the aim of the ADF has been to provide small resources, like loans, that enable the recipients to be self-reliant and build a sense of self-worth.

In 1997, after undergoing severe budgetary and staff reductions, the ADF committed itself to a comprehensive reexamination of its mission and a complete reengineering of its programming and support processes. The mandate was simple—reposition the ADF to assure its long-term viability and convincingly demonstrate the unique and essential contributions it makes within the United States's larger economic-assistance strategy toward Africa. When President Bill Clinton traveled to Africa in 1998 he found evidence of the ADF's successful programs in the countries he visited. As Africa shifted to the forefront of U.S. foreign policy concerns, U.S. leaders found that the small but successful ADF was already paving the way for beneficial relations with African nations.

Ugandan President Yoweri Museveni (waving). *While Museveni has been credited with liberalizing his country's economy, he has also been unwilling or unable to stop the execution of children convicted of participation in rebel forces. Critics question whether or not the ADF should contribute funds to a country with such unchecked civil unrest.*

(Agence France Presse/Corbis-Bettmann)

CURRENT POLITICAL ISSUES

One of the great strengths of the African Development Foundation (ADF) is that it enfranchises the poor in self-help activities at the local level, enhancing opportunities for community development. Because the ADF deals with grassroots organizations rather than governments, which are subject to change, development programs belong to the people they are designed to help. Assistance is targeted at those most in need of it, and the ADF is able to promote and reinforce U.S. policies in African nations without the attitude of superiority that has plagued U.S. relations with Africa for years. It assists in building democracies from the bottom up, working on the premise that if people are thriving, totalitarian dictatorships or military regimes cannot gain a foothold. Critics have claimed, however, that many of the programs assist undemocratic governments in sub-Saharan Africa.

Case Study: Uganda's Rocky Road to Democracy

Uganda has been transitioning to a constitutional democracy and a free-market economy. It has recovered remarkably in the last ten years from the social and economic devastation that resulted from autocratic rule and civil-war leadership. During U.S. President Bill Clinton's visit to Uganda, he observed many of the grassroots efforts that were instrumental in changing the government from Idi Amin's totalitarian regime into a more stable government.

However when compared to long-time democracies of the Western world, some human rights gaps remained. For example, in 1998, because of the pressures of civil unrest, children less than 15 years old awaited execution on death row. According to a March 1998 *Sunday Telegraph* article, children had become "the main source of manpower for the various rebel armies in their eleven-year campaign to overthrow President [Yoweri] Museveni's government.'' Although Museveni privately expressed outrage concerning the children on death row, nothing was done to alleviate the situation. The government did, however, liberalize its economy and unleash the private sector because, as Museveni stated, "without economic growth there can be no sustainable development."

But Uganda is still a poor country divided by civil unrest. The per capita income is $220, and although ADF programs have generated more than five percent economic growth annually since 1989, reaching ten percent in 1997 (one of the highest growth rates in the world), the poverty rate is still high. Relatively few Ugandans are literate and the nation's infrastructure is underdeveloped, so employment opportunities are limited. HIV and AIDS infection rates have reached devastating proportions, further complicating economic restructuring and reform. Critics of U.S. policy point to situations such as Uganda's and ask why organizations like the ADF are involved in countries with comparatively low human

FAST FACTS

In 1996 the ADF funded 33 new grant projects in 11 countries at a cost of $5 million.

(Source: *ADF Report to Congress*, 1998.)

rights and living standards and high levels of civil unrest. They say such programs support shaky regimes and do nothing to promote human rights.

In the first five years that the ADF worked in Uganda, though, grassroots-level programs were instrumental in raising the standard of living of the people and in calming civil unrest. The ADF supported a silkworm cooperative, with training in production and processing, that enabled its members to earn in one month more than the average Ugandan farmer makes in one year. Ugandan silk is now prized for its high quality. Another program boosted vanilla production and marketing of vanilla products through the U.S.-based McCormick spice company. The ADF has also been instrumental in the construction of water systems in several villages, providing thousands of Ugandans with safe drinking water and sanitary facilities.

SUCCESSES AND FAILURES

The African Development Foundation (ADF) prides itself on getting big results from small investments, and it offers many success stories as proof. ADF-supported small businesses in Zimbabwe are now generating $6.6 million a year, more money than the ADF invested in the country over an 11-year period. An ADF-sponsored community bank in Ghana has become a model for community banks throughout that nation, and the Lesotho government implemented community agriculture initiatives that resembled ADF programs.

FUTURE DIRECTIONS

Africa stands poised on an era of development and growth. The African Development Foundation (ADF), with its innovative programs and unique grassroots focus, will assist in the development of the sub-Saharan countries as they morph into economically competitive, stable democracies. Agriculture and resource development are the new goals of the ADF.

AGENCY RESOURCES

The African Development Foundation's Web site at http://www.adf.gov provides updates on project developments throughout Africa. Additional information about the agency may be obtained by sending a written request to the public affairs officer at the African Development Foundation, 1400 I St. NW, Washington DC 20005, or calling (202) 673-3916 or E-mailing info@adf.gov.

AGENCY PUBLICATIONS

The African Development Foundation's congressional presentation, including its programs overview, budget, and strategies for aiding different countries, may be viewed on its Web site at http://www.adf.gov/docs/cpfinal1.html. Also, the congressional charter that established the foundation may be viewed on-line at http://www.adf.gov/docs/ADF_ACT.html.

BIBLIOGRAPHY

Lees, Caroline. "International: Boy Soldier 'Traitors' Face Death in Uganda." *Sunday Telegraph,* London, 22 March 1998.

Rich, Bruce. "Ideas: Nations to World Bank." *Newsday,* 1 August 1993, p. 34.

"Secretary Albright Has It Right!" Africa News Service, 5 January 1998.

"Summary: The African Growth And Opportunity Act (H.R. 1432)." Africa News Service, 23 May 1997.

"U.S. Africa Aid Decision Nears." Africa News Service, 28 August 1996.

"U.S./Africa Trade Bill Excerpts And Comments." Africa News Service, 18 March 1998.

Agency for Health Care Policy and Research (AHCPR)

WHAT IS ITS MISSION?

According to the agency, the mission of the Agency for Health Care Policy and Research (AHCPR) is "to generate and disseminate information that improves the quality, medical effectiveness, and cost of health care and the health care system." The AHCPR is a relatively new agency and as such, is still exploring the parameters and scope of its mission. The AHCPR aids in informed decision making by providing consumers, health care providers, and policymakers with objective, up-to-date information on health care issues.

HOW IS IT STRUCTURED?

The Agency for Health Care Policy and Research (AHCPR) is an operating division within the U.S. Department of Health and Human Services (HHS), a cabinet-level department. An administrator, appointed by the president and approved by the Senate, directs the AHCPR. Six AHCPR offices handle the policy, financial, grant-making, planning, and other administrative work of the agency. Eight centers conduct and support health care and health services research in the areas of health care technology, outcomes and effectiveness, primary care, organization and delivery, cost, financing and access, quality measurement and improvement, information technology, and health information dissemination.

The National Advisory Council for Health Care Policy, Research, and Evaluation provides the administrator with advice and recommendations on priorities for the national health services research agenda. The 24-member

PARENT ORGANIZATION: Department of Health and Human Services
ESTABLISHED: December 31, 1995
EMPLOYEES: 250 (1997)

Contact Information:

ADDRESS: 2101 E. Jefferson St.
Rockville, MD 20852
PHONE: (301) 594-6662
TDD (HEARING IMPAIRED): (888) 586-6340
FAX: (301) 594-2800
E-MAIL: info@ahcpr
URL: http://www.ahcpr.gov
ADMINISTRATOR: John M. Eisenberg

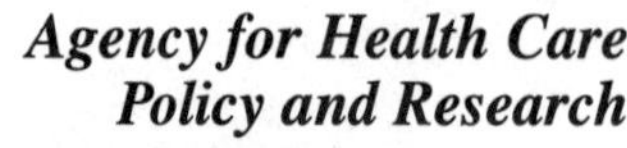

Agency for Health Care Policy and Research

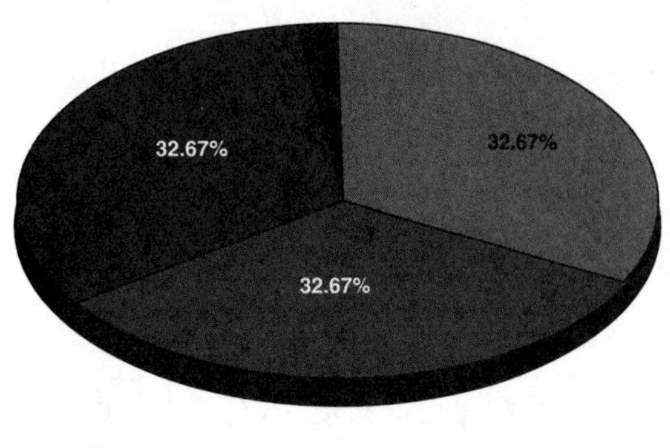

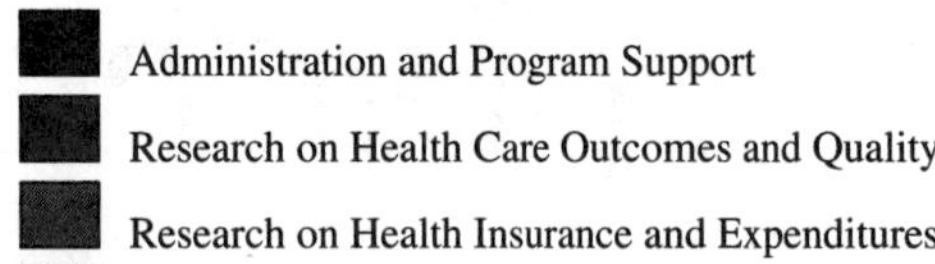

panel is composed of 17 private-sector experts representing health care plans, providers, purchasers, consumers, and researchers, and seven representatives of federal agencies that address health care issues. Private-sector members are appointed by the HHS secretary and serve three-year terms.

PRIMARY FUNCTIONS

The Agency for Health Care Policy and Research (AHCPR) carries out its mission by conducting and supporting, through grants, research that creates the science base to guide improvements in health care practices, policies, plan choices, insurance, and costs. The AHCPR also conducts and supports research designed to determine health care needs of consumers, and the agency helps policymakers make decisions regarding the quality and type of health care systems. The AHCPR also measures, monitors, and evaluates the quality and delivery of health care.

The AHCPR is the health services research arm of the Public Health Service. It works closely with other federal health agencies including the National Institutes of Health, which is the biomedical research arm of the Public Health Service. The AHCPR funds research projects of federal, state, and local governments; educational institutions; and individual fellows.

PROGRAMS

The eight centers within the Agency for Health Care Policy and Research (AHCPR) conduct and fund dozens of research programs related to their particular fields of research. For example, the Center for Health Care Cost, Financing, and Access generates information on issues related to the cost and financing of health care, health insurance coverage, and access to care. The center identifies barriers to services and suggests ways to improve quality of care. The agency is guided by its studies, like its HIV Cost and Service Utilization Study, a national survey that provides estimates of the cost of medical and related services for persons with HIV/AIDS.

The Center for Health Information Technology promotes greater use of computers to improve the quality and effectiveness of medical care and to reduce its cost by using computerized decision-support systems in everyday clinical practice. Projects in this area include designing, implementing, and evaluating a drug-monitoring system and testing a computerized system to facilitate information exchanges between bone marrow transplant experts and the primary care physicians who provide follow-up care to transplant patients.

One of the AHCPR's highest priorities is providing consumers with science-based, easily understandable information that will help them make decisions about their own health care, including choosing quality health plans and services. Through its Guidelines program, the AHCPR's Center for Health Information Dissemination publishes free pamphlets for consumers on health care issues including elective surgery, prescription medicines, health care plans, and treatment options for a number of diseases and conditions.

BUDGET INFORMATION

The 1998 budget for the Agency for Health Care Policy and Research was approximately $90 million. The AHCPR's budget is allocated entirely by Congress. Some AHCPR research projects involve partnerships with private-sector organizations, but AHCPR's share of costs are paid for by these organizations. About two percent of AHCPR's budget is spent on administration and program support cost. The remaining funds are divided roughly into thirds and allocated to research on health care systems cost and access, research on health insurance and expenditures, and research on health care outcomes and quality.

HISTORY

Before 1989 the National Center for Health Services Research was the federal government's source for information related to health care. But in the mid- to late-1980s, public concern over health care cost and quality and policymakers' need to address these concerns exceeded the scope of that agency's services. The Agency for Health Care Policy and Research (AHCPR) was created in 1995 by absorbing the National Center's programs and establishing new research initiatives in all areas of health care including technology and information dissemination. The reorganized agency was created to serve policymakers, consumers, health care providers, health plan providers, researchers, and health plan purchasers like employers and unions.

FAST FACTS

AHCPR studies "identified 11 warning signs for death from pneumonia that can help physicians provide intensive treatments faster."

(Source: AHCPR. "Improving Health Care Quality Through Research and Education," September 4, 1998.)

CURRENT POLITICAL ISSUES

Despite its newness, the Agency for Health Care Policy and Research (AHCPR) and its programs have been at the center of controversies resulting from the conflicting interests of its clients. Consumers want high-quality, effective care and comprehensive health care coverage plans. But while health care coverage providers want to offer this, they are businesses, ultimately concerned with generating profits. As such, they must balance the coverage they offer with their own financial needs. Health maintenance organizations (HMOs) particularly have been accused of compromising high-quality care by limiting the amount of tests and treatments approved under HMO plans, a cost-cutting measure designed to increase profits. Government policymakers, too, must balance interests, those of their grassroots-level voters with those of the major campaign donors whose businesses and organizations operate in their districts or states.

At the center of such issues is the AHCPR. The agency is charged with conducting science-based research and providing factual information to its clients. Yet the AHCPR relies on government funding, allocated by consumers' representatives, often for partnership programs that rely on the participation of health care providers and health plan providers. The agency strives to provide objective, honest, and scientifically sound information, however AHCPR's information is often publicized by its clients to serve their own purposes. For example, consumer advocate groups will publicize an AHCPR study that indicates health care quality is dropping, while a health care provider will publicize a study that puts providers in a more favorable light.

Case Study: The AHCPR Back Pain Study

In 1995 the AHCPR published a report on the findings of a study involving more than four thousand back pain cases, with several findings contradicting long-held beliefs about treatment of acute back pain. Specifically, the report indicated that ibuprofen and aspirin were as effective in treating back pain as prescription muscle relaxants, cost less, and had fewer side effects. The report recommended moderate exercise instead of bed rest, and the AHCPR suggested doctors wait four weeks before ordering tests unless signs of nerve injury or bone disease were present. Traction, massage, acupuncture, and supportive back belts were found to have no proven value in eliminating back pain. Finally, the study pointed out that eighty percent of patients suffering from lower back pain recovered with or without an operation, indicating that back surgery is overused in treating back pain.

Publication of the report resulted in a flurry of compliments and criticisms. Consumer advocates saw the results as justification for health plan providers to refuse to cover the more expensive back pain treatments. Health care providers and health plan providers were justified in their belief that money and time spent on treating back pain could be reduced with no adverse effects for patients. Manufacturers of products recommended in the report widely publicized the findings. Producers of products found to be of little use in treating back pain criticized the study as being too limited or inconclusive.

Only time can determine the long-term validity of the AHCPR's study, but at the very least the agency fulfilled its mission of generating and disseminating health care information. Consumers, health care providers, and insurers now have more information about back pain treatment options, possibly offering a way for sufferers of back pain to avoid unnecessary drugs and surgery. But insurers would suffer a mountain of negative publicity if the study were used to back up decisions not to cover back pain treatments.

SUCCESSES AND FAILURES

The Agency for Health Care Policy and Research (AHCPR) has enjoyed several notable successes, especially in the area of reducing health care costs. For example, in 1995 the agency published a report on the impact on cost and quality of health services research. The three central findings of the report indicated that AHCPR products have reduced costs, that lower costs often mean higher quality because they are the result of efforts to identify costs that can be cut without affecting quality, and that information can serve as a substitute for regulation by encouraging better and more cost-effective care without the burden of government regulation.

Assuming they affect one patient in five, the AHCPR claims its recommendations can result in annual savings of $132 million in regard to stroke prevention therapies, $8.5 million in regard to preconception and prenatal care for diabetic women, and $27 million in regard to on-call medical care to terminally ill patients living at home. The agency has disseminated more than 25 million copies of clinical practice guidelines which address symptom assessment, testing recommendations, and treatment options. When Utah's Intermountain Health Care tested AHCPR ulcer-prevention guidelines in one of its hospitals for six months, it found that using the guidelines saved $240,000.

FUTURE DIRECTIONS

Because it is a relatively new agency, many Agency for Health Care Policy and Research (AHCPR) projects are still in the developmental stage or in early phases of implementation. One AHCPR priority is to establish a comprehensive Internet source for clinical practice guidelines. The new National Guideline Clearinghouse is to make available a full range of guidelines on treatments for specific medical conditions. It will also compare and contrast the recommended treatment guidelines as well as provide summaries of areas of agreement and disagreement.

Another priority for the AHCPR is to develop "report cards" for consumers requesting information on quality, service, and cost issues. This will help consumers evaluate health care systems and plans. In 1997 the AHCPR initiated the first phase of a five-year project by sending surveys to consumers to determine what they want to know when choosing health care providers and insurance plans. Later phases of the project will include translating consumer questions into measurable objectives and developing a process for monitoring, evaluating, and publicizing report card measurements.

AGENCY RESOURCES

The Agency for Health Care Policy and Research (AHCPR) research portfolio on topics such as managed care, physician practices, computers and health care, and primary care issues is available on-line at http://www.ahcpr.gov:80/research/. Information on AHCPR research can also be requested by calling (301) 594-6662.

The AHCPR operates the Computerized Needs-Oriented Quality Measurement Evaluation System (CONQUEST), a quality-improvement software tool that helps users identify, understand, evaluate, and select measures to assess and improve clinical performance. CONQUEST diskettes and user's guides are available free-of-charge from the AHCPR Publications Clearinghouse, PO Box 8547, Silver Spring, MD 20907, or call 1-800-358-9295.

AGENCY PUBLICATIONS

The Agency for Health Care Policy and Research (AHCPR) publishes free consumer guides about the benefits and risks of treatments for specific medical conditions. Topics include smoking cessation, pain management, heart failure, post-stroke rehabilitation, and lower back pain. Guides may be viewed on-line at http://www.ahcpr.gov:80/guide or they may be ordered by calling 1-800-358-9295. The agency also publishes other consumer information including *Checkup on Health Insurance Choices,* designed to help consumers select health insurance plans and *Questions to Ask Your Doctor Before You Have Surgery,* designed to help consumers make decisions about surgery. These publications and a list of other titles can be ordered by calling 1-800-358-9295.

BIBLIOGRAPHY

Gaus, Clifton R. "Health Services Research: Now More Than Ever." *Journal of the American Medical Association,* 12 July 1995.

Hagland, Mark. "Clifton Gaus: Administrator of the Agency for Health Care Policy and Research (Interview)." *Hospitals and Health Networks,* 20 July 1995.

Jones, Laurie, and Deborah Shelton Pinkney. "Help on the Way for Treating Growing HIV Epidemic." *American Medical News,* 7 February 1994.

Kent, Christina. "Smoking Cessation Guidelines Successful—If Used." *American Medical News,* 14 October 1996.

Lloyd, Farrell, et al. "The AHCPR Unstable Angina Algorithm in Practice." *Journal of the American Medical Association,* 26 March 1997.

Matson, Mandy. "Good News for Bad Backs." *Reader's Digest,* May 1995.

Prager, Linda O. "Agency Shifts Focus on Guidelines Work to Research." *American Medical News,* 9 December 1996.

———. "Policy Research Agency Faces Its Own Cost/Benefit Analysis." *American Medical News,* 4 September 1995.

Agency for International Development (USAID)

PARENT ORGANIZATION: Independent; merger with Department of State slated for 1998
ESTABLISHED: 1961
EMPLOYEES: 2,847

Contact Information:

ADDRESS: 320 21st St. NW
Washington, DC 20523-0001
PHONE: (202) 647-1850
FAX: (202) 216-3524
E-MAIL: pinquiries@usaid.gov
URL: http://www.info.usaid.gov
ADMINISTRATOR: J. Brian Atwood

WHAT IS ITS MISSION?

The U.S. Agency for International Development (USAID) was created to provide economic and humanitarian aid to foreign nations and to advance the economic interests of the United States in the process. The organization benefits the international community in four venues: economic growth, environmental quality, democracy, and humanitarian aid. This mission is called "promoting sustainable development," because the methods employed foster self-reliance of the assisted nations.

HOW IS IT STRUCTURED?

The U.S. Agency for International Development (USAID) is an independent agency that operates under the guidance of the Department of State. USAID and its sister organization, the Overseas Private Investment Corporation, combine to form the U.S. International Development Cooperation Agency, whose acting director is the USAID administrator.

USAID is organized into five functional areas: the Bureau for Humanitarian Response, the Bureau for Africa, the Bureau for Asia and the Near East, the Bureau for Latin America and the Caribbean, and the Bureau for Europe and the New Independent States. Within each national location served, USAID maintains one of three types of country organizations: missions, offices, or sections of the embassy. Missions are located in countries where USAID involvement is extensive and is expected to continue. Over time, as a country becomes increasingly self-reliant, USAID gradually rolls back its opera-

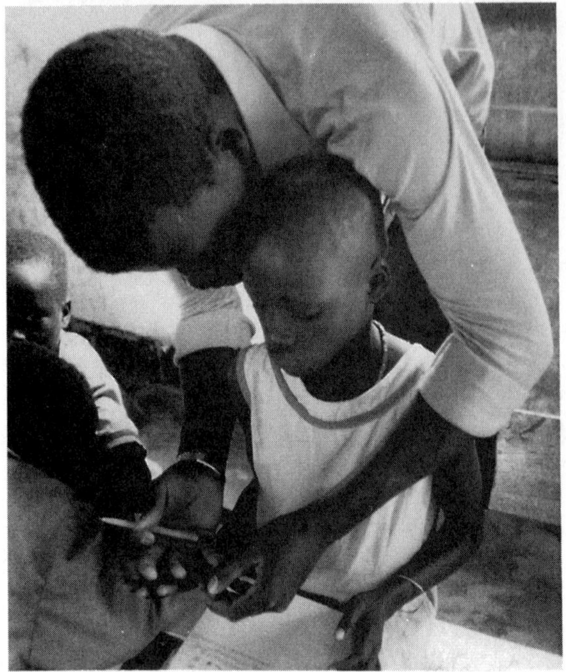

Achieving USAID's objective of a reduction in the rate of child labor in developing countries would mean that children would have more time to focus on education.
(AP/Wide World Photos)

tion within that territory. When a country accomplishes sufficient economic progress and no longer requires a USAID mission, a representative office is established. Representative offices also operate in countries where the need and nature of USAID support and involvement is less acute.

A section of a U.S. embassy is maintained in countries where USAID involvement is of a limited nature or where USAID operations are near completion and are being phased out. In general, USAID programs are of a bilateral nature (between two countries). There are some programs however, that involve multiple nations. These multilateral programs are administered by USAID regional offices in Nairobi, Kenya, and Cote D'Ivoire, Abidjan. Each regional office is under the direction of a regional director. Additionally, USAID maintains five development assistance coordination and representation offices. These are located in Rome, Italy; Paris, France; Manila, Philippines; Tokyo, Japan; and Geneva, Switzerland.

USAID administrative bureaus include the Bureau for Global Programs, Field Support and Research; the Bureau for Legislative and Public Affairs; the Office of Equal Opportunity Programs; the Office of the General Counsel; the Office of the Inspector General; and the Office of Small Disadvantaged Business/Minority Resources Center. USAID operations fall under the direction of the Bureau for Policy and Program Coordination, which operates under the Bureau for Management. The Bureau for Management and the USAID administrator coordinate their individual functions through the Quality Council.

PRIMARY FUNCTIONS

The U.S. Agency for International Development (USAID) operates within the superstructure of the International Development Cooperation Agency. Most USAID projects are funded under this agency through Overseas Private Investment Corporation investments. This arrangement allows U.S. businesses to make a profit on aid to foreign nations. Because of USAID's reciprocity arrangements, approximately three-quarters of USAID money goes to pay contracts to U.S. businesses.

USAID provides assistance in five critical aspects of national development: population and health, economic growth, environmental protection, democratization, and post-crisis transitions. Prior to establishing a field mission USAID first determines a country's eligibility by evaluating its commitment to democracy, social reform, and economic upgrading. Once committed to a mission the agency teaches family planning, HIV/AIDS prevention, and sanitation methods, while dispensing vaccines and rehydration therapy to children. In so doing, USAID relief saves millions of lives each year. USAID sponsors voter education programs and monitors elections as the peoples of recipient nations are encouraged to develop multiple political parties. Energy conservation experts, contracted through USAID, work with local officials in developing programs to control pollution and preserve the environment.

USAID responds to urgent situations with disaster assistance response teams, which are often mobilized in conjunction with the U.S. armed services to deliver relief supplies to disaster victims worldwide. Nations experiencing political crisis or catastrophic natural disaster can rely on team deployments to bring food and other emergency supplies as quickly as possible.

PROGRAMS

Money invested in the U.S. Agency for International Development (USAID) assists foreign nations and benefits U.S. concerns. For example, in 1996 a program to improve electric service in the Ukraine led to a partnership between the Kentucky Utilities Co. and the Dniproenergo service abroad. It is this reciprocity of purpose that enables USAID programs to benefit developing nations and the United States simultaneously. USAID's Lessons Without Borders program takes a different approach toward fostering the reciprocal design of U.S. foreign aid.

Lessons Without Borders

Lessons Without Borders is a USAID initiative to recapture, assess, and recycle the information and lessons learned through the agency's overseas programs. This unique program brings together representatives from underdeveloped and assisted nations and representatives from U.S. communities. They come together at international conferences to discuss and resolve common issues like development of microenterprise, HIV/AIDS prevention, and childhood vaccination. Following a 1994 conference in Boston, Massachusetts, city officials traveled to Jamaica to observe community awareness programs to reduce teen pregnancy and discourage violence. A similar conference in Seattle, Washington, led to collaborations in problem resolution between Zimbabwe, Egypt, the Philippines, and the United States. During the 1994 inaugural conference for Lessons Without Borders, in Baltimore, Maryland, U.S. Vice President Al Gore said, "Here we are truly helping ourselves, bringing the lessons we've paid for to our own doorsteps."

BUDGET:

Agency for International Development

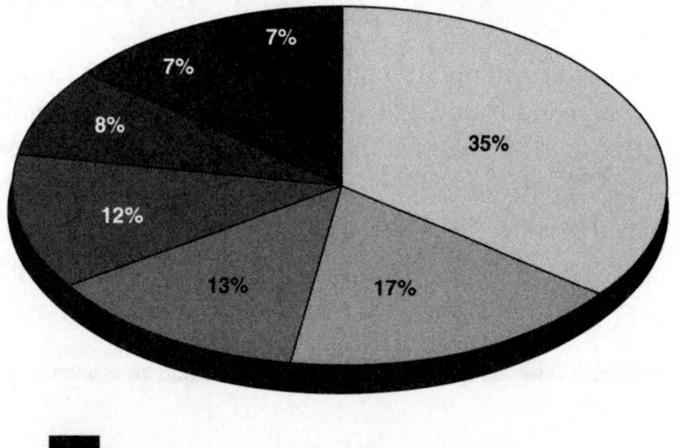

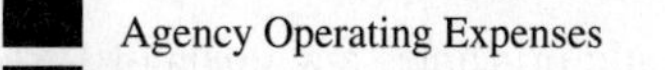

Agency Operating Expenses

Development Funds for Eastern Europe

Child Survival and Disease Programs Fund

Agricultural Supplies and Food Monies for Developing Countries

Development Funds for the Newly Independent States

Development Assistance

Economic Support Fund

BUDGET INFORMATION

The USAID budget is apportioned by Congress from U.S. tax dollars. Its budget was an estimated $6.97 billion in 1998. The bulk of USAID funds, $2.42 billion in 1998 (35 percent of the USAID budget), were designated for the Economic Support Fund. Additionally, development funds for the Newly Independent States and eastern Europe received $925 million (13 percent) and $465 million (7 percent) respectively. Another major budget item for USAID was development assistance, which was appropriated $1.17 billion or 17 percent of USAID's budget. Funding for Public Law 480 (P.L. 480) Title II, which mandates agricultural supplies and food monies for developing countries, received $837 million or 12 percent of the budget. The Child Survival and Disease Programs Fund received $550 million (8 percent of the USAID budget) in 1998. This fund is specially allocated to fund immunization, health, and nutrition programs—including sanitation and water programs. An additional sum of $479 million (7 percent) was budgeted for agency operating expenses and for compensation and retirement payments for over 2,500 USAID employees. The remaining USAID funds were devoted to international disaster assistance, P.L. 480 Title III funds, and credit programs for enterprise development and urban and environmental credit.

OPIC, which provides financial services to USAID, is funded separately from USAID. OPIC funds totaled approximately $30 million in 1998. The funds were designated for administrative expenses.

HISTORY

After World War II (1941–45), the Marshall Plan went into effect to assist the recovery of the war-torn nations of Europe. President Harry Truman endorsed this need for development cooperation between nations during his inaugural address in 1949. Ultimately the European recovery extended into the 1950s, and by 1961, under the administration of President John F. Kennedy, a new Foreign Assistance Act was passed to perpetuate U.S. aid indefinitely. The act, which established the U.S. Agency for International Development (USAID), was amended in 1969 and again in 1980. The USAID program has been reevaluated by every president since that time. Nevertheless, regardless of political party affiliation and budget constraints, the program has persevered. The program was subjected to extensive scrutiny for potential elimination in 1993 and again in 1995 during development of government downsizing programs by Congress and President Bill Clinton. However neither attempt was successful.

Women in Development

In addition to addressing problems of food supply and health care, USAID has noted that in many lesser-developed countries women are relegated to an inferior status. In some cases these circumstances pose a jeop-

FAST FACTS

According to opinion polls most Americans believe that foreign aid is one of the largest items in the federal budget. Some believe that the foreign aid budget uses as much as 20 percent of total tax dollars. In reality USAID uses far less than one percent.

(Source: Agency for International Development. "PR Newswire," June 16, 1998.)

ardy to the democratic principles and goals of USAID. Without USAID's intervention, educational programs have been frequently denied to women in some assisted countries. For this reason USAID established the Office of Women in Development in 1974 to encourage and ensure the involvement of women in USAID programs. The office has proved critical to the undertaking of strategic initiatives to address the issue of gender bias, especially in education, and child labor.

CURRENT POLITICAL ISSUES

Comparatively, U.S. foreign aid policies and programs are ambitious, but some critics question the true motives behind USAID and similar programs. They are not humanitarian or ecologically driven, but economically driven, critics say. For example, the U.S. government contends its involvement in the Middle East and Northern Africa aims at furthering freedom and democracy. Instead, it has been suggested, the United States is on a mission of opportunism, seeking to keep millions of barrels of crude oil flowing to North America. Additional criticism has been leveled against USAID with the discovery of extreme famine conditions in areas served by USAID programs. These discoveries made some question the viability and competency of such large-scale programs in general.

Case Study: Somalia

Early in the 1990s the United States became involved in an extensive intervention operation to bring food to the starving population of Somalia, a nation of six million people with a literacy rate of 24 percent. But relief efforts were forcibly intercepted by political leaders who halted all humanitarian supplies coming into the country. The United Nations intervened to stop this, and U.S.-led military forces mobilized to assist with the delivery of emergency supplies to Somalia, late in 1992. Some members of the U.S. forces died while carrying out this mission, and less than one year later the humanitarian mission turned into a battlefield.

Two bloody confrontations broke out between U.S. Army rangers and followers of Mohammed Farrah Aidid in the Somalian capitol of Mogadishu late in 1993. The attacks happened within four days of one another, leaving 16 rangers dead and 89 wounded. Two hundred Somalis also died and hundreds were wounded. Additionally, the corpse of one U.S. victim was dragged through the streets and defiled, and a severely injured U.S. helicopter pilot was taken prisoner. The prisoner, Michael Durant, relayed a message to the U.S. public, as reported by *Time* magazine: "When you don't live here, you can't understand what's going on in this country. We Americans have tried to help. But at one point things turned bad."

Public Impact

The Somalia incident made it clear that USAID programs could pose a threat to Americans, and many began to question the value versus the cost of foreign assistance. Ken Menkhaus, writing for the Middle East Policy Council, summarized the issue; "Few topics inspire more cynicism among seasoned observers of international politics than foreign assistance to Somalia." Menkhaus went on to dub Somalia a "graveyard of foreign aid," and the incident served as justification for legislators to devise drastic reforms in contemporary foreign aid programs. Specifically, USAID embarked on a series of foreign policy reforms known as the Greater Horn of Africa Initiative, which focused on conflict prevention, especially in less stable regions. The initiative also shifted a significant burden back to the region in distress.

SUCCESSES AND FAILURES

Although a significant portion of U.S. Agency for International Development (USAID) dollars are spent directly on programs that benefit a foreign populace, statistically speaking, USAID programs like Lessons Without Borders reflect improvements in the quality of life for American children in addition to children of other nations. What is more, USAID immunization programs are credited with saving three million lives each year: USAID brought measles immunizations for children in India up to eighty percent from one percent. The global vaccination rate also exceeded eighty percent, boosting it 37 percent in 1984. USAID estimates one million children are saved every year through oral rehydration therapy, which combats deadly infant and childhood diarrhea. Though the treatment is widely available in the United States, it not as available worldwide. Additionally, USAID's family-planning programs have reached fifty million couples, and new HIV/AIDS prevention programs operate in dozens of countries around the world.

FUTURE DIRECTIONS

One of the biggest gaps between the United States and nations of Africa, Asia, Central America, and South America is access to technology. In 1998 the United States held 55 percent of the World Wide Web market share even though it makes up only about 4.5 percent of the total world population. Realizing the significance of this disparity, the U.S. Agency for International Development (USAID) launched the five-year Leland Initiative in mid-1998. This $15 million series of funds for less developed countries will concentrate on improving the library resources of 21 nations. Mali, Korea, and Chile are the first countries slotted to receive this aid.

AGENCY RESOURCES

The U.S. Agency for International Development (USAID) Web site at http://www.info.usaid.gov/ is an excellent source of information about the agency's programs. The Global Education Database at http://www.info.usaid.gov/educ_training/ged.html was developed by USAID to provide worldwide education information in an easy-to-use electronic format. For more information contact USAID's Center for Human Capacity Development, Room 3.09, U.S. Agency for International Development, Washington, DC 20523. The agency's Women in Development office can be contacted by writing to Room 3.08-042U Ronald Reagan Building, Washington, DC 20523-3801, by E-mailing dsedigi@usaid.gov, by calling (202) 712-0570, or by faxing (202) 216-3173.

AGENCY PUBLICATIONS

The U.S. Agency for International Development (USAID) publishes an annual *Agency Performance Report,* and its strategic plan titled *Strategies for Sustainable Development.* For copies write to the USAID Information Center, Ronald Reagan Building, Washington, DC 20523-0016 or call (202) 712-4810. The agency also publishes a quarterly newsletter, *USAID Developments,* which can be accessed on-line at http://www.info.usaid.gov/pubs. To order hard copies write to the USAID Bureau for Legislative and Public Affairs, Washington, DC 20523-0056, send E-mail to pinquiries@usaid.gov, or call (202) 647-1850. Some USAID materials are available on-line at http://www.info.usaid.gov/about/.

GENDERACTION is a newsletter that is published quarterly by USAID's Women in Development division. For copies write to WID/USAID, Room 3.08-042U Ronald Reagan Building, Washington, DC 20523-3801, send E-mail to dsedigi@usaid.gov, call (202) 712-0570, or fax (202) 216-3173.

BIBLIOGRAPHY

Adams, Patricia. *In the Name of Progress: The Underside of Foreign Aid.* Toronto: Energy Probe Research Foundation, 1991.

Duffy, Michael, J.F.O. McAllister, Bruce van Voorst, and Marguerite Michaels. "Anatomy of a Disaster." *Time,* 18 October 1993, p. 40.

Henry, Clement M. "Promoting Democracy: USAID at Sea or Off to Cyberspace?" Middle East Policy Council, 1997.

Lumsdaine, David Halloran. *Moral Vision in International Politics: The Foreign Aid Regime, 1949–1989.* Princeton: Princeton University Press, 1993.

Menkhaus, Ken. "U.S. Foreign Assistance to Somalia: Phoenix from the Ashes?" Middle East Policy Council, 1997.

Meyer, William H. *Human Rights and International Political Economy in Third World Nations.* Westport, Conn.: Praeger, 1998.

Sobel, Richard, ed. *Public Opinion in U.S. Foreign Policy: The Controversy Over Contra Aid,* Lanhan, Md.: Rowman & Littlefield, 1993.

Thompson, Paul B. *The Ethics of Aid and Trade: U.S. Food Policy, Foreign Competition, and the Social Contract.* Cambridge, England: Cambridge University Press, 1992.

Tisch, Sarah J. *Dilemmas of Development Assistance: The What, Why, and Who of Foreign Aid.* Boulder, Colo.: Westview Press, 1994.

Agency for Toxic Substances and Disease Registry (ATSDR)

PARENT ORGANIZATION: Department of Health and Human Services
ESTABLISHED: 1980
EMPLOYEES: 380

Contact Information:

ADDRESS: 1600 Clifton Rd. NE
Atlanta, GA 30333
TOLL FREE: (800) 447-1544
FAX: (404) 639-0522
E-MAIL: atsdric@cdc.gov
URL: http://atsdr1.atsdr.cdc.gov:8080
ACTING ADMINISTRATOR: Claire V. Broome, M.D.
ASSISTANT ADMINISTRATOR: Barry L. Johnson, Ph.D.

WHAT IS ITS MISSION?

According to the agency, the mission of the Agency for Toxic Substances and Disease Registry (ATSDR) is "to prevent exposure and adverse human health effects and diminished quality of life associated with exposure to hazardous substances from waste sites, unplanned releases, and other sources of pollution present in the environment." Since its creation the ATSDR's mission has expanded to include more public awareness and education projects involving hazardous substances in households and nature, not just those related to toxic waste sites. The ATSDR's role as a research agency in regard to the health effects of toxic substances has also grown to include numerous partnerships with state, local, and federal agencies.

HOW IS IT STRUCTURED?

The Agency for Toxic Substances and Disease Registry (ATSDR) is an operating agency within the U.S. Department of Health and Human Services (HHS), a cabinet-level department in the executive branch of the federal government. ATSDR administrative offices include the Office of Federal Programs, the Office of Program Operations and Management, the Office of Policy and External Affairs, and the Office of Regional Operations. The agency is headquartered in Atlanta, Georgia, with an office in Washington, D.C., and ten regional offices across the country. The director of the Centers for Disease Control and Prevention is the administrator of the ATSDR and is nominated by the president and confirmed by the Senate.

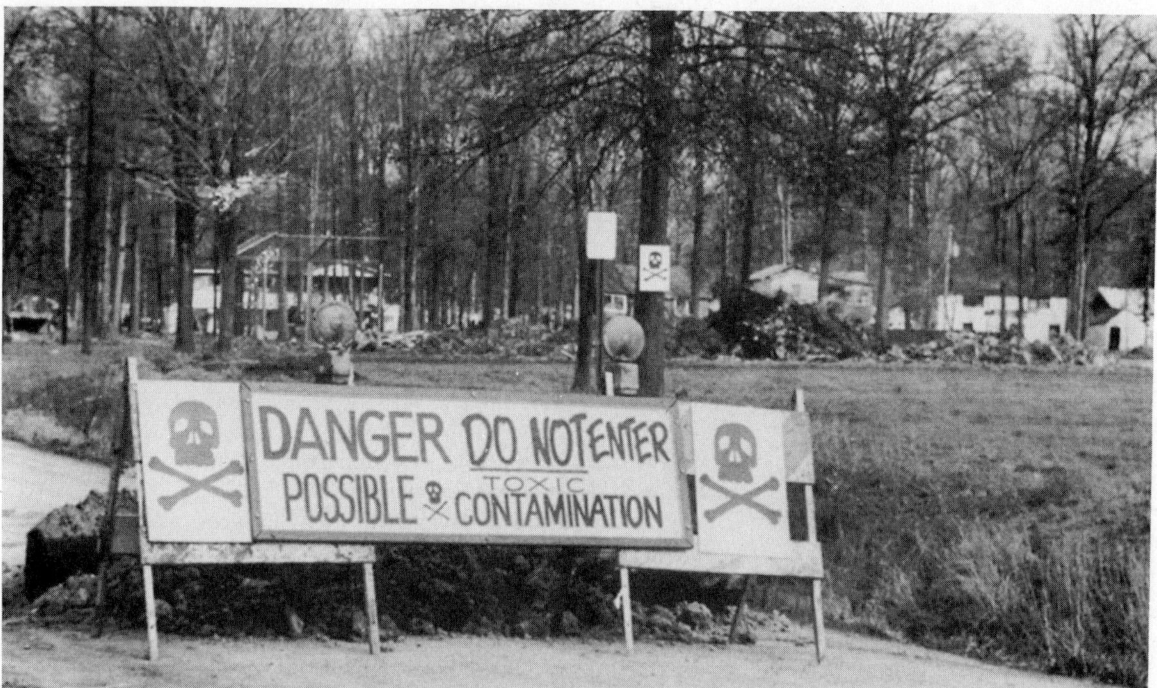

One of the most alarming incidents of toxic contamination in the United States occurred in an area known as the Love Canal (New York state) in the mid-1970s. It was discovered that thousands of tons of toxic chemicals were buried insecurely under or near the residential area. (AP/Wide World Photos)

The agency executes its operations through four program-specific divisions. The Division of Health Assessment and Consultation (DHAC) assesses all sites on the national priorities list of hazardous sites, and it provides consultations on health issues related to exposure to toxic substances to the Environmental Protection Agency and to state and local administrators. The Division of Health Education and Promotion (DHE) conducts programs for health professionals and communities on the health effects of hazardous substances. The Division of Toxicology (DT) identifies hazardous substances, conducts research, and coordinates activities associated with toxicological profiles and research. The Division of Health Studies (DHS) coordinates activities associated with epidemiological studies, investigations of human exposure to hazardous substances, and the national registry of people exposed to toxic substances.

PRIMARY FUNCTIONS

The Agency for Toxic Substances and Disease Registry (ATSDR) assesses the presence and nature of health hazards at sites on the national priorities list of hazardous sites and at other sites when emergencies occur. The agency then helps prevent or reduce further exposure to hazardous substances and the illnesses that result from exposure. The agency also conducts research to expand what is known about the health effects of exposure to hazardous substances. It maintains registries of people who have been exposed to hazardous substances for the purpose of long-term follow-up studies.

State and local governments, as well as federal agencies like the Environmental Protection Agency and the Centers for Disease Control and Prevention, rely on the ATSDR for research and assessment information. The ATSDR trains and educates through its programs, and it provides research data for communities affected by health problems related to hazardous substances. Training for first responders is provided by the ATSDR to ensure adequate response to public health emergencies.

PROGRAMS

Each division of the Agency for Toxic Substances and Disease Registry (ATSDR) operates programs related to its specific role. For example the Division of Health Assessment and Consultation performs a public health assessment after it investigates and reviews information about hazardous substances at a site. In 1996 this division, in collaboration with 22 state health depart-

BUDGET:

Agency for Toxic Substances and Disease Registry

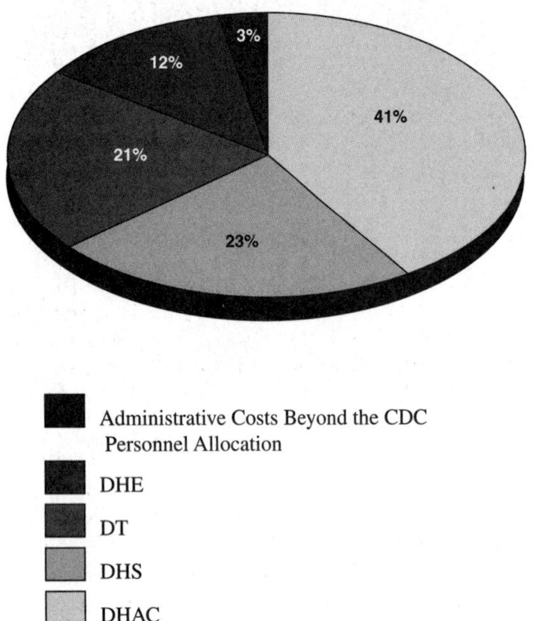

ments, prepared public health assessments of 75 new sites, 58 sites already under review, and 55 sites assessed earlier in the agency's existence. From the information in public health assessments, the ATSDR has been able to make observations about the types of contaminants that threaten public health, the environmental elements most affected by contaminants, and ways people are exposed to contaminants. These observations allow other divisions of the ATSDR and other agencies to create specific plans for preventing exposure and treating people who have been exposed.

The Division of Health Education and Promotion provides funding and technical assistance to determine educational needs and deliver programs in communities experiencing the health effects of exposure to hazardous substances. In 1996 this division implemented health education activities at eighty hazardous waste sites. The type and scope of these activities is determined by the needs of people at each site. Studies of the Jasper County Superfund site in southwest Missouri showed that children in the area, where lead-zinc was mined, had high blood lead levels. The health education division established an areawide blood-screening program in cooperation with the local public health department. It also developed a Girl Scouts badge program so scouts would learn about the environmental issues in their area and teach younger scouts. The same information was incorporated into the Girl Scouts Wider Opportunity program in 1997, in which thirty senior scouts from across the nation learned about environmental hazards.

BUDGET INFORMATION

The 1997 budget for ATSDR was approximately $64 million. ATSDR receives its funding through the Environmental Protection Agency (EPA) and its personnel allocation through the Centers for Disease Control and Prevention (CDC). Funding for federal facility sites is negotiated with the Department of Defense (DOD) and the Department of Energy (DOE), depending on which department is responsible for a site. The budgets of EPA, CDC, DOD, and DOE are allocated by Congress and include line item funding amounts for ATSDR. In 1996 DOD contributed approximately 15 percent of ATSDR's total budget and DOE contributed approximately 9 percent.

ATSDR's funds are mainly distributed to its four operating division with approximately 41 percent to DHAC, 23 percent to DHS, 21 percent to DT, and 12 percent to DHE. The remaining 3 percent of the budget covers administrative costs beyond the CDC personnel allocation.

HISTORY

In 1980 Congress enacted the Comprehensive Environmental Response, Compensation, and Liability Act, commonly known as Superfund legislation, as a means of locating, assessing, and cleaning up sites contaminated by hazardous substances. The Agency for Toxic Substances and Disease Registry (ATSDR) was created to implement the health-related sections of the act that protect the public from hazardous wastes and spills. The ATSDR originally focused on assessing public health dangers, exploring relationships between exposure to hazardous substances and illnesses, providing literature on health effects of hazardous substances, and assisting health care providers with the medical care and testing of people exposed to hazardous substances.

By 1983 the agency was established as a separate agency of the Public Health Service. In 1984 the ATSDR was authorized to conduct public health assessments as requested by the Environmental Protection Agency, states, or individuals. The ATSDR also began to help the Environmental Protection Agency decide which substances should be regulated and at what levels those substances threaten human health.

Following the reauthorization of Superfund in 1986 under the Superfund Amendments and Reauthorization Act, the agency received major new mandates. The reauthorization act broadened the ATSDR's responsibilities to include establishment and maintenance of toxicological databases, dissemination of more information, and creation of educational programs for health care professionals. By the late 1980s the ATSDR had become the federal government's lead agency for investigating and responding to the health effects of exposure to all forms of hazardous substances.

In 1988 the ATSDR was required to report to Congress on the health effects of medical waste. In 1990 a similar report was required of the Environmental Protection Agency in cooperation with the ATSDR on the adverse effects of water pollutants on people and wildlife. Also in 1990, the ATSDR was assigned to a task force to research methods of identifying and assessing risks to human health from exposure to air pollutants. Legislation enacted in 1992 assigned the ATSDR to a cooperative effort with the Environmental Protection Agency and the Department of Housing and Urban Development to conduct a public education program on lead contamination from household substances. In 1995 the agency's increased responsibilities resulted in its elevation to operating division status within the HHS.

CURRENT POLITICAL ISSUES

In the mid-1980s minority activists sparked a campaign to make the public and government aware of the health needs of minorities. National health statistics documented that African Americans, Hispanics, American Indians, and Alaskan Natives suffered disproportionately from preventable diseases and higher death rates at younger ages than white Americans. However, the impact of the environment, particularly of toxic and hazardous wastes, on the health of minority populations had not been specifically investigated or characterized. Activists asked the government to address this issue as part of a larger project aimed at minority health issues.

Opponents pointed out that targeting federal dollars to programs for specific populations was unnecessary because the Agency for Toxic Substances and Disease Registry (ATSDR) already provided public health assessments for all citizens. In addition, they believed federal funds should focus on cleanup efforts and that states and local health care systems should address health effects.

Those who supported the proposed study believed existing statistics showing the higher incidence of other health problems for minorities indicated a strong possibility that they would also have more negative health effects from exposure to hazardous substances. Citizens and officials on this side of the issue insisted that if minorities were at greater risk of exposure and resulting illnesses, the ATSDR must respond.

The ATSDR did initiate a minority health project focused on demographics, health perspectives, health communications, and health education. The effort was expanded into a minority health program in 1990 and has grown since then to address issues related to minority health and the environmental justice movement. Projects like the Minority Health Professionals Foundation, the Hispanic American Initiative, and the Mississippi Delta Project allow the ATSDR to respond more appropriately to the health and education needs of minority communities exposed to and affected by exposure to hazardous substances.

Case Study: The Mississippi Delta Project

The Mississippi Delta Project is a partnership of governments, academia, private-sector organizations, and community residents who focus on identifying and reducing the impact of environmental hazards. The program targets a 219-county strip along the Mississippi River in Arkansas, Illinois, Kentucky, Louisiana, Mississippi, Missouri, and Tennessee. About eight million people, including some three million people of color, populate the region. The region's identified environmental hazards include mercury contamination in surface waters, pesticide runoff, seasonal degradation of air quality, environmental and health consequences of natural disasters, toxic release from waste sites, lead-based paint in older structures, and chemical spills.

Through the active participation of the project's stakeholders, the Mississippi Delta Project works to meet or surpass environmental standards, promote community awareness, and establish safe methods for disposing of hazardous wastes in the region. The ATSDR also works through the project to determine associations between hazardous substances and adverse human health outcomes in minority populations. The project also aims to increase the number and diversity of people in professions associated with environmental health. This includes assisting with curriculum development, convening seminars and workshops in toxicology and related subjects, and providing short-term training for professionals on identifying and preventing environmental hazards. Community partnerships provide culturally- and regionally-sensitive pollution prevention and health education programs. Program participants include the ATSDR, the Environmental Protection Agency, the Centers for Disease Control and Prevention Office of Minority Health, and the Centers for Disease Control and Prevention National Center for Environmental Health.

SUCCESSES AND FAILURES

In 1996 the Agency for Toxic Substances and Disease Registry (ATSDR) completed a study investigating the interaction between lead and osteoporosis in women who were employed at the Bunker Hill lead-smelting facility in Silver Valley, Idaho, in the 1970s. The study provided information about the effects of lead on women who are going through menopause. The study found that women employed at the facility had significantly higher blood and bone lead levels than women in a comparison group. As the former workers aged, their bone density also decreased at a faster rate. Further, the female workers were more likely to report diagnoses of hypertension, anemia, arthritis, and osteoporosis, all conditions associated with increased exposure to lead.

The ATSDR recommended that the subjects be followed to assess health risks in the future and that they be considered for medical monitoring. Information from the study was provided to health professionals and officials and to government agencies working with patients and sites with high lead levels. The women in the study were given medical counseling and information on estrogen replacement therapy and calcium supplements to decrease bone absorption and, therefore, release of lead from bone.

The ATSDR has also completed the first phase of the Great Lakes Human Health Effects Research Program through which the ATSDR funded nine institutions researching the human health impact of eating fish from the Great Lakes region. Their studies have provided the ATSDR and health agencies with essential information on the types and levels of contaminants that humans are exposed to and with studies that evaluate the continuing effects of these contaminants.

FUTURE DIRECTIONS

The Agency for Toxic Substances and Disease Registry (ATSDR) will broaden its efforts to educate health care professionals about the health effects of exposure to hazardous substances. This will be done through pilot projects like the Howard University Environmental Medicine Rotation which will ultimately create a group of physicians trained to recognize environmental emergencies and evaluate and treat those exposed. These physicians will also be able to provide insight to the ATSDR to help improve the agency's training and education projects.

The ATSDR also aims to create a more user-oriented approach to public health assessments through its Public Health Assessment Enhancement Initiative. The initiative promotes closer cooperation between the ATSDR and the Environmental Protection Agency, state and local environmental and health departments, and community members. The initiative is intended to ensure that the ATSDR's public health activities are better integrated into cleanup efforts and are more responsive to health and community concerns.

FAST FACTS

More than 924,000 people in the United States live within a one-mile radius of sites that were the subject of 1996 public health assessments.

(Source: Agency for Toxic Substances and Disease Registry, 1997.)

AGENCY RESOURCES

HazDat is an on-line database of hazardous substance releases and health effects, which is maintained by the Agency for Toxic Substances and Disease Registry (ATSDR). It includes information about site characteristics, contaminants found, community health concerns, exposure routes, impact on populations, and site activities. HazDat also includes data from the Environmental Protection Agency and the Comprehensive Environmental Response, Compensation, and Liability Information System. This can be accessed via the Internet at http://atsdr1.atsdr.cdc.gov:8080/hazdat.html#A3.1.

The ATSDR Science Corner is a gateway to environmental health information and resources. Its primary focus is to find and share global information resources on the relationships between exposure to hazardous substances and human health. This site can be accessed online at http://atsdr1.atsdr.cdc.gov:8080/cx.html.

AGENCY PUBLICATIONS

The Agency for Toxic Substances and Disease Registry (ATSDR) publishes a quarterly newsletter, *Hazardous Substances & Public Health,* which contains information about ATSDR activities, research reports, resources, health studies, and related programs and projects. The newsletter can be viewed on-line at http://atsdr1.atsdr.cdc.gov:8080/HEC/hsphhome.html or ordered by phone by calling (404) 639-5040 or faxing (404) 639-0560. Write to the newsletter's staff at Hazardous Substances & Public Health, ATSDR, 1600 Clifton Rd. NE, MS E33, Atlanta, GA 30333, or send E-mail to thw3@cdc.gov.

BIBLIOGRAPHY

Bonfatti, John F. "Verdese Carter Park Lead Results Released." *Oakland Post,* 29 October 1995.

"EH Update." *Journal of Environmental Health,* 1 January 1995.

Friede, Andrew, and Patrick W. O'Carroll. "CDC and ATSDR Electronic Information Resources for Health Officers." *Journal of Environmental Health,* 1 November 1996.

Gist, Ginger L., JeAnne Burg, and Timothy Radtke. "The Site Selection Process for the National Exposure Registry." *Journal of Environmental Health,* 1 January 1994.

Manns, Leslie D. "Regulation of On-Site Medical Waste Incinerators in the United States and the United Kingdom." *Journal of Economic Issues,* 1 June 1995.

Silver, Ken. "The Yellowed Archives of Yellowcake." *Public Health Reports,* 13 March 1996.

Wendt, Richard D., et al. "Evaluating the Sensitivity of Hazardous Substances Emergency Events Surveillance." *Journal of Environmental Health,* 1 May 1996.

Bureau of Alcohol, Tobacco, and Firearms (ATF)

PARENT ORGANIZATION: Department of the Treasury
ESTABLISHED: July 1, 1972
EMPLOYEES: 3,911

Contact Information:

ADDRESS: 650 Massachusetts Ave. NW
Washington, DC 20226
PHONE: (202) 966-7777
FAX: (202) 927–8500
E-MAIL: atfmail@atfhq.atf.treas.gov
URL: http://www.atf.treas.gov
DIRECTOR: John W. Magaw
DEPUTY DIRECTOR: Bradley A. Buckles

WHAT IS ITS MISSION?

As a law enforcement organization within the U.S. Department of the Treasury, the Bureau of Alcohol, Tobacco, and Firearms (ATF) is dedicated to reducing violent crime, collecting revenue from the sale of controlled substances, and reducing the incidence of arson and terrorism. The ATF enforces and regulates controlled substances that pose a threat to public health and safety. It also enforces federal laws relating to alcohol, tobacco, firearms, explosives, and arson. The bureau suppresses and prevents crime and violence through enforcement, regulation, and community outreach; by ensuring fair and proper revenue collection; by providing fair and effective industry regulation; by supporting federal, state, local, and international law enforcement; and through training programs that support criminal and regulatory enforcement functions.

HOW IS IT STRUCTURED?

The Bureau of Alcohol, Tobacco, and Firearms (ATF) falls under the Department of the Treasury, and its headquarters are in Washington, D.C. The ATF is headed by a director who is supported by a deputy director, a chief counsel, and an associate director for the bureau's Office of Law Enforcement. Assistant directors head the offices of Inspection, Liaison and Public Information, Management, Science and Information Technology, and Training and Professional Development.

Twenty-four criminal enforcement field divisions implement agency policies and coordinate regulatory and criminal law enforcement investigations. Field divisions assist federal, state, and local law enforcement offices in handling crime related to alcohol, tobacco, firearms, explosives, and arson. Another bureau division, the ATF Laboratories, analyzes vast numbers of alcohol and tobacco samples and other forensic evidence.

Two ATF facilities provide a clearinghouse of information specific to the bureau's mission. The National Tracing Center provides critical assistance to federal, state, and local law enforcement in their investigations of weapons used in violent crimes. For example, the bureau might trace a weapon's serial number or provide ballistics research. The Firearms and Explosives Licensing Center processes all federal license applications and operating permits for businesses engaged in the production of firearms and explosives.

Alcohol-related crimes, now the responsibility of the ATF, were once the responsibility of the Internal Revenue Service (IRS). During the Prohibition (1919-34) large quantities of illegal alcohol were seized and destroyed by agents.

(Courtesy of the Library of Congress)

PRIMARY FUNCTIONS

As a law enforcement agency, the objectives of the Bureau of Alcohol, Tobacco, and Firearms (ATF) are to maximize compliance with laws and to investigate violations of them, within its jurisdiction. The ATF suppresses illegal trafficking, possession, and use of firearms, destructive devices, and explosives. It also investigates arson, narcotics traffickers who use firearms and explosives, and interstate trafficking of distilled spirits and cigarettes. When possible the ATF helps federal, state, and local law enforcement agencies reduce crime and violence.

Regulatory enforcement entails ensuring full collection of tax revenue due from legal alcohol, tobacco, firearms, and ammunition manufacturing and sales. The bureau also prevents illegal transaction practices like deception, bribery, and improper health warnings. The ATF ensures that certain individuals cannot obtain licenses or permits, that explosives storage facilities are safe, and that federal, state, and local government agencies resolve problems of revenue protection. Also, the ATF maintains an audit trail so that firearms and explosives can be traced. Five district offices oversee regulatory enforcement in the Southeast, North Atlantic, Southwest, Midwest, and West.

PROGRAMS

The Bureau of Alcohol, Tobacco, and Firearms (ATF) combats crime through a variety of programs. The Industry Regulation and Partnership Program encourages members of the explosives industry to work together to develop prevention strategies, and it conducts seminars to provide current information on laws and regulations pertaining to explosives and their potential for illegal use. As a part of the ATF's strategy, the Explosives Program provides vital resources to local communities to investigate explosives incidents and arson-for-profit schemes. This program saves the insurance industry, and ultimately the public, millions of dollars in fraudulent claims annually. To investigate explosives incidents and arson, the ATF uses national response teams, international response teams, and arson task forces. These teams consist of ATF special agents, auditors, technicians, laboratory personnel, and dogs.

The Firearms Program pursues a combined regulatory and enforcement strategy. Investigative priorities focus on armed violent offenders and career criminals, narcotics traffickers, narco-terrorists, violent gangs, and domestic and international arms traffickers. The Achilles and Violent Offenders Program functions through task forces composed of ATF special agents, inspectors, and other federal agents. Task forces work in neighborhoods with the highest number of incidents of gang-related violence, drug trafficking, homicides, and other violent crimes. Project Lead also targets illegal firearms traffickers. It is an automated information system that analyzes information gathered by the ATF's National Trac-

BUDGET:

Bureau of Alcohol, Tobacco, and Firearms

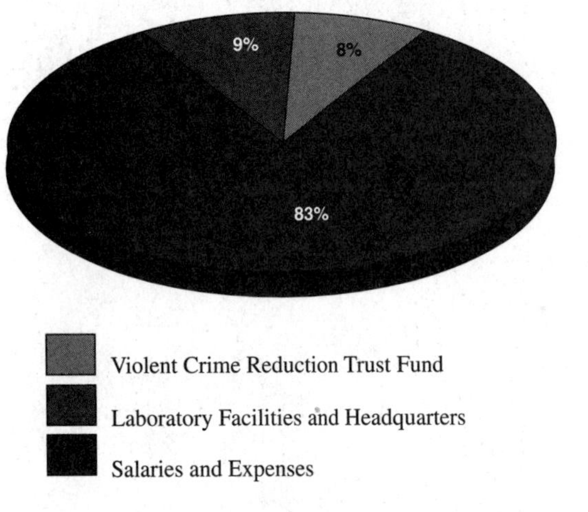

Violent Crime Reduction Trust Fund
Laboratory Facilities and Headquarters
Salaries and Expenses

ing Center. When crime-related firearms are traced, information concerning when the firearm entered the hands of the criminal and who provided that firearm to a criminal can be gathered. The ATF's goal is to eliminate the flow of firearms to violent criminals in order to reduce the overall violent crime rate.

In the area of prevention the ATF supports the Gang Resistance Education and Training (GREAT) program. Born in 1992, this program aims to reduce violence and gang activity in the Phoenix, Arizona, metropolitan area. GREAT is a school-based program in areas where gang activity exists or is emerging.

Alcohol and tobacco programs are in place to ensure the collection of excise taxes and accurate deposit and accounting for the taxes, to prevent criminal entry into the alcohol or tobacco industry, and to suppress label fraud, commercial bribery, diversion, smuggling, and other unlawful practices. The ATF's Revenue Management programs include a variety of activities and functions in connection with the processing, auditing, and recording of tax returns; the preparation of monthly operating reports; and the handling of accounting for deposits and payments for taxes, licenses, permits, and fees from the alcohol, tobacco, firearms, ammunition, and explosives industries.

BUDGET INFORMATION

The annual budget of the Bureau of Alcohol, Tobacco and Firearms is approximately $602 million. Of this appropriation 83 percent, or $497 million, is spent on salaries and expenses. The Violent Crime Reduction Trust Fund accounts for 8 percent, or $50.4 million, and Laboratory Facilities and Headquarters receives 9 percent, or $55 million.

HISTORY

The Bureau of Alcohol, Tobacco, and Firearms (ATF) recently marked its twenty-fifth anniversary as a bureau, yet it traces its history to the earliest days of federal law enforcement. The first alcohol tax was levied to pay debts left over from the American Revolution (1775–83). When outraged citizens staged the Whiskey Rebellion of 1794, President George Washington was forced to raise 15,000 troops to restore order and invoke the federal government's right to enforce such taxes. In 1863 the federal government needed revenue to pay for the American Civil War (1860–65) and so levied a tax on all distilled spirits. This action led to the creation of government offices that have grown into the Internal Revenue Service and the ATF. Collection of alcohol-related revenues continued until Congress passed the Eighteenth Amendment to the Constitution (1919), beginning the era of Prohibition.

With the criminalization of alcohol came the need for a bureau to enforce the law. At that time the Internal Revenue Service was given jurisdiction over enforcement of laws related to the illicit manufacture, sale, and transportation of alcohol. By the mid-1920s alcohol-related crimes necessitated the creation of the Bureau of Prohibition, which pursued the mobsters and racketeers who were building their criminal empires. Prohibition was repealed in 1934 with passage of the Twenty-first Amendment. Consequently, federal agencies were reorganized again and the Alcohol Tax Unit was established as a division of the Bureau of Internal Revenue.

Prohibition era criminal activity did not end but merely found new sources to profit from. Increases in the incidence of gun-related crimes led to the 1934 National Firearms Act, which specifically addressed the control of weapons used by criminals, for example, machine guns and sawed-off shotguns. The Alcohol Tax Unit was given new responsibilities as a result of its unique experience with both regulation of controlled substances and enforcement of those regulations. In the coming years similar legislation added tobacco and explosives to the responsibilities of this agency and gave it the title of Alcohol, Tobacco, and Firearms Division, which was part of the Internal Revenue Service. In 1970 more legislation, primarily the Organized Crime Control Act, produced studies that illustrated how the Alcohol, Tobacco, and Firearms Division was responsible for a widening spectrum of activities that were clearly distinguishable from those of the Internal Revenue Service. In 1972 the ATF was officially created and designated as a distinct division within the Department of the Treasury.

The ATF marked its twenty-fifth anniversary in 1997 surrounded by controversy. The agency came under intense scrutiny by political and private organizations as a result of the deaths of agents and civilians in several highly-publicized agency actions. The agency has also been accused of becoming increasingly militaristic and confrontational in its style of investigation. The ATF explains this trend by referring to the increasingly violent nature of crimes and the battle-oriented title of the national "War on Drugs," in which the ATF has been a high-profile participant. During the mid-1990s the agency's activities were thoroughly investigated by the U.S. attorney general. The director was replaced and a reorganization and retraining of key personnel ensued.

FAST FACTS

More Americans were murdered with firearms in the four years between 1988 and 1991 than were killed in battle during the Vietnam War.

(Source: Department of Defense. "Defense Almanac/FBI Uniform Crime Reports," 1998.)

CURRENT POLITICAL ISSUES

The Bureau of Alcohol, Tobacco, and Firearms (ATF) has been the focus of a series of investigations beginning in the early 1990s as a result of incidents that resulted in the deaths of ATF agents and suspects. Two highly publicized incidents, known by their location, are Waco, Texas, and Ruby Ridge, Idaho. These two incidents prompted Senate investigations, a storm of criticism by groups like the American Civil Liberties Union, and a reexamination of the role of federal law enforcement activities in an increasingly crime-sensitive nation. One explanation for an alleged increase in militarization of the ATF is that the agency is responding to an increasingly violent era in which the drug war and terrorist activities have forced it to take more drastic action in fighting crime. Accusations of ATF misconduct range from inappropriate behavior on the part of agents, to destruction of property and improperly conducted raids. The most serious accusation is the needless loss of life at both Waco and Ruby Ridge.

Case Study: Ruby Ridge and Waco

Ruby Ridge, Idaho, is normally an idyllic setting. It is also a place where some Americans have gone to escape the encroachment of government and culture upon their lives. The Weaver family had sought this kind of refuge in Idaho. Randy Weaver, a self-described white separatist, came to the attention of the ATF because of his association with the Aryan Nation, a neo-Nazi white supremacist organization. The ATF used an informant to purchase illegal weapons from Randy Weaver. Accusations of entrapment surrounded this initial ATF activity. Weaver ignored trial dates related to the sale of firearms, which ultimately led to the August 21, 1992, shootings that took the life of a U.S. marshall as well as Weaver's wife and his son.

Simultaneously, ATF agents were investigating a religious group called the Branch Davidians in Waco, Texas, whose members were believed to be stockpiling significant numbers of firearms. The ATF raided the compound on February 28, 1993, resulting in the deaths of four ATF agents and six Branch Davidians. This led to a standoff, followed by a second raid on April 19, 1993, during which a fire at the compound killed 81 people, including 23 children. The televised incident was thoroughly investigated by a Senate subcommittee and the U.S. attorney general. The investigations revealed the ATF had an exaggerated profile of the group. They also concluded that not only was the raid inappropriately militaristic, it was poorly executed.

U.S. Attorney General Janet Reno, at the time only recently confirmed, was involved in the final decision to end the standoff that resulted in the fire. Her hope was that agents would rescue the children still within the compound. The deaths of Davidians, particularly the children, caused Reno significant regret and distress. Following the investigations, two ATF supervisors, Chuck Sarabyn and Phillip Chojinacki, were dismissed, although they were later reinstated at a lower rank. The conclusion of the incident ushered in the appointment of a new director, G. R. Dickerson, who said before a Senate subcommittee, "the line between vigorous law enforcement, which I demand, and overzealous law, which I deplore, is a thin one, but it is one which we are determined to follow."

Public Impact

The impact of these incidents on society in general has been significant. Investigations of militia groups and federal response to them is under intense scrutiny. Federal law enforcement agencies are increasingly required to account for their actions. Interest groups already critical of the federal government's regulation of firearms have used the incidents to crusade against enforcement of laws they deem unconstitutional. For example, the National Rifle Association has used the actions of the ATF to advance its anti-gun control message. Opinion of federal law enforcement took a negative turn as a result of these incidents. In the wake of Ruby Ridge and Waco came the Comprehensive Terrorism Prevention Act of 1995, a bill that strengthened the powers of federal law

FAST FACTS

Licensed firearms dealers sell an estimated 7.5 million guns per year, including 3.5 million handguns.

(Source: Bureau of Alcohol, Tobacco, and Firearms, 1998.)

enforcement authorities in their pursuit of terrorists. However, politicians and citizens alike question the ability of agencies like the ATF to use those powers wisely. Perhaps the most tragic aftermath of Waco was the bombing of the Alfred Murrah Federal Building in Oklahoma City, Oklahoma, in which 168 people died. The incident is considered to have been a revenge attack on the federal government for its actions against the Branch Davidians.

SUCCESSES AND FAILURES

A string of arsons, primarily against black churches in the South, prompted the Bureau of Alcohol, Tobacco, and Firearms (ATF) to create the National Church Arson Task Force. To date the ATF has launched 429 investigations into church arsons. It has made arrests in thirty percent of the cases, nearly twice the amount for arson in general. There have been 110 convictions related to 77 arsons since January 1995.

Fears of a racially-motivated conspiracy have not, as yet, been supported by the task force. Although some of the arsons were committed by extremists, the majority were the result of a wide variety of causes. The crimes are extremely difficult to investigate, and many of the six hundred recorded cases will go unsolved. Federal agencies continue to investigate, educate church leaders, and develop strategies to combat this trend.

FUTURE DIRECTIONS

CEASEFIRE is a new firearms enforcement program that takes advantage of state-of-the-art technology. The program will utilize a unique ballistic comparison system known as the Integrated Ballistic Identification System, which will allow firearms technicians to digitize, catalog, and automatically sort bullet and shell casing marks. This will allow the Bureau of Alcohol, Tobacco, and Firearms (ATF) to accelerate investigations into the use of firearms in criminal activities. The system will be linked to the National Tracing Center, a clearinghouse for firearms data providing 24-hour assistance to federal, state, local, and foreign enforcement agencies in tracing guns used in crimes.

AGENCY RESOURCES

The Bureau of Alcohol, Tobacco, and Firearms (ATF) Web site, at http://www.atf.treas.gov, provides a variety of information regarding the structure, funding, and programs related to the agency's law enforcement activities surrounding controlled substances.

AGENCY PUBLICATIONS

The Bureau of Alcohol, Tobacco, and Firearms (ATF) publishes a number of documents that either explain the goals and progress of programs or provide regulatory information to citizens involved in the sale or purchase of controlled substances. General publications include the *Youth Crime Gun Interdiction Initiative,* the *National Church Arson Task Force First Year Report for the President,* and the *Church Threat Assessment Guide.* Other ATF publications explain compliance with federal regulations in relation to alcohol and tobacco sales. Among publications specific to firearms and explosives are the *List of Explosive Materials* and the *Federal Firearms Regulation Reference Guide.* Other ATF publications provide specific compliance with federal tax law. ATF forms and publications are available by writing to the ATF Distribution Center, PO Box 5950, Springfield, VA 22150-5950, or by calling (703) 455-7801. ATF publications can also be viewed and printed by visiting the agency's Web site at http://www.atf.treas.gov.

BIBLIOGRAPHY

Butterfield, Fox. "Report Links Crimes to States with Weak Gun Control." *New York Times,* 4 April 1997, p. A14.

Johnston, David. "Senate Report Faults F.B.I. and Other Agencies on Idaho Incident." *New York Times,* 22 December 1995, p. A35.

Morganthau, Tom. "Fires in the Night." *Newsweek,* 24 June 1996, p. 28.

———. "Janet Reno Confronts Waco's Bitter Legacy." *Newsweek,* 15 May 1995, p. 26.

Vizzard, William J. *In the Crossfire: A Political History of the Bureau of Alcohol, Tobacco, and Firearms.* Boulder, Colo.: Lynne Riemer Publishers, 1997.

"Waco's Unlearned Lessons." *New York Times,* 31 July 1995, p. A12.

Bureau of Economic Analysis (BEA)

WHAT IS ITS MISSION?

As the nation's accountant, the Bureau of Economic Analysis (BEA) collects, integrates, and interprets a variety of economic data in order to present a complete picture of the U.S. economy. BEA data is used to provide information on economic issues like regional development, economic growth, and the strength of the U.S. economy in the global market. In sum, it is the BEA's job to track the U.S. economy and make its findings available to the government and the public.

PARENT ORGANIZATION: Department of Commerce
ESTABLISHED: January 1, 1972
EMPLOYEES: 420

Contact Information:

ADDRESS: Department of Commerce
Washington, DC 20230
PHONE: (202) 606-9900
FAX: (202) 606-5310
URL: http://www.bea.doc.gov
DIRECTOR: J. Steven Landefeld
DEPUTY DIRECTOR: Rosemary D. Marcuss

HOW IS IT STRUCTURED?

The Bureau of Economic Analysis (BEA) along with the Bureau of the Census, falls under the Economics and Statistics Administration, which is part of the Department of Commerce and is led by the undersecretary for economic and statistical analysis. The director of the BEA reports directly to the undersecretary.

In addition to the office of the director and its associated administrative offices, the BEA has two significant officials involved in formulating and determining the course of the bureau's work, the chief statistician and the chief economist. The chief statistician is responsible for seeing that the statistical methods used by the bureau to study its data lead to accurate analysis. The chief economist is responsible for making valid interpretations and projections based upon the BEA's data. The BEA also includes associate directors for the BEA's three program areas: national income, expenditures, and wealth accounts; regional economics; and international economics.

PRIMARY FUNCTIONS

The BEA's chief function is to study the U.S. economy. The BEA not only studies the economy as a whole, but through its various programs it breaks the economy down to study trends across states, industries, and people. In addition the BEA prepares extensive reports on the economy. Many commonly cited figures, such as the gross national product or gross domestic product were developed by the BEA to describe how the U.S. economy is performing. Through a substantial network of computer information services and print and electronic media, the BEA distributes much of its information at no charge to the public.

PROGRAMS

The BEA divides its programs into three primary areas, represented by the associate directors for national income, international economics, and regional economics. Within these program areas the BEA operates programs intended to provide a picture of the various sectors of the U.S. economy.

The national income program collects data and reports on the national income and product accounts, which includes the numbers for the gross domestic product, the BEA's measure of how the U.S. economy as a whole has performed. The national income and product accounts provide a quantitative view of the production, distribution, and use of the goods and services produced in the United States. This program also prepares estimates of the total personal income in the United States, along with the nation's tangible wealth and gross product by industry.

International economics programs include the study of U.S. international transactions (balance of payments) with foreign countries and the exports and imports of goods and services. Using survey-based data, the bureau tracks U.S. investments abroad and foreign direct investment in the United States. Regional economic accounts include the gross state products, total and per capita personal income for each state, and total and per capita personal income for each county and metropolitan area in the United States. The bureau also prepares projections for regional economic activity, and its information allows comparison between different regions in the United States.

BUDGET INFORMATION

For budgeting purposes, the BEA, the policy support staffs of Economic and Statistical Analysis, and STAT-USA, the office's statistical electronic bulletin board, are all federally budgeted together under "Economic and Statistical Analysis." A small part of this budget is covered by subscriptions to STAT-USA or BEA publications, but most of the funds are acquired through congressional appropriations. The estimated 1998 budget for the BEA was about $42.3 million.

HISTORY

At the initiative of Commerce Secretary Herbert Hoover, balance of payments accounting for the United States was begun in 1921 in order to provide information about the role of the United States in the world economy. During the same year, the first publication of the *Survey of Current Business* was released.

The Great Depression of the 1930s led to the realization that more information about the nation's economy was necessary in order to predict and avoid further national financial disasters. In 1933 the first official continuing series on national income was completed by the Commerce Department under the direction of economist Simon Kuznets and released in the *Survey of Current Business*. The national accounting system devised by Kuznets later earned him a Nobel Prize and is structurally the same system used by the BEA today.

During the 1940s, the Bureau of Foreign and Domestic Commerce introduced estimates of the gross national product (GNP) to measure the effect of World War II (1939–45) on the U.S. economy. In 1946 the Office of Business Economics, the BEA's predecessor, supplemented the annual balance of payments estimates with quarterly estimates. The GNP, or total amount of goods and services sold in the United States, became the benchmark by which the U.S. economy was measured. In the 1950s the first estimates of GNP adjusted for inflation, or the constant-dollar GNP, were introduced to provide a better measure of economic growth. Later in that decade, the bureau turned its attention to U.S. economic involvement in other countries, conducting a census of U.S. business investments abroad and surveying business enterprises under foreign ownership.

An Expanded Role

The role of the regional and international programs grew remarkably during the 1960s. Quarterly estimates of personal income by state and annual estimates at the sub-state level were published for the first time, and a consistent set of regional and demographic projections were developed. The economy of the 1970s, characterized by inflation, structural change, new international considerations, and concern with the environment, led to similar rapid changes in the Department of Commerce. In 1972, under President Richard Nixon, the Bureau of Economic Affairs and the Bureau of the Census were established within a single office within the Department of Commerce and their functions were defined much as they are today.

During the 1970s the BEA expanded and improved information on prices in the national accounts, took over business cycle indicators and devised an inflation-adjusted system for analyzing them, took responsibility for the survey of business capital spending, and began work on a system to account for capital stocks and depreciation in its indexes. In 1975 estimates of personal income for all U.S. counties were published for the first time. The practice of foreign investment increased dramatically in the mid-1970s, leading to legislation that required the BEA to conduct periodic surveys of U.S. direct investment abroad as well as foreign investment in the United States. Environmental legislation provided the BEA with additional responsibilities, leading to significant levels of spending for pollution abatement and control.

FAST FACTS

The Gross Domestic Product of the United States was a little over $7 trillion for the first quarter of 1997—the first time in history the GDP had reached that mark.

(Source: Bureau of Economic Analysis. "NIPA archives," 1997.)

The 1980s and 1990s

The U.S. economy underwent further changes in the 1980s, and the BEA struggled to keep its measures meaningful. A new price index was created for computers, for example, to account for rapid technological changes, and experimental estimates of gross state product by industry were first published in 1985. These estimates increased the ability of regional economists to study economic competitiveness and the effects of state economies on changes in the national economy. As the economy became increasingly service oriented and less oriented to manufacturing, the bureau conducted a 1987 benchmark survey of transactions in services. The resulting statistics supported U.S. efforts to include trade in services in international trade negotiations.

Throughout the 1980s and 1990s, the changes undergone by the economy—dominated by a shift toward trade in services rather than goods and the rapid growth of technology—were so radical that some critics began to question the use of the old standard of economic performance, the GNP. Officials and economists began to tinker with it. Over time it came to be known as the gross domestic product (GDP), to better reflect the sector of the economy being measured. In 1996 the BEA's computation of the GDP was revised in a complex statistical scheme to make the GDP more accurately reflect the nation's economy. Using chain-weighted instead of fixed-weighted figures, the bureau attempted to make the GDP a more flexible measure. (Chain-weighted figures are expressed in real dollars adjusted for inflation and market changes, whereas fixed-weighted figures are expressed in one sum of current dollars not adjusted for inflation.) The GDP is now expressed by the bureau not in constant dollars, but in terms of an index, a dramatic change in the way the U.S. economy is evaluated.

CURRENT POLITICAL ISSUES

The gross domestic product (GDP) has become the benchmark by which the U.S. economy is evaluated, and the BEA is the agency in charge of computing the GDP and publishing a detailed report on its contents. Probably no economic figure is more important in the United States; the GDP is the foundation on which government budgeting and public policy are established. The GDP is a measure of the total amount of money spent on goods and services produced in the United States. Its simplified interpretation by economists and politicians equates to the notion that, the more money that is spent in the United States, the more disposable income that exists in the hands of Americans. Therefore, a high GDP is an indicator of a strong economy.

Case Study: Statistical Problems with the GDP

In its most basic sense, the GDP was flawed from the start in terms of the way its numbers were compiled and weighted. The BEA used to calculate the rate at which the economy grew by using real GDP, a figure that was adjusted for inflation. The underlying assumption is that prices and characteristics of goods and services don't change very quickly in relation to each other. The technological explosion of the 1990s makes this assumption obsolete, however, as revealed in an example given by Susan Dentzer in the July 1997 issue of *U.S. News and World Report.*

Until recently the BEA's methods assumed the average new car and a sophisticated personal computer would both have cost about $16,400 in 1987. In 1995 the BEA's methods assumed that the computer and the car still cost the same, although a car would cost closer to $20,000 and a computer's cost would be closer to $4,500. When the government added up all the cars and computers sold, it overstated the value of computer sales in relation to cars. This problem led to serious distortions in computing the overall worth of goods sold in the United States. The BEA's 1996 switch to a chain-weighted rather than a fixed-weighted GDP made some adjustments for this problem. While addressing the statistical difficulties associated with its economic yardstick, however, the

BIOGRAPHY:
Simon Kuznets

American Economist (1901–1985) American economist, researcher, and author Simon Kuznets won the Nobel Prize in 1971 for pioneering the use of a nation's gross national product as a means of analyzing economic growth. This economic structure remains the national accounting system still used by the Bureau of Economic Analysis to this day. Kuznets's fields of specialization included the study of economic growth, development, and planning; economic theory and policy; the economics of technological change; and demographic economics. In addition to researching these subjects, Kuznets taught them as well. Kuznets was particularly interested in the relationship between a population's size and traits and long-term economic growth. His research was not limited to the United States. Kuznets analyzed the national income and growth data of a number of industrialized nations. Through his research Kuznets uncovered what he called "new truths" about the relationships that exist in the world. He did so by applying a more commonsense, rational approach to economics, instead of using more formal, traditional economic models. An example of "new truth" is the discovery that there is a relationship between long-term economic growth in a society and the distribution of income within that society.

bureau has been hesitant to address the much larger social and economic problems underlying the GDP.

The use of the GDP has been criticized in terms of philosophy and economic theory, but this criticism has peaked in recent years in light of the rapid changes taking place in the U.S. society and its economy. The GDP is an accurate numerical measure of how much Americans buy, but it inevitably comes up short when used to measure the actual quality of life in the United States. In the past decade, while economic experts have pointed to a booming GDP as evidence of relative economic prosperity, some Americans have still complained of hardship.

Critics of the GDP argue that the way the policy establishment measures the economy, and the way Americans actually experience it, are two completely different things. This difference, according to GDP critics, is a product of a fundamental flaw in the thinking behind the GDP. The problem with using mere consumption or investment as a measure of prosperity is that it does not take into account what is being consumed or invested in. A few examples quickly expose this problem.

A person living in a high-crime neighborhood might purchase a security system out of fear of being victimized. In terms of GDP, the money spent on this equipment equals economic prosperity. The increasing number of prison construction projects, undertaken as a result of our growing crime problem, are also added into the GDP. But are these expenses indicative of a healthy, prosperous society? Everything produced and sold is not necessarily indicative of prosperity; more production and purchasing does not automatically equal greater economic well-being. In the GDP, money that is spent fighting diseases, combating social problems like drug abuse, and cleaning up after environmental and natural disasters is tallied by the BEA as economic growth, for the sole reason that money has been spent.

Another criticism of the GDP is more subtle—by including only the part of the economy that is transacted through money, it ignores the dynamics of the household. As more married couples find it necessary for both to work in order to support a household, more money is spent on child care. As families become increasingly pressed for time, more money may be spent on going out to eat, rather than having a meal at the family table. As household functions are replaced by purchased services, the GDP rises, indicating a positive upswing, when in reality the family dynamic may indicate otherwise.

Critics of the GDP also argue that a measure of economic prosperity should make distinctions between the costs and benefits of the goods and services consumed. It must also begin to value the dynamics of the household and the state of the natural environment, both of which are beyond a monetary price. Government has been resistant to adopt such changes, however. An economic measure must be both scientific and value-free, officials argue, and any attempt to gauge how the economy actually affects people would involve making assumptions about the way Americans should live. The government can fix problems concerning the actual numbers of the GDP, but it is hesitant to begin presuming how to measure quality of life.

It is in these philosophical terms, however, that critics have attacked the GDP. To leave social and environmental costs out of the compilation of the GDP, they say, does not avoid value judgements. Instead, it implicitly makes the judgement that crime, the breakdown of families, underemployment, and the loss of free time are irrelevant to the economic picture.

FUTURE DIRECTIONS

The BEA's need to improve GDP and related data loom large, and the bureau recognizes this. The National Academy of Sciences has released two studies exploring how U.S. systems for collecting and analyzing data have fallen behind the times. The BEA is now focusing on improving the accuracy of chain-weighted figures and other economic measures. The BEA is also taking part in an international effort to agree on common definitions used for collecting data on portfolio investments and other economic matters. Participating countries will modify data collection systems to improve consistency and fill gaps in coverage. By creating a more standardized system of data exchange, the BEA hopes to increase the accuracy of its international data. In addition, the bureau has set a number of customer service goals that involve increasing the accuracy, reliability, and timeliness of BEA data. An improved computer system resulting in a wider range of electronic access to data is a significant goal for the bureau.

AGENCY RESOURCES

Those seeking additional information about the work of the BEA should contact the Public Information Office, Bureau of Economic Analysis, Department of Commerce, Washington, DC 20230; phone (202) 606-9900. In addition to the BEA's comprehensive Web site, two other on-line resources exist for accessing BEA data: FEDSTATS, a set of links to federal statistical resources on the World Wide Web at http://www.fedstats.gov, and STAT-USA at http://www.stat-usa.gov, a service allowing users to access data from many providers at a single Web site. Some of STAT-USA's information is available only to subscribers. The BEA also sells CD-ROMs containing data and tables from the national economic, social, and environmental data bank and the regional economic information system. These can also be ordered through the public information office.

The BEA has created the BEA regional facts (BEARFACTS) database, available via the BEA Web site at http://www.bea.doc.gov. A project of the Regional Economic Measurement Divisions, BEARFACTS offers computer-generated narratives providing information on the personal income of states and counties, including per capita personal income, total personal income, total personal income broken down into components, and earnings by industry. The narratives are brief and easy to read, and provide an attractive alternative to poring over numerous charts and tables.

AGENCY PUBLICATIONS

Two regularly produced BEA publications are the *Survey of Current Business,* the BEA's monthly journal containing estimates and analyses of U.S. economic activity, and the *User's Guide to BEA Information,* which describes BEA products, tells how and where to order them, and offers directions for other information requests. Both of these and many other BEA publications can be downloaded from the BEA Web site at http://www.bea.doc.gov, or print versions can be ordered from the Public Information Office, Bureau of Economic Analysis, Department of Commerce, Washington, DC 20230; phone (202) 606-9900. Paid subscriptions are also available. The vast number of BEA reports and publications are collections of data with titles such as *Fixed Reproducible Tangible Wealth in the United States, 1925–89* and *Regional Multipliers: A User Handbook for the Regional Input-Output Modeling System (RIMS II).* Many of these can be downloaded from the BEA Web site.

BIBLIOGRAPHY

Cobb, Clifford, Ted Halstead, and Jonathan Rowe. "If the GDP Is Up Why Is America So Down?" *Atlantic Monthly,* October 1995, pp. 59–78.

Cooper, James C., and Aaron Bernstein. "Suddenly, the Economy Doesn't Measure Up: The Government's New Statistics Make the Gains of the '90s Look Weak." *Business Week,* 31 July 1995, pp. 74–6.

Dentzer, Susan. "The Growing Mysteries of the GDP." *U.S. News and World Report,* 30 October 1995, p. 67.

Eisner, Robert. "What Counts and How to Count It." *Wall Street Journal,* 12 November 1996, p. A22.

Evans, Mike. "Minor Player, Major Impact." *Industry Week,* 17 July 1995, p. 76.

Rowe, Jonathan. "Replace the GDP." *Washington Monthly,* January–February 1996, pp. 34–6.

Shaikh, Anwar M., and E. Ahmet Tonak. *Measuring the Wealth of Nations: The Political Economy of National Accounts.* New York: Cambridge University Press, 1994.

"Statistics Producer's Corner." *Business Economics,* January 1996, pp. 65–6.

"User's Guide to BEA Information." *Survey of Current Business,* April 1996, pp. 88–132.

Bureau of Engraving and Printing (BEP)

PARENT ORGANIZATION: Department of the Treasury
ESTABLISHED: August 29, 1862
EMPLOYEES: 2,877

Contact Information:

ADDRESS: 14th and C Sts. SW
Washington, DC 20228
PHONE: (202) 874-3019
URL: http://www.bep.treas.gov
DIRECTOR: Larry Rolufs

WHAT IS ITS MISSION?

The Bureau of Engraving and Printing (BEP) is the federal government's source for secure financial documents such as bills, securities, notes, and postage. Their most familiar products are the paper money and postage stamps Americans use every day, but the BEP also produces other securities and notes for the government. It is the BEP's mission to produce these securely and cost-effectively and to make them as difficult to counterfeit as possible.

HOW IS IT STRUCTURED?

The BEP is headed by a director who is appointed by the Secretary of the Treasury. The director's office is located in Washington, D.C., where the bureau is headquartered. The Washington facility was the only location for the printing of secured documents until 1991 when the BEP completed a modern, high-volume, secure documents manufacturing plant in Fort Worth, Texas. The Texas facility provides currency to western Federal Reserve Banks while the Washington, D.C., facility supplies the rest of the country.

The BEP is staffed by a wide variety of personnel. Among them are administrative and maintenance personnel, printing press operators, and engravers. Although engravers make up only a small percentage of BEP staff, they are highly skilled artisans who apprentice for years in preparation for the design and production of the images on BEP documents. The nature of the products manufactured by the BEP requires that the agency maintain high standards of security. BEP facilities are carefully guarded, personnel are monitored, and equipment is frequently inventoried.

PRIMARY FUNCTIONS

The BEP manufactures financial documents and other secured documents used to conduct business. The bureau designs and prints a variety of secured documents, including U.S. paper currency, Federal Reserve notes, U.S. postage stamps, Treasury securities, identification cards, naturalization certificates, other special security documents, and items such as White House invitations. All of the bureau's products are designed and manufactured with special features designed to foil attempts to counterfeit them.

PROGRAMS

The BEP does not operate any programs per se, as the production of secured documents is its only major function. In addition to producing secured documents the BEP researches ways to improve them, especially how to make them more difficult to counterfeit. Due to its expertise in this area, the BEP is often called upon to advise federal agencies on document security.

The BEP does maintain some programs for the public including facility tours, redemption of damaged currency, and sale of specialty items like uncut sheets of money. Tours are only available at the Washington, D.C., branch of the bureau. The Office of Currency Standards will redeem at face value any U.S. currency that has been so mutilated that less than half the bill remains or is so badly damaged that it is no longer recognizable as currency.

BUDGET INFORMATION

The approximate budget appropriated by Congress for the BEP was $469 million in 1998. The bulk of this sum, $371 million or 79 percent, of the total BEP budget, was spent on the process of printing currency. Other programs that were allocated money in the BEP budget were postage printing, $67 million or 14 percent; purchase of operating equipment, $30 million or 6 percent; and plant alterations and experimental equipment, $1 million or 0.2 percent.

HISTORY

In the early years of U.S. history, paper currency was not issued by the federal government. Instead, federal currency consisted entirely of coin, and on a local level many used notes of credit issued by their banks for day-to-day transactions. The BEP traces its beginnings to August 29, 1862, when six men and women worked in a basement room of the Treasury building preparing $1 and $2 U.S. notes. These early notes, known as greenbacks for the color of ink used, were printed by private banks for the Department of the Treasury, which issued the first paper currency of the United States in 1862 as part of its plan to finance the Civil War (1860–65).

After the war the BEP continued to grow. Initially it only handled some of the nation's currency needs, with private companies also printing bills under contract with the government. By 1877 however, the BEP had demonstrated the ability to do the job as well as any contractor and became the sole manufacturer of U.S. paper currency and a number of other official documents. As the Treasury printing facility grew so did concerns regarding the safety of the facility from the threat of fire. The flammable combination of chemicals and paper in the printing process led to a unique solution. In 1877 the Plate Printer Force, which included experienced firemen, formed a fire brigade to protect BEP property. The group held drills every Saturday in preparation for an emergency.

From 1877 forward, the greatest challenge the BEP has faced has been keeping up with demand. Automation has played an important role in the methods used to print documents, and the BEP started using automated machinery as early as 1898. Equipment speed increases since that time allowed the BEP to print 38 million notes per day in the 1990s.

BUDGET:

Bureau of Engraving and Printing

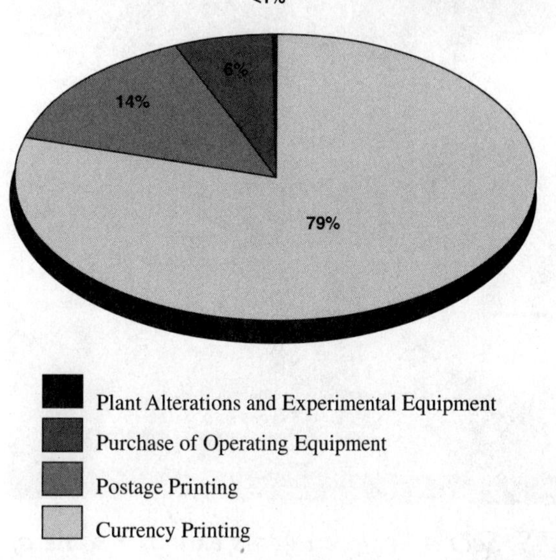

Plant Alterations and Experimental Equipment
Purchase of Operating Equipment
Postage Printing
Currency Printing

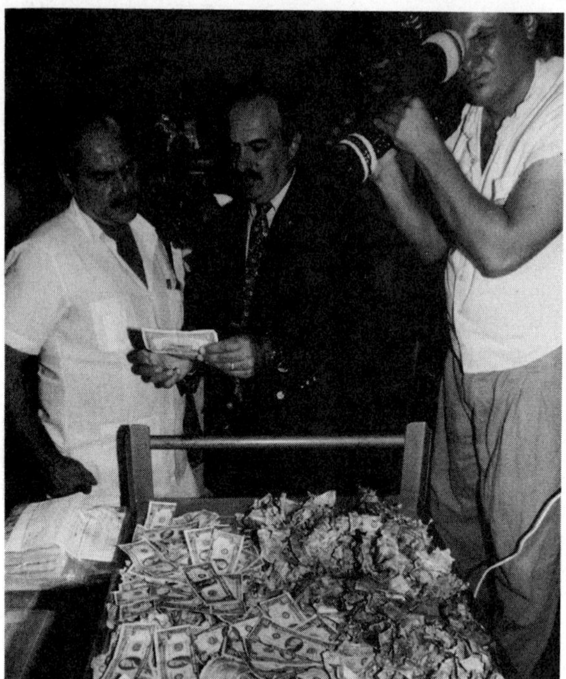

U.S. Secret Service agents examine some of the over $100,000 in seized counterfeit money. The BEP uses special anti-counterfeiting measures such as watermarking, embedded security thread, and color-shifting ink. *(Photograph by Joshua Roberts. UPI/Corbis-Bettmann)*

The bureau took over the printing of all revenue stamps in 1876 and began printing postage stamps in 1894, the last major addition to its product line. The BEP has often been called on to print special documents, particularly during wartime. During World War I (1914–18) the BEP printed 500,000 Liberty Bonds a day. During World War II (1939–45) it printed two million War Savings Bonds a day. The BEP also printed special currencies during World War II for use in Hawaii and any captured territories, and it made worn-looking currency for Americans operating behind enemy lines in the Philippines. Since the 1950s the BEP has not been called upon to print anything more unusual than the stamps and cash Americans use every day, but its headquarters remains one of Washington's most popular tourist attractions.

CURRENT POLITICAL ISSUES

The BEP operates primarily as a manufacturing division of the Department of the Treasury. It relies on outside companies to provide specialized materials and, in some cases, it works on a contract basis. The lucrative contract for supplying paper was granted for 117 consecutive years to the Massachusetts family-owned firm Crane & Company. The company had been negotiating the contract with Treasury officials yearly and were audited to ensure the accuracy of cost-to-profit ratio of the contract.

Case Study: The Crane & Company Paper Contract

In 1984 the Competition and Contracting Act forced the BEP to open the contract process to new bidders. Crane & Company's potential loss of the contract gained attention by Massachusetts politicians who investigated whether the new plan was financially sound. They were angered to find that within the contract process the BEP was offering $100 million in incentives to companies who bid for the paper contract. The financial incentive was meant to attract new bidders that did not have the necessary equipment; the money was to be used for the purchase of the specialized equipment. The argument between Treasury officials and Senate politicians focused on the contract process and the risks versus benefits of using multiple paper suppliers. Arguments were made on both sides concerning the security issues and government costs associated with opening the bidding process.

Working against Crane & Company were questions raised by the Treasury about paper prices from 1988 to 1991, which led to a five-year investigation. As a result the Treasury requested that the Justice Department issue a subpoena for Crane & Company records. While the investigation continues the Treasury must proceed with accepting bids in a competitive process that is meant to bring goods and services to the BEP at the best possible price.

SUCCESSES AND FAILURES

Improving the security of U.S. currency is a priority for the BEP. Working with the National Academy of Sciences, the Federal Reserve Bank, and the U.S. Secret Service, the BEP considered more than 120 security features before deciding on the final design of the new series of currency that went into circulation in 1996.

Some of the changes to the new $100 bill designed to defeat counterfeiters are: a security thread that glows red under ultraviolet light, a watermark that is visible only when held up to a light, micro printing within the phrases "USA 100" and "United States of America," and color-shifting ink that looks green when viewed straight on but black when viewed from an angle. These new security measures are meant to combat counterfeiters who have taken advantage of high-quality color copying machines and other printing equipment in order to duplicate secured documents. In the first year of issuance the

U.S. Secret Service found that the 1996 $100 bills were counterfeited one-eighteenth as often as the older bills, although the newer bills represented only one-third of the bills in circulation.

FUTURE DIRECTIONS

The BEP is still in the process of introducing its new Series 1996 currency. This is a process that is expected to take some years, as it takes time to replace widely circulated bills such as the $20, $5, and $1. As it introduces this new series the BEP will continue to focus its efforts on security measures used in the printing of currencies and on upgraded automation in its production facilities. By lowering the cost of manufacturing currency the U.S. government clears a higher profit on each note printed.

AGENCY RESOURCES

A variety of information about the BEP is available at the agency's Web site at http://www.bep.treas.gov. The site contains information regarding sales to the public, tours, procurement, administration, and damaged currency redemption.

AGENCY PUBLICATIONS

Other than U.S. paper money the BEP produces a few publications, most of which deal with counterfeiting. Educational materials on the Series 1996 currency and counterfeiting, including a CD-ROM, VHS tapes, and pamphlets, can be ordered on-line at http://www.bep.treas.gov/business/orderform or write to New Designs For Your Money, Federal Reserve Bank of Kansas City—Omaha Branch, PO Box 3958, Omaha, NE 68103-0958. Some of these materials are also available at Federal Reserve Banks. The BEP also produces a number of items for sale to the public including uncut currency, copies of the Gettysburg Address, and portraits of U.S. presidents. All of these products are available for purchase on-line at http://www.bep.treas.gov/catalog/index.cfm.

FAST FACTS

The BEP produces 38 million notes a day with a face value of approximately $541 million.

(Source: Bureau of Engraving and Printing. "Fun Facts," 1998.)

BIBLIOGRAPHY

Gaouette, Nicole. "A Family Firm's Fight for Rags to Riches Contract." *Christian Science Monitor*, 12 March 1997, p. 1.

Lamb, David. "The Budget Stalemate: Crisis Fails to Slow U.S. Money Presses." *Los Angeles Times*, 4 January 1996, p. A12.

Lipkin, Richard. "Guarding Against Fake Money." *Consumers' Research Magazine*, 1 May 1996, p. 19.

McClellan, Doug. "Desktop Counterfeiting." *Technology Review*, 12 February 1995, p. 38.

Royce, Knut. "Mystery of the Missing Money." *Newsday*, 11 February 1996, p. A31.

———. "Made in China: Something Fishy About 1934 Bills with 80s Signatures." *Newsday*, 12 February 1997, p. A07.

Bureau of Export Administration (BXA)

PARENT ORGANIZATION: Department of Commerce
ESTABLISHED: October 1, 1987
EMPLOYEES: 390

Contact Information:

ADDRESS: 14th St. & Constitution Ave. NW
Washington, DC 20230
PHONE: (202) 482-2721
FAX: (202) 482-2421
URL: http://www.bxa.doc.gov
UNDERSECRETARY: William A. Reinsch
ASSISTANT SECRETARY: R. Roger Majak
ASSISTANT SECRETARY: F. Amanda DeBusk

WHAT IS ITS MISSION?

According to the undersecretary of the Bureau of Export Administration (BXA), the BXA "enhances the nation's security and its economic prosperity by controlling exports for national security, foreign policy, and short supply reasons. [It] administer[s] the Export Administration Act by developing export control policies, issuing export licenses, and prosecuting violators."

HOW IS IT STRUCTURED?

The BXA is a bureau within the Department of Commerce, and its administrator holds the title of undersecretary for export administration. The administrative functions of the bureau are centered in a single Office of Administration, which conducts affairs such as budgeting, personnel, public affairs, and congressional relations.

The BXA has two operating units, export administration and export enforcement. Export administration functions are divided among five primary units, two of which control exporting of specific materials, the Office of Chemical and Biological Controls and Treaty Compliance and the Office of Nuclear and Missile Technology Controls. The Office of Strategic Trade and Foreign Policy Controls implements export controls under an international agreement dealing with conventional weapons; it is also the Commerce Department office responsible for controlling exports to countries with histories of terrorist activity. Ensuring the U.S. defense industry can meet national security requirements and analyzing the impact of U.S. export controls on U.S. industrial competitiveness is the function of the Office of Strategic Industry and Economic Security. The Office of Exporter Services counsels exporters, conducts export control seminars, and administers export license applications.

The Office of Export Enforcement investigates violations of Export Administration regulations and works with officials to prosecute violators. Special agents in Washington, D.C., and in the Office of Export Enforcement's eight field offices are empowered to make arrests, carry firearms, execute search warrants, and seize goods that are about to be illegally exported. Other enforcement offices are the Office of Enforcement Support, which assists the field offices and the export licensing office by gathering and distributing information about problem exporters, and the Office of Antiboycott Compliance, which implements the antiboycott provisions of the Export Administration regulations. The antiboycott provisions were adopted to require U.S. firms to refuse to participate in foreign boycotts that the United States does not sanction, for example the Arab League boycott of Israel.

Two other offices serve significant and unique functions. The Office of Chief Counsel for Export Administration is a unit of attorneys who provide legal counsel and services for all BXA programs including representing the agency in administrative enforcement proceedings. The Nonproliferation and Export Control Cooperation Team coordinates Department of Commerce efforts to help other countries develop or strengthen export controls and stop the proliferation of certain goods and technology to potentially dangerous countries.

PRIMARY FUNCTIONS

The BXA's mandate is to implement the legislation that created it, the Export Administration Act (1987), including all boycott provisions. In particular it monitors the export of industrial products and technology that could be used in a military capacity. Further, it ensures compliance with treaties that impose requirements on U.S. industry, such as the Chemical Weapons Convention. In accordance with the Defense Production Act, the bureau analyzes and protects the Defense Department's industrial and technology base by controlling the export of high- technology goods to ensure that the United States remains secure and by promoting exports to ensure the United States remains competitive in expanding markets. The bureau also works with countries emerging from the former Soviet Union—Ukraine, Kazakhstan, Belarus, and Russia—to develop export control systems and dismantle existing defense systems.

Finally, the BXA is a primary resource for exporters in the United States. It processes license applications, maintains the Export Administration regulations database, and conducts seminars and conventions that outline correct export procedures for businesses. The BXA also maintains an international entities list of end-users who have been deemed risky, meaning they are believed to be involved in developing weapons or the missiles used to deliver them. Exporters are prohibited from delivering goods to these entities without a license.

FAST FACTS

The BXA's powers of enforcement are substantial: an individual who violates export laws can be imprisoned for up to ten years, and a company can be fined up to $1 million.

(Source: Bureau of Export Administration. "Antiboycott Compliance Requirements," 1997.)

PROGRAMS

Individual programs within the BXA are, for the most part, divided between enforcement and administration functions. The safeguards verification program conducts numerous on-site verification trips around the world to examine how U.S. exports are being used. Another enforcement program, visa application review, attempts to prevent unauthorized access to controlled U.S. technology or technical data by noncitizens visiting the United States.

Other BXA programs include the defense industrial base programs, through which the BXA conducts research and analysis on the development of critical technologies, the effect of imports on national security, and industrial capabilities. These projects provide data and recommendations to government policymakers and industry leaders to help maintain and increase U.S. defense and economic security. To conduct its assessments the BXA designs surveys of specific technologies or industries and releases them in a series of Critical Technology Assessments. Recently assessed areas include semiconductor materials and artificial intelligence.

BUDGET INFORMATION

The BXA's budget authority is granted through congressional appropriations. In 1998, the agency's budget was approximately $47 million. The BXA spends nearly equal amounts on its two main areas of operation; 47 percent of the budget was spent in the area of export administration, and 47 percent in export enforcement. The remainder of the budget, about 6 percent, was spent on management of the bureau and policy coordination.

HISTORY

The concept of controlling exports to certain countries reached a critical point in the years following World War II (1939–45), when the United States joined Belgium, France, Italy, the Netherlands, Luxembourg, and the United Kingdom to form the Coordinating Committee on Multilateral Export Controls. The committee's purpose was to curtail exports to "rogue" or enemy nations that, as Germany had done prior to the war, become powerful through strategic trade. In 1949 the first Export Control Act was passed in the United States. Two years later the Battle Act prohibited U.S. aid to any country that allowed exports of strategic materials to Communist bloc countries. In 1969, in response to a growing international trade deficit, the Export Administration Act replaced the 1949 legislation. The new act specifically endorses trade in peaceful goods, but it also imposes controls on exports of high-technology products and commodities.

Restructuring

By the late 1970s, due largely to the U.S. business community's inexperience in dealing with centrally-planned economies such as those of the Soviet Union and China, the U.S. trade deficit was soaring. Struggling to centralize control of the situation, Congress passed the Trade Reorganization Act to establish a new national export policy. The act created the International Trade Agency and combined, for the first time, responsibility for both promoting and policing exports. Export control programs and licensing were conducted by an agency within the International Trade Agency, the Trade Administration. Licensing procedures were balanced to serve national security and foreign policy goals while minimizing adverse effects on the balance of trade. Strict enforcement of export controls resulted in more criminal and administrative penalties against violators.

International trade practices, especially those of Japan, became a dominant U.S. concern in the 1980s. When steps were taken to eliminate the barriers that U.S. companies faced in foreign markets, it became clear that having a single agency promoting and policing trade did little to encourage the interest of potential foreign trading partners. The Department of Commerce created a new agency, the Bureau of Export Enforcement, in 1987. The new agency took on the functions of the former Trade Administration and new responsibilities.

The BXA was charged with analyzing, formulating, and implementing export control policy to prevent the loss of commodities and technologies that would harm U.S. national security by benefiting the military capabilities of adversarial nations. It was also made responsible for securing voluntary support from the business community, preventing violations of export laws through close supervision of licensing activities, and deterring violations through the use of criminal and administrative punishments.

CURRENT POLITICAL ISSUES

The BXA is an arm of government whose primary concern is the protection of national security. As such, it is often placed in an unpopular position; it must tell individuals and businesses with goods for sale that for security reasons they are not allowed to market or sell their products or services abroad. The BXA is therefore often at odds with the defense industry—designers and producers of high-tech weaponry—whose products are desired by countries lacking the technological infrastructure of the United States. As technology advances, the list of products and services that have the potential to threaten U.S. security grows, and questions continue to be raised about the government's role in controlling the exports of certain technologies.

Case Study: Encryption Technology

Cryptography, the science of making and breaking codes for secret messages, is nearly as old as the written word. However, the still-developing technology of data encryption, which uses computer software to scramble and unscramble sensitive information (such as bank accounts and other financial activities), has sparked continuing controversy in the United States. In the early 1990s encryption technology became a useful way for securing information that could be passed through the Internet or other computer networks. As it has become more advanced, the software used to encode and decode information has become more complex. The idea of exporting advanced software that could encode information and make it inaccessible to the government was immediately threatening to the U.S. defense community; encryption technologies were classified as "munitions," and their export was prohibited.

But companies like Netscape, Microsoft, and IBM had much to gain from the fast-growing international demand for secure data. The Internet was changing quickly, and if manufacturers of encryption software wanted to keep up with the competition, they argued, these export controls needed to be relaxed. It didn't take long for academics, attorneys, and computer entrepreneurs to protest the policy of equating encryption products with military weaponry.

President Bill Clinton's administration understood the potential gain for U.S. businesses that the encryption products market represents, but it firmly believed that when used outside the United States encryption products could jeopardize U.S. foreign policy and national security interests. One of the administration's first solutions was the "Clipper" initiative, which allowed export of encryption products as long as the software keys were deposited with the FBI or another law enforcement agency. This solution, it was argued, would allow business to profit from the sale of encryption products while permitting possible government recovery of any encoded information.

The Clipper initiative was roundly criticized not only by the computer industry but also by the American Civil Liberties Union, which equated it to giving the police the key to one's bank account. The American Civil Liberties Union made the argument that encryption is speech and should be protected by the First Amendment to the Constitution. Though favored by the defense and law-enforcement communities, Clipper didn't last long. It became clear to the Clinton Administration that consumers would not want a product to which the U.S. government held the keys.

In May 1997 the BXA announced that it would allow the export of the strongest available data encryption products to support electronic commerce around the world. It also announced the future publication of new regulations that would allow the export of the highly-complex products specifically designed to support financial transactions. In addition the regulations would allow the export of powerful, nonrecoverable, commercially-available data encryption products for interbank and similar transactions, provided the manufacturers make a commitment to develop recoverable products. The 1997 announcement was provisional and still left many questions unanswered, but it was a step toward the eventual deregulation of encryption exports.

SUCCESSES AND FAILURES

In recent years the BXA has worked to keep its regulations current, a requirement that demands more from the BXA than from nearly any other regulatory agency. For example, in 1992 the BXA defined a computer capable of running at 195 million theoretical operations per second (MTOPS) as a supercomputer subject to strict export controls. Just a few years later, personal computers that exceeded that performance were being sold for less than $2,000 at retail stores and through mail order catalogs, making previous export controls pointless as well as harmful to U.S. computer manufacturers. The BXA adapted to this rapid change and continues to update its controls on high performance computers, semiconductors, telecommunications equipment, and chemical mixtures.

FUTURE DIRECTIONS

The end of the Cold War created a complex world with indistinct battle lines between competing countries. The United States now faces more ambiguous threats, including terrorism and the proliferation of weapons of mass destruction in a handful of smaller rogue states. At the same time, the rapid spread of technology in a global economy has made critical items widely available and increased the number of nations capable of producing advanced technology.

The BXA's response to these changed circumstances is to generally tighten export controls, but it lists four priorities for future export administration. First, it intends to reform the export licensing process so that all relevant agencies can participate in a review of sensitive transactions while ensuring that U.S. exporters are not placed at a disadvantage. Second, the BXA intends to streamline controls in order to focus on the items that pose the greatest threat to national security. The agency will also seek to clarify its regulations so that exporters can better understand their obligations and improve compliance. Finally, the BXA intends to work internationally to strengthen multilateral control systems.

AGENCY RESOURCES

General inquiries about the BXA should be directed to the Office of Public Affairs, Room 3897, 14th St. & Constitution Ave. NW, Washington, DC 20230; phone (202) 482-2721. The complete Export Administration regulations database can be accessed on the Internet at http://bxa.fedworld.gov.

AGENCY PUBLICATIONS

The BXA's *Critical Technology Assessments,* along with many other national security reports, can be ordered through the National Technical Information Service by calling (703) 487-4650. The BXA also publishes the *Guide to Small Business,* a handbook that describes various export assistance programs offered to small and medium-sized businesses. A free copy of the guide can be ordered using the E-mail form on the agency's Web site at http://www.bxa.doc.gov.

BIBLIOGRAPHY

Clinton, Bill. "Letter from President Clinton." *Business America*, September 1996, pp. 4–6.

Deieso, Don. "Industry Advisors for Environmental Export Programs." *Business America*, April 1996, p. 30.

Johnson, Robert L., John R. Liebman, and Rauer Meyer. *Export Controls in the United States*. Orlando: Harcourt Brace & Company, 1985.

Koch, Elizabeth. "Confronting a Crisis: Clipping Clinton's Encryption Policies." *Reason,* November 1996, p. 22.

Lader, Philip. "Export Ease." *Entrepreneur*, October 1995, p. 98.

Magnusson, Paul. "High-Tech Exports: Is the Dam Breaking?" *Business Week*, 4 June 1990, pp. 128–30.

Markoff, John. "U.S. to Ease Rules on Export of Finance Encryption Technology." *New York Times*, 9 May 1997, p. A15.

Mehta, Stephanie. "More Start-Ups Pursue Exporting Strategies." *Wall Street Journal*, 16 July 1996, p. B2.

National Academy of Sciences, et al. *Finding Common Ground: U.S. Export Controls in a Changed Global Environment*. Washington, D.C.: National Academy Press, 1991.

National Research Council, Office of International Affairs Staff. *Dual-Use Technologies & Export Administration in the Post-Cold War Era*. Washington, D.C.: National Academy Press, 1994.

Pikus, Irwin M. *Breaking Down the Barricades: Reforming Export Controls to Increase U.S. Competitiveness*. Washington, D.C.: Center for Strategic & International Studies, 1994.

Bureau of Indian Affairs (BIA)

WHAT IS ITS MISSION?

The Bureau of Indian Affairs (BIA) is entrusted with the safety, supervision, and economic development of American Indians and Alaskan Natives living on tribal lands held in trust by the federal government. The primary goals of the bureau are to provide for educational opportunity and economic advancement for American Indians. It is the mission of the BIA to see that tribal welfare and stability are an integral part of federal policy.

HOW IS IT STRUCTURED?

The Bureau of Indian Affairs (BIA) is a division of the Department of the Interior. The assistant secretary for Indian affairs is the director of the agency and is appointed by the president in conjunction with the secretary of the interior. The assistant secretary for Indian affairs is responsible for policy and program administration. The deputy commissioner of Indian affairs oversees the operation of 12 area offices, 83 agency offices, three subagencies, six field stations, and two irrigation project offices. The director of the Office of Indian Education has authority over the 26 education line offices.

The 12 area offices assist the Office of the Assistant Secretary with administrative functions such as budget allocation and service delivery. Area offices are divided geographically, and the directors of each area are appointed to their positions by the assistant secretary for Indian affairs. However, because of proposed congressional budget cuts and federal government streamlining, the area offices may be reorganized into fewer regional

PARENT ORGANIZATION: Department of the Interior
ESTABLISHED: 1824
EMPLOYEES: 10,694

Contact Information:

ADDRESS: 1849 C St. NW
Washington, DC 20240
PHONE: (202) 208-7163
FAX: (202) 208-6334
URL: http://www.doi.gov/bureau-indian-affairs.html
ASSISTANT SECRETARY: Kevin Gover

BUDGET:
Bureau of Indian Affairs

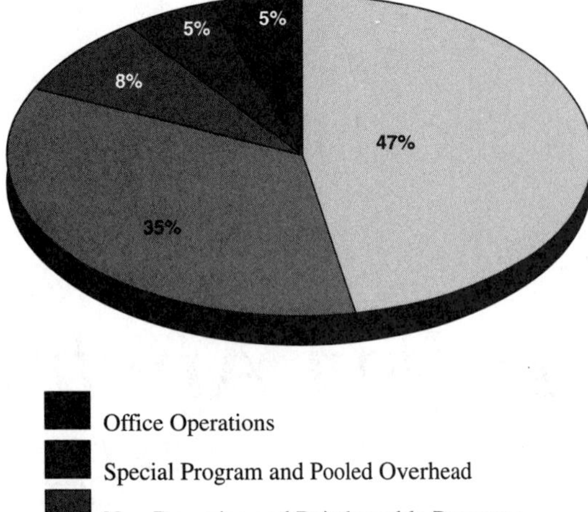

- Office Operations
- Special Program and Pooled Overhead
- Non-Recurring and Reimbursable Programs
- Other Recurring Programs Including Educational Programs
- Tribal Courts, Law Enforcement, Social Services, Adult Vocational Training, and Housing Repairs

PRIMARY FUNCTIONS

As the principal link between the federal government and American Indian tribes, the BIA assists in the administration of 53 million acres of land held in trust for tribes by the federal government. The BIA provides services and aid to approximately 753,000 American Indians and Alaska Natives. To be eligible for land and services a tribe must be one of the approximately 550 federally-recognized American Indian tribes or one of the two hundred native Indian villages in Alaska.

Federally-recognized tribes are expected to have an elected governing body and a constitution subject to approval by the secretary of the interior. The BIA encourages each tribe to assume administration of reservation programs. Each tribe then sets its own rules to determine who is eligible to vote and to be an enrolled member of the tribe. This is particularly important regarding the Indian Self-Determination and Education Assistance Act (1975), which directs the BIA to allocate federal funds that are in turn disbursed internally on reservations by their tribal governments.

Because of the diversity of American Indians, the BIA seeks to offer Indian peoples educational opportunities responsive to their needs and cultural backgrounds. The BIA operates an American Indian school system of 168 schools and gives financial assistance to public school systems that have substantial American Indian student enrollment. The BIA also works with tribal governments, government agencies, and nongovernmental agencies to assist American Indian economic development. The bureau also helps tribes preserve their natural resources.

PROGRAMS

Tribal Priority Allocations, Indian Health Services, and Indian Educational Services are among the programs designed to aid in the advancement and security of American Indians. BIA area offices disburse funds required to support programs that include tribal governmental operations; general assistance to Indians whose incomes are below state standards; child welfare programs that provide assistance to abandoned or neglected children and prevent the separation of Indian families; higher-education scholarships; law enforcement, detention services, and community fire protection; maintenance of more than twenty million miles of roads on reservations; and housing repairs for Indian families.

The Branch of Acknowledgment and Research is the program through which tribes submit petitions requesting federal acknowledgment of Indian tribal status. Petitions are filed with the hope of developing a government-to-government relationship between tribal representatives and the BIA. Agency staff provide petitioners with technical assistance, administer regulations, and defend tribal-recognition decisions in appeals and court cases. Staff are skilled in anthropology, genealogy, and history and use these disciplines to provide accurate evaluation of petitions. Every three years the Branch of Acknowledgment publishes in the *Federal Register* the list of federally-recognized American Indian tribal governments.

BUDGET INFORMATION

For fiscal year 1998, Congress appropriated approximately $1.61 billion for the BIA; this included an increase of about $70 million from the previous year for the agency. The increase in the budget reflected the growing need tribes have to provide basic reservation programs in the areas of tribal governments, educational programs and facilities, and infrastructure such as road and utilities maintenance.

Only 10 percent of the budget is spent on administrative overhead with 90 percent going directly to tribal offices. As many as half the existing offices may be closed as a result of these cuts.

BIOGRAPHY:
Ada E. Deer

Activist (b. 1935) A life-long advocate for social justice, Ada E. Deer was the first woman to head the Bureau of Indian Affairs (BIA). Deer's native heritage came from her father, who was nearly full-blooded Menomonee Indian. Her career as a social worker and leader in community and political organizations, and her successful fight to restore federal recognition to the Menomonee tribe, attest to her commitment to human rights. When Deer took on the post of assistant secretary in 1993, she inherited an agency infamous for its bureaucracy and historically poor relations with tribes. She contended with budget reductions and conflict among tribes and localities over land management, water resources, tribal recognition, education, and religious freedom. She encouraged tribes to work cooperatively with businesses, organizations, and government entities, with the ultimate goal of helping the tribes regain economic self-sufficiency. Deer's tenure through 1997 was filled with significant successes. She helped bring about U.S. government recognition of more than 220 Alaska Native villages. She also saw an increase in the number of self-governing tribes and was instrumental in the reorganization of the BIA. Deer has lived up to her motto, "one person can make a difference." During her fight to regain federal recognition of the Menomonee tribe in the 1970s Deer said to a *Washington Post* reporter: "mainly I want to show people who say nothing can be done in this society that it just isn't so. You don't have to collapse just because there's a federal law in your way. Change it!"

programs on an annual basis. Tribal Priority Allocations received approximately $759 million of the budget for tribal spending priorities. This translated into 47 percent of the BIA's operating budget spent to support tribal courts, law enforcement, social services, adult vocational training, and housing repairs on more than 200 reservations.

Other recurring programs were allocated $558 million or 35 percent of the BIA's budget. Education programs accounted for the largest segment of this money; they received more than $450 million. Maintaining 185 Indian schools accreditation and providing safe transportation for 52,000 students is a priority for the BIA. Non-recurring and reimbursable programs were apportioned approximately $133 million or 8 percent and special program and pooled overhead $73 million or 5 percent of the budget. The BIA allotted a $86 million for office operations, $46 million (3 percent) for central office operations and $40 million (2 percent) for area office operations.

HISTORY

Initially the Indian Affairs division of the U.S. government was established as part of the War Department. As the federal government expanded and matured, Indian Affairs was transferred to the Department of the Interior in 1849. At this time the primary function of this department was the acquisition of Indian lands and the containment of the Indian people and their culture.

In 1867 Congress created the Peace Commission, devoted to persuading Indians to settle on reservation land in exchange for government benefits. When the Peace Commission failed, the U.S. Army enforced compliance. During this period the federal government promoted a policy of cultural assimilation of the American Indians. Through education and missionary efforts the federal government hoped to transform these tribal nomadic peoples into independent Christian farmers. Indian children were removed from families and put in schools where they were taught the foundations of Western civilization.

Under President James K. Polk the reservation policies began in earnest. Indians who refused to be relocated were hunted by the military and forced onto reservations in the Oklahoma Territories. By the 1880s government officials, military officers, Christian reformers, and congressional leaders agreed that allowing tribal land holdings should end.

The political status of American Indians began to improve in the 1930s under President Franklin D. Roosevelt's New Deal. Tribal governments gained legal recognition and began to gain legal sovereignty over tribal lands, allowing them to develop reservations and manage the lands in accordance with their own needs. However, strides in self-determination did not completely end federal supervision in areas such as land use,

FAST FACTS

In 1990 the Bureau of the Census reported the state most populated with American Indians was Oklahoma with 252,089, and the least populated was the District of Columbia with 1,432.

(Source: Department of Commerce. Bureau of the Census: 1990 Census.)

water rights, and government-sponsored social service programs.

Some tribes were able to promote their culture, their art, and their spirituality and thus bring jobs and money to the reservation, but other tribes were not as successful and struggled with chronic poverty and reliance upon federal aid. From the time the federal government separated the BIA from the War Department, the policy has been one of containment, aid, and education.

In 1977 the Office of Assistant Secretary for Indian Affairs was created within the Department of the Interior to centralize the federal government's policymaking and advocacy functions with respect to Indians. During his tenure President Bill Clinton appointed Ada Deer, a Menomonee Indian who for years pursued federal recognition for her tribe, assistant secretary for Indian affairs.

CURRENT POLITICAL ISSUES

Severe economic conditions and lack of legal resources on the part of Indian tribes has contributed to environmental crises on the land owned by Indian peoples and on the land that has been entrusted to them by the Bureau of Indian Affairs (BIA). As a result these lands are often targeted by industries seeking development opportunities. In some cases tribes have allowed resource development projects on their lands in return for economic benefits only to find years later that the jobs they were promised were temporary and the negative environmental impact to their land significant and long lasting.

Historically, American Indians have been strong conservationists and leaders in protecting the land and its wildlife. However, they frequently are without legal documentation and support for regulating land use. Environmental restrictions on Indian lands are sometimes weaker than on federal, state, and private lands in the same region. A mining project or waste disposal plan that elsewhere would not pass a federal environmental impact study is not under the same jurisdiction on Indian-held land, making such a project more feasible and less costly. As a result, corporations have been known to target reservations for the placement of toxic waste dumps that would face stricter governmental regulation and perhaps community opposition if located elsewhere.

Case Study: Mohawk Tribe Fights Effects of Abandoned Factories

Populated by the Mohawk tribe for centuries, the lands at their St. Regis, New York, reservation provided abundant hunting, fishing, and farming. However, the St. Lawrence River traverses the reservation, and Canadian and U.S. factories lining the riverbanks have severely polluted the reservation's water supply. Mohawks living on the reservation lands began to notice the effects of the pollution on the river and on their own health and livelihoods. As the effects of the pollution accumulated, fishing jobs and income were lost and tribal members were advised by scientists to avoid eating fish from the river and food irrigated by the river water. In addition, since the opening of a General Motors foundry in the 1940s the rate of diabetes among Mohawks has increased to twice that of the national average. Foundries are a main source of polychlorinated biphenyls (PCBs).

After five decades of suffering the effects of pollutants the Mohawk tribe took action. In 1990 the tribe passed a resolution implementing water quality standards intended to reduce the flow of toxic waste onto the reservation. Initially the Environmental Protection Agency was receptive to these standards, but conflicts arose as the Environmental Protection Agency negotiated increases in allowable levels of PCB contaminants at dump sites, saving General Motors $15 million in cleanup costs.

American Indian leaders have declared that the practice of such negotiations constitutes environmental injustice. Angry response to the trend of exposing tribal members to high levels of pollution has contributed significantly to the emergence of the environmental justice movement. Supporters of the movement seek to educate the public and fight the practice of exposing low-income peoples and minorities to excessive pollution when these citizens have neither the finances nor the legal tools to oppose such contamination.

In February 1994 President Bill Clinton identified environmental justice as a top administrative priority by requiring all federal agencies, including the BIA, to include achievement of environmental justice as part of their mission statement. The executive order has added substance to the many environmental battles being fought around the country. Outside the executive branch, however, the trend in federal government policy is toward deregulation of environmental standards, allowing states to determine their own criteria.

SUCCESSES AND FAILURES

The BIA, in cooperation with other organizations, seeks to support solutions to environmental and economic problems faced by American Indians. For example, in 1994 a massive forest fire decimated an area of Blackridge, Colorado, destroying thousands of acres of ancient piñon trees. In conjunction with Global ReLeaf Forest Partners and the Bureau of Indian Affairs, Southern Ute tribal members reforested the area with 63,000 piñon trees. Wages to the reforesters were provided by corporate-sponsored donations to the BIA.

As part of the BIA's efforts to provide quality education to American Indians, partnerships like the Southern Ute reforestation project represent a major cooperative success. Another initiative is the Four Directions project, which was created to bring computer technology to Indian schools. In 1997 Secretary of the Interior Bruce Babbit announced a significant donation from Microsoft Corporation. Eight Indian schools around the nation were given computers and software, allowing the schools to share learning resources, improve communications, and give students valuable experience with information-age technologies.

FUTURE DIRECTIONS

Education of American Indian children and development of new educational opportunities for them are top priorities of the BIA. The Office of Indian Education was charged with drafting a plan to reform, reinvent, and restructure Indian education programs. The plan covers 1997-2002 and is called Goals 2000. The plan's primary focus is promotion of lifelong learning among American Indians. The bureau also seeks to replace aging buildings with new facilities.

AGENCY RESOURCES

Information about the BIA can be obtained by contacting the Public Affairs Office, Bureau of Indian Affairs, Department of the Interior, Washington, DC 20240 or by phoning (202) 208-3710. The BIA Web site at http://www.bia.gov contains extensive information on the operations of the BIA and the status of American Indians.

AGENCY PUBLICATIONS

The following publications explaining American Indian issues are available from the Superintendent of Documents, Government Printing Office, Washington, DC 20402: *Answers to Your Questions About American Indians, Indian Land Areas, Famous Indians, American Indian Calendar,* and *The States and Their Indian Citizens.* Additionally, BIA publications such as the *BIA Strategic Plan* and its *1996 BIA Customer Satisfaction Report* are available on-line at the BIA Web site at http://www.doi.gov/bureau-indian-affairs.html.

BIBLIOGRAPHY

"American Bureau of Indian Affairs Labelled Worst Government Department." *Akwesasne Notes*, Spring 1995, p. 108.

"Burgers or Blackjack? Indian Development." *The Economist*, 12 March 1994, p. A35.

Clines, Francis X. "The Pequots." *New York Times Magazine*, 27 February 1994, p. 49.

Deer, Ada E. "Biography of Assistant Secretary for Indian Affairs." *Current Biography,* September 1996, p. 14.

Ferrara, Peter J. "Choctaw Uprising." *National Review*, 11 March 1996.

Monk, Nina. "Two Armed Bandits." *Forbes*, 22 May 1995, p. 151.

Nylan, Paul. "Measure to Give More Control to Tribes OK'd by Panel." *Congressional Quarterly Weekly Report*, 28 May 1994, p. 1398.

Satchell, Michael. "The Worst Federal Agency: Critics Call Bureau of Indian Affairs a National Disgrace." *U.S. News and World Report*, 28 November 1994, p. 161.

Van Biema, David. "Bury My Heart in Committee." *Time*, 28 September 1995, p. 48.

Walsh, Catherine. "Most Americans Are Not Aware of the 'Special Relationship' Between the U.S. Government and Native American Tribes." *Perspectives*, 14 October 1995, vol. 173, no. 11.

Bureau of International Labor Affairs (ILAB)

PARENT ORGANIZATION: Department of Labor
ESTABLISHED: December 31, 1959
EMPLOYEES: 70

Contact Information:

ADDRESS: 200 Constitution Ave. NW
Washington, DC 20210
PHONE: (202) 219-6061
URL: http://www.dol.gov/dol/ilab
DEPUTY UNDER SECRETARY: Andrew James Samet

WHAT IS ITS MISSION?

The agency describes its mission as follows: "The Bureau of International Labor Affairs (ILAB) carries out the Department of Labor's international responsibilities and assists in formulating international economic, trade, and immigration policies affecting American workers." It is responsible for coordinating the Department of Labor's involvement with policy making in international labor issues and works with a variety of other federal agencies, elected U.S. representatives, and foreign countries. The ILAB creates and coordinates policies related to workers' rights and international labor standards and assists in efforts to implement these policies.

HOW IS IT STRUCTURED?

The ILAB is an independent agency within the Department of Labor. It is run by a deputy under secretary who is appointed by the president. The ILAB is made up of five offices with separate areas of responsibility: International Economic Affairs, International Organizations, Foreign Relations, National Administrative Office, and the Child Labor Group. The International Economic Affairs is further divided into trade policy, international commodities, foreign economic research, and immigration policy and research.

PRIMARY FUNCTIONS

Each office of the ILAB has its own responsibilities. The stated mission of the International Economic Affairs is that "through membership on executive branch committees concerned with foreign economic policy, the Department participates in formulating international trade, investment, and economic policy; advising the President on the labor implications of trade and immigration legislation; and negotiating and administering international trade agreements." The International Economic Affairs advises the president and his advisers on the impact of their decisions about international labor issues on U.S. workers. For example, it was involved in the discussions and negotiations of the North American Free Trade Agreement (NAFTA) with Mexico and Canada.

The International Organizations's main responsibility is to participate in two very important international organizations, the Organization for Economic Corporation and Development and the International Labor Organization. The Organization for Economic Development is an organization of different countries who meet to discuss ways of coordinating their economies for their mutual benefit. The International Organizations's main responsibility within the Organization for Economic Development is to participate on the Employment, Labor, and Social Affairs Committee, which is concerned with issues such as employment, immigration, industrial relations, statistics, women's issues, and social policy.

The International Organizations also participates in the International Labor Organization, an agency within the United Nations. One of its main interests is to oversee "a large program of technical assistance to developing countries and research on all aspects of the world of work, as well as the development and supervision of international labor standards." The primary goal of this initiative is to help poorer countries develop their economies by formulating and implementing a set of standards that will protect workers and ensure the nation's economic success.

In contrast, the Office of Foreign Relations offers a more practical, hands-on approach by offering technical assistance to countries that are making the transition from Communism to a more democratic government and free market economy. The Office of Foreign Relations delivers a variety of resources, including training in particular work skills, financial help through funding or grants, technology such as computers, and personnel to help companies solve labor-related problems. In addition, the Office of Foreign Relations is concerned with furthering U.S. foreign policy objectives and promoting the export of U.S. products and services. It also conducts research to discover any skills or methods used overseas that might be adapted to address U.S. work-related problems. Much of this office's activities are funded by other organizations such as the Agency for International Development, the World Bank, and the government of Saudi Arabia.

The Office of Foreign Relations has a number of advisers in various regions around the globe such as Africa, the Far East, Europe, Latin America, and Asia. Their purpose is to "analyze internationally recognized worker rights, participate in the formulation of U.S. foreign policy, and support DOL domestic programs." Also, as a member of the Board of the U.S. Foreign Service, the deputy under secretary helps determine assignments for foreign service officers and assists in their recruitment and training. The Office of Foreign Relations and the Foreign Service often work together and share information about significant labor issues and events.

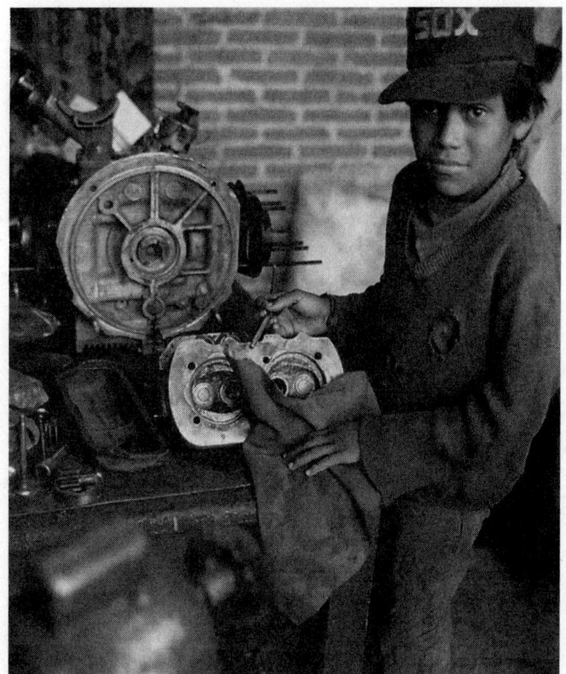

ILAB's Child Labor Group uses congressional funds to help investigate and abolish the use of child labor throughout the world. This young boy works in an auto repair shop in Mexico. (Courtesy of the International Labor Organization)

The National Administrative Office was created as a result of the North American Free Trade Agreement, a trade agreement between the United States, Canada, and Mexico with the purpose of increasing the amount of trade between these countries and lower trade barriers. As part of this agreement, each country was required to create its own National Administrative Office to help implement the treaty and serve as a source of information and communication between the countries involved. For example, Mexico can get information about Canada's labor laws by contacting Canada's National Administrative Office.

The Child Labor Group was created in 1993 as a result of a public concern about the use of child workers throughout the world. As a result of studies conducted by the Child Labor Group three major reports have been

FAST FACTS

Japan's economy is providing less and less of the food necessary to support its people and is therefore relying more on imports. Only 5.2 percent of the workforce are farmers, whose average age is 60.

(Source: Frank Gibney, Jr. "The Bubble Bursts." *Time,* April 28, 1997.)

published since 1994 on specific aspects of child labor. *By the Sweat and Toil of Children Vol. 1* reviews countries and industries that use child labor to produce products for export to the United States. *By the Sweat and Toil of Children Vol. 2* looks at the number of children working in foreign countries who produce agricultural products for export into the United States. This report also studies the use of children as slave labor or as prostitutes.*The Apparel Industry and Codes of Conduct: A Solution to the International Child Labor Problem?* examines the role of child labor in producing garments for U.S. consumption, and it evaluates the effects of voluntary codes of conduct adopted by U.S. manufacturers.

PROGRAMS

The ILAB operates a number of programs within each of its five main divisions. Many of these efforts involve negotiation or advisory functions. The ILAB is concerned with getting labor policies accepted and implemented; each of the ILAB's main divisions approaches this goal differently. For example, the Office of Foreign Relations is currently advising the government of Romania on how to automate its Ministry of Labor. The Office of Foreign Relations is also helping the government of Turkey improve employment services for its citizens, and it is helping set up a system that will help find employment for the former soldiers in Bosnia-Herzegovina. The office has also helped the government of Saudi Arabia set up a vocational education system for its people. The Child Labor Group has been responsible for administering an $8.1 million congressional grant for the prevention of child labor through the International Programme on the Elimination of Child Labor.

In 1990 the Office of Foreign Relations launched a special labor assistance program for the countries of Central and Eastern Europe in order to help the slowly developing European countries as they emerged from under Communist rule. The program provided advice, personnel, and technology such as computers. The Office of Foreign Relations sponsored four regional workshops in Latin America and the Caribbean to study industrial problems such as employee treatment, how to increase exports, and how to identify their places in the global market.

The National Administrative Office is a crucial element in the successful implementation of the North American Free Trade Agreement (NAFTA). The agreement is one of the most significant economic international agreements of recent years because it affects so many people in three nations and is meant to foster the economic growth of all North America. In 1998 the National Administrative Office received a complaint from some Mexican factory workers that their attempts to organize a union were met with harassment and threats from a competing union. Fifty of these workers were allegedly fired for complaining about poor safety and health conditions, a clear violation of NAFTA, which required Mexico to be responsible for protecting workers' rights. As a result, the National Administrative Office brought public attention to the violations and pressured the Mexican government to act. The Mexican Supreme Court issued two decisions supporting the right of workers to unionize, and the government of Mexico agreed to provide additional funding to further enforce labor law.

BUDGET INFORMATION

The budget of the ILAB is alloted as a portion of departmental management's budget through the Department of Labor. Departmental management was allocated an estimated $186 million in 1998. Of this amount, the ILAB accounted for approximately $12 million.

HISTORY

Following World War II (1939–45) many of the agencies within the Department of Labor had to be reorganized in order to respond to changing times. Programs were cut and agencies were created, changed, or abolished. Many returning veterans left the military in order to seek jobs, and the Department of Labor was responsible for making this transition as easy and as effective as possible. In addition, as a result of the United States's new role as a world leader and major participant, the Department of Labor thought it was necessary to create an agency that would focus primarily on economic and labor issues on the international level. In 1947 Secretary of Labor Schwellenbach created the Office of International Labor Affairs whose primary purpose was to exchange information with other countries about labor issues. In 1959 the office was renamed the Bureau of International Labor Affairs (ILAB).

The ILAB continued to advise the Department of Labor on international issues and to focus on a number of primary goals: (1) technical assistance to poor and underdeveloped countries, such as training on labor-management relations, running employment services, administering safety and labor laws within industries (in 1957 more than 760 foreign citizens participated in these programs); (2) collection of statistical data about workers in other countries, such as comparisons of wages and benefits and the costs of goods, all to determine how the United States could best compete with other countries and promote a thriving world economy; (3) participation in the International Labor Organization, a major forum and vehicle of communication between nations, as well as one of the best avenues for the United States to influence world labor. The Department of Labor has participated in the International Labor Organization since 1934.

Today the ILAB is a flexible organization that responds to changing economic and political climates. Some of its divisions and programs are new and were created in response to specific needs (for example, the National Administrative Office and the Child Labor Group). Nations once isolated within the framework of Communism are now joining a global economy connected by new telecommunications technologies. At the same time, formerly poor and undeveloped nations are increasing their ability to compete on a global scale. The piece of legislation that has most dramatically effected the ILAB in recent years is NAFTA. Contentiously debated in Congress for years before it was finally passed, NAFTA immediately became a centerpiece of ILAB responsibility. The creation of the National Administrative Office pushed the United States even more decisively into a leadership role and increased the importance of the ILAB's mission.

CURRENT POLITICAL ISSUES

As the widespread use of child labor became more apparent to the U.S. public in the 1990s, the Child Labor Group was created within the ILAB in order to study and assess the extent and severity of the problem. Although incidences of child labor are prevalent and on the rise, there is no universal agreement on its definition nor on the best methods to stop it.

Case Study: Child Labor in the International Marketplace

Although most countries ban the use of child labor, the International Labor Organization estimates between 100 and 200 million incidents, mostly in India, Africa, and Latin America. The International Labor Organization has set an international standard that prohibits anyone under 15 years of age from working, however it allows children as young as eleven to do light work in some countries. There is, however, no clear definition of what light work entails, nor do many countries keep statistics on children under a certain age.

This lack of information makes the ILAB's job of setting standards and stamping out abuses especially difficult. Within the United States there is a fairly clear consensus that child labor must be stopped, but many other countries do not agree. In India, for instance, poverty is often so severe that children and their families would not survive if children were not permitted to work; banning cheap labor would further threaten the country's economy. Other societies may be less concerned about the welfare of children who are from racial or ethnic backgrounds they consider inferior.

Some believe that the United States does not have the right to dictate labor practices to other countries, but others counter that is exactly what the United States should do as a world leader. Some have suggested economic measures such as banning the sale of all goods imported into the United States that have been produced by child labor. Others argue that such a ban will only hurt poorer countries' economies and cause the children to suffer indirectly.

The ILAB's first report, *By the Sweat and Toil of Children Vol. 1*, published in September 1994, summarizes the controversy and asserts that experts in the International Labor Organization, United Nations International Children's Education Fund, and other organizations disagree on how best to deal with the problem of child labor. Some advocates for children's rights recommend abolishing all child labor immediately and argue that many countries already have the resources but lack the political resolve to provide compulsory education and enforce minimum age laws. Others, however, recommend first abolishing the most abusive forms of child labor and strictly regulating other practices for those who must work to survive. They believe that child labor in some regions must be viewed in the larger context of a country's overall development. All agree that some practices, such as child prostitution, bonded labor, and dangerous working conditions, must be abolished immediately.

Public Impact

As a result, the ILAB has published three more reports *By the Sweat and Toil of Children* (Vols. 2, 3, and 4), and it hopes to compile more accurate statistics on the occurrence of child labor, especially the use of children under age 12. Through the International Labor Organization, the ILAB also continues to try to use the power of the United States to exert international pressure and find a solution to this problem.

FUTURE DIRECTIONS

When the National Administrative Office investigated allegations that pregnant women in Mexico were being fired or denied employment in violation of NAFTA, it determined that the rules regarding pregnancy are not clear under the agreement. The National Administrative Office therefore recommended that in the future, the Office of the Secretary of Labor should meet with the Office of the Social Welfare of Mexico in order to work out differences in screening practices and standards for employment eligibility for pregnant women.

AGENCY RESOURCES

Information about the National Administrative Office and its activities is available in the form of reports and documents from the National Administrative Office Information Center by writing to the Information Officer, U.S. National Administrative Office, ILAB, Room C-4327, Department of Labor, Washington, DC 20210 or by calling (202) 501-6653, extension 22. A list of facts that may be requested is available on the Internet at: http://www.dol.gov/dol/ilab/public/aboutilab/org/fxdemand.htm.

AGENCY PUBLICATIONS

"Foreign Labor Trends" provides factual information on all aspects of labor in many foreign countries. This publication and others concerning the work of the Office of Foreign Relations are available by writing to the Office of Foreign Affairs, ILAB, Room S-5325, Department of Labor, Washington, DC 20210. Other publications about the National Administrative Office's work include: *North American Agreement on Labor Cooperation, (NAALC), NAALC Public Submissions Files*, and *Labor Law — Mexico and Canada.* These and other publications can be obtained by writing to the Information Officer, U.S. National Administrative Office, ILAB, Room C-4327, Department of Labor, Washington, DC 20210 or by calling (202) 501-6653, extension 22. They are also available on the Web at http://www.dol.gov/dol/ilab/public/media/pub/publcnao.htm.

By the Sweat and Toil of Children Vols. 1–3 are available from the Child Labor Group, ILAB, Room S-5303, Department of Labor, Washington, DC 20210; phone at (202) 208-4843 or by E-mail at jaffe-maureen@dol.gov. The series is also on the Internet at http://www.dol.gov/dol/ilab/public/aboutilab/org/child.htm. Other publications can be obtained by writing to the Bureau of International Labor Affairs, 200 Constitution Ave. NW, Washington, DC 20210, or by calling (202) 219-6061.

BIBLIOGRAPHY

"Alas, Slavery Lives." *Time*, 22 March 1993.

Charnovitz, Steve. "Promoting Higher Labor Standards." *Washington Quarterly*, Summer 1995, pp. 167–90.

"Danger on the Job." *Futurist*, July 1993.

Gibney, Frank Jr. "The Bubble Bursts." *Time*, 28 April 1997.

Hawken, Paul. "Social Waste." *Mother Jones*, March 1997.

Norton, Rob. "Why Asia's Collapse Won't Kill the Economy." *Fortune*, 2 February 1998, pp. 26–7.

Prashad, Vijay. "Contract Labor: The Latest Stage of Illiberal Capitalism." *Monthly Review*, October 1994, pp. 19–26.

Ridgeway, James. "Happy Days Are Here Again?" *Village Voice*, 13 January 1998.

Sjoberg, Amy. "This Just In: Global Labor: A Magazine of International Labor Issues." *Utne Reader*, November 1993.

Stokes, Bruce. "Here's What They Skipped." *National Journal*, 19 March 1994, pp. 669–70.

Bureau of Labor Statistics (BLS)

WHAT IS ITS MISSION?

The stated mission of the Bureau of Labor Statistics (BLS) is to be a "fact-finding agency for the Federal Government in the broad field of labor economics and statistics." The BLS is a national agency that collects and analyzes and then makes available statistical data about the U.S. economy to the public and the federal government, as well as to state and local governments.

HOW IS IT STRUCTURED?

The BLS is an agency within the Department of Labor, which falls under the authority of the executive branch. The BLS is a large agency headed by a commissioner, whom the president appoints, and a deputy commissioner. Its eleven main offices are: Quality and Information Management Staff; Administration; Compensation and Working Conditions; Employment Projections; Employment and Unemployment Statistics; Field Operations; Prices and Living Conditions; Productivity and Technology; Publications and Special Studies; Research and Evaluation; and Technology and Survey Processing.

Within most of these offices are smaller divisions which handle more specific tasks. For example, the Office of Employment and Unemployment Statistics has three other offices, and the Office of Prices and Living Conditions has six separate divisions.

The smaller divisions within the offices each handle specific tasks. For example, the Office of Current

PARENT ORGANIZATION: Department of Labor
ESTABLISHED: March 4, 1913
EMPLOYEES: 2,600

Contact Information:

ADDRESS: 2 Massachusetts Ave.
Washington, DC 20212
PHONE: (202) 606-5886
TDD (HEARING IMPAIRED): (202) 606-5897
FAX: (202) 606-7890
E-MAIL: blsdata@bls.gov
URL: http://stats.bls.gov/blshome.htm
COMMISSIONER: Katherine G. Abraham

FAST FACTS

The survey used to collect data for the Consumer Price Index tracks the prices of approximately 95,000 items in 22,000 retail outlets nationwide.

(Source: Jeff Gelles. "Economists Argue Over CPI's Accuracy." Knight-Ridder/Tribune News Service, January 30, 1997.)

Employment Analysis under the Office of Employment and Unemployment Statistics analyzes the current workforce by detailed criteria such as sex, race and ethnicity, and level of education. It also studies shifting patterns in employment in various regions. Under the Office of Compensation and Working Conditions, the Office of Safety, Health and Working Conditions gathers and studies statistics on health and safety conditions of workplaces throughout the country.

PRIMARY FUNCTIONS

The BLS collects data that Congress has determined is relevant and necessary to understand how the U.S. economy is working. Data collected by the BLS is then used to help government policymakers and other people in the public sector to better understand the economy. These statistics have far-reaching effects on the economy, and allow economists and analysts to adjust prices, judge the effects of inflation, and determine the poverty line. Groups that depend on these statistics on a regular basis include Congress, the president and his administration, the Department of Labor, and various businesses and professional associations.

The BLS addresses many different questions, including: What are the costs of goods? How have prices gone up or down? How many people are unemployed? Are wages going up or down? Are American workers better off than they were in the previous year? The BLS must also continually update methods of gathering and analyzing statistics so that they are reporting the most accurate and objective data possible.

BLS employees include economists, statisticians, computer specialists, writers and editors, staff support, and many others. In one form or another, these workers are involved in conducting surveys of Americans, studying the results and then preparing the information for publication in press releases, bulletins, or by publication in the *Monthly Labor Review*, the main publication of the BLS. The BLS also provides specific reports and data directly to Congress and various governmental agencies.

BLS employees attempt to study and understand who is working where, what kind of people are doing what kind of work, and how much money is being made and spent. They look for overall patterns and trends in the attempt to provide the government and the public with information that will help them to make decisions that will keep the economy healthy.

PROGRAMS

Most BLS programs are concerned with surveying and tracking statistics about the U.S. workplace. The main programs are run by the offices of Employment and Unemployment; Prices and Living Conditions; Compensation and Working Conditions; Productivity and Technology; and Employment Projections. There are also a number of international programs. Under the Office of Employment and Unemployment, the Current Employment Statistics Program keeps track of the number of people working or not working. Its stated purpose is to be "a monthly survey conducted by state employment security agencies in cooperation with the Bureau of Labor Statistics. The survey provides employment, hours and earnings estimates based on payroll records of business establishments."

The Office of Prices and Living Conditions operates the Producer Price Index, a national survey that measures the average changes in the price of goods sold in the United States. The Producer Price Index gathers information from a variety of industries, including mining, manufacturing, agriculture, fisheries, forestry, and service sectors. The Producer Price Index allows government and businesses to follow and forecast trends in the economy and judge the effects of inflation. This office operates a number of similar programs, such as the Consumer Price Index, International Price Index, and the Consumer Expenditure Survey.

The Office of Compensation and Working Conditions keeps track of the number of injuries, illnesses, and deaths in the U.S. workplace. This information is used to determine what industries have the highest health risks so that government and businesses can then focus their attention and resources toward lowering those risks. This office also operates an Employee Benefits Survey, the Occupational Compensation Survey, the National Compensation Survey, and the Employee Cost Trends Survey.

BUDGET INFORMATION

The estimated budget appropriated by Congress for BLS in 1997 was $372 million. When divided according to the amounts spent on the activities of the overall general programs, these amounts fell into seven general categories: labor statistics, $163 million; prices and cost of living, $102 million; compensation and working conditions, $56 million; executive direction and staff services, $23 million; productivity and technology, $7 million; and employment projections, $5 million. Also included in this budget was $16 million earmarked for the revision of the CPI. Changes will be made in the CPI's methods for the collection and processing of data.

Out of the total budget of $372 million, it is estimated that the largest expenditures will be $121 million on personnel compensation; $27 million on rental payments for use of privately owned office facilities; $10 million for payment of research and development contracts to private companies for specific jobs; and $6 million for the purchase of equipment.

BUDGET:

Bureau of Labor Statistics

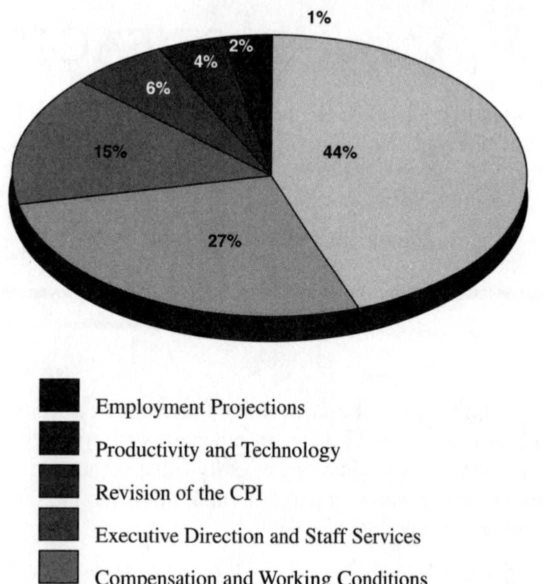

Employment Projections
Productivity and Technology
Revision of the CPI
Executive Direction and Staff Services
Compensation and Working Conditions
Prices and Cost of Living
Labor Statistics

HISTORY

The history of the BLS began with the formation of the Department of Labor, its parent organization, which was created by Congress and approved by President William Howard Taft in 1913 "to foster, promote and develop the welfare of working people, to improve their working conditions, and to enhance their opportunities for profitable employment." The need for the Department of Labor arose out of a struggle in the late 1800s between big businesses and labor organizations, each vying for control over how U.S. workers would be treated. The federal government finally stepped in and created the Department of Labor in order to regulate the workplace and balance the rights of workers with the needs of the economy.

At first the department was made up of four bureaus: the Bureau of Labor Statistics, the Bureau of Immigration, the Bureau of Naturalization, and the Children's Bureau. Since then the department's role has changed with the needs of workers and with the constantly varying economy. The BLS grew in size and importance as the country and the world grew and the need for economic data increased. It became well known around the world for providing very accurate economic statistics.

Today, the BLS is the only surviving agency of the original four, and its function has remained the same. The issues and activities of the BLS are consistently influenced by changing political trends and ideas, as could be expected in an economy as large and volatile as that of the United States, making the BLS the target of frequent controversy. The work of the BLS has a significant impact on the economy of many other countries but, for the most part, its role has not changed.

CURRENT POLITICAL ISSUES

In collecting statistics the BLS uses a variety of complicated surveys intended to give an accurate overall view of current trends in the workplace. The BLS attempts to study trends that are not always clear-cut or easily identifiable in an active and complex economy. Though many BLS reports have a huge impact on the economy as a whole, affecting millions of people, the accuracy of methods it uses to gather information have been questioned.

Case Study: Consumer Price Index

One of the main purposes of the Consumer Price Index (CPI) is to measure changes in the costs of all goods and services purchased by the average urban U.S. household. The CPI keeps track, on a monthly and yearly basis, of price changes of the items used in everyday life, from automobiles to shoes, heating oil, and vegetables. With these statistics the BLS can then keep track of inflation (the overall increase in costs) and predict how much it will cost to operate businesses, maintain households, and maintain life-styles.

To gather these statistics, the BLS sends out workers to check on prices across the country. Workers go to various stores each day, week after week, and check the

FAST FACTS

On average, in 1997 there were roughly 129.5 million employed and 6.7 million unemployed workers in a total U.S. force of 136.2 million. The average unemployment rate was approximately 5%.

(Source: Bureau of Labor Statistics, 1998.)

prices on an array of predetermined items, such as cereal in a grocery store, bicycles in a department store, kitty litter, and the cost of having a cavity filled at the dentist. These prices are compared month after month, and increases or decreases are noted.

Proponents of the CPI say that these measurements are very accurate. Opponents, however, claim that the measured items change so much from month to month that accurate comparison cannot be made. For example, when the price-checker for the BLS goes back to the same store to check the price of the same kitty litter and finds that brand no longer exists and a slightly different brand for a slightly higher price is being offered instead, is this comparison an accurate measurement of an increase in the cost of kitty litter? Or is this just a different price for a different product? And when this unlike comparison happens with thousands of products across the nation, can it be an accurate measurement of price changes? The BLS claims that it carefully considers such changes and figures them into the formula, but opponents claim that the CPI overstates inflation by more than one percent every year.

Public Impact

The consequences of a mere one percentage point error in the enormous U.S. economy are vast. Social Security payments to the elderly are tied to the CPI so that recipients' incomes keep pace with rising prices. If these increases are not accurate, the elderly may have trouble surviving. Tax brackets are also determined by the CPI, adjusted up or down with inflation in order to prevent someone who makes more money one year from jumping to a higher tax bracket even if in real terms the money cannot buy as much because prices have also increased. In other words, families could pay thousands more in taxes if the CPI is incorrect. Companies and workers use the CPI to determine salaries, based on how much it costs and will cost to live. The CPI is used to determine what incomes are above and below the poverty level. As a result, it is used to determine who is eligible for many social welfare benefits such as food stamps and Medicaid. A change of one percent could mean loss of benefits for those close to the poverty level.

As a result of this controversy, a Senate commission was appointed by Congress to study the matter, and $16 million was appropriated by Congress from the federal budget for the study and revision of the CPI.

SUCCESSES AND FAILURES

The BLS, in conjunction with the American Statistical Association, will continue to offer the Senior Research Fellow Program, which is funded by a grant from the National Science Foundation. Its purpose is to provide academic scholars the opportunity to work at the BLS and study the methods and problems encountered in gathering statistical information. These scholars use the BLS facilities and work with BLS staff on solving industries' problems.

The BLS is the largest organization in the world that deals with labor statistics. As a result, the BLS conducts a unique series of seminars every year to bring together industry professionals, statisticians, economists, analysts, and others who use such data from all over the world. These seminars, conducted at the BLS International Labor Statistics Center in Washington, D.C., focus on the methods of collecting and analyzing labor statistics and help to improve the gathering and interpretation of data on a worldwide basis.

FUTURE DIRECTIONS

Most of the BLS's future goals involve refining methods for obtaining statistical information and improving the analysis of that information. A primary goal is to improve the quality of the Consumer Price Index. Money has been appropriated by Congress from the federal budget for this purpose, and a Senate commission has made recommendations for what direction the revision should take.

Included among the improvement of these methods is a goal to increase coordination with other federal, state, and international statistical agencies by continually updating the BLS Internet site and by making more information available to these bodies over the Internet. In addition, the Interagency Council on Statistical Policy, which includes members of various federal statistical agencies, has brought agencies together with the BLS's cooperation to share information and plan future surveys. As part of this effort to stay current in the gathering of data, many BLS computer systems are being upgraded with more modern equipment.

AGENCY RESOURCES

Information can be obtained from BLS offices from 8:30 A.M. to 4:30 P.M. E-mail inquiries should be sent to blsdata@bls.gov, and information specialists are available at (202) 606-5886. Information may also be obtained directly from any BLS regional office, whose phone numbers and addresses are available at http://stats.bls.gov/regnhome.htm or by writing the Bureau of Labor Statistics, Publications Sales Center, PO Box 2145, Chicago, IL 60690.

Many BLS documents are available from the federal depository libraries. For a location near you check http://www.access.gpo.gov/su_docs/dpos/adpos003.html. Phone numbers for nearby locations can be found in the telephone directory. Other documents and information are available at the BLS Web site at http://stats.bls.gov/blshome.htm.

AGENCY PUBLICATIONS

The BLS regularly publishes a great deal of information on labor statistics. A good place to start looking for the publications that interest you are at their Web site at http://stats.bls.gov/blshome.htm or at the Publications and Research Papers Web site at http://stats.bls.gov/opbhome.htm. The BLS also publishes many of its monthly statistics and reports in the *Monthly Labor Review*. Articles from past issues are available at the BLS Web site or at your local public library. A variety of news releases, reports, and summaries are available free-of-charge while supplies last from any of the eight regional BLS offices. To contact the nearest office, look for phone numbers and addresses at http://stats.bls.gov/regnhome.htm, write the Bureau of Labor Statistics, Publications Sales Center, PO Box 2145, Chicago, IL 60690, or call the information specialists at (202) 606-5886.

BIBLIOGRAPHY

Banks, Howard. "Job Trends Across the Millennia." *Forbes*, 6 January 1992, p. 35.

Barrett, Wayne. "Pataki's Job Hoax." *Village Voice*, 30 January 1996, pp. 11–2.

Church, George J. "The Work Ethic Lives!" *Time*, 7 September 1987, pp. 40–2.

Epstein, Gene. "Economic Beat: The History of Her." *Barron's*, 18 August 1997, p. 36.

Forsyth, Randall W. "Current Yield: The Government Cuts 150,000 More Jobs from May Payrolls and the Market Loves It." *Barron's*, 2 June 1997.

Gelles, Jeff. "Economists Argue over CPI's Accuracy." *Knight-Ridder/Tribune News Service*, 30 January 1997.

Paulson, Mary. "Web Statistics 101." *PC Magazine*, 21 January 1997, p. 66.

Pollitt, Katha. "Let Them Eat Numbers." *Nation*, 30 December 1996, p. 8.

Tweed, Vera. "What's Up On The Web." *Business and Health*, August 1997, pp. 37–8.

Whaples, R. M. "Bureau of Labor Statistics." *Choice*, 1997, pp. 72–3.

Whiteley, Sandy. "Career Guide to America's Top Industries by the Bureau Of Labor Statistics." *Booklist*, 1 December 1993, p. 708.

Zaldivar, R. A. "Why The Accuracy of the Consumer Price Index Is Such a Big Deal." *Knight-Ridder/Tribune News Service*, 11 March 1997.

Bureau of Land Management (BLM)

PARENT ORGANIZATION: Department of the Interior
ESTABLISHED: July 16, 1946
EMPLOYEES: 9,650

Contact Information:

ADDRESS: 1849 C St. NW
Washington, DC 20240
PHONE: (202) 452-5125
FAX: (202) 208-3435
URL: http://www.blm.gov
DIRECTOR: Pat Shea

WHAT IS ITS MISSION?

According to the Bureau of Land Management (BLM), its mission is "to sustain the health, diversity and productivity of federally owned public lands for the use and enjoyment of present and future generations." The bureau promotes the sustainable use of public lands by private business so that their productivity can produce an economic return for the American people. Furthermore, the bureau promotes public safety for the millions of Americans who visit public lands for recreational purposes.

HOW IS IT STRUCTURED?

The Bureau of Land Management (BLM) is one of the bureaus that make up the Department of the Interior. It consists of headquarters in Washington, D.C., and five national support and service centers. These are the National Interagency Fire Center, the National Training Center, the National Applied Resource Sciences Center, the National Human Resources Management Center, and the National Business Center. Additionally, the BLM operates 12 state offices, 59 district offices, and 140 resource offices.

The BLM also utilizes a system of advisory councils to assist in the development of management plans and policies. The advisory councils work closely with state government agencies, as well as nongovernmental agencies when appropriate.

PRIMARY FUNCTIONS

The BLM manages all aspects of the use and protection of the public lands under its care, including maintaining their infrastructure, ensuring their safety, and making their resources available to the public. Timber, solid minerals, oil and gas, geothermal energy, wildlife habitat, endangered plant and animal species, rangeland vegetation, recreational and cultural resources, wild and scenic rivers, and designated conservation and wilderness areas are some of the many varied resources managed by the bureau.

The BLM provides the physical and legal means for access to public lands by private-sector businesses. Land use is monitored and fees are collected from applicants. For example, ranchers have long used public lands to graze livestock when their own grasslands will not support their herds. Historically, this type of arrangement between applicants who seek raw materials and the federal government has been a beneficial one, with low fees promoting land use, which in turn spurs the economy.

The BLM is responsible for building and maintaining the infrastructure on public lands, including roads and bridges, and for controlling erosion. The bureau also provides information on the history, nature, and quality of public lands.

Each year more citizens discover public lands as a source of recreation. The BLM is responsible for a variety of public safety issues related to the use of these natural attractions. Although most citizens abide by the established rules and regulations, law enforcement has become a major program of the bureau. BLM rangers monitor public lands and issue citations when appropriate. The BLM works closely with other law enforcement agencies, particularly sheriffs, to make sure public lands are not misused. For example, public lands have been used illegally to cultivate or produce illegal substances such as marijuana. In other cases antiquities and artifacts have been illegally removed from public lands. Rangers and sheriffs are increasingly on the lookout for vandalism and other illegal acts.

The Bureau of Land Management is responsible for enforcing the many laws regulating the use of public lands. The Antiquities Act of 1906, the National Wilderness Act of 1964, the National Historic Preservation Act of 1966, the Wild and Scenic Rivers Act of 1968, the Wild Free Roaming Horse and Burro Adoption Act of 1971, the Endangered Species Act of 1973, the Sikes Act of 1974, the Federal Land Policy and Management Act of 1976, the Archaeological Resources Protection Act of 1979, and the Native American Graves Protection and Repatriation Act of 1990 all set forth procedures for the legal use of public lands, and it is the BLM's role to enforce statutory procedures.

About 75 percent of northern spotted owls live on federal lands. With the passage of Option 9 that allows increased forestry in California's old-growth redwood forests, the future of these nearly extinct birds is in jeopardy. *(Photograph by John and Karen Hollingsworth. U.S. Fish and Wildlife Service)*

PROGRAMS

The sustainable use of America's grasslands has become an environmental issue because of the negative impact of overgrazing. In response, the BLM has established resource advisory councils to develop strategies to promote sustainable management of this valuable resource. The Public Land Survey System is a legal foundation within the BLM that manages public land records, assists tribal governments in managing their energy and mineral resources, and shares fire management capabilities with other agencies.

The BLM administers the Central HAZMAT Fund, which is responsible for remediation and cleanup of hazardous waste substances, pollutants, and contaminants in accordance with the Comprehensive Environmental Response, Compensation, and Liability Act. The BLM, under the guidance of the Department of the Interior, is now required to manage the cleanup of hazardous substance releases on its lands and at its facilities.

BUDGET:

Bureau of Land Management

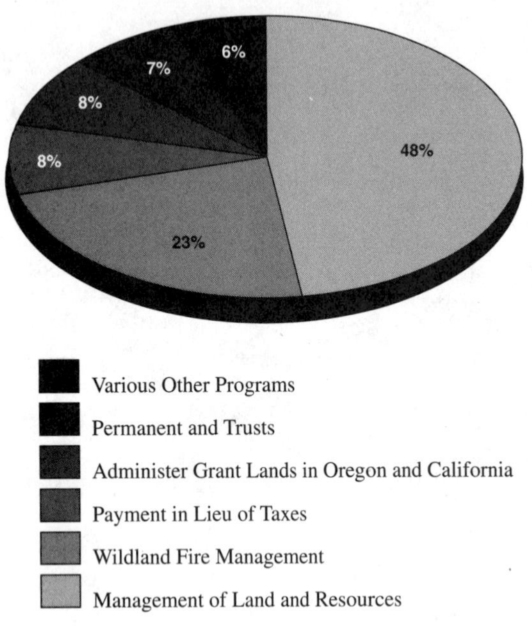

- Various Other Programs
- Permanent and Trusts
- Administer Grant Lands in Oregon and California
- Payment in Lieu of Taxes
- Wildland Fire Management
- Management of Land and Resources

BUDGET INFORMATION

The estimated 1998 budget appropriation from Congress for the BLM was $1.21 billion. This represented a slight increase of $31.9 million from the 1997 budget. Even though demands on the bureau have increased, the BLM is under pressure to run the agency at, or below, funding levels of previous years due to political pressures to reduce the federal government's budget deficit.

BLM spent $587 million on management of land and resources, accounting for 48 percent of the budget. Wildland fire management required funding at $280 million, accounting for 23 percent of the budget. Payment in lieu of taxes, which disburses funds to states who lose tax base as a result of the federally owned lands, was allotted $101 million for 8 percent of the budget. Another $101 million and 8 percent was spent to administer grant lands in Oregon and California. Seven percent or about $90 million was allocated to permanent and trusts.

The remaining 6 percent of the budget was divided among various programs such as Central HAZMAT (1 percent), a program that removes toxic materials from federal lands. The bureau also continues to acquire small portions of land and allocated $9 million (1 percent) to these purchases. Finally, the BLM spent $43 million on the Forest Plan in 1998. This long-term plan is redirecting its funding from planning and reforestation to implementation of experimental techniques in adaptive management of forests and surveying of forest species and habitat.

HISTORY

As pioneers moved westward across the continent, they passed by vast areas of land that were considered unsuitable to their needs and became known as "the lands that nobody wanted." These inhospitable lands might not have attracted settlers, but the resources within those lands provided the building materials of great U.S. cities and the foundation of the economies of the western states. It was the role of the government to survey and assess these lands for future development.

Initially two government agencies handled the primary responsibilities that came with these lands. Through the consolidation of the General Land Office (created in 1812) and the Grazing Service (formed in 1934), the Bureau of Land Management (BLM) was established on July 16, 1946. The Federal Land Policy and Management Act of 1976 provided a basic mission statement for the bureau and established policy guidelines and criteria for the management of public lands and resources administered by the bureau.

Initially the BLM was responsible for managing public land use by focusing on the extraction of livestock forage, timber, and energy and mineral commodities. Over the last 20 years the agency has had to broaden the scope of its management to include supervising outdoor recreation and scenic landscapes, preserving the natural and cultural heritage, and developing communication facilities, waste disposal operations, and land for use in filmmaking. The BLM has had to redirect its main focus from consumption of natural resources to the health and sustainability of the vast and dynamic ecosystems that make up the public lands.

CURRENT POLITICAL ISSUES

Although the mission of the BLM is straightforward, public land stewardship, the political issues are vast and complex. Should the BLM be a service to industries whose goal is to make a profit, or should it be an environmental agency whose job is to protect and preserve the country's natural heritage? This battle is fought over and over wherever the BLM is active and there are conflicts over public land use. In 1996, for example, BLM director Jim Baca was removed from his position by the Department of the Interior with the acquiescence of the President Bill Clinton administration. This was widely recognized as a political decision made to quiet the complaints of pro-business interests in the western states.

Baca was interested in seeing the BLM impose environmental restrictions on business, and that created a serious political problem.

Over the decades BLM policies have provided for the low-cost use of resources such as grazing lands for livestock and low fees for timber and mining rights. Critics argue that low fees are a way of subsidizing these industries. Industry argues that low federal land-use fees are the only way to offset the high cost of extracting resources in remote areas. The Clinton administration ran a campaign with a strong environmental platform, and through the appointment of Bruce Babbitt as secretary of the interior a distinctive plan of environmental reform was intended. However, the implementation of environmental reform has been extremely difficult because of the protests of private–interest groups whose profits are at stake. Consequently the Clinton administration has pursued a middle road in conflicts over land management.

Case Study: Option 9

Where environmental sustainability is at stake, it is the government's responsibility to develop and implement long-range solutions to conflicts over resources. Option 9 is a federal plan mediated by the Clinton administration to resolve the growing conflict in California over the fate of the last 4 percent of old-growth redwood forests. Because BLM lands are subject to the Endangered Species Act, environmentalists used studies showing that logging these forests would further endanger the nearly extinct spotted owl. The logging industry was equally adamant over the protection of business interests.

The resolution did not make either side, the environmentalists or the private-interest groups, particularly happy. The plan opened up areas of forest for logging; it also protected some areas of the spotted owl habitat. The plan sought to mitigate the effects of current and future logging restrictions by providing federal money for contracts that would bring aid to local economies suffering from loss of jobs and revenue. The process of developing alternative economies to replace logging is slow and is often met with resistance. However, tourism, hunting, fishing, and other recreational activities are increasingly the alternatives looked to for economic support.

Public Impact

Option 9 will affect California's citizens in a variety of ways. First, it allows the BLM to continue to work with businesses in the logging of public lands, thus creating jobs and keeping lumber companies in business. Timber interests argue that if entire areas were restricted as habitat for endangered species, timber supplies would go down and the cost of specific types of timber, like redwood, would increase as it already has because of environmental regulations. For areas where jobs are actually lost as a result of Option 9, the BLM administers a program called Jobs in the Woods, which subsidizes jobs where logging has been restricted.

FAST FACTS

Public lands under the supervision of the BLM produce 33 percent of the nation's coal, 8 percent of its natural gas, and 5 percent of its oil.

(Source: Bureau of Land Management, 1998.)

A second impact is the effect continued logging will have on the environment. Environmentalists opposed to logging the last ancient redwood groves in California continue the struggle to save this natural monument for future generations. As areas are opened up for logging, organized groups of environmentalists see no alternative but to protest by disrupting the efforts to remove the trees. This will result in arrests and inevitably cost the BLM money for law enforcement activity.

The passage of Option 9 will also likely affect ecosystems interconnected with the redwood forests. The streams found within the old growth forests are the spawning grounds for another endangered species, the Coho salmon. As the forests are logged, streams are damaged, fish do not reproduce, and fishermen lose; one group's gain is another's loss. Federal agencies like the BLM and the Department of the Interior will increasingly look to scientific studies to shed light on environmental problems, then bring the different interest groups together to search for lasting solutions.

SUCCESSES AND FAILURES

The Wild Free Roaming Horse and Burro Adoption Act of 1971 was implemented to protect the health of animals suffering the effects of overpopulation, primarily in the arid lands of Nevada, which could not always support them. The adoption program provides tracking, herd management practices, and adoption opportunities. More than 125,000 animals have been adopted through the program, allowing the approximately 40,000 animals left living in the wild to have adequate water and forage and thus lead healthier lives.

The BLM received criticism in 1997, however, when it was discovered that some of the adopted animals were sold to slaughterhouses. After completing a full investigation, the agency tightened tracking methods to follow up on adopted animals and instituted penalties for program violations. Another successful aspect of the program is the involvement of federal prisoners in the training of wild horses. Providing horses with humane treatment and prisoners with meaningful work has made this aspect of the program a dual success.

FUTURE DIRECTIONS

Traditionally the National Park Service, not the BLM, has managed and operated national monuments, but recently this has begun to change. On September 18, 1996, the president created by proclamation the Grand Staircase-Escalante National Monument, a 1.7–million-acre landscape in south-central Utah containing some of the most stark and beautiful stone canyons in the United States. This new monument is to be cared for by the BLM, and more monuments may be placed under its control in the future. This new responsibility of the BLM demonstrates the changing demands on the use of public lands and the evolving sentiment for their stricter stewardship, changes that the BLM will have to respond to.

AGENCY RESOURCES

Information about the BLM can be obtained from the Office of Public Affairs, Bureau of Land Management, Department of the Interior, Washington, DC 20240; phone (202) 452-5125. The Office of Public Affairs can also provide the address and phone number of the BLM's Information Access Centers. These centers provide information on the nature, location, and primary use of public lands by region and state.

AGENCY PUBLICATIONS

Included among BLM publications are an annual publication, *Public Land Statistics,* and *Discover the Past.* These documents provide various statistical and historical data regarding public lands and are available from the Superintendent of Documents, Government Printing Office, Washington, DC 20402.

BIBLIOGRAPHY

Department of the Interior. "Secretary Babbitt Signs Agreement to Promote Economic Development for Alaska Natives and to Protect the Kenai River." 13 May 1997.

Knickerbocker, Brad. "Saving Land—and Ranchers Who Work It." *Christian Science Monitor,* 10 January 1996, p. 1.

———. "Swimming Up Stream to Save the Salmon." *Christian Science Monitor,* 15 May 1997, p. 10.

Oppenheimer, Todd. "The Rancher Subsidy." *Atlantic Monthly,* January 1996, p. 26.

Ross, Chris. "Go West Young Mappers: Geographic Information and Geographic Positioning Systems Technology Makes It Possible for the BLM to Locate Thousands of Dangerous Abandoned Mine Sites Scattered across the Deserts of Nevada." *American City and County,* October 1994, p. 30.

Wilkinson, Tom. "Why Megadump May Be Neighbor of Desert Park." *Christian Science Monitor,* 25 February 1997, p. 3.

Bureau of Prisons (BOP)

PARENT ORGANIZATION: Department of Justice
ESTABLISHED: May 14, 1930
EMPLOYEES: 31,633 (1999)

Contact Information:

ADDRESS: 320 First St. NW
Washington, DC 20534
PHONE: (202) 307-3082
URL: http://www.bop.gov
DIRECTOR: Dr. Kathleen M. Hawk Sawyer

WHAT IS ITS MISSION?

The mission of the Federal Bureau of Prisons (BOP) has two essential aspects. First, the bureau is charged with protecting society by segregating criminals from the public. Second, it has a mandate to provide humane confinement of prisoners, including opportunities for rehabilitation and self-improvement. The late Chief Justice Warren Burger summed up the essence of the BOP in this statement, "When society places a person behind walls and bars . . . it has an obligation—a moral obligation—to do whatever can reasonably be done to change that person before he or she goes back into the stream of society."

HOW IS IT STRUCTURED?

The BOP, like many other bureaus in the Department of Justice, is subdivided into many smaller groups and has four administrative offices, six divisions, a training institute, and a wholly owned government industry.

Offices and Administrative Divisions

The Executive Office of the Director oversees all BOP operations and functions. Three subordinate offices—the offices of General Counsel, Program Review, and Internal Affairs—coordinate BOP administration.

The BOP Administrative Division is responsible for administering the BOP budget, for facilities planning,

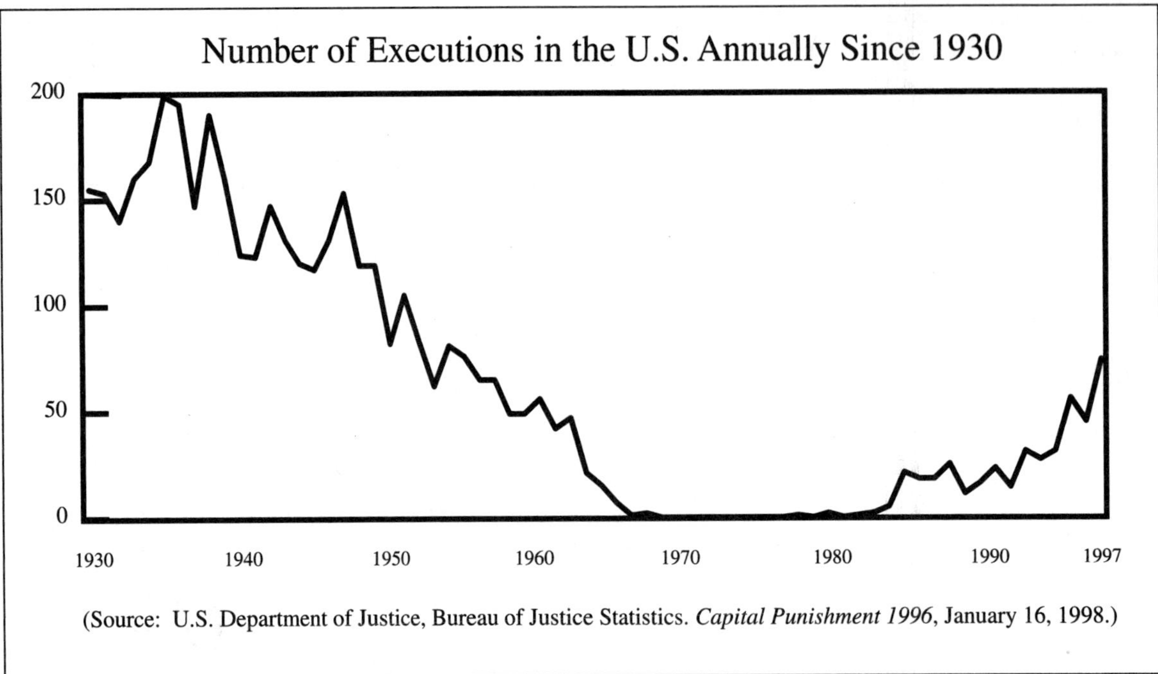

(Source: U.S. Department of Justice, Bureau of Justice Statistics. *Capital Punishment 1996*, January 16, 1998.)

staffing, and procurement. The five remaining divisions address inmate needs and services. The Community Correction and Detention Division addresses the needs of community-based facilities and the privatization of correctional facilities. The Correctional Programs Division oversees matters of inmate security and welfare. The Health Services Division manages farm and food operations for corrections facilities. Health Services also oversees medical and psychiatric facilities, environmental issues, and occupational health matters. The Information, Policy and Public Affairs Division provides information and research services and performs public relations for the bureau. Finally, the bureau's Human Resource Management Division handles personnel and recruitment matters.

Special Programs

The BOP also oversees two special programs. The first is UNICOR, a wholly owned corporation of the federal government. Traditionally known as Federal Prison Industries, Incorporated (FPI), UNICOR provides employment and on-the-job training in a variety of industries, including manufacturing and service-based industries, for inmates. It also sponsors vocational and experimental training programs.

The BOP's National Institute of Corrections (NIC) provides nationwide training for correctional personnel and services to foreign governments. The NIC prison division, community corrections division, and administrative offices are in Washington, D.C.; the jails division, training academy, and information center are located in Longmont, Colorado.

Regional Centers

BOP management centers are distributed throughout the United States. Regional offices are located in Annapolis, Maryland, Kansas City, Missouri, Philadelphia, Pennsylvania, Dallas, Texas, Atlanta, Georgia and Dublin, California. There are also two regional staff training centers in Glynco, Georgia, and in Aurora, Colorado.

PRIMARY FUNCTIONS

The BOP is responsible for the security, welfare, and rehabilitations of inmates within the federal prison system. A prison is defined as a place where sentenced offenders are confined to serve out their sentences in restitution to society for crimes committed, as opposed to a jail which is a confinement area for arrestees who are awaiting court proceedings such as arraignment or trial. Except in rare cases, BOP facilities are used to incarcerate only federal offenders. Federal offenses are defined by their scope. They generally occur on an international level, involve the federal government (such as espionage), or were committed across state boundaries. In dealing with crimes at the federal level, BOP interacts with law enforcement agencies worldwide as well as with the individual states and U.S. territories to provide training and guidance in prison management and inmate supervision.

BOP Training Program

Inherent in prison management is the need to address the health and welfare needs of the federal prison population as well as critical security issues. The BOP provides extensive field training for staff employees and formal training programs at the NIC. Initial training routines are reinforced by follow-up cross-training assignments in active field work. BOP staff members rotate responsibilities and alternate among prison facilities as well as between the various security levels of facilities within the system.

The NIC coordinates with other federal agencies to develop training programs and technical assistance for specialized corrections programs. In conjunction with the U.S. Department of Health and Human Services, the NIC addresses the unique problems of doubly diagnosed inmates—individuals who suffer from both mental illness and substance abuse. The NIC develops training and technical assistance programs for juvenile authorities in alliance with the Office of Juvenile Justice and Delinquency Prevention, and the Office of Justice Programs works with NIC to disburse grants for correctional facilities under the Violent Crime Control and Law Enforcement Act of 1994.

A Secure Environment

The BOP must also provide a secure environment for the protection of both inmates and society. Inmate activity is continually supervised to protect inmates not only from each other but also from themselves. The security level of prisons can vary considerably. For example, minimum security prisons are sometimes referred to as "country clubs" because prisoners are not constrained within a locked environment.

Inmate Welfare

Health and welfare are other important aspects of inmate care. The BOP provides medical and recreational facilities for inmates within the confines of the prison walls, and BOP staff members include medical and mental health professionals. The BOP also offers programs to counteract drug abuse among prisoners, more than half of whom are drug offenders.

The BOP's Office of Research and Evaluation conducts research, maintains statistics, studies trends, and evaluates conditions and practices in a continuing effort to improve inmate conditions and to foster a rehabilitative environment within the prisons.

BOP employees provide administrative and supervisory support for UNICOR (the Federal Prison Industries), a self-sufficient corporation staffed by inmates that teaches skills in manufacturing and service-based industries.

FAST FACTS

While Alcatraz was a federal penitentiary, there were seven attempted prison breaks from the ultra-secure facility. All seven ended in failure. On June 11, 1962, however, three convicts successfully vanished from the island, and no trace of any of them was ever found. The case was reopened in 1989 after a detailed account of the mystery was presented on network television, but it was never solved.

(Source: Don DeNevi. *Riddle of the Rock.* Prometheus Books, Buffalo, N.Y.: 1991.)

PROGRAMS

BOP programs range from inmate welfare and rehabilitation to staff training and research. One of the oldest and most impressive BOP programs is the inmate rehabilitation program, which focuses on teaching industrial skills that can be used when inmates are released back into society.

Federal Prison Industries (FPI)

The FPI program has many purposes. In addition to providing on-the-job industrial training, the prison industries program affords incentives and opportunities for prisoners to spend their time in productive pursuits. FPI's core enterprise is a wholly owned government corporation called UNICOR, which is completely self-sustaining and typically earns enough money from sales of its merchandise to pay its own overhead and show a profit. The company has returned more than $80 million in excess profits to the U.S. Treasury in just over six decades of operation.

UNICOR employs approximately 25 percent of all BOP inmates in a variety of jobs in assorted industries. UNICOR policies provide incentives to learn, to earn, and to prepare for a normal and productive life in the mainstream of society. Statistics indicate that program participants have significantly decreased recidivism (return to criminal behavior and prison).

FPI manufactures an impressive array of products: furniture, clothing, bedding, protective wear, and machinery components. UNICOR services include remanufacturing, data entry, and printing as well.

BUDGET:
Bureau of Prisons

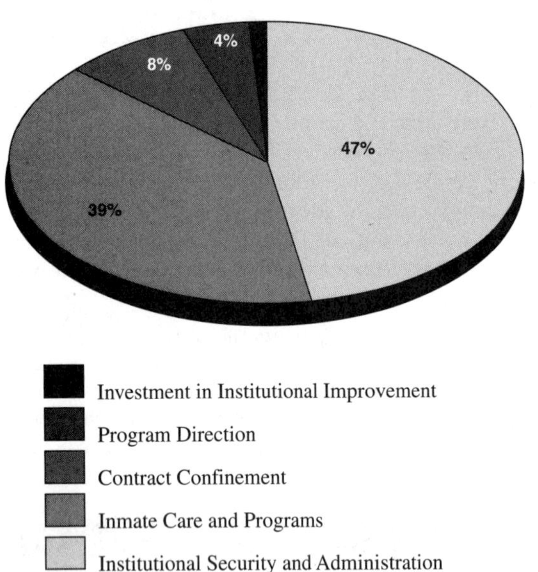

BUDGET INFORMATION

In 1999 Congress appropriated an estimated $3.1 billion to the federal prison system. An additional $27 million in funding was appropriated from the Violent Crime Reduction Trust Fund, according to provisions of the Department of Justice Appropriations Act of 1998. Federal Prison System funds go toward institutional security and administration ($1.48 billion or 47 percent of the total budget), inmate care and programs ($1.12 billion or 39 percent), contract confinement ($255 million or 8 percent), program direction ($140 million or 4 percent) and investment in institutional improvement ($44 million or 1 percent). These amounts do not include compensation for approximately 26,000 inmate employees of UNICOR.

Commissary Trust Fund and UNICOR

The prison system commissary facilities are financed through a system of trust-revolving funds. These funds underwrite the budgets of federal prison commissaries and insure the availability of working capital for that purpose. Profits derived from commissary operations are used to purchase items for communal recreational facilities for prisoners. In a similar fashion UNICOR, a wholly owned government corporation, is financially self-sufficient. Since the establishment of UNICOR in 1934, the corporation has, in fact, returned $82 million in excess income to the U.S. Treasury.

The total UNICOR budget for 1999 was $523 million, including operational expenses, employee compensation for inmates, civilian personnel, costs of goods and services, facilities, and equipment. According to statute (5 U.S.C. 3109) a prescribed maximum of UNICOR capital is designated for administrative overhead costs, not to exceed $3.27 million of corporate funds.

HISTORY

The BOP was created under an act of Congress in 1930 by President Herbert Hoover to consolidate the operations of all federal prisons. Federal prisoners were first incarcerated in state-run facilities using funds appropriated by the U.S. attorney general and then disbursed to the states. The prisoners in turn were hired out as contract labor until Congress outlawed the "leasing" of prisoners in 1887. In 1895, the first federal penitentiary in the United States opened at Leavenworth, Kansas, the first of three such prisons initiated by the Three Prisons Act of 1891. A second prison in Atlanta opened in 1902, and in 1907 the territorial prison camp at McNeil Island in Washington state was converted into the third federal penitentiary. By 1930 there were seven federal prisons.

Early Twentieth Century Prison Management

Early penitentiaries were operated by the Department of Justice under the control of a single federal superintendent of prisons. In practice, however, each prison was an autonomous operation controlled by a single warden. Individual prisons received their funding directly from Congress, and wardens were typically appointed as a result of political favoritism. In many cases, these wardens had few qualifications for their position, and little interest in their duties. As a result, the earliest federal prisons were poorly run and were often guilty of gross improprieties. Prisoners were treated with needless brutality, and there was little concern for their physical well-being or mental condition. Worst of all, there was no one to intercede on behalf of prisoners who suffered at the hands of corrupt wardens.

During the 1920s conditions in the federal prisons were very poor. Overcrowding became commonplace as overwhelming numbers of Americans were incarcerated for violating the prohibition laws. These extreme conditions eventually led to the creation of the Federal Bureau of Prisons in 1930. Reformist Sanford Bates, the federal superintendent of prisons at that time, became the first director of the new Bureau of Prisons. He was a firm administrator, and an innovative leader who guided the new bureau for seven years. During his tenure, prison employees became members of the federal civil service, a critical improvement which effectively eliminated the bureau's reputation of indulging political favoritism. James V. Bennett, Bates's assistant, ultimately succeeded him as director. A highly charismatic man, he is credited with founding the FPI during his tenure as assistant director. Bennett served as director until 1964, and he is remembered for his dynamic approach to prison administration.

FPI was founded in 1934 to provide on-the-job training for inmates as well as to encourage a positive and productive environment to foster rehabilitation. This self-sufficient corporation was renamed UNICOR in 1978. UNICOR realized over $250 million in gross sales in 1985; but in spite of its success, the 101st Congress moved to minimize the program in 1989. The program was salvaged intact only as a result of BOP's efforts.

Modern BOP

Meryl Alexander replaced Bennett in 1964 and continued the bureau along a course set by his predecessor. In 1970 Alexander's executive aide, Norman A. Carlson, became director and he served for 17 years. Carlson was replaced by J. Michael Quinlan in 1987, and in 1992 Kathleen M. Hawk Sawyer took over the post.

BOP directors have established a reputation as administrators of a capable and resourceful federal institution and have maintained high morale among bureau staffers. Custodial officers transfer posts frequently, alternating between minimal security camps such as the one in Allenwood, Pennsylvania, and "super-maximum-security" facilities such as the penitentiary in Marion, Illinois. In addition, every BOP staff member regardless of age or sex, including office personnel, is required to undergo basic training, so they will be prepared to deal with emergencies. This unique policy was seen in action during a hostage-taking incident at the federal penitentiary at Atlanta in 1987.

CURRENT POLITICAL ISSUES

The Constitution specifically prohibits the imposition of cruel and unusual punishment under the Eighth Amendment. As the United States enters the twenty-first century, the majority of Americans concur that the Eighth Amendment precludes exotic tortures such as flagellation or impalement; but there is much room for controversy between these antiquated punishments and modern prison facilities. The death penalty is a topic of much controversy. Political conservatives aver that capital punishment is the only deterrent to murder and that people will not resort to murder for fear of being put to death. Advocates of prison reform, however, maintain that contemporary prisons are antiquated chambers of horror and that compassion and humane treatment is the only viable means of eliminating crime in any society. Reformists contend that violent criminals must be treated for their violent tendencies and should never be isolated in sterile regimented environments nor alienated from human contact. Reform advocates maintain that any method of execution intrinsically constitutes cruel and unusual punishment and deprives the individual of the inalienable right to life as defined in the Declaration of Independence. Above all, the prison reform movement upholds the importance of educating convicted offenders and presenting them with viable opportunities for rehabilitation and reentry into society.

Case Study: Wilbert Rideau

In 1993 a 51-year-old convicted murderer, Wilbert Rideau, was the subject of several magazine articles for his outspoken opinions on prison reform. Rideau was originally sentenced to death, but on appeal his punishment was reduced to life in prison for a brutal murder and hostage-taking incident following a bank robbery. Rideau, an eighth-grade dropout, committed the crime at the age of 19. In 1993, after 31 years of incarceration, he was earning seven cents an hour at the Louisiana State Penitentiary as editor-in-chief of the prison magazine of the Louisiana Department of Public Safety and Corrections.

Under Rideau's control the magazine came to national attention for its professional quality as well as for Rideau's assertive editorials on prison reform. He was credited with exposing inhumane conditions at the Angola State Penitentiary and with bringing about critical improvements in the living conditions of the inmates there. As Rideau confided to *Time* reporter Richard Woodbury, in the August 23, 1993, issue: "Crime is a social problem, and education is the only real deterrent. . . . Look at all of us in prison: we were all truants and dropouts. . . . Look at your truancy problem, and you're looking at your future prisoners. The length of a prison sentence has nothing to do with deterring crime . . . [I know, because] I've lived with criminals for 31 years."

Public Impact

Rideau's ironic circumstance as a critic of the penal environment whose life was spared by the appeals court illustrates the position of BOP, especially with respect to the Federal Prison Industries program. Over the years the program has come under fire by private enterprise and conservative politicians alike, but BOP maintains that the FPI is effective at maintaining order and improving prison conditions. Statistics show that the FPI in conjunction with the many BOP social programs, most notably drug abuse treatment and counseling, is effective in reducing recidivism as well.

Barbara Dority, President of Humanists of Washington, lamented in 1993 that "the United States now imprisons over a million Americans . . . this is an astonishing number of American citizens being kept in cages." Dority further upheld the importance of education in preventing crime, contending that one cause of escalating violence can be traced to the priorities and value system of modern society—a typical public school system spends an average of $4,000 per student per year compared with $26,000 spent on every prison inmate in the same locale.

FUTURE DIRECTIONS

In consideration of future needs, the BOP's Office of Research and Evaluation conducts research on aspects of social science that are relevant to both prison management and inmate welfare. The purpose of such research is to solve current problems and answer questions that might improve BOP in coming years. Prominent areas of research encompass a wide assortment of issues. Studies of prison classification systems are used to determine better ways of assigning security levels to prison inmates. Drug treatment evaluation studies help to assess the effectiveness of critical drug treatment programs. Between 1970 and 1998, the percentage of sentenced drug offenders in the prison population rose from 16.3 percent to 59.1 percent, an increase of more than 42 percent. Other studies evaluate the effectiveness of BOP intensive confinement centers, commonly known as boot camps.

AGENCY RESOURCES

Certain information concerning federal inmates is a matter of public record under the Freedom of Information Act. For inmate information, call the Federal Inmate Locator at (202) 307-3126. Archived inmate data (prior to 1982) is available from the Office of Communications and Archives, 320 First St. NW, Washington, DC 20534, or by calling (202) 307-2934. Inquiries regarding non-federal inmates should be directed to the appropriate state department of corrections.

The BOP Library houses domestic (U.S.) and foreign publications, government documents, statistical information, periodicals, and organizational publications about prisons and inmates. Convenient document access is provided through an automated card catalog and CD-ROM databases. The library is located at the Central Office, Building 500, on the 7th floor. Visitors' hours are from 9 A.M. to 5 P.M., Monday through Friday. The library phone number is (202) 307-3029, or fax for information at (202) 307-5756. Send mail to the Federal Bureau of Prisons Library, 320 First St. NW, Bldg. 500, 7th Fl., Washington, DC 20534. BOP materials circulate to the public at large through the interlibrary loan program. Information is available at local libraries.

Available records of the BOP archives include annual reports, official speeches and correspondence, and UNICOR records. Also available are photographs, videos, and other memorabilia—including case files of the most infamous federal felons. Research aids in the BOP archives also refer researchers to related materials in the National Archives and Records Administration collection. Contact the Federal Bureau of Prisons Archives at 320 First St. NW, Bldg. 500, 7th Fl., Washington, DC, 20534.

The BOP Library hosts a Web site at http://www.bop.library.net. The site features a searchable library catalog, general information and library policies, and information about the BOP archives and periodicals collection.

AGENCY PUBLICATIONS

The BOP publishes an annual "State of the Bureau" report containing statistical data, activities reports, and a facilities directory. Individual reports often spotlight one or more topics of timely concern. The 1993 report contained an article entitled "A Day in the Life of the Bureau of Prisons." Program evaluation and planning was featured in the 1992 report, and drug treatment programs were discussed in 1991.

The *Federal Prisons Journal,* published between 1989 and 1994, presented articles on prison management as well as information about the BOP. Back issues are available from the BOP Office of Public Affairs at (202) 307-3198.

BIBLIOGRAPHY

Adint, Victor. *Drugs and Prison.* New York: Rosen Publishing Group, 1995.

Colt, George Howe, and John Loengard. "The Most Rehabilitated Prisoner in America." *Life.* March 1993, p. 68.

DeNevi, Don. *Riddle of the Rock.* Buffalo, New York: Prometheus Books, 1991.

Dority, Barbara, "Americans in Cages." *Humanist,* November–December 1993, p. 36.

Encyclopedia of American Prisons. New York: Garland Publishing, 1996.

Hjelmeland, Andy. *Prisons: Inside the Big House.* Minneapolis: Lerner Publications Company, 1996.

Keve, Paul W. *The McNeil Century: The Life and Times of an Island Prison.* Chicago: Nelson-Hall, 1984.

Morris, Norval, and David J. Rothman, eds. *The Oxford History of the Prison.* New York: Oxford University Press, 1986.

Oliver, Marilyn Tower. *Prisons: Today's Debate.* Springfield, N.J.: Enslow Publishers, 1997.

Bureau of Reclamation (BOR)

WHAT IS ITS MISSION?

The Bureau of Reclamation (BOR) is the largest supplier and manager of water in the 17 western states. Its mission is to develop, protect, and conserve water, and related resources in an environmentally and economically sound manner. Reclamation projects are designed to protect local economies and preserve natural resources and ecosystems through the effective use of water resources.

HOW IS IT STRUCTURED?

The Bureau of Reclamation (BOR) is a division of the Department of the Interior (DOI) that works closely with other DOI divisions and related federal agencies. BOR is administered by a commissioner who is nominated by the president and confirmed by the Senate. The commissioner's office is responsible for policy development and overseeing the uniform application of standards to implement those policies throughout the agency. This office, with staff located in Washington, DC, and Denver, Colorado, provides the line management for BOR's program activities.

Working under the commissioner's supervision are six directors and managers responsible for administrative programs. The secondary level of management is composed of five regional directors who are in charge of area offices throughout the western states.

The Program Analysis Office (PAO) in Denver provides expert resource management advice to the commissioner, commissioner's office directors, and BOR regional directors. It also represents the BOR within the

PARENT ORGANIZATION: Department of the Interior
ESTABLISHED: July 8, 1902
EMPLOYEES: 6,049

Contact Information:

ADDRESS: 1849 C St. NW, Rm. 7654
Washington, DC 20240-0001
PHONE: (202) 208-4662
URL: http://www.usbr.gov
COMMISSIONER: Eluid Martinez

The Glen Canyon Dam, located on the upper Colorado River in northern Arizona, has generally been considered a great success. The dam, completed in 1963, created Lake Powell in southern Utah, which generates electricity for millions of people in six states and provides recreational opportunities for thousands of tourists. (AP/Wide World Photos)

Department of the Interior on policy matters. Most of its work is accomplished by teams using staff from its service center and from regional and area offices. BOR's operations office in Denver consists of a research director and a Dam Safety Office.

The Reclamation Service Center (RSC) provides scientific, engineering, research, laboratory, administrative, and human resources management services, including the development of programs, procedures, and standards to support BOR's water resources management program and assigned Interior Department programs. The RSC also provides these services to other federal agencies as assigned. The RSC is divided into four major offices: the Technical Service Center, the Management Services Office, the Human Resources Office, and the Administrative Service Center. Reclamation project facilities in operation include 355 water storage reservoirs, 69,400 miles of canals and other water conveyances and distribution facilities, 300 recreational sites, and 58 hydroelectric power plants.

PRIMARY FUNCTIONS

BOR manages water resources indispensable to the communities, industries, and agriculture of the arid western states. Water management facilities include dams (which also produce hydroelectric power), reservoirs, canals, pumping plants, and flood control facilities. Careful management of these water supplies allows for economic development and reduced financial losses caused by adverse weather patterns. The bureau also has an environmental mandate to aid in the protection of fish and wildlife whose habitats are dependent upon BOR—managed water and land.

In addition, the BOR manages partnerships with various entities such as state and local governments, American Indian tribes, and developers seeking invaluable water resources. Water resources in the possession of the federal government are bought and sold much like other commodities. However, legal and historical water rights issues are often involved in the transference of water resources from watershed to end user.

Because of increasingly limited federal funds and costly environmental regulation, new BOR projects must be economically justified and environmentally compatible with federal regulation. New projects often take years of scientific study and legal debate before any construction is begun.

PROGRAMS

Water resource programs managed by BOR are divided into the following areas: Facility Operation, Facility Maintenance and Operation, Water and Energy Management and Development, Fish and Wildlife Management and Development, and Land Management and Development.

Ongoing programs include the operation of dams, reservoirs, canals, and flood control and energy production facilities. Important programs include the Central Valley Project Restoration Fund, which was created to preserve wildlife habitats and restore fish populations, specifically through the Anadromous Fish Restoration Plan. The fund provides for acquisition of water for wildlife refuges and construction of fish hatcheries and other facilities.

BOR will also play an important role in the completion of the California Bay-Delta Ecosystem Restoration Project, designed to conserve and protect one of the most unique and delicate environments in the world.

FAST FACTS

BOR is the largest water supplier in the United States, bringing water resources to more than 31 million people and irrigating approximately 10 million acres of agriculturally productive land.

(Source: Bureau of Reclamation. "Press Release," March 27, 1997.)

BUDGET INFORMATION

The budget of the BOR appropriated by Congress in 1997 was approximately $948.3 million. Ongoing programs, which include dams, canals, and hydroelectric power plants account for $763 million, or 80 percent, of the budget. New projects, loans, and restoration funds account for the remainder of the budget.

Between 1992 and 1996, BOR's budgetary authority was reduced by $174 million, and its work force was reduced by 20 percent. BOR's Strategic Plan was prepared assuming a relatively flat budget with increases accounting only for inflation. Even though the budget remains flat the demands on the BOR resources continue to grow. The population in western states has grown significantly and developers continue to plan communities and other projects that require water and power.

HISTORY

Reclamation was defined by early settlers as the practice of claiming rain and snow runoff, or wasted water, and storing it for use in the dry seasons. Farmers in western states suffering from seasonal water shortages set about developing irrigation projects, but few succeeded because of poor engineering and lack of funds.

State representatives, motivated by the potential of such projects, looked to the federal government for assistance with large-scale irrigation projects that, with the government's help, could be properly designed and funded. In 1900 the West's irrigation issues found their way into the politics of the Republican and Democratic Parties. Consequently, Congress approved the Reclamation Act of 1902, which granted then secretary of the interior Ethan Allen Hitchcock the authority to further study, locate, and construct irrigation works in the West.

Hitchcock established the U.S. Reclamation Service within the U.S. Geological Survey (USGS). The new Reclamation Service studied potential water development projects in each western state with federal land. Revenue from the sale of federal lands was the initial source of the program's funding. The directives of the secretary would have the power to limit or promote homesteading, mining, mineral leasing, or removal of timber, stone, or gravel in specific regions. Based upon these directives Department of the Interior water projects would have a powerful impact on land values and financial speculation of all kinds, a major aspect of the development of the western frontier.

From 1902 to 1907 the Reclamation Service began approximately 30 projects in western states. Then, in 1907, the secretary of the interior separated the Reclamation Service from the USGS and created the Bureau of Reclamation, an independent bureau within the Department of the Interior. In the bureau's early years many projects encountered problems: some land was found to be unsuitable for irrigation, settlers were inexperienced in irrigation farming, and land speculation resulted in settlement patterns in areas where irrigation was not feasible. Some project repayment programs met with default because of unforeseen land–preparation and facilities–construction costs that were not balanced by the final value of the crops produced.

In 1924, in the face of increasing settler unrest and financial problems for the reclamation program, the government-sponsored "Fact Finder's Report" investigated reclamation projects. The Fact Finders Act, passed in late 1924, sought to resolve some of the financial and other problems associated with the early projects.

In the 1920s economic growth in the western states fueled debates among state and federal politicians concerning public versus private electric power generation. Arguments for public power prevailed when, in 1928, Congress authorized the Boulder Canyon Project (the Hoover Dam). For the first time large appropriations began to flow to the BOR from the funds of the U.S. Treasury. This began a significant period of project construction that, although interrupted briefly by World War II (1939–45), continued through the 1970s.

The last authorization for major construction projects occurred in the late 1960s. After this point two conditions restricted the authorization of new projects: Americans became concerned with the environmental impact of large–scale water development projects and the cost of large–scale water and power projects increased dramatically.

The first and only failure of a major BOR dam, that of the Teton Dam in 1976 as it filled for the first time, shook the bureau badly. The catastrophe led to the development of a strong dam-safety program designed to prevent such problems in the future. The failure of Teton Dam, along with a budding environmental movement and the announcement that President Jimmy Carter had created a "hit list" on water projects, profoundly affected the direction of BOR's programs and activities. President Carter's "hit list" eliminated funding for specific projects with high costs, negative environmental impact, and political association. Since that time obtaining authorization for new BOR projects has been difficult.

BOR frequently works with stakeholders to promote negotiation in developing new water policy. Partnerships among water users are becoming more common as the BOR works to bring competing interests together around this shared resource.

CURRENT POLITICAL ISSUES

Every new large-scale water reclamation initiative is subject to extensive review. Democrats, in heeding environmental arguments against new construction, have been criticized as slowing progress and hampering business. Republicans, taking a more economically minded approach, have been less critical of large-scale water projects that promote growth and improve economic conditions.

Case Study: Animas-La Plata Dam

Southern Colorado is a high-desert environment that is home to resort areas, expanding communities, and the Southern Ute and Ute Mountain Indian tribes. In 1988 Congress ordered the restoration of American Indian water rights in the region, giving tribes the legal footing to pursue the completion of the Animas-La Plata Dam which was intended to provide water, revenue, and development opportunities for the tribes. The project stalled, however, because of its possible environmental impact on the region.

The Sierra Club Legal Defense Fund filed a federal lawsuit to stop the project on grounds that it would alter the flow of the Animas River and further damage the habitat of endangered species of fish. This claim was studied by the U.S. Fish and Wildlife Service and by the Bureau of Reclamation. Also, BOR scientists were required to submit updated studies on the environmental impact of the project. In 1996 their report was deemed inadequate by the Environmental Protection Agency (EPA).

These studies delayed the projected construction start date, and gave opponents in government plenty of time to build their case against the project. They argued that the anticipated benefits of the dam were outweighed by its estimated cost, which is in the hundreds of millions of dollars. However, if the project is not begun in a timely manner, as mandated by legislators, American Indian tribes could seek legal action against the federal government, which could result in millions of dollars spent in court and legal fees.

Time passed, but the controversy around the Animas-La Plata Dam only grew. A 1995 study by the BOR found that the project would return only 36 cents for each dollar invested. The EPA determined that if the project were carried through, it would result in violations of the Clean Water Act in the areas downstream. Critics also began to question how much the project would benefit American Indian tribes, as they would receive only one third of the newly available water. In 1997 a proposal to cut funding for the project altogether was accepted in the U.S. House of Representatives, but failed in the Senate. In spite of growing criticism, the project has continued forward.

SUCCESSES AND FAILURES

The Glen Canyon Dam, located on the upper Colorado River in northern Arizona, has changed the river drastically. The dam, completed in 1963, created Lake Powell in southern Utah and a hydroelectric power-generating facility within the dam. The lake has provided recreational opportunities for thousands of visitors while providing the water used to generate electricity for millions of people in six western states. The dam has also helped foster a $22 million-a-year river rafting industry on the Colorado, allowing people to enjoy the Grand Canyon while riding the river.

Scientists and environmentalists have watched over the years since the completion of the dam as the composition of the Colorado River and the canyon wall habitat have altered from their original state. The end of seasonal floods created a clearer, colder river. Wildlife and vegetation, once stripped from the canyon walls each spring, now remain year-round, and beaches, once washed away in the flooding, now make good places for campsites.

However, changes in the water temperature have led to the endangerment of native fish species, which have been replaced by species that can tolerate the lower temperatures. The Department of the Interior, following its mandate to conserve and protect the environment, devised a plan to release water from Lake Powell to recreate flood conditions natural to the canyon. In March 1996 Glen Canyon Dam began to release water into the Colorado River at 45,000 cubic feet per second, enough to fill a football stadium in seven minutes. BOR officials continued the flooding for a week and then reduced the flow. Downriver, hundreds of scientists studied the effects of the flooding on wildlife and geology.

On hand to observe the impact were scientists from the Colorado River Energy Distributors Association, a consortium of one hundred utilities that buy power from the BOR. The reason for the association's participation is that plans to alter the flow of water through the dam's turbines could reduce the dam's electrical output by 25 percent, costing millions of dollars in lost power consumption. Even though revenues will be affected, the association agrees with the strategy and supports the plan to bring environmental equilibrium back to the Colorado River.

FUTURE DIRECTIONS

The BOR released a revised strategic plan during July 1997 that outlines its administrative strategies for a five-year period, 1997–2002. The plan outlines the commissioner's goals and objectives for the future and ways the agency will continue to pursue positive partnerships among legislators, the public, and its own employees. Broadening the mission of the BOR is an important goal as the agency branches into new areas of activity. Of particular importance are areas such as water supplies for growing urban populations, water rights for American Indian tribes, fish and wildlife protection, and environmental restoration through endangered-species recovery.

Balancing these goals will be the greatest challenge to the BOR. Urban populations of the western states have grown to almost 10 times what they were at the beginning of the century. The BOR has developed safe water supplies for the public and will continue to do so. However, while the public's need for water has grown, so has its awareness of the environmental trade-off of large-scale public works projects. The challenge facing BOR is to continue in its present role as water and power supplier while enhancing its environmental research. BOR will continue to balance environmentally sound strategies against financial considerations. For example, the agency has studied ways to raise the temperature of the Colorado River. The cost of one proposed plan that would alter intake pipes on the Glen Canyon Dam is estimated at $100 million.

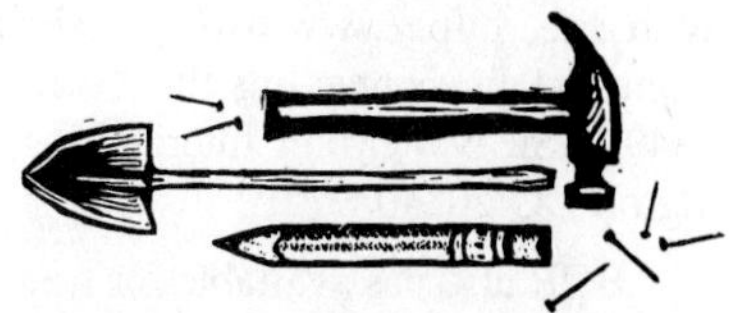

GET INVOLVED:

In the western states water is a scarce resource. Changing weather patterns can cause drought conditions in some areas, causing millions of dollars in damage to crops and adversely affecting electricity production. Water conservation awareness is promoted by BOR to educate the public on how to treat this important resource. BOR offers information on ways to conserve reclamation water at the Web site http://ogee.do.usbr.gov/rwc/intro.html. In addition BOR offers a program for educators and students, "Learning to Be Water Wise and Energy Efficient." The program offers instructional materials and describes products like water-saving shower heads and leak detectors. BOR's 21 area offices also provide an annual implementation plan reflecting local needs and concerns. Water users can request assistance for planning and implementing water-efficient practices, testing and demonstrating innovative techniques, and learning about relevant existing and new technology. For more information contact BOR at (202) 208-4662.

AGENCY RESOURCES

For more information on the Bureau of Reclamation, access the BOR Web site at http://www.usbr.gov/main. Information may also be obtained by sending a request in writing to Public Affairs Division, Bureau of Reclamation, Department of the Interior, Washington, D.C. 20240-0001 or by phoning (202) 208-4662.

AGENCY PUBLICATIONS

The Bureau of Reclamation publishes scientific reports on hydrology and related aspects of water resources management. Some recent publications include *Dams and Public Safety*, *Water Measurement Manual*, *Flood Hydrology Manual*, and *Ground Water Manual*. These books are available by contacting the U.S. Government Printing Office, Superintendent of Documents (SUPDOCS) at (202) 512-1800, or the National Technical Information Service (NTIS), 5285 Port Royal Rd., Springfield, VA 22161; phone 1-800-553-6847. The BOR also publishes an overview of the history and science of the agency titled *Written in Water*. This publication is available for viewing at the agency's

Web site, http://www.usbr.gov. Printed copies can be requested by contacting the Office of Public Affairs, 1849 C St. NW, Main Interior, Rm. 7060-MIB, Washington DC 20240-0001.

BOR also has available for free loan films that illustrate bureau projects. Titles include *How Water Won the West*, *Challenge At Glen Canyon Dam*, and *Hydropower: A 20th Century Force*. Films are available by contacting the Visual Communication Services of the Bureau of Reclamation, PO Box 25007, D-1500, Denver, CO 80225; phone (303) 236-6973.

BIBLIOGRAPHY

Balzar, John. "The Old and the River." *Los Angeles Times,* 11 May 1997, p. A-1.

Brown, Matthew. "Provocative Proposal to Drain Lake Powell Could Make Waves." *Los Angeles Times,* 19 January 1997, p. B-1.

Clifford, Frank. "Controlled Flood to Replenish Grand Canyon." *Los Angeles Times,* 24 March 1996, p. A-1.

Long, Michael. "Grand Managed Canyon." *National Geographic,* July 1997, p. 114.

Miller, Ken. "Water Agency Warns 1995 'Could Be Extremely Alarming'." *Gannett News Service*, 7 December 1994.

Sahagun, Louis. "GOP Victory Proves a Watershed for Controversial Reservoir Project." *Los Angeles Times,* 27 December 1994, p. A-5.

Ward, Janet. "100 Years of Public Works: 1894–1994." *American City & County,* 1 September 1994, p. 74.

"Warnings Issued After Break in Folsom Dam." *Los Angeles Times,* 18 July 1995, p. A-3.

Bureau of the Census

PARENT ORGANIZATION: Department of Commerce
ESTABLISHED: March 6, 1902
EMPLOYEES: 5,400

Contact Information:

ADDRESS: Department of Commerce
Washington, DC 20233
PHONE: (301) 457-3030
TOLL FREE: (301) 457-4067
FAX: (301) 457-3670
E-MAIL: pio@census.gov
URL: http://www.census.gov
ACTING DIRECTOR: James F. Holmes
DEPUTY DIRECTOR: Bradford R. Huther

WHAT IS ITS MISSION?

The mission of the Census Bureau is to collect and provide punctual, relevant, and reliable data about the people and economy of the United States. The bureau's long-standing purpose has been to provide the official statistics required for effective governing as authorized by the Constitution, but its scope of responsibility has grown to include the provision of products and services to the public. It aims to succeed through innovative management and customer service.

HOW IS IT STRUCTURED?

The Bureau of the Census is one of two agencies (the Bureau of Economic Analysis is the other) under the supervision and control of the Economics and Statistics Administration, a Department of Commerce mission area led by the under secretary for economics and statistics. Although it is directly controlled by the director of the Census Bureau, bureau policy and program direction is influenced by the under secretary.

The hierarchy of the Census Bureau is the result of more than two centuries of individually added missions and programs, and as such it is complex and sprawling, especially for a smaller agency. In addition to the Office of the Director, census operations are apportioned among two principal associate directors—one for internal affairs, one for programs—eight associate directors, and more than 40 separate offices.

The associate director for communications falls under the direct supervision of the Office of the Direc-

BUDGET:

Bureau of the Census

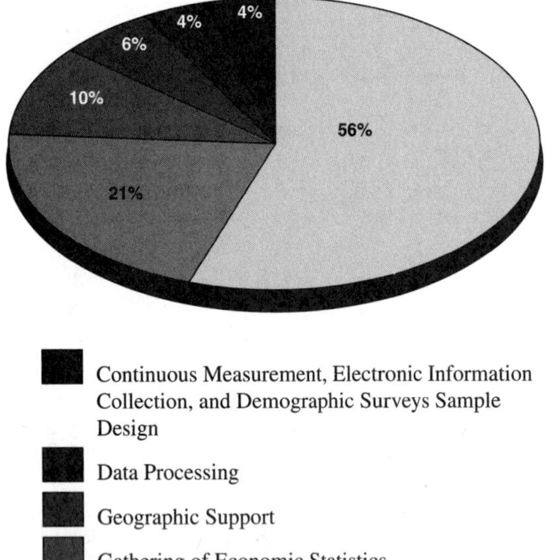

Continuous Measurement, Electronic Information Collection, and Demographic Surveys Sample Design

Data Processing

Geographic Support

Gathering of Economic Statistics

Salaries and Expenses

Demographic Statistics Programs

tor. The offices in this area include the Public Information Office and the Congressional Affairs Office, and they are responsible for maintaining good congressional, public, and customer relations.

The associate directors for Administration, Information Technology, and Field Operations are under the supervision of the principal associate director and chief financial officer. The offices in these areas are mostly concerned with administrative activities such as budgeting, policy making, and employment. The Customer Services Office is considered an administrative office and is under the supervision of the associate director for administration. The bureau's field operations are administered through 12 regional agencies located nationwide.

The associate directors for Demographic Programs, Decennial Census, Economic Programs, and Methodology and Standards are under the supervision of the Principal Associate Director for Programs. The many offices in the program areas are responsible for planning, conducting, marketing, and distributing the results of the bureau's various surveys. The Computer-Assisted Survey Research Office, which helps individuals in investigating specific research questions, is also in this area.

PRIMARY FUNCTIONS

The Census Bureau's primary business is large-scale surveys and censuses and any activities that support this ultimate end. It takes a census of the population and housing every 10 years and a census of agriculture, state and local governments, manufacturers, industry, and transportation every five years. The agency designs surveys and instruments used for collecting information; processes information once it is received; disseminates survey results through publication, the Internet, CD-ROM production, and other media; and conducts research and data analysis that support the bureau's capabilities.

The Census Bureau also serves state and local governments as an agency for hire, conducting special censuses at their request and expense. It produces statistical compendia, catalogs, guides, and directories that are useful in locating information on specific subjects. At the request of private citizens, the bureau conducts searches for a fee of decennial (10-year) census records and furnishes certificates for use as evidence of age, relationship, or place of birth.

PROGRAMS

The bureau's two primary programs are the decennial census, which is mailed to families and focuses on population and housing, and the five-year (quinquennial) economic censuses, which are more diverse in form and are mailed to businesses. The decennial census is conducted in years ending in "0" (Census 2000), and economic censuses are conducted in years ending in "2" and "7." Economic censuses contain inquiries about employment, payroll, output, and other questions that vary according to the company's economic sector.

In response to growing social and economic concerns, a number of special census programs have been added in recent years to the economic census. For example, the Business Owners Survey, conducted as a follow-up to the economic census, provides periodic data that describe and compare women, minority, and non-minority male business owners and their businesses. Responses to this survey are mandatory, and the survey is partially funded by the Minority Business Development Agency and the Small Business Administration.

BUDGET INFORMATION

The bureau's budget in 1998 was approximately $709 million. This is considerably larger than the bureau's traditional budget, mostly because of the agency's preparations for Census 2000, its comprehensive end-of-millennium survey. Most of the bureau's budget authority is received through congressional appropriations, but some costs are offset by collections from the survey and location services offered by the bureau.

Because of the costs involved in Census 2000, the conduct of demographic surveys has taken on prominence in the bureau's budget; about $397 million or 56 percent of spending is done for demographic statistics programs. The second largest amount of the budget is allocated to salaries and expenses with 21 percent of the budget. The gathering of economic statistics accounts for 10 percent of the budget. The remainder of the bureau's budget was allocated to geographic support, 6 percent; data processing, 4 percent; and continuous measurement, electronic information collection and demographic surveys sample design, 4 percent.

FAST FACTS

According to the census population clock, the U.S. population grows as follows: one birth every 8 seconds; one death every 14 seconds; one international migrant entering every 37 seconds; and one federal U.S. citizen returning from abroad every 4,063 seconds. These figures combine to yield a net gain of one person every 13 seconds in the United States.

(Source: U.S. Census Bureau, 1998.)

HISTORY

A decennial census has been a part of American life since the founding of the United States. A decennial inventory is prescribed by article I, section 3 of the Constitution in order to apportion seats among the states in the House of Representatives. "The actual enumeration shall be made within three years after the first meeting of the Congress of the United States, and within every subsequent term of ten years, in such manner as they shall by law direct." The first census was conducted in 1790.

Initially, there was no permanent agency charged with conducting the decennial census. Every ten years, a temporary organization would be established to conduct the census, and disbanded once its work was completed. As the country grew in size, so did the task of the census agencies. For many years few changes were enacted within the census programs. What evolved was the number and type of questions included in the census survey. Over time, questions reflecting economic and social concerns were added; for example, inquiries into income, employment, and school attendance. The bureau also developed entirely new censuses over the years—a census of manufacturers in 1810, of agriculture and mining in 1840, and of governments in 1850.

A Permanent Agency

Complaints about the inefficiency of temporary census agencies mounted during the last half of the nineteenth century. A permanent Bureau of the Census was established by the Census Act of 1902, which created a continuing organization responsible for the current statistics and service work. The act also firmly established strict rules concerning the confidentiality of census returns—rules which gave the Census Bureau unique standing among government agencies in terms of protecting information provided by citizens.

In the years that followed, the bureau gradually expanded as it developed new programs and surveys for each new census. Major expansions occurred during and after World War II (1939–45), when the bureau began to conduct surveys for other government agencies, for a fee. It was also during this period that the agency began to gather current statistics. After the enactment of Public Law 671 in 1948, the bureau had the authority to issue smaller surveys as necessary to maintain an accurate statistical picture of the United States.

Advances in science, statistics, and technology have greatly affected the way census information is collected and processed. The statistics research in areas such as sample design, response research, survey design, and systems analysis resulted in one of the bureau's most significant procedural changes. Beginning with the 1960 census, data was collected by mail, rather than by direct questioning. In the economic censuses, Social Security and Internal Revenue Service records were used to supply mailing addresses.

Most census officials and workers agree that the shift to mail has improved the quality and detail of the information collected, but others have argued that the method virtually insures the undercounting of certain people in the United States. As long as census figures are used to formulate government policy at all levels the undercounting of certain groups will remain a subject of debate.

CURRENT POLITICAL ISSUES

The U.S. government does not gather census information out of mere curiosity. Census data categories are used by federal agencies to uncover job discrimination and school segregation and to parcel out large amounts of financial aid. Because the way people are counted affects the boundaries and composition of state and congressional districts, political observers from both sides are very vigilant of the way the census is conducted.

The 1990 census was estimated to have missed 1.6 percent of the population, or more than 4.3 million people. Because of the nature of census head-counting, a higher proportion of U.S. populations who are transient and who have variable work histories and living arrangements are "differentially undercounted," or missed by census-takers. These populations are overwhelmingly ethnic and racial minorities; a post-census statistical sampling indicated that about 4.5 percent of African Americans were undercounted in 1990. The undercount figure proved unacceptable to both the bureau and Congress, and the bureau is under much pressure to improve its accuracy with Census 2000.

Case Study: Census 2000 and Race

The census has a long, often confusing, and sometimes comical history of differentiating between Americans in terms of race and ethnicity. Early in census history, census-takers were given diagrams of nose, eye, and lip shape along with other physical descriptions intended to help them to determine the "race" of interviewees.

The census has been less standard in other ways; every single census since the first in 1790 has handled race in a different way, resulting in a confusing jumble of racial categories that enter and leave the census vocabulary according to the effectiveness of political lobbying efforts. Past categories include "part Hawaiian," "mulatto," "octoroon (one-eighth black)," "Hindu," and "Japanese." Sometimes these classifications serve only to bewilder census respondents. A classic example is the 1970 census, which included the category "South American" on its census form to indicate persons with racial or ethnic ties to the continent of South America. Over one million residents of Mississippi, Alabama, and other southern states checked the "South American" box.

The 1990 census used a 20-year-old system with four racial categories: black, white, Asian, and American Indian, along with two ethnic categories (Hispanic and non-Hispanic), and a catch-all "other" category for respondents who did not see themselves accurately described on the census form. The bureau later considered an additional racial category for the 2000 census form: "multiracial."

Since the last state law barring interracial marriages was struck down by the Supreme Court in 1967, such marriages have tripled, and births to interracial couples have doubled. The children of these couples do not conform to the categories on the census form, and there is a growing movement for them to be counted as multiracial. This movement has much support among the general population but it also has some surprising critics.

The National Association for the Advancement of Colored People (NAACP) and the National Council of La Raza, a Hispanic advocacy group, are strongly opposed to the new census category because those who label themselves "multiracial" on the census will no longer belong to the black or Hispanic political base. The "multiracial" category sparked some bitter debates in Washington, but parents of multiracial children argue that such self-identification is optional and merely offers people the choice to identify themselves as they see themselves rather than as assigned by arbitrary census categories.

SUCCESSES AND FAILURES

It is difficult to point to a specific program achievement of the Census Bureau, because the results of censuses themselves are used by other agencies to launch programs and initiatives. However, one characteristic that has made it unique among similar agencies around the world is its strict statutory protection of all individual information collected. Part of the 1902 Census Act, the bureau's long-standing record of keeping census responses confidential has helped the bureau achieve high response rates to questions that most people view as highly personal.

FUTURE DIRECTIONS

The goals proposed by the Census Bureau in its 1997–2001 Draft Strategic Plan are rather broad when compared with those of other agencies. The bureau names four strategic goals. It aims to achieve greater customer satisfaction with bureau products and services, and to provide better customer access to census data. By improving technology and statistical methods, it seeks greater productivity. One of its more specific goals is to have a management information system in place by 2000 that will allow the agency to know its costs, understand its processes, share information easily, and quickly redistribute resources.

The Census Bureau also hopes to achieve better public perception and cooperation through developing partnerships and implementing a marketing strategy for its products. Internally, the agency hopes to achieve a more diverse, efficient, and skilled workforce through flexible management, a rewards system, and a communications strategy.

These goals have in common a concentrated effort toward assuring the quality and popularity of the 2000 Census—one of the largest undertakings in the bureau's history—and the implementation of new technology to assist in organizing, analyzing, and communicating within the bureau.

AGENCY RESOURCES

General information about the work of the Census Bureau can be obtained from the Public Affairs Office,

Bureau of the Census, Department of Commerce, Washington, DC 20233; phone (301) 457-3030. For more specific statistical information, visit the bureau Web site, where the census databases CenStats and CenStore can be accessed. CenStat is a Web-based data service that provides access to Census Bureau databases, including some CD-ROMs, and access to all census publications released within the last year. CenStore provides information about products (CD-ROMs, maps, computer tapes, and publications) sold by the Census Bureau and the U.S. Government Printing Office.

Information seekers can also access the National Technical Information Service (NTIS) at http://www.fedworld.gov/ntis/ntishome.html. Specific census searches can be conducted through the personal search unit of the bureau: PO Box 1545, Jeffersonville, IN 47132.

AGENCY PUBLICATIONS

The Census Bureau's catalog of publications is so vast that it can often be difficult to locate desired materials. Categories of census publications include Agriculture, Business, Foreign Trade, General Reference, Governments, and more. Census publications take on many forms: books of general interest such as *History of the Economic Censuses* and *Statistical Abstract of the United States* as well as simple statistical reports such as "Marital Status and Living Arrangements: March 1995" and brochures such as "America's Agriculture: Highlights of U.S. Agricultural Activity." The Census Bureau's monthly newsletter, *Census and You*, contains articles summarizing reports and data files.

Some Census Bureau publications can be downloaded from the agency Web site, but they are also available from several sources. The customer services office of the bureau can be reached by mail at U.S. Department of Commerce, Bureau of the Census, Customer Service, Washington, DC 20233; phone (301) 457-4100. Census publications can also be ordered from the United States Government Printing Office or downloaded from the NTIS Internet site.

BIBLIOGRAPHY

Beech, Hannah. "Don't You Dare List Them as 'Other.'" *U.S. News and World Report*, 8 April 1996, p. 56.

Choldin, Harvey N. *Looking for the Last Percent: The Controversy over Census Undercounts*. New Brunswick: Rutgers University Press, 1994.

Crispell, Diane. "This is Just a Census Test." *American Demographics*, February 1996, pp. 13–15.

Edmonston, Barry, and Charles Schultze, eds. *Modernizing the U.S. Census*. Washington, D.C.,: National Academy Press, 1994.

Fulkerson, Jennifer. "The Census and Privacy." *American Demographics*, May 1995, pp. 48–54.

Garland, Susan B. "Census 2000: You Can Count on this Fight to Get Ugly." *Business Week*, 28 April 1997, p. 50.

Hodgkinson, Harold. "What Should We Call People? Race, Class, and the Census for 2000." *Phi Delta Kappan*, October 1995, pp. 173–78.

"The Other Census Bureau." *American Demographics*, April 1996, p. 4.

Reid-Green, Keith S. "The History of Census Tabulation." *Scientific American*, February 1989, pp. 98–103.

Roush, Wade. "A Census in Which All Americans Count." *Science*, 1 November 1996, pp. 713–14.

"Sampling Isn't Counting." *Wall Street Journal*, 22 May 1997, p. A14.

Bureau of the Public Debt (BPD)

PARENT ORGANIZATION: Department of the Treasury
ESTABLISHED: June 30, 1940
EMPLOYEES: 1,800

Contact Information:

ADDRESS: 999 E St. NW
Washington, DC 20239
PHONE: (202) 219-3300
E-MAIL: OAdmin@bpd.treas.gov
URL: http://www.publicdebt.treas.gov
COMMISSIONER: Richard L. Gregg

WHAT IS ITS MISSION?

According to the agency, the mission of the Bureau of the Public Debt (BPD) is "to borrow the money needed to operate the federal government and to account for the resulting debt. In a nutshell, we borrow by selling Treasury bills, notes, and bonds, as well as U.S. Savings Bonds; we pay interest to our investors; and, when the time comes to pay back the loans, we redeem investors' securities. Every time we borrow or pay back money, it affects the outstanding debt of the United States. It's important that we keep careful track of the amount of this debt." Also, the BPD is responsible for creating strategies that will ensure the payment of debt and seeks new opportunities for raising the money necessary to run federal government programs.

HOW IS IT STRUCTURED?

The Bureau of the Public Debt is a bureau under the Department of the Treasury. Principal offices of the BPD are located in Washington, DC, and Parkersburg, West Virginia. The Washington, DC offices consist of the Office of the Commissioner and Deputy Commissioner. There are also seven subordinate units under the direction of an assistant commissioner: Financing, Public Debt Accounting, Securities and Accounting Services, Administration, Savings Bond Operations, and Automated Information Systems. The Division of Procurement is located in Parkersburg, West Virginia.

The commissioner, who is appointed by the president and confirmed by the Senate, reports to the assistant secretary of Fiscal Affairs in the Department of the Treasury. The BPD, the Fiscal Assistant Secretary's Office, and the Financial Management Service form the Treasury Department's Fiscal Services division. On its own the BPD does not have any public policy decision-making authority.

During World War II, patriotic posters encouraged the general public to invest money in bonds to support the U.S. war effort. *(Courtesy of the National Archives and Records Administration)*

PRIMARY FUNCTIONS

The bureau is involved in six primary activities: commercial book-entry securities, direct access securities, savings securities, government securities, market regulation, and public debt accounting.

Invested with authority by Congress and the Constitution, the BPD acts as a fiscal service of the Department of the Treasury to determine the methods of debt creation and limit the amount and composition of the public debt. Using financial tools, the Bureau of Public Debt borrows money, primarily from individuals and corporations, which is then used to pay for the activities and services of the federal government. These tools consist of secured documents such as Treasury bills, notes, and bonds. Such secured documents are individually registered and accounted for by the BPD. These documents act as a contract between the owner and the U.S. government showing that money has been lent to the government. Over time these documents provide a financial return on the original purchase price, although it is usually lower than from other investment methods. The incentive to the buyer is the guarantee offered by the government, which means that these investments are generally considered extremely safe.

Bonds are marketed to the public through a nationwide network of federal issuing and paying agents. Working with the Bureau of the Public Debt, Federal Reserve banks operate as agents of the BPD by managing the sale and redemption of U.S. bonds.

The bureau also conducts annual sales and education campaigns all over the United States through its contacts with more than 150,000 companies, banks, federal, state, and educational organizations. While conducting these campaigns the BPD promotes the sale and retention of savings bonds through timesaving services such as payroll deduction savings plans. In this way the bureau provides a financial service to consumers looking to support the federal government through their investment.

Acting as a financial regulatory agency, the BPD implements regulations which govern transactions within the government securities market. Regulations provide for investor protection and promote a fair market for government securities.

Exact financial reporting describing the public debt is required by federal law and is used for budget purposes by many government departments. The BPD provides daily and periodic reports on the composition and size of the public debt. This information is made available to the public for comparison with other governmental financial indicators that are critical in understanding the overall financial operations of the federal government.

PROGRAMS

The U.S. Savings Bond program makes bonds available to the public through Federal Reserve banks and other financial institutions. Bonds provide investment opportunities for the general public as well as for companies, banks, and other organizations. Savings bonds are a secure low-paying investment whose values are determined by their interest rates. In May of 1997 the Treasury sought to boost sales of these bonds by increasing yields, simplifying interest rates, and continuing the sale of small denominations.

BUDGET INFORMATION

The Bureau of Public Debt operates on a budget of approximately $169 million. The bureau maintains its staff and administrative offices and performs public debt financing with this level of funding. The entire budget is

FAST FACTS

The Bureau of the Public Debt borrows approximately $2 trillion annually to help fund the federal government.

(Source: Bureau of the Public Debt, July 1997.)

used by the administration of the bureau in support of its government-financing activities.

HISTORY

The first public debt incurred by the federal government was largely the result of money borrowed to finance the American Revolution. The earliest public debt statutes were financial statements agreed upon by legislators. Such statements were made public and lawful by an act passed in August of 1790 authorizing the payment of the foreign debt, funding of existing domestic debt, and the assumption of debts from several states. This act also gave the president the authority to borrow money on the credit of the United States for those purposes. The president then delegated his authority to the secretary of the Treasury. With the development of a public debt administration under way, Congress provided for the placement of federal loan commissioners throughout the states.

In 1861, as Civil War threatened the Union, Congress authorized the secretary of the Treasury to borrow money for government use without the involvement or permission of the president. A period of heavy financing activity followed as the first Treasury bonds were issued. Such bonds guaranteed repayment of the value plus interest to the owner, and sales were used to fund the war effort. Congress continued this borrowing strategy for the next 50 years by legislating borrowing for specific government activities, such as constructing the transcontinental railroad, building the Panama Canal, and financing the war with Spain.

During World War I, with passage of the First Liberty Bond Act of 1917, the president regained the authority to issue bonds and notes. The act also gave the secretary of the Treasury increased discretion in determining the financial mechanics, the terms, conditions, and interest on bonds, notes, and securities. The work of financing the federal government greatly expanded during this period. In response the secretary of the Treasury developed an intergovernmental relationship with the Federal Reserve banks, which would operate as fiscal agents allowing them to carry out financial transactions of bonds, notes, and securities on behalf of the Treasury Department and the Bureau of the Public Debt. By providing public access to Treasury Department financial services, the Bureau of the Public Debt was free to focus on accounting, reporting, and other administrative functions of the system. Because of the program's success the secretary of the Treasury expanded and reorganized the Bureau of Public Debt in order to prepare for inevitable federal expenses of an expanding nation.

The Bureau of the Public Debt was officially established on June 30, 1940, as part of the Reorganization Act of 1939. The bureau would be put to the test as United States military involvement in World War II resulted in a tremendous economic burden on the federal government. This problem was solved in part by the introduction of war bonds. Popular with Americans looking for a way to support the war effort by investing in their country, the bonds were effectively managed and raised billions of dollars. During the 1930s and 1940s, the BPD began to issue bonds in lower denominations, encouraging average-income investors and allowing more Americans the opportunity to save money by investing in the government.

The victory of Allied forces gave a boost to the U.S. economy and increased financial confidence. Millions of Americans took advantage of the postwar economic boom to invest in federal securities and the bureau expanded its nationwide offices. As the role of Treasury bonds in the American economy increased, a network of Federal Reserve banks, commercial financial institutions, industrial organizations, and post offices all participated in the service or sale of Treasury bonds. During this peak period, 10,000 staff were employed at the Chicago office alone for calculating, accounting, and servicing the public debt.

In 1957 advances in electronic accounting technologies became available and consequently brought about a major consolidation of the agency's staff. The BPD became one of the first government offices to successfully use computers to increase efficiency and lower costs. By 1975 offices in Parkersburg, West Virginia, and Washington, D.C., were able to administer all programs with a skeleton staff.

Between 1975 and 1995 the Treasury and Federal Reserve system continued to rely on advancing technologies and accounting systems to offer financial services tailored to the needs of the government and its investors, the American people.

CURRENT POLITICAL ISSUES

The mission of the BPD is to raise money for the day-to-day operation of the federal government. While the vast majority of this capital is obtained through loans and bond sales, a small percentage is actually donated to the BPD by private citizens. This drive to reduce the national debt has drawn attention to government spending practices.

Case Study: The People of the United States vs. the National Debt

As long as the United States has had a national debt, individual citizens have tried to help erase it. In 1961 the BPD began accepting donations made specifically to combat the debt. Few believed that such contributions would actually erase the debt. Rather, the BPD had created a means for individuals to show voluntary monetary support for their country. The "fundraiser" was a public relations success. Donations continued to roll in and the IRS included how-to instructions in its 1982 tax booklet. The following year, 3,570 taxpayers sent close to $350,000 to help reduce the debt. Currently, donors are asked to write separate checks payable to the BPD.

Since 1961 the BPD has accepted $57 million from Americans who wanted to reduce the debt. While this figure sounds impressive, it would pay for roughly 90 minutes of interest on the $5.5 trillion debt. After peaking in 1983, donations declined throughout the 1990s. The 1996 fiscal year saw donations reach only 25 percent of their 1983 levels. If this rate of contribution is maintained, the current national debt (excluding interest) will be erased in approximately 64,700 years.

SUCCESSES AND FAILURES

Under the guidance of the BPD and the secretary of the Treasury, the savings bond program played an important role in U.S. economic history. Launched in March 1935, the bond was named Series A after the secured documents which would be printed for a limited time. Unofficially these securities became known as "baby" bonds. Issued in denominations from $25 to $1,000, they were sold at 75 percent of face value and accrued interest at the rate of 2.9 percent per year. That interest compounded for their 10–year maturity period. The bonds were the first ever to be available and practical for the nonprofessional investor. Series A bonds were offered from March 1935 through the remainder of that year, and Series B bonds were offered in 1936. Series C bonds were offered both in 1937 and again in 1938, and Series D bonds were sold from the beginning of 1939 through April 1941. The BPD borrowed a total of $3.9 billion through the issue of Series A through D savings bonds, providing important capital for the federal government during the Great Depression.

By 1941, with U.S. involvement in World War II on the horizon, the BPD released the Series E bond. These bonds, promoted to support the war effort and encourage individual savings, were a financial success during the wartime economy and offered the added economic bonus of controlling inflation during this period of economic instability. The Savings Bonds programs and the War Bonds program helped to finance the federal government during a period of increased scope and growth, and government spending on services could not have proceeded as it did without this important financial tool. In addition, the program succeeded in encouraging increased savings by the public for everything from retirement to college education for children. By combining public savings with investment in government, two primary features of these programs, the BPD helped to prime the U.S. economy for a future which included the largest accumulation of capital by any country during the twentieth century.

FUTURE DIRECTIONS

The BPD plans to pursue its mission through better management of information technology. The BPD is promoting a service-oriented data processing program that will be an integral part of future operations and management. The BPD will continue to operate a computer center in Parkersburg, West Virginia, while expanding networks of smaller computers distributed throughout Public Debt offices.

An important aspect of the future data environment within the federal government is systems compatibility. The BPD will be constructing data processing systems compatible with the Federal Reserve system that will be directly connected to the Federal Reserve communications network. Goals for the project are compatibility of software and communication utilities to optimize the exchange of data, improved sharing of information among federal offices, improved data security, and increased opportunity for employees in both the Federal Reserve system and Bureau of the Public Debt to interact with shared computer-based applications in either organization. The goal is to become the primary source of direction and guidance on debt accounting, reporting, and analysis for the U.S. Treasury and the federal government. By increasing the efficiency of these financial systems and reducing the time it takes to provide information to policymakers and administrators, the federal government intends to improve its financial planning and reduce the cost of managing investment programs linked to the public debt.

AGENCY RESOURCES

The BPD offers a recorded message which provides information on Treasury bill, note, and bond offerings, auction results, and U.S. Savings Bond information at (202) 874-4000. For more information on BPD activities, contact the Public Affairs Officer, Office of the Commissioner, Bureau of the Public Debt, Washington, DC 20239-0001; phone (202) 219-3302. For up-to-date information on the exact amount of the public debt, see the BPD's Web site at http://www.publicdebt.treas.gov.

AGENCY PUBLICATIONS

The Treasury Bulletin, available on-line from the Financial Management Service at http://www.treas.gov, categorizes ownership of U.S. government securities by types of investors—for example, the public, federal reserve banks, foreign investors, or corporations. This publication explains the composition of the public debt and its relationship to economic conditions.

BIBLIOGRAPHY

Egerton, Judith. "ABC's of Investing in T-Bills." *Gannett News Service,* 17 August 1994.

"Melon Bank/FMS: Secure Electronic Commerce Takes a Major Step Forward in the U.S." *M2 Presswire,* 25 July 1997.

Peake, Charles F. "The Dollar, Family Saving, and Government Policy." *National Forum,* 1 June 1995, p. 6.

Quinn, John Bryant. "Personal Business: Staying Ahead: Inflation Protection Bonds Offer Interesting Opportunity." *Atlanta Journal and Constitution,* 23 December 1996, p. E03.

Scheer, Steven. "Bond Market Fears Grow as U.S. Treasury Auctions Shrink." *Reuters Business Report,* 23 May 1997.

Stern, Linda. "Should You Buy the New Real Bonds?" *Reuters Business Report,* 14 January 1997, p. 5.

Waggoner, John. "Grabbing Juicy Yields: Treasury Auction Draws New Crowd." *USA Today,* 10 August 1994, p. 1.

Willette, Anne, and Sandra Block. "Inflation-Proof Notes: Safe, but Small Returns." *USA Today,* 24 January 1997, p. 5.

Centers for Disease Control and Prevention (CDC)

PARENT ORGANIZATION: Department of Health and Human Services
ESTABLISHED: July 1, 1946
EMPLOYEES: 6,900

Contact Information:

ADDRESS: 1600 Clifton Rd. NE
Atlanta, GA 30333
PHONE: (404) 639-3311
TOLL FREE: (800) 311-3435
E-MAIL: netinfo@cdc.gov
URL: http://www.cdc.gov
DIRECTOR: Jeffrey P. Koplan, M.D.
DEPUTY DIRECTOR: Claire V. Broome

WHAT IS ITS MISSION?

According to the agency, the mission of the Centers for Disease Control and Prevention (CDC) is "to promote health and quality of life by preventing and controlling disease, injury, and disability." As the nation's prevention agency, the CDC works with partners throughout the nation and the world to detect and investigate health problems, conduct research to improve prevention activities and treatment options, and provide leadership and training to the health care community.

HOW IS IT STRUCTURED?

The CDC is an agency of the Department of Health and Human Services, a cabinet-level department in the executive branch of the federal government. In addition to the director's office, the CDC contains 11 major operating components: the National Center for Chronic Disease Prevention and Health Promotion; the National Center for Environmental Health; the National Center for Health Statistics; the National Center for Human Immunodeficiency Virus (HIV), Sexually Transmitted Disease (STD), and Tuberculosis (TB) Prevention; the National Center for Infectious Diseases; the National Center for Injury Prevention and Control; the National Institute for Occupational Safety and Health; the Epidemiology Program Office; the Office of Global Health; the Public Health Practice Program Office; and the National Immunization Program.

Approximately two-thirds of CDC employees work at the CDC headquarters in Atlanta or at other locations

BUDGET:

Centers for Disease Control and Prevention

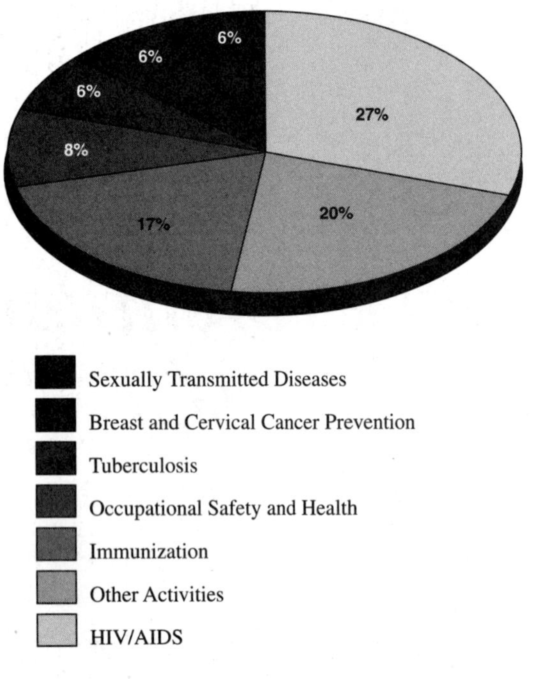

Sexually Transmitted Diseases
Breast and Cervical Cancer Prevention
Tuberculosis
Occupational Safety and Health
Immunization
Other Activities
HIV/AIDS

in the area. The remainder of CDC employees work at one of 10 CDC facilities throughout the country.

PRIMARY FUNCTIONS

The CDC conducts research into the origin and occurrence of diseases and develops methods for their control and prevention. The CDC also works closely with other federal agencies, such as the National Institutes of Health, and particularly with state and local health departments, to develop and administer programs on injury awareness and prevention, immunizations, chronic disease prevention, environmental health problems, and training for public health workers. National data on health issues are collected, analyzed, and disseminated by the CDC. The CDC serves as a leading repository of information and resources in the health care and prevention field. The CDC also serves as a consultant to other nations battling health problems and participates in international efforts to investigate, quarantine, and work toward eradication of communicable diseases.

PROGRAMS

Each division of the CDC operates research programs on issues ranging from infant mortality, environmental hazards, and nutrition monitoring, to motor vehicle accidents, youth suicide, and refugee health. Prevention and training programs based on research results are developed and implemented through individual operating components.

The CDC programs that have received a great deal of attention and have been the subject of much political debate are those related to HIV/AIDS research and prevention. The CDC has been at the forefront of research into the origin, cause, effects, spread, and prevention of HIV and AIDS.

Other CDC programs include the Behavioral Risk Factor Surveillance System (BRFSS) and the Youth Risk Behavior Surveillance System (YRBSS). The BRFSS is a state-based continuous telephone survey program to monitor health behaviors and knowledge regarding several safety and prevention topics. The YRBSS is a national school-based survey system that measures youth risk behaviors like smoking, drug use, and incidents of violence to track trends, modify programs, and inform policymakers.

The Comprehensive School Health Education program helps develop and disseminate curricula that address the physical, mental, emotional, and social dimensions of youth health. "Be Proud! Be Responsible!" is a five-hour program for youths ages 13 to 18 emphasizing the development of refusal skills, negotiation skills, and other skills that reduce risky behaviors for HIV infection.

BUDGET INFORMATION

The CDC budget is developed by the director and allocated by Congress. The 1998 CDC budget was approximately $2.4 billion. The majority of the CDC budget (89 percent) was allocated to its operating divisions. These most notably included: HIV/AIDS, 27 percent; immunization, 17 percent; occupational safety and health, 8 percent; tuberculosis, 6 percent; breast and cervical cancer prevention, 6 percent; and sexually transmitted diseases, 6 percent. The remaining funds were allocated to other activities, such as preventive-health block grants (6 percent) and health statistics (3 percent).

HISTORY

The CDC's roots lie in the Malaria Control in War Areas (MCWA) program, created in 1942 to develop a malaria control program for military bases and essential war industries. After World War II (1939–45), the

MCWA expanded to become a center for efforts to eradicate communicable diseases, and it was renamed the Communicable Disease Center in 1946. Veterinary and epidemiology divisions were added during the late 1940s.

In the 1950s emphasis shifted from insect control to medicine and biomedical science. Programs in venereal disease and tuberculosis were developed. The CDC also began to expand its activities beyond the bounds of infectious disease to include areas such as nutrition, chronic disease, and occupational and environmental health. To reflect this broadened role, a 1967 name change to National Communicable Disease Center was followed in 1970 by a change to the Center for Disease Control. The name was changed to the plural *Centers* in 1980, and then to its current designation—Centers for Disease Control and Prevention—in 1992.

By the 1970s public health experts believed they had nearly triumphed over infectious disease. Smallpox and polio were on the way to extinction, and improved antibiotics, sanitation methods, and pesticides had reduced the incidence rate of tuberculosis, cholera, and malaria. Over the following two decades, however, more than 20 other diseases caused by pathogens (bacteria or viruses) were identified, including HIV, Ebola, Lassa fever, Marburg virus, and hantavirus.

Researchers pointed the finger at modern society. As people pushed farther and farther into the rain forests of South America and Africa, they came into contact with microbes that had probably been circulating among animals for centuries. These same animals were taken from jungles for zoos and sport hunting. In the age of air transportation and migration to urban areas, infected animals and people could quickly transmit diseases to all corners of the world. Overuse or improper use of antibiotics killed off weak disease microbes but left hardier strains to develop—strains that were resistant to known drug treatments.

At the same time, human defenses were crumbling. Although deaths from infectious diseases rose 56 percent from 1980 to 1992, budget cuts had reduced the number of infectious-disease experts working at the CDC from 13 to six by 1995. Of the five labs worldwide that observed the intense safety precautions necessary to work with Biohazard Level-4 (BL-4) viruses (the most deadly, contagious, and incurable), only the BL-4 lab at the CDC was operational. Because of budget cuts, the other facilities had deteriorated or lacked personnel. In the past, samples thought to be less dangerous could be passed to the CDC's next most secure facilities, the BL-3 labs. By 1995 the CDC was reluctant to pass infectious-disease work to its BL-3 lab because the buildings had deteriorated so badly that inspectors had urged they be condemned. A request for funds to build a new BL-3 lab had been approved by Congress in 1994, but approval was rescinded in 1995.

Political groups also differed on the role of the CDC in coordinating responses to infectious-disease outbreaks.

The CDC quarantined monkeys and employees at the Texas Primate Center when it was discovered in 1996 that one of the monkeys at the breeding center was a carrier of the Ebola virus. Here a CDC worker in protective gear feeds the monkeys. The virus killed two monkeys, but was successfully contained by the quarantine. (AP/Wide World Photos)

Some groups argued that incidents in other countries were the responsibility of the World Health Organization. Other groups claimed that the CDC must play a major role because of the need for its BL-4 lab and expert personnel. It was also argued that the CDC had a stake

FAST FACTS

About 2.1 million Americans died from cigarette smoking in 1990 through 1994—an average of 430,700 per year. In fact, one in every five deaths in the United States is smoking-related.

(Source: Centers for Disease Control and Prevention. "Facts About Cigarette Mortality," May 23, 1997.)

in infectious-disease outbreaks anywhere in the world, because the chances they could spread to the United States were increasing. Within the United States the same arguments over control involved the CDC and state and local public health agencies.

The CDC maintains that incidents of infectious disease should be treated as health issues, not political issues. Effective responses to ensure the public safety requires three elements: recognition of syndromes and identification of and access to patients for study, resources for field investigation to determine the source of infection and mode of transmission, and laboratory diagnosis that aids the other elements and helps determine the appropriate course of action. Cooperation without regard for geography, funding sources, or political agenda—from all involved agencies—is necessary to effectively control infectious disease. In an era of shrinking budgets and increased needs, the CDC will be challenged to continue to make the system work.

CURRENT POLITICAL ISSUES

The CDC struggles to balance effective responses to health issues with reduced federal spending and support. Nowhere is this struggle more evident than in the battle against infectious diseases.

Case Study: Hantavirus in Four Corners

Merrill Bahe's girlfriend, her brother, and the brother's girlfriend had been stricken with sudden respiratory illnesses. Both women died. On May 14, 1993, Merrill Bahe was on his way to his girlfriend's funeral when he found himself gasping for air and was suddenly overcome with fever, headache, and respiratory distress. Minutes later, he was pronounced dead at the Indian Health Center in Gallup, New Mexico.

Attending physician Dr. Bruce Tempest was struck by the victim's youth and relative good health, and he remembered a similar case he had discussed with a colleague at another Indian Health Services (IHS) facility. He then took three decisive steps to treat the situation as more than a routine case of unexplained illness.

Tempest called in the state medical examiner to perform autopsies on all three victims. The autopsies showed that the young people's lungs were so fluid filled that they weighed twice as much as would normally be expected. Tempest also got on the phone to other IHS doctors in the Four Corners area (so called because the borders of four states meet in the region) and compiled a list of five other healthy young people who had recently died of acute respiratory distress. The third step was to call in the New Mexico Department of Health (NMDH) to begin testing autopsy samples and reviewing medical charts in an effort to determine the source of the illness.

An IHS epidemiologist, Dr. Jim Cheek, was also assigned to the case. Within days he had a list of 10 other suspected cases, but none of his theories of origin had panned out. The state labs were unable to find evidence of flu or any other common viruses or bacteria. Cheek contacted his friend Rob Breimen, the CDC's top epidemiologist, and faxed him files on the cases on May 24, the same day the NMDH sent bulletins to all the state's physicians describing the illness and requesting immediate notification of new cases. On May 27 the IHS and the state of New Mexico formally requested CDC assistance.

The CDC sent epidemiologist Dr. Jay Butler and two assistants to the Four Corners region. There they met with colleagues from the IHS, the NMHD, and the University of New Mexico to create a possible list of causes based on symptoms and progression of the illness. A similar gathering was being held at the CDC headquarters, and both groups came up with the same possibilities: an unknown chemical toxin, a new virulent flu strain, a new sheep bacterium, anthrax, hemorrhagic fever virus, Hantaan virus, or something completely unknown. CDC officials soon ruled out toxic chemicals because they were not known to cause fevers, and they decided to begin testing samples from patients from the Four Corners area for antibodies for all the possible viruses.

Tribal medicine men and elders of the Navajo Nation were consulted in an unprecedented integration of community members in an investigation. The elders provided investigators with vital information, noting that the mouse population was unusually large that year. Further investigation showed a tenfold increase in the deer mice population.

On June 2, with the death toll up to 12 and the onset of 21 more suspected cases, public panic was growing. The CDC took the unprecedented step of sending a CDC information officer to the Four Corners area to coordinate public relations. By then the field team included more than one hundred scientists, physicians, animal trappers, and paraprofessionals.

On June 3 the CDC lab determined what was causing the illnesses and deaths when antibodies from a family of viruses called hantaviruses reacted with blood samples from patients. An even stronger reaction occurred when patient blood samples were injected into mice, proving the virus was contagious and could grow in mice. Rodent samples from the area confirmed that a new strain of hantavirus was the culprit. The CDC realized that the species of deer mice that carried the virus were known to live all over the United States, with the exception of the deep South, and it began to prepare public education materials.

The CDC again collaborated with state and local health officials and communities to educate the public about transmission prevention and safety measures and to identify drugs that could halt the illness if taken early enough. Identification of the particular strain of hantavirus, named Muerto Canyon (Valley of Death), also was the starting point for the long process of developing improved drug treatments and, eventually, a vaccine.

Public Impact

Between 1993 and 1997, 156 Americans in 25 states died from hantavirus pulmonary syndrome. CDC officials worked in tandem with state and local health agencies to alert the public to risks, provide information on safety precautions, and provide symptom and treatment information to physicians.

Hantaviruses, as well as other infectious disease microbes, have always existed, but the danger of human infection has increased as rodent populations have exploded and funds for rodent extermination have been cut by as much as 50 percent in some states and most urban areas. Hantaviruses are not contagious from person to person, but many "new" infectious diseases are.

FUTURE DIRECTIONS

The CDC's National Immunization Outreach program will strive to meet and maintain its goal of having every American child fully immunized by age two. New partnerships are being formed with corporations such as McDonald's, Proctor and Gamble, and K-Mart to provide financial support for immunization projects and for public information about them.

The CDC will also work with the EPA and the Department of Agriculture (USDA) to develop an early-warning system for outbreaks of illnesses caused by food-borne pathogens and to develop proper treatment plans and contamination controls.

AGENCY RESOURCES

The CDC divisions maintain information repositories with statistics, resources, and research that relates to their field of expertise. Directories can be viewed on-line at http://www.cdc.gov or requested by calling (404) 639-3311. The CDC also provides the AIDS Hotline at 1-800-342-2437, the STD Hotline at 1-800-227-8922, and the TB voice information system at (404) 330-1231.

AGENCY PUBLICATIONS

CDC publications are available on thousands of health and disease topics, research updates and conclusions, injury control and prevention measures, treatment options, and environmental health issues. Reports include *Home and Leisure Injuries in the United States, Suicide in the United States 1980–1995, Emerging Infectious Diseases, The ABC's of Healthy Child Care,* and *Health Information for the International Traveler.* CDC publications can be viewed and ordered on-line at http://www.cdc.gov; request a catalog by contacting the CDC at (404) 639-3311.

BIBLIOGRAPHY

Blair, Kathleen. "CDC, EPA Issue Drinking Water Guidance for People with Weakened Immune Systems." *Journal of Environmental Health,* 1 September 1995.

"CDC Report Documents First Ever Decline in AIDS Deaths in the U.S." US Newswire, 27 February 1997.

Close, William T. *Ebola.* New York: Ivy Books, 1991.

Garrett, Laurie. *The Coming Plague.* New York: Penguin Books, 1994.

Lemonick, Michael. "Atlanta, Plagues: Guerrilla Warfare Infectious Disease Can Strike Anywhere, Anytime." *Time,* 18 September 1996, p. 58.

McCormick, Joseph B., and Susan Fisher-Hoch. *Level 4: Virus Hunters of the CDC."* Atlanta: Turner Publishing, 1996.

Morse, Stephen. "Controlling Infectious Diseases." *Technology Review,* October 1995, pp. 54–8.

Parascandola, John. "From MCWA to CDC: Origins of the Centers for Disease Control and Prevention." *Public Health Reports,* 21 November 1996, p. 549.

Reed, Mack. "Deadly Dust." *Los Angeles Times,* June 1996, p. B1.

Rochell, Anne. "CDC at 50." *Atlanta Journal and Constitution,* January 1996, p. H02.

Central Intelligence Agency (CIA)

PARENT ORGANIZATION: Independent
ESTABLISHED: September 18, 1947
EMPLOYEES: Due to the secretive nature of the CIA's operations, figures on the number of employees working for the agency are not available to the general public.

Contact Information:

ADDRESS: Washington, DC 20460
PHONE: (703) 482-1100
FAX: (703) 482-1739
URL: http://www.odci.gov/cia
DIRECTOR: George J. Tenet
EXECUTIVE DIRECTOR: David W. Carey

WHAT IS ITS MISSION?

The Central Intelligence Agency (CIA) is the principal agency responsible for gathering information and intelligence on matters of national security and foreign affairs. This intelligence is intended to aid the management of crises, conduct of war, and formulation of policy. The CIA also cooperates with other government agencies to counter the attempts of other nations to gather intelligence on the United States, a process called counterintelligence. Additionally, it engages in "special activities, and other functions related to foreign intelligence and national security as directed by the President."

HOW IS IT STRUCTURED?

The CIA is an independent agency within the executive branch of government. It is part of a broad network of organizations known as the U.S. intelligence community. Other organizations which make up the intelligence community include the National Security Council (NSC), the Federal Bureau of Investigation (FBI), the Drug Enforcement Administration (DEA), and the intelligence corps of the army, navy, and air force, among others. Each of these agencies gather information in its area of expertise and provides its findings to the CIA, which serves as the overall coordinator of the information. The national intelligence effort is led by the director of central intelligence (DCI), who also serves as the head of the CIA. The DCI is appointed by the president upon the approval of the Senate and serves as the principal adviser to the president on intelligence matters. Although the position has no direct authority over any of the other intelligence agencies, the DCI provides broad organizational oversight so that there is no overlap in each of the agency's intelligence-gathering efforts or conflicts of interests between organizations. The DCI is also responsible for presenting the findings of these coordinated efforts to the president on a daily basis.

Daily operations at the CIA are overseen by an executive director. As an independent agency, the CIA is accountable to intelligence oversight committees within Congress.

The DCI creates special task forces or centers as needed to address high-priority issues including counterterrorism, international organized crime, or nonproliferation of weapons of destruction.

PRIMARY FUNCTIONS

The main function of the U.S. intelligence community, and the CIA in particular, is to provide necessary information to the political and military bodies that manage critical national security interests. To this end, the CIA supports the information needs of the president, cabinet officials, Congress, and military forces in the field.

Through visible means the CIA is charged with gathering the information necessary to keep the nation's leaders forewarned of potential dangers and impending crises that affect the immediate interests of the government and its citizens. The CIA is also responsible for monitoring long-standing threats posed by countries who have a history of terrorist activities, illegal arm sales, stockpiling weapons of mass destruction, drug trafficking, or economic fraud.

The CIA engages in covert actions at the request of the president and usually due to recommendations made by the NSC. On its Internet home page, the CIA explains that covert actions are deemed necessary when "U.S. foreign policy objectives may not be fully realized by normal diplomatic means and when military action is deemed too extreme an option. Therefore, the Agency may be directed to conduct a special activity abroad in support of foreign policy such that the role of the U.S. Government is neither apparent nor publicly acknowledged."

PROGRAMS

Two main programs of the CIA include the Directorate of Science and Technology (DS&T) and the Center for the Study of Intelligence (CSI). The DS&T is responsible for developing new and innovative technologies to assist in the process of gathering intelligence. Through research, analysis, and technical innovation, the division serves as the lead agency within the intelligence community for improving the quality and methods for gathering information. In addition, the program develops intelligence devices for officers' use in the field.

FAST FACTS

Although the CIA states that it does not keep secret files on U.S. citizens, it does admit that names may appear in its records as a result of "routine business" individuals may have with the agency. Under the Freedom of Information Act and the Privacy Act of 1974, individuals can request any files compiled about them or groups they are affiliated with. However, the CIA can also refuse a request for information if they believe the response would threaten national security.

(Source: Central Intelligence Agency, 1997.)

The CSI supports research and publishing within the intelligence field by providing fellowships to intelligence professionals and scholars that result in the publication of manuscripts. It also builds collaborative relationships with academic institutions and scholars through conferences, seminars, and sponsorship of CIA Officer in Residence programs at universities throughout the United States.

BUDGET INFORMATION

During the budgeting process each year, the president presents Congress with an itemized budget outlining each government agency's financial needs. However, due to the secrecy under which the CIA operates, a detailed budget is not itemized for the budgeting process and the total budget of the CIA is classified information. The total estimated budget for 1998, however, was $26.7 billion. Most of the CIA's money is channeled through other departments, particularly the Department of Defense and the State Department, as part of those agencies' discretionary money, and to further protect the CIA from exposing details of its allocations. The Office of Management and Budget is aware of the CIA's budget requests and a few congressional members appointed to intelligence oversight committees are also informed. One aspect of the CIA's budget that is known is its Retirement and Disability System Fund. This fund was allocated $197 million in 1998.

HISTORY

After the Japanese bombing of Pearl Harbor that initiated U.S. involvement in World War II (1939–45), a congressional committee determined that the United States could have anticipated and might have prevented the attack if all the intelligence information available had been gathered and analyzed. Although mechanisms for military and political intelligence were in place after the war, Congress also saw the need for a centralized intelligence bureau that documented the activities of foreign governments in order to better protect national security interests. To this end, Congress passed the National Security Act in 1947, which resulted in the creation of the CIA. Many of its operations had been preceded by the Office of Strategic Services (OSS), which had conducted espionage and counterespionage during the war.

Initially the CIA spent most of its resources on collecting intelligence gathered by other agencies, but by the 1950s, when Communist North Korea invaded South Korea, the CIA reorganized and resources were redirected to the agency's own covert intelligence operations.

As the fear of communism began to escalate, the nation entered the period known as the Cold War and the CIA was thought to be the country's best defense against the perceived Soviet threat. During this era, which lasted more than 40 years, the Soviet Union and the United States vied for influence over emerging governments and nations. As the world's two major political powers, each country sought to dominate the other in terms of developing political allies with each determined to extend its sphere of influence and support throughout the world. As a result, the CIA's covert operations continued to grow. Some of its earliest efforts resulted in the overthrow of a democratically elected president in Guatemala who was feared by the U.S. government because of his leftist politics. Another early CIA operation, accomplished by clandestine means, was the installation of the Shah of Iran in power, an important pro-American victory.

In the early 1960s the CIA lost favor with the U.S. public because of its involvement in an invasion of Cuba (the "Bay of Pigs" incident). In 1961 a group of Cuban exiles who had been trained by the CIA invaded Cuba in an attempt to overthrow the Marxist government led by Fidel Castro. The Cuban military overwhelmed the invaders and many were taken captive or killed. The U.S. role in the incident was quickly revealed, and the operation's dismal failure outraged the American public. Within a year, however, the CIA had discovered and photographed Soviet missile sites in Cuba with warheads aimed at the United States. The discovery led to the Cuban Missile Crisis, considered a victory for the United States when President John F. Kennedy ordered Cuba blockaded, forcing the Soviets to withdraw their missiles.

Since the 1960s the CIA has remained a controversial agency due to such actions as its attempt to install a non-Communist government in Vietnam during the late 1960s, its involvement in the Watergate scandal in the 1970s, and other concerns that the CIA was involved in foreign assassination plots, surveillance of U.S. antiwar protesters, and other actions that fell far outside its legal authority.

CURRENT POLITICAL ISSUES

Allegations that the CIA was involved in illegal activities were eventually discovered after an internal report known as the "Family Jewels List" was leaked to the *New York Times* at the end of 1974. In the report the CIA admitted that it had conducted large-scale illegal spying operations by using wiretaps and surveillance techniques and intercepting the mail of randomly monitored American citizens. A congressional committee found further evidence of illegal activity during the same period. Since then the agency has struggled to improve its reputation.

Case Study: Iran-Contra Scandal

Some of the most damaging evidence about the CIA's illegal covert actions was uncovered in investigations of the U.S. government's role in funding paramilitary operations in Nicaragua and illegal arms sales to Iran. In 1986 an independent counsel concluded that top officials in President Ronald Reagan's administration were involved in providing assistance for military activities to Nicaraguan contra rebels, even though such aid had been strictly prohibited by Congress. In addition, it was found that the illicit funds were raised through the sales of arms to Iran, another direct violation of U.S. law and government policy. The case broke when Eugene Hasenfus was taken into captivity by the Nicaraguan government after his plane, loaded with military supplies for the contras, was shot down. He later admitted to the government soldiers that he was employed by the CIA. One month later the secret sale of U.S. arms to Iran was reported in a Lebanese publication. It was subsequently discovered that some of the proceeds from the arms sales had been diverted to the Nicaraguan contras.

As it further investigated the case, the independent counsel found widespread efforts by senior Reagan administration officials to conceal the truth about their knowledge of and support for the operations. In the end 14 high-ranking officials were indicted, including four CIA officials. One official's case was dismissed when the Bush administration refused to declassify information needed for his defense. During his administration President George Bush interceded and pardoned the remaining CIA officials who had been charged, allowing them to avoid trial.

Public Impact

In theory and by law, the CIA is accountable to the president and to Congress. Special committees within Congress are directly responsible for oversight of the CIA, yet the Iran Contra affair operated outside the government's system of checks and balances. Of the fourteen individuals indicted by the independent counsel, three were charged with withholding information from Congress, three were charged with aiding and abetting in the obstruction of Congress, and five were charged with directly lying to Congress. Those involved committed unlawful acts that undermined fundamental constitutional principles, and each also played a role in undermining the U.S. public's faith in government.

SUCCESSES AND FAILURES

In an effort to rebuild its reputation and restore public faith, the CIA made a major policy commitment in 1992 to reevaluate its climate of secrecy. Since that time, the agency has adopted an "openness" policy which has resulted in the release of formerly classified material. For example, the CIA released its records on the 1954 covert operation that resulted in the overthrow of Guatemala's president. In 1996 the CIA held a symposium on declassification of its secret files. At that time, the CIA admitted that the costs of secrecy had grown excessive, especially in light of the end of the Cold War and the clandestine operations that dominated that era. In its Winter-Spring 1997 newsletter, the Center for the Study of Intelligence (CSI) announced that it would continue to publish and release once-classified information—such as the Bay of Pigs records—and make the documents available through the National Archives and Records Administration.

FUTURE DIRECTIONS

In a February 5, 1997, statement before the Senate Select Committee on Intelligence, then Acting Director of Central Intelligence George J. Tenet explained "that as we survey today's world, core threats which dominated our national security for fifty years have ended or receded. In their place, however, is a far more complex situation that holds at least five critical challenges as we bring this century to a close and usher in the next. As was the case fifty years ago, these challenges will require the best from the intelligence community in helping defend American interests and support American leadership."

Acting Director Tenet went on to identify several key threats: the transformation of Russia and the growing political power of China; the hostile policies of nations such as North Korea, Iran, and Iraq; transnational issues such as terrorism, drug trafficking, and growing international crime rings; the Middle East, Southeast Asia, and other regions perceived to present a threat of conflict; and nations where human suffering is widespread, such as Burundi and Bosnia, and where the ability to cope with ensuing crises will demand ongoing intelligence and monitoring. These challenges, Tenet explained, will be the issues that dictate the CIA's future operations.

AGENCY RESOURCES

The Public Affairs Office of the CIA handles all information that is available to the public. A visit to the CIA Web site at http://www.odci.gov/cia will provide access to press releases, speeches, and testimonies before Congress.

The Center for the Study of Intelligence (CSI) serves as the CIA's primary information source by supporting research and publishing within the intelligence professions. It publishes *Studies in Intelligence*, an unclassified version of a booklet based on a quarterly classified one that contains articles on a number of intelligence subjects from Nazis to UFOs as well as historical and opinion pieces. Recent issues may be obtained by accessing the CSI Web site at http://www.odci.gov/csi. Back issues of *Studies in Intelligence* can be ordered from the National Archives at (301) 713-7250.

AGENCY PUBLICATIONS

Many of the CIA's publications are classified but the agency releases a wide variety of publications for public access. *The World Factbook* is a comprehensive guide that offers a political, economic, environmental, and geographic profile of almost every country in the world. The CIA also publishes the monthly *Chiefs of State,* which profiles foreign leaders throughout the world. These and other publications can be obtained at the CIA's Internet site at http://www.odci.gov/cia/publications/pubs.html or by mailing a request to the Superintendent of Documents, PO Box 371954, Pittsburgh, PA 15250-7954 or phoning (202) 512-1800.

BIBLIOGRAPHY

Ellis, Rafaela. *The Central Intelligence Agency*. Broomall, Pa.: Chelsea House Publishers, 1988.

Kluger, Jeffrey. "CIA ESP: The CIA's Experimental Psychic Program." *Discover*, April 1996, p. 34.

Marchetti, Victor L., and John D. Marks. *The CIA and the Cult of Intelligence*. New York: Alfred A. Knopf, 1974.

Merida, Kevin. "Lawmakers Press the Drug Conspiracy Issue." *Emerge*, December 1996, p. 26.

"On CIA, Once More: Abolish the Damned Thing." *National Catholic Reporter*, 6 September 1996, p. 20.

Shenon, Philip. "CIA Evidence Suggests a Wider Spread of Nerve Gas in Gulf War." *New York Times*, 19 March 1997, p. B10.

"Spies Like Us." *The Nation*, 7 October 1996, p. 3.

Stockwell, John. *In Search of Enemies: A CIA Story*. New York: W. W. Norton & Co., 1978.

Commodity Futures Trading Commission (CFTC)

PARENT ORGANIZATION: Independent
ESTABLISHED: 1974
EMPLOYEES: 580

Contact Information:

ADDRESS: 1155 21st St. NW
Washington, DC 20581
PHONE: (202) 418-5000
TDD (HEARING IMPAIRED): (202) 418-5513
FAX: (202) 418-5525
URL: http://www.cftc.gov
CHAIRMAN: Brooksley E. Born

WHAT IS ITS MISSION?

Through its primary activity, the regulation of futures and options trading, the Commodity Futures Trading Commission (CFTC) promotes healthy economic growth, protects customers' rights, and ensures fairness and integrity in the marketplace. To meet this goal, it also analyzes and interprets important economic issues that affect or are influenced by futures trading.

HOW IS IT STRUCTURED?

The CFTC is an independent regulatory agency. The commission consists of five commissioners appointed by the president with the advice and consent of the Senate. The commissioners serve staggered five-year terms. The president designates one commissioner to serve as chairman. By law, no more than three commissioners may belong to the same political party. The commission develops and implements agency policy and direction; all actions of CFTC divisions must be approved by a majority vote of the commissioners.

Of the commission's five major operating units, two exist primarily to serve legal and administrative functions. The Office of General Counsel, the commission's legal adviser, represents the CFTC when an appeal is filed to protest a regulatory or disciplinary action and in certain other cases. General counsel staff also review significant legislative and administrative matters presented to the commission and advise the commission on the application and interpretation of important statutes such as the Commodity Exchange Act.

Farm product prices at the Chicago Board of Trade, circa 1920. Chalkboards were replaced with electronic displays in 1967. *(Courtesy of the Chicago Board of Trade)*

The Office of the Executive Director manages the administrative functions and policies of the agency. This office supervises the allocation and use of agency resources, formulates the CFTC budget, and develops and maintains the automated information systems of the agency. A significant office under the direction of the executive director is the Office of Proceedings, which provides a forum for handling customer complaints against National Futures Association registrants. (Any company or individual that acts on behalf of a customer or gives trading advice must apply for registration through the National Futures Association, a self-regulatory organization approved by the CFTC.) The Office of Proceedings also hears and decides enforcement cases brought against the commission.

The main work of the CFTC is divided among three operating units: the Division of Economic Analysis, the Division of Enforcement, and the Division of Trading and Markets. The Division of Trading and Markets oversees the compliance activities of the commodity exchanges and the National Futures Association. It conducts sales practice audits and trade practice surveillance, reviews exchange applications, oversees the ethics training of industry professionals, drafts regulations governing the operation of the National Futures Association and all exchanges, and develops policies governing interna-

WHAT IS A FUTURE?

A futures contract is an agreement to buy or sell, at some time in the future, a specific amount of a commodity at a specific price. Perhaps the simplest example is an arrangement between a corn grower and a beef cattle rancher who uses corn for feed. Instead of waiting until the time the corn is needed, when either party may be subject to an unfavorable price fluctuation, the two enter into a contract that provides for the delivery of corn to the rancher at a specified date, at a specified price. Either party can cancel its involvement in the contract by selling it to a third party prior to the agreed-upon delivery date.

The futures markets involve basically two types of contractors: "hedgers" are typically farmers who enter into a futures contract to ensure against price fluctuations; "speculators" trade in futures contracts themselves, in the hope of making a profit. For example, a speculator who buys a grain futures contract at $5 a bushel and later sells the contract at a rate of $5.50 a bushel is making a profit of $.50 per bushel. Speculators help stabilize futures markets by increasing the number of buyers and sellers on the market; however, futures trading has become so complex that only a very small percentage of contracts result in the actual delivery of the product being traded.

An option on a commodity futures contract gives the buyer the right to convert the option into a futures contract—the buyer is purchasing the option to buy and can decline prior to the agreed-upon date if prices are unfavorable. Futures are typically traded in a diverse number of goods, including agricultural commodities such as grain, meat, and poultry; lumber; metals; and petroleum. Futures trading has also expanded into the markets of financial products such as gold, foreign currency, U.S. Treasury bonds and notes, and even stock indexes.

---

tional transactions. The Division of Economic Analysis works to ensure that markets remain competitive by detecting and protecting against price manipulation. The division conducts daily market surveillance to detect price distortion, congestion, or manipulation; it also provides economic analyses for enforcement investigations and litigation. The Division of Enforcement investigates and prosecutes alleged violations of CFTC regulations and the Commodity Exchange Act. Violations of the Commodity Exchange Act or other federal laws may be referred to the Department of Justice for prosecution. The division also provides detailed legal and technical assistance to international authorities, U.S. attorneys offices, and other federal and state regulators.

In addition to its Washington, D.C., headquarters, the CFTC maintains regional offices in cities that have commodity exchanges: New York, Chicago, Kansas City, and Minneapolis. An office in Los Angeles supports the commission's enforcement functions.

PRIMARY FUNCTIONS

The CFTC's primary activity is to review the terms and conditions of proposed futures contracts to ensure the integrity of U.S. futures markets. The commission conducts daily market surveillance and in an emergency has the authority to order a commodity exchange to restore an orderly market in any futures contract being traded. The commission also serves several important customer-protection functions. It requires registrants to disclose all market risks and past performance information to prospective customers, it requires customer funds to be kept in separate accounts from those maintained by companies for their own use, and it requires that customer accounts be adjusted at the close of trading each day to reflect the current market value. The commission also oversees the supervisory systems, sales practice compliance programs, and mandatory ethics training courses of all registrants.

Commodity exchanges add to federal regulations by making their own rules governing trade orders, the clearance of trade, price limits, disciplinary actions, business conduct standards, and floor trading practices. These rules can be implemented or changed only upon CFTC approval. The commission may also direct an exchange to alter its rules or practices; it regularly audits the compliance programs of each exchange.

PROGRAMS

Most of the CFTC's programs are a function of its legislative mandate, the Commodity Exchange Act of 1936 as amended. For example, its Audit and Review Program, administered through the Division of Trading and Markets, protects market participants by monitoring the market oversight activities of the National Futures Association and futures exchanges. The program also supervises reporting requirements and the compliance programs for disclosure and keeps track of the risks to individual companies and the marketplace from external events that disrupt the market.

Another example of the CFTC's legislative mandate is the Reparations Program, run by the Office of Proceedings. The Reparations Program resolves customer–broker disputes. If a customer is unable to resolve a dispute with a futures broker who was registered with the CFTC at the time of the alleged wrongdoing or at the time the claim is filed and the customer believes the account executive or brokerage firm violated the Commodity Exchange Act or CFTC rules and caused a financial loss, the customer may file a complaint with the Reparations Program. Typically, a reparations case is resolved within six to eight months.

BUDGET INFORMATION

The CFTC's spending authority is granted through congressional appropriations. In 1998 the CFTC budget was approximately $58 million. The largest portion of the CFTC budget, $23 million, or 40 percent, was spent on enforcement activities. Trading and market activities accounted for $17 million (28 percent) while market surveillance, analysis, and research accounted for $11 million (19 percent). The remaining 13 percent of the budget was divided between the Office of General Counsel (8 percent) and the Office of Proceedings (5 percent).

BUDGET:

Commodity Futures Trading Commission

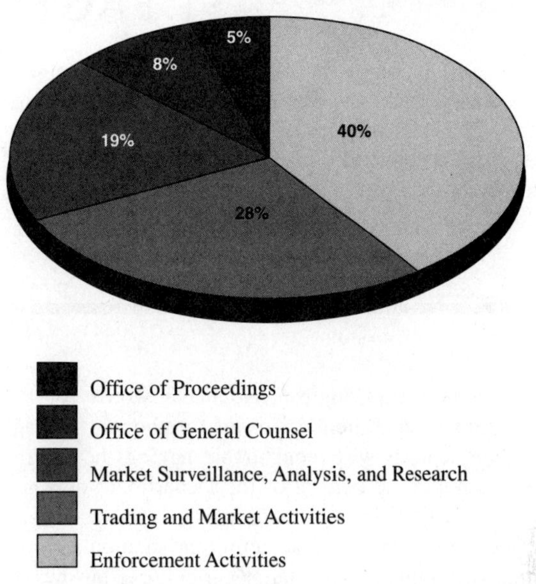

HISTORY

Organized commodity markets emerged in the United States as early as the late 1700s to handle the buying and selling of corn, wheat, livestock, and other farm commodities. These exchanges were cash markets involving contracts for immediate delivery of, and payment for, the commodities sold. It did not take long for farmers to learn that these exchanges were an impractical business. They were generally held at the same time each year, just after the fall harvest, and contracts for delivery overwhelmed available transportation and storage facilities. Prices of goods generally fell sharply owing to the great supply. In the following spring, supplies typically fell to insufficient levels, and prices skyrocketed.

Traders began using "forward contracts" to organize agricultural buying and selling more efficiently. Forward contracts guaranteed the prices of the goods that were to be delivered on a specified date. Forward markets allowed farmers to space deliveries throughout the year without worrying about seasonal price fluctuations and guaranteed buyers a solid price, thus reducing financial risk for both parties. In the late nineteenth century, forward trading had expanded to such an extent that the trading of many commodities had become standardized, with agreements that tended to specify commonly used delivery dates and typical quantities of goods.

The CFTC Supersedes the Commodity Exchange Authority

These standardized contracts became officially normalized in the United States in 1936 with the passage of the Commodity Exchange Act. This legislation created within the Department of Agriculture a bureau known as the Commodity Exchange Authority, which assumed regulatory authority of U.S. commodity exchanges and required them to register with the Commodity Exchange Authority. A distinction was made between forward contracts and futures contracts, which are contracts traded on registered exchanges. The distinction made the trading of off-exchange forward contracts illegal, because of the increasing potential for swindles and scams to be carried out on the futures market and the potential for these contracts to create substantial price swings.

For 38 years the Commodity Exchange Authority was generally considered to be an effective control to the futures market, but in the 1970s two events provided evidence to the contrary. First, exchanges began developing futures contracts for foreign currencies, stock indexes, bonds, and other investment products. These financial futures were not effectively regulated by the Commodity Exchange Act. In 1973 about one-third of contracts traded involved unregulated commodities. Second, in July 1972 the Soviet Union contracted to buy more than 8.5 million tons of U.S. grain, including one-fourth of that year's total wheat crop. It was the largest single grain transaction in U.S. history and resulted in a domestic shortage of farm products, an explosion in the cost of food, and, in effect, a transfer of many U.S. taxpayers' dollars to the Soviet Union.

FAST FACTS

The CFTC regulates the activities of 241 commodity brokerage firms, 49,308 salespersons, 8,993 floor brokers, 1,288 floor traders, 1,317 commodity pool operators, 2,523 commodity trading advisers, and 1,507 introducing brokers.

(Source: Commodity Futures Trading Commission. "About the CFTC," 1997.)

Members of Congress had harsh words for the Agriculture Department's lack of forethought in handling the sale. It was thought that having the futures markets under the control of the Department of Agriculture constituted a conflict of interest and was also an ineffective means of counteracting the manipulation of commodities markets by large agricultural businesses or even foreign countries. The debate surrounding the sale eventually resulted in the Commodity Futures Trading Commission Act of 1974, which established an independent agency to regulate all trading in commodity futures. The commission established by the act, and its functions are nearly identical in structure to the commission that exists today.

Beginning in the 1990s, the complexity of futures contracts increased and the types of futures traded became diversified. Futures traditionally included agricultural commodities such as corn and wheat but over time began to include energy commodities such as natural gas as well as "financial instruments" such as foreign currencies. Such changes led to a perceived duplication of efforts between the CFTC and another independent regulatory agency, the Securities and Exchange Commission, which regulates the trading of stocks, bonds, and other securities. The result was a call for the consolidation of the two agencies, which continues today as a point of political debate.

CURRENT POLITICAL ISSUES

Many CFTC rules were put into place when most exchange clients were farmers and other small-volume buyers and sellers of agricultural products. Now, however, most futures trading is done by large firms and professional investors who are extraordinarily knowledgeable about these markets and for whom, they argue, regulation is inappropriate. The increasing trade in financial and stock index futures, many believe, has led to increased volatility and speculation. In addition, increased innovation in the creation of financial products by these professional investors has led to a number of products that appear to fall into a gray area between futures and stocks. Because of its regulatory structure the CFTC has had difficulty making timely decisions about the status of some of these contracts, and as a result many of its enforcement actions undertaken in the 1990s have failed to hold up in court.

Another difficulty resulting from the proliferation of different types of financial futures and contracts is the unavoidable duplication of the activities of the CFTC and the Securities and Exchange Commission, the independent agency that oversees the trading on U.S. stock exchanges. In fact, the one CFTC-regulated exchange, the New York Futures Exchange, is itself a part of the New York Stock Exchange, which is regulated by the Securities and Exchange Commission.

Case Study: CFTC and Securities and Exchange Commission Consolidation

The call for consolidation of the CFTC and the Securities and Exchange Commission began in the late 1980s when the CFTC's lack of success in dealing with market innovations became obvious. A number of bills had been introduced since 1990 to bring about the merger, but political infighting has stalled the process. Prominent futures traders have publicly praised the CFTC's efforts, not out of real support but because they fear even tougher market restrictions under Securities and Exchange Commission control. Opponents of the merger argue that the futures market is no more volatile than it ever was and that only a very small percentage of futures contracts would currently fall under the jurisdiction of the Securities and Exchange Commission. Furthermore, they assert that the innovations in financial products, which have created a number of hard-to-classify investment contracts, would be suppressed by the all-powerful agency resulting from the proposed merger.

Officials at both the Securities and Exchange Commission and the CFTC, however, see the move as inevitable and necessary, pointing out that the United States is the only country with two separate agencies overseeing its financial markets. The political climate of the 1990s, calling for smaller government and reduced budgets, also seemed to favor the merger. In reality the merging of the $60 million CFTC budget with the $310 million Securities and Exchange Commission budget would create a negligible savings for taxpayers, but in 1997 the merger seemed compatible with both Democratic Vice President Al Gore's program for downsizing government and the Republicans' pledge to trim the budget wherever possible.

SUCCESSES AND FAILURES

In response to the expanding use of the Internet and on-line services in the financial services industry, the CFTC has made an effort to make use of on-line resources, especially in the area of enforcement. Computer technology provides a new means for familiar frauds and scams in the futures market, and the CFTC has attempted to keep up by making use of this technology itself. In 1996 the Division of Enforcement posted a virtual "wanted" poster on the commission's World Wide Web page calling for information about defendants in CFTC injunctive actions whose whereabouts were unknown. The site features a form people can use to E-mail any information they might have about specific violators of federal laws and CFTC regulations.

FUTURE DIRECTIONS

The CFTC's greatest potential challenges for the future lie in the arena of agricultural commodities. The passage of the 1996 farm bill, which eased marketing regulation and government subsidies of agricultural commodities, and congressional ratification of international trade agreements (the General Agreement on Tariffs and Trade and the North American Free Trade Agreement) that have set the stage for gradual removal of tariffs and other price protections, have increased the probability of greater volatility in feed and grain prices. At the same time, because of the demand for smaller government prevalent in U.S. politics, the CFTC is not likely to gain greater regulatory control over these potential market fluctuations.

It is in the best interest of farmers and agribusiness to learn how to manage these yield and price risks on their own now that the taxpayer-financed safety net is being phased out. Subject to the 1996 farm bill the CFTC and the secretary of agriculture are responsible for developing and maintaining an educational program that will teach financial risk management to American farmers. Efforts to establish this mandated program are under way.

AGENCY RESOURCES

For more information on the CFTC, contact the Office of Public Affairs, Commodity Futures Trading Commission, Three Lafayette Center, 1155 21st St. NW, Washington, DC 20581; phone (202) 418-5080. Some CFTC records or information requests can be routed through the Office of the Secretariat, available by calling (202) 418-5100.

AGENCY PUBLICATIONS

The CFTC publishes a number of brochures intended for the general public, including "Glossary: The Language of the Futures Industry," "Futures and Options: What You Should Know Before You Trade," and "Economic Futures of Commodity Futures Trading." Sanctions undertaken by the commission are also released periodically, along with numerous reports including the commission's annual report, weekly advisory, and quarterly review. Many of the commission's releases are available for downloading at the CFTC Web site at http://www.cftc.gov. For a list of other CFTC publications, contact the Office of Public Affairs, Commodity Futures Trading Commission, Three Lafayette Center, 1155 21st St. NW, Washington, DC 20581; phone (202) 418–5080.

BIBLIOGRAPHY

Broder, John M. "Wide Open Once Again? Chicago Exchanges Seek to Lessen Yoke of Regulation." *New York Times*, 4 June 1997, p. C1.

"The CFTC's Uncertain Future." *The Economist*, 28 October 1995, pp. 93–4.

"CFTC Will Require Firms to File Statements Sooner." *Wall Street Journal*, 22 January 1997, p. B5.

Einhorn, Cheryl Strauss. "Here Comes the SECFTC." *Barron's*, 1 January 1996, p. MW12.

Johnson, Philip McBride. *Commodities Regulation*. Boston: Little, Brown, 1989.

Koprowski, Gene. "Regulatory Activism is in the Futures for CFTC." *Insight on the News*, 13 November 1995, pp. 18–9.

Louthold, Raymond M., Joan C. Junkus, and Jean E. Cardier. *The Theory and Practice of Futures Markets*. New York: Free Press, 1989.

Lucchetti, Aaron, and Jeffery Taylor. "Bid to Overhaul Futures Trading Sparks Debate." *Wall Street Journal*, 18 February 1997, p. C1.

Mayer, Martin. "Trading in the Closet: Commodity Regulators Propose Allowing Private Deals." *Barron's*, 5 December 1994, pp. 56–7.

McKinney, Bob. *Regulation of the Commodities, Futures & Options Markets*. Colorado Springs: Shepard's/McGraw-Hill, 1995.

Understanding Commodity Futures Trading. Grove City, Pa.: Center for Futures Education, 1994.

Congressional Budget Office (CBO)

PARENT ORGANIZATION: Congress
ESTABLISHED: February 24, 1975
EMPLOYEES: 232

Contact Information:

ADDRESS: Ford House Office Bldg.
Second and D St. SW
Washington, DC 20515
PHONE: (202) 226-2600
FAX: (202) 226-2714
URL: http://www.cbo.gov
DIRECTOR: June E. O'Neill
DEPUTY DIRECTOR: James L. Blum

WHAT IS ITS MISSION?

The Congressional Budget Office (CBO) is a support agency charged with helping Congress to fulfill its role in the federal budgeting process. The mission of the CBO is to provide Congress with reports, estimates, and analyses that the legislature needs to make economic and budget decisions. The CBO's reputation for professionalism rests on the fact that these reports and analyses are objective and nonpartisan. The CBO does not make recommendations on economic or fiscal policy.

HOW IS IT STRUCTURED?

As an agency in direct support of the Congress, the CBO is led by a director who is selected jointly by the Speaker of the House of Representatives and the president pro tempore of the Senate. The director is usually chosen from a list of candidates supplied by the House and Senate budget committees, and the appointment is based solely on the candidate's fitness for the job, regardless of political affiliation. The director's term of office is four years, with no limit on the number of terms a director may serve. Either house of Congress may remove a director by resolution, although this has never happened.

The director of the Congressional Budget Office is charged with seeing that all duties of the organization, as specified by law, are performed efficiently, in the manner most useful to Congress. The director appoints all CBO staff, including the deputy director, and all appointments are based on competence rather than partisan affiliation. For purposes of pay and benefits, all CBO staff are technically considered to be employees of the House of Representatives, even though they work for both houses of Congress. The director is assisted by a general counsel, who interprets applicable laws, analyzes proposed legislation, and reviews procurement actions. The Administration and Information Division provides internal management and administrative support services to the entire CBO staff as well as to the director. This division also handles editorial and library services as well as the production and distribution of the many CBO products.

The CBO's staff is organized into seven different divisions, each led by an assistant director and each of which corresponds to the types of reports and analyses it generates. When it was established, the organization's functions were divided into separate budget and program analysis staff in order to more easily reach the twin goals of budgetary assistance and policy analysis. Policy and program analyses are prepared by four different divisions, each of which represents a broad area of legislative concern: Natural Resources and Commerce, Health and Human Resources, National Security, and Special Studies (which examines specific issues related to the budget process). Recent Special Studies analyses have included reports on the line-item veto, privatization of government-sponsored enterprises, and federal pay. The policy and program analysis divisions employ about one-third of the CBO's staff.

The three divisions that help Congress to plan and formulate the annual federal budget are the Macroeconomic Analysis Division, the Budget Analysis Division, and the Division of Tax Analysis. Macroeconomics is the study of the economy as a whole, and the Macroeconomic Analysis Division prepares the CBO's economic projections, analyzes the effects of economic policy, and advises the Congress in general on such macroeconomic issues as employment, production, saving, trade, and inflation. The reports of the Macroeconomic Analysis Division provide the Budget Analysis Division with the information it needs to produce cost estimates for individual bills, as well as its "scorekeeping" task, i.e., checking the results of budget bills against figures targeted by Congress. The Tax Analysis Division estimates and projects tax revenues and analyzes the U.S. tax structure.

FAST FACTS

The Balanced Budget Act of 1997 is set to balance the budget by 2002; if it succeeds, this will be the first balanced budget since 1969.

(Source: Congressional Budget Office. "Fact File," 1998.)

PRIMARY FUNCTIONS

Some of the CBO's activities are statutory tasks, or duties required by law; others are carried out at the request of congressional committees. According to the legislation that created the CBO, the Budget and Impoundment Control Act of 1974, the CBO must give top priority to requests from the House and Senate budget committees. Priority is then given to requests from the two appropriations committees, the House Committee on Ways and Means and the Senate Committee on Finance, and then to all other congressional committees. The CBO will typically handle requests from individual legislators only to the extent that its limited resources allow.

The CBO's services can be grouped into four broad categories. First, it helps Congress develop a plan for the budget by developing an annual report, which provides economic and budget projections for the next 10 years. It also makes shorter-term projections for major economic variables such as gross domestic product, unemployment, and inflation. To give the Congress a baseline for measuring the affects of proposed changes in tax and spending laws, the agency projects how different policy decisions might affect the budget. The president's budget is also analyzed in comparison to see how its revenue and spending proposals would affect these baseline projections.

The second group of CBO duties are designed to help Congress stay within its budget plan once it has been drafted and passed into law. The CBO is required to develop a cost estimate for virtually every bill reported to congressional committees to show how the bill would affect spending or revenues over the next five years or more. One of the CBO's most important, and often controversial, tasks is "scorekeeping," or keeping track of the amount of spending associated with each budget-related bill to make sure it is operating within the bounds originally set for it. The CBO scorekeeping system observes all bills that affect the budget from the time they are reported out of committee to the time they are passed into law. The office also prepares three sequestration reports every year. These reports estimate whether proposed spending levels in a bill will exceed the limits set by Congress, and if this is the case the CBO will recommend how much money should be sequestered or set aside to eliminate any excesses.

The Unfunded Mandates Reform Act of 1995 assigned the CBO an additional task, to help Congress assess unfunded mandates or financial burdens that are placed on state or private agencies by federal legislation. For example, a federal law may impose clean-air requirements on certain states, regions, or industries without providing any funds to help the agencies meet these new standards. The new requirement is considered an unfunded mandate. The CBO gives authorizing committees a statement about whether certain bills contain unfunded mandates, and, if the five-year cost of these mandates exceeds a certain level, it provides an estimate of these costs and an explanation of how it arrived at these figures.

Finally, the CBO is responsible for analyzing specific program and policy issues that affect the federal budget and the economy. The analyses cover a variety of federal activities: budget analysis, economic policy, natural resources and commerce, health and human resources, and national security. Although the CBO uses them to examine current policies, suggest other approaches, and project how alternatives would affect the budget and the economy, it must adhere to its requirement to be nonpartisan. It does not offer recommendations on policy in these studies.

BUDGET INFORMATION

The 1998 budget appropriated by Congress for the CBO was about $25 million. Of its total expenditures, the largest share—more than 80 percent—goes toward the salaries and expenses of the personnel who work for the agency. The second largest component of the budget was computer costs, which were allotted around 11 percent of the budget. The remainder of the budget was spent on costs associated with printing and distributing the many reports and analyses compiled by the CBO.

HISTORY

The Congressional Budget Office (CBO) was created in 1974 with the passage of the Congressional Budget and Impoundment Control Act. The act was designed to give Congress more control over the nation's finances and to counter growing presidential power in budgeting. Before the Budget and Impoundment Control Act, only the president had a complete source of data on the budget and the economy.

The old authorization-appropriations process, which had been the congressional budgetary tradition for more than 50 years, had become increasingly unpopular by the 1970s. The process divided the budget into 13 parts that were never considered or examined as a whole. As a result, spending was more difficult to control, and the federal deficit grew considerably. President Richard Nixon, criticizing Congress as irresponsible, began to impound or refuse to spend money that Congress had appropriated for the budget. Defying Nixon's intrusion into the budgeting process, Congress in 1972 created the Joint Committee on Budget Control.

Although created with bipartisan support, the committee proved to be unobjective in its interests because it was composed of individual members from the House and Senate. Republicans on the committee argued strenuously for balancing the budget, whereas liberal Democrats wanted to debate the imbalance of government spending on defense compared to that spent on social programs. The committee had not actually replaced the old system but had merely made the process more contentious and complicated by adding a new process of debate.

The Budget and Impoundment Control Act was designed to be a solution to both of these problems: by creating the CBO, Congress would arm itself with the kind of expert budgetary support that the president received through the Office of Management and Budget (OMB) and would provide Congress with independent, nonpartisan reports and estimates of the effects of planned budget measures. The act also created the House and Senate budget committees, to which the CBO would be primarily responsible and which would report budget resolutions to their respective houses and follow a strict timetable for action. In addition, the presidential practice of impoundment was banned, replaced by two options; the president could request that Congress temporarily delay spending (deferral), or he could request a permanent elimination of certain spending items (recision).

The CBO began its operations in February 1975. Opinions of the resulting budget process were mixed. Although the information gathered by the CBO was generally presented in an objective manner, it was interpreted along political lines by opposing Democratic and Republican legislators. Initially the new budgeting process did little to restrain spending; it merely accommodated the totals reached by the actions of the different spending committees.

Later legislation was passed with the intent of refining this process, and the CBO played an important role in assuming newly mandated tasks. The Balanced Budget and Emergency Deficit Control Act of 1985 (amended in 1987), the Budget Enforcement Act of 1990, the Unfunded Mandates Reform Act of 1995, and the Balanced Budget Act of 1997 each added specific responsibilities to the CBO's staff. In each case the CBO's additional duties were designed with the ultimate goal of helping Congress limit federal spending and bring the budget process under control.

CURRENT POLITICAL ISSUES

Although CBO information is intended to serve Congress in making its budget decisions, it is often used to make political arguments. At times, the office is accused of bending information for members of Congress. For example, when the House Education and Labor Committee proposed a bill in 1988 that would raise the minimum wage from $3.35 to $5.05 over a period of five years, the CBO estimated that the higher wages could lead to higher consumer prices and a loss of nearly 500,000 jobs. The committee, which was chaired and dominated by Democratic members, was unhappy with the CBO's first report, and another version was submitted four days later that did not refer to the bill's effect on the economy. In instances such as this, it is clear that the CBO's objective analysis is misrepresented or obscured by those in Congress whose agendas are not served by it. In most cases, however, the reports of the CBO serve as a kind of moderating point of factual reference for the political debates that take place in Congress.

Case Study: The 1998 Budget Surplus

When it was finally signed into law in 1997, the Balanced Budget Act was heralded as a definitive end to deficit spending on the part of the federal government. In other words, the government was required by law to stop spending more money on programs than it earned in taxes and revenue during the year. The legislation targeted 2002 as the year in which revenue and expenditures in the U.S. budget would finally be roughly equal. Americans were surprised, then, in 1998 when President Bill Clinton and later the CBO announced that the 1998 budget would result in a budget surplus—the government would earn more than it spent.

Before the amount of the surplus could be accurately estimated, Republicans and Democrats in Congress began arguing over how the surplus should be spent. Republicans wanted to use it to cut taxes and pay for the retirement of federal workers, whereas many Democrats wanted to use it to increase entitlement programs such as Medicare. Very few legislators argued for, or even mentioned, what many analysts and critics considered a top priority—the reduction of the national debt.

Clinton challenged Congress to "save Social Security first" by using the surpluses to invest in the entitlement trust fund that was projected to go broke in 2029. The administration then used the new budget figures to predict a total of $218 billion in budget surpluses over the next five years and drafted a budget proposal for the coming years in which more would be spent on programs in areas such as education and law enforcement. It took a few weeks for the CBO to issue its more modest estimate: over the next five years, there would really be only about $100 billion in surplus funds. Republicans in Congress criticized the Clinton administration as irresponsible but still voiced their ideas for how this budget surplus should be spent.

Throughout the political debate, however, it was unclear to most Americans what was meant by "budget surplus." Because the CBO is required by law to reveal the accounting methods it uses to arrive at its estimates, it was soon revealed that what was being called a surplus was not really a surplus at all. To make its estimates correspond to those of the president's budget office, the CBO was basing them on a document called the Unified Federal Budget, which included "revenue" from the Social Security trust fund and other government trust funds. The unified budget understates the liabilities (debts) of the federal government according to the change in value of government retirement programs in a given year. Money in federal retirement accounts is not available to be appropriated by Congress for other programs. In contemporary terms, a unified budget that is "balanced" still represents a total deficit of more than $100 billion in the federal budget.

SUCCESSES AND FAILURES

Because the CBO does not make policy or carry out programs, its success can only be measured by the accuracy of its forecasts and analyses. The office's renowned objectivity has nearly always made its estimates more realistic and precise than those of either Congress or the president. The CBO almost always estimates higher costs than the president's budget office, and the CBO figure is usually closer to the mark. For example, in nine out of 10 years between 1982 and 1992, the CBO estimated that adoption of the president's budgetary proposals would result in much higher deficits than those estimated by the administration. During this period the CBO's estimate was an average of $22 billion higher than the administrations estimate.

FUTURE DIRECTIONS

The Balanced Budget Act of 1997 presents new challenges to the CBO, and its projections will become crucial for federal agencies seeking funding in the coming years. Discretionary spending, or spending by agencies beyond that necessary to meet obligations mandated by law, is generally controlled by annual appropriation bills. The CBO bases its projections on the most recent appropriations as well as on the statutory limits placed on future appropriations. The Balanced Budget Act of 1997 sets strict limits on discretionary spending for fiscal years 1998 through 2002.

By placing a cap on spending, the Balanced Budget Act forces various agencies and programs to compete more vigorously for funding. According to the terms of the new legislation, discretionary spending limits are enforceable through sequestration or through automatic spending cuts in all programs subject to that limit. The accuracy of the CBO's projections will be critical in deciding the fiscal well-being of many agencies.

AGENCY RESOURCES

The CBO's Web site at http://www.cbo.gov contains detailed information about all of the agency's responsibilities and activities as well as its organization and staffing. Many of the most recent CBO reports are available at this site as well. For further information about the CBO, contact the general information number at the Administration and Information Division at (202) 226-2600.

AGENCY PUBLICATIONS

The CBO's most widely-read and distributed publication is its annual report, but the office also produces many cost estimates, studies and reports, testimonies, and other documents. Among the dozens of CBO documents are titles such as *An Analysis of the President's Budgetary Proposals for Fiscal Year 1999*, *The Proposed Tobacco Settlement: Issues from a Federal Perspective*, *Monthly Budget Review*, and *The Economic and Budget Outlook: Fiscal Years 1999–2008.*

The CBO distributes its reports to all members of Congress and makes unclassified documents available to the public at no charge. Those interested may request a list of publications or a specific report by calling (202) 226-2809 or by writing to the Administration and Information Division, Ford House Office Building, Second and D Sts. SW, Washington, DC 20515. Many CBO publications can be purchased from the Superintendent of Documents at the U.S. Government Printing Office. For information about exact costs and ordering, call (202) 512-1800, E-mail gpoaccess@gpo.gov, or write the Superintendent of Documents, U.S. Government Printing Office, Washington, DC 20402.

BIBLIOGRAPHY

"The Balancing Act." *The Economist*, 1 February 1997, p. 32.

The Congressional Budget Office. "The Balanced Budget Act of 1997." Fact File, 1998.

Forbes, Steve. "Bad Math Adds up to Bad Policy." *Forbes*, 6 May 1996, p. 23.

Georges, Christopher. "CBO Doubts Clinton on Size of Surpluses." *Wall Street Journal*, 4 March 1998, p. A3.

———. "Congressional Analysts Now Predict Budget Surplus in Current Fiscal Year." *Wall Street Journal*, 11 February 1998, p. A2.

Guide to Congress. Washington, D.C.: Congressional Quarterly, 1994.

Hager, George. "War Over Predictions Goes On Despite History of Bad Calls." *Congressional Quarterly Weekly Report*, 29 March 1997, pp. 735–6.

Hollings, Ernest F. "Beltway Accounting." *New York Times*, 9 October 1997, p. A19(N), p. A31(L).

Williams, Walter. *The Congressional Budget Office: A Critical Link in Budget Reform*. Seattle: University of Washington, 1974.

Congressional Research Service (CRS)

PARENT ORGANIZATION: Library of Congress
ESTABLISHED: 1970
EMPLOYEES: 740

Contact Information:

ADDRESS: 101 Independence Ave. SE
Washington, DC 20540
PHONE: (202) 707-7904
FAX: (202) 707-4446
DIRECTOR: Daniel Mulhollan

WHAT IS ITS MISSION?

The Congressional Research Service (CRS) works exclusively and directly for all members and committees of Congress. The published mission of the CRS is "to provide comprehensive and reliable analysis, research and information services that are timely, objective, non-partisan, and confidential, thereby contributing to an informed national legislature." Since its creation, the CRS's mandate has expanded to include in-depth policy analysis, use of electronic information systems, and providing seminars and in-person briefings to members of Congress.

HOW IS IT STRUCTURED?

The CRS is a division of the Library of Congress, which is the national library, originally established to meet the informational needs of Congress. The CRS is headed by a director and has four administrative offices: special programs, operations, policy, and research coordination. The research divisions of the CRS are: American law, economics, education and public welfare, environment and natural resources policy, foreign affairs and national defense, government, and science policy research. The CRS has two reference divisions, the Congressional Reference Division and the Library Services Division. The CRS is located in the James Madison Memorial Building of the Library of Congress in Washington, D.C., and it maintains reference centers in all congressional office buildings. In order to carry out its broad research goals, the professional staff of the CRS includes attorneys, defense and foreign affairs analysts, economists, engi-

BUDGET:

Congressional Research Service

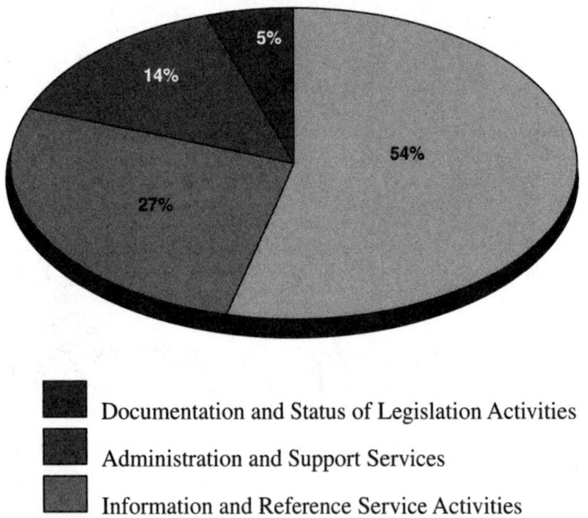

neers, librarians, physical and behavioral scientists, political and social scientists, and public administrators.

PRIMARY FUNCTIONS

The CRS works as the reference and research arm of Congress. Its services, documents, and collections are not available to the public. As the researchers for Congress, the CRS is called on to present the most up-to-date and unbiased information available, and to do so confidentially and outside the influence of partisan politics. In addition to answering specific requests for information from congress members, the CRS conducts a number of programs intended to provide all Congress members with up-to-date information on a variety of important issues.

PROGRAMS

The CRS uses several methods to provide research and information to Congress. Much of its research is done in response to specific requests from particular Congress members. These requests generate policy analyses, statistical reports, background studies, and other reports on a given topic. The CRS also presents seminars and briefings to Congress and congressional committees. The CRS supplements these individual requests for information through two programs: the Info Pak Program and SCORPIO. Info Packs are collections of CRS products and carefully selected materials from outside sources that are sent to legislators. These materials provide background information on issues of interest to congressional members. SCORPIO is an on-line system that provides Congress with the most current information on topics including summaries of all bills before Congress and their status. This information is updated daily.

BUDGET INFORMATION

CRS had a 1997 operating budget of approximately $62 million, entirely allocated by Congress. Policy analysis and research activities account for approximately 54 percent of total expenditures; documentation and status of legislation activities are 5 percent; information and reference service activities are 27 percent; and executive direction, administration and support services receive 14 percent of total funds.

HISTORY

The Library of Congress was created to serve the information and research needs of Congress so that legislators could make knowledgeable decisions on the issues before them. By 1914 U.S. society had grown so complex and the responsibilities of the federal government had grown so complicated that Congress established a separate division of the Library of Congress, the Legislative Reference Service, to assist it in its work. The Legislative Reorganization Act of 1970 renamed the division the Congressional Research Service and specified the CRS's responsibilities. The Reorganization Act also required the CRS to expand its analytical capabilities to meet the needs of Congress, especially service to congressional committees. Today the CRS provides a full range of research and information services to Congress and its committees.

CURRENT POLITICAL ISSUES

The advances of the information age have given the CRS powerful new tools. Telephone lines have become data highways, allowing researchers to access material on the other side of the globe. It is this free flow of information however, which has created a minor controversy surrounding the CRS.

Case Study: Public Access to the Congressional Research Service

For years the CRS existed to serve the needs of Congress. However, some Congress members asserted that the public should have access to the same resources. The Freedom of Information Act and the fact that the CRS is publicly funded were used to support this argument. In March 1998 Senator John McCain (R-Ariz) introduced a bill that would have opened the CRS archives to the public.

CRS reports had been available in some form to the public for some years. However, they could only be obtained after a lengthy wait or through a third-party vendor at an inflated cost. McCain's bill would move all nonclassified CRS documents into the public domain, available through the Library of Congress Web site. CRS Director Daniel Mulhollan spoke out against this proposal, claiming it would jeopardize the impartial nature of the group. Other members of Congress came to the support of Mulhollan, pointing out that the CRS was designed to serve the needs of hundreds, not millions, of people. The bill, S.1578, eventually died in committee, but not before gathering a number of supporters. Congress may have to learn to share the CRS in the future.

Public Impact

If CRS archives are opened the public will gain access to one of the premier research institutes in the nation. However, opponents claim that there are too many negative repercussions to justify this move. Before making documents more open to the public, issues ranging from scholastic integrity to copyright and libel laws would need to be addressed. Ultimately, two needs must be weighed against each other. One is the need for Congress to have informed opinions about key issues. The other is the public's need to see how those opinions were formed. Balancing these two needs will determine the future direction of the CRS.

SUCCESSES AND FAILURES

The CRS has used new information technology to deliver its products and services to Congress more quickly and efficiently than ever before. Using the SCORPIO on-line system, the CRS can deliver up-to-the-minute information on proposed legislation and provide any changes or actions involving legislation on a daily basis. Individual requests for research and information can be processed immediately and many requests receive same-day responses. Members and committees of Congress can also request and receive information from any location, thus eliminating a wait for materials to be delivered.

FUTURE DIRECTIONS

The CRS has initiated a program to make some of its materials available to libraries and special-interest groups on CD-ROM, which may be purchased on a subscription basis. The CD-ROMs will include information on current topics of national and international interest. This program is the first step in making CRS materials more accessible to the public.

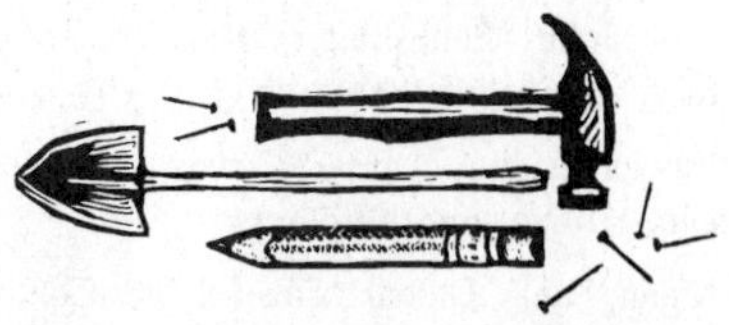

GET INVOLVED:

The Congressional Research Service has internship opportunities available for undergraduate and graduate students to assist in performing research and reference services to members of Congress. Interns typically work three months to a year and there is no financial compensation. Interns assist with research and reference activities and may help in the development, planning, and coordinating of seminars and briefing programs for members and committees of Congress and their staff. Call the CRS volunteer coordinator at (202) 707-7641 for information on how to become a CRS intern.

AGENCY RESOURCES

Requests for CRS products and services can only be made by members of Congress and are not readily available to the general public. University Publications of America offers major CRS studies to libraries on a subscription basis. Contact your local library to determine if it subscribes to this service.

AGENCY PUBLICATIONS

Penny Hill Press offers CRS publications to the public for a fee. Subscribers to its Congressional Research Report may request copies of more than 1,000 CRS studies for $3 each, with a minimum order of five documents. A subscription to Congressional Research Report costs $190 per year. Nonsubscribers pay $47 per order. To order publications or a subscription, contact Penny Hill Press by telephone at (301) 229-8229, by fax at (301) 229-6988, or by E-mail at pennyhill@clark.net.

BIBLIOGRAPHY

Clifford, Frank. "Rival Studies Intensify Debate on Dump Site." *Los Angeles Times,* 16 July 1997.

Cole, John. "Publishing at the Library of Congress: A Brief History." *Publishing Research Quarterly,* 1 June 1996.

Lawler, Andrew. "Panel Considers Radical Funding Cuts." *Science,* 10 November 1995.

Mann, Paul. "Global Arms Exports Continue Decline." *Aviation Week & Space Technology,* 2 September 1996.

Manzo, Kathleen Kennedy. "Lack of Diversity Spurs Call For Reform In Public Policy Posts." *Black Issues In Higher Education,* 2 February 1994.

Phipps, Polly. "An Experimental Consumer Price Index for the Poor." *Monthly Labor Review,* 1 September 1996.

Consumer Product Safety Commission (CPSC)

WHAT IS ITS MISSION?

The stated mission of the Consumer Product Safety Commission (CPSC) is "to protect the public against unreasonable risks of injuries and deaths associated with consumer products." The goal of the CPSC is to keep families, and especially children, safe in their homes. While the CPSC has the authority to regulate consumer products and impose penalties on manufacturers who do not comply with regulations, usually the CPSC encourages voluntary compliance and works to create partnerships with manufacturers. With the advent of computer technology, the CPSC has broadened its mission to include timely consumer notification of product warnings and recalls.

HOW IS IT STRUCTURED?

The Consumer Product Safety Commission is an independent federal regulatory agency headquartered in Bethesda, Maryland. The commission is made up of as many as five commissioners who are appointed by the president with the advice and consent of the Senate. The president appoints one of the commissioners to act as chairman and one commissioner to act as vice chairman.

The CPSC has six offices that work beneath the five commissioners: the secretary, congressional relations, the general counsel, the inspector general, equal opportunity and minority employment, and the executive director. Reporting to the Office of the Executive Director are nine branches: two directorates, five offices with no reporting directorates or divisions, and two offices with reporting

PARENT ORGANIZATION: Independent
ESTABLISHED: May 14, 1973
EMPLOYEES: 487

Contact Information:

ADDRESS: East West Towers
4330 East West Highway
Bethesda, MD 20814
PHONE: (301) 504-0580
TOLL FREE: (800) 638-2772
TDD (HEARING IMPAIRED): (800) 638-8270
E-MAIL: info@cpsc.gov
URL: http://www.cpsc.gov
CHAIRMAN: Ann Brown

A Consumer Product Safety Commission poster warns that drawstrings on children's clothing can be dangerous. (AP/Wide World Photos)

directorates or divisions. The directorates for field operations and administration and the offices of human resources management, budget, planning and evaluation, information and public affairs, and information services are seven of the nine that assist the Office of the Executive Director. The final two offices have their own subsidiaries. The Office of Compliance heads the divisions of administrative litigation, corrective actions, and regulatory management. The Office of Hazard Identification and Reduction heads the directorates for economics, engineering sciences, epidemiology and health sciences, and laboratory sciences.

PRIMARY FUNCTIONS

The CPSC works to reduce the risk of injury and deaths from consumer products by developing voluntary safety standards with industries, issuing and enforcing mandatory standards when necessary, and banning consumer products if no standards would effectively protect the public. The CPSC also conducts research on potential product hazards and the deaths, injuries, diseases, and economic losses associated with consumer products. The commission is responsible for obtaining the recall or repair of hazardous products as well as informing and educating the public about product hazards and recalls. The CPSC has jurisdiction over more than 15,000 consumer products, while other products, such as cars, drugs, food, firearms, and pesticides are regulated by other federal agencies such as the Department of Transportation, the Food and Drug Administration, and the Department of the Treasury. The CPSC also occasionally works with other federal agencies to help enhance product safety for the public. For example, since 1998 National Highway Traffic Safety Administration's product recalls have been published opposite CPSC product recalls in the *Consumer Product Safety Review.*

PROGRAMS

CPSC activities and programs involve investigating reports of unsafe products, working with industry on voluntary safety standards, assisting businesses with standards compliance, and educating the public about safe use of products and product recalls. Even though the CPSC must sometimes create and impose mandatory standards on an industry, the agency prefers to work cooperatively with industries whenever possible to ensure consumer safety. An example of this kind of collaborative effort is the CPSC/Customs Compliance Program. Through this program the CPSC and the Customs Service have stopped more than twenty million hazardous fireworks and 500,000 defective toys from entering the United States.

The CPSC and Customs investigators screen incoming products and test suspect products in CPSC laboratories. Products that do not comply with regulations are seized, and CPSC staff oversees their reconditioning and recalls previously distributed shipments. In an attempt to cooperate with the program, the fireworks industry has developed a safety certificate plan for its products, and the toy industry has made greater efforts to inform its members of CPSC requirements and to meet those requirements. Many individual firms have developed or improved their own testing and quality control programs with assistance from the CPSC.

The CPSC also operates the Small Business Ombudsman Program, which provides a liaison to small businesses to answer inquiries and give advice on compliance and regulations under the jurisdiction of the CPSC. The Small Business Ombudsman Program also provides technical assistance to small businesses attempting to resolve compliance problems. The program also provides information on CPSC activities that will affect small businesses through voluntary and mandatory standards.

In addition to its widespread publications program to educate consumers about product safety, the CPSC has developed several program initiatives with manufacturers to give consumers a better understanding of product safety issues. One such program is the Baby Safety Shower Program developed by the CPSC and the Gerber Products Company. The program encourages individuals and community groups to host baby showers that have home safety themes for future and new parents. The program provides materials that describe safe practices for caring for children such as sleeping, bathing, and travel practices as well as information about products that are safe for infants and children. Baby safety checklists of home safety tips are available as well as ideas for games and prizes that promote safety information.

BUDGET INFORMATION

The CPSC operates on a budget appropriated for it by Congress. The agency requested a budget of $46.5 million for 1999. Compliance and enforcement activities receive 35 percent of total funds. Hazard assessment and reduction activities receive 20 percent of total funds. Seventeen percent of the budget is allocated to the activities related to hazard identification, testing, and analysis. Consumer information, including publications and programs, receives 13 percent of the CPSC budget funds. Fifteen percent of the total budget is allocated to agency management including the operation of three regional offices and many of the activities of approximately 130 field staff members working throughout the country.

BUDGET:

Consumer Product Safety Commission

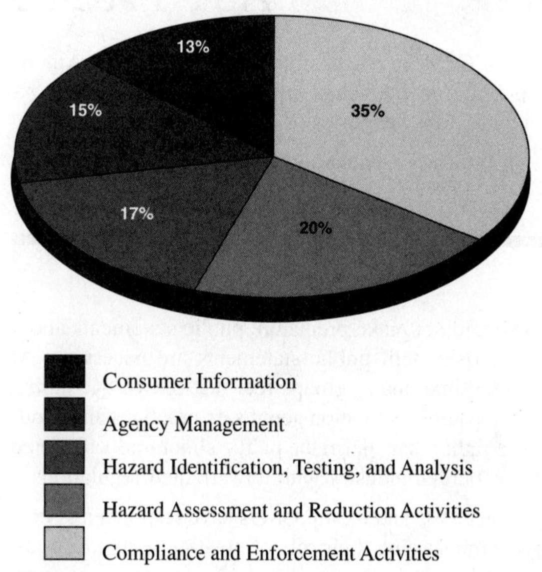

HISTORY

Until 1973 consumer products other than very dangerous items such as vehicles and firearms were subject to only a few government regulations. But in the 1960s and early 1970s, several trends emerged that demonstrated a growing need for greater federal involvement in the regulation of consumer products. First, the number of consumer goods, especially those marketed to homeowners with increasing disposable income and those marketed for children, were growing at an unprecedented rate. Second, more consumer goods were being manufactured or imported from outside the United States and were not always in compliance with industry standards set for products produced domestically. Finally, the number and power of consumer advocate groups who wanted the government to protect the safety of citizens rather than the interests of industry were increasing. Manufacturers had previously developed their own standards of product safety or had their products certified as safe by independent organizations, but many Americans felt industry would not place safety before profit.

In response to growing consumer concerns, Congress passed the Consumer Product Safety Act in 1973, which created the Consumer Product Safety Commission (CPSC). The original mandate stressed not only regulations and compliance but also the need for a widespread consumer information system. In the 1980s the CPSC was required to emphasize the development of voluntary standards with the cooperation of industries whenever possible, an emphasis intended to promote the growth of industry, lessen government regulation of business, and still protect consumers.

CURRENT POLITICAL ISSUES

Since its creation the CPSC has been accused of creating excessive and costly regulations that hamper industry's growth and ability to stay profitable. Some groups believe that the CPSC has expanded its original mandate of protecting consumers from unreasonable risk too far into the realm of preventing the possibility of injury. Critics believe that the need for the CPSC should be evaluated, and they advocate that at minimum its activities should be reformed. Suggested recommendations for improving the CPSC include developing clear and consistent guidelines to determine when products should be recalled, eliminating recalls of products thought to be potentially hazardous when there is no evidence of injuries, improving the scientific research basis for product safety evaluation by using the cost-effective services of independent laboratories, and instituting cost-benefit studies of the effect CPSC actions will have on industry and consumers when compared to the risks involved.

Critics of the CPSC also believe that the commis-

FAST FACTS

The CPSC is responsible for protecting the American public from the risk of injury and death from approximately 15,000 categories of consumer products.

(Source: Consumer Product Safety Commission, 1998.)

sion should not make premature public statements about product risks until public statements are necessary. At the same time, many groups feel that the CPSC should stress consumer education about safe practices and product use rather than alarm the public about undocumented risks or burden industry with unwarranted regulations.

The CPSC and its supporters have responded to critics by emphasizing their role of creating voluntary standards rather than imposing excessive government regulations. Voluntary standards use the industry's own expertise and strike a balance between the manufacturers' interests and consumer safety. The CPSC has participated in the development of more than three hundred voluntary standards while imposing only fifty mandatory standards.

The CPSC's position on recalls is that potentially hazardous products must be redesigned before injuries occur because preventing injuries is part of protecting consumers from risk. The CPSC often relies on consumer information to alert the agency to hazardous products, and so it must warn of possible hazards to increase awareness of products that must be handled safely. While the CPSC is aware that recalls are costly to businesses and consumers, its first priority is to "protect the public from risk without being primarily concerned about the expense of recalling potentially unsafe product."

As long as the needs of consumers and industry conflict, the CPSC must strike a balance between the two. The CPSC has worked to create a less antagonistic system of establishing and enforcing standards by increasing the role of industry in its activities. At the same time, it attempts to respond to consumer concerns without rashly acting on every suspected hazard before the risk is carefully evaluated.

Case Study: Bunk Bed Safety Standards

In 1994 Victoria Morris put her nephew, two-and-a-half-year-old Nicholas Mayernik, on the top bunk of her son's bunk beds for a nap. She checked on the boy periodically, and when she returned to the room about half an hour after putting Nicholas in bed, she found him trapped under the bed's guard rail, hanging feet down with his face pressed against the mattress. Nicholas was rushed to the hospital but was later pronounced dead from suffocation.

The child's death was one of at least 45 fatalities and thousands of serious injuries associated with bunk beds since 1990. Bunk bed injuries had often occurred with little notice, but Nicholas's relatives and relatives of other bunk bed accident victims pressed the CPSC to conduct an investigation. The agency found that 17 of 85 manufacturers were selling bunk beds with obvious entrapment hazards. Recalling the beds would not necessarily resolve the problem, because the safety standards for bunk beds are voluntary, and there are no penalties for companies who do not comply.

In 1995 the CPSC concluded that the bed did not meet the voluntary standards which included provisions to guard against entrapment, warning labels, and design specifications. The manufacturers of the bed did recall them and were sued by Nicholas' parents, but they declared bankruptcy before a settlement was reached.

The Mayernik family continued to pressure the CPSC to create mandatory safety regulations for bunk beds. CPSC staff noted that 538,530 metal bunk beds had been recalled between December 1993 and October 1994. After completing their review the CPSC declined to make the bunk bed safety rules mandatory because the industry had met the necessary criteria, adequate voluntary standards and reasonable compliance. The 17 companies with hazardous beds redesigned the beds to comply with the voluntary standards. In 1996 the CPSC revised the voluntary standards to further avoid the strangulation and entrapment hazards of bunk beds and published new consumer education materials related to bunk bed safety. The Mayerniks and many other groups continue to advocate mandatory bunk bed safety regulations, but the industry continues to support the voluntary standards.

SUCCESSES AND FAILURES

While the CPSC faces many ongoing issues related to safety regulations, its work has resulted in many cooperative agreements with industry and the reduction of injuries and deaths involving consumer products. In 1994 the CPSC approached the venetian blind industry with figures showing that at least one child a month was being strangled by the loops at the end of the product's cords. The industry agreed to address the problem voluntarily with the CPSC's assistance and to replace the loops with safety tassels or rods that protect children. The number of accidents involving children and venetian blinds has been significantly reduced, and more than 35 children's lives will be saved over a five-year period, according to the commission. While not all product safety issues that the CPSC addresses result in voluntary compliance by industries, the CPSC is generally successful in confronting industries with possible hazards and receiving full cooperation in correcting the problem. Its ratio of voluntary to mandatory compliance is six to one.

The CPSC has also had great success in increasing consumer education through its Video News Release Program, which produces and distributes videos with specific product safety information for broadcast on national television and to the target audiences most likely to come in contact with the featured product. Video News Release Program tapes about flammable skirts, fleece, and bean bag chairs reached over 187 million viewers and generated more than 55,000 follow-up telephone calls to the CPSC Consumer Hotline.

FUTURE DIRECTIONS

A future goal of the CPSC is providing more and better safety information to consumers. In addition to publications and information on the CPSC Internet site, CPSC Chairman Ann Brown has launched a long-range media plan in which commission members will appear regularly on national morning news shows and contribute monthly articles to national magazines. Telephone lines available to consumers will be tripled. Due to the record sales of candles for home use and the resulting increase of related injuries, the CPSC will pursue meetings with the National Candle Association to explore the possibility of voluntary standards involving candle-related fires.

AGENCY RESOURCES

The CPSC operates a consumer hotline for citizens to report unsafe consumer products, and product-related injuries or to obtain product safety information and general information about CPSC activities. The hot line number is 1-800-638-2772 or 1-800-638-8270 for hearing-impaired citizens. The CPSC also operates an Internet site just for children titled "4 Kids." Visitors to the site can obtain safety information on products and activities of special interest to young people. Users can also visit the "Talk to Us" site and give their opinions and ideas on helping young people learn more about product safety. The "4 Kids" site can be accessed at http://www.cpsc.gov/kids/kids.html, and "Talk to Us" is at http://www.cpsc.gov/talk. The National Injury Information Clearinghouse provides statistics and information relating to the prevention of injury and death associated with consumer products. It can be contacted by telephone at (301) 504-0424, by fax at (301) 504-0025, or by E-mail at info@cpsc.gov.

AGENCY PUBLICATIONS

The CPSC produces a variety of publications related to consumer product safety. The monthly *Consumer Product Safety Review* informs the public of recent CPSC activities. Other publications include "Home Safety Checklist for Older Consumers," "Bicycle Safety," "Super Sitter," "Chain Saw Safety," "Skateboards Fact Sheet," and many other topics from poison prevention to holiday safety. Publications are free-of-charge, and lists of them are available on the Internet at http://www.cpsc.gov/cpscpub/pubs/pub_idx.html and http://www.cpsc.gov/kids/kids.html. Information can also be obtained from the Office of Information and Public Affairs, Consumer Product Safety Commission, East West Towers, 4330 East West Highway, Bethesda, MD 20814 or by phoning (301) 504-0580. News releases and some other information can be obtained from the CPSC's fax-on-demand service by faxing (301) 504-0051 with a request for information.

BIBLIOGRAPHY

Adams, Susan. "Baby May Burn, but her Pj's Won't." *Forbes*, 30 December 1996.

Berlau, John. "Is CPSC's Bat 'Corked?" *Consumers' Research Magazine*, July 1996.

Brown, Ann. "Data Show Success of Childproof Caps." *The Wall Street Journal*, 4 June 1997.

"CPSC Recalls Tippy Chair for Home Repair." *Consumer Reports*, October 1996.

Emert, Carol. "Burlington Coat Agrees to Pay Fine by CPSC." *WWD*, 29 May 1996.

Mulrine, Anna, Traci Watson, Erin Strout, and Stephaine Ingersoll. "Window Blinds That Can Poison Kids." *U.S. News and World Report*, 8 July 1996.

Owens, Jennifer. "Big Stores Endorse CPSC's Call for Team to Battle Flammability." *WWD*, 5 June 1997.

"Product Recalls: Less Than Meets the Eye. Who Took the Consumer Out of Consumer Protection?" *Consumer Reports*, November 1994.

"Pushing for Product Recalls." *Consumer Reports*, November 1995.

"Thumbs Up for Cotton Pj's." *Parents Magazine*, November 1996.

Corporation for National and Community Service (CNS)

PARENT ORGANIZATION: Independent
ESTABLISHED: September 21, 1993
EMPLOYEES: 557 employees; 1,000,000 volunteers

Contact Information:

ADDRESS: 1201 New York Ave. NW
Washington, DC 20525
PHONE: (202) 606-5000
TOLL FREE: (800) 942-2677
TDD (HEARING IMPAIRED): (202) 565-2799
FAX: (202) 565-2777
URL: http://www.cns.gov
CHAIR: Bob Rogers
CHIEF EXECUTIVE OFFICER: Harris Wofford

WHAT IS ITS MISSION?

According to *The United States Government Manual 1997/1998*, the mission of the Corporation for National and Community Service (CNS) is to "engage Americans of all backgrounds in community-based service which addresses the Nation's educational, public safety, human, and environmental needs to achieve direct and demonstrable results. In so doing, the Corporation fosters civic responsibility, strengthens the ties that bind us together as a people, and provides educational opportunity for those who make a substantial service contribution."

HOW IS IT STRUCTURED?

The CNS was established in 1993 by President Bill Clinton and Congress as a federal corporation governed by a 15-member bipartisan board of directors appointed by the president with the advice and consent of the Senate. The National and Community Service Act of 1993 not only created the CNS but also authorized the newly formed corporation to assume the programs and authorities previously administered under ACTION (a program formerly charged with domestic volunteer service), monitor the Points of Light Foundation, and assist in funding the America Reads program. Ex-officio members of the board are the secretaries of agriculture, defense, education, health and human services, housing and urban development, interior, and labor; the attorney general; the Environmental Protection Agency administrator; and the chief executive officer of the CNS. The main headquarters of the CNS is in Washington, D.C. State CNS offices in all fifty states and territories work closely with communities to establish programs and assign and monitor volunteers.

PRIMARY FUNCTIONS

The Corporation for National and Community Service (CNS), created by the National and Community Service Act of 1993, is charged with increasing the role of community service throughout the United States. The CNS provides grants to states, localities, and community groups to fund projects and provide college-age volunteers and senior service volunteers with small stipends to defray tuition costs or loan repayments or to assist with living expenses. Grants are announced through the *Federal Register* and are awarded to more than 350 state or community programs that best use the services of the volunteers and enhance the community. Programs are also supported by public-private partnerships as well as by funding from Congress.

AmeriCorps volunteers stack firewood for use in the winter of 1995. After cuts in federal heating aid, some Vermonters needed assistance to combat the cold winter weather. (AP/Wide World Photos)

PROGRAMS

The main programs under the control of the CNS are AmeriCorps, Learn and Serve America, and the National Senior Service Corps. The AmeriCorps initiative has three components: AmeriCorps*State and National, which is administered through grant awards, and AmeriCorps*VISTA and AmeriCorps*National Civilian Community Corps, which are both run directly by the CNS.

AmeriCorps

AmeriCorps*State and National volunteers provide direct services in education, public safety, human needs, and the environment. It is from this pool of volunteers that the national literacy program America Reads draws its tutors. Other volunteers serve as mentors for teenage parents, provide victim assistance and help for homebound and disabled persons, initiate environmental projects, and restore national parks. Full-time state and national volunteers serve at least 1,700 hours and not more than 12 months to earn an education award, and part-time members serve 900 hours over two years (or if enrolled in college, three years) to be eligible for an education grant. Volunteers are given a living expenses allowance of $7,640, health insurance, and child care assistance. They can be in the program for only two years and can earn two $4,725 education awards to pay off school loans or cover tuition for college, graduate school, or vocational training. The CNS grants funds for AmeriCorps*State and National through the state commissions on national service, which in turn make subgrants to community programs.

AmeriCorps*VISTA (Volunteers in Service to America) began in 1965 as a full-time service program that addresses poverty and poverty-related issues. The CNS funds VISTA directly but contracts with community public and private agencies to ensure that the VISTA volunteers serve in antipoverty activities and as organizers to enhance the community's capacity for fighting poverty after they are gone. VISTA volunteers receive a stipend for living expenses and child care and can elect to receive $1,200 at the end of their service in lieu of an education or tuition or reimbursement.

AmeriCorps*National Civilian Community Corps (AmeriCorps NCCC) volunteers work with communities to promote civic pride and responsibilities. The volunteers, whose ages range from 18 to 24, are nationally recruited and trained in three main areas: NCCC values, service learning models, and the best in military techniques. All these serve to increase the volunteer's leadership skills as they are assigned to projects in education, public safety, human needs, and environmental needs. NCCC volunteers reside at closed or downsized military facilities. The program is administered directly by the CNS.

BUDGET:

Corporation for National and Community Service

1%

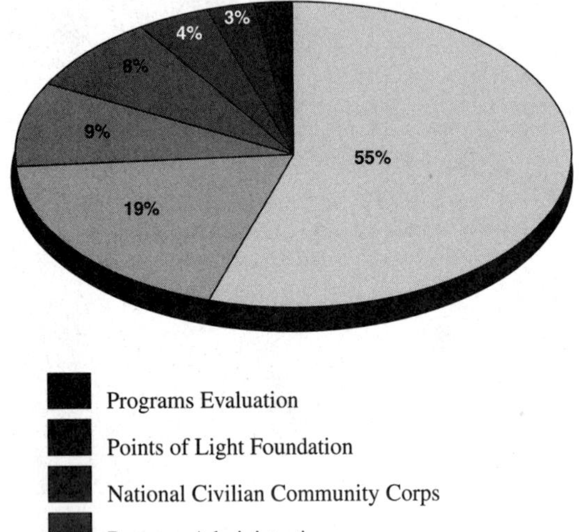

- Programs Evaluation
- Points of Light Foundation
- National Civilian Community Corps
- Program Administration
- Innovation Assistance
- Learn and Serve America
- National Service Trust
- AmeriCorps Program

Learn and Serve America

Through grants to state educational agencies, colleges, and nonprofit organizations, Learn and Serve America supports service learning by students from kindergarten through graduate school. Divided into school-based and community-based components, Learn and Serve America's focus is to build a firm foundation of service-oriented learning in every school in America. Both components seek to increase the opportunities for youth to serve their communities in volunteer efforts that make a difference in the quality of life. The program also stresses lifelong commitment to the concepts and actions of volunteerism in the community.

National Senior Service Corps

Divided into three areas—the Foster Grandparents Program, Senior Companions, and the Retired and Senior Volunteer Program—the National Senior Service Corps is a network of federally-funded programs that helps those age 55 and above find service opportunities in their own communities. Foster Grandparents offers support to children with special needs, coupling a senior with a child or family and providing a $2.45 per hour stipend, with meals and transportation. Senior Companions provide aid to elderly persons who, although living independently, need assistance in their everyday activities. They receive the same stipend as Foster Grandparents. The small stipend provides an excellent tool to bring persons on a low or fixed income into the program. The Retired and Senior Volunteer Program brings seniors into a variety of part-time, unpaid services such as tutoring, adult education computer classes, leading museum tours, and assisting in classrooms.

BUDGET INFORMATION

Congressional allocations to the CNS budget totaled approximately $657 million in 1998. The largest portion of the budget, $364 million and 55 percent of the total CNS budget, was allocated to the AmeriCorps program. In addition the National Service Trust received $123 million or 19 percent of the budget. Other programs receiving allocations were Learn and Serve America (9 percent), NCSA program administration (4 percent), National Civilian Community Corps (3 percent) and the Points of Light Foundation (1 percent). Innovation assistance (8 percent) and programs evaluation (1 percent) also received CNS funds.

HISTORY

The CNS was established in 1993 as a fulfillment of a campaign promise by President Bill Clinton to institute and revitalize the United States's long-standing commitment to community service. President Franklin D. Roosevelt's successful Civilian Conservation Corps put thousands of Depression-era crews to work at public service occupations such as expanding the national parks and building the highway infrastructure. During its first 35 years, President John F. Kennedy's Peace Corps sent more than 140,000 volunteers overseas as unofficial ambassadors to work with developing nations in such areas as agriculture, education, and health care issues. Clinton's goal in establishing the CNS according to Harris Wofford, chief executive officer of the CNS, was to "rekindle the spirit of service" in Americans.

The CNS met with controversy from its beginning in the form of Republican opposition to Clinton's desire to ensure a legacy of volunteerism leading into the twenty-first century. After an easy initial passage into law during the Democratic-controlled Congress of 1993, the CNS grew quickly and experienced financial troubles during its first years. Once the Republicans gained control of Congress in 1994, they twice voted to shut down the CNS in order to eliminate its programs. Clinton saved the corporation by threatening to veto any bill that included the elimination of the CNS. The attacks by the Republican opposition, especially during the CNS's early years, were intense. Speaker of the House Newt Gingrich referred to CNS participants as "useless" and "dangerous" and claimed that the program was "coerced volunteerism." Senator Charles Grassley (R-Iowa) blasted the program when it was only halfway through its first year, according to the *Washington Times*, stating "Taxpayers are paying far more for this program than advertised. We're told we're getting a good government program. Instead it appears to be a Great Society-style boondoggle." He insisted that the government was paying $27,000 per volunteer, as opposed to its declared $18,000. The General Accounting Office agreed with the assessment, and this created confusion and turmoil over the continued existence of the CNS.

Once Clinton appointed Harris Wofford, a former Democratic senator from Pennsylvania, to head the organization, audits and fiscal improvements were set in place almost at once. "We've had some mistakes," Wofford told *USA Today*, "but while the storm was over Capitol Hill, the grass roots got stronger." As Wofford gained control of the agency and committed to reducing the cost per volunteer to $15,000 per year by 1999, even critics came to appreciate the value of CNS programs.

On January 19, 1998, President Clinton introduced a bill to reauthorize the CNS with expanded funding and authority to increase the scope and substance of its three program areas. The goal of this reauthorization was to ensure that the CNS would continue to have a positive impact on the way Americans assist other Americans.

CURRENT POLITICAL ISSUES

One of the major political issues that has haunted the CNS was that it was perceived as a large, ineffective government bureaucracy. Opponents were concerned about what appeared to be runaway costs and maintained that paying the volunteers a stipend would disparage the concept of volunteering.

Case Study: Paid Volunteerism

The stipend offered by the CNS to its volunteers became the first real controversy surrounding the new agency. Because many volunteers received stipends (for example, those in AmeriCorps, Senior Companions, and Foster Grandparents), critics claimed that the programs corrupted the spirit of volunteerism. "Paid volunteerism will discourage the real thing—precisely the type of perverse incentive that is the hallmark of the welfare state," wrote John Walters, president of the New Citizenship project in *Investor's Business Daily*. Others feared that the program would become a kind of indentured servitude. Because the maximum time that anyone could be in AmeriCorps was two years, the program was not a permanent subsidy or way of life, but it took the first few years to prove this to critics. The stipends were minimal and slated mostly for completing higher education. The health insurance that covered the AmeriCorps volunteers was basic but gave them peace of mind and allowed them to concentrate on completing the public service work for which they were trained and ready.

Even Senator Grassley, who was vehement in his denunciation of the program in its initial years, changed his mind. Once he saw the positive results that the program had in his own constituency, he admitted that CNS programs were useful and withdrew his opposition. He went on to agree with supporters of the CNS, who pointed out that the programs were making a difference in cities and small towns.

The CNS has brought renewed focus to public service and volunteerism. When Clinton and former presidents George Bush, Jimmy Carter, and Gerald Ford joined together to kick off a nationwide campaign for volunteerism, the CNS and its programs played an important role in renewing a spirit of helping fellow Americans.

SUCCESSES AND FAILURES

Some of the CNS's more conspicuous successes involve AmeriCorps. AmeriCorps members mentored inner-city children, delivered meals to shut-ins and AIDS patients, built playgrounds, counseled domestic violence victims, built low-income housing, and cleaned polluted rivers and creeks, to name a few of the many projects that existed in its first years. Senior Corps members volunteered thousands of hours at private homes as companions, trained adults on computer skills, and acted as foster grandparents to children in need. Learn and Serve America programs instilled the concept of public service as a duty and privilege in schoolchildren, college students, and postgraduate students throughout the country.

AmeriCorps Accomplishments

In Atlanta, Georgia, 24 AmeriCorps volunteers working with Habitat for Humanity undertook to construct a ninety–dwelling housing development for the poor. By the end of the first year they had completed 44 homes, something that public housing authorities had never accomplished. The reason is that the AmeriCorps members coordinated and focused the efforts of more than five thousand unpaid volunteers. About twenty miles outside Washington, D.C., the Arthur Capper Senior Apartments had been in dire need of renovation and rehabilitation for more than ten years. Working under the auspices of the Department of Housing and Urban Development, 24 AmeriCorps volunteers repaired, plastered, and painted the complex, working to bring it up to code.

In thousands of projects around the country, AmeriCorps volunteers provide the leadership to communities

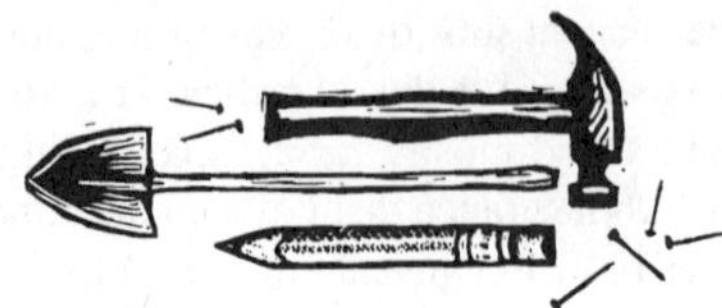

GET INVOLVED:

As the CNS is a service-based organization, there are many ways to get involved with its activities. For general information about how to become a part of AmeriCorps programs, visit the CNS Web site at http://www.cns.gov/americorps/index.html. For specific information about applying for the AmeriCorps*VISTA program, call 1-800-942-2677 or visit the Web site at http://www.cns.gov/americorps/ac_vista_join.html. Information on applying for Learn and Serve America grants can be found at http://www.cns.gov/learn/index.html or by calling (202) 606-5000. To become involved in the America Reads program, visit http://www.cns.gov/areads/over3pg.html or call 1-800-USA-LEARN. For high school juniors and seniors who are interested in community service and wish to receive a higher education scholarship for their efforts, contact the National Service Scholarship office at 1-888-275-5018 or visit http://www.nationalservice.org.

To find out about other service opportunities, visit http://www.cns.gov/resources/links.html#state for direct links to state agencies and volunteer organizations or call 1-800-942-2677.

to take on projects that might otherwise seem impossible. The program benefits both the workers and the community. Clinton's goal when he introduced the idea of national service in 1988 to the Democratic National Leadership Council was "to instill civic pride, encourage responsibility, expand national educational opportunities, and provide help to communities," according to *USA Today*. If the response from communities where AmeriCorps volunteers worked was any indication, his goals were met.

Foster Grandparents

Too often lost in the controversy over AmeriCorps, another part of the CNS was often overlooked. The National Senior Service Corps had more than 500,000 senior volunteers, both paid and unpaid, in communities throughout the country. One area that is key to the success of the Senior Corps is the Foster Grandparents Program. Mary Nims, director of the Wayne County, Michigan, Foster Grandparents Program, told the *Michigan Chronicle* that being a foster grandparent often gives seniors "a purpose to get up in the morning . . . to be needed and useful . . . to make a contribution . . . to give their love to someone." An example from Wayne County illustrates the way the program functions throughout the country.

George O'Neal, a senior in the Detroit area, became a foster grandparent to Eddie, a severely disabled six-year-old. O'Neal considered Eddie's family his surrogate family and in turn was treated by Eddie's family like a grandfather. He worked with the family for seven years. After the child died, O'Neal continued his community service by volunteering at Aurora Psychiatric Hospital for Children.

FUTURE DIRECTIONS

The future of the CNS was introduced to Congress on January 19, 1998, as a bill to be enacted that would provide more Americans the opportunity to serve, give more authority over national service programs to the states, strengthen partnerships with traditional volunteer organizations, and codify agreements made with Congress and other entities to reduce costs and streamline national service. Some of the changes introduced in the bill included reduced costs per AmeriCorps member; supported innovative national service programs like the AmeriCorps Challenge Scholarships and the high school National Service Scholarships; new opportunities for individuals to participate in national service; broader age and income guidelines for National Senior Service Corps participants to expand the pool of older Americans available to serve their communities; and a simplified administration of Learn and Serve America so that states and communities can provide opportunities for students to learn through service. To ensure that Americans embrace the concept of volunteerism and have the necessary outlets through which to focus their civic responsibility, the CNS restructured itself to embrace more people at reduced costs and with less bureaucracy.

AGENCY RESOURCES

Each state has an office of the CNS and various programs that are specific to the individual state. Interested persons can contact 1-800-942-2677 for more information about what is occurring in each state or visit the CNS Web site at http://www.cns.gov, where state commissions and other volunteer activities are listed.

AGENCY PUBLICATIONS

CNS publications include *The AmeriCorps Member Handbook 1998, AmeriCorps NCCC Can Aid Your Community, The Corporation for National Service Strategic*

Plan, 1997–2002, inspector general reports, and annual reports. These and other publications from the CNS are available on-line at http://www.cns.gov, or by calling 1-800-942-2677. For publications write to CNS, 1201 New York Ave. NW, Washington DC 20525.

BIBLIOGRAPHY

Byrd, Stephen. "Valleywide; AmeriCorps Seeks Local Volunteers." *Los Angeles Times*, 15 May 1997, p. B-3.

Carlson, Margaret. "The General's Next Campaign. . . ." *Time*, 17 March 1997, pp. 28+.

Ferguson, Ellyn. "Cisneros Praises Lafayette." *Gannett News Service*, 24 April 1996, p. FLA.

Foskett, Ken. "Well-intentioned and Endangered." *Atlanta Journal and Constitution*, 11 September 1995, p. C/01.

Garrett, Echo Montgomery. "Money Newsline: Do it Now." *Money Magazine*, 1 October 1993, p. 17.

Keen, Judy. "What People are Saying About AmeriCorps." *USA Today*, 8 June 1995.

Larson, Ruth. "Grassley Blasts High Cost of AmeriCorps." *Washington Times*, 17 July 1995, p. 13.

"Official Business: A Second Career in Public Service." *AsianWeek*, 13 February 1997, p. PG.

Stone, Andrea. "AmeriCorp Making a Difference." *USA Today*, 21 November 1996, p. 10A.

Waldman, Steven. "Americorpse: Newt's War on National Service." *New Republic*, 13 November 1995, p. 22.

Wofford, Harris, and Stephen Waldman. "AmeriCorps: Expendable or Valuable?" *Washington Times*, 25 August 1996, p. B3.

Council of Economic Advisers (CEA)

PARENT ORGANIZATION: Executive Office of the President
ESTABLISHED: 1946
EMPLOYEES: 35

Contact Information:

ADDRESS: Old Executive Office Bldg.
Washington, DC 20502
PHONE: (202) 395-5084
FAX: (202) 395-6958
URL: http://www.whitehouse.gov/WH/EOP/CEA/html/CEA.html
CHAIRMAN: Janet M. Yellen
CHIEF OF STAFF: Michelle M. Jolin

WHAT IS ITS MISSION?

The mission of the Council of Economic Advisers (CEA) is to analyze and appraise the national economy and to provide policy recommendations to the president that will encourage economic growth and stability. To carry out certain parts of its mission, the council assists in the preparation of the president's economic reports to the Congress. In all its activities, the CEA is intended to be a nonpartisan agency that is concerned only with reporting facts and trends.

HOW IS IT STRUCTURED?

The CEA is an agency within the organizational structure of the Executive Office of the President. It has remained one of the smallest federal agencies for more than 50 years. The council itself consists of a chairman and two members, each of whom is appointed by the president with the advice and consent of the Senate. Most of the members of the council are professional economists, typically selected from the academic community.

The chairman of the council participates directly in cabinet and presidential policy meetings to offer advice and recommendations. Although each of the three members, along with the council staff, plays some role in forming policy recommendations, the opinions offered by the director in these high-level meetings represent the positions of the director alone; he or she is responsible for establishing the positions taken by the council. In other words, the director is not meant to serve as a mouthpiece for any group but as a professional individual who counsels the executive branch of the U.S. government. Although the president and the heads of federal departments often welcome the council's advice, they are under no obligation to accept it. The other two members of the council direct research activities of the council in particular economic fields, represent the council at meetings with other agencies, and generally work with the chairman to formulate the council's economic advice.

The CEA's small professional staff is selected under the final authority of the director. A group of about ten economists, who are typically professors on temporary leave from their universities, serve as senior staff economists who specialize in specific areas of economics. They are served in turn by a roughly equal number of junior staff economists, who are usually advanced university graduate students. These staff economists typically serve only a year or two in the council and then return to their respective academic institutions. Four or five members of the council staff serve permanently as economic statisticians who assist the economists in the collection and interpretation of economic data.

This unusual organizational status—the academic rather than political nature of the CEA staff—was designed to ensure that the staff of the council is concerned primarily with identifying facts and trends in the economy rather than with satisfying any professional or political ambitions. The academic background of council and staff members also generally ensures a higher level of economic sophistication and a familiarity with current developments. Council staff are also able to use their links to the academic community to obtain expert advice on technical issues. The one important drawback to this arrangement is that staff members often come to Washington, D.C., without much experience in the bureaucratic process of government decision making. Most scholars, however, are able to adapt and contribute substantially to policy debates.

FAST FACTS

The CEA has remained one of the smallest federal agencies for more than 50 years: the number of senior economists on its staff has rarely exceeded 18 to 20, in a staff that has stayed between 35 and 40 total personnel.

(Source: Roger B. Porter. *American Economic Review,* May 1997.)

PRIMARY FUNCTIONS

The way the Council of Economic Advisers (CEA) functions within the presidential administration has varied widely with each administration since the council's creation in 1946. In general, the council briefs the president on overall economic policy objectives and what programs need to be implemented; it is charged with keeping the president informed on major policy issues (unemployment, inflation, environmental impacts, and international economic issues, for example) on a continuing basis. One of the agency's statutory functions is preparing an annual economic report for submission to the president, as well as the formalized *Economic Report of the President*, which is submitted to Congress every January. To compile these reports, the CEA employs its staff of economics experts to research and analyze information on a variety of economic developments and trends that are impacting the nation. In addition, it looks for any economic factors that might interfere with the president's fiscal policy plans.

At times the council has also chaired an interagency group that makes economic projections. This group has been called "the Quadriad" when it includes the head of the Federal Reserve, the Secretary of the Treasury, the CEA chairman, and the director of the president's Office of Management and Budget. The group has been referred to as "the Troika" when it has included the CEA, Treasury, and Office of Management and Budget heads. The CEA typically participates in cabinet-level domestic policy discussions on such issues as tax reform, regulation or deregulation, trade, and budget reform. A CEA function that has gained prominence in recent years is the appraisal of economic policies and programs of the federal government.

BUDGET INFORMATION

In 1998, the CEA's total budget was about $4 million. Nearly all of the council's budget was spent on salaries for council and staff members; the rest was spent on researching and preparing the advice reports that are submitted to the executive branch and Congress.

HISTORY

The Council of Economic Advisers (CEA), an organization charged with the generalized review of economic policy, was created in 1946 for a very specific purpose: to help the nation's economy change after World War II (1939–45) from a high-production wartime economy to a civilian economy, without a loss in stability or employment. The legislation that created the CEA, the

Employment Act of 1946, was designed to provide employment opportunities for those who were returning to civilian life and to promote production and purchasing power.

To help the administration of President Harry S. Truman carry out the provisions of the Employment Act, Congress created the CEA. The creation of an independent professional council had never before been established to supply an objective overview of the economy to the president, and the provision that the Senate had the power to confirm the president's nominees to the council led many to suppose that the Employment Act was an attempt to reassert congressional control over economic policy making.

Truman seemed to suspect this also; he had not proposed the creation of the CEA, and although he publicly praised the Employment Act as a "commitment to take any and all measures necessary for a healthy economy," he was not quick to appoint his own council of economic advisers.

Early Years

Truman's eventual nominee for chairman, Edwin G. Nourse, was an academic professional who would come to raise questions about the CEA's role in the administration. Nourse, a moderate conservative, found himself at odds with the other two members of the council, Leon Keyserling (the vice chairman) and John Clark, both of whom were more liberal than Nourse and therefore more in tune with Truman's policies. Even though Nourse insisted repeatedly that the council's function was to assist the president in a strictly behind-the-scenes advisory capacity, Keyserling and Clark insisted on testifying publicly before the congressional Joint Committee on the Economic Report (later renamed the Joint Economic Committee). To Nourse, this put the council in the awkward position of having to argue the administration's economic policies with Congress.

Nourse's fear was borne out in 1948; as the presidential elections neared Keyserling and Clark expressed a wish to testify on behalf of the administration's programs. When they were encouraged to do so by Truman, disagreement broke out in the ranks of the council and its staff, which soon split into two factions. Already observers in Congress were proposing a restructuring of the council. Nourse soon resigned his chairmanship, which was assumed by Keyserling. As an attempt at congressional control of the president's economic policy the CEA had proved a failure, but under Keyserling the CEA did show promise as a source of economic information and analysis that could prove valuable to future presidents.

Changes

By the time President Dwight Eisenhower took office in 1953, the CEA was in trouble. Congressional Republicans were unhappy with the role Keyserling's council had served in the Truman administration and were uncertain about whether they wanted to continue funding it. Eisenhower himself expressed a desire for the kind of advice that could be provided by the CEA but said he preferred that the agency return to its previous form as a nonpolitical body whose primary mission was to provide advice based on fact.

Shortly after taking office, the president issued a reorganization plan that made the chairman, not the three-person council, the focus of CEA contact with the president. The vice chairman position was eliminated, and the sole responsibility for CEA recommendations was given to the newly appointed chairman, Arthur F. Burns.

The reorganization also created the Advisory Board on Economic Growth and Stability, a kind of economic subcabinet that involved agency heads in the process of economic advice. Burns and the CEA were to coordinate task forces and interagency groups that would address specific issues within the administration. The CEA's role in these sessions would be to project the possible implications of legislation proposed in the cabinet and by other agencies and to advise the agency heads of the effects of alternatives. This type and form of advisement has been assumed to some extent by every subsequent presidential administration.

Since the Eisenhower Administration, the council's status in presidential cabinets has changed remarkably with each new administration. Some CEA chairs have been objective and staunchly nonpolitical, whereas others have been mouthpieces for the president's economic plans. Chairmen under presidents Richard Nixon, Ronald Reagan, and Bill Clinton, in particular, were regarded mostly as persuasive advocates of the president's policies rather than as speakers of economic truths. Regard for the standing of the CEA has depended largely on the objectivity and professionalism of its chairman.

Despite the shifting status of the CEA certain trends have remained since Eisenhower's reorganization, and the council's role appears to have changed entirely from its original mandate of stabilizing the economy and creating employment. The stabilization role has shifted to the Federal Reserve, which influences the national economy through its regulation of factors such as interest rates and the money supply. The CEA has become better known for its ability to project the effects of laws and programs proposed by the administration. In effect the CEA lets the administration know which proposed programs are likely to be a waste of money, and it proposes modification or elimination of such programs.

CURRENT POLITICAL ISSUES

The CEA is unusual among government agencies in that it is forced to reestablish its influence at the beginning of each administration. The most crucial issue now facing the CEA has to do with the agency's role in delivering economic policy advice to the president. When the Employment Act of 1946 was signed by Truman, there was widespread fear that the end of World War II would plunge the U.S. economy back into the conditions of the Great Depression. The CEA was created to provide a level of expert economic advice that did not previously exist in the executive branch or its departments in order to prevent this from happening. When Eisenhower set the precedent for establishing a separate economic advisory board that would include representatives from the cabinet agencies, he unknowingly created a need for the cabinet agencies to employ at least one person who would understand the scholarly and technical explanations or criticisms that the CEA might offer when evaluating the various regulations or subsidies proposed by the executive departments.

Since then, agencies have usually had their own economic experts on staff to examine the effects of proposed legislation. For example, the Environmental Protection Agency's chief economist might attend meetings of the National Economic Council to argue the economic benefits of environmental regulations. The CEA no longer has a monopoly on economic expertise, and of course it can no longer be the only executive agency to advise the president. If it claims that a specific tax policy will hurt certain taxpayers, for example, several agency economists—from the Treasury, the Federal Reserve, the Office of Management and Budget, or others—might take issue with the CEA's stance. Because the council represents no political interest, it is sometimes ignored.

When he took office in 1993, President Bill Clinton appeared to acknowledge this by immediately creating the National Economic Council, an agency for the coordination of economic policy that includes many presidential aides and cabinet representatives. The National Economic Council was designed as a partisan agency, intended to monitor and ensure the implementation of Clinton's economic policy agenda. As a contributor to the operations of the National Economic Council, the CEA was often forced to play along in order to survive. Many observers asked why the council continued to exist at all. With economists scattered throughout the executive branch, was it too cluttered to justify including the CEA?

Not long after CEA Chairman Joseph Stiglitz assumed his post in 1995, the House Appropriations Committee announced its intent to "zero out" or eliminate the CEA's budget. The CEA would certainly not have been the first agency within the Executive Office of the President to be cut; nearly forty executive office agencies had been eliminated since 1939. Some believed, however, that the CEA continued to survive only because it made a small target for congressional budget cutters. When called in front of the committee to justify the CEA's $3.4 million budget, Stiglitz replied that the savings from just one of the bad economic policies the CEA had prevented—such as expensive subsidies for the development of high-definition television or supersonic land transport—would be enough to finance a permanent endowment for the CEA.

In making his argument, Stiglitz acknowledged the dramatic change in the CEA's role in shaping economic policy. The agency is no longer the central source of economic advice for the president. It is not likely to serve as a proponent of any agency's proposed programs; there are too many agency economists to fill that role. But Stiglitz and other defenders of the CEA believe that the proliferation of economists throughout the executive branch has intensified, rather than decreased, the need for the CEA. The council works for no agency; ultimately, its members and staff return to universities rather than climb a political ladder. They can and do serve primarily as economic troubleshooters, exposing risky or unsound investments of the government's money. Although there are many good economists in the executive branch's individual agencies, it is the CEA that is in the best position to represent the interests of the public and of future generations of taxpayers.

SUCCESSES AND FAILURES

Responsibility for making economic forecasts and projections is scattered among several federal agencies, but throughout its history the council has shaped economic policy in ways that probably could not have been achieved by other organizations. For example, much of the negotiating between the executive branch and Congress over proposed legislation is based on technical estimates of certain provisions in bills. A good example was the Clean Air Act amendments of 1990, when bargaining between the administration of President George Bush and the Senate relied almost entirely on the cost estimates of many of the regulatory provisions contained in the amendments.

Aside from the traditional friction between congressional Democrats and Republicans concerning environmental regulation, sharp differences of opinion existed between different agencies within the executive branch, most notably the Environmental Protection Agency, the Office of Management and Budget, and the Department of Energy. They tend to disagree on the costs of additional regulatory burdens on Americans. Throughout these negotiations the CEA was generally viewed as the most neutral and competent source of reliable technical estimates.

FUTURE DIRECTIONS

Most economic scholars believe that the CEA's most important contribution to the administration is to point out the likely effects of proposed economic policies in terms of cost and efficiency. In the years ahead, the council faces new policy directions in many aspects of economic policy, including the budget, the redesign of the Medicare system, trade policy, and changes to the federal tax system. In each of these areas the CEA's analysis is likely to be an important element in making sound decisions.

AGENCY RESOURCES

The CEA's Internet site, http://www.whitehouse.gov/WH/EOP/CEA/html/CEA.html, contains a detailed explanation of the council's structure, function, and history along with most of the CEA's recent publications. For further information about the council and its work, contact the staff office at (202) 395-5084.

AGENCY PUBLICATIONS

Probably the most widely read publication released by the Council of Economic Advisers is the *Economic Report of the President,* which is submitted to Congress at the beginning of each year. The council also publishes a number of scholarly studies, called "white papers," on various economic policy topics. Recent white papers include "The Economics of Child Care," "Educating America: An Investment for Our Future," and "U.S. Trade Policy with Japan: An Update." The CEA also collaborates with the congressional Joint Economic Committee in publishing *Monthly Economic Indicators* , a statistical summary of macroeconomic trends such as employment, trade, and price indexes. All of the most recent of the CEA's publications are available for viewing or downloading from the CEA Internet site at http://www.whitehouse.gov/WH/EOP/CEA/html/publications.html. For information on ordering printed copies, contact the council's staff office at (202) 395-6958.

BIBLIOGRAPHY

Berry, John M. "CEA: Jobless, Inflation Rates Sustainable." *Washington Post*, 11 Feb 1997, p. D1.

Cabinets and Counselors: The President and the Executive Branch. Washington, D.C.: Congressional Quarterly, 1989.

"Department of Debunkery: Economic Policy Advice." *The Economist*, 18 Jan 1997, pp. 71–2.

Feldstein, Martin S. "The Council of Economic Advisers: from Stabilizatoin to Resource Allocation." *American Economic Review* , May 1997, pp. 99–102.

Porter, Roger B. "Presidents and Economists: The Council of Economic Advisers." *American Economic Review*, May 1997, pp. 103–6.

Sobel, Robert, and Bernard S. Katz, eds. *Biographical Directory of the Council of Economic Advisers*. Westport, Conn.: Greenwood Publishing, 1988.

Solow, Robert M. "It Ain't the Things You Don't Know That Hurt You, It's the Things You Know That Ain't So." *American Economic Review*, May 1997, pp. 107–8.

Stein, Herbert. "In Praise of (Some) Government Workers." *The Wall Street Journal*, 5 March 1996, p. A14.

Stiglitz, Joseph E. "Looking Out for the National Interest: the Principles of the Council of Economic Advisers." *American Economic Review*, May 1997, pp. 109–13.

Council on Environmental Quality (CEQ)

PARENT ORGANIZATION: Executive Office of the President
ESTABLISHED: January 1, 1970
EMPLOYEES: 23

Contact Information:

ADDRESS: 722 Jackson Pl. NW
Washington, DC 20503
PHONE: (202) 395-5750
FAX: (202) 456-2710
URL: http://www.whitehouse.gov/CEQ
CHAIRMAN: Kathleen A. McGinty

WHAT IS ITS MISSION?

The Council on Environmental Quality (CEQ) is "a top-level advisory group concerned with all aspects of environmental quality—wildlife preservation, parklands, land use, population growth, as well as pollution." The CEQ works to ensure that federal agencies give proper consideration to the effects their actions will have on the environment and that they obey the National Environmental Policy Act of 1969. The CEQ and the Environmental Protection Agency are to "work in close harmony, reinforcing each other [to] encourage productive and enjoyable harmony between man and his environment."

HOW IS IT STRUCTURED?

The CEQ is a part of the Executive Office of the President of the United States. The council is headed by a chairperson, who is appointed by the president with Senate approval. The council office includes nine associate directors, a chief of staff, a deputy chief of staff, a general counsel, an assistant general counsel, an administrative officer, and multiple special assistants. The agency's administrative staff make up the smaller Office of Environmental Quality (OEQ). Defining the difference between these two entities is difficult because in addition to staff, their operations also overlap. The CEQ chair serves as the OEQ director, the OEQ provides administrative assistance to CEQ, and the entire operation is housed in one office.

FAST FACTS

Scientists project the global mean temperature may increase by as much as 6 degrees by the end of the twenty-first century. Many plants and animals would be threatened by this accelerated climate change because they might not be able to adapt quickly enough to survive.

(Source: International Panel on Climate Change, 1998.)

PRIMARY FUNCTIONS

The council assists and advises the president in developing environmental policies and proposing environmental legislation at the national and international levels. Each year the CEQ compiles an Environmental Quality Report for the president that includes information about critical environmental issues and trends. The CEQ coordinates with and advises government offices and agencies on matters of environmental quality. The CEQ differs from the Environmental Protection Agency (EPA), the government's largest environmental agency, in that the EPA operates to accomplish ends whereas CEQ responsibilities are limited to providing advice and guidance to groups like the President's Committee of Advisors on Science and Technology Policy and the Industrial Council. The CEQ assists in developing environmentally sound plans of action. Before 1977 the CEQ handled the filing of Environmental Impact Statements. That responsibility was transferred to the EPA, though the CEQ still monitors the process, furnishes guidelines, and arbitrates disputes.

PROGRAMS

The CEQ does not operate any programs per se; its primary purpose is to monitor the activities of other agencies and advise them. When the CEQ does act, it is usually as part of a group of agencies. With its very small staff, the CEQ does not conduct major initiatives; its role is limited to organizing and sometimes leading temporary task forces or special commissions organized around specific issues.

The CEQ was heavily involved in the White House Initiative on Global Climate Change, which ended in 1998. The initiative was formed to determine the best strategy for reducing the worldwide emission of greenhouse gases. The initiative developed the policy that the United States successfully argued for at the 1997 international conference on global warming in Kyoto, Japan. The council also participates in an Environmental Technology Task Force, established by the CEQ in 1996 to coordinate with the President's Council on Sustainable Development. The task force provides outreach support to the populace, serves as an information clearing house, and supports the administration in matters relevant to environmental technology.

BUDGET INFORMATION

CEQ funds are appropriated by Congress, with the stipulation that no other funds be used to support the council. The council operated on a budget of approximately $3 million in 1998. The CEQ budget may vary drastically from one year to the next, to accommodate fluctuations in staffing. The CEQ budget for 1999 was estimated to be $3.02 million, marking a 50 percent increase from 1997. The increase was to accommodate a staff expansion that occurred in 1998.

The CEQ budget is primarily used for staff salaries. After salaries are paid, the remainder of CEQ budget resources are allocated to the CEQ Management Fund, which is designated to study contracts sponsored by CEQ in conjunction with other agencies.

HISTORY

The CEQ was founded in 1969 as part of the National Environmental Policy Act of 1969. This legislation established the CEQ and the Environmental Protection Agency (EPA) and provided for systematic reorganization of environmental control activities. The act further abolished the Domestic Council and terminated the Citizens' Advisory Committee on Environmental Quality. The powers of the Domestic Council were reverted to the president of the United States, at that time Richard M. Nixon, and the council replaced the advisory offices. The Office of Environmental Quality, the CEQ's administion, was established by the Environmental Quality Improvement Act of 1970.

The Evolution of Environmental Awareness

The CEQ made progress under President Gerald Ford with aggressive measures to assess the economics of pollution control in terms of cost/benefit ratios. Many studies were performed by the CEQ during these years, especially regarding key environmental issues like climate changes and deforestation. The CEQ continued to flourish under President Jimmy Carter, whose council of 49 employees came to be known for its meticulous assessment of issues in the Environmental Quality Report compiled each year.

Interest in the CEQ waned during the 1980s, however, and President Ronald Reagan cut the staff to eight people. Reagan's successor, George Bush, brought staffing back up to 31, but the council seats were never filled, except for the position of chairman. President Bill Clinton cut the staff again, leaving fewer than 25 employees. The CEQ drew criticism during the Clinton Administration, in part for its lackluster performance. The Senate rallied support to abolish the council, but its efforts never came to fruition.

CURRENT POLITICAL ISSUES

To a large degree environmental problems are the results of human activities. Worldwide, resources are depleted and polluted as businesses, governments, and citizens carry out their day-to-day activities. Forests are cut down, fossil fuels are burned, and plastics that nature can never break down are buried in landfills within the earth, to name only a few. Such issues tend to attract a flurry of attention when their impact is brought to light.

Global warming, the gradual increase in the world's average temperature, became a prominent issue in the 1990s. A small number of scientists argue that global warming is not occurring, or that if it is, it is a natural temperature cycle the Earth undergoes periodically. However, most agree that global warming is occurring, at least partly because of the "greenhouse effect," the entrapment of poisonous gases within the Earth's atmosphere, thought to be a result of the burning of oil, coal, and natural gas by factories, cars, and the like. The problems associated with global warming include gradual erosion of coastlines due to rising sea levels and aggravated periods of drought and flood.

Case Study: The White House Initiative on Global Climate Change

In 1995 the Intergovernmental Panel on Climate Change (IPCC), fostered by the United Nations (UN), published a comprehensive report on the effects of greenhouse gases on the earth's atmosphere. In response to the IPCC study the CEQ undertook the White House Initiative on Global Climate Change. By 1997 the White House Initiative was in full operation.

In conjunction with the White House Initiative, the president invited a panel of noted scientists to Washington to discuss the issues and possible solutions. Three months later the White House hosted a national briefing on climate change for weather forecasters. Later that year the president attended an international convention in Kyoto, Japan, at which world leaders discussed their positions on the issue. More than 160 nations were represented in this effort to finalize negotiations for an international agreement on climate change.

In a series of related events, including press briefings, goodwill tours, and a special session of the UN, the administration lobbied for aggressive action by the global community to forestall the effects of global warming. On January 31, 1998, Clinton unveiled plans for a program to ward off the effects of global warming and spur the economy in the process. Clinton proposed a combination of tax incentives, accelerated research programs, and reductions in industrial energy consumption to retard the greenhouse effect.

According to the Clinton plan, consumers would be encouraged to purchase energy-efficient vehicles in return for hefty income tax credits. Energy-efficient home appliances, heaters, and air conditioners would also qualify to earn tax credits under the plan. The government in turn would make a commitment to support research and development of technologies to make these devices highly effective.

SUCCESSES AND FAILURES

Scientific innovations and increased efforts to educate the public about the critical issues of environmental protection have reaped many benefits during the years since the inception of the CEQ and the Environmental Protection Act. Russell Peterson, who chaired the CEQ from 1973 to 1976, wrote in the *25th Anniversary Report of the CEQ (1994–1995)*, "Twenty-five years ago, almost nobody knew what the word 'ecology' meant. Twenty-five years ago, there were few graduates of any environmental science or law program. There has been a major increase in courses and graduates. There are still companies who will oppose environmental regulation, so we have to keep educational programs going."

In the same report former Senator Gaylord Nelson of Wisconsin commented that "when something is complicated, you don't get a revolution overnight. There is no other issue like the environment that has the political, economic, technical, and cultural ramifications and that involves every discipline of science. If it took us 25 years to ban smoking in airplanes [could we] have solved all the problems in the environment [in that time]? When you contrast that, it's revolutionary what has happened in the past 25 years."

FUTURE DIRECTIONS

Future efforts will focus on preventing pollution as well as on refining existing environmental controls. Michael Deland, the CEQ chair under President George Bush, emphasized that as the world and new technologies grow more complex, so do pollution problems. The challenge, he said, will be to examine their effects on the health of people and the environment.

During the Clinton Administration ten factors were identified for reinventing environmental regulations. A key point is the need to shift efforts from reactive (cleanup) measures to proactive (preventive) controls. Additionally the CEQ will be looking at how governments, businesses, and people will share responsibility for cleaning up and preventing environmental problems. Specifically the agency will likely investigate economic factors, performance-based regulations such as accountability standards, and the use of market incentives to foster environmental concern.

AGENCY RESOURCES

The CEQ hosts NEPANet on the World Wide Web at http://ceq.eh.doe.gov/nepanet.html. This is a comprehensive source of environmental protection information featuring EnviroText, a search program that provides access to regulations, tribal codes, treaties, statutes, and international agreements. NEPANet includes links to Duke University NEPA courses, case law reviews, EIS files, CEQ annual reports, the NEPA bibliography, and more. Additional information may be obtained by writing to the CEQ at Information Office, Council on Environmental Quality, 722 Jackson Pl. NW, Washington, DC 20503, or by calling (202) 395-5750.

AGENCY PUBLICATIONS

CEQ publications offer information and assistance for implementing environmental controls and for complying with mandates of the National Environmental Protection Act. These publications typically take the form of memorandums, guidelines, and answers to frequently asked questions. Available titles include "Where & How to File an Environmental Impact Statement," "Environmental Impact Statements Available for Review," "Pollution Prevention," and "Guidance Regarding the NEPA Regulations." Information concerning these publications is available on the CEQ NEPAnet Web site at http://ceq.eh.doe.gov/nepanet.html. Specific requests for information may also be obtained by writing to the Information Office, Council on Environmental Quality, 722 Jackson Pl. NW, Washington, DC 20503, or by calling (202) 395-5750.

The Environmental Technology Task Force supports projects, distributes publications, and furnishes information on educational resources. The task force makes information available via the Internet at http://www.whitehouse.gov/CEQ/etask.html. Its "Agenda for Action" is available through the Education for Sustainability Working Group at 1-800-363-3732.

The CEQ Environmental Quality Report provides assessments of environmental conditions, new technologies, and government activities. The 1970 report, for example, focused on global climate change; tropical deforestation was addressed in 1978; and the implications of biological diversity were discussed in the 1980 report. These reports are at least partly intended to catalyze change among the U.S. public and around the world.

BIBLIOGRAPHY

Connor, D. M. *Constructive Citizen Participation: A Resource Book (4th ed.).* Victoria, BC: Development Press, 1992.

Council on Environmental Quality. "25th Anniversary Report of the CEQ (1994–1995)."

Gibbons, Boyd. *CEQ Revisited: The Role of the Council on Environmental Quality.* Henry M. Jackson Foundation, 1995.

Glantz, Michael H. *Currents of Change: El Niño's Impact on Climate and Society.* Cambridge University Press, 1996.

Gribbin, John. *The Hole in the Sky: Man's Threat to the Ozone Layer.* Toronto and New York: Bantam Books, 1988.

Johnson, Brian J. "Slime or No Slime?" *Progressive,* July 1996, p. 6.

Ladd, Everett Carl, and Karlyn H. Bowman. *Attitudes Toward the Environment: Twenty-five Years After Earth Day.* Washington, D.C.: American Enterprise Institute, 1995.

MacDonald, Gordon J. "Assessing the U.S. Environment." *Environment,* March 1996, p. 25.

McLachlan, John A., and Steven F. Arnold. "Environmental Estrogens." *American Scientist,* September–October 1996.

Roan, Sharon L. *Ozone Crisis: The 15-Year Evolution of a Sudden Global Emergency.* New York: John Wiley and Sons, 1989.

Defense Nuclear Facilities Safety Board (DNFSB)

PARENT ORGANIZATION: Independent
ESTABLISHED: September 29, 1988
EMPLOYEES: 140

Contact Information:

ADDRESS: 625 Indiana Ave. NW, Ste. 700
Washington, DC 20004
PHONE: (202) 208-6400
TOLL FREE: (800) 788-4016
FAX: (202) 208-6518
E-MAIL: mailbox@dnfsb.gov
URL: http://www.dnfsb.gov
CHAIRMAN: John T. Conway
VICE CHAIRMAN: A. J. Eggenburger

WHAT IS ITS MISSION?

The Defense Nuclear Facilities Safety Board (DNFSB) was created in 1988 as an independent agency for the oversight of all activities within the Department of Energy's nuclear weapons complex that have the potential to affect nuclear health and safety. The board does this through the review of operations, practices, and events that occur at Department of Energy defense nuclear facilities. The Department of Energy's defense nuclear facilities include sites across the United States where nuclear materials related to defense are processed, stored, or disposed. Examples of this nuclear material include fuel for navy submarines, the nation's strategic inventory of tritium gas, the plutonium cores of nuclear weapons, and radioactive waste awaiting treatment.

HOW IS IT STRUCTURED?

The DNFSB is an agency of the Department of Energy under its nuclear weapons division. Ultimately, responsibilities and decision-making powers for designing, constructing, operating, or decommissioning any of the Department of Energy's defense nuclear facilities rest with the secretary of energy, with input from the Department of Defense. The DNFSB has no power to issue orders, and unlike other government agencies with a board structure, such as the Securities and Exchange Commission or the Commodity Futures Trading Commission, its decisions do not bear the weight of regulatory authority. Its decisions do not, in effect, become law. Rather, the DNFSB makes recommendations to the Department of Energy; the law that authorizes the board

A mushroom cloud towers 60,000 feet over Nagasaki, Japan. The city was devastated by a U.S. atomic bomb on August 9, 1945, the second atomic bomb used in warfare.

(Courtesy of the National Archives and Records Administration)

merely requires "appropriate and timely resolution of DNFSB recommendations." Because of the potentially disastrous consequences involved in working with nuclear materials, however, DNFSB recommendations are not taken lightly by the Department of Energy. The department's interactions with the board are managed through a departmental representative to the DNFSB.

The board itself is composed of five members who are appointed by the president with the advice and consent of the Senate. Board members are appointed from among U.S. citizens who are respected experts in the field of nuclear safety. These five board members are the agency's final decision-making body; all recommendations are formulated in their ultimate form, drafted, and transmitted to the Department of Energy by these five members. Administrative support is provided to the board by an office that is divided into the functions of human resources, finance and administration, and acquisition and information management. The Office of the General Counsel serves as the board's primary legal adviser and, among other legal functions, helps it draft recommendations.

Most of the support staff involved in DNFSB's activities, however, are employed in the technical bureau that carries out the board's field activities. All board recommendations, in the areas of operational safety, process engineering, standards development, and others, begin with the observations and analyses of technical staff specialists from this office. In many cases reports to the board come from representatives who have been assigned to specific sites. The Savannah River site in South Carolina, the Hanford Nuclear Reservation in Washington, and the Rocky Flats plant in Colorado are among the defense nuclear facilities where site representatives operate. Site representatives advise the board on overall safety and health conditions at defense nuclear facilities. They also conduct board reviews and evaluations related to design, construction, operation, and decommissioning of facilities. They interact with site management teams and participate in meetings with state and local agencies, the public, and industry officials.

PRIMARY FUNCTIONS

According to the mandates of the legislation that created the DNFSB, the board is generally directed to review and evaluate the standards relating to design, construction, operations, and decommissioning of the Department of Energy's defense nuclear facilities and to recommend to the secretary of energy those specific measures that should be adopted to ensure public health and safety. The board reviews the design and construction of all new Department of Energy defense nuclear facilities and analyzes facility design and the operational data gathered by its technical field experts.

In periodic meetings, most of which the public is encouraged to participate in, the board arrives at its recommendations. These recommendations are transmitted to the secretary of energy and made available to the Department of Energy. The board attempts to assist the department in the following ways: by helping it develop safety standards, by ensuring standards are translated clearly and consistently for Department of Energy management and contractors, by raising the technical expertise of the department, and by assisting and monitoring the department's Office of Environment, Safety, and

Health. The DNFSB is also responsible for identifying imminent or severe threats to public health and safety at Department of Energy defense nuclear facility sites. In the event that such a threat is perceived, the board transmits recommendations directly to the president and the secretaries of energy and defense.

PROGRAMS

Under the terms of the legislation that created it, the DNFSB is not authorized to intervene directly into the affairs of the Department of Energy. The board is considered an "action forcing" agency that exists to supervise and advise the Department of Energy on nuclear safety. The results of DNFSB recommendations typically emerge after a series of meetings and consultations. For example, the Senate Armed Services Committee, in drafting the board's appropriations legislation, directed the DNFSB "to raise the technical expertise of the Department substantially." In 1996 board actions to address this problem included a public meeting and issuance of a technical report, which led to a joint Department of Energy/DNFSB conference. As a result the Department of Energy initiated the first rigorous review of the technical qualifications of its senior technical safety managers. Additionally, the Department of Energy hired 56 new staff members under its service authority.

Another example of actions forced by the DNFSB occurred after its 1996 review of a 50-year-old plant at the Hanford Nuclear Reservation in Washington. The board discovered an air filter in the exhaust system that had degraded due to age and accumulated radiation exposure, and three previously used filter units were being isolated by water seals, a method that does not adequately isolate airborne radioactivity. As a result of the board's findings, the Department of Energy replaced the old filter and constructed a new system for isolating the previously used filters. The new system provided a more reliable physical barrier between the contaminated filters and the environment.

BUDGET INFORMATION

The DNFSB's annual budget is acquired through congressional appropriation legislation and totaled about $17 million in 1997. About half of the board's budget is spent on the salaries of the personnel involved in the board's evaluations and implementations; the other half is spent on employee benefits, facilities rentals, and various services (such as consulting and production) provided to the board by agencies and private companies.

FAST FACTS

As a result of the arms reduction treaties signed by the United States, about 15,000 U.S. nuclear weapons will be retired by the early twenty-first century. This amounts to about 60 pounds of surplus plutonium to be disposed of.

(Source: "Nuclear Arms Cleanup." *CQ Researcher*, June 24, 1994.)

HISTORY

Nuclear fission was first used for U.S. national defense on August 6, 1945, with the explosion of an atomic bomb over Hiroshima, Japan. Along with the second bomb, dropped three days later over Nagasaki, Japan, the United States killed more than 220,000 people. This remains the only known use of nuclear devices in combat. The use of nuclear technology to create weapons and fuel for defense applications, however, has grown rapidly since then. Throughout the Cold War, when the Soviet Union was perceived as a powerful military threat to the United States, the U.S. military industrial complex underwent a remarkable buildup. New weapons and nuclear applications were developed throughout a period of nearly fifty years.

Throughout this period, the Department of Energy and its predecessor agencies operated the nation's defense nuclear weapons complex without independent, external oversight. The work of the Department of Energy seemed to reach a critical point in the late 1980s when safety problems at some of the sites began to surface with alarming regularity. Of particular concern was Rocky Flats, a plant outside Denver, Colorado, that created the plutonium pits, constituting the core of nuclear weapons. Repeated incidents of radiation pollution and worker exposure eventually prompted the government to close the facility in 1989.

It was becoming increasingly clear to Congress that significant public health and safety problems were accumulating. Part of the problem was that private contractors had been hired to operate facilities, but the Department of Energy had failed to manage and oversee their operations; the department was not enforcing health and safety measures. The most significant outcome of these concerns was the creation of the Defense Nuclear Facilities Safety Board in 1988. This new agency was to serve as an independent oversight organization within the executive branch, charged with advising the secretary of energy on nuclear safety issues. By fall of 1989 the initial five members of the board had been appointed by the president and confirmed by the Senate, and staff recruitment efforts at the new agency were under way.

Within a matter of months, however, the defense nuclear complex in the United States underwent a transformation. Almost concurrent with the collapse of the Soviet Union, which brought the Cold War to an abrupt end in 1992, the United States and the Soviet Union negotiated the historic Strategic Arms Reduction Treaties (START I and II), which reduced the nuclear weapons capabilitites of both countries. With the end of the Cold War, the mission of the Department of Energy's nuclear defense complex shifted. It had been dedicated to the production of plutonium and tritium and the fabrication, assembly, and testing of nuclear weapons. Its new mandate was to manage the remaining weapons stockpile, dismantle nuclear weapons, and bring nuclear weapons testing to a halt. The department also faced the task of bringing many facilities to a safe shutdown condition and cleaning up the radioactive contamination that had accumulated during the complex's nearly fifty years of weapons production.

As a result the DNFSB has had to shift its mission and direction. It has devoted significant attention to ensuring the safe stabilization of residues and waste produced during the nuclear arms buildup and it established a framework for integrated safety management programs across the defense nuclear complex. It has also attempted to stimulate Department of Energy progress in developing the technical expertise of its own staff in order to make the department's operations at nuclear facilities safer and more self-sufficient.

CURRENT POLITICAL ISSUES

The effort to clean up harmful radioactivity that resulted from the nuclear arms race is still in its beginning stages, with experts predicting it will take up to 75 years and cost taxpayers anywhere from $230 billion to $500 billion. If the cost reaches the high end of these estimates, cleanup will have cost more than the research, build up, detonation, and testing that brought on the situation ($375 billion in adjusted dollars). One slow down that the cleanup effort invariably faces is the coordination of the entities involved. The Department of Energy, the private contractors, the DNFSB, state officials, and in some cases the Environmental Protection Agency (EPA) must all work together toward a common goal, perhaps not an unreasonable expectation but certainly a bureaucratic one with many competing interests.

Case Study: The Hanford Nuclear Reservation

The Department of Energy's Hanford Site, just outside Richland, Washington, was the United States's original plutonium production complex and the source of the plutonium used in the bombs detonated over Japan. But the START treaties and the end of the Cold War has rendered the site useless, transforming the government reservation half the size of Rhode Island into a complex of decaying buildings and contaminated facilities that costs tens of millions of dollars each year to be kept stable and safe.

The Department of Energy began deactivating and cleaning up Hanford in 1989, yet still in 1996, 15,000 employees were working in the 1,400 places where environmental safety work had begun or was needed. Although more than $8 billion has already been spent, workers there acknowledge that little permanent cleanup has been accomplished, and the most serious problems at Hanford have not yet been addressed. The site has extensive soil and water contamination, some of which has made its way into the Columbia River, and large volumes of radioactive waste remain stored in old, rusting metal containers.

The difficulty of collaboration between the Department of Energy and the DNFSB has stymied progress at Hanford, partially because of the complex legal agreement the Department of Energy entered into for cleanup of the site. The contract, known as the tri-party agreement involves the Department of Energy, the Environmental Protection Agency, and the State of Washington. It sets up a detailed schedule for cleaning up the area, with most of the job to be completed by the year 2018. The main private contractor hired by the Department of Energy to clean up the site, Westinghouse, fell far behind schedule and exceeded the estimated costs to the extent that the Department of Energy is at risk of being sued for billions of dollars by the State of Washington.

With no end to the cleanup in sight, the billions of dollars involved in the project have attracted workers in the fledgling nuclear deactivation and cleanup industry. In a seemingly contradictory effort, the district's representative, Richard Hastings, tried to protect the cleanup work, paid for by tax dollars, that has brought prosperity to his area while also pushing for a balanced budget and tax cuts. Hastings found himself at odds with many fellow Republicans who were working to change the federal laws behind the tri-party agreement in order to avoid a costly lawsuit. At almost the same time, the Clinton Administration cut the Department of Energy's nuclear cleanup funding by $4.4 billion. Having no force of law, DNFSB recommendations have fallen victim to political forces and funding shortages.

SUCCESSES AND FAILURES

Success at the DNFSB is achieved each time a recommendation induces Department of Energy action that prevents a serious nuclear accident. In 1996 the board became concerned that explosive amounts of hydrogen gas were accumulating in tanks that contained plutonium solution at the Rocky Flats Environmental Technology Site in Colorado. The board review concluded that the tanks might not be properly ventilated, and at the board's urging the Department of Energy took gas samples from several tanks. The samples confirmed the presence of hydrogen gas at concentrations of up to fifteen times the minimum explosive limit. The possibility of an explosion in such a tank posed a very serious safety concern to workers at the plant. But this was avoided when the Department of Energy took DNFSB's recommended corrective actions to purge and ventilate the tanks.

FUTURE DIRECTIONS

The DFNSB's objectives for the future are aimed at shaping Department of Energy standards and operations. Included among the objectives outlined in its strategic plan are successful management of the nation's stockpile of nuclear weapons and components and the management of hazardous by-products of nuclear weapons production. Also the DNFSB supports the continued improvement of Department of Energy technical expertise and the formation of a standards-based integrated safety management program at defense nuclear facilities. The agency will also work with the Department of Energy, helping it to properly characterize, stabilize, process, and safely store surplus plutonium, uranium and other actinides, residues, spent fuel, and wastes from nuclear weapons.

AGENCY RESOURCES

General inquiries about the DNFSB should be directed to the agency's public information branch at PO Box 7887, Washington, DC 20044. The phone number is 1-800-788-4016. The DNFSB's Web site at http://www.dnfsb.gov also has a number of links to information about the Department of Energy, nuclear safety, and other related government agencies.

AGENCY PUBLICATIONS

Board publications of interest to the general public include the agency's annual reports to Congress and its *Strategic Plan 1997–2001*, which are available at the board's Web site at http://www.dnfsb.gov. The board also publishes trip reports on visits to defense nuclear facilities, as well as weekly reports from site representatives at specific locations. Other board publications include board recommendations, technical documents that are included in agency correspondence, and public speeches, statements, and remarks made by DNFSB members. Many of these are also available through the board's Web site. For further information about DNFSB publications contact the Public Information Office at PO Box 7887, Washington, DC 20044.

BIBLIOGRAPHY

Aeppel, Timothy. "Untidy Cleanup: Mess at A-Bomb Plant Shows What Happens if Pork Gets in the Way." *Washington Post*, 28 March 1995, p. A1 (W).

Defense Nuclear Facilities Safety Board. *Strategic Plan FY 1997–2002*. Washington, D.C.: DNFSB, 1997.

General Accounting Office. *Nuclear Safety: The Defense Nuclear Facilities Safety Board's First Year of Operation: Report to Congressional Requesters*. Washington, D.C.: Government Printing Office, 1991.

Hecker, Siegfried S. "Retargeting the Weapons Laboratories." *Issues in Science and Technology*, Spring 1994, pp. 44–7.

"Nuclear Arms Cleanup." *CQ Researcher*, 24 June 1994, pp. 554–75.

Wald, Matthew L. "Factory Is Set to Process Dangerous Nuclear Waste." *New York Times*, 13 March 1996, p. C19 (N).

Zorpette, Glen. "Hanford's Nuclear Wasteland." *Scientific American*, May 1996, pp. 88–97.

———. "Keeping the 'Tiger' at Bay: With Fewer Experts and Facilities, the DOE Is Trying New Ways of Preventing Nuclear Accidents." *Scientific American*, July 1996, pp. 36–7.

Department of Agriculture (USDA)

ESTABLISHED: May 15, 1862
EMPLOYEES: 104,000

Contact Information:

ADDRESS: 14th St. & Independence Ave. SW
Washington, DC 20250
PHONE: (202) 720-2791
TDD (HEARING IMPAIRED): (202) 720-2600
FAX: (202) 690-0228
E-MAIL: agsec@usda.gov
URL: http://www.usda.gov
SECRETARY OF AGRICULTURE: Dan Glickman
DEPUTY SECRETARY OF AGRICULTURE: Richard Rominger

WHAT IS ITS MISSION?

When it was first established more than 130 years ago, the mission of the United States Department of Agriculture (USDA) was "to acquire and diffuse among the people of the United States useful information on subjects connected with agriculture . . . and to procure, propagate, and distribute among the people new and valuable seeds and plants." This core mission of improving and maintaining farm income has expanded as a result of larger crop yields to include a number of supplemental goals, especially in the area of expanding markets abroad for agricultural products. To assist farmers, the USDA has added missions such as forecasting the weather, promoting rural economic development, promoting exports, and guaranteeing credit.

To aid U.S. consumers the department regulates food safety through inspection and grading services, promotes the teaching of home economics, encourages an adequate diet for all Americans, and regulates marketing systems. The USDA also works with farmers to protect the soil, water, and forests in order to maintain production capacity, keep agricultural products safe for consumption, and enhance the environment.

HOW IS IT STRUCTURED?

The Department of Agriculture is a cabinet-level agency and is part of the executive branch of the U.S. government. The USDA is led by a secretary who is appointed by the president and confirmed by Congress. The primary missions of the USDA are carried out by six major bureaus, which are led by administrators bearing the title of undersecretary. These are the bureaus of Natural Resources and Environment; Farm and Foreign Agricultural Services; Rural Development; Food, Nutrition, and Consumer Services; Food Safety; and Research, Education, and Economics. Each of these bureaus plays a significant role in formulating USDA policy, and most have a broad range of responsibilities that involve the operation of other federal agencies, such as the Bureau of Natural Resources and Environment's responsibility for the U.S. Forest Service.

To carry out its work the USDA relies on the support of departmental administration staff, along with the Office of the Chief Financial Officer, the Office of Congressional Relations, the Office of Inspector General, the Office of General Counsel, the Office of Executive Operations, and the Office of Communications.

Marketing and regulatory programs not concerned with food safety are handled by a separate office under the leadership of the assistant secretary for marketing and regulatory programs. Also affiliated with the USDA, but operating independently (using sources other than the USDA budget for funding), are the USDA Graduate School, a continuing education program offering career training to adults, and the Alternative Agricultural Research and Commercialization Center, which provides and monitors financial aid for developing and marketing new nonfood and nonfeed products made from agricultural and forestry materials.

FAST FACTS

The USDA's food assistance, nutrition, and health care support programs directly help one in six Americans.

(Source: Department of Agriculture. "The People's Department," 1997.)

PRIMARY FUNCTIONS

The USDA is the liaison between U.S. farmers and their government, and its activities revolve around regulating, improving, and promoting agricultural products. In doing so, the department works with government to develop policy and with farmers to help them adhere to policy and improve their products and their farming and ranching methods. The USDA, therefore, directly serves all Americans by ensuring the quality of their food. To accomplish its vast responsibilities, the USDA has several agencies and divisions working under it, each with a specific focus.

Research

The USDA's research activities span a broad spectrum of topics, and its findings guide virtually all other activities and goals. Through research the USDA seeks to find new technologies to improve production of agricultural products; to find new uses for products; to improve crop varieties and livestock species; to improve food safety, quality, and supply; and to develop farming techniques that better protect the environment and natural resources. To do this the department studies the economy, production levels, and the supply and demand of agricultural products. Such information is used by the government in making policy decisions and by farmers in planning their planting, feeding, breeding, and marketing.

Stabilizing Farmers and Their Commodities

The USDA stabilizes farmers and their communities by monitoring the market prices for their goods and attempting to keep the prices stable. As market prices are directly related to supply and demand, the USDA must monitor that too. When necessary, the USDA supports agricultural prices and income and adjusts production levels. This is primarily accomplished through commodity loans and purchases, which are geared toward providing farmers with interim financing and balancing distribution of their products. The purchasing of agricultural products by the government also helps maintain market prices.

The department helps new and disadvantaged farmers in several ways. It offers credit and direct and guaranteed loans for farm ownership, operating costs, or to help farmers recover from the effects of a natural disaster. Catastrophic crop insurance is made available as well as basic loss insurance to cover losses due to less serious events like drought, frost, or disease. Additional specialized assistance programs are developed to help farmers in areas that are declared disaster areas. For example, the USDA may help a farmer pay to replace cattle feed if a substantial amount has been destroyed by a disaster. Additionally, rural economies and quality of life are enhanced with USDA infrastructure projects. Improving water and wastewater systems, telecommunications, electricity, housing, technical assistance, and business development initiatives are a few ways the USDA attempts to accomplish this.

Promoting Agricultural Products

The USDA seeks to make farming and ranching more stable and profitable through traditional marketing techniques designed to maintain the competitive position of U.S. products in the global economy. For example, the

FAST FACTS

Since 1980, USDA scientists have developed more than seven hundred new or improved varieties of fruits, vegetables, and other crops.

(Source: Department of Agriculture. "The People's Department," 1997.)

department disseminates market news, advises on such things as rural transportation issues, and provides patent-type protection for new plant varieties. The department also attempts to combat unfair competition, find new markets for agricultural products, and expand exporting opportunities.

Conservation

Since agriculture depends so heavily on the environment and natural resources, farmers and ranchers need to protect these resources in order to protect their own futures. The USDA develops programs that compensate farmers and ranchers for protecting highly-erodible or otherwise sensitive acreage. For example, the department may "rent" such an area in return for the farmer growing a protective cover of grass or trees instead of soil-depleting crops. Other conservation methods include developing and demonstrating farming methods that conserve land, water, forests, and other resources to the greatest extent possible. Two USDA agencies, the Forest Service and the Natural Resources Conservation Service, share responsibility for the stewardship of 75 percent of the country's total land area. These agencies extensively study and predict the effects of farming practices so that conservation methods can be adopted.

Food Safety and Nutrition

In order to maintain the integrity of U.S. agricultural products, the USDA seeks to ensure that U.S. meat, poultry, and produce is wholesome, unadulterated, safe, and properly labeled and packaged. To do so the USDA inspects slaughter and processing facilities and product samples. Inspectors evaluate the presence of chemical residues, disease-causing pathogens, additives or other foreign matter, sanitation levels, handling practices, and processing methods. Additionally, the USDA inspects imports. To prevent problems from occurring, the USDA attempts to keep foreign pests and diseases out through quarantine practices and pest and disease eradication programs.

Finally, the USDA does much to help the citizens of the world attain an adequate, nutritious diet. The department helps develop nutrition guidelines and standards and disseminates such information with the intent of encouraging Americans to choose healthy foods. USDA nutrition assistance programs, for instance the Food Stamp program and the Special Supplemental Nutrition Program for Women, Infants, and Children, serve one in six Americans. Additionally, the USDA donates food to domestic and international food banks for the hungry.

PROGRAMS

USDA programs are the means by which the department carries out many of its functions, like conserving natural resources and ensuring food safety, quality, and availability. Programs are carried out by the USDA agency that focuses on a given mission. For example, the Farm Service Agency runs programs that stabilize wheat, corn, and cotton markets. Such commodity stabilization programs typically provide loans, payments, or purchases to growers who are experiencing price instability. Similar programs include the Grain Reserve Program, which provides extended loans and storage payments to growers who agree to hold some grain in reserve, and the Noninsured Crop Disaster Assistance Program.

Programs in the USDA's marketing mission area include the Market Promotion Program, which provides assistance to trade promotion organizations to help fund their market development activities overseas, especially in markets where the United States encounters unfavorable trade practices by foreign competitors or importers. For the protection of consumers, Food, Nutrition, and Consumer Services administers the National School Lunch Program, which provides financial assistance to public and nonprofit private schools in operating nonprofit school lunch programs. This mission area also runs the Food Stamp and Food Distribution programs.

BUDGET INFORMATION

The USDA's authority to commit funds of the U.S. Treasury is normally granted by Congress through appropriations acts. In submitting the budget, the president requests Congress to appropriate or otherwise provide the amount of budget authority needed to carry out recommended USDA programs. The estimated budget for the USDA in 1998 was approximately $83 billion, making up about 5 percent of the total federal budget of $1.653 trillion. About 44 percent of the department's budget goes to food, nutrition and consumer services, 34 percent to farm and foreign agricultural services, 12 percent to rural development, and 6 percent to natural resources and environment. The remainder, about 4 percent, is divided among food safety; research, education, and economics; marketing and regulatory programs; and departmental or administrative activities.

About three-fourths of the money spent by the USDA is devoted to meeting the obligations of its mandatory programs. These programs, including the majority of food assistance programs, some conservation programs, and commodity programs, are required by law. The other one-fourth of USDA expenditures are spent on discretionary programs, including the Special Supplemental Nutrition Program for Women, Infants, and Children (WIC), food inspection, soil and water conservation, and management of the national forests.

BUDGET:

Department of Agriculture

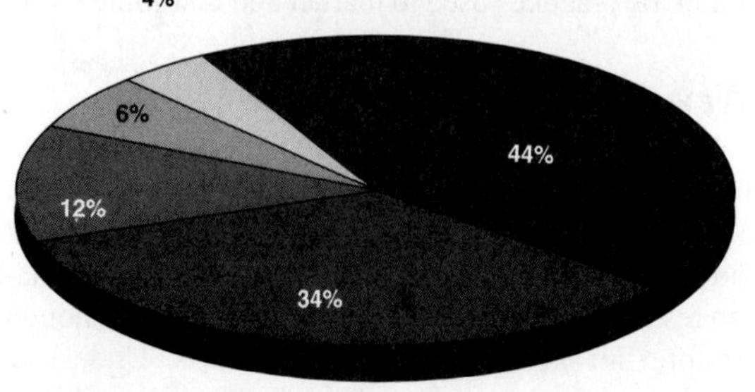

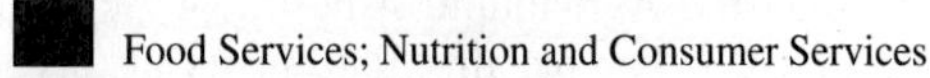

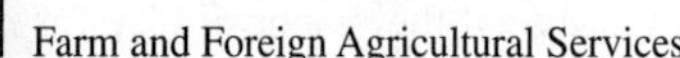

Rural Development

Natural Resources and Environment

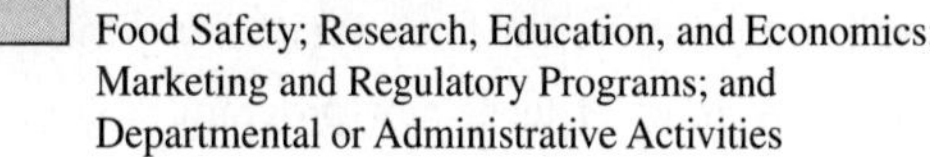

Percentage of Federal Budget

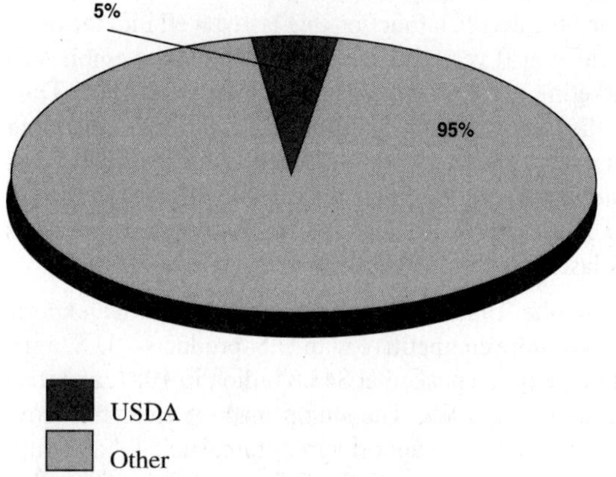

USDA

Other

HISTORY

Proposals for an agricultural branch of the federal government were made as early as 1776. In 1796 President George Washington recommended such an agency, and in 1819 the Secretary of the Treasury gave the idea momentum by asking naval officers and ambassadors overseas to send home seeds and better breeds of domestic animals. The U.S. Patent Office soon created an agricultural division for collecting agricultural statistics, conducting investigations, and distributing seeds. Over the next few decades, many farmers and community leaders, later led by the U.S. Agricultural Society, continued to urge that agriculture be represented by a separate agency.

Early Years

The goals of this movement were realized on May 15, 1862, when President Abraham Lincoln created the U. S. Department of Agriculture (USDA). The law that created the USDA authorized its commissioner (until 1889 the USDA was led by a commissioner rather than a cabinet-level secretary) to collect statistics; conduct experiments; and collect, test, and distribute new seeds and plants. The department's purpose was, in its conception, very broad: "to acquire and to diffuse among the people of the United States useful information on subjects connected with agriculture in the most general and comprehensive sense of the word." The first commissioner of this new department, Pennsylvania dairyman Isaac Newton, planted his first experimental crops on the Washington Mall.

The department's research function expanded slowly until the appointment of Secretary James Wilson in 1897. Wilson served 16 years in office under four different presidents, and he made the department into one of the world's great research institutions, focusing primarily on increasing crop yields and improving efficiency in livestock production. Wilson also organized a number of new bureaus, including the U.S. Forest Service. By 1912 the department's size, in personnel and expenditures, was seven times larger than it had been at the time of Wilson's appointment.

The diverse research activities of the department provided the information needed for regulatory functions, and the two were often carried out in close relation. For example, after outbreaks of contagious animal diseases occurred in 1884, resulting in the barring of U.S. meat from some European markets, the department investigated the disease and was given the authority to control the movement of livestock in interstate commerce. This was the first of many regulatory powers granted to the agency, and this action set the precedent for the development of federal standards and grades for farm products and the practices used to market and distribute them.

A New Era

Beginning with World War I (1914–18), the twentieth century brought a series of economic situations that shifted the department's focus. By the time the Great Depression hit in 1929, it was obvious that the emphasis on research, regulation, and marketing was not enough to restore the incomes of rural Americans. Under the leadership of Secretary Henry A. Wallace, the USDA worked to get the Agricultural Adjustment Act signed into law in 1933. For the first time in its history, the department was assigned the responsibility for administering a program that would provide direct economic assistance to farmers. The same circumstances that created this legislation would lead to the creation of programs and agencies for ensuring better rural credit facilities, soil conservation, and loans for rural electrification.

Although most of these new programs were aimed at farm welfare and production, it was soon apparent that urban Americans as well were suffering from an insufficient food supply. The department worked with welfare agencies to set up programs for distributing surpluses among the needy, a function that lasted well into the post-World War II years. The department began to emphasize marketing and distribution, rather than production. During the 1960s and 1970s its attention turned to ensuring that every American was sufficiently fed, and the Food Stamp Program was created to enable poorer families to buy necessary food. This consumer-centered emphasis has lasted to the present day.

In the 1980s European grain and animal exports became more competitive with U.S. products—U.S. agricultural exports peaked at $43.8 billion in 1981, and then declined until 1987. The slump made it clear that government efforts to support agriculture, such as farm subsidies, were not the kind of financial incentives that would extend U.S. exports into an increasingly global marketplace. Instead, U.S. leaders began to propose agricultural policy that would be responsive to changing market forces. By 1988 the U.S. had signed a trade accord with Canada that would initiate free trade in all commodities, including farm products. Similar negotiations with Mexico began in 1990.

In 1993 the United States ratified two major free-trade agreements, the North American Free Trade Agreement (NAFTA) and the General Agreement on Tariffs and Trade (GATT). Each treaty would lower trade barriers for U.S. products in Canada, Mexico, and Europe, thereby enhancing the export prospects for U.S. agriculture. By 1996 U.S. agricultural exports had set a new record of $59.8 billion. In order to insure continued success in agricultural exports, Congress passed the 1996 Federal Agriculture Improvement and Reform (FAIR) Act, informally known as the 1996 farm bill. The main focus of the farm bill's many provisions was to make USDA farm programs more reliant on worldwide market signals, and more efficient and flexible in dealing with sudden changes in market conditions.

CURRENT POLITICAL ISSUES

Much has changed in American society since President Lincoln created the Department of Agriculture in 1862. Urban expansion and several economic crises among farmers nationwide have greatly altered the way of life for most Americans. As a result, citizens and legislators alike have shown an increasing desire to streamline or eliminate many of the department's programs.

Department officials, as well as advocates from the scientific community, say the changing nature of American agriculture and society is further reason to spend money on research and development, especially in areas where public safety is an issue, for example the quality of the food supply. As the Department of Agriculture attempts to reorganize itself to fit into this era of "smaller government," it struggles with the dilemma of where and how cuts will be made in its budget.

Case Study: Regulating Organic Labeling

Organic farming involves the raising of livestock and crops without the use of chemical pesticides, herbicides, fertilizers, or other artificial means. Rather, organic farming relies on naturally occurring pest predators and fertilizers, and the natural needs and behavior of livestock are accommodated to a greater extent. The goal is to produce choice-quality, healthy products of high nutritional value while protecting the environment and ensuring the long-term fertility of the land.

When the organic farming movement began to take shape in the first half of the twentieth century, it had little momentum. Organically grown crops and livestock yield less than their conventionally farmed counterparts and, in turn, organically grown foods cost more. Therefore, organic farming was unattractive to many producers and consumers. The USDA, therefore, paid little attention to this small agricultural sector.

By the end of the twentieth century, organic farming came to prominence in concert with the animal rights, environmental protection, and healthy-living movements, gaining popularity as more and more consumers became concerned about what they were putting into the environment and their own bodies. It was at this time that the USDA started to take notice of this growing segment of the agriculture-based economy.

Its primary concern was the need to regulate organic growers as there was considerable variation in their practices, attitudes, and philosophies. There was also the potential for fraud—an unscrupulous farmer could produce higher-yielding non organic crops but call them organic to get a higher price. Just as the Food and Drug Administration established standards that must be met in order for products to be labeled "low-fat," the USDA sought to set the standards by which farmers must adhere in order to label their products "organic."

The Organic Foods Production Act, passed in 1990 as part of the Food, Agriculture, Conservation, and Trade Act (also known as the 1990 farm bill), initiated development of such standards. The act's purpose was "(1) to establish national standards governing the marketing of certain agricultural products as organically produced products; (2) to assure consumers that organically produced products meet a consistent standard; and (3) to facilitate interstate commerce in fresh and processed food that is organically produced."

Support from the organic industry was strong, especially since the bill established the National Organic Standards Board to include consumers and representatives from the organic industry who would work with the secretary of agriculture in developing a list of allowed synthetic and prohibited natural substances for use in producing products labeled "organic." Fourteen board members were appointed in January 1992, and the National Organic Standards Board started developing its recommendations by forming subcommittees to focus on major issues. Six committees were formed: crops standards; livestock and livestock products standards; processing, packaging, and labeling standards; accreditation; international issues; and materials. The board issued recommendations two years later, including specifications on the use of antibiotics and parasiticides (dewormers) in livestock, emergency crop spraying situations, and breeding methods. Three recommendations, however, sparked political debate. When the USDA unveiled its long-awaited draft of proposed rules in 1997, the document contained wording that implied that the USDA supported the use of biosolids, ionizing radiation (irradiation), and genetically engineered organisms, all of which are procedures that the National Organic Standards Board opposed.

Biosolids are the treated sewage sludge that can be used as fertilizer. The USDA justified its position by citing that "the EPA [Environmental Protection Agency] defines biosolids as the primarily organic residuals, produced by current wastewater treatment processes that treat domestic sewage, that can be beneficially recycled. Under current EPA regulations, such recycling can include land application of biosolids to provide primary plant nutrients and micronutrients to crops and vegetation produced in agriculture and to improve soil characteristics by providing necessary moisture and/or organic matter to enhance soil tilth. Over the years, EPA, USDA, and FDA [Food and Drug Administration] have issued joint policy statements that have endorsed the beneficial utilization of biosolids on land for purposes that include the production of fruits and vegetables."

The National Organic Standards Board had protested use of municipal sludge on grounds that it is synthetic and could be contaminated with toxic household and industrial pollutants and synthetic materials such as PCBs, cadmium, and lead, which are prohibited in organic production systems.

Irradiation is the process of exposing foods to radiation to eliminate the pathogens that cause food borne illnesses. On this, the USDA's proposal said "the application of ionizing radiation as a sanitation or preservation treatment currently is permitted by FDA for a wide range of agricultural products. Additionally, a request to permit the use of ionizing radiation on red meat products was recently approved by FDA."

The board, however, had opposed irradiation, saying that "the long-term effects of consuming irradiated foods are unknown. Irradiation introduces radioactive material to organic products and as such is a synthetic process neither needed nor desired by the organic industry. Irradiation is a band-aid approach that treats the symptoms of potential contamination rather than addressing and eliminating sources of contamination that can be managed by good manufacturing and handling practices." Likewise, the National Organic Standards Board opposed the sanctioning of genetically-modified organisms as "organic" on grounds that "genetic engineering, particularly recombinant DNA technology, is a process that never would occur in nature and is presently inconsistent with the principles of organic production. Additionally, the long-term effects on the environment and human health are unknown."

On this the USDA's proposal cited a Senate report that said "as time goes on, various scientific breakthroughs, including biotechnology techniques, will require scrutiny for their application to organic production. The committee is concerned that production materials keep pace with our evolving knowledge of production systems." The USDA added: "in the time since the OFPA [Organic Foods Production Act] was passed, GEOs [genetically engineered organisms] and their products have assumed a more significant role in agricultural production. The policy of the United States Government is that GEOs and their products should be regulated based on risk, not on how they are produced."

For each of these disputed points, the USDA solicited public commentary as to whether or not the procedures should be permitted or prohibited or, in the case of genetic engineering, allowed on a case-by-case basis. Immediately thereafter, the organic community responded, flooding the USDA with more than 250,000 letters, postcards, and petition signatures. Some letters were personally written while others were part of letter-writing campaigns sponsored by groups like Working Assets, Organic Farmers Marketing Association, Save Organic Standards–the Campaign for Food Safety, American Natural Hygiene Society, Center for Science

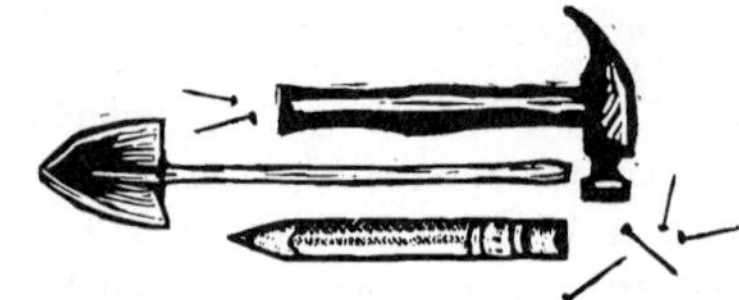

GET INVOLVED:
Second Harvest

Second Harvest, a nationwide network of food banks, is the largest charitable hunger relief organization in the United States. With the assistance of citizen volunteers and student organizations, the organization's food pantries, soup kitchens, and homeless shelters serve nearly 26 million people each year. In 1995 Second Harvest distributed 811.3 million pounds of food to hungry people across the country. To volunteer at any of Second Harvest's two hundred food banks or one of the fifty thousand charitable agencies associated with Second Harvest, call (312) 263-2303. Although it is the largest and most extensive program of its type in the United States, Second Harvest is not alone in its food distribution efforts. For information about programs nationwide, or to find the program nearest you, call the USDA's toll-free hot line at 1-800-GLEAN-IT.

in the Public Interest, Onion River Food Co-op, Harvest Cooperative Supermarkets, Petaluma Poultry Processors Inc., Organic Watch, and the San Francisco Bay Area Food Community. The department also held another round of public meetings.

The headline on a May 8, 1998, USDA press release read: "USDA to make fundamental changes in revised proposed rule on organic standards." The department directly attributed the decision to do so to the public's response. "The bulk of the extraordinary number of comments opposed including the products of biotechnology, the use of irradiation in food processing, and the application of biosolids (municipal sludge) in organic food production," the release said. "Biotechnology, irradiation, and biosolids are safe and have important roles to play in agriculture, but they neither fit current organic practices nor meet current consumer expectations about organics, as the comments made clear... Therefore, these products and practices will not be included in our revised proposal, and food produced with these products and practices will not be allowed to bear the organic label."

Public Impact

In itself, establishing standards for organic farming and labeling will serve the public in several ways. First, consumers will gain a definitive answer as to what exactly is in such products or how they were produced. A high level of security in this should prevail as the Organic Foods Production Act has the force of law. That is, producers found to be fraudulently claiming to have produced organic products can be prosecuted by the federal government. Additionally, the establishment of standards should open new international markets, particularly those that require organic products to be government certified as such.

The outcome of the political dispute over the three points of contention also illustrates that activism can affect change. The number of responses the USDA received—275,603—is only about 0.1 percent of the U.S. population. Further, the public victory will serve to preserve the integrity of the "organic" label.

SUCCESSES AND FAILURES

One of the USDA's most obvious successes is the effectiveness of the Animal and Plant Health Inspection Service. The agency's fight against one of California's most destructive pests, the Mediterranean fruit fly, or Medfly, was begun in the spring of 1994. The Preventive Release program distributes 125,000 sterile Medflies per square mile weekly over a 2,155-square-mile area that includes portions of Los Angeles, Orange, San Bernardino, and Riverside counties. No Medfly infestations have been detected in southern California since the program's inception, despite ongoing detection programs. The Medfly program is one illustration of the intensity and comprehensiveness of the Animal and Plant Health Inspection Service's inspection and pest control efforts, which keep the United States relatively safe from the kinds of diseases and contaminations that sometimes strike in other countries, such as the 1996–97 outbreak of "mad cow disease" (bovine spongiform encephalopathy, or BSE) in England.

FUTURE DIRECTIONS

The opening up of the global marketplace will guide much of the USDA's coming initiatives. New markets will open for agricultural products, but the USDA will have to work to ensure that U.S. products are competitive with those of other nations also seeking to gain a foothold in new markets. With the opening of the U.S. market to imports, the USDA will need to strengthen its inspection services and learn about new animal and plant diseases that the United States has not yet had to deal with.

Also, the USDA will be working to use the breakthroughs in genetic engineering to farmers' and ranchers' advantage, while also monitoring their effects on farmers and their products. And the department will have to help farmers and ranchers deal with global warming issues. Not only does global warming change the environment that farmers and ranchers depend on, but initiatives to control global warming almost guarantee that the price of fuel will be on the rise. This would increase operating costs for farmers and ranchers but would not bring any additional value to their products, making them less profitable to produce.

AGENCY RESOURCES

The USDA offers educational, organizational, and financial assistance to consumers and their families in such fields as rural housing, farm operations, and nutrition. The USDA's main contact is the Office for Public Affairs at (202) 720-2791. Videotapes on a variety of agricultural subjects are available through the Video and Teleconference Division. For a listing of cooperating film libraries, call (202) 720-6072. Information is also available electronically via the World Wide Web at http://www.usda.gov/news/howto/howto.htm. Specific requests for information should be mailed to U.S. Department of Agriculture, 14th and Independence Ave. SW, Washington, DC 20250.

AGENCY PUBLICATIONS

The many and varied publications of the USDA include a periodical news publication, *The USDA News*, as well as the *Agriculture Fact Book 1997*, and the online pamphlet "A Citizen's Guide to Food Recovery." Most publications can be located through the Public Affairs Office. To order USDA publications for sale, contact the Government Printing Office, Superintendent of Documents, by telephoning (202) 512-1800 or visit the World Wide Web at http://www.access.gpo.gov/su_docs/sale.html.

BIBLIOGRAPHY

Caswell, Julie A. *Economics of Food Safety*. New York: Elsevier, 1991.

Chun, Janean. "Contract Players." *Entrepreneur*, 24, no. 13 (December 1996): p. 42.

Gardner, Gary T. *Shrinking Fields: Cropland Loss in a World of Eight Billion*. Washington, D.C.: Worldwatch Institute, 1996.

Marshall, Eliot. "An All-You-Can-Eat Genome Project." *Science*, 277 (15 August 1997): p. 889.

Paddock, Joe. *Soil and Survival: Land Stewardship and the Future of American Agriculture*. San Francisco: Sierra Club Books, 1986.

Spaid, Elizabeth Levitan. "Minority Farmland Eroded by USDA Discrimination." *The Christian Science Monitor*, 89, no. 25 (31 December 1996): p. 3.

Tarrant, John. *Farming and Food*. New York: Oxford University Press, 1991.

"USDA/FDA Info Center Established to Reduce Foodborne Illness Risks." *Journal of Environmental Health*, 58 (September 1995): pp. 38–9.

Department of Commerce (DOC)

ESTABLISHED: February 14, 1903
EMPLOYEES: 31,600

Contact Information:

ADDRESS: 14th St. and Constitution Ave. NW
Washington, DC 20230
PHONE: (202) 482-2000
TDD (HEARING IMPAIRED): (202) 482-4670
FAX: (202) 482-0077
E-MAIL: opaosec@doc.gov
URL: http://www.doc.gov
SECRETARY OF COMMERCE: William M. Daley

WHAT IS ITS MISSION?

The Department of Commerce's mission is to promote job creation, economic growth, sustainable development, and improved living standards for Americans by working in partnership with business, universities, communities, and workers. It encourages, serves, and promotes the nation's international trade and technological advancement. The department's mission statement involves three strategic themes: building for the future and promoting U.S. competitiveness in the global marketplace; keeping the United States competitive by remaining at the vanguard of science and technology; and providing effective management and stewardship of our nation's resources and assets in order to ensure sustainable economic opportunities.

HOW IS IT STRUCTURED?

Although it is the smallest cabinet-level agency, the Department of Commerce's broad range of missions and objectives has divided it into a large number of offices and bureaus, each designed to fulfill specific objectives of the department's mission: the Economics and Statistics Administration (ESA), the Bureau of Export Administration (BXA), the Economic Development Administration (EDA), the International Trade Administration (ITA), the Minority Business Development Agency (MBDA), the National Oceanic and Atmospheric Administration (NOAA), the National Telecommunications and Information Administration (NTIA), the Patent and Trademark Office (PTO), and the Technology Administration (TA). These offices bear primary responsibility for

BIOGRAPHY:
Herbert Hoover

31st President of the United States (1874–1964) Before Herbert Hoover entered politics he had gained a reputation as a dynamic businessman and ardent philanthropist. A wealthy mining engineer, Hoover became a millionaire before he turned 40. He first turned to public service during World War I when he headed the Commission for Relief in Belgium. In 1920 he was appointed secretary of commerce by President Warren Harding and continued to serve as secretary under Calvin Coolidge until 1929. During his tenure, Hoover created the Federal Radio Commission, which eventually became the Federal Communications Commission. In effect, Hoover shaped the broadcast industry. Shortly after he became president, America faced the crisis that would cast a shadow over Hoover's entire term. On October 24, 1929, the stock market crashed, which sparked a downward economic slide that led to the Great Depression. Economic conditions worsened throughout Hoover's administration. He attempted to increase loans to businesses, stabilize food prices, and encourage businesses to maintain employment and wages. He also refused to provide direct federal aid to the unemployed and dispossessed. Such a stance was in keeping with Hoover's belief in individualism and his fear of direct intervention programs sponsored by the federal government. But the public did not understand. Hoover lost nearly all his political support and he overwhelmingly lost his bid for reelection in 1932.

Hoover disappeared from the public eye for a time only to resurface in 1947 when he accepted President Truman's offer to lead the Commission on the Organization of the Executive Branch. Hoover remained active in the Republican Party until his death, at age 90, in 1964.

formulating department policy and operating programs associated with their operations; the U.S. Census Bureau, for example, operates under the authority of the ESA.

The Office of the Secretary is the main administrative office of the department. Many staff offices under the secretary's direct control are devoted to establishing and maintaining open relations with government officials and the public—for example, the Office of Business Liaison and the Office of White House Liaison. The secretary is also served by the offices of deputy secretary; general counsel; and inspector general; and the assistant secretaries of administration, legislative, and intergovernmental affairs; and public affairs.

Promoting a better understanding between business and consumers is the responsibility of the Office of Consumer Affairs, another administrative office. This office educates consumers and seeks to improve the quality of business services.

Another office under the secretary's direct control is the Office of Small and Disadvantaged Business Utilization, which differs from the MBDA in that its function is primarily administrative. It serves as the focal point for the department's efforts to increase contracts and awards to small, minority, and female business owners. It also ensures that an equitable number of commerce programs involve contracts with such businesses.

PRIMARY FUNCTIONS

One of the most versatile agencies in the U.S. government, the Department of Commerce administers programs to prevent unfair foreign trade competition, offers assistance and information to increase U.S. competitiveness in the world economy, provides socioeconomic statistics and analyses for business and government planners, and provides research and support for the increased use of scientific and technological development.

The department works to improve understanding of the earth's physical environment and oceanic resources, grants patents and registers trademarks, develops policies and conducts research on telecommunications, and assists in promoting domestic economic development and the growth of minority businesses. As varied as the department's services are, they are all related to the goal of working with the business community to foster economic growth and create new jobs.

PROGRAMS

The department operates many programs intended specifically to help Americans and businesses succeed. For example the Manufacturing Extension Partnership is a network of extension centers and experts who provide tech-

BUDGET:
Department of Commerce

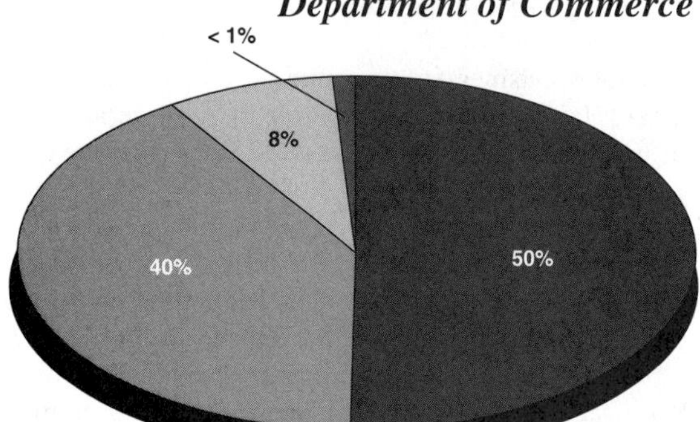

Education, Training, Employment, and Social Services

Community and Regional Development

Advancing and Regulating Commerce and Housing Credit

The National Oceanic and Atmospheric Administration's (NOAA) Operations in Natural Resources and the Environment

Percentage of Federal Budget

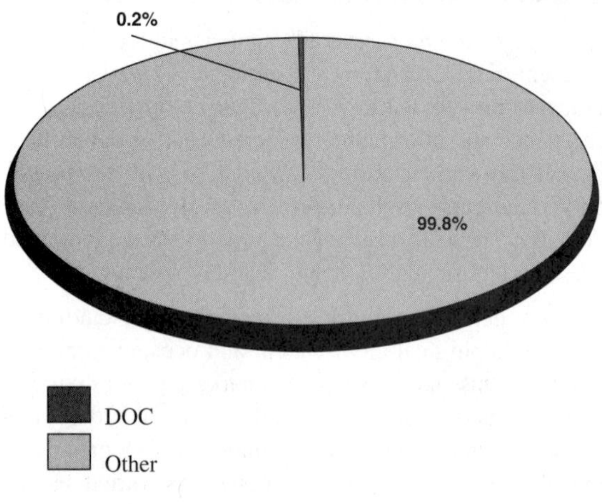

DOC

Other

nical and business-related assistance to small manufacturers adopting new technologies. The Public Telecommunications Facilities Program extends the delivery of public telecommunications services to U.S. citizens and seeks to increase ownership and management of these facilities by women and minorities. The Trade Adjustment Assistance Program provides technical assistance to certified firms and industries that have been economically damaged by the impact of decreasing imports.

BUDGET INFORMATION

In 1998 Congress appropriated the Commerce Department a budget of approximately $4 billion. The department's budget made up approximately 0.2 percent of the total federal budget of $1.653 trillion. Due to its diverse and extensive range of responsibilities (such as managing U.S. fish stocks, protecting the environment and endangered species, and predicting weather), the National Oceanic and Atmospheric Administration's (NOAA) operations in natural resources and the environment account for roughly half of the department's budget.

Most of the remainder of the budget, about 40 percent, goes to programs in the area of advancing and regulating commerce and housing credit. Of the programs in this area, the Bureau of the Census (15 percent) and the International Trade Administration account for most of the expenditures; the Census expenditures have grown remarkably in preparation for the decennial (2000) census. About 8 percent of the budget goes to community and regional development programs operated by the Economic Development Administration. A very small amount, less than 1 percent, goes to education, training, employment, and social services.

Nearly all of the department's budget is discretionary; that is, its activities and expenditures are not due to mandates required by law. Over the years, this has made the department a prime target for congressional efforts at cutting the budget—in 1996, many Republicans in Congress promoted the idea of eliminating the department entirely.

HISTORY

Early in the twentieth century, President Theodore Roosevelt and numerous government and business leaders believed the United States was not keeping up with its industrial competitors in promoting foreign trade. Out of this concern, the Department of Commerce was established in 1903 with George Cortelyou as its first secretary. The department absorbed many of the functions that had been previously scattered among other agencies. In its early years, officials often wondered what effect, if any, the new agency was having on the goal of increasing overseas trade; many of its formative years were spent resolving interdepartmental arguments and jealousies about priorities and funding.

During the administration of President Woodrow Wilson, the department gained some momentum under Secretary of Commerce William Redfield, who was able to negotiate, with some degree of success, the bureaucratic problems that plagued the department. (The Department of Commerce did not yet have its own building, and its eight units were scattered in Washington.) A new force of overseas commercial representatives was recruited from both the commerce and state departments, and branch offices were opened in several cities. During World War I (1914–18), the department's successes included innovative programs and research activities to aid in the war effort.

The Hoover Years

During the administrations of Warren Harding and Calvin Coolidge, the Department of Commerce was led by the energetic Herbert Hoover, under whom the department became a vast source of information and advice for U.S. industry and finance. The department also offered much assistance to U.S. business leaders in the form of advertising packaging for the export of goods.

Despite Hoover's enthusiasm his leadership suffered from profound inconsistencies. Hoover denounced other world powers for monopolizing critical natural resources such as rubber, yet he dreamed of U.S. control. He criticized foreign cartels and their manipulation of prices but defended U.S. tariff barriers on imports. This contradictory policy led to several squabbles with European powers and set a precedent for almost every administration since—presidents Jimmy Carter and Ronald Reagan imposed boycotts and economic bans against Soviet goods despite international opposition.

Another problem during the Hoover years was that existing laws and department rules did little to reduce the degree of speculation in foreign ventures, the investments that eventually led to the Great Depression, which brought the ruin of many investors. The Department of Commerce could only warn against the practice. In fact, the department did not oppose the surge in foreign investment as long as it was private in nature and served economically-productive ends. When the Great Depression hit in the late 1920s, U.S. foreign trade was at its lowest level since before World War I.

Rebuilding U.S. Trade

Following the Great Depression, the Department of Commerce assisted President Franklin Roosevelt's New Deal programs in rebuilding the U.S. economy. Together with restoring the economy's domestic infrastructure, the commerce and state departments collaborated on new trade agreements with foreign nations. Foreign trade suffered a setback with the approach of World War II (1939–45) however; and during this time armaments dominated the trade scene. The U.S. government became the top purchaser of U.S. arms production.

After the war, promotion of U.S. trade overseas changed remarkably. Efforts were concentrated on rebuilding war-torn areas, but this time such efforts were dominated by government rather than private investment. Indeed, a legacy of Roosevelt is the government's expanded role in economic planning and manipulation. Export controls went into place, and as the Cold War intensified the Department of Commerce promoted trade outside the Communist bloc. This was at least partially aimed at strengthening ties with and the positions of Western, democratic nations in an effort to build a unified front against Communist threats. By the 1950s serious concern over increasing foreign competition surfaced, and this unfavorable balance of trade has been a problem for the United States ever since.

Trade restrictions against Communist countries were relaxed with the cooling off of the Cold War. But the global economic changes of the 1980s and 1990s further intensified the competition for imports. The fall of the Soviet empire and its subsequent struggle to adopt a market economy coincided with the rise of Asian nations as economic powers, most notably Japan. The Department of Commerce faces the challenge of strengthening the U.S. economy through expanded trade while maintaining economic stability in a more-highly integrated and sometimes volatile global economy.

FAST FACTS

Exports support 11.5 million American jobs and have been responsible for one-third of U.S. economic growth since 1993.

(Source: Department of Commerce. "Statement of Policy Governing Department of Commerce Overseas Trade," 1998.)

CURRENT POLITICAL ISSUES

U.S. foreign trade is a particularly heated political issue. Basic market studies reveal that the United States, a nation that comprises just four percent of the world's population, is characterized by the following: an aging population and a low population growth rate; a mature economy that will develop slowly, not by leaps and bounds; and an economy that is driven by capital and technology. In contrast, many other nations in the world in the 1990s are characterized by the following: growing middle classes (and therefore growing consumer bases); rapid economic growth; ongoing industrialization; and greater accumulated wealth.

Economic power is growing worldwide, and the U.S. will probably not continue to enjoy its historical dominance in trade. The Department of Commerce sees its challenge as taking advantage of the growing economic opportunities around the world. Meeting this challenge, however, is not without obstacles—many of them involving American domestic politics.

Opening trade between two countries involves lowering tariffs and other barriers to imports as well as improving access for services trade. Simply stated, the corporate interests of the nation stand to profit greatly from the removal of trade barriers, while the working class is faced with an increased danger of losing jobs to cheaper foreign production.

Case Study: The North American Free Trade Agreement (NAFTA)

In January 1994 the United States, Canada, and Mexico implemented the North American Free Trade Agreement (NAFTA), a region-wide agreement to gradually eliminate tariffs and other barriers to trade, improve access for services trade, and create a consensus on rule-making, dispute settlement, investment, and intellectual property rights.

The signing of NAFTA created considerable debate nationwide. Corporate representatives praised it as a step toward free trade and a more open and competitive market, while advocates of blue-collar, middle-class U.S. workers denounced it as a blow to job security. The presidential candidate for the Reform Party, Ross Perot, warned Americans to be prepared for the "giant sucking sound" of jobs disappearing south across the Mexican border.

In its first year, U.S. export performance in North America did show substantial improvement, but it is also true that the Mexican labor force, whose wages are considerably lower (in 1997 the average starting wage at an assembly plant in Nuevo Laredo was 69 cents an hour), enjoyed much greater growth than its U.S. counterpart. In the future, job displacement could be significantly higher as tariffs continue to fall and trade grows.

NAFTA's effect on U.S. politics is perhaps best illustrated by the presidential campaign of 1996. The candidates—President Bill Clinton and Republican challenger Bob Dole—had both supported NAFTA but were conspicuously silent about the effects of the agreement. But the Clinton administration, hoping to avoid the loss of blue-collar votes in key Midwest states, took action. A NAFTA clause allowing Mexican trucks to make deliveries in border states was suspended, officially because of safety and drug trafficking issues, but more likely because of pressure from the powerful International Brotherhood of Teamsters labor union. Also, Florida vegetable growers were satisfied when the administration pressured Mexico to stop shipping $800 million worth of low-priced tomatoes daily into the United States. The White House no doubt noted that Florida had 25 electoral votes, while Mexico had none. As NAFTA continues to open trade between the U.S. and Mexico, the question of whether cheaper goods are enough to compensate for the loss of jobs will likely remain a significant political issue.

SUCCESSES AND FAILURES

The effects of Department of Commerce actions are typically complex and difficult to categorize as successful or not, especially when considering things like trade in which an advantage for one party is troublesome for another. Perhaps the clearest examples of the beneficial efforts of the Department of Commerce are its achievements in foreign tourism. Between 1961 and 1969 the U.S. Travel Service successfully increased the number of foreign visitors to the United States by 230 percent. By 1981 the number of foreign visitors further increased 1,400 percent, to 23 million. These visitors spent an estimated $14 billion. The Office of Travel and Tourism has since been absorbed by the International Trade Administration, but the number of foreign visitors continues to increase yearly. In 1996 39.2 million people visited the United States from Mexico, Canada, and overseas and spent just over $90 billion.

FUTURE DIRECTIONS

The Department of Commerce is undergoing several significant changes as it approaches the twenty-first century. According to its 1997 Strategic Plan, the department intends to adapt to the general environment of downsizing and resource limitations that all federal agencies must face by linking many of the activities involved in the departmental mission; for example, the department will coordinate the activities of the NOAA and the EDA to provide economic and technical assistance to distressed fishing communities while working to restore fish stocks to sustainable levels.

The department's clearest challenges lie in adapting to the remarkable changes in the global economy. The department intends to capitalize on the export opportunities opening up for U.S. businesses; according to its 1997 policy statement governing overseas trade missions, fully 96 percent of the potential consumers of U.S. goods and services are outside U.S. borders. The administration's goal is to increase U.S. exports to $1.2 trillion—double the 1992 amount—by 2000.

To increase exports the department intends to strengthen its cooperation with private business to carefully design and execute specific overseas trade missions in order to open markets, secure export and investment opportunities for U.S. businesses, and showcase U.S. products and technology around the world. In addition, the department plans to implement a rigorous authorization process for proposed trade missions to insure they succeed as planned. It also seeks to increase federal trade assistance aimed at small- and medium-sized businesses.

AGENCY RESOURCES

One of the department's most important information sources is the National Technical Information Service (NTIS), administered by the department's Technology Administration. The NTIS is the nation's largest central clearinghouse and government resource for scientific, technical, engineering, and other business-related information. For on-line access of NTIS documents, researchers may connect to FedWorld, a bulletin board service at http://www.fedworld.gov/. For information on how to order NTIS products call 1–800–553–6847 or send E-mail to Orders@ntis.fedworld.gov. NTIS titles are also available through http://www.ntis.gov in a new venture with the Government Research Center. For further information about the Department of Commerce or its operating programs contact the Office of Public Affairs at (202) 219-3605.

AGENCY PUBLICATIONS

Each of the department's operating programs produces many publications, including periodicals such as *Commerce Business Daily* and *Minority Business Today*, books such as the *Statistical Abstract of the United States*, and pamphlets such as "Tornado Safety." A list of publication contacts is available by fax from (202) 501-1191 ("Flash Facts").

These and other publications are announced in the weekly *Business Service Checklist*, which may be purchased from the Government Printing Office by calling (202) 783-3238. NTIS titles are also available through http://www.ntis.gov in a new venture with the Government Research Center.

BIBLIOGRAPHY

Breaking New Ground in U.S. Trade Policy. New York: Committee for Economic Development, 1991.

Cooper, Helene. "U.S. Trade Deficit Fell $6.47 Billion in Quarter but Rose 11.4% for Year." *Wall Street Journal,* 14 March, 1997, p. 128.

Desler, James. "New Metropolitan Export Figures Reveal Importance of Trade to Nation's Cities." *Business America,* November 1996, pp. 4–6.

Lenz, Allen J. *Beyond Blue Horizons: U.S. Trade Performance & International Competitiveness in the 1990s.* Westport, Conn.: Greenwood Publishing Group, 1990.

Rogowski, Ronald. *Commerce & Coalitions: How Trade Affects Domestic Political Alignments.* Princeton, N.J.: Princeton University Press, 1990.

Rosenberg, Mark B., ed. *The Changing Hemispheric Trade Environment: Opportunities and Obstacles.* Miami, Fla.: Florida International University, Latin American and Caribbean Center, 1991.

Sanger, David E. "Commerce Department Sets New Guidelines for Trade Missions." *New York Times,* 4 March 1997, p. A11.

"Taking the Politics out of Trade Missions." *Business Week,* 17 March 1997, p. 128.

Department of Defense (DoD)

ESTABLISHED: August 10, 1949
EMPLOYEES: 1.5 million on active duty in the armed forces; 1 million members of the reserve components; 900,000 civilian employees

Contact Information:

ADDRESS: Office of the Secretary
The Pentagon
Washington, DC 20301
PHONE: (703) 545-6700
FAX: (703) 697-2577
URL: http://www.dtic.mil/defenselink
SECRETARY OF DEFENSE: William S. Cohen
DEPUTY SECRETARY OF DEFENSE: John J. Hamre

WHAT IS ITS MISSION?

The fundamental mission of the Department of Defense (DoD) is to provide the military forces, agencies, and field activities needed to deter war and protect the security of the United States.

HOW IS IT STRUCTURED?

The DoD is a cabinet-level agency under the executive branch of the U.S. government. The department is headed by the secretary and deputy secretary of defense. Immediately under them is the Office of the Secretary of Defense, the Department of the Army, the Department of the Navy, the Department of the Air Force, the Joint Chiefs of Staff, the Unified Combatant Commands, and the Inspector General.

The secretary of defense is the primary defense policy adviser to the president, who is commander in chief of U.S. armed forces. The secretary of defense is responsible for formulating general defense policy and related policies and for executing approved policy. The secretary exercises authority, direction, and control over the DoD. Under the Office of the Secretary are various defense agencies and field activities that help fulfill the secretary's purpose, including the Office of Acquisition and Technology and the Office of Personnel and Readiness.

There are 15 defense agencies, and each is under the control of a particular office led by an administrator within the Office of the Secretary (the Ballistic Missile Defense Organization and the Defense Logistics Agency, for example, are supervised by the under secretary for acquisition and technology). The National Imagery and Mapping Agency and the National Security Agency, however, report directly to the secretary of defense. Agencies serve various purposes—many are combat-support agencies; others are oriented to policy or finance—but all are designed to fulfill some element of the mission of the DoD.

Likewise, the nine field activities of the DoD are supervised by administrators within the Office of the Secretary. For example, the American Forces Information Service, a defense field activity, is directed by the assistant secretary for public affairs, whereas the Defense Medical Programs Activity is led by the assistant secretary for health affairs.

The military departments are the Department of the Air Force, which seeks to defend the United States through control and exploitation of air and space; the Department of the Army, which operates the land combat and service forces along with such aviation and water transport as may be needed for these forces; and the Department of the Navy, which combines the Marine Corps with naval aviation forces to form the U.S. land- and sea-based military forces. Each military department is organized under its own secretary, who is responsible to the secretary of defense for the operation and efficiency of the department. The secretary of defense has ultimate control and authority over the military departments.

The nine Unified Combatant Commands are designated either geographically (e.g., the Atlantic Command) or by function (e.g., Strategic Command). Each is an interservice unit of military forces led by a commanding officer who is responsible to the president and the secretary of defense for accomplishing the military missions assigned to the command. The operational chain of command runs from the president to the secretary of defense to the commanders of the unified combatant commands. The chairman of the Joint Chiefs of Staff functions within the chain of command by passing on orders from the president or secretary of defense to the commanders.

The Joint Chiefs of Staff are led by the chairman, who is the principal military adviser to the president, the secretary of defense, and the National Security Council. Other members of the Joint Chiefs are military advisers who may provide additional information on request and who may submit their advice when it does not agree with that of the chairman. The Joint Chiefs of Staff assist in providing for the strategic direction and planning of the armed forces but have no executive authority to command combatant forces.

The Inspector General (IG) is responsible for serving as an independent and objective office that scrutinizes the operations of the DoD. The IG also analyzes how the DoD manages its functions and proposes methods of improving efficiency within the department.

PRIMARY FUNCTIONS

The DoD, through the secretary of defense and the president, is responsible for formulating and executing the defense policies of the United States. With the assistance of the Joint Chiefs of Staff, the Defense Department allocates resources to fulfill strategic plans, compares the capabilities of American and allied armed forces with those of potential adversaries, and assigns responsibilities within the armed forces.

The Departments of the Army, Air Force, and Navy are responsible for maintaining and operating land, air, and water-borne military forces for the United States. Each department contains numerous units devoted to accomplishing its task of carrying out the tasks assigned to them by the secretary of defense and the president. These missions may comprise humanitarian or combative objectives.

The secretary of defense and the Joint Chiefs of Staff are the primary advisers to the president concerning the military defense of the United States. With the help of support staffs, the secretary and the Joint Chiefs research and analyze information on situations around the world in which military intervention may be a necessity. They assist in devising policy that will result in the successful accomplishment of American objectives as established by the president.

The Unified Combatant Commands are responsible for executing the orders originating from the president and the secretary of defense. Coordinating their efforts with those of the Departments of the Army, Air Force, and Navy, the commands oversee missions after being assigned personnel from the necessary armed forces by the secretary of defense. The defense agencies and field activities are responsible for maintaining the health and preparedness of military personnel and with researching and developing new and advanced defense capabilities. Their functions are more limited in scope than those of the other sections of the DoD but are equally vital.

PROGRAMS

Most DoD programs are carried out by defense agencies or field activities divisions. The Office of Civilian Health and Medical Program of the Uniformed Services, for example, is one of the 15 defense field activities. It provides medical care to active duty and retired service members and their dependents and survivors. The Defense Department's development of ballistic missile defense systems is carried out by the Ballistic Missile Defense Organization, a defense agency.

There are a few programs, however, that are run directly by the Office of the Secretary of Defense. One of the most significant is the National Security Education Program (NSEP), created by the National Security

BUDGET:
Department of Defense

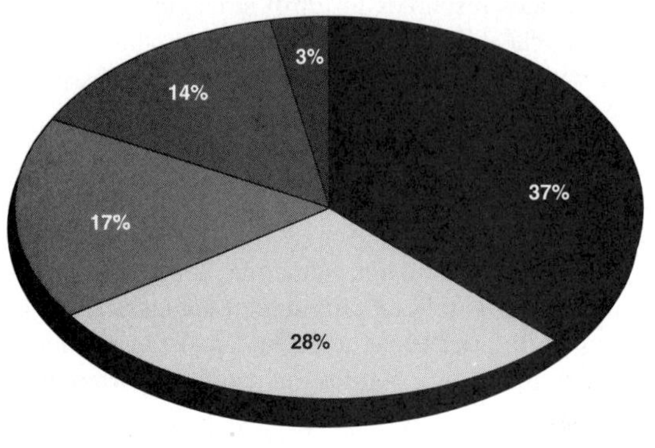

Construction of Military Facilities and Family Housing for Military Personnel

Research and Development

Acquiring New Weapons and Upgraded Capabilities for Modernization

Preserving Force Readiness and Supporting Ongoing Military Operations

Operation and Maintenance of Existing Programs, Forces, and Facilities

Percentage of Federal Budget

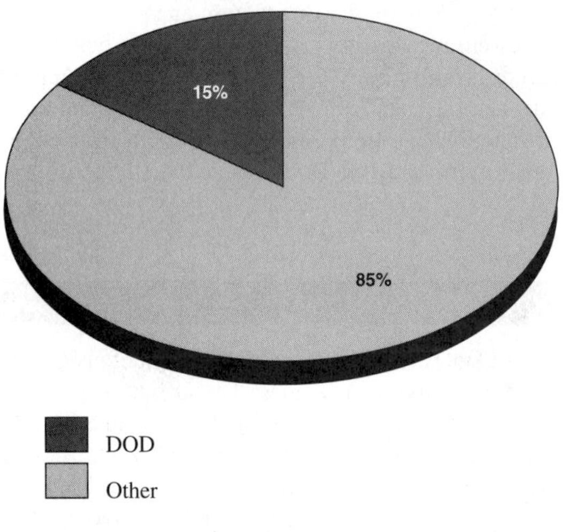

DOD

Other

Education Act of 1991. The NSEP is a grant program designed to underwrite the education of students who might some day help the United States remain engaged in global issues. It aims to develop a staff of professionals with expert knowledge of language and culture who will be able to help the United States make sound decisions on global issues related to U.S. security. The program awards scholarships to undergraduates for study abroad, fellowships to graduate students, and grants to U.S. institutions of higher education.

The DoD is also involved in international programs such as the North Atlantic Treaty Organization (NATO), an alliance of 16 independent nations that are committed to one another's defense. The North Atlantic Treaty was signed in Washington, D.C., on April 4, 1949, creating an alliance of 12 independent nations. Four more European nations later agreed to the treaty between 1952 and 1982. The DoD participates in this alliance by stationing its forces at military bases in Europe, conducting cooperative military and peacekeeping exercises such as the NATO intervention in the Bosnia crisis, and by participating in the planning and development of the European security structure.

BUDGET INFORMATION

For 1997 the DoD budget, which is part of the president's annual budget, totaled approximately $250 billion. The DoD budget accounted for about 15 percent of the federal government's total of $1.653 trillion.

The largest portion of the DoD's budget, about 37 percent, is spent on the operation and maintenance of existing programs, forces, and facilities. Approximately 28 percent is spent on preserving force readiness and supporting ongoing military operations. The DoD spends about 17 percent of its budget on acquiring new weapons and upgraded capabilities for modernization. Fourteen percent of the budget is spent on research, development, testing, and evaluation. The construction of military facilities and family housing for military personnel accounts for a little more than 3 percent of the budget.

HISTORY

Before World War II (1939–45) the U.S. armed forces were led by two separate departments: the War Department, which was concerned with land forces and had been created in 1789, and the Navy Department, established in 1798 to run the nation's sea forces. World War II, however, demonstrated the need for a unity of command and interservice cooperation of land, sea, and air forces, both at home and in foreign countries where U.S. armed forces were stationed. As a result, the National Military Establishment (NME) was established by the National Security Act of 1947.

International developments following the war also suggested the need to revise the structure of U.S. defense. Extensive technological changes in weapons systems and

BIOGRAPHY:

Mary Walker

Physician and Reformer (1832-1919) Dr. Mary Edwards Walker practiced medicine during the Civil War, attempted to change the way women were expected to dress, and was the first and only woman to receive the Congressional Medal of Honor. Walker attended Syracuse Medical College, and practiced medicine with her husband in Columbia, Ohio, and Rome, New York. When the Civil War broke out she offered her services to the medical corps but was turned away because of her gender. After working for two years as an unpaid volunteer, Walker was finally acknowledged and granted a salary. In 1865 she was captured and imprisoned, but was returned safely after being exchanged for a Confederate soldier. For this bravery and devotion General William Sherman recommended that she be awarded the Congressional Medal of Honor, which President Andrew Jackson presented to her on November 11, 1865. In her personal life, Walker was viewed as quite scandalous. She scorned conventional female attire, wore trousers, and was an ardent proponent of "dress reform." Such nontraditional behavior during a time in which women were expected to demonstrate more socially submissive ways, tended to alienate her. At one point she even made a living by performing in sideshows. After being alerted to this type of conduct, the Federal Board of Medal Awards withdrew her medal on June 3, 1917. Walker, however, refused to give up her medal and wore it until she died three years later at the age of 67. On June 10, 1977, through the efforts of her family and members of Congress, Walker's medal was restored.

the advent of new warfare capabilities, such as the atomic bomb and air power, required development and deployment decisions based solely on national security needs rather than on the desires of a particular armed service. It also became clear that the United States would be called upon to play a much more active role in future world events, a policy much different from its previous detachment before World War II. The need for a national defense policy, one that would be formulated in anticipation of international developments, became urgent.

Unfortunately, the National Security Act of 1947 was not as strong as President Harry Truman had envisioned. Although the act established the post of secretary of defense, the new administrator, former Navy Secretary James V. Forrestal, soon discovered that his powers to direct and control the nation's defense were insufficient to promote unity within the NME. The nation's armed forces had long maintained an interservice rivalry that had been considered healthy until the army, navy, and air force began to compete for funds and resources.

On August 10, 1949, an executive agency, the Department of Defense, replaced the NME by amendments of the National Security Act. The three service branches became military departments, rather than executive departments under the amendments, and the secretary of defense was granted "direction, authority, and control over the Department of Defense."

Further Changes

The 1949 amendments presented substantial improvements, but continued interservice rivalry over roles, missions, weapons, and budgets, along with the Korean War (1950–53), made clear the need for further strengthening of the secretary of defense's power to unify. In accordance with the recommendations of his advisers, President Dwight D. Eisenhower submitted Reorganization Plan #6 to Congress, and it was quickly enacted into law in June 1953. The plan abolished several agencies, including the Munitions Board and the Research and Development Board, and transferred their functions to the secretary of defense. The plan also authorized six additional assistant secretaries to serve the Office of the Secretary and granted the chairman of the Joint Chiefs of Staff greater power to select and lead the Joint Staff.

The changes brought about by Eisenhower's reorganization plan were dramatic, but it took only a few more years for them to prove insufficient as well. In scientific and technological accomplishments, the United States had fallen behind the Soviet Union, as was shockingly evident upon the launch of the first Sputnik satellite into space in October 1957, and many held the Defense Department responsible. President Eisenhower and his advisers blamed the lack of progress on inefficiency and duplication of efforts growing, once again, out of interservice rivalry.

FAST FACTS

In 1863 Congress made the Medal of Honor a means of decorating soldiers who distinguished themselves by their bravery in action. Since then almost 3,400 men and one woman have received the award.

(Source: American Forces Information Service. "Armed Forces Decorations and Awards," 1997.)

New legislation proposed by Eisenhower and passed by Congress in 1958 granted the defense secretary authority to transfer, consolidate, or outright abolish certain functions. The secretary was also given the authority to reassign noncombat functions, along with the authority to reassign procurement, production, and operational control of new weapons systems to a particular service. Finally, the defense secretary had the control needed to effectively lead the DoD. Along with the secretary of state, the defense secretary became, and has remained, one of the two most important individuals in the cabinet.

The amendments of 1958 were the last major revisions of the National Security Act of 1947. Since then other organizational changes have been made. For instance, a 1977 law established two under secretary positions, for policy and for research and engineering.

When the Soviet Union collapsed in 1992, the United States no longer had a single powerful enemy toward which its defense policies and installations were focused. Instead, the DoD began to base its policies and strategies on the idea that threats to national security could now come from any part of the world, with very short notice. Reorganizations of the U.S. defense structure were initiated in order to make the military more streamlined, flexible, and efficient. In 1995, in line with these objectives, the Defense Department initiated its Base Realignment and Closure (BRAC) initiative, which would reduce the number of active military bases in the United States and combine the functions of others.

In 1997, the DoD announced it would launch reforms that would rethink the way the defense structure was managed. The Defense Reform Initiative (DRI), introduced by Secretary of Defense William Cohen, was to be an attempt at consolidating and strengthening the installations and forces of the Defense Department, in large part by applying the business management practices of the private sector to the DoD command structure.

CURRENT POLITICAL ISSUES

One of the most serious issues facing the DoD is the increasing role and presence of women in the armed forces. The role of female personnel did not appear to be significant until the 1980s, when women first started joining the military in significant numbers, and it was not until the Clinton administration that women soldiers were routinely accepted into combat situations. Women now serve on warships and fly combat planes but are still held back from front line infantry, armor, and artillery units. The military has gone to great lengths to accommodate the presence of women in the military, but, for a variety of reasons, the armed forces have a long way to go before there is complete gender integration.

Physical Differences

One of the most difficult problems for the military involves the basic anatomical differences between men and women. In order to be an effective fighting force, the infantry depends on "units" of interchangeable soldiers. Women are on average about five inches shorter than men, have 37 percent less muscle mass, have lower aerobic capacity, and carry a lighter skeleton. Many military officials argue that as a result most women are simply unfit for, say, an artillery position, in which soldiers are routinely called upon to lift shell casings that weigh nearly one hundred pounds. Male soldiers often complain that training exercises have been modified to soften the blow for female recruits. An obstacle course at one training ground was renamed the "confidence course," and female recruits were often not held to an objective standard but were asked to perform timed exercises in which they were to do the best they could. This new emphasis on self-esteem and cooperation, rather than competition and survival, has led critics to claim that the military's approach to training women recruits is a form of political correctness that has been adopted from the civilian culture but has no place in a military culture where the stakes are so high. As long as women are held to a different standard, they claim, the military will have two unequal classes of soldiers.

Case Study: The USS Acadia

Another problem accompanying the increasing number of women in the military has arisen in the peacetime operations of forces, when recruits, between 18 and 25 years old, are housed far from home in ships, coed tents, or barracks and subjected to long periods of loneliness, boredom, or stress. Sex between superior officers and subordinates is strongly prohibited in the military, but sex between personnel of equal rank is permitted. This has presented the military with a new, unanticipated problem—pregnancy. The rate of pregnancy in the military is already high and shows no signs of decreasing. On the USS *Acadia*, a navy ship mockingly called "the Love Boat" by members of the press, 36 of the 360 women sailors aboard had to be evacuated during a tour of the Persian Gulf because they had become pregnant.

Case Study: Tailhook Connection and Aberdeen Proving Ground

Perhaps the most disturbing problem facing the military is the discrimination and harassment encountered by women in a traditionally male culture that has used hazing to shame or bully weaker members into meeting a certain standard. Unfortunately, many male officers and enlisted men have chosen to harass women recruits for entirely different reasons. The 1990s seemed to reveal one scandal after another, from the sexual harassment of female naval personnel at the navy's Tailhook Convention in 1991 to the sexual harassment and rape of female recruits by male drill instructors at the army's Aberdeen Proving Ground in 1996. One instructor, Sgt. Delmar Simpson, was convicted on 18 counts of rape involving female recruits. It is clear from these events that much progress is yet to be made in the sexual attitudes of the military culture; Pentagon surveys reveal that about 75 percent of women in the military have experienced some form of sexual harassment.

The scandals have made many people wonder whether the integration of women into the armed forces is a failed experiment. Conservatives maintain that armies exist to fight and win wars, not to be test cases for social engineering. But in practical terms there is no turning back; the armed forces would not be able to meet its recruitment quotas without women, who now make up nearly 15 percent of the military, in contrast to 2 percent at the end of the Vietnam War.

SUCCESSES AND FAILURES

The United States suffered its greatest military failure and humiliation in the Vietnam War. American objectives never seemed clear and were often changed in the middle of operations as a result of domestic political pressures. The American public became strongly opposed to the war effort, and tens of thousands of U.S. service personnel were killed in the conflict. To this day, many Americans are skeptical of U.S. military involvement in foreign conflicts that do not appear to have a direct effect on U.S. interests.

It was not surprising, then, that Americans were skeptical in the fall of 1990 when President George Bush began to make public statements threatening war against the Iraqi regime of Saddam Hussein, who had orchestrated an August 2 invasion and occupation of the small nation of Kuwait. As U.S. military forces built up in the Persian Gulf and in nearby Saudi Arabia, many members of Congress and the public denounced the war threat as a move to protect the supply of crude oil. Kuwait was an oil-producing nation, and many believed its invasion could be the first in an Iraqi campaign to corner the international oil market. President Bush and members of the administration, however, insisted that if a war were fought it would be fought primarily to restore the freedom and independence of the innocent people of Kuwait. Political analysts and members of Congress theorized that the Bush administration's apparent support for Hussein's rise to power denoted a remarkable failure in defense intelligence and that war could have been avoided if the administration and the Defense Department had used foresight.

Whatever miscalculations might have led to the war, and whatever its primary political objectives, there is no disputing that the Persian Gulf War was a remarkable military success. The war, which began with the U.S. invasion of Baghdad on January 17, 1991, ended a little more than five weeks later. The United States lost 148 soldiers in the war; the Iraqis lost approximately 100,000.

FUTURE DIRECTIONS

During the 1990s, Secretary of Defense William Cohen and Chairman of the Joint Chiefs of Staff General John Shalikashvili set out to develop a plan for the future of the armed forces. The plan, called Joint Vision 2010, is a template for how the U.S. armed forces will achieve better effectiveness in joint military operations. In a 1997 speech, Secretary Cohen summed up the strategic objectives of the plan. The first is to shape the global security environment in ways that promote and protect U.S. interests. The second is to maintain a strong, ready force that will be able to respond quickly and decisively when those interests are threatened. Departmental advisers have determined that in the future U.S. armed forces must be capable of fighting and winning two major theater wars nearly simultaneously. This will ensure a responsible approach to deterring opportunism by nations that might seek to gain advantage while the United States is engaged in a war elsewhere. The third objective of Joint Vision 2010 is to prepare for such threats, largely through taking advantage of the revolution in information technology. Joint Vision 2010 asserts that technology will transform the way our forces fight.

The authors of Joint Vision 2010 reached several conclusions. If the plan is carried out the way it was envisioned, U.S. forces will be smaller, more streamlined, more versatile, and more agile. They will need fewer weapons platforms and will be able to direct lethal fire to the appropriate targets, causing less collateral damage (accidental damage to people or property not targeted in a specific military attack), less "friendly fire" (detonation or weapons discharge accidentally directed toward one's own troops), and fewer casualties. They will be able to surprise and overwhelm the enemy, and end battles quickly on their own terms. The DoD believes that the key to successfully fulfilling the promise of Joint

Venture 2010 is to maintain a balanced focus, one that looks at the dangers and opportunities of the present day as well as the potential risks and events of the future.

AGENCY RESOURCES

Further information about the DoD can be obtained through the Office of the Assistant Secretary for Public Affairs, The Pentagon, Washington, DC 20301; phone (703) 695-2113, or through a public affairs officer at the nearest military installation. Information about particular branches of service can be obtained from the following offices: Office of the Director of Public Affairs, Department of the Air Force, 1670 Air Force Pentagon, Washington, DC 20330, (703) 697-6061; Office of the Chief of Public Affairs, Department of the Army, Washington, DC 20310, (703) 694-0741; Office of Information, Department of the Navy, Washington, DC 20350, (703) 697-7391; Commandant and Director of Public Affairs, U.S. Marine Corps, Washington, DC 20380, (703) 614-1492.

Each defense agency also has its own public affairs office, which can be accessed through the assistant secretary's office or the nearest military installation. A great deal of information is available through DefenseLINK at http://defenselink.mil/, the Defense Department's World Wide Web information service. Links include the Defense Fact File at http://www.dtic.mil/defenselink/factfile and the Armed Forces Information Service at http://www.dtic.mil/defenselink/afis.

AGENCY PUBLICATIONS

The DoD offers a vast array of publications, from the armed services newspaper *Stars and Stripes*, to magazines for specific service members such as *Marines* magazine and *Soldier: The Official U.S. Army Magazine*. Other publications intended for servicemen but available to the public include the *Army Weapon Systems Handbook* and the *Cooperative Threat Reduction Handbook*. The department also makes a number of pamphlets, public statements, and statistical reports available to the public, such as "The Pentagon," an informational brochure; the *Organization and Functions Guidebook*; and the *Annual Report to the President and the Congress*.

Many defense publications are available on-line through either DefenseLINK or the National Technical Information Service (http://www.fedworld.gov/ntis/ntishome/html). Other publications are available through the Superintendent of Documents, Government Printing Office, Washington, DC 20402; phone (202) 512-1800.

BIBLIOGRAPHY

Barry, John and Evan Thomas. "At War Over Women." *Newsweek*, 12 May 1997, pp. 48–49.

Borger, Gloria, et al. "Losing Time?" *U.S. News and World Report*, 16 December 1996, p. 19.

Fulghum, David A., and Paul Mann. "Military Modernization with a Budget Boost." *Aviation Week and Space Technology*, 30 September 1996, p. 28.

Kapstein, Ethan. *Downsizing Defense*. Washington, D.C.: Congressional Quarterly Books, 1993.

Krauss, Clifford. "Pentagon Priority Remains Readiness over New Arms." *New York Times*, 28 January 1997, p. A8.

Manigart, P. *Future Roles, Missions, & Structures of the Current Forces in the New World Order: The Public View*. Commack, N.Y.: Nova Science Publishers, Inc., 1995.

"Money Dictating Defense." *Navy Times*, 19 May 1997, p. 26.

Pulley, John. "DoD Faces Privatization, Downsizing." *Federal Times*, 6 January 1997, p. 15.

Redesigning Defense: Planning the Transition to the Future U.S. Industrial Base. Washington, D.C.: Congress of the United States, Office of Technology Assessment, 1991.

Ricks, Thomas E. "The Great Society in Camouflage." *Atlantic Monthly*, December 1996, pp. 24–29.

Sherlock, Richard J. "New Realities, Old Pentagon Thinking." *Wall Street Journal*, 24 April 1997, p. A18.

Smith, Perry M. *Pentagon: The Insider's Guide to the Potomac Puzzle Palace*. McLean, Va.: Brassey's, 1993.

Willis, G. E. "Perry Reviews the Army of the Future." *Army Times*, 18 November 1996, pp. 29–30.

Department of Education (DOE)

WHAT IS ITS MISSION?

The Department of Education states that its mission is to "ensure equal access to education and promote educational excellence throughout the nation." It supports and complements the efforts of states, local school systems, parents, and students to improve the quality of education. Historically the aim of the department was to support institutions of higher learning. In the twentieth century, its mission expanded to provide leadership in establishing public high schools and elementary schools as a means of providing educational opportunities to all Americans. Efforts by the Department of Education to ensure access to educational opportunities for all children regardless of race, gender, or disability are a direct result of efforts ranging from civil rights legislation of the 1960s to the Americans with Disabilities Act enacted in 1990.

HOW IS IT STRUCTURED?

The Department of Education (DOE) is a cabinet-level department that operates within the executive branch of the federal government and is directed by the secretary of education who is nominated by the president and confirmed by Congress. The department has ten administrative offices that perform external relations, budget, operational, financial and legal functions. Its seven program offices are Bilingual Education and Minority Languages Affairs; Civil Rights; Educational Research and Improvement; Elementary and Secondary Education; Postsecondary Education; Vocational and Adult Education; and Special Education and Rehabilitative Services.

ESTABLISHED: May 4, 1980
EMPLOYEES: 4,900

Contact Information:

ADDRESS: 600 Independence Ave. SW
Washington, DC 20202
PHONE: (202) 708-5366
TOLL FREE: (800) 872-5327
URL: http://www.ed.gov
SECRETARY OF EDUCATION: Richard W. Riley

FAST FACTS

Department of Education financial aid programs help over seven million students attend college annually.

(Source: Department of Education. http://www.ed.gov (1998).)

The department's ten regional offices are headed by a regional representative of the secretary of education. The regional offices serve as liaisons to state, local, and private education organizations and promote federal education policies and initiatives.

PRIMARY FUNCTIONS

In the United States, education is primarily a state and local responsibility. The federal government fills in the gaps in state and local support for education when critical national needs arise. The DOE provides leadership to address issues in American education by creating partnerships such as the Family Involvement Partnership for Learning, a long-term agreement with states, communities, and more than 130 national organizations that represent schools, parents, employers, and religious groups to provide support to families to help their children learn.

The DOE collects and shares information on education to help decision makers improve their schools. For example, in 1994 the department published *Strong Families, Strong Schools*, which summarizes 30 years of research on increasing family involvement in education. This information was used by states and local school districts to make decisions about creating and funding family involvement activities such as reading clubs, field trips, and in-home visits.

The federal government funds about 75 percent of all financial aid for college students, and helping families pay for college is a primary function of the DOE. The nation's economic productivity relies on a well-trained workforce, and its social and political structure relies on well-informed citizens.

The department also helps local schools and communities meet the needs of their students with funds to improve safety in schools, attract and train better teachers, promote drug-free schools, and increase parent involvement.

The DOE's Office of Civil Rights is responsible for enforcing the federal laws that prohibit discrimination by recipients of federal education funds on the basis of race, color, national origin, gender, disability, or age.

PROGRAMS

The Department of Education operates more than 200 programs that touch on every level and area of education. DOE programs include those that collect and disseminate information on schools and teaching, such as the Eisenhower National Clearinghouse for Mathematics and Science Education (ENC) and the Educational Resources Information Center (ERIC). The DOE prints and processes the Free Application for Federal Student Aid (FAFSA), the form used to determine financial aid for college students. Federal financial aid is delivered from the federal government through the DOE's Pell Grant program and two major student loan programs. The Federal Pell Grant Program makes grants averaging $1,500 to nearly four million postsecondary students annually. The William D. Ford Direct Loan Program provides $10 billion in direct federal loans to more than 1,500 schools and more than 2.1 million students and parent borrowers. The Federal Family Education Loan Program provides loan subsidies and guarantees against default on loans made to students by private lenders.

Goals 2000 is the department's flagship education program to help parents, teachers, and community leaders improve their schools by raising academic standards, addressing safety and discipline issues, attracting and training better teachers, and improving parent involvement.

Title I programs help disadvantaged children through preschools, tutors, equipment, and mentoring. The Safe and Drug Free Schools program addresses the growing crises of violence and drugs in schools through drug abuse and violence prevention programs. DOE grant programs enable schools to meet the needs of students with disabilities in programs serving children from birth to age 21.

The School-to-Work Opportunities Act is administered jointly by the Department of Education and the Department of Labor and provides funding for states and communities to create job readiness programs. Students in these programs combine school-based and work-based learning in preparation for employment.

BUDGET INFORMATION

Congress allocates the entire budget of the DOE and has approved moderate annual increases as education has become a top priority for the nation. The DOE contributes 5 percent to the nation's total educational expenditures with the other 95 percent being paid by state and local funds.

From a 1997 budget of approximately $33 billion, 39 percent was spent on post-secondary education, mainly student financial aid. Thirty-one percent of DOE funds are spent on elementary education programs; 20 percent on special education and rehabilitative services; and 9 percent on other services including vocational and adult education, educational reform, and educational research. About 1 percent of the DOE budget is spent on administrative costs. The Department of Education's budget makes up approximately 2 percent of the total federal budget of $1.653 trillion.

BUDGET:

Department of Education

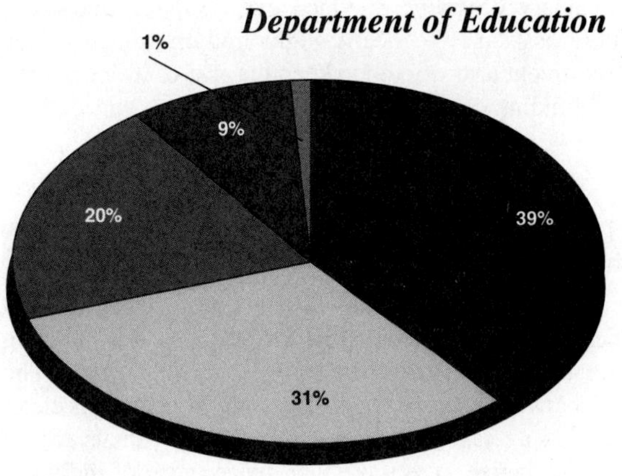

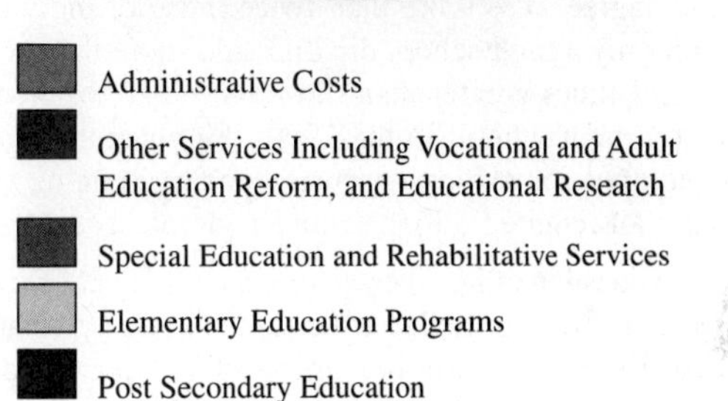

Percentage of Federal Budget

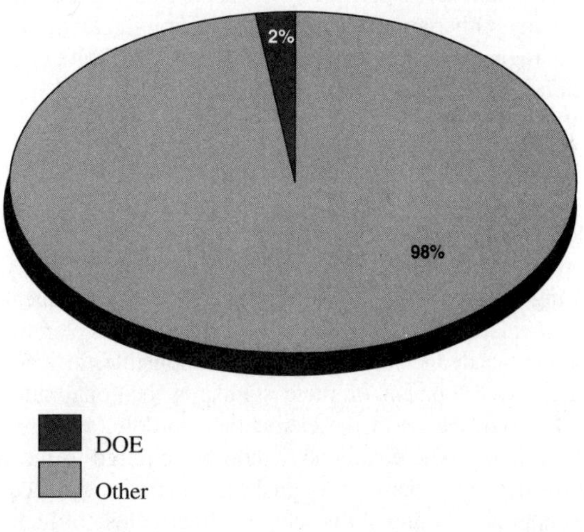

DOE
Other

HISTORY

The original Department of Education was created by Congress in 1867 to collect information on schools and teaching that would help the states establish effective school systems. About a year later, it was abolished and its functions transferred to a new Office of Education in the Department of the Interior. Legislation in 1890 gave this office responsibility for supporting the original system of land grant colleges and universities. Vocational education became the next major area of federal aid to schools in 1917, and the 1946 George-Barden Act focused on agricultural, industrial, and home economics training for high school students. Throughout this period, however, the office remained a relatively minor agency which primarily concerned itself with collecting statistics.

World War II (1939–45) led to a significant expansion of federal involvement in education. The G.I. Bill provided financial assistance to more than eight million veterans returning from the war for postsecondary education. When the Soviet Union beat the United States in launching the first satellite (*Sputnik I*) in 1957, Congress responded in part by passing the National Defense Education Act in 1958 to improve America's science and math programs. This began what would soon be a massive expansion of the Office of Education. Civil rights legislation in the 1960s called for the office to ensure equal access to education for all including women, the handicapped, and African Americans. The Elementary and Secondary Education Act of 1965 had the office providing assistance to low-income school districts.

Led by the National Education Association (NEA), educators claimed for many years that federal educational activities deserved full and individual membership in the cabinet. By 1970 the Office of Education, now part of the Department of Health, Education, and Welfare, had a larger budget than many cabinet departments. Despite criticism from those who believed that the federal government should not be involved in education, the Office of Education became the Department of Education in 1980.

This new status was not without controversy, however, and when Ronald Reagan became president in 1981, he sought to eliminate the new department. The DOE survived, but with reduced staff and budgets. Many educational programs remained under the control of other agencies, so that the department never truly became the controlling agency for federal education policy that its supporters had envisioned.

In the 1990s the DOE's elementary and secondary programs served 15,000 school districts and more than 50 million students attending more than 85,000 public schools and 26,000 private schools each year. Its postsecondary programs provided grants, loans, and work study assistance to nearly eight million students. The department also worked to keep the size of its workforce and funding down, with some success.

CURRENT POLITICAL ISSUES

In an era of international economic competition and increasing use of technology, Americans are realizing that a good education is more important than ever. The link between education and economic well-being is clear. In 1994 average annual earnings for individuals with a college degree were more than twice those of individuals with only a high school diploma and more than two-and-a-half times greater than those who had not graduated from high school. In the 1990s, 89 percent of new jobs required some form of postsecondary training and virtually all required a high school diploma.

The question of how best to prepare young people for the world of work or higher education is a highly volatile political issue. Education is a priority for American citizens and politicians alike, but the role of the federal government—in particular, the DOE—is hotly debated. Some groups advocate a larger role for the DOE through legislation and expanded programs. These groups see education as a national responsibility to ensure a strong national economy. Other groups support downsizing the DOE and encouraging states and local school districts to resolve educational issues based on community needs.

Case Study: National Education Standards

President Bill Clinton's 1997 State of the Union address outlined a ten-point education plan that placed the Department of Education at the heart of controversy by calling for an initiative to develop high national education standards. The DOE supports the president's plan for national academic standards and is responsible for leading the development of these standards. National standards would be set at the elementary, middle, and high school levels where students would be required to meet performance standards in English, mathematics, science, and applied learning skills such as effective use of technology and communication skills. National education standards are intended to challenge high-achieving students and identify those who need additional assistance.

While such standards have been supported by many segments of the education community, some groups fear that the influence of the DOE will broaden and ultimately prove detrimental to schools at the local level. It has been suggested that DOE regulations have created a need to increase nonteaching staff just to handle required paperwork. Other groups feel that standards are meaningless in improving education outcomes and that competition between schools, with parents allowed to choose the school their children attend, is the preferred method. These groups feel that the DOE can do more to improve education by cutting national programs that they believe don't work, like bilingual education, and allowing those dollars to be spent on improving local schools, training teachers, and creating more classrooms. The argument between increasing federal involvement and reducing federal requirements will continue to place the DOE in the line of fire from parents, educators, and Congress.

SUCCESSES AND FAILURES

The DOE has claimed a victory in the approved budget allocation for increasing direct federal loans to college students. The direct loan program reduces bureaucracy and cuts out middlemen in the student loan process. Direct lending is expected to save taxpayers $6 billion to $8 billion by 2000. However, many universities are wary of, and opting out of, the program, citing past government defaults on loans. The 1994 School-to-Work Opportunities Act, administered jointly by the Department of Education and the Department of Labor, provides funding to every state and to interested communities to develop school-to-work programs.

The DOE has also provided over $2 billion annually to assist one million adults with disabilities in finding employment and living independently. Over 200,000 individuals are placed each year in jobs that enable them to earn 80 percent of their total income and therefore reduce their reliance on public assistance.

School-to-work partnerships are also increasing through DOE support and guidelines. Mentoring programs link students with business leaders, and job shadowing programs allow students to follow the activities of people working in specific employment areas. Job preparation classes, apprenticeships, and credits for work experience allow students to begin the transition to the workforce with improved skills.

FUTURE DIRECTIONS

Secretary of Education Richard Riley developed a common agenda for the Department of Education based on President Clinton's 1997 State of the Union address. Family involvement in education will be a top priority, focusing on ways to involve parents and siblings in learning experiences at home and in school. The DOE will also be leading the America Reads Challenge, a national effort to make sure every child can read well and independently by the end of the third grade.

Training on and the use of technologies will also be a focal point for the DOE well into the twenty-first century. In 1996 President Clinton asked Congress to fund a

$2 billion, five-year Technology Literacy Challenge to connect every school and classroom in the United States to the Internet, provide computer access to all students and teachers, develop software and on-line learning as part of the school curriculum, and provide teachers with training to enable them to help students learn through technology.

Technology Innovation Challenge Grants encourage school systems, colleges, universities, and businesses to collaborate on projects that create new ways of learning through technology. Each federal grant dollar must be matched by more than three local dollars, and each project will creatively integrate technology to improve teaching and increase learning.

AGENCY RESOURCES

The Department of Education houses a vast amount of information for teachers, administrators, students, parents, and others with a stake in education. The department's Educational Resources Information Center (ERIC) can be contacted by phone at 1-800-538-3742 or via the Internet at http://ericir.syr.edu. Information and publications about DOE programs and activities is available by calling 1-800-872-5327. Many DOE publications are available through the DOE Web site at http://www.ed.gov.

AGENCY PUBLICATIONS

DOE publications include "Student Guide to Financial Aid," "Excelling in Math and Science," "What Should I know About ED Grants?" and "Guide to U.S. Department of Education Programs." Newsletters, publications for parents, and education statistics are also available. Contact the DOE by mail at 600 Independence Ave. SW, Washington, DC 20202, by telephone at 1-800-872-5327, or contact the DOE's Web site at http://www.ed.gov.

BIBLIOGRAPHY

Applebome, Peter. "New Call for Support of Clinton on Schools." *New York Times*, 19 February 1997.

Burd, Stephen. "Still Waiting for Student Aid; Delays Leave High School Seniors in the Lurch." *Chronicle of Higher Education*, 3 May 1996.

Dority, Barbar. "The Ideology of Cultural Conformity." *The Humanist*, May–June 1995, p. 37.

"Education Department Orders Georgia School District to End Racial Tracking." *Jet*, 3 July 1995, p. 22.

Healy, Patrick. "Education Department Urges Public Colleges to Keep Affirmative Action Programs." *Chronicle of Higher Education*, 3 May 1996.

Leiter, Lisa. "Education Expelled?" *Insight on the News*, 3 July 1995, p. 20.

Leonard, Bill. "From School to Work." *HR Magazine*, July 1996, p. 74.

Marsh, Ann. "Uncle Scam." *Forbes*, 3 June 1996, p. 12.

"President Announces Grants for Computers in Classrooms." *New York Times*, 9 February 1997.

"A Quick Look at the Current State of the Teaching Profession: Teachers 10 Years After *A Nation at Risk*." *Education Digest*, December 1996.

Wells, Robert Marshall. "GOP Plan Would Close Doors of Department in a Year." *Congressional Quarterly Weekly Report*, 27 May 1995.

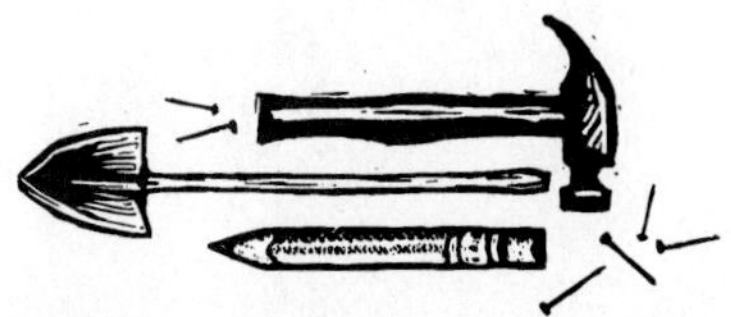

GET INVOLVED:

The America Reads Challenge is a program instituted by President Bill Clinton with the intended result that every child in the United States be able to read well and independently by the third grade. There are many ways to get involved with this vital initiative. Read to a child for 30 minutes once a week or volunteer for an area literacy program. Encourage book-borrowing at the local library or other outside-of-school reading by establishing or participating in an elementary school reading program.

Department of Energy (DOE)

ESTABLISHED: October 1, 1977
EMPLOYEES: 18,555

Contact Information:

ADDRESS: 1000 Independence Ave. SW
Washington, DC 20585
PHONE: (202) 586-5000
URL: http://www.doe.gov
SECRETARY OF ENERGY: Bill Richardson

WHAT IS ITS MISSION?

As stated by the Department of Energy (DOE), its mission is "to contribute to the welfare of the nation by providing the technical information and scientific and educational foundation for technology, policy and institutional leadership necessary to achieve efficiency in energy use, diversity in energy sources, a more productive and competitive economy, improved environmental quality, and a secure national defense." The DOE provides the framework for a comprehensive national energy plan that encompasses energy, national security, environmental management, science, and technology research and programs. In recent years the DOE's mission has expanded to include long-term planning for nuclear power and weapons waste in light of growing dependence on nuclear energy and the reduction of nuclear weapons stockpiles.

HOW IS IT STRUCTURED?

The DOE is a cabinet-level department and is part of the executive branch of the federal government. At the head of the DOE is the secretary, who is responsible for the overall planning, direction, and control of all departmental activities. The secretary is appointed by the president and confirmed by the Senate. The DOE contains several offices that focus on internal and nontechnical responsibilities including Field Management; Congressional and Intergovernmental Affairs; Policy and International Affairs; Environment, Safety, and Health; Human Resources and Administration; Inspector General; General Counsel; Public Affairs; Hearings and

Appeals; Chief Financial Officer; and Economic Impact and Diversity. These offices perform financial, administrative, personnel, and public relations functions for the DOE. Offices that provide technical direction and support and oversee large budget programs are divided into three main categories: energy, weapons/waste cleanup, and science and technology.

The DOE is headquartered in Washington, D.C., and has eight operations offices and two field offices throughout the United States. The DOE also controls five power administrations in the United States that market and transmit electric power. In addition, the Federal Energy Regulatory Commission is an independent regulatory organization within the DOE.

FAST FACTS

The DOE's Partnerships for Affordable Housing will install energy efficiency improvements in at least one million low- to moderate-income housing units by 2000, achieving average efficiency increases of 20 to 30 percent.

(Source: Department of Energy. "News Briefs," 1997.)

PRIMARY FUNCTIONS

The DOE was created to deal with the national problem of dwindling supplies of coal, oil, and natural gas and the increasing dependence on foreign sources of fuel. It is responsible for fostering more-efficient technologies for the utilization of energy resources, sponsoring efforts to explore and utilize alternative energy resources, and regulating energy production. The DOE is also involved with nuclear weapons and nuclear energy programs, the result of a historical pattern of placing nuclear technology under scientific rather than military control.

Energy research and regulation are the primary functions of the DOE. It also provides information on the impact of energy needs and consumption to other segments of the federal government and to state governments. The DOE also works with other government departments to reduce energy waste in federal programs. Close collaboration with federal agencies such as the Environmental Protection Agency (EPA), the Nuclear Regulatory Commission (NRC), and the Bureau of Mines is necessary to create energy plans that meet a variety of needs and interests. The DOE must juggle the conflicting interests of consumers, environmentalists, industry, and government in pursuing sound energy policies, programs, and technology.

PROGRAMS

The DOE operates programs that research and develop nuclear technologies; waste disposal systems; solar, wind, and natural gas resources; and energy information resources. For example, the Federal Energy Management Program helps federal agencies find ways to save energy, use renewable energy sources, and conserve water by developing partnerships between agencies and private utility companies.

Other programs include the Motor Challenge, a collaborative effort between the DOE and the automotive industry to develop engines that are more energy efficient and environmentally sound. The Radioactive Waste Management Program and the Stockpile Stewardship and Management Program oversee the maintenance of nuclear weapons and the disposal of nuclear waste materials.

The Pollution Prevention Program (PPP) provides government agencies, industry, and the public with information on how to reduce pollutants, reuse and recycle materials, and treat, store, and dispose of waste. The DOE has established goals for reducing the generation and release of toxic chemicals, all types of waste, and pollutants, by December 31, 1999. The comprehensive program contributes to savings in waste treatment, storage, and disposal costs and lowers health risks to workers and the public pollution prevention activities include development of new uses for existing chemicals, chemical substitutions, development of new materials and techniques, more efficient use of materials, recycling and conservation. Trash disposed as low-level radioactive waste at the Fernald Environmental Management Project was reduced through the Green is Clean program created with the assistance of PPP. Uncontaminated office trash is separated from radioactive waste and put in green bags by employees as they exit the work place. The green bagged waste is disposed at much lower cost than radioactive waste.

BUDGET INFORMATION

The DOE develops its budget and the president then presents it to Congress for approval and allocation. In 1998 the budget appropriated to the DOE was approximately $16.5 billion, making up about 1 percent of the total federal budget of $1.653 trillion. Seventy percent of the DOE budget is spent on atomic-energy defense activities, with 27 percent of the department's total budget going to environmental restoration and waste management; 25 percent to weapons activities; and the remaining 18 percent to other atomic-energy defense activities such as waste disposal and facilities closure projects. The other 30 percent of the DOE's budget is spent on science research (13 percent), energy supply research (6 percent), energy conservation (4 percent), and other activities (7 percent).

BUDGET:

Department of Energy

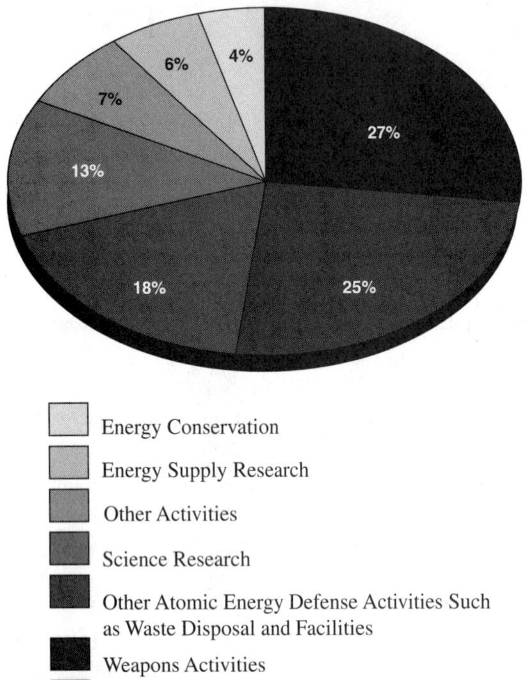

Percentage of Federal Budget

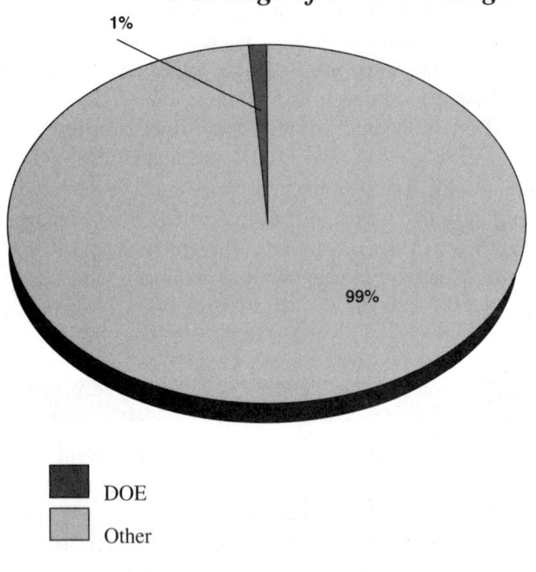

HISTORY

Two long-standing traditions were integrated with the creation of the DOE during a time of modern crisis. The first tradition consisted of allocating responsibility for non-nuclear energy research, development, regulation, pricing, and conservation over several government departments and agencies. Although various offices had a piece of the energy "pie," there was little coordination of activities and policies. Also, Americans maintained that the federal government should play a limited role in formulating or regulating national energy policies except in times of emergency, as in the days of fuel rationing during World War II (1939–45). The nation relied on private industry to fulfill the country's energy needs and required government intervention only when the free market was threatened. Fuel and the energy it produced were relatively abundant and cheap.

The second tradition that dictated American energy policy was the role of the federal government in nuclear energy. Beginning in 1942 the government sponsored the Manhattan Project, which not only created nuclear weaponry but also introduced nuclear technology that could be used for civilian energy purposes. With the creation of the U.S. Atomic Energy Commission in 1946, nuclear power became a commercial and scientific concern beyond the scope of military control.

What brought these two traditions together were the energy crises of the 1970s. Predictions that the United States's massive use of fuel and its dependence on foreign sources would create such crises, as well as recommendations for a coordinated government policy on energy, were ignored when things were going smoothly. Oil embargoes, limited or no fuel at gas stations, emergency conservation measures, and escalating fuel prices brought the message home. The nation that wanted the federal government to stay out of the energy business now held the government responsible for the energy crises and demanded action to improve the situation. Thus the DOE was created in 1977 to bring energy related activities and programs and incorporate nuclear technology as a key component to providing an alternative energy source within the United States.

Through the years the DOE has weathered changing roles and expectations. President Jimmy Carter's administration (1977–80) encouraged the growth of the DOE as energy provider, regulator, and research organization. President Ronald Reagan (1981–88) and President George Bush (1989–92) saw the DOE in danger of being dismantled as the federal government's role in regulation and direct service was downsized or abolished. During the 1980s the primary function of the DOE was to encourage and support the growth of the nuclear power industry. In the late 1980s and early 1990s, the DOE became responsible for the consequences of the rapid growth of nuclear energy plans and activities. Environmentalists questioned the safety of nuclear power sites in the wake of the Three Mile Island (near Harrisburg, Pennsylvania) and Chernobyl (Ukraine) nuclear facility accidents. Energy could not be supplied at the expense of human safety and at the risk of environmental damage.

FAST FACTS

Hazel O'Leary, secretary of energy from 1993 to 1997, was the first African American woman to hold a cabinet post.

(Source: Jacob Heilbrunn. "Over a Barrel." *New Republic*, October 7, 1996.)

CURRENT POLITICAL ISSUES

The DOE's activities and responsibilities lie at the heart of many complex political issues. As the American economy continues to grow, so too does pressure on the DOE to continue to create and improve energy systems that fuel the nation's industries. Yet a growing awareness of the environmental impact of reliance on fossil fuels demands that energy be supplied through more environmentally sound processes than in the past. Attempts to expand use of alternative energy sources have been met with great opposition by petroleum companies seeking to protect their industry.

In the rapid expansion of nuclear power facilities in the 1980s safety and regulatory compliance were often sacrificed in the rush to lessen U.S. dependence on foreign oil. Today the DOE bears the responsibility of reorganizing nuclear energy facilities and cleaning up nuclear contamination in plants and at materials sites, while maintaining an adequate energy supply.

Case Study: Maywood Cleanup Project

From 1916 to 1959, the Maywood Chemical Works in Bergen County, New Jersey, extracted radioactive thorium (an element used in industry and electronics and as atomic fuel) from sand for commercial use. During its operations, waste from the plant was removed in the form of mulch and fill material and spread through migration via an open stream. Thorium waste settled onto commercial and residential properties along the stream. The Stepan Co. acquired the Maywood Chemical works in 1959 and began cleaning up thorium waste in 1963. From 1966 through 1968 the Stepan Co. removed contaminated material and buried it in three pits on the property. Based on results of an Atomic Energy Commission survey in 1969, the property was certified for use with no radiological restrictions. In 1980, a new survey confirmed the presence of radioactive materials throughout the property. In 1985, the Department of Energy acquired a tract of land to use as an interim storage area to expedite cleanup efforts. The estimated total radioactive waste is 302,000 cubic meters. By 1996, 27,000 cubic meters of contaminated material had been excavated and stored at the DOE temporary storage facility at Maywood.

Additional DOE cleanups will be completed in two phases and are expected to be finished by 2000. Phase 1 will concentrate on residential, municipal, and state-owned properties. Phase 2 will address commercial, industrial, and government properties. In addition to cleanup at the site, the DOE must arrange for the disposal of contaminated materials. The current plan is to ship the radioactive waste by rail to a DOE storage facility in Utah.

The risk to the residents of the area is thought to be minimal because thorium presents a health risk only if large quantities are ingested. However, because the site includes so much publicly accessible land such as parks, the community's desire for efficient cleanup is great.

Public Impact

Citizens near the Maywood site and many other contaminated sites throughout the United States continue to pressure the DOE. Reassurances that health risks are often minimal are not enough. The need for storage facilities is increasing as residents fight having such facilities located near their towns. Voters are organizing efforts to encourage politicians and DOE officials to allocate more funds to clean-up efforts and safe waste disposal and storage.

SUCCESSES AND FAILURES

President Bill Clinton challenged the federal government to keep American families secure in a new economy, protect the environment, lead the fight for peace and freedom in the world, reform government, and renew schools. The DOE rose to these challenges in a variety of ways: retraining workers displaced through downsizing; producing a medical isotope for cancer patients; and continuing the trend of reducing gasoline prices. The DOE also accelerated cleanup activities at 14 sites throughout the nation. DOE officials participated in removing Chernobyl contaminants from food and milk

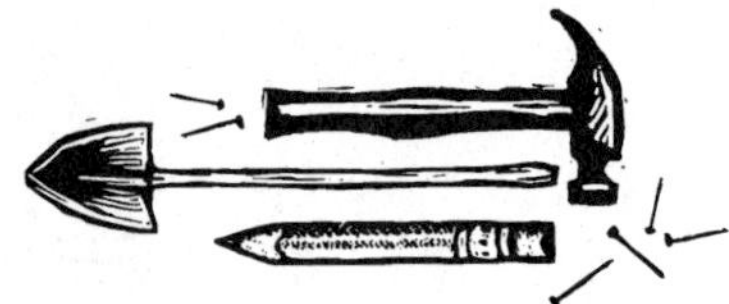

GET INVOLVED:

- Many nuclear energy facilities offer tours of their sites and opportunities for local citizens to get involved through advisory boards and focus groups. Contact the DOE at (202) 586-5000 to locate nuclear energy production sites. Visit a local site and get involved as a community representative.
- The DOE funds thousands of programs that provide weatherization services to the homes of low-income families and senior citizens, such as sealing windows and caulking cracks in basements and attics. Call the DOE to find out about these weatherization services and to volunteer some time.

in the Ukraine and dismantled more than two thousand nuclear weapons in 1995 and 1996. More than 20 teacher-student research teams will share millions in federal funds to advance the nation's coal-science knowledge, and seven thousand disadvantaged students will receive excess DOE education-related equipment through math and science programs.

A major failure of the DOE was the demise of the proposed superconducting supercollider project to build the world's largest particle accelerator, the basic research tool for studying the nature of matter and energy. Approved for construction by President Reagan in 1987, the process of collecting site, research, and construction proposals began in 1988. Budget constraints slowed the funding process for several years. Despite support from President Clinton and former Secretary of Energy Hazel O'Leary, the project, already under construction near Dallas, Texas, was defunded in 1993 due to reports of mismanagement and rising costs. The Republican-majority Congress viewed the project as a symptom of the overgrown federal system.

FUTURE DIRECTIONS

Former Secretary of Energy Frederico Peña stated in his 1997 confirmation hearing that the DOE will develop strategies that address both energy consumption and production, maintain the safety of the nation's nuclear deterrent without testing, and reduce unnecessary DOE regulation of national laboratories. According to its strategic plan, the DOE will also streamline processes and seek to privatize major functions. Top priority will be creating a safe, efficient, and prompt cleanup of nuclear weapons sites.

AGENCY RESOURCES

DOE resources, science and technical information, and databases can be accessed through the DOE's Internet site at http://www.doe.gov. The Energy Information Administration (EIA) maintains a comprehensive data and information program on energy resources and reserves, energy production and technologies, and statistics. The EIA can be accessed on-line at http://www.eia.doe.gov, by calling (202) 586–8800, or by writing to NEIC/EIA, 1000 Independence Ave. SW, Washington, DC 20585.

The Energy Efficiency and Renewable Energy Clearinghouse (EREC) provides information on the full spectrum of renewable energy and energy efficient technologies to consumers, teachers, and students. EREC maintains lists of organizations that will supply educators with energy-related booklets, audiovisual materials, software, and equipment. All publications are free and may be requested by calling 1–800–353-3732 or contacting EREC in writing at PO Box 3048, Merrifield, VA 22116.

AGENCY PUBLICATIONS

The DOE publishes a wide variety of reports and pamphlets. Of special interest to students are the booklets "Energy Education Resources" and "Energy Information Sheets." For information on these publications and many others, contact the DOE Office of Public Information at (202) 586-5575 or access the DOE home page at http://www.doe.gov/.

BIBLIOGRAPHY

Davidson, Keay. "Nuclear Fuel Rod Arrivals in Bay to be Semi-Secret." *San Francisco Examiner*, 2 May 1997.

Glass, David. "Growing International Markets." *Genetic Engineering News*, 15 October 1996.

Hann, Rosin. "Educating Feddie." *New Republic*, 3 February 1997.

Heilbrunn, Jacob. "Over a Barrel." *New Republic*, 7 October 1996.

Kozloff, Keith, and Olatokumbo Shobowale. *Rethinking Development Assistance for Renewable Electricity Sources*. Washington D.C.: World Resources Institute, 1994.

Lewin, David. "Look for the Union Label." *Journal of NIH Research*, 1 December 1996.

Wald, Matthew. "Peña Headed for Another Sprawling Department." *New York Times*, 21 December 1996.

Department of Health and Human Services (HHS; DHHS)

ESTABLISHED: May 4, 1980
EMPLOYEES: 59,000

Contact Information:

ADDRESS: 200 Independence Ave. SW
Washington, DC 20201
PHONE: (202) 619-0257
TDD (HEARING IMPAIRED): (404) 331-2205
E-MAIL: hhsmail@os.dhhs.gov
URL: http://www.os.dhhs.gov
SECRETARY OF HEALTH AND HUMAN SERVICES:
Donna E. Shalala

WHAT IS ITS MISSION?

According to its Web site, the Department of Health and Human Services (HHS or sometimes DHHS) is "the U.S. government's principal agency for protecting the health of all Americans and providing essential human services, especially for those who are least able to help themselves." To meet these objectives, the HHS provides services to infants, children, youth, low income families (families whose income falls at or below federal poverty guidelines), Americans in need of health care, and senior citizens. HHS agencies provide medical insurance, improved education, regulation of food and drugs, and numerous other services to millions of Americans. Together, the agencies of the HHS work toward the goals of breaking the cycle of poverty and achieving optimal mental and physical health for all Americans.

HOW IS IT STRUCTURED?

The Department of Health and Human Services is a cabinet-level department within the executive branch of the federal government. The secretary of the HHS oversees all aspects of the department and is an adviser to the president on issues related to the department. The secretary is appointed by the president and confirmed by the Senate.

The HHS has nine internal divisions: Management and Budget, Planning and Evaluation, Legislation, Public Affairs, General Counsel, Office for Civil Rights, Inspector General, and the Departmental Board of Appeals. These divisions perform administrative, legal, financial, and legislative functions for the department.

FAST FACTS

The percentage of children living in extreme poverty in the United States has doubled since 1975; as of 1997 it was 10 percent, or 6.3 million children. The ranks of the "poor" include one in every five children in the United States.

(Source: Elizabeth Gleick. "The Children's Crusade: a 60s-Style Campaign Aims to Put Kids First in This Year's Budget Battles and the Presidential Race." *Time*, June 3, 1996.)

The operating divisions of the HHS are divided into two categories: the Public Health Services Division and the Human Services Division. The Public Health Services Division agencies include the National Institutes of Health, the Food and Drug Administration, the Centers for Disease Control and Prevention, the Agency for Toxic Substances and Disease Registry, Indian Health Service, Health Resources and Services Administration, Substance Abuse and Mental Health Services Administration, and the Agency for Health Care Policy and Research. The Human Services Division agencies include the Health Care Financing Administration (which administers the Medicare and Medicaid programs), the Administration for Children and Families, and the Administration on Aging.

The U.S. Office of Consumer Affairs is located administratively in the HHS, but the director of that office reports to the president.

The HHS is headquartered in Washington, D.C., and maintains ten regional offices throughout the country. Each agency within the HHS operates a variety of programs, and many of these programs have headquarters and regional offices.

PRIMARY FUNCTIONS

The HHS is responsible for administering a wide range of programs in the fields of health care and social services and providing information on these issues to the president and the Congress. The department includes more than 300 programs that provide services to the widest range of populations, from infants to senior citizens. The HHS works closely with state and local governments, and many HHS-funded services are provided at the local level by state or county agencies or through private-sector grantees.

The Public Health Services Division of the HHS operates primarily through research and regulation. Its primary function is to prevent or lessen the effects of malnutrition, illness, substance abuse, and mental illness on Americans. The agencies in this branch of the HHS are not often seen directly intervening in the lives of Americans. Instead, they research cures for common diseases and disorders, develop new treatment methods for substance abusers, and ensure that the drugs available at the supermarket will help, not harm, those who take them.

The Human Services Division of the HHS also works to help Americans maintain their mental and physical health, but it does so by providing education, food, treatment, and direct monetary assistance to those who need help securing their basic needs. These agencies are trying to prepare or assist Americans in taking care of themselves.

PROGRAMS

There are a number of programs under the auspices of the various HHS agencies and bureaus. Major HHS programs include the Office of Family Assistance's Temporary Assistance for Needy Families (TANF) program, formerly the Aid to Families with Dependent Children (AFDC) program. TANF provides direct financial assistance to low-income families and assistance with child care and transportation costs.

Through the Health Care Financing Administration, the HHS also administers the Medicare and Medicaid programs which provide health insurance to about one in every five Americans. Medicare provides health care coverage to 37 million elderly and disabled Americans. Medicaid, a joint federal-state program, provides health care coverage for 36 million low-income persons, including 17.6 million children. Medicaid also pays for nursing home coverage for low-income senior citizens, covering almost half of the total national spending for nursing home care.

Another HHS program, the Child Support Enforcement program under the Office of Child Support Enforcement, has been expanded to require that parents provide primary financial support to their children whenever possible. Partnerships with state and local law enforcement agencies have resulted in stiffer penalties for parents who are delinquent in child support payments.

BUDGET INFORMATION

The HHS budget is allocated by Congress and is one of the largest department allocations at approximately

$359 billion in 1998. It made up about 22 percent of the total federal government budget of $1.653 trillion. Just over 83 percent of the entire HHS budget is spent on Health Care Financing Administration (HCFA) programs. The primary expenditures within HCFA are the Medicare program, which provides health insurance to elderly and disabled Americans, and the Medicaid program, which provides health insurance to low-income Americans.

Approximately 10 percent of the HHS budget is spent on other agencies in the Human Services Division, such as the Administration for Children and Families and the Administration on Aging. Roughly 7 percent of HHS funds are spent on all the agencies and programs within the Public Health Service Division of HHS, such as the National Institute of Health, the Food and Drug Administration, and the Indian Health Service.

BUDGET:

Department of Health and Human Services

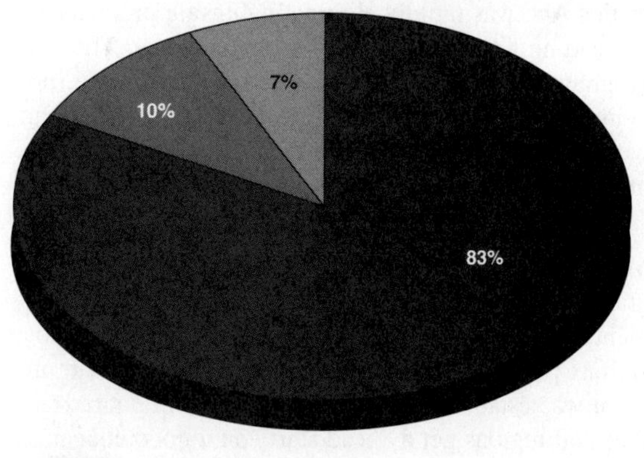

Agencies and Programs

Other Agencies in the Human Services Division

Health Care Financing Administration (HCFA) Programs

Percentage of Federal Budget

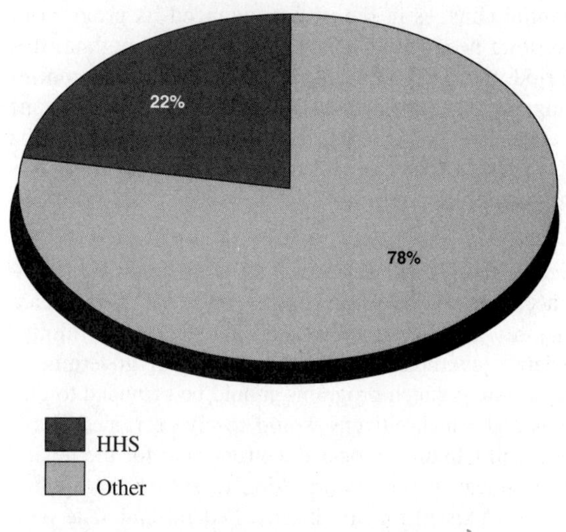

HHS

Other

HISTORY

The roots of the Department of Health and Human Services go back to the earliest days of the nation, when the first marine hospital, a forerunner of the Public Health Service (PHS), was established in 1798 to care for sailors. In 1887 the federal government opened a one-room laboratory in the marine hospital on Staten Island, New York, marking the beginning of the National Institutes of Health. By the early 1900s the marine hospitals had become the Public Health Service, and the one-room hygiene laboratory had been expanded to research all of the most pressing medical concerns of the day.

The Bureau of Chemistry was the forerunner of the FDA, begun under President Abraham Lincoln in 1862, with his appointment of Charles Wethril as the first chief chemist of the Department of Agriculture. Wethril and the other chemists who followed him lobbied Congress for many years to pass laws regulating the content of food and drugs. In 1902 Congress passed the Biological Control Act to ensure the purity of serums and vaccines used to treat human diseases. This act, enforced by the PHS, was followed in 1906 by the landmark Food and Drugs Act and the Meat Inspection Act, to be enforced by the Department of Agriculture.

By 1930 the Bureau of Chemistry had been replaced by the Food and Drug Administration (FDA), and the hygiene laboratory became the National Institute of Health. In 1939 the Federal Security Agency (FSA) was established, bringing together the NIH, the FDA and related agencies, education programs, and a new program called the Social Security Agency (SSA), which had been created by the Social Security Act of 1935. The FSA would eventually become the Department of Health and Human Services.

During World War II (1939–45) much of the FSA was focused on helping the war effort. Treatments were sought for maladies common to soldiers, and studies were conducted to ensure the safety of workers in the defense industry. In 1946 the Communicable Disease Center was established, later to become the Centers for Disease Control and Prevention.

After World War II the FSA began to develop into the agency now known as the HHS. The National Institute of Health became the National Institutes of Health, reflecting the establishment of many specific programs within the institute that began with the National Cancer Institute in 1937. The NIH also began its program of sponsoring private research through the use of grants, which has characterized its work since. The FDA, its power expanded in 1938 by the Food, Drug and Cosmetics Act, was rapidly eliminating unsafe products and misleading advertising from the marketplace. The SSA program began to operate on an ever larger scale, providing thousands and then millions of older Americans with benefits. In 1953 the FSA was renamed the Department of Health, Education and Welfare (HEW).

In 1965 HEW gained several new major programs. Medicare and Medicaid, the federal government's programs to help the elderly and poor pay for medical treatment, quickly joined Social Security as the largest social welfare program in the United States. The Head Start program was established to help children from poorer families and regions get a "head start" on a good education.

The 1970s and 1980s saw more organizational changes. The Health Care Financing Administration (HCFA) was established in 1977 to administer Medicare and Medicaid, moving these programs out of the SSA. In 1980 the education branch of the HEW was removed to become the cabinet-level Department of Education, and the HEW was renamed the Department of Health and Human Services. In 1985 the SSA became an independent agency. The HHS also saw substantial changes in the way it managed its program of assisting needy children and families. Throughout this period, the HEW/HHS faced the difficulties of continuing its mission as funding was lowered, questions were raised, and it struggled to effectively manage the bureaucracy that came with some of the government's largest public programs.

During the 1990s the role of the Department of Health and Human Services, in fact its continuing existence, was an ongoing controversy. The Republican-majority Congresses advocated a reduced and limited federal government, with state and local governments determining which programs should be provided to citizens and which citizens would receive services. President Bill Clinton advocated a strong role for the federal government in service provision to ensure that quality services existed for all citizens. Federal and state partnerships constantly reevaluate the delicate balance of federally funded and regulated programs that are administered locally and must be responsive to community needs and priorities.

Nowhere is this disagreement more evident than in the controversy over welfare programs that resulted in the passage of the Personal Responsibility and Work Opportunity Reconciliation Act of 1996 (PRWORA). Income assistance programs, like Aid to Families with Dependent Children (AFDC), were intended to provide temporary financial assistance to families to sustain a basic standard of living. However, many families—indeed generations of families—came to rely on federal assistance programs as their permanent source of income, food, and health care. The minimal income assistance that the programs provided was not enough to raise a family's standard of living or help a family acquire quality housing, however, and areas with high poverty rates did not have a large enough tax base to provide funding for quality schools. Thus, federal welfare programs came to be identified with maintaining, and sometimes increasing, poverty and its effects.

CURRENT POLITICAL ISSUES

The PRWORA was an uneasy compromise between President Clinton and the Republican-dominated Congress. The PRWORA created looser federal guidelines for income assistance programs, enabling states to have more control over the design and implementation of assistance programs. Time limits on the availability of assistance, work requirements, and eligibility requirements were among the criteria many states imposed on program recipients.

Supporters of the PRWORA, and subsequent supporting legislation, point to the reduced number of people on state welfare rolls as a sign that the new laws were successful in motivating people to move from welfare to work. Also, costs went down, and state and local governments were able to administer programs that were responsive to the needs and priorities of their communities.

Groups opposed to the PRWORA believed that eliminating the federal guarantee of income assistance to families removed the safety net from those least able to help themselves: children. Children of parents who are unable or unwilling to adapt to requirements for assistance suffer greatly if financial assistance is denied or terminated, opponents said. They also pointed to the fact that quality day care for children whose parents are required to work, often in low-paying, unskilled jobs, is often unavailable or unaffordable.

In response to groups opposed to the PRWORA, President Clinton committed to strengthening and creating family support programs through the Department of Health and Human Services. The HHS is charged with expanding and increasing access to social programs that assist and support families. Initiatives like those for the prevention of substance abuse and child abuse; those providing health and nutrition services to expectant mothers, infants, and children; and Head Start have become a primary focus of the HHS.

Case Study: Head Start

Head Start was created in 1965 as a preschool program to provide services to low-income children and their families. In addition to education, Head Start provides a variety of health and social services and promotes parent involvement as the foundation of the program. Grants for Head Start programs are awarded to local agencies by the HHS, which issues guidelines and regulations for the programs. Over the years, Head Start has grown in every state and in Puerto Rico and serves more than 800,000 children and their families. To qualify for Head Start services, family income must be at or below federal poverty guidelines. Thirty percent of Head Start employees are parents whose children have participated in Head Start programs, and assistance with college expenses is often provided to employees. The mission of Head Start is "to break the cycle of poverty by ensuring that disadvantaged children are prepared to succeed in school and by assisting parents in improving their life and job readiness skills."

The HHS plans to increase the impact of Head Start by boosting enrollment, expanding services to younger children, and creating community partnerships that help parents move from welfare to work. Recent research points to the importance of infant care and stimulation in the development of the brain and learning abilities. Head Start Infant/Toddler programs will seek to meet these needs. Family Service Centers are also being created where parents can receive literacy training, substance abuse counseling, and job readiness services. Parent involvement is an essential component of every Head Start program. Meaningful parent involvement provides an opportunity for parents to learn and practice new problem-solving skills and model these skills for their children.

Support for Head Start is fairly strong among both Democrats and Republicans. However, many politicians continue to question the government's expanding role as a service provider. Many others feel Head Start should be moved to the Department of Education, claiming it is an education program with limited social services. Opponents of the program claim that its value is minimal. They cite studies which show that the academic gains of Head Start children level off at about third grade. Proponents of Head Start respond that these studies are limited, as they focus only on academic measures without measuring social gains such as the lower delinquency, drop-out, substance abuse, and pregnancy rates of Head Start children. Advocates claim that these areas prove the value of Head Start as a social, as well as educational, program.

SUCCESSES AND FAILURES

The HHS has had several successes in the health field. Through the National Institutes of Health (NIH), quality research, information, and care for a variety of health needs has become readily available and continues to advance. Information on and treatment of cancer and AIDS has become a priority for the NIH and flourishes under HHS leadership after many years of slow progress. New dietary guidelines and food-labeling systems publicized by the Food and Drug Administration have created a nationwide focus on nutrition. Efforts to immunize children are more effective than they have been in decades.

The human services sector of the HHS operates programs that successfully meet the needs of millions of Americans. Medicare, Medicaid, Head Start, and meals for senior citizens are examples of programs that significantly improve the quality of life for recipients. Under the Child Support Enforcement program's new income tax refund offset program, the federal government may deduct the overdue amount of child support from the tax refunds of parents whose payments are delinquent. In 1995 alone more than $1 billion in delinquent child support was collected and returned to more than 1.2 million families.

FUTURE DIRECTIONS

The HHS Strategic Plan of 1997 (available at http://aspe.os.dhhs.gov/hhsplan) outlines many of the specific areas of concern to the department. One goal on which the HHS places particular emphasis is the reduction of tobacco use among Americans, particularly among America's youth. It is the department's goal to reduce tobacco usage by the young by 50 percent by 2005. All of the major agencies within the HHS are involved in accomplishing this mission. The FDA will play a key role as it enforces laws that restrict the availability of tobacco to minors. The NIH will sponsor research to find out why young people begin and continue to smoke, as well as research into a genetic basis for nicotine addiction. The CDC and other agencies will initiate an educational campaign with the purpose of informing all Americans of the negative health effects of tobacco. Through it all, the HHS plans to remain at the forefront of health research, care, and technology.

This is only one of the many issues facing the HHS. Drug resistant disease strains, the spread of infectious and sexually transmitted disease, and the needs of a large aging population will create enormous problems for the department in the years ahead. The implementation of new laws on welfare assistance to children and families will also require a major effort by the HHS, and by other government agencies such as the Department of Labor. Problems exist within the department as well, with streamlining and reform of the huge Medicare program a serious concern.

AGENCY RESOURCES

The HHS has a vast amount of information on its programs, resources and statistics. Information can be

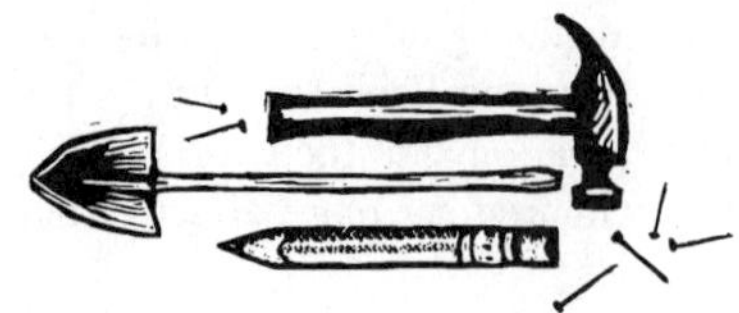

GET INVOLVED:

In 1996 the Elderly Nutrition Program (ENP) provided 127 million meals to 2.3 million senior citizens in group settings and 173 million meals to 877,000 homebound senior citizens. ENP meals provide more than half the recommended daily nutrients to participants. The program also gives clients opportunities for social interaction. Contact the Administration on Aging at (202) 401-4541 to find a local senior nutrition program and volunteer as a server or delivery person.

obtained by contacting the HHS by phone at (202) 619-0257 or on-line at http://www.os.dhhs.gov. Catalogs of department resources are also available by mail from the Information Center, Department of Health and Human Services, 200 Independence Ave. SW, Washington, DC 20201; phone (202) 619-0257.

Healthfinder is a consumer health resource Web site located at http://www.healthfinder.gov/. Healthfinder leads users to publications, addresses, databases, Web sites, and support groups related to thousands of health issues.

AGENCY PUBLICATIONS

HHS publications include reports such as "Preventing Drug Use Among Children and Adolescents," "Trends in the Well Being of Children and Youth," "The Role of Protease Inhibitors in Arresting HIV Growth," and "Vegetarian Diet Impact on Hypertension." Informational guides and pamphlets include "Girl Power!," "Marijuana: Facts for Teens," "Media Violence: Tips for Parents," and "Recognizing Suicidal Behavior." Write to the Information Center, Department of Health and Human Services, 200 Independence Ave. SW, Washington, DC 20201, or call (202) 619-0257.

BIBLIOGRAPHY

"Change in Entitlement Status for Welfare Could Swamp Cities." *Nation's Cities Weekly*, 25 March 1996, p. 13.

DeParle, Jason. "A Sharp Decrease in Welfare Cases is Gathering Speed." *New York Times*, 2 February 1997.

Geier, Thom. "Young and Abused." *U.S. News and World Report*, 30 September 1996, p. 24.

Gleick, Elizabeth. "The Children's Crusade: a 60s-Style Campaign Aims to Put Kids First in this Year's Budget Battles and the Presidential Race." *Time*, 3 June 1996, p. 30.

"HHS Removes Race as Barrier to Adoptions of Minority Children." *Jet*, 15 May 1995, p. 4.

Katz, Jeffrey L. "Head Start Reauthorization Calls for New Standards." *Congressional Quarterly Weekly Report*, 16 April 1994, p. 896.

Kent, Christina. "Long-Awaited Tobacco-Control Rules Get Tepid Praise." *American Medical News*, 5 February 1996, p. 6.

Lewis, Anne C. "What Teens Smoke." *Education Digest*, December 1996, p. 72.

Seachrist, Lisa. "Government Guidelines Okay Vegetarian Diet." *Science News*, 6 January 1996, p. 6.

Thibodeau, Patrick. "Welfare Agencies Off Schedule." *Computerworld*, 3 March 1997, p. 28.

Department of Housing and Urban Development (HUD)

WHAT IS ITS MISSION?

The Department of Housing and Urban Development (HUD) was established to address the nation's housing needs. In addition, HUD is responsible for ensuring fair housing opportunities for all U.S. citizens and is engaged in a broad spectrum of programs designed to improve the quality of life in communities throughout the United States. HUD also administers mortgage insurance programs; provides rent subsidies to low- and moderate-income families who otherwise would be unable to afford adequate housing; provides funds for construction of new public housing and rehabilitation of existing units; and addresses cases of discrimination in public housing.

HOW IS IT STRUCTURED?

HUD is a cabinet-level agency and is part of the executive branch of government. It is led by a secretary who is appointed by the president and confirmed by Congress. The secretary formulates policy recommendations for the president; coordinates with other agencies to ensure that where there is program overlap, consistent policy directions are made; works with the private sector to encourage participation in meeting a specific community's housing and economic development needs; ensures nondiscrimination in housing; and provides general oversight of HUD's Federal National Mortgage Association.

Staff offices include the Small and Disadvantaged Business Utilization Office, which is responsible for overseeing contracts made with disadvantaged and

ESTABLISHED: November 9, 1965
EMPLOYEES: 11,466

Contact Information:

ADDRESS: 451 7th St. SW
Washington, DC 20410
PHONE: (202) 708-0417
TDD (HEARING IMPAIRED): (202) 708-1455
FAX: (202) 708–0299
URL: http://www.hud.gov
SECRETARY OF HOUSING AND URBAN DEVELOPMENT: Andrew Cuomo

FAST FACTS

There are an estimated 600,000 homeless Americans living on the streets and in shelters every day. HUD's homeless assistance programs have provided assistance to an estimated two million families and individuals since 1987.

(Source: Department of Housing and Urban Development. "Questions and Answers about HUD," 1998.)

minority businesses. The Office of Administrative Law Judges hears and decides on cases related to federal housing discrimination. The HUD Board of Contract Appeals rules on all appeals concerning HUD actions, including disciplining mortgagees, awarding grants and contracts, and offseting tax refunds of people indebted to the agency. The Office of Federal Housing Enterprise oversees the financial safety of the Federal National Mortgage Association (FNMA) and the Federal Home Loan Mortgage Corporation (FHLMC).

HUD also has 10 field offices, which are each directed by a regional representative of the secretary. The secretary's representative oversees the daily operations of the field office and ensures that responsibilities assigned to them by the secretary are carried out. Field offices are located in Massachusetts, New York, Pennsylvania, Georgia, Illinois, Texas, Kansas, Colorado, California, and Washington.

HUD also operates 80 community offices throughout the United States. Local offices manage subsidized housing units and create programs intended to address community needs, such as opportunities for youth employment or economic self-sufficiency programs for adults. Because it is interested in meeting community needs at a local level, HUD frequently contracts with nonprofit organizations, mortgage companies, and housing authorities in order to better serve the public.

PRIMARY FUNCTIONS

As a cabinet agency, HUD makes policy recommendations to the president and designs legislation to bring before Congress. Through legislation and a budget provided by Congress, HUD fulfills its primary goal of helping communities improve the quality of life through better housing for America's most disadvantaged populations: the working poor, ethnic minorities, people with AIDS, the elderly, and the homeless. It does this through a number of different initiatives, most of them centering around providing adequate housing by several different means. For low-income citizens, HUD provides vouchers that can be used to purchased housing. Additionally, HUD funds regional and local organizations to subsidize housing for those that could not otherwise afford it. It also provides mortgage guarantees so lower income Americans can afford to buy homes and provides funds for renovation and for the construction of new housing. The department also offers homes that have had their HUD mortgages foreclosed upon, often at prices that low- or middle-class incomes can afford.

HUD attempts to make American citizens as well informed as possible about a variety of housing issues. Using pamphlets, hot lines, and on-line materials, HUD disseminates information on how to buy a home, what to do if the mortgage on the home you own is foreclosed, the dangers of lead-based paint, land sales, home improvement and other topics. Additionally, HUD informs tenants of rented property of their rights under law and what to do if a renter/buyer or potential renter/buyer of property is discriminated against. The enforcement of anti-discrimination laws in regard to housing falls under the jurisdiction of HUD.

HUD also serves as the primary voice for urban issues in the executive branch of government. HUD's research arm, the Office of Policy Research and Development, serves as a major source of information and analysis regarding housing and community development issues. It studies issues affecting urban populations and works with regional and local organizations to come to resolutions on how to deal with problems such as urban sprawl and stagnation.

PROGRAMS

HUD operates a number of different programs in an attempt to fulfill its mission of "a decent, safe, and sanitary home and suitable living environment for every American" (HUD Web site). Many of its programs are centered around the construction, rental, and purchase of housing. HUD also has programs to build housing for the poor and underprivileged, to assist people in making their rent payments, and to make it easier for people to get mortgages.

HUD has a number of different programs for funding new construction. Through the Community Development Block Grants (CDBG) program, HUD provides funds to state and local governments to carry out their own construction and revitalization plans. The Home Investment in Affordable Housing (HOME) program also funds new construction and housing rehabilitation, as well as assists first-time homebuyers. HUD also has a number of programs to help the homeless find a place to live, and has programs to assist other groups of people with special housing needs, including the elderly and the handicapped.

In addition to building and fixing homes, HUD programs help people to pay for existing housing. Through its Section 8 housing programs, HUD provides subsidies (rental assistance) to families with limited incomes. The Government National Mortgage Association (GNMA), often called Ginnie Mae provides federal guarantees for mortgage loans, making it easier for low- and middle-income families to become homeowners. Through its Office of Federal Housing Enterprise Oversight, HUD also oversees the Federal National Mortgage Association (Fannie Mae) and the Federal Home Loan Mortgage Corporation (Freddie Mac), which are two government-backed private organizations designed to help those with lower incomes get mortgages.

BUDGET INFORMATION

Budgetary recommendations from HUD's secretary and the president are proposed to and approved by Congress. HUD's total operating budget for 1998 was approximately $34 billion, making up about 2 percent of the total federal budget of $1.653 trillion. Major program expenses include Section 8 and rental assistance at 30 percent; CDBG and economic development programs at 24 percent; development, repair, and modernization of public housing units at 22 percent; homeownership opportunities at 11 percent; and housing programs for disadvantaged populations, including the disabled, the elderly, American Indians, AIDS/HIV patients, and the homeless at 4 percent. The remaining funds, about 9 percent of the budget, are expended on personnel expenses, fair housing activities, research and development, and other discretionary expenses.

BUDGET:
Department of Housing and Urban Development

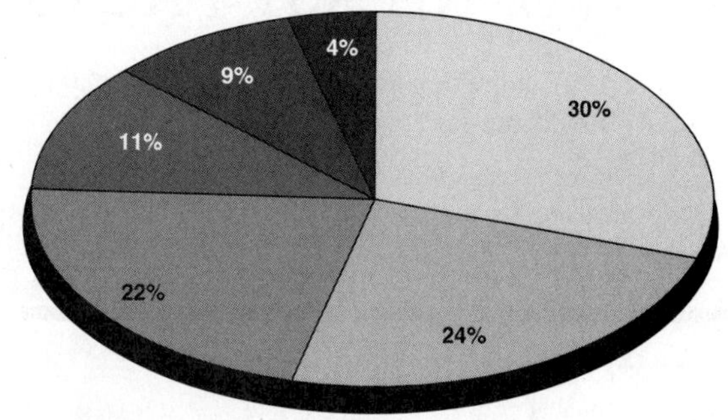

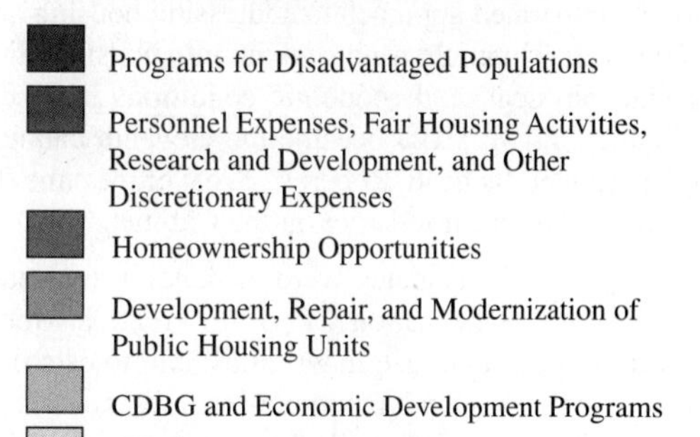

Percentage of Federal Budget

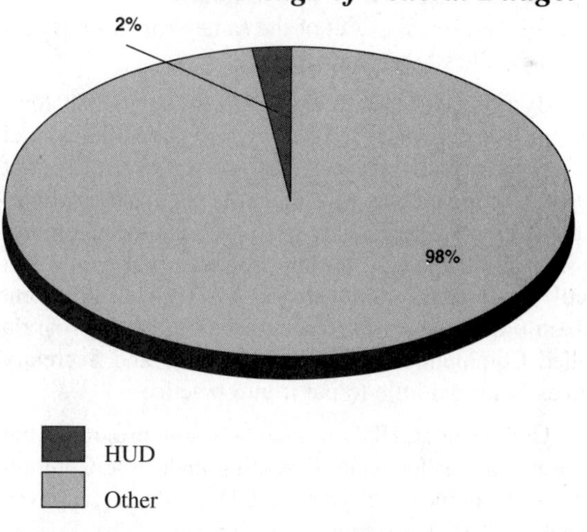

HISTORY

During their presidencies, John F. Kennedy and Lyndon Johnson both presented plans to Congress to establish an agency to deal with the nation's housing needs, and both of their initial proposals were voted down by Congress. However, Congress did recognize the need to better respond to changing demographics in the country. By the early 1960s, 70 percent of the nation's population resided in cities and outlying suburbs. With this dramatic shift from previous decades when the majority of the population resided in rural areas, the issue of urban crowding became a very real concern. The government faced such problems as housing shortages, pollution, and lack of public transportation and needed to find a solution.

Before HUD was established a number of agencies were responsible for addressing these issues, but because various departments handled the problems, disjointed solutions were offered. For example, a public housing unit would be constructed, but it would be located far away from important services such as transportation, hospitals, and businesses. Upon establishing HUD as part of President Johnson's War on Poverty in 1965, Congress hoped

FAST FACTS

As of 1997, more Americans than ever were paying over half of their pre-tax income for housing.

(Source: Richard Ravitch. "The Unhoused: A Looming Housing Crisis and How to Fix It." *New Republic,* January 27, 1997.)

to form an integrated approach to addressing housing and community development needs, taking into consideration the social, physical, and economic conditions that help communities thrive. HUD became the eleventh cabinet-level department. Its head, Robert C. Weaver, became the first African American to serve on the Cabinet.

HUD's initial mandates were to develop rent subsidy programs for the nation's poor; to create a Model Cities program to revitalize inner cities; and to establish a program for low- and moderate-income families to become homeowners. What all of these programs had in common was the goal of making affordable housing available to everyone. The Civil Rights Act of 1968, often called the Fair Housing Act, outlawed housing discrimination, and made HUD responsible for enforcing its statutes. The Housing Act of the same year made it easier for families to get mortgages.

By 1972, HUD was building more than 500,000 low-income housing units a year, mostly under the Model Cities program. President Nixon, however, did not approve of the federal government's large-scale involvement in housing. In January 1973, he announced a moratorium on all federal housing programs that would last until the Carter administration (1977–81). President Nixon did create a new revenue sharing grant program called Community Development, but he and Secretary James Lynn did little to put it into practice.

Under Carter, HUD resumed housing programs, but on a much smaller scale. Operating under the Community Development Program, HUD produced approximately 100,000 housing units per year. The Reagan administration once again brought cutbacks to HUD. Throughout the 1980s, HUD built only about 50,000 units per year. Meanwhile, the inflation of the 1970s and 1980s led to high interest rates which made it difficult for HUD's mortgage programs to be truly effective.

By the 1990s, HUD was viewed as a poorly run agency. Public housing developments were notoriously crime ridden and lacked important services. The National Academy of Public Administration found HUD to be so poorly managed that it recommended to Congress that the entire department be dismantled. While HUD was not dismantled, a long period of reform did begin. By the latter half of the 1990s, HUD had regained some of the respect it had lost, in large part due to the efforts of Secretary Henry G. Cisneros, who was appointed by President Bill Clinton in 1993. Cisneros reorganized HUD, created a smaller department, and took action on some of the agency's most outstanding embarrassments. For example, under Cisneros's leadership, some of the nation's most dangerous and decaying public housing units were dismantled and replaced with new units strategically located near critical community services.

CURRENT POLITICAL ISSUES

As of the needs of today's American citizen becomes more complicated, Critics often target offices such as the Department of Education and HUD, claiming that the interests of both groups would be better served at the local, rather than federal level. While HUD continues to draw its share of negative commentary, its dramatic work with the Chicago Housing Authority has silenced some opposition.

Case Study: Resurrecting the Chicago Housing Authority

The Chicago Housing Authority (CHA) was formed to provide temporary homes for low income families who could not afford "decent, safe, sanitary dwellings." As time went on, the temporary arrangement became permanent. Generations of families began to depend on the CHA and it became the second largest public housing organization in the United States.

Crime, drugs, and welfare abuse went nearly unchecked for years. The properties themselves fell into ruin. CHA "projects" such as Cabrini Green and the Robert Taylor homes achieved infamy as the nation's most dangerous public housing complexes. The CHA could no longer effectively provide dwellings that were decent, safe, or sanitary and drastic measures were needed to reverse the decades of decay. HUD attempted to take control of the agency in 1987, but their efforts were resisted by Chicago Mayor Harold Washington. Since it was the mayor who had ultimate control over the leadership and operation of the CHA, there was little HUD could do.

In May of 1995, the board of directors of the CHA resigned as a statement to call attention to the desperate state of affairs in Chicago's public housing. HUD took control of the CHA with the full approval of Chicago's Mayor Daley. Using a recovery team to assess the areas in need of immediate attention was the first step after the federal takeover. The team concluded that the major problems were the housing projects themselves. Seven of America's ten poorest urban neighborhoods exist within CHA complexes and the complexes served as a way to isolate the urban poor. It was this concentration that had been undermining the CHA for years. "You can drive for almost four miles along south State Street and never leave the shadow of public housing," said former HUD Secretary Henry Cisneros. HUD embarked on a program to refurbish buildings that were worth saving and to demolish those that were not.

Over the next three years, HUD tore down over 1,200 units, with another 3,000 marked for demolition. Two thousand units were repaired and five hundred new units were constructed. Three hundred of these new units were "scattered sites" developments, subsidized housing integrated into existing neighborhoods. This was done in an attempt to move away from the "project" concept of old. These radical changes, costing approximately $50 million, have made a difference.

HUD publishes a yearly review of the nation's public housing. Prior to federal takeover the CHA had never received a passing grade. In 1998, the CHA passed and was removed from HUD's list of most troubled housing authorities. HUD Secretary Andrew Cuomo announced that, because of this success, control of the CHA would pass back to the city of Chicago in 1999.

Public Impact

HUD strives to de-ghettoize public housing, such as it existed in Chicago. The destruction of high-rise housing projects is the first step down this road. The integration of public housing into existing, stable neighborhoods is the next. Finally, HUD wishes to privatize as much public housing management as possible. This would allow communities to become self-sufficient and perhaps return to the days when public housing was seen as a temporary solution.

SUCCESSES AND FAILURES

HUD's efforts to improve the quality of living in the nation's public housing stock has resulted in not only the removal of some of its most deplorable units but also in a new vision for building stronger communities and extending economic opportunities to the seven million families assisted by HUD's rental assistance program. As part of its new direction, HUD created the Family Self-Sufficiency (FSS) Program as a partnership with local housing authorities to help residents achieve a greater measure of financial independence. Participating families work closely with local housing authority staff to design a contract that provides the necessary tools for residents to be better equipped to enter the job market. To support these efforts, participants may receive child care stipends, transportation assistance, education and job skills training, or whatever they and the local housing authority agree will make their self-sufficiency plan successful. Implemented before welfare reform became a priority of the Clinton administration, the FSS Program is considered to be an important model for redirecting public assistance programs.

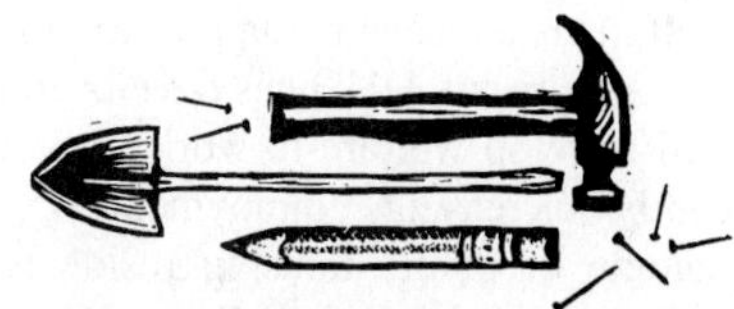

GET INVOLVED:

A Community in Action

The Willamette Valley is the headquarters of Oregon's billion-dollar agricultural industry, and Marion County is the valley's top-producing county. Marion is also home to 40 percent of the state's entire farmworker population. This segment of the population had long coped with a chronic lack of available, affordable housing. In 1993 a consortium of nonprofit organizations and representatives of the farmworker community began negotiations with HUD and the local housing authority to construct apartment units that would not only address the issue of affordable housing but also serve as a community center for farmworker families by providing other essential services. As of early 1997, 52 units with affordable rents were constructed, housing 300 individuals. In addition residents also initiated a Youth Leadership Development Group, creating a forum for young people to meet to discuss social, family, and cultural issues. Youth have held fundraisers that resulted in the construction of a community basketball court. In addition, these young residents have become advocates for further farmworker housing development in the Marion area by participating at local city council meetings and public forums, offering testimony about the positive changes they have experienced since moving to their new home.

Youthbuild

Students can become directly involved in HUD activities through Youthbuild, the agency's program to assist low-income youth in receiving the education and job skills necessary for greater economic opportunities. The program provides leadership development training and provides opportunities for youth to participate in community development efforts at the local level. For further information about Youthbuild, contact the Community Connections program at 1-800-998-9999.

FUTURE DIRECTIONS

HUD is increasingly being called upon to design opportunities for public housing residents who rely on welfare as a means of support to move into the job market. As a result, HUD has developed grant programs that will develop welfare-to-work projects aimed at significantly increasing employment opportunities and the income of public housing residents in seven targeted cities across the United States. Grants will provide job training and educational opportunities, loan funds for residents to borrow from in order to establish their own businesses, support for child care and transportation, and homeownership counseling. For example, in Long Branch, New Jersey, funds will be used to establish a small business training program and to establish a microloan fund and a credit union. HUD will provide child care, transportation, employment counseling, and educational courses for participants.

AGENCY RESOURCES

HUD's Office of Policy Development and Research (PDR) publishes thousands of documents on housing and community development issues. In addition, the PDR provides other HUD departments and programs with the necessary statistical and analytical information necessary in developing policy recommendations. In 1978 the PDR created HUD-USER, a complete information source of housing and community development information for researchers and policymakers. HUD-USER is also available for the general public to utilize. For further information about HUD-USER and its information resources, contact the PDR at (202) 708-1600.

AGENCY PUBLICATIONS

HUD publishes thousand of brochures, reports, and other publications annually. *Renewing America's Communities from the Ground Up* by former HUD Secretary Henry Cisneros is an interesting report on the department's vision for the social and economic conditions necessary for communities throughout the United States to thrive. A synopsis of the report is available on-line; copies of the full report can be obtained from HUD. Other publications of interest include *Cityscape,* HUD's periodic journal dedicated to sharing the latest innovations and research in housing and urban development issues, and *Why America's Communities Need a Department of Housing and Urban Development.*

Other popular HUD publications include information on building technology, financing homeownership, affordable housing, and housing markets and demographics. All publications may be ordered directly from HUD's Web site at http://www.hud.gov or by contacting the PDR at (202) 708–1600.

BIBLIOGRAPHY

Brooke, James. "Indian's Cruel Winter of Aid Cuts and Cold." *New York Times,* 27 January 1997, p. A1.

"HUD Tired of CHA Failures." *Chicago Tribune*, 28 May 1995.

Loeb, Penny. "The Unsheltered Life: The Factors Behind the Nation's Acute Shortage of Affordable Housing." *U.S. News and World Report,* 11 November 1996, p. 28.

"Mayor Getting Ready to Bring CHA Home." *Chicago Tribune*, 30 August 1998.

Nagourney, Adam. "For a Political Son, Forging An Identity." *New York Times,* 21 December 1996, p. A11.

"Officially, HUD Takes Over CHA." *Chicago Tribune*, 31 May 1995.

Price, Erica. "Community Connections: Your Link to Community Building Resources." *Nation's Cities Weekly,* 23 September 1996, p. 7.

Ravitch, Richard. "The Unhoused: A Looming Housing Crisis and How to Fix it." *The New Republic,* 27 January 1997, p. 10.

Terry, Don. "Chicago Housing Agency to be Taken Over by U.S." *New York Times*, 28 May 1995.

Department of Justice (DOJ)

WHAT IS ITS MISSION?

The Department of Justice (DOJ) is self-described as "the largest law firm in the nation," and its primary client is the United States government. The DOJ represents the government in federal cases and investigates and prosecutes violations of federal law. In addition, the DOJ is charged with protecting the public interest and the safety of the nation and is responsible for overseeing the federal correctional system and developing crime prevention programs.

HOW IS IT STRUCTURED?

The Department of Justice is a cabinet-level agency and is part of the executive branch of government. The department is organized into the following offices: Executive Direction and Management, Investigatory and Law Enforcement, Legal and Policy, and Litigation.

The Executive Direction and Management Offices include the Office of the Attorney General, Deputy Attorney General, and the Solicitor General. The attorney general heads up the Department of Justice. Considered the chief law enforcement officer of the federal government, the attorney general is responsible for representing the United States in legal matters and providing legal advice to other heads of departments as needed.

The attorney general is assisted in her efforts by assistant attorneys general. The attorneys general are housed within the Litigation Office and oversee six major divisions within the Department of Justice, including the Antitrust, Civil, Civil Rights, Criminal, Environment and Natural Resources, Tax, and U.S. Attorneys. Through

ESTABLISHED: June 22, 1870
EMPLOYEES: 107,277

Contact Information:

ADDRESS: 10th St. and Constitution Ave. NW
Washington, DC 20530
PHONE: (202) 514-2000
TDD (HEARING IMPAIRED): (800) 514-3883
FAX: (202) 514-4371
URL: http://www.usdoj.gov
ATTORNEY GENERAL: Janet Reno

FAST FACTS

According to a 1996 RAND corporation study, the number of serious crimes prevented by every $1 million spent incarcerating repeat felons is 61; the number prevented by every $1 million spent on high-school graduation incentives is 258.

(Source: *Harper's Magazine,* February 1997.)

these divisions, the DOJ serves as an advocate and enforcer for other cabinet-level departments.

The Antitrust Division is dedicated to ensuring free market competition within the United States economy. It is responsible for enforcing antitrust laws that affect nearly every type of industry and all levels of an industry's operations.

The Civil Rights Division serves as legal counsel and defense for the federal government when its actions are challenged. The division is involved in defending and litigating on behalf of various federal programs and functions. The Civil Rights Division is responsible for protecting the civil rights of the nation's citizenry by enforcing federal laws that ban discrimination based on race, sex, ability, or religion. For example, the Housing and Civil Enforcement Section of the Civil Rights Division is responsible for enforcing the Fair Housing Act, which prohibits discrimination in housing. As a result, the section can act on behalf of individuals when a complaint has been filed with the Department of Housing and Urban Development.

The Criminal Division develops, enforces, and supervises the application of criminal law. The division also monitors sensitive programs such as the Witness Protection Program.

The DOJ describes its Environment and Natural Resources Division as "the nation's environmental lawyer." The division is charged with representing the United States in cases where federal lands and natural resources are at risk.

The Tax Division provides legal services to its principal client, the Internal Revenue Service (IRS). The division also defends the federal government in cases that involve issues such as contended tax refunds or collection actions.

The last major division, the U.S. Attorneys Division, conducts most trial work when a branch of the federal government is involved in a court case.

The Investigatory and Law Enforcement Offices deal with the DOJ's crime control and prevention programs. They include the Federal Bureau of Investigation (FBI), Wanted Fugitives, the Federal Bureau of Prisons, and other offices dedicated to criminal intelligence, international police relations, and prisons. The Legal and Policy Offices are responsible for formulating policy recommendations and advising on legal issues pertinent to the DOJ's mission. In addition, the department is home to a number of well-known bureaus including, the Immigration and Naturalization Service (INS), the Drug Enforcement Administration (DEA), and the U.S. Marshals Service.

PRIMARY FUNCTIONS

Guiding the DOJ are two major mandates, which are to aid and assist the U.S. government in all legal matters and to serve as the country's chief enforcement agency, ensuring the safety and protection of its citizenry. The *United States Government Manual* describes the DOJ's main functions as follows: "Through its thousands of lawyers, investigators, and agents, the Department plays a key role in protection against criminals and subversives, in ensuring healthy competition of business in our free enterprise system, in safeguarding the consumer, and in enforcing drug, immigration and naturalization laws. The Department also plays a significant role in protecting citizens through its efforts for effective law enforcement, crime prevention, crime detection, and prosecution and rehabilitation of offenders."

The DOJ makes policy recommendations and suggests legislative directions to the president. Other functions include prosecuting or defending the U.S. government in civil cases; prosecuting in criminal cases on behalf of the government; determining which cases should be appealed when the U.S. government has lost; and collecting debts owed to the federal government which it otherwise has been unable to collect.

PROGRAMS

The Department of Justice is responsible for an enormous number of programs and bureaus. In addition to the FBI, the Immigration and Naturalization Service, the Drug Enforcement Agency, and the U.S. Marshals Service, the department operates the Bureau of Prisons, the United States National Central Bureau, the United States Parole Commission, the Office of Special Investigations, and the Community Relations Service, among others.

The Community Relations Service (CRS) was created under the DOJ after the Civil Rights Act of 1964 was passed. According to its mission statement, its purpose is "to prevent and resolve community conflicts and reduce community tensions arising from actions, policies, and practices perceived to be discriminatory on the basis of race, color, or national origin."

The service is designed not only to resolve conflicts but to prevent them. The CRS provides training at the request of local or state officials or when the service itself feels its assistance is necessary. The service also provides support for refugee resettlement programs. Since 1982, the service has been involved in assisting Haitian and Cuban immigrants upon their release from the Immigration and Naturalization Service (INS). The CRS provides shelter and child welfare services and seeks to reunite families who may have been separated during their processing or retainment period with the INS.

The U.S. Marshals Service is also a major program of the DOJ. As the oldest federal enforcement agency, the Marshals Service provides critical services that include protecting judges, jurors, and other trial participants involved in federal court cases; tracking and taking into custody federal fugitives; administering the Federal Witness Security program; transporting federal prisoners between facilities; carrying out court orders and arrest warrants; cooperating with the Asset Forfeiture Program by seizing and selling the property of criminals; and providing training for new and senior marshals at its training academy.

BUDGET INFORMATION

The department's budget for fiscal year 1998 was an estimated $18.9 billion, approximately 1 percent of the total federal budget of $1.653 trillion. In addition to allocations from Congress, the DOJ receives funding from a special anticrime trust account ($5.2 billion) and fees from activities such as border crossings ($2 billion).

Over 50 percent of the budget—or $9.9 billion—is allocated for law enforcement programs. This category also includes personnel expenses for the entire department. It is expected that some of this funding will be used for additional staffing, including 363 new hires for the Drug Enforcement Administration, 144 for the Federal Bureau of Investigations, and 56 for the U.S. Attorney's office.

Other major expenditures within the department include $6.2 billion for litigation activities; $340 million for the Legal Services Corporation; $227.5 million for juvenile crime programs, including special courts and crime prevention programs; $36 million for the FBI's laboratory; and $29.5 million for a new counterterrorism program that was created in response to the bombing of the federal building in Oklahoma City.

BUDGET:

Department of Justice

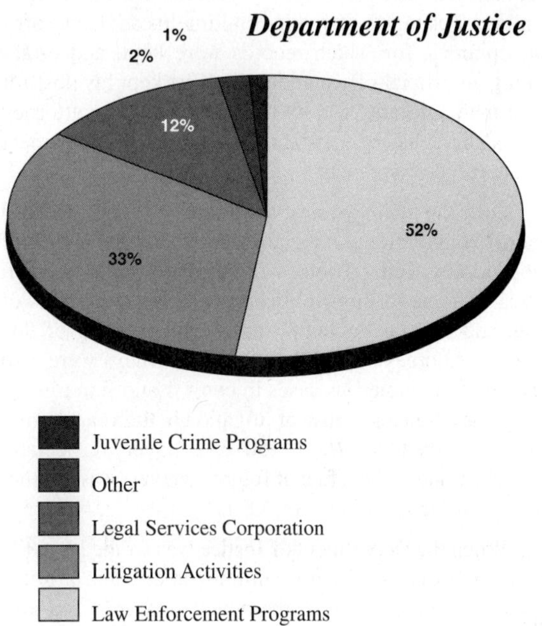

Percentage of Federal Budget

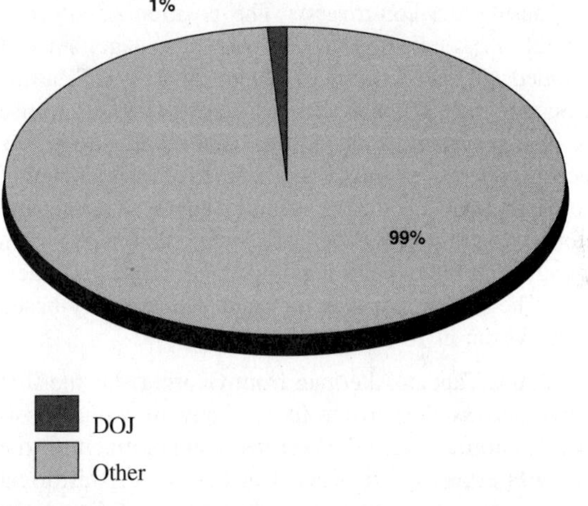

HISTORY

While the Department of Justice was not formed until 1870, its history begins in 1789. It was in that year that President George Washington appointed Edmund Randolph to be the first attorney general of the United States. One of the original cabinet posts, the attorney general was charged with serving as a legal adviser to the president and other department heads, and representing the United States in any lawsuits against the nation that were tried before the Supreme Court.

Initially, the attorney general was a relatively minor position. Government was still small, its needs for legal representation few. The powers and responsibilities of the post were poorly defined, and early attorneys general did little more than provide advice upon request; the position was really only considered part-time. In 1817, William Wirt became attorney general. He instituted a number of changes, including limiting his advice to official opinions, for which records were kept, and establishing an official office and staff. Wirt kept his post for more than a decade, and by the time he left the attorney generalship it had been established as the law department of the executive branch.

Over the next 40 years, the attorney general worked against congressional reluctance to expand the Office of the Attorney General into a full-fledged department. It inherited some responsibilities from the Departments of State and Interior, including the commissioning of law officers. Attorneys general and U.S. attorneys were also busy arguing numerous cases in court. Land fraud in the West was a frequent cause of litigation in the years before and during the Civil War (1960–65). Slavery, especially the slave trade and the fate of fugitive slaves, was another issue of some legal concern.

When the Department of Justice was formed in 1870 during Ulysses S. Grant's administration, the attorney general became its leader, the new department was also officially charged with the supervision of all federal law officers and attorneys, the control of immigration, and the investigation of federal crimes. The appointment of the attorney general to head the Department of Justice did cause some controversy. The position of attorney general was viewed as one of great patronage, since it included the appointment of federal judges, U.S. attorneys, and marshals. The attorney general's ability to use the justice system to his political party's advantage has been a concern ever since. Another area of concern within the department was the fee system. Federal marshals and attorneys were paid on a per case basis, encouraging them to engage in many petty legal actions, or else go underpaid. The fee system was replaced with a salary-based wage system in 1897.

Amos Tappan Akerman from Georgia was the first individual assigned to the increasingly important position of attorney general. Akerman's appointment to the post was especially significant in light of the historical context. With the end of the Civil War just five years past, the nation was still recovering, and the appointment of a Southerner served as a symbol of a renewed commitment to build a united republic. During Akerman's tenure the Department of Justice was primarily involved in investigating violations of Reconstruction laws. Working with the Army, the department investigated and attempted to stop the increased violence against African Americans.

The Modern Era

The end of the nineteenth and beginning of the twentieth centuries saw Department of Justice attorneys heavily involved in anti-trust actions under the Sherman Anti-Trust Act of 1890. The Anti-Trust Division of the department continued to monitor the growth of corporations throughout the twentieth century, and occasionally took legal action to stop mergers. During World War I (1914–18), it fell to the Department of Justice to enforce a number of new laws. The Neutrality Acts were the most difficult to oversee, but they ended when the United States entered into the war. Meanwhile, the Bureau of Investigation took charge of enforcing laws against sedition and espionage. In 1924 the department was rocked by scandal, when Warren Harding's attorney general, Harry Daugherty, was forced to resign amid reports of mismanagement and payoffs.

During the 1940s and 1950s the Department of Justice was involved in the so-called Red Scare, along with several other agencies and congressional committees. Using methods that some have since harshly criticized, a number of suspected Communists and other subversives were prosecuted. It was also during the 1950s that the department established a Special Group on Organized Crime to coordinate the federal law enforcement campaign against organized crime. This despite the opposition of Federal Bureau of Investigation (FBI) Chairman J. Edgar Hoover, who denied the existence of organized crime in the United States. Robert Kennedy, who became attorney general in 1961, made organized crime the department's number one priority. His best known success was the 1967 conviction of Teamsters Union President James Hoffa for jury tampering.

The major political upheavals of the 1960s and 1970s, such as the Vietnam War, mass demonstrations, and the Civil Rights movement, changed the face of the Department of Justice dramatically. New legislation, such as the Civil Rights Act of 1964 and the Voting Rights Act of 1965 directly impacted the department's responsibilities. The department had created a Civil Rights Division in 1957, in part as a response to the *Brown vs. Board of Education* case of 1954 which found segregated schools to be unconstitutional. This Division quickly became heavily involved in the protection of African American voters in the South.

Richard Nixon had campaigned for office on a crime prevention platform, and his presidency saw the powers of the Department of Justice greatly expanded. However, the scandal surrounding the Watergate break-in and cover up gravely harmed the reputation and image of the Department of Justice. Three attorneys general resigned during the crisis, one of whom, John Mitchell, was later convicted of conspiracy, obstruction of justice, and perjury.

During the 1980s the Department of Justice continued to grow in size and influence in part because a campaign against illegal drugs became a national priority. During the 1990s the DOJ was often in the news and underwent much public scrutiny. In 1993 President Bill Clinton appointed Janet Reno the first female attorney general. A few months later federal agents were involved in the controversy filled siege of a religious cult at Waco, Texas, which ended in a fire and dozens of deaths.

Throughout the decade the department was also embroiled in a series of political controversies surrounding President Clinton and his administration. For example, there were concerns that the Democratic Party had violated political fundraising laws during the campaigns of 1996, including President Bill Clinton's successful campaign for reelection. Attorney General Janet Reno opened a DOJ investigation, but many called for her to appoint an independent counsel, outside of the direct control of the DOJ, to investigate the issue. Reno refused, leading to accusations that she was abusing her power as attorney general, in order to protect the president who appointed her.

CURRENT POLITICAL ISSUES

As the largest law firm in the country, the DOJ serves as counsel for all its citizens by representing their needs in law enforcement and prosecution. Just as private lawyers range in their foci, from medical malpractice to civil rights to criminal law and everything in between, so too do DOJ lawyers, investigators, and agents. It is the department's responsibility to protect against criminals and subversion, ensure free enterprise and competition, safeguard the consumer, and enforce drug, immigration, and naturalization laws. The difference is, the DOJ does not take up matters of limited interest. Rather, the DOJ approaches issues that have an impact on a great many people.

Case Study: Keeping Microsoft in Check

In 1990 the Federal Trade Commission (FTC) began an investigation of Microsoft, the world's leading supplier of operating systems software designed for IBM and IBM-compatible personal computers (PCs). A computer's operating system controls the computer and any attached devices like a mouse, keyboard, and disk drive. The FTC was investigating Microsoft's acquisition and maintenance of monopoly power in that market, but it never filed complaint against Microsoft because the commission never came into full agreement that such a move was justified. Thus, the commission suspended further investigation.

The antitrust division of the DOJ took over where the FTC left off. In addition to reviewing FTC files, the department issued 21 civil investigative demands to Microsoft and third parties, reviewed one million pages of documents, conducted more than 100 interviews, and deposed 22 persons, including Microsoft Chairman Bill Gates.

In July 1994, the department filed a civil antitrust complaint to prevent and restrain Microsoft from using exclusionary and anticompetitive contracts to market its personal computer operating system software, in violation of Sections 1 and 2 of the Sherman Act. Microsoft was charged with unlawfully maintaining a monopoly of operating systems and unreasonably restraining trade of the same product by others.

Original equipment manufacturers (OEMs) supply the computer itself, generally pre-installed with an operating system so that the unit is ready to use upon purchase. But the DOJ charged that Microsoft used unique contract terms to deter OEMs from installing other operating systems during the life of their contracts with Microsoft.

Specifically, Microsoft's contracts required OEMs to pay Microsoft a royalty for each computer sold with an x86 class microprocessor, whether or not the OEM included a Microsoft operating system, a different operating system, or no operating system. This was known as a per processor license.

Additionally, the DOJ charged, Microsoft further excluded other software competition by forcing major OEMs into long-term contracts, by requiring minimum commitments, and by crediting unused balances to future contracts, thereby extending the contract term and discouraging OEMs from installing non-Microsoft operating systems.

A second practice that fell under DOJ scrutiny was Microsoft's use of nondisclosure agreements with certain independent software vendors (ISVs), the companies that provide applications software (word processors, games, etc.) to run "on top of" Microsoft's operating system. Microsoft had provided only some ISVs with advance test versions of its newest operating system, so that they could develop their software to be compatible with that operating system. In such situations however, Microsoft imposed nondisclosure agreements, which restricted the ISVs from working with any other operating systems companies.

These issues were resolved between Microsoft and the DOJ in June 1995, at which time both parties agreed to a consent decree, effective for six and one-half years. The decree prohibited Microsoft from entering into per processor licenses, licenses with a term exceeding one year, licenses containing a minimum commitment, and restrictive nondisclosure agreements. Microsoft was also prohibited from using other exclusionary practices including lump-sum pricing and variants of per processor licensing. The decree applies to Microsoft's most popular operating systems products, MS-DOS, Windows, and Windows 95.

In October 1997 the DOJ brought Microsoft to court for violating the consent decree. The action the DOJ opposed was that Microsoft required OEMs to license Microsoft's Internet Explorer along with, and as a condition of, licensing its Windows operating systems. According to the DOJ's petition, "Conditioning its Windows licenses on OEMs licensing Internet Explorer is precisely the sort of improper use of Microsoft's market power to protect and extend its monopoly that this Court's Final Judgment sought to prevent and which it expressly prohibits."

Public Impact

The Antitrust Procedures and Penalties Act, known as the Tunney Act, specifically requires that an antitrust consent decree be "in the public interest." By taking Microsoft to court for alleged anticompetitive practices, the DOJ sought to secure, in the public interest, the benefits of competition. By keeping Microsoft in check consumers should notice higher quality, more innovation, competitive pricing among like products, and more variety. With eighty percent of U.S. public schools hooked up to the Internet and 40 percent of homes running a computer (*Consumer Electronics, U.S. Sales, 1997*, Electronic Industries Association), the DOJ's cases against Microsoft have the potential to affect millions of Americans.

SUCCESSES AND FAILURES

In 1996 the Federal Bureau of Investigation (FBI), under the auspices of the Department of Justice, was able to peacefully resolve an 81-day standoff with the Montana Freemen, an antigovernment paramilitary organization that had taken hostages in its efforts to pressure the government into negotiations. The standoff was closely watched and was a critically important success for the FBI after a 1992 incident in Ruby Ridge, Idaho, in which extreme right-wing tax resisters engaged in a shootout with federal agents. In that incident, a woman and her child were shot to death and the remaining family members filed and won a wrongful death suit against the government.

FUTURE DIRECTIONS

Since his election in 1992, President Clinton has worked closely with the Department of Justice to address the increased incidence of violent crimes committed in the United States. During his first term, President Clinton proposed legislation based on recommendations from the DOJ that called for sweeping reforms in the criminal justice system. Known as the Crime Bill, this legislation also took a tougher position on juvenile justice issues. In his State of the Union address in 1997, President Clinton announced "full-scale assault on juvenile crime."

To this end, the Department of Justice was charged with formulating policy recommendations and suggesting legislation related to youth violence and gang activities. As part of its effort, the DOJ prepared a four-part strategy: try youth as adults when they have committed violent crimes; impose curfews and keep schools open for extended hours for youth who have nowhere else to go; expand existing restrictions of gun sales to juvenile delinquents, prohibiting the sale of guns to those convicted of violent crimes even after they are of legal age; and reform the juvenile justice system to deal with young offenders more effectively.

AGENCY RESOURCES

The Office of Justice Programs (OJP) serves as the department's primary source of information through its on-line Justice Information Center (http://www.ncjrs.org). This information clearinghouse includes the most extensive source of information on criminal and juvenile justice in the world.

One of OJP's popular home pages on the World Wide Web is the Bureau of Justice Statistics, where the latest information on topics such as drug use rates and data on firearms can be found. This site is located at http://www.ojp.usdoj.gov/bjs.

AGENCY PUBLICATIONS

The Department of Justice and its many agencies publish thousands of information resources each year. Frequently requested publications include the *FBI Law Enforcement Bulletin; Law Enforcement and Management Statistics;* and *U.S. Supreme Court Opinions.* For further information on these and other DOJ publications, call (202) 514–2000.

BIBLIOGRAPHY

"At War With Microsoft." *Economist*, 23 May 1998.

Caplan, Lincoln. "Serenely Against the Tide." *New York Times*, 25 November 1996, p. 45.

"Doctors Given Federal Threat on Marijuana—U.S. Acts to Overcome States Easing of Law." *New York Times*, 31 December 1996, p. A1.

Dunn, Lynn. *The Department of Justice*. New York: Chelsea House Publishers, 1989.

Garland, Susan B. "Justice vs. Microsoft: Who's Got the Edge?" *Business Week*, 28 May 1998.

"The Guns of October." *U.S. News and World Report*, 4 November 1996, p. 16.

"Justice Department to Join Case Against California's Affirmative Action Ban." *Jet*, 13 January 1997, p. 12.

Koprowski, Gene. "Justice Makes Radio Waves." *Insight on the News*, 27 January 1997, p. 42.

Nossiter, Adam. "Early Reports of Abuses Cited in Citadel Inquiry—Handling of Harassment Case is Criticized." *New York Times*, 22 January 1997, p. Al0.

"Why Reno's Tin Ear is No Longer a Virtue," *Time*, 28 April 1997, p. 35.

Department of Labor (DOL)

WHAT IS ITS MISSION?

The Department of Labor (DOL) was established in 1913 to protect the interests of and strengthen the rights of working people, and to improve workplace conditions for the employed. To achieve these goals, the DOL deals with a broad range of programs designed to promote the well-being of workers, including job safety, workers' compensation, unemployment insurance, fair labor practices, and job training opportunities.

HOW IS IT STRUCTURED?

The DOL was the ninth cabinet-level department created and remains part of the executive branch of government. The department is led by a secretary who is appointed by the president. The secretary serves as the principal adviser to the president on the development of labor policies designed to ensure safe working conditions, protect employees' rights, and advance employment opportunities. The DOL consists of eight administrative offices, including the Office of the Secretary, Office of Administrative Law Judges, Office of the Assistant Secretary for Administration and Management, Office of the Assistant Secretary for Policy, Office of the Chief Financial Officers, Office of the Inspector General, Office of Small Business Programs, and the Office of the Solicitor.

In addition, nine bureaus are responsible for carrying out the primary goals of the DOL. These are the Bureau of International Labor Affairs, Bureau of Labor Statistics, Employment Standards Administration, Employment and Training Administration, Mine Safety and Health Admin-

ESTABLISHED: March 4, 1913
EMPLOYEES: 15,412

Contact Information:

ADDRESS: 200 Constitution Ave. NW
Washington, DC 20210
PHONE: (202) 219-5000
FAX: (202) 219-8822
URL: http://www.dol.gov
SECRETARY OF LABOR: Alexis M. Herman

FAST FACTS

The DOL administers and enforces over 180 federal laws, affecting 10 million employers and 125 million workers.

(Source: U.S. Department of Labor. "Major Statutes of the U.S. Department of Labor," 1997.)

istration, Occupational Safety and Health Administration, Pension and Welfare Benefits Administration, Veterans' Employment and Training Service, and Women's Bureau. Each bureau plays a significant role in determining policy and enforcing existing labor laws.

PRIMARY FUNCTIONS

Fostering the welfare of workers is the goal of the DOL. To this end, the department administers and enforces approximately 200 laws that address specific labor and workplace issues. For example, the DOL initiated the Fair Labor Standards Act which suggests standards for the minimum-wage rates. The department also sets limitations on the circumstances under which wages can be garnished or withheld. Through its Occupational Safety and Health Administration bureau, the department sets rules and regulations for employers so that workplaces are safe, free from hazards, and, in cases where they must use hazardous materials, workers are protected to the fullest extent possible. The DOL's Employment Standards Administration oversees the Family and Medical Leave Act which requires employers with 50 or more employees to provide an unpaid 12-week leave of absence for a worker when there is a birth or adoption of a child or a serious illness involving the employee or a family member.

Other functions involve regulating pension programs, monitoring certain reporting practices within labor unions, working with veterans, and assisting employees subject to plant closings. The DOL also provides support for populations that are often the target of unlawful or discriminatory working conditions, such as children, women, and minorities.

PROGRAMS

The DOL is responsible for a broad range of programs, with each division dedicated to certain aspects of U.S. workers' welfare. For example, the Women's Bureau was established in 1920 to serve the interest of working women. Today, over 60 million women are in the labor force and the bureau continues to dedicate itself to ensuring that women's voices are being heard and that their issues are reflected in public policy. Specifically, the Women's Bureau keeps women updated about their rights in the workplace; designs and promotes policy initiatives that benefit working women; conducts research and analyzes information about working women; and serves as a voice for women to the president, Congress, and the U.S. public. Issues of concern to the bureau include fair and equitable wages, balancing work and family demands, fair treatment on the job, and equal opportunities for advancement. In 1997 the Women's Bureau held its first summit, which was an opportunity for working women across the United States to discuss solutions to some of the most pressing workplace issues for women. The summit served as a place for policymakers and workers to meet face to face in locations across the country. Recommendations from the gathering offered new directions for addressing issues such as equitable pay, continuing educational opportunities, and discrimination issues.

Saving lives, preventing injuries, and protecting the health of Americans at work is the purpose of the DOL's Occupational Safety and Health Administration (OSHA). As a result of the Occupational Safety and Health Act of 1970, OSHA is charged with setting protective job-site standards, enforcing those standards, and assisting employers and employees through technical assistance and educational programs. OSHA's standards for on-the-job safety are developed by engineers, physicians, educators, and technicians. Inspection teams throughout the country work with employers to encourage compliance with OSHA standards, and in some cases, enforce penalties when workplaces are not implementing protective measures. OSHA also works with employees so that they become familiar with the specific safety and health issues in their work environment.

An example of OSHA in action includes its efforts to address a new category of on-the-job injuries known as repetitive stress injuries (RSI). RSIs result when workers must repeat the same motion throughout the day, do the work in an awkward position, use a great deal of exertion at the job, or any combination of these risk factors. Workers who experience RSIs may be unable to perform their jobs or even simple household tasks. RSIs are one of the fastest growing workplace injuries, costing employers more than $20 billion for 2.73 million workers' compensation claims in 1993.

According to 1994 Bureau of Labor Statistics data, nursing home workers have one of the highest rates of occupational injuries and illnesses among all U.S. industries. Only meat-products processing and motor vehicle/equipment manufacturing industries rank higher. Forty-two percent of nursing home injuries result from back injuries when lifting residents. Back injuries average more than $8,400 each in workers' compensation expenses alone. To address these issues OSHA has launched a program to work specifically with nursing home operators and employees on how to protect and prevent back injuries.

BUDGET INFORMATION

The 1998 Department of Labor budget was $35.7 billion, slightly more than 2 percent of the entire federal budget of $1.653 trillion. Of this amount $10.6 billion was allocated for discretionary programs that come under the theme of Lifelong Learning in the 21st Century. These programs, intended to increase the skill base of all U.S. workers and to maintain safety standards include: the $2.4 billion Youth Jobs initiative for summer employment and learning and employment opportunities, especially for noncollege bound youth; $5 billion for Jobs-to-Jobs, to assist workers affected by changes in the economy, such as workers who have been displaced due to plant closings and relocations; $2.1 billion for Welfare-to-Jobs programs promoting economic self-sufficiency; and $1.1 billion in worker protection programs such as pension security and continuing health insurance or portability.

Mandatory funding in 1998 was estimated to reach $25 billion, with approximately $24 billion devoted to unemployment insurance. The remainder is dedicated to workers' compensation, and enforcing occupational safety and health mandates and other statutes.

BUDGET:
Department of Labor

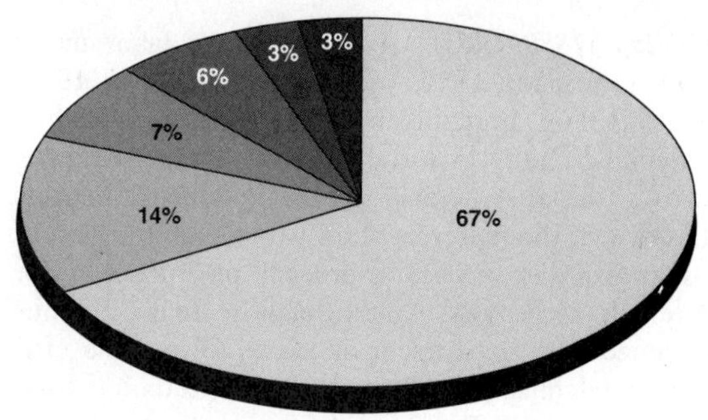

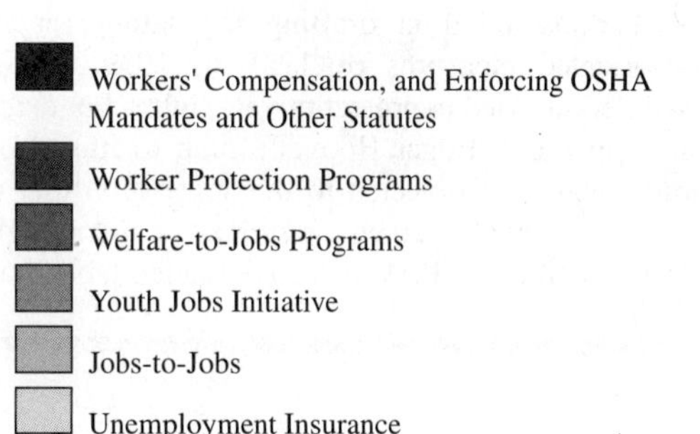

Percentage of Federal Budget

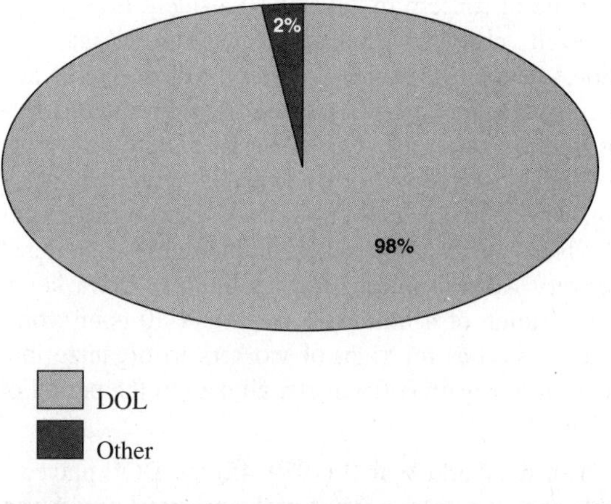

HISTORY

The DOL was established in 1913, "to foster, promote, and develop the welfare of working people, to improve their working conditions, and to enhance their opportunities for profitable employment." Initially, the DOL consisted of four agencies that had previously been part of the Department of Commerce and Labor (which now became simply the Department of Commerce): the Bureau of Labor Statistics, Bureau of Immigration, Bureau of Naturalization, and the Children's Bureau. Created after 50 years of campaigning by organized labor for its voice in the government, the department was intended to promote reasonable working hours, fair pay, safe working conditions, cooperative labor and management relations, and to fight discrimination on the job. These issues have continued to be the focus of the department throughout its history.

The DOL's first nationwide program came during World War I (1914–18), when it was called upon to help organize U.S. industry and labor to support the U.S. war effort. The DOL created the War Labor Administration (WLA) to mobilize workers to contribute to the war effort by working in shipbuilding factories and defense plants. Through the WLA, the DOL set policies on wages, recruited women and minorities for work in the defense industry, and worked on improving the safety conditions and other employment-related problems so that the workforce could better support the war effort.

The practices of the WLA became the foundation on which much of the department's later programs were based. After a decade of prosperity, the DOL faced great

BIOGRAPHY:

Frances Perkins

Politician (1880–1965) As secretary of labor under President Franklin D. Roosevelt from 1933 to 1945, Frances Perkins drafted New Deal legislation including the Social Security Act and the Fair Labor Standards Act. As the first female cabinet member, Perkins believed that she represented all women, and felt enormous pressure to succeed in order to pave the way for her female successors. As the labor secretary Perkins reorganized the Department of Labor to increase efficiency, modernize procedures, and restore its integrity. When the National Recovery Administration and other early New Deal initiatives came under attack by the courts, Perkins aided in drafting legislation for the reform-oriented measures of 1935 to 1939. During wartime Perkins tried to protect private rights. For example she opposed J. Edgar Hoover's plan to fingerprint all immigrants, and objected to the suggestion that all men, and possibly all women, be subject to an industrial and agricultural draft. Perkins also defended labor standards, particularly championing the forty-hour work week and payment for overtime. Agreeing with the Children's Bureau that a young mother's primary responsibility was to her children, she lobbied against government-sponsored day care centers as a wartime measure. The American Federation of Labor and the Congress of Industrial Organizations thoroughly supported her. On Inauguration Day 1945, Perkins tried to resign from her post but deferred to the wishes of an obviously ill Roosevelt. Upon Roosevelt's death President Harry Truman asked her to stay on, and in September 1946 Truman appointed her to the Civil Service Commission, a post she held for seven years.

challenges with the onset of the Great Depression in 1932. The high unemployment rates of the Great Depression were of concern to the DOL. President Franklin D. Roosevelt charged Secretary Frances Perkins, the nation's first female cabinet secretary, with designing key reform and relief programs. The DOL played an important role in Roosevelt's New Deal by administering the Civilian Conservation Corp's unemployment relief program. The department also played a role in forging closer links between industry and labor through the National Recovery Administration. The abolition of child labor, the institution of a minimum wage and 40-hour workweek, as well as the right of workers to organize into unions and bargain collectively, all date to the period of the New Deal.

During World War II (1939–45) the DOL played a much smaller role than it had in the previous world war. None of the special war labor agencies established during the war were administered by the DOL. However, during this period, the DOL assisted these new agencies while working to maintain labor standards, in the face of tremendous pressure on the wartime economy.

After World War II, the focus of the DOL shifted towards guaranteeing the safety of workers and protecting minorities against job discrimination. While the WLA had considered workplace safety issues, it wasn't until 1958 that the department began to take the lead in developing job-safety legislation. Slowly, laws were passed to regulate working conditions for various employment sectors, ranging from dock workers to miners. The DOL's role in assuring safety and enforcing health standards increased dramatically when OSHA passed in 1970.

During the 1950s the labor department began to address employment discrimination against women, minorities, and people with disabilities. Since then, formulating policy to provide equal opportunities and equal pay has became a priority within the DOL. The 1960s saw the passage of civil rights legislation, which affirmed the right of all Americans to equal opportunity in employment, and the DOL worked to insure that these rights were upheld. President Lyndon Johnson's war on poverty in the mid–1960s saw an expansion of the DOL's role in aiding the poor and unemployed, especially in the area of job training and placement.

Since 1970, the DOL has focused its efforts on improving its services rather than enacting new programs. Having seen rapid expansion of its duties, especially with the passage of OSHA, the department tried to determine how best to administer its duties. At times heavily criticized for its extensive regulations and bureaucracy, especially during the administration of President Reagan (1981–89), the DOL has worked to improve its efficiency at all levels.

CURRENT POLITICAL ISSUES

The DOL was founded without a clear mandate. While most people agreed that an organization should exist to guarantee worker safety and security, few had any idea of how to bring this about. The constitutionality of previous labor laws had been challenged before the Supreme Court and laws governing child labor and a minimum wage for women had been struck down. By 1936, the Department of Labor was an organization that had goals but no clear way to meet them.

Case Study: Minimum Wage Law

Franklin Roosevelt asked Frances Perkins to be Secretary of Labor in 1933, promising that there would be a reform of labor laws. Perkins was a strong supporter of minimum wage and limiting child labor. She consulted with a team of lawyers, drafting several bills in the hope that one might survive a court challenge. After seeing most of these bills die before the U.S. Supreme Court, Perkins held one final strategy back.

The strategy was a general labor practices act. After it was scrutinized by a team of White House lawyers, the bill was introduced on the House floor on May 24, 1937. One year and close to a dozen revisions later, the bill was signed into law as the Fair Labor Standards Act (FLSA). It effectively ended child labor, set a minimum wage of twenty-five cents an hour, and created the standard 40-hour workweek.

The impact of the FLSA was initially felt only by those people engaged in interstate commerce, about one-fifth of the workforce. As time passed, the FLSA was expanded to cover farming and retail jobs. A 1966 amendment added schools, nursing homes, and the construction industry. By the 1970s, the effects of the FLSA had been felt by virtually all workers in the United States. The minimum wage has been increased 26 times in the history of the FLSA through 1997.

Each increase requires an act of Congress and must be signed into law by the president. For each hour in excess of 40, a worker would receive "time and a half" pay of 150 percent of the standard hourly wage. On September 1, 1997, the minimum wage in the U.S. rose to $5.15, up from the base rate of $4.25, and an interim rate of $4.75. The increase was hotly debated in Congress with opponents saying it was unaffordable for some businesses. However, Congress approved the new standard and as a result, nearly 10 million hourly-paid workers received the increase, adding an additional $1,800 per year to their annual income. In arguing for the increase, proponents noted that for many families, an additional $1,800 annually meant the equivalent of seven months of groceries, one year of health care costs, nine months worth of utility bills, or even a full year's tuition at some colleges. In addition, a study conducted by the Department of Health and Human Services suggested that 300,000 people would move above the poverty line as a result of the increase, including 100,000 children living in poverty.

FUTURE DIRECTIONS

The DOL will continue its efforts to address workplace inequities by convening meetings such as the Women's Summit, which seek new solutions to persistent problems regarding unequal wages and disproportionate educational and career advancement opportunities.

Another major initiative of the DOL is the effort to move more U.S. citizens off welfare assistance and into employment and training programs. To this end, the DOL has developed a One-Stop Career Center System program to centralize information about employment and training programs available to the public. These centers, currently being developed or planned in each of the 50 states, will offer access to all the available services under such programs as the Job Training Partnership Act, Unemployment Insurance, and the Senior Community Service Employment Program. Job seekers will be able to access information about the program that best serves their needs, whether they be entering the work force for the first time, returning to work after an extended leave, or seeking opportunities to train in a new field as a result of plant closures or downsizing of companies.

AGENCY RESOURCES

The Bureau of Labor Statistics (BLS) is the principal information agency for the DOL. The BLS gathers, analyzes, and disseminates information related to labor, wages, employment rates, job growth indicators, and more. The BLS also serves as the main source of employment statistics for the DOL. For further information, contact the BLS at (202) 606-5886 to speak directly with an information specialist. For general information about the DOL, contact its Office of Public Affairs at (202) 219-8211 or write to the U.S. Department of Labor, Office of Public Affairs, 200 Constitution Ave., NW, Room S-1032, Washington, DC 20210.

AGENCY PUBLICATIONS

The DOL publishes hundreds of pamphlets, press releases and reports each year, on subjects ranging from employee benefits studies to women in the workplace to how to find a job. One of the DOL's annual products is the *Occupational Outlook Handbook*. Published by the BLS, it features information about leading employment fields, how to find a job and what factors to consider before accepting a job offer. The Bureau of International Labor Affairs, which studies child labor practices worldwide, has published *By the Sweat and Toil of Children: The Use of Child Labor in American Imports*. The report examines the use of children in the manufacturing of household items imported to the United States. These and most other DOL publications are available through the BLS Chicago office, which can be contacted at (312) 352-1880 or Bureau of Labor Statistics, Publications Sales Center, P.O. Box 2145, Chicago, IL 60690.

Many DOL publications are available on-line, either in the DOL's on-line library at http://www.dol.gov/dol/public/library.html or on the Web sites of DOL's agencies, accessible through the DOL's home page at http://www.dol.gov.

BIBLIOGRAPHY

"If You're Going to Downsize, Do It Gently: Interview with U.S. Labor Secretary Robert Reich." *Sales and Marketing Management*, September 1996, p. 118.

Moskowitz, Rachel, and Drew Warwick. "The Job Outlook in Brief: 1994–2005." *Occupational Outlook Quarterly*, Spring 1996, p. 2.

"Productivity in 1996 Up." *New York Times,* 12 March 1997, p. C4.

Schlesinger, Jacob M. "Inflation's Pace Slowed During January." *Wall Street Journal*, 20 February 1997, p. A2.

Stinson, Joseph. "Beyond Shop Talk: Reinventing High School." *Electronic Learning*, February 1996, p. 18.

"Welcome to the Department of Labor: Benefits and Services at a Glance." Washington, D.C.: U.S. Department of Labor, 1997.

Department of State (DOS)

WHAT IS ITS MISSION?

According to the official statement published by the Department of State, its mission is "to ensure national security by building and maintaining international alliances, and defusing and preventing crises; advance the economic interests of the American people by promoting free trade and assisting American businesses; promote democratic values and respect for human rights; and provide protection to Americans abroad and control access to the United States." The Department of State (DOS) is the primary foreign relations branch of the United States government and advises the president on all matters of foreign affairs.

HOW IS IT STRUCTURED?

The DOS, a cabinet department under the umbrella of the executive branch, is the lead United States foreign affairs agency. It is led by the secretary of state who is appointed by the president and confirmed by Congress. The secretary and the deputy secretary oversee the activities of its many bureaus, offices, embassies, consulates, missions, posts, and delegations around the world. Personnel include political appointees, as well as career Civil Service and Foreign Service professionals.

The DOS's five undersecretaries advise the secretary, oversee most of the department's day-to-day operations, and are each responsible for managing the major areas of DOS activity. These major areas are called groups. The five groups are: Political Affairs, Economic and Agricultural Affairs, Arms Control and International

ESTABLISHED: July 27, 1789
EMPLOYEES: 24,608

Contact Information:

ADDRESS: 2201 C St. NW
Washington, DC 20520
PHONE: (202) 647-4000
TDD (HEARING IMPAIRED): (800) 877–8339
FAX: (202) 647-7120
E-MAIL: secretary@state.gov
URL: http://www.state.gov
SECRETARY OF STATE: Madeleine K. Albright

FAST FACTS

The executive appointment of Madeleine K. Albright as Secretary of State makes her the first woman to fill this high-ranking position.

(Source: Department of State, 1998.)

Security Affairs, Management, and Global Affairs. Each group contains a number of individual bureaus and offices that administer the functions of the group in specific geographical or subject areas.

In addition to the many activities carried out by its own personnel, the DOS also oversees several other governmental agencies involved in foreign affairs. These agencies include: the Arms Control and Disarmament Agency (ACDA), which manages U.S. participation in arms control treaties; the U.S. Agency for International Development (USAID), which provides economic and humanitarian aid to other countries; and the U.S. Information Agency (USIA), which explains and gains support for U.S. policy among the public of foreign nations. The permanent representative to the United Nations for the United States is a position that is also administered by the State Department.

The State Department Abroad

The United States maintains 250 diplomatic and consular posts around the world. Located in these countries are embassies that are headed by ambassadors, each of whom is appointed by the president. Ambassadors are posted in 164 countries and serve as personal representatives of the president. Ambassadors are also responsible for negotiating agreements between the United States and host countries, explaining and distributing United States policy, and maintaining friendly relations with the host country's government and people.

The State Department also operates consulates in many foreign countries; consulates are headed by consuls. While ambassadors are primarily concerned with the leaders and people of the nation hosting their embassy, consuls exist to protect and represent the interests of American citizens who are visiting or living in a host country. They can issue passports, help Americans find legal assistance, notarize documents, provide U.S. tax forms, and otherwise assist Americans in need.

PRIMARY FUNCTIONS

The Department of State heads up diplomatic relations between the United States and approximately 180 countries. The State Department does much of its work through U.S. embassies, which are located in the foreign nations. Likewise, foreign nations have embassies in the United States, primarily in Washington, D.C. The work of the department is ultimately determined by the president. However, the president does collaborate with the secretary of state and DOS representatives, whose task it is to examine the situations of a given nation and make policy recommendations. General goals of foreign policy include peacekeeping; economic development, both foreign and domestic; and attention to global problems.

One of the central concerns of the State Department in matters of diplomacy is to promote peaceful interactions between foreign countries and the United States. It coordinates its efforts with other like-minded countries in countering the proliferation of nuclear weapons by encouraging countries not to acquire them or test them. It also attempts to prevent regional crises by becoming involved in negotiations between warring parties and providing economic aid for development in regional hot spots. It supports international peacekeeping and humanitarian efforts, such as the United Nations, by curtailing violence and assisting refugees and victims of disasters around the world.

By creating trade agreements and international partnerships and developing markets for U.S. exports, the State Department is committed to increasing the magnitude of both the U.S. and global economies. Representatives from other countries meet with department officials to establish arrangements that are beneficial to all; this increases the amount of U.S. exports, which in turn creates new markets and jobs for American workers. The department places special emphasis on developing countries as they are the fastest growing market for U.S. goods.

A number of global problems directly affect the United States and have become a major focus for the State Department. Environmental issues, like the threat of global warming, have caused the department to turn its attention to countries whose actions have a direct effect upon the world's environment. For instance, the State Department has attempted to help the Brazilian government find other ways to sustain its economy without destroying its valuable rain forests. Additionally, the department has dedicated a great deal of effort toward eliminating international terrorism and drug trafficking through enforcement cooperatives set up with other nations.

In addition to its work in diplomacy, the State Department also provides helpful services to Americans travelling or living abroad. It issues passports and disseminates a variety of useful information such as the approved methods of conducting business abroad, travel or emergency situation advisories, and medical insurance. Additionally, the State Department helps to ensure that American citizens who have been arrested in other countries are treated humanely and receive a fair trial. For foreigners wishing to enter the United States, the State Department is responsible for issuing visas to those that qualify.

PROGRAMS

The Department of State has several programs devoted to helping young people learn more about foreign affairs. In early 1998 the Geography Learning Site on the Internet was created. Its mission is to be an interactive resource for students in grades kindergarten through 12. The Web site contains numerous maps showing the location of various State Department embassies and consulates as well as information about the department and some of the issues it focuses on. In an effort to stay current with recent events, the site is updated and its functionality has been increased.

The State Department also runs a variety of programs to recruit interested people into the Foreign Service. One of these programs is the Foreign Affairs Fellowship Program, directed toward undergraduate students in their sophomore year. The fellowship provides funding for junior, senior, and first year of graduate school for qualified applicants. In exchange, participants commit to pursue a graduate degree in international studies as well as at least a four-and-a-half year assignment as a Foreign Service officer. Selection of those participating is based on undergraduate grade point average, leadership skills, and an interview with Foreign Service staff.

Created in 1964 the Art in Embassies Program (AIEP) is devoted to showcasing American visual artists in the residences of U.S. ambassadors around the world. Museums or private individuals lend (or occasionally donate) pieces of American art for a period of three years. During this time, the thousands of visitors passing through a residence will be able to appreciate these symbols of American culture. The State Department shows its appreciation of the lenders and donors by placing a commemorative tablet next to each piece that includes the museum's or person's name.

BUDGET:

Department of State

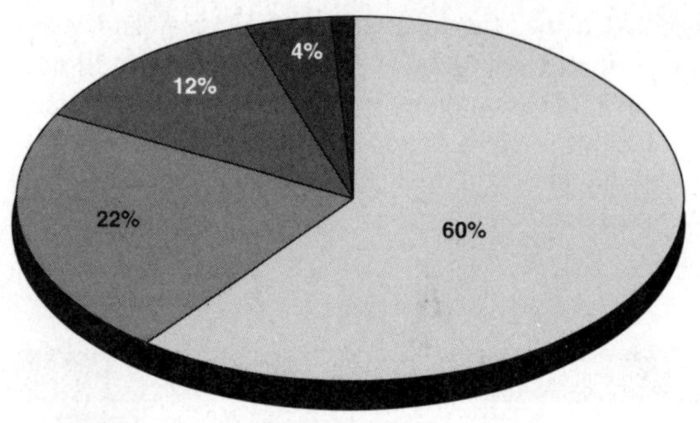

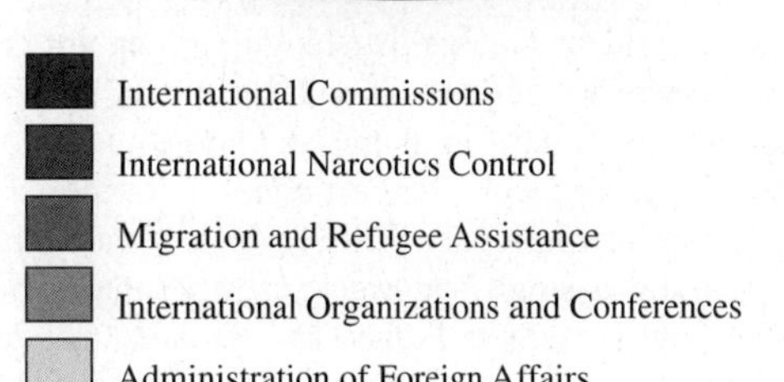

Percentage of Federal Budget

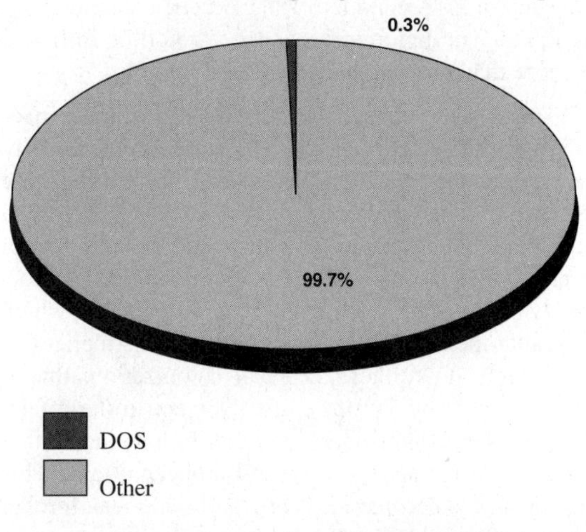

BUDGET INFORMATION

In 1998 Congress appropriated a budget of approximately $5.5 billion to the State Department. This made up about 0.3 percent of the estimated 1998 total federal budget of $1.653 trillion.

The administration of foreign affairs made up the largest portion ($3.01 billion or 60 percent) of the State Department's budget. This money includes $1.64 billion (30 percent of the total State Department's budget) for diplomatic and consular programs, $537 million (10 percent) for various foreign affairs trust funds, $398 million (7 percent) for security and maintenance of U.S. missions, $352 million (6 percent) for foreign affairs salaries and expenses, $236 million (4 percent) for the Foreign Service retirement and disability fund, $86 million (2 percent) for the capital investment fund, and $27 million (1 percent) for the Office of the Inspector General.

Other monies within the State Department budget were directed toward international organizations and conferences ($1.21 billion or 22 percent of the total State Department budget); migration and refugee assistance ($650 million or 12 percent); international narcotics control ($216 million or 4 percent); and international commissions such as the International Boundary and Water Commission, United States and Mexico ($43 million or 1 percent). The remaining funds within the State Department budget were divided among U.S. emergency refugee and migration funding, narcotics interdiction, and the Asia Foundation.

HISTORY

From President George Washington's appointment of the first Secretary of State, Thomas Jefferson, in 1789, the protection of American interests at home and abroad has been the department's highest concern. In the years following the Revolutionary War (1779–83), the United States was still a small and weak nation compared to European powers such as France and Britain. President Washington's foreign policy, therefore, concentrated on avoiding U.S. involvement in international affairs. Indeed, Washington was committed to a policy of American neutrality. The advice he gave in his farewell address at the end of his second term, that America should avoid any military or diplomatic alliances, would be followed for more than one hundred years.

This is not to say that the State Department was inactive during the early decades of U.S. history. One early success was the Louisiana Purchase in 1803, when the United States negotiated the purchase of all the land between the Appalachian Mountains and the Mississippi River from France. In 1823 President Monroe put forward what became known as the Monroe Doctrine, which stated that the United States considered the Americas to be off-limits to further European colonization, that it would oppose any European involvement in the affairs of the Western Hemisphere, and that in turn the United States would not involve itself in European affairs. This position would become the bedrock of American foreign policy until World War I.

The 1840s saw the annexation of, then independent, Texas. This in turn triggered a war with Mexico in 1846, from which the United States emerged quite successful. The Treaty of Guadalupe Hidalgo, negotiated in 1848 by Chief Clerk of the Department of State Nicholas P. Trist, ended the war and gave the United States control over California and New Mexico. This, combined with an agreement with Britain over the northwestern border between the United States and Canada, established the present-day borders of the continental United States. Meanwhile, the United States began to involve itself in trade and diplomacy with Asia, securing a treaty with China and in 1853 forcing Japan to open its ports to U.S. trade.

The Civil War (1860–65) saw the United States withdraw almost entirely from international affairs. By the end of the war the United States was well on its way to being one of the world's great military and industrial powers. It continued to abide by the Monroe Doctrine, however, and for the rest of the nineteenth century concerned itself primarily with discouraging European involvement in the Western Hemisphere.

As the twentieth century dawned, the United States began to assert itself in foreign affairs as it never had. While still avoiding involvement in the politics of Europe, the United States was successful in its aims for greater power in the Pacific and in Latin America. Further, in the late 1890s, the United States was able to encourage most of the nations trading with China to agree to an Open Door policy in which they would allow equal access to that country's trade. In 1903 and 1904, the United States secured the rights to build what would become the Panama Canal.

The year 1914 saw the beginning of one of the most terrible armed conflicts the world has ever seen, World War I. By the end of the war, the United States had broken its long policy of avoiding European entanglements, and sent troops to fight with France and Britain against the Germans. The terrible losses suffered during World War I greatly influenced American foreign policy, further reinforcing that involvement in European affairs should be discouraged. President Wilson's cherished idea of a League of Nations, although intended to discourage war, was rejected by Congress. The United States entered into a period of what is called isolationism, attempting to cut itself off from involvement with other nations. The United States did want to reduce the threat of future war, but not if doing so would require a commitment of U.S. power. One famous treaty, authored in 1927 by Secretary of State Frank Kellogg and French Foreign Minister Aristide Briand and thus called the Kellogg-Briand Pact, proposed to outlaw war entirely, but many of its signatories soon broke their pledges not to engage in hostilities.

During the 1930s Adolf Hitler rose to power in Germany. While Hitler led Germany on a path of expansion, most other nations, including the United States, did little to stop him. War was to be avoided at all costs. In the end, however, what would soon become known as World War II erupted. The United States initially stayed out of this conflict, but by the time Japan attacked Pearl Harbor in 1941 the United States had already established its Lend-Lease agreement with Britain that would become the basis of its wartime economic aid to the Allies.

After four years of fighting, the Axis powers (Germany and its allies) had been defeated, and the United States found itself, along with the Soviet Union, as one of the two supreme military powers in the world. Rejecting its earlier position of noninvolvement in European affairs, the United States sought a new course. Enter Secretary of State George C. Marshall. Marhsall developed a massive economic aid program for the nations of

BIOGRAPHY:

George C. Marshall

General and Statesman (1880–1959) A career soldier and statesman, George C. Marshall was best known for developing the Marshall Plan that rebuilt Europe after World War II. Marshall had seen active duty during World War I, and had risen to the position of army chief of staff during World War II. In 1945 President Harry Truman called Marshall out of retirement to mediate an end to the civil war in China. Even though the mission ultimately failed, in 1947 Truman asked Marshall to be his secretary of state. By the late 1940s U.S. leaders were fearful of Communism. Specifically, because Communism had gained control in several countries in Western Europe, the United States believed the nations that had still not recovered from World War II were the most vulnerable. Secretary of State Marshall put out a call to action. Marshall enunciated a plan to help Europe recover economically, and, in the process, regain political strength. The Marshall Plan proved a great success. The United States supplied money and materials, while the noncommunist European nations banded together to solve their problems without turning to a new political system. An economically healthy Western Europe defeated postwar hunger, resumed trade with the United States, and, integral to goals of the plan, they rejected Communism. Marshall resigned as secretary of state early in 1949, but when the North Korean Communists invaded South Korea in June 1950, Truman again ended Marshall's retirement by convincing him to take the post of secretary of defense. For his lifelong efforts, Marshall received the Nobel Peace Prize in 1953.

Europe that had been devastated by World War II. This program, called the Marshall Plan, allowed the nations of Western Europe to rebuild industry quickly in the decades following the war, ensured their goodwill toward the United States, and set the United States down a new road as a leader in world affairs. The success of the Marhsall Plan, and post-war efforts to strengthen Western Europe against the military threat of the Soviet Union, led to the formation of the North Atlantic Treaty Organization (NATO). This historic agreement further shifted U.S. foreign policy, promoting permanent United States alliances with key western European nations.

In the decades following World War II, the United States engaged in what became known as the Cold War, a long period of mutual hostility with the Soviet Union. The 1950s, 1960s, and 1970s found the United States involved in two wars and several smaller military conflicts, as it sought to prevent any expansion of Soviet power. While tensions were at times very high, the United States and the Soviet Union never fought each other directly, and in the 1970s tensions eased to the point that arms reduction treaties were signed. In the 1980s, tensions rose again. The Cold War culminated not in a military action, however, but in the collapse of the Soviet Union at the end of the decade. As the U.S.S.R.'s member republics broke away, for the most part peacefully, to become independent nations, the United States declared its foreign policy of the preceding forty years a success.

In 1990, after 45 years of political struggle NATO announced that the Cold War was over, marking a new era in United States foreign policy formulation under the Bush, and then Clinton administrations. This new era has been described as one in which international relations are globalizing in scope, a shift from the previous era in which two primary superpowers competed for supremacy, and their relations dominated the international scene. In a strange turnaround, the DOS is now pressured to provide economic aid to the former Soviet Republics in order to promote democracy and stabilize the economies of the region. As nations reshape themselves outside of the politically intense atmosphere of the Cold War, the United States has remained focused on developing strong relationships with other democratic, free market economies throughout the world.

CURRENT POLITICAL ISSUES

The Clinton administration has made the reform of the federal government a priority. Under the guidance of Vice President Al Gore's National Performance Review initiative the State Department is redefining its role, reorganizing specific bureaus, and adapting the department to the changing requirements of foreign policy management. For example, the Arms Control and Disarmament Agency is to be integrated into the State Department's Arms Control and International Security Affairs. Other agencies are slated to be integrated or reorganized as the federal government tries to accomplish more with less money. Increasingly there is pressure for the executive and legislative branches of government to cooperate on foreign affairs. Congressional support is key as the effort to streamline government can become bogged down in partisan politics, each party promoting its own political agenda at the expense of forward momentum in government business. Meanwhile, critical foreign policy decisions are brought before Congress regularly. As the State Department struggles to refine its methods and streamline bureaucracies; critical priorities remain. Arms control, in particular, continues to dominate high levels of U.S. foreign policy.

Case Study: Chemical Weapons Ban Approved

The State Department, in conjunction with other international organizations, monitors weapons of mass destruction throughout the world. For over 20 years, spanning the Reagan, Bush, and Clinton presidential administrations, the U.S. State Department has been working toward the establishment of a treaty to ban chemical weapons. The Chemical Weapons Convention, is just such a treaty.

The Chemical Weapons Convention (CWC) called for its signatories to eliminate their stockpiles of chemical weapons, to restrict the sale of certain chemicals used to make weapons to non-signatory nations, and provided for inspections of the signatory nation's chemical plants to make sure they were in compliance. Senate Democrats solidly supported the treaty, but a significant group of Republicans, including Senate Foreign Relations Committee Chairman Jesse Helms (R-N.C.) did not.

A number of different issues combined to generate Republican opposition to the CWC. Critics questioned the effectiveness of its inspection measures, claiming that since the necessary facilities for production could be so small, and the materials needed are so widely available, any inspection could be avoided. Another complaint was that the nations considered the greatest chemical weapons threats to the United States—Libya, North Korea, Iraq—were not signatories to the treaty, and thus would not be bound by it. Thus the critics felt that U.S. participation would not really work to reduce the threat of chemical weapons, but only siphon away tax money toward new international organizations, and lead to higher costs for U.S. chemical companies that would have to deal with international inspectors.

Supporters of the treaty, including prominent Republicans from the Bush and Reagan administrations, insisted that the treaty would be effective. They stressed that no treaty was perfect, and did not deny that the CWC would be difficult to fully enforce. They emphasized that the United States would have to worry about the non-signatory nations whether they ratified the treaty or not, and that if the treaty was ratified it would at least play a role in ensuring that most of the mandates were carried out effectively. Republicans remained unwilling to accept the treaty as it stood, however, and proposed several amendments. The State Department and other Clinton administration figures insisted that the amendments were unacceptable, as most of them would have required a renegotiation of the treaty that the other signatories had no interest in undertaking.

On April 24, 1997, with only five days left to go before the CWC went into effect with or without the United States, President Clinton and the Democrats in the Senate agreed to a number of concessions, which gained enough Republican support to ratify the treaty. The CWC was ratified without any changes, but Congress was given control over how much money the United States would pay to its administrative body, the Organization for the Prohibition of Chemical Weapons. Another part of the deal concerned U.S. foreign policy agencies. Senator Helms had long sought to have the three largest independent foreign policy agencies, the Arms Control and Disarmament Agency, U.S. Agency for International Development, and the U.S. Information Agency, incorporated into the Department of State. As part of the compromise to get the CWC ratified, it was agreed that all three of these agencies would be brought under DOS control.

Public Impact

Approval of the CWC treaty ensures United States participation in the international movement of some 89 nations to outlaw the development, production, sale, purchase, stockpiling, or use of chemical weapons. This convention will establish an international agency to collect data and conduct inspections intended to verify compliance with those prohibitions. The Chemical Weapons Convention will seek to eliminate the use of weapons of mass destruction for the purpose of war. Supporters believe that the ban will strengthen the international movement against chemical weapons, thus lowering the chances that U.S. military forces will be exposed to chemicals as the result of armed conflict. Critics remain concerned, however, that the treaty will fail to prevent the manufacture of chemical weapons while at the same time providing a false sense of security against chemical attacks.

SUCCESSES AND FAILURES

The relationship between the United States and China is an example of a controversial success for the State Department. A communist nation and a nuclear power, China was once regarded as one of the greatest threats to U.S. national security. Since President Richard Nixon paved the way for diplomatic relations with China in 1972, the State Department has supported a policy of friendly relations, despite widespread criticism of China's human rights record. In the 1990s, with a strengthened economy and the world's largest population, China emerged as a major force in international affairs and a potentially huge market for U.S. goods.

At stake are millions of dollars in exports and other trade-related issues. The U.S. trade deficit with China has reached $40 billion. The astounding growth of the Chinese economy, 10 percent annual growth, makes it one of the most enticing investment opportunities of the 1990s. The State Department can point to these factors and call their policy toward China successful. A vocal minority of critics, however, can point to China's continued human rights abuses and communist government, and call the State Department's success a qualified one.

FUTURE DIRECTIONS

The State Department is faced with a rapidly changing theater of world events in which the political assumptions of the Cold War era are no longer appropriate in the development of current foreign affairs policy. Secretary of State Madeleine K. Albright promotes a global perspective on international relations and an approach to conflict resolution and economic development that emphasizes U.S. cooperation with other nations, as well as international organizations. Of great importance will be strengthening the role of the United States in the United Nations. There will also be increased reliance on the success of the North Atlantic Treaty Organization in order to promote democracy, human rights, economic stability, and international crises prevention. The foreign policy objective of the United States can be described as one that strives to shape the world to be consistent with distinctly American core values, a world made up of open societies and free markets. The primary foreign policy challenges of the twenty-first century will be arms control and sustainable economic development on the international scene.

AGENCY RESOURCES

The State Department's Public Information Division, Public Information Service at (202) 647-6575 provides fact sheets and policy statements on department activities. The Office of Public Information at (202) 647-8677 will provide press release statements, as well as specific publications on international arms control and the progress of the Chemical Weapons Convention. Information on the State Department is also available by accessing the comprehensive Web site at http://www.state.gov. While in Washington, D.C., visit the Department of State's public reading room, which offers unclassified and declassified documents for inspection. The reading room is located at 2201 C St. NW., Washington, D.C.; phone (202) 647-8484.

AGENCY PUBLICATIONS

Dispatch, the official magazine of U.S. foreign policy, is among the many publications that shed light on U.S. foreign relations. It is published weekly by the Office of Public Communication, Bureau of Public Affairs, U.S. Government Printing Office. For information call (202) 512-1800. *American Foreign Policy* is an annual volume containing current official public statements that explain the objectives of U.S. foreign policy. The series includes texts of major official messages, addresses, statements, reports and communications by White House, Department of State, and other federal government agencies involved in the foreign affairs process.

The DOS through the Bureau of Consular Affairs provides a number of pamphlets to educate travelers including *A Safe Trip Abroad*, *Tips for Americans Residing Abroad*, *Your Trip Abroad*, and *Passports: Applying for Them the Easy Way*. For information on these and other publications call (202) 512-1800. Also, information on how and where to apply for a passport is available by calling Passport Services at (202) 647-0518.

BIBLIOGRAPHY

Albright, Madeleine K. "Blueprint for Bipartisan Foreign Policy." *New York Times*, 26 January 1997, p. E13(N).

———. "The United Nations, NATO and Crises Management." *U.S. Department of State Dispatch*, 29 April 1997, p. 219(4).

"The Clinton Administration's Policy on Reforming Multilateral Peace Operations." *U.S. Department of State Dispatch*, 16 May 1994, p. 315(7).

Doherty, Carroll J. "Albright Wields Persuasive Powers at Confirmation Hearing." *Congressional Quarterly Weekly Report*, 11 January 1997, p. 133(2).

Erlanger, Steven. "Albright Picks Two Longtime Diplomats for Two Posts." *New York Times*, 23 January, 1997, p. A9(L).

———. "China Grows, Russia Shrinks, Albright Juggles." *New York Times*, 12 January 1997, p. E18(N).

Levitin, Carl. "Russian Parliament Ratifies Chemical Weapons Treaty." *Nature*, 13 November 1997.

Meyers, Steven Lee. "Albright is Given Bush's Support on Chemical Weapons." *New York Times*, 9 February 1997, p. 4(n).

———. "State Dept. Set for Reshaping, Pleasing Helms." *New York Times*, 18 April 1997, p. A1.

Mitchell, Alison. "Clinton Makes Final Push on Chemical Arms Treaty." *New York Times*, 23 April 1997, p. A10.

———. "How the Votes Were Won: Clinton's New G.O.P. Tactics." *New York Times*, 25 April 1997, p. A1.

Department of the Air Force (USAF)

PARENT ORGANIZATION: Department of Defense
ESTABLISHED: September 18, 1947
EMPLOYEES: 750,000

Contact Information:

ADDRESS: 1670 Air Force Pentagon
Washington, DC 20330-1670
PHONE: (703) 697-6061
FAX: (703) 614-5794
E-MAIL: usaf@af.pentagon.mil

WHAT IS ITS MISSION?

The Air Force defines its mission simply: "to defend the United States through the control and exploitation of air and space."

HOW IS IT STRUCTURED?

The U.S. Air Force (USAF), a component of the U.S. Department of Defense along with the army and the navy, is led by the secretary of the air force, a civilian administrator who is appointed by the president and supervised by a military chief of staff. The secretary is responsible to the president and to the secretary of defense through the representation of the Joint Chiefs of Staff (JCS) of the Department of Defense. The secretary is responsible for ensuring the current and future readiness of the air force to accomplish its mission, and for overseeing the recruiting, training, and equipping of air force personnel. The air force is headquartered in the Pentagon, Washington, D.C., where the secretary is assisted by an undersecretary, a deputy undersecretary, and a number of assistant secretaries whose offices serve specific operations such as space, manpower, and acquisition. The Office of the Secretary includes a general counsel, auditor general, inspector general, administrative assistant, public affairs director, legislative liaison director, and a number of statutory boards and committees.

Professional assistance is provided to the secretary, undersecretary, and assistant secretaries (the secretariat) by the Air Staff, a headquarters functional organization under the chief of staff, United States Air Force. The chief of staff is the senior uniformed air force officer

A B-2 bomber, designed with advanced stealth technology, is difficult to detect with radar. Critics question if they are worth a cost of $2 billion per plane. *(U.S. National Aeronautics and Space Administration/NASA)*

responsible for the organization, training, and equipping of air force personnel; he or she is appointed by the president, usually for a four-year term. The chief of staff is directly responsible to the secretary of the air force for the efficiency and operational readiness of the USAF and is a member of the Joint Chiefs of Staff. Air Staff functions are specialized into clearly defined areas involving the management of the air force, including logistics, personnel, plans and operations, intelligence, and command, control, communications, and computers. A significant member of the Air Staff is the chief master sergeant of the air force, who serves as an adviser to the secretary and the chief of staff on matters concerning the general welfare, effective use, and career progress of the enlisted members of the air force.

The air force's eight major commands, 37 field operating agencies, three direct reporting units, and their subordinate elements make up the field organization that is charged with carrying out the air force mission. There are also two reserve components, the Air Force Reserve and the Air National Guard. The major commands are organized on a functional basis in the United States (Material Command, Space Command, and so forth) and on a geographical basis overseas (Pacific Forces, Forces in Europe). The individual commands are responsible for accomplishing designated phases of air force activities and organizing and equipping their subordinate elements for assigned missions. In descending order of command, operating elements of major commands include numbered air forces, wings (considered the basic unit for generating and employing combat capability), groups, squadrons, and flights.

Field operating agencies are other air force subdivisions; they report directly to headquarters. Each agency is assigned a special mission, smaller in scope than a major command, and carries out its activities under the operational control of a headquarters functional manager. Direct reporting units (the Air Force Academy, 11th Wing, and Operational Test and Evaluation Center) are also responsible to headquarters, but are not under headquarters operational control because of a unique mission, legal requirements, or other factors.

PRIMARY FUNCTIONS

The air force's primary responsibility is to provide aircraft and missile forces necessary to prevent or fight a general war, along with the land-based air forces needed to establish air superiority, to restrain the enemy, and to provide air support of ground forces in combat. The air force is also responsible for providing the primary aerospace forces for the defense of the United States against air and missile attack; for this reason, it assists the National Aeronautics and Space Administration (NASA) in conducting the nation's space program. The air force

BUDGET:

Department of the Air Force

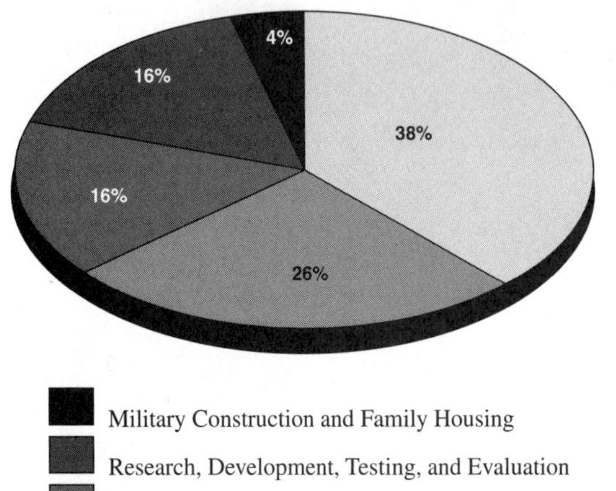

- Military Construction and Family Housing
- Research, Development, Testing, and Evaluation
- Procurement of New Aircraft and Weaponry
- Training, Administration, and Equipage of Personnel
- Operation and Maintenance of Aircraft, Equipment, and Facilities

also supplies the primary airlift capability for use by all U.S. military services and is the major space research and development agency for the Department of Defense.

PROGRAMS

The air force is involved in numerous programs, the list of which is continually updated and revised. Programs involve specific aircraft, organizations, space research and utilization, and the development of weapons. One air force space-related program is the Defense Meteorological Satellite Program (DMSP), conducted by the 6th Space Operations Squadron at Offutt Air Force Base in Nebraska. The two operational DMSP satellites are in polar orbits at about 458 nautical miles, collecting weather data for U.S. military operations. The satellites provide continuous visual and infrared imagery of cloud cover over an area of 1,600 nautical miles. Other sensors provide atmospheric vertical profiles of moisture and temperature. Military forecasters use these data to monitor and predict weather patterns. The DMSP satellites are also capable of evaluating the impact of the ionosphere's electromagnetic charges on early missile warning systems and long-range communications.

The air force also conducts several programs in specialized areas, such as the Thunderbirds, which could most accurately be called a public relations program. The Thunderbirds, the air force's demonstration squadron, perform precision aerial maneuvers that demonstrate the capabilities of air force high-performance aircraft (Lockheed Martin F-16 Fighting Falcons) to people throughout the world. A Thunderbirds air demonstration is a mix of formation flying and solo routines. The Thunderbirds are headquartered at Nellis Air Force Base in Nevada.

BUDGET INFORMATION

The Air Force budget, a component of the entire Department of Defense budget request, was approximately $61 billion in 1997. The largest amount of the Air Force budget, 38 percent, went to the operation and maintenance of aircraft, equipment, and facilities. After that, 26 percent was spent on the training, administration, and equipage of military personnel; 16 percent was allocated for the procurement of new aircraft and weaponry; 16 percent was spent on research, development, testing, and evaluation; and military construction and family housing accounted for about 4 percent of the budget.

HISTORY

The U.S. Air Force had its roots in turn-of-the-century efforts at technology assessment. In January 1905, the War Department considered an offer from two Dayton, Ohio, inventors—Orville and Wilbur Wright—to provide the government with a heavier-than-air flying machine.

The role in warfare of airships had not yet been proved. The Army Signal Corps' balloon section, inspired by the use of balloons by French revolutionaries for scouting purposes in 1794, served with mixed results during the Spanish-American War (1898). A previous Signal Corps contract for an airplane, with Samuel P. Langton, resulted in tests that ended in a spectacular dive into the Potomac River. For the time being, the government declined the offer of the Wright brothers.

The attitude of the government soon changed. The Wright brothers received their patent in 1906, and President Theodore Roosevelt urged the corps to contract with them. The first airplane was delivered in 1909. In 1911 Congress voted its first appropriation for military aviation.

The First World War

The importance of military aviation was proved in World War I (1914–18), when balloons were used for artillery spotting, dirigibles for bombing, and airplanes for bombing as well as reconnaissance over enemy territory. Great battles between "knights of the air" provided the world with romantic and legendary stories. At the time of the United States' declaration of war against Germany in 1917, however, the army's aviation section was sadly lacking. Its 1,200 officers had no knowledge of the air war in Europe, and its 250 airplanes and five balloons were not likely to last long in combat. However, when France asked the United States to provide an air force of 4,500 planes and 50,000 men, the government hastily agreed. The result was chaos and a miserable failure on the part of the Signal Corps. On Armistice Day, November 11, 1918, there were 740 U.S. aircraft at the front in France, and most of these planes were European-made.

The important role played by air power in World War I led to a movement in the 1920s and 1930s to create an independent air force in the United States modeled after the structure of Great Britain's Royal Air Force (RAF). But army leaders saw the role of the airplane primarily as a weapon for supporting the infantry. Local commanders, none of them aviators, ran the air forces assigned to them. A series of boards and commissions studied the issue of reorganization, with no meaningful result.

The Age of Liberation

World War II (1939–45) ushered in the true age of liberation for American air power. Early reports from the European front were testimony to the dominant role of the airplane in modern warfare. In staff talks with the Americans, the British always included RAF representatives as well as leaders from the army and the navy, and the United States was forced to respond in kind with its own air representative. The Army Air Forces (AAF), during the World War II expansion, became the world's most powerful air force.

The AAF's first priority in the war was to launch a strategic bombing offensive in support of the RAF in Germany. After a slow and costly start, the Eighth Air Force had pounded the German industrial infrastructure to ruins by the end of the war. In the war against Japan, General Douglas MacArthur made his advance by leapfrogging the air forces from island to island. The AAF also helped Admiral Chester Nimitz's carriers make their way across the Central Pacific to support Allied forces in Burma and China. Long-range B-29 Superfortresses were used to bomb Japan's home islands and eventually dropped the atomic bombs on Hiroshima and Nagasaki that brought the war to a definitive end.

An Independent Force

Independence for the air force was inevitable after World War II. It was finalized by the National Security Act of 1947, which transferred the AAF from the Department of the Army (formerly the War Department) to a new Department of the Air Force. The newly created Department of Defense, at first a loose confederation of armed forces that acted as budgetary rivals, became more authoritative and centralized during and after the Korean War (1950–53).

In response to the new Soviet nuclear threat, the air force developed its first intercontinental ballistic missiles (ICBMs) during the 1950s. By 1960 the long-range bomber force had been cut back, and more than one thousand ICBMs were in place. After the Vietnam War (1959–75), however, the strategy of deterrence that had led to the ICBM buildup began to seem an obvious doctrine of mutually assured destruction, and the Soviet Union and the United States entered into their first arms reduction talks in 1972.

Twenty years later, as the Soviet Union collapsed, the air force had already begun to change its emphasis from long-range ICBMs and bombers to a more precise, technologically driven approach. Much of the technology under development was untested, but the 1991 Persian Gulf War, fought to liberate the small nation of Kuwait from an Iraqi invasion, provided the air force with an opportunity to evaluate its new systems. The war was brief and involved relatively few civilian casualties, and in large part the new technology employed by the air force—involving laser-guided missiles ("smart" bombs), radar-jamming devices, and virtual data and communications systems—proved successful.

FAST FACTS

The traditional call sign for the presidential aircraft—Air Force One—was first used in September 1961 to identify the C-118 aboard which President John F. Kennedy flew.

(Source: Department of the Air Force. "Air Force One Fact Sheet," 1998.)

CURRENT POLITICAL ISSUES

The United States spends far more of its citizens' tax dollars on defense than does any other nation in the world. In 1994 the U.S. defense budget was $285 billion, compared to $80 billion for Russia and $27 billion for China. Although most Americans are in favor of a strong defense, the rapid increase in defense costs has alarmed many members of the public and Congress.

What is most disturbing to these people is the way in which certain projects are awarded to private defense contractors, which have developed much of the military's high-tech weaponry and communications systems. Projects designed to fit certain defense needs for a certain time period have tended to take on a life of their own once they are under way, allegedly propelled by corporate contributions to members of Congress. Members of the House and Senate defense appropriation committees—the members of Congress who decide which projects to develop—were given $8.5 million in military-related political action committee (PAC) and individual contributions in 1993 and 1994. Critics ask whether these contributions provide an incentive for lawmakers to encourage continued work on certain projects, perhaps even after the projects have proved to be ill-advised.

Case Study: The B-2 Bomber

The air force's B-2 bomber, popularly known as the "stealth" bomber, was designed in secrecy beginning in 1980. The new plane was billed as the ultimate penetrating bomber, capable of delivering nuclear weapons to targets deep within the Soviet Union—the Cold War enemy of the United States—during a prolonged nuclear conflict. The builder of the B-2, an aerospace contractor named Northrop, originally estimated the final cost for each plane at $550 million making the B-2 the most expensive aircraft in history.

When the B-2 was revealed to the public in 1989, the Soviet Union was undergoing grave changes. Its ultimate collapse in 1992 virtually eliminated the B-2's primary mission. Northrop, now Northrop-Grumman, and a few Defense Department officials had to sell the B-2 to the American public as a highly necessary conventional bomber with a global reach. However, most members of the defense community no longer wanted anything to do with the project; Northrop-Grumman appeared to have engaged in some questionable accounting procedures in its original estimates, and it was now clear that the price of a single B-2 bomber would be more than $2 billion. In a 1995 study commissioned by Congress, the Institute for Defense Analysis concluded that the fall of the Soviet Union had made the B-2 unnecessary. Even many conservatives believed that the air force should concentrate on what its new bomber force should look like instead of financing the B-2.

Despite the unwillingness of the Pentagon and the air force to continue development of the B-2, Northrop-Grumman's influence on certain members of Congress was too strong to keep the program down. It had subcontracted the provision of parts and service among 3,400 subcontractors located in 48 states—each of them eager to let their congressional representatives know how valuable the B-2 was to the constituency. As a result of their efforts, along with the strength of military-industrial PACs, members of Congress found the funds to give Northrop-Grumman a down payment on twenty more B-2 aircraft, the final one of which would be delivered in 2003. Congress was giving the air force an aircraft it did not even want—a plane that was too expensive and had never been tested in battle.

SUCCESSES AND FAILURES

The air force's involvement in Operation Desert Storm, the U.S. military operation during the Persian Gulf War, illuminated the new directions being undertaken in war strategy and tactics. The war's quick conclusion—the conflict lasted barely five weeks—was effected in large part by the sophisticated weaponry and communications networks that had been developed since the last major U.S. conflict, the Vietnam War. U.S. infantry relied heavily on air force sorties to take out key Iraqi military targets such as heavily fortified command and communications centers, missile launch sites, radar facilities, and airports and runways. The air force and coalition forces, at the end of ten days, had launched 10,000 sorties, and much of Iraq's power to make war had been crippled or destroyed.

Many of the devices used in this display of air power were newly developed; some of them, such as the satellites used for the Global Positioning System, were still under development at the time of the Gulf War but nevertheless proved useful. The Defense Meteorological Support Program helped to accurately predict the weather in the region, which was the worst in that area in 14 years. The air force's Mission Support intelligence system provided charts, maps, and other vital data to pilots, who were generally briefed for a mission in about four hours—it took about two days for mission planning in Vietnam. The use of precision-guided munitions provided pilots with weapons of unprecedented accuracy and deadliness; during the last weeks of the war, laser-guided bombs destroyed two hundred Iraqi tanks each night.

FUTURE DIRECTIONS

The changing nature of world politics, particularly of the post-Cold War realities for U.S. foreign policy, have presented the military with the unique challenge of changing its entire defense structure and philosophy. The U.S. defense structure has changed from one in which the nation faced a known adversary and easily predicted threats to one involving unpredictable opponents whose challenges are poorly understood. The creation of nuclear, biological, and chemical weapons is on the rise, as is the information technology used in weapons systems. Information itself has become both a weapon and a target.

As part of the Defense Department's plan to meet these new challenges, the air force has recently published

Global Engagement: A Vision for the 21st Century Air Force. The study describes a new type of force to be employed in the future, one that is more flexibly organized and able to bring intense firepower to bear over global distances within hours. With U.S bases abroad being curtailed, the air force will have to project power increasingly from the continental United States. The force is already transitioning from an air force into an air and space force, with American dominance of the medium of space. The total forces will need to achieve clear information superiority and be able to attack the information infrastructure of the enemy. Such operations will generally require a smaller, more specialized, more expert air force that relies heavily on reserve forces and civilian operatives.

AGENCY RESOURCES

Questions that are not answered by the extensive fact sheets offered on the air force's Web site can be directed to the Public Affairs Resource Library, 1690 Air Force Pentagon, Washington, DC 20330-1690; phone (703) 697-4100. Historical information about the air force can be obtained from the Air Force History Support Office, 500 Duncan Ave., Box 94, Bolling AFB, Washington, DC 20332; phone (202) 404-2264.

The air force has also recently made available a service called Facts on Demand, which allows customers to request and receive information by fax. The toll-free service operates 24 hours a day; it requires a touch-tone phone and, of course, a fax machine. Users dial 1-800-422-USAF and, following recorded instructions, request document number 1,000, which is a list of all the documents available on the service. Users may then redial and request other documents by number.

AGENCY PUBLICATIONS

Official magazines of the air force include *Airman*, the air force's flagship publication; *Air Force Magazine*, *Airpower Journal*, *Air Chronicles*, and the *Almanac of the Air Forces of the Americas*. Other periodical publications include the *Air Force Policy Letter*, a monthly digest of leadership messages from senior officials on air force issues, and the annual *Air Force Issue Book*, a blueprint that explains how the air force will reach its goals and initiatives. Special studies released by the air force include titles such as *Global Engagement*, *National Missile Defense—the Minuteman Option*, *Our Nation's Air Force*, and *Roswell Incident—Report of Air Force Research*. A great many air force publications are accessible from the air force Web site at http://www.af.mil. For further publications information, contact the Public Affairs Resource Library at 1690 Air Force Pentagon, Washington, DC 20330-1690; phone (703) 697-4100.

BIBLIOGRAPHY

Black, Ian. *Desert Air Force*. Osprey Aerospace, 1992.

Bond, David F. "U.S. Air Force Streamlining Plan Features Command Mergers, Headquarters Staff Cuts." *Aviation Week and Space Technology*, 23 September 1991, p. 64.

Boyne, Walter J. *Beyond the Wild Blue: A History of the United States Air Force, 1947–1997*. New York: St. Martin's, 1997.

Dellums, Ronald V. "Stealth Bombing America's Future." *The Nation*, 2 October 1995, pp. 350–52.

Fogleman, Ronald R. "Getting the Air Force into the 21st Century: The Ability to Model and Simulate Combat." *Vital Speeches*, 1 May 1995, pp. 434–38.

———. "Strategic Vision and Core Competencies: Global Reach-Global Power." *Vital Speeches*, 1 December 1996, pp. 98–100.

Goyer, Robert. "50 years of the USAF." *Flying*, August 1997, pp. 100–102.

Kelly, Orr. *From a Dark Sky: The Story of U.S. Air Force Special Operations*. Novato, Calif.: Presidio, 1996.

Krepenevich, Andrew F., Jr. "The Air Force at a Crossroads." *Issues in Science and Technology*, Winter 1996, pp. 42–48.

Larrabee, J. Whitfield. "Black Holes: How Secret Military and Intelligence Appropriations Suck Up Your Tax Dollars." *The Humanist*, May–June 1996, pp. 9–15.

McPeak, Merrill A. "Restructuring the Air Force: Organize, Train, and Equip." *Vital Speeches*, 15 November 1991, pp. 69–72.

Moorman, Thomas S., Jr. "The Future of the United States Air Force Space Operations: The National Security Dimensions." *Vital Speeches*, 15 March 1994, pp. 325–29.

Department of the Army (USA)

PARENT ORGANIZATION: Department of Defense
ESTABLISHED: June 14, 1775
EMPLOYEES: 1,315,000 (495,000 active combat forces; 367,000 Army National Guard; 208,000 Army Reserve; 245,000 civilian workforce)

Contact Information:

ADDRESS: The Pentagon
Washington, DC 20310
PHONE: (703) 545-6700
FAX: (703) 697-2519
URL: http://www.army.mil
SECRETARY OF THE ARMY: Louis Caldera
CHIEF OF STAFF OF THE ARMY: Gen. Dennis J. Reimer

WHAT IS ITS MISSION?

The Department of the Army's stated mission is "to organize, train, and equip active duty and reserve forces for the preservation of peace, security, and the defense of our nation." The army is the component of the national military team that focuses on land operations, but its activities also include aviation and water transport in the course of mobilizing its personnel. Its total force is charged with preserving the peace and security and providing for the defense of the United States, its territories, commonwealths, and possessions, and any areas occupied by the United States. If necessary, the total force is obligated to overcome any nations responsible for aggressive acts that imperil the peace and security of the United States. The army also administers certain environmental engineering programs and provides military assistance (such as natural disaster relief) to federal, state, and local government agencies.

HOW IS IT STRUCTURED?

The Department of the Army is a military department of the U.S. Department of Defense. It is headed by a civilian secretary of the army, who is subject to the direction, authority, and control of the commander in chief (the president) and the secretary of defense. The secretary of the army is responsible for all affairs of the army, including its organization, administration, operation, and efficiency. The army is headquartered at the Pentagon, Washington, D.C.

The staff that helps fulfill the purpose of the Office of the Secretary of the Army (the secretariat) includes

Soldiers make their way through barbed wire during Operation Desert Storm.

(Reuters/Corbis-Bettmann)

the secretary's principal assistants—the undersecretary of the army, numerous assistant secretaries, the general counsel, several directors and chiefs, the auditor general, the chairman of the Army Reserve Forces Policy Committee, and others. Certain civilian functions, such as accounting, acquisitions, inspection, and information management, are also under the control of the army secretariat. The secretariat is guided in its decision making by the Army Policy Council, the senior policy advisory council of the army.

The military staff of the secretary of the army (the army staff) is presided over by the chief of staff of the army. The chief of staff is the principal military adviser to the secretary of the army and is responsible for planning, developing, executing, reviewing, and analyzing army programs. The chief of staff is directly responsible to the secretary of the army for the efficiency of the army, its preparedness for military operations, and plans related to these purposes. The army staff's duties include preparing for the deployment of the army and for activities—such as recruiting and supplying—that will assist in the execution of any power, duty, or function of the secretary or the chief of staff; investigating and reporting on the efficiency of the army and its preparations; acting as the secretary's agent in coordinating the action of all organizations of the army; and other duties prescribed by the secretary.

The program work of the army is carried out at Army Headquarters, the Pentagon, by the 15 major commands (MACOMs) of the army and at approximately 200 army installations worldwide. By far the most complex and varied program comprises the functions grouped under the heading "military operations and plans." Other army program areas are personnel; reserve components; intelligence; research, development, and materiel acquisition; logistics; engineering; civil functions; medical; inspection; religious; legal; public affairs; and history.

Each MACOM is led by a commanding general. Some of the MACOMs are classified according to function (U.S. Army Intelligence and Security Command; U.S. Army Recruiting Command), and others are named geographically (U.S. Army Europe and Seventh Army, Germany; U.S. Army Pacific Command). Some MACOMs are subject to the authority of others at certain times. For example, the commanding general, U.S. Army Forces Command, commands all assigned active army forces in the continental United States, the five continental U.S. armies, and assigned Army Reserve Troop Program Units in the continental United States and Puerto Rico.

PRIMARY FUNCTIONS

The programs of the army, despite their apparent diversity, are for the most part focused on the organization, training, and equipping of active-duty and reserve

BUDGET:

Department of the Army

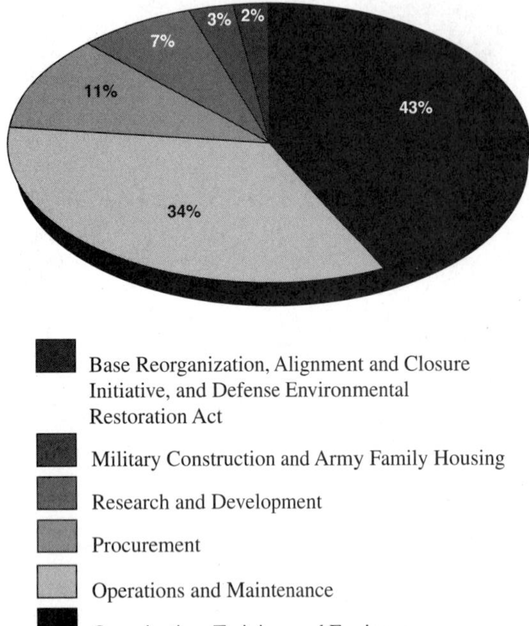

forces to fulfill the army's mission. Among the more prominent of its vast military operations are national security affairs, strategy formation, operational readiness and mobilization, electronic warfare, nuclear and chemical matters, and intelligence activities.

In addition, the army also administers programs aimed at improving the quality of civilian life. These programs are concerned with protecting the environment, improving waterway navigation, controlling flood and beach erosion, and developing water resources. On occasion—usually in times of great need, such as recovery from natural disasters—the army also lends military service and relief assistance to state and local governments.

PROGRAMS

The army is involved in numerous programs designed to serve specific functions of its mission. Programs involve specific training issues, organizations, research and study, weapon and equipment development, medicine, communications, or any of the army program areas.

One program fundamental to the army's mission, the Battle Command Training Program (BCTP), based at Fort Leavenworth, Kansas, uses computer simulation to lead realistic, stressful training operations for army corps, division, and brigade commanders and their staffs. Each BCTP consists of three events: the battle command seminar, the warfighter exercise (WFX), and the "take home package," or debriefing. The BCTP conducts about 35 simulated battles each year.

Some army programs are required by law. The Congressional Special Interest Medical Research Programs, for example, are administered by the U.S. Army Medical Research and Materiel Command. The organization is chartered to perform and sponsor medical research in areas such as breast cancer, neurofibromastosis, osteoporosis, ovarian cancer, and prostate cancer, that have been mandated by Congress.

One of the more unusual programs administered by the army is the Personnel Exchange Program (PEP). PEP soldiers are assigned to a 24–month tour of duty with another country's army. Currently PEP is involved in an exchange program with the Schools of Other Nations (SON) in Australia. SON soldiers are assigned for either six or 11 months to attend the Australian Command and General Staff College or the Joint Services Staff College.

The army also plays an active role in civil functions. The Army Corp of Engineers administers the Civil Works Program (CWP), dating back to 1824. The CWP is the nation's major federal water resources development program. It involves engineering works such as major dams, reservoirs, levees, harbors, and many others. These works are designed to protect cities from floods, supply water for municipal and industrial use, generate hydroelectric power, and provide recreational resources, among other functions.

BUDGET INFORMATION

The Army's budget, a component of the Defense Department's annual budget, is acquired through congressional appropriations of tax revenues. The Army's budget appropriated for 1998 was a little over $60 billion, 43 percent of which was spent on the organization, training, and equipage of personnel. Army operations and maintenance of existing facilities and equipment accounted for another 34 percent of the budget, while the procurement of new weapons, anti-weapons, and communications systems accounted for 11 percent. Seven percent of the budget is spent on research, development, testing, and evaluation of projects; 3 percent was spent on military construction and Army family housing. The Army's operations in fulfillment of two recently enacted initiatives, the Base Reorganization, Alignment and Closure Initiative and the Defense Environmental Restoration Act, each accounted for about 1 percent of the Army budget.

HISTORY

The army is unusual among government agencies in that it is older than the nation itself. During the colonial period many colonists gained military experience while serving with British soldiers in the imperial battles over North America, from roughly 1689 to 1763. Colonial military service during the French and Indian War (1754–63) proved especially valuable in forming a national army during the American Revolution (1775–83).

In June 1775, two months after the American Revolution began in Massachusetts, the Second Continental Congress established the Continental Army and appointed George Washington as commander in chief. In 1781 the Office of the Secretary of War was created to lead the army bureaucracy. Upon the realization of national independence in 1783, Congress reduced the army to fewer than 700 troops. This practice—proportioning force strength according to the pressures of war—is one of the most enduring legacies passed down from the Continental Army.

The War Department was established in 1789, the year the U.S. Constitution was ratified. Throughout the first half of the nineteenth century many patterns were set for the army's future, such as use of a dual system of regular forces and citizen-soldiers and the employment of an executive agency (the War Department, later the Department of Defense) to lead the nation's military affairs. Throughout the conflicts of this period—most notably the War of 1812 and the Spanish-American War (1898)—the army showed improvements in training, organization, and command.

The army grew during the American Civil War (1860–65) to a strength of nearly 1.1 million troops in 1865. The war's enormous casualty rate has been blamed on three factors: failure of the army to adapt to new, long-range efforts; the efforts of commanders on both sides to fight decisive, "Napoleonic" battles; and the intrusion of politics on army decision making. From the 1870s to the 1890s the army's strength was usually less than 25,000 troops.

The Early Twentieth Century

The first years of the twentieth century were highlighted by accomplishments of the army's medical and engineering personnel in Central America. In Cuba and Panama, yellow fever and malaria were virtually eliminated as epidemic threats, allowing the Panama Canal to be completed in 1914.

Upon the U.S. entry into World War I (1914–18), the War Department's general staff was expanded from 19 to nearly 1,100 officers. About 3.7 million troops served in the army during 1917 and 1918; nearly 70 percent of these were drafted under the Selective Service Act, passed in May 1917. The army did not contribute much in the way of Allied strategy, but the army's size and firepower and the offensive mind-set of the U.S. forces helped turn the tide of the war against the German army. Following the armistice on November 11, 1918, U.S. forces were quickly demobilized, reducing the army to a strength of about 214,000 troops in 1920.

FAST FACTS

The army's soldiers have been awarded almost 24,000 Congressional Medals of Honor, more than all the other armed forces combined.

(Source: United States Army Center of Military History, September 1998.)

The 1920s was a decade of frugality in government spending, and the army further reduced its members. In the late 1930s the Army Air Corps (later the Army Air Forces and the U.S. Air Force) received funds for expansion, but when World War II (1939–45) began, air and ground forces were insufficient. Thanks to the Selective Service and Training Act of 1940, the army's strength was quickly expanded, to a peak strength in 1945 of 8.3 million personnel. By the end of the war, the U.S. army was the most powerful in the world. During the Korean War (1950–53) the U.S. army became the dominant member of the United Nations (UN) coalition and bore the principal logistical responsibility for the ground war.

The Post-World War II Army

The National Security Act of 1947 was intended to integrate national security policy making and put an end to interservice (army/navy) squabbling for influence and funding. It was a landmark measure in the structuring of the American national defense, but it fell short of achieving its main objectives and had to be reshaped several times before details were satisfactorily worked out. The act created the National Military Establishment, made up of the Office of the Secretary of Defense and the Departments of the Army, Navy, and Air Force. Later amendments officially established the Department of Defense.

During the post-war administration of President Dwight D. Eisenhower (1953–61), emphasis in defense planning was placed on strategic nuclear weapons and air-naval delivery systems; the army's conventional ground warfare took a backseat in defense policy as the administration looked to the threat of its new enemy, the Soviet Union. The army, trying to keep up with the new technology of defense, developed such tactical weapons as surface-to-air missiles, atomic artillery, attack helicopters, and personnel carriers. However, the army, trained primarily for conventional warfare, never completely adjusted to the tactics of counterinsurgency used by its opponents in the Vietnam War (1959–75). This conflict proved to be a painful lesson in the need to keep the army prepared for flexible responses.

Judging from the results of the Persian Gulf War (1991) the army did learn some valuable lessons during the Vietnam War; adapting quickly to warfare in a desert environment, the army's ground offensive brought the war to a quick and decisive conclusion, with relatively few civilian casualties.

CURRENT POLITICAL ISSUES

The most urgent peacetime issue for the army today is a problem that has been experienced to some degree by each of the armed forces: the increased integration of female service personnel into almost every functional unit of the military. Women's service in the armed forces dates back to before the First World War, but until recently the functions of female personnel were strictly proscribed. For example, they were initially limited to serving in the Army Nursing Corps. In the 1990s, however, as female personnel became increasingly integrated into the strategic and tactical structures of defense, the traditional male warrior culture of each of the armed forces demonstrated a clear inability to handle this integration. Highly publicized accounts of sexual harassment and discrimination began to emerge from the military in the early 1990s, including the well-publicized 1991 Tailhook scandal, in which several navy women were crudely harassed by their male colleagues.

Case Study: The Army's Troubles

These problems have been especially serious in the army. Charges of harassment seemed almost ubiquitous by November 1996, when news of the "Aberdeen rape ring" first came to light. At the Aberdeen Proving Ground in Maryland, a training facility for army recruits, 19 female victims charged that they had been repeatedly harassed, abused, intimidated into unwanted sex, and forcibly raped by men at the post—including drill instructors. In many cases female recruits were threatened with death if they exposed the pattern of abuse; at least one of the women attempted suicide.

Once the accusations had been registered and sorted through, 20 noncommissioned officers at Aberdeen came under investigation. One of the offending drill instructors, Drill Sgt. Delmar Simpson, was later convicted on several counts of rape; cases against other personnel remain unresolved. To its credit the army responded quickly to the accusations, perhaps having learned from the navy's disastrous attempts to cover up the Tailhook scandal. A telephone hot line was set up to collect other rape and sexual-harassment complaints; within the first week 4,000 calls were fielded and of these, 500 were considered serious enough to warrant investigation. Formal investigations were undertaken at seven other army installations, and some resulted in criminal charges against drill instructors. Other investigations revealed that several recruiting sergeants had become sexually involved with teenage girls who had visited army recruiting stations. The problem seemed to have permeated all levels of the army.

The situation took a bizarre turn a year later. Army Secretary Togo West, acting on the problem, appointed a panel to review the army's sexual harassment policies. An obvious choice for the panel was Sergeant Major of the Army Gene McKinney. As sergeant major of the army, McKinney was the army's top enlisted man and was considered the chief of staff's top adviser on all matters relating to the army's enlisted soldiers.

In February 1997, not long after McKinney's appointment to this commission, disturbing charges were leveled at the sergeant major himself by his former public relations assistant, Sgt. Maj. Brenda L. Hoster. Hoster claimed McKinney had sexually assaulted her in a hotel room in Hawaii in April 1996, kissing her, grabbing her, and asking her for sex. Hoster said after she had reported the incident to superiors, they took no action and she was forced into early retirement after they repeatedly ignored her pleas for a job transfer. When McKinney was named to the panel that would decide the army's future policies on sexual harassment, she said she could remain silent no longer and was compelled to make her charges public.

Hoster's charges were initially met with skepticism. By the summer of 1997, however, McKinney's career was in serious trouble—five other women, emboldened by Hoster's charge, had come forward with similar charges against McKinney. One of these women claimed McKinney had forced her into having unwanted sex. The case was quickly taken up by the military courts. With his career in jeopardy, McKinney, an African American, contended the army was engaging in a racist investigation of unsubstantiated charges. In the meantime, McKinney was removed from the policy-making commission and was placed on suspension.

SUCCESSES AND FAILURES

Although the army's military operations tend to receive much of the public's attention, it is often small, behind-the-scenes advancements that make dramatic and lasting changes to the way the army operates. For example, in 1990 the army began to consolidate its communications planning and information management functions into one suite of software at one physical location. Known as Integrated System Control (ISYSCON), the project combines the functionality of all existing communications network planning and management systems using modern hardware and software development techniques. The result has been an overall streamlining of army communications and management systems and the compilation of a "reuse" software library, which has been utilized by a number of army agencies, for a cost savings of close to $1 million.

FUTURE DIRECTIONS

In 1996 the chairman of the Joint Chiefs of Staff published *Joint Vision 2010,* which provided a template for the evolution of U.S. armed forces into the twenty-first century. *Army 2010,* the army's contribution, is a blueprint for how the army will contribute to the fulfillment of Joint Vision 2010. The basic idea put forth is that in today's complex global environment, the army will need to be strategically mobile—able to be deployed rapidly to wherever it is needed. To meet these challenges the army has redistributed its forces, closed and realigned bases, and improved the integration of active and reserve components. The army is transforming from a "forward deployed" force during the Cold War, when it was prepared to project power against the Soviet Union, to a "capabilities based" force with the ability to project power worldwide.

AGENCY RESOURCES

Because of the high volume of information requests received by the Army Community Relations Team, information requests are preferred in writing. Write to the Office of the Chief of Public Affairs (Attn. Community Relations Team), Army 1500 Room 2E, 641 The Pentagon, Washington, DC 20310; phone (703) 695-5469.

The National Archives has historical operational information on army units. For military information dated before 1941, contact the National Archives One at (202) 501-5390. For military information from 1942 and forward, contact the National Archives Two at (301) 713-7250.

ArmyLINK News, an on-line service of the Department of Defense, contains current Office of Public Affairs press releases and maintains an accessible historical database of previous releases. The site address is http://www.dtic.mil/armylink. The Army News Service posts releases from the Pentagon as well as from army public affairs offices worldwide on its own Web site (http://www.dtic.mil/armylink/news).

AGENCY PUBLICATIONS

The army releases countless publications each year. Among the most prominent are periodicals such as *Soldiers*, the army's official magazine, and *Military Review*, a forum for the open exchange of ideas on military affairs. Many army offices and organizations publish their own periodicals, many of which are accessible on-line through the army Web site.

A host of army brochures and manuals (for instance, "Weather Support for the U.S. Army," "Ophthalmic Services," "Army National Guard Computer Center") are available on-line from the U.S. Army Publications Agency (USAPA) at http://www.asappc.hoffman.army.mil.

Many publications cannot be ordered from the USAPA without clearance. Information seekers should then turn to the National Technical Information Service (NTIS) searchable site for army manuals and publications (http://www.ntis.gov/databases/armypub.htm). NTIS also makes available more than 60,000 army manuals and regulations on CD-ROM. The NTIS sales desk can be telephoned at (703) 487-4650.

BIBLIOGRAPHY

"Army Expands Combat Support." *Aviation Week and Space Technology*, 18 September 1995, pp. 56–7.

Bentayou, Frank. "Cyber Soldiers." *The American Legion*, August 1996, pp. 20–4.

Ganoe, William A. *The History of the United States Army*. Temecula, Calif.: Reprint Service Corporation, 1993.

Kagan, Frederick W., and David T. Fautua. "Could We Fight a War If We Had To?" *Commentary*, May 1997, pp. 25–9.

"Okinawa's Rethink." *The Economist*, 19 July 1997, p. 39.

Ricks, Thomas E. "About Face: U.S. Infantry Surprise." *Wall Street Journal*, 6 January 1997, p. A1.

Schmitt, Eric. "Women in the Army Face Wide Bias, 2 Inquiries Find," *New York Times*, 31 July 1997, p. A1.

Sciolino, Elaine. "The Army's Problems with Sex and Power." *New York Times*, 4 May 1997, p. E4.

Stanton, Shelby L. *Soldiers: A Portrait of the United States Army*. Charlottesville, Va.: Howell Press, 1991.

Vistica, Gregory L. "Rape in the Ranks," *Newsweek*, 25 November 1996.

William, John A., and Sam C. Sarkesian, eds. *The U.S. Army in a New Security Era.* Boulder, Colo.: Lynne Rienner Publishers, 1990.

Zurick, Tim. *Army Dictionary and Desk Reference.* Mechanicsburg, Pa.: Stackpole Books, 1992.

Department of the Interior (DOI)

ESTABLISHED: March 3, 1849
EMPLOYEES: 71,338 (1997)

Contact Information:

ADDRESS: 1849 C St. NW
Washington, DC 20240
PHONE: (202) 208-3171
URL: http://www.doi.gov
SECRETARY OF THE INTERIOR: Bruce Babbitt

WHAT IS ITS MISSION?

The Department of the Interior (DOI) is charged with the protection and conservation of federally owned land and water resources for the use and enjoyment of future generations. In addition, the DOI is authorized to sell, lease, and manage federal lands for the purpose of providing a source of revenue for the federal government. The DOI is also responsible for providing sound scientific analysis in order to prepare Americans for natural disasters. The DOI also serves and protects American Indians, Alaskan Natives, and the inhabitants of U.S. Pacific Island territories through the administration of land trust systems, educational programs, and economic assistance.

HOW IS IT STRUCTURED?

The Department of the Interior (DOI) is a cabinet-level agency headquartered in Washington, D.C. The DOI is headed by the secretary of the interior who is responsible for the development and implementation of U.S. natural resource policies. The Office of the Secretary includes the offices of Deputy Secretary, the Assistant Secretaries, the Special Trustee for American Indians, the Solicitor, and the Inspector General. Individual bureaus and offices are headed by a director or an assistant secretary. The Office of the Assistant Secretary provides advice on earth science policy to the secretary and represents the DOI in interagency efforts on a wide range of scientific issues. Special assistants, such as the White House Liaison, support the authority and responsibilities of DOI staff.

The DOI is composed of nine primary divisions: the National Park Service (NPS), Bureau of Land Management (BLM), Bureau of Indian Affairs (BIA), Bureau of Reclamation (BOR), Fish and Wildlife Service (FWS), United States Geological Survey (USGS), Minerals Management Service (MMS), Office of Surface Mining, and Office of Insular Affairs. These bureaus, offices, and services are responsible for the sound management of natural resources located within the United States. Each division is directed by an assistant secretary who operates under the supervision of the secretary of the interior.

The DOI also administrates resources and parks in U.S. territories such as the Virgin Islands, Guam, American Samoa, the Northern Mariana Islands, and Palau and provides funding for development to the Marshall Islands and the Federated States of Micronesia.

PRIMARY FUNCTIONS

As the nation's principal conservation agency, the DOI is responsible for more than 549 million acres of public lands which account for approximately 28 percent of the total U.S. land area. DOI staff manage the use and protection of U.S. natural resources and develop strategies to solve legal, logistical, and environmental conflicts related to air, land, water, and wildlife. The DOI exercises control over federal lands through the enforcement of laws and regulations that guide the use and consumption of U.S. natural resources.

Interior Department staffs are largely composed of administrators and professional civil service employees. The bureaus and divisions of the DOI are staffed by a wide variety of personnel from administrators to park rangers to field scientists to computer programmers. Field personnel are involved in the preservation, protection, and study of natural resources as well as education programs designed to inform the public about the complex environment and natural history throughout the United States.

In addition to its administrative and policy-making functions, a primary function of the DOI is the survey, study, and analysis of federal lands. The DOI, through its supervision of the USGS provides quantitative analysis of the North American continent and beyond through topographical maps and satellite imagery. Scientific data assembled by the USGS provides the federal government with information which can be used to administrate U.S. boundaries where legal and environmental disputes may occur. For example, the publication of exact maps of U.S. coastal waters is very important to the U.S. fishing industry. The role of this bureau is also to provide up-to-date information and alert appropriate authorities when natural disasters are imminent. The USGS has provided significant information for the study of earthquakes and volcanic activity which pose serious threat to life and property around the world.

The DOI is also responsible for providing safe access and enjoyment of U.S. parks and other federal lands that are open to recreational use. The NPS, the BLM, and other divisions of the DOI offer public access to federal lands which contain vast areas of pristine wilderness. DOI staff manage federal lands and make public access to those lands possible through the operation of campgrounds, trails, access roads, and other types of facilities.

PROGRAMS

The DOI's nine primary divisions are responsible for policies and programs that promote the management, study, and use of U.S. natural resources. The U.S. Fish and Wildlife Service (FWS) is responsible for the management and protection of wildlife and resources owned by the federal government. The FWS oversees approximately 442 wildlife refuges, 150 waterfowl production areas, and a network of wildlife laboratories and fish hatcheries. Two FWS initiatives, the National Wildlife Refuge system and the Endangered Species Act, address losses of habitat and species thereby preserving the quality of America's unique wildlife and landscapes.

The DOI administers the National Park Service (NPS) which is responsible for public access to and protection of approximately 340 national parks, scenic monuments, rivers, seashores, recreation areas, and historic sites. An example of an NPS program is the Vanishing Treasures initiative. Under the guidelines of this initiative, the NPS administers funding used to maintain American Indian archeological sites. For example, the NPS will use funds for the preservation and maintenance of the dwellings of the Anasazi Indians in the arid southwest which deteriorate each year due to natural weathering and other causes. Preservation of irreplaceable cultural and historic resources for the education and enjoyment of future generations is part of the DOI's mission.

The Bureau of Land Management (BLM) administers policies and programs regarding public land use. BLM lands are leased for mining, timber harvest, and cattle grazing as well as offered to the public for recreational use. The BLM assesses, monitors, and aids in the sound use of natural resources under its jurisdiction. Through the BLM the federal government leases land for development and resource extraction. Government regulation of these resources has a huge impact on companies in competition for natural resources. The DOI relies upon the BLM to implement policy and monitor the use of public lands for recreational use as well as for lawful extraction of valuable natural resources by companies.

The Bureau of Indian Affairs (BIA) administers the American Indian reservation system which holds specific lands in trust for legally recognized American Indian and Alaskan Native tribes. Approximately 50 million acres of land are held in trust for Native Americans. Revenues

BUDGET:

Department of the Interior

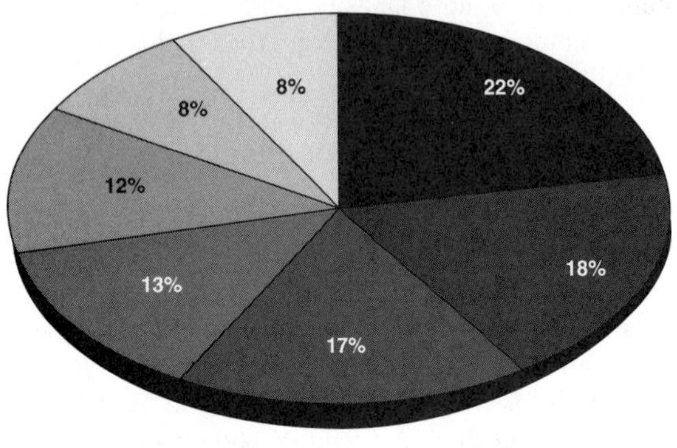

Departmental Offices, Including Salaries and Expenses

Bureau of Reclamation

Bureau of Land Management

Fish and Wildlife Service

Bureau of Indian Affairs

National Park Service

Others, Such as the U.S. Geological Survey, Minerals Management Service, Office of Surface Mining, and Land Acquisitions, Maintenance, and Exchanges

Percentage of Federal Budget

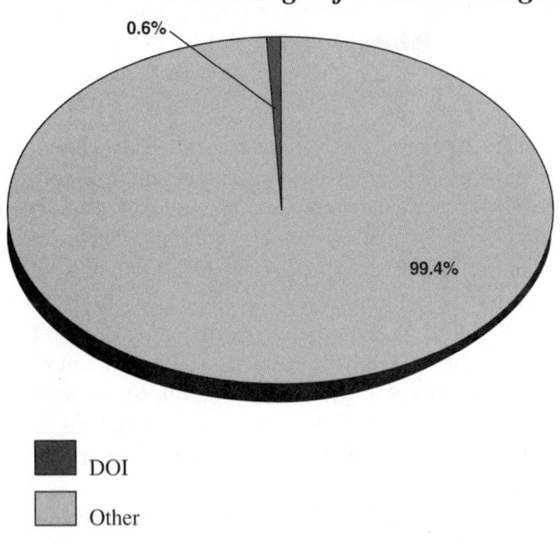

DOI

Other

generated through coal, oil, and mineral leases are disbursed to Native American tribal landowners and governments by the BIA. The BIA is also responsible for coordinating policy between the federal government and tribal governments. In addition, the BIA is responsible for distribution of funding for programs which promote education and economic development.

The Bureau of Reclamation (BOR) is responsible for water resources in the semi-arid western states. The BOR manages rivers and dams which support hydroelectric production facilities. Scientific management of scarce water resources impacts urban development, river recreation, farming, and the production of hydroelectric power. The BOR, in conjunction with other DOI divisions, provides the department with critical data and expertise in managing water resources and the multiple demands placed on that resource.

The U.S. Geological Survey (USGS) was initially charged with mapping the United States as the federal government acquired vast western lands. Over time the USGS developed into an important scientific research agency. It provides a wide variety of information for use in natural resource decision making. For example, under the direction of the USGS, the National Water Quality Assessment Program provides scientific analysis of water quality conditions for 75 key metropolitan areas within the United States.

BUDGET INFORMATION

In 1998 the approximate budget of the Department of the Interior was $10.4 billion, making up about 0.6 percent of the total federal budget of $1.653 trillion. The majority of the department's budget is composed of funding to the National Park Service (18 percent), the Bureau of Indian Affairs (17 percent), the Fish and Wildlife Service (13 percent), the Bureau of Land Management (12 percent), and the Bureau of Reclamation (8 percent). Others, such as the U.S. Geological Survey (7 percent), Minerals Management Service (7 percent), land acquisitions, exchanges, and maintenance (5 percent), and Office of Surface Mining (3 percent) compose the other 24 percent of the department's programming budget. Departmental offices, including salaries and expenses, make up the remaining 8 percent of the budget.

Highlighted in the budget are increases for the Fish and Wildlife Service, with enforcement of the Endangered Species Act receiving $11.4 million, a 15 percent increase for that program. Among these budget priorities is the restoration of specific landscapes whose deteriorating ecologies are a danger to the economic health and sustainability of nearby communities. For example the Florida Everglades Restoration Fund will receive $400 million until the year 2001. In combination with other federal monies, allocations will be spent on habitat restoration, land acquisition, and scientific research. The

California Bay-Delta ecosystem supports the production of 45 percent of the nation's fruits and vegetables. Taking into consideration the economic impact of poor water quality in the region, President Clinton signed the California Bay-Delta Environmental Enhancement and Water Security Act authorizing $143.3 million a year for three years. This money will be combined with voter approved state funding that will be spent restoring and improving this valuable water resource.

FAST FACTS

According to the Department of the Interior, over 275 million people visited America's national parks in 1998.

(Source: Department of the Interior, 1998.)

HISTORY

The Treasury Department was originally responsible for many of present-day DOI functions. Vast new lands acquired as a result of the Louisiana Purchase of 1803, the Mexican War (1846–1848), and the 1848 Treaty with Great Britain by which the United States acquired the Oregon Territory made the responsibilities of the Treasury greater than its offices could handle. Legislators decided to address the problem by creating the DOI by an act of March 3, 1849. Transfered to the DOI were the General Land Office, the Office of Indian Affairs, the Pension Office, and the Patent Office. Over the decades, there was significant debate among cabinet and congressional leaders over the exact role of the DOI within the federal government. In general, the DOI has expanded upon its original duties—the sale and lease of federal lands—to focus more on conservation and protection of the U.S. natural resources.

For at least a century the DOI's policy of resource management reflected the more general public sentiment that natural resources were limitless. Gradually Americans realized that the natural resources of the United States were not inexhaustible. President Theodore Roosevelt, concerned by the uncontrolled development of the western United States in the late 1800s and early 1900s, established many national parks and forests. Roosevelt's goal was not to stop development, however, but to manage it, and to ensure that something of the natural heritage of the United States would be preserved. At the same time that he was expanding the national forests, Roosevelt also encouraged the construction of dams and irrigation systems.

The environmental movement of the 1960s and 1970s built on the conservationist concerns of Roosevelt. In an attempt to manage the impact of industrialization on the environment, the Environmental Protection Agency (EPA) was established. This bold new regulatory agency gave legal recourse to government and private agencies seeking to combat pollution and environmental degradation. While not a part of the DOI, the establishment of the EPA reflected a major change in the attitude of the government toward the resources and land of the United States, a change which greatly impacted the DOI. From the 1960s onwards, protection of the environment has become one of the determining factors in DOI activities.

However, environmentalists experienced a formidable opponent in James G. Watt, Secretary of the Interior under President Ronald Reagan from 1981 to 1983. Watt was appointed to the DOI specifically for his anti-regulatory, pro-development stance regarding public land use and had spent past years working with political action groups for the elimination of environmental regulations. He held the opinion that industrial and commercial development was more important than environmental concerns. After an eight-month investigation, Watt came under fire from Congress and the House Appropriations Committee. As secretary of the interior he had placed a freeze on the NPS's land acquisition activities, initiated a plan to sell millions of acres of federal land to private bidders, and leased extensive offshore areas to oil companies for drilling. The House Appropriations Committee also found that DOI policies allowed private companies to reap windfall profits from an illegally operated federal coal leasing program. Watt's racially insensitive remarks and disparaging references to American Indians made him a political outcast among Republicans. President Ronald Reagan and other key Republicans accepted Watt's resignation feeling that he could not successfully pursue policy objectives as secretary of the interior.

Although environmentalists, such as members of the Sierra Club, were encouraged by the resignation of such an anti-regulatory secretary of the interior, Watt was quickly replaced by Reagan appointee William Clark, a judge with links to Reagan from his days in California, who had no experience with natural resources but who could defend the DOI in legal matters.

Successive presidential administrations sought to promote a positive relationship with environmentalists. This was a politically successful election strategy to woo younger voters that were sympathetic to environmental concerns. The Clinton administration's appointment of Bruce Babbitt as secretary of interior represented an effort to promote a pro-conservation environmental agenda. Initially Babbitt's appointment encouraged environmentalists who hoped that the administration was serious about strengthening conservation policies. However, Babbitt's early popularity deteriorated when he unveiled his solution for water management conflicts, particularly regarding grazing fees. Environmental advocates came to realize that Babbitt's appointment did not necessarily mean that the sweeping changes promised during the presidential campaign would be instituted. Instead environmentalists found that policy initiatives continued to favor private enterprise's extraction of natural resources. Political debate continues over the role of the DOI and the impact of federal policies on environmental issues.

Protection of habitat and species versus economic prosperity for families is frequently the focus of controversy. Federal environmental regulations come increasingly under attack by citizen action groups as being inconsistent and out of touch with the needs of local businesses and communities. Today the DOI continues to struggle to balance political, economic, and environmental interests.

CURRENT POLITICAL ISSUES

The president has the authority to designate specific sites within the United States as national monuments. The designation allows the president to determine how the site is to be protected and whether there will be any special circumstances regarding use of the site. Such an executive designation does not require full congressional support.

National monuments are chosen for their historical, biological, archeological, or environmental significance. These sites are visited by millions of Americans each year. The designation is meant to provide for the preservation of the site and the sharing of historical and cultural values. The designation of a new site is often greeted with popular support by the states or cities in which they are located. National monuments can draw tourists and create income for local communities. However, when there are competing interests involved, the designation of a protected area can be a source of political conflict.

Case Study: Creation of the Grand Staircase-Escalante National Monument

In 1997 President Clinton designated the Grand Staircase-Escalante a national monument in Utah. Various plans for such a designation had been discussed within the DOI for many years. Secretary of the Interior Bruce Babbitt supported designation of the monument and called it a positive act of land stewardship by the federal government. Environmental groups applauded the effort to protect some 1.7 million acres of the most remarkable and uniquely beautiful landscape in the West. Opponents of the plan included private energy companies, which were supported by Utah Senator Orin Hatch. Senator Hatch called the act, "an example of federal arrogance."

Senator Hatch, a group of western Republicans, and some Democrats spoke out against the designation of the national monument in Utah claiming that there was no proper discussion held with Utah political representatives. Utah's Republican officials were most concerned with a loss in projected tax revenues to the state. Secretary of the Interior Babbitt countered that the plan had been public for months and the process was open.

The monument designation prohibits mining and other commercial development on protected lands. Some private companies already owned leases for land occupied by the Grand Staircase-Escalante, which would now be protected by national monument status. Led by Senator Hatch, Republicans acted quickly to oppose the termination of leases already in progress. Republicans sought to amend the Antiquities Act of 1906, an act championed by President Theodore Roosevelt which formed the legal basis for national monument designation. Political pressure by Republicans and private companies holding lease rights was successful in obtaining guarantees that leases purchased before the designation would be honored, which would allow for minerals exploration to take place. In response, environmental groups, such as the Southern Utah Wilderness Alliance, sought public support, as well as legal action, to oppose minerals exploration of the site. The designation of the Utah monument brought initial praise to President Clinton for his willingness to protect the site from development. For many environmental groups the government's honoring of preexisting leases has tarnished that success.

DOI officials predict that the numbers of visitors to the monument will grow. In order to meet the demands of tourists and enterprises, the DOI allocated $5 million to the Bureau of Land Management (BLM) to plan and prepare for multiple uses. Accommodations will need to be made for recreational use as well as roads and infrastructural improvements for private companies to gain access for energy exploration. The Clinton administration has accepted the multiple use concept for the national monument as a means of smoothing the political opposition among Utah's politicians. Although discouraged by the setback, environmental groups are organizing to stop development of the national monument's mineral resources.

SUCCESSES AND FAILURES

The Endangered Species Act of 1973 represents a milestone in the regulatory activities of the federal government. The act was established to conserve and protect the biological diversity of animal and plant life. After being extensively researched by DOI scientists, species thought to be nearing extinction are placed on the endangered species list. When a species is placed on the list, its habitat is monitored and plans are developed to promote the health and well being of the species. If the species is further endangered through some private or public activity, the act offers legal recourse for individuals or groups outside of the government to protect the species.

In 1994 the DOI reintroduced the gray wolf into Yellowstone National Park. This was a milestone in the return of an endangered species to its natural habitat. Although the reintroduction of the wolf furthers wildlife conservation, neighbors of the park are less supportive of the plan. Ranchers bordering Yellowstone cite the cost of lost livestock as a primary argument against the reintroduction of this predatory species. Environmentalists see the reintroduction of the species as a step toward ensuring health of the entire ecosystem and its wildlife.

When public land use is an issue, a single animal or plant being added to the endangered species list can be blamed for lost jobs and revenues. This was the case when the spotted owl of the Pacific Northwest was added to the list. The spotted owl's habitat is in old growth redwood forest and is also a highly desired timber harvest area. As timber companies came closer to harvesting timber from the region, environmentalists averted their venture by getting the spotted owl, an inhabitant of that forest, categorized as an endangered species. This proved to be the beginning of a long battle between lumber companies and environmentalists. Finally the Clinton administration set about finding a way to mediate the crisis and came up with a plan titled Option 9, which divided contested lands into protected zones and harvest zones. Another important part of the plan was the introduction of salvage logging, which called for leaving the older trees but allowing the removal of damaged or dying trees. The role the federal government played in mediating this conflict is the first of its kind. The plan has been touted as a success by the Clinton administration and the DOI. Unfortunately the regulation has produced criticism from both environmentalists seeking habitat conservation and private companies seeking to continue logging practices.

FUTURE DIRECTIONS

The secretary of the interior and members of the Senate Appropriations Subcommittee Interior and associated agencies are moving forward with implemention of a fee demonstration project. New fee structures will be implemented at approximately 5 percent of the federally owned recreation sites. Of 1,880 recreational sites managed by the National Park Service (NPS), Bureau of Land Management (BLM), and the U.S. Fish and Wildlife Service (FWS), 106 of them have been identified as eligible for fee increases. Funds generated by the project are intended for repairs and improvements to roads, restrooms, campgrounds, nature trails, and increased visitor safety.

Historically fees collected at park and recreation sites have been directed to the Department of the Treasury and distributed by Congress through the appropriations process. The test fee demonstration project authorized by the Omnibus Consolidated Recessions and Appropriations Act of 1996 allows specific collecting sites to keep up to 80 percent of the new fees on site and direct the remaining 20 percent to be disbursed to the sites in the most need. The plan is that the nominal fee increases plus more effective distribution should provide funds to compensate for budget shortfalls. In addition, the Interior Department hopes that the funds will help those parks most visited by Americans.

Partnerships with state, local, and private interests are a major focus of the DOI. By fostering these partnerships the DOI intends to further conservation goals and extend scarce government resources. Examples of these kinds of partnerships are evident in large-scale restoration projects such as those operating in the Florida Everglades and the California Bay Delta.

Habitat Conservation Plans, or HCPs, is another example of how the DOI seeks to use partnerships to boost conservation of natural resources. HCP's call for land protection and acquisition costs to be disbursed locally, again preserving federal funds. However, in order to institute the process, the DOI has budgeted $6 million per year for HCP administration. Improved coordination between DOI offices and programs, such as the FWS, the BLM, and the NPS, should build confidence in the partnership model. In 1996 the DOI had approved 197 HCPs and 200 more were in development stages. The DOI intends to have 400 HCPs functioning or in negotiation by the end of 1998.

In 1997 President Clinton announced plans for the DOI to improve public awareness of water quality, specifically of toxic contaminants and other pollutants which may be present in water systems throughout the nation. Implementation of the plan will be conducted by a collaboration between the Environmental Protection Agency (EPA), the National Oceanic and Atmospheric Administration (NOAA), and the U.S. Geological Survey (USGS). The USGS is managing the National Water Assessment Program which will collect and distribute water quality data. Collection sites provide data from streams, lakes, and reservoirs located throughout the United States. The USGS will distribute the data via the Internet, and the publication of fact sheets are available by contacting USGS Earth Science Information Centers around the nation.

Providing information to the public is a major focus of the DOI and is part of its improved customer service. Another element of this goal is the DOI's intention to reduce bureaucracy and reduce the amount of time it takes for businesses to effectively operate where permits, leases, or other types of federal documentation are required. The goal is part of an overall effort by the Clinton administration to improve access to federal government services for citizens and private companies. This goal is federally mandated by the Government Performance and Results Act. The DOI has instituted programs and strategic plans throughout its bureaus and offices in order to comply with that effort.

AGENCY RESOURCES

A wide variety of information is available about the DOI and its offices and bureaus via the Internet. Information on mapping, earth science, education resources, and research data is available at the U.S. Geological Survey (USGS) site at http://www.usgs.gov. Or visit the Bureau of Land Management (BLM) Web site for information on the 270 million acres under federal management at http://www.blm.gov. Also at the BLM site are descriptions of the wild horse and burro adoption programs. The U.S. Fish and Wildlife Service (FWS) provides information about its conservation programs and activities at http://www.fws.gov. Information and updates about the National Wildlife Refuge System, the Endangered Species Program, Coastal Ecosystems, and National Wetlands Inventory are also available at that site. The National Park Service (NPS) site, at http://www.nps.gov, provides information on the 365 sites where camping and/or recreation are available.

AGENCY PUBLICATIONS

U.S. Geological Survey (USGS) publishes technical and scientific reports and maps, described in the monthly periodical *New Publications of the USGS*, with yearly supplements; *Publications of the USGS, 1879–1961*; *Publications of the USGS, 1962–1970*; and a variety of nontechnical publications described in General Interest Publications of the USGS.

Maps are sold by the Branch of Distribution, USGS, Box 25286, Denver Federal Center, Denver, CO 80225, phone (303) 236-7477. Information about the status of USGS mapping in any state as well as availability of maps by other federal and state agencies can be obtained from any USGS Earth Science Information Center. Call 1-800-USA-MAPS.

NPS publications available to the public include: "Access National Parks, A Guide for Handicapped Visitors;" "Lesser Known Areas of the National Park System;" a natural history series, a scientific monograph series, an official handbook series, and the Publications in Archeology series. "National Parks of the United States," a guide and map is available from the Consumer Information Center, Pueblo CO 81009. For information on scientific, cultural, and technical publications and publications which describe historic preservation, natural landmarks, and outdoor recreation, write the National Park Service, P.O. Box 37127, Washington D.C., 20013-7127, or telephone (202) 208-4747. You can also visit the NPS Web site at http://www.nps.gov for extensive information regarding park sites.

BIBLIOGRAPHY

Babbitt, Bruce. "Science: Opening the Next Chapter of Conservation History." *Science*, 31 March 1995, p. 1954.

"Back to the Future." *Science World*, 9 December 1994, p. 20.

Freedman, Allan. "After Interior's Smooth Ride, Some Issues Left Behind." *Congressional Quarterly Weekly Report*, 5 October 1996, p. 2858.

———. "House Passes Interior Bill, But Difficulty Lies Ahead Despite Small Steps Toward White House Position, Disputes Remain on Funding, Tribal Taxation, Parks." *Congressional Quarterly Weekly Report*, 22 June 1996, p. 1748.

Hamilton, Joan. "Babbitt's Blunder." *Sierra*, May–June 1994, p. 44.

———. "Babbitt's Retreat." *Sierra*, July–August 1994, p. 52.

Nelson, Robert H. "Environmental Creationism." *Forbes*, 8 April 1996, p. 76.

O'Connel, Kim A. "Congress Slashes Interior Spending, President May Veto Bill that Takes Dead Aim at Resources." *National Parks*, November–December 1995, p. 18.

Richardson, Valerie. "Alone on the Range." *National Review*, 30 May 1994 p. 24.

Short, Henry, and Jay B. Hestbeck. "National Biotic Resource Inventories and GAP Analysis." *BioScience*, September 1995, p. 535.

"U.S. Bills Firms $273.6 Million on Oil Royalties; Interior Department Alleges Nine Oil Companies Underpaid in 1980–83." *Wall Street Journal*, 6 January 1997, p. B5B.

Department of the Navy (USN)

PARENT ORGANIZATION: Department of Defense
ESTABLISHED: October 13, 1775
EMPLOYEES: 700,000

Contact Information:

ADDRESS: The Pentagon
Washington, DC 20350
PHONE: (703) 545-6700
E-MAIL: help@chinfo.navy.mil
URL: http://www.navy.mil
SECRETARY OF THE NAVY: John H. Dalton
UNDERSECRETARY OF THE NAVY: Jerry MacArthur Hultin
CHIEF OF NAVAL OPERATIONS: Adm. Jay L. Johnson

WHAT IS ITS MISSION?

Subject to the direction of the president of the United States or the secretary of defense, the U.S. Navy's primary mission is to protect the United States by the effective prosecution of war at sea. This mission, which involves the U.S. Navy's Marine Corps component, includes the seizure or defense of advanced naval bases, the support of all military departments of the United States, and the maintenance of freedom of the seas.

HOW IS IT STRUCTURED?

The navy is a component force of the U.S. Department of Defense, a cabinet-level agency reporting directly to the president. The secretary of the navy is a civilian appointed by the president as head of the Department of the Navy and is responsible for its operation, organization, function, and efficiency. The secretary is assisted in this function by other members of the executive administration, including the civilian executive assistants—the undersecretary of the navy, the assistant secretaries, and the general counsel of the navy. Each civilian executive assistant is assigned a particular area of responsibility and serves as the principal adviser to the secretary in that area.

The navy secretariat is rounded out by the staff assistants, which include the naval inspector general, the auditor general of the navy, the chief of information, the judge advocate general, and the heads of other boards and offices established by law or by the secretary for the purpose of assisting the secretary or the civilian executive

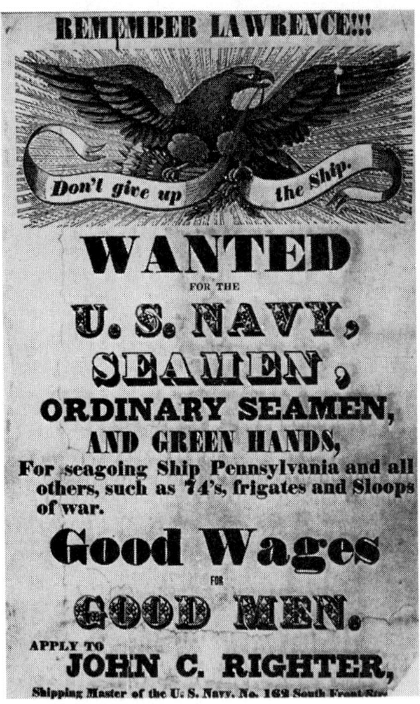

A Navy recruiting poster recalling the War of 1812. *(Courtesy of the Library of Congress)*

assistants. Examples of such boards or offices are the Naval Criminal Investigative Service and the Office of Naval Records.

The military and operating personnel of the navy are led by the chief of naval operations, who commands certain central executive organizations, assigned shore activities, and the operating forces of the navy. The chief of naval operations takes precedence above all officers of the naval service and is the navy member of the Joint Chiefs of Staff. The chief of naval operations plans for and provides the manpower, materials, weapons, facilities, and services to support the needs of the navy.

The naval operations necessary to carry out the Department of the Navy's role in upholding and advancing the national policies and interests of the United States are the responsibility of the operating forces of the navy. These include the several fleets, seagoing forces, Fleet Marine Forces, and other assigned Marine Corps forces; the Military Sealift Command; and other forces as may be assigned by the president or the secretary of the navy. The major fleets are the Pacific and Atlantic Fleets. The Military Sealift Command provides ocean transportation for personnel and cargo of all components of the Department of Defense; it also operates underway-replenishment ships and other vessels providing mobile logistical support and sometimes operates ships in support of scientific projects and other programs for federal agencies.

Other major commands of the operating forces of the navy are the Naval Forces, Europe; the U.S. Naval Forces Central Command; the Naval Special Warfare Command; the Operational Test and Evaluation Force; and the Naval Reserve Force.

The operating forces of the navy are further divided into numerous offices and bureaus that serve to support the navy's primary mission, such as Naval Medicine, Air Systems, Naval Personnel, Oceanography, Space Command, Cryptology, and Naval Doctrine Command. In time of war the U.S. Coast Guard is considered an operating unit of the navy, and is commanded by the chief of naval operations; during peacetime the Coast Guard is a part of the Department of Transportation.

PRIMARY FUNCTIONS

Nearly all peacetime naval operations are focused on recruiting, training, organizing, and equipping the operating forces of the navy. Assistance to civilian organizations is infrequent, but navy ships are often allowed to become a part of federally supported research activities or other government programs. The Bureau of Naval Medicine sometimes cooperates with civil authorities in matters involving public health disasters and other emergencies, in addition to its primary mission of maintaining and safeguarding the health of U.S. Navy and Marine Corps personnel.

The Space Command identifies fleet operational requirements for space systems and helps prepare the navy for extended future involvement in space. The Naval Meteorological Command, an invaluable research unit for both the military and the academic community, examines how naval operations are influenced by the physical environment and applies its findings to the development of technology and methods for improving those operations.

PROGRAMS

The Navy maintains fleets in the Pacific, the Atlantic, and the Indian Oceans and also in the Mediterranean and Arabian Seas and the Persian Gulf. These fleets are generally made up of both surface ships and submarines, as well as aircraft if an aircraft carrier is part of the fleet.

The navy maintains numerous onshore bases, including air bases for patrol and attack aircraft, base camps for marine units, and ports where navy ships can be resupplied and repaired. The navy also carries out an active nationwide recruiting program and operates an academy for officer training at Annapolis, Maryland.

The navy conducts both scientific and military research, often in cooperation with other government agencies or private businesses. Most of the navy's military research is concerned with the development of new technologies and weapons systems. One advanced military project was the V-22A Osprey. Developed by Bell-Boeing, the Osprey is a multimission aircraft that combines vertical takeoff and landing capability with high-speed, high-altitude flight. The aircraft operates as a helicopter when taking off and landing, but once the Osprey is airborne, the engine casings on each wingtip rotate forward, converting it into a high-speed, fuel-efficient turboprop plane. The Osprey is designed to serve as either a search-and-rescue or assault-transport craft, operating from air-capable ships or onshore bases.

One of the navy's largest nonmilitary research programs is the oceanography program conducted by its Oceanography Command. The program utilizes five major scientific disciplines to investigate the nature and behavior of the ocean environment in which the navy operates. Those sciences are hydrography, which involves charting the oceans and establishing navigational references; oceanography, especially water-volume characteristics such as underwater acoustics, water dynamics, and corrosion; meteorology, the study of atmospheric characteristics such as winds and currents or radar-refractive indices; astrometry, which seeks to determine the position and motion of celestial bodies as they relate to navigation; and precise time, involving the determination and provision of precise time and time intervals for use in navigation and command, control, and communications.

BUDGET INFORMATION

The Navy budget, a component of the Department of Defense's budget, was $75.6 billion in 1997. Operation and maintenance of the Navy and Marine Corps, in addition to the reserve forces, accounts for approximately 31 percent of this budget, and the training, outfitting, and equipage of the military personnel of these forces accounted for about 31 percent as well. Another 23 percent of the Navy budget was spent on the procurement of aircraft, ships, weapons, ammunition, and other equipment or facilities, and 10 percent was spent on research, development, testing, and evaluation of new programs, systems, equipment, or facilities. Other elements of the budget, which together accounted for about 2 percent of the Navy's expenditures, included military construction and family housing, the National Defense Sealift Fund, environmental restoration, and base realignment and closure.

HISTORY

Navies were important throughout the colonial period in determining the fate of European empires in North America, and the 1775 commissioning of a navy by the Continental Congress was a natural step in the American Revolution (1775–83). The Continental Navy played a decisive role in the British decision to abandon the American colonies, but it was quickly dismantled after the war.

BUDGET:

Department of the Navy

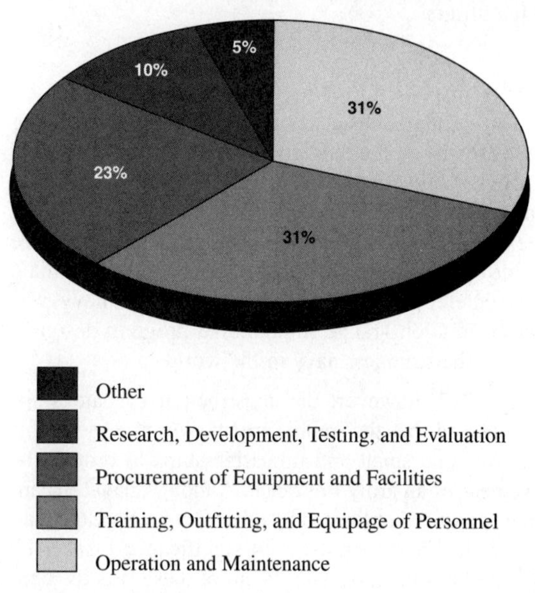

During the 1790s, however, interest in an American fleet was revived by the seizure of American merchant ships by Barbary pirates from North Africa, as well as British and French privateers. When the French refused to stop this practice, Congress established the Department of the Navy in 1798 and carried out an undeclared naval war with France. By the time the conflict had ended, the foundations had been laid for the U.S. Navy.

President Thomas Jefferson called for reduced military spending and a defensive naval policy, but it was not long before the North African state of Tripoli began further harassment of American merchant ships. It took the U.S. Navy four years, from 1801 to 1805, to defeat Tripoli. An even greater challenge came during the War of 1812, which was fought largely at sea against the powerful Royal Navy of Britain. Although the U.S. Navy was too small to prevent the British from concentrating assaults on the coastal cities of Washington, Baltimore, and New Orleans, U.S. naval commanders led a number of impressive victories on inland waters.

From 1815 to 1861 the navy maintained squadrons all over the world, with the primary goal of protecting

American overseas commerce. The American Civil War (1860–65) saw an increase in the navy's total strength from less than 50 to about 700 active ships, but the navy declined in importance soon after the war because of postwar demobilization, the fading importance of the merchant marine, and a shrinking American interest in foreign affairs.

A New Naval Vision

During the 1880s a different type of ship was being built by the navy: the modern steel cruiser. Although initially built for the traditional mission of protecting American commerce and attacking enemy shipping, the United States began in the 1890s to develop a battleship force capable of defeating a hostile fleet. By the time the United States entered World War I (1914–18), the navy was engaged in a long-range shipbuilding program designed to create the strongest navy in the world.

In 1917, however, the construction of battleships was delayed by the more urgent wartime need for destroyers and small antisubmarine ships to protect the movement of an army to France. Although naval expansion was somewhat limited by other factors after the war, the navy had made a number of significant advances by 1941; perhaps the most significant of these was the construction of a strong force of aircraft carriers that rivaled battleships as the navy's major offensive weapon. Long-range submarines, designed for a potential conflict with Japan, were another important development.

During World War II (1939–45), Chief of Naval Operations Ernest J. King emerged as one of the strongest leaders in the navy's history. One of his achievements was to direct significant attention to the Pacific theater, despite the agreement among British and American officials to assign first priority to the defeat of Germany. The navy took part in the largest naval war in U.S. history by undertaking a submarine campaign that ruined Japan's merchant shipping and by employing its carrier aircraft in the aerial bombardment of the enemy's home islands. At the end of World War II, the U.S. Navy was by far the most powerful in the world.

The Postwar Navy

Following World War II the absence of potential enemy fleets and the growing belief that nuclear weapons made navies obsolete led to a clear reduction in naval strength. A general rearmament, brought on by the Cold War and the Korean War (1950–53), renewed the navy's strength; by the 1960s the service operated a powerful, modern fleet built around the backbone of its aircraft carrier fleet. The navy also constructed a large force of submarines capable of firing long-range nuclear missiles, which became an essential part of the U.S. nuclear deterrent.

From 1964 to 1973 the navy was involved in the Vietnam War (1959–75). The navy deployed ships and small craft to inland Vietnamese waters, and its carriers participated in the extended air campaign against North Vietnam. The effort was extremely unpopular with the American public and was ultimately unsuccessful.

Two significant events occupied the navy in the early 1990s—the Persian Gulf War (1991) and the fall of the Soviet Union. The navy's carrier aircraft were instrumental in the heavy aerial bombardment that enabled U.S. ground forces to bring the Persian Gulf War to a swift end, but the end of the Cold War presented new challenges to the navy that have yet to be fully resolved. The navy has begun to recreate its mission and to rethink the structure of a naval force that was specifically built over the last 50 years to defeat an enemy that no longer exists.

CURRENT POLITICAL ISSUES

After World War II the aircraft carrier was considered the backbone of the naval fleet; carriers were involved in some of the epic battles of World War II, such as the Battle of Midway and the Battle of the Coral Sea. It has remained a status symbol for the navy and a significant element of the navy's post-Cold War strategy. Advocates of the aircraft carrier maintain that the navy's ability to carry out U.S. military strategies depends heavily on its ability to supply tactical air power at sea and to deliver weapons quickly where and when the president commands. An aircraft carrier group, with one or more aircraft carriers, one hundred or more warplanes, and dozens of other warships and support vessels, can be deployed quickly and can be used to execute a wide variety of missions. However, the aircraft carrier is an enormously expensive weapon and has for years been the target of public and congressional criticism.

Case Study: The USS Harry Truman and the USS Ronald Reagan

The Navy's USS *Nimitz* class nuclear-powered aircraft carriers are the largest and most expensive ships in the world. Since the USS *Nimitz* was launched in 1977, the navy has built six more carriers in its class, with two more scheduled to be built. With the end of the Cold War and changes in naval tactics, many observers are beginning to question the reason for building these warships.

In addition to the price of building a single *Nimitz*-class aircraft carrier (approximately $4.5 billion), a contingent of one hundred seagoing aircraft must be built to serve on the carrier. Several other ships, destroyers and cruisers to protect the carrier and long-range supply ships to travel with the aircraft carrier group must be built or reassigned from other duties for each new carrier. These additional ships and planes boost the construction price of an aircraft carrier group to around $10 billion—not including another $2 billion each year to operate the group. With the navy's budget in decline after the end of the Cold War, it is likely that cash spent building the next two *Nimitz* carriers—the USS *Ronald Reagan* and USS *Harry Truman*—will require a transfer of funds from other navy programs, leaving each carrier without enough planes and escort ships to fully complement it.

Critics of the aircraft carrier do not deny that it has a legitimate role in the execution of a national security strategy, but even before the fall of the Soviet Union, its status as the backbone of the navy's operating forces was questioned. In recent decades the increasing vulnerability of carriers to submarine attacks caused the costs of defending each carrier to outweigh most of the benefits of the offensive air power carried on each ship. Many critics, including high-ranking navy officers, have argued that the attack submarine long ago replaced the aircraft carrier as the capital ship of the navy, just as the carrier replaced the battleship during World War II. Sea-launched cruise missiles—tested and proved during the Persian Gulf War—have given frigates, destroyers, and cruisers the long-range striking power that was once associated only with aircraft carriers. In addition, the development of vertical takeoff and landing aircraft such as the Osprey means that smaller, more versatile ships will be able to carry aircraft.

The real obstacle to trimming the carrier force is Congress; carriers take years to build and involve hundreds of subcontractors nationwide, who do not want to see the navy's aircraft carrier contracts disappear. This provides a powerful political incentive for members of Congress to keep the carrier program going—a situation that prompted a 1996 editorial in *Fortune* magazine referring to the aircraft carrier as "90,000 tons of prime pork."

FAST FACTS

The oldest commissioned ship in the navy is the USS *Constitution*, a wooden, three-masted frigate that was used in the American Revolution (1775–83). In 1997 the restored *Constitution* sailed for the first time in 116 years.

(Source: Department of the Navy, 1998.)

SUCCESSES AND FAILURES

The navy makes significant peacetime contributions to civil authorities in responding to emergencies. When TWA Flight 800 crashed into the Atlantic Ocean off the New York coast in July 1996, the navy immediately became involved in the salvage operation. Navy teams coordinated both the civilian and military crash-site mapping efforts. A total of 149 active and reserve navy divers participated in the recovery of victims, the location and retrieval of flight data and voice recorders, and the recovery of more than 90 percent of the wreckage. The navy's amphibious ships *Oak Hill* and *Trenton* served as floating command posts and wreckage-retrieval platforms.

FUTURE DIRECTIONS

The U.S. Navy and the Marine Corps began publishing installments in a series, . . . *From the Sea*, in 1992 to describe their combined vision for the twenty-first century. They have updated this description every two years, and the 1997 installment, *Enduring Impact . . . From the Sea*, is the navy's contribution to *Joint Vision 2010*, a 1996 statement of the Joint Chiefs of Staff describing the joint forces of the twenty-first century.

The navy is perceived by many to be struggling to clearly state a post-Cold War mission. Its 1997 posture statement, *Enduring Impact*, does not delineate the navy's plans for integration into *Joint Vision 2010*, but it does describe a naval force shaped for joint operations. It stresses the need for a "forward deployed" force that will be able to respond quickly, with considerable firepower, to conflicts around the world. Many of the navy's future capabilities are described as being the result of new technological developments and capabilities—for example, the ability to network navy command and control systems that are fully interoperable with joint command and control systems.

AGENCY RESOURCES

The Navy Office of Information maintains public affairs centers that provide written, audio, and photographic feature material about fleet personnel, units, and activities. For the nearest center, call the office at (703) 697-5342. Other information about the Navy is available from the Navy Department Library, located at the Naval Historical Center, Washington Navy Yard Bldg. 44, 901 M St. SE, Washington, DC 20374; phone (202) 433-4132. Founded in 1800 the library has a vast collection that includes valuable historical documents and manuscripts; information on shipbuilding, navigation, naval customs, traditions, stations, yards, and bases; and much more.

A valuable on-line source of information is Navy OnLine, the "technical gateway" to the navy's other on-line resources, available at http://www.ncts.navy.mil/

nol/. Links to other naval-related Web sites, news and information services, and search engines are also accessible at this Web site.

AGENCY PUBLICATIONS

Navy publications oriented toward the public include *Enduring Impact . . . From the Sea*, the navy's 1997 posture statement; *All Hands*, the navy's monthly magazine; and *Direct Line*, a newsletter from the master chief petty officer of the navy. These publications can be viewed at the navy's Web site, http://www.navy.mil. For subscription information, contact the Superintendent of Documents, U.S. Government Printing Office, Washington, DC 20402. The navy also has many publications that, although intended for an internal audience, are also available to the public. These include the *Navy News Service*, *Marine Corps News*, and *Chips*, the navy's technical journal. Information on these and similar publications is available on-line at http://www.navy.mil/nol.

The National Technical Information Service (NTIS) also makes some navy publications available, such as older budget documents, posture statements, and internal studies. For information or a list of these items, call the NTIS at (703) 487-4650.

BIBLIOGRAPHY

Butterfield, Fox. "*Constitution*, Under Sail, Evokes a Century Past." *New York Times*, 22 July 1997, p. A8.

Ebbet, J., and Marie-Beth Hall. *Crossed Currents: Navy Women from WWI to Tailhook.* McLean, Va.: Brassey's, 1993.

Gourley, Scott. "Special Weapons and Tactics of the Navy SEALS." *Popular Mechanics*, November 1995, pp. 51–6.

Gray, Colin S. *The Navy in the Post-Cold War World: The Uses & Values of Strategic Sea Power.* University Park: Pennsylvania State University Press, 1994.

Harrigan, Anthony. "The U.S. Navy: Guardian of the Pacific." *Vital Speeches*, 1 Aug 1996, pp. 614–7.

Krapinovich, Andrew F. "Transforming the Navy's War-Fighting Capabilities." *Issues in Science & Technology*, Fall 1996, pp. 28–32.

Kushlan, James P. "Flagship Encounter." *American History*, November–December 1996, pp. 51–6.

Santelmann, Neal. "How to Train a SEAL." *Forbes*, 5 May 1997, pp. S129–134.

Thorpe, Helen. "Naval Gazing." *Texas Monthly*, May 1997, pp. 64–8.

Ullman, Harlan K. *In Harm's Way: American Seapower & the 21st Century.* Silver Spring, Md.: Bartleby Press, 1991.

Vistica, Gregory. "Anchors Aweigh." *Newsweek*, 5 February 1996, pp. 69–72.

Department of the Treasury (The Treasury; DOT)

ESTABLISHED: September 2, 1789
EMPLOYEES: 148,089

Contact Information:

ADDRESS: 1500 Pennsylvania Ave. NW
Washington, DC 20220
PHONE: (202) 622-2000
E-MAIL: opbmail@treas.sprint.com
URL: http://www.ustreas.gov
SECRETARY OF THE TREASURY: Robert E. Rubin

WHAT IS ITS MISSION?

The stated mission of the Department of the Treasury (DOT) is "to formulate and recommend economic, fiscal and tax policies; serve as financial agent of the U.S. government; enforce the law; protect the President and other officials; and manufacture coins and currency." As the chief banking and economic institution of the federal government, it plays a critical role in the success of economic activities in both the private and public sectors.

HOW IS IT STRUCTURED?

The Department of the Treasury is composed of two main branches—the Office of the Secretary and the bureaus. The secretary of the treasury is the chief financial officer of all offices and bureaus of the Treasury and a high-ranking cabinet officer who counsels the president of the United States on financial matters. As the second-highest ranking cabinet officer, the secretary formulates and recommends financial, economic, and tax policy, both domestic and international. Management of the public debt is also within the secretary's responsibilities. The secretary also serves as the chair *pro tempore* (temporary chairperson) of the Economic Policy Council and is the U.S. Governor of the International Monetary Fund, the International Bank of Reconstruction and Development, the Inter-American Development Bank, the Asian Development Bank, and the African Development Bank. In addition to broad management and policy responsibilities, the secretary is accountable to Congress and is required to submit periodic reports, which describe in detail the government's fiscal operations and expenses.

The secretary also publishes the government's annual report, which provides financial information for congressional review. This report provides the numerical foundation for political and economic debate on the direction and health of the government and the overall economy.

Treasury business is implemented by the deputy secretary, undersecretaries, and assistant secretaries in charge of their respective offices including domestic finance, international affairs, enforcement, financial institutions, economic policy, legislative affairs and public liaison, and tax policy and analysis. Specific offices within these departments are headed by directors who report to the assistant secretaries, who in turn report to the secretary of the treasury. Other high-level positions include the general counsel and the inspector general, who handle legal and internal affairs respectively.

The Treasury's broad-ranging responsibilities are divided among bureaus and agencies. The Financial Management Service implements departmental goals by providing information or services to federal government agencies, taxpayers, and other governments. The following bureaus and offices manage treasury policy and U.S. law enforcement: U.S. Customs Service; U.S. Secret Service; Bureau of Alcohol, Tobacco and Firearms; the Federal Law Enforcement Training Center; and the Office of Foreign Assets Control. The Bureau of Engraving and Printing and the United States Mint are responsible for the production of currency, postage, certificates, and other controlled documents necessary to conduct government business. The Office of the Comptroller of the Currency, an integral part of the national banking system, oversees the execution of laws related to nationally chartered banks, trust activities, and banking operations.

PRIMARY FUNCTIONS

The duties of the Department of the Treasury are carried out by its departmental offices and its 13 bureaus. The departmental offices are essentially responsible for directing policy and managing the DOT and its units. In addition, these offices advise the president and Congress on financial, trade, and tax matters. However, 98 percent of the DOT's workforce is involved in the operating bureaus that carry out the specific operations assigned to the department.

One of the DOT's major functions is as collector and disburser of federal funds. Both the Financial Management Service and the Internal Revenue Service (IRS) work to collect the money from tax payers necessary for the federal government to operate. The tax revenues that the IRS gathers fund 95 percent of all federal actions. The Financial Management Service is also responsible for distributing more than $1 trillion to various departments and federal agencies so that they can perform their functions.

Managing and establishing policies for the nation's banks also falls under the DOT's responsibilities. The Office of the Comptroller of Currency (OCC) and the Office of Thrift Supervision (OTS) work together in this capacity. The OCC charters and manages banks throughout the country, while the OTS analyzes their stability.

The Department of the Treasury is also responsible for creating and managing U.S. currency. The Bureau of Engraving and Printing designs and prints the range of dollar bills and postage stamps available for use in commerce while the U.S. Mint designs and stamps the coins.

The DOT has several functions associated with the area of law enforcement. Its Bureau of Alcohol, Tobacco, and Firearms (ATF) works to license alcohol, tobacco, and guns as well as eliminate illegal buying and selling of these products. The ATF is also responsible for working with other federal and local law enforcement agencies to analyze bombings and arsons. The U.S. Customs Service monitors both goods and people entering and exiting the country to make sure that all laws regarding their passage are being followed. Instructing a variety of federal law enforcement officers is the responsibility of the Federal Law Enforcement Training Center. The function of the Financial Crimes Enforcement Network is to pursue anti-money laundering interests both domestically and internationally by analyzing various databases of financial information and coordinating efforts with other law enforcement organizations to halt illegal actions. The Internal Revenue Service is responsible for enforcing tax laws and pursuing those people and businesses that attempt to evade paying their taxes. The Bureau of Engraving and Printing and the United States Secret Service coordinate efforts to stop the counterfeiting of U.S. currency both domestically and abroad.

One of the most visible functions of the DOT is that of the protection given by the United States Secret Service (USSS). The USSS works not only to safeguard the president and vice president and their immediate families but also presidential candidates and visiting dignitaries. USSS protection of the president and his family lasts for ten years after he finishes his final term.

PROGRAMS

The Department of the Treasury runs a wide variety of programs primarily through its various bureaus. The Bureau of Alcohol, Tobacco, and Firearms (ATF), for example, instituted the Youth Crime Gun Interdiction Initiative (YCGII) in 1997. This program is dedicated to understanding and destroying the illegal gun market that fuels many of the violent crimes committed by youth. The YCGII researches various aspects of the market such as what sort of guns are used in youth crimes and how they might have been procured. Using this information, the YCGII attempts to identify the market and what resources and materials it would take to dispose of it. Almost 30 cities participate in the YCGII program, coordinating efforts between local law enforcement agencies and ATF officials.

Programs by the Internal Revenue Service (IRS), another bureau of the Department of the Treasury, include the Problem Solving Days programs. During one or more days of each month, the IRS staffs its local offices in most states with tax experts to answer the questions of those attempting to understand the complicated process of paying federal taxes or to resolve outstanding tax difficulties. The general public is welcome to either visit or phone the office that is closest. Tens of thousands of people have taken advantage of this service since it was instituted in November 1997.

BUDGET INFORMATION

The 1998 budget appropriated by Congress to the Department of the Treasury was approximately $389.3 billion. This amount accounted for 24 percent of the total federal government budget of $1.653 trillion. The Treasury obtained another $16 billion through intrafund transactions and offsetting receipts, bringing its total spending to $405.3 billion. By far the largest portion of the Treasury budget was spent on the interest that accumulated on the public debt in 1998. This amounted to 89 percent, or $362.1 billion, of the 1998 Treasury budget.

The next largest portion of the Treasury budget, $32.7 billion (8 percent), was allocated to the Internal Revenue Service. Most of the remainder of the budget was allotted to the Financial Management Service ($5.8 billion or 1 percent) and the U.S. Customs Service ($2.2 billion or 0.5 percent).

BUDGET:

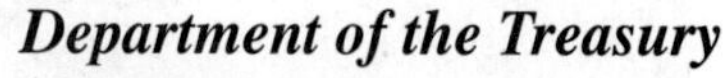

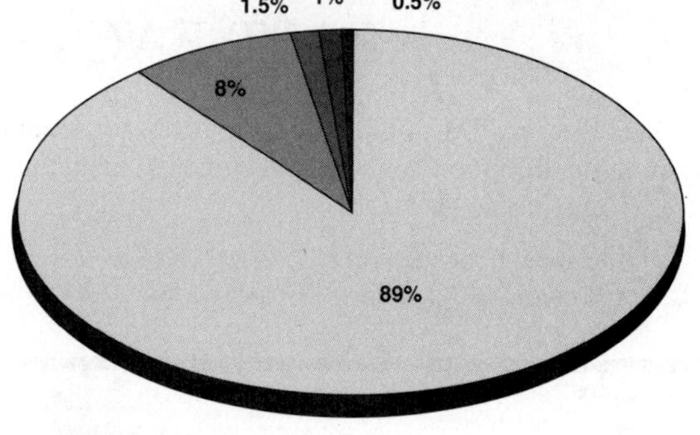

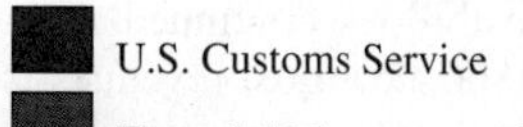

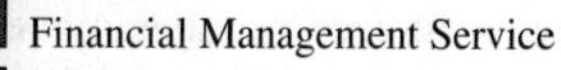

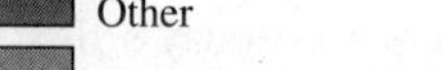

Internal Revenue Service

Interest on the Public Debt

Percentage of Federal Budget

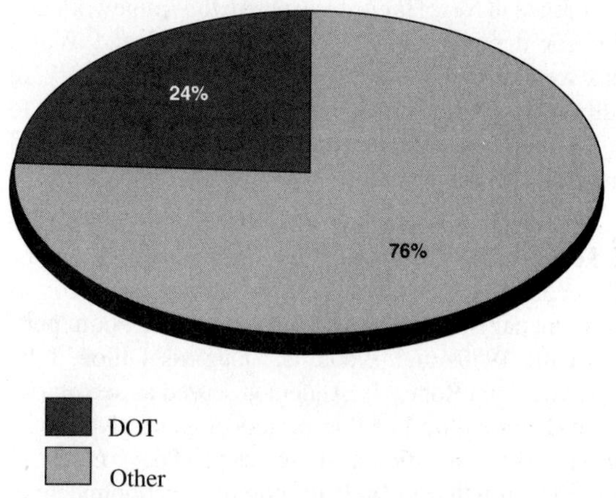

DOT

Other

HISTORY

The Office of the Treasurer was established in 1777 and was initially responsible for the receipt and custody of government funds. As the new republic continued to grow, it quickly became clear that a centralized bureau with greater authority was necessary not only to manage the nation's finances but also to provide leadership in setting its fiscal policy in order to plan the country's financial future. As a result, the Department of Treasury was one of the first cabinet-level departments established in 1789 during the first session of Congress.

President George Washington appointed Alexander Hamilton the Treasury Department's first secretary. Hamilton's contributions to building the government's early financial policies are still recognized today. He was instrumental in solidifying the Bank of the United States, which issued money in the government's name. The financial success of the new government was critical to instilling popular trust in the new government. Hamilton is also credited with establishing the high degree of political influence associated with the position and set a precedent for the Treasury secretary to serve as one of the president's top advisers.

FAST FACTS

The Treasury Department is responsible for annually printing 40 billion controlled documents, including currency and postage.

(Source: *Congressional Quarterly's Guide to the Presidency*, Congressional Quarterly, Inc. 1996.)

The Treasury's responsibilities continued to grow during the Civil War era (1860–65). Lost revenues from seceded Southern states forced the development of a national banking system. During this period, the Bureau of Internal Revenue, the precursor of today's IRS, was established, and the government also began printing paper currency, a role it still plays today.

Following the world wars, the U.S. became more involved in foreign trade and played a leadership role in establishing international banking systems. Specifically, the Treasury played a key role at the 1944 Bretton Woods Conference in New Hampshire, where the framework and rules for the International Monetary Fund and World Bank were created. Since then, the Treasury secretary, in addition to domestic responsibilities, has continued to play a major role in the pursuit of U.S. international financial interests.

The years following World War II (1939–45) were marked by economic growth and financial stability in the U.S. economy. The U.S. Treasury is recognized for its steady management of the ensuing economic boom periods of the 1950s and 1960s. C. Douglass Dillon, John W. Snyder, and Robert B. Anderson served as secretaries of the Treasury during this period of general political conservatism and financial security. They managed domestic growth and built up complex economic relationships with other countries based on loans and commercial relationships. During this period, often referred to as the Cold War due to the tense relationship between the U.S. and the Soviet Union, the Treasury was influential in managing the financial policies necessary to fund military services and equipment. Cold War spending encouraged confidence in the U.S. economy, which in turn supported the growth of investment in America by foreign economies, increasing economic links between countries eager to put their capital to work.

The previous period of economic growth began to slow in the 1970s. Rising prices and falling wages caused concerns and serious economic speculation on the long-term effects of Treasury and Federal Reserve policies, specifically the effect of interest rates on borrowing and saving. The Carter administration increased the flow of new money into the economy to fight inflation; and of equal concern the now-sluggish economy's growing recession.

This combination of events allowed Republican Ronald Reagan to launch a successful campaign for the presidency which focused on the economic failures of the Carter administration. Under Reagan, the Congress and the Treasury lowered taxes to encourage commerce and drastically reduced the federal budget by cutting a wide variety of programs. Reagan promoted a straightforward economic theory whose real impact on the overall economy is still a matter of debate. He deregulated many financial industries, freeing up the movement of capital but also setting the stage for a later catastrophic collapse of hundreds of savings and loan organizations throughout the United States. The economy did benefit from a return to the Cold War spirit by the $2.2 trillion spent on military services and programs, an important linchpin in President Reagan's foreign policy initiatives, but his policies dramatically increased the federal budget deficit. Reagan's vice president and later successor George Bush managed to maintain the spirit of Reagan's economic policy while increasing taxes, but the extent and scope of the federal deficit did not become apparent until the early 1990s.

By 1995, several years into the Clinton administration, economic indicators were stronger than in previous years, quieting concerns over inflation and recession. The security of a strong economy encouraged debate in Congress and the Senate on how best to improve the efficiency of the Treasury through technical and administrative improvements.

CURRENT POLITICAL ISSUES

Each president has an economic plan designed to promote confidence and financial growth. These plans are usually hotly debated among the different political parties whose economic forecasting and perspectives are often radically opposed. The dominant government financial issue of the 1990s was the federal budget deficit whose origins lay in the policies of the Reagan and Bush administrations, and which grew to $5.4 trillion in 1997. Democrats and Republicans, conservatives and liberals, and economists of various schools all present different models for solving the deficit problem. Between presidential and congressional leadership, these governmental forces balance political maneuvering and economic interpretation to provide solutions that will ultimately be their legacy to future generations.

With the assistance of the secretary of the Treasury, the president must present a federal budget to Congress each year for approval. Under the guidance of the Clinton administration, the Democrats, presented a deficit reduction plan, that included dramatic cuts in the Department of Defense budget and a Rebuilding Government Program designed to streamline government agencies across the board. These efforts seemed to have the desired effect: the Clinton administration's economic policies were strengthened by a 1995 budget windfall of $135 billion, due largely to a strong economic upswing. In spite of this unexpected revenue, important federal programs including health care, education, agriculture subsidies, and research and development are still subject to congressional spending cuts. The Clinton administration hopes to strengthen the economy through federal spending in health care and education while providing modest tax cuts to middle-income Americans. This economic agenda, designed to support middle-income taxpayers, is sometimes at odds with Republican economic strategies which seek to cut government spending dramatically as well as cut taxes in an effort to promote economic growth.

FAST FACTS

The national debt increased at a rate of $256 million per day during 1998. If you are an American citizen, your share of the national debt is about $20,550.

(Source: Bureau of the Public Debt, 1998.)

Case Study: Whose Taxes Should Be Cut?

One of the most debated and politically charged issues is the capital gains tax that is levied when an individual sells an asset such as real estate or stocks at a profit. Democrats have traditionally supported a capital gains tax as a means of raising revenue from wealthier households and minimizing additional burdens on middle- and lower-income families who tend not to generate income from such transactions. Republicans have argued that such a tax against wealthy households places a burden on all sectors in the economy, because it diverts money from being invested.

Usually opposed on the issue, Republicans and Democrats united under the Clinton administration to approve a capital gains tax cut. Democrats felt such a compromise was necessary in order to gain Republican support for other political issues. Together, both parties worked out agreements for implementing the cuts while supplementing programs that support middle- and low-income citizens.

Public Impact

Republicans argue that the capital gains tax cut increases investment in the economy, creating economic growth and jobs. They cite studies showing that one-third of all taxpayers realized a capital gain as a result of some financial activity in the last ten years. Supporters of a higher capital gains tax argue that while one-third of all taxpayers may have realized a profit from the sale of an asset, individual profits vary widely, and other studies indicate that five percent of the nation's household tax bills are significantly impacted by the capital gains tax cut.

Adjustments in tax rates are an important means of manipulating the deficit because taxes directly increase or decrease government revenue. Manipulation of tax rates creates a distinct public impact as citizens absorb the cost of government through income tax, sales tax, and excise taxes. Although Republicans and Democrats reached a compromise on the capital gains tax, it may again emerge as a means of raising government funds, and with it, the question will be raised of who should be taxed and at what cost.

SUCCESSES AND FAILURES

One significant event in international finance was the Clinton administration's handling of the Mexican financial crisis of 1994. During the early 1990s Mexican banks lost control of debt management and inflation, bringing the country to the brink of economic instability. The Clinton administration had previously fully committed itself to the North American Free Trade Agreement (NAFTA) in an attempt to bring renewed economic growth to the United States and its economic partners, most notably Mexico. In order to avert economic disaster for U.S. businesses that had invested heavily in the Mexican economy, a loan bailout was devised. Developed and implemented by the U.S. Treasury and administered by the Economic Stabilization Fund, it provided Mexican authorities with $20 billion in funds under the terms of four specific agreements. Mexico was under pressure to successfully restructure its short-term debt and strengthen its entire banking system. In addition, it agreed to route all crude oil revenues through a Federal Reserve Bank account in New York. If Mexico could not meet its financial obligations, those funds would be claimed as payment. If loans were paid on time, the money would be made available to the Bank of Mexico. Mexican authorities were also obligated to pursue a rigorous program of economic restructuring to restore financial stability and report periodically on their progress. The Mexican economy showed signs of progress, and loans were repaid on time, making this bailout a successful program in international aid and financial assistance that has directly affected U.S. jobs, immigration interests, and national security.

FUTURE DIRECTIONS

Secretary of the Treasury Robert Rubin announced plans to modernize the financial management techniques of the Treasury, believing that the federal government could save the consumer up to $15 billion a year by making financial services more efficient and increasing competition. According to Rubin, "The time has come to modernize the rules of our financial service system." Secretary Rubin also states, "Such a move must be done with regard for safety and soundness to benefit the broad range of users of financial services: consumers, small businesses, communities, and state and local governments."

Such modernization will focus on the IRS. Secretary Rubin testified before the Senate Subcommittee on Government Management, Information and Technology about the impact of technology on the IRS. An emphasis on technically trained personnel and the introduction of new technologies are expected to increase the efficiency and customer service of the IRS. Among the strategies is the use of outside contractors to work on modernizing the tax system and expansion of its capabilities for electronic filing (19 million returns were filed electronically in 1996). Such trends will continue as the IRS and the Department of the Treasury work to simplify tax filing, strengthen the security of private tax information, and improve customer service.

AGENCY RESOURCES

The Treasury Library is located in Room 5030, Main Treasury Bldg., 1500 Pennsylvania Ave. NW., Washington, DC 20220; phone (202) 622-0990. Within the library is a reading room that offers a variety of information regarding the Treasury and its bureaus. The Public Affairs and Public Liaison offices are available by phone at (202) 622-2960 to answer general questions about Treasury activities. Documents concerning events, policy news, and recent speeches are available via fax at (202) 622-2040. Information on financial services, tax information, government regulations, and law enforcement is available via the Treasury Web site at http://www.ustreas.gov.

General information about the production, value, and collection of money (numismatics) and postage (philately) is available by calling the Bureau of Engraving and Printing, Office of Communications, at (202) 874-3019.

For those interested in visiting the Treasury building in Washington D.C., tours can be arranged by calling (202) 622-0809. A virtual building tour is also available on-line at http://www.ustreas.gov/archives where visitors can view photos of rooms and art pieces. The Treasury building is steeped in historical significance. Many of it offices and rooms are maintained as they were originally built and provide an interesting glimpse of the Treasury's place in American government.

AGENCY PUBLICATIONS

The *Treasury Bulletin* is published for the general public and contains narrative, tables, and charts describing financial news and issues. Call for a copy at (202) 874-9913 or send a request by E-mail to treasury.bulletin@fms.sprint.com. The Financial Management Service has comprehensive statistical and customer service information at its Web site at http://www.ustreas.gov.

Other publications include the Annual Report, which is available both via the Treasury's Web site and in printed form through the Government Printing Office.

BIBLIOGRAPHY

Hurtado Robert. "Inflation Data Helps to Lift Bond Prices: 30 Year Treasury's Yield Falls to 7.07%." *New York Times*, 2 April 1997, p. D20.

Ireland, Doug. "Robert Rubin, Reignmaker: Rubin Is the Most Powerful Treasury Secretary Since Alexander Hamilton." *The Nation*, 10 March 1997, p. 19.

Lane, Randall, and Lawrence Minard. "The View from the Treasury." *Forbes*, 30 December 1996, p. 45.

Norton, Rob. "Rubin's Just Another Bad Wizard." *Fortune*, 27 November 1995, p. 54.

Ulmann, Owen, Mike McNamara, and Lee Walczak. "Why the GOP Loves to Hate Bob Rubin." *Business Week*, 10 March 1997, p. 32.

Walsh, Kenneth. "Treasury's New Age Liberal: Why Robert Rubin Has Taken the Lead in Making Urban Policy." *U.S. News and World Report*, 14 February 1997, p. 27.

Zuckerman, Gregory. "Bond Prices Ease as Investors Look to Release of CPI Data for a Sense of Economy's Strength. (Consumer Price Index)" *Wall Street Journal*, 15 April 1997, p. C19.

Department of Transportation (DOT)

ESTABLISHED: October 15, 1966
EMPLOYEES: 100,518

Contact Information:

ADDRESS: 400 7th St. SW
Washington, DC 20590
PHONE: (202) 366-4000
FAX: (202) 366-7777
E-MAIL: dot.comments@ost.dot.gov
URL: http://www.dot.gov
SECRETARY OF TRANSPORTATION: Rodney E. Slater
DEPUTY SECRETARY OF TRANSPORTATION:
Mortimer L. Downey

WHAT IS ITS MISSION?

The stated mission of the Department of Transportation (DOT) is "to assure the coordinated, effective administration of the transportation programs of the Federal Government." Dedicated to developing safe and efficient means of transportation, the DOT currently coordinates 10 different operating agencies as a way of ensuring decentralized power in the transportation industry.

Efficiency is DOT's chief goal in moving people and goods. The department focuses on safety and environmental concerns and is a strong supporter of free enterprise within the transportation industries. The core mission of DOT is to help move the federal government into the twenty-first century by providing first-rate transportation programs that achieve consistent operational success. In coordination with environmental researchers and energy conservationists, DOT strives to improve transportation resources in large metropolitan areas, where they are needed the most.

HOW IS IT STRUCTURED?

The Department of Transportation is the third-largest cabinet-level agency and is part of the executive branch of the U.S. government. DOT is led by a secretary appointed by the president and confirmed by Congress. DOT oversees 10 agencies: the Coast Guard (USCG), Federal Aviation Administration (FAA), Federal Highway Administration (FHWA), Federal Railroad Administration (FRA), National Highway Traffic Safety Administration (NHTSA), Federal Transit Administra-

BUDGET:

Department of Transportation

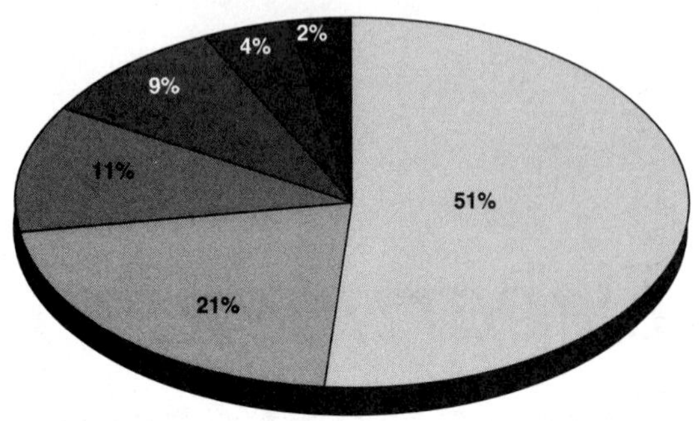

- National Highway Traffic Safety Administration
- Federal Railroad Administration
- Mandatory Obligations for Federal-Aid Highways
- U.S. Coast Guard
- Federal Transit Administration
- Federal Aviation Administration
- Federal Highway Administration

Percentage of Federal Budget

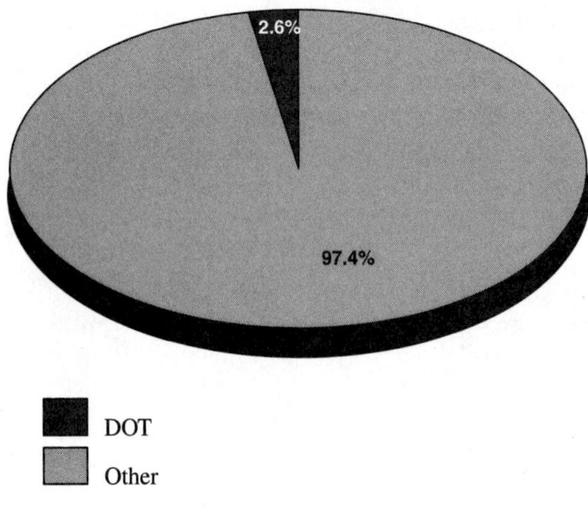

- DOT
- Other

tion (FTA), Saint Lawrence Seaway Development Corporation (SLSDC), Maritime Administration (MARAD), Research and Special Programs Administration (RSPA), and Bureau of Transportation Statistics (BTS). Each of these agencies has various responsibilities within the transportation field and most are concerned with one or more specific modes of transport. For example, the FAA oversees all air commerce in the United States and investigates all air traffic matters.

In carrying out its daily functions and duties, DOT interacts with other offices such as the Office of Civil Rights, Board of Contract Appeals, Executive Secretariat, Office of Small and Disadvantaged Business Utilization, Office of Intelligence and Security, Office of Public Affairs, General Counsel, Assistant Secretary for Transportation Policy, Assistant Secretary for Aviation and International Affairs, Assistant Secretary for Budget and Programs and Chief Financial Officer, Assistant Secretary for Governmental Affairs, Assistant Secretary for Administration, and Office of Inspector General.

Also included in DOT's organizational structure is the Office of Intermodalism. The purpose of this office is to help research and develop new transportation systems and provide support for existing systems. This office also serves as the principal adviser for the department when it formulates policy and management systems.

PRIMARY FUNCTIONS

DOT establishes policies and programs that facilitate efficiently run transportation systems. Through its 10 agencies, DOT regulates the industries responsible for developing these systems and often investigates ineffective or unsafe designs concerning a particular mode of transport. In the automobile industry, for example, the department, through its NHTSA, develops specific guidelines for automobile safety using experiments that test air bag restraint systems and seat belts. In addition DOT administers the safety laws relating to airplanes, boats, rail cars and engines, and other means of transport. As well as enforcing safety laws, DOT investigates major transportation accidents in an effort to protect the public from future mishaps. The department also conducts research and educates the public in order to promote its transportation programs.

PROGRAMS

The programs of DOT are as numerous and varied as the agencies that administer them. For example, the FTA's programs include the Capital Program, which assists in the financing and improvement of mass transportation in urban areas. The money from this program is allocated in three ways: (1) 40 percent is used for the modernization of transportation services; (2) 40 percent for the construction of new transportation systems; and (3) 20 percent for the repair and purchase of buses and related equipment.

Programs in another DOT agency, the FHWA, include the Highway Safety Program, which provides funding on the state and local levels for activities such as removing hazardous obstacles from roadsides, remarking pavement, and upgrading railroad crossing signals. The FHWA also manages the Federal Lands Highway Program, which provides funding to repave and improve more than 80,000 miles of federally owned roads that are open to public travel.

BUDGET INFORMATION

The DOT's 1998 budget was approximately $42.8 billion and made up about 2.6 percent of the total federal budget of $1.653 trillion. Most of that budget went into DOT's ten umbrella agencies. Approximately 51 percent of the DOT's overall budget, was given to its largest agency, the Federal Highway Administration. In comparison, some of the nine remaining agencies received much less: the Federal Aviation Administration received $9.1 billion, the Federal Transit Administration received $4.8 billion, and the U.S. Coast Guard received $3.9 billion.

Other functions receiving portions of the DOT's budget are mandatory obligations for federal-aid Highways ($1.6 billion), the Federal Railroad Administration ($732 million), and the National Highway Traffic Safety Administration ($333 million).

HISTORY

The federal government has been responsible for regulating transportation in the United States since the late nineteenth century. The Interstate Commerce Commission (ICC) was created in 1887 to regulate rates and tariffs on the massive railway system that boomed after the American Civil War (1860–65). Even though the ICC helped the federal government control the railroads, the need for a larger, more comprehensive federal agency was apparent once other modes of transport were invented and developed.

People began to travel farther and faster during the twentieth century via the automobile and the airplane, and the need became apparent for a cabinet-level transportation administration to meet the demands of a growing economy. Federal transportation policy was often dictated by world events such as World War I (1914–18), the Great Depression (1929–40), and World War II (1939–45), however no single federal agency was responsible for creating a national transportation policy. It was not until the 1950s, when President Dwight Eisenhower initiated construction on the Interstate Highway System, that the idea of one executive-level transportation agency took root.

In his 1963 State of the Union address, President John F. Kennedy told the nation that a new executive-level transportation agency must be developed or the United States would face serious economic adversity.

FAST FACTS

In 1997 there were 6.76 million police-reported accidents on U.S. highways in which 41,967 travelers died.

(Source: National Highway Safety Administration. "Traffic Safety Facts," 1998.)

The federal government relied too heavily upon fragmented federal agencies to administer transportation policy, and the result was chaotic; too much bureaucracy and too much money was being spent on transportation systems that were never fully developed. On October 15, 1966, President Lyndon Johnson signed the act creating the DOT, a cabinet-level agency responsible for creating and regulating policy for the entire transportation industry in the United States.

Transportation Policy in the First Decade

The first mode of transportation targeted by DOT was the airline industry. In 1968 Congress amended the Federal Aviation Act of 1958, giving the FAA, an agency controlled by DOT, authority to establish new aircraft noise standards. A year later the National Transportation Policy Act was passed, establishing major environmental requirements for building transportation facilities, such as airports. In 1971 DOT created Amtrak, an intercity rail passenger service that would operate across the United States. Other major transportation policies created by DOT during the 1970s included setting the national maximum speed limit at 55 miles per hour; establishing a new computerized air traffic control system for all major airports; obtaining grants to develop mass transit in seven U.S. cities; establishing the Railroad Revitalization and Regulatory Reform Act of 1976, which loosened economic regulations on the rail industry; and establishing a new department, the Office of Small and Disadvantaged Business Utilization, which helps women and minorities create their own businesses in the transportation industry.

The Second Decade and Beyond

During the 1980s and 1990s DOT's focus moved toward establishing more safety guidelines and tariff regulations. In 1980 DOT launched its first nationwide campaign against drinking and driving. In 1984 the national minimum drinking age of 21 was established as a way to curb drinking-related fatalities on U.S. highways. That same year, in legislation originally created by DOT, the Shipping Act of 1984 was signed into law by President Ronald Reagan, restructuring regulations covering all U.S. waterborne foreign trade. Also in 1984 DOT enforced guidelines for automobile manufacturers, requiring them to equip all passenger cars with either air bags or automatic safety belts by 1989. In 1988, Pathfinder, the first automobile in-vehicle navigation system in the United States, was financed and developed with the help of DOT in hopes of improving traffic flow in the greater Los Angeles area.

DOT's improvement of resources and technology continued into the 1990s. One of the most significant acts of this era was President George Bush's signing of the $155 billion Intermodal Surface Transportation Efficiency Act (ISTEA) of 1991. The goal of this bill was to create more than 400,000 transportation-related jobs in six years. The Persian Gulf War (1991) also saw DOT agencies perform their finest work in years. Both the U.S. Coast Guard and the MARAD activated special sealift ships that helped deliver American troops into battle, making DOT responsible for the largest, most concentrated military lift operation since World War II. Also during this era, more in-vehicle navigation system experiments were under development. Nicknamed SMART CARS and TravTek, these intelligent transportation systems were designed to offer alternate routes for drivers when traffic became congested.

CURRENT POLITICAL ISSUES

Since modern transportation systems have always had difficulty meeting U.S. population demands, DOT has faced extreme criticism in policing transportation security and safety standards. Many critics have charged DOT with a "wait and see" policy when dealing with major transportation accidents. The airline and automobile industries, in particular, fall victim to public scrutiny, especially when an intensive investigation follows the aftermath of a major tragedy.

Case Study: The ValuJet Crash

On the afternoon of May 11, 1996, ValuJet Flight 592 bound for Atlanta crashed while returning to Miami International Airport after the pilots reported smoke in the cockpit. Both pilots and 108 passengers were killed when the DC-9 jet burst into flames and crashed nose first into the Florida Everglades. NTSB investigators were at first unsure about what caused the tragedy. They soon learned, however, that several oxygen generators (canisters used by airlines as emergency oxygen systems and filled with flammable sodium chlorate) were stored in the jet's forward cargo hold. Originally, it was thought that these canisters were empty, but investigators later concurred that the generators labeled as empty could have been active. Somehow, the investigators surmised, these generators set off a flash fire in the cargo area by mixing with grease, oil, and other flammable materials inside the jet.

Public Impact

DOT's investigation into the ValuJet accident created more questions than answers. The crash focused attention on the entire airline industry, asking whether "discount" airlines such as ValuJet, which offered a low-cost alternative to the more-established airlines, were a threat to air travel safety. Critics believed that ValuJet and other discount airlines often used older aircraft in commuter flights as a way of saving overhead costs. Aircraft maintenance inspection was also scrutinized; planes flown by low-cost airlines such as ValuJet, it was learned, were often carelessly examined or not examined at all.

DOT's Office of the Inspector General took over the case when it was learned that ValuJet and SabreTech, an aircraft-maintenance company that supplied the oxygen generators, might have deliberately misled investigators about the status of the oxygen canisters. Later, Inspector General Mary Schiavo created a controversy when she declared that she would avoid flying ValuJet, even after her boss, Transportation Secretary Frederico Peña, stated the airline was safe to fly. Schiavo eventually resigned from office, saying she felt the department and its investigators were "soft" and did not adequately investigate the case.

Although DOT has since banned the storing of oxygen generators in aircraft cargo holds, many critics believe the ValuJet investigation revealed an agency that is simply too disorganized and undisciplined to regulate the transportation industry. Critics asked why such accidents still occur if DOT was created with the intent of forming strong, decisive transportation policy.

Case Study: Air Bag Safety

Following the ValuJet tragedy, the department learned to be more responsive to public and media scrutiny. A good example of this new-found attitude was DOT's response to the public outcry over the improper inflation of automobile air bag restraint systems.

During the late 1980s, air bag restraint systems became standard in most American-built automobiles. The inflatable device activated during serious frontal collisions, allowing front-seat passengers extra protection from devastating injury. To critics everywhere, air bags were widely viewed as the solution to automobile safety problems. Since 1991 air bags have been credited with saving approximately 1,600 lives. But during this time the device has also been blamed for the deaths of 51 people. In one reported case in 1996, a child was decapitated by a rapidly inflating air bag.

Eager to respond to growing public concern over the air bag issue, DOT issued a statement in November 1996 guaranteeing that it would ensure that more advanced air bag systems be installed in future automobiles. The biggest concern the agency promised to address was the speed with which air bags inflated and whether this rapid inflation led to harmful injury. Many consumer groups believed this was the case, and DOT promised the public that by 1999, all air bag systems in cars would be "smarter." In alliance with the three major auto makers, DOT began to experiment with air bag systems that would contain multiple ultrasound sensors, allowing a computer to determine the size and position of an occupant, and that would inflate in stages, depending on the severity of the crash. This newer design would prevent air bags from activating inappropriately.

The DOT also proposed a rule which would require dealers to permanently deactivate air bags in a vehicle upon the request of its owner. This proposal was forcefully opposed by auto manufacturers and dealers. They believed that allowing permanent deactivation would send the wrong message to consumers, implying that air bags are unsafe, when in fact the vast majority of passengers will benefit from the presence of an air bag. Dealers also feared they would be held liable for injuries suffered by those whose air bags they had disabled. A compromise was reached, and in December of 1997 a new rule was adopted by the NHTSA. The rule called for the dealer installation of cut-off switches for air bags, if requested by the car's owner. These switches allow air bags to be activated and deactivated by the owner whenever he wishes, as opposed to the original proposal of permanently disabling air bags.

Public Impact

The public response to DOT's actions was overwhelming. After the air bag redesign proposal was announced, calls from people who wanted to learn more about air bag safety flooded the department's telephone hot lines. When cut-off switches became available in 1998, thousands of Americans had them installed in their cars. Consumer groups from across the United States applauded DOT for its active participation in solving the air bag safety issue.

FUTURE DIRECTIONS

"The Future Starts Here" is the title of DOT's 25th anniversary report, which outlines the agency's goals for the twenty-first century. The development of a "smart car/smart highway" system is one of DOT's major goals for increasing efficiency in automobile transportation. The department has long proposed the idea of a computerized in-vehicle navigation system that would eventually replace the human driver. Such systems are under development; a select number of cars can be equipped with in-vehicle monitors that tell the driver what routes to take. The department wants to continue experimenting with this new technology in hopes of introducing a driverless motor vehicle.

DOT is also working on magnetic levitation trains as a high-speed alternative for commuters. High-speed trains are widely used in such countries as Japan and France, and DOT wants to develop a similar transportation system that will alleviate major traffic woes in heavily populated urban areas such as Los Angeles.

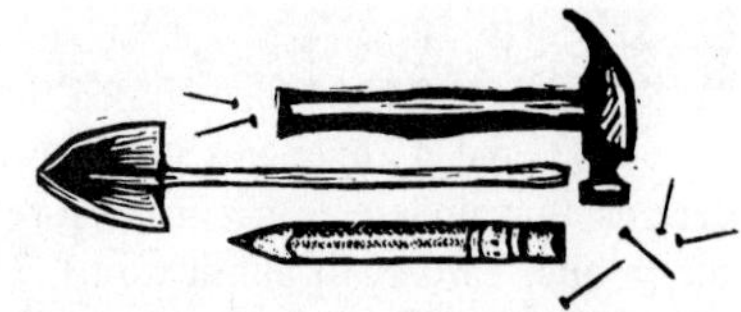

GET INVOLVED:

Many educational programs are offered by the various Department of Transportation agencies. These programs teach local groups and members of the business community the importance of safety in the transportation industries. Aviation Medical Training is one such program that is currently offered to the general aviation community; for more information call (405) 954-6212. Other safety training programs are available from the National Transit Institute at (908) 932-1700. The Transportation Safety Institute also fields questions about safety training at (405) 949-0036, extension 361.

AGENCY RESOURCES

DOT answers consumers' questions through a number of different telephone hot lines. For general airline difficulties such as lost luggage or complications with airfare rates and service, DOT offers the Air Travel Consumer Complaint Hotline at (202) 366-2220. The Aviation Consumer Hotline is also set up to inform consumers about regulations concerning carry-on baggage, aircraft certifications, and airport facility operations; this toll-free number is 1-800-322-7873. The Aviation Safety Hotline offers consumers a chance to report violations of federal aviation regulations; this hot line number is also toll-free at 1-800-255-1111.

For questions about mechanical defects in automobiles or information about any automobile recall, DOT offers the toll-free Auto Safety Hotline at 1-800-424-9393. Any complaints about waste, fraud, or abuse of transportation facilities can be reported to DOT's inspector general at 1-800-424-9071. For questions concerning maritime and water safety, consumers can use the Boating Safety and Consumer Hotline at 1-800-368-5647.

AGENCY PUBLICATIONS

DOT and its agencies produce a number of publications that update transportation-related programs for the public. Two such publications, *The National Transportation Initiative: A Progress Report* and *Air Bag Safety: Hearing Before the Committee on Commerce, Science, and Transportation*, are available at local libraries or through the Government Printing Office (GPO) at (202) 512-1800. Other related publications, such as transcripts of recent speeches by the secretary of transportation, can be obtained from the GPO or from DOT's World Wide Web site at http://www.dot.gov.

BIBLIOGRAPHY

Anderson, Joshua P., and Arnold M. Howitt. "Clean Air Act SIPs, Sanctions, and Conformity." *Transportation Quarterly*, Summer 1995, p. 67.

"Clinton Proposes Rule on Car Seats for Children." *New York Times*, 16 February 1997, p. A19.

Dean, Alan L., and James M. Briggs. "The Department of Transportation Comes of Age: The Nixon Years." *Presidential Studies Quarterly*, Winter 1996, pp. 209–15.

"Department of Transportation." *Financial World*, 25 October 1994, p. 66.

Greenwald, John. "The Air-Bag Safety Saga." *Time*, 2 December 1996, p. 40.

"Highways Become Safer." *The Futurist*, January/February 1994, pp. 51–2.

Kerwin, Kathleen. "GM Pickups: The Issue is Safety, Not Regulation." *Business Week*, 12 December 1994, p. 95.

Resh, Robert E. "Air Bags." *Scientific American*, June 1996, p. 116.

Stout, David. "Slater Wins Confirmation for Position in the Cabinet." *New York Times*, 1 February 1997, p. A22.

Sullivan, John. "Standards for Gas Pipelines Unchanged Years After Blast." *New York Times*, 9 April 1997, p. A1.

Department of Veterans Affairs (VA)

ESTABLISHED: March 15, 1989
EMPLOYEES: 266,274

Contact Information:

ADDRESS: 810 Vermont Ave. NW
Washington, DC 20420
PHONE: (202) 273-4900
URL: http://www.va.gov
SECRETARY OF VETERANS AFFAIRS: Togo D. West, Jr.

WHAT IS ITS MISSION?

The Department of Veterans Affairs (VA) was established by an act of Congress in 1989 to replace the Veterans Administration, which was founded in 1930. The continuing mission of the VA is to assist and provide for veterans and the families of veterans. The programs of the VA are designed to benefit veterans and their families by providing them with disability benefits, pensions, and health care. By administering the National Cemetery System (NCS), the VA also maintains responsibility for and recognition of deceased veterans. The VA's motto, a quote from Abraham Lincoln, states that the VA exists to "care for him who shall have borne the battle, and for his widow and his orphan."

HOW IS IT STRUCTURED?

The VA is a federal department that is part of the executive branch and has cabinet rank. Its head official, the secretary of veterans affairs, is appointed by the president and confirmed by Congress. As the second largest of the cabinet-level departments, the VA is divided into three major administrative blocks: the Veterans Benefits Administration (VBA), the Veterans Health Administration (VHA), and the NCS. These organizations carry out the majority of the VA's work, from determining and disbursing veterans' compensation and pensions to treating the medical needs of veterans and their families to maintaining the national cemeteries. Each organization has a central office under the management of the secretary of veterans affairs and individual field branches.

FAST FACTS

From the time of the American Revolution (1775–83), 40 million men and women have served in the U.S. armed forces.

(Source: Department of Veterans Affairs, 1997.)

The secretary of veterans affairs and the deputy secretary of veterans affairs oversee the operations of the entire department. Those functions that are not covered by one of the three main divisions (VBA, VHA, or NCS) are the responsibility of five assistant secretaries in the areas of management, human resources and administration, policy and planning, public and intergovernmental affairs, and congressional affairs.

Other offices include the Board of Veterans' Appeals, the Board of Contract Appeals, the Center for Minority Veterans, the Center for Women Veterans, and Veterans Service Organizations Liaison. These handle the remainder of veteran-related issues and provide special services that focus on the needs of women and minority veterans as well as veterans' legal claims.

PRIMARY FUNCTIONS

The primary functions of the VA are to aid veterans and to assume responsibility for their welfare and that of their families, in recognition of their service to the United States. The main forms of assistance provided by the VA are payments for disability or death, pensions, medical treatment and health care facilities, and other related services to maintain and promote veterans' quality of life.

Individual programs within the department offer education, transitional help for returning veterans, information assistance, loan guaranty, and life insurance policies. For example, to assist members of the armed forces serving with *Operation Joint Endeavor* in Bosnia, the VA has designated specific members of various offices to serve as contacts for Bosnia-related activities. These range from plans to host a video satellite conference for the entire department on health issues in Bosnia to coordinating veterans' admissions to medical treatment facilities with the Department of Defense (DoD). The VA works closely with the DoD in many of its functions.

Within the VA, the VHA conducts medical research, on both disease and health care delivery systems. It is known primarily for its studies on post-traumatic stress disorders, aging, and Alzheimer's disease, as well as its research on drug addiction, alcoholism, and schizophrenia. Credited with developing the cardiac pacemaker and the CT scan, the VA also has placed emphasis on rehabilitating the blind. The NCS cares for veterans' posthumous needs by providing burial sites and grave markers.

The VA is also a legal authority to which veterans can appeal. The Board of Veterans' Appeals and the Board of Contract Appeals hear and decide benefits claims and disputes over contracts awarded to companies by the VA. Both the VBA and the VHA involve the department in litigation ranging from unsettled veterans' claims to health care malpractice suits.

The VA also assumes an advocacy role for veterans. In addition to an assistant secretary for congressional affairs, the VA has a veterans' affairs committee in Congress. Legislation that relates to the VA includes bills concerning disability payments, the VA's budget, educational benefits, home loans, employment for veterans, hospital construction, and other topics. For instance, Undersecretary for Health Kenneth Kizer testified before Congress about the illnesses of Persian Gulf War (1991) veterans.

PROGRAMS

The VA provides three major services: financial compensation, health care, and national cemetery maintenance. The VBA conducts programs related to the fiscal welfare of veterans and their families. These include assistance with applying for benefits, aid in resolving housing problems, evaluation of disability claims, and disbursement of pensions and compensation allowances. In the Loan Guaranty program, the VA assesses veterans' eligibility and handles the various loan operations. Education and vocational rehabilitation including counseling, training, and employment, are other support services under the VBA.

The VHA provides health care to eligible veterans and their families. It operates 173 medical centers, 39 domiciliaries, 376 outpatient clinics, 131 nursing home care units, and 205 Vietnam veteran outreach centers in the United States, the commonwealth of Puerto Rico, and the Republic of the Philippines, according to *The United States Government Manual 1996/97*. The VHA also pays for treatment for veterans at non-VA facilities and for dental outpatient services. In addition to being a significant research institution in the medical and health care fields, the VHA educates and trains professionals within the medical and dental fields.

The NCS operates the nation's cemeteries and offers eligible veterans and active service members burial sites in national cemeteries for themselves and their families. The NCS also provides grave markers and headstones for service members, reservists, and National Guard members with twenty years' qualifying service. As well as helping states to establish and expand current veteran's cemeteries, it executes the Presidential Memorial Certificate Program for deceased veterans or service members with an honorable discharge standing. The NCS oversees all national cemeteries except for Arlington National Cemetery, which is under the auspices of the Department of the Army.

In addition to its main services, the VA has instituted numerous special programs for specific needs, such as a toll-free hot line for information and assistance about illnesses thought to be related to the Persian Gulf War. The Center for Minority Veterans and the Center for Women Veterans exist to help minority and female veterans use current programs to their full advantage. In addition the VA seeks to establish new policies and services with minority and female veterans in mind. The Center for Minority Veterans conducts research on minority veterans' needs in relation to the effectiveness of current programs and helps to develop and implement programs at all levels, with an emphasis on how minority veterans can benefit from them. It also evaluates complaints against the department related to minority issues and serves as an information resource.

The VA also has designed a program for alternate dispute resolution and mediation to operate within VA facilities. Its resources include documentation, systems for managing conflict and dispute, communication principles, and a reading list.

Department of Veterans Affairs

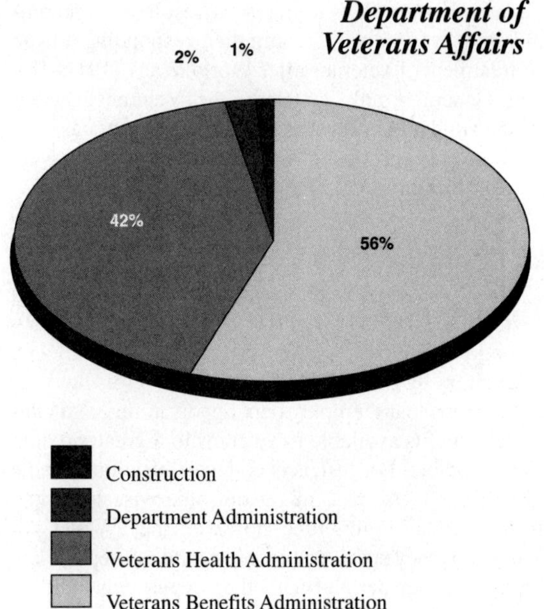

Construction
Department Administration
Veterans Health Administration
Veterans Benefits Administration

Percentage of Federal Budget

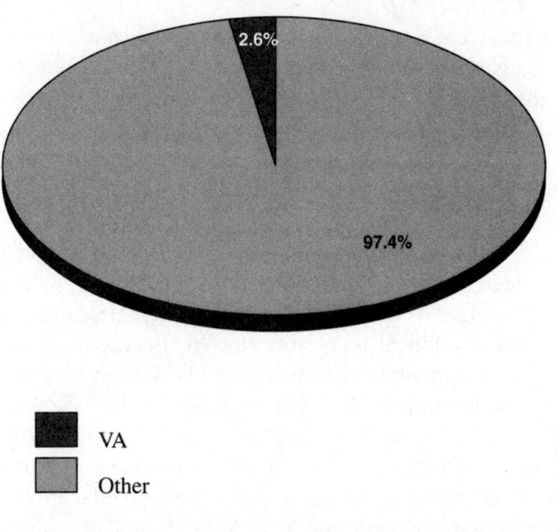

VA
Other

BUDGET INFORMATION

Funding for the VA's programs, including loans and benefits payments, comes from federal taxpayers' money. Each year, Congressional committees appropriate certain funds to the department. Additional monies may be acquired by the passing of legislation to allocate funds for specific programs beyond the VA's approved budget.

The VA was appropriated an estimated $42.7 billion in 1998, making up about 2.6 percent of the total federal budget of $1.653 trillion. Much of this money was split between two major programs, the Veterans Health Administration and the Veterans Benefits Administration. The Veterans Benefits Administration received almost $24 billion, approximately 56 percent of the VA's budget. Compensations and pensions (48 percent of the total VA budget) compromised the largest amount of this money, with readjustment benefits (3 percent) and other benefits programs (5 percent) taking up the rest. The Veterans Health Administration received $18.1 billion, approximately 42 percent of the VA's budget. Medical care (41 percent of the total VA budget) was the primary use of the money, with 1 percent going to other health programs such as medical and prosthetic research and medical administration. The other programs allocated money from the VA budget are department administration (2 percent) and costruction (1 percent).

HISTORY

President Herbert Hoover established the Veterans Administration (VA) by Executive Order 5398 on July 21, 1930. This independent agency was created by consolidating the U.S. Veterans Bureau, the Bureau of Pensions, and the National Home for Volunteer Soldiers. The Board of Veterans' Appeals followed in 1933.

The Veterans Bureau had been established under President Warren G. Harding as a result of a recommendation by a citizens' committee responding to the poor treatment of veterans after World War I (1914–18). Under General Frank T. Hines, the Veterans Bureau gained a solid, positive reputation with Congress as well as with veterans groups. It later became part of the Veterans Administration, with Hines still in leadership.

The GI Bill of Rights

The Servicemen's Readjustment Act of 1944 (also known as the GI Bill of Rights) was passed unanimously by Congress and was signed by President Franklin D. Roosevelt on June 22, 1944. The purpose of this law was to make home loans, employment opportunities, and educational benefits available to veterans to a greater extent than ever before. For instance, college education became available for many who might not otherwise have had that option. During this time, however, the VA was not given war agency status and therefore did not receive the personnel and materials that other departments did to implement these new benefits. Administrative problems arose when the VA tried to meet all the demands.

VA Leadership

President Harry S Truman replaced Hines with General Omar N. Bradley, who reorganized the VA, focused on the specific needs of World War II (1939–45) veterans, and made the VA more capable of serving veterans effectively. As part of the changes, the U.S. government established the Department of Medicine and Surgery, followed by the Department of Veterans Benefits in 1953. That same year President Dwight D. Eisenhower appointed a new VA administrator, initiating the policy of changing the administration every time a president of a different political party was elected. Because various presidents appointed administrators like Joseph Cleland, who lost multiple limbs when he fought in the Vietnam War (1959–75), the VA's leadership could identify with the needs of other veterans. The VA continued its active service of providing benefits, insurance, and educational and employment opportunities to millions of veterans and their families from both world wars, the Korean War (1950–53), and the Vietnam War. The VA also gained responsibility for the National Cemetery System in 1973, with one exception: the Department of the Army continues to oversee Arlington National Cemetery.

Reorganization and Renaming

The late 1980s proved a transitional time for the federal veterans' organizations. In 1988 President Ronald Reagan signed a bill that gave the agency cabinet-level status. Effective March 15, 1989, the U.S. government combined the Veterans Administration, the Department of Medicine and Surgery, and the Department of Veterans Benefits into one Department of Veterans Affairs. The Department of Medicine and Surgery became the Veterans Health Services and Research Administration, an organization within the VA that was renamed the Veterans Health Administration in 1991. The Veterans Benefits Administration succeeded the Department of Veterans Benefits as the third section of the VA. The establishment of the VA's cabinet-level status in 1989 made it the fourteenth department in the cabinet.

CURRENT POLITICAL ISSUES

The medical services of the VA are regarded by the public as a model of social health care. As the only health care provider at the national level, the VA makes crucial decisions about funding, eligibility, and type and availability of medical treatment. Described as an "inefficient and wasteful bureaucracy" in an article in *Insight on the News* magazine, the VA's medical treatment programs have been subject to the question of reform, particularly because the system is federally funded. Public opinion about the VA's services varies—it receives commendation for the education and training it sponsors and the significant medical research it conducts but is criticized for the condition of its health care facilities and for its administration. Because the VA is a federal department, its attempt to reorganize for greater efficiency is a significant concern.

Another challenge the VA faces is how to respond to veterans suffering from Gulf War syndrome. Since U.S. involvement in the Persian Gulf War in 1991, veterans of that war have complained of numerous physical ailments; many attribute their symptoms to their service during that time. Although studies have been done by the Pentagon, the Presidential Advisory Committee on Gulf War Veterans' Illnesses, and the Centers for Disease Control and Prevention (CDC), interpretations of their research appear contradictory. The public has raised questions of a cover-up by the Department of Defense regarding servicemen's exposure to poisonous gases while in the Gulf. There are also reports of veterans being ordered to have vaccinations that were not approved by the U.S. Food and Drug Administration (FDA). In addition to the complaints to the VA about symptoms believed to be related to Gulf War syndrome, birth defects allegedly related to exposure during the war have occurred in children born to men and women who served in the war. The VA has responded by setting up a telephone hot line and a home page on the Internet that has information on research, programs, and assistance for affected veterans.

Case Study: The Cost of Gulf War Syndrome

Approximately 697,000 men and women served their country as part of Operation Desert Storm during the Persian Gulf War in 1991. When they came home they returned as American heroes. For almost 10 percent of those soldiers, however, their private battles were just beginning. These are the 70,000 veterans who have complained to the VA or to the Pentagon of suffering from symptoms of Gulf War syndrome, a mysterious condition producing such symptoms as chronic fatigue, joint ache, loss of mental focus, and problems with digestion. Nausea, hair loss, respiratory difficulties, and birth defects in their children have been cited as other complications. With such a wide variety of symptoms and little understanding of the cause, diagnosis for many veterans has been impossible. There is some speculation that Gulf War syndrome does not exist, despite the complaints.

Many of those suffering have not been able to claim benefits. Unless veterans can show that they became ill within two years of returning from the Persian Gulf, they are not eligible for compensation, according to Public Law 103–446, passed in 1994. This qualifier excludes 95 percent of those veterans who have applied for medical assistance from the Department of Veterans Affairs in connection with Gulf War syndrome.

Although clear answers about the condition and its cause have not been found, Congress is investigating options to allow increased compensation for affected veterans. Until those options become law, however, these soldiers will continue to fight against an undiagnosed condition that worsens their lives and for the medical benefits they need to improve them.

SUCCESSES AND FAILURES

In its pursuit of a more efficient and effective bureaucracy, the VA has begun to rework its health care system. Multiple instances have evidenced the need for reform, as many VA patients have experienced problems. For example, one veteran continued to complain of weakness and stomach pain more than three months after his abdominal surgery. Not only had a VA surgeon left a sponge inside the veteran's body which later caused an infection, but a VA radiologist misread the x ray, which kept doctors from determining the cause of the problem. The cost of damages was $100,000. In another case, a health care center had to go through two years of hearings and paperwork to permanently remove a depressed VA nurse, considered to be a threat to patients, from duty. Poor and inefficient procedures apparently are part of the problem.

One success is the Central Region Contract Service Center, located at the Clement J. Zablocki Veterans Administration Medical Center in Milwaukee, Wisconsin. One of the VA's reforms at the center was to streamline the way supplies are purchased for the VA's facilities and programs by consolidating the contract process into one regional location. Buying in bulk for multiple hospitals has made wholesale supply contracts possible as well.

FUTURE DIRECTIONS

Continued reform of the VA's health care programs and treatment facilities will be of major public and political interest in years ahead. The undersecretary for health for the VHA, Dr. Kenneth Kizer, has designed a plan to reorganize the health care system into a series of 22 Veterans Integrated Service Networks. Optimal results would include improved efficiency and access for veterans, more accountability, and increased quality of care. With fewer than 10 percent of eligible veterans taking advantage of the VA's benefits, a change in the structure of the system may seem necessary.

AGENCY RESOURCES

For general information about the VA, contact the Office of Public Affairs at (202) 273-5700. Audiovisual productions can be requested through the Chief of Media Services (032B) at (202) 482-6793 or (202) 482-6794. The VA can be accessed electronically via its home page on the Internet at http://www.va.gov. The VA Research Project database, which gives details on the VA's medical, rehabilitation, and health services research, can also be accessed through the VA's home page.

A toll-free number has been set up for veterans to obtain information regarding the debt that they owe to the VA: 1-800-827-0648. The Debt Management Center can be accessed by E-mail at vadmc@mm.com or by calling 1-800-827-0648.

The VA keeps all its records through the VA Records Center and Vault. For information about obtaining records, veterans should contact the VA regional office nearest them.

Information on the VA's policy and programs relating to Bosnia's *Operation Joint Endeavor* can be found through the Office of the Assistant Secretary for Policy and Planning (008) at (202) 273-5033. The VA's Persian Gulf veterans information help line is 1-800-749-8387.

AGENCY PUBLICATIONS

The VA publishes several pamphlets and reports available to the general public. *The Annual Report of the Secretary of Veterans Affairs* is available through the Reports and Information Service (008C2) of the VA. Regarding benefits, the pamphlet "Federal Benefits for Veterans and Dependents" can be purchased from the Superintendent of Documents, Government Printing Office, Washington, DC 20402. *A Summary of Department of Veterans Affairs Benefits* can be acquired from any regional office of the VA. For information on national cemeteries and veterans' eligibility for burial, *Internments in VA National Cemeteries*, VA NCS-IS-1, is available through the National Cemetery System (402B2) at the

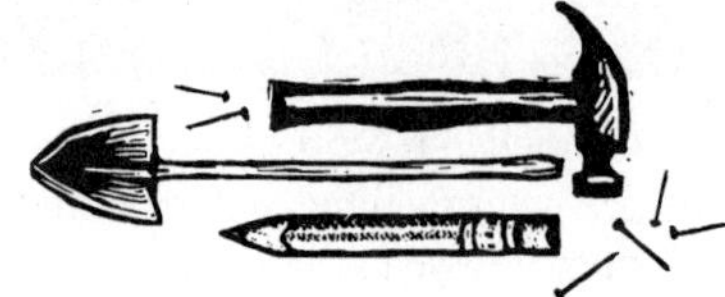

GET INVOLVED:

The Student Volunteer Program of the VA provides opportunities for students under age 19 to serve as part of a VA medical center's treatment team. Through voluntary service at a local VA medical facility, students can gain experience in a variety of fields, such as audiology and speech pathology, nursing, occupational and physical therapy, research, and social work. Not only do the student volunteers receive hands-on training at the medical facility and function as liaisons to the community, but the veterans benefit from the students' participation as well. The James H. Parke Memorial Youth Scholarship Award for college is also funded by the VA. Interested student volunteers can contact the VA Voluntary Service Office through the VA home page at http://www.va.gov or contact a local VA health care Voluntary Service staff member to learn more about the criteria for nomination.

Department of Veterans Affairs. *The Board of Veterans Appeals Index* is available on microfiche from Promisel and Korn, Inc., Suite 480, 7201 Wisconsin Ave., Bethesda, MD 20814; phone (301) 986-0650.

BIBLIOGRAPHY

Bauman, Robert E. "Can Government Run a Health Care System?" *USA Today*, January 1995, pp. 10–13.

Fisher, Elliott S., and Gilbert Welch. "The Future of the Department of Veterans Affairs Health Care System." *Journal of the American Medical Association*, 22 February 1995, pp. 651–6.

Hanson, Gayle M. B. "Is It Time to Overhaul VA Hospitals?" *Insight on the News*, 3 July 1995, pp. 8–12.

Home From Desert Storm. Green Bay, Wis.: Recovery Enterprises, 1991.

Hudson, Derek, and Kenneth Miller. "The Tiny Victims of Desert Storm." *Life*, November 1995, pp. 46–59.

Iglehart, John K. "Reform of the Veterans Affairs Health Care System." *New England Journal of Medicine*, 31 October 1996, pp. 1407–12.

Kizer, Kenneth W., and Garth L. Nicolson. "Is the Government Taking the Right Approach Toward Gulf War Illness?" *Insight on the News*, 27 January 1997 pp. 24–28.

Lasson, Kenneth. *Your Rights As a Vet.* New York: Pocket Books, 1981.

Masci, David. "Cuts All Over—Except the VA." *Congressional Quarterly Weekly Report*, 15 July 1995, p. 2067.

O'Dell, Richard E. *The Viet Vet Survival Guide: How to Cut Through the Bureaucracy and Get What You Need and Are Entitled To.* New York: Facts on File, 1986.

Shay, Jonathan. *Achilles in Vietnam: Traumatic Stress and the Undoing of Character.* New York: Simon and Schuster, 1994.

"VA Told to Compensate Disabled." *Modern Healthcare*, 20 February 1995, p. 28.

Drug Enforcement Administration (DEA)

PARENT ORGANIZATION: Department of Justice
ESTABLISHED: July 1, 1973
EMPLOYEES: 7,464

Contact Information:

ADDRESS: 700 Army-Navy Dr.
Arlington, VA 22202
PHONE: (202) 307-1000
FAX: (202) 307-7965
URL: http://www.usdoj.gov/dea
ADMINISTRATOR: Thomas A. Constantine

WHAT IS ITS MISSION?

The Drug Enforcement Administration (DEA) describes itself on its Internet homepage as, "the lead agency responsible for the development of overall drug enforcement strategy, programs, planning, and evaluation." Specifically the DEA is responsible for enforcing laws related to illegal drugs; identifying and bringing to trial individuals and groups involved in drug trafficking; and developing proactive strategies to reduce the level of illegal drugs available in the United States and worldwide. In recent years the DEA has sought opportunities to form partnerships with community agencies working with youth in order to discourage illegal drug use.

HOW IS IT STRUCTURED?

The DEA is an agency within the Department of Justice (a cabinet-level department), and is part of the executive branch of government. Led by an administrator, the DEA's major offices include the Office of Congressional and Public Affairs, the Office of Chief Counsel, and the Office of Administrative Law Judges. There are also six major divisions within the DEA. These are the Inspection, Operations, Human Resources, Intelligence, Operational Support, and Financial Management divisions.

The Intelligence Division maintains the Intelligence Center located in El Paso, Texas. This site serves as a key data-gathering and monitoring station for drug trafficking along the U.S.-Mexico border. Other international locations of primary concern to the DEA include

A Los Angeles police officer stands guard over 20 tons of cocaine. Seized from a U.S. warehouse in 1989, this cocaine had a street value of $6.7 billion. At the time, it was the largest cocaine bust ever made. (Photograph by Joshua Roberts. UPI/Corbis-Bettmann)

South America and Southeast Asia where there is a proliferation of acreage dedicated to growing crops that are used in the manufacture of drugs that are illegal in the United States. In addition, the DEA operates its Training Center in Quantico, Virginia, as part of the administration's Human Resources Division. Ongoing training is conducted there for new DEA employees, as well as advanced training for senior agents.

Key to the DEA's success is the strength of its relationships with local, state, and international law enforcement agencies. To this end, the DEA has at least one office in each of the 50 states, as well as 71 offices in 44 foreign countries. Under advice from the Secretary of State and U.S. embassies, the DEA is assigned responsibility for developing working relationships and strategies with its counterparts overseas. The DEA also operates seven laboratories and drug-testing facilities at locations throughout the United States.

PRIMARY FUNCTIONS

The DEA's primary function is to reduce the supply and demand for illegal drugs in the United States. The administration's methods for achieving this goal include enforcing existing laws under the Controlled Substances Act (originated in the 1970s), which regulates the manufacture and distribution of legally produced controlled substances; investigating and providing the necessary evidence to prosecute major offenders of federal drug laws; and seizing and forfeiting the assets, including cash and other valuables, of individuals or groups that were gained from illicit drug trafficking.

Other methods used for curtailing drug trafficking include collecting, analyzing, and publishing data on drug-related activities. This information is then shared with other law enforcement agencies. In some instances local, state, and international sources provide the DEA with information.

The DEA also works with all levels of drug enforcement agencies on reduction efforts, such as crop eradication or substitution. It provides assistance and works cooperatively with authorities on cases where there may be an overlap in jurisdiction or where one authority's sphere of influence is limited.

PROGRAMS

In order to accomplish its overall mission of reducing the supply of and demand for illegal drugs in the United States, the DEA operates or takes part in a number of specific programs. These programs fall into the following major divisions: Enforcement Operations, Intelligence, Demand Reduction, Diversion Control, and Aviation Operations.

The Demand Reduction program seeks to educate the public about the negatives of drug use. The DEA's Diversion Control program is charged with preventing the illegal sale of controlled but legal substances, such as prescription medication. Usually it is physicians or pharmacists who steal legal drugs for their own consumption or illegal sale and falsely prescribe medication.

The Intelligence division of the DEA is responsible for collecting, analyzing, and dispersing information on drug trafficking for the entire U.S. law enforcement system. It gathers information through federal and local law enforcement agencies.

In Enforcement Operations, many DEA agents work in cooperation with state and local task forces, drawing on local expertise to capture drug criminals, while using their own expertise to help combat the violence that typically surrounds the illegal drug trade. The DEA maintains 19 special Mobile Enforcement Teams to assist local authorities, in dealing with acute situations. Beyond these partnership programs, the DEA also has a great number of agents assigned to its own, independent, drug enforcement activities. These activities generally focus on stopping drugs coming into the United States from the foreign countries where they are manufactured. Agents are stationed along the U.S.–Mexico border and in major ports, such as Miami, Florida, for this purpose. The DEA also acts in cooperation with law enforcement agencies in 50 foreign countries, to stop the production of drugs at their source.

The Aviation Operations program supports Intelligence and Enforcement activities. Aircraft are used for surveillance and for intercepting drugs moving into the United States by air or sea.

BUDGET INFORMATION

In 1998 the DEA operated with a budget of approximately $1.14 billion. This budget was divided with 59 percent going toward enforcement activities, 34 percent for investigative support, and the remaining 7 percent devoted to program direction.

HISTORY

It wasn't until the 1930s that the concern with drug use warranted the creation of a federal agency to deal with enforcement issues. To this end President Herbert Hoover established the Federal Bureau of Narcotics (FBN) in 1930. Priority was given to stop the flow of opiate-based drugs, such as morphine and heroin, into the United States. The FBN agents were placed at key ports of entry where they attempted to confiscate illegal drugs.

BUDGET:

Drug Enforcement Administration

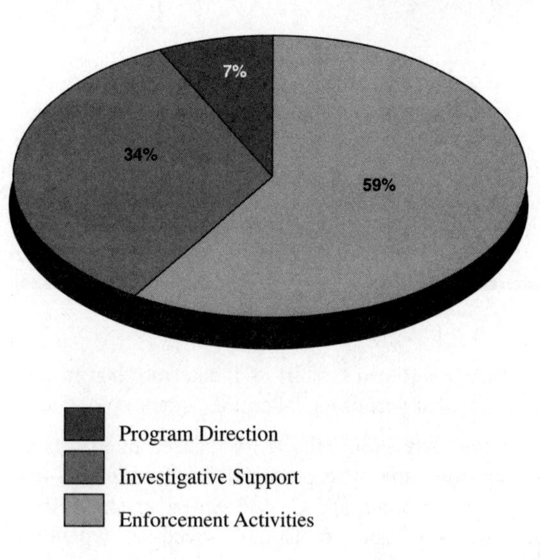

By 1936 the use of marijuana had substantially increased, correlating to the economic and social devastation of the Great Depression (1929–40). As a result, Congress passed the Marijuana Tax Act of 1937, which categorized marijuana and hashish as illegal drugs.

Following World War II (1939–45) cocaine, which had not been widely used in the past, began arriving in the United States in large quantities. Congress, rather than continuing to consider each drug separately, gave the FBN the power to determine for itself which drugs should be classified illegal. As drug use in the United States continued to increase, especially in the 1960s, the Bureau of Drug Abuse Control was established to control stimulant and hallucinogenic drugs.

In 1970 the Drug Abuse Prevention and Control Act passed, establishing new categories for controlled substances that were based on the dangerous side effects of each drug, its potential for abuse, and whether it had any legitimate uses. During this same period, the resources allocated by Congress to fight illegal drug use and trafficking grew dramatically and culminated with the demise of existing drug agencies and the creation of the DEA in 1973.

Over the next 20 years, the DEA grew in size as drugs, and violent drug–related crimes, became more prevalent. In the 1980s, a new form of cheap cocaine, often called "crack," became available. Crack became very popular, and in many areas of the country powerful and well armed gangs battled for control over its sale.

FAST FACTS

According to a survey conducted in 1995, 12.8 million Americans admitted to using an illegal drug during the same month they were interviewed.

(Source: Substance Abuse and Mental Health Services Administration. "National Household Survey on Drug Abuse," 1996.)

The DEA was forced to shift its focus from heroin trafficking to what was often called the "crack epidemic."

In the early 1990s, the DEA focused its efforts on bringing down the most powerful drug producers—the drug cartels of South and Central America. This "Kingpin strategy" had some remarkable successes. Operation Green Ice was an undercover operation that, upon its conclusion in 1992, led to the arrest of 140 suspected drug criminals, many of them high level money managers and traffickers. Under new leadership in 1994, the DEA shifted its efforts from attacking the powerful cartels to assisting local law enforcement groups that were being overwhelmed by violent drug crimes.

CURRENT POLITICAL ISSUES

Throughout the DEA's history, for every law passed in favor of more restrictive drug laws, there are opponents who argue in favor of laws that are more tolerant. According to some, easing up on restrictions is the answer to deterring many of the criminal activities that surround the drug trade. Proponents of drug legalization contend that being under the influence of narcotics does not automatically lead the drug user to commit violent crimes. For example, a study of 118 murders in New York City involving crack cocaine users found that only one of the murders was classified as psychopharmacological, or due to the fact that the user was under the influence of narcotics.

Those in favor of legalization argue that crime and drugs are related because of the illegal black market element. In the attempt to capture the greatest profits, violence, which often results in murder, is rampant among rival dealers. Proponents of legalization also argue that crimes such as robberies and theft are often committed by addicts who need large sums of money to pay for drugs that demand a high "street price." By eliminating the black market, those in favor of legalization believe that the profits of the drug trade would be greatly reduced, as well as the cost of the drug to the user. This would lessen the profit incentive of illicit drug trafficking and the crimes associated with the trade.

Another question has been raised in the debate about drug legalization: using illegal drugs for medicinal purposes. Marijuana, in particular, has been hotly debated. The DEA takes the stance that there are no compelling reasons for its use as a prescription drug. Many patients, suffering from AIDS and various forms of cancer, argue that the medical use of marijuana is the only relief from the physical pain and nausea they experience on a daily basis.

Case Study: Legalization of Marijuana

Voters in California and Arizona passed precedent setting ballot initiatives in 1996 which legalized the prescription use of marijuana. The legislation in California allowed doctors to write prescriptions for their patients whose symptoms were not alleviated by traditional medicines. Prescriptions for marijuana could be filled at buying clubs. While some patients used buying clubs before the new law was passed, the new law would specifically protect doctors and patients from arrest.

Responding to the new laws, the DEA announced in a press release that its mission would by no means be altered and it would continue to target large drug traffickers at home and abroad. It was initially unclear if the buying clubs would become targets of DEA operations, but in late 1996 federal agents raided several clubs, and charged their operators with violation of federal drug laws. This highlights the fact that, regardless of what voters in California and Arizona wanted, federal law still prohibited the cultivation, sale, or use of marijuana.

Marijuana is listed as a Schedule I substance, meaning that it has a high potential for abuse and has no medical use. As long as it remains Schedule I, federal officials say they will continue to arrest those who grow or sell it. Many organizations of physicians have called for marijuana to be made a Schedule II substance. Such drugs, which include cocaine and morphine, are also considered to have a high potential for abuse, but can still be legally prescribed by doctors and sold to prescription holders. Officials at the DEA and the Office of National Drug Control Policy stated that more research is required to determine if marijuana has legitimate medical uses.

The DEA remains firm in its position that legalization of drugs, for any reason, is a grave mistake and will directly undermine the agency's efforts to curtail drug trafficking in the United States. It will require action by the Food and Drug Administration (FDA), or by Congress, to change marijuana's legal status. While the FDA is studying the issue, it will likely be many years before any decisions are made. Meanwhile, federal prosecution of the buying clubs continued, and in February 1997 the

State Supreme Court of California determined that, even under the new state laws established by the medical marijuana initiative, the cultivation and sale of marijuana was still illegal.

SUCCESSES AND FAILURES

In September of 1992 the DEA's two-year undercover operation, known as Operation Green Ice, culminated in the seizure of over $50 million and the arrests of over one hundred criminals, including two high-ranking Colombian cartel members. The operation was considered a major blow to one of the world's most powerful drug manufacturing groups. More than one hundred agents and police agencies in six countries were involved. Key to the entire investigation was Heidi Landgraf, a 37-year old agent, who, for two years, assumed a false identity as Heidi Herrera, a multi-million dollar money launderer. For her efforts, Landgraf received the DEA's Administrator's Award for outstanding services. No longer able to work undercover since her real identity became known, Landgraf continues to work for the DEA at its San Diego office and is responsible for media relations and drug prevention and education programs.

FUTURE DIRECTIONS

While Green Ice and similar operations have been successful for the DEA, some feel that they have come at the cost of badly needed aid for local law enforcement. Much of America's violent crime is believed to be drug related, and in some locations violent drug–trafficking gangs are more than the local police can handle. The DEA has rededicated itself through programs such as its Mobile Enforcement Teams, to provide assistance at a local level. The DEA will continue to combat the largest and most dangerous drug cartels, while it helps to eliminate the local drug dealers that can destroy a community.

In addition, the DEA is continuing to seek new ways of reaching youth, the largest population of new drug users. Through its publications and other outreach and educational efforts, the DEA hopes to reach young people before they begin using drugs.

AGENCY RESOURCES

The Office of Congressional and Public Affairs responds to requests for information from the public. Contact them at, Public Affairs Section, Drug Enforcement Administration, Department of Justice, Washington, DC 20537; phone (202) 307-7977. The DEA's Internet home page (http://www.usdoj.gov/dea) is another excellent source of information; it includes a statistics page called "Drug Data" that contains survey findings on trends such as "Rise in Teen Drug Use" and "Problems Facing Teens."

AGENCY PUBLICATIONS

Drugs of Abuse is published jointly by the DEA and the National Guard. The purpose of the periodical is to educate people regarding the physical effects of drug abuse and its effects on individuals and society as a whole.

Get it Straight is also published by the DEA. Intended for teenage audiences, the publication was initiated by a DEA employee whose own child was working on a drug prevention project at school. What began as one individual's project resulted in the DEA holding focus groups with adolescents around the country to gauge their level of awareness and the accuracy of their knowledge regarding drugs. *Get it Straight* serves as an educational tool and contains activities for individual students or entire classrooms. These and other publications are available online at http://www.usdoj.gov/dea/pub.htm.

BIBLIOGRAPHY

Andelman, David A. "Cleaning Up the Kingpins." *Regardie's Magazine*, May–June, 1994, p. 130.

Baum, Dan. "Rx: Marijuana," *The Nation*, 2 December 1996, p. 5.

McAllister, J. F. "Getting In the Way of Good Policy." *Time*, 7 November 1994, p. 50.

"Mexico Rebuffs U.S. on Arms for Drug Agents." *New York Times*, 26 December 1996, p. A5.

"The War on Drugs is Lost." *The National Review*, 12 February 1996, p. 34.

Economic Development Administration (EDA)

PARENT ORGANIZATION: Department of Commerce
ESTABLISHED: 1965
EMPLOYEES: 260

Contact Information:

ADDRESS: Room 7800B
14th St. and Constitution Ave. SW
Washington, DC 20230
PHONE: (202) 482-5081
FAX: (202) 482-5112
URL: http://www.doc.gov/eda
ASSISTANT SECRETARY : Phillip A. Singerman
DEPUTY ASSISTANT SECRETARY: Wilbur F. Hawkins

WHAT IS ITS MISSION?

The Economic Development Administration (EDA) seeks to generate jobs, help retain existing jobs, and stimulate industrial and commercial growth in economically distressed areas of the United States. Guided by the principle that distressed communities must be given control over their own economic and revitalization strategies, the EDA makes assistance available to rural and urban areas of the nation experiencing long-term economic deterioration and its symptoms, such as low income levels and high unemployment. The agency also helps communities experiencing sudden and severe economic distress, such as those associated with the economic impacts of natural disasters or the closing of military installations and other federal facilities.

HOW IS IT STRUCTURED?

The EDA is a bureau of the U.S. Department of Commerce. Its administrator bears the title of assistant secretary for Economic Development and reports directly to the secretary of commerce. The EDA operates through a network of headquarters and more than 50 regional offices throughout the country. Other than the Office of the Assistant Secretary and its associated administrative offices, the EDA's organizational structure is based entirely on the forms of financial assistance it offers through its programs.

PRIMARY FUNCTIONS

Virtually all of EDA's activities involve the distribution of financial resources (government grants) to communities and organizations that successfully demonstrate a need. Grants are provided for public works and development facilities, planning and coordination, defense conversion, and other financial help that may reduce unemployment in economically distressed areas.

Public works grants support infrastructure projects (road-building, power grids, etc.) that will foster the establishment or expansion of commercial businesses, supporting the creation and retention of jobs.

Planning grants support the design and implementation of effective economic development policies and programs by local development organizations in states, communities, and American Indian tribes nationwide. EDA planning grants operate in 385 economic development districts.

Technical assistance grants provide technical information and knowledge that will support local industry studies, operational assistance, natural resource development, and export promotion. In addition, EDA funds a network of 68 university centers to integrate programs of higher education into the local community. University centers exist primarily to provide technical assistance to promote economic development.

Defense economic adjustment grants assist communities adversely affected by Department of Defense base closures and defense contract cutbacks as well as Department of Energy realignments. EDA grants help these communities rebuild and diversify their economic foundations.

The Trade Adjustment Assistance Program, through its nationwide network of 12 trade adjustment centers, provides technical assistance to companies and industries that are certified to have suffered economically from the impact of international trade competition and therefore have experienced a decrease in imports.

Economic adjustment grants help communities accommodate a gradual erosion or a sudden change in economic conditions that have the potential to damage the underlying economic base. These grants include post-disaster economic recovery grants and grants to communities faced with a decline in natural resources.

Research, evaluation, and demonstration funds are used to support studies of the causes of economic distress and to discover ways of counteracting or preventing it entirely.

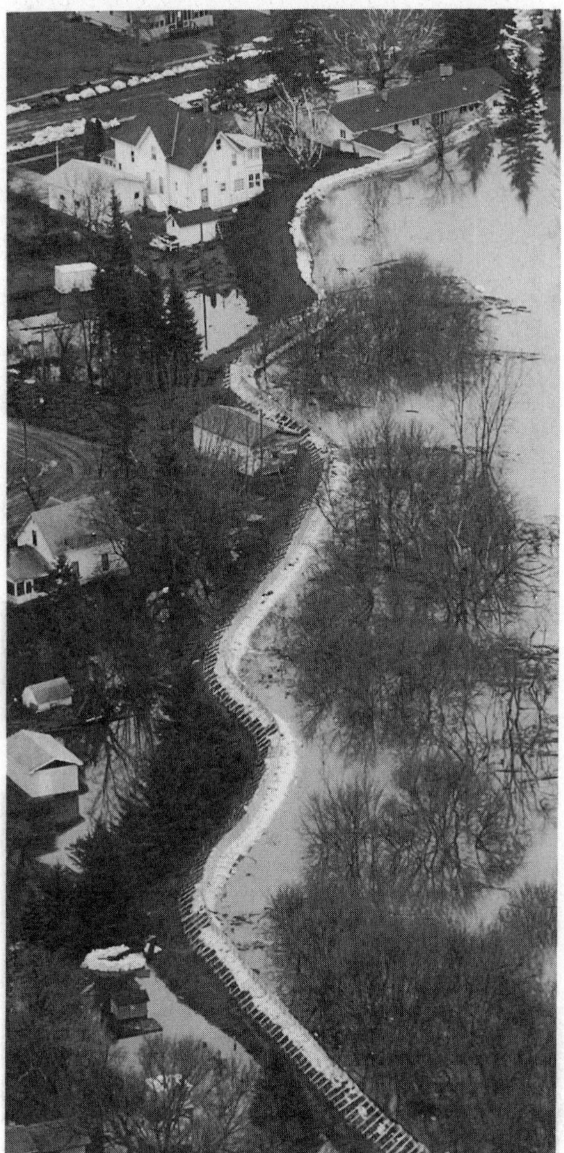

A dike built by residents and volunteers protects Drayton, North Dakota, from the floodwaters of the Red River. The EDA's Levee Restoration Program is an important source of aid for flood relief and rebuilding efforts. (AP/Wide World Photos)

PROGRAMS

Each funding category within the EDA is made up of many individual projects and initiatives that have applied for and been approved to receive EDA funds. Economic adjustment grants, for example, have been extended to fishing communities in the Northeast, where stocks have declined in recent years; coal communities in Appalachia; and timber and salmon areas in the Pacific Northwest. The Northwest Timber Initiative, included in the 1998 federal budget, was designed to support President Clinton's Forest Plan, which involves realigning many of the timber-based economies of the Pacific

BUDGET:
Economic Development Administration

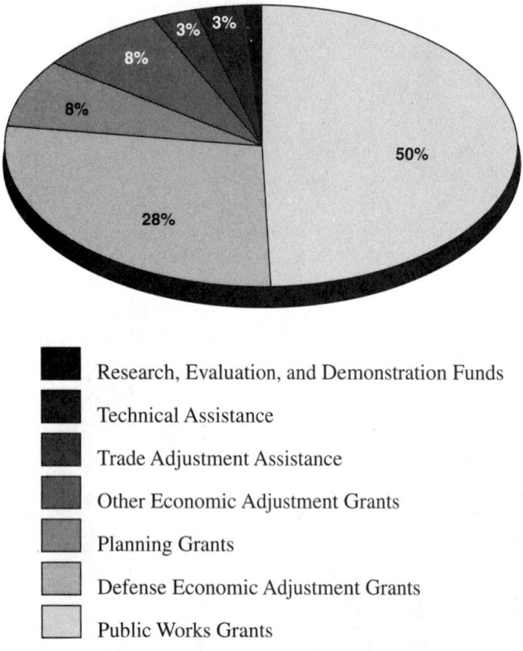

Northwest. The EDA also provides post-disaster assistance to areas affected by presidentially-declared disaster areas, such as areas of the Red River Valley affected by the spring floods of 1997.

EDA often forms partnerships to address specific problems and many of its projects involve other government agencies. The administration is currently working with the U.S. Army Corps of Engineers to support EDA's Levee Restoration Program, associated with the Midwest floods of 1993 and the Northwest floods of 1996. One of the most notable examples of such partnerships is the Office of Economic Conversion Information (OECI), an operation jointly administered by the EDA, the Commerce Department's Economics and Statistics Administration, and the Department of Defense. The OECI is a clearinghouse of information needed to anticipate, plan for, and respond to defense downsizing, most of which occurred as a result of the Department of Defense's Base 1995 recommendation to realign or close 146 military bases nationwide. OECI information is made available to communities, industries, and workers affected by such closures or realignments.

The EDA also has a program to encourage private investment in commercial development, the Revolving Loan Program. By providing the initial capital for revolving loans from banks or other companies within or associated with distressed communities, EDA helps leverage private capital for investment in the communities. Upon repayment of these loans, principal and interest stay in the community for re-lending and further economic development.

BUDGET INFORMATION

EDA's assistance programs are funded almost entirely through congressional appropriation of federal tax revenues, and in 1998 was budgeted an amount of about $343 million. Two EDA programs account for a majority of the budget: public works grants, which account for approximately 50 percent of EDA's budget, and defense economic adjustment grants, which are 28 percent of EDA expenditures.

Planning grants and other economic adjustment grants each account for 8 percent of the EDA budget, while trade adjustment assistance and technical assitance each account for 3 percent. Research, evaluation and demonstration funds make up less than 1 percent of the administration's expenses.

HISTORY

The EDA was created in 1965 under the terms of the Public Works and Economic Development Act, an effort to target federal resources to economically distressed areas and to help develop local economies in the United States. It was mandated to assist rural and urban communities that were isolated from the mainstream economy and lagged in terms of economic development, industrial growth, and personal income. During its early years, EDA organized its district and regional commissions and established the criteria for selecting projects to be funded. In 1969, the growing regional commissions were given separate administrative offices.

Over the next decade and a half, EDA acquired several new responsibilities. Emergency assistance became a responsibility of the EDA in the summer of 1972, when the eastern seaboard was ravaged by Hurricane Agnes. Congress designated $55 million for assistance to rebuild the affected communities. In 1974, the administration took on responsibility for long-term development aid to the states as well as economic adjustment assistance to respond to economic dislocations such as plant closings.

Jumbled Responsibilities

Throughout the 1970s and the 1980s, the EDA's charges continued to grow. In 1975, EDA was assigned responsibility for the Job Opportunities Program, a measure designed to assist areas with high-unemployment. A year later, it received the demanding assignment of administering an antirecessionary Local Public Works Program that would eventually involve more than 10,000 projects and $6 billion in federal funds. The EDA's Trade Adjustment Assistance Program was also initiated during this period.

At times, however, the priorities of the EDA seemed to be lost in the government's efforts to provide assistance to projects that would not be funded by other agencies. Some EDA projects seemed to have little to do with the EDA's initial mandate; it provided, for example, funding for facilities involved in the 1980 Olympic Games at Lake Placid, New York, and also instituted a $10 million program to increase energy efficiency in public buildings, while its own budget was shrinking.

FAST FACTS

From 1992 to 1996, EDA invested more than $2 billion in the nation's distressed communities, resulting in the creation or retention of more than 825,000 jobs.

(Source: U.S. Department of Commerce. "Department of Commerce Budget in Brief," 1997.)

A More Focused Direction

Throughout the 1980s and at the outset of the 1990s, the EDA lacked formal authority to carry out its missions. Republican Presidents Ronald Reagan and George Bush repeatedly targeted the EDA for elimination, arguing that EDA grants amounted to "pork barrel" handouts to states with the most powerful lobbyists and congressional representatives. However, due to pressure from Democratic congressional leaders, most notably Senate Appropriations Chairman Robert Byrd, a senator from West Virginia, the EDA continued to be funded.

A sharp budget cut in 1981 forced the EDA to reevaluate some of the ways its grant money was being used. Immediately after the 1981 budget cuts, the administration began to phase out its business loan program. In the mid-1980s, EDA leadership decided to return to the administration's roots by placing priority on helping distressed rural areas, the primary target of program expenses during the EDA's early years. The administration emphasized funding for the most distressed areas, and for projects that would receive significant support from cost-sharing sources such as state and local governments or private industry. Before long, the EDA's Revolving Loan Program began to ease some of the administration's financial burden. In a political climate which emphasized smaller government, the EDA was forced to turn to such partnerships, especially with private businesses, in order to continue its assistance to distressed communities.

After the Defense Department's 1995 Base Realignment and Closure (BRAC) initiative, the Clinton administration saw the EDA as a means of softening the blow to communities whose economies had relied on military installations. EDA grants to these communities and the formation of the OECI were quickly implemented.

CURRENT POLITICAL ISSUES

Though Presidents Reagan and Bush were the first executives to strongly oppose what they saw as the "pork barrel politics" behind EDA grants, they were by no means the first to recognized this particular aspect of American government. The phrase "pork barrel politics" is derived from the pre-Civil War practice of distributing salt pork to slaves from huge barrels. By the 1870s, congressmen were referring to regularly dipping into the "pork barrel" to obtain funds for popular projects in their home districts. Pork barrel politics has become a popular term for the way in which members of Congress try to protect their electoral bases by directing funds for federal projects, such as dams, roads, military bases, and other grants to their home states or districts. A member of Congress with a reputation for taking care of his or her constituents can be difficult to defeat in the U.S. electoral system. While such projects and grants constitute only a small part of the total federal budget, their usefulness in reelection campaigns makes them important factors in congressional politics. In voting on funding for such federal grant programs, members tend to focus on benefits to their states or districts.

During the conservative administrations of Presidents Reagan and Bush, EDA programs were cited as particularly blatant examples of handouts to states and localities. Even though President Clinton used the EDA to give relief to communities hurt by base closures, the agency is still often cited as an example of pork barrel politics.

Citizens Against Government Waste (CAGW), a government watchdog group, carries out a campaign against political pork and its annual *Congressional Pig Book Summary* chronicles wasteful government projects. One of the primary crusaders for the EDA during the Reagan and Bush presidencies, Senator Robert Byrd of West Virginia, is a common target of CAGW criticism. As one of Congress's most senior members, his influence over the distribution of federal funds illustrates some of the problems of the committee system by which Congress operates. Many projects require powerful committee advocate funding—pork serves as a way to protect incumbent congressmen and entice local constituents with their own money. When the appropriations process is abused for the purposes of gaining favor with voters, critics charge pork barrel politics can result in the unfair and inefficient distribution of federal funds.

Many of the EDA's projects serve communities legitimately suffering from economic hardships that are beyond their control. The relative absence of debate about EDA assistance to communities hurt by the BRAC was proof of the legitimacy of its mission. But in the hands of legislators more eager to score points with their home districts than to equitably spend federal funds, the EDA may be in danger of resembling what some critics have described as the "Congressional Cookie Jar."

SUCCESSES AND FAILURES

As part of its current redirection toward technology-based jobs, EDA has been instrumental in creating opportunities in this growing field, primarily for urban communities. For example, EDA invested grant funds in the renovation of an existing building in Baltimore, Maryland, for use as a technological incubator by several tenants at Johns Hopkins Bayview Medical Center. EDA and the City of Baltimore also joined to construct a two-story manufacturing building that would house the Maryland Bioprocessing Center, which EDA estimates has generated more than 1000 jobs and $42 million in new capital investment.

FUTURE DIRECTIONS

As part of a nationwide movement toward streamlining and "right-sizing" government, EDA is in the process of cutting its staff and shifting personnel from headquarters to field operations in order to improve customer service. The administration is also streamlining its regulations to better serve customers; 200 specific regulations have already been deleted, a reduction of about 62 percent.

Two major trends appear poised to exert powerful influences on EDA in the coming years—the explosion of technology and technology-based industry, and increased imports resulting from two international trade agreements, GATT/WTO and NAFTA. These two treaties will likely lead to increased client caseloads for the Trade Adjustment Assistance Program, and a move toward higher technology firms will occur while basic industries such as clothing and footwear decline in the face of international competition. Part of EDA's response is already under way—the costshare required of participating companies has been increased, the once-complex process of certifying a community as economically "injured" has been simplified, and new guideline and documentation procedures have been adopted.

AGENCY RESOURCES

General questions about the work of the EDA can be directed to the Office of Public Affairs at (202) 482-5112 or the appropriate regional office. Some information relevant to the Trade Adjustment Assistance Program is available through the Department of Commerce's Trade Information Center, available by telephone at 1-800-872-8723 or on-line at http://www.ita.doc.gov/tic. Information made available through the Office of Economic Conversion Information can be accessed by telephoning the OECI at 1-800-345-1222.

AGENCY PUBLICATIONS

The EDA periodically issues notices on the availability of funds for its programs as well as requests for proposals through the *Federal Register*, which is available on-line at the Government Printing Office access site at http://www.access.gpo.gov/su_docs/aces/aces140.html.

BIBLIOGRAPHY

"Aid to 'Empowerment Zones' Set." *Facts on File*, December 1994, p. 980.

Barblinger, Anne. "Federal Aid for Rural Economic Development." *The Annals of the American Academy of Political and Social Science*, September 1993, pp. 155–64.

Barlas, Stephen. "'Zone' Proposals Get a New Look." *American City & County*, November 1996, p. 16.

Barrier, Michael. "Base Closings: The Last Roundup." *Nation's Business*, April 1996, pp. 62–63.

Darlin, Damon. "A New Flavor of Pork." *Forbes*, 5 June 1995, pp. 146–47.

Fulton, William. "The Political Magic of Pork." *Governing*, December 1995, p. 66.

Mayer, Virginia. "Economic Development Goes Off the Federal Budget Scales." *Nation's Cities Weekly*, 5 February 1990, p. 10.

Mills, Mike. "House Approves Measure to Reauthorize EDA." *Congressional Quarterly Weekly Report*, 14 May 1994, p. 1210.

Path to Smarter Economic Development: Reassessing the Federal Role. Washington: National Academy of Public Administration, 1996.

Pressman, Jeffrey L., and Aaron B. Wildaysky. *Implementation: How Great Expectations in Washington are Dashed in Oakland*. Berkeley: University of California Press, 1984.

Schatz, Thomas A. "Pork-Barrel Spending: A Raw Deal in Any Form." *Insight*, 21 March 1995, p. 32.

Employment and Training Administration (ETA)

PARENT ORGANIZATION: Department of Labor
ESTABLISHED: November 15, 1975
EMPLOYEES: 1,600

Contact Information:

ADDRESS: Francis Perkins Bldg.
200 Constitution Ave. NW
Washington, DC, 20210
PHONE: (202) 219-6050
URL: http://www.doleta.gov
ASSISTANT SECRETARY: Raymond L. Bramucci

WHAT IS ITS MISSION?

The mission of the Employment and Training Administration (ETA) as stated on the agency's Web site is to "contribute to the more efficient and effective functioning of the U.S. labor market by providing high quality job training, employment, labor market information, and income maintenance services primarily through state and local workforce development systems."

HOW IS IT STRUCTURED?

The ETA is an agency within the Department of Labor (DOL), which falls under the executive branch of the U.S. government. The ETA is headed by an assistant secretary who works under the secretary of labor. There are eight main divisions under the assistant secretary: the Office of Financial and Administrative Management, the Office of Regional Management, the Office of Policy and Research, the Unemployment Insurance Service, the United States Employment Service, the Office of Job Training Programs, the Office of Work-Based Learning, and the Bureau of Apprenticeship and Training.

These offices handle the five major areas of responsibility in the ETA: employment security, job training, planning and policy development, financial and administrative management, and regional management. The ETA has offices throughout the United States and its responsibilities are vast. Each of the eight central offices has numerous offices and divisions within it that help perform various aspects of its duties. For example, the Office of Financial and Administrative Management con-

FAST FACTS

According to the Clinton administration, between 1992 and 1996 more than 8.5 million new jobs were created.

(Source: David Francis. "Upbeat Job, Wage News: Is White House Right?" *Christian Science Monitor*, March 4, 1996.)

tains five suboffices: the Office of the Comptroller, the Office of Grants and Contract Management, the Office of Information Resources Management, the Office of Management Support, and the Office of Human Resources. Even these suboffices have a web of supporting departments; for example, the Office of the Comptroller includes the Division of Budget and the Division of Accounting.

PRIMARY FUNCTIONS

The ETA operates a variety of programs that help Americans find and keep jobs. The agency trains individuals who need to learn specialized skills in order to qualify for specific jobs. It sometimes offers financial assistance to people while they are in training programs. It also provides income to people who are out of work and looking for employment. The agency helps businesses and communities create job opportunities for students who are entering the workforce. The ETA helps employers find qualified workers and individuals find employment. These functions are offered through specific programs in ETA offices located throughout the United States. Individuals can contact these regional offices to learn which programs are available.

PROGRAMS

Programs run by the ETA are designed to accomplish the agency's wide range of responsibilities. For example, the Job Corps offers training and educational opportunities to qualified young people so that they can find jobs and pursue careers. The Job Corps offers training in a variety of fields such as carpentry, health services, welding, computer science, and heavy-equipment operation. The Job Corps also works with local colleges to help students earn General Equivalency Diploma (GED) certification. There are Job Corps centers throughout the country and individuals who are accepted into the program usually live on the center's campus for anywhere from six months to two years. It is also possible for participants to commute to a Job Corps center during the day while living in a nearby community.

Also operated as a part of the Job Corps is the School-To-Work (STW) program. STW offers instruction that is geared toward educating students for jobs in the workplace. Employers and industries play a part in designing the curriculum; instructors who are familiar with the necessary job, prepare classroom assignments that teach students what they will need to know when they enter the workforce.

Programs for Employers

A number of ETA programs are also available to help employers operate better in the marketplace, including assistance in locating qualified workers through the STW program and the Job Bank. Tax credits are also offered to employers when they hire certain workers, such as those who have been receiving long-term public assistance and are looking to join the workforce.

Tax incentives are also available to employers who invest in Enterprise Zones, specific areas of the country that need development. These economically depressed zones are found in both urban and rural areas and are in need of services such as banks and grocery stores. The ETA provides tax breaks to those employers willing to start businesses in these troubled communities and hire workers from that area.

Also available free to businesses is current information about the U.S. marketplace, such as statistics on salaries in a specific industry. This type of information can help employers determine where to locate branches of a current business or if it is advisable to start up new businesses.

Other Programs

The Apprenticeship program, operated by the Bureau of Apprenticeship and Training (BAT), offers assistance to industries that provide on-the-job training programs. These programs help people learn and train to do their jobs while getting paid at the same time.

The ETA also operates another program called Unemployment Compensation that offers payments to workers who have lost their jobs. These workers might have been laid off because of company downsizing (decreasing its size in order to stay competitive) or because their company went out of business. The money these workers receive is meant to help them while they look for other employment. The federal government and individual states work together to implement this program.

BUDGET INFORMATION

In 1997 the estimated amount of money appropriated by Congress from the overall budget of the United States for the operation of the ETA was $4.728 billion. This represented an increase from the 1996 estimated appropriations of $3.947 billion.

The areas of the 1997 budget that received the largest part of the funding were as follows: $1.142 billion went to the Job Corps program, an increase from the 1996 figure of $1.096 billion. Approximately $1.232 billion, up from $939 million in 1996, went to helping workers who had lost their jobs; $947 million went to help train workers for specific jobs, while in 1996 the figure was $830 million; and $871 million went to a training program to help youth work during the summer months, while in 1996 this area received $635 million.

BUDGET:

Employment and Training Administration

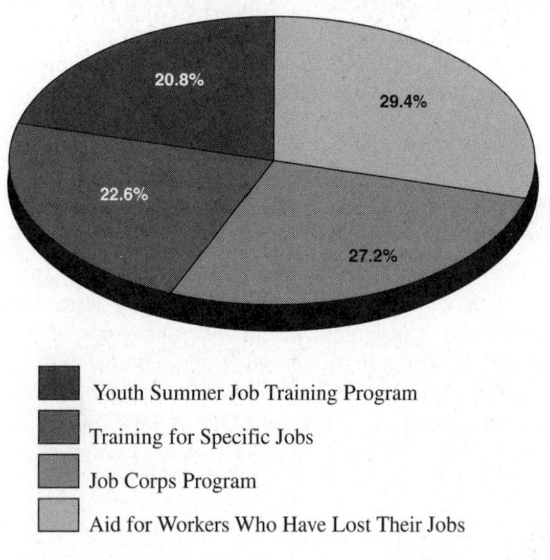

Youth Summer Job Training Program
Training for Specific Jobs
Job Corps Program
Aid for Workers Who Have Lost Their Jobs

HISTORY

After World War I (1914–18), the government feared that the great number of veterans returning to the workforce would not be able to find jobs. The wartime United States Employment Service (USES) remained to help place people in jobs, and a new agency, the Bureau of Apprenticeship and Training (BAT), was established to train veterans and other workers for the jobs that were available. These agencies proved inadequate to deal with the massive economic difficulties of the 1930s, and many new agencies such as the Civilian Conservation Corps and the Works Progress Administration were formed under President Franklin Roosevelt in an attempt to boost employment levels.

Most of the new agencies created to fight the Great Depression were disbanded during or shortly after World War II (1939–45). The economy was going through major changes as veterans returning from war were looking for work, and there were worries that an end to high wartime production levels would cause another depression. The USES was reorganized and became, along with the Unemployment Insurance Service, the Bureau of Employment Security (BES). The fears of another depression proved groundless, however, as the economy boomed. Unemployment levels were low throughout much of the 1950s.

By the early 1960s new technologies, especially those in the areas of aerospace and electronics, began to rapidly develop. Inflation rates rose and with them, unemployment. The government became concerned that workers might be getting left behind in the surge of these new technologies. President John F. Kennedy at the time described his concern about technology getting ahead of the country's ability to supply workers as "the number one domestic concern of the United States in the 1960s." As a result, the Office of Manpower, Automation, and Training (OMAT) was created. OMAT's purpose was to enforce two pieces of legislation: the Area Redevelopment Act of 1961 (ARA) and the Manpower Development and Training Act of 1962 (MDTA), both meant to address the needs of workers looking to stay abreast of the latest technological innovations. ARA and MDTA were specifically intended to channel money into areas of the country that were in need of financial help and to provide training to unemployed workers. The Manpower Administration (MA) was also created, to act as an umbrella agency and oversee the implementation of OMAT's burgeoning legislative responsibilities as well the duties of the BES and the BAT. As part of the Johnson administration's "War on Poverty" of the mid-1960s, the programs and duties of the MA continued to increase.

Beginning with the Johnson administration's "War on Poverty" in the mid–1960s, new laws were regularly passed to help the Manpower Administration address the needs of the changing economic climate. Some of these include the Economic Opportunity Act of 1964, which established the Job Corps program, and the Older Americans Act of 1965. Under the Nixon administration, the DOL was reorganized to more efficiently handle its expanding duties. In 1975, the name of the Manpower Administration was changed to the Employment and Training Administration (ETA), although none of its programs or responsibilities were altered.

During President Ronald Reagan's administration, the U.S. economy experienced rampant inflation and high unemployment rates. The economy spiraled downward into a recession as the 1980s drew to a close. However, when President Bill Clinton entered office in 1992, he pledged to concentrate his efforts on supporting job growth throughout the country. He asked the ETA to turn its focus toward the young people of the United States. He initiated programs to aid teenagers find work in the summer and moved to increase funding to the Job Corps. The ETA grew to become the largest agency within the DOL; in 1998 and 1999 it accounted for more than 90 percent of the total DOL budget.

CURRENT POLITICAL ISSUES

The ETA oversees large programs that affect millions of people. As a result its management duties are complex and expensive. The policies and goals of the ETA are also strongly influenced by the political climate of the day. Thus, the effectiveness of some of its work is often the center of controversy. One of the ETA's most controversial areas has been the Jobs Corps program.

Case Study: Job Corps

The Jobs Corps is the largest and most expensive employment training course in the country with an annual budget that consistently exceeds $1 billion. There are just under 125 centers throughout the country that have given training to 1.5 million young people between 16 and 24 years of age since it began in 1964.

Proponents claim that while the program is by no means perfect, it has been a success. Approximately 70 percent of its graduates get jobs and many participants go on to college. Congressional findings report that "for every dollar the federal government pours into Job Corps, it pockets $1.46 in decreased welfare outlays, criminal processing costs, and boosted tax receipts" (*Christian Science Monitor* February 2, 1995).

Opponents of the program, such as Senator Nancy Kassebaum (R-Kansas), say that the cost of running the program is too high. They say that it is fraught with waste, abuse, and a high dropout rate. Others claim that many centers are plagued by gangs, drugs, and violence. A report by Larry King, union representative for the National Federation of Federal Employees stated that 85 percent of workers in Job Corps centers had been assaulted by students in one 18-month period.

Public Impact

The Job Corps program has come under greater scrutiny by Congress in recent years with some members seeking to eliminate the program altogether. Advocates, however, are pushing for increased funding. In 1995 the Clinton administration lobbied to double the number of Job Corps centers by the year 2000. Funding has increased as a result of the controversy, although not as much as advocates had hoped, from an estimated $1.246 billion in 1996 to an estimated $1.300 billion in 1997.

With an increasing budget, the Job Corps is expanding to meet the needs of more communities throughout the United States. Construction of four new Job Corps centers in Massachusetts, Florida, Illinois, and California is expected to be concluded by June 1999.

FUTURE DIRECTIONS

The ETA has set a goal to focus on expanding the One-Stop Career Center System, a program helping people seeking jobs, and hopes to continue to make this a decentralized program that is operated mainly by individual states instead of a large federal center. The program incorporates federal and state resources and information into one convenient location. The ETA is creating this system in conjunction with the local state employment services already in operation in most states. The ETA believes that this decentralization will make it easier and more convenient for people to obtain information. At these centers, individuals can find job listings and information on careers and training. Legislation from the Workforce Investment Act of 1998 will also help the effort by combining a multitude of federal programs into several concentrated sources of funding.

AGENCY RESOURCES

To obtain more information about the ETA and its various programs, access the agency's Web site at http://www.doleta.gov; send a request in writing to Employment and Training Administration, Francis Perkins Bldg., 200 Constitution Ave. NW. Washington DC 20210 or phone (202) 219-6050.

For information about the Apprenticeship program, write the Bureau of Apprenticeship and Training (BAT), U.S. Department of Labor, 200 Constitution Ave. NW, Washington, DC 20210, or call (202) 219-5921. The BAT is also available on the Web at http://www.doleta.gov/bat/index.htm. You may also contact the nearest BAT Regional Office; information on the office nearest you can also be obtained at http://www.doleta.gov/bat/sobat.htm.

The national job banks can be accessed on the Web at http://www.usajobs.opm.gov/ or by contacting your local State Employment Service Office listed in your local telephone book.

AGENCY PUBLICATIONS

The ETA Web site offers a number of its publications at http://www.doleta.gov. These include a variety of fact sheets about ETA programs, press releases on current ETA initiatives, and news events. For more information on what is available, write the main office at Employment and Training Administration, Francis Perkins Bldg., 200 Constitution Ave. NW, Washington, DC 20210 or call (202) 219-6050. Some of the titles available from the ETA are "Tips for Finding the Right Job," "Work-based Learning," "Your Guide to Job Corps," and "Employment and Training for America's Homeless."

BIBLIOGRAPHY

Cue, Eduardo. "Government as Youth Employer." *U.S. News and World Report*, 29 September 1997.

Dillinger, William C. "Job Corps to the Rescue." *Audubon*, May 1995.

Francis, David. "Upbeat Job, Wage News: Is White House Right?"*Christian Science Monitor*, 4 March 1996.

Galbraith, James K. "The End of Economics?" *Nation*, 29 September 1997.

Glassman, James K. "Lonely Unemployment Line." *U.S. News and World Report*, 22 December 1997.

Jacobsen, J. P. "Black Unemployment: Part of Unskilled Unemployment." *Choice*, October 1997.

Kaslow, Amy. "Corps for Troubled Youths Now Finds Itself in Trouble." *The Christian Science Monitor*, 2 February 1995.

Schiff, Lenore. "It Just Goes On and On." *Fortune*, 27 October 1997.

Employment Standards Administration (ESA)

PARENT ORGANIZATION: Department of Labor
ESTABLISHED: 1972
EMPLOYEES: 3,400

Contact Information:

ADDRESS: 200 Constitution Ave. NW
Washington, DC 20210
PHONE: (202) 219-6191
FAX: (202) 219-6191
URL: http://www.dol.gov/dol/esa/welcome.html
ASSISTANT SECRETARY: Bernard E. Anderson

WHAT IS ITS MISSION?

The stated mission of the Employment and Standards Administration (ESA) is "to enhance the welfare and protect the rights of, and generate equal employment opportunity for, American workers, and to provide the best possible program for income replacement, medical treatment and rehabilitation for injured workers." The ESA protects workers throughout the country by offering benefits and aid while at the same time enforcing the laws that empower those standards.

HOW IS IT STRUCTURED?

The ESA is the largest agency within the Department of Labor (DOL). It falls under the executive branch and is headed by an assistant secretary who is appointed by the president. Under the assistant secretary is the Equal Employment Opportunity Unit, the Office of Public Affairs, and the Office of Management Administration and Planning. In addition, the following divisions are responsible for the four major program areas of the ESA: Wage and Hour Division (WHD); Office of Federal Contract Compliance Programs (OFCCP); Office of Workers' Compensation Programs (OWCP); and the Office of Labor-Management Standards (OLMS). Under each of these divisions is a regional director who oversees from five to ten regional offices located in major urban areas, such as Boston, Massachusetts, New York, New York, Philadelphia, Pennsylvania, Dallas, Texas, Denver, Colorado, and San Francisco, California.

The ESA is responsible for enforcing many federal laws dealing with child labor, equal opportunity for minorities in the workplace, and the minimum wage. Pictured here are workers assembling garments in a New York City garment factory. (AP/Wide World Photos)

PRIMARY FUNCTIONS

The ESA states that its primary function is to enforce and administer the laws which set workplace standards for "wages and working conditions, including child labor, minimum wages, overtime and family and medical leave; equal employment opportunity in businesses with federal contracts; and workers' compensation for certain employees injured on their jobs." For the most part these tasks are handled by the WHD, OFCCP, OWCP, and OLMS.

The WHD sends employees out to conduct surveys and inspect industries throughout the country to make sure they are complying with the wage laws. For example, the WHD enforces the law requiring workers to be paid at least the minimum wage for forty or fewer hours of work per week. The WHD then contacts any employers who are in violation and ensures compliance through warnings, fines, and other law enforcement methods. The WHD focuses extra attention on repeat violators such as the nursing home and health care industries, the garment industries, and onion and garlic growers. In addition, the WHD studies its findings to be sure that standards continue to be up to date.

A number of significant pieces of legislation give the WHD its mandate, such as the Fair Labor Standards Act (FLSA), the Family and Medical Leave Act of 1993 (FMLA), the Migrant and Seasonal Agricultural Workers Protection Act (MSPA), and the Employee Polygraph Protection Act.

The OFCCP's goal is to ensure that there is no discrimination in the workplace and that all Americans have an equal chance to work for government contractors regardless of race, religion, disabilities, minority status, or other factors. The OFCCP states that its function is "assuring that employers doing business with the federal government comply with the equal employment opportunity and affirmative action provisions of their contracts." Three main legal mandates of the OFCCP are Executive Order 11246, Section 503 of the Rehabilitation Act of 1973, and the affirmative action provisions of the Vietnam Era Veterans's Readjustment Assistance Act and the FMLA. The OFCCP investigates violations of the laws and enforces compliance. One of its most prized enforcement methods is to encourage voluntary participation by making examples of employers who are compliant. It also communicates with the civil rights community and meets with labor leaders to discuss issues.

The OWCP's purpose is to see that federal employees receive disability compensation benefits that are due them. These benefits include "wage replacement, medical treatment, vocational rehabilitation and other benefits to certain workers or their dependents who experience work-

BUDGET:
Employment Standards Administration

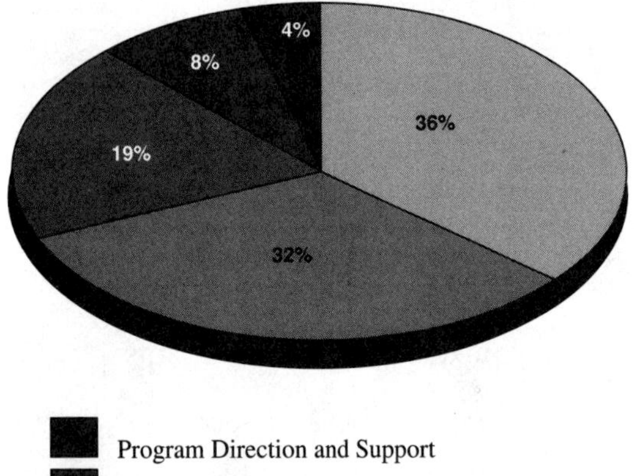

Program Direction and Support
Labor-Management Standards
Federal Contractor EEO Standards Enforcement
Federal Programs for Workers' Compensation
Enforcement of Wage and Hour Standards

related injury or occupational disease." Three major pieces of legislation give the OWCP its mandate: the Federal Employees' Compensation Act of 1916, the Longshore and Harbor Workers Compensation Act of 1927, and the Black Lung Benefits Act of 1977. These acts supply benefits such as compensation for maritime workers injured or killed on the job, medical benefits and monthly support payments to retired coal miners, and disability payments to federal workers injured or killed on the job.

The OLMS is responsible for assuring that labor organizations which represent employees in private industries treat their members according to "basic standards of democracy and fiscal responsibility." The OLMS is responsible for administering and enforcing the provisions of the Labor-Management Reporting and Disclosure Act of 1959 (LMRDA), the Civil Service Reform Act of 1978, and the Foreign Service Act of 1980. These legislative mandates protect federal employees and make sure that their representatives, their unions, treat them fairly.

PROGRAMS

The ESA, under its four main divisions, operates a wide variety of programs requiring a vast and complicated bureaucracy. Its programs reach Americans in all walks of life from union members to medical workers, coal miners, federal office workers, migrant workers, farmers, and nursing home workers and they affect a great number of workers' benefits such as wages, health insurance plans, and disability plans.

One of the ESA's most important programs is enforcement of antidiscrimination legislation. Specifically, under the OFCCP, the ESA makes sure that no one is discriminated against because of sex, race, or religious beliefs under federal equal employment opportunity laws. It also monitors compliance with the government's affirmative action laws by requiring that contractors analyze their own businesses to make sure that no one is being discriminated against and that there is an appropriate balance in the number of minorities employed. The OFCCP then conducts it own investigations to discover any violations or to follow up on any complaints. Then the OFCCP makes sure that corrective action is taken by the contractors.

Another of the ESA's mandates is the Family and Medical Leave Act of 1993 (FMLA). The ESA states that the FMLA "entitles eligible employees to take up to 12 weeks of unpaid, job-protected leave in a 12-month period for specified family and medical reasons." The act defines who is eligible to take leave and how health benefits will apply during the leave; it guarantees that an employee can return to the job after leave; and it protects employees from any negative effects as a result of requesting or taking leave. The WHD will also investigate any complaints of violations of the FMLA, and if necessary, the DOL will take legal action to enforce compliance.

BUDGET INFORMATION

The 1998 congressionally appropriated budget for the ESA was approximately $332 million. Most of the ESA's budget was allocated to enforcement of wage and hour standards (36 percent of the ESA budget) and federal programs for workers' compensation (32 percent). Other monies were directed toward federal contractor Equal Employment Opportunity (EEO) standards enforcement (19 percent), labor-management standards (8 percent) and program direction and support (4 percent).

HISTORY

The ESA began in 1971 as the Workplace Standards Administration (WSA) and was renamed the Employment Standards Administration in 1972. It combined four major program areas—the WHD, the OFCCP, the OWCP, and the OLMS—under one agency. Each of these agencies was separately created at different times before being brought under the umbrella of the ESA. As one of the major divisions of the DOL, the ESA shares the DOL's primary mission to improve and monitor the U.S. workplace. The history of the ESA is the history of the DOL and the government's increasing efforts to safeguard workers and keep the economy healthy.

The first of these four divisions was the OWCP, created in 1916 under the DOL to administer claims to qualified employees; it was part of the DOL's earliest administrative structures. A more significant earlier division was the WHD, whose mission was to take a more active role in improving workers' wages and conditions. It was established under the DOL in 1938 with the passage of the Fair Labor Standards Act (FLSA).

Work conditions before that time were unregulated and often dangerous. For example, in the mining industry children of all ages were often employed to work in small spaces in the mines. The FLSA established a national minimum wage of twenty-five cents an hour, limited a regular work week to forty hours, and prohibited anyone from working who was under sixteen years of age. Since then, the WHD has become responsible for enforcing many more laws created to safeguard the workplace, such as the Davis Bacon Act, the Service Contract Act, the Migrant Seasonal Agricultural Workers Protection Act (MSPA), the Farm Labor Contractor Registration Act, and the Employee Polygraph Protection Act. Today its regulations affect nearly 113 million workers.

The WHD was followed in 1965 by the OFCCP, which drew its mandate directly from the Equal Employment Opportunity Act (EEO), the Rehabilitation Act of 1973, and the affirmative action provisions of the Vietnam Era Veterans Readjustment Assistance Act of 1974.

The fourth of these major divisions to be created was the OLMS, reestablished as part of the ESA in 1996, although its mandate arose from earlier legislative acts, primarily the Civil Reform Act of 1978 and the Labor-Management Reporting and Disclosure Act of 1959 (LMRDA). This division of the ESA went through a number of reorganizations and renamings. Its original name was the Bureau of Labor-Management Reports (BLMR) in 1959. It was then renamed the Labor-Management Services Administration (LMSA) in 1963, then became part of the Office of the American Workplace (OAM) in 1993. With the demise of the OAM, it eventually became the OLMS and a part of the ESA in 1996.

FAST FACTS

Despite ESA standards for employment, employers can still set all sorts of rules that may seem unfair. In Dallas, Texas, home of the Dallas Cowboys football team, a grocery store worker was fired for wearing the sweatshirt of an opposing football team.

(Source: Barbara Ehrenreich. "Zipped Lips." *Time,* February 5, 1996.)

CURRENT POLITICAL ISSUES

The actions of the ESA affect millions of American workers every day and thus affect the state of the economy. Few major changes are made in the agency's policies and standards without much debate and controversy. Usually, the president and Congress get directly involved, and questions of how to safeguard the workplace and economy are frequently divided sharply along political lines. Because the economy is always changing, the same debate often arises again and again. A good example of such a recurring controversy is the federal standard for the minimum wage as upheld by the WHD within the DOL.

Case Study: The Minimum Wage

In 1997, amid heated controversy, a bill was proposed by the Clinton administration and subsequently passed by Congress to raise the minimum wage from $4.25 to $5.15 per hour. In addition, in the year 2000, this bill provides for a further increase to $6.15. Proponents of raising the minimum wage want to increase it further, while opponents think that it has already been raised too far. Both sides continue to lobby for their own point of view. The WHD—as part of the ESA and the DOL and as executors of the Clinton administration's objectives—strongly favored the hike.

Proponents claim that workers today do not make enough money at the minimum wage to survive. They say that increasing the hourly rate will help the economy by increasing tax revenues, keeping people off public welfare roles, and giving them more money to spend. They claim that the higher rate in the year 2000 will only elevate workers to the official poverty level of $12,800 per year, the minimum amount that an average family in United States needs to survive. Even making $5.15 an hour, a worker today takes home less than $200 a week after taxes. These proponents claim that 71 percent of minimum wage workers are adults, and 58 percent of those are female. They say that 57 percent of the income from those wages goes to families who make up the bottom 40 percent of the income scale.

On the contrary, opponents claim that most minimum-wage workers are teenagers whose main source of income is their parents. They claim that any increase would come from employers who are already financially burdened and fear that many small businesses would not be able to survive such an increase in costs. They point out that in the years immediately after the 1997 increase, nearly 380,000 jobs were eliminated. Opponents believe that the marketplace should be left as free as possible to determine its own wage levels.

Public Impact

Whether a direct effect of increased minimum wage or not, the U.S. unemployment rate fell in the years immediately following the 1997 increase. By 1998 nearly 10 million workers enjoyed the benefit of the 90 cent increase. The total number of employed people grew by 267,000 every month in 1998 for a total of 137 million workers. From 1996 to 1998, there was a shortage of workers, and employers were forced to keep wages high in order to attract workers. When a positive economy no longer supports higher wages, the debate about whether to raise the minimum standard will no doubt be raised again.

SUCCESSES AND FAILURES

The WHD has formed a partnership with the Occupational and Health Safety Administration (OSHA) to educate the poultry industry about its requirements for compliance with government standards, and together they perform survey-type investigations to assess compliance. Also in 1997 compliance surveys were performed in the onion and garlic farming industry, the Southeast hotel and motel industry and the New York garment manufacturing industry. A main component of these efforts is reinvestigation ensuring that the required measures have been followed. Enforcing compliance in these particular industries has been a continual problem for the ESA.

FUTURE DIRECTIONS

The ESA likes to reward industries that successfully comply with labor laws and make them positive role models. To this end the OFCCP states that it will continue to acknowledge these companies by means of Exemplary Voluntary Efforts (EVE) and Opportunity 2000 awards which are presented annually. In addition, the OFCCP "will again award the Exemplary Public Interest Contribution Award (EPIC), first presented in 1994, to organizations whose activities support the mission of OFCCP. Letters of recognition will also be sent to federal contractors who are identified by the OFCCP staff as deserving acknowledgment."

AGENCY RESOURCES

The ESA can be found on the Web at: http://www.dol.gov/dol/esa/welcome.html. The national office can be reached by writing to the Employment Standards Administration, c/o U.S. Department of Labor, 200 Constitution Ave. NW, Washington, DC 20210 or by calling (202) 219-6191. Regional offices are listed in local telephone directories.

AGENCY PUBLICATIONS

A variety of reports, press releases, and articles are available at the ESA Web site at http://www.dol.gov/dol/esa/welcome.html. The ESA also offers free posters which advertise its missions and standards. Posters are available, for example, that explain the minimum wage law or employees' rights under the FMLA.

BIBLIOGRAPHY

Alter, Jonathan. "Washington Washes Its Hands." *Newsweek*, 12 August 1996, pp. 42–4.

"Bare Minimum." *Economist*, 28 September 1996.

Behar, Richard. "Guess Gets Pressed." *Fortune* , 11 November, 1996.

Corney, Mark. "Good Investment Or Bad Business?" *Times Educational Supplement*, 20 September 1996.

Ehrenreich, Barbara. "Zipped Lips." *Time*, 5 February 1996.

Francis, David R. "Minimum Wage Hike Didn't Raise Jobless." *The Christian Science Monitor*, 3 June 1994.

Henderson, David R. "The Squabble Over The Minimum Wage." *Fortune*, 8 July 1996, pp. 28–30.

Judis, John B. "TRB from Washington: Bare Minimum." *New Republic*, 28 October 1996.

Norton, Rob. "The Minimum Wage Is Unfair." *Fortune*, 27 May 1996.

Ridgeway, James. "Let Them Eat Whoppers." *Village Voice*, 2 July 1996.

Silverstein, Ken. "Congress's Beach Boys." *Nation*, 12 January 1998, pp. 21–3.

Wood, Daniel B. "Debate Escalates Over 'Living Wage' as Antipoverty Tool." *The Christian Science Monitor*, 17 October 1996.

Wright, E. Assata. "Waging Battle For Decent Pay." *Village Voice*, 18 June 1996, pp. 10–2.

Environmental Protection Agency (EPA)

PARENT ORGANIZATION: Independent
ESTABLISHED: December 2, 1970
EMPLOYEES: 17,900

Contact Information:

ADDRESS: 401 M St. SW
Washington, DC 20460
PHONE: (202) 260-2090
TDD (HEARING IMPAIRED): (202) 260-3658
FAX: (202) 260-0279
E-MAIL: Public-Access@epamail.epa.gov
URL: http://www.epa.gov
ADMINISTRATOR: Carol M. Browner
DEPUTY ADMINISTRATOR: Fred J. Hansen

WHAT IS ITS MISSION?

The Environmental Protection Agency's (EPA) stated mission is "to protect public health and safeguard and improve the natural environment—air, water, and land—upon which human life depends." It is dedicated to controlling and reducing pollution in the areas of air, water, solid waste, pesticides, radiation, and toxic substances. Its obligation is to coordinate an integrated attack on environmental pollution in cooperation with state and local governments.

To accomplish its mission, the EPA strives to ensure that federal environmental laws are implemented and enforced fairly. It also makes sure that environmental protection is an important consideration in policies formulated by other U.S. agencies. The EPA attempts to base its efforts at reducing environmental risk on the best available scientific information, and it aims to secure full access to this information for communities, citizens, businesses, and state and local governments so that they may become full participants in preventing pollution and protecting human health.

HOW IS IT STRUCTURED?

The EPA is an independent agency that falls under the executive branch but does not carry cabinet department status. For carrying out its stated missions, the EPA has four offices that are devoted primarily to formulating policy and operating programs in their areas of expertise: the Office of Air and Radiation; the Office of Prevention, Pesticides, and Toxic Substances; the Office of

FAST FACTS

Since the EPA's creation, more than 1 billion pounds of toxic pollution have been prevented from entering our nation's waters.

(Source: The Environmental Protection Agency. "Twenty-Five Years of Environmental Progress at a Glance," 1998.)

Water; and the Office of Solid Waste and Emergency Response. Most of the agency's programs and initiatives are implemented through these offices.

Another important office within the EPA is the Office of Research and Development, which oversees the EPA's national laboratories and coordinates the EPA's national research policy. Research grants and fellowships are offered through this office in order to encourage environmental research.

Because cooperation and good relations are such an important part of achieving the agency's goals, three offices are devoted to maintaining good relations with both potential partners and potential critics: the Office of Communications, Education, and Public Affairs; the Office of Regional Operations and State/Local Relations; and the Office of Congressional and Legislative Affairs.

The administrative, legal, and financial duties of the agency are carried out and assisted by a number of offices, including the Office of General Counsel, the Office of Administration and Resources Management, and the Environmental Appeals Board. The EPA's Office of Enforcement and Compliance is responsible for ensuring that the nation's environmental laws are not being broken.

Included in the EPA's organizational structure is the Office of the Inspector General. The inspector general is appointed by the president and exists to watch over the EPA. The Office of the Inspector General reviews the financial and administrative affairs of the EPA and investigates any allegations of misconduct.

The EPA also has 10 regional offices throughout the country that are responsible for working with headquarters to develop local programs. Each office is led by an administrator who designs and carries out an environmental plan for the region. The regional offices are located in Boston, Massachusetts; New York, New York; Philadelphia, Pennsylvania; Atlanta, Georgia; Chicago, Illinois; Dallas, Texas; Kansas City, Missouri; Denver, Colorado; San Francisco, California; and Seattle, Washington.

PRIMARY FUNCTIONS

The EPA develops policies and programs to control environmental pollution, and it develops and enforces standards for compliance with these policies. In addition, the agency supplies direction, support, and training to regional communities to assist them in meeting EPA guidelines. In the area of hazardous waste treatment, the EPA develops policies and regulations, manages cleanup programs, performs economic impact assessments, and develops guidelines for community preparedness. The agency regulates pesticides and monitors pesticide levels in food, people, and animals. It develops and enforces policies for the control of toxic substances and estimates the effects of new and existing chemicals on the environment. In addition to these operations, the EPA also conducts a national research program aimed at the technological control of pollution.

PROGRAMS

The EPA has a hand in literally dozens of programs at the local, state, and national levels. Among the largest and best known of these is Superfund, which accounts for about 20 percent of the agency's budget. Superfund is a trust fund set up to pay for the cleanup of abandoned warehouses or places of business where hazardous wastes have been left behind. Superfund personnel are on call to respond at a moment's notice to chemical emergencies, accidents, or releases. A similar program is the Brownfields Initiative, a program for restoring to use any abandoned or underused commercial facility where real or perceived environmental contamination exists.

The EPA is also involved in a number of programs that make use of partnerships with industry, state or local governments, or communities. The Environmental Finance Program (EFP) attempts to bridge the gap between the growing costs of environmental protection and the ability of state and local governments to meet these costs. It also helps communities develop creative approaches to funding environmental projects. The Partners for the Environment Program attempts to reach out to communities, universities, and small and large businesses to address environmental issues.

The EPA also administers several geographically specific programs, such as the Puget Sound initiatives, designed to help ease the environmental strain of recent population growth in the Seattle/Puget Sound region.

BUDGET INFORMATION

The EPA's budget in 1998 totaled slightly over $7 billion. Nearly 50 percent of that budget goes to the agency's operating programs; 30 percent goes to water infrastructure financing as part of State and Tribal Association Grants (STAG), and approximately 20 percent goes to the Superfund program. A small percentage of the budget (less than 1 percent) goes to the Leaking Underground Storage Tank Trust Fund (LUST).

Of the funds spent on operating programs, nearly half go to either state grants or to research. In the area of environmental programs, most of the available funds are devoted to cleaning up environmental and drinking water, and then, in descending order: air, hazardous waste (excluding Superfund), toxic substances, pesticides, and radiation. A significant portion of the operating programs budget is spent on multimedia and communications used to illustrate various environmental principles to various parties.

BUDGET:

Environmental Protection Agency

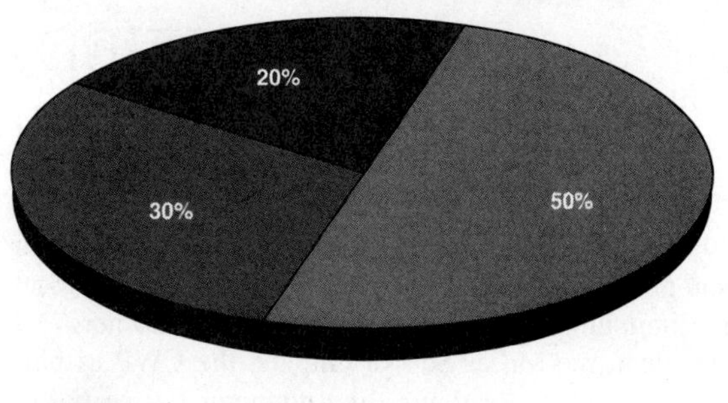

Superfund Program

Water Infrastructure Financing

Operating Programs Including State Grants and Research

HISTORY

The EPA was created on December 2, 1970, under the Nixon administration's Reorganization Plan No. 3, which brought together nearly 6,000 employees from 15 government programs that already existed under three departments: the Department of Health, Education, and Welfare; the Department of Agriculture; and the Department of the Interior.

Upon the EPA's inception, President Richard Nixon called for a comprehensive system of waste management that would be centrally administered. Although the agency's first administrator, William Ruckelshaus, attempted to center the agency on a few functional offices, the plan for centralization soon encountered difficulties. One reason for this failure was that the aims of different offices were simply too diverse; air pollution specialists and water pollution experts, for example, were pursuing different activities and tended to have little contact. Coordinating their activities seemed impractical. Another reason was legislative—the programs tended to have differing legal foundations, and in the years immediately following 1970, new laws further increased and diversified the agency's obligations. Congress expanded the agency's responsibilities for solid wastes in 1970 and for pesticides in 1972. A noise bill was passed in 1972, a drinking water act in 1974, and a toxic substances control act in 1976. In addition to these, the EPA took on considerable obligations for research.

Ruckelshaus, a former Department of Justice official, had become most comfortable presiding over attorneys, and during his administration the tone of the agency's work was set—the emphasis tended to be on enforcement rather than research and prevention. This focus created difficulties on two fronts: the agency spent much time and money in court and often found itself on the defensive after industries brought lawsuits fighting regulation, and relatively little progress was made in actually cleaning up the environment.

Finally, the courts limited the discretionary behavior of the EPA bureaucracy. Issues were decided case-by-case, and environmental law was interpreted using different principles at different points in time. Pollution control began to be evaluated against a standard of costs and benefits—the costs of preventing pollution, it was believed, should not outweigh the benefits of the effort. In 1977 Congress further revised air and water pollution control statutes, requiring the EPA to take into account technological innovation, economic impact, employment impact, and other factors that would affect industry's ability to comply with and meet the deadlines of environmental law.

Since the difficult times following its origins, the EPA has begun to reevaluate how it interacts with industry and the public. A variety of programs have been tested and implemented to anticipate and prevent environmental problems as well as to enforce environmental law. In some ways, the EPA is returning to President Nixon's intended mission for it: a coordinated and inclusive effort to control pollution in all its forms.

CURRENT POLITICAL ISSUES

One of the most politically sensitive issues for the EPA has been "environmental racism," now more widely

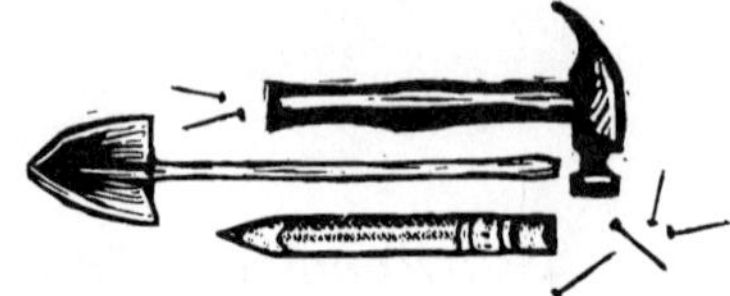

GET INVOLVED:

A Community Success in Virginia

In 1994, the Environmental Education Center at the Miller School in Charlottesville, Virginia, teamed with local government agencies in Albemarle County to form the Community Watershed Project (CWP). Teachers and students at the Miller School initiated the CWP as part of an EPA grant for controlling nonpoint source pollution. It is a coordinated program involving entire communities to monitor and control the runoff that ends up in streams. Schools serve as the hub of each watershed team, and interested citizens are encouraged to join with local schools to participate in stream monitoring and other activities.

The steps in the CWP program were as follows: a map was made of watersheds for each community in the area; workshops were held to train teachers in stream monitoring, storm drain stenciling, and other skills; and a Student Water Congress was held consisting of middle school and high school students from around the area who made individual presentations about their home watersheds. The CWP has since expanded to involve faculty and students at the University of Virginia, and its efforts now include collaboration with land developers to insure that development does no further damage to local streams.

To find out how you might play a role in developing a program similar to the CWP, start by locating watersheds in your area on a map provided by the Office of Water, located on the Web at http://www.epa.gov/surf.

---

known as "environmental justice." The main argument of the environmental justice movement is that particular communities in the United States, primarily those composed of minorities and the poor, have been forced to bear disproportionate external costs associated with industrial processes. Poor and minority communities, the movement argues, are systematically discriminated against in the siting, regulation, and remediation of industrial and waste facilities.

The environmental justice movement is not new—as early as the late 1970s, community leaders attempted to bring the perceived injustice before the public—but it has only recently begun to have much of a direct political influence on EPA policy making and enforcement. The study most often associated with this issue, conducted by the Rev. Benjamin Chavis of the United Church of Christ in 1987, concluded that a high percentage of waste sites and polluting industries were deliberately placed in minority neighborhoods. Studies since have suggested that there is some truth to this argument; it seems obvious that the poor do bear proportionately more of this toxic burden, but the underlying reasons appear to be more complicated than is claimed by members of the environmental justice movement. Economics and lack of political influence may have more to do with the problem than overt racism.

Whatever the causes, it is clear to American political leaders that to ignore the implications of the environmental justice movement, and to thereby appear insensitive to the plight of minority communities, is unwise. The most dramatic political event to arise from the movement occurred in February 1994, when President Bill Clinton issued an executive order on environmental justice. The order required federal agencies, and in particular the EPA, to demonstrate that their programs and policies do not unfairly cause environmental risk for the poor and minorities, and it created an interagency task force to insure that environmental justice policies are implemented promptly.

Case Study: Escambia

In 1996 the Pensacola, Florida, neighborhood of Escambia began to notice disturbing coincidences in its community. It seemed to the people of Escambia that they had been suffering from a frighteningly high incidence of birth defects and cancer deaths. Since 1990 the predominantly African American community of only 358 families had lost about 50 individuals to cancer.

The houses and apartments of Escambia bordered a 26-acre Superfund toxic waste site where an industrial company had soaked pine logs in chemical preservative to make telephone poles and pilings. After President Clinton's 1994 executive order on environmental justice, the EPA decided to make Escambia its pilot project for the new policy. Arsenic, dioxin, lead, and other toxic substances were found at dangerous levels in a handful of residential yards near the Superfund site. An assessment by the Florida Health Department concluded that only a few families living next to the site faced any serious health risks. The EPA offered to finance the relocation of 66 families, but the residents of Escambia refused the offer, saying the move would divide the community and leave those remaining on worthless land that bordered a Superfund site. The agency shied away from moving the entire community, citing unreasonably high costs.

Eventually, after much discussion and argument, the political pressures on the EPA were too great to ignore, and the agency agreed to pay for the relocation of all 358 families. Two hundred fifty-eight of these families lived in an apartment complex where toxic levels were shown to be well below the level considered harmful by regulators, but to have refused assistance to them would have been politically damaging to both the EPA and the Clinton administration.

The government's decision on Escambia is likely to increase demands from other communities for either faster cleanup or total relocation of neighborhoods in toxic areas. Relocations on the scale of Escambia will not be possible nationwide; the EPA's Chief Administrator, Carol Browner, estimates that one in four Americans lives within four miles of a toxic waste site.

SUCCESSES AND FAILURES

One of the EPA's most dramatic successes has been its campaign to remove lead particulates from the air. Due primarily to the EPA's efforts to eliminate lead from gasoline and to place limits on specific industrial sources of lead, airborne lead emissions have decreased by 98 percent since 1970.

FUTURE DIRECTIONS

The "New Directions" section of the EPA's 25th anniversary report claims that the agency is seeking to change in two major areas. First, the EPA is exploring new ways in which to implement its programs in order to make operations fairer, faster, and more cost-effective. Instead of taking the offensive approach and focusing primarily on punishment and enforcement, the EPA wants to take a more flexible, active approach, forming partnerships with states, tribes, and regulated businesses or entities to find cheaper, more effective solutions.

The EPA also appears determined to change the way it manages the environment, preferring to view entire ecosystems rather than handling air, water, and solid waste as distinct problem areas. The agency is determined to break through the red tape and legal barriers that make implementing such an integrated approach difficult at the facility, industry, and community levels.

AGENCY RESOURCES

One of the most comprehensive sources of EPA information is the National Center for Environmental Publications and Information (NCEPI), a central repository for all EPA documents. The NCEPI has more than 5,500 titles in paper or electronic format and can be accessed from the ageny's Web site at http://www.epa.gov/ncepihom/index.html.

Agency dockets contain public records of information used in the rulemaking or policies of the EPA and include *Federal Register* notices, public comments, and transcripts of public hearings. A charge is imposed for copies more than 226 pages long. To contact the Information Management and Services Division, call (202) 260-5914.

For general research assistance, contact the EPA's Headquarters Information Resource Center (IRC), a link between program offices, information resources, and the public. The IRC can be contacted at (202) 260-5921 or by E-mail at Public-Access@epamail.epa.gov.

Also available is INFOTERRA, an international environmental referral and research network of about 170 countries. INFOTERRA is coordinated by the United Nations (UN) and is headquartered in Nairobi, Kenya, but its U.S. national focal point is located at EPA Headquarters. INFOTERRA/USA can be contacted at (202) 260-5917 or by E-mail at Library-infoterra@epamail.epa.gov.

AGENCY PUBLICATIONS

The EPA's publications include periodicals such as *Contaminated Sediment News*, informational pamphlets such as "Household Hazardous Waste Management," and official reports such as "Small Community and Wastewater Treatment." Publications can be ordered through NCEPI on-line or by calling 1-800-490-9198. Other sources of EPA publications include the EPA National Library Network Program, INFOTERRA, and the Government Printing Office.

BIBLIOGRAPHY

Ackerman, Frank. *Why do We Recycle?: Markets, Values, and Public Policy.* Washington, D.C.: Island Press, 1997.

Bald, Jim. "Think Green." *Overdrive*, pp. 49–54.

Caldwell, Lynton Keith. *Environment as a Focus for Public Policy.* Texas A & M University Press, 1995.

Corn, David. "A Bad Air Day." *Nation*, 24 March 1997, pp. 16–19.

Fairley, Peter. "Hazardous Waste." *Chemical Week*, Vol. 159, no. 1, p. 9.

Gray, Robert. "Washington News." *Water Engineering and Management*, Vol. 44, no. 4, p. 6.

Kirsch, Robert. "Find Out What the New EPA Reform Initiatives Mean for You." *Boston Business Journal*, Vol. 17, no. 1, pp. 31–2.

Regan, Mary Beth. "The Dust-up Over Fine Air Pollutants." *Business Week*, 24 March 1997, p. 203.

"U.S. Scales Back Estimates on Air Rules." *New York Times*, 3 April 1997, p. A22.

Equal Employment Opportunity Commission (EEOC)

PARENT ORGANIZATION: Independent
ESTABLISHED: July 2, 1965
EMPLOYEES: 2,586

Contact Information:

ADDRESS: 1801 L St. NW
Washington, DC 20507
PHONE: (202) 663-4900
TOLL FREE: (800) 669-4000
TDD (HEARING IMPAIRED): (800) 669-6820
URL: http://www.eeoc.gov
CHAIRMAN: Paul M. Igasaki
GENERAL COUNSEL: Clifford Gregory Stewart

WHAT IS ITS MISSION?

The mission of the Equal Employment Opportunity Commission (EEOC), as stated in its 1997–2002 Strategic Plan, is "to ensure equality of opportunity by vigorously enforcing general legislation prohibiting discrimination in employment. It uses investigation, conciliation, litigation, coordination, regulation in the federal sector, education, policy research and provision of technical assistance to achieve this end." The EEOC seeks to free the workplace from discriminatory practices on the basis of race, color, religion, national origin, sex, age, or disability. It promotes equal opportunity via administrative and legislative guidelines and supports its actions and rules through the enforcement of civil rights laws.

HOW IS IT STRUCTURED?

The EEOC is an independent agency that falls under the executive branch of the federal government. It is composed of five commissioners and a general counsel, all of whom are appointed by the president and confirmed by the Senate. Each commissioner's term is for five years, and each term is staggered so there is continuity on the commission. The general counsel serves for four years. Of the five commissioners, one is appointed chairman, who also serves as the CEO, and one vice chairman. The role of the commission is to make policy and approve most of the litigation. Commissioners can also initiate investigations. The general counsel decides whether to litigate individual claims under Title VII of the Civil Rights Act of 1964 (Title VII), the Age Discrimination in Employment Act of 1967 (ADEA), the Americans with Disabilities Act (ADA), or the 1991 Civil Rights Act.

The main headquarters of the commission is in Washington, D.C. and there are 50 field offices. The EEOC has work-sharing agreements with Fair Employment Practices Agencies (FEPA), which are state and local government agencies that work under contract with the EEOC to process charges of discrimination. This relieves some of the EEOC's work and financial demands, as FEPA's are only partially funded by the EEOC. Additionally, the EEOC works with other federal agencies associated with ensuring civil rights, such as the U.S. Civil Rights Commission, the Department of Education's Office of Civil Rights, the Labor Department's Office of Federal Contract Compliance Programs, and the Department of Justice's Civil Rights Division.

PRIMARY FUNCTIONS

The EEOC develops policies and guidelines to eliminate workplace discrimination. It also investigates complaints, initiates or joins employment litigation, and enforces the various mandates and acts passed by Congress to ensure that Americans in the workforce receive fair treatment by their employers and fellow employees. The EEOC is authorized to enforce the primary federal laws that prohibit employment discrimination. These statutory authorities include: Title VII of the Civil Rights Act of 1964, the Age Discrimination in Employment Act of 1967, the Equal Pay Act of 1963, Title I of the Americans with Disabilities Act of 1990 (ADA), Section 501 of the Rehabilitation Act of 1973, and the Civil Rights Act of 1991.

In addition to investigating over 80,000 complaints each year, the EEOC works in partnership with state and local agencies to develop alternatives to litigation. In particular, it sponsors programs, seminars, and roundtables to educate businesses and workers in an attempt to prevent discrimination before it happens.

PROGRAMS

The EEOC operates a number of programs to help the federal government and businesses deter discrimination in employment practices. The EEOC Technical Assistance and Training Programs were authorized under the EEOC Education, Technical Assistance and Training Revolving Fund Act of 1992, which allows the EEOC to charge reasonable fees to cover the cost of providing specialized education and training about equal employment opportunity laws. The purpose of these seminars, which are either a full day or a half day, is to teach employers and federal agencies how to keep discrimination complaints from happening and, if they do occur, how to effectively deal with them. Areas that are covered include sexual and racial harassment, ADA issues, national origin and immigration discrimination, and age discrimination.

Because of an enormous backlog of cases and complaints, the Alternative Dispute Resolution Program (ADR) was developed to keep discrimination complaints of a less-serious nature from reaching the litigation stage. The ADR's goal was to resolve cases quickly, through mediation between parties, and not have them enter the legal system where they might take years to resolve.

BUDGET:

Equal Employment Opportunity Commission

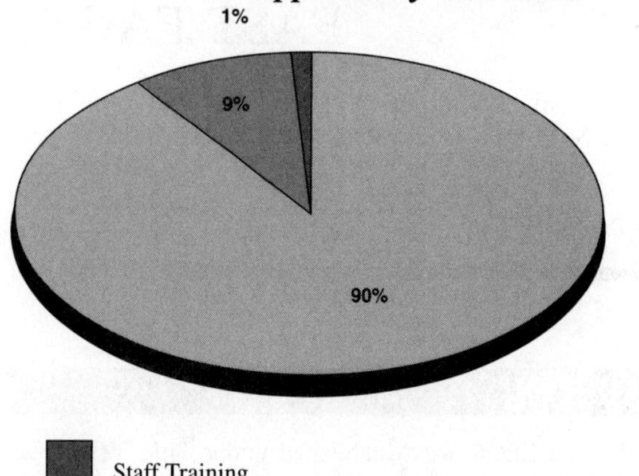

Staff Training

Litigation Support, New Technology, and Related Cost

Personnel Costs and Rent

BUDGET INFORMATION

The EEOC was appropriated a $239.7 million budget in 1997. This includes over $27 million for state FEPA offices to assist in compliance actions. Since the EEOC depends heavily on its investigative, enforcement, and legal personnel, the majority of the budget (90 percent) is spent on personnel costs and rent for the 50 field offices. 9 percent is used for litigation support, new technology, and related costs while the remaining 1 percent of the budget is spent on ongoing training for EEOC staff. The number of staff members dropped from 3,390 in 1980 to 2,680 in 1997, while the enforcement obligations rose substantially with the addition of the ADA; the 1991 Civil Rights Act, especially in its regard to sexual harassment; and other statutory responsibilities.

FAST FACTS

From 1995 to mid-1997 the EEOC collected more than $425 million for victims of discrimination; 80 percent was the result of mediation.

(Source: EEOC's Strategic Plan 1997–2002.)

HISTORY

The EEOC was established under Title VII of the Civil Rights Act of 1964 to investigate and conciliate all claims of discrimination in the workplace on the basis of race, color, national origin, sex, and religion. (It actually began operations July 2, 1965.) The Civil Rights Act of 1964, signed by President Lyndon B. Johnson, was enacted as a bipartisan effort to redress centuries of bias against minorities and to give them true equality under the laws of the United States. The Civil Rights Act was one of the most influential measures taken by this nation to combat discrimination in all sectors of society. As part of the historic and sweeping reforms of this act, the EEOC became an integral part of the nation's attempts to ensure that all persons have freedom, equality, justice, and opportunity.

Originally, the EEOC investigated and attempted to administratively reconcile the various discrimination actions that were brought before it. That is, while the EEOC investigated cases of discrimination and made determinations, it could only recommend steps to eliminate the problem. It had no authority to enforce the recommendations.

By 1972 Congress realized the EEOC needed authority to take action, so the EEOC was given the power to bring litigation against cases that it could not settle out of court. Additionally, when Congress extended Title VII to cover federal employees, the EEOC was given the responsibility of ensuring that federal workers are afforded the same rights as state and local workers. Thus, the mandate of the EEOC was expanding so it has authority to fight discrimination in the private and public sectors and to make certain that issued directives are followed.

In the ongoing fight against discrimination in the workplace, Congress passed legislation that addressed issues of pay inequity and age discrimination. In 1978 the powers of the EEOC were again increased when it was given full responsibility to enforce the Equal Pay Act of 1963 (EPA) and the Age Discrimination in Employment Act of 1967 (ADEA).

When the Americans with Disabilities Act (ADA) was passed by Congress in 1990, the EEOC was again called upon to serve as the enforcement agency to ensure the end of what then-President George Bush called "the unjustified segregation and exclusion of persons with disabilities from the mainstream of American life." In 1991 the EEOC's mandate further expanded to include a damages remedy for Title VII and the ADA.

CURRENT POLITICAL ISSUES

Some of the many issues the EEOC has confronted in the 1990s are language-rights discrimination, sexual harassment, nonsexual harassment, mental health discrimination, and cases of religious bias. The focus of EEOC priorities, however, often shifts as the presidential administration and congressional bodies change. And, because the EEOC commissioners and chairman are appointed by the president and Congress, the commission often reflects the existing political climate. For instance, former EEOC Chairman and current Supreme Court Justice Clarence Thomas firmly disagreed with the policy of affirmative action; therefore, under his tenure other anti-discrimination actions were pursued.

Case Study: Del Laboratories

One of the best examples of the EEOC at work is its involvement with the sexual harassment case at Del Laboratories. For 25 years, according to *Newsday* (September 17, 1995), Dan K. Wassong, the CEO of Del Labs, harassed his administrative assistants, all of whom were women. He verbally abused them, made their work environment hostile, and made unwelcome physical advances. Over the 25 years, dozens of women quit or were fired by Wassong. Many complained to Del officials but got nowhere, because the person about whom they were complaining was the CEO. Until he hired a young woman named Jonneigh Adrion, no one was able to successfully confront him.

Determined not to allow Wassong to destroy her self-esteem, Adrion set in motion a plan to stop him. She gathered all the information she could, contacting all the former assistants. She discovered that each of these women was willing to testify against Wassong, even though the statute of limitations for their own claims was long expired. Along with a coworker, Lucy Pelligrino, who was hired by Wassong in March 1992 and subjected to the same abuse, Adrion approached lawyers, who told her that her case was impossible. Nonetheless, Adrian and Pelligrino persevered. They quit their jobs and contacted the EEOC. When the EEOC attorney and investigator corroborated the stories of the two women, they discovered that many former aides to Wassong were willing to testify against him, even though they were not party to the suit. In 1994 the EEOC filed a lawsuit in the names of Adrion, Pelligrino, and twelve others. Adrion told *Newsday*, "I was afraid of what he might do. . . . He had the resources to do almost anything."

Faced with possible testimony of at least 34 former assistants, Wassong and Del Laboratories settled the case for $1.19 million for the plaintiffs. It was the largest settlement ever achieved in a sexual harassment case to that date. Wassong never admitted guilt, but Del Labs was required to conduct training and set up an 800 number complaint line. Wassong was required to undergo personal training. The case sent a clear message that the EEOC will pursue discrimination in the workplace, even if it leads to the CEO of a major corporation.

FAST FACTS

As of 1997 a woman in the workforce earns 71 cents for every dollar earned by her male counterpart.

(Source: Equal Employment Opportunity Commission, 1998.)

SUCCESSES AND FAILURES

Perhaps the greatest success the EEOC has accomplished with its rigorous pursuit of bias in the workplace is the sensitization of many American firms. It has caused businesses to reevaluate their employment practices, whether it means removing an offensive calendar from a wall or respecting the diversity of culture, language, and ethnicity in the workforce. Even when the EEOC's lawsuits are defeated in court, the very presence of such actions causes businesses to reflect on their own practices.

The commission is not without its detractors. Because the EEOC is required to investigate complaints of race, sex, age, and other types of discrimination filed by employees against their employers, it is often on the hot seat when it comes to fulfilling its obligations. In 1996 alone, the agency received more than 90,000 complaints based on race, ethnicity, and gender. The backlog of cases at times can exceed 100,000, which the EEOC attributes to increasing responsibilities coupled with a shrinkage of staff. Therefore, the commission is accused of not responding quickly to complaints, and some feel violations will continue without redress since the EEOC is so busy.

Other critics question how the EEOC focuses its attention. Groups ranging from African Americans, Latinos, and Asian Americans, to individuals with mental health problems, feel their needs are ignored by the agency as it pursues high-profile cases. To counter these critics, the EEOC established policies and offers training to help employers and their employees learn how the EEOC interprets the complex sets of laws it upholds and enforces. To help resolve this problem, the agency initiated the Alternative Dispute Resolution Program, discussed earlier. It is designed to eliminate costly and time-consuming litigation for cases that can be settled in a less-formal forum than the court system. The benefits of such mediation are that cases can be resolved more quickly and, more important, the victims of discrimination do not have to suffer through a long legal process.

In a 1997 interview that appeared in *USA Today*, then-EEOC Chairman Gilbert Casellas answered critics by commenting, "The bottom line is that this agency will never be popular. We don't give away money and we enforce the law."

FUTURE DIRECTIONS

The future of the EEOC is inextricably linked with the changes that face the American workforce: an aging workforce, multiculturalism in the workplace, language issues, and ongoing issues of harassment, sexual or nonsexual, by nonemployees as well as fellow workers, to name a few. New rules will be established to assist employers in making certain that no one is discriminated against because of his or her religious beliefs. Initiatives such as an evaluation of the EEOC's enforcement program, which brought about the National Enforcement Plan and commissioner-run task forces to investigate the practices of the agency, will be at the forefront of all new initiatives. Restructuring of the enforcement programs, development of newer and more relevant education and technical assistance programs, and establishment of a close working relationship with employers, unions, advocates, civil rights groups, and federal employees will focus the limited resources of this small but powerful agency to prepare it for an increased role in eliminating bias and discrimination in the workplace of the twenty-first century.

AGENCY RESOURCES

Each state has a field office of the EEOC. There is a general toll free number to call, which will automatically connect the caller to the nearest field office: 1-800-669-4000 (TDD 1-800-669-6820). The EEOC headquarters can be reached by calling (202) 663-4900 or (202) 663-4494 (TDD). To receive updates on the latest meeting of the EEOC commissioners, which is usually held the second Tuesday of each month, call (202) 663-7100. Meetings are also open to the general public. More information about the EEOC can be found on its World Wide Web site at http://www.eeoc.gov.

AGENCY PUBLICATIONS

Included among the many publications available from the EEOC are "Compliance Manual Section 902: Definition of the Term 'Disability'" (1995), "EEOC Enforcement Guidance on Non-Waivable Employee Rights under EEOC Enforced Statutes" (1997), and "Enforcement Guidance on Sex Discrimination in the Compensation of Sports Coaches in Educational Institutions" (1997).

EEOC publications (including the texts of the laws enforced by the EEOC, facts about employment discrimination, and enforcement guidance and related documents) are available free of charge and can be obtained by writing the U.S. Equal Employment Opportunity Commission, Publications Information Center, PO Box 12549, Cincinnati, Ohio 45212-0549; or call 1-800-669-3362 (voice); 1-800-800-3302 (TDD); or fax (513) 791-2954.

BIBLIOGRAPHY

Amour, Stephanie. "EEOC's Departing Chief Reviews Gains, Criticisms." *USA Today*, 10 November 1997.

Anderson, Peg L., et al. "Learning Disabilities, Employment Discrimination and the ADA." *Journal of Learning Disabilities*, 1 April 1995.

Cacas, Samuel R. "Language Rights Loom Larger than Ever in America's Workplace." *AsianWeek*, 21 October 1994.

Davis, Ann. "Who Can't Work? Courts Take Hard Line. . . ." *Newsday*, 27 July 1997.

Falk, William B. "Them Vs. The CEO." *Newsday* , 17 September 1995.

Harrigan, Susan. "Under Fire." *Newsday*, 11 October 1992.

Jaroff, Leon. "Assembly-Line Sexism? Charges of Abusing Women—and Angry Denials—Rock a Midwestern Mitsubishi Plant." *Time*, 6 May 1996.

Kezman, Diana L. et al. "Harassment by Non-Employees: How Should Employers Respond." *HR Magazine*, 1 December 1996.

Litvan, Laura M. "EEOC Turns to Mediation." *Nation's Business*, 1 June 1995.

Price, David Andrew. "English-Only Rules: EEOC Has Gone Too Far." *USA Today*, 28 March 1996.

Schneid, Thomas D. *The Americans with Disabilities Act: a Practical Guide for Managers*. New York: Van Nostrand Reinhold, 1992.

"You'll Be Hearing From My Lawyer." *The Economist*, 21 June 1997.

Export-Import Bank of the United States (Ex-Im Bank)

WHAT IS ITS MISSION?

The mission of the Export-Import Bank of the United States (Ex-Im Bank) is to create and maintain private sector jobs through exports of the nation's goods and services. This goal involves three major areas of activity: supplementing the commercial financing of export activities with government subsidy, absorbing the risks of nonpayment of loans incurred by private lending institutions, and meeting export competition posed by foreign competitors. In order to meet these primary objectives, the Ex-Im Bank offers numerous loan, guarantee, and insurance programs to support transactions that would not be available to U.S. businesses without its assistance.

HOW IS IT STRUCTURED?

The Ex-Im Bank is an independent agency operating under the authority of the Export-Import Bank Act of 1945. It is led by a board of directors which includes a president and chairman, a first vice president and vice chair, and three other directors, all of whom are appointed by the president with the advice and consent of the Senate. The United States trade representative and the secretary of commerce also serve on the board as *ex officio* (non-voting) members. The board of directors is responsible for making primary policy and program decisions affecting the Ex-Im Bank. They are assisted by their chief legal adviser, the general counsel; the chief financial officer, who is responsible for advising the board on the bank's available resources and monitoring the status of its loans; and the chief of staff, who man-

PARENT ORGANIZATION: Independent
ESTABLISHED: February 2, 1934
EMPLOYEES: 420

Contact Information:

ADDRESS: 811 Vermont Ave. NW
Washington, DC 20571
PHONE: (202) 565-3946
TOLL FREE: (800) 565-3946
TDD (HEARING IMPAIRED): (202) 565-3377
FAX: (202) 565-3380
URL: http://www.exim.gov
PRESIDENT AND CHAIRMAN: James A. Harmon
VICE PRESIDENT AND VICE CHAIR: Jackie M. Clegg

BUDGET:

Export-Import Bank of the United States

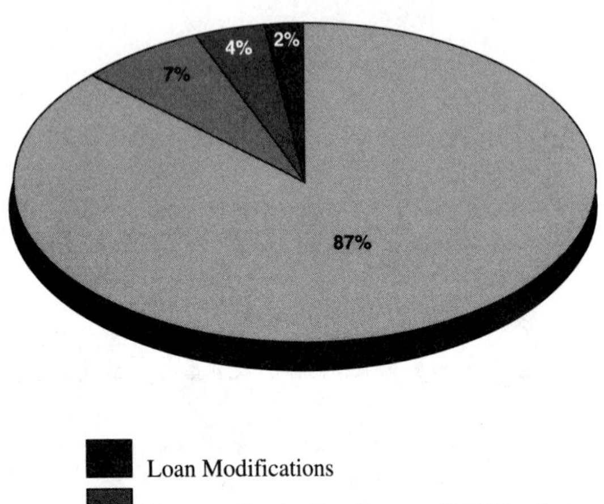

Loan Modifications
Loans to Foreign Purchasers of U.S. Products
Administrative Expenses
Guaranteeing Loans

ages the interactions of the many Ex-Im Bank offices and their personnel.

The bank's programs are carried out through numerous offices, the most significant of which is the Export Finance Group, which provides direct credit loans, bank or major financial institution guarantee of repayment, and export insurance against repayment to foreign and domestic obligors (organizations that have taken out loans). Another important office, Process Development, assists both domestic and international businesses in developing their own export programs, independent of subsidy. Because the Ex-Im Bank receives thousands of applications each year and must manage all documents relevant to these applications, a separate Office of Information Management and Technology plays an important role in the agency's operations.

Functions designed to serve specific agency goals are carried out by a number of separate offices, including the Office of Congressional and External Affairs, the Office of Broker Relations and Product Development, the Office of Country Risk Analysis, and the Office of Administrative and Management Services.

PRIMARY FUNCTIONS

The activities of the Ex-Im Bank are varied and diverse but can be grouped under four broad areas of export financing: working capital guarantees, export credit insurance, loan guarantees, and direct loans. By extending working capital guarantees to lenders, the Ex-Im Bank provides creditworthy small- and medium-sized businesses with the capital they need to buy, build, or produce products for export sale. The Ex-Im Bank also provides credit insurance to U.S. exporters in order to protect them against the risks of a foreign buyer defaulting on payment.

One of the Ex-Im Bank's most important functions is the provision of loan guarantees. By protecting private U.S. lenders against the risk of nonpayment, loan guarantees encourage more U.S. sales to foreign buyers. On a smaller scale, the bank also provides direct loans to foreign buyers to provide financing for their purchases from U.S. exporters. Under the amended Export-Import Bank Act, the agency may lend at rates that are competitive with foreign export credit agencies, but it may not compete with commercial lenders within the United States.

PROGRAMS

The Ex-Im Bank implements many different programs designed to promote economic growth through exports. Some programs are broadly applied and fundamental to the agency's mission; for example, the Export Credit Insurance Program helps U.S. exporters develop and expand overseas sales by protecting them against a possible loss if a foreign buyer or debtor defaults on payment for political or commercial reasons. The Medium and Long Term Loan Program is a foreign buyer credit program; the Ex-Im Bank establishes a credit and repayment schedule by reaching a credit agreement with a foreign buyer, and the disbursements go directly to the U.S. exporter.

Among these broad programs are smaller programs designed to serve specific groups, especially small businesses. The Working Capital Guarantee Program assists small businesses in acquiring working capital to fund their export activities. The program guarantees 90 percent of the principal and interest on loans extended by commercial lenders to eligible U.S. exporters. The Ex-Im Bank has also established an Environmental Exports Program which increases the level of support it provides to exporters of environmentally beneficial goods and services as well as to exporters participating in foreign environmentally beneficial projects. The program grants a special level of support to exporters in conjunction with either the Insurance Program or with loan and guarantee programs. Other specialty Ex-Im Bank programs include Aircraft Finance and Engineering Finance.

BUDGET INFORMATION

About half of the Export-Import Bank's budget is supplied by collections from its loan accounts; the other half is provided through congressional appropriation of tax revenues. In 1997 the Ex-Im Bank's total spending authority was about $980 million, but about $300 million of that was "unobligated," or placed in reserve for possible future loans. Of the $680 million spent by the Ex-Im Bank, by far the largest portion—87 percent—was spent on guaranteeing loans made by private-sector banks to foreign purchasers of U.S. products, or on guaranteed loans to U.S. producers seeking to enter export markets. 7 percent of the budget was spent on administrative expenses; 4 percent on direct loans to foreign purchasers of U.S. products, and a little under 2 percent on loan modifications such as refinancing.

FAST FACTS

The Ex-Im Bank estimates that it supported more than $15 billion in U.S. exports in 1997.

(Source: Export-Import Bank. "1997 Annual Report," 1997.)

HISTORY

The Export-Import Bank of Washington, predecessor to the Export-Import Bank of the United States, was inspired by the economic conditions of the 1930s when exports were seen as a stimulus to economic activity—a desperately needed stimulus for the economy of the Great Depression. Initially the bank was intended to be a trade-oriented by-product of U.S. recognition of the new Soviet Union. Loans were never made to the Soviet Union due to unsettled debts, however, and the Ex-Im Bank extended its operations to other international markets. The rationale behind the bank's existence was the failure of private-sector banks to sustain the financing needs of export trade and the uneven competition created by the export financing programs of foreign nations. Before World War II (1939–45), the bank operated with little controversy.

Under wartime conditions, Congress greatly expanded the Ex-Im Bank's lending authority to support the governments and banks that were negatively affected by the war effort. After the war the need for international economic assistance, especially involving the reconstruction of Europe and Japan, became the driving force behind the Ex-Im Bank's mission. The bank's legal status had to be altered somewhat to fit this mission; its proposed role became to serve as a principal instrument for implementing the post-war economic policy of the United States. The Export-Import Bank Act of 1945 established the bank as a permanent statutory agency, providing the basic framework for the Ex-Im Bank of today.

Changing Finance Needs

In 1954 members of the public and the U.S. Senate began to question whether the Ex-Im Bank's focus should turn from foreign aid to direct export financing for U.S. manufacturers. Under a reorganization plan initiated by President Dwight D. Eisenhower, the bank's programs became more trade-oriented. During the administration of John F. Kennedy, the bank's emphasis became the maximization of favorable trade balances with foreign nations. President Kennedy directed the president of the Ex-Im Bank to design a new program that would place U.S. exporters on a basis of full equality with their foreign competitors. The bank was eventually reorganized to meet this demand.

In 1968 the bank's name was officially changed to the Export-Import Bank of the United States. In the context of the Vietnam War (1959–75), the Export-Import Bank Act was amended to place foreign policy-based limitations on the lending practices of the bank. Generally, financial support for any exports to Communist or enemy countries, or defense articles or services to underdeveloped countries, were prohibited. Other 1968 amendments, however, further increased the bank's trade promotion capabilities by authorizing up to $500 million in lending and credit authority at any one time. By the end of President Lyndon Johnson's administration, the Ex-Im Bank was on the verge of its modern role in which it would increasingly respond to growing exports from major industrial competitors such as Japan and Europe.

The Modern Era

The Nixon and Carter administrations oversaw an Ex-Im Bank that was increasingly active in trade promotion with expanding programs and lending authority. During this period expenditures for program activities expanded to five times their 1969 rate, but the bank's net income dropped sharply—the low interest rates at which the bank financed its loan programs were lowering its profits. Under 12 years of the conservative leadership of Presidents Ronald Reagan and George Bush, the programs of the Ex-Im Bank were strongly criticized as unjustified expenditures of taxpayers' money, given the increasingly negative relationship between lending authority and net income. The Ex-Im Bank's programs were seen as entitlement programs for private businesses, a concept rejected by both administrations.

The Clinton administration brought the Ex-Im Bank back to life, however; the bank was a key component of the president's National Export Strategy (NES), an aggressive effort at capturing foreign markets in a rapidly growing global economy. Under the NES, the Ex-Im Bank assisted exporters in their effort to target big emerging markets and business sectors worldwide. The policies of the NES granted the Ex-Im Bank the greatest program authority in its history.

CURRENT POLITICAL ISSUES

The Ex-Im Bank was created during the Depression, a time of dire economic need for U.S. businesses, and the stimulus it provided proved useful for the nation's business interests. During the Reagan administration the programs of the Ex-Im Bank were criticized by members of U.S. political and business communities, who believed that a Depression-era agency designed to provide economic stimulus was no longer needed. This criticism continued throughout a period in American politics marked by ongoing criticism of wasteful government spending.

In the summer of 1997 a number of conservative and liberal Ex-Im Bank critics began a movement to refuse the renewal of the Ex-Im Bank's charter, effectively ending its programs. In order to make their case the bank's critics attacked two of the main arguments posed by the Ex-Im Bank and its supporters: that the bank is necessary for providing support in instances of "market failure," (filling the gap when the private market does not provide services similar to Ex-Im Bank's), and that it counteracts subsidized export finance activities of foreign competitors.

"Market Failure"

The Ex-Im Bank provides services and loans to countries or projects when the private market will not. Critics argue that there are usually good reasons why the private market will not provide loans or guarantees in such cases, and the Ex-Im Bank should heed these warnings about risky investments. They also point out that many of the companies subsidized by Ex-Im Bank programs are not in danger of failure and could easily provide the means for foreign investment by themselves. In 1997 the bank approved $500 million of financing for gas field development projects in the Arab nation of Qatar that would benefit, among other U.S. contractors, Mobil Corporation, one of the wealthiest corporations in the world.

The most serious attack on the "market failure" argument is that the Ex-Im Bank often works to delay the development of foreign markets rather than promote them. In the early 1990s, the bank approved a $5.6 billion loan to Mexico's state-owned oil monopoly, PeMex. Because of PeMex's immense power, the Mexican government has been reluctant to open up the oil market to competition, and the Ex-Im Bank's loan was denounced by Mexican economists as a move designed to prevent real market reform in Mexico.

Counteracting Competition

Supporters of the Ex-Im Bank also argue that the bank's programs serve to level the playing field in international markets. Foreign governments are subsidizing the competition of U.S. companies, they say, and the support provided by the Ex-Im Bank's programs enables U.S. businesses to keep up. Critics point out that there are in fact lessons to be learned from these competitors—in Western European countries, which have for many years supported their exports at levels higher than in the United States, unemployment is nearly twice as high as in the United States, and the governments are experiencing structural problems brought on by years of regulatory and welfare policies. The argument that exports produce jobs does not appear to be true in these countries, especially in the public sector.

It is also worth noting, critics say, that while the agency is fond of pointing out that 80 percent of its individual transactions involve small businesses, by far most of the Ex-Im Bank's actual funds are used to benefit large, politically powerful corporations such as Boeing, Motorola, and AT&T—companies that have abundant resources for exporting their products, even in the face of fierce competition. In most cases the playing field already appears favorable for U.S. businesses, and for many critics, the Ex-Im Bank should save tax money by withdrawing support from already prosperous corporations.

SUCCESSES AND FAILURES

One of the Ex-Im Bank's clearest successes involves the loss rate involved in its loans, or the amount of principal and interest that the bank fails to recover in a given year. Since 1980 the Ex-Im Bank's loan loss ratio has been about 1.9 percent. From 1984 to 1995 U.S.-insured commercial banks experienced a 6 percent loss rate on loans extended to foreign governments and a 3.3 percent rate on loans to individuals under credit card plans.

FUTURE DIRECTIONS

In response to critics who call for nonrenewal of the agency's charter, the Ex-Im Bank hopes to further develop its program assistance to small- and medium-sized exporters in the United States. The Ex-Im Bank claims its efforts in this area are a great success, noting that more than 80 percent of its transactions currently involve small businesses. In reality, this percentage accounts for only about 20 percent of the total dollar volume of all the Ex-Im Bank's financing—meaning that 80 percent of the bank's financing goes to a relatively small number of large corporations. In the future additional assistance to small businesses will be top priority for the Ex-Im Bank.

AGENCY RESOURCES

The Ex-Im Bank's Web site at http://www.exim.gov contains a list of multiple links to other sites useful for those seeking further information about trade, exports, finance, business, government bodies, and international organizations. For further information about the Ex-Im Bank, contact the International Business Development Office at 1-800-565-3946.

AGENCY PUBLICATIONS

Ex-Im Bank publications consist primarily of informative booklets or pamphlets that are grouped by program area. Titles include the "Services for Small Businesses Fact Sheet," the "Ex-Im Bank User's Guide Order Form," "Environmental Exports Program," and "A New Approach to Project Finance." Copies of these publications can be downloaded from the Ex-Im Bank's Web site at http://www.exim.gov. For more information about publications, contact the Business Development Group at 1-800-565-3914.

BIBLIOGRAPHY

Andelman, David. "America's Financier to the World." *Management Review*, October 1994, pp. 29–31.

Baron, David P. *The Export-Import Bank: An Economic Analysis*. New York: Academic Press, 1983.

Chimerine, Lawrence. "Don't Quench the Export Fire." *New York Times*, 27 April 1997, p. F12.

Feinberg, Richard E. *Subsidizing Success: The Export-Import Bank in the U.S. Economy*. New York: Cambridge University Press, 1982.

Greider, William. "The Ex-Im Files: How the Taxpayer-Funded Export-Import Bank Helps Ship Jobs Overseas." *Rolling Stone*, 8 August 1996, pp. 51–57.

Hillman, Jordan Jay. *The Export-Import Bank at Work: Promotional Financing in the Public Sector*. Westport, Conn.: Quorum Books, 1982.

Maynard, Roberta. "Ex-Im Bank Debuts Loan Guarantee Program." *Nation's Business*, November 1996, p. 10.

Mehta, Stephanie N. "Export-Import Bank, Meeting Criticism, Acts to Give More Help to Small Firms." *The Wall Street Journal*, 8 February 1996, p. B2.

Rodriguez, Rita, ed. *The Export-Import Bank at Fifty : The International Environment and the Institution's Role*. Lexington, Mass.: Lexington Books, 1987.

Stern, Paula. "Reorganizing Government for Economic Growth and Efficiency." *Issues in Science and Technology*, Summer 1996, pp. 67–73.

Farm Credit Administration (FCA)

PARENT ORGANIZATION: Independent
ESTABLISHED: 1933
EMPLOYEES: 318 (1999)

Contact Information:

ADDRESS: 1501 Farm Credit Dr.
McLean, VA 22102-5090
PHONE: (703) 883-4000
TDD (HEARING IMPAIRED): (703) 883-4444
FAX: (703) 790-3260
E-MAIL: info-line@fca.gov
URL: http://www.fca.gov
CHAIRMAN: Marsha Pyle Martin

WHAT IS ITS MISSION?

The mission of the Farm Credit Association (FCA) is to assure the reliability and solvency of the Farm Credit System (FCS) and the various farm credit securities, for borrowers and investors alike. This mission reflects the government's responsibility of insuring the financial stability of the agricultural sector of the economy.

HOW IS IT STRUCTURED?

The FCA is an independent agency consisting of a three-member board. Each member is appointed by the president, with Senate approval; no more than two members may be from the same political party. Each serves a single, staggered six-year term. One member is designated, by the president, to be chairperson and CEO. FCA board members also serve on the Farm Credit System Insurance Corporation (FCSIC) board, however the FCA chair may not head the FCSIC.

The FCA, headquartered in McLean, Virginia, maintains a field office in Bloomington, Minnesota; Dallas, Texas; Denver, Colorado; and Sacramento, California. The FCS also operates cooperatives and other financial institutions, self-regulatory bodies, and trade associations under the authority of six farm credit banks. Each district's Farm Credit Bank oversees four types of financial institutions: federal land bank associations, production credit associations, agricultural credit associations, and federal land credit associations. Additionally there is a Bank for Cooperatives and an Agricultural Credit Bank. FCS peripheral corporations, also under the regulation of the FCA, provide a variety of services to these banks.

Only the Farm Credit Corporation (FCC) operates independently of the FCA. The FCC is a trade association that represents lending institutions and protects the cooperative interest of farmers at the national and district levels. Accordingly, it turns to the FCA to work with Congress on behalf of the agricultural community, and the FCA regulates FCC member institutions.

The FCA staff is organized into seven divisions: the Office of Examination, the Office of Congressional and Public Affairs, the Office of Policy and Analysis, the Office of General Counsel, the Office of Inspector General, the Office of Resources Management, and the Office of Secondary Market Oversight.

The Office of Policy and Analysis performs risk analysis for FCS lending and develops policies and regulations accordingly. Similarly the office evaluates the FCA's ability to perform its function. The Office of Examination monitors FCS financial institutions to insure they remain financially solvent and capable of providing services as chartered.

The Office of Secondary Market Oversight oversees the Federal Agricultural Mortgage Corporation known as Farmer Mac, a secondary market for real estate loan securities. Unlike treasury bonds and other government securities, Farmer Mac securities are not backed by the U.S. government. Accordingly, this office performs risk-based analysis and oversight management.

The FCA Office of Resources Management provides internal administrative support and staff in key areas: payroll, personnel, budgeting, communications, procurement, document processing, and information technology. The Office of Inspector General is an internal auditor that operates independently in investigating FCA operations and programs. This office assesses the economic impact of FCA actions, keeping Congress apprised and making recommendations.

The Office of Congressional and Public Affairs handles communications between the Office of Inspector General and Congress and between the FCA and the public. This office also seeks public feedback concerning proposed legislation and farm policies. Essentially the office funnels incoming and outgoing information, serving as a public relations arm of the FCA in addition to a Congressional liaison.

FCA interactions with government agencies are handled by the Office of General Counsel, which operates in conjunction with the Department of Justice specifically to provide legal resources and inter-agency services for the FCA in matters involving the U.S. Department of Agriculture (USDA) and other federal agencies. The Office of General Counsel also mediates legal and policy disputes affecting FCA policy enforcement.

FAST FACTS

In 1996 Farm Credit Leasing, a member corporation of the farm credit system that leases equipment to rural cooperatives and producers, was rated the eighth-largest independent leasing company in the United States.

(Source: Farm Credit Administration. "About Farm Credit Leasing," 1997.)

PRIMARY FUNCTIONS

The FCA is the independent federal regulator of the Farm Credit System (FCS), a self-sustaining agricultural lending organization. The FCA is responsible for the efficient operation and financial reliability of the Farm Credit System and its individual entities. This puts the FCA in a position of responsibility for the reliable performance of a multitude of banking corporations, each with a specialized function.

The FCA first of all is responsible for the solvency of the 48 federal land banks associations (FLBAs), which provide farmers with access to 40-year amortized loans. As borrowers repay loans, the FLBAs continually reinvest the returns into the stock of the local lending associations. This creates a system whereby farmers who borrow acquire cooperative ownership in the regional farm credit banks.

In addition to FLBAs, the FCA regulates 31 federal land credit associations (FLCAs) plus dozens of production credit associations (PCAs) and agricultural credit associations (ACAs). FLCAs make long-term non-real estate loans, while PCAs provide short-term credit. ACAs furnish loans of various duration, as needed. So while FCS banks and lending institutions furnish such credit to the agricultural community, the FCA is responsible for their solvency.

Several regulatory and evaluative functions help insure the solvency of the FCS and its member institutions. For example the FCA reviews and resolves legal issues, enforces statutes, creates and maintains charters for FCS lending institutions, and examines lenders. In doing so the FCA identifies and avoids excessive risk factors, conditions that imply financial instability.

The complex cash flow scheme of FCS farm securities illustrates the scope of responsibilities of the FCA as the regulating agency of the Farm Credit System. The origin of FCS funding is the FCBFC, the FCS fiscal agent in New York that obtains investment collateral for the FCS by selling securities to the public. This means the FCS raises money through the FCBFC when it allows the public to share in the profits from farm loans through the purchase of securities on the stock exchange, similar to the means by which corporations raise money by offering common stock to the public.

The FCS maintains a secondary securities corporation, Farmer Mac (the Federal Agricultural Mortgage Corporation), which guarantees payment on FCBFC securities by purchasing loans from FCS lenders and using the interest from the loans to fund new loans for agricultural borrowers. These new loans generate new capital, which is used to underwrite the original investment securities. The surplus, or profit, fuels the cash flow cycle and becomes the funding source for even more loans.

The FCA is accountable for the integrity and profitability of this securities operation as well as individual lenders within it. One safeguard is the Farm Credit System Financial Assistance Corporation (FCSFAC), which insures that government assistance funds, or "bail-out" capital, go into the FCS. It is a proactive investment entity that is also regulated by the FCA.

PROGRAMS

The FCA's key role as examiner of FCS institutions involves a comprehensive program of procedures, guidelines, and clear communication between regulator and lenders, an ongoing process of formal and informal communications with lenders and corporations. The FCA refers to this as "regulatory oversight." According to law all institutions are examined annually, except FLBAs which are examined every three years. Agency guidelines require appraisal of specific criteria: capital, asset quality, management, earnings, and liquidity. This criteria, called a CAMEL rating, encourages objective assessments.

The examination process includes a review of the lender's documents, such as meeting minutes of the lender's board of directors, business plans, memorandums and other correspondence, and financial reports. The FCA's risk-based approach requires that potential risk factors be pursued and documented, with follow-up investigation when warranted by circumstance.

The agency holds conferences and interviews with the board of the lending institution, during which the examiner identifies perceived and potential weaknesses that must be addressed in order to minimize risk factors. After completing the examination the examiner creates summary and conclusion documents. FCA examiners draw up a series of workpapers for every FCS institution under examination. These include off-site reports and other documentation, along with examination results. They are indexed and held on file by the FCA as part of the ongoing regulatory process required for each institution. Specific topics for documentation include past performance, FCA compliance assurance, work evaluation, institutional trends, and elaboration of perceived weaknesses of the institution.

The FCA's quality assurance program mandates persistent supervision of examiners, cross-referencing of documentation, scrupulous review of records for accuracy, adequacy, and content, and a final supervisory review of all matters. Specific areas of investigation are clearly defined by the FCA including, but not limited to, credit administration, loan portfolio management, review of assets, and allowance for loan losses.

BUDGET INFORMATION

In order for the FCA to keep pace with the ever changing farm economy, Congress budgets more than $30 million each year into a revolving fund to the FCA for administrative expenses. The FCA then levies assessments against the financial institutions within its authority. The money collected from assessments is then deposited into the revolving fund. In this manner the FCA maintains a self-funded operation at no expense to the U.S. taxpayer.

The FCA operating budget for 1999 was $35.9 million. Over 80 percent of the FCA funds for 1999 were allocated toward human resources (personnel costs) for risk identification activities and corrective actions. Less than 20 percent of the 1999 FCA budget went to regulatory activities and policy maintenance functions.

HISTORY

The Farm Credit Administration (FCA) was established in 1933 as a single source that links farm bureaus, organizations, legislative measures, and administrations. Farmers had formed cooperatives and alliances much earlier, helping themselves on a more local level through organizations like the Grange, the National Farmers' Alliance and Cooperative Union of America, and the Farmers' League. By the 1900s this "farm bloc" had matured into an impressive political force within the U.S. Congress, but during the early years of the twentieth century all legislative proposals supported by it were rejected. Government, too, had established an earlier resource for farmers, the Federal Farm Board. Born in 1929, the board was endowed with $500,000 as a revolving seed fund to finance loans to farming cooperatives and otherwise subsidize the farm economy. However the stock market crash of 1929 came soon after and brought on the Great Depression, which destroyed many farmers as well as the federal board.

Birth of FCA

By 1933 the Farm Board's accrued losses totalled more than $300,000—nearly depleting the revolving fund. New farm legislation was urgently needed, and with federal dollars at stake, the issue received immediate attention. The Agricultural Adjustment Act (AAA) of 1933 established the FCA to replace the financially-depressed Federal Farm Board and created the Commodity Credit Corporation (CCC) to issue subsidy loans to farmers on a collateral system based on surplus agricultural product. The AAA framework consisted of an independent FCA system of credit and collateral, investment of farm surplus, and payment of market subsidies by the government to farmers. These principles formed the rudiments of the modern farm credit system.

The depression conditions of the 1930s promoted the Bankhead-Jones Farm Tenancy Act (1937), which created the Farm Security Administration (FSA) under the USDA. The goal of the FSA was to increase land ownership among countless tenant farmers by funding low-interest 40-year mortgage plans for agricultural real estate. The FCA was then also placed under the jurisdiction of the USDA as a matter of convenience in 1939.

Although the value of farm goods rose predictably under the wartime economy, prices plummeted once again during the post-war years. The government responded with emergency and disaster relief programs, low-income mortgage services for tenant farmers, a dairy surplus buy-back program that eventually grew to be the School Milk Program, and "Food for Peace," which reduced the mounting surplus of farm goods by sending them to less-developed countries after they had been purchased by the government.

Farm Boom and Farm Bust

Beginning with the Farm Credit Act (1953), the FCA regained independence from the USDA, but it kept control of the FSA, which gradually emerged as a fully independent and cooperative organization owned by farmer-borrowers. The decades following saw an explosion of the farm economy. Contributing to the boom were farm credit policies, expanded over the years to allow for cheaper credit for the agricultural community, a response to the dramatic rise in the value of farmland. The farm credit boom was followed by a "bust," an economic crisis, during the 1980s. By 1984 the crisis became evident as farm credit institutions nationwide approached insolvency at an alarming rate, which farmer-bankers and Congress spent the next 14 years trying to resolve. A series of legislation passed during the late 1980s resulted in comprehensive restructuring of the farm credit system, primarily through consolidation. Between 1983 and 1998 the total number of credit institutions reduced by 77 percent. The total number of banks similarly declined.

Production credit associations and federal land credit associations were combined into more efficient agricultural credit associations that could lower costs. The 12 banks for cooperatives were merged into the lone National Bank for Cooperatives, and other banks merged to create CoBank (Agricultural Credit Bank), which operates internationally. Federal land banks and federal intermediate credit banks, the original farm credit institutions, were consolidated into 6 farm credit banks. After years of government funding and restructuring of the FCS, the farm credit crisis was declared over in spring of 1998 by FCA Chairwoman Marsha Pyle Martin.

CURRENT POLITICAL ISSUES

During the latter half of the twentieth century, large non-farming corporations bought farm land at an alarming rate for the main purpose of *not* farming the land in order to reap federal soil conservation subsidies. These affluent non-agricultural industrial organizations succeeded further in transforming very minimal amounts of acreage into thriving crop harvests through the use of high technology and costly automated farming machinery. The extensive use of automation led to devastating repercussions and rampant unemployment in the farm labor market throughout the United States. What was worse was that control over agricultural product supply, the goal of soil conservation programs, was over time redirected into the hands of food processing companies and others in the food distribution channels. This seriously impacted the small, private farmers who were increasingly unable to compete.

Case Study: The Farm Credit Crisis

In mid-1983, with 37 banks in the farm credit system and more than $80 billion in outstanding loans, the competency of the FCA grew suspect because it had an unusually low rate of loss on loans—less than one-half of one percent. Congressional critics maintained that the low rates were not the result of prudent business practice, but were rather due to sluggish lending practices. The FCA responded by extending greater credit than ever before. However the credit was based on inflated land valuations resulting from soil conservation programs, which skewed the appraised value of unused land. By the mid-1980s the FCS was experiencing excessive loan defaults from small farmers. What appeared on paper to be an agricultural boom, was in reality a fragile farm credit structure, ready to collapse at any time. But few paid heed because the FCS, completely solvent since 1968, appeared to be running more smoothly than ever.

Early in 1985 a series of reports affirmed that the FCS was indeed in serious financial trouble. The losses from loan defaults had mounted, and by late September the Louisville district went public with a request for financial assistance from the government. The Louisville district was only one example. Several institutions throughout the nation were believed to be on the brink of collapse.

The administration in Washington was slow to respond. The FCS was thought to have billions in collateral, and any government farm credit "bail-out" would require use of federal tax dollars. In reality, however, the FCS was financially helpless, with most of its collateral in land holdings that would not bring their appraised values if sold for liquidation. Congress pressured the FCS to consolidate its credit institutions in order to reduce overhead, and to privatize farm credit. Farmers' cooperatives and the FCA fought these recommendations for fear of losing local autonomy and independence. To a large extent the non-agricultural population remained passive over the crisis. Some saw it as a fair outcome for farmers who had been receiving government payments for not working their land.

But as despair ran rampant throughout the agricultural community, Congress eventually responded. Key among the solutions was the consolidation or "downsizing" of the farm credit system. The number of credit institutions declined by 77 percent between 1983 and 1998. The production credit associations and federal land bank associations were merged into agricultural credit associations. The 12 farm credit districts were reduced to 6. One National Bank for Cooperatives emerged from the consolidation of 12 banks for cooperatives. The federal intermediate credit banks and the federal land banks were consolidated into 6 farm credit banks.

The Farm Credit System Capital Corporation (FCSCC) was created in 1985 to provide government-backed technical and financial assistance to distressed institutions. The new Federal Agricultural Mortgage Corporation, known as Farmer Mac, was authorized under the Agricultural Credit Act (1987) as a secondary market to buy loans from lenders and resell the loans as securities in order to provide a source of new income for loan capital. Also, the Farm Credit System Insurance Corporation was established to insure farm securities against losses.

Over time the FCS repaid all government-sourced emergency capital infusions and the agency retained its independent cooperative status. By the first quarter of 1998 emergency conditions had ebbed to the point that the FCA publicly declared that the farm credit crisis was resolved. FCA Chairwoman Marsha Pyle Martin was quoted in the *Fort Worth Star-Telegram* as having said, "the system is in the best financial condition in its history."

FUTURE DIRECTIONS

The FCA looks to the future with specific hopes and concerns. In the wake of the farm credit crisis of the 1980s the agency aims to re-affirm its independence, specifically through the elimination of federal support by 2002. It may be impeded in this goal, however, since the farming population has decreased. Small farms are simply not successful ventures. An upward trend in land valuations poses a risk as well, as a high land valuation increases risk to lenders because land values in no way reflect profits.

FCA staff will be trained as capital markets experts and will devise initiatives to minimize loan risk among FCS institutions. These goals may be expedited as the FCA develops databases on CD-ROM for faster, more efficient access to information. This will improve risk analysis procedures for the FCA, and lenders and borrowers within the farm credit system.

AGENCY RESOURCES

For information on upcoming FCA events contact the FCA Office of Congressional and Public Affairs at (703) 883-4056 or E-mail info-line@fca.gov. A number of database series in the custody of the National Archives and Records Administration (NARA) provide a comprehensive information base regarding the history of agriculture in the United States. Available files include historical information concerning land use, research findings, corporate involvement, and rural population demographics. Many NARA-held database files are available for purchase; for further information or for documentation regarding available reference material, contact the Center for Electronic Records, National Archives at College Park, 8601 Adelphi Rd., College Park, MD 20740-6001; phone (301) 713-6645; fax (301) 713-6911; or E-mail cer@nara.gov.

Statutory information including FCA regulations, statutes, and board policies are published on the Internet by the FCA. Information is excerpted from Statutes-at-Large, U.S. Code, the Federal Register, and the Code of Federal Regulations. Access this site at http://www.fca.gov/handbook.nsf or E-mail reg-comm@fca.gov for further information.

AGENCY PUBLICATIONS

To obtain a copy of an FCA examiner's report, call (703) 883-4030, or E-mail burrj@fca.gov. The most recent semi-annual reports are posted on the Internet through links to the FCA home page at http://www.fca.gov/. For FCA Quarterly Reports, executive summaries, and other articles call (703) 883-4401. "Where Have All the Customers Gone?" is an FCA publication that discusses recent trends and offers insight into the recent drops in the farm credit market share. "The Director's Farm Credit System Institutions" is an FCA handbook for credit institution directors, and special reports, strategic plans, and updates on farm credit financial conditions are also available. For literature, write to the Farm

Credit Administration Office of Congressional and Public Affairs, 1501 Farm Credit Dr., McLean, VA 22102-5090, or call (703) 883-4056.

BIBLIOGRAPHY

Adams, Jane. *The Transformation of Rural Life: Southern Illinois, 1890–1990.* Chapel Hill: University of North Carolina Press, 1994.

Allen, Kristen, ed. *Agricultural Policies in a New Decade.* Washington, D.C.: Resources for the Future and National Planning Association, 1990.

Clarke, Sally H. *Regulation and the Revolution in United States Farm Productivity.* New York: Cambridge University Press, 1994.

Greene, Leonard M., Martin A. Luster, and Rael Jean Isaac. "Why Must Farms Use Migrant Labor?" *New York Times,* 3 June 1998, p. A26(N), A24(I).

Hansen, John Mark. *Gaining Access: Congress and the Farm Lobby: 1919–1981.* University of Chicago Press, 1991.

Luttrell, Clifton B. *The High Cost of Farm Welfare.* Washington, D.C.: Cato Institute, 1989.

Mann, Susan Archer. *Agrarian Capitalism in Theory and Practice.* University of North Carolina Press, 1990.

Silverstein, Kenneth. "Capital Needed for Rural Development." *American City & County,* June 1996, p. 10.

Slaybaugh, Douglas. *William I. Myers and the Modernization of American Agriculture.* Ames, Iowa: Iowa State University Press, 1996.

Sunbury, Ben. *The Fall of the Farm Credit Empire.* Ames, Iowa: Iowa State University Press, 1990.

Farm Service Agency (FSA)

PARENT ORGANIZATION: Department of Agriculture
ESTABLISHED: 1994
EMPLOYEES: 15,900

Contact Information:

ADDRESS: 1400 Independence Ave. SW
Washington, DC 20250
PHONE: (202) 720-5237
FAX: (202) 690-2828
URL: http://www.fsa.usda.gov
ADMINISTRATOR: Keith Kelly
ASSOCIATE ADMINISTRATOR: Randy Weber

WHAT IS ITS MISSION?

Although the programs and activities of the Farm Service Agency (FSA) of the U.S. Department of Agriculture (USDA) are numerous and varied, its missions remain relatively focused. The FSA seeks to stabilize the income of American farmers, to help farmers conserve land and water resources, and to provide credit to new or disadvantaged farmers and ranchers.

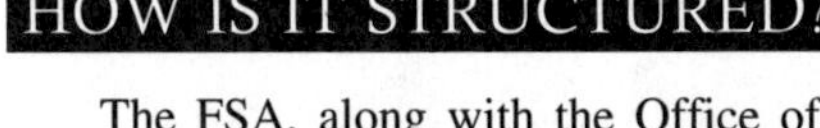

HOW IS IT STRUCTURED?

The FSA, along with the Office of Risk Management and the Foreign Agricultural Service, is an agency within the Farm and Foreign Agricultural Services (FFAS) mission area of the Department of Agriculture. The administrator of the FSA reports to the FFAS undersecretary. The administrator's staff includes several offices that assist with policy making, administration, and communications: the Executive Secretariat, Civil Rights and Small Business Utilization, Legislative Liaison, Public Affairs, and Economic and Policy Analysis.

FSA operations are divided among five different areas of operation, each of which is led by a deputy administrator. The management unit handles the budgeting, financial management, personnel, and information technology needs of the entire agency. Because FSA operations are carried out through individual states, an important operating unit within the FSA is Program Delivery and Field Operations. All state, area, and county offices are included in this unit. In each state, operations are supervised by a state committee of three to five members. In each of approximately 2,500 agricultural counties in the United States, a county committee of three farmers is responsible for local administration.

Responsibility for FSA programs is divided among the remaining three operating units: Farm Programs, Farm Loans, and Commodity Operations. Farm Programs include emergency assistance to farmers, price-support programs, and conservation and environmental programs.

The FSA works closely with another government agency, the Commodity Credit Corporation (CCC), which is responsible for gathering and distributing surplus agricultural commodities, such as corn, wheat, cotton, and honey, in the United States. The CCC finances the conservation and commodity programs of the FSA. Commodity operations are conducted through the FSA's Kansas City Commodity Office, which seeks to stabilize commodity prices through commodity loans, direct purchases of commodities, and payments to eligible producers. For most commodities, loans and payments are made directly to producers on the unprocessed commodity through the FSA's county offices.

PRIMARY FUNCTIONS

The FSA administers farm commodity stabilization and resource conservation programs and makes loans through a network of state and county offices. For the FSA's commodity stabilization programs, the agency provides the operating personnel to the CCC, which supports the prices of some agricultural commodities through loans and purchases. Farmers are provided with interim financing, which helps maintain balanced and sufficient supplies of farm commodities throughout the year. For most commodities, loans and payments are made directly to producers on the unprocessed commodity through the FSA's county offices. The CCC also supports prices by buying surplus items at announced prices to be stored for distribution as part of the USDA's emergency, international food aid, or domestic food aid programs.

The FSA offers direct and guaranteed farm ownership and operating loan programs to farmers who are temporarily unable to secure private commercial credit. In many cases these are beginning farmers who do not have the net worth to qualify for credit. Farmers who qualify obtain their credit by having the FSA guarantee up to 90 percent repayment to the commercial lender. If the farmer cannot even qualify for a loan guarantee, the FSA makes direct loans. These loans are made and serviced by an FSA official who provides credit counseling and supervision to direct borrowers by evaluating the farming operation.

To help preserve and improve the wealth and promise of American farmlands, the FSA also conducts conservation programs designed to provide incentives for farmers to restore and protect the nation's land and water resources.

PROGRAMS

The FSA conducts many different programs in each of its mission areas. The Farm Ownership Loans program, targeting beginning farmers, is available to all beginning farmers who meet eligibility requirements.

The most significant conservation program conducted by the FSA is the Conservation Reserve Program (CRP), a joint effort with the USDA's National Resources Conservation Service (NRCS). The CRP aims to save the nation's most fragile farmlands by encouraging farmers to stop growing crops on highly erodible and other environmentally sensitive land. After planting a permanent vegetative cover, the farmer is paid an annual rental payment by the USDA.

The most varied FSA programs are the commodity stabilization programs, which involve different terms and conditions for each commodity area. Generally they are intended to ensure adequate supplies of the commodities, allow for changes in the cost of production, and ensure a level of farm income to maintain productive capacity sufficient to meet future needs. The Dairy Price Support Program, for example, establishes a "support price" for dairy commodities, and then authorizes the purchase of surpluses at that price by the CCC. In the future the program will also provide for a "recourse loan program" to be available to commercial processors of eligible dairy products to ensure price stability and guarantee stable inventories.

BUDGET INFORMATION

The FSA budget, a component of the USDA budget, is funded partly through congressional appropriation, but its commodity programs and conservation programs are funded through the Commodity Credit Corporation. The projected 1999 FSA budget is approximately $20 billion. Of this $20 billion, 72 percent of the budget is for commodity programs, 14 percent is for farm credit programs, and 9 percent is for conservation programs.

HISTORY

Government assistance to farmers dates back to before 1900 in the United States, but the first focused effort took root during the Great Depression of the 1930s, when farm poverty, especially that of the tenant class, received a great deal of attention. The Agricultural Adjustment Administration (AAA), created by legisla-

BUDGET:

Farm Service Agency

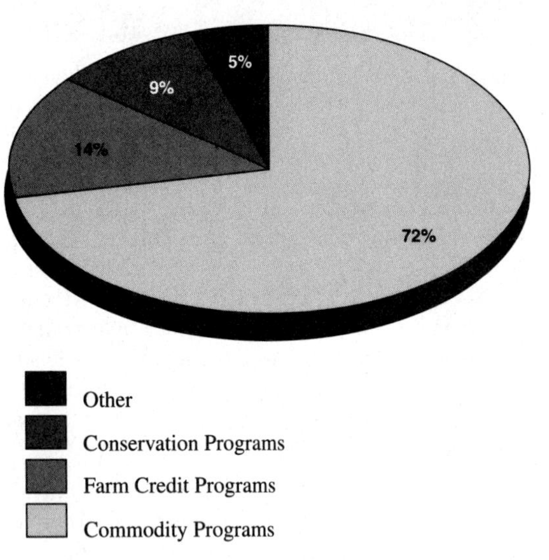

tion in 1933, established the state and county administrative structure used by present-day farm programs. The AAA was built around two major program divisions: the Division of Production and the Division of Processing and Marketing.

In July 1937 Congress passed the Bankhead-Jones Act, which authorized federal loans to farm tenants for the purpose of buying farmland. To administer these loans, Secretary of Agriculture Henry A. Wallace established an agency known as the Farm Security Agency, which, by employing such unusual programs as cooperative living arrangements and medical cooperatives, would prove to be one of the USDA's most politically controversial agencies.

The AAA was amended in 1938 to revise certain production and marketing provisions of the original legislation, and a general reorganization of the USDA was executed that fall. In addition, 1938 introduced complex changes in conservation, crop support, and marketing legislation. Through the various agencies created by these new laws, the federal government became the primary decision maker for U.S. farmers.

After the Japanese attack on Pearl Harbor in 1941, the War Food Administration (WFA) was organized to meet the increased food needs. The WFA reorganization grouped production, supply, and marketing authorities under a central agency that coordinated the flow of basic commodities. The WFA was disbanded after the war and its field services were maintained by the Production and Marketing Administration.

Peace-time production levels proved to be nearly as difficult to handle as those of the war effort, however. The overproduction of certain commodities threatened to cause dramatic drops in farm income levels. The increased food needs of war-torn foreign countries helped absorb some of the surplus, but oversupply continued to be a problem. In 1953 a dramatic USDA reorganization made further changes in the powers and duties of the price support and supply management agency. Now called the Commodity Stabilization Service (CSS), the new agency operated with an increased emphasis on farm income. Conservation programs were initiated, among them the first programs involving taking land out of production for prescribed periods of time. In 1961 the agency was renamed the Agricultural Stabilization and Conservation Service (ASCS).

It was also during this time that the Farm Security Administration was disbanded and replaced by the Farmers Home Administration (FMHA), a change legislated in 1946. The FMHA assumed responsibility for farm improvement loans, emergency assistance, and other forms of financial aid to farmers, but the radical cooperative arrangements instituted by the Farm Security Administration, always unpopular with political conservatives, were terminated.

It was not until 1994 that an attempt at centralizing the government's farm programs was carried out: the Consolidated Farm Service Agency was created by the secretary of agriculture in the fall of 1994 to assume several functions of the ASCS, the FMHA, and another agency, the Federal Crop Insurance Corporation (FCIC). In 1995 the name Farm Service Agency became official, and with the federal farm legislation of 1996, most of the functions that the FSA had assumed from the FCIC were once again reshuffled to a newly created USDA agency.

CURRENT POLITICAL ISSUES

Since the Great Depression, U.S. agricultural policy has attempted to keep farmers working and citizens fed through a number of assistance programs. Farm subsidies such as price supports, tariffs, and deficiency payments—direct cash payments made by the federal government to farmers when commodity prices fall below a fixed rate—were once targeted to a small number of underprivileged farmers. In recent years, however, because of the complex political processes involved, federal subsidy programs seem to have grown to favor a small number of wealthy, politically powerful leaders in agribusiness. Since 1986 farm subsidies have cost U.S. taxpayers a staggering $400 billion. In 1996 it was estimated that the median farm family earned about $2,000 a year more than the average nonfarm family.

The Federal Agricultural Improvement and Reform Act of 1996, popularly known as the 1996 Farm Bill, did

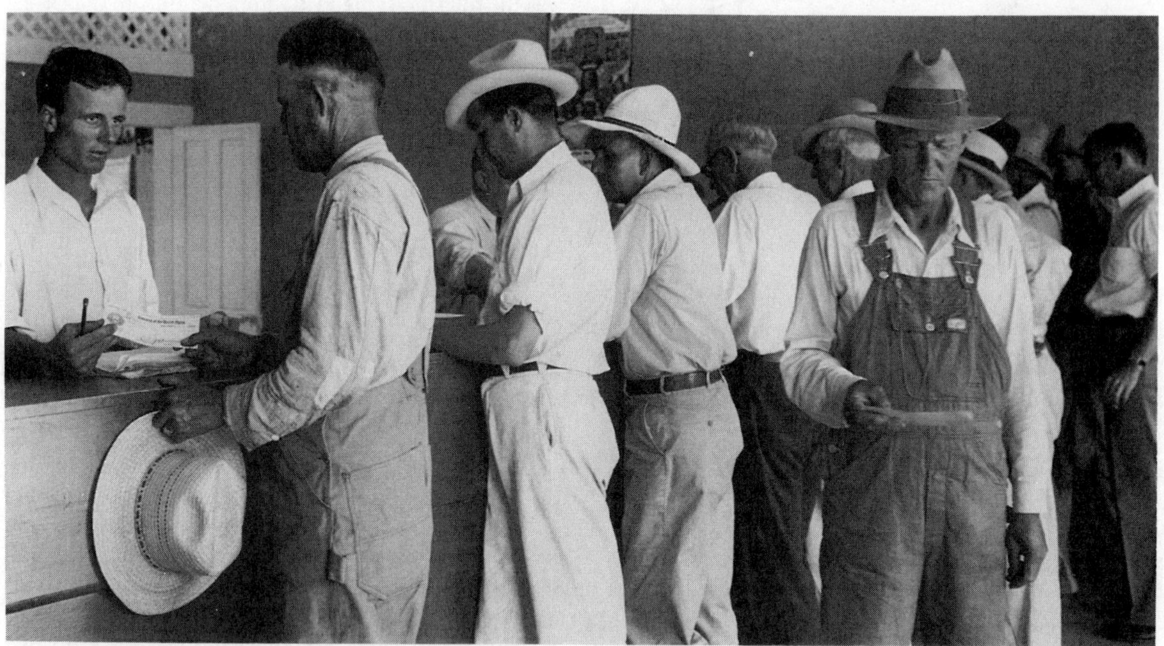

Texas farmers collect benefit checks from the Agricultural Adjustment Administration (AAA) during the Great Depression. The AAA was the direct forerunner of the modern FSA. (Photograph by George W. Ackerman. Corbis Corporation)

away with what many members of Congress and the public considered to be the most obnoxious use of taxpayers' money: deficiency payments. The new law was a long-awaited reform of a government assistance program that had grown outdated and increasingly expensive to the American public. But growers of some commodities—most notably sugar—were politically powerful enough to threaten the passage of the entire 1996 legislation as it was written and were therefore exempted from many of the bill's provisions. For the time being, these growers managed to escape the sweeping reforms that were provided by the bill.

Case Study: Sugar Subsidies

Sugar growers in the United States constitute one of the most powerful and well-funded industries in U.S. agriculture. By 1996 FSA loan programs for the sugar industry cost taxpayers about $120 million each year. Import restrictions on foreign sugar, an "indirect" type of subsidy, keep the price of sugar high—doubling it in 1996 from 11 cents per pound to more than 22 cents. The General Accounting Office estimates that this artificially inflated price costs U.S. consumers more than $1.4 billion each year.

As the 1996 Farm Bill was being discussed, sugar cane growers were unpopular for an additional reason: growers in Florida, many of them millionaires, had covered about 500,000 acres of swampland near Everglades National Park with crops. These growers diverted water that had been flowing into the Everglades to water their fields, dumping pesticides, herbicides, and phosphorus back into the water supply. The pollution created an algae bloom the size of Rhode Island in Florida Bay that is still seeping toward the Florida Keys to the Atlantic, where it is contributing to the destruction of vast stretches of North America's only coral reef.

For these reasons, it would have seemed clear that federal subsidy of the sugar industry would inevitably be discontinued as part of the 1996 Farm Bill. However, the sugar industry is a powerful lobbying group in Washington, and many in Congress feared losing a chance at reelection if the industry's support were withdrawn. The sugar industry was also supported by Midwestern corn and sugar beet growers, because high sugar prices would increase the demand for their alternative sweeteners. The entire bill was in danger of being brought down by these interests.

A solution of sorts was quickly introduced by Senator (and then presidential candidate) Bob Dole, who added a rider to the bill that appropriated $200 million for restoration of the Everglades and Florida Bay. The action seemed to conciliate aggressive reformers enough to pass the bill into law—without withdrawing the 60-year-old subsidy for sugar.

FAST FACTS

In 1995 it was estimated that farmers dump 40 billion pounds of fertilizer and 500 million pounds of pesticides on fields annually.

(Source: Jonathon Tolman. "Poisonous Runoff from Farm Subsidies." *Wall Street Journal*, September 8, 1995.)

SUCCESSES AND FAILURES

The 1996 Farm Bill brought about changes in the operation of the FSA that were passionately debated. Several reforms mandated by the bill were intended, at least in part, to remedy the unintended environmental consequences of FSA crop subsidies. For example, the FSA had reimbursed farmers for the difference between the market price of a given commodity and the government's guaranteed price, which was nearly always higher. Farmers were thus given an incentive to increase their production in order to increase their subsidies. To counteract the oversupply that might result from this program, the FSA required farmers participating in the program to set aside acreage not to be cultivated. The irony was this: farmers were being given an economic incentive by the FSA to maximize yields on fewer acres. They invariably did this by dumping tons of fertilizers and pesticides onto their producing lands. These chemicals ran off the lands during rains and eventually found their way into community water supplies.

Responding to estimates that eliminating farm subsidies such as these deficiency payments could result in a 35 percent reduction in pesticide use and a 29 percent reduction in fertilizer use per acre, the USDA and Congress decided to make some changes. Under the 1996 Farm Bill, the FSA removed this critical link between support payments and farm prices—but only for a limited number of specific commodities. Powerful lobbyists representing other commodities—sugar, for example—were able to exempt themselves from these new terms.

FUTURE DIRECTIONS

The 1996 Farm Bill has resulted in a reorganization and consolidation of various program areas involving the FSA. One of the most significant changes within the FSA was the transfer of the FCIC from the FSA to the Office of Risk Management. Although the FSA still has responsibility for emergency assistance to uninsured farmers who have experienced a catastrophic loss, the agency is in the process of transferring most of its crop insurance functions to the new office.

The new law will also gradually phase out price supports of certain commodities by removing the link between income support payments and farm prices (the difference between the government's guaranteed price and the actual market price of a given commodity). Instead of support payments, farmers may sign up to receive a series of "transition payments"—fixed amounts, paid out over a period of seven years, that will help them become independent of government subsidy.

The law also mandates budget restrictions that the USDA will have to act creatively to meet. Already, field offices of three USDA agencies—the FSA, Natural Resources Conservation Service (NRCS), and the Rural Development—have been combined into a network of one-stop USDA service centers. Nonfederal employees at these service centers numbered about 9,900 for the USDA's 1998 budget, but the law reduces that number to 4,900 by the year 2002. Obviously, one of the greatest challenges for the FSA is to come up with a way to deliver its programs with such limited resources.

For now, the FSA's plans include two objectives: to reach consensus with the leaders of the congressional and executive branches on issues involving the FSA's role in the delivery of agricultural production programs, and to assist the secretary of agriculture's study examining the FSA and the NRCS for further opportunities to coordinate and reduce the cost of delivering customer services.

AGENCY RESOURCES

For further information about the FSA and its programs, contact FSA Public Affairs, PO Box 2415, STOP 0506, Washington, DC 20013; phone (202) 720-5237. For information on commodity sales and purchases, contact the FSA Commodity Office, PO Box 419205, Kansas City, MO 64141; phone (816) 926-6364. Information on the FSA is also available at all county offices, which are usually listed in the governmental/public organization sections of telephone directories under U.S. Department of Agriculture, Farm Service Agency.

AGENCY PUBLICATIONS

FSA publications include lengthy reports such as *Agricultural Statistics 1995–1996* and *USDA, Farm Service Sweetener Market Data*. The agency also publishes a bimonthly publication, *FSA News*, that is primarily of interest to FSA employees. The publications likely to be most useful to the general public, however, are the background and fact sheets released by the agency, with titles such as "Commodities," "Dairy Indemnity Payment Program," "Feed Grains," and the "Conservation Reserve Program." Many of these are available for downloading at the FSA Web site, http://www.fsa.usda.gov. For further information about FSA publications, contact the public affairs staff at (202) 720-5237.

BIBLIOGRAPHY

Benenson, Bob. "Plan to Trim Agencies, Staff Clears its First Hurdle." *Congressional Quarterly Weekly Report*, 12 February 1994, pp. 325–26.

Bovard, James. *The Farm Fiasco*. San Francisco: ICS Press, 1989.

"Farm Service Agency: How Federal Farm Programs Operate." *Congressional Digest*, April 1996, pp. 99-101.

"The Farmbelt Breaks Free." *Economist*, 12 July 1997, pp. 21–2.

Greenwald, John. "Sugar's Sweetest Deal: The Landmark Farm Bill Left Sugar Subsidies Standing. Reformers Wonder What Went Wrong." *Time*, 8 April 1996, p. 34.

Hosansky, David. "Details of 1996 Farm Bill." *Congressional Quarterly Weekly Report*, 4 May 1996, p. 1243.

Luttrell, Clifton B. *The High Cost of Farm Welfare*. Washington, D.C.: Cato Institute, 1989.

Manning, Richard. "The Sweet Smell of Subsidies: The Grass May be Greener in Canada, but U.S. Farm Policy Spreads the Green Around." *Harper's*, April 1996, pp. 64–5.

"Not So Mad Cows." *New Republic*, 15 April 1996, p. 7.

Pippert, Paul. "A Glimpse at Farming Without Subsidies." *Successful Farming*, March 1996, p. 15D.

Porter, John, and Arlan Strangeland. "Should Congress End Sugar Subsidies? (Pro and Con)." *American Legion Magazine*, July 1988, p. 10.

Federal Aviation Administration (FAA)

PARENT ORGANIZATION: Department of Transportation
ESTABLISHED: August 1958
EMPLOYEES: 48,903 (1997)

Contact Information:

ADDRESS: 800 Independence Ave. SW
Washington, DC 20591
PHONE: (202) 267-8521
FAX: (202) 267-5039
URL: http://www.faa.gov
ADMINISTRATOR: Jane F. Garvey

WHAT IS ITS MISSION?

The mission of the Federal Aviation Administration (FAA), according to its published mission statement, is to provide "a safe, secure, and efficient global aerospace system that contributes to the national security and the promotion of U.S. aerospace safety." Safety is the FAA's main priority: its activities—regulation, inspection, certification, and air traffic control—are meant to make commercial and private civil aviation as safe as possible.

The FAA is also charged with the development of civil aeronautics. In addition, it is responsible for promoting a healthy environment through the implementation of air and noise pollution standards for the aerospace industry.

HOW IS IT STRUCTURED?

The FAA is a regulatory agency in the Department of Transportation. It is headed by an administrator who is appointed by the president and confirmed by the Senate. The FAA administrator serves a five-year term of office.

There are seven major departments, each headed by an associate administrator and responsible for a specific area of agency oversight or administration. They are Commercial Space Transportation, Airports, Civil Aviation Security, Regulation and Certification, Air Traffic Services, Research and Acquisitions, and Administration. These departments are further divided into smaller offices for various subspecialties.

In addition to general administrative responsibilities, the associate administrator for administration oversees the FAA's 10 major field organizations, which include nine regional offices and the Mike Monroney Aeronautical Center, the FAA's school for air traffic controllers in Oklahoma City, Oklahoma.

In 1997, 35,788 of the agency's 48,903 employees were involved in air traffic control to a certain degree. The next largest segment of the FAA's workforce was the 5,819 personnel engaged in regulation and certification.

PRIMARY FUNCTIONS

The FAA performs several vital functions in the exercise of its mission. It is responsible for operating and maintaining the nation's air traffic control (ATC) system; for regulating all areas of civil aviation and for enforcing compliance with its rules and regulations; for ensuring the security of the civil aviation system, including its aircraft, airports, and the airways; for safeguarding the environment; and finally, for overseeing a program of research and development to make the U.S. system one of the world's most technologically advanced.

Air Traffic Control

The FAA's first and most important duty is the operation, maintenance, and regulation of the nation's air traffic control (ATC) system. One component of this system is a nationwide web of navigational aids that enables pilots to find airports and land, even when weather is particularly bad. A second component of the ATC is the men and women who are air traffic controllers. Aided by radar and sophisticated computer programs, air traffic controllers are the traffic directors of the air. They control the number of planes in the air at a particular time as well as the movements of aircraft in the air and on the ground. The FAA has divided the ATC into distinct areas of responsibility. Different groups of controllers are responsible for aircraft on the ground, in the airspace over an airport, and en route between airports. As aircraft leave one area of control and enter another, they are "handed off " to the next controller.

Certification

The FAA is the main regulatory agency for the U.S. aviation industry. Its rules and regulations extend into every area of civil flight in the country. All pilots and aircraft mechanics must be certified by the FAA. Pilot certificates specify what type of plane a pilot may fly, which types of airports may be used, how many passengers may be carried, how far a pilot may fly from the home airport, and whether the pilot may fly under instrument as well as visual flight rules. The FAA certifies air traffic controllers as well and maintains a school for them, the FAA Academy in Oklahoma City, Oklahoma.

FAA regulations require that all aircraft built and flown in the United States meet specific construction, maintenance, and safety standards. All new aircraft designs are tested while they are in prototype; manufacturing processes, together with quality control standards, must be approved; finally, individual aircraft are issued an airworthiness certificate. Once aircraft are built, the FAA requires that they meet specific maintenance schedules.

Security

Since the 1960s the FAA has been responsible for overseeing the security of airports and aircraft. Airports and airlines are required to meet specific security guidelines issued by the agency. Passengers and hand baggage, for example, must be screened before they are allowed on a plane. The Office for Aviation Research conducts research into advanced techniques for detecting explosives.

Other Functions

The FAA promulgates noise standards for aircraft, helps airports develop noise abatement plans, and works closely with the Environmental Protection Agency to cut pollution from aircraft engines. The FAA manages a fund that is used to make grants to localities for every phase of airport development: construction, design, lighting, firefighting, land acquisition, and so forth. The FAA has been a leader in providing training to aviation specialists from other nations. The agency has trained nearly eight thousand foreign aviation professionals. Through its research programs, the FAA looks for ways to improve air navigation; a recent advance uses satellite-based technologies. It also researches more accurate weather prediction, new flight technologies, and more effective ATC technologies.

PROGRAMS

The FAA's Airport Improvement Program has been in operation since 1983. Under its provisions, the agency provides grants-in-aid to public-use airports. The money can be used for a variety of purposes, such as construction, safety improvements, airport rescue and fire-fighting equipment purchases, noise abatement measures, land acquisition, and installation of lighting and navigational aids. A goal of the program is to ensure that future airport capacity meets the nation's needs. More than $2 billion was allocated to the program in fiscal year 1998.

The FAA is in the early stages of implementing a technology known as Global Positioning System (GPS), a satellite-based navigational aid that is expected to eliminate the need for ground radar. Under this project, which carries high priority at the agency, 24 satellites will provide pilots and air traffic controllers with a three-

BUDGET: *Federal Aviation Administration*

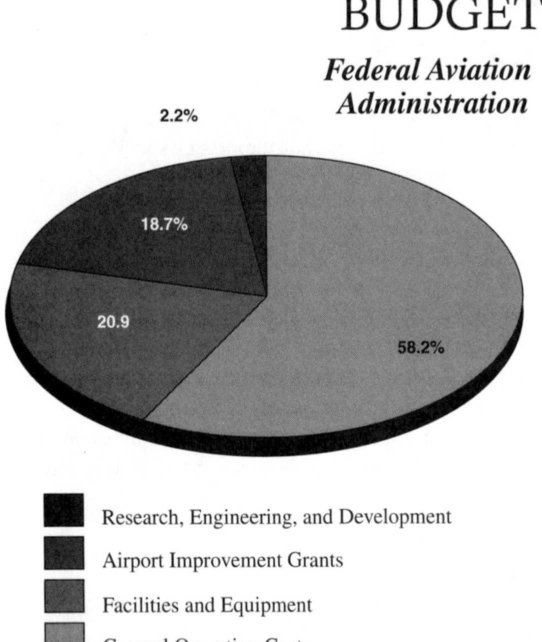

Research, Engineering, and Development
Airport Improvement Grants
Facilities and Equipment
General Operation Costs

dimensional picture of multiple aircraft in a specific U.S. airspace. Once in place, it is expected to improve American air traffic technology to a marked degree. In March 1996 a directive of President Bill Clinton established GPS as "a national utility."

The FAA has other programs to develop and deploy state-of-the-art weather prediction technology known as Doppler radar to warn pilots of inclement conditions; to research new ways to detect bombs and explosives at airports; and to modernize the agency's nearly obsolete air traffic control system through its Capital Investment Plan.

BUDGET INFORMATION

The total budget of the FAA for 1998 was $9.1 billion. The budget covers all FAA salaries, administration, research, and the national air traffic control system. General operation costs at the agency accounted for about $5.3 billion of the budget; this included funds for air traffic services and airspace safety. The next largest portion, about $1.9 billion, went to facilities and equipment. The rest was divided between airport improvement grants ($1.7 billion) and research, engineering, and development ($199 million).

About $3.4 billion was appropriated from general government funds; the remaining $5.7 billion came from the Airport and Airways Trust Fund. Monies in the fund come from a 10 percent tax that is imposed on all airline tickets sold in the United States. The tax is intended to make the FAA as self-supporting as possible. Under the law that established the fund, the use of its monies for specific purposes must first be approved by Congress. In 1997 the tax was extended for another 10 years.

HISTORY

Federal regulation of aviation has its origins in the Air Commerce Act of 1926. The act gave the Department of Commerce responsibility for the regulation of pilots and aircraft, for setting up a system of airways and navigational aids, and for fostering air commerce in general. The legislation was strongly backed by the infant aviation industry, which recognized the need for safety standards if it was to achieve its full commercial potential. The Aeronautics Branch was founded to carry out these new duties, with William P. MacCracken as its first head.

In its first decade, the Aeronautics Branch dealt with the fundamental issues of civil flight. It took over a program for the construction of lighted airports that the U.S. Postal Service had begun for its air mail service. Radio beacons were built to improve navigation, and radio communication with aircraft was developed. More important, as the number of planes in the sky increased, the first air traffic control system was organized by a group of airlines. In 1936 the Bureau of Air Commerce took over many of the ATC centers, adding new centers across the nation. At that time, air traffic control was in its primitive stage, relying on telephones, blackboards, little wooden markers pushed across maps, and "best estimates" of a plane's actual location in the air. The Aeronautics Branch was renamed the Bureau of Air Commerce in 1934.

In 1938 regulation of aviation was removed from the Commerce Department with the creation of the independent Civil Aeronautics Authority (CAA). Two years later responsibility for flight regulation was split between the CAA and the Civil Aeronautics Board (CAB). CAA was put in charge of air traffic control, certification, and safety enforcement; CAB was responsible for formulating safety regulations, for regulating commercial aviation, and for investigating accidents. When the split was made, both agencies were again put under the administration of the Commerce Department, but CAB answered directly to the president.

By the end of World War II (1939–45), aviation in the United States was undergoing major changes. The CAA had taken over most of the nation's ATC system. Radar promised to become an important tool for controlling airspace. ATC improvements were especially important. Between 1945 and 1955 passenger rates climbed from 6.7 million to 38 million. Congress, however, refused to appropriate money that would have enabled the FAA to upgrade its ATC system with radar.

Only after a series of midair collisions—the most catastrophic occurred over the Grand Canyon in 1956 when 128 people died—did Congress approve the funds for the modernization. By mid-1960 the introduction of radar was well under way.

Federal Aviation Act

The Federal Aviation Act of 1958 transferred the CAA's functions to a new, independent body called the Federal Aviation Agency (FAA), with Elwood Queseda, a retired air force general, as its first administrator. The act was meant to strengthen safety regulation by removing it from political and commercial influences. The act also gave the FAA responsibility for promoting air commerce in the United States.

In 1966 the Department of Transportation Act renamed the agency the Federal Aviation Administration and transferred it to the newly created Department of Transportation (DOT). The congressmen who had sponsored the FAA Act of 1958 maintained that depriving the agency of its independence was a step backward, that being in DOT would interfere with efficient regulation. Nonetheless, the law was passed more or less as originally drafted. With increasing concern over noise pollution and hijacking in the late 1960s, the agency was given responsibility for regulating noise abatement and security on aircraft and at airports.

The Airport and Airways Trust Fund was created in 1970 to finance technical improvements in the FAA's ATC and navigation system as well as improvements to the nation's airports. Money for the fund was derived from a surcharge levied on airline tickets. Approximately 75 percent of the agency's budget is drawn from this fund.

Deregulation

Automation of the FAA's air traffic control system continued during the 1970s as new radar and computer systems were installed. These changes came at an opportune time for travelers because two momentous events were about to occur in aviation. In 1978 Congress deregulated the airlines. Routes were no longer assigned to airlines; ticket prices were no longer regulated by the government; and the CAB ceased to exist. Deregulation resulted in the founding of several new airlines, the onset of price wars, and a dramtatic increase in the number of people who traveled by plane. The sudden growth placed a heavy strain on the FAA: there were more airlines, planes, and pilots to certify and many more planes occupying the same amount of airspace.

The Air Traffic Controllers Strike

These rapid, destabilizing changes occurred just before another critical event: a strike by the Professional Air Traffic Controllers Organization (PATCO). For months PATCO had been engaged in unsuccessful contract negotiations with the FAA. The union was trying to obtain better working conditions for air traffic controllers, primarily less overtime and better equipment. In August 1981, seven months after its contract expired, PATCO went on strike. President Ronald Reagan called the strike illegal under the Civil Service Reform Act and gave the controllers 48 hours to return to work or be fired. Most ignored the ultimatum, and Reagan fired 11,345 air traffic controllers out of about 16,200 then employed in U.S. civil aviation. The system was on the verge of collapse. The FAA struggled to fill the gap with nonstrikers, administrative personnel, military controllers, and retirees. Tight restrictions were placed on the frequency of flights; those restrictions lasted more than three years. It was not until after 1985 that the FAA had the ATC system operating at what it considered full capacity once again.

FAST FACTS

Jane Garvey is the first woman to head the Federal Aviation Administration and is the third administrator who does not fly.

(Source: *Aviation Week and Space Technology*, August 8, 1997.)

Attempts at Modernization

In the 1990s the FAA attempted unsuccessfully to modernize its outdated ATC system. After nearly 10 years, the National Airspace System Plan (NAS), which had been drawn up to provide for modernization, was abandoned and replaced in 1991 with the Aviation System Capital Investment Plan (CIP). Both plans had multibillion-dollar budgets, were poorly managed, and ultimately ran years behind schedule. The FAA fell under intense criticism from consumer groups and government officials in the mid-1990s, a situation that was exacerbated by a series of highly publicized airline crashes. The criticism peaked after the ValuJet crash in June 1996, and Anthony Broderick, the most powerful nonappointed FAA administrator, was forced to resign.

CURRENT POLITICAL ISSUES

The FAA has been the target of much criticism in recent years for a perceived lack of commitment to air safety. Critics have focused on the agency's core activities: the air traffic control system and the regulation of the airlines. They contend that the ATC system seems

FAST FACTS

The five busiest FAA airport traffic control towers in 1996, in descending order, were O'Hare International in Chicago, Dallas/Fort Worth International, Los Angeles International, Atlanta International, and Metropolitan Airport in Detroit.

(Source: Federal Aviation Administration. *FAA Administrators Fact Book*, 1998.)

---

somehow to resist the FAA's efforts or ability to modernize it, whereas deep-seated institutional forces in the FAA have made its regulatory work less than ideal.

Case Study: Modernizing Air Traffic Control

The nation's ATC computer technology is responsible for telling controllers what planes are in the airspace that the controller is monitoring, where those planes are located, and how fast they are flying. Most of these computers were installed in the 1960s and 1970s, and they have been upgraded very little in the intervening years. In an age when most computers are PCs that utilize semiconductors and integrated circuitry, ATC computers are old mainframes that still rely on vacuum tubes. The FAA, in fact, is the nation's largest purchaser of vacuum tubes, spending some $19 million a year on them. This equipment is even used in the busiest U.S. airports—O'Hare Airport in Chicago and John F. Kennedy Airport in New York, for example.

Much of this equipment has been operated 24 hours a day, seven days a week for 20 years or more, and it has started to wear out. Controllers describe wire so brittle it breaks as soon as it is touched. As would be expected, the equipment breaks down regularly, despite its critical importance to flight safety. In 1995 and 1996, JFK Airport in New York lost power, computers, and communications on multiple occasions for up to five hours and 49 minutes. O'Hare Airport in Chicago, the nation's busiest airport, experienced similar outages. The president of the eastern region of the National Air Traffic Controllers of America, Joseph Fruscella, told *Time* in 1996, "There is not one day that goes by without our losing radar or radio communications with an aircraft."

Public Impact

When ATC computers go down, controllers cannot monitor the movement of the aircraft in their assigned airspace. They no longer have vital information on the planes' movement or location. Barry Krasner of the National Air Traffic Controller Association described a typical situation to *Time*: "You have to visualize a radar screen showing two planes aimed at each other from 50 miles away. Your equipment goes down for six minutes. When the equipment comes back up, where are those two airplanes? The answer is that they are two miles apart, nose to nose, with a closure rate of 800 mph and less than five seconds to make a course correction." Controllers are given some training to deal with these outages, but few think it is sufficient.

The FAA has had modernization plans in the works since 1983, just after the PATCO strike. The aim was to fully automate the system with computers and make air traffic controllers more expendable. The new system would introduce state-of-the-art computer systems and cost $2.5 billion. It was supposed to be completed in 1996. In 1988 the General Accounting Office reported that several plan milestones had been missed and that the program was already two and a half years behind schedule. In November 1990 the FAA scrapped the planned system and introduced one that was even more complex—and more expensive. Its cost was estimated at $39.9 billion. In 1994 FAA Administrator David Hinson recognized that the plan was completely out of control and canceled it. Hundreds of millions had been spent, but there was no new system to show for it. By the beginning of 1998 the Global Positioning System had been introduced, but the old computers were still in place, still breaking down. Neither the administration nor the Department of Transportation has taken any decisive action on the issue.

Case Study: ValuJet and the Dual Mandate

Critics have long recognized a conflict in the FAA's mission: it is supposed to *regulate* and *promote* civil aviation at the same time. The agency, however, has seemed far more committed to looking out for the interests, especially the financial interests, of the aviation industry than to regulating it. Newly recommended regulations were rejected by the agency as not cost effective or injurious to a weakened industry. The FAA, it was charged, was too close to the commercial interests it was supposed to be regulating; the aviation industry's costs had become the paramount consideration in regulating safety issues. This conflict came to a head with the ValuJet crash in 1996.

ValuJet was a new airline that specialized in low-fare, bare-bones flights, cutting corners in the areas that most affected flight safety. For example, it allegedly hired the least-experienced pilots and mechanics, neglecting maintenance and pressuring pilots to fly under conditions in which other planes remained on the ground. Between 1993 (the first year of ValuJet's operation) and 1996, the airline experienced an unusually high number of accidents and near accidents. When DOT Inspector

General Mary Schiavo brought it to the attention of FAA inspectors, she was told the agency was unaware of the spate of ValuJet accidents and that its planes had been inspected approximately five thousand times and no problems had been found. The accidents, the FAA maintained, were unrelated. The year before, however, ValuJet had applied to the Department of Defense for a troop transport contract. The DOD condemned the airline's safety record and procedures in an internal report and rejected the application.

Despite the inspector general's recommendations, the DOD's condemnation, and ValuJet's record, both the DOT and the FAA publicly defended the company, calling it as safe as any other airline. Secretary of Transportation Federico Peña even booked a flight on the airline and called it perfectly safe. After Schiavo went to the FAA and the DOT to urge tighter controls over the airline, she was allegedly told that ValuJet lobbyists were already working to undo her efforts.

Public Impact

On May 11, 1996, three months after the airline's record had been pointed out to the FAA without any results, a ValuJet plane crashed in the Florida Everglades. All 110 people on board were killed. The FAA continued to insist that the airline was safe, merely "unconventional," and refused to ground it. Within a month, however, it was revealed that FAA inspectors in Atlanta had sent a memo to Washington in February 1996 recommending that ValuJet be grounded. It was ignored in Washington. When the FAA began daily inspections of ValuJet aircraft a couple weeks after the crash, it had to ground so many of its planes that the airline had to cut its flight schedule in half. In the summer of 1996 all of the airline's planes were grounded. The FAA administrator finally admitted that FAA inaction was partly to blame for the ValuJet problem. In the subsequent wave of negative publicity, Anthony J. Broderick, an associate administrator who was considered the real power in the FAA, was forced to retire.

In the wake of the ValuJet controversy, the secretary of transportation formally requested that Congress change the language of the FAA Act to remove the wording that makes the FAA responsible for the promotion of aviation. Congress amended the law in the fall of 1996. It is unclear how effective such a change will be. Only four months after the crash—under pressure from Congress, the aviation industry, and ValuJet and its investors—the DOT and the FAA allowed the airline to resume service.

SUCCESSES AND FAILURES

One of the most successful programs in recent FAA history is the agency's Central Flight Control System, which coordinates all the commercial flights in the nation—more than 100,000 a day. It avoids air traffic problems when bottlenecks or hazardous situations can be foreseen by holding planes on the ground until the situation is safer.

For example, if a heavy snowstorm were expected in New York City in the early evening, the Control System Command Center, located in Herndon, Virginia, would put a hold on flights departing from the West Coast and due to arrive in New York around the same time as the snow. Flights from the East Coast or Midwest scheduled to arrive in New York before the storm hits would be allowed to take off as planned. By doing this rather than allowing the planes to pile up in airspace, safe conditions are maintained. It also cuts costs and pollution because aircraft on the ground consume far less fuel than those circling an airport in the air.

The FAA's environmental program, despite a slow start, is showing positive results. The agency requires that airlines phase out older jet engines and replace them with newer models that are cleaner and quieter. As of September 1997 implementation of the plan was ahead of schedule for the fifth consecutive year, and the agency predicted that by 2000 all of the older engines would be replaced by newer ones.

FUTURE DIRECTIONS

An important challenge facing the FAA is clearly to define its functions and responsibilities and then pursue them with vigor. Some projects, like the plan to modernize the ATC system, have been plagued by overambitious goals and by managers unable to see the complex projects through to completion. Some critics believe the agency needs to trim back and work at developing more limited, achievable goals. It must also plan, test, and implement new systems more effectively. This will not be easy. The FAA's workforce is shrinking while commercial aviation is steadily growing.

Incidents like the ValuJet crash in 1996 did much to erode public confidence in the FAA. To win that confidence back, the agency will have to distance itself from the airlines, as it began to do when the DOT requested that promoting commercial aviation be struck from the FAA mandate. At the same time it will have to regulate the industry more proactively and aggressively.

One proposal for making the agency more effective is to remove it from DOT supervision and restore its independence. That action would free the FAA from political agendas within the DOT, remove the DOT from all regulatory activity, and center regulatory authority in the FAA itself. On the other hand, the FAA would no longer be subject to oversight by offices like that of the DOT inspector general.

Another proposal is to remove air traffic control from the FAA and place it in a separate agency or privatize it. Proponents of the privatization plan claim it would make the national ATC system self-supporting and would free the federal government of the tremendous financial strain of paying for the system's modernization. Still others, citing the German system, claim that a private ATC system would also be more efficient. Germany has had a private system since 1993, and delays in German flights have dropped 25 percent with no apparent impact on safety. Privatization is unlikely in the United States, however. Advocates in the White House and FAA lobbied unsuccessfully for such a plan and it died a quick death.

AGENCY RESOURCES

The FAA maintains two hot lines for the public. The FAA Consumer Hotline takes complaints about FAA regulations as they affect travelers: for example, carry-on luggage restrictions or airport security procedures. Complaints regarding FAA services can also be made on the hot line. The number is 1-800-322-7873, or (202) 267-8592 in the District of Columbia.

The FAA Safety Hotline has been set up to take from airline employees reports of violations of FAA regulations. The identity of all callers is held in strict confidence. The number is 1-800-255-1111, or (202) 267-8590 in the District of Columbia. Consumers with questions or complaints about airline services—for example, ticketing, scheduling, or flight delays—should call DOT Consumer Affairs at (202) 366-2220.

General questions regarding the FAA, as well as Freedom of Information requests, should be directed to FAA Public Affairs, 800 Independence Ave. SW, Rm. 119A, Washington, D.C. 20591. Telephone inquiries can be made at 202-267-3883.

The FAA rules and regulations can be found in the *Code of Federal Regulations*, Title 14, parts 4–199. A copy can be found in the DOT Library with other FAA reports; publications on aviation safety; and other scientific, academic, and federal publications on aviation. The library is open Monday through Friday, 9 A.M. through 4 P.M. Its address is DOT Library, Transportation Administrative Services Center (TASC), 400 7th St. SW, Rm. 2200, Washington, D.C. 20590; phone (202) 366-0746.

The DOT Office of Informational Aviation has a listing of the current fares for all airlines that offer international service, including special promotional fares like super-saver fares. It can be contacted at (202) 366-2414.

AGENCY PUBLICATIONS

The FAA Public Inquiry Center publishes the "Guide to Federal Aviation Administration Publications." It can be requested by writing the FAA Public Inquiry Center, 800 Independence Ave. SW, Washington, D.C. 20591, or by phoning (202) 267-3484.

Aviation Forecast Information is an annual publication that presents a 12-year forecast on many aspects of aviation, including passengers, cargo, aircraft production, air traffic control, and general and military aviation. Statistical information on aircraft in the United States is published in *Aircraft Information*. Both publications can be obtained from the FAA Public Inquiry Center.

The FAA has published a multivolume history of federal civil aviation policy in the United States. The books also trace the growth of civil aviation and the air traffic control system. Titles include Nick A. Komons, *Bonfires to Beacons: Federal Civil Aviation Policy under the Air Commerce Act, 1926–1938*; John R. Wilson, *Turbulence Aloft: The Civil Aeronautics Administration Amid Wars and Rumors of Wars*; Stuart Rochester, *Take-off at Mid-Century: Federal Civil Aviation Policy 1953–1961*; Richard J. Kent, Jr., *Safe, Separated, and Soaring: A History of Federal Civil Aviation Policy, 1961–1972*; and, Edmund Preston, *Troubled Passage: The Federal Aviation Administration During the Nixon-Ford Term, 1973–1977*. All historical titles can be purchased from the Superintendent of Documents, U.S. Government Printing Office, Washington, D.C. 20402. Credit card orders can be placed by calling (202) 512-1800.

BIBLIOGRAPHY

Cohen, Adam. "Can We Ever Trust the FAA?" *Newsweek*, 1 July 1996.

Cook, Gareth. "Uncle Sam's Not-So-Friendly Skies." *Washington Monthly*, January/February 1996.

Hughes, David. "FAA Inspection System Works, But Challenges Loom." *Aviation Week & Space Technology*, 18 August 1997.

Lane, Randall. "FAA, Inc." *Forbes,* 26 August 1996.

Nadar, Ralph, and Wesley J. Smith. *Collision Course: The Truth about Airline Safety*. Blue Ridge Summit, Pa: TAB Books, 1994.

Ott, James. "FAA Funding Crisis Bolsters Ticket Tax."*Aviation Week & Space Technology*, 10 February 1997.

———. "FAA Users Attack Political Winds that Pull Agency Apart."*Aviation Week & Space Technology*, 18 August 1997.

———. "Intense Scrutiny Shapes New Direction of FAA." *Aviation Week & Space Technology*, 18 August 1997.

Proctor, Paul. "Public Opinion, Not Safety, Shaping FAA Enforcement."*Aviation Week & Space Technology*, 18 August 1997.

Regan, Mary Beth. "Can Jane Garvey Pull the FAA Out of Its Dive?" *Business Week*, 21 July 1997.

Schiavo, Mary. *Flying Blind, Flying Safe.* New York: Dutton, 1997.

Scott, William B. "FAA Pilots Claim Managers Risk Safety." *Aviation Week & Space Technology*, 18 August 1997.

Shifrin, Carole. "FAA Reforms Set in Motion." *Aviation Week & Space Technology*, 1 April 1996.

Smolowe, Jill. "Out of Control Tower." *Time*, 19 February 1996.

Federal Bureau of Investigation (FBI)

PARENT ORGANIZATION: Department of Justice
ESTABLISHED: July 26, 1908
EMPLOYEES: 25,516

Contact Information:

ADDRESS: 935 Pennsylvania Ave. NW
Washington, DC 20535
PHONE: (202) 324-3444
TDD (HEARING IMPAIRED): (202) 324-2333
FAX: (202) 324-4705
URL: http://www.fbi.gov
DIRECTOR: Louis J. Freeh
DEPUTY DIRECTOR: William J. Esposito

WHAT IS ITS MISSION?

The Federal Bureau of Investigation (FBI) is the nation's principal investigative authority. As a branch of the U.S. Department of Justice, the FBI's mission is to investigate federal crimes, protect the nation against terrorist activities, and provide leadership and support to all levels of law enforcement agencies throughout the country.

The FBI also provides intelligence services at the request of the president via executive orders. For example, the FBI is responsible for running security checks on the backgrounds of nominees for sensitive government posts, such as White House staff or key Department of Justice positions.

HOW IS IT STRUCTURED?

The FBI is a division of the Department of Justice and part of the executive branch of government. The bureau is led by a director who, together with the deputy director, is responsible for overseeing all activities at the FBI's central headquarters in Washington, D.C.

Operating out of FBI headquarters are the bureau's nine divisions and four main offices. The nine divisions represent the key functions and services of the FBI and include the Criminal Justice Information Services, Training, Personnel, Information Resources, National Security, Criminal Investigations, Laboratory, Finance, and Inspection units. Each division is headed by an assistant director.

The four offices provide program support and include the Office of Public and Congressional Affairs,

BUDGET:

Federal Bureau of Investigation

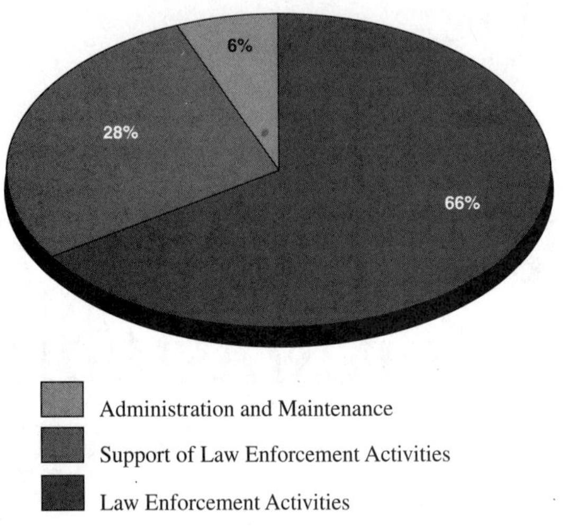

the Office of the General Counsel, the Office of Equal Employment Opportunity Affairs, and the Office of Professional Responsibility. Each office is led by an executive within the FBI.

Key to carrying out the goals and objectives of the bureau are its field offices located in 56 cities in the United States and Puerto Rico. The activities of the field offices are the responsibility of the assigned special agent in charge, except in New York and Washington, D.C., where due to the size and scope of the office's jurisdiction, a higher-ranking assistant director in charge heads the office. In addition, the FBI supervises four field installations with two offices designated as Computer Support Centers and two as Information Technology Centers.

Finally, due to the growth in international criminal activity against the United States, the FBI has expanded its operations to include 23 foreign liaison posts located in U.S. embassies. Any investigation the FBI wishes to conduct overseas must meet with the approval of the host country and the U.S. Department of State. Special Agents assigned to international posts are assigned the title of Legal Attaché.

PRIMARY FUNCTIONS

The FBI investigates, and if possible, attempts to prevent more than two hundred kinds of federal crimes. One of the FBI's most important duties is to maintain U.S. national security against threats from within the borders of the United States. For example, the FBI is the primary counterintelligence agency of the United States, meaning that it is responsible for protecting the United States from spies and saboteurs. The FBI is also responsible for investigating individuals applying for certain sensitive federal jobs, including White House staff, U.S. court candidates, and FBI special agents. The bureau is in charge of the federal government's counterterrorism efforts, leading the defense against hostage taking, hijackings, bombings, and nuclear extortion. While the U.S. Secret Service is responsible for protecting the president, the FBI is the agency that investigates attacks on the president, vice president, or members of Congress. Acting on the orders of Congress or the president, the FBI also gathers information about any other activities that are perceived to pose a threat to U.S. national security.

National security issues are by no means the sole focus of the FBI's efforts. The bureau is responsible for the investigation of kidnappings, bank robberies, environmental crimes, theft of government property, transportation of stolen goods across state lines, sexual exploitation of children, crime on American Indian reservations, crimes committed on board aircraft, election law violations, bank fraud and embezzlement, and a host of other federal crimes. The FBI takes special interest in drug-related offenses and organized crime, with special task forces devoted to investigating these matters.

The FBI also provides laboratory services for criminal investigations conducted by local and state law enforcement agencies which otherwise would not have access to or experience with cutting-edge technology. In addition, the FBI does provide training opportunities for these same agencies so that smaller law enforcement agencies are better able to expand their local laboratory's capacity.

PROGRAMS

The FBI's Criminal Investigation Division serves to protect the United States from major safety threats and is the umbrella under which all investigations take place. Upon conducting an investigation, the FBI presents its findings to officials within the Department of Justice who must then decide whether or not to prosecute the case. Top priority cases include counterterrorism, drugs and organized crime, foreign counterintelligence, violent crimes, and financial crimes.

Another key department within the FBI is its Laboratory Division. The FBI lab provides the scientific data necessary to support all bureau investigations. As one of the most comprehensive forensic (crime) labs in the world, the FBI lab conducts and analyzes DNA testing, chemistry profiles, photography samples, and firearms identification services, among others.

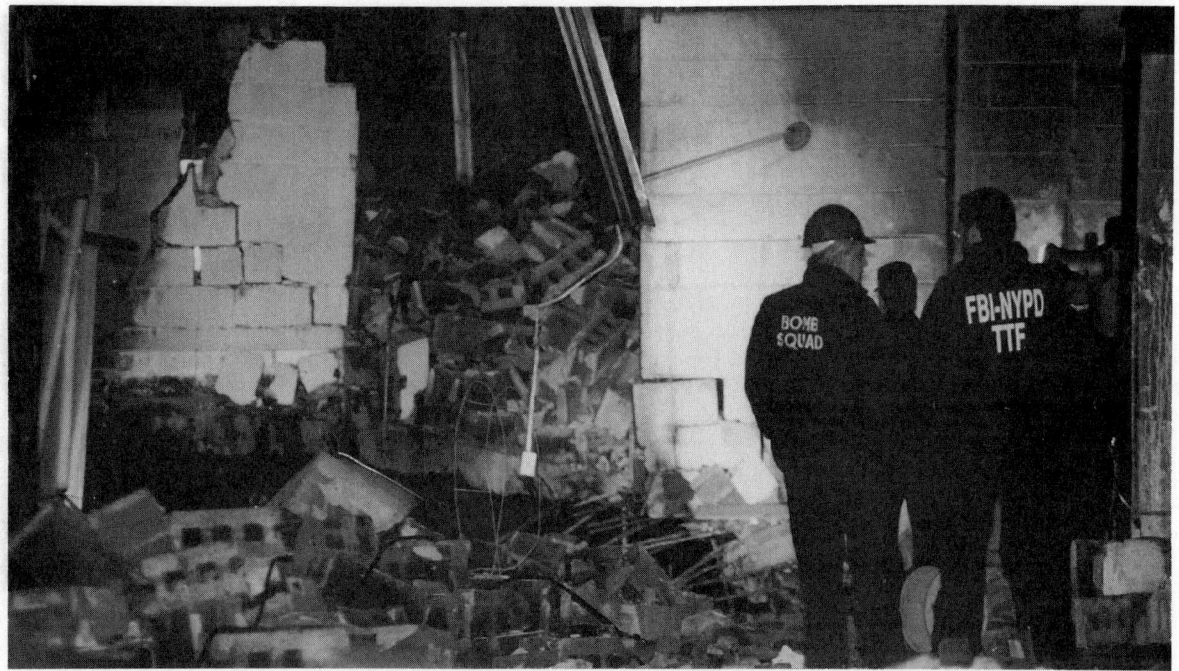

FBI agents view rubble in a parking garage below the World Trade Center in New York City. A bomb planted there by terrorists in February 1993 killed 6 people, injured 652, and caused millions of dollars of structural damage to the building itself. (Reuters/Corbis-Bettmann)

Finally, the FBI operates many other programs such as the national Violent Criminal Apprehension Program and the locally based Community Outreach Program as part of its overall mission to ensure law enforcement and public safety in communities throughout the United States.

BUDGET INFORMATION

The FBI's budget is submitted to Congress as part of the DOJ's overall request. In a year of budget cuts the FBI has seen increases of up to 25 percent. In fiscal year 1997, the FBI's budget climbed to $2.9 billion, allowing the agency to establish additional field offices, hire 3,600 new employees, and install an advanced computer system.

The majority of the FBI's funds, 66 percent, are used for law enforcement activities, including counter-terrorism efforts and other investigation. Support of law enforcement activities requires another 28 percent of the budget. Included in this part of the budget is the FBI lab, which has come under fire for mismanagement issues. It is scheduled to receive $36 million, up from $8 million in the previous year's budget. The remaining 6 percent of the agency's funding goes towards administration and maintenance.

HISTORY

In 1908 Attorney General Charles J. Bonaparte created a corps of special agents to serve as the investigative arm of the DOJ. Not until 1935, after several name changes, did the Federal Bureau of Investigation receive its present name. During its early years, the FBI dealt with only a few existing federal violations, including bankruptcy fraud, banking practices, and antitrust laws.

During World War I (1914–18), the Bureau of Investigation, as it was known, and its agents were given responsibility for espionage and sabotage and worked closely with the Department of Labor to investigate infiltration of war enemies into the U.S. wartime labor force.

In the 1920s the Gangster Era of law enforcement began after the institution of prohibition laws (legislation making the manufacturing and sale of alcohol illegal). Bank robberies and the incidence of kidnapping crimes increased dramatically, but initially special agents were not allowed to be involved in these cases, as the crimes were not considered federal violations. With the passage of federal kidnapping laws in 1932 and other legislation, Congress granted FBI agents greater authority in making arrests and the right to carry firearms.

World War II (1939–45) saw further increases in the bureau's jurisdiction as it expanded to include international intelligence gathering. As a result of the Cold War

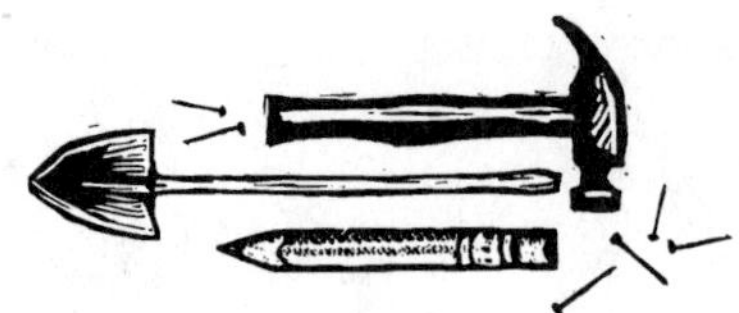

GET INVOLVED:

The Community Outreach Program (COP) offers opportunities for FBI employees to work closely with communities on prevention programs and other collaborative efforts designed to reduce crime rates. For example, COP coordinators from each of the FBI's 56 field offices work on programs such as Adopt-A-School, providing mentors and support to students, or the Junior Special Agent program, which encourages students to consider careers in law enforcement by bringing them face-to-face with special agents. A new venture developed under the COP's auspices is a partnership with the Drug Enforcement Agency, Marine Corps, and National Guard that offers a science education program for at-risk youth. To find out more about these programs, contact the FBI field office nearest you.

and a growing national fear of communism, the FBI began conducting background investigations on individuals nominated to key positions within the executive branch. The FBI was also allowed to conduct background checks on existing federal employees. Although these investigations were carried out in the name of national security, they perpetuated an atmosphere of fear and suspicion; even though federal employees were told not to report unfounded claims, they were also urged through FBI materials to report any "subversive activities."

In the 1960s Congress continued to expand the jurisdiction of the bureau so that it could play a greater role in investigating civil rights violations and organized crime. The Vietnam War (1959–75) was also being waged during this period. The number of Americans who objected to U.S. involvement in the war continued to grow, and the government was faced with one of the most widespread levels of dissent in U.S. history.

The end of the Vietnam War became the common goal of many peace, social justice, and human rights organizations. However, this growing movement of war protesters and resisters greatly threatened the FBI's sense of law and order. Although the majority of those who participated in efforts to end the war were nonviolent, other more radical groups formed that the FBI asserted had a "romance with violence." In public statements, the FBI began to portray the entire antiwar movement as a threat to national security. In 1966, in an interview with *PTA Magazine*, FBI Director J. Edgar Hoover lashed out at the antiwar movement, stating that the U.S. government was being attacked by "a new style in conspiracy—conspiracy that is extremely subtle and devious and hence difficult to understand . . . a conspiracy reflected by questionable moods and attitudes, by unrestrained individualism, by nonconformism in dress and speech, even by obscene language, rather than by formal membership in specific organizations."

By the mid 1970s the FBI's reputation had suffered due to its role in the antiwar movement. Clarence Kelly, appointed the FBI's director in 1978, vowed to restore the public's faith in the FBI and instituted a Quality Over Quantity Management program.

In the 1980s and 1990s the FBI faced an increased level of international crime, including dramatic increases in terrorist incidents worldwide. The United States experienced two devastating terrorist attacks during these years on its own soil. The World Trade Center in New York was bombed by foreign terrorists, killing six civilians and injuring hundreds more, and the bombing of the federal building in Oklahoma City by U.S. terrorists killed more than 100 people, including 19 children.

CURRENT POLITICAL ISSUES

The FBI handles more than 600,000 forensic examinations a year and more than two million fingerprint comparisons. The proper handling of evidence and management of the laboratory are critical and provide the evidence that makes possible the conviction of terrorists and others suspected of federal crimes.

Case Study: FBI Laboratory Investigation

In April 1997 the Department of Justice's Inspector General Michael Bromwich released a report that questioned the credibility of the FBI's laboratory procedures and practices. Ten lab workers responsible for handling many critical lab examinations were found to be inept and their actions inexcusable. An FBI lab examiner admitted that he conducted tests that were beyond his expertise, and in another case the same employee stated that fibers from a suspected killer's wig used as evidence were later identified as hair from the doll of the child who had been murdered. These and other disclosures led Bromwich to conclude in his report that lab employees had "reached conclusions that incriminated the defendants without a scientific basis."

Public Impact

In an April 15, 1997, press release Deputy Director William Esposito responded to the inspector general's findings by saying, "While the problems in the Lab are serious and should not have occurred, the FBI has no reason to believe that any pending or future cases have been compromised." What Esposito did not address, and what alarmed critics, are the cases that have already been tried in which evidence was handled by the lab workers who were faulted in the report. Of greatest concern are cases in which defendants were convicted but may now be able to call for retrials or appeal their cases. A great deal of the lab's staffing and forensic resources will be spent in responding to these motions, so that the FBI's increased funding in 1998 will be spent on correcting previous errors and not on advancing the agency's other critical programs.

SUCCESSES AND FAILURES

In 1993, an explosion at the World Trade Center cost dozens of lives and millions of dollars in structural damage—the first time that foreign terrorism had exacted such a heavy toll in the United States. By the end of 1994, four suspects had been apprehended by the FBI, and each received a 240-year prison term and a $500,000 fine. It was also ruled that any money the criminals received for interviews or books would be turned over to the families of the six people killed in the bombing. However, David Williams, an explosives expert involved in the investigation of the bombing, was condemned in Bromwich's report for presuming the suspects' guilt without substantial evidence to back up his claims and for "tailoring" his testimony during the trial. As a result, convictions in the World Trade Center bombing may be eligible for appeal.

FUTURE DIRECTIONS

In mid-1997 the bureau announced that for the first time it would hire a scientist from outside the FBI to head the bureau's laboratory. The bureau will devote more resources to improving its forensics laboratory in order to prevent mistakes that have occurred in the past.

The FBI is also planning major changes for its National Crime Information Center (NCIC), a sophisticated computer system that allows law enforcement agencies in all 50 states to conduct searches and receive timely information about missing persons, stolen autos, federal fugitives, and missing guns within a matter of minutes.

The NCIC has greatly assisted the efforts of local and state authorities in their ability to identify and apprehend criminals. Through its NCIC 2000 program, the FBI is seeking to expand the benefits and successes of the existing system. The new system will allow electronic transmissions of photographs and mug shots and will also provide for an automated fingerprint matching system that can determine the true identity of a suspect when an alias or false identification is being used. These capabilities will be available with software that the FBI will provide free of charge to law enforcement agencies nationwide. Local agencies will be responsible for purchasing hardware to be installed in individual patrol cars. The FBI expects NCIC 2000 to be in operation by July 1999. The mainframe computer will be located at the FBI's new facility in Clarksburg, West Virginia.

AGENCY RESOURCES

The Criminal Justice Information Services Division (CJIS) is the FBI's main information clearinghouse for all its criminal justice information resources. The CJIS houses the world's largest fingerprint files and the criminal histories of thousands of known convicted felons and fugitives.

The ABC Radio Network also features a weekly program on the bureau's activities, "FBI, This Week," which offers a one-minute report on the agency's current investigations or findings. It is distributed weekly via satellite and can be heard across the United States.

AGENCY PUBLICATIONS

The FBI publishes its own monthly periodical, *FBI Law Enforcement Bulletin*, which can be reviewed online at http://www.fbi.gov/leb/leb.html. To subscribe, contact the Superintendent of Documents, PO Box 371954, Pittsburgh, PA 15250–7954; or call the Government Printing Office at (202) 512–1800; or fax at (202) 512–2250. In addition, the CJIS Division publishes national crime reports offering criminal statistics and overviews, such as the annual *Crime in the United States* and a *Special Report on Hate Crimes*. These are available on-line at the FBI's Web page at http://www.fbi.gov/ and through the CJIS's SEARCH Web page, at http://www.search.org. To order by phone, call 1-888-827-6427.

BIBLIOGRAPHY

Collins, James. "The Weight of the Evidence," *Time*, 28 April 1997, p. 37.

Gibbs, Nancy. "Under the Microscope," *Time*, 28 April 1997, p. 28.

Hargrove, Jim. *The Story of the FBI*. Chicago: Children's Press, 1988.

Tully, Andrew.*Inside the FBI*. New York: McGraw-Hill, 1980.

Wilson, Charles. "New Vision: Criminal Justice Education for Students," *FBI Law Enforcement Bulletin*, March 1997.

Zoner, Sharon. "Teen Court," *FBI Law Enforcement Bulletin*, March 1997.

Federal Communications Commission (FCC)

PARENT ORGANIZATION: Independent
ESTABLISHED: 1934
EMPLOYEES: 2,271 (1995)

Contact Information:

ADDRESS: 1919 M St. NW
Washington, DC 20554
PHONE: (202) 418-0200
TDD (HEARING IMPAIRED): (202) 632-6999
FAX: (202) 418-2830
E-MAIL: fccinfo@fcc.gov
URL: http://www.fcc.gov
CHAIRMAN: William E. Kennard

WHAT IS ITS MISSION?

Established in 1934, the Federal Communications Commission (FCC) acts in the public's interest by promoting fair competition within communications industries. According to the FCC, "the mission of this independent agency is to encourage competition in all communications markets and to protect the public interest. In response to direction from the Congress, the FCC develops and implements policy concerning interstate and international communications by radio, television, wire, satellite, and cable."

HOW IS IT STRUCTURED?

The FCC is an independent agency that falls under the executive branch of the federal government. It is composed of five commissioners, who are appointed by the president and confirmed by the Senate. To guard against political bias, the commissioners cannot all be members of the same political party, and their time in office is staggered in five-year terms to prevent undue influence from the president. One of the five commissioners serves as chairman. The chairman acts as chief executive officer for the commission, but the daily operations management is generally delegated to the FCC's managing director. The chairman represents the FCC before the government, and each of the commissioners has individual responsibilities beyond participating in the decision-making process of the commission as a whole. They meet together regularly in open and closed meetings and may call special meetings as well. The commission is required by law to hold at least one meeting per month that is open to the public. In addition to the official actions that occur at these meetings, the commissioners may make formal decisions by circulating documents among themselves for individual review.

Within the FCC, there are six main divisions: the Mass Media Bureau, the Common Carrier Bureau, the Compliance and Information Bureau, the Wireless Telecommunications Bureau, the Cable Services Bureau, and the International Bureau. Secondary offices include the Office of Public Affairs, the Office of Legislative and Intergovernmental Affairs, the Office of the Inspector General, the Office of Plans and Policy, the Office of Administrative Law Judges, the Office of Communications Business Opportunities, the Office of Workplace Diversity, the Office of Engineering and Technology, and a Review Board.

PRIMARY FUNCTIONS

The FCC is unique in that its function is quasi-legislative and quasi-judicial. It is responsible for determining and enforcing regulations and establishing policies for all of the communications industries, both interstate and international. Additionally, the FCC is charged with making sure that the consumer is protected and represented in decisions regarding the television, radio, cable, wire (telephone), and wireless arenas. The organization's Mass Media Bureau is the source of all broadcast permits and licenses, and its Office of Engineering and Technology provides expertise in new technological opportunities and coordinates the private and commercial use of the spectrum (the range of radio frequencies used in the transmission of sound, data, and television).

PROGRAMS

Beyond the duties of the individual commissioners, the operations of the FCC as an agency are carried out by the various bureaus and offices. The Common Carrier Bureau is responsible for regulating interstate wire systems. It primarily deals with the policies and services of, and competition between, domestic telephone carriers. *The United States Government Manual 1996–1997* classifies "common carriers" as "companies, organizations, or individuals providing communications services to the public for hire, who must serve all who wish to use them at established rates." The Common Carrier Bureau also oversees the telegraph business.

The programs of the Mass Media Bureau regulate the broadcast industry, which includes mainly television and AM (amplitude modulation) and FM (frequency modulation) radio. Permits and licenses are obtained through this bureau, and it is charged with enforcing national policies and requirements for television and radio communications. In the same way, the Cable Services Bureau regulates all cable television systems, as well as collects data and acts as an advisory resource to the government and the public.

The Wireless Telecommunications Bureau determines policy and procedures for the private and commercial use of wireless communication, such as pagers, cellular telephones, and special types of mobile radios. It is responsible for executing laws and policies related to using radio for safety purposes, both on land and in the air. The management of amateur radio operation falls under programs run by the Wireless Bureau. Spectrum auctions, in which sections of the spectrum (the range of frequencies) are sold for use by members of the private sector, also come under its auspices. The Wireless Bureau does retain and manage portions of the spectrum for public use.

The Compliance and Information Bureau functions mainly through its regional and field staff as well as the central office. Its programs primarily involve enforcing FCC policies and regulations and educating the public about how to comply with FCC standards. In addition to searching out violators, field crews also detect distress communications from airplanes or ships.

The key programs relating to communications across or beyond national boundaries are administered by the International Bureau. It develops and carries out the principal policies and regulations of all satellite communications and of telecommunications that are specifically international. In particular, the Telecommunications Division of the International Bureau handles policymaking and training in connection with the global information infrastructure (GII) plan which aims to integrate local, regional, and national networks to create a worldwide information network. This network would facilitate the transfer of various forms of information like graphics, video, and sound. The Satellite and Radio Communication Division handles both the earth-based and the space satellite facilities. Another significant function of the International Bureau is to represent the FCC in negotiations of multinational agreements on radio frequency usage and at international conferences. This bureau also conducts research programs on international communications development.

Other programs established by the FCC include the Lifeline and Link Up assistance programs. Lifeline provides matching state and federal funds to qualified low-income consumers to help decrease the cost of monthly telephone bills. The Link Up program grants federal money to qualified low-income consumers to reduce the initial costs of local telephone connection.

BUDGET INFORMATION

Funding for the FCC and its operations comes from the federal treasury. Each year, the president proposes a

FAST FACTS

The Federal Communications Commission's list of employment needs includes attorneys, electronics engineers, economists, accountants, administrative managers, computer specialists, and clerical help. What the list does not include are communications professionals.

(Source: *The United States Government Manual 1997/98.*)

budget for the FCC, and Congress appropriates certain funds. In addition, the FCC collects fees from the companies it regulates. In 1998 the FCC was appropriated approximately $187 million. Portions of the budget include funding for the Corporation for Public Broadcasting, the National Telecommunications and Information Agency, and the Information Infrastructure Grant program.

HISTORY

The first federal act to regulate broadcast communications dates back to 1912, with the passage of the Radio Communications Act. This ruling mandated radio licenses, obtained from the U. S. Department of Commerce and Labor, for all transmissions. When the heavy, random usage of multiple frequencies resulted in poor-quality transmissions, the industry requested that the government regulate airwave use.

FCC Is Created in 1934

The Federal Radio Commission was established by the Radio Act of 1927. This body preceded the creation of the Federal Communications Commission by Congress in 1934, at the proposal of President Franklin Roosevelt. The FCC combined the functions of the Federal Radio Commission with the telephone and telegraph policies previously regulated by the Interstate Commerce Commission and the Office of the Postmaster General. Originally a seven-member commission, the FCC in its early years produced a major, formal study of the telephone industry, which led to attempts to decrease rates on long-distance telephone calls. Finally, the agency concentrated on regulating broadcast communications.

The FCC strictly limited entry into the broadcast industry. Because the ratings system of measuring viewers determines financial success in broadcasting, the FCC did not have to govern rates. Perhaps because of the closed nature of the industry and its self-regulation by ratings, federal regulations have not been applied to broadcast services nearly as much as to the services of other industries. This self-contradicting role of the FCC may be due in part to the 1934 act, which set out conflicting responsibilities for the agency. Although one section states that the FCC can revoke a broadcasting license if the programming is not in accordance with "public interest, convenience, or necessity" (Section 309), another prohibits the FCC from censoring content except in instances of "obscene, indecent, or profane language" (Section 326).

Exercising Regulatory Powers

The 1940s saw the FCC take a proactive role in the regulation of broadcast services, including forcing the breakup of the National Broadcasting Company (NBC) into two networks, NBC and ABC (American Broadcasting Company). It also published the *Blue Book*, in which it addressed the federal regulation of programming content for the first time. This push for censorship did not last, partly because the FCC lacked the necessary funds and personnel.

In the late 1940s and 1950s, the independent regulatory powers of the FCC were threatened by outside sources, as lines between the industry and the commission blurred. In 1947, for instance, the Chairman of the FCC left his position to become a vice president at NBC. Another threat came from the executive and legislative branches of the federal government during the McCarthy era, when members of Congress and certain officials pressed the FCC to refuse licenses to stations with so-called "Communist" leanings.

A decade later, the FCC still could not effectively use its authority. This was demonstrated by the agency's inactive role in stopping the television quiz show scandals of the 1950s, in which selected quiz show participants—usually good-looking—were given answers, thereby creating artificial winners in order to heighten interest and viewership, as well as the resulting advertising advantages. The schemes were finally outlawed by Congress. Instead of assuming a dominant role in regulating programming during the 1960s, the FCC required that content be determined by local stations, according to public need, rather than viewer preference. Although the commission technically regulated content by this action, it actually placed responsibility for content on the local stations. The FCC attempted to limit the scope of the networks in 1970 by requiring additional time for local broadcasts, but the decision backfired when the networks simply reran syndicated programs rather than lose money on local programs.

Telecommunications Act of 1996

With the passing of the Telecommunications Act of 1996, Congress established three rights for newcomers to the telecommunications industry: (1) the right to pay a fair price and compete with a local carrier's service; (2) the right to pay a fair price and combine new elements with those of a previously established network; (3) and the right to fair prices in terminating their services with a network already in a market and interconnecting their own services and facilities. This law created a competitive marketplace for local exchange and provided for deregulation of the telephone industry. Long-distance companies can now move into local service, and in a reverse scenario, local carriers can offer long-distance services as well. Although establishing a free-market policy in telecommunications would seem to benefit both telephone companies and consumers, the government, the industry, and the public all have reason to be concerned about the potential impact of major consolidation. The 1998 AT&T Corp.-SBC (American Telephone and Telegraph and Southwestern Bell Corporation, Inc.) merger, and others that are likely to follow, could bring back monopolies that span both the local and the long-distance markets. At the same time, some question whether an all-inclusive telecommunications company is needed to compete in the global market.

The Telecommunications Act of 1996 requires that quality service be provided to all segments of the public at fair, reasonable rates. Service also must be made more available, particularly in rural, low-income areas and areas where costs for service are high. Furthermore, every telecommunications service has a responsibility to contribute to this universal service in some way, supported by federal and state mechanisms. The goal of this initiative is to increase access to quality, affordable telecommunications services and, specifically, to provide advanced telecommunications services to all schools, including libraries and classrooms, and to health care providers.

FAST FACTS

The Mass Media Bureau of the FCC oversees licenses of 12,020 radio stations and 1,543 television stations.

(Source: Federal Communications Commission. "Who and What Is the FCC?" 1998.)

CURRENT POLITICAL ISSUES

The massive growth of information technology has made the FCC and its decisions relevant to every person. Not only is the agency charged with protecting the public interest, but it is responsible for managing and regulating domestic and international communications systems and policies. Another issue that has prevailed throughout the FCC's history is censorship. Some commissions have taken an authoritative stand, but others have been more liberal.

Case Study: Censorship in the 1990s

In the 1990s, the FCC attempted to involve the television industry in determining regulatory policy. Rather than mandating a set of predetermined standards for a TV ratings system, the FCC considered a proposal submitted by the television industry as encouraged by Congress. This proposal allows television networks to set standards for rating programs containing "sexual, violent or other indecent material about which parents should be informed before it is displayed to children" (Section 551 of the Telecommunications Act of 1996). The industry also agreed to broadcast these ratings.

The FCC must continue to evaluate public opinion on the proposed rating system and then accept or reject it. If the industry's plan is rejected, the FCC must set up a committee to research and develop a TV ratings system with guidelines. This scenario of government and industry working together reflects the responsibility of the industry to the public while maintaining voluntary consent on limits to freedom of expression.

Another related instance of united effort is the congressional mandate (through the Telecommunications Act of 1996) to require an electronic mechanism called a V-chip to be placed on all television sets made after February 1998, allowing viewers to block programs of a particular rating. The guidelines for implementation, however, have been left to the FCC to determine with electronics manufacturers.

Children's television programming also has raised the question of FCC regulation. Certain educational standards already exist, but regulating the amount of violence in children's programming remains a major concern. The V-chip was supposed to allow parents to regulate this themselves, but critics claim that the rating system developed by the broadcast industry is not specific enough for parents to be able to judge the violent content of a program. Senator Ernest Hollings (D-SC) proposed a bill in 1997 that would prohibit violent programming during the hours that children would be most likely to watch television (6:00 AM to 10:00 PM), except for programs that are specifically rated for their violent content, and can be blocked electronically by parents. A similar bill was later introduced in the House of Representatives, but neither had been accepted by 1998.

In contrast to the television ratings controversy, television broadcasters and the FCC have been able to cooperate effectively on the issue of liquor advertising. When manufacturers of hard liquor decided to lift their voluntary ban on broadcast advertising in November 1996, the FCC chairman declared that the commission might require that television stations choosing to broadcast the ads to also air public service announcements against alcohol. Some questioned this statement as a return to the Fairness Doctrine, a proactive FCC policy that reflected a strong use of regulatory authority. It had stated, for instance, that if ads promoting products harmful to children were broadcast, ads against that product also had to be aired. Following the FCC's inquiry into liquor advertisements, and with pressure in the form of a bill presented in Congress to create a mandatory standard, the major televisions networks voluntarily agreed not to air ads for hard liquor.

SUCCESSES AND FAILURES

Unlike most government agencies, the FCC has been able to return money to the federal government. By auctioning the rights to the wireless spectrum, the FCC earned $23 billion for the U.S. Treasury in four years. Even with selling parts of the spectrum to the private sector, the agency has retained a certain portion of the spectrum for public use.

The passage of the Telecommunications Act of 1996 was viewed by some as a major success for the FCC. The resulting changes in the communications industries and policies governing telecommunications could be key factors in improving the public's access to information and technology in the twenty-first century. In the words of former FCC chairman Reed Hundt, "That's what the 1996 act was all about: creating a telecommunications system that is better, faster, and more powerful throughout our country, and bringing our country the economic and social benefits that even better telecommunications will bring. . . ."

In reality, telecommunications since the 1996 law was passed has not necessarily brought benefits to the public. According to the Bureau of Labor Statistics, cable TV rates rose 7.8 percent, local phone rates went up 0.9 percent, and long-distance rates were up 3.7 percent within the year. Although the Telecommunications Act supposedly encouraged competition, with the potential for more companies to offer better services and lower rates, mergers equaled $103 billion 18 months after the law's passage, with others pending. Representative Billy Tauzin, chairman of the House Telecommunications Subcommittee, said in an interview by *The Flint Journal,* "I hope the next chairman (after retiring FCC chairman Reed Hundt) will help reinvent the FCC, downsize it and make it more friendly to users and the economy." One journalist noted that if broadcasting networks were allowed to use part of their allotted spectrum space for multiple channels rather than having to use it to broadcast the high-definition television (HDTV) signal, then they, like cable companies, could charge for additional services.

FUTURE DIRECTIONS

Besides working to establish universal access to information, one way in which the FCC is determining the direction of communications for the future is by its requirement to implement digital broadcasting. In 1997 the FCC ruled that all broadcasters must begin to use the digital spectrum, which uses cable wiring to transmit signals rather than airwaves. Television networks and local stations may choose to broadcast a single signal that requires an HDTV for reception, or they can split the digital spectrum and broadcast over several channels with a quality slightly less than that of HDTV. Although manufacturers of television sets are pushing for HDTV because it will require people to purchase new TVs rather than adding a digital converter to their regular sets, networks are undecided.

The FCC already has amended its original decision to require digital broadcasts for all television stations by 2006. Instead, only those network affiliates in the country's top 10 markets were required to produce digital broadcasts by the end of 1998. The FCC's role in this transition will prove instrumental, not only in how the networks change their broadcast medium but also in how the United States fares in the competition for technology advancement.

AGENCY RESOURCES

General information on the programs of the FCC and how the public can participate in decisions on specific issues can be obtained from the Public Service Division of the FCC at (202) 418-0200. For inquiries about employment, contact the Chief of the Personnel Resources Division at (202) 418-0130. Public information can be accessed at the FCC's headquarters in Washington, D.C., by fax-on-demand at (202) 418-2830, or on the Internet at http://www.fcc.gov. Information regarding the licenses of specific broadcast stations and operating information can be found at the individual stations. FCC regulations and rules are available through the FCC Library, (202) 418-0450. For press releases, contact the Office of Public Affairs at (202) 418-0500. Further information on the specific services of the FCC can be obtained from the chief of the bureau or office related to particular programs.

AGENCY PUBLICATIONS

Although the FCC does not produce any regularly published items for the public, like a newsletter, it does offer several general reference items including its annual report, a glossary of telecommunications terms, and information about the commission's structure and general activities. These are available through the FCC by phoning (202) 418–0500 or (202) 418–2555 (TTY). Documents from specific FCC bureaus and offices are published on a daily basis and can be obtained through the U.S. Government Printing Office at (202) 512–1800.

BIBLIOGRAPHY

Barnouw, Erik. *A Tower in Babel: A History of Broadcasting in the United States.* Vols. 1–3, 1966, 1968, 1970.

Barrett, Amy. "Musical Chairs at the FCC." *Business Week,* 9 June 1997, p. 32.

Forbes, Steve. "Uncle Sam: Underwriting Smut." *Forbes* 159, No. 7 (7 April 1997): 28.

"Free Airwaves." *PC Magazine* 16, No. 5 (4 March 1997): p. 10.

Shafroth, Frank. "FCC Panel Will Set Aside Radio Spectrum for Local Public Safety: Move Marks Key Victory in Ongoing Fight." *Nation's Cities Weekly* 20, No. 14 (7 April 1997): 1–2.

Stern, Christopher. "FCC Regs Fueling Debate." *Variety* 365, No. 9 (6–12 January 1997): N2.

"The War Over Net Access Fees." *PC Magazine* 16, No. 8 (22 April 1997): 10.

Federal Deposit Insurance Corporation (FDIC)

PARENT ORGANIZATION: Independent
ESTABLISHED: January 1, 1934
EMPLOYEES: 8,000

Contact Information:

ADDRESS: 550 17th St. NW
Washington, DC 20429
PHONE: (202) 393–8400
TOLL FREE: (800) 934-3342
TDD (HEARING IMPAIRED): (800) 925-4618
E-MAIL: ombudsman@fdic.gov
URL: http://www.fdic.gov
CHAIRMAN: Donna Tanoue

WHAT IS ITS MISSION?

According to the *The United States Government Manual 1997/98*, the Federal Deposit Insurance Corporation (FDIC) "promotes and preserves public confidence in U.S. financial institutions by insuring bank and thrift deposits up to the legal limit of $100,000; by periodically examining state-chartered banks that are not members of the Federal Reserve System for safety and soundness as well as compliance with consumer protection laws; and by liquidating assets of failed institutions to reimburse the insurance funds for the cost of failures."

The vision of the FDIC as stated in its *1997–2002 Strategic Plan* is "to assure that the FDIC is an organization dedicated to identifying existing and emerging risks to the deposit insurance funds."

HOW IS IT STRUCTURED?

The FDIC is managed by a bipartisan five-member board of directors that includes a chairman, a vice chairman, and an appointive director. The comptroller of the currency, who supervises federally chartered or national banks, and the director of the Office of Thrift Supervision, who supervises federally chartered savings and loan associations are also members of the board. All five are appointed by the president and confirmed by the Senate.

The eight divisions of the FDIC that carry out the mandate of the FDIC to protect the safety of the nation's banks are the Division of Supervision (DOS), which is responsible for conducting both off-site reviews and on-site examinations of financial institutions; the Division of Compliance and Consumer Affairs (DCA), which conducts bank examinations and reviews bank compliance with federal laws intended to promote consumer protection, fair lending, and community reinvestment; the Division of Resolutions and Receiverships (DRR), which is called into action when a bank or savings institution is identified as a potential failure; the Legal Division, which drafts regulations and prepares enforcement actions in support of the bank supervision and consumer protection programs; the Division of Research, which studies stock trends, home buying, and other indicators to determine how they might affect the banking industry's performance; the Division of Insurance, which studies trends that the Division of Research has uncovered and tries to determine potential bank failures and find ways to prevent them; the Division of Administration, which oversees the FDIC staff, purchasing equipment and services, the hiring of new employees, and providing other corporate support; the Division of Finance, which monitors and manages the FDIC's money and accounting and audits participatory banks to ensure that the correct insurance deposit premiums are being paid on time; and finally, the Division of Information Management, which maintains the FDIC communications and computer systems, develops new information management systems and databases when needed, and creates FDIC applicable software. Eight regional offices with 80 smaller offices accommodate bank examiners when needed.

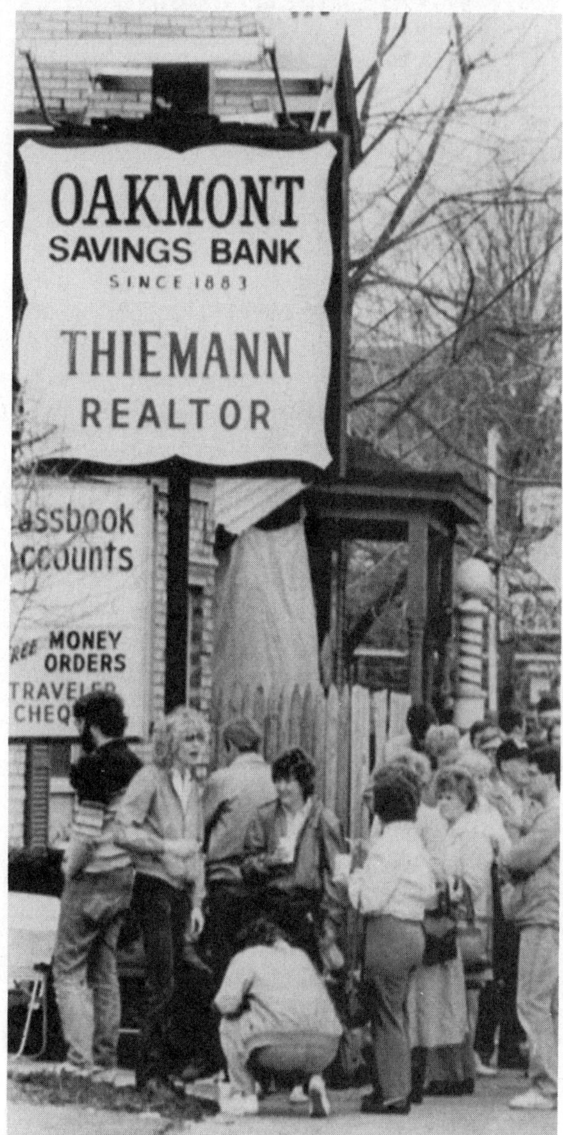

During the 1980s, scenes like the one pictured here, where hundreds of customers gather outside Oakmont Savings and Loan to withdraw their funds, were common across the country. (UPI/Corbis-Bettmann)

PRIMARY FUNCTIONS

The FDIC insures and supervises deposits at more than 11,191 banks and savings and loan (S & L) institutions each year as well as examines and supervises the practices and procedures of more than six thousand banks that are not members of the Federal Reserve System. The examinations consist of checking for compliance with consumer laws such as the Truth In Lending Act, Mortgage Disclosure Act, and Community Reinvestment Act and ensuring the soundness and safety of the depositors' money. If a bank or savings association fails, it is closed by its chartering authority, and the FDIC is named as its receiver. It is the FDIC's function to either find a healthy institution to take over the failed bank or to pay the depositors their insured funds (up to $100,000). The FDIC also approves mergers and consolidations, acquisitions, the opening of new branches, improving main offices, issuing enforcement actions for violations, and reporting changes in ownership or control of a bank.

PROGRAMS

The FDIC operates two main programs—the Bank Insurance Fund (BIF) and the Savings Association Insurance Fund (SAIF). Each division of the FDIC works toward ensuring that these two main programs receive the most current research on trends and are examined regularly to ensure proper banking practices and the safety of depositor's accounts.

One of the major programs operated by the FDIC is in anticipation of the Year 2000 computer issue. This problem is inherent in all computer systems for which the changing of the century was not anticipated. The calen-

FAST FACTS

From 1994 to 1997 the FDIC was led by Ricki Helfer, the first woman appointed to the position in the history of the organization and the first to chair any federal banking agency.

(Source: Federal Deposit Insurance Corporation, 1998.)

dars of these computers will register the date only until the end of 1999. At this time, instead of progressing to January 1, 2000, these computers will revert to January 1, 1900. The anticipated confusion and alarm over this possible problem in financial institutions prompted the FDIC to develop and distribute a plan to avoid the crisis.

In a statement issued to all CEOs of financial institutions that come under the authority of the agency, the FDIC, in its capacity as bank examiner, said it has expanded its review of data processing servicers to focus on Year 2000 issues and that affected institutions will be notified of the results of the reviews. Although the FDIC will inform its institutions of significant weaknesses, according to the statement, "neither the FDIC nor other federal regulators will certify a servicer as Year 2000 compliant. Institutions are expected to solicit, from the servicer, information sufficient to form an independent conclusion of the servicer's Year 2000 readiness."

Some of the steps the FDIC undertook to ensure the success of an institution's readiness for Year 2000 include an on-site review of Year 2000 compliance at each institution it supervises by June 30, 1998. The review assesses progress in establishing, implementing, and monitoring a Year 2000 plan, efforts to monitor the progress of data servicers, software providers, and other vendors, and the impact of the Year 2000 problem on credit risk.

BUDGET INFORMATION

The operating budget of the FDIC in 1998 was $1.36 billion. This reflected a reduction of $255 million from 1997 due to an effort on the part of the FDIC to consolidate offices and programs more efficiently. The FDIC is not operated on funds appropriated by Congress. It derives income from the insurance premiums paid by member banks to the Bank Insurance Fund (BIF) and by S&Ls to the Savings Association Insurance Fund (SAIF)—until 1995 known as the FSLIC. The amount of the premiums are determined by an assessment of the deposits held by those banks. The FDIC also derives income from the interest on the investment of its surplus funds in government securities. Congress has authorized that the FDIC may borrow up to $30 billion from the Treasury Department to cover deposit insurance losses. Since 1980 deposits have been insured for up to $100,000.

HISTORY

As a result of the bank failures of the Great Depression, President Franklin D. Roosevelt and Congress created the Federal Deposit Insurance Corporation (FDIC) to help restore the country's confidence in its banking system. By 1932, with a 25 percent unemployment rate in the United States, depositors began to withdraw their savings from banks in order to survive. In many cases, the banks, which had overextended themselves in the purchase of stocks, loans to failing farms, and other bad investments that had been steadily losing value since the great crash of 1929, did not have the assets to cover the depositors' withdrawals. This caused widespread panic as frantic depositors demanded their money. In 1933 President Roosevelt temporarily closed the banks to stem the tide of outgoing deposits and to save the remaining banks from closing permanently.

In 1933 Congress passed the National Banking Act, which created the FDIC as a temporary agency and gave it the authority to regulate and supervise some banks and to provide deposit insurance. On January 1, 1934, the FDIC was operational. Like other insurance companies, the FDIC charged member banks premium payments that were prorated upon the number of deposits held within each institution. In turn, it guaranteed that depositors accounts were protected initially for $2,500 and by the middle of 1934, $5,000. After the failure of nine FDIC insured banks occurred in 1934, the first depositor was paid. Another insurance agency was founded under the National Housing Act in 1934 along the lines of the FDIC: the Federal Savings and Loan Insurance Corporation (FSLIC) was to serve as a supervisory agency over the S&Ls that were limited to home loans.

Banks continued to close throughout the remainder of the 1930s, but those depositors who banked with institutions insured by the FDIC were reimbursed up to $5,000 of their deposits. This helped restore confidence in the American banking system, and by 1939 fewer banks were closing and some were even showing profits again. By 1950, during the economic boom that followed World War II (1939–45) the FDIC increased the deposit coverage to $10,000 per depositor per bank.

By 1974 the FDIC was insuring up to $40,000. In 1975 and 1977 Congress passed the Home Mortgage Disclosure Act of 1975, and the Community Reinvestment Act of 1977 made home loans available to lower income families and neighborhoods. Congress charged the FDIC to examine nonmember state (as opposed to national) banks to ensure compliance with the new laws.

The deposit insurance rose to $100,000 in 1980. This raise in the deposit insurance was fortunate because the 1980s were to prove to be a stressful time for banking. More than 1,600 banks failed in this decade—more banks than during the 1930s or at any other period in the FDIC's history.

Parallel to the problems besetting the FDIC were the problems being encountered by the FSLIC and its member S&Ls. According to *History of the Eighties*, an analysis published in 1997 by the FDIC, the increasing number of bank failures had "no single cause or short list of causes. Rather it resulted from a concurrence of various forces working together to produce a decade of banking crises." Three of the main reasons banks failed were untimely regional recessions, legislative deregulations, and excessive risks without adequate supervisory authority. By 1984, for the first time since it began in 1933, the FDIC paid out more than it received. For the next eight years, this was to be the norm. Despite the bank failures however, no depositor lost a penny on federally insured funds.

By 1990, economic analysts realized that the banking crisis was still deepening. They warned that "any major failure, or series of failures, could wipe out the insurance funds of the FDIC" which stood at less than $13 billion of insurance for more than $2 trillion of deposits (*Christian Science Monitor*). Congress authorized the FDIC to borrow $30 billion from the U.S. Treasury if needed. Tighter controls over banking practices, more audits of banks to resolve problems at their onset, and larger national banks that could cover regional recessions through a use of their assets were solutions to the crisis in banking that were established over the next decade.

Parallel to the banking crises, but of far greater magnitude, were the failures in the country's S&Ls. Congress passed legislation in 1980 that basically deregulated S&Ls, allowing them to offer checking accounts and credit cards—services that were available in commercial banks. By 1982 this trend continued, with allowing S&Ls to invest in commercial real estate and land development deals, to offer money market accounts, and even to own land development companies. By the mid-1980s the S&Ls had overextended themselves, taken too many risks on questionable loans, and were failing, leaving the FSLIC to pay depositors. The FSLIC was in dire trouble and insolvent by the end of the decade.

Congress stepped in and made sweeping changes. They dissolved the FSLIC and gave the FDIC authority over savings and loan associations. Congress created a temporary agency, the Resolution Trust Corporation (RTC), to clean up the mess made by the savings and loan associations. The normal staffing levels of the FDIC hovered at around eight thousand employees, but with inclusion of the RTC staff it swelled to more than 22,000 by 1992. At the end of 1995 the RTC had completed its mandate and was dissolved, having accomplished much in the way of reselling property and restoring depositors' belief in the stability and solvency of the S&Ls. The remaining business was given to the FDIC to complete.

At the FDIC, two offices were established, the Banking Insurance Fund (BIF) and the Savings Association Insurance Fund (SAIF), to accept the premiums paid by the banks and the S&Ls to the FDIC. After more than a decade of turmoil and problems, the FDIC returned to its former size and to a more solvent and focused banking industry. The RTC's work continued under the authority of the FDIC, which now received all the remaining properties affected by the S&L failures, as well as ones from bank failures. A new era of bank mergers and consolidations began under the guidance of the FDIC. By the late 1990s the FDIC's insurance fund was fully restored.

CURRENT POLITICAL ISSUES

For most of its history, the FDIC was a benign insurance agency that guaranteed the safety and stability of American banks and gave depositors a feeling of confidence in the banking community. The 1980s, however, was a period of sweeping change in the perception of the safety and stability of the nation's banks. The failure of more than 1,600 banks and the S&L debacle were warnings that unless banking regulations were examined and updated, other problems such as these could occur. The consolidation and mergers of many smaller banks into larger, more fiscally sound institutions; the legislation permitting major banks to open branches in all regions of the country; and the increased supervision of the banks were established to eliminate potential problems.

Case Study: Understanding Deposit Insurance

How well do bank employees and depositors understand what the FDIC insurance covers? *Money* magazine found that many individuals, bank employees, and even staff members of the FDIC did not always understand what the insurance covered. Computer consultant Alan Naisuler came to *Money* in 1993 with a disturbing tale. He had asked an officer at his bank if the $100,000 account that he held in his name in trust for his mother and his own $40,000 account were both covered by the FDIC. He was told that they were by the bank officer. He found out differently when the bank failed and was closed the following year. The FDIC only covered $100,000. Under the rules set forth by the FDIC, an account in trust did not qualify as a separate account so the consultant was $40,000 over the limit. Since the FDIC was able to arrange a sale of his bank to another more solvent bank, the customer was able to get some of his money back, but he still experienced a loss of more than $13,000. "The officer who advised me had an FDIC sign on her desk. I thought I was safe," he told *Money*.

Still angry over what he considered inadequate knowledge of FDIC rules, Naisuler started to wonder if other banks and S&Ls were as ignorant of the FDIC rules as was his own. He visited 79 banks and thrifts in the Boston area, posing as a prospective depositor. He asked them all the question that led him to lose money: "Would two accounts, one in his name, and one in his name in trust for his mother, each qualify for full separate FDIC coverage?" He even persuaded the bankers to give him the answer in writing by pretending to have a broken finger and needing them to write the information. He found that 85 percent of the banking staff he asked (67 out of 79) gave him the wrong answer.

Money verified Naisuler's results in an independent survey. Posing as ordinary depositors, *Money* reporters contacted 273 large and small banks in 14 different states and asked them five questions. Only 33 representatives (12 percent) were able to answer all five questions. Even FDIC officials in regional offices were unable to answer all of the questions. (Washington headquarters' FDIC personnel got all five right.) These results shocked *Money*, which reported its findings to both the banks and to the FDIC. Although the FDIC found that the lack of knowledge and training of bank employees regarding FDIC rules was a serious problem, they admitted that bank examiners did not review the training of employees during audits. They responded with a letter to all banks and thrifts urging training and sent out explanatory brochures.

These measures were too late in some instances. There are few avenues for people to regain losses caused by bank negligence. Even the 5th Circuit Court of Appeals placed obstacles in the path of persons trying to recover their money when the loss resulted from bad advice. The court ruled that the wrong advice must have been given in writing at the time the account was opened and it must have been approved by the bank's board of directors and included in the bank's official records. If a depositor opened an account and was simply told the wrong thing, the depositor was left to suffer the consequences.

SUCCESSES AND FAILURES

For more than 60 years the FDIC has insured depositors' money in banks. When the agency began during the worst years of the Great Depression, its goal was to give the American people a renewed sense of security in their financial institutions. Even during the turbulent 1980s when bank failures numbered in the thousands, the FDIC kept its commitment and paid depositors their insured amounts. From this and the close watch now kept on uninsured banks by FDIC examiners, Americans can once again feel confident about the strength and security of their financial institutions.

FUTURE DIRECTIONS

As 2000 approaches and computer systems are expected to experience problems the FDIC is developing software and contingency plans to ensure that all member banks and thrifts are able to make the transition smoothly and without interruption. The FDIC will also provide regulations and insurance to banks as they begin to transact business electronically, with depositors completing their transactions on-line.

AGENCY RESOURCES

To find out more about the FDIC, visit its Web site at *http://www.fdic.gov* or call the consumer hot line at 1-800-934-3342. Information is also available by writing FDIC, 550 17th St. NW, Washington DC 20429.

AGENCY PUBLICATIONS

The FDIC publishes a number of handbooks for both consumers and bankers, brochures, newsletters, press releases, and a banking journal, the *FDIC Banking Review*, which is available on-line and in hard copy as well. Other publications include *Quarterly Banking Profile, Summary of Deposits (Data Book), Real Estate Survey*, and *Statistics on Banking*. These are all available on-line or by writing FDIC, Office of Corporate Communications, 550 17th St. NW, Washington DC 20429.

BIBLIOGRAPHY

Belsky, Gary. "Money Update: First, the Federal Savings." *Sports Illustrated*, 1 October 1991, p. 29.

Denver, Jonathan Beaty. "Running With a Bad Crowd." *Time*, 1 October 1990, p. 36.

"The Effect of the FDIC Act of 1991 on Bank Stocks." *Journal of Financial Research*, 1996.

Federal Deposit Insurance Corporation. *History of the 80s: Lessons for the Future*. Government Printing Office, 1997.

Halverson, Guy. "Bank Trouble Threatens FDIC." *Christian Science Monitor*, 26 September 1990.

Hornik, Richard. "Business Breaking the Bank, Taxpayers Beware." *Time*, 24 September 1990, p. 66.

Kane, Edward J. "Re-regulating Rural Banks: Discussion." *American Agricultural Economics Association*, pp. 751–7.

Kobliner, Beth, and Lisa Fickenscher. "Banking: What Banks Don't Know Can Hurt You." *Money*, 1 March 1993, p. 144.

Mazumdar, Sumon C. "Bank Regulations, Capital Structure and Risk." *Journal of Financial Research*, 22 June 1996, p. 209.

O'Connell, Vanessa. "Exclusive Rating: The Best Bank in America." *Money*, 1 June 1995, p. 126.

Stavins, Joanna. "Can Demand Elasticities Explain . . . ." *Federal Reserve Bank of Boston*, 1996.

"Wealth Effects of Enforcement Actions." *Journal of Financial Research*, 1996.

Federal Election Commission (FEC)

PARENT ORGANIZATION: Independent
ESTABLISHED: April 14, 1975
EMPLOYEES: 297

Contact Information:

ADDRESS: 999 E St.
Washington, DC 20463
PHONE: (202) 694-1100
TOLL FREE: (800) 424-9530
TDD (HEARING IMPAIRED): (202) 219-3336
E-MAIL: rwerfel@fec.gov
URL: http://www.fec.gov
VICE CHAIRMAN: Scott E. Thomas

WHAT IS ITS MISSION?

According to the *The United States Government Manual (1997–98)*, "The Federal Election Commission (FEC) has exclusive jurisdiction in the administration and civil enforcement of laws regulating the acquisition and expenditure of campaign funds to ensure compliance by participants in the federal election campaign process. Its chief mission is to provide public disclosure of campaign finance activities and effect voluntary compliance by providing the public with information on the laws and regulations concerning campaign finance."

HOW IS IT STRUCTURED?

The FEC is composed of six members, appointed by the president and confirmed by the Senate. Each member serves a six-year term, and two seats are subject to appointment every two years. By law no more than three commissioners can be members of the same political party, and at least four votes are required for any official commission action. This structure was created to encourage nonpartisan decisions. The chairmanship of the commission rotates among the members each year, with no member serving as chairman more than one time during his or her term.

The general counsel, staff director, and inspector general administer execution of the mandates of the FEC. The general counsel and staff are responsible for policy, litigation, enforcement of FEC rules and public funding, ethics, and special projects. The staff director manages all administrative functions: election administration,

CAMPAIGN CONTRIBUTION LIMITS

The following contribution limits are set forth by the Federal Election Campaign Act:

- An individual may give $1,000 per election to a candidate or a candidate committee; $20,000 per year to a national party committee; and $5,000 per year to any other political committee. Total contributions per calendar year may not exceed $25,000.
- A multi-candidate committee may give $5,000 per election to a candidate or a candidate committee; $15,000 per year to a national party committee; and $5,000 per year to any other political committee. There is no limit on total contributions. (A multi-candidate committee is a political committee that has at least 51 contributors, has been registered for at least six months, and has made contributions to at least five candidates for federal office.)
- Any other political committee may give $1,000 per election to a candidate or a candidate committee; $20,000 per year to a national party committee; and $5,000 per year to any other political committee. There is no limit on total contributions.

NOTE: If a contributor gives to a committee knowing that a substantial portion will be used to support a particular candidate, then the contribution counts as a contribution to a specific candidate and therefore counts against the donor's limit. The per election limits apply to each individual election, which means that primaries, runoffs, and general elections are considered separate elections and therefore have separate contribution limits. Limits apply to the total value of money, goods, services, loans, endorsement of loans, and any other type of contribution given.

Prohibited Campaign Contributions

- No contribution may come from the treasury of a corporation, labor organization, or national bank.
- Federal government contractors are prohibited from contributing to any election. The prohibition does not apply to personal contributions made by employees, partners, shareholders, or officers.
- No contribution may be made by one person in the name of another.

NOTE: Prohibitions apply to contributions to or from political committees. They apply whether or not the contribution was solicited and regardless of the type of contribution made or the purpose for which it was used. Committee treasurers are responsible for ensuring that all contributions are legal.

---

reports to Congress, audits, information, personnel, the press office, data systems development, and planning and management. The inspector general and staff monitor FEC activities to ensure complete adherence to campaign finance laws.

PRIMARY FUNCTIONS

The FEC administers and enforces the Federal Election Campaign Act (FECA), the statute that governs the financing of federal elections. Outlined in the FECA are the rules for how elections are to be conducted, what amounts of money can be donated by an individual or a corporation to a particular candidate, and the boundaries of the FEC's monitoring and enforcement powers. Regulation of federal campaign funding came from congressional judgment that a representative form of government needed protection from the influence of unlimited and undisclosed political contributions. The laws were designed to ensure that candidates in federal elections were not "bought," or indebted to a narrow group of people.

The FEC ensures that campaign contributions are within the legal limits mandated by the law. This means that "hard money" or money that is directly given to a candidate cannot exceed specified limits. "Soft money," which has no dollar limit, is paid to an organizational group, such as the Democratic Committee or Republican National Committee. The money is then funneled by the committee to candidates. The main source of soft money is Political Action Committees (PACs) that were created to allow corporations, labor unions, and similar organizations to make donations to a party or candidate. The FEC closely monitors PACs because their financial clout is significant. The FEC oversees more than 8,000 PACs.

The commission regulates the public financing of presidential elections by certifying federal payments to primary candidates, general election nominees, and national nominating conventions. It also audits recipients of federal funds and may require repayments to the U.S. Treasury if a political committee makes non-qualified campaign expenditures.

The Commission also ensures public disclosure of campaign finance activities reported by PACs supporting federal candidates. Committee reports, filed regu-

FAST FACTS

Each citizen filling out a 1040 federal income tax form is given the opportunity to contribute three tax dollars to the Presidential Election Campaign Fund. Approximately 33 million taxpayers check the "yes" box every year.

(Source: Federal Election Committee. "$3 Dollar Tax Checkoff," 1998.)

larly, disclose sources of campaign money and how it is spent. The reports are compiled and placed on public record within 48 hours of receipt.

PROGRAMS

Although the FEC's primary duty is to monitor elections, it also makes an effort to keep Americans informed on elections, campaign financing, and related issues. In addition to press releases and the information on its Web site at http://www.fec.gov, the FEC sponsors a number of conferences each year. Topics generally covered include fundraising, reporting, registering and voting in elections, and PACs.

BUDGET INFORMATION

The FEC was appropriated $31.6 million by Congress in 1998. The majority of this money was spent on staff salaries. Other areas receiving money from the budget were civilian personnel benefits, General Service Administration rental payments, communications, and computer equipment.

HISTORY

Early in its history the United States became concerned with election regulations. According to the *Twenty Year Report* issued by the FEC, the first political campaign that was financed was conducted in 1791 when Alexander Hamilton's supporters "published competing newspapers designed to sway the electorate. These minimal expenditures set the tone for campaigns over the next several decades." In 1832 Andrew Jackson's presidential campaign again changed how campaigns were financed when one of the first special interest groups, the privately–owned Bank of the United States, spent heavily to support Jackson's opponent Henry Clay because they feared Jackson would revoke the bank's charter. Pre-Civil War campaign expenditures were moderate, though, compared to the expenditures of later years.

By 1896 excesses in campaign financing and corruption came to light through the efforts of muckraking journalists who reported on how corporations bought candidates and votes. President Theodore Roosevelt declared: "all contributions by corporations to any political committee or for any political purpose should be forbidden by law." These revelations led to a series of laws over the next century designed to curb special interest influence on U.S. elections. Some of the more notable acts (and there were many dealing with all aspects of campaign financing reform) included: the Tillman Act (1907), which prohibited corporations and national banks from contributing money to federal campaigns; three years later the first campaign disclosure legislation; the Hatch Act (1939) and its 1940 amendments, which gave Congress the power to regulate primary elections and limited the amount of campaign contributions and expenditures for congressional elections; and the Taft-Hartley Act (1947), which barred labor unions and corporations from making contributions to candidates in federal elections.

Congress's passage of the Federal Election Campaign Act of 1971 fundamentally changed the federal campaign finance laws. Provisions required full reporting of campaign contributions and expenditures. It also allowed corporations and labor unions to form Political Action Committees (PACs) for which they could solicit contributions. PACs are prohibited from contributing directly to publicly financed federal election campaigns; but may support a candidate through independent spending—such as by paying for television commercials. The 1971 laws also required full disclosure of contributions and limited advertising in the media. The Revenue Act, also passed in 1971, allowed citizens to donate a dollar by way of their income tax return to a general campaign fund, which was to be divided among eligible presidential candidates. By 1976 enough tax money had accumulated to fund the 1976 Presidential election, the first publicly-funded federal election in U.S. history.

There was no group or agency charged with monitoring or enforcing newly enacted laws. Amendments to the FECA established the Federal Election Commission (FEC) in 1975. The first FEC commissioners were sworn in on April 14, 1975. Aside from the usual efforts to circumvent campaign finance laws, special interest groups challenged the laws in court. The Supreme Court in *Buckley v. Valeo* (1976) upheld contribution limits but struck down expenditure limits because they restricted the "quantity of campaign speech," which subsequently effects free speech as guaranteed by the Constitution.

Campaign financing laws are continuously examined and revised in an effort to guarantee freedom yet protect the American public from corruption.

One of the more obvious attempts to circumvent election laws was the efforts of an Arkansas restaurateur to funnel funds, allegedly from a foreign government, to the Democratic National Committee in what appeared to be an influence buying scheme. The twists and turns of the money were daunting with checks made in names other than the contributors, corporate donations and such. Similar situations have forced the FEC to be ever vigilant in enforcing the laws. The remainder of the 1970s found the FEC struggling to enforce new rules such as limiting honoria (gifts) for speaking engagements by federal office holders, eliminating any additional "personal use" of funds by Congress, and monitoring the presidential dollar donations.

As it evolved, the FEC also became a "customer" driven agency. Much time and effort were spent educating the public about elections, encouraging compliance with the legal limits, monitoring federal election spending, and providing opinions and documents to congressional staff who made the laws. The FEC tried in the 1980s and 1990s to maintain a strong, watchful eye on the various aspects of funding, including "soft money," and the complete disclosure of information regarding funding. Many Administrative Orders (AOs) have been issued concerning all aspects of campaign financing and, according to the *Twenty Year Report*, there are more than 12 million pages available on this topic for public review.

CURRENT POLITICAL ISSUES

One of the most heated and troubling issues facing the FEC has been the amount of "soft money" that has been contributed to federal campaigns. Senators Fred Thompson (R-TN) and John Glenn (D-OH) held hearings from 1997 through 1998 concerning the effects and scope of the soft money funds that were being shifted to federal elections, particularly the 1996 presidential campaigns. The FEC was the primary agency under fire during these investigations.

Case Study: PACs and the President

When Senators Thompson and Glenn convened their bipartisan subcommittee hearing in 1997, there was great optimism that there would emerge from these hearings a new set of campaign finance directives that would reform the current laws and set limits on soft money contributions. While many politicians felt the hearings were an indictment of the Democratic Party, it was made clear at the outset that both parties and their involvement with PACs and soft money would be examined thoroughly. Thompson promised that by the fall of 1997 there would be comprehensive reforms presented to the Senate for consideration.

Allegations of influence peddling from a foreign government, contributions from the Chinese government to the Clinton campaign, illegal campaign contributions to Vice President Albert Gore from a Buddhist temple, and questionable campaign fund-raisers were among the issues to be investigated. The media broadcast stories of foreign money being donated to the Democratic Party, hidden funds, and illegal uses of funds. Evidence found in the course of the media investigations was taken into consideration when the subcommittee formulated its questions for the hearings.

Before the hearings began President Bill Clinton requested that the FEC move to ban soft money and began a firestorm of debate over who has the authority to dictate soft money issues, the Congress or the FEC. The reason the President asked for this ban was to try and control whose money is donated to a national committee. Thus, by the time the hearings began, there was a negative and pessimistic outlook as to what they would accomplish.

As the hearings progressed, it became apparent that the FEC was overworked and under budgeted and staffed to adequately monitor all the federal campaign contributions that were given to both presidential and congressional campaigns. The subcommittee found that the FEC, which was in charge of monitoring these investigations, did complete their tasks but took a long time to finish reports and order fines and other punishments. For instance, the FEC took seven years to complete the report on President George Bush's 1988 campaign and, although the FEC found illegal campaign contributions, chose to fine the president's committee rather than seek criminal charges.

Public Impact

The Senate ultimately deadlocked in the fall of 1997. Although the subcommittee did not recommend substantial changes in the campaign finance laws, it did focus the attention of the public on the excesses that occurred under the guise of fundraising. It also became apparent that while there has been a public demand for campaign finance reform, this demand was tempered with a concern for civil liberties and the rights of individuals to work for and sponsor a candidate. In order to address these concerns, groups such as the American Civil Liberties Union (ACLU) recommended reforms that could benefit both the candidates and the individual giver while limiting direct influence of PACs on candidates. Some of the reforms suggested by the committee to the FEC and Congress have included elimination of soft money, offering candidates discounted television access for their commercials, and limiting the amount of PAC money that can be given to candidates. These restrictions would not impinge on individuals' rights to free speech as covered by the First Amendment.

FUTURE DIRECTIONS

One of the FEC's most important plans for the future is to use the Internet to provide better access to campaign finance information to the public. Users will soon be able to peruse up-to-date information on which candidates received money from which individuals and PACs and the candidates that specific individuals and PACs contributed to. Individuals and PACs contributing over $200 to federal political committees will be listed as well. Additionally, images of actual campaign finance reports that were added to the Web in early 1998 will include all those dating back to 1993. All of these services will be made accessible through the FEC's Web site at http://www.fec.gov.

AGENCY RESOURCES

The Information Services Division provides information and assistance to federal candidates, political committees, and the general public. This division answers questions on campaign finance laws, conducts workshops and seminars on the law, and provides publications and forms. For information or materials, call 1-800-424-9530. The Office of Public Records, at 999 E Street NW, Washington, DC 20463 provides space for public inspection of all reports and statements relating to campaign finance since 1972. It is open weekdays from 9 a.m. to 5 p.m. and has extended hours during peak election periods. The public is invited to visit the office or obtain information by calling 1-800-424-9530. The library contains a collection of basic legal research resources, that emphasize political campaign financing, corporate and labor political activity, and campaign finance reform. It is open to the public on weekdays between 9 a.m. and 5 p.m. For further information call 1-800-424-9530.

AGENCY PUBLICATIONS

The FEC publishes a number of brochures for individuals and groups that describe the campaign finance laws, voting rights, and personal contributions. Some of the titles include: *Citizens Guide to Contributions and the Law*, *Financial Information about Candidates, Parties and PACs*, *Help for Candidates*, and *About Elections and Voting*. Many of the publications are available in Spanish. To obtain these and other FEC documents, sign onto the Web site at http://www.fec.gov or request a catalog from the FEC Information Services by calling 1-800-424-9530 or writing 999 E Street NW, Washington, DC 20463.

BIBLIOGRAPHY

Clinton, William J. "Letter from the President to Members of the Federal Election Commission." *M2 PressWIRE*, 3 March 1998.

Dowd, Ann Reilly. "Money and Politics: Look Who's Cashing in on Congress: Tales from the Money Trail." *Money*, 1 December 1997, pp. 128+.

Federal Election Committee. *Twenty Year Report 1975–1995*. Washington, D.C., 1996.

Gullo, Karen. "Once-Illegal 'Soft Money' Taints Political Climate: 'Soft' Contributions Again Raising Queries on Curbing Big-Money". *Rocky Mountain News*, 12 October 1997, p. 14A.

"A Look at Campaign Funding." *Gannett News Service*, 7 March 1997.

Murphy, Laura W. "The ACLU vs. Public Citizen: A Debate on Campaign Finance," *The Progressive*, 1 December 1997, pp. 20(3).

Sammon, Bill. "Funds for Democrats Hid from FEC by Union." *Washington Times*, 26 October 1997, p. 7.

Federal Emergency Management Agency (FEMA)

PARENT ORGANIZATION: Independent
ESTABLISHED: March 31, 1979
EMPLOYEES: 2,600 (1998)

Contact Information:

ADDRESS: 500 C St. SW
Washington, DC 20472
PHONE: (202) 646-4600
TDD (HEARING IMPAIRED): (800) 462-7585
URL: http://www.fema.gov
DIRECTOR: James Lee Witt

WHAT IS ITS MISSION?

According to its "Strategic Plan 1997–2007," the mission of the Federal Emergency Management Agency (FEMA) is "to reduce loss of life and property and protect our nation's critical infrastructure from all types of hazards through a comprehensive, risk-based, emergency management program of mitigation, preparedness, response and recovery." FEMA is the response crew that comes to the aid of the public when a large area of the country is hit by a severe storm, hurricane, fire, or other disaster that causes damage to houses, roads, buildings, bridges, and other structures. FEMA also maintains a state of readiness to respond to potentially dangerous problems such as an accident at a nuclear power plant or a flood resulting from dam failure.

HOW IS IT STRUCTURED?

FEMA is the independent cabinet-level agency that manages the president's Disaster Relief Fund, the source of most federally funded disaster assistance. The director of FEMA is appointed by the president and approved by Congress. Along with the director, a deputy director and a chief of staff administer the nine central offices, ten regional offices, five directorates, and two administrations that comprise FEMA.

FEMA's central offices work out of the Washington, DC, headquarters. Five of them are primarily engaged in internal functions of the agency; they are the Office of Human Resources Management, the Office of Equal Rights, the Office of Financial Management, the

Office of General Counsel, and the Office of Inspector General. The central offices that deal with public matters are the Office of Congressional and Legislative Affairs, the Office of Emergency Information and Media Affairs, the Office of Policy and Regional Operations, and the Office of National Security Affairs. The regional offices each serve several states specifically by helping them prepare a plan to respond to disasters, develop mitigation programs, and meet other needs when major disasters occur. They also assist the regions in meeting national program goals and supporting policy development.

FEMA directorates work together in response to emergencies. Each represents a step of the emergency response process: the Mitigation Directorate, the Response and Recovery Directorate, the Preparedness Directorate, the Operations Support Directorate, and the Information and Technical Services Directorate.

The Federal Insurance Administration, under the Office of the Director, engages in flood-related activities. It runs the National Flood Insurance Program, which offers federal flood insurance through private insurers. The program also aims to educate people about flooding and the importance of having flood insurance. The United States Fire Administration (USFA) and its National Fire Academy were created by the Federal Fire Prevention and Control Act of 1974. The Federal Insurance Administration states that its mission is "to provide leadership, coordination and support for the Nation's fire prevention and control, fire training and education, and emergency medical services activities." The USFA attempts to curb the United States's fire death rate, which is one of the highest per capita in the industrialized world; each year fire injures more than 25,000 people, kills about 5,000 people (100 of whom are firefighters), and causes more than $9 billion in direct property losses.

FEMA works with more than 25 federal departments and agencies and innumerable regional disaster management agencies. More than 4,000 disaster assistance employees (DAEs) stand ready to serve when they are needed at a disaster site. DAEs are federal government employees who volunteer and receive training to help FEMA. Their service may span a few days to several weeks and they may be called upon two or three times a year depending on their specialty and the number of disasters that arise. FEMA also sends limited assistance to disaster victims outside the United States.

PRIMARY FUNCTIONS

FEMA is the central agency within the federal government that handles emergency disaster management, a process that begins even before disaster strikes. The "disaster life cycle" involves prevention, preparedness, response, and recovery. While disaster prevention is not always possible, some accidents, like chemical explosions, hazardous materials spills, and fires, can be prevented. Often prevention measures are simple, such as the installation of smoke detectors

Preparedness and Mitigation

FEMA works directly with communities to help them prepare for disaster, particularly those that are prone to them, like the southeastern coastal states that are frequently hit by hurricanes. FEMA may recommend the type of windows a building should have or train emergency managers at its National Emergency Training Center. At the training center trainees are taught emergency management planning, flood plain management, hazardous materials planning, dam safety, and multi-hazard response planning. The agency also offers independent study courses in disaster preparedness, disaster assistance, and hazardous materials, which are available to the general public for free. FEMA also develops detailed response plans for serious man-made disasters, such as those that might occur at a commercial nuclear power plant or a U.S. Army chemical stockpile site.

FEMA considers pre-disaster planning an important step in the disaster life cycle and encourages states and localities to plan for emergencies, make resources available to provide facilities and purchase equipment for disaster response, provide emergency personnel training, sponsor preparedness exercises, and keep their constituencies informed. The Preparedness, Training and Exercise Directorate coordinates such activities.

Mitigation is a type of preparedness and an attempt to break the disaster-rebuild-disaster cycle. The goal of mitigation is to lessen the impact of disasters upon families, homes, communities, and the economy by reducing or eliminating long-term risk to people and property from natural hazards and their effects. Mitigation measures can be as complicated as reengineering bridges to withstand earthquakes or as easy as encouraging people to purchase flood insurance to replace belongings. Developing, adopting, and enforcing stricter building codes and standards is an important, widely used mitigation technique. In fact, communities that apply for federal emergency flood insurance are required to adopt more stringent ordinances, like floodplain management requirements aimed at controlling future use of flood plains.

Response

Response begins when disaster threatens. It is FEMA's process of mobilizing and positioning emergency equipment; helping people get out of danger and obtain food, water, shelter, and medical attention; and restoring damaged services, especially important ones like telephone services, transportation routes, and hospitals. A state or local government requests federal aid when it cannot do these things on its own. The first step is for the government, often the president, to declare an area to be a disaster area or make an emergency declaration. Federal assistance usually takes the form of money but could include resources from any federal department or agency.

Recovery

After a disaster occurs, much rebuilding, or recovery, is needed. Clearing debris, repairing roads and bridges, restoring water and sewer services, and rebuilding homes and businesses are all part of this process. Federal disaster assistance takes three forms: individual assistance is made available to individuals, families, farmers, and businesses and includes such things as loans, grants, emergency housing, tax relief, and unemployment assistance; public financial assistance is made available to states, localities, and nonprofit groups for the restoration of public systems and facilities; and matching mitigation funds are available to states and localities for projects that eliminate or reduce an area's vulnerability to a hazard.

PROGRAMS

FEMA programs range as much in diversity as the scope of disasters that can occur. But the majority of its programs clearly emphasize training and community involvement. For example, FEMA's Community and Family Preparedness Program (CFP) seeks to educate, advance, and support emergency managers, firefighters, volunteers, teachers, and other professional disaster preparedness educators by amassing a common body of knowledge and materials for use in training and organizing communities. The CFP specifically developed a training package on how to organize and manage a community and family preparedness program.

Additionally FEMA operates a free independent study program, available to the public through the Internet, which offers courses such as "Hazardous Materials: A Citizen's Orientation" and "Animals in Disaster—Awareness and Preparedness." FEMA's Emergency Management Institute offers classes to the general public as well as specialized training; for example, it runs the Multi-hazard Building Design Summer Institute, which offered instruction in earthquake mitigation and fire safety design.

Project Impact

Project Impact is a multifaceted, community-based, pre-disaster prevention program. It activates communities to prevent, prepare for, and handle disasters, with the ultimate goal being to protect the economic well-being of the community. For example, Napa, California, instituted a local sales tax increase to fund flood reduction efforts, and a Home Depot store in Deerfield Beach, Florida, has a Project Impact aisle and provides educational and informational materials on how to make buildings disaster resistant. As FEMA Director James Lee Witt said to the National Press Club at the June 3, 1998, Project Impact National Kick-Off, "Our studies show we can save up to $2 in disaster relief costs for every $1 investment in prevention." The four steps Director Witt outlined for becoming disaster resistant are: create Project Impact partnerships, identify local risks, prioritize prevention actions designed to mitigate risks, and make good on action plans.

BUDGET:
Federal Emergency Management Agency

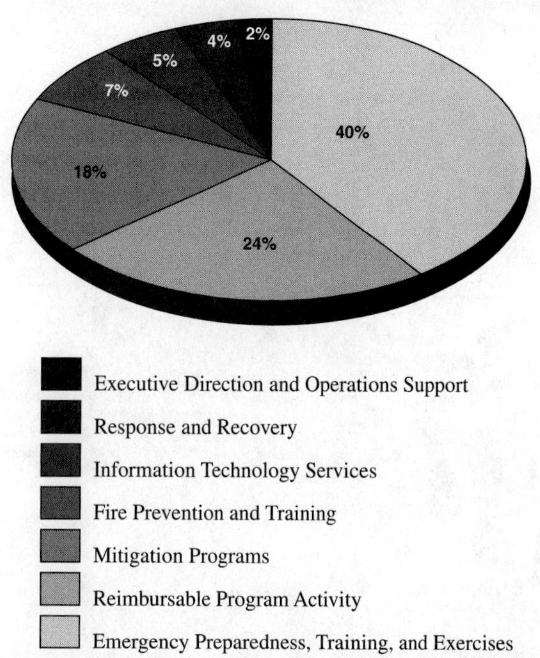

BUDGET INFORMATION

In 1998 Congress appropriated $320 million for the daily operation and training of FEMA personnel. Of this amount $128 million or 40 percent was directed toward emergency preparedness, training, and exercises. Reimbursable program activity accounted for $76 million or 24 percent. Additionally funds went toward mitigation programs ($57 million or 18 percent), fire prevention and training ($22 million or 7 percent), information technology services ($16 million or 5 percent), and response and recovery ($13 million or 4 percent). The remaining portion of the FEMA budget was spent on executive direction and operations support.

Hurricane Hugo was one of the most devastating storms of the 1980s. Dozens of pleasure boats lie jumbled together, swept onto the Isle of Palms off the coast of South Carolina. FEMA was widely criticized for its ineffective response to Hurricane Hugo. *(Photograph by Tom Salyer. Reuters/Corbis Bettmann)*

In addition to its operating budget, each year Congress sets aside money to be used for emergency relief as necessary. This sum can vary a great deal from year to year, as the cost of the previous year's relief efforts are assessed. In 1998 Congress appropriated approximately $2.6 billion to the President's Disaster Relief Fund. $100 million was also allocated to the Emergency Food and Shelter Program.

HISTORY

FEMA was established by Executive Order 12127 on March 31, 1979, consolidating the nation's emergency-related programs. When President Jimmy Carter began the agency, its primary mission was to help the country recover in the event of a nuclear attack; the nation was at the height of the Cold War with the now defunct

Soviet Union. According to the *Gannett News Service* FEMA's primary function was to "help the country to recover from a nuclear attack and to help ensure the government continued to operate in a nuclear war." Helping people recover from disasters was its secondary function.

From 1982 until 1991, 78 percent of FEMA's budget was allocated to national security. *Newsday* reported that for every dollar FEMA spent on disasters, $12 was spent on secret security programs. Expenditures included maintaining bomb shelters and underground facilities, watching over the United States's chemical weapons, and developing a 300-vehicle mobile communications fleet that would be used to maintain communications during an enemy attack. About one third of FEMA's staff was assigned to this project and the budget for it was submitted to Congress as classified due to its relation to national security. FEMA's focus was not on earthquakes or hurricanes and their effects on the lives of Americans.

FEMA's response to natural disasters during this time was usually ineffective. For instance, in 1991 the city manager in Homestead, Florida, needed hand-held radios for his emergency crews to communicate with each other on the ground after Hurricane Andrew destroyed the phone lines. FEMA responded by sending high tech vans capable of communicating with aircraft halfway around the globe but not capable of contacting the next street. The lack of confidence in FEMA's ability to handle disasters was so great that President George Bush sent the secretary of transportation to coordinate relief efforts rather than rely on FEMA.

A shift came when President Bill Clinton took office. In 1993 President Clinton appointed James Lee Witt as the director of FEMA. Mr. Witt, unlike his predecessor, had actual disaster relief experience. Director Witt began the transformation of FEMA from an agency primarily concerned with national defense to one that proactively assisted people experiencing disasters. Funding for defense activities was reduced from 70 percent to 11 percent of the budget; the remaining funds were reserved for disaster relief and preparedness programs. Those high-powered vans became mobile communications centers; warehouses were filled with emergency supplies such as tents, generators, plastic sheeting, and food. Training programs were established to assist in disaster preparedness and FEMA became proactive in anticipating problem areas and acting to mitigate the effects of a disaster. Its new focus breathed new life into a dying agency and created a new and vibrant source for disaster relief.

FAST FACTS

A month after President Bill Clinton signed a disaster declaration at the request of California Governor Pete Wilson for damage caused by the 1998 El Niño storms, FEMA issued checks totaling $10,745,583 to more than 7,000 storm victims.

(Source: Federal Emergency Management Agency, 1998.)

CURRENT POLITICAL ISSUES

After years of criticism and debate over its viability, FEMA has proved itself an agency that has shifted its focus and improved its ability to meet the challenges of its mandate. With a new emphasis on preparedness, the mismanagement and distrust that were prevalent during the days of hurricanes Hugo and Andrew began to recede as FEMA improved its services and therefore its image.

Case Study: Preparing for Hurricane Erin

In 1995, three years after Hurricane Andrew killed 55 people and caused $30 billion in damage, Hurricane Erin headed toward the east coast of Florida, prompting Florida Governor Lawton Chiles to declare a state of emergency. Projections identified Erin as a Category Two hurricane with winds up to 95 mph. A hurricane warning was issued for Florida's southeastern coast, a flood watch was issued for all of east-central Florida, and a tornado watch was put into effect. Though it was not yet apparent whether or not federal assistance was going to be needed, FEMA moved in.

FEMA immediately opened shelters for the 650,000 people in coastal Florida who were forced to evacuate their homes before Erin made landfall. The Region IV Regional Operations Center (ROC) in Atlanta, Georgia was activated and a FEMA emergency response team of disaster experts was deployed. A Mobile Emergency Response Support (MERS) detachment with radio and phone communications equipment and power generators was stationed in central Florida, and FEMA representatives joined the three Florida State Rapid Impact Assessment Teams (RIATs) that were activated and stationed in Orlando. U.S. Army Corps of Engineers representatives were also waiting at the FEMA Region IV ROC and at Florida's Emergency Operations Center (EOC) in Tallahassee. Additionally, the FEMA Headquarters Emergency Support Team Information and Planning section was activated.

FEMA Director Witt was in continual contact with President Clinton and Governor Chiles. A defense coordination officer was made available to deploy Department of Defense resources, FEMA staff in Washington, DC were on call, and other agencies were contacted and put on standby. To keep the public informed, Director Witt gave live radio interviews the evening before Erin was to hit and the ROC director was interviewed for a television news segment that aired that night.

Erin came early on August 2, knocking down trees and causing more than 200,000 Florida Light and Power customers lost power. The number of outages plus the downed foliage made it difficult to get to downed power poles, lines, and transformers. The major impact of Erin, despite the fact that it was downgraded to a tropical storm, was expected to come from the remaining heavy wind and rain that would cause flooding in already saturated areas. Based on the projected path of the storm, Louisiana's EOC and communications network stood by waiting.

Responding to and Recovering From Erin

Two of the three RIATs were activated to perform a quick-needs assessment with assistance from FEMA representatives. Six Preliminary Damage Assessment (PDA) Teams (joint FEMA, state, and local teams for individual assistance) went into the affected area, and six more waited for the storm to play out. FEMA reported that 11,353 people had checked into 140 shelters where 10,900 meals had been served. The military activated an additional EOC, and a dispatch of joint service preparedness liaison officers were sent to the FEMA ROC and Florida's EOC. FEMA also began to review emergency flood insurance policies, checking to see how many properties in the affected area were covered.

FEMA's efforts received much publicity; the Fox Television "Morning News Show" was broadcast from FEMA Headquarters. New information about Erin was posted frequently on FEMA's Web site, including news releases, situation reports, maps, and links to related Internet sites. FEMA Radio Network carried hurricane public service announcements and sound bites from FEMA officials.

Florida continued its recovery process. Two state roads and a bridge were closed, a railroad trestle was washed out, and a cruise ship with 11 crew members on board had sunk. Eighty more shelters opened, housing a total of 27,690 people. By this time 24,223 meals had been served at 54 mobile and 219 fixed feeding sites. In the afternoon, Florida Power reported that 172,000 customers still did not have power, although 186,655 customers had their power restored.

On August 3, shortly after Governor Chiles submitted a request for a major disaster declaration for individual and public assistance for several counties, the White House issued a statement that said, "We pray for a quick recovery. To help that process get underway, I have tonight signed an emergency declaration for the state of Florida and have asked James Lee Witt, the director of the Federal Emergency Management Agency, to coordinate all efforts to save lives and protect the health, safety and property of those effected. There are already FEMA trucks loaded with plastic sheeting, chain saws, generators and other tools headed for the impacted area. Director Witt will go to Florida first thing in the morning, inspect the damage and report back to me."

The Florida RIATs finished damage assessment on the east coast of Florida and was redeployed to the panhandle area to start assessments there. Along with Governor Chiles and the FEMA region IV director, Director Witt himself inspected damaged areas. Governor Chiles requested "search and rescue assets; emergency communications assistance; generators and water pumps; engineering assistance to restore critical facilities; public works support; mass care supplies including ready-to-eat military meals, infant formula, tents, cots and blankets, bottled water, portable toilets and hygiene items; plastic sheeting and furring strips for temporary roof repairs; disaster medical assistance teams, and other types of support," according to a FEMA press release.

As the critical life- and property-threatening stages of Erin passed, FEMA wrapped up its efforts. The MERS detachment departed for home base, shelters on Florida's east coast closed, and residents returned to their homes.

Before responding to Erin, FEMA had been criticized for slow response time and highly bureaucratic recovery processes. The agency had not yet embraced the broader mission of emergency management beyond nuclear disaster but began to do so after a director with extensive experience in emergency management took office. The dramatic difference was best exemplified by the communications trucks that had been almost useless during earlier disasters, but were reconfigured to open direct communications for rescue workers. FEMA had successfully lived up to its mandate and helped the residents of Florida survive a difficult time.

FUTURE DIRECTIONS

FEMA is dedicated to reducing response time to disasters. For instance, it plans to reduce the time taken to provide individuals with FEMA disaster housing assistance from an average of ten days to an average of eight days after the individual registers for assistance. FEMA also has the goal of acting on requests from disaster victims for water, food and shelter within 12 hours after a disaster occurs.

FEMA wants to increase its partnerships with voluntary, state, local, and other federal agencies to increase the responsiveness that each agency has in answering to a disaster. Too often in the past, FEMA has been accused of foot-dragging and slow response time when people are in need. By creating strong partnerships with agencies like the Red Cross and state disaster agencies, FEMA hopes to demonstrate the redirection of its mission and commitment to its goals.

AGENCY RESOURCES

FEMA can be contacted by writing to the Federal Emergency Management Agency, 500 C Street SW, Washington, DC 20472. One of the most important tools that FEMA maintains is the updated Web site at http://www.fema.gov, which contains information regarding disasters and FEMA's disaster preparedness status. When a disaster has struck or is anticipated, FEMA normally establishes hot lines in the affected areas. FEMA educates the public about prevention, provides educational resources to teachers and has an on-line interactive Web site for students, http://www.fema.gov/kids. The site also features a virtual library and an archive of *Impact,* a newsletter for FEMA employees.

AGENCY PUBLICATIONS

FEMA releases hundreds of publications each year on preparing for and recovering from disaster. Among them are: *Arson in the United States*; *Hurricane Tracks, Damage Predictions and Resource Deployments*; *Against the Wind: Protecting Your Home from Hurricane and Wind Damage*; and *Through Hell and High Water: Disasters and the Human-Animal Bond.* These documents are available on-line at http://www.fema.gov or by calling the FEMA Publications Center at 1-800-480-2520.

BIBLIOGRAPHY

Baker, David R. "FEMA Freezes Quake Aid for Bottle Village." *Los Angeles Times,* 8 February 1997, p. B 4.

Becker, Tom, and Robin Rauzi. "Quake-Repair Funds Ok'd for El Portal." *Los Angeles Times,* 14 January 1998, p. B 1.

"Bomb Threat Took Up Most FEMA Funds." *Newsday,* 22 February 1993, p. 15.

"Bond Angered by Lack of FEMA Accountability." Capitol Hill Press Releases, 20 October 1997.

Booth, Cathy. "Catastrophe 101: Will the Government Learn." *Time,* 14 September 1992, p. 42.

"FEMA Efforts to Minimize Disaster Damages." Congressional Testimony, 28 January 1998.

Lipman, Larry. "Washington Bureau, Around the South: Storm Preparation." *Atlantic Constitution,* 2 August 1995, p. B04.

McCarthy, Sheryl. "Keep Politics Out of FEMA." *Newsday,* 3 February 1993, p. 8.

Ryan, Richard A. "FEMA Rebuilds from a Major Disaster—Its Reputation." Gannett News Service, 12 July 1997, p. S11.

Wheeler, Larry. "Computer Program Manager Lauds Forecasting Ability in Hurricane Erin." Gannett News Service, 4 August 1995.

Yan, Ellen, and Michael Slackman. "FEMA Won't Pay on Flight 800." *Newsday,* 17 April 1997, p. A30.

Federal Energy Regulatory Commission (FERC)

PARENT ORGANIZATION: Department of Energy
ESTABLISHED: October 1, 1977
EMPLOYEES: 1350

Contact Information:

ADDRESS: 888 1st St. NE
Washington, DC 20426
PHONE: (202) 208-0055
TDD (HEARING IMPAIRED): (202) 208-0345
FAX: (202) 208-2320
E-MAIL: Public.ReferenceRoom@ferc.fed.us
URL: http://www.ferc.fed.us
CHAIRMAN: James J. Hoecker

WHAT IS ITS MISSION?

According to its published mission statement, the Federal Energy Regulatory Commission (FERC) exists "to oversee America's electric utilities, natural gas industry, hydroelectric projects, and oil pipeline transportation system." Since FERC's creation in 1977, its role has evolved from that of a limited regulatory agency to that of a leader in the regulatory reform process needed to foster healthy competition in the energy industry and create more consumer choices.

HOW IS IT STRUCTURED?

FERC is an independent regulatory commission within the Department of Energy, which is a cabinet-level agency that reports directly to the president of the United States. The commission has five members, who serve staggered terms: one member is appointed by the president, with the advice and consent of the Senate, each year. Members can be reappointed. Each commissioner has an equal vote on regulatory matters and no more than three commissioners may belong to the same political party. One member is designated by the president to serve as the chairman and acts as FERC's administrative head.

The administrative offices of FERC include those of the chief accountant, general counsel, secretary, chief financial officer, and the Office of Economic Policy. The Office of Administrative Law Judges provides legal service to the commission on regulatory matters. FERC's Office of External Affairs serves as the primary source of information regarding energy regulatory matters for public, federal, state, and local government agencies and for public- and private-interest groups. FERC's three program divisions are pipeline regulation, electric power regulation, and hydropower licensing.

PRIMARY FUNCTIONS

FERC administers numerous laws and regulations involving energy issues. It oversees the transportation of natural gas and oil by pipeline and in interstate commerce as well as the transmission and wholesale sales of electric energy in interstate commerce. Retail sales of electricity to end-use customers such as home owners and businesses are regulated by state-run public utility commissions. The licensing and inspection of private, municipal, and state hydroelectric projects is also FERC's responsibility.

Through its programs and regulations, FERC attempts to keep the price of energy at reasonable and reliable rates, in part by encouraging competition in the energy industry. FERC sets the rates that oil pipelines may charge for their transportation services. It also works to ensure the safe use of pipelines and hydroelectric dams.

PROGRAMS

FERC conducts numerous programs, most of which fall into its three major program divisions: pipeline regulation, electric power regulation, and hydropower licensing. All of FERC's programs are focused on carrying out the inspections and regulations established by the commission.

FERC's Pipeline Regulation Division (PRD) regulates the rates and practices of oil pipeline companies engaged in interstate transportation. The division's objective is to establish reasonable rates to encourage maximum use of oil pipelines, which are a relatively inexpensive means of bringing oil to markets. The PRD ensures that oil shippers have equal access to pipeline transportation and equal service conditions on pipelines as well as reasonable rates. Transportation of natural gas by interstate pipeline is also regulated by the PRD. The PRD's primary programs are its Pipeline Certificate program, which regulates the construction, operation, and eventual decommissioning of oil pipelines, and its rate regulation programs.

The Electric Power Regulation Division (EPRD) oversees wholesale electric rates and service standards as well as the interstate transmission of electricity, ensuring that wholesale and transmission rates charged by utilities are reasonable and not preferential. The commission also reviews utility pooling agreements through the EPRD. The sales of electricity that are regulated by the EPRD

BUDGET:

Federal Energy Regulatory Commission

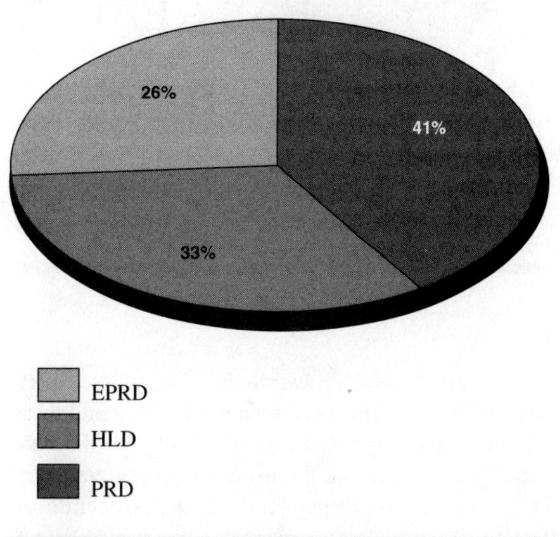

regulates electricity sales by one public utility to another or by a public utility to a municipality or a cooperative. Public utilities, municipalities, or cooperatives that purchase wholesale electricity can then resell the electricity to individual customers.

The Hydropower Licensing Division (HLD) regulates nonfederal hydroelectric power projects that affect navigable waters, occupy U.S. lands, use water or water power at a government dam, or affect the interests of interstate commerce. The work of the HLD includes project licensing, compliance activities, and reviews of projects proposed by other federal agencies. The HLD's Dam Safety Program is responsible for inspecting dams under the FERC's jurisdiction to ensure that they are constructed and operated safely.

BUDGET INFORMATION

The projected 1999 budget allocated by Congress to FERC is approximately $197 million. Expenditures for the three program areas are about 26 percent of funds for EPRD, 33 percent of funds for HLD, and 41 percent of funds for PRD. Approximately 61 percent of each program area's funds are spent on employee salaries and benefits.

FERC recovers all of its operating costs through fees and annual charges. Revenues from these sources offset the congressional appropriations and result in no cost for

FAST FACTS

The interstate oil pipeline network consists of more than 200,000 miles for a total investment of more than $20 billion.

(Source: John Harmon. "Let It Flow." *Atlanta Journal and Constitution,* October 31, 1995.)

FERC to the federal government. Generally FERC receives revenues that exceed its appropriation and these excess funds are deposited as trust funds for the next operating year. Therefore the users and beneficiaries of FERC's services actually pay for the agency's operations.

HISTORY

In 1877 the U.S. Supreme Court ruled that there is a distinction between conventional private property and private property affected with the public interest. Opening the door to government regulation of public utilities and commerce, the Court gave the Illinois state legislature the right to fix grain prices to protect farmers whose access to markets was being limited by the private owners of grain elevators on Lake Michigan, who controlled access to shipping. The first federal commission with authority to fix prices and regulate businesses concerned with the public interest was the Interstate Commerce Commission (ICC), established in 1887.

At about the same time, the telephone and the electric lamp were invented, and soon the concept of a business associated with the public interest was applied to electricity, gas, and telephone companies. Because most of the companies providing these services did business within a limited area, their rates and practices were overseen by emerging state regulatory commissions.

After the establishment of the ICC, there was little expansion in federal regulation until the 1930s. Although the Federal Power Commission (FPC) was created in 1920, it had little authority until it became heavily involved in the regulation of interstate electricity in 1935 and in the regulation of natural-gas sales in 1938. The FPC created a quasi-judicial process of regulation in which energy issues were reviewed and decided on a case-by-case basis. Complaints or recommendations reviewed by the FPC tended to involve public utility management and the industry. Because consumers ultimately bought their power from local public utilities, their concerns were referred to state commissions.

After the energy crises of the 1970s, consumers increasingly demanded that the federal government take a more active role in energy regulation and create a national energy policy. The Department of Energy Organization Act of 1977 created a cabinet-level department to establish and oversee U.S. energy policy. This act also abolished the FPC and created FERC to replace it. In 1978 Congress passed the National Energy Act, which gave FERC a specific regulatory role and provided guidelines for its activities. The Energy Policy Act of 1992 further extended FERC's responsibilities.

CURRENT POLITICAL ISSUES

On April 24, 1996, FERC issued two orders, effective on July 9, 1996. Order No. 888, entitled "Promoting Wholesale Competition Through Open Access Nondiscriminatory Transmission Services By Public Utilities," requires all public utilities that own, control, or operate electricity transmission facilities to provide open access to other companies to use those facilities to transmit electricity. The second order, Order No. 889 entitled "Open Access Same Time Information Systems and Standards of Conduct" requires utilities to develop an Internet-based bulletin board system to provide information about the availability of transportation capacity on electricity transmission lines.

The goal of these two new rules was to begin the largest transformation in the electric power industry since the passage of the Federal Power Act in 1935. The orders allow any interested company or cooperative to purchase, for a reasonable charge, wholesale electricity and transmit it through existing lines to resell to individual customers. This creates choices for consumers in the electric power industry, ending a 90-year-old monopoly system. FERC estimates that the new open access initiatives, once fully implemented, will save consumers between $3.8 and $5.4 billion annually. Before Orders 888 and 889 were issued, utilities that owned and operated electricity transmission systems essentially controlled their respective markets, and could monopolize prices despite regulations.

When the orders were announced, debate over their merit broke out in Congress and among consumer groups and utility companies. Supporters of the orders welcomed the opportunity for consumers to make choices about their utility providers, believing that prices would go down as competition increased. Many groups also predicted that creating open access to power lines would encourage utilities to expand other services sent along the same lines, such as cable television and telephone services.

Opponents of the orders found many flaws in the idea of open access. Consumers may be overwhelmed by too many choices or possibly face constant solicitation from utility companies, much like the barrage of phone company sales pitches. The utilities feared huge losses, particularly if their biggest business customers were the first targets of rivals. Environmentalists feared a widespread return to the use of coal, a fuel that produces massive amounts of pollution, to produce cheaper electricity for resale. And consumers in low-cost energy states worried that their power might be shipped elsewhere, raising their own costs.

Implementing the new open access rules is a complicated process that will take the electric power industry many years to complete. Orders 888 and 889 were only intended to begin this process, spurring state legislatures and Congress into action, and preparing the electric power industry for changes to come. FERC has successfully completed this goal. By 1998, six states had passed legislation requiring power companies to allow open access, and electric power companies were preparing, some more reluctantly than others, for a new era of competition.

SUCCESSES AND FAILURES

Through the introduction of improved technology, FERC has continued its efforts to provide the public and its own staff with the most effective means of gathering and using information. The move to a new building in 1996 allowed FERC to accommodate new technologies through fiber-optic cable. This expanded technology enabled FERC to create an Internet site, an electronic bulletin board system, and the Remote Public ACCESS (RPA) system, which provides the public with access to commission records and dockets.

FERC is also encouraged by the increased competition and reduced rates in the natural gas industry. These activities are the direct result of FERC's revision of rules governing the industry in 1993, which broke up several pipeline monopolies. In 1990 wholesale gas prices were an average of $2.10 per million cubic feet of pipeline. In 1996 prices averaged $1.35 per million cubic feet of pipeline.

FUTURE DIRECTIONS

In the future FERC will work to further utilize its electronic communications capabilities to streamline its activities and the regulatory process. Systems are being developed that would allow public utilities and other FERC customers to submit reports, documents, and proposals through electronic pathways. Information regarding regulations, investigations, and legal proceedings could also travel immediately from FERC to industry.

AGENCY RESOURCES

FERC operates the Hotline Enforcement Task Force, at (202) 208-1390, for complaints or questions concerning gas and electric power companies or to report violations of FERC regulations.

The Public Reference Room (PRR) is the commission's main source for meeting the public's information needs. It contains FERC records, documents, research studies, and energy guidelines. The Public Reference Room is located at 888 1st St., NE, Washington, DC 20426. The PRR can be contacted by phone at (202) 208-1371, by fax at (202) 208-2320, or via the Internet at http://www.ferc.fed.us/ofc/pubrefrm.

The Government Printing Office (GPO) is another source of information about FERC, as well as many other government agencies. Its Government Information Locator Service (GILS) Web site is a good place to find more information on specific aspects of FERC; it is located at http://www.access.gpo.gov/su_docs/gils/gils.html.

AGENCY PUBLICATIONS

FERC publications include commission orders, tariff information, hearing transcripts, and reports filed by regulated entities. Titles of information brochures include "A Guide to Public Information at the Federal Energy Regulatory Commission" and "Inside FERC." All publications can be ordered from FERC's Public Reference Room by phone at (202) 208-1371, by fax at (202) 208-2320, or via the Internet at http://www.ferc.fed.us/ofc/pubrefrm.

BIBLIOGRAPHY

Barcella, Mary Lashley. "Natural Gas in the Twenty-first Century." *Business Economics,* 1 October 1996.

Bradford, Peter A. "Electric Bargain's Cost Is Dirty Air." *Newsday,* 18 April 1996.

Collins, Scott. "New Rule Won't Cut Energy Bills Soon." *Los Angeles Times,* 3 May 1996.

Gordon, Craig. "A Freer Market for Ratepayers?" *Newsday,* 3 February 1997.

Harmon, John. "Let It Flow." *Atlanta Journal and Constitution,* 31 October 1995.

Kraul, Chris. "Merger of Two Major Southland Utilities Ok'd." *Los Angeles Times,* 26 June 1997.

Moyer, R. Charles. "The Future of Electricity." *Business Economics,* 1 October 1996.

Smith, L. David. "Deregulation Spreads Competition Abroad." *Modern Power Systems,* 1 May 1996.

Stein, Hank. "FERC Final Rule Opens Up Stranded Cost Debate." *Modern Power Systems,* 1 June 1996.

Federal Highway Administration (FHWA)

PARENT ORGANIZATION: Department of Transportation
ESTABLISHED: October 3, 1893
EMPLOYEES: 3,620

Contact Information:

ADDRESS: 400 7th St. SW
Washington, DC 20590
PHONE: (202) 366-0660
FAX: (202) 366-3302
URL: http://www.fhwa.dot.gov
ADMINISTRATOR: Kenneth R. Wykle

WHAT IS ITS MISSION?

The Federal Highway Administration (FHWA) describes its mission thus: "We continually improve the quality of our Nation's highway system and its intermodal connections. We carry out this mission by providing leadership, expertise, resources and information in cooperation with our partners to enhance the country's economic vitality, the quality of life and the environment." The FHWA oversees highway transportation in its broadest scope. Its goal is to coordinate motor transportation with rail, marine, and air modes of transportation, to achieve the most effective balance of transportation systems and facilities possible.

HOW IS IT STRUCTURED?

The Federal Highway Administration is a federal regulatory agency in the Department of Transportation (DOT). It is headed by an administrator appointed by the president and confirmed by the Senate. The administrator is accountable to the secretary of transportation and is responsible for carrying out the agency's mission and supporting the DOT's goals and objectives.

The FHWA's Washington headquarters include the Intelligent Transportation Systems Joint Program Office (ITS/JPO), the Office of Program Development, the Office of Research and Development, the Office of Safety and System Applications, and the Office of Motor Carriers (OMC). The ITS/JPO is responsible for planning and overseeing the implementation of the Intelligent Transportation Systems, a major highway initiative of the

The FHWA's Federal-Aid Highway program provides billions of dollars to individual states to build and maintain highways, like this one in Detroit, Michigan.

(Photograph by Brian Merrill)

DOT. The Program Development Office administers most of the highway federal aid programs and assists in the design and construction of highways. The Office of Research and Development is responsible for developing new methods and materials of highway construction. It works closely with the academic and private business sectors. The Office of Safety and Systems Applications advises the federal highway administrator on highway safety, traveler information systems, and traffic management. The OMC develops and distributes standards for the trucking industry; they include standards for the size and weight of trucks and for the transport of hazardous materials on highways.

In addition to its Washington headquarters, the FHWA has nine regional offices throughout the United States. They provide technical expertise to state and local highway officials, evaluate the effectiveness of FHWA programs, and carry out inspections of motor carriers. The agency is further subdivided into 55 division offices, whose primary responsibility is administering federal aid and federal lands programs.

PRIMARY FUNCTIONS

The FHWA's most important function is managing of the Federal-Aid Highway Program. The multibillion-dollar program provides the states with money for planning, building, and maintaining interstate and other federal highways, as well as some state highways. The program also provides money for highway beautification and environmental projects. Through its federal aid program the FHWA regulates the design and construction of highways; highways built under the program must adhere to agency standards.

The agency promulgates safe operating standards for commercial motor carriers and inspects trucks at carrier facilities as well as on the road. The FHWA issues safety regulations that cover approximately 330,000 carriers and 36,000 shippers of hazardous materials. The agency can impose civil and criminal penalties for violations of its regulations.

The FHWA establishes national standards for a commercial vehicle driver license, including a test of driver skills for commercial vehicles. It can revoke the licenses of drivers guilty of serious offenses, for example, driving while intoxicated or under the influence of drugs. The FHWA also maintains a national database of commercial driver license information.

FHWA experts advise state and local transportation agencies on a variety of highway issues, including the construction, design, and maintenance of roads and bridges, the design of "intelligent" transportation systems, environmental protection, highway and motor

FAST FACTS

The Transportation Research Board and the Federal Highway Administration estimate that by 2010 traffic congestion on freeways in the United States will have quadrupled, making the rush hour periods longer and longer. The time spent in jams will increase by 5.6 billion hours, and the cost of delay will increase by $41 billion per year.

(Source: "No Room, No Room." *The Economist*, December 6, 1997.)

safety, and highway project evaluation. The National Highway Institute (NHI), the technical training organization of the FHWA, provides specialized training to state and local highway employees. In addition to its instructional training programs, which are also available to private individuals and select foreign nationals, the NHI offers fellowships for research and education related to highway safety. The institute is located in Arlington, Virginia.

FHWA labs carry out a range of research on new highway technologies, processes, and materials. One area of importance is the development of new long-lasting pavement materials that will prevent the formation of ice in freezing weather.

PROGRAMS

Many of FHWA activities are carried out through agency programs. The most important of these are the Federal-Aid Highway Program, the Federal Lands Highway Program, and the Motor Carrier Safety Program.

The Federal-Aid Highway (FAH) Program was set up to develop an economically efficient, environmentally sound transportation system that can provide the basis for economic competition in the global marketplace. The FAH provides financial assistance to the states for planning, constructing, and maintaining highways. The major beneficiary of the program is the 161,000 mile-long National Highway System (NHS). The NHS consists of 42,500 miles of interstate highways, important rural highways, urban freeways, the Department of Defense's Strategic Highway Network, and roads connecting the NHS to intermodal facilities. Under the program's financing, the federal government pays 90 percent of the costs of improvements to the interstate system; states pay 10 percent. The program also provides 75 percent federal funding for improvements on about 800,000 miles of additional roads in the United States. The program provides money for regular repair or replacement of roads as they deteriorate. Monies from the Federal-Aid Highway Program are available for acquiring property and relocating people dislocated by highway construction, improving access to the handicapped, preserving natural or historic sites, and encouraging minority and disadvantaged businesses to participate in highway construction.

The Federal Lands Highway Program administers the construction of roads on land owned by the federal government. It includes eight thousand miles of park roads and parkways in the National Park system and 49,000 miles of roads into and on Indian lands. The program is run jointly by the FHWA, the National Park Service, and the Bureau of Indian Affairs. Altogether the program provides money for the funding of more than 80,000 miles of federally owned public roads serving federal lands. Besides executing the Federal Lands Highway Program, the Federal Lands Highway Office (FLH) oversees the Defense Access Road Program. The program provides for the construction and maintenance of state and local roads to military installations and is funded by the Department of Defense.

Motor carrier programs of the FHWA are aimed at achieving safety and uniformity among national motor carriers—companies that deliver freight by truck. As part of the programs the agency reviews truck size- and weight-enforcement programs in the states and works toward uniform safety regulations, inspections and fines, licensing, registration and taxation requirements, and accident data for motor carriers. States that participate in the International Registration Plan and the International Fuel Tax Agreement are eligible for motor carrier program grants for technical assistance, training, and equipment. The agency's Motor Carrier Safety Assistance Program performs hundreds of thousands of roadside inspections annually that result in the decommissioning of thousands of vehicles and drivers for safety regulation violations.

The FHWA cooperates on a number of highway safety programs with state and local governments and the National Highway Traffic Safety Administration (NHTSA). The two agencies cosponsor the Red Light Running program, aimed at reducing disregard for traffic signals in the nation. The agency has developed a highway safety construction program that funds the removal of roadside obstacles, the identification and correction of hazardous locations, and the elimination of hazards at railroad crossings. The strategic safety reform program supports driver training, judicial outreach programs, and research to support regulatory initiatives.

The Intelligent Transportation Systems (ITS) program was implemented to develop, test, and evaluate advanced electronic systems to regulate the flow of traffic in order to reduce congestion and improve safety on highways. Various agencies, including the DOT and the NHTSA, participate with universities and private industry. An ITS incentive program has been proposed that would provide the states with funding to develop their own uniform, integrated ITS.

BUDGET INFORMATION

The FHWA's budget for 1998 totaled $22.88 billion, just over half of DOT's total budget. The budget proposed for 1999 decreased FHWA's appropriation slightly to $21.85 billion. The $21.5 billion earmarked for Federal-aid Highway Program accounts for the lion's share of FHWA's 1999 budget: $496 million was requested for research and development; $250 million of that was to be used for the Intelligent Transportation System Program.

Most of the money budgeted to FHWA comes from the Highway Trust Fund. Revenues in the Fund come from the motor fuel tax and other taxes paid by highway users. The 1998 fund receipts were estimated at $26.15 billion. FHWA administers funding of other government agencies by the Highway Trust Fund. The Bureau of Transportation Statistics and Amtrak, for example, both receive monies from the fund.

HISTORY

The Federal Highway Administration was founded October 3, 1893, as the Office of Road Inquiry, an agency in the Department of Agriculture. The Office was established following a meeting of the National League for Good Roads, a lobbying group dedicated to the passage of national road legislation. The agency's budget was increased to $30,000 in 1903 and it was made a permanent agency within the Agriculture Department.

The agency's name was changed to the Office of Public Roads in 1905. Over the next decade the agency took over responsibility for highway bridges and developed an experimental federal aid program for the construction of post roads. Passage of the Federal-Aid Road Act in 1916 authorized the first federal aid for highways, a total of $75 million over five years. The federal government and states were to share the costs equally, and the states would oversee planning and construction, subject to federal approval.

In 1918 the agency became the Bureau of Public Roads (BPR). Because of World War I (1914–18), only 17.5 miles of roads had been completed under the 1916 act. In 1919 the U.S. Army mounted a convoy to move vehicles from Washington, D.C. to San Francisco, a trip that took two months. The convoy dramatically illustrated the importance of a good system of roads for the defense of the nation.

The Federal Highway Act, signed into law by President Warren Harding on November 9, 1921, set aside federal funds for a system of roads that would cross state lines and be at least 18 feet wide. The first system of numbered U.S. highways was established by the BPR in 1925.

In 1933 the administration of President Franklin Roosevelt began establishing public works projects, including road building, in response to the Great Depression. In 1935 U.S. Highway 30, the first paved transcontinental road, was completed. In 1939 the BPR, renamed the Public Roads Administration, was transferred to the Federal Works Agency. That year a report entitled "Toll Roads and Free Roads" was presented to Congress; it contained the first formal plan for a free interstate highway system. In 1944 Congress passed the Federal-Aid Highway Act, which approved the establishment of the 64,000-kilometer National System of Interstate Highways.

The interstate system gained its first real momentum during the administration of President Dwight D. Eisenhower. In 1956 Eisenhower signed the Federal-Aid Highway Act, which provided the first major funding for the interstate system. It specified that the federal government would fund 90 percent of the highway system's costs. It also created the Highway Trust Fund to provide the money for construction, with revenues coming from taxes on gasoline and tires and fees levied on trucks and buses. The interstate system took 25 years to complete and cost $129 billion.

The construction of the interstate system did not take place without controversy and protest. In the late 1950s, allegations of corruption and waste led to congressional hearings that eventually exonerated the BPR and the interstate program. Other groups protested the effect the roads would have on the natural and urban environments. Eventually, compromise was reached: the FHWA agreed to do environmental impact studies of its projects, and the Department of Transportation Act of 1966 placed restrictions on road construction in parks, wildlife refuges, and other natural areas. The Federal Highway Act of 1973 ended controversial urban plans and replaced many with mass transportation projects.

Congress responded to the oil crisis of the middle 1970s by enacting a maximum speed limit of 55 miles per hour, which remained in force until 1995. Congress took steps in 1983 to finance the restoration of the nation's highways and bridges when it passed the Surface Transportation Act. The law added five cents to the gasoline tax, the first gas tax increase in 21 years.

In 1986 the Commercial Motor Vehicle Act gave the FHWA authority to create national standards for truck and bus driver licenses. The act established uniform standards for testing drivers, created a central clearinghouse for driving records, and established mandatory penalties for serious traffic violations and felony convictions.

The National Transportation Plan (NTP) was developed in 1990 under the leadership of transportation secretary Samuel Skinner. It called for the designation of a National Highway System (NHS) consisting of the interstate system and other significant roads. The Intermodal Surface Transportation Efficiency Act (ISTEA) of 1991 implemented many aspects of the NTP. The ISTEA provided funding for many traditional highway projects like road and bridge construction. It recognized that transportation can be more than just the automobile and included provisions for bicycling and walking as well as for high-tech developments like intelligent vehicle and highway systems and high-speed rail. It expressed the nation's commitment to intermodal transportation, a system that unifies highway, rail, water, and air modes to promote economic well being and reduce energy consumption.

CURRENT POLITICAL ISSUES

The Federal Highway Administration deals with many highway issues: the construction of interstate highways, maintenance and repair of highways and bridges, highway safety, regulation of trucks, and the role of highways in the nation's intermodal transportation system. The Highway Trust Fund, established to help pay for the interstate highway system, later became the source of financing for almost all the activities of the FHWA. Questions arose, however, regarding whether or not that money should be used exclusively for highway projects and if so, should as much of the money as possible be put to use.

Case Study: The Highway Trust Fund's Untouchable Millions

Established in 1956, the Highway Trust Fund contains revenues that were drawn primarily from gasoline taxes and were earmarked specifically for the construction and maintenance of the Interstate Highway System. By the late 1980s, however, the fund was bringing in billions of dollars annually, and it caught the eye of politicians concerned about the growing federal budget deficit. In 1993 Congress increased the federal gas tax by 4.3 cents per gallon and stipulated that the extra money was to be used for paying off the federal debt.

The extra tax drew protests from groups that maintained that gas tax monies should be used only for highway projects. They were unable to get the act repealed, so they focused on getting the additional funds redirected to pure highway expenditures, arguing that there would be extra billions available every year for work on the nation's highways, which had been neglected for decades. Congress agreed and on October 1, 1997, President William Clinton signed a law directing that the 4.3 cents per gallon be deposited in the Highway Trust Fund. Since then all federal gas tax revenues—18.4 cents per gallon in all—have been deposited in the fund.

It is estimated that those additional funds will bring $74.2 billion in new revenues into the trust fund between 1998 and 2007. Unfortunately the 1997 law did not indicate how the new money could be spent. Since the money had not been specifically designated for any specific purpose, the new revenues began adding up, unavailable to anyone.

Public Impact

People of driving age use the highway system nearly every day of their lives, often spend an hour or more each day driving, and are frustrated by bad roads or highway repairs that cause traffic tie-ups for months on end. The interstate system is deteriorating at an alarming rate. The DOT reports that 26 percent of the highways are in poor or mediocre condition and must be repaired soon if they are to remain usable. Another 34 percent were rated "fair," meaning they also needed work, but not quite as urgently. Traffic levels, especially in urban areas, long ago outstripped the capacity of many roads. Roads that are inadequate and in disrepair lead to gridlock, wasted fuel, aggressive driving, and fatal accidents. Thirty-one percent of highway bridges are structurally deficient or obsolete.

As the Road Information Program (RIP), a private lobbying group in Washington, has pointed out, making road improvements can save lives. After declining steadily between 1988 and 1992, traffic-related fatalities increased every year through 1996. Widening a lane by one foot, according to the RIP, can reduce fatalities by 12 percent. Widening a lane by two feet can reduce fatalities by 23 percent. Ironically, while money sits unspent and unspendable in the Highway Trust Fund, the DOT has estimated that the government would have to increase its investment in highways by $20 billion a year for 20 years just to maintain them in the poor condition in which they already exist. To actually improve them would take increases of $40 billion annually.

SUCCESSES AND FAILURES

Without a doubt, the greatest success of the Federal Highway Administration and its predecessor agencies is the Interstate Highway System. It has justifiably been called the nation's largest public works project and the greatest nonmilitary construction program in world history. It consists of 42,795 miles of highway, without a single grade crossing or traffic light. Accounting for just one percent of the nation's highways, it carries 21 percent of the nation's traffic. Almost two million acres of land had to be acquired for the entire system. If laid end to end the interstates would loop two times around the equator. In addition, the system provided a model for cooperative work between the federal government and the 50 states.

The FHWA is also a model of how a federal agency can open doors to leadership positions to minorities. In the mid-1990s the FHWA had an African American administrator, Rodney Slater, and a female deputy administrator, Jane Garvey. (Both were later given positions of greater responsibility: Slater was named secretary of transportation and Garvey became the administrator of the Federal Aviation Administration). The agency brought in its first four female division administrators, its first female regional administrator, its first Latino regional administrator, and its first African American regional administrator. Between 1993 and 1996 minority representation in senior executive service in the agency rose from 20 percent to 31 percent.

FUTURE DIRECTIONS

The FHWA has two major issues to contend with in the future. First, the growing population is expected to lead to a 50 percent increase in traffic in the next decade, with concomitant increases in energy consumption and pollution. The fastest-growing group in the population will be the elderly, who will have both time and money to spend driving the nation's highways. Despite trumpeted trends toward telecommuting, the FHWA believes that most Americans will continue to go to work in their private autos until well into the twenty-first century. Trucking, a lifeblood of the economy, will continue to increase as well.

The second issue is that the American highway system is reaching its capacity. Roads are no longer able to handle the volume of traffic, and there is nowhere to expand them. To adapt, the FHWA is relying on the National Highway System and the Intelligent Transportation Systems (ITS) program to make the best use of its existing resources. The ITS program is aimed at developing a system in which vehicles and highways are equipped with a sophisticated network of sensors, actuators, and computers that modulate traffic and reduce congestion. Roads will sense traffic patterns and adjust the timing of traffic signals; vehicles will sense other travelers on roads and maintain safe distances, adjust speed, or brake automatically; weather conditions will be monitored by satellite and transmitted to the intelligent highway for processing. Research on the ITS has been undertaken by a broad-based consortium of federal agencies, businesses, and university labs, and the participation of private-sector business and academia is essential to achieving this end.

AGENCY RESOURCES

A great deal of information on FHWA programs and standards, together with select agency publications and reports, is available at the FHWA Web site at http://www.fhwa.dot.gov. Highway statistics are also available from the FHWA Office of Highway Information Management, 400 7th St. SW, Washington, DC 20590 or by calling (202) 366-0180. Docketed material can be viewed in the Docket Room of the FHWA Law Library between the hours of 8:30 A.M. and 3:30 P.M. The Docket Room is located in Room 4232 at FHWA Washington headquarters. Its phone number is (202) 366-1387. A large selection of material on general transportation topics is available in the DOT Library, located in the Transportation Administrative Services Center (TASC), 400 7th St. SW, Rm. 2200, Washington, DC 20590. The library can be reached by telephone at (202) 366-0746. It is open Monday through Friday from 9 A.M. until 4 P.M. Information on the National Highway Institute can be obtained at the NHI Web site, http://www.nhi.fhwa.dot.gov/, or by writing NHI, Customer Service, 901 N. Stuart St., Ste. 300, Arlington, VA 22203

AGENCY PUBLICATIONS

Read Your Road is full of facts about the U.S. highway system its signs and signals, as well as safe-driving tips. It is available free of charge from FHWA Public Affairs, (202) 366-0660. Many publications are available from the FHWA's Web site at http://www.fhwa.dot.gov/. Information on other FHWA publications can be obtained from the FHWA Office of Highway Information Management, 400 7th St. SW, Washington, DC 20590 or by calling (202) 366-0180.

BIBLIOGRAPHY

Fahey, James P. "How the Highway Trust Fund Has Changed and the Impact On Road and Bridge Funding Needs." Washington, D.C.: The Road Information Program, 1998.

The Federal Highway Administration: Who We Are & What We Do. Washington, D.C.: Federal Highway Administration, 1996.

"Federal Law Won't Let Atlanta Build New Highways. State Law Won't Fund Anything but New Highways." *Atlanta Constitution*, 13 June 1997.

"The Future FHWA." *Public Roads,* Spring 1996.

Government Accounting Office. "Transportation Infrastructure—Review Of Project Selection Process for Five FHWA Discretionary Programs," 5 December 1997.

Hastalis, Steven. "Asphalt Nation: How the Automobile Took Over America and How We Can Take It Back." *Reason*, 1 January 1998.

Koepp, Stephen. "Gridlock! Congestion on America's Highways and Runways Takes a Grinding Toll." *Time*, 12 September 1988.

Labatut, Jean, and Wheaton J. Lane, eds. *Highways in Our National Life: A Symposium*. Princeton, N.J.: Princeton University Press, 1950.

Moore, Thomas. "How to Cut the Budget: The Federal Government Can Cut the Deficit—And Promote Commerce More Effectively—If It Stops." *Fortune*, 1 April 1985.

"No Room, No Room." *Economist*, 6 December 1997.

Owen, Wilfred, and Charles L. Dearing. *Toll Roads and the Problem of Highway Modernization*, Washington, D.C.: Brookings Institution, 1951.

Perry, Nancy J. "Good News About Infrastructure." *Fortune*, 10 April 1989.

Rose, Mark H. *Interstate: Express Highway Politics, 1939–1989.* Knoxville: University of Tennessee Press, 1990.

Shogren, Elizabeth. "Clinton Offers Plan for Tolls on Interstates." *Los Angeles Times*, 13 March 1997.

Slater, Rodney E. "The National Highway System: A Commitment to America's Future," *Public Roads*, Spring 1996.

Smith, David C. "Closing the Technology Gap." *Public Roads*, 1 January 1997.

Weems, Christopher. "The Interstate Highway System: 40 Years of Driving to the Future." *Atlanta Inquirer*, 7 December 1996.

Weingroff, Richard F. "Highway Excellence—100 Years And Beyond." *Public Roads*, Autumn 1993.

———. "Milestones." *Public Roads*, Spring 1996.

Wiemer, Bob. "Outrageous Roads a Source of Road Rage." *Newsday*, 16 February 1998.

Wiseman, Paul. "Highway Bill Is a Road to Community Projects." *USA Today*, 9 June 1998.

Zaccagnino, William. "Technology for Work and Travel." *Public Roads*, Spring 1996.

Federal Judicial Center

WHAT IS ITS MISSION?

The stated mission of the Federal Judicial Center is "to further the development and adoption of improved judicial administration" in the courts of the United States. The goal of the Federal Judicial Center is to improve the efficiency of the U.S. courts through research, analysis, education, and training.

HOW IS IT STRUCTURED?

The Federal Judicial Center falls under the judicial branch and was created to advise the Judicial Conference of the United States, which is responsible for setting the national policy of the federal judiciary. The conference is composed of the chief judges from each judicial circuit and a district judge from each of the 12 geographical circuits, together with the chief judge of the Court of International Trade.

The center has a board which is chaired by the chief justice of the United States and includes two circuit judges, three district judges, one bankruptcy judge, and the director of the Administrative Office of the U.S. Courts. The board appoints the center's director and deputy director, and the director then appoints the center's staff. At the end of each year, the board is required to submit a report of its recommendations to the Judicial Conference for consideration.

The center is made up of five divisions and two offices: the Court Education Division; the Judicial Education Division; the Planning & Technology Division; the Publications & Media Division; the Research Division;

ESTABLISHED: 1967
EMPLOYEES: 138

Contact Information:

ADDRESS: One Columbus Circle NE
Washington, DC 20002-8003
PHONE: (202) 273-4000
URL: http://www.fjc.gov
DIRECTOR: Rya W. Zobel

the Federal Judicial History Office; and the Interjudicial Affairs Office. Each division is run by a director, and each office is run by a chief. Together these divisions and offices work together to implement the center's many education, research, technology, and planning activities.

PRIMARY FUNCTIONS

The goals of the center fall into three broad categories: (1) conducting and promoting research on federal court organization, operations, and history; (2) conducting and promoting orientation and continuing education and training programs for federal judges, court employees, and others; and (3) developing recommendations about the operation and study of the federal courts.

Under the first of these categories, the center is specifically directed by federal statute to assist the Judicial Conference with research and planning on how to more effectively operate the court systems. The center also encourages persons and institutions outside the agency to study and research the courts and cooperates with state judiciaries to help them research and study their administration of justice. Under this category, the center also promotes the study of the history of the federal judicial system and facilitates the archiving of all court records.

Under the second category, the center is directed by statute to provide education and training for all judicial employees and others who are directly involved with the operation of the judicial branch. In addition, the center provides information to people working in foreign court systems so that they may better understand how justice is administered in the United States.

Under the third category, the center is directed by statute to develop and make recommendations to the Judicial Conference for improvements in the administration of the federal courts, encompassing all of the duties and goals of the first two categories.

PROGRAMS

Most of the center's programs are involved with education, training, and research in one form or another, and each of the five divisions operates a variety of programs specific to its individual task. For example, the Court Education Division develops and administers training and education programs for nonjudicial court personnel, including orientation workshops, continuing education, training for special types of jobs, and long-term leadership programs.

The Judicial Education Division, on the other hand, develops and administers similar education and training programs for judicial employees, such as judges and court attorneys. The Planning and Technology Division is responsible for studying technology and its impact and use in the judicial system. Its activities involve operating current technology, studying emerging technologies, aiding individual courts with technical assistance, and giving advice on planning the use of such technology. The Publications and Media Division produces a variety of publications and media programs for use in the center's other divisions, as well as a wide array of manuals, outlines, and periodicals that are available to the public.

The Federal Judicial History Office works with the National Archives and the Administrative Office of the U.S. Courts to record and make available court records as well as compile an ongoing history of the courts. The Interjudicial Affairs Office serves as a clearinghouse of information for research done at the center. It also works with state judicial systems and with foreign judicial and legal officers through programs such as the center's Visiting Foreign Judicial Fellows program, which helps to educate foreign court personnel on the workings of the U.S. court system.

BUDGET INFORMATION

In 1997 the budget appropriated by Congress, under the Judiciary Appropriations Act of 1997, for the operation of the Federal Judicial Center was $17.5 million. This reflects a steady decline in the FJC's budget since 1992 from an overall budget of $18.9 million.

The budget is divided into three main categories: education and training, which receives approximately $10 million; research and technology, which receives approximately $4 million; and administration and support services, which receives approximately $3 million of the total.

HISTORY

Originally, in the 1800s, the court system of the United States was simple enough that not much concern was given to its administration and management. As the country grew and the number of court cases steadily increased, the judicial system became increasingly more complex. The courts, therefore, began to seek out better and more efficient methods for operating the system which included how hiring would be done, what technology to use or not to use, what rooms or buildings to meet in, who cleans the rooms and repairs equipment, who answers phones, and how bills are paid.

At first, from the late 1800s through the early 1900s, such administrative responsibilities fell under the auspices of the Department of Justice. In 1939, however, Congress created the Administrative Office of the United States Courts (AO) and delegated these tasks to them.

However, the number of court cases and the complexity of the U.S. court system continued to escalate over the years, and the judicial system felt an ongoing and ever-increasing need to find better and more efficient ways to handle the overload. By the 1960s, it was determined that a separate organization was needed to handle the more complex tasks.

The Federal Judicial Center was created in 1967 specifically to study and analyze the methods and procedures used in the court systems and to educate members of the courts while leaving the AO to manage practical details. To date, the center's efforts have grown to involve 1,300 programs that reach more than 30,000 participants per year.

FAST FACTS

In 1996, the center provided 1,500 educational programs for more than 38,000 federal judge and court participants.

(Source: The Federal Judicial Center. *1996 Federal Judicial Center Annual Report*. Washington, D.C., 1996.)

CURRENT POLITICAL ISSUES

The center faces many complex challenges in the administration of U.S. justice, including how to apply the ever-changing world of technology effectively in the court system. The center must also deal with the evolving needs of society through a complex system of study and research and education. The center must respond to many variables, such as the passage and implementation of new legislation or the most recent interpretations of the Constitution by the U.S. Supreme Court. The challenge for the center is to stay up to date with its research and analysis and to offer current and effective suggestions for improvement.

One of the center's significant areas of concern is the jury system. A flawed jury system can have monumental consequences for the administration of justice in the United States.

Case Study: Juries

In the 1990s with the number of high-profile court cases such as the trial of the Menendez brothers, the Rodney King trial, and the O.J. Simpson trial, a debate has arisen over whether the jury system as it is now applied is working. Specifically, questions have arisen about jury nullification (when a jury votes the way it wishes despite the evidence presented in a trial). Observers question whether or not jury nullification is occurring at all; whether or not it should be prevented; how to prevent it; what message is being sent by the citizens who participate in nullification; and whether or not these citizens represent other groups in society. The center studies these issues to determine if justice is being fairly and effectively handed out and to make suggestions for fixing the problem if it exists.

Some members of the legal profession and the public at large believe that juries vote according to what their conscience tells them is right, disregarding whatever evidence is presented, and that to do so is their right as citizens. It is an exercise of their free speech, a way to express their concerns and to have an effect on the system.

Other people argue that disregarding the evidence and the rules of the courts, basing a verdict on bigger issues such as race or class, and then meting out justice according to personal beliefs is a dangerous practice that would mean that no person is safe from the whims of his neighbors. Many innocent people would go to jail, and many guilty people would go free. Still others are not convinced that jury nullification takes place at all or often enough to cause any real impact.

Public Impact

The center's problem is to answer these questions and then educate members of the judiciary, as well as the public, about the best methods for handling juries. The center has responded by creating programs such as "Improving Jury Selection and Juror Comprehension," a conference of experts who compare notes and analyses and then offer their conclusions to members of the judiciary in a series of workshops. "Called to Serve," a video, is used to educate prospective jurors about their duties.

Should the U.S. jury system be changed in some way in response to the issue of jury nullification, the effect would be profound and far-reaching, prompting debate about the correctness of previous and future verdicts as well as about the very nature of justice itself. Such questions will not be easily answered nor will changes be quickly effected. This continuing debate reflects society's view of crime and punishment at its most basic level and will continue to be a major area of research, analysis, and education for the center.

SUCCESSES AND FAILURES

In the District of Columbia, a multimedia info kiosk system called "The Court Connection" has been developed to improve public access to information. This kiosk provides direct access to court docket information, procedures for filing petitions, and official forms which can then be printed out for use.

In 1996, the center also developed "Security Awareness in the Federal Courts," a video that helps court employees understand and handle security problems when and before they arise during court proceedings.

FUTURE DIRECTIONS

The center's future projects involve educating participants in the most effective methods for the administration of justice. One of the center's top priorities is to help the courts better manage federal death penalty cases and the death penalty appeals that come from state court systems by organizing and summarizing all the different administrative methods that have been used and then making this information available to the courts. This effort will include collecting all applicable court records and the experiences of various judges, as well as recording all the different policies and procedures courts have used to handle these cases.

AGENCY RESOURCES

Information about the Federal Judicial Center is available from any of its five divisions and two offices. These are most easily accessed by calling the recorded message and office directory at (202) 273-4000 or by writing the Federal Judicial Center, Thurgood Marshall Federal Judiciary Building, One Columbus Circle NE, Washington, DC 20002-8003. Information is also available electronically via the World Wide Web at http://www.fjc.gov.

AGENCY PUBLICATIONS

Single copies of most of the publications of the Federal Judicial Center are available free of charge by calling (202) 273-4153 or by fax at (202) 273-4025. These include *The Federal Courts and What They Do* and *Welcome to the Federal Courts*. More than 40 selected publications are available electronically via the World Wide Web at http://www.fjc.gov; including *Reference Manual on Scientific Evidence*, *Manual for Complex Litigation, Third*, and *Survey on the Federal Rules of Bankruptcy Procedure*.

BIBLIOGRAPHY

Champagne, Anthony. "The Impact of Judicial-Selection Method on State-Supreme-Court Policy: Innovation, Reaction, and Atrophy." *Annals of the American Academy of Political & Social Science*, January 1997, pp. 198–199.

Cooper, N. Lee. "Don't Get Trampled by Media Circus." *ABA Journal*, February 1997, p. 8.

Geyh, Charles Gardner. "Paradise Lost, Paradigm Found: Redefining the Judiciary's Imperiled Role in Congress." *New York University Law Review*, November 1996, pp. 1165–1250 .

Neff, David. "Judging the Justices." *Christianity Today*, 9 December 1996, pp. 14–15.

Puro, Steven. "The Federal Courts: Challenge and Reform." *Library Journal*, January 1997, p. 122.

Ratliff, William. "Judicial Reform: The Neglected Priority in Latin America." *Annals of the American Academy of Political & Social Science*, March 1997, pp. 59–71.

Reske, Henry J. "Pondering Judicial Independence." *ABA Journal*, February 1997, p. 92.

Saari, Peggy. "Reasonable Doubts: The O.J. Simpson Case and the Criminal Justice System." *Antioch Review*, Fall 1996, pp. 494–495.

Stein, Robert A. "Help in High-Profile Trials." *ABA Journal*, February 1997, p. 93.

Zuckerman, Mortimer B. "A Good Idea Gone Wrong." *U.S. News and World Report*, 16 December 1996, pp. 78 (80).

Federal Labor Relations Authority (FLRA)

PARENT ORGANIZATION: Independent
ESTABLISHED: January 1, 1979
EMPLOYEES: 216

Contact Information:

ADDRESS: 607 Fourteenth St. NW
Washington, DC 20424-0001
PHONE: (202) 482-6560
FAX: (202) 653-5091
URL: http://www.flra.gov
CHAIRMAN: Phyllis N. Segal

WHAT IS ITS MISSION?

According to the Federal Labor Relations Authority (FLRA) Web site, its mission is "to promote stable and constructive labor-management relations that contribute to an efficient and effective government." The FLRA embraces the philosophy of conflict resolution and discourages contentious behavior between parties involved in disputes. The FLRA employs an introspective, self-evaluative operating strategy, in order to adapt dynamically to the changing needs of the federal labor force. It maintains ongoing self-improvement programs that continually upgrade FLRA staff mediation skills, in order to minimize the need for adjudicatory proceedings.

HOW IS IT STRUCTURED?

The FLRA, as it was established by the Civil Service Reform Act of 1978, operates as a complement to the Office of Personnel Management (OPM). The OPM, as defined by statute, oversees the management of federal human resources. The FLRA and a second review agency, the Merit Systems Protection Board (MSPB), are charged with conflict resolution within the federal employment ranks. The FLRA specifically is the authority for resolving labor-management disputes within the federal work force. Decisions of the FLRA are not subject to further appeals in most cases. This system ensures a form of checks and balances among the civil service personnel agencies, specifically between the OPM and the FLRA.

FAST FACTS

Historically, approximately 95 percent of all unfair labor practice charges within the FLRA's jurisdiction have been filed by unions; less than 5 percent were filed by individual employees.

(Source: Federal Labor Relations Authority, 1998.)

The FLRA is an independent organization composed of three distinct functional groups: the Board of the Federal Labor Relations Authority (also called the Authority), the Office of the General Counsel, and the Federal Service Impasses Panel. The FLRA also includes two foreign services groups: the Foreign Service Impasse Disputes Panel and the Foreign Service Labor Relations Board.

The president of the United States appoints each of the three members of the Authority; these board members serve terms of five years each. The president also assigns one of the appointed board members as chair of the FLRA. The chair serves simultaneously as the chair of the Foreign Service Labor Relations Board and as a member of the president's National Partnership Council. The FLRA domestic functions are divided between the three-member board or Authority and the Federal Service Impasses Panel.

The foreign services divisions of the FLRA, established by the Foreign Service Act of 1980, include the Foreign Service Impasse Disputes Panel and the Foreign Service Labor Relations Board. The five members of the Foreign Service Impasse Disputes Panel are part-time appointees selected by the FLRA chair. The chair also appoints the three members of the Foreign Service Labor Relations Board.

The FLRA Office of the General Counsel operates independently of the domestic and foreign services divisions. The general counsel, who serves a five-year term, is a presidential appointee and must be approved by the Senate. The Office of the General Counsel is also the managing head of the seven regional FLRA offices—in Atlanta, Georgia, Boston, Massachusetts, Chicago, Illinois, Dallas, Texas, Denver, Colorado, San Francisco, California, and Washington, D.C.

All FLRA organizational divisions are supported by one FLRA staff. The staff of the Federal Service Impasses Panel also supports the Foreign Service Impasse Disputes Panel.

PRIMARY FUNCTIONS

The FLRA oversees the administration of labor-management relations programs for up to two million federal employees worldwide. Specifically it is responsible for the 1.1 million of these employees who are exclusively represented by one of over two thousand bargaining units. The FLRA insures the stability and constructive character of labor-management relations, which in turn fosters effective operations within the federal work.

The FLRA is responsible for hearing arbitration appeals submitted by either unions representing federal employees or the agencies that employ them. If a union and an agency disagree over an employee grievance, the two sides go to a third party arbitrator to settle their dispute. After an arbitrator makes a decision, either party has the option of filing an appeal with the FLRA. If an appeal is filed, the FLRA reviews the determination and decides to enforce all, part, or none of that decision. Unless there is an unfair labor practice involved in the case, the FLRA's conclusion is final and may not be argued in any court.

The FLRA is also involved in negotiations between labor unions and the management of agencies through its Federal Service Impasses Panel. After attempting to resolve disputed issues themselves, agencies or unions may submit these issues to the Impasses Panel for review. The Impasses Panel suggests both informal and formal procedures by which the two parties could resolve their differences. If this is unsuccessful the Impasses Panel will then impose a resolution upon the two parties which is binding unless both agree that it will not be. The conclusions the Impasses Panel reach cannot be appealed.

The FLRA also oversees the unionization of federal employees within an agency. Issues that arise between the employees that are organizing and the agency management can be referred to one of FLRA's Regional Offices. The Regional Office conducts elections to determine whether or not employees want to be represented by a union and, if they do, which union will represent them. The Regional Office also holds meetings between labor and agency management to ensure that all representation matters are resolved. If there are any issues upon which the employees and the employers cannot agree, the Regional Office Director will hold a hearing and make a conclusion based on the information provided during that hearing. If either party is not pleased with the Regional Office's decision, it may be appealed to the Authority. The Authority will then decide to uphold the entire decision, part of it, or none of it. No further appeal to any court will be permitted after the Authority reaches a decision.

The FLRA Office of General Counsel (OGC) investigates unfair labor complaints. The OGC has the authority to bring charges against alleged unfair federal employers. The OGC also oversees the operations of the seven regional FLRA offices nationwide. These offices negotiate issues between employee union representatives and employers in attempts to avert the need for intervention by the OGC in Washington, DC. An unresolved conflict may be referred to the main office of the FLRA for adjudication. Decisions rendered under these circumstances are final and therefore not subject to appeal.

The Foreign Service Labor Relations Board is specifically responsible for the resolution and adjudication of labor-management relations within the U.S. Information Agency, the Agency for International Development, the Department of State, the Department of Agriculture, and the Department of Commerce.

PROGRAMS

In the majority of cases before the FLRA, employee complaints are referred by a collective bargaining unit when negotiations with an employer reach an impasse. In every case, and regardless of the circumstances, the FLRA procedures and awards must comply with prescribed statutes under the Code of Federal Regulations. These can become very time consuming and costly.

In consideration of containing costs and other factors, the FLRA implemented a program called Collaboration and Alternative Dispute Resolution (CADR) in 1996. CADR dictates uniform guidelines and aggressively encourages the resolution of all issues through negotiation rather than adjudication. CADR guidelines affect FLRA functions on an agency-wide basis. Within the OGC, the CADR prescribes the implementation of training sessions and other educational services to thousands of federal employees each year. The substance of CADR training deals with targeting and correcting conditions of potential altercation before formal disputes erupt.

The ultimate goal of CADR is to discourage agencies and bargaining units from lapsing into a pattern of "frequent filing" or persistent requests for dispute arbitration. It is also important for all parties to resolve issues voluntarily prior to trial whenever possible, because the decision of an FLRA administrative law judge in many cases is final. FLRA decisions are likewise final in matters involving union representation. By seeking FLRA arbitration, both the employer and the bargaining unit relinquish control of a situation.

BUDGET INFORMATION

The FLRA budget is relatively stable from year to year. In 1999 the FLRA was allocated approximately $22.586 million by Congress. About $18 million (over 78 percent) was designated for salaries and for personnel benefits. Approximately $3 million was budgeted to rental and miscellaneous expenses and the remainder, $1 million, was allocated for travel and transportation.

Additionally the FLRA raised money to support the various training programs associated with CADR through fees charged to third-party (nonfederal) program participants.

HISTORY

The U.S. government's earliest involvement with personnel management dates back to 1883 when Congress authorized the creation of a Civil Service Commission. That commission remained in effect for nearly 100 years, until the Jimmy Carter administration when the Civil Service Reform Act of 1978 was passed. The act, also called the Federal Service Labor-Management Relations Statute, was inspired in part by the exposure of an unprecedented level of corruption amongst federal employees during the presidential administration of Richard M. Nixon. The act became effective on January 1, 1979 and dissolved the Civil Service Commission of 1883.

Some functions of the defunct commission were delegated to the Equal Employment Opportunity Commission (EEOC). Three new personnel management bodies were established to replace the commission: the Office of Personnel Management (OPM), the Merit Systems Protection Board (MSPB), and the Federal Labor Relations Authority (FLRA). The FLRA was established under Title VII of the Civil Service Reform Act, to oversee the certification of federal employees' bargaining units and to handle labor-management issues. The Foreign Services divisions of the FLRA were created the following year under the Foreign Service Act of 1980.

The newly established FLRA was highly visible during President Ronald Reagan's administration in the 1980s. In 1981 a major dispute over working conditions and wages flared up between the Federal Aviation Administration and the Professional Air Traffic Controllers' Organization (PATCO). Around that same time, a similar confrontation within the Immigration and Naturalization Service (INS) was threatened but failed to materialize in the wake of the repercussions of the PATCO incident.

Again in 1985, the leaders of three U.S. postal workers' unions were relieved of their duties—Vincent R. Sombrotto, Kenneth T. Blaylock, and Moe Biller were cited under the Hatch Act for using their authority within the unions to endorse the democratic presidential candidate, Walter Mondale, during the campaign of 1984.

When President Bill Clinton came into office in 1992, he created labor/management councils to facilitate employee negotiations directly with government employers in order to reduce the need for arbitration. He also created the National Partnership Council by an executive order and made the FLRA chair plus three union leaders serve as members of the council. The council gives the federal union representatives a direct voice to the Congress. Clinton also signed a law permitting federal employees to endorse political campaigns outside of the work place. He failed to get legislation passed that would have prevented the federal government from entering into an agreement with a contractor during a union dispute if permanent replacement workers were hired by the employer.

CURRENT POLITICAL ISSUES

It is impossible to generalize regarding the substance and nature of the many cases that routinely go before the FLRA and its various arbitration panels and adjudicatory channels. For example, at issue before the FLRA in recent years were a variety of cases involving suspension and/or termination of employment for a multitude of reasons—improper use of government E-mail facilities, complaints about management, and changing one's mind after voluntary resignation. However, the cases that bring the FLRA the greatest publicity are those in which their decisions affect the lives of the general public.

Case Study: PATCO

In 1981 the FLRA was in the middle of an historic confrontation between the federal air traffic controllers' union, called the Professional Air Traffic Controllers Organization (PATCO), and the administration of President Ronald Reagan. PATCO came forward with a list of grievances that included job stress, which, they claimed, impaired their ability to function in a reliable manner and thus jeopardized commercial airline safety. When negotiations failed PATCO members walked off the job on August 3, 1981, in direct defiance of federal law which forbids federal employees to resort to a strike as a negotiation tactic.

After a swift review of the case, the FLRA stepped in and decertified the union. The decertification of PATCO meant that the union and its leaders were stripped of all authority to represent federal employees to the FLRA in the course of any labor dispute. Without the FLRA's protection, the Federal Aviation Administration (FAA), PATCO members' employer, was free to fire PATCO strikers without fear of recourse. Within two days of the walkout by PATCO members, on August 5, the 11,345 striking members of the decertified union were dismissed by the FAA, and PATCO leaders were jailed for violating federal law.

Without delay the FAA hired 13,000 replacement workers. *Time* reported, "No labor conflict in recent years ended more dramatically than the collision between ... [the federal government] and the Professional Air Traffic Controllers Organization." The PATCO replacements later organized themselves into the National Air Traffic Controllers Association and filed for certification with the FLRA.

Public Impact

These events shocked many who had come to believe that unionism could guarantee job security. Some found it especially upsetting to think that workers could be fired for striking over working conditions, particularly where public safety was at issue. However many Americans were gratified to know that the federal government would uphold the law that precludes strikes among federal employees. Regardless of circumstances, the potential inconvenience of any civil service strike affects virtually all of the general public. The airline industry suffered considerable loss of business due to airport slowdowns caused by inadequate staffing in the nation's control towers, despite the swift retaliation of the FLRA and FAA. Some commercial airline companies reported as much as a twenty-five percent slowdown in business due to the inadequacies in the national air traffic control system. One smaller airline ceased operations altogether because it was unable to compete with the limited facilities imposed by the strike.

FUTURE DIRECTIONS

The FLRA has occasionally been plagued by long delays in decision-making during the arbitration, mediation, and representation processes. In an effort to end these delays, the FLRA is turning to new information technology to assist them. The FLRA is making plans to transfer as much of the information needed to process its decisions to the World Wide Web. In early 1998, the FLRA took an important step in this direction by making many of the forms necessary for its services available at its Web site.

AGENCY RESOURCES

For more information about the FLRA, access the FLRA's Web site at http://www.flra.gov, send a written request to Public Information Office, Federal Labor Relations Authority, 607 Fourteenth St., NW, 4th Floor, Washington, DC 20424-0001, or call (202) 482-6540.

Information is available on FLRA hearings and cases—dockets and decisions—by contacting the Office of Case Control, Federal Labor Relations Authority, 607 Fourteenth St., NW, 4th Floor, Washington, DC 20424-0001, or by calling (202) 482-6540. The hours of service are from 9:00 A.M. to 5:00 P.M., eastern standard time (EST), Monday through Friday. The office should be called in advance to ensure that the viewing of this information is possible.

The Federal Service Impasse Panel offers assistance in resolving impasse issues between federal agencies and employee representatives. Information is available from the Federal Service Impasses Panel, Federal Labor Relations Authority, 607 Fourteenth St., NW, 4th Floor, Washington, DC, 20424-0001, or by calling (202) 482-6540.

The Federal Labor Relations Library contains information on the FLRA and labor-management relations in the federal service. The collection is limited and appointments to enter the library are recommended. Contact the Federal Labor Relations Library, Federal Labor Relations Authority, 607 Fourteenth St. NW, 4th Floor, Washington, DC 20424-0001. Hours of service are from 9:00 A.M. to 5:00 P.M., EST, Monday through Friday. The telephone number is (202) 482-6552 and the fax number is (202) 482-6659.

AGENCY PUBLICATIONS

The FLRA furnishes the following free publications: "Federal Service Labor-Management Statute," "A Guide to the Federal Service Labor-Management Relations Statute," and the "Annual Report of the Federal Labor Relations Authority and the Federal Services Impasses Panel." FLRA publications are available from the Public Information Office, Federal Labor Relations Authority, 500 C St. SW, Washington, DC, 20424. The phone number for ordering is (202) 382-0711.

The following publications provide information on negotiating impasses "Guide to Hearing Procedures of the Federal Services," "Impasses Panel," "Subject Matter Index," "Table of Cases," and the "Annual Report." For copies contact Federal Service Impasses Panel, Federal Labor Relations Authority, 500 C St. SW, Room 215, Washington, DC, 20424, or phone (202) 382-0981.

BIBLIOGRAPHY

Crawford, James. "Blacklist Goes To Washington." *Mother Jones*, June 1984, p. 10.

Hubbartt, William S. *The New Battle Over Workplace Privacy.* New York: American Management Association, 1998.

Ingraham, Patricia W., and Carolyn Ban, eds. *Legislating Bureaucratic Change: the Civil Service Reform Act of 1978.* Albany, N.Y.: State University of New York Press, 1985.

Kenny, John J., and Linda G. Kahn. *Primer of Labor Relations.* (24th Ed.) Washington, D.C.: Bureau of National Affairs, Inc., 1989.

Novack, Janet. "We took 'em to the Woodshed." *Forbes*, 22 November 1993, p. 43 (2).

Pedeliski, Theodore B. "Privacy and the Workplace: Technology and Public Employment," *Public Personnel Management*, Winter 1997, p. 515 (13).

Pincus, Laura B., and Clayton Trotter. "The Disparity between Public and Private Sector Employee Privacy Protections." *American Business Law Journal*, Fall 1995, pp. 51–89.

Troy, Leo. *The New Unionism in the New Society: Public Sector Unions*. Washington, D.C.: George Mason University Press, 1994.

"Unhappy Again: The Air Controllers Reorganize." *Time*, 6 October 1986, p. 59.

Wallihan, James. "Too Little, Too Late: The Limits of Standalone Arbitration in Discharge Cases." *Labor Studies Journal*, Spring 1996, p. 39 (22).

Federal Maritime Commission (FMC)

PARENT ORGANIZATION: Independent
ESTABLISHED: 1961
EMPLOYEES: 140

Contact Information:

ADDRESS: 800 N. Capitol St. NW
Washington, DC 20573
PHONE: (202) 523-5707
FAX: (202) 523-5785
URL: http://www.fmc.gov
CHAIRMAN: Harold J. Creel
MANAGING DIRECTOR: Edward Patrick Walsh

WHAT IS ITS MISSION?

According to the agency, the mission of the Federal Maritime Commission (FMC) is to "ensure the Nation's interests are met through an efficient, economic, and nondiscriminatory ocean transportation system that is free of unfair foreign maritime trade practices."

HOW IS IT STRUCTURED?

The FMC is an independent agency under the executive branch of the U.S. government. The FMC's five commissioners are appointed for five-year terms by the president with the advice and consent of the Senate. No more than three commissioners may be from the same political party. From these five members, the president chooses a chairman, who must be approved by the Senate. The FMC is headquartered in Washington, D.C., and has four area representatives around the nation who ensure the rules of the FMC are followed by all commercial shipping into or out of the United States.

The chairman and commissioners oversee the agency and establish the rules. Reporting to them are six offices: the Office of the Secretary, the Office of the Managing Director, the Office of the Inspector General, the Office of the General Counsel, the Office of Administrative Law Judges, and the Office of Equal Employment Opportunity. The secretary and managing director oversee daily operations and offices and the inspector general maintains audit capabilities and sees that proper procedures are maintained financially and legally. The general counsel and the Office of Administrative Law

Judges assist in advising the commissioners in regard to the legal operations of the FMC. The Office of Equal Employment Opportunity works to ensure that the FMC is fair in its hiring practices. Under the auspices of the managing director are bureaus that are responsible for handling the commission's work: the Bureau of Economics and Agreement Analysis, the Bureau of Enforcement, the Bureau of Tariffs, and Certification and Licensing.

PRIMARY FUNCTIONS

According to the FMC, it "regulates the waterborne foreign commerce of the United States, ensures that U.S. international trade is open to all nations on fair and equitable terms, and protects against unauthorized, concerted activity in the waterborne commerce of the United States." To accomplish these tasks the FMC's duties are split among the agency's various offices.

In addition to offering legal advice to the FMC, the Office of General Counsel (OGC) is responsible for the FMC's international affairs. If the OGC becomes aware of practices in foreign countries that may be unfair to U.S. shipping carriers, its duty is to advise the FMC what should be done. This advice may include penalties to the foreign countries in question or restrictions on what goods can be shipped from or to those countries. Additionally, the OGC maintains a list of carriers operated by foreign governments; the rates at which these carriers ship goods is closely watched to ensure that the carriers do not abuse the privilege of their position.

The main function of the Office of Informal Inquiries and Complaints and Informal Dockets (OIIC) is to help complaintants avoid the often lengthy and complicated process of filing a more formal complaint with the FMC. To this end, the OIIC helps individuals resolve their problems with shipping carriers in several ways. The OIIC attempts to eliminate any problems that may have resulted in delays of the arrivals or departures of shipments. Also, if any money was improperly collected from an individual by a shipping carrier, the OIIC works with the two parties to recover and return the funds. The OIIC helps carriers resolve problems with contract negotiations with shipping associations. Finally, the OIIC assists people who are moving overseas to ensure they receive their possessions in a timely manner.

The Office of Administrative Law Judges investigates alleged violations of the Shipping Act of 1984. The FMC or private parties (such as goods carriers or individual citizens) may make such a complaint. A judge from this office first hears the assertions of both parties to decide if there is enough evidence of a transgression to warrant continuing. If so the judge attempts to negotiate an agreement. If this does not work the judge hears the case and determines who is correct. A judge's decision can be appealed or reviewed by the FMC.

FAST FACTS

In 1997 the FMC received approximately 10,000 service contracts and 29,000 amendments to existing contracts from the U.S. shipping industry.

(Source: Federal Maritime Commission. "Remarks of the Honorable Harold J. Creel Jr. before the Agriculture Transportation Coalition, San Francisco, California." June 26, 1998.)

The Bureau of Enforcement has two main functions: to monitor and investigate carriers for possible abuses and to adjudicate formal proceedings against them. In a formal proceeding the bureau identifies the regulatory issues involved and bureau attorneys serve as legal advisors to the FMC. To guarantee the statutes and regulations administered by the FMC are followed, the Bureau of Enforcement also checks shipping carriers and ports. The bureau keeps a close watch to ensure violations, such as illegal rebating of shipping rates, improper describing of shipped goods, or shipping without a proper license, do not occur. When the bureau discovers a violation, it serves a notice to the violator and possibly enters into formal proceedings.

The Bureau of Economics and Agreement Analysis evaluates agreements between shippers and their destination ports. The bureau ensures that the companies maintain standards of competition and do not abuse antitrust laws. In addition, the bureau appraises current economic trends, keeping track of carrier pricing and the commercial and economic activity in the areas of major U.S. trade.

The Bureau of Tariffs, Certification, and Licensing has several functions. It licenses freight carriers, certifies that the owners and operators of carrier ships take proper responsibility for accidents, and preserves all tariff filings.

PROGRAMS

The highly specialized FMC bureaus run programs parallel to their specializations. For example, the Bureau of Enforcement operates an enforcement program. The monitoring of shipping practices done by the Bureau of Economics and Agreement Analysis constitutes the commission's program for encouraging competition in the industry.

The Bureau of Tariffs, Certification, and Licensing runs several programs. One of these, the Automated Tariff Filing System (ATFI), is the FMC's primary means of tracking information on shipping rates for the public, information that all U.S. common carriers are required to make available. The Bureau of Tariffs, Certification, and Licensing also maintains the Regulated Persons Index, which contains vital information on waterborne carriers and terminal operators whose positions fall under the regulation of the FMC. The index includes their names, addresses, and phone and fax numbers. Most of this data is available to the general public but some is designated as confidential.

BUDGET INFORMATION

Congress appropriated $15 million for the FMC in the 1998 budget. The FMC's budget is fairly equally divided among the areas of formal proceedings; operations and administration; economics and agreement analysis; tariffs, certification, and licensing; and enforcement. Presently the money for the FMC's budget comes from the taxpayer-supported federal budget. Legislation introduced in 1998 is attempting to shift the funding to a system that is supported solely by user fees.

HISTORY

In 1961 the FMC was established to ensure U.S. goods shipped overseas received fair treatment and, conversely, that foreign goods shipped to the United States were fairly tariffed and received once they arrived on U.S. docks. According to FMC Chairman Harold Creel, "the Commission has been around in one form or another since early in this century, 1916 to be precise. For years we performed our duties while operating within the present-day Maritime Administration. In 1961, the FMC was created as an independent regulatory agency—Congress saw the wisdom of separating our regulatory functions from MarAd's responsibility to subsidize and promote the U.S. flag fleet."

The 1970s and 1980s brought a substantial decline in the number of operating U.S. ocean-borne carriers. With industry experts viewing this as indicative of a failing shipping industry, changes in certain regulations had to be made for U.S. carriers to compete internationally. Under President Ronald Reagan the Shipping Act of 1984 was passed overwhelmingly by Congress, drastically changing the ways the shipping industry and the FMC operated. One of the purposes of the act was to reduce government intervention and regulatory costs. Antitrust restrictions on specific companies were dropped, allowing U.S. ocean-borne carriers to set shipping rates and divide routes among themselves. This relieved the FMC from regulating companies in regard to trust laws.

Often Americans are not aware of the FMC's impact on shipping tariffs until they travel on a cruise ship or buy an import, both of which require tariff payment. However the FMC's involvement in U.S. trading affairs became somewhat more noticeable in the late 1990s. In particular, in 1997 the FMC threatened to charge Japan $100,000 per ship per day unless the Japanese opened their ports to U.S. goods. This brought the relatively small regulatory agency into the limelight of international politics. The next year the agency was asked by Congress and U.S. carriers to target China, another major trading partner, with accusations of unfair trading policies. Because of their complaints, the FMC took action and began negotiations with Chinese shipping officials to reduce restrictions on the U.S. shipping industry faced when dealing with China.

CURRENT POLITICAL ISSUES

Throughout 1997 the FMC found itself at the center of a controversy that nearly threw trans-Pacific shipping into a tailspin. As policymakers debated and negotiated, the FMC stood ready to impose fines, impound ships, and thereby disrupt trade operations between two major trading nations.

Case Study: Japanese Tariffs on U.S. Imports

While the United States has maintained an open-door policy regarding Japanese goods entering the country, a reciprocal agreement has not existed in Japan. While the U.S. marketplace includes many Japanese-made goods, like cars, electronics, watches, and computers, Japanese markets have either charged high tariffs on U.S. goods or not allowed some, like cars and other high priced items, into the country. The United States had difficulty negotiating a trade agreement that it felt balanced its interests equitably with Japan's.

In response to negotiations that failed to open Japanese ports to U.S. goods, the FMC imposed fines of $100,000 per ship, per day for Japanese carriers arriving in U.S. ports. When the Japanese refused to pay the millions in accumulated fines, the FMC ordered a shipping ban to go into effect October 17, 1997. The ban would have forbidden Japanese container ships from entering U.S. ports and impounded those already there. This ban would have interrupted billions of dollars worth of trade. It also spurred U.S. and Japanese officials, who prior to the threat were at an impasse, to reach a tentative agreement that modified the cumbersome and costly rules that shipping to Japan entailed. President Bill Clinton took the opportunity to state to the *Los Angeles Times*, "We have always pressed Japan for a firm commitment to liberalize trade in its ports and today they have done just that."

The negotiators scrambled to send a copy of their agreement to the FMC in order to avert the shipping ban from going into effect. The agreement modified some of Japan's laws such as "prior consultation," a regulation that forced shippers to inform the Japan Harbor Transportation Association (JHTA) of any changes in routes, pricing, or other plans. The agreement set up a framework that allowed shippers to bypass the JHTA and streamlined licensing for foreign companies.

Public Impact

If the shipping ban on Japanese goods had gone into effect, it would have had an impact on the type and price of items that Americans could purchase. The FMC's proposed ban and its results would also have affected U.S. businesses. According to Gill Roeder, marketing director for APL Ltd., speaking to the *L.A. Times,* "any substantive breakthrough in the current monopolistic and anti-competitive environment of Japan's ports would be welcomed." APL Ltd. operates American President Lines which has shipped cargo to Japan since 1867 and has to deal with Japan's anticompetitive, closed-door policies.

FUTURE DIRECTIONS

As one of several federal agencies involved in international trade, the FMC is watching the European Community (EC) in hopes of developing a closer shipping relationship with it. While obstacles stand in the way, the FMC and the U.S. shipping industry remain hopeful that upcoming talks will help circumvent their difficulties and result in mutually beneficial shipping relations.

AGENCY RESOURCES

More information about the FMC and its role in U.S. shipping can be obtained at its Web site at http://www.fmc.gov. On the Web site are copies of FMC decisions, its strategic plan, and agreements. A *Public Information Handbook,* the Annual Report, or other information can be obtained from the FMC library by writing to the FMC at 800 N. Capitol St. NW, Washington, DC 20573.

AGENCY PUBLICATIONS

The following records are generally available for inspection and copying upon written request to the Office of the Secretary: tariffs, agreements in effect and newly filed agreements that have been noticed in the *Federal Register*, a list of passenger vessel certifications of financial responsibility, and a list of licensed ocean freight forwarders. Also, to the extent not otherwise exempt from disclosure, the following materials are available through the commission's electronic reading room: final opinions and orders, statements of policy and interpretation adopted by the commission, and administrative staff manuals and instructions to staff that affect the public. Information can also be obtained by calling (202) 523-5793 or faxing (202) 523-4372.

BIBLIOGRAPHY

Barr, Cameron. "U.S. Slaps $100,000 Tax on Japanese Ships in Latest Trade Dispute." *The Christian Science Monitor*, 12 March 1997, p. 9.

Iritani, Evelyn. "U.S., Japan Defuse Trade Fight."*Los Angeles Times,* 18 October 1997, p. A–1.

Kempster, Norman, and Robert A. Rosenblatt. "Maritime Agency's Big Splash Helped Break Up Trade Logjam." *Los Angeles Times,* 18 October 1997, p. A-12.

Pine, Art. "U.S. to Answer Japan's Port Policies With Penalty Fees." *Los Angeles Times,* 27 February 1997, p. D-1.

Remarks of the Honorable Harold J. Creel, Jr., Chairman Federal Maritime Commission Before the Economic Strategy Institute. Washington, D.C., 6 November 1997.

Federal Mediation and Conciliation Service (FMCS)

PARENT ORGANIZATION: Independent
ESTABLISHED: 1947
EMPLOYEES: 290

Contact Information:

ADDRESS: 2100 K St. NW
Washington, DC 20427
PHONE: (202) 606-8100
FAX: (202) 606-4216
URL: http://www.fmcs.gov
DIRECTOR: John Calhoun Wells

WHAT IS ITS MISSION?

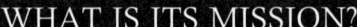

According to its "Strategic Plan 1997–2002," the mission of the Federal Mediation and Conciliation Service (FMCS) is "promoting the development of sound and stable labor-management relations; preventing or minimizing work stoppages by assisting labor and management in settling their disputes through mediation, advocating collective bargaining, mediation and voluntary arbitration as the preferred processes for settling issues between employers and representatives of employees; developing the art, science and practice of conflict resolution, and fostering the establishment and maintenance of constructive joint processes to improve labor-management relationships, employment security and organizational effectiveness."

HOW IS IT STRUCTURED?

The director, appointed by the president with the advice and consent of the Senate, heads the FMCS. This person sets policy and is the agency's liaison to government and organized labor; the director also assists in mediation of major disputes. Two deputy directors assist and advise the director in matters of policy, mediation, agency representation, and management. Five regional offices and 75 field offices carry out FMCS policy and programs and respond to mediation and arbitration requests.

National Office Departments

The Office of Mediation Information, or Notice Processing, keeps track of labor contract expirations and documents progress or steps taken to reach new contract agreements. The information from case tracking is used to compile statistics and reports, as well as answer contract expiration notice queries that are submitted under the Freedom of Information Act. The Office of Alternative Dispute Resolution Services provides dispute consultation, mediation training, mediation services, and follow-up work. The Office of Arbitration services keeps an inventory of arbitrators qualified to handle labor-management disputes and appoints an arbitrator when appropriate. The International Affairs Office performs the above tasks but in foreign nations.

The Grants Office funds the establishment, operations, and activities of joint labor-management committees designed specifically to improve labor relations, productivity, or other aspects of management-labor cooperation. Applicants for funding should be under formal bargaining agreements, and a review board determines if a grant will be awarded.

The Office of the General Counsel handles the legal needs of the FMCS, such as protecting the agency's mediators from being forced to testify in court (mediators are protected by client privilege). This office also reviews congressional testimony and proposed legislation that can impact the agency's mission or work.

The Office of Administration, the Office of Budget, and the Office of Finance support the management and operations of the FMCS by administering hiring, employee benefits, contracts, records management, and budgeting. An education and training coordinator designs programs to develop employee skills. The Public Affairs Office handles internal and external communications, including media and public relations.

The FMCS at the Field Level

Each of the five regional offices is headed by a regional director who is the region's liaison to the national leadership. This person has close ties with his or her region's labor-management community and elected officials. There are two directors of mediation service in each region who report to the regional director. These directors of mediation work with a team of about twenty mediators. The mediators compose the largest percentage of FMCS employees. They work directly with FMCS clients, mediating contract or other labor-management disputes.

PRIMARY FUNCTIONS

The FMCS works to prevent disruptions in the flow of interstate commerce caused by labor-management disputes by providing mediators to assist disputing parties in the resolution of their differences. The FMCS offers it services in mediating labor-management disputes to any industry affecting interstate commerce that has employees represented by a union whenever in its judgment, such dispute threatens to cause a substantial interruption of commerce. This may be either on its own motion or at the request of one or more of the parties to the dispute. FMCS mediation efforts are directed toward the establishment of sound and stable labor-management relations on a continuing basis, thereby helping to reduce the incidence of work stoppages. The mediator's basic function is to encourage and promote better day-to-day relations between labor and management, so that issues arising in negotiations may be faced as problems to be settled through mutual effort rather than issues in dispute.

Each division in the FMCS focuses on a different aspect of mediation. The Dispute Mediation division mediates contract negotiations between employers and unions that represent employees in the private, public, and federal sectors. The Preventive Mediation division provides services and training in cooperative processes to help labor and management break down traditional barriers and build better working relationships. The Alternative Dispute Resolution division offers services and training in joint problem solving that can be used in lieu of courtroom litigation, agency adjudication, or traditional rule-making by federal, state, and local governments. Arbitration Services maintains a computerized roster of qualified, private-sector arbitrators, retrievable by geographical area, professional affiliation, occupation, industry experience, or other specified criteria, who are able to mediate labor-management disputes in throughout the country.

The Labor Management Relations Act requires that parties to a labor contract must file a dispute notice if agreement is not reached 30 days prior to a contract termination or reopening date. The notice must be filed with the FMCS and the appropriate state or local mediation agency. The FMCS is required to avoid the mediation of disputes that would have only a minor effect on interstate commerce if state or other conciliation services are available to the parties.

PROGRAMS

The FMCS runs several programs designed to involve more people in labor-management relations. For example, the FMCS sponsors a National Labor Management Conference every two years which is open to the public. The conference features discussion groups and panel speakers on such topics as multicultural issues in arbitration hearings, how to build a labor-management partnership to avert layoffs, and the impact of external law on traditional arbitration issues. More formal training is available through FMCS mediation and conflict resolution training programs. Participants learn about mediation, such as the tools used and the ethics of the negotiation process; mediation facilitation (e.g. how to convey neutrality or maintain composure in difficult situations);

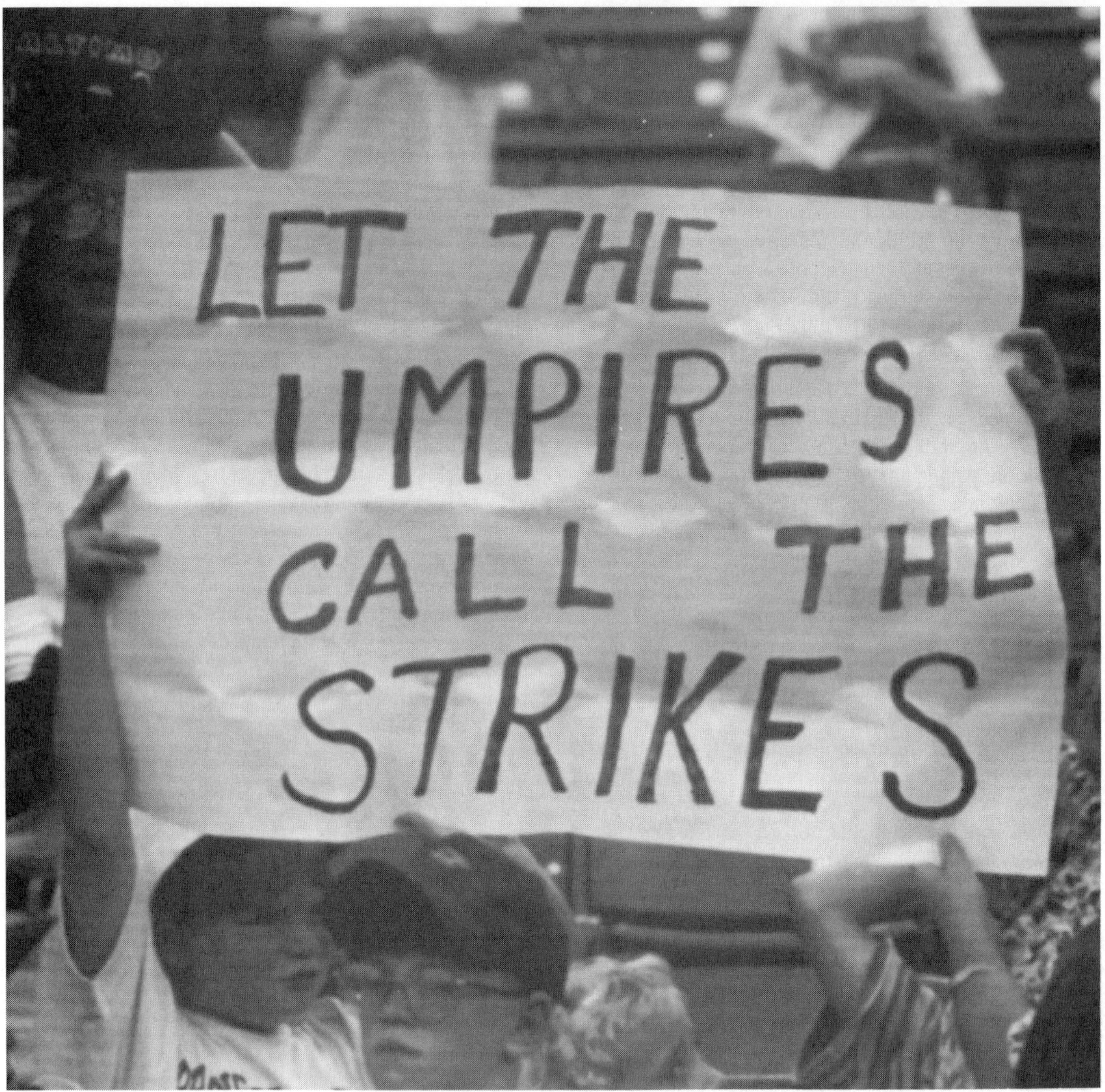

When professional baseball players went on strike in 1994, the FMCS, and eventually Congress and the president, helped to negotiate a settlement. Five months before the strike began, fans were protesting against the growing possibility of a players' strike.
(AP/Wide World Photos)

interest-based bargaining (how to do it and how it differs from traditional bargaining); and conflict resolution and mediation in a diverse workplace where multicultural issues are discussed, such as the impact of stereotyping, prejudices, and discrimination in the workplace.

The Labor-Management Grants Program

The Labor-Management Grants Program offers opportunities for labor and management to reach reconciliation before a work stoppage or strike results. This program was mandated by the Labor-Management Cooperation Act of 1978, which requires the FMCS to provide assistance in the establishment and operation of labor-management committees organized in a plant, area, government agency, or other industry that falls under the auspices of this program. The committees are charged with improving communications with respect to subjects of mutual interest to management and labor, with the goal of improving labor-management relationships, job security, organizational effectiveness, and economic development.

Committees may receive up to $100,000, but the grant amount depends on the specific nature, needs, and duration of the committee. There are seven major areas of committee focus that are considered appropriate for grant application: improving communication between labor and management, providing workers and employers with opportunities to study and explore innovative joint approaches to achieving organizational effectiveness, assisting workers and employers in solving problems of mutual concern not applicable to resolution within the collective bargaining process, studying ways to eliminate potential problems which reduce competitiveness and inhibit economic relations, enhancing the involvement of workers in making decisions that affect their working lives, expanding and improving working relationships between workers and managers, and encouraging free collective bargaining by establishing continuing mechanisms for communication between employers and their employees through federal assistance in the formation and operation of labor-management committees.

BUDGET INFORMATION

In 1998 Congress appropriated approximately $33.5 million to the FMCS. Most of the FMCS budget was directed toward dispute and preventive mediation services. The remaining fraction of the FMCS budget was directed toward management and administrative support, labor-management cooperation projects, and arbitration services.

HISTORY

The 1947 Taft-Hartley Act amendments to the National Labor Relations Act (NLRA) state that "sound and stable industrial peace and the advancement of the general welfare, health, and safety of the nation and of the best interest of employers and employees can most satisfactorily be secured by the settlement of issues between employers and employees through the processes of conference and collective bargaining between employers and the representatives of their employees; the settlement of issues between employers and employees through collective bargaining may be advanced by making available full and adequate governmental facilities for conciliation, mediation, and voluntary arbitration. [sec. 201.]"

This policy prompted Congress to create the FMCS to minimize interruptions of business that grew out of labor disputes and to settle labor and management disputes through conciliation and mediation. For over 50 years the FMCS served at the forefront in mediating disputes, providing preventive measures, mediating collective bargaining contract negotiations, providing binding arbitration if necessary, and settling disputes.

Much of the FMCS's work is done away from the glare of media scrutiny, but its results are often touted on the news. Over the years it has been granted more authority over various aspects of public and private mediation and taken on disputes among many of the United States's largest corporations and unions. In the late 1940s and early 1950s labor underwent radical changes with the consolidation of the American Federation of Labor (AFL) and the Congress of Industrial Organizations (CIO) into the AFL-CIO, and the expulsion of the Teamsters from the federation. At that time unions were considered hotbeds of Communism and often treated as anti-American during the Red Scare of the 1950s. Gradually the FMCS was given more power to arbitrate and mediate disputes between the growing unions and management. This was the true beginning of the three-way partnership among labor, management, and government. Labor was trying hard to keep corruption from within its ranks, but Congress realized that without federal intervention, this would prove difficult.

By 1959 various labor acts were passed to ensure labor remained open and aboveboard. Although strikes and work stoppages were inevitable in many cases as management and labor each failed to see the other's point of view, the FMCS was given more leeway to step in and resolve issues before they resulted in a work stoppage. This came about due to a 1974 change in the 1947 Taft-Hartley Act. The change required labor and management to give the FMCS 30 days notice prior to the start of any contract negotiations. This allows FMCS mediators the opportunity to intervene if necessary to ensure negotiations proceed smoothly.

In the 1970s FMCS mediators were also called in to assist negotiations between the Department of the Interior and American Indian tribes for land rights and were able to establish a conciliated agreement between them. This was the beginning of the alternative dispute resolution component of the FMCS.

In 1997 the FMCS was involved in the successful resolution of the United Parcel Service (UPS) and International Brotherhood of Teamsters strike. It was under the auspices of the mediators who were willing to stay at the bargaining table, that an agreement was reached before the strike severely impacted the economy. Under Director John Calhoun Wells, the FMCS's role was broadened to include raising economic consciousness in order to transform industrial relations from an adversarial to a cooperative relationship.

CURRENT POLITICAL ISSUES

Critics of the FMCS have complained that it takes too long for federal mediators to become involved in the

FAST FACTS

The owners of major league baseball teams announced that the 1994–95 strike cost them $700 million for the games not played in 1994 and another $300 million due to the delay in starting the 1995 season.

(Source: *Monthly Labor Review*, March 1, 1997, pp. 21–7.)

collective bargaining process, resulting in long, drawn-out negotiations. Mediators for the FMCS try to persuade parties to make concessions but, unlike arbitrators, they have no power to impose a settlement. Usually mediators are trainers and conciliators who aim to bring about workplace harmony and are more effective when involved in the negotiation process early.

Case Study: Strike Three and You're Out!

For 232 days in the summer, fall, and winter of 1994 and 1995, one of the biggest strikes in the history of professional sports dominated the news. The strike of Major League Baseball players caused billions of dollars in losses for both team owners and players, and caused fans to become disillusioned by the controversy over money. FMCS mediators attempted to bring about an equitable settlement for all, but since they could not enforce their mediation recommendations, their efforts were greatly hampered.

A number of labor disputes from the late 1970s through the early 1990s precursed the strike of 1994–1995. This adversarial stance between the owners and the players set the stage for the tremendous strike that began August 12, 1994. Free agency, salary caps, and revenue sharing were the opening issues to be negotiated. Although talks on these matters had begun two years earlier, no consensus between owners and players had been reached. By walking out on August 12, the baseball players maximized the negative impact of the strike on the owners. The bulk of the players' salaries had already been paid—the owners, however, had not been able to recoup their outlay, which was expected from the huge television contracts, especially during the playoff season. The initial negotiations were very hostile.

At the beginning of the strike, both sides agreed to accept mediation by the FMCS. They went through several mediators, including Director John Wells; however, both sides were so entrenched in their respective positions that there was no progress towards a settlement. The mediators suggested that the owners become involved in the negotiations rather than rely on hired negotiators, but this did not bring about a resolution to the dispute. A former director of the FMCS, Fred Usery, was then assigned the negotiations but even his efforts did not bring about conciliation between the warring factions. The players thought that his proposal was overly favorable to the owners. Finally, President Bill Clinton threatened to intervene with the consent of Congress. It took these threats, combined with a federal judge's order to end the stalemate, to establish a new contract in which concessions were made by both owners and players.

Many viewed the baseball strike as rich people fighting richer people to become even richer and both sides in the dispute tarnished the image of professional baseball. The role of the mediator was to try and cut through the side issues and bring out the real areas of contention to disputants and allow them to work through them. Without both sides agreeing to binding arbitration, the mediator's role remained as an adviser who guides the process of negotiation. The FMCS was unable to bring negotiations to a close successfully with this limited ability.

SUCCESSES AND FAILURES

The FMCS uses both its success and failures to demonstrate to bargaining parties what effect strikes and effective management have on the health and well-being of an organization. The FMCS sponsors yearly labor-management seminars where successful organizations share their stories and strategies about their relations. Under the auspices of the FMCS, communication by management sharing business information and labor's effort to improve relations even when disagreements threaten to disrupt the workplace, have led to a partnership of sorts that embraces competing and common interests. With FMCS training and assistance, management and labor share a vision for their mutual interests shaping a successful future.

In 1996 McDonnell Douglass and the International Association of Machinists were brought together in Representative Richard Gephardt's office and after a marathon bargaining session, Director Wells wrested agreements from both sides and concluded the bargaining with new contracts.

On July 31, 1997, the FMCS entered negotiations between UPS and the International Brotherhood of Teamsters six hours before a strike deadline. There were three weeks of mediated negotiation, with many session lasting around the clock, before an end was brought to the largest national strike in two decades. The FMCS director, deputy director, and field mediator led the parties through 80 hours of bargaining over five days.

Finally, just after midnight on August 10, an agreement was announced for a new five-year contract.

FUTURE DIRECTIONS

In the years to come the FMCS plans to build on the foundation of its internal reinvention. They are committed to becoming more results-oriented. The focus will be to strengthen performance, to improve quality of services, and to provide an expanded range of conflict resolution services to all customers. It is hoped that not only FMCS customers but the executive branch, the Congress, the taxpayers and the public at large will benefit.

AGENCY RESOURCES

To find out more about the services offered by the FMCS, contact a regional office or the main headquarters at (202) 606-8100. FMCS information can also be found on-line at http://www.fmcs.gov. There you will find press releases of current FMCS projects, a copy of the magazine *The Mediator,* and news about upcoming labor-management conferences, training sessions, and seminars.

AGENCY PUBLICATIONS

The FMCS publication *FMCS Arbitration Services: Self-governing in the Workplace*, the *49th Annual Report,* and the annual journal *The Mediator* are available from the agency and any Government Printing Office (GPO) store, which can be found in federal buildings across the country. For more information concerning these or any other brochures and publications offered by the FMCS, please write to the Federal Mediation and Conciliation Service, 2100 K Street NW, Washington, DC 20427, or call (202) 606-8100. Publications are also available on-line at http://www.fmcs.gov.

BIBLIOGRAPHY

Alexander, Steve. "Honeywell, Strikers to Meet Again this Morning." *Star Tribune*, 12 February 1998, pp. 3D.

"Federal Mediation and Conciliation Service Forty-ninth Annual Report." *1996 Performance*, Washington, D.C.: Government Printing Office, 1997.

Federal Mediation and Conciliation Service Strategic Plan, Washington, D.C.: Government Printing Office, 1997.

"Kaiser Permanente Asks Federal Mediators to Help Jumpstart Bargaining with Nurses' Union in Northern California. " *Business Wire*, 26 January 1998.

Kellogg, Carole. "UPS Strike Settled; Home Edition." *Los Angeles Times*, 25 August 1997, p. B4.

Kurkjian, Tim. "Like a Plague, the Major League Baseball Strike Has Infected." *Sports Illustrated,* 23 January 1995, p. 70.

Lawsky, David. "UPS Chairman, Teamsters President in Last-Ditch Talks." *Reuters Business Report*, 31 July 1997.

Mitchell, Cynthia. "UPS Pilots Agree to Pact Raising Pay 27%." *Atlanta Journal and Constitution*, 18 March 1998, pp. D1.

Noble, Marty. "Baseball, It's Baseball on Hold." *Newsday*, 25 September 1994, p. 13.

Staudohar, Paul D. "The Baseball Strike of 1994-95." *Monthly Labor Review*, 1 March 1997, pp. 21–7.

Federal Railroad Administration (FRA)

PARENT ORGANIZATION: Department of Transportation
ESTABLISHED: October 15, 1966
EMPLOYEES: 750

Contact Information:

ADDRESS: 400 7th St. SW
Washington, DC 20590
PHONE: (202) 366-4000
URL: http://www.fra.dot.gov
ADMINISTRATOR: Jolene M. Molitoris
DEPUTY ADMINISTRATOR: Donald M. Itzkoff

WHAT IS ITS MISSION?

According to its published mission statement, the Federal Railroad Administration (FRA) "promotes rail safety throughout the U.S. railroad system and encourages policies that help rail realize its full potential." Further, the FRA is committed to "working as a partner with all associated with the U.S. railroad industry, making rail transit safe for both employees and the traveling public, and promoting environmentally sound rail transportation."

HOW IS IT STRUCTURED?

The FRA is a regulatory agency of the Department of Transportation (DOT). It is headed by an administrator who is appointed by the president and confirmed by the Senate. Directly under the administrator is the deputy administrator, who is responsible for overseeing the establishment of FRA strategic policy and its safety enforcement initiatives.

The administrator is supported by four associate administrators, each responsible for a major area of regulation or policy. The associate administrator for safety oversees the agency's most important regulatory activities. The office is responsible for ensuring railroad safety in a variety of areas, including trains, signals, brakes, and the transportation of hazardous materials. Over four hundred safety inspectors work out of the FRA's eight regional offices, and the agency has certified an additional 130 state inspectors. The associate administrator for railroad development is responsible for both the agency's research and development programs and its financial aid programs for the nation's railroads. Finally, there is an associate administrator for administration and finance and an associate administrator for policy.

PRIMARY FUNCTIONS

The FRA's primary function is the administration and enforcement of federal laws and regulations regarding railroad safety. The Rail Safety Act of 1970 is the most important law that falls within its jurisdiction. It gives the agency authority over track maintenance, railroad equipment standards, and the transport of hazardous materials. The FRA investigates all serious railroad accidents. As part of its safety activity, it develops campaigns to educate the public about rail safety.

The FRA conducts and supports research and development related to intercity ground transportation. The goal of the agency's various research projects is to improve the efficiency and safety of the nation's railroads, as well as to ensure that railroads remain a commercially viable transportation resource. The FRA conducts tests on advanced and conventional systems at the Transportation Test Center, a 50-square-mile facility in Pueblo, Colorado, managed by the Association of American Railroads.

The agency administers a number of financial assistance programs for railroads. These programs provide grants and loans to freight and passenger lines on a national, regional, and local basis. The primary recipients of FRA aid are Amtrak (the National Railroad Passenger Corporation) and the railroads that serve the "Northeast Corridor" between Boston and Washington, DC.

The FRA is responsible for formulating national railroad policy. The agency bears primary responsibility for integrating rail transportation into the entire national system of waterways, roads, and air routes as described in the plan for the DOT's Intermodal Transportation System.

PROGRAMS

The FRA's programs encompass a broad range of railroad issues. Its research and development programs work toward a better understanding of the human factors involved in train design and operations, advanced train control technology, and safety issues connected with high-speed rail systems. The agency also administers various education and public awareness programs; for example, its "Expect a Train" campaign, which promotes safety at railroad crossings.

BUDGET:

Federal Railroad Administration

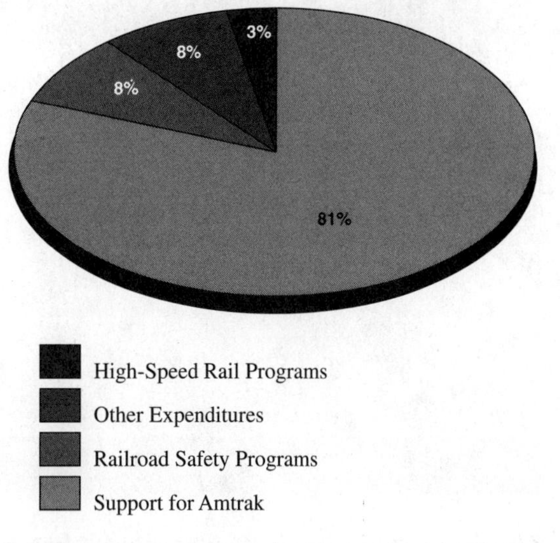

High-Speed Rail Programs
Other Expenditures
Railroad Safety Programs
Support for Amtrak

Safety Assurance and Compliance Program

The Safety Assurance and Compliance Program (SACP) is the FRA's primary safety program. Implemented in 1995, the SACP is a new form of regulation in which the FRA works on safety cooperatively with railroad companies and unions. In the first step of the SACP, teams of FRA regulators, railroad administrators, and workers work together to develop a safety profile that provides an overview of safety strengths and weaknesses, accident patterns, and other safety concerns for each railroad. The principle behind the program is to identify systemic problems that will enable the railroad community to avoid individual problems.

After the safety profile has been developed, it is presented to railroad management. They consider the issues presented and formulate a Safety Action Plan (SAP), which is submitted to the FRA. The SAP describes how the railroad intends to deal with safety problems outlined in the safety profile. The FRA reviews the SAP and either approves or rejects it. If the plan is approved, the agency notifies the company as to how corrective measures will be monitored. Once the SAP is in place, FRA regulatory activity in a company is focused on compliance with the plan. Regular safety assessment inspections are carried out, in cooperation with company management and labor, to establish whether a company is complying with the terms of its SAP.

High-speed trains, such as this one in Japan and others in use in Europe, are being considered by the FRA. It is hoped that high-speed trains running between major U.S. cities could compete with air travel and automobiles, thereby reducing costs and traffic while increasing safety. (Courtesy of the Library of Congress)

Next Generation High-Speed Rail Program

High-speed ground transportation (HSGT) is a transportation system being designed for use between cities that are one hundred to five hundred miles apart. The speed of various systems already in use in Europe and Japan ranges from 100 to 300 miles per hour. These speeds would enable trains to compete with airplane and automobile transportation. Implementation of HSGT systems on high-use routes would reduce air traffic congestion and highway traffic, and contribute to greater safety in the nation's transportation system.

An early high-speed system was developed along the Northeast Corridor. Trains now travel between Boston and Washington, DC, at speeds between 125 and 150 miles per hour. Other new technologies related to high-speed rail are being tested by the FRA. These include nonelectric locomotives and new types of grade crossings. Radio-based train control systems being researched could, according to the agency, lower the cost of new rail systems to as little as $2 to $3 million per mile, nearly 80 percent lower than the current cost of the upgrade of the Northeast Corridor.

BUDGET INFORMATION

The FRA budget in fiscal year 1998 totaled $732 million, just under 2 percent of the total for the Department of Transportation that year. The Clinton administration requested $751 million for fiscal year 1999. Over 80 percent of the FRA budget consists of appropriations that support Amtrak, the National Railroad Passenger Corporation. It received $594 million in 1998. Another $20 million was appropriated for the agency's high-speed rail programs. The FRA's railroad safety programs received $57 million in 1998. The Clinton administration has proposed that, beginning in 1999, all of the FRA's safety activities be paid for in full by fees collected from railcarriers.

HISTORY

In 1893 Congress enacted the first railroad safety law. It protected workers on locomotives and railroad cars. Over the next 40 years, laws were passed governing a variety of other railroad safety issues, including hours of service, accident reporting, signals, and locomotive inspections. These laws were enforced by the

Interstate Commerce Commission (ICC) until 1967, when they were taken over by the newly created Federal Railroad Administration in the Department of Transportation.

A number of serious railroad accidents in the late 1960s led to the passage of a comprehensive railroad safety law in 1970, the Federal Railroad Safety Act (FRSA), which gave the FRA full rule-making authority over all areas of railroad safety. The FRSA also authorized the FRA to issue emergency safety orders and compliance orders. In 1975 Congress passed the Hazardous Materials Transportation Act, which authorized the DOT to regulate the transportation of hazardous materials in all types of transportation; the FRA was given specific authority over its transportation by railroad.

After a period of comprehensive training, the first federal railroad inspectors went to work for the FRA in 1974. At that time, one of the worst problems facing the American rail system was its badly deteriorated tracks; it was estimated that it would cost some $4 billion to bring them back into serviceable condition. That same year a tanker car exploded in Decatur, Illinois, killing 10 people. The accident led to sharp public criticism of the FRA at a time when the agency was also under criticism from the railroad industry. Congress and the media called for much stricter rules while the industry complained about fines, which were nearly twice as high in 1974 as in 1973.

Congress decided in 1976 to fund high-speed rail in the Northeast Corridor, from Boston to Washington, DC. Responsibility for the project was split between the FRA and Amtrak, with the former overseeing administration and design of the new system and the latter its construction and operation. Although the system was eventually completed, the division of authority, compounded by the FRA's lack of experience in the area, led to months of delay in work approvals and enormous budget overruns.

The Staggers Rail Act, passed in 1980, deregulated the railroad industry after more than 50 years of control by the ICC. Railroads were allowed to set their own rates based on market forces. The act led to a consolidation of the industry; unprofitable companies were bought by larger ones. Allowed to cease unprofitable operations, railroads concentrated service on the most profitable areas, and the total length of track in the United States decreased by some 41 percent.

In 1986 the General Accounting Office (GAO) released a report criticizing the FRA's inspections. The GAO called the agency's procedures ineffective. Inspectors did not concentrate on the areas with the greatest potential for danger and did not use their authority to issue safety violations. The number of total inspections, the GAO found, had declined significantly since 1984.

Despite deregulation, train accidents decreased by over 75 percent between 1978 and 1993. Nonetheless, major accidents periodically occur and usually call into question the quality of the FRA's inspection. For example, after 47 people died when an Amtrak train derailed on a damaged bridge in 1993, it was revealed that the agency had rejected a plan 14 years earlier to install sensors that could have prevented the accident. In another accident in 1991 a Southern Pacific train derailed in northern California, spilling toxic chemicals into the Sacramento River, killing all life in a 45-mile stretch of the river. It was one of the worst railroad accidents to date. The FRA and the NTSB both called for stricter rules governing hazardous materials. In the investigation afterward, however, it was revealed that three weeks earlier an FRA inspector had canceled an inspection of the Southern Pacific yard where the wrecked train was from. The inspector said the railroad had complained about too-frequent inspections. Close ties between the agency and the railroad industry have been criticized often. Critics point out that railroad managers frequently take jobs in the FRA, and FRA officials leave the agency to take jobs in the railroad industry. Critics maintain that this pattern creates a coziness between regulator and regulated that leads to lax enforcement.

FAST FACTS

A train traveling 50 mph takes a mile-and-a-half to stop.

(Source: Federal Railroad Administration, 1998.)

In 1993 President Clinton signed the Government Performance and Results Act into law. The act required federal agencies to adopt strategies used by private corporations to increase efficiency. It also called for agencies to focus on results rather than punishment in their regulatory practices. To comply with the new guidelines, the FRA implemented its Safety Assurance and Compliance Program (SACP) in 1995. The SACP stressed cooperation with industry in achieving railroad safety. The program has been criticized, notably by the NTSB and the GAO. The NTSB stressed the need for continuing traditional on-site inspections to ensure the compliance of companies with federal safety standards, whereas the GAO noted a 23 percent drop in inspections in the mid-1990s. The drop occurred in all areas of FRA oversight: track, equipment, signals, hazardous materials, and operating practices.

CURRENT POLITICAL ISSUES

The Clinton administration made safety a major priority of its Department of Transportation. With railroad

FAST FACTS

About one thousand people die each year as a result of grade-crossing accidents and trespassing.

(Source: "Keeping Safety on Track." *Federal Times*, November 10, 1997.)

accidents in decline for nearly three decades, the FRA seemed to be overseeing a house that was, by and large, in order. Then in the summer of 1997 the Union Pacific Railroad experienced three bad accidents in two months' time and the FRA had to intervene.

Case Study: The Union Pacific Accidents

After its takeover of the Southern Pacific, the Union Pacific became the nation's largest railroad. The merger caused numerous problems. Shippers and their customers complained about enormous quantities of freight that were backlogged. Union Pacific (UP) simply did not have the resources to cope with an increase of demand in the mid-1990s. No one believed, however, that because of this the railroad had serious safety problems. Then came three accidents in quick succession: in June two trains collided in San Antonio, Texas, resulting in four deaths; a week and a half later two Union Pacific trains crashed near Delia, Kansas; at the end of August four parked locomotives rolled away from a siding and crashed into an oncoming freight train.

Following the last crash, the FRA announced an unprecedented, two-week round-the-clock investigation of Union Pacific. More than one hundred agency inspectors were put on the case, investigating safety along the 36,000 miles of Union Pacific line. The day the investigation began *another* UP train derailed in Texas. In the second week in September the FRA ordered Union Pacific to immediately remedy a number of serious breakdowns in safety procedure that had taken place. Twelve additional inspectors were assigned to the case in October, and more were added in November after five crewmen were killed in two more UP accidents.

The agency used its new SACP cooperative style of investigation with Union Pacific, eliciting the cooperation of company management and workers. After the initial inquiry, the FRA presented UP with a list of its recommendations. The FRA's final report detailed a list of widespread deficiencies: UP-Southern Pacific corporate culture stressed efficiency at the cost of safety; the staff was often inadequate and badly managed; employees were overworked; dispatching centers were understaffed; supervisors often ordered trains moved with defective equipment despite crews' protests; management harassed employees who insisted on safety regulations and intimidated them into silence; the drug and alcohol program was not correctly implemented; and the company's fleet of locomotives was improperly maintained.

In September 1997, following a team audit of Union Pacific in which more than 85 federal and state safety inspectors took part, the FRA met with UP management and labor unions to set up another SACP. Under the terms of the program, Union Pacific management was expected to develop a safety action plan based on the problems the FRA had found and to prepare a proposal of its own for dealing with the conditions that had led to the accidents. Finally the FRA obtained a signed commitment from Union Pacific and its labor organizations pledging themselves to address the safety problems discovered in the various team audits.

By March 1998, under the leadership of the FRA, a number of steps had been taken to alleviate the problems at Union Pacific. A steering committee, composed of company management, labor, and the FRA, had been established to oversee the UP safety program. Additional dispatchers and trainmen were hired. Engine and yard employees were given the option of taking a rest day after seven consecutive days of working. Union Pacific created the position of director of alertness, to monitor worker fatigue issues. In the meantime Union Pacific continues to be inspected, both by the FRA and the National Traffic Safety Board (NTSB), which opened its own independent investigation into the railroad's problems.

SUCCESSES AND FAILURES

The FRA maintains that the SACP initiative is thus far a great success. By spring 1998 the FRA had organized programs at most of the major railroads in the United States. Involving management and labor in the problem-evaluation process has, according to the FRA, altered the sometimes adversarial relationship that previously existed between the agency and the industry. The program also helped lessen the FRA's workload and enabled problems to be identified before they reach the critical stage.

The FRA's primary responsibility is railroad safety, and that has been improving steadily for decades. According to agency data, the total number of railroad accidents between 1978 and 1993 decreased by 75 percent. Between 1993 and 1997 the decline continued, although not as dramatically. Total railroad fatalities fell by 18 percent; crossing fatalities by 28 percent; employee casualties by 46 percent; and train accidents, not counting motor vehicle-train collisions, by almost 11 percent.

FUTURE DIRECTIONS

The FRA is investigating the implementation of the Nationwide Differential Global Positioning System (NDGPS) for the nation's railroads. The Department of Transportation plans such systems for the nation's entire transportation system. Once the system is fully implemented, satellites and onboard equipment will enable controllers to track the movement of trains, planes, boats, and motor vehicles. Once a system is in place for the rail system, train dispatchers will know precisely where every train in the country is at any given time, and they will know when situations arise that could lead to accidents well before the accidents actually take place, so steps can be taken to avert them.

The FRA, together with the Surface Transportation Board (STB), has developed a requirement for future railroad mergers. Companies will be required to develop a Safety Integration Plan (SIP) describing exactly how they intend to address safety problems connected with their merger. The FRA developed the concept and presented it to the STB at the height of the investigation into Union Pacific. After the STB accepted the recommendation, the two agencies set out to develop joint rules for safety integration planning as a precondition for all future mergers, acquisitions, and consolidations. CSX and Norfolk Southern Railroads were the first companies to be asked to write up an SIP before their joint acquisition of Conrail was approved. Careful advance planning, it is hoped, will prevent the kind of serious problems encountered at Union Pacific.

AGENCY RESOURCES

The FRA releases railroad statistics and reports regularly. The public affairs office can provide further information on material currently available and how to obtain it. The FRA public affairs office is located in the Department of Transportation Building at 400 7th Street SW, Washington, DC 20590. Its telephone number is (202) 632-3124. FRA dockets are maintained by the FRA chief counsel. Dockets can be viewed in Room 8201 of the DOT Building between 9:00 A.M. and 5:00 P.M. Monday through Friday. Further information can be obtained by calling (202) 632-3198. FRA rules and regulations can be found in the *Code of Federal Regulations*, Title 49, Parts 200–299.

Operation Lifesaver, sponsored by the FRA, is an educational program aimed at reducing deaths and injuries at railroad crossings. The program has produced a series of videos targeted at drivers, police and fire fighters, school bus drivers, and schoolchildren. Other materials are available for teachers. They can be obtained by calling 1-800-537-6224 or writing to Operation Lifesaver, Inc., 1420 King St. #401, Alexandria, VA 22314. Information is also available at the FRA Web site at http://www.fra.gov. The Education Page at the FRA's Web site includes a number of materials for elementary school teachers about trains, railroads, and safety, including lesson plans, puzzles, games, and instructions for building a miniature steam engine.

AGENCY PUBLICATIONS

The FRA publishes railroad accident statistics annually. They include the *Accident Incident Bulletin*, the *Highway-Rail Crossing Accident/Incident and Inventory Bulletin*, and the *Trespasser Bulletin*. The agency also has publications on its safety programs and its high-speed ground transportation research programs. These publications, as well as information about other publications, are available from the FRA public affairs office by writing to the Office of Public Affairs, Federal Railroad Administration, Department of Transportation, 400 7th St. SW, Washington, DC 20590. Some can be read on-line at the FRA Web site at http://www.fra.gov.

BIBLIOGRAPHY

Banks, Bill. "Ex-Engineer Right on Track with Safety Message." *Atlanta Journal and Constitution*, 14 August 1997.

Department of Transportation. "FRA Releases Safety Report on Union Pacific Railroad Audit." *M2 PressWIRE*, 26 February 1998.

Fumo, Paige. "Plan for St. Louis to Chicago High-Speed Rail Inches Along." *St. Louis Post-Dispatch*, 16 March 1998.

Larson, Kelli M. "Hazmat on the Rails: A Closer Look." *Environmental Solutions*, 1 October 1996.

Longman, Phillip J. "Blood on the Tracks." *U.S. News and World Report*, 27 October 1997.

"Union Pacific Heavily Criticized at Hearing Transportation: Head of Troubled Railroad Says He Hopes to Have Service Woes Resolved in a Month." *Los Angeles Times*, 28 October 1997.

"U.S. to Probe Railroad Over Fatal Crashes Safety." *Los Angeles Times*, 28 August 1997.

Wheeler, Larry. "Many U.S. Railroad Crossings Have Not Been Inspected for Years, Federal Data Show." Gannett News Service, 4 December 1997.

———. "Railroad Crossings." Gannett News Service, 16 December 1996.

Federal Reserve System (The Fed)

PARENT ORGANIZATION: Independent
ESTABLISHED: December 23, 1913
EMPLOYEES: 25,000

Contact Information:

ADDRESS: 20th St. and Constitution Ave.
Washington, DC 20551
PHONE: (202) 452-3000
FAX: (202) 452-3819
URL: http://www.bog.frb.fed.us
CHAIRMAN: Alan Greenspan
VICE CHAIRMAN: Alice Rivlin

WHAT IS ITS MISSION?

When it was first established by the Federal Reserve Act of 1913, the Federal Reserve's mission was defined rather narrowly: "to furnish an elastic currency, to afford means of rediscounting commercial paper, to establish a more effective supervision of banking in the United States, and other purposes." Commercial paper refers to short-term, unsecured promissory notes (a signed document containing a written promise to pay a stated sum to a specified person or organization at a specified date) issued by commercial firms, financial companies, or foreign governments. Since then, the Federal Reserve System has broadened its mission to include the formulation and administration of policy for the nation's credit and monetary affairs. The Fed supervisory and regulatory functions are intended to help maintain the banking industry in sound condition, able to respond to the country's international and domestic financial needs and goals.

HOW IS IT STRUCTURED?

The structure of the Fed is designed by Congress to give it a broad perspective on the economy and on economic activity in all parts of the country. It is composed of a central governmental agency—the Board of Governors—and twelve regional Federal Reserve Banks.

The Board of Governors, headquartered in Washington, DC, is composed of seven members appointed by the president with the advice and consent of the Senate. It has broad powers of supervision over the Fed, and determines general monetary, credit, and operating policies. It also formulates the rules and regulations necessary to carry out the purposes of the Federal Reserve Act under which the System was created.

The Federal Open Market Committee (FOMC), is a major component of the Fed. It oversees open-market operations, which is the main tool by which the Fed influences money-market conditions and the growth of money and credit. Open-market operations—the purchases and sales of government securities in the freely competitive market—of the Reserve Banks are conducted under regulations adopted by this committee.

The FOMC is composed of the seven members of the Board of Governors, along with five of the twelve Reserve Bank presidents. The president of New York's reserve bank is a permanent member, and the other presidents serve a one-year term on a rotating basis. All the presidents participate in discussions, but only the five FOMC presidents may vote on policy decisions. By law, the FOMC determines its own internal organization; by tradition, it elects the chairman of the Board of Governors as its chairman and the president of the Federal Reserve Bank of New York as its vice chairman. Formal meetings are held eight times a year in Washington, and informal consultations are held as needed.

The Board of Governors is guided in its decision-making by three advisory committees. The Federal Advisory Council confers with the Board of Governors on general business conditions, and is required to meet in Washington at least four times a year. The Consumer Advisory Council advises the Board on its responsibilities under such consumer protection laws as Truth in Lending, Home Mortgage Disclosure, and Equal Credit Opportunity. The third committee, the Thrift Institutions Advisory Council, meets with the Board to discuss developments relating to thrift institutions (savings banks, savings and loan associations, and credit unions), the housing industry, and mortgage finance.

The 12 Federal Reserve Banks are located in Atlanta, Boston, Chicago, Cleveland, Dallas, Kansas City, Minneapolis, New York, Philadelphia, Richmond (VA), San Francisco, and St. Louis. Branch banks are located in 26 other cities. The tools of the Fed's monetary policy are carried out by the 12 regional Reserve Banks. They issue currency, extend credit to depository institutions, and act as depositories and fiscal agents of the United States. In general, they exercise all banking functions specified in the Federal Reserve Act.

PRIMARY FUNCTIONS

The Fed's responsibilities fall into four main categories. By influencing money and credit conditions in the U.S. economy to encourage full employment and stable prices, it conducts the nation's monetary policy. It attempts to maintain the stability of the financial system and to restrain the extreme fluctuations that arise in financial markets. Examples of the Fed's activities in this regard are its adjustment of lending interest rates (interest rates charged by lending institutions for consumer loans such as mortgages or car loans) and the imposition of reserve requirements—the amount of money that must be kept on deposit at financial institutions.

In order to ensure the safety and soundness of the nation's banking and financial system, and to protect the credit rights of consumers, the Fed supervises and regulates banking institutions. It also provides financial services to the U.S. government, to the public, financial institutions, and foreign official institutions; for example, it plays a significant role in conducting the nation's payment system.

In order to understand the Fed's functions, it is important to understand the four basic tools at its disposal for regulating the money supply and the U.S. economy. The Fed engages in open-market operations. In order to supply bank reserves that will support the credit and money needed for long-term growth, and that will accommodate seasonal demands of customers and businesses, the System may buy or sell securities (stocks) on the open market.

The Fed changes reserve requirements, the amount of money banks are required to keep on reserve—that is, they are not allowed to lend or invest that money, but must keep it on hand as security. When reserve requirements are high, there is less money circulating in the economy, and the economy is slowed.

It sets the terms of credit for certain types of loans. By regulating the guidelines for who may and may not receive certain types of loans, the Fed guards against banks granting loans to those who are a bad risk for defaulting, or failing to repay a loan.

The Fed also raises or lowers the discount rate. The discount rate is the interest rate charged by banks that lend money to other banks. When the rate is raised by the Fed, the higher cost of doing business with other banks is passed on to bank customers who apply for loans—the interest rates charged for their loans are raised in turn. When interest rates are higher, people are less willing to take out a loan, and economic activity is slowed. This chain reaction is inevitable and is why one usually hears of the Fed "raising interest rates" rather than simply raising the discount rate.

BUDGET INFORMATION

Because the Federal Reserve is intended to operate independently, its budget authority is not granted through congressional appropriations; each level, from national to local, is responsible for the budgeting of its resources. The Board of Governors and the Federal Reserve Banks

BUDGET:

Federal Reserve System

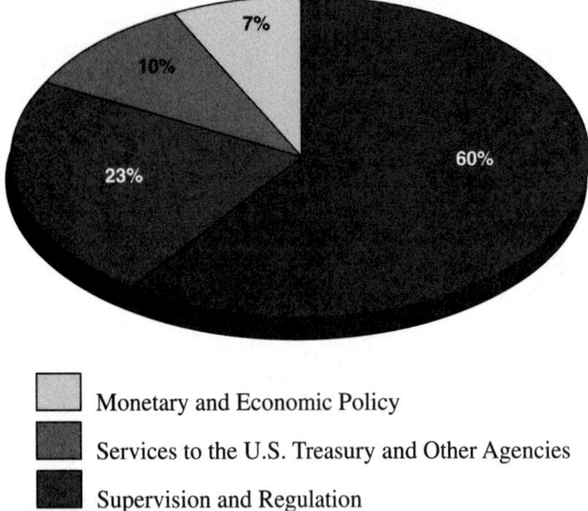

have separate budgets and budgeting processes, but each draws from the same funds. In 1998, the entire Federal Reserve System had a budget of $2.24 billion.

Approximately half of the Reserve's expenditures are offset by revenues it gets from performing paid services, the most significant of which are commercial checks ($605 million in 1997) and fund transfers ($97 million). The remainder of expenditures are covered by the earnings on the Reserve's portfolio of U.S. government securities, which in 1997 earned an estimated $20.7 billion. This substantial sum is more than enough to cover the Reserve's needs, and each year its excess earnings are transferred to the Treasury.

Out of the $2.24 billion budgeted by the Federal Reserve for 1998, 91 percent goes to Reserve Banks, and 9 percent goes to the Board of Governors. The system's expenditures are divided into four basic operational areas: monetary and economic policy (7 percent), services to the U.S. Treasury and other government agencies (10 percent), services to financial institutions and the public (60 percent), and supervision and regulation (23 percent).

HISTORY

Before the Fed was created, the United States suffered from periodic financial panics that contributed to many bank failures, business bankruptcies, and generalized economic downturns. A severe 1907 crisis, in which banks extended too much credit to consumers in order to keep up with a boom in spending, seriously depleted the supply of currency available to the public. Cash reserves were so low that banking officials were reluctant to pay out currency in any amount—without it, the banks would lose their security and collapse. Though many similar financial crises had occurred prior to this one, the 1907 panic led to the formation of the National Monetary Commission, which proposed the creation of an institution that would counter financial disruptions of these kinds. After a period of debate, Congress passed the Federal Reserve Act, which was signed into law by President Woodrow Wilson on December 23, 1913. The act established the Federal Reserve Board, whose purposes of oversight and regulation were not yet clearly defined.

It soon became clear that the act had broader implications for national economic and financial policy. The system that the act created had been intended to be little more than the coordinator of the Federal Reserve banks created by the act, and to play a passive role, merely controlling the "discount rate," or interest rate at which banks could lend each other money. The powers of the Federal Reserve Board to force changes in a particular bank's discount rate were not clear during the first 20 years of the system's operation. Another problem was that though the system was intended to operate independent of political concerns, its board included the secretary of the treasury, whose departmental interests tended to dominate the board's policies. From 1913 to 1933, the influence of the Federal Reserve Board was limited.

Reshaping the System

The economic collapse of the 1930s, which caused the Great Depression, exposed two weaknesses of the Federal Reserve Act. The monetary and banking theories were not sound, and the policies resulting from these theories were too simplistic and did not allow for centralized control over monetary policy. The depression forced dramatic changes in the Fed's operations. It brought about the Banking Act of 1935, which centralized power in the renamed Board of Governors of the Federal Reserve System. The new board was given power over open-market operations through the formation of the Federal Open Market Committee, and it was also given a stronger authority to control discount rates.

The first chairman of the new board, Mariner Eccles, served for more than 12 years, and was a powerful force in determining monetary policy. However, the board continued to have difficulties dealing with the dominance of the Treasury Department in monetary matters. The arrival of World War II (1939—1945) highlighted these differences. When the war was over, the Treasury pressed for low-interest rates to ease the servicing of wartime debts. The board, however, feared the inflation that these lower rates might bring about.

Finally, in 1951, the Treasury and the board signed an agreement, the Treasury-Federal Reserve Accord,

BIOGRAPHY:
Alan Greenspan

Chairman of the Federal Reserve Board (b. 1926) As chairman of the Federal Reserve Board Alan Greenspan commandeers U.S. monetary policy. In doing so he exercises a power that stretches beyond U.S. borders. When he speaks the world listens; stock markets and the value of the U.S. dollar overseas rise or fall, depending on the content of his message. As head of the Federal Reserve Board Greenspan oversees an institution that was created by Congress in 1913 to manage the nation's money supply and centralize and strengthen the regulation of banks. Greenspan chairs a presidentially-appointed board of governors that makes policy for Federal Reserve district banks and helps determine the lending practices of all deposit-taking institutions in the United States. Greenspan favors a *laissez faire* philosophy, which allows economic conditions to self regulate rather than having them respond to government intervention. However some economists argue that Greenspan has taken the hands-off principle too far, that he has not acted strongly enough when the economy has suffered dips. On the other hand, he has been praised for recognizing that many of the factors driving the U.S. economy have less to do with monetary policy and more to do with fiscal policy, which is largely the domain of the president and Congress. Greenspan has said that changes in tax policy and decisions regarding the U.S. deficit will affect the long-term health of the economy far more than any monetary policy ever could.

which set the board free to follow a monetary policy separate from the financing needs of the Treasury Department. The Treasury's desires regarding interest rates were no longer the driving force behind policy decisions. Historically, however, the board's independence has only gone so far; the monetary policies of the Board of Governors have typically proven to be integrated and compatible with the larger economic policies set by the president.

Later Trends

The objectives of the Board of Governors were shaped as the system developed, and a few appeared to take precedence over time: economic growth in line with the economy's potential to expand, a high level of employment, stable prices, and moderate long-term interest rates. Since the 1960s, especially, the board has tended to see its main task as stabilizing the dollar both at home and abroad. Typically this has been done through the regulation of interest rates, both in domestic and international lending, in a way that has kept the extension of credit from overextending the cash reserves available to secure such loans.

Though Congress has in recent decades tended to criticize the Fed for operating with too much independence, Congress' actions have tended to support more centralized control of the U.S. economy and money supply. The Financial Institutions Reform, Recovery, and Enforcement (FIRRE) Act of 1989, for example, actually strengthened the Fed's ability to effect enforcement of its regulations on thrift institutions. In 1991, Congress further expanded the Fed's supervision of the U.S. operations of foreign banks.

CURRENT POLITICAL ISSUES

The Fed's activities regarding interest rates are always hotly debated, because among the Fed's tools for controlling the economy, they are the most easily understood, and most directly felt, among consumers and business interests. In the mid-1990s, fluctuations in a booming stock market created concern at the Board of Governors, because many stocks were considered to be overpriced, and many stock purchases were being made on credit. To slow the economy, the Fed raised interest rates in May of 1997, and predictably, corporate interests around the country responded negatively. A less robust economy typically hurts corporations in the short run by undercutting profits, and many corporate representatives argued that the change in rates was unjustified, given the strength of the economy.

However, economic slowdowns can also have the effect of eventually bringing down long-term interest rates and keeping inflation in check. Defending the Board's decision, chairman Alan Greenspan said: "For the Federal Reserve to remain inactive against a possible buildup of insidious inflationary pressures would be to sanction a threat to the job security and standards of living of too many Americans . . . It is clear from our history that surges in growth financed by excessive credit creation threaten the underlying stability of our economy."

FAST FACTS

In 1996, Federal Reserve Banks distributed $406.2 billion in currency, and destroyed $148.4 billion in unfit (counterfeit) currency.

(Source: The Federal Reserve System. "Purposes and Functions," 1997.)

AGENCY RESOURCES

One of the most comprehensive information resources offered by the Fed is the National Information Center of Banking Information, which provides comprehensive information on banks and other institutions for which the Fed has a supervisory, regulatory, or research interest. The NIC includes the organizational structure of financial institutions, as well as financial information for some of those institutions. Historical information is available on the structure of all the institutions. Financial information is available for selected time periods. The National Information Center can be reached on the World Wide Web at http://www.ffiec.gov/nic/.

For further information about the organization, structure, history, or functions of the Federal Reserve System, contact the Office of Public Affairs, Board of Governors, Federal Reserve System, (202) 452-3204.

AGENCY PUBLICATIONS

The Fed's publications include *The Federal Reserve System—Purposes and Functions*, articles published in the monthly periodical *Federal Reserve Bulletin*, and books such as *The U.S. Economy in an Interdependent World*. A number of short pamphlets are also available, including "Consumer Handbook to Credit Protection Laws" and "Making Sense of Savings." Information about publications can be obtained from the Martin Building of the Board's headquarters, (202) 452-3244.

BIBLIOGRAPHY

Baer, Herbert, and Sue F. Gregorash, eds. *Toward Nationwide Banking: A Guide to the Issues*. Federal Reserve Bank of Chicago, 1986.

Broaddus, Alfred. *A Primer on the Fed*. Federal Reserve Bank of Richmond, 1988.

Currency and Coin Responsibilities of the Federal Reserve: A Historical Perspective. The Federal Reserve Bank of Cleveland, 1989.

Feinman, Joshua. "Reserve Requirements: History, Current Practice, and Potential Reform." *Federal Reserve Bulletin*, June 1993, pp. 569–89.

Foust, Dean. "Political Hardball Inside the Fed." *Business Week*, 30 September 1996, p. 38.

Goodfriend, Marvin. "Why We Need an Accord for Federal Reserve Credit Policy." *Journal of Money, Credit, and Banking*, August 1994, pp. 572–85.

Lewis, Michael. "Club Fed: Power over the Economy Resides in the Hands Not of the President but of Alan Greenspan." *New York Times Magazine*, 21 April 1996, p.22.

McTague, Jim. "Fears at the Fed: Its Payment System Meets the Internet." *Barron's*, 11 December 1995, p. 29.

Russell, Etta. *Basic Principles of Constitutional Money: A Textbook for High Schools & the General Public on the Federal Reserve Conspiracy*. New York: Gordon Press Publishers, 1980.

Spong, Kenneth. *Banking Regulation: Its Purposes, Implementation, and Effects*, 3rd ed. Federal Reserve Bank of Kansas City, 1990.

Federal Trade Commission (FTC)

WHAT IS ITS MISSION?

The primary mission of the Federal Trade Commission (FTC) is to preserve competition within the U.S. economy, and to prevent the free enterprise system from being burdened by monopoly or trade restraints. The FTC also seeks to keep business from being corrupted by deceptive or unfair trade practices. The commission's objective has two main elements: the protection of consumers from unfair trade or promotion activities and the encouragement of competitive forces in the economy.

HOW IS IT STRUCTURED?

The FTC is an independent administrative agency that reports its actions to Congress. The commission itself is composed of five members, each appointed by the president with the advice and consent of the Senate, who serve seven-year terms. To ensure the commission's independence, no more than three of its members may be members of the same political party. One appointed commissioner is designated chairman by the president and is responsible for the FTC's administrative management.

The commission's chief operating officer and manager is the executive director, whose office is responsible for such administrative matters as budget, personnel, and information management. The Office of the Executive Director is also charged with overall FTC program and policy execution. The commission's regional offices operate under the general management of this office.

Another important officer at the FTC is the general counsel, the commission's primary legal officer and

PARENT ORGANIZATION: Independent
ESTABLISHED: September, 1914
EMPLOYEES: 710

Contact Information:

ADDRESS: 6th St. and Pennsylvania Ave. NW
Washington, DC 20580
PHONE: (202) 326-2222
TDD (HEARING IMPAIRED): (202) 326-2502
FAX: (202) 326-2496
E-MAIL: crc@ftc.gov
URL: http://www.ftc.gov
CHAIRMAN: Robert Pitofsky
COMMISSIONER: Sheila F. Anthony
COMMISSIONER: Mozelle W. Thompson
COMMISSIONER: Orson Swindel

FAST FACTS

The FTC has the authority to issue and enforce distinct trade regulation rules. For example, the "Cooling-Off Rule" states that consumers have the right to cancel purchases of $25 or more that are made from door-to-door sales, or from any place other than the seller's usual place of business, within three days.

(Source: *The United States Government Manual, 1997/98.*)

adviser. The Office of the General Counsel represents the FTC in court and provides legal counsel to the commission, its operating bureaus, and other offices.

There are three operating bureaus within the FTC: the Bureau of Competition, the Bureau of Consumer Protection, and the Bureau of Economics. The Bureau of Competition is the FTC's antitrust arm, whose mission is to prevent business practices that restrain competition. The Bureau of Economics provides economic analysis and support to the commission's casework and rulemaking in order to ensure that the commission considers the economic impact of its actions. It also analyzes the impact of government regulation on competition and consumers.

The Bureau of Consumer Protection's mission is to protect consumers from unfair, deceptive, or fraudulent market practices. The bureau enforces a variety of consumer protection laws enacted by Congress as well as commission-formulated trade regulation rules. It contributes to the commission's ongoing efforts to inform Congress of the impact of proposed actions on consumers. One of the most important offices of the agency, the Office of Consumer and Business Education, is housed in this bureau.

The FTC's ten regional offices are in Atlanta, Boston, Chicago, Cleveland, Dallas, Denver, Los Angeles, New York, San Francisco, and Seattle. Their program activities, coordinated through the Bureaus of Competition and Consumer Protection, include conducting investigations and litigation; providing advice to state and local officials on the implications of approved FTC actions; recommending cases; and coordinating activities with state, local, and regional authorities. The frequent consumer conferences and workshops staged by the FTC are sponsored through these regional offices.

PRIMARY FUNCTIONS

The commission's efforts to promote competition include preventing general trade restraints such as price-fixing agreements; boycotts; illegal combinations of competitors (collusion); the payment or receipt of illegal brokerages; and discrimination among competing customers in the furnishing or providing of services or facilities used to promote the resale of a product. It also attempts to block corporate mergers, acquisitions, or joint ventures when such practices or arrangements may substantially reduce competition or create a monopoly.

The second part of the FTC's mission, consumer protection, involves the prevention of false or deceptive advertisements of consumer products and services in general, and foods, drugs, cosmetics, and therapeutic devices in particular. The commission works to ensure truthful labeling of textiles, wool, and fur products; regulates the packaging and labeling of consumer commodities covered by the Fair Packaging and Labeling Act; supervises the registration and operation of associations of U.S. exporters engaged in export trade; fights against telemarketing scams; and works to achieve accurate credit cost disclosure by consumer creditors. In addition, the FTC protects consumers against the circulation of inaccurate or outdated credit reports, and offers other protections mandated by the Fair Credit Reporting Act.

The FTC's purpose is not to punish but to prevent practices outlawed by federal trade regulation. Its primary means of exercising this authority is the "cease and desist" order that warns a business to stop such practices. In general, compliance is achieved through voluntary cooperation derived from FTC staff advice, advisory opinions issued by the commission, or guides and policy statements published and released by the FTC.

An order to cease and desist, along with other possible corrective actions such as restitution or divestiture, becomes final 60 days after the date it is served upon a respondent. During that period, the respondent may petition an appropriate U.S. court of appeals to contend the order. After a cease-and-desist order becomes effective, the respondent is sued by the U.S. government in a federal district court for recovery of the civil penalty, which can be no more than $10,000 for each violation. When the violation continues, each day of its continuance is considered a separate violation.

PROGRAMS

Many of the FTC's programs are preventive in nature and are carried out through the Bureau of Consumer Protection. For example, the Consumer Privacy Initiative is an ongoing effort to bring consumers and businesses together to address privacy issues posed by the emerging on-line marketplace. Another FTC initiative is the Joint Venture Project, which teams the FTC with the Department of Justice to determine whether antitrust guidance (guidelines which prevent unfair business practices) to the business community can be improved through clarifying and updating antitrust polices regarding joint ventures and other forms of competitor collaborations.

The FTC sometimes finds it necessary to investigate deceptive or fraudulent marketing practices. When it does so, it coordinates a joint federal/state antifraud law enforcement effort, or "sweep." Such programs have included Operation Senior Sentinel, a 1996 program targeting telemarketing practices designed to defraud senior citizens of their savings, and Project $cholar$cam, a crackdown on organizations that fraudulently offered scholarship information in exchange for fees. Another enforcement initiative is Operation Mousetrap, which targets deceptive invention promotion companies.

BUDGET INFORMATION

The FTC's budget authority comes from a combination of congressional appropriations and fees collected for premerger notification filings under the Hart-Scott-Rodino Antitrust Improvements Act of 1976. In 1998 the commission's budget was about $107 million, which was allocated to the commission's two mission areas, consumer protection (52 percent) and maintaining competition (48 percent). Congress appropriates $28 million of the total budget from tax revenues, all of which goes toward consumer protection. The remaining $79 million of the budget is financed through premerger notification fees.

HISTORY

The turn from the nineteenth to the twentieth century was marked by the influence of "robber barons" and other big business trusts on U.S. markets. Large companies such as the steel trust, railroad trust, and oil trusts dominated the U.S. economy. The first federal antitrust law, the Sherman Antitrust Act, was passed in 1890, but in the early twentieth century there was serious debate about whether the law was adequate to protect the public from inflated monopoly prices and other economic harm. At about the same time, a movement began to protect customers from unfair business practices such as fraudulent or deceptive representations. The overriding concern was that the free enterprise system on which the U.S. economy had been based was not working.

The result of these concerns, the Federal Trade Commission Act of 1914, granted the FTC unprecedented authority to investigate, publicize, and prohibit all unfair methods of business competition. From the start, the public was distinctly divided on the potential benefits of the law, and as a result the history of the FTC has been a history of explosive political divisions. In its first decade, the commission made little progress in stopping unfair competition; it was hampered by the courts, who denied the FTC the right to specifically define "unfair" competition, and by businesses who refused to submit their records to the FTC. By 1925 the FTC had taken a less regulatory, more cooperative attitude toward business—which some charged was in direct opposition to its mandate.

In 1935, President Franklin Roosevelt revitalized the agency with renewed antitrust activity and the beginnings of a solid consumer protection program. For the next 15 years, a series of laws expanded and strengthened the commission's powers, granting it enforcement authority over price concessions, deceptive advertising, and certain types of anticompetitive mergers.

New Directions and "Consumerism"

After World War II, the FTC's activities began a trend toward emphasizing consumer protection and away from a prosecutorial approach to antitrust. The FTC chairmen during the Eisenhower, Kennedy, and Johnson administrations attempted to pursue a more moderate course, combining industry guidance with voluntary procedures and reserving litigation for extreme cases. These policies appeared to conflict, however, with the public's attitude.

Prior to his assassination, President Kennedy's words and actions helped create a wave of social criticism against American consuming habits and the nation's preoccupation with television, cigarettes, automobiles, and other products. Many blamed this social crisis on manipulation by corporations. Critics of the FTC lodged a still-familiar complaint: the FTC tended to concentrate its efforts on trivial matters, failed to set priorities, and was run by professional incompetents who could not agree on the commission's mandate. In 1969 protesters led by consumer advocate Ralph Nader demanded the resignation of Chairman Paul Rand Dixon and a complete overhaul of the commission's policies, practices, and staff. Further criticisms led to President Richard Nixon's program of "consumerism in America" and his appointment of Chairman Caspar Weinberger, who centralized control of caseload decisions in the chairman and top-level personnel and strengthened the authority of the field offices.

Conservative Attacks

When the American economy faltered in the late 1970s, the FTC experienced the strongest attack ever on its authority. Conservative critics charged that the commission's consumerism campaign had gone too far and that its rulings carried the authority of congressional legislation. Business interests complained that the FTC's rulings added unnecessarily to manufacturers' and consumers' costs. A movement to slash the FTC budget and stop the commission's investigations of the petroleum and car manufacturing industries was set in motion. Throughout the 1980s and early 1990s, under the administrations of Presidents Ronald Reagan and George Bush, a consumer-oriented FTC, Congress, and conservative administrations remained at odds. Not until the mid-1990s, when new technologies threatened to introduce new and unanticipated consumer scams to the U.S. marketplace, did many people began to view the FTC as a useful tool for controlling certain business activities.

CURRENT POLITICAL ISSUES

One of the FTC's most urgent challenges today is the rapid expansion of the Internet as a global marketplace. Still relatively unregulated, commerce on the Internet in general, and on the World Wide Web in particular, attracts ethical as well as unethical business. One-third of the estimated 15 million Web sites on-line are corporate home pages. The legislative process has simply not been able to keep up with the progress of technology.

As on-line technology matures and becomes more interactive, marketers will be able to track a person's on-line activities, generate consumer profiles, and make personalized appeals to individual consumers, something no other advertising medium has ever been able to do. The use of on-line marketing tools, and their increasing sophistication, has raised two particular concerns regarding children. First, it is generally recognized that children know more about the Web than most parents, which makes it difficult for parents to observe or control their children's activities on-line. Furthermore, the Center for Media Education (CME), an organization founded in 1991 to improve the quality of electronic media, estimates that in 1996 children under 12 spent $14 billion, teenagers another $57 billion, and together these groups influenced $160 billion of their parents' annual spending. This expenditure represents a market segment that is not likely to be taken lightly by marketers, and it makes many critics uneasy that much of this marketing activity takes place without parental supervision. Even more than television, critics argue, computer technology undermines the power of the family and the authority of parents to make decisions.

Second, unlike adults, young children are not able to assess inquiries that appear on-line. For the promise of a prize or free membership in what is presented as an exclusive club, children are often asked on-line to answer invasive market-research questions—not only about their preferences and the buying habits of their parents, but in some cases about those of their friends. Parents have not been aware of the extent to which cleverly disguised marketing devices are imposed upon their children, and critics argue that the collection of such personal data is exploiting children's natural curiosities.

Case Study: KidsCom

In May of 1996 the CME filed a formal complaint with the FTC urging the commission to investigate a Web site called "KidsCom" that was allegedly deceiving children by posing as an educational and entertainment Web site while actually collecting data, conducting market research, and advertising particular products. CME requested that a cease-and-desist order be imposed immediately on SpectraCom, the Milwaukee marketing company that maintained the site.

At the site, children were asked about TV viewing habits, product preferences, hobbies, ambitions, and the interests of their families. The complaint described a "Graffiti Wall" where children were lured with the promise of interacting with other children from all over the world, but where they were merely asked further personal questions about preferences and interests. In another area, "New Stuff for Kids," the company allegedly implied that it had reviewed games and had chosen the best ones. In fact, SpectraCom required a minimum product donation of $1,000 from each game manufacturer in exchange for describing and listing its products on the site. This exchange was not described on-screen, and the CME charged that KidsCom promoted only the products of its corporate sponsors.

A little more than a year after the KidsCom complaint was lodged, the CME and the Consumer Federation of America (CFA) joined the Federal Trade Commission in staging the Public Workshop on Consumer Information Privacy, which urged the commission to take steps to protect children's privacy on-line. The organizations argued that it was necessary for the FTC to formulate guidelines for obtaining parental consent when personally identifiable information is collected from children and requiring full disclosure from companies about their information collecting activities.

Although the FTC had spent years defining traditional approaches to consumer deception and fraud, on-line privacy for children was an issue over which it did not yet have formal authority. The agency needed time to investigate and ensure its own authority to regulate in such circumstances. In July of 1998 the FTC presented its findings in *Privacy On-Line: A Report to Congress.* Examining the issue of on-line privacy in general, and the solicitation of information from children in particular, the FTC concluded that it did not have the authority to regulate the Internet to ensure privacy. The FTC stated that industry self-regulation will be key to the protection of on-line consumers' privacy. KidsCom, for example, avoided action by the FTC by voluntarily altering its Web site to eliminate its deceptive product endorsements, and by requesting permission from a child's parents before releasing any information gathered on-line to a third party. Despite successes such as this, however, the FTC concluded its report by saying that new laws were needed, empowering the FTC to regulate on-line information gathering.

SUCCESSES AND FAILURES

In strictly economic terms, what is good for business often costs more for consumers, and vice versa. The FTC's actions therefore usually provoke a complaint from at least one party, depending on the situation. The commission's most widely acknowledged successes, then, are actions whose results cannot be measured in mere dollar value. For example, in 1997 the FTC worked to ensure that no single biotechnology company could monopolize research and development and innovation in gene therapy, a technology with the potential to produce new lifesaving therapies for diseases such as cancer and cystic fibrosis. The move to distribute this extraordinary power among competitors ensured wider access to the knowledge necessary to develop the technology and received praise from both the general public and the business community.

FUTURE DIRECTIONS

The 1990s have been marked by remarkable and rapid changes in many sectors of the economy, and as a result the FTC faces two trends that present significant challenges. While globalization and information technologies have created potentially great benefits for consumers, they have also raised new consumer protection concerns such as on-line fraud, the loss of privacy, international telemarketing scams, and the relatively new crime wave of "identity theft," in which thieves armed with a victim's personal information can charge large quantities of merchandise and services in the victim's name. In the FTC's strategic plan for the years 1997-2005, the commission acknowledges the need to find cost-effective ways of dealing with these new problems before they become commonplace. It also points out, however, that continued rapid increases in cross-border and Internet fraud could reduce the commission's ability to meet its consumer protection goals.

The FTC's mission to maintain competition is also complicated by the acceleration of technological development—which causes unpredictable shifts in the type of business conduct that the commission must evaluate—together with an "ongoing merger wave of historic proportions." Business mergers can make businesses more efficient, and most do not harm competition. But anticompetitive mergers can raise consumer costs by millions of dollars a year, and as more mergers are filed, more demand is placed on the resources of the FTC to evaluate their market impact. So far the commission has been successful in keeping up with the merger trend, but it anticipates further strain on its capacities and is in the process of formulating its responses to future markets.

AGENCY RESOURCES

The FTC's primary information resource for reports, speeches, rules, consumer and business brochures, or other general information is the Public Reference Branch, Room 130, FTC, Washington, DC 20580; phone (202) 326-2000. For information about the FTC's educational print and broadcast projects, contact the Office of Consumer and Business Education, Room 403; (202) 326-3650. The FTC library has 120,000 volumes on legal, economic, and business subjects, as well as 1,000 periodicals and an interlibrary loan service. The library is in Room 630; phone (202) 326-2395.

The Office of Consumer and Business Education also maintains two on-line information resources. ConsumerLine offers the full text of about 150 consumer protection publications, a collection of ongoing consumer information initiatives, and Consumer Alert!, a service to warn consumers of current issues in the markets. BusinessLine offers the full text of several business advisements and other business assistance publications as well as a number of business education campaigns. Both services are available at the FTC's site on the World Wide Web at http://www.ftc.gov.

AGENCY PUBLICATIONS

The FTC publishes a number of general information brochures, including "How to Resolve Consumer Disputes" and "66 Ways to Save Money"; a line of periodic staff reports, including "Fighting Consumer Fraud: The Challenge" and the "Campaign and Price Check: A Report on the Accuracy of Checkout Scanners"; and publications intended for educating businesses, including "A Business Guide to the FTC Mail," "Telephone Order Merchandise Rule," and "Complying with the Telemarketing Sales Rule." Many of these publications are available for downloading from ConsumerLine or BusinessLine.

BIBLIOGRAPHY

Donlan, Thomas G. "Market Discipline or Tyranny? Competition Need Not be Active to be Effective." *Barron's*, 28 April 1997, p. 55.

Eisner, Marc Allen. *Antitrust and the Triumph of Economics: Institutions, Expertise, and Policy Change*. Chapel Hill, N.C.: University of North Carolina, 1991.

Freundlich, Naomi. "A Booster Shot for Gene Therapy." *Business Week*, 20 January 1997, pp. 92-93.

"Globalization Leads FTC to Review Antitrust Rules." *Wall Street Journal*, 3 June 1996, p. A3.

Mackay, Robert J., James C. Miller III, and Bruce Yandle. *Public Choice and Regulation : A View from Inside the Federal Trade Commission.* Stanford, Calif.: Hoover Institution Press, 1987.

Murphy, Patrick E. and William L. Wilkie, eds. *Marketing and Advertising Regulation: the Federal Trade Commission in the 1990s.* South Bend, Ind.: University of Notre Dame, 1990.

"New Antitrust Plans by U.S." *New York Times*, 20 October 1994, p. D2.

"Price Fixing Plays a More Visible Hand." *Sales and Marketing Management*, December 1995, p. 11.

Roberts, Johnnie. "Antitrust: The Friendly Giant." *Newsweek*, 19 February 1996, p. 49

Teinowitz, Ira. "FTC Chairman Seeking Voluntary Web Rules." *Advertising Age*, 10 June 1996, p. 42.

Yang, Catherine. "When Protectionism Wears Camouflage." *Business Week*, 2 June 1997, p. 50.

Federal Transit Administration (FTA)

PARENT ORGANIZATION: Department of Transportation
ESTABLISHED: July 1, 1968
EMPLOYEES: 496

Contact Information:

ADDRESS: 400 7th St. SW
Washington, DC 20590
PHONE: (202) 366-4043
FAX: (202) 366-3472
URL: http://www.fta.dot.gov
ADMINISTRATOR: Gordon J. Linton

WHAT IS ITS MISSION?

The mission of the Federal Transit Administration (FTA) is "to ensure personal mobility and America's economic and community vitality by supporting high quality public transportation through leadership, technical assistance and financial resources." It promotes economically viable, environmentally sound mass transit as a means of decreasing congestion on highways and in urban areas and provides transportation for those unable to drive automobiles. The agency carries out this mission primarily through its grant and planning programs for states, cities, and rural areas.

HOW IS IT STRUCTURED?

The Federal Transit Administration is an agency in the Department of Transportation (DOT). It is headed by an administrator appointed by the president and confirmed by the Senate. The administrator oversees all FTA activities and is responsible for maintaining liaisons between the agency and Congress and other agencies within the DOT and the federal government. The FTA administrator answers to the transportation secretary.

Under the Office of the Administrator is a deputy administrator and nine operational offices. The most important operational office is the Office of Program Management, which is responsible for administering the FTA's grants and financial assistance programs. It also assists the FTA's field offices as well as the transit industry and the states in grant program administration. The Office of Planning manages financial, organizational, and

Public mass transportation, such as this light rail train in Denver, Colorado, is the focus of the FTA. (AP/Wide World Photos)

technical aspects of FTA programs. It also provides expert assistance on transportation planning, environmental impact, and public involvement in transportation issues. The Office of Research, Demonstration, and Innovation provides technical assistance and training to states, communities, and private industry. Other operational offices are the Executive Secretariat, the Office of Administration, the Office of Budget and Policy, the Office of Civil Rights, the Office of Public Affairs, and the Chief Counsel. FTA programs are implemented on a regional and local level through 10 regional offices. They are the FTA's main point of contact with state, local, and transit industry officials.

PRIMARY FUNCTIONS

The FTA's primary purpose is to improve mass transit throughout the United States. The agency manages all federal mass transit programs. FTA activities include grant assistance to state and local governments as well as private transit companies. The agency also offers assistance with training, planning, research and development, and solving technical problems connected with the operation of mass transportation systems.

FTA grant programs finance a broad range of mass transit activities. They include funding for new transit systems, the purchase of vehicles or equipment, the maintenance or expansion of existing transit systems, funding for the development of transit systems for the elderly and handicapped, and funding to state and local government and to the transit industry for planning, research, and development. FTA grants are the primary source of financial assistance for localities planning and developing mass transit.

The FTA is also an important source of technical expertise. The agency assists communities in planning mass transit projects, and research carried out or funded by FTA provides an important base of knowledge for future transit projects. Research areas include traffic management, crime as it relates to public transportation, mass transit safety, and transportation technology.

PROGRAMS

The two most important grant programs administered by the FTA are the Major Capital Investments Program and the Grants in the Urbanized Area Formula Program. Grants in the latter program are awarded to public agencies in urban areas that want to improve or replace existing mass transit facilities. Monies are allotted from a formula based on population and population density. Under the terms of the program, the federal government pays 80 percent of the net project cost.

The Major Capital Investments Program funds the construction of new mass transit rail systems as well as extensions of existing rail systems. The federal government pays 80 percent of total costs in this program; state and local governments must fund the remainder. Cities and regions compete for funding according to criteria developed by the FTA. Both the Major Capital Investments Program and the Urbanized Area Formula Program are funded by the Mass Transit Account of the Highway Trust Fund.

The FTA administers programs to ensure that mass transportation is available for those who rely on it most. The Elderly and Persons with Disabilities Program provides money to states, localities, and private organizations for specialized transportation services for elderly and disabled individuals. Funded projects include buses with lifts and folding seats for wheelchair users and elevators or special ramps in subways or streetcar systems. Transit companies that provide transportation for the elderly and disabled are also eligible for grants. Monies are distributed according to the number of elderly and disabled people in an area. In general, the federal government pays 80 percent of the costs of special vehicles.

The Access to Jobs Program provides funding to state and local governments, as well as to private nonprofit organizations. Grant money can be used to plan, develop, and operate special transportation systems that ensure access to jobs and job training for welfare recipients. Grant criteria include the severity of the transportation problem for welfare recipients in an area, the quality of the area's performance in other welfare reform programs, and the level of the area's collaboration with agencies providing employment opportunities for individuals on welfare. The FTA provides 50 percent of a project's cost.

The FTA's Transit Benefit Program was designed to encourage employees to commute to work by means other than motor vehicles with a single occupant. The program promotes Section 132 of the Internal Revenue Code, which allows employers to write off up to $65 per month per employee when money is provided for travel to work by mass transit or vanpool. Under the IRS code, employees need not report the subsidy on their returns.

The FTA provides the funding for the National Transit Institute at Rutgers University. Based on the National Highway Institute of the Federal Highway Administration (FHWA), the institute offers training programs in the management of transit systems, transportation planning, environmental factors, land acquisition, mass transit engineering, and the efficient operation of transit systems.

FAST FACTS

Traffic congestion in major metropolitan areas costs more than $40 billion annually in wasted time and fuel. Without public transit the nationwide costs in these metropolitan areas would be $15 billion higher because of increased gridlock on major roadways.

(Source: Federal Transit Administration, 1998.)

BUDGET INFORMATION

The total budget appropriated by Congress and enacted for the FTA in 1998 was $4.8 billion. This amount represented just over 10 percent of the Department of Transportation's budget for that year. The FTA's appropriation is the third highest in DOT, after the Federal Highway Administration and the Federal Aviation Administration. More than 92 percent of the FTA budget was used for its transit grant programs.

The agency's requested budget of $4.7 billion for 1999 was slightly less than the previous year; grants account for 96 percent of those monies. Much of the FTA's budget is funded by the Mass Transit Account of the Highway Trust Fund, a fund comprised of money collected through gasoline taxes. The Clinton administration has proposed that in 1999 the FTA be funded exclusively by the Mass Transit Account of the Highway Trust Fund.

HISTORY

The federal government's first involvement in transit funding was the Housing Act of 1961. The act provided for loans to state and local governments that could be used to purchase transportation equipment, such as buses, trains, and streetcars. It also instituted a grant program for transportation planning and research. A new agency, the Federal Office of Transportation, was established under the Housing and Home Finance Agency (HHFA) at the same time. Its function was to determine a role in transportation for federal government.

In April 1962 President John F. Kennedy proposed a program of federal capital grants for mass transit. The Urban Mass Transportation Act of 1964, now known as the Federal Transit Act, was the legislation enacted by Congress. The act established programs for matching grants, technical assistance, and research, to be funded by the federal government. In 1965 when HHFA was moved into the newly formed Department of Housing and Urban Development (HUD), the Office of Transportation was renamed the Urban Transportation Administration (UTA). Three years later on July 1, 1968, it became the Urban Mass Transportation Administration, the forerunner to the Federal Transit Administration, and was transferred to the Department of Transportation.

The Surface Transportation Assistance Act, signed into law by President Ronald Reagan in 1982, expanded the sources of funding for transit projects. The law stipulated that a penny per gallon gasoline tax be earmarked for mass transportation projects. The same law established the Mass Transit Account, a special fund in the Highway Trust Fund. Nearly all FTA projects and operating costs are today funded from this account, and the Clinton administration has proposed that the agency's entire budget be drawn from it beginning in 1999.

A significant step was taken in 1991 when President George Bush signed the Intermodal Surface Transportation Efficiency Act (ISTEA) into law. The act was a first step toward the development of the so-called National Intermodal Transportation System, in which all modes of transportation, roads, rail, water and air, would be integrated in an economically efficient and environmentally sound system. The ISTEA included provisions for highway construction, highway safety, and mass transportation. The law increased to 58 percent the funds available to the FTA from the Mass Transit Account.

The ISTEA tightened restrictions on planning transportation projects. The only projects that could be funded under the new law were those that could demonstrate that sufficient revenues were currently available or would be available in the foreseeable future. The law also required that the public be actively and formally involved in the planning of all funded transit projects. To ensure that mass transit planning conforms to ISTEA standards, the Federal Highway Administration (FHWA) and the FTA are required to jointly evaluate planning in all communities with populations of more than 200,000. Finally, the ISTEA changed the name of the agency from Urban Mass Transportation Administration to the Federal Transit Administration.

In 1992 the General Accounting Office (GAO) completed a study of the FTA's grant management oversight. Both the GAO and the Inspector General of the DOT found a number of weaknesses in the FTA oversight of grant recipients. The FTA was strict in awarding grants but paid only superficial attention to how grants were used afterward. The GAO found that the FTA rarely used the enforcement mechanisms at its disposal to compel grant recipients to make corrections. The potential misuse of federal funds that the study implied led the GAO to classify the FTA as a high-risk federal program area. In 1995, following recommendations by GAO, the FTA centralized its oversight functions in a single new department, the Office of Oversight, and began taking a more proactive role in monitoring how federal transit funds were being used. Despite some continued shortcomings, the GAO removed the high-risk designation in 1995, and in a follow-up report issued in 1998 praised the progress the FTA had made in its grants oversight.

CURRENT POLITICAL ISSUES

Building a public transportation system is one of the most expensive propositions a local government can undertake. In addition to enormous construction costs, equipment must be purchased, land acquired, environmental impact studied, parking and energy infrastructure planned, and approval of voters won. Such projects often require creative planning, organization, and cooperation on the part of federal, state, regional, and local offices. But when it collides with traditional procedures, innovation can bring its own problems. A case in point is the plan to extend the transit system in the San Francisco Bay area to its airport.

Case Study: The San Francisco-BART Extension

The Bay Area Rapid Transit System (BART) is a typical metropolitan transit system serving communities throughout the San Francisco Bay area. Even as the first lines of the BART system were being completed in the early 1970s, public authorities considered an extension to San Francisco airport. The need for an expansion of BART became increasingly obvious in the 1990s. The airport was the fifth busiest in the nation and was implementing a $2.3 billion expansion that was expected to lead to a jump of 21 million in annual passengers by 2006. Consequently motor traffic to the airport on area expressways, which already often exceeded capacity, was expected to rise by 52 percent by 2010, bringing with it significantly higher levels of air pollution. Because of its potential to reduce traffic congestion and air pollution, Governor Peter Wilson named the BART project one of California's top three transportation priorities.

BART applied for FTA funding in the early 1990s and was awarded $568.5 million for two projects, one of which was the airport extension. As in other mass transit projects, the FTA's role was to provide federal money and monitor the project's real progress against the construction schedule presented by the local authority in its first grant application. The traditional role of the local public authority, in this case BART, was to develop the transit plan from the ground up and manage all work from start to finish. BART, however, with the FTA's blessing, took a different approach. It adopted a procedure called "design-build contracting." Under this procedure contractors do more than simply build under the supervision of an area's public authorities. Once they win the bid, they are given full responsibility for their portion of a project and manage every aspect from start to finish. Public agencies provide oversight.

This had a significant effect. Mass transit projects normally cost hundreds of millions of dollars to build. The federal government pays the lion's share, but state and local governments are responsible for contributing as well. In the case of BART, the state of California, local communities, and the San Francisco airport had to come up with about $417 million dollars for the project. Like most communities, San Francisco found it very difficult to reach a consensus on the need to spend so much money for public transportation. But BART's design-build contracting approach resulted in savings estimated at between 30 and 50 percent. BART also estimated that the approach would lead to significant time savings as well. These savings made it much easier to win voter approval for the project. It also took the day-to-day management of the project out of the hands of local authorities and put it in the hands of private business at a time when government was being urged to cut its responsibilities in the private sector. Approving the BART plan in June 1997, the FTA called it one of the most innovative it had seen.

But the new approach brought its own set of problems as well. After the plan was approved, for example, discrepancies arose between BART's original financing plan and the agreement actually implemented by BART and the FTA. BART's first plan was based on the accelerated construction schedule that the design-build contracting made possible. It assumed that federal payments would be made over a six-year period. The plan agreed to by the FTA, which was used to more traditional time frames for mass transit projects, spread federal payments out over an eight-year period. The result is that the project will spend money faster than it gets it from the federal government. By 1999, two years before the line is scheduled to be completed, the project is expected to encounter severe funding shortages.

The GAO has reported that total shortfalls could be as high as $290 million; somehow BART has to come up with 10 percent of those costs. BART was hit with another bill when it awarded the first contracts in 1997. Even the lowest bids were so much higher than BART's projections that they overran all the allotted contingencies—money specifically set aside to cover higher-than-projected costs. BART officials claimed to be delighted that the bids were not even higher. Although these new expenses seemed to cast doubt on BART's "innovative" project management, the FTA did not intervene. The agency let BART officials work on making up the deficits on their own, a decision the GAO believed at first might be wrong because it could cause the entire project to grind to a halt.

However, less than a month after the contracts were awarded at the higher rates, the financial community made a great show of confidence in BART. A $350 million bond issue floated by the transit agency was given a AA rating by all three major investment institutions—Standard & Poors, Moody's, and Fitch IBCA. The bonds sold out within two hours of being put on the market. The FTA's wait-and-see stance had been validated at the last moment.

Once the bonds had been issued, construction on the airport extension picked up and the project seemed to take on new life. Ground was broken in November 1997, and the power lines were raised for the track into the airport in early 1998. BART predicts the entire project will be completed on schedule in late 2001. Only time will tell if the extension can be finished on time. The FTA's experience with BART has demonstrated that there is a place for change and innovation in mass transit. It need not lead to squandered federal funding or interminable delays. It has also shown that public works can be carried out efficiently by a relatively independent private sector with only a moderate level of FTA and public oversight.

SUCCESSES AND FAILURES

The FTA's Persons with Disabilities Program has contributed significantly to the ability of the disabled to use public transportation in the United States. As a result of the program, more than two-thirds of American buses used for mass transit are fully accessible to the handicapped. Accessibility to light rail systems, such as streetcars and subways, has also been improved through the financing of special ramps and elevators.

FUTURE DIRECTIONS

FTA research programs are dedicated to developing transportation that is both safe and environmentally friendly. Examples include hybrid electric buses, commuter rail control systems that increase the safety of passengers and workers, and new propulsion systems powered by fuel cells and batteries. Among the institutions whose work in these directions the FTA supports are the Transit Cooperative Research Program, the National Transit Institute, and University Transportation Centers.

The FTA sees as part of its future mission not only improving transit infrastructure and transportation systems but also fostering a positive image for public transit in America. As such it plans partnership with other organizations to identify customer needs in areas such as safety and security and to enhance the public's awareness and perception of transit. Other proposed programs include basic information, a national media campaign, town hall meetings, promotional programs, and participation in legislative and other policy forums.

AGENCY RESOURCES

Information about FTA programs can be obtained by contacting the agency's public affairs office at 400 7th St. SW, Washington, DC 20590. The office can be reached by phone at (202) 366-4043. Information is also available on-line at the FTA Web site, http://www.fta.dot.gov.

Information regarding public transportation for persons with disabilities is available from the FTA Office of Civil Rights' toll-free Americans with Disabilities Act Assistance Line at 1-888-446-4511 or (202) 366-0153. The TDD number is 1-800-877-8339.

Questions about the FTA's Transit Benefit Program can be obtained from the Office of Policy Development, TBP-10 Federal Transit Administration, 400 7th St. SW, Rm. 9310, Washington, DC 20590; phone (202) 366-4060; or fax (202) 366-7116.

AGENCY PUBLICATIONS

FTA publications are distributed by the Office of Training, Research, and Rural Transportation. Information regarding publications can be obtained by writing the office at 400 7th St. SW, Rm. 6107, Washington DC 20590, or by calling (202) 366-4995.

BIBLIOGRAPHY

"BART Board OKs Biggest SFO Contracts." *Business Wire*, 11 February 1998.

"BART Bonds a Best Seller." *Business Wire* , 11 March 1998.

"BART Breaks Ground for SFO Extension." *Business Wire*, 2 November 1997.

Bernick, Michael. *Transit Villages in the 21st Century*. New York: McGraw-Hill, 1997.

Federal Transit Administration. *This Is FTA*. Washington, D.C., 1993.

General Accounting Office. *Actions Needed for the BART Airport Extension*. Washington, D.C., 1996.

———. *Surface Infrastructure: Costs, Financing and Schedules for Large-Dollar Transportation Projects*. Washington, D.C., 1998.

Markman, Jon D., and Richard Simon. "L.A.'s Subway Has Dug a Hole for Itself in Congress." *Los Angeles Times*, 11 September 1996.

Martin, James D. "Intermodal Transportation: Evolving toward the 21st Century." *Transportation & Distribution*, 1 February 1996.

Food and Drug Administration (FDA)

PARENT ORGANIZATION: Department of Health and Human Services
ESTABLISHED: 1930
EMPLOYEES: 9,150 (1997)

Contact Information:

ADDRESS: 5600 Fishers Ln.
Rockville, MD 20857
PHONE: (301) 443-1544
TOLL FREE: (800) 532-4440
FAX: (301) 443-3100
E-MAIL: execsec@oc.fda.gov
URL: http://www.fda.gov
ACTING COMMISSIONER/LEAD DEPUTY COMMISSIONER FOR OPERATIONS : Michael A. Friedman, M.D.

WHAT IS ITS MISSION?

The Food and Drug Administration (FDA) is a public health agency that aims to protect American consumers primarily in the areas of foods, drugs, and cosmetics. The FDA's mission statement describes the organization as "a team of dedicated professionals working to protect, promote and enhance the health of the American people." This agency enforces the Federal Food, Drug, and Cosmetic Act, as well as other public health laws. In particular, it ensures that foods for people and animals are wholesome and sanitary, cosmetics are not dangerous, and medicines are safe and effective. The FDA also checks the safety of electronic products that emit radiation, such as microwave ovens. In addition, it regulates the labeling of all of these products to ensure that the information presented to consumers is truthful and accurate.

HOW IS IT STRUCTURED?

The FDA is an agency in the Public Health Services Division of the Department of Health and Human Services. It is run by a commissioner who is appointed by the president and approved by Congress. In addition, there are four deputy commissioners, who report directly to the commissioner.

The FDA is divided into five main offices. The first is the Office of the Commissioner. This office supervises the activities of the other offices. It consists of the commissioner and the deputy commissioners, as well as the executive secretary, chief counsel, chief mediator and ombudsman, and the Office of Special Investigations.

FAST FACTS

The cost of food poisoning to the nation, based on direct medical expenses, lost wages and productivity, and industry loss of tainted food products, is estimated at $1 billion to $10 billion annually.

(Source: Paula Kurtzweil. "Inside FDA: Center for Food Safety and Applied Nutrition." *FDA Consumer*, April 1997.)

The Office of Operations is the largest branch of the FDA. It oversees product reviews and is the liaison between the FDA and the Department of Health and Human Services and other government agencies. It consists of six centers: the Center for Biologics Evaluation and Research, the Center for Devices and Radiological Health, the Center for Drug Evaluation and Research, the Center for Food Safety and Applied Nutrition, the Center for Veterinary Medicine, and the National Center for Toxicological Research. In addition, there is the Office for Orphan Products Development, which develops products to treat rare diseases; the Office of Regulatory Affairs, which ensures that products comply with federal laws; and the Office of Science, which directs the scientific development of the agency.

A third main branch of the FDA is the Office of Policy. This office oversees the broad policy objectives of the FDA, including international policies. It works with similar agencies in other countries and with the United Nations to develop international product standards.

Another main unit is the Office of External Affairs. It consists of seven offices, which work with other organizations and special interest groups outside the FDA. Such organizations include U.S. health profession organizations, the World Health Organization, foreign governments, the Department of Agriculture, the Bureau of Alcohol, Tobacco, and Firearms, and Congress. In addition, this branch handles public affairs, including all media relations, and works with groups with special health concerns, such as Acquired Immunodeficiency Syndrome (AIDS), cancer, and women's health issues.

A fifth branch of the FDA is the Office of Management and Systems, which handles all of the business affairs of the agency. It consists of five offices, which oversee financial management, personnel, property management, information technology, and planning and evaluation for the agency.

The headquarters of the FDA are in Washington, D.C., though there are district and local offices in 157 cities throughout the United States. The agency regulates almost 95,000 businesses across the country.

PRIMARY FUNCTIONS

The structure of the FDA is somewhat complicated because of its numerous activities and the large number of products it regulates. However, the function of the agency can be summarized by its three main activities: product safety, inspections and legal sanctions, and scientific expertise. The FDA's purpose is to ensure that the food, cosmetics, and drugs that are publicly available are safe, as mandated by the Food, Drug, and Cosmetic Act and other laws that the FDA enforces. To do this, the FDA establishes health and safety guidelines for manufacturers of foods and drugs. It sets the standards that these products must meet. Such products are then thoroughly reviewed by FDA scientists before being allowed on the market. In addition, the FDA regulates the labels on these products to ensure that they are correct and informative for the consumer.

The FDA also inspects manufacturing facilities, collects samples for examination, and conducts tests to ensure that manufacturers are following government regulations. The agency employs more than 1,000 investigators and inspectors, who visit more than 15,000 facilities a year to check on product safety and proper labeling. Companies that violate federal regulations on product safety are usually asked to voluntarily correct the problem. For example, the FDA may ask a company to recall an unsafe product. If a company refuses to comply with FDA suggestions to correct an unsafe product, then the FDA seeks legal sanctions, including criminal penalties, against the manufacturers and distributors of the product.

PROGRAMS

Each office of the FDA administers a variety of programs at the federal, state, and local levels. For example, the Office of Regulatory Affairs has field offices across the country so that the FDA can more closely monitor companies' activities. It also sponsors a program of state management conferences to coordinate FDA activities with state officials.

Another important FDA program is MedWatch, the Medical Products Reporting Program. It is the means by which new safety information about foods and drugs is quickly passed on to the medical community. It also serves to educate health professionals about how to look for unexpected problems and how to report such problems to the FDA.

The Office of Special Health Issues handles FDA activities regarding serious health problems such as AIDS, cancer, and Alzheimer's disease. The office has programs to inform patients about the FDA drug approval process and clinical trials of new medications. It also presents patient views to the FDA and participates in national policy debates and developments regarding special illnesses and the people they affect.

The Office of Women's Health promotes women's health issues. It sponsors both research and outreach programs. Important research areas for women include pregnancy, sexually transmitted diseases, and breast implants. Outreach programs focus on providing consumers with information on women's issues such as breast-feeding and mammography. In addition, this office ensures that the FDA testing and regulations are fair regardless of gender.

BUDGET INFORMATION

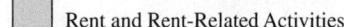

The FDA's 1997 budget was $921 million, which was less than 1 percent of the total budget of the Department of Health and Human Services. The largest shares of the FDA's budget went to the areas of human drugs (27 percent) and food and cosmetics (21 percent). The rest of the money was distributed as follows: devices and radiological products, 17.4 percent; biologics, 13.3 percent; veterinary medicine, 4.1 percent; the National Center for Toxicological Research, 3.4 percent; rent and rent-related activities, 2.5 percent; and other activities, 9.7 percent.

BUDGET:

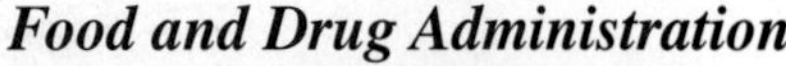

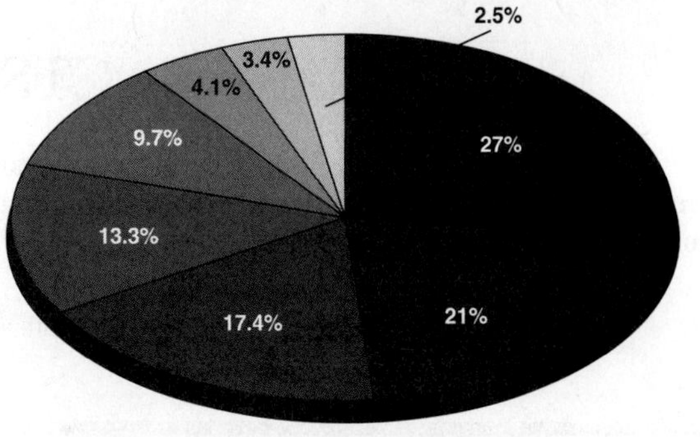

HISTORY

The regulation of food in the United States dates back to a Massachusetts food law in 1785; the federal regulation of drugs began in 1848. By the late 1800s there was a growing national movement for a federal law to prohibit misbranding and adulteration of food and drugs. In 1898 the Pure Food Congress was held in Washington, D.C., to discuss this issue. It was led by Dr. Harvey W. Wiley, a researcher of food adulteration with the Department of Agriculture, who would later become the first commissioner of the FDA.

Congress first allocated money to the development of federal food standards in 1902. Four years later the Food and Drug Act of 1906 and the Meat Inspection Act were signed into law by President Theodore Roosevelt. Wiley was appointed the first administrator of these acts. It was not until 1927 that the first agency was formed to enforce this kind of legislation. It was called the Food, Drug, and Insecticide Administration, but in 1930 the name was changed to the Food and Drug Administration.

The first Food, Drug, and Cosmetic Act was passed by Congress in 1938. It expanded the role of the FDA to include cosmetics and therapeutic devices. It also implemented a new system of drug regulation whereby new drugs had to be proved safe before marketing, and it allowed the FDA to conduct factory inspections. In 1939 the FDA issued the first federal food standards which covered tomatoes, tomato puree, and tomato paste.

Over the next few decades the FDA proved to be a flexible organization that could adapt to new technological developments and organizational changes. For example, in 1951 a congressional investigation of chemical safety in foods and cosmetics prompted the need for effective controls for pesticides, food additives, and colors. Pesticide regulation was increased with the Pesticides Amendment of 1954, which set safety limits for pesticide residues on raw agricultural products. The FDA continued to regulate pesticides until 1970, when the Environmental Protection Agency was established and took over this area.

In the 1960s the government's commitment to public safety was renewed with the passage of the Consumer Bill of Rights, signed into law by President John F. Kennedy. This bill ensured for consumers the right to safety, the right to be informed, the right to choose, and the right to have their concerns and opinions heard by the government. The FDA assumed significant responsi-

FAST FACTS

The FDA regulates more than $1 trillion worth of products, which account for 25 cents of every dollar spent annually by American consumers.

(Source: *The Food and Drug Administration: An Overview*. Food and Drug Administration Publication No. BG95-13. July 15, 1997.)

bility in fulfilling the intended goals of this bill. For example, in 1966 the Child Protection Act gave the FDA control over hazardous toys. In the same year the Fair Packaging and Labeling Act was also passed to ensure that products were honestly and informatively labeled.

The FDA has continued to keep up with technological and medical changes. Some examples of this effort include implementing the regulation of radiation from electronic products in 1971. Also, in 1977 the agency issued warning labels on the artificial sweetener saccharin. In 1985 the FDA approved the first AIDS blood test in an effort to protect patients from infected donors. Two important FDA regulations of the 1990s include the Nutrition Label and Education Act of 1990, which requires all packages to have nutrition labels, and the Mammography Quality Standards Act of 1992, which requires all mammography facilities to be federally certified.

CURRENT POLITICAL ISSUES

In a 1996 article in *Newsweek*, outgoing FDA commissioner David Kessler wrote that "the two chief causes of preventable death in the United States are poor diet and smoking." Although the FDA has always supported education and food regulations to ensure good nutrition, the battle over smoking has been much more difficult. The tobacco industry is a profitable business that contributes greatly to the U.S. economy and has much political influence in Congress. Therefore, even though health professionals have known about the dangers of smoking for years, it has been difficult to pass federal regulations against it. Public opinion against smoking has been increasing, and there have been several lawsuits attempting to hold the tobacco industry accountable for tobacco-related illnesses. Because much of the smoking debate has focused on whether or not tobacco is an addictive "drug," the FDA has played a large role in this discussion.

Case Study: Children and Tobacco

In August 1996 the FDA announced the first-ever proposal to regulate tobacco in the United States. Instead of targeting smokers directly, the agency focused on prevention. The FDA rule sought to reduce the availability and appeal of tobacco to children. Despite the fact that the sale of tobacco products to children under 18 years old is illegal in every state, tobacco use among minors increased in the 1990s. The FDA reports that every day about three-thousand young Americans become regular smokers.

In 1995 President Clinton called smoking a "pediatric disease" and supported FDA efforts to regulate children's access to tobacco products. Between 1995 and 1996 there was much public and political debate over whether and how this should be done, and by August 1996 the FDA had presented its new regulations.

The FDA limited the availability of tobacco to children by requiring anyone under age 27 to present a photo ID before purchasing tobacco products, banning cigarette vending machines, and banning free samples of cigarettes or packs of less than 20 cigarettes, known as "kiddie packs." In addition, the FDA helped to restrict the tobacco advertising seen by children by prohibiting billboards near schools and playgrounds. It also limited advertising appeal by restricting advertising to black-and-white text only. This was an important restriction because it meant eliminating all color advertisements, including those with well-known characters such as "Joe Camel" and the "Marlboro Man," which were especially fascinating to children. The FDA also forbade the sale or free distribution of products, such as caps or bags, with the names of any tobacco products and prohibited brand-name sponsorship of sporting or entertainment events by tobacco manufacturers.

The new regulations went into effect in February 1997. Manufacturers of tobacco products, advertising agencies, and convenience stores sued the FDA because they believed the agency did not have the proper authority to regulate cigarettes and tobacco products. On April 25, 1997, the federal district court in Greensboro, North Carolina, ruled that the FDA did have the authority to restrict access to tobacco products under the Food, Drug, and Cosmetic Act; however, the constitutionality of the advertising restrictions was still questioned. In July 1997 the tobacco industry finally agreed to the advertising restrictions as part of a global settlement with 40 state attorneys general who were suing the tobacco industry for medical costs associated with smoking.

Once all of the FDA regulations regarding children and smoking are in place, the agency hopes to cut tobacco use by minors in half within seven years.

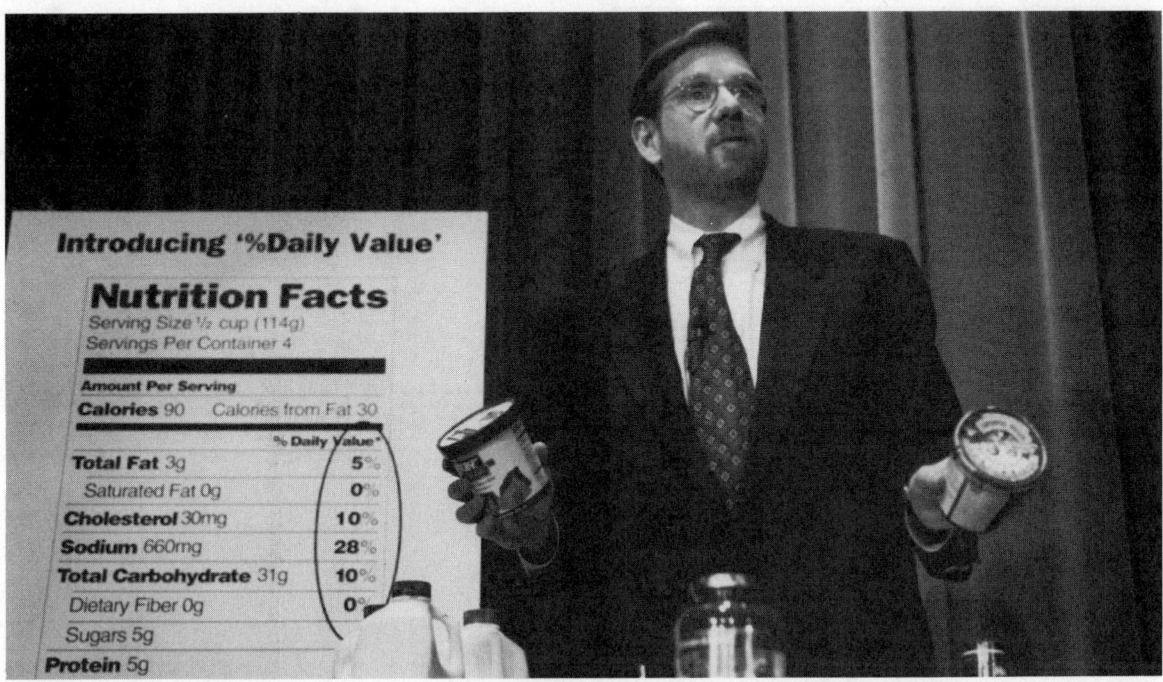

Former FDA Commissioner David Kessler discusses food labeling requirements at a 1994 press conference. The FDA is responsible for ensuring that the food, cosmetics, and drugs sold in the United States are wholesome and sanitary, and that the labeling of these products is truthful and accurate. (Photograph by J. Scott Applewhite. AP/Wide World Photos)

FUTURE DIRECTIONS

The stated vision of the FDA for the year 2000 is "to maximize public health protection while minimizing regulatory burden." It aims to be a strong science-based agency that will uphold safety standards, protect consumers, and promote public health. Specifically, the FDA will continue its fight against children's smoking. In addition, growing public concern for greater food inspection and safety research will be a top priority of the FDA, as will the regulation of new diet pills that will soon replace those taken off the market.

AGENCY RESOURCES

The FDA has a wealth of information on its Web site at http://www.fda.gov and in its publications, which can be ordered by calling (301) 443-1544. Important FDA phone numbers include the 24-hour emergency number at (301) 443-1240, the Consumer Information Hotline at 1-800-532-4440, and the Seafood Hotline at 1-800-332-4010. The FDA archive of agency reports, press releases, and other information is located at http://www.fda.gov/opacom/archives.html. There are also two electronic reading rooms available on-line. One is for dockets containing information on new FDA rules and is available at http://www.fda.gov/dockets/default.htm. The other, for Freedom of Information requests and information not readily available to the public but which can be specially requested, is available at http://www.fda.gov/foi/foia2.htm or by writing to FOI Staff, 5600 Fishers Ln., Room 12A-30, Rockville, Maryland 20857.

AGENCY PUBLICATIONS

The FDA publishes a wide variety of brochures, flyers, and audiovisual materials for consumers. A catalog of consumer publications can be found on the FDA Web site at http://www.fda.gov/opacom/7pubs.html. This includes a section of "easy-to-read" publications. The official magazine of the FDA is the *FDA Consumer*. Issues dating back to 1985 are available on-line, and printed copies of all issues are available through the Government Printing Office at (202) 512-1800. The *FDA Consumer* magazine features "On the Teen Scene" articles written especially for teenagers. Other publications include the *FDA Medical Bulletin*, *FDA Enforcement Report*, and *FDA Almanac*.

BIBLIOGRAPHY

Bader, Greg. "FDA Ties Up Doctor's Research on Cancer." *USA Today*, 10 February 1997, p. 15A.

Centers for Disease Control and Prevention. *Preventing Tobacco Use Among Young People: A Report of the Surgeon General.* Washington, D.C.: U.S. Government Printing Office, 1994.

Cohn, Bob, and Bill Turque. "Firing Up the Politics of Teen Smoking." *Newsweek*, 21 August 1995.

Kerr, Kathleen. "Fen-Phen Reports Unheeded/FDA Didn't See Link." *Newsday*, 22 December 1997, p. A06.

Kessler, David. "'We've Fought the Good Fight.'" *Newsweek,* 19 December 1996.

Kurtzweil, Paula. *Can Your Kitchen Pass the Food Safety Test?* FDA Publication Number 96-1229. November 1996.

Lynch, Barbara S., and Richard J. Bonnie, eds. *Growing Up Tobacco Free: Preventing Nicotine Addiction in Children and Youths*. Washington, D.C.: Institute of Medicine, National Academy Press, 1994.

Reed, Lawrence W. "How a Food Safety Myth Became a Legend." *Consumers' Research Magazine* Vol. 78 (February 1995): 23–4.

Sinclair, Upton. *The Jungle*. New York: Doubleday, Page & Co., 1906.

Williams, Rebecca D., and Isadora Stehlin. *Breast Milk or Formula: Making the Right Choice for Your Baby.* FDA Publication Number 97-2307. December 1996.

Food and Nutrition Service (FNS)

PARENT ORGANIZATION: Department of Agriculture
ESTABLISHED: August 8, 1969
EMPLOYEES: 1,700

Contact Information:

ADDRESS: 3101 Park Center Dr.
Alexandria, VA 22302
PHONE: (703) 305-2286
TDD (HEARING IMPAIRED): (800) 828-1120
FAX: (703) 305-2908
URL: http://www.usda.gov/fcs
UNDER SECRETARY: Shirley Robinson Watkins
DEPUTY UNDER SECRETARY: Julie Paradis

WHAT IS ITS MISSION?

The primary goal of the Food and Nutrition Service (FNS) is to secure access to nutritious, healthy diets for all Americans—a goal pursued through direct food assistance and nutrition education. The programs of the Food and Nutrition Service focus on providing needy persons with access to a more nutritious diet and improving the eating habits of the nation's children. By providing an outlet for the distribution of food purchased under farmer assistance authorities, the FNS satisfies its secondary objective of helping America's farmers.

HOW IS IT STRUCTURED?

The Food and Nutrition Service is an operating unit of the Food, Nutrition, and Consumer Service, a mission area of the United States Department of Agriculture (USDA). Its chief administrator holds the title of under secretary of agriculture for Food, Nutrition, and Consumer Services. The Office of the Under Secretary, along with its associated offices, are responsible for most of the administrative and policy-related work at the FNS.

The operating bureaus of the FNS are divided into four program areas. The Food Stamp Program and the Special Supplemental Program for Women, Infants, and Children (WIC) are the two largest programs at the FNS and are conducted as individual operating units. Another program unit, Food Distribution Programs, is responsible for programs that distribute agricultural commodities to needy populations. Programs in this area include the Nutrition Program for the Elderly, the Food Distribution

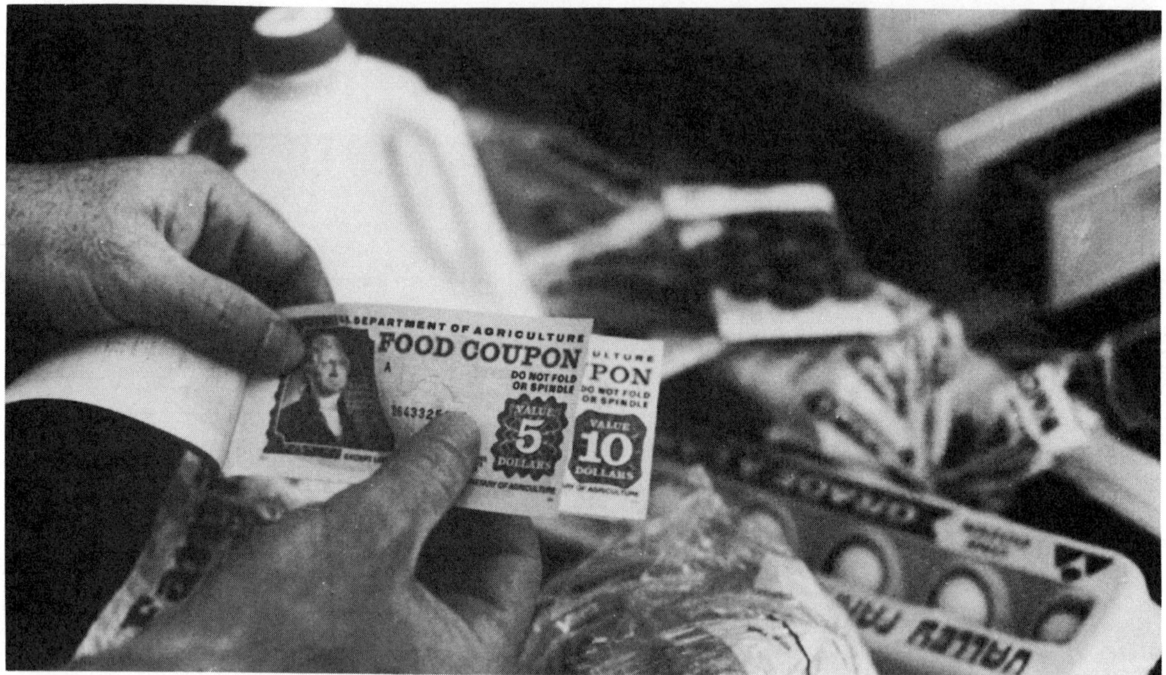

The FNS's Food Stamp program is one of the federal government's primary means of providing food aid. Approximately 21.5 million Americans received food stamps in 1997. (UPI/Corbis-Bettmann)

Program on Indian Reservations and the Trust Territories, and the Commodity Supplemental Food Program. The operating unit with the greatest number of programs is Child Nutrition Programs, which is responsible for the National School Lunch Program, the School Breakfast Program, and other programs devoted to improving the diet of low-income children.

The FNS is assisted in its work by the Office of Analysis and Evaluation, which studies the participation in FNS programs, the success of the programs, and compliance with program guidelines. The Office of Analysis and Evaluation publishes periodic reports on these issues, as well as profiles of the populations that participate in food assistance programs.

Another important office, the Center for Nutrition Policy and Promotion (CCNP), was formed in 1994 and includes members of the FNS as well as other USDA agencies. The CCNP is responsible for developing and coordinating nutrition policy within the USDA, as well as assessing the cost-effectiveness of government-sponsored nutrition programs on food consumption, food expenditures, food-related behavior, and nutritional status. The CCNP prepares periodic updates on the cost of family food plans and the cost of raising children and investigates techniques for effective nutrition communication for Americans. The staff of the center is composed primarily of nutritionists, nutrition scientists, and economists, all of whom were chosen from other USDA agencies for their expertise.

PRIMARY FUNCTIONS

The FNS is the arm of the Department of Agriculture that coordinates consumer education and outreach activities, encourages customer involvement in USDA policy making, and makes sure that the USDA adequately addresses consumer concerns and interests. The programs of the FNS provide supplemental foods and nutritional education to low-income infants and children; pregnant, postpartum, and breast-feeding women; and elderly people who are vulnerable to malnutrition. Food distributed by the FNS is purchased from farmers and distributors by the Department of Agriculture.

In all its programs, FNS works in partnership with the states, which determine the administrative details regarding the distribution of food benefits and the eligibility of participants. In most cases FNS funds are distributed in the form of cash grants to state agencies or recognized Indian tribes, which further apportion the funds to localities, where they are used to buy food and pay administrative costs. Under the education and training programs of the FNS, funds are granted to the states to collect and disseminate nutrition information to children, as well as to conduct in-service training of food service and teaching personnel.

PROGRAMS

The FNS administers a total of 15 food assistance programs, the cornerstone of which is the Food Stamp Program. This program provides direct food assistance to needy Americans by either issuing monthly allotments of coupons that are redeemable at retail food stores or, increasingly, providing benefits through electronic benefits transfer (EBT). EBT allows food stamp customers to use a plastic card, similar to a bank card, to buy groceries by transferring funds directly from a food stamp benefit account to the retailer's account. Eligibility and allotments are based on household size, income, financial assets, and other factors.

Another important FNS program is the Special Supplemental Program for Women, Infants, and Children, or WIC. The goal of WIC is to improve the health of low-income pregnant and postpartum women and of infants and children up to five years old. WIC supplies participants with vouchers that can be redeemed at food stores for specific foods—typically foods rich in the nutritional sources that are frequently lacking in the diets of low-income mothers and their children.

The FNS's focus on the health of low-income children is made clear through the variety of programs designed to maintain healthy diets. These programs include the National School Lunch Program, the School Breakfast Program, the Summer Food Service Program, the Child and Adult Day Care Food Program, the Homeless Children Nutrition Program, and the Special Milk Program for Children, which provides milk to children in schools, summer camps, and childcare institutions that have no federally supported meal program.

BUDGET INFORMATION

The FNS budget is a component of the budget for the entire Department of Agriculture, which is granted almost entirely through congressional appropriations. Of the 1997 FNS budget of over $39 billion, about two-thirds (66 percent) is spent on the Food Stamp Program. Child nutrition programs account for about 23 percent of the budget; 10 percent is spent on the WIC program; and about 1 percent is spent on commodity assistance programs.

HISTORY

The U.S. Department of Agriculture began in the late nineteenth century as a research-oriented agency that was intended to provide technical assistance to farmers. The economic collapse of the 1930s, however, shifted the department's focus to financial assistance; programs created in response to the Depression included improved rural credit facilities, aid for poverty-stricken farmers to acquire property, and loans for rural electrification.

It did not take long for the USDA to realize, however, that the Depression affected city dwellers as well as rural farmers. Many people were unable to purchase sufficient food. It was in response to this poverty that the USDA, working with welfare departments, established programs for distributing food to the needy in both rural and urban areas. Marketing and distribution, rather than mere production, became the emphasis concerning agricultural products. The primary means of food assistance during the Depression was the Needy Family Program, which evolved into the present-day Food Distribution Program on Indian Reservations and the Trust Territories. Another present-day program, the National School Lunch Program, also has its roots in Depression-era efforts to help children from low-income families.

The Food Stamp Program was inaugurated as an experimental project by Secretary of Agriculture Henry Wallace on May 16, 1939, but was terminated on March 1, 1943, because of high war-time employment and food rationing. After World War II (1939–45) and the Korean War (1950–53), however, the USDA again directed particular attention to marketing problems. In 1954 Congress reauthorized the Food Stamp Program in the Agricultural Trade Development and Assistance Act. The provisions

BUDGET:

Food and Nutrition Service

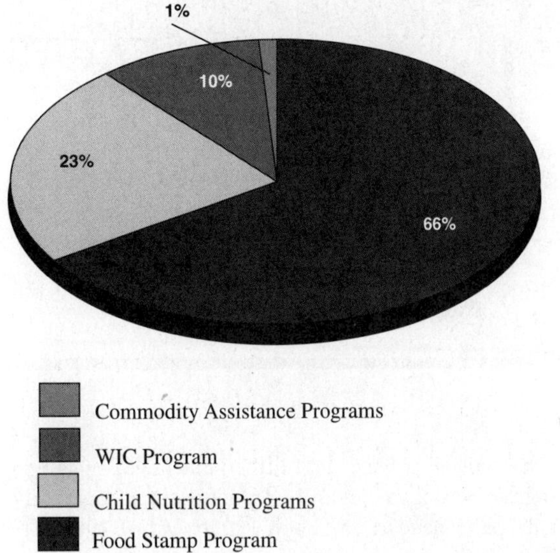

FAST FACTS

The Food Stamp Program does not allow participants to buy any of the following with food stamp benefits: alcoholic beverages, tobacco, lunch counter items or foods to be eaten in the store, vitamins, medicines, pet foods, or any nonfood items (except seeds and plants).

(Source: Food and Nutrition Service. "Nutrition Program Facts," 1998.)

of the legislation were not fulfilled until 1961, when the program was again begun on a pilot basis; it was finally made permanent by the Food Stamp Act of 1964. The USDA's Special Milk Program for Children began its first operations in 1955.

Throughout the 1960s and 1970s, the USDA turned its attention to ensuring that every American family had sufficient food. It was determined that to do this a single administration should oversee the USDA's food assistance programs, and the Food and Nutrition Service was established on August 8, 1969. Programs added to the USDA during this period of expansion included the School Breakfast Program (1966), the Summer Food Service Program (1968), the Child and Adult Day Care Food Program (1975).

These programs underwent several revisions during the 1980s but experienced no dramatic changes until 1994, when a restructuring of the USDA was undertaken and the Food and Nutrition Service was eliminated. Its functions were assumed by the Food and Consumer Service. The USDA launched an ambitious nationwide program, the School Meals Initiative for Healthy Children, which centered on updated nutrition standards for school meals as recommended in the department's *Dietary Guidelines for Americans*. The new regulations went into effect during the 1996–97 school year. In 1996 the Healthy Meals for Children Act, which expanded schools' menu-planning options and reinforced the requirement that all school meals must meet the Dietary Guidelines, was passed.

Despite these program expansions, however, the attitude of the American public toward welfare programs in general, and some food assistance programs in particular, began to change during the 1990s. Increasingly, it seemed, taxpayers wanted to see evidence of some responsibility on the part of welfare program participants and to see them demonstrate a willingness to work to support their families. The reasons for this apparent change in public opinion were uncertain, but the political establishment was quick to act on it. The Personal Responsibility and Work Opportunity Reconciliation Act, also known as the Welfare Reform Act, was passed in 1996. The legislation placed some restrictions on FNS assistance programs, especially the Food Stamp Program. In general, it tightened eligibility requirements by placing certain conditions on the granting of food assistance to participants.

In late 1997 the agency underwent a name change from the Food and Consumer Service back to the Food and Nutrition Service. In a December 1, 1997, news release, Under Secretary Watkins commented, "Nutrition is the foundation of this agency's programs. Putting nutrition in the title emphasizes the importance of nutrition in the administration of the food assistance and nutrition education programs for our customers."

CURRENT POLITICAL ISSUES

In 1996 Congress passed one of the most sweeping welfare reform laws in U.S. history, the Personal Responsibility and Work Opportunity Reconciliation Act of 1996. The new welfare law was the product of a political climate in America that had become increasingly critical of people who allegedly took advantage of the various federal public assistance programs. Although the extent of such abuses was unknown, it was true that USDA inspectors were working before the passage of the bill to root out violators who engaged in illegal practices such as trafficking in food stamps (exchanging stamps for cash). In 1996, Under Secretary for Food, Nutrition, and Consumer Services Ellen Haas denounced traffickers as literally taking food out of the mouths of hungry families.

Congress, anxious to cut the federal budget, was able to make President Bill Clinton acknowledge that federal welfare programs were often inefficiently administered, misused by participants, and in some cases inadvertently structured to encourage dependence on government assistance rather than self-reliance. The new law was designed to emphasize jobs rather than benefits to force welfare recipients into some form of employment that would help support them and their families. It was also intended to localize control of these programs—instead of making the distribution of benefits a federally administered responsibility, the new law issued funds in the form of "block grants" (single lump sums) to each of the states, to be used for welfare benefits as was deemed appropriate by each state government.

The law dramatically affected FNS nutrition programs, especially the Food Stamp Program, which was eventually forced to deny benefits to about two million people. The law was composed of nine titles; titles IV and V, dealing with immigrants and food stamps, accounted for most of the $54 billion in savings proposed by the law. Critics of the legislation denounced it as a serious blow to the well-being of the nation's poor children who relied on program benefits for basic nutrition.

Case Study: The Food Stamp Program

When the 1996 welfare law was passed, the Food Stamp Program had long been one of the nation's costliest public assistance programs. Procedures for establishing the eligibility of applicants were complicated and time-consuming and were therefore expensive to execute. Some of the federal regulations caused confusion at the local level, where circumstances were often quite different from those envisioned by the writers of food stamp regulations.

The program distributed benefits in the form of paper coupons, which were offered to retailers, which then sent the coupons in to the government for redemption. This system was easily abused, with widely publicized reports of theft and fraud. Sometimes, unprincipled retailers accepted food stamps from customers for unauthorized items such as alcoholic beverages or tobacco—because the government required no documentation of how the stamps were actually spent. There were also cases of criminal networks in some cities that specialized in the circulation of (often stolen) food stamps from liquor stores and other illegal traders in the coupons.

The new law came down hard on food stamp recipients, preventing any able-bodied adult between the ages of 18 and 50 from collecting food stamps for more than three months out of a three-year period unless they worked at least 20 hours a week. The law also encouraged the conversion from paper coupons to a more easily controlled electronic benefits transfer (EBT), to reduce incidents of theft and fraud.

The law had its opponents—including the Clinton administration's assistant secretary for children and families in the Department of Health and Human Services, who resigned after the law was passed. While acknowledging that fraud and abuse had been taking benefits away from hungry families and children, the FNS and other critics, many of them representatives of the medical profession, argued that the new welfare law did just as much harm with its overall reduction in funding. They pointed out that the new legislation did not make an allowance for the low employment in the areas in which many food stamp recipients lived. They also argued that without skills, it would be impossible for former welfare recipients to find work in these areas. The law did not address this point; it left such concerns up to the states, which were invited but not required to seek waivers for recipients who lived in areas with high unemployment. Leaving such an important point up to loose interpretation by state governments, critics said, was irresponsible and potentially harmful to the children of the nation's poorest families.

SUCCESSES AND FAILURES

There are many overwhelmingly positive statistics often mentioned in conjunction with FNS programs. The WIC program, for example, has helped to improve the health and nutrition of thousands of pregnant and postpartum women, and their young children; studies have also shown that it has saved from $1.77 to $3.13 in Medicaid dollars for each dollar spent on prenatal WIC benefits. The Summer Food Service Program feeds two million children each year during school vacation periods. The School Breakfast Program feeds 6.6 million children. In terms of sheer numbers, the successes of FNS programs are impressive at first glance.

A study compiled in 1995 by the Food Research and Action Center—a private national nonprofit organization dedicated to eliminating hunger and malnutrition in the United States—presented some even more staggering numbers, however, and the results were not as positive. The study, named the Community Childhood Hunger Identification Project, claimed that about four million U.S. children under the age of 12 go hungry at least part of the year. Furthermore, the study found, almost 10 million additional children in low-income families are at risk of hunger and its health consequences. The study did not take a stance on whether the FNS's programs were at fault for the huge number of hungry children in the United States, either because of inefficiency in their administration or simply because of lack of resources.

FUTURE DIRECTIONS

Most of the FNS's immediate future will be spent on restructuring its program operations to conform to the provisions of the 1996 Welfare Reform Act. In particular, many states participating in the Food Stamp Program, in an effort to stem incidences of fraud and misuse, will convert their food stamp issuance to electronic benefits transfer (EBT) systems. EBT allows food stamp customers to use a plastic card, similar to a bank card, to buy groceries by transferring funds directly from a food stamp account to the retailer's account. Currently 23 states are using EBT to issue at least part of their food stamp benefits, and 27 others and the District of Columbia are in some stages of planning or implementing EBT. The Welfare Reform Act requires all states to convert to EBT issuance by 2002.

AGENCY RESOURCES

General inquiries about the work of the FNS should be directed to the Office of Governmental Affairs/Public Information, 3101 Park Center Dr., Rm. 805, Alexandria, VA 22303; phone (202) 305-2286. For nutrition information, a significant source is the Food and Nutrition Information Center (FNIC), maintained by the

National Agricultural Library. The FNIC's holdings include books, journals, and audiovisual materials covering a wide range of topics, from children's literature to technical nutrition information. The FNIC can be accessed on-line at http://www.nal.usda.gov/fnic; by E-mail at fnic@nal.usda.gov; by telephone at (301) 504-5719; or by regular mail at Food and Nutrition Information Center, National Agricultural Library, Rm. 304, 10301 Baltimore Ave., Beltsville, MD 20705.

Another important source of information is the National Food Service Management Institute (NFSMI) Clearinghouse, maintained by the National Agricultural Library and the University of Mississippi. The NFSMI Clearinghouse provides information on research and findings concerning all aspects of food service programs. The NFSMI Clearinghouse's information services include quick answers to factual questions, referrals to other organizations, photocopies of journal articles, and lending services. For further information about the NFSMI Clearinghouse, call 1-800-321-3054.

AGENCY PUBLICATIONS

Most FNS-related publications of general interest to the public, such as "Promoting Healthy Food Practices," "Exploring Foods with Young Children," and "Creating Healthy Menus," are available through either the Food and Nutrition Information Center or the National Food Service Management Institute Clearinghouse. Contact FNIC at (301) 504–5719; or at Food and Nutrition Information Center, National Agricultural Library, Rm. 304, 10301 Baltimore Ave., Beltsville, MD 20705; the NFSMI Clearinghouse can be reached at 1-800-321-3054. The FNS posts reports on its research and findings, including "Understanding the Food Choices of Low Income Families," and "WIC Dynamics Study Volume I: Final Report," on its Web site for downloading at http://www.usda.gov/fcs.

BIBLIOGRAPHY

"America's Hungry Children." *New York Times*, 17 October 1996, p. A19.

Avruch, Sheila, and Alicia Puente Oackley. "Savings Achieved by Giving WIC Benefits to Women Prenatally." *Public Health Reports*, January–February 1995, pp. 27–35.

General Accounting Office. *Food Assistance: Potential Impacts of Alternative Systems for Delivering Food Stamp Program Benefits*. Washington, D.C., 1995.

Gleick, Elizabeth. "To Be Leaner or Meaner? A Congressional Proposal to Eliminate Nutrition Programs Raises an Outcry." *Time*, 6 March 1995, pp. 44–45.

Hunter, Beatrice Trum. "Updating School Lunches." *Consumer's Research Magazine*, October 1996, pp. 8–9.

Lutterback, Deborah. "Food Stamp Fallout." *Common Cause Magazine*, Spring 1995, pp. 8–11.

"No Free Lunch." *New Republic*, 10 April 1995, p. 7.

Nutrition Reform: How Much Will It Cost if Kids Go Hungry?" *Consumer Reports*, June 1995, p. 390.

Ohls, James C., and Harold Besbout. *The Food Stamp Program: Design Tradeoffs, Policy, and Impacts*. Washington, D.C.: Urban Institute Press, 1993.

Postrel, Virginia L. "Food Fight." *Reason* , June 1995, pp. 4–5.

Swarns, Rachel L. "For Now, Few are Going from Food Stamps to Soup Kitchens." *New York Times*, 5 July 1997, sec. 1, p. 13.

Food Safety and Inspection Service (FSIS)

WHAT IS ITS MISSION?

The Food Safety and Inspection Service (FSIS), a public health agency of the U.S. Department of Agriculture (USDA), is responsible for ensuring that the nation's commercial supply of meat, poultry, and egg products is safe, healthy, and correctly labeled and packaged.

HOW IS IT STRUCTURED?

The FSIS is the sole agency of the USDA's food safety mission area, and because of this there is often some confusion about the roles of the administrator of the FSIS and the nominal "director" of food safety, the under secretary for food safety. The under secretary reports to the secretary of agriculture on the operations of the FSIS; his or her responsibility is primarily as a representative. The administrator is the official who directly manages the operations and functions of the agency itself; this official is the primary decision maker for all areas of the FSIS's operations. Important offices under the administrator's direct control are the Legislative Liaison staff and the Food Safety Education and Communications staff.

The FSIS is further divided into four major offices, each led by a deputy administrator: the Office of Management; the Office of Public Health and Science; the Office of Field Operations; and the Office of Policy, Program Development, and Evaluation. The Office of Management handles administrative functions such as budgeting, personnel management, and administrative services. The Office of Public Health and Science con-

PARENT ORGANIZATION: Department of Agriculture
ESTABLISHED: June 17, 1981
EMPLOYEES: 9,900

Contact Information:

ADDRESS: 1400 Independence Ave. SW
Washington, DC 20250
PHONE: (202) 720-7943
TOLL FREE: (800) 535-4555
FAX: (202) 720-9063
E-MAIL: fsis.webmaster@usda.gov
URL: http://www.usda.gov/agency/fsis
ADMINISTRATOR: Thomas J. Billy
DEPUTY ADMINISTRATOR: Alberta Frost

Meat inspectors examine hogs at a Chicago, Illinois, meat packing house, circa 1900. *(Library of Congress/Corbis Bettmann)*

ducts FSIS research and contains all related divisions, such as the Food Hazard Surveillance Division and the Chemical and Toxicological Division.

The Office of Policy, Program Development, and Evaluation is the office that constantly analyzes the FSIS's approach to food safety and coordinates activities with other food safety organizations from the local to the international level. Both the Animal Production Food Safety Program and the FSIS's participation in the international Codex Alimentarius Commission are under the control of this office.

Before the FSIS undertook its dramatic reorganization in 1996, roughly 90 percent of its resources were devoted to its Office of Field Operations, which organizes and supports meat inspections and enforcement actions at plants nationwide. Once involving 18 districts, the field services have been consolidated into fewer than ten.

PRIMARY FUNCTIONS

Under the provisions of the Federal Meat Inspection Act and the Poultry Products Inspection Act, the FSIS inspects all meat and poultry sold in the United States, including imported products. Inspectors check animals before, during, and after slaughter; they prevent diseased animals from entering the food supply and examine carcasses for visible defects that can affect safety and quality. The FSIS also inspects products during processing, handling, and packaging. To address more specific concerns, inspectors sometimes test for the presence of pathogens or chemical residues, often with the support of the agency's three field laboratories. The service also conducts continuous inspection of the production of liquid, dried, and frozen egg products.

The FSIS sets the regulatory standards for a range of activities associated with the production of meat and poultry products, including the operation of all plant facilities and equipment; labeling; slaughter and processing activities; storage; and the use of ingredients, compounds, and additives for preparing and packaging meat and poultry products. The FSIS is authorized to take any necessary compliance actions to protect the public, including detention or recall of products, or, in some rare cases, referral for criminal prosecution.

The service continually tests samples of meat, poultry, and egg products for microbial and chemical contaminants to monitor trends for enforcement purposes. It operates state programs for the inspection of meat and poultry products sold in intrastate commerce and also conducts numerous consumer education activities, anchored by the toll-free Meat and Poultry Hotline, to answer the public's questions about labeling and safe handling of meat, poultry, and egg products.

PROGRAMS

One of the most important FSIS programs is the Animal Production Food Safety Program (APFSP), a collaborative program that concentrates on the link between animal production and slaughter and processing operations. The APFSP staff works with producers, researchers, and others to identify scientifically based practices to reduce potential chemical, physical, and microbial public health risks. The role of the APFSP in the USDA's food safety mission is to work with other federal agencies that share food safety responsibilities (i.e., the Food and Drug Administration) to ensure that efforts are coordinated and to create collaborative opportunities for both public and private investment in APFSP risk reduction.

The FSIS is also involved in an international effort called Codex Alimentarius. The Codex Alimentarius Commission provides a forum where member countries and international organizations can meet and exchange information and ideas about food safety and trade issues; it also articulates food standards that can be used to facilitate international trade. There are 156 member countries of Codex Alimentarius.

BUDGET INFORMATION

The FSIS budget, which was approximately $589 million in 1998, is a component of the entire USDA budget. Only about one-third of the FSIS budget is appropriated by Congress; the rest is supplied primarily by user fees, charged to recover the costs of inspection provided beyond regularly scheduled operations or on holidays. The bulk of the FSIS budget, about 84 percent, was spent on the process of food inspection. Approximately 8 percent was spent on inspection grants to states, 6 percent on operating the service's three laboratories, 2 percent on import/export inspection and about 1 percent on field automation and information management, the telecommunications link among members of the workforce.

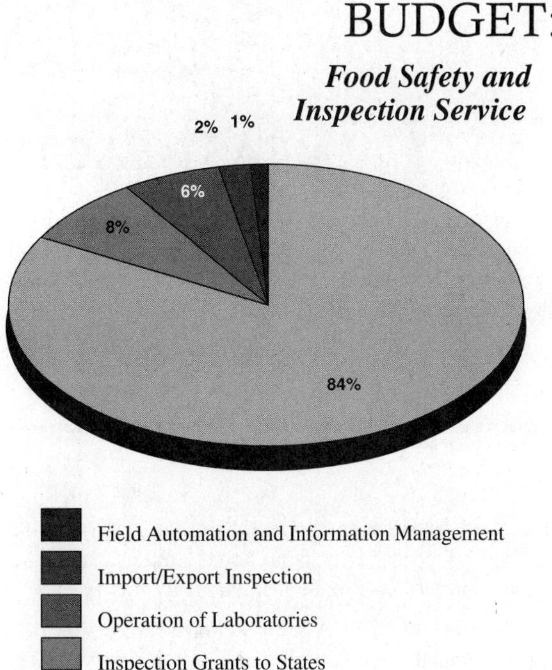

HISTORY

Before to the passage of the Meat Inspection Act of 1906, meat inspection in the United States was carried out in a very elementary way, usually by local butchers. In the early 1880s, however, the press began to focus its attention on the problem of quality and purity of food products sold to the public. Public condemnation of the slaughterhouses and meatpacking plants of Chicago was especially sharp and the subsequent damage to the industry's meat exports caused Chicago packers and processors to develop an improved inspection system in cooperation with health authorities.

The first federal attempt at protecting the public was an 1891 law, amended in 1895, that granted the secretary of agriculture the authority to implement a preslaughter inspection program that would prevent the transport of any cattle, hogs, or sheep across state lines or international borders. The law, which had nothing to do with animals after they had been killed, was a first step but did nothing to satisfy the demands of the American public for an adequate national system of meat inspection. The press continued to direct attention to the unsanitary manner in which packing houses were operated.

The Jungle

In 1906 public opinion reached a tipping point with the publication of *The Jungle*, a book written by Upton Sinclair. Although written as social critique, an attack on the plight of poor meatpacking workers, Sinclair's depictions of the appalling practices typical in Chicago slaughterhouses served to thoroughly disgust the American public. Committees were dispatched by the secretary of agriculture and President Theodore Roosevelt to investigate the Chicago packing industry, and the reports were not favorable. The comprehensive Meat Inspection Act was passed on June 30, 1906, giving the USDA the authority to conduct antemortem inspections (of live animals), postmortem inspections (after slaughter), and product inspection (in all stages of processing).

A federal meat inspection service was now in place, but poultry inspection was not covered by the Meat Inspection Act. As the poultry-processing industry developed throughout the 1920s, some voluntary programs evolved, funded by poultry slaughter and processing plants. It wasn't until 1957 that a Poultry Products Inspection Act was passed containing provisions similar to those in the Meat Inspection Act, and 1968 amendments to the law gave the USDA the authority to inspect poultry and poultry products.

Intrastate Commerce and Legislative Consolidation

The Meat and Poultry Inspection Acts applied to animals slaughtered and processed for interstate and foreign commerce, but did nothing in terms of intrastate commerce or regarding slaughterhouses and processors selling meat in strictly local areas. Regulation of these sales was the responsibility of various state and local authorities and was not well coordinated. The Wholesome Meat Act of 1967 provided for a state-federal cooperative program to regulate this area of commerce.

The passage of the Wholesome Meat Act led to the consolidation of all previous legislation—the Meat Inspection Act and its amendments, the Humane Slaughter Act of 1958, and the Poultry Products Inspection Act and its amendments—into a single Federal Meat Inspec-

FAST FACTS

Nationwide, about 7,400 FSIS inspectors carry out inspection laws in 6,200 plants, visually examining more than six billion poultry carcasses and 125 million livestock carcasses each year.

(Source: Food Safety and Inspection Service. "What Does FSIS Do?" 1998.)

tion Act. Antemortem inspection of all cattle, swine, sheep, and goats, as well as horses, mules, and other equine animals, was made mandatory by this law.

In 1981 the USDA's inspection service was officially named the Food Safety and Inspection Service. The growth of processing plants led to the passage of the Processed Products Inspection Improvement Act of 1986, which transferred some inspection responsibility to the processors themselves. In 1994, under the provisions of the Egg Products Inspection Act, the FSIS took on the responsibility for inspecting and regulating egg products.

CURRENT POLITICAL ISSUES

Government food safety oversight at the federal level is divided between the USDA's FSIS, which regulates the meat, dairy, poultry, and egg industries, and the independent Food and Drug Administration (FDA), which regulates essentially everything else, including seafood. Critics attack this divided effort, citing duplication of activities and the inefficient use of government resources. These critics, President Bill Clinton's administration, and officials at both the USDA and the FDA are pushing for more government authority to force the recall of contaminated products, to hire more inspectors, and to step up bacteriological testing at critical points in the processing of food.

Case Study: E. Coli *Outbreaks*

President Clinton's food safety initiative was a reaction to an alarming trend of foodborne pathogens in the United States in the 1990s. Outbreaks related to FSIS-regulated products included the 1993 *E. coli* outbreak on the west coast, which resulted in the death of at least four children, and a similar case in Colorado during the summer of 1997. In both cases a harmful strain of *E. coli* had been present in ground beef eaten as hamburger. The Colorado case led to the recall of 25 million pounds of ground beef by the producer Hudson Foods of Columbia, Nebraska, and further harm was prevented.

The FSIS reaction to the *E. coli* outbreak in Colorado was a great success, unlike its reaction to a similar outbreak in 1993. The FSIS discovered the problem quickly because of FoodNet, its new active surveillance approach. The health department in the state of Colorado, where the outbreak occurred, notified the FSIS of several confirmed cases of illness caused by *E. coli* bacteria, and an FSIS laboratory isolated the pathogen from an opened package of ground beef patties collected from a patient's freezer and from unopened packages from the marketplace. The FSIS quickly removed the contaminated product from the marketplace and from consumer homes, stopping what could have been a large outbreak.

In addition to these cases numerous other outbreaks of illness caused by food—including fruits, vegetables, seafood, ice cream, and juices contaminated with such harmful organisms as cyclospora, hepatitis A virus, or salmonella—have been recorded since 1991. Scientists and scholars point out likely reasons for this recent rise in contaminated food. First, an increasingly global economy involving the constant transport of food products across national boundaries makes it more difficult to stop harmful organisms. The United States imports much more food than it used to, and safety concerns have increased in recent years. Second, the food-processing industry is increasingly becoming the domain of centralized corporations. Although this might make it easier for the government to monitor food safety because the total number of processors is low, it also ensures that when something goes wrong, as it did at Hudson Foods, the resulting contamination is widespread.

But hiring more inspectors and stepping up testing and regulation simply isn't the answer, according to some scientists, who say the media's and the public's criticism of the FSIS for the 1993 and 1997 *E. coli* outbreaks is misplaced. It is simply very difficult to eliminate the *E. coli* organism from all red meat, and any degree of testing and inspection is still just an examination of a very small part of a supply of meat. In fact, meat testing and inspection is a practice that epidemiologist Michael Osterholm, quoted in a September 1997 *Newsweek* article, likens to "sticking your hand in one part of the haystack and saying the whole stack is free of needles."

Public Impact

Many epidemiologists agree on the answer to this problem: irradiation, which attacks bacteria with low-level radiation. Epidemiologists consider irradiation to be the key to reducing the risk of food-induced illness in the United States, and it is a proven technology that has been endorsed by the World Health Organization (WHO) and other international agencies. Irradiation is already used in virtually all of the spices sold in the United States. But the word *irradiation* rings alarm bells for many people in the United States, and activist groups are opposed to the practice, despite the scientific evidence of its effectiveness and its harmlessness to humans. As late as 1997 the FDA was still cautiously considering the possibility of approving irradiation of food products, but the food industry, fearing the anger of activist groups, remained reluctant to use irradiation as a disease-preventing tool. To some public health officials, however, food irradiation is an unavoidable and necessary advance in disease prevention.

FUTURE DIRECTIONS

The FSIS is undergoing a dramatic change in both its operational philosophy and its organizational structure. In the traditional meat and poultry inspection system, the finding that a product was not adulterated or contaminated was based on FSIS inspectors' visual and olfactory examination of the product itself. The traditional method of enforcement then was for inspectors to document deficiencies, which the plants or establishments would then correct. Recent outbreaks of illness, some rather serious, forced the FSIS in 1995 to reevaluate its approach to inspection and prevention. The agency's deliberations have resulted in a new organizational philosophy based on prevention rather than detection of problems; this change in direction was enforced in the spring of 1997 with President Clinton's Food Safety Initiative.

The new system is designed to rely on science rather than visual inspection. The goal is to target and reduce harmful bacteria in raw products and to make use of newly developed rules concerning Hazard Analysis and Critical Control Points (HACCP) programs—procedures designed to identify dangerous exposure points during the transport, slaughter, storage, or processing of animal carcasses. All plants in the United States will be required to have HACCP programs. The new plan sets interim targets for pathogen reduction in slaughter plants, requires microbial testing to meet those targets, and requires plants to implement three food safety interventions in its processing.

The FSIS is still in the process of streamlining, training, and redirecting its resources to reflect this change. In addition, the agency will need to accommodate the provisions of President Clinton's Food Safety Initiative, an effort that will involve FSIS collaboration with other agencies such as the Food and Drug Administration FDA and the Centers for Disease Control (CDC).

AGENCY RESOURCES

General inquiries about the work of the FSIS can be directed to the FSIS Food Safety Education and Communications Staff, Rm. 1175-South Bldg., 1400 Independence Ave. SW, Washington, DC 20250; phone (202) 720-7943. Another important source of information is the Food and Nutrition Information Center (FNIC), a service provided by the USDA's National Agricultural Library. The FNIC contains extensive bibliographies, resource lists, and fact sheets on the topics of human nutrition, food service management, and others. Several FSIS-related databases are accessible through the FNIC, including Foodborne Illness Educational Materials and HACCP Training Programs and Resources. The FNIC's Web site is http://www.nal.usda.gov/fnic. The center may also be contacted at FNIC, 10301 Baltimore Ave., Rm. 304, Beltsville, MD 20705; phone (301) 504-5719.

The FSIS's Meat and Poultry Hotline, 1-800-535-4555, is a toll-free telephone service that helps consumers prevent food—related illness, specifically by answering their questions about safe storage, handling, and preparation of meat and poultry. The hot line also answers all types of questions related to the mission of the FSIS—meat and poultry inspection, product recalls, enforcement, and so forth.

AGENCY PUBLICATIONS

The FSIS makes available to the public a number of fact sheets, news releases, and brochures related to food safety, such as "Is Pink Turkey Meat Safe?" "Focus On Cutting Board Safety," and "Food Safety During Disasters." A recently developed publication of particular use to the general public is the agency's *Food Safety Educator* newsletter, a quarterly periodical exploring current issues in food safety. The FSIS also issues a few technical publications (e.g. *Food Safety Research Agenda: Directions for the Future*) and a number of background papers on specific technical issues, such as *Reorganization of the Food Safety and Inspection Service* and *Revised Labeling Requirements for "Fresh" Raw Poultry Products.* Most publications can be accessed on the FSIS Web site at http://www.usda.gov/agency/fsis, but other food safety-related publications are available through the Food and Nutrition Information Center at http://www.usda.nal.usda.gov/fnic.

BIBLIOGRAPHY

Agres, Ted. "How U.S. Government Meat Tests Keep Our Food Chain Safe." *R&D*, July 1996, pp. 29–30.

"FDA & USDA Working Hand in Hand." *Progressive Grocer*, May 1996, p. 197.

Hunter, Beatrice Trum. "Simple Ways to Prevent Foodborne Illness." *Consumers' Research Magazine*, August 1997, pp. 25–28.

Janofsky, Michael. "U.S. Proposing Greater Powers on Food Safety." *New York Times*, 30 August 1997, p. 1.

Krantz, Michael. "An Inedible Beef Stew." *Time*, 1 September 1997, p. 34.

"Making Food Safer." *New York Times*, 14 May 1997, p. A18.

Morganthau, Tom. "E. Coli Alert." *Newsweek*, 1 September 1997, pp. 26–32.

Patton, Barbara J. *Food Safety*. Vero Beach, Fla.: Rourke Corporation, 1995.

Raybon, Donna. "Mad Cow Disease: Cause for Concern?" *Countryside & Small Stock Journal*, September–October 1996, pp. 16–17.

Sanson, Michael. "How Do You Spell Food Safety? HACCP." *Restaurant Hospitality*, March 1996, pp. 109–110.

Foreign Agricultural Service (FAS)

PARENT ORGANIZATION: Department of Agriculture
ESTABLISHED: 1953
EMPLOYEES: 900

Contact Information:

ADDRESS: 1400 Independence Ave. SW
Washington, DC 20250
PHONE: (202) 720-7115
TDD (HEARING IMPAIRED): (202) 690-3955
FAX: (202) 720-1727
E-MAIL: info@fas.usda.gov
URL: http://www.fas.usda.gov
ADMINISTRATOR: Lon Hatamiya
ASSOCIATE ADMINISTRATOR: Timothy Galvin

WHAT IS ITS MISSION?

The Foreign Agricultural Service (FAS) programs are designed to build and maintain the competitive position of exported U.S. agricultural, fish, and forest products in the global marketplace. The FAS is also responsible for the Department of Agriculture's international food assistance programs.

HOW IS IT STRUCTURED?

The Foreign Agricultural Service (FAS) is an agency of the U.S. Department of Agriculture (USDA). It is headed by an administrator who reports to the under secretary of agriculture for Farm and Foreign Agricultural Services, who in turn reports to the secretary of agriculture. The administrator and the associate administrator are assisted by the general sales manager in overseeing FAS programs.

The Office of the General Sales Manager is responsible for directing the agricultural functions of the Food for Peace Program, export credit guarantee programs, and direct sales of surplus commodities that are owned by the Commodity Credit Corporation (CCC), the USDA's institution for guaranteeing agricultural exports. The FAS program bureau that handles most of these functions, Export Credits, is led by a deputy administrator who reports to the general sales manager.

The FAS is divided into four other program areas, each of which is led by a deputy administrator: International Trade Policy, Foreign Agricultural Affairs, International Cooperation and Development, and Commodity

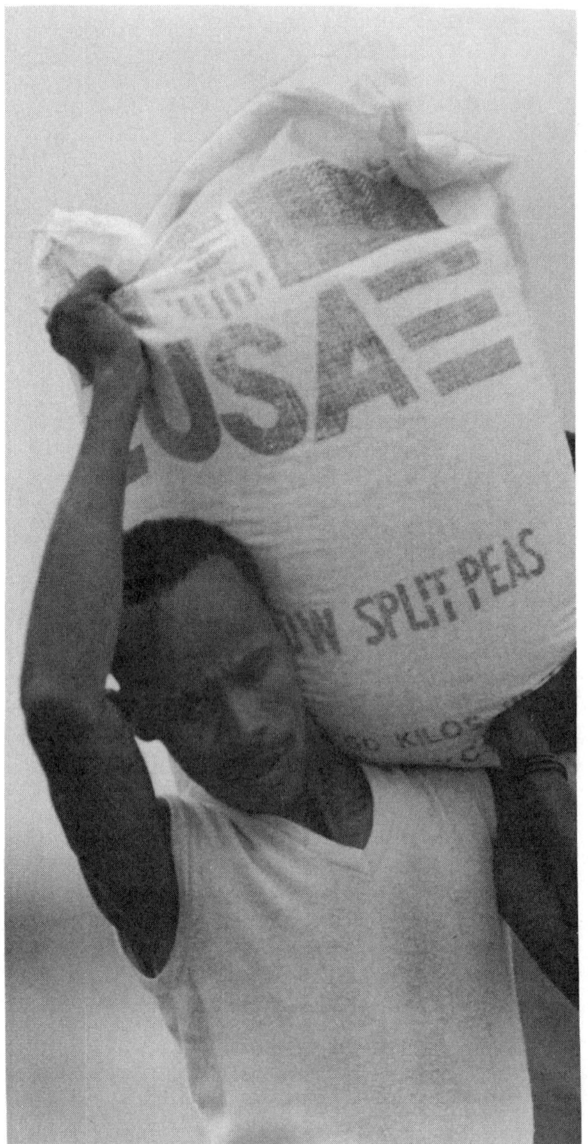

A Kenyan worker loads a bag of split peas from the United States onto a truck. The United States is the world's largest food aid donor. *(Photograph by Pat Hamilton. Reuters/Corbis-Bettmann)*

and Marketing Programs. International Trade Policy coordinates and directs the USDA's responsibilities in international trade agreement programs and negotiations and maintains an ongoing effort to reduce foreign trade barriers.

Through Foreign Agricultural Affairs, the agency's area officers and overseas attachés follow foreign governmental actions that affect the market for U.S. agricultural commodities.

The USDA's participation in international organizations, its research and scientific exchange programs, and its technical assistance programs are administered by International Cooperation and Development. Commodity and Marketing Programs, the FAS's largest bureau, develops and conducts marketing operations for agricultural commodities in five different areas (forest products; grain and feed; dairy, livestock, and poultry; oilseeds and products; and tobacco, cotton, and seeds). This bureau also conducts production assessments and crop estimates in these areas.

PRIMARY FUNCTIONS

Most FAS activity focuses on building markets overseas for U.S. farm products. The FAS maintains a worldwide agricultural intelligence system through an attaché service that posts professional agriculturalists in more than 75 countries. These attachés represent the Department of Agriculture and provide information on the agricultural policies of foreign governments; analyses of supply and demand; descriptions of commercial trade relationships; and market opportunities. Attaché reports are analyzed by the FAS staff in Washington. During international trade negotiations, the FAS provides the staff and support for representing the U.S. agricultural interest.

Under legislative mandate, the FAS also has the responsibility to provide U.S. agricultural exporters with commercial financing support through the Commodity Credit Corporation (CCC), the USDA's institution for guaranteeing agricultural exports. The credit guarantee programs are designed to expand or maintain foreign markets for U.S. agricultural commodities. Several FAS export assistance programs are designed to counter the adverse effects of the unfair trade practices of foreign competitors.

The FAS's International Cooperation and Development (ICD) program area increases the competitiveness of U.S. agriculture by providing linkages to world resources and international organizations. By sharing agricultural knowledge, the FAS provides tools to help build stable economies. The FAS manages programs to exchange technologies between U.S. and international scientists, support collaborative research, provide technical assistance and professional development and training programs to lower-income nations, and organize overseas trade and investment missions.

The FAS conducts several foreign food-assistance programs, including the agricultural functions of the Food for Peace Program (Public Law 480) and the Food for Progress Program. Some foreign aid involves the donation of CCC surplus commodities to people or nations in crisis.

PROGRAMS

Many of the FAS's most important programs are carried out as mandated by past legislation. For example, the Export Enhancement Program (EEP) is operated under the authority of the amended Agricultural Trade Act of 1978 and the Federal Agricultural Improvement and Reform (FAIR) Act of 1996. The EEP's primary goal is to help products produced by American farmers meet competition from countries that subsidize their agricultural exports, especially in the European Union. Under the program, the USDA pays cash bonuses to exporters, effectively allowing them to sell U.S. agricultural products in certain countries at prices below the exporter's cost of acquiring them from the producers. Other FAS export programs include the Supplier Credit Guarantee Program (SCGP), the Market Access Program, the Foreign Market Development Program, the Facility Guarantee Program, and the Dairy Export Incentive Program.

FAS food aid programs, which provide for the sale and donation of agricultural products to underdeveloped countries, are similarly a result of major legislation: Public Law 480, also known as the Food for Peace Program; the Food for Progress Act of 1985, and the Agricultural Act of 1949. The FAS also operates a number of programs in the areas of import information, technical assistance and exchange, and trade data acquisition.

BUDGET:

Foreign Agricultural Service

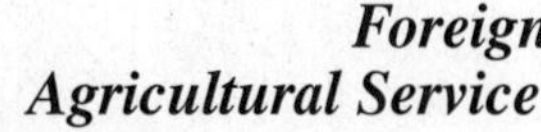

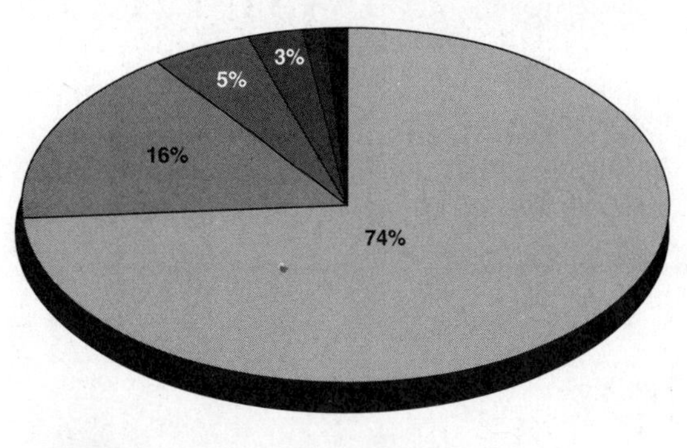

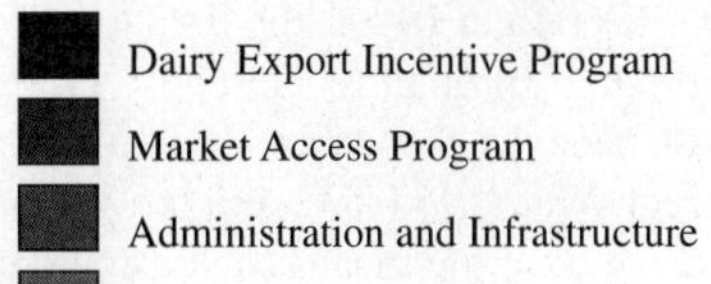

BUDGET INFORMATION

The FAS budget is a component of the budget for the entire USDA, which is granted largely through congressional appropriations. The FAS's projected 1999 budget is $6.216 billion. Much of this money is set aside for use in specific programs as needed, and may not be used if not warranted by market conditions. Approximately 74 percent of the FAS budget is devoted to the Export Credit Guarantee Program. Food aid programs, including Food for Peace and Food for Progress, take up 16 percent of the budget. The Export Enhancement Program receives 5 percent of the budget. The Market Access Program and the Dairy Export Incentive Program each use 1 percent of the agency's budget, and the remaining 3 percent is devoted to administration and infrastructure.

HISTORY

Since the earliest days of its history, the Department of Agriculture attempted to discover and maintain export markets for U.S. farmers. However, the USDA's efforts in this area were generally recognized as a scattered number of small programs without a central focus. The difficulties suffered by farmers during the Great Depression made apparent the need for centrally administered export activities. The Office of Foreign Agricultural Relations was established at the USDA in 1939 and served to coordinate all activities relating to the export of farm commodities. The office's initial focus was on providing foreign market intelligence to domestic farmers and agriculture professionals.

The Agricultural Act of 1949 strengthened the USDA's support of agricultural exports by providing price supports for certain commodities. Over the years, these price supports have been revised, retracted, and reinstated to fit the market conditions of the times, but price guarantees and export credit to U.S. farmers have remained the key ingredients in the USDA's efforts at improving international market access for American farm commodities.

In 1953 Secretary of Agriculture Ezra Taft Benson reorganized the USDA. The Office of Foreign Agricultural Relations was abolished and was replaced with the Foreign Agricultural Service. The FAS expanded activities designed to increase exports and initiated its involvement in international organizations such as the Agency for International Development and the Food and Agriculture Organization of the United Nations. The FAS administered import quotas on foreign agricultural goods

FAST FACTS

Crops from nearly one-third of U.S. farm acreage go to overseas consumers.

(Source: Foreign Agricultural Service. "About FAS," 1997.)

and provided the government with information for trade negotiations.

Throughout the 1960s and 1970s, the FAS turned its attention to marketing problems abroad. Foreign economies that had been weakened by World War II (1939–45), the Korean War (1950–53), and the Vietnam War (1959–75) did not have the means to accommodate agricultural imports, and the FAS sought to provide technical assistance to those nations to increase their self-sufficiency and stability. In the 1980s this trend continued, and the goals of FAS food aid and export assistance programs became irreversibly intertwined: without stable economies, developing countries could not establish reliable markets for agricultural commodities, and without some form of assistance, these economies could not be stabilized. FAS programs attempted to balance aid programs with conditions for repayment, commodity storage, and agricultural training that would make developing countries more promising long-term export targets.

Before long, U.S. legislators, responding to rapid economic growth around the world, realized the potential for improved agricultural export markets. The Federal Agricultural Improvement and Reform (FAIR) Act of 1996 made several changes to agricultural trade programs. While tightening the repayment conditions of some foreign credit programs, the 1996 Farm Bill also required that the CCC make at least $1 billion available for direct credit or credit guarantees to emerging markets around the world between 1996 and 2000.

Food Aid

U.S. foreign food assistance began not long after the formation of the FAS with the 1954 initiation of the Food for Peace Program (Public Law 480). The law authorized the sale of food surpluses to developing nations and the emergency donation of these surpluses in times of urgent need, such as famine or natural disaster. In 1961 a separate office was set up by executive order to handle the USDA's foreign aid programs. The Food for Peace Act of 1965 renewed these authorizations but included provisions intended to promote the self-reliance of underdeveloped nations. Eligibility for U.S. agricultural aid was established by several criteria, including the use of land resources for food production, the development of agricultural industry, the initiation of agricultural training and instruction, and voluntary population control.

As part of the 1985 Farm Bill, another program, Food for Progress, was initiated. Food for Progress authorized the CCC to finance the sale and exportation of agricultural commodities on credit terms or, on a grant basis, to support developing countries that were emerging democracies. Under the provisions of the program, only those countries that had clearly demonstrated a commitment to introducing or expanding a free-enterprise system into their agricultural commodities could be eligible for aid.

The 1996 Farm Bill made several changes to the food aid programs of the FAS. It amended some credit programs to include private organizations as well as foreign governments and reduced the grace period for the repayment of credit. It also amended the Agricultural Act of 1980 to establish a Food Security Commodity Reserve and raised the reserve's emergency release authority for urgent humanitarian relief in the case of disasters. All food aid programs, including Food for Peace and Food for Progress supports, were generally reauthorized by the 1996 Farm Bill through 2002.

CURRENT POLITICAL ISSUES

Since the earliest days of its food-relief efforts, the United States has been the world's largest supplier of international food aid. The programs under which the government is granted authority to grant that aid, however, are built upon several requirements for eligibility. The Food for Progress Program, for example, authorizes food relief only to developing countries with a proven commitment to establishing democratic governments and free-market economies. The Food for Peace Program allows a little more latitude, however; under the provisions of Title II of the program, the FAS has the authority to lend food aid to virtually any foreign government in times of emergency or crisis.

In certain cases, however, whether the U.S. government should exercise this authority becomes an issue that sparks debate across the country. Following the Persian Gulf War of 1991, the United States used its international political clout to establish an embargo of virtually all goods and services to its enemy, Iraq, until certain concessions were met. Many members of the international community felt that the U.S. conditions were arbitrary and served only to mask the real purpose behind the blockade—to deprive the Iraqi people of even the most basic commodities, including food and medicine, until they became desperate enough to overthrow their dictator, Saddam Hussein. The practice of using food aid as a political weapon is nearly always roundly denounced by critics, who point out that the people who suffer from the deprivation are the common people who have committed no wrongs. Government officials and people with political power, whom such embargoes are designed to punish, always find a way to eat well.

Case Study: North Korea

At the beginning of the 1990s, the small communist nation of North Korea created the greatest foreign policy threat the United States had seen since the Cuban missile crisis. Always an isolationist country that had followed an ethic of self-reliance, or *juche*, North Korea became increasingly dangerous after the collapse of its former allies, the Soviet Union and associated European socialist countries. When North Korean plans to develop nuclear weapons and use them as a military threat against South Korea became known, the United States stepped in to negotiate an agreement for helping North Korea develop its nuclear power program, while verifying that the technical assistance was not being used to manufacture weapons. The deal helped the United States to establish relations with one of the most mysterious, closed societies in the world. When the country's stern dictator, Kim Il Sun, died in 1994, his son, Kim Jong Il, took over and immediately downplayed the *juche* ideology. Soon it became clear that North Korea, although still a powerful country that posed a military threat to its neighbors, was a country whose extreme isolation had placed it on the verge of collapse.

North Korea's political and economic turmoil were worsened by devastating floods in 1995 and 1996 that wiped out or damaged almost one million acres, or 20 percent of the country's farmland. The greatest threat to the regime became famine; by 1997 the country lacked half of the cereal and grain supply it needed to feed itself. The government responded by cutting rice rations to a half-bowl of rice per person per day. It became likely that the North Korean people, beginning with the children and the elderly, would begin to die in large numbers.

Typically, in times of famine the United States supplies one-third of the food needed, transferring commodities from the CCC or the FAS to the World Food Program, which distributes it to the people in need. But in this case U.S. response was slow; by 1997 it had supplied only 1 percent of the food aid North Korea said was needed. Congress seemed to be withholding food in order to punish North Korea for its isolationism and occasional belligerence. Those who opposed aid did so on the grounds that it was bad policy to supply food to an enemy nation, one of the world's last communist strongholds, that might divert food aid to its army. It was even argued that the famine was made up by a cynical government that wanted to use food aid either as a stockpile for a future attack or as a political bargaining chip to initiate peace talks with the United States and South Korea.

Alarming reports from observers in North Korea, however, made it plain that the famine was real and far advanced. Many communities were reported to be without dogs and cats because pets had been consumed for food. To supplement their small rice ration, people were eating a weak soup made by boiling tree bark. Many children were balding from malnutrition, and there were even a few isolated reports of cannibalism. The North Korean government itself seemed to confirm the famine by broadcasting recipes for boiling grasses. Such incidents increased the public outcry against U.S. reluctance to lend food aid to the people of North Korea—it was not the government who was being punished, but North Korea's innocent citizens, especially the children.

By the summer of 1997 an increase in food aid to North Korea was still merely being discussed by the United States—and with conditions: food was held out as a possible reward to be given if North Korea agreed to a U.S.-South Korean proposal for peace talks. North Korea's leaders were aware that they needed foreign aid to stay in power but had shown a remarkable resistance to these kinds of tactics, which they, and an increasing number of international advocates, saw as cruel bullying. They refused the conditional offer of food aid, and the famine continued to worsen.

Beginning in the fall of 1997, several events occurred that changed the stances of both governments. Throughout a period of several months, a number of high-level North Korean officials fled the country and publicly expressed concern for the future of their homeland. A few of these defectors offered to reveal secrets about North Korean arms sales. With such highly-publicized evidence of famine in North Korea, the U.S. State Department had little choice but to compel greater contribution to the World Food Program, and in February 1998, the United States pledged 200,000 tons of food to ease the crisis. Similarly, the prospect of having state secrets revealed by top diplomats was disagreeable to North Korea's leaders; eventually, they agreed at least in principle to hold talks with their South Korean neighbors.

In April 1998 North and South Koreans met for the first time in almost four years, breaking the long and hostile silence. With the famine in North Korea far from over, President Bill Clinton pledged in July to send $250 million in surplus U.S. grain to the North Korean people.

FUTURE DIRECTIONS

The Federal Agriculture Improvement and Reform Act, or FAIR Act, also known as the 1996 Farm Bill, involved many provisions that the FAS will be implementing over the next several years. The law was designed to make FAS's export programs more efficient and flexible and to expand export opportunities for American farmers while taking into account the terms of international agreements formed in 1995 at the Uruguay

Round of trade talks, where the World Trade Organization (WTO) was created. Among the provisions of the FAIR Act was to require that between 1996 and 2002 the Commodity Credit Corporation make not less than $1 billion of direct credit or credit guarantees available to emerging international markets for agricultural commodities. The FAS is working with other USDA agencies to determine what these markets are and the CCC is determining how to allocate these resources.

AGENCY RESOURCES

For further information about the work of the FAS, contact the Information Division, FAS, Rm. 5074, USDA, Washington, DC 20250; phone (202) 720-7115. The FAS Web site at http://www.fas.usda.gov is also a good information source; it contains numerous links to sites offering varied information about agricultural exports, international agricultural organizations, and other public and private food-relief programs.

AGENCY PUBLICATIONS

One of the most prominent FAS publications is *AgExporter*, a monthly magazine for businesses selling farm products overseas. *AgExporter* provides tips on exporting, descriptions of markets with the greatest sales potential, and information on USDA export assistance. Other FAS publications include the *FAS Export Directory*, along with attaché reports, food market briefs, food market overviews, and monthly summaries of export credit activities. The FAS also publishes a number of fact sheets on its programs, services, and policies; these fact sheets and several other publications are generally available on the FAS Web site at http://www.fas.usda.gov. For further information about FAS publications, contact the Information Division, FAS, Rm. 5074, USDA, Washington, DC 20250; phone (202) 720-7115.

BIBLIOGRAPHY

Bovard, James. "Plowing Deeper: The New Farm Law Continues the Freedom to Farm Washington." *Barron's*, 15 April 1996, p. 58.

Budiansky, Stephen. "Subsidies Are Dead, Long Live Subsidies." *U.S. News and World Report*, 19 February 1996, p. 36.

Hosansky, David. "After Spats on Price Supports, Farm Spending Moves Easily." *Congressional Quarterly Weekly Report*, 15 June 1996, pp. 1666–68.

Ingersoll, Bruce. "New Farm Law Gives USDA Tools to Expand Exports." *Wall Street Journal*, 12 April 1996, p. A11A.

Kilman, Scott. "Turning the Soil." *Wall Street Journal*, 16 June 1996, p. A1.

Mongelluzzo, Bill. "U.S. Farm Bill Expected to Spur Cotton Exports." *Journal of Commerce and Commercial*, 17 April 1996, p. 1A.

"New Head of Foreign Ag Service Wants to Help Small Exporters." *Successful Farming*, November 1994, p. 29.

"Peace for Food." *Maclean's*, 21 April 1997, p. 27.

Rudnitsky, Howard. "A Healthy Crop." *Forbes*, 5 June 1995, p. 62.

Sanderson, Fred H., ed. *Agricultural Protectionism in the Industrialized World*. Washington, D.C.: Resources for the Future, 1990.

Thirtle, C., J. Harrington, and R. Loader. *Agricultural Price Policy: Government & the Market*. Lanham, Md.: Bernan Associates, 1992.

Foreign Service

PARENT ORGANIZATION: Department of State
ESTABLISHED: May 24, 1924
EMPLOYEES: 7,700 full-time; 9,500 Foreign Service nationals

Contact Information:

ADDRESS: PO Box 9317
Arlington, VA 22219
PHONE: (703) 875-7252
FAX: (703) 875-7243
URL: http://www.afsa.org/index.html
DIRECTOR GENERAL: Edward W. Gnehm, Jr.

WHAT IS ITS MISSION?

Members of the Foreign Service represent U.S. interests abroad. Foreign Service officers work in tandem with employees of other agencies that have missions abroad to implement U.S. foreign policy. Secretary of State Madeleine K. Albright emphasized during a budget briefing in 1997 that "America's strength depends not only on a world class military, but on world class diplomacy."

HOW IS IT STRUCTURED?

The director general of the Foreign Service is appointed by the president, with the advice and consent of the Senate, and serves under the Department of State's under secretary for management. The individual also fills the post of director of personnel for the department. However, candidates for appointment to the Foreign Service are reminded by the department that the Foreign Service is not a single organization, but one whose members might work for the department, the United States Information Agency (USIA), or several other departments or programs within the federal government.

In each nation where the United States maintains an embassy or a consulate, members of the Foreign Service help make up what is known as the "country team." Country teams are headed by the chief of mission and may be composed of hundreds of Foreign Service officers, specialists, and nationals, as well as representatives of other U.S. agencies, or be composed of fewer than a dozen individuals, depending on the size of the nation and its strategic and economic importance. The U.S.

embassy in Saudi Arabia is one of the largest, with more than nine hundred American employees.

A chief of mission is generally an ambassador who acts as the president's personal representative in the country in which he or she serves. Ambassadors are among those at the highest levels of Foreign Service employment. They must be well informed about government activities and operations of the host country and be knowledgeable about the nation's history and culture, its economic system, and its political institutions. They are expected to become skilled in speaking the language of the host country.

There are three career stages for Foreign Service officers: junior officer (or Foreign Service officer—career candidate), career officer, and senior Foreign Service officer. Only the most experienced and capable career officers reach senior Foreign Service status, where they play a major role in the creation, coordination, and implementation of U.S. foreign policy. Junior officers will serve at least their first two assignments abroad, including one as a consular officer protecting the interests of Americans overseas and issuing visas to residents of foreign countries who plan to enter the United States.

Career officers select a "cone" or area in which they will specialize for most or all of their years in the Foreign Service. Cones can have administrative, consular, political, or economic focuses. An exception to this career path exists for officers in the USIA, which serves as its own cone. The public diplomacy functions of the USIA are carried out by public affairs, information, and cultural affairs officers.

Individual overseas assignments for Foreign Service officers range from 18 months to four years. Members of the Foreign Service must be willing to serve anywhere in the world, from war zones in the Middle East, the Balkans or Africa, to the remote island republics of the Pacific Ocean.

Missions abroad also rely on Foreign Service nationals. These are local residents with language skills and cultural expertise who are essential to the transient American staff. Their careers often rival and surpass those of their Foreign Service colleagues in length.

PRIMARY FUNCTIONS

The primary role of the Foreign Service is to ensure that U.S. missions abroad are staffed with the best people available to represent the interests of the Department of State, other federal agencies, the president, and the American people. The functions of Foreign Service officers vary according to specific assignment and circumstance. Diplomatic and negotiating skills are employed to help establish peace, protect the safety of American citizens, and open new markets for U.S. companies.

Ambassadors

An ambassador's day might begin before breakfast, with language lessons of the host country. After arriving at the embassy, the ambassador might review overnight communications from around the world, then begin a heavy schedule of meetings. For Thomas R. Pickering, ambassador to the Russian Federation, those meetings often focused on international peacekeeping efforts, U.S. aid to former republics of the Soviet Union, and the expansion of business opportunities for the more than six hundred U.S. companies operating in Russia. Pickering traveled extensively throughout Russia and as ambassador was called upon to host visits by many U.S. officials, including the president, vice president, and members of Congress.

Foreign Service Officers

Members of the Foreign Service assist with the full range of responsibilities that must be carried out to effectively represent the interests of the United States and its citizens abroad. Foreign Service officers support Americans overseas by finding medical help, locating missing travelers, and assisting in international child custody disputes. They also play a major role in activities of the ambassador, from negotiating treaties to combating international terrorism:

- In August 1990, when Iraq ordered the closing of all embassies in Kuwait following its "annexation" of that nation, Deputy Chief of Mission Barbara Bodine and seven other members of the U.S. embassy staff remained behind. The embassy stayed open for another 137 days serving as a temporary sanctuary until more than four hundred Americans, plus nationals from 30 other countries, could be evacuated.
- Foreign Service officer Susan Crais Hovanec and U.S. Ambassador Peter W. Galbraith embarked on a mission of creative yet dangerous diplomacy when they received permission from local authorities in 1995 to enter war-torn areas of the Balkans. They invited 35 journalists, including representatives of CNN, ABC, and CBS, to join them. The reporters had previously been denied access to the region, but their presence on the mission served as a warning to the warring parties that their actions and atrocities would be monitored and shown to the world.
- In 1977 Foreign Service officer F. A. "Tex" Harris persisted in delivering accounts of human rights violations in Argentina, sending full details to Washington in spite of efforts by some superiors to "put a more favorable 'spin'" on his human-rights reporting. He jeopardized his career to ensure that top-level U.S. officials received complete information related to the Argentine military's war on its nation's own citizens. In 1993 Harris received the Department of State's highest recognition, its Distinguished Honor Award, for his efforts more than 15 years earlier.

PROGRAMS

The personnel mission of the Foreign Service means that a primary function of the agency is the recruitment and training of new Foreign Service officers. In addition, programs administered by the Department of State, in some cases overseen by the director general of the Foreign Service, support Foreign Service members assigned abroad.

Foreign Service written examinations are given annually, with registration forms usually available at many college and university career placement centers or from the Department of State's Recruitment Division. The comprehensive exam is staged at more than two hundred sites across the United States and at U.S. embassies and consulates. It is taken by as many as 12,000 people each year, with only one in five generally scoring high enough to take a follow-up oral exam.

The Foreign Service Institute of the Department of State has as its major function the training of Foreign Service officers, although the program actually serves more than 40 government agencies. The institute offers three hundred courses at its National Foreign Affairs Training Center. Topics include the environment, terrorism, and human rights. Training in more than 60 languages is provided, with Russian, Spanish, French, German, and Arabic in greatest demand. Tajik and Uzbek are among the newest additions.

While abroad, Foreign Service officers and their families may need special assistance to help their lives proceed smoothly. The Family Liaison Office helps spouses maintain a career and find work in the country. The Office of Overseas Schools ensures a good education for children of Foreign Service members, at either local or American-sponsored schools. The Office of Medical Services helps protect the health of Foreign Service members and their families, especially in areas where the quality of local medical care is unreliable.

FAST FACTS

Foreign Service officers serve in 164 U.S. embassies around the world.

(Source: *United States Government Manual 1997/98.*)

BUDGET INFORMATION

A line item does not exist in the federal budget that specifies funding of the Foreign Service. Operations of the Foreign Service and the wages of its domestic and overseas employees are embedded in the International Affairs Budget, which was appropriated $19 billion by Congress in 1998. The diplomatic and consular programs of the Department of State, from which the Foreign Service draws most of its budget, were allocated slightly more than $1.7 billion.

During the middle part of the 1990s, funding for foreign affairs programs of the Department of State remained essentially flat. Faced with a growth in consular workloads, an increase in the number of crises abroad, and a rise in inflation rates in many overseas locations, the department was forced to reduce costs by cutting more than 2,500 employees from its workforce and closing over 30 embassies and consulates.

HISTORY

The Foreign Service was formally established by Congress early in the twentieth century, but the actual foreign service mission of the United States dates back to the American Revolution (1775–83). The origin of the Foreign Service is closely linked to that of the Department of State, especially from the revolutionary period through World War I (1914–18).

In 1775, following the outbreak of war with England, a committee representing the Continental Congress contacted allies in Europe in hopes of gaining their support. In 1789, after independence was won, Congress created the Department of Foreign Affairs (soon renamed the Department of State). Its responsibilities included advising the president on foreign policy and foreign relations.

A basic framework for the diplomatic and consular services that would eventually be provided by U.S. embassies worldwide was established in 1856. However, it took another 68 years, ending with the tremendous loss of life in World War I, for the United States to decide that it must become more involved in international affairs. This prompted the official creation of the U.S. Foreign Service by the Rogers Act (1924) to better represent the country's political and economic interests abroad. The Foreign Service Act of 1946 expanded the agency's responsibilities to include the entire federal government, not just the Department of State, and the Foreign Service Act of 1980 strengthened its recruitment and training activities.

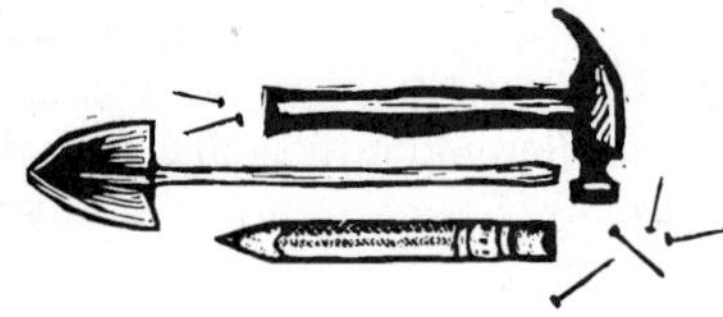

GET INVOLVED:

- Diplomats Online was created by the American Foreign Service Association (http://www.afsa.org/afsadol/index.html) to facilitate exchange between the public and Foreign Service employees. You can access E-mail links to both active and retired Foreign Service personnel to learn about the activities of Foreign Service officers and explore the issues they face.
- The Foreign Affairs Fellowship Program was established in 1990 to help undergraduate and graduate students prepare for a career in the Foreign Service. Approximately 10 fellowships are awarded each year to students who have an interest in a career in the Foreign Service, meet specific academic requirements, and plan to study international affairs at the graduate level. Applications or information can be requested from the Foreign Affairs Fellowship Program, The Woodrow Wilson National Fellowship Foundation, PO Box 2437, Princeton, NJ 08543.
- Information about Foreign Service examinations can be obtained by writing to the Department of State's Recruitment Division, PO Box 9317, Arlington, VA 22219, or calling (703) 875-7490.

CURRENT POLITICAL ISSUES

The Foreign Service and its members face fundamental changes in the nature of worldwide diplomacy that affect how they go about their jobs. Political alliances continue to shift following the end of the Cold War—a period of escalated ideological tension between the United States and the Soviet Union following World War II (1939–45)—while environmental issues cross many national borders. Yet possibly the biggest political issues facing the Foreign Service are internal.

Case Study: Conflict within the Foreign Service

The interests of the United States and its citizens suffer to the extent that their representatives abroad—members of the U.S. Foreign Service—do not reflect contemporary American society based on gender, race, and ethnic background. Dr. Allan E. Goodman, executive dean of the School of Foreign Service at Georgetown University, stated in 1997 that U.S. interests heavily depend on working with and in countries and markets where American diversity should be an asset. He believes that the manner in which people have been recruited to join the Foreign Service has excluded large segments of U.S. society, including women, Catholics, Jews, most eastern and southern European groups, Hispanics, Asians, and African Americans.

Support for Dr. Goodman's contention was voiced in 1997 by native Virgin Islander and career ambassador Terence Todman. Todman was awarded one of the Department of State's highest honors, the Director General's Cup, yet he lamented, "we had fewer African Americans in the Foreign Service in '96 than we did in '83, both in absolute and relative numbers." Further support came in the form of a book, *Journey Into Diplomacy: A Black Man's Shocking Discovery*, by former Foreign Service officer Leaford C. Williams, published at about the same time.

Allegations of sexual discrimination have also been made against the Foreign Service. A grievance filed by Foreign Service officer Alison Palmer in 1971 was expanded into a lawsuit in 1976 but was not resolved for many more years. In an article prepared for the *Foreign Service Journal* in 1996, Dan Kubiske wrote that Palmer's case "would take two full decades to settle—the same number of years as the average FSO's career."

Federal law and various affirmative action policies of the Foreign Service and agencies employing Foreign Service officers are intended to provide greater opportunity for Americans of all backgrounds and to ensure that the country's interests overseas are better represented. It is required by statute today that intensive recruitment efforts be undertaken to ensure that the Foreign Service "reflects the cultural and ethnic diversity of the United States," and the Department of State has declared that its American workforce serving in the Foreign Service must be "truly representative of the American people, while its employment practices must demonstrate the U.S. commitment to the principles of fairness and equal employment opportunity."

FUTURE DIRECTIONS

The Foreign Service is expected to invest heavily in technology in the future, in "a library of databases, expert systems, simulations and web services, plus cybrarians and knowledge managers to design effective decision-support systems," reported David Pearce Snyder and Gregg Edwards in the *Foreign Service Journal* (May 1997). This strategy stems partly from such complex issues as worldwide population growth and the impact of people on the environment that now face members of the Foreign Service. Even traditional issues such as the suppression of terrorism and controlling international drug traffic, Snyder and Edwards added, "are not easily resolvable by a couple of precision air-strikes and an offshore bombardment." Effective diplomacy will require increased access to information, which technology can help provide.

AGENCY RESOURCES

One of the best sources of information about the Foreign Service is the Internet Web site of the Department of State at http://www.state.gov. Included are overviews of the duties and career paths of Foreign Service officers, along with extensive background about diplomacy and specific policy issues confronted by Foreign Service members. In addition, the Web site provides information specific to approximately 80 U.S. diplomatic and consular posts, most of them embassies. The Foreign Service operates a 24-hour career information line for persons seeking information about employment opportunities call (703) 875-7490. Unclassified and declassified documents of the Foreign Service can be inspected in a public reading room operated by the Department of State, located at 2201 C Street NW, Washington, DC. The telephone number is (202) 647-8484.

AGENCY PUBLICATIONS

The Foreign Service and the State Department issue a variety of publications focusing on foreign affairs and foreign relations, travel abroad for Americans, and aspects of Foreign Service employment. Consular information sheets are prepared for all countries and cover issues such as health conditions, political disturbances and areas of instability; also included are the addresses of U.S. embassies and consulates. The information sheets are free and can be accessed on-line at http://travel.state.gov. *Key Officers of Foreign Service Posts—A Guide for Business Representatives* assists American businesses active in or interested in the international market. The *United States Department of State Dispatch*, published 10 to 12 times a year, includes updates on U.S. treaty actions and ambassadorial appointments. *Dispatch* is among the many resources released annually on *U.S. Foreign Affairs on CD-ROM. A Career in the Foreign Service* offers an overview of diplomatic and consular service. For information on these and other publications and materials, write to Public Information, Bureau of Public Affairs, Department of State, Rm. 5831, Washington, DC 20520, or call (202) 647-6575.

BIBLIOGRAPHY

Albright, Madeleine K. "The United States and Assistance to Post-Conflict Societies." *Department of State Dispatch,* December 1997.

Claussen, Eileen B. "U.S. Foreign Policy and the Environment: Engagement for the Next Century." *SAIS Review*, Winter-Spring 1997.

Hecht, David. "Human Rights-Mauritania: 'Slavery' Persists, Or Does It?" *International Press Service English News Wire,* 9 December 1996.

Krebsbach, Karen, ed. *Inside a U.S. Embassy: How the Foreign Service Works for America.* Washington, D.C.: American Foreign Service Association, 1996.

Mak, Dayton, and Charles Kennedy. *American Ambassadors in a Troubled World.* Westport, Conn.: Greenwood Press, 1992.

McClen, Nancy E. *Women in Foreign Policy: The Insiders.* New York: Routledge, 1993.

Miller, Robert Hopkins. *Inside an Embassy: The Political Role of Diplomats Abroad.* Washington, D.C.: Congressional Quarterly, 1992.

Mortensen, Ronald. "Beyond the Fence Line: Lessons from 21 Years Overseas." *HR Magazine,* 1 November 1997.

Newsom, David D. *Diplomacy and the American Democracy.* Bloomington, Ind.: Indiana University Press, 1988.

Rafshoon, Ellen. "Does Humor Play a Role in Diplomacy?" *Foreign Service Journal,* January 1997.

Shapiro, Harold. "Learning from Failure." *Foreign Service Journal,* December 1997.

Snyder, David Pearce, and Gregg Edwards. "The Future of World Affairs." *Foreign Service Journal*, May 1997, p. A16.

Steigman, Andrew L. *The Foreign Service of the United States.* Boulder, Colo.: Westview Press, 1985.

Forest Service

PARENT ORGANIZATION: Department of Agriculture
ESTABLISHED: February 1, 1905
EMPLOYEES: 36,800

Contact Information:

ADDRESS: Auditors Bldg.
201 14th St. SW
Washington, DC 20250
PHONE: (202) 205-1661
TDD (HEARING IMPAIRED): (202) 855-1000
FAX: (202) 205-1610
URL: http://www.fs.fed.us
CHIEF: Mike Dombeck
ASSOCIATE CHIEF: David G. Unger

WHAT IS ITS MISSION?

As set forth in law, the U.S. Forest Service has the responsibility for national leadership in forestry. The agency promotes the health, productivity, diversity, and beauty of forests and associated lands; provides technical and financial assistance wherever it is needed—domestically or internationally—for protection and management of forests and rangelands; and provides work, training, and education in forestry to the public.

HOW IS IT STRUCTURED?

The Forest Service is one of the largest agencies within the U.S. Department of Agriculture (USDA). The under secretary for natural resources and environment is responsible for indirect authority over the Forest Service, but the primary administrator is the chief, who supervises and controls the general direction of Forest Service programs and policy. The forest service consists of several divisions: Administration, Programs and Legislation, National Forest System, State and Private Forestry, Research, and International Forestry. Each of these divisions is led by a deputy chief who reports to the chief. The Office of Administration includes several staffs that exist to serve the agency's internal functions, such as the Office of Information Services and Technology, the Office of Civil Rights, and the Office of Fiscal and Accounting Services. The Office of Programs and Legislation includes staffs that serve to support and promote the policies and programs of the Forest Service; activities such as resource planning, budgeting, collaboration with Congress, and policy analysis are conducted through this office.

The Office of Research develops the science and technology needed to protect, manage, use, and sustain the country's 1.6 billion acres of forest and rangeland. The research is conducted through a network of seven forest experiment stations, along with the Office of Research's Forest Products Laboratory (FPL) in Madison, Wisconsin, and the International Institute of Tropical Forestry, located in Puerto Rico.

The U.S. commitment to natural resource conservation around the world is discharged by the Office of International Forestry, which provides assistance to other countries that promote sustainable development and global environmental stability. The international forestry effort involves input and support from all Forest Service units, along with other government agencies, for policy development, training and technical assistance, research and scientific exchange, and disaster relief.

PRIMARY FUNCTIONS

Through the work of the National Forest System, the Forest Service manages national forests and rangelands and protects them as much as possible from wildfire, pest and disease epidemics, erosion, floods, and water and air pollution. It regulates the harvest of timber on national forest lands and provides access to these lands for the public. It leads a cooperative effort with state and private interests to protect the resources of nonfederal forests and rangelands, and it expands this responsibility with its International Forestry division to provide similar assistance around the world.

The Forest Service performs basic and applied research focusing on three major components: understanding the structure and function of forest and rangeland ecosystems; understanding how people perceive and value the protection and use of natural resources; and determining which methods of protection, management, or use are most appropriate for sustainable production and use of the world's natural resources.

The agency also operates a number of human resources programs, including the Youth Conservation Corps and the Volunteers in the National Forests programs. The Forest Service works with the Department of Labor on several programs that involve American citizens, both young and old, in forestry-related programs.

PROGRAMS

The Forest Service and its divisions operate a number of programs with a wide variety of purposes. By far its most controversial is the timber sale program, which allows the harvesting of timber from National Forest System lands and regulates these harvesting activities. Other programs with broad applications include the Forest Health Monitoring Program, which provides information needed for ecosystem management and the protection of the nation's forests, and the Forest Health Protection Program, which utilizes this information.

The agency also operates more geographically specific conservation programs, usually in conjunction with state or local administrations. One example is the Interior Columbia Basin Ecosystem Management Project, which is a collaborative effort to develop a management strategy for the public lands encompassed by the Columbia River Basin. The Forest Service is also involved in international efforts to restore native populations of Brazilian mahogany.

Several human resources programs, involving both volunteer and paid conservation work, are also organized and operated by the Forest Service. These programs achieve millions of dollars worth of conservation work while providing participants with benefits such as training, paid employment, and worthwhile outdoor experience.

BUDGET INFORMATION

The total budget of the National Forest Service in 1997 was $3.48 billion. Most of the agency budget comes from congressional appropriations; some comes from offsetting receipts from the sale of timber.

Most of the Forest Service budget is spent on the National Forest System (54 percent) and firefighting efforts (22 percent). State and private forestry accounts for roughly the same percentage of expenditures as the reconstruction and construction of trails, roads, and facilities; about 7 percent. Slightly more, about 8 percent, is spent on forest and rangeland research. Together, the International Forestry Program and land acquisition account for much of the remainder of the budget.

HISTORY

The preservation of forests became increasingly important to Americans toward the end of the nineteenth century. Shortly after the first Arbor Day in 1872, the federal government enacted the Timber Culture Law, which sought to encourage forestation by requiring the planting and growing of a certain number of trees as consideration for a deed to a quarter section of land (160 acres) in the public domain. Increased public concern led to the creation of the Division of Forestry (DOF) in the Department of Agriculture in 1881. The DOF was authorized to study forest conditions and disseminate forest information.

BUDGET:
Forest Service

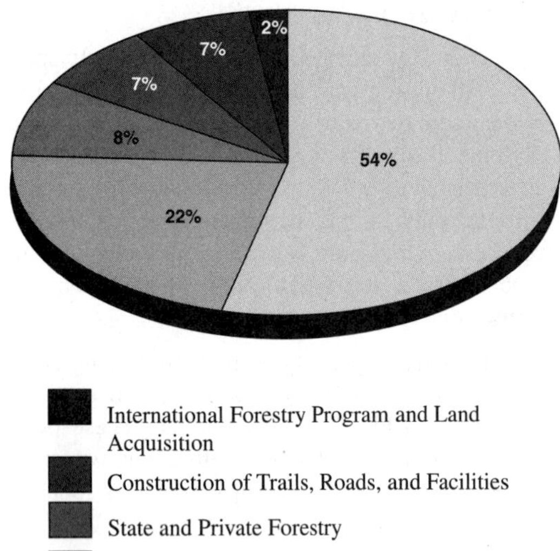

- International Forestry Program and Land Acquisition
- Construction of Trails, Roads, and Facilities
- State and Private Forestry
- Forest and Rangeland Research
- Firefighting Efforts
- National Forest System

In 1891 influenced by the DOF's first ten years of research, Congress authorized the president to withdraw portions of public lands and designate them as "forest reserves." During the next six years, Presidents Benjamin Harrison and Grover Cleveland set aside about 39 million acres of these reserves. Although the DOF created these reserves, the agency placed in charge of the reserves was the General Land Office of the Department of the Interior, which employed no trained foresters and had no plan for protecting and managing the reserves. Gifford Pinchot, who became the head of the DOF in 1898 and is considered to be the first native U.S. professional forester, strongly criticized this arrangement.

With the help of President Theodore Roosevelt, Pinchot drove Congress to change the situation, finally succeeding in 1905 when legislation was enacted authorizing the transfer of control of the reserves to the DOF. The agency had grown considerably since 1881 and had been renamed the Bureau of Forestry in 1901. Soon after the transfer of these reserves, it was renamed the Forest Service. Two years later the forest reserves were renamed "national forests."

The Modern Forest Service

The new Forest Service's program became one of the great campaigns of the twentieth century, a movement for the conservation of forests and natural resources led by Pinchot and supported by President Theodore Roosevelt. During these years the Forest Service adopted a number of principles and practices that it maintains to this day; its belief that the best use of the forests is to provide the greatest good to the greatest number of people over the long run is still a guiding principle. That credo led to the agency's timber management program, which provided for the sale of mature timber from public lands where there was demand and where the considerations of silviculture (forest agriculture) permitted cutting. The Forest Service also adopted a systematic effort to protect the national forests against forest fires, introduced a program of forest research, and in 1908 began establishing forest experiment stations, which were to become important centers for solving forest- and range-related problems in various regions of the United States.

Another product of the Pinchot era was a growing resentment in the western United States of the restrictions imposed by the Forest Service. The national forests restricted agriculture and mining and caused large portions of land to be withdrawn from states' tax bases. These criticisms influenced Congress in 1907 to prohibit any further additions to national forests in several western states without the consent of Congress. In 1908 Congress determined that national forest states should receive 25 percent of the receipts from forest uses for allocations to schools and roads in counties where the forests were located.

After Pinchot

"The Father of American Forestry" fell prey to politics in 1910; after clashing with the secretary of the interior over how to manage the public lands of Alaska, Gifford Pinchot was dismissed by President Howard Taft. The event, however, did not affect the growth of the Forest Service. Over the next 15 years or so, the agency developed its emphasis on federal and state cooperation in forestry and fire prevention. The McSweeney-McNary Act of 1928 launched an even more comprehensive program of forest research and authorized the first of the agency's national surveys of forest resources.

During the New Deal era, after the stock market crash of 1929, the Forest Service's role expanded even further as the principal cooperating agency with the Civilian Conservation Corps. From 1933 to 1942 the Forest Service organized and supervised the efforts of more than one million workers engaged in tree planting, fighting forest fires, and improving recreational facilities. At the same time the Prairie States Forestry Project cooperated with farmers in the Great Plains states to improve farm conditions. These programs were predecessors of Forest Service human resources operations. In 1945 the Cooperative Forest Fire Prevention Campaign introduced Smokey the Bear, who became one of the best-known advertising symbols in the United States. Within a few

Once considered harmful, scientists now believe that occasional fires are natural and healthy for forests. Based on this information, the Forest Service is reevaluating its approach to forest fire management and is developing new methods for coping with wildfires. (Photograph by Robert J. Huffman. Field Mark Publications)

years, the agency began to play a greater role in the affairs of international forestry. The Forest Service continued to expand.

The Forest Service reached a landmark in 1974 with the passage of the Forest and Rangeland Renewable Resources Act. The act, which required the agency to conduct periodic analyses of present and predicted forest usage, along with demands and supplies of forest and range resources, represented the first congressional realization that natural resources management can succeed only when planning and funding are done on a long-term basis.

Events at the end of the twentieth century have called into question two of the strongest traditions of the Forest Service: its timber sales program and its approach to fighting forest fires. Antilogging activists in the United States have become increasingly vocal in their opposition to cutting trees on public lands. In 1997 the one-hundredth anniversary of timber companies' first access to national forest land, dozens of Seattle, Washington, protesters gathered to call for an end to commercial logging on public lands, citing wildlife habitat damage and a corrupt system that had become driven by profit.

The Forest Service's policies and activities dealing with wildland fire fighting have also undergone change; science surveys have shown that the agency's long history of overzealous fire fighting has resulted in the dangerous accumulation of brushy clutter and dry, dead fuel along many forest floors. Such buildup was thought to be responsible for the huge Yellowstone National Park fire of 1988 and the rash of fires across the United States during the drought and record-breaking heat of the summer of 1988. The Forest Service's current policy on wildfire is that fire is a critical natural process that must be integrated into plans for resource management.

CURRENT POLITICAL ISSUES

When the Forest Service was created in 1905, it was placed under the USDA. At that time trees were considered a crop that could theoretically be planted, harvested, and replanted. For many years the logging of federal lands was avoided, not out of principle but because of concern of an excess supply of timber. During the latter part of the twentieth century, however, the U.S. demand for wood products ushered in extensive private logging of national forests. The Forest Service's timber program had long been criticized, but it was not until the 1990s that perceived corruption reached proportions that caused many critics to call for an end to the logging of public lands.

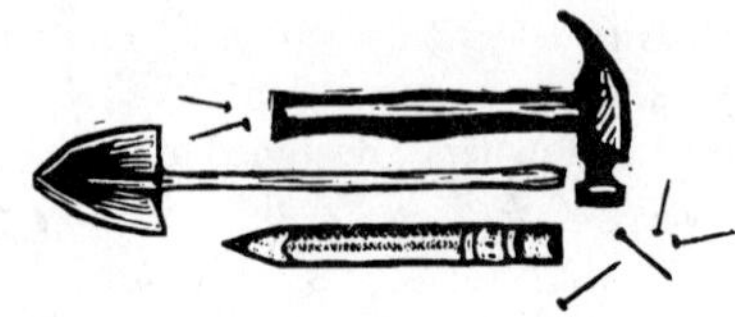

GET INVOLVED:

The Forest Service, through its many human resources programs, offers a number of opportunities for volunteer involvement in the national forests or rangelands. Information on opportunities to get involved in such activities as trail work or campground hosting is available through the periodical "Helping Out in the Outdoors," a directory of more than 500 volunteer positions and internships on U.S. public lands. Published by the American Hiking Society in cooperation with the Forest Service, the directory can be purchased for $7 per copy. To order, contact the American Hiking Society, PO Box 20160, Washington, DC 20041-2160; phone (703) 255-9304; fax (703) 255-9308.

Case Study: The Logging Controversy

Revenue from the Forest Service's timber program and its treatment within the federal budgeting process appears to play a big role in the agency's image problems. Agency officials establish an annual timber-sale goal, put in their budget requests, and then work to ensure that the budgeted sales targets are met. Falling short of a sales target means having to return some of the federal money granted through appropriations and not being able to ask for a higher appropriation the following year. Thus the Forest Service has for years found it necessary to allow private loggers into the national forests. In its mission statement the Forest Service professes to seek sustainable agricultural practices that adhere to silvicultural principles, but as early as the 1960s logging companies found sustainable logging practices less profitable than "clear-cutting" (taking every tree in a given area). Thus, ironically, clear-cutting became known as the unofficial federal timber-harvest policy.

The irony of the agency's dependency on the logging industry does not stop there. An investigation by the Natural Resources Defense Council in the late 1980s revealed that the Forest Service had actually made a profit only three times in its history: in 1955, 1956, and 1969. With costs such as the $30,000–per-mile logging roads required to allow private access to national forests, the Forest Service was doomed to lose money.

Case Study: Salvage Timber

In 1976 a law was passed that allowed trees burned in wildfires to be sold by the Forest Service as salvage timber. The law was intended to give the Forest Service the flexibility to sell small amounts of timber to needy customers, even if such sales were not budgeted. But when forest fires began sweeping the western United States in 1987 an opportunity arose to generate millions of dollars in salvage profits. In 1988 salvage receipts accounted for 7 percent of federal timber sales; by 1993 salvage accounted for 42 percent of the sales.

When record wildfires again swept the western national forests in the summer of 1994, President Bill Clinton expressed an interest in saving the public forests from what the administration viewed as a "health crisis" caused by overmature forests dense with dead and dying trees and brush. The administration talked of "treatment" and "stewardship" instead of logging, but the "treatment" initiative soon spiraled out of control. In a rider to the initiative, the 104th Congress authorized the Forest Service to sell not just dead and dying trees but "associated" green trees that were undamaged. President Clinton intended to veto the rider but was forced by political pressures to give in. Vice President Al Gore later called the signing of the rider the Clinton administration's "biggest mistake."

The day the salvage rider was signed—July 27, 1995—arsonists set fire to 20,000 acres of the Gila National Forest in New Mexico. Firefighters on the ground later complained that the Forest Service provided little air support. Customarily, the agency provides chemical drops that slow fires and make ground work safer for firefighters. At least one plane flying over the flames that day, it was alleged, was there not for air support but to map out an area for a salvage sale.

SUCCESSES AND FAILURES

An indisputable Forest Service success has been the work of its Forest Products Laboratory (FPL) in Madison, Wisconsin. Since its establishment in 1910, the FPL has become the world's outstanding institution for the scientific study of wood and its uses. The laboratory conducts research and technology transfer programs in areas such as fiber and particle products; wood bonding systems; fire safety; pulp, paper, and packaging; and protection from biodeterioration. The laboratory also publishes its findings to meet the needs of the general public, industry, regulatory agencies, and state and private foresters.

FUTURE DIRECTIONS

The Forest Service's Course to the Future, part of its 1997 Strategic Plan, described the agency's plan for providing sustainable forest benefits to the American people and to the world. The Course to the Future established four goals for the agency: to ensure the health and diversity of ecosystems while meeting the needs of the people; to improve deteriorated ecosystems on National Forest System lands by developing the science and technology needed for effective restoration; to meet the multiple-use needs of the American people within the limitations of maintaining ecosystem health and diversity; and to improve organizational effectiveness by creating and maintaining an atmosphere in which people are respected, trusted, and valued.

AGENCY RESOURCES

General information requests can be directed to the Public Affairs Office, Forest Service, Department of Agriculture, PO Box 96090, Washington, DC 20090; phone (202) 205-1760. Inquiries can also be sent to the appropriate regional office. The Forest Service also offers an extensive library of informational and educational videos about such topics as fire, recreation, the history of the Forest Service, and ecosystem management. Video loans are free; the only cost to the user is return postage. A limit of ten videotapes can be borrowed at one time. Send requests to the Forest Service Video Library, c/o Audience Planners, 5341 Derry Ave., Ste. Q, Agoura Hills, CA 91301; phone 1-800-683-8366; fax (818) 865-1327.

Also available is INFOSouth, an on-line library and information service specializing in forestry information. INFOSouth is a cooperative operation involving both the Forest Service and the University of Georgia Libraries and offers access to libraries throughout the world. INFOSouth's Internet address is http://wwwfs.libs.uga.edu.

AGENCY PUBLICATIONS

The Forest Service's publications include books and pamphlets about how to use forest products, such as *Quality Drying of Softwood Lumber* and *Sawing and Related Processes*; pamphlets such as "Tax Tips for Forest Landowners," designed to assist private forestry; and a variety of books for the general citizenry, including *A Guide to Your National Forests*, *Fishing Your National Forests*, *Woodframe House Construction*, and *Silvics of North America, Volume I: Conifers*. To obtain copies, address requests to USDA Forest Service, Auditors Bldg., Washington, DC 20250, Attn: PAO, Publications; phone (202) 205-0957; fax (202) 205-0885.

BIBLIOGRAPHY

Bass, Rick. "The War on the West." *Harper's*, February 1996, pp. 13–5.

Hodges, Glen. "Dead Wood." *Washington Monthly*, October 1996, pp. 12–8.

Langston, Nancy. *Forest Dreams, Forest Nightmares: The Paradox of Old Growth in the Inland West*. Seattle: University of Washington Press, 1996.

McLean, Herbert E. "Hot Logs: Timber Theft on the National Forests." *American Forests*, September–October 1994, pp. 17–22.

Nelson, Robert M. "The Future of the National Forests." *Society*, November–December 1996, pp. 92–7.

Rauber, Paul. "Improving on Nature." *Sierra*, March–April 1995, pp. 44–54

Roberts, Paul. "The Federal Chainsaw Massacre." *Harper's*, June 1997, pp. 37–51.

Smith, Darrell M. *The Forest Service: Its History, Activities and Organization*. New York: AMS Press, 1980.

Steen, Harold K., ed. *Origins of the National Forests*. Durham, N.C.: Duke University Press, 1992.

Williams, Ted. "Only You Can Postpone Forest Fires." *Sierra*, July–August 1995, pp. 36–46.

General Accounting Office (GAO)

PARENT ORGANIZATION: Congress
ESTABLISHED: 1921
EMPLOYEES: 3,500

Contact Information:

ADDRESS: 441 G St. NW
Washington, DC 20548
PHONE: (202) 512-3000
FAX: (202) 512-7726
E-MAIL: majordomo@www.gao.gov
URL: http://www.gao.gov
COMPTROLLER GENERAL: James F. Hinchman

WHAT IS ITS MISSION?

The General Accounting Office (GAO) seeks to ensure honest and efficient management of public funds and full accountability throughout the federal government. As the investigative arm of Congress, the GAO serves the public interest by providing the public, Congress, and federal policymakers with accurate information, nonpartisan analysis, and objective recommendations on the use of public resources. In essence, the GAO is the primary watchdog of the federal government within the government.

HOW IS IT STRUCTURED?

Under the Budget and Accounting Act of 1921, the agency is under the control and direction of the comptroller general of the United States, who is appointed by the president with the advice and consent of the Senate for a term of 15 years. This is a longer term than that of any other nonjudicial officer in the federal government and is designed to firmly establish the independence and nonpartisan integrity of the GAO's work. Once appointed, a comptroller general cannot be removed from office except by a joint resolution of both the House of Representatives and the Senate following an initial notice and a hearing.

The Office of the Comptroller General is assisted in its functions by a deputy comptroller general, a principal assistant comptroller general, and two assistant comptroller generals, one in charge of operations and one responsible for the GAO's planning and reporting. Other support and administrative functions, including human resources, public affairs, special investigations, and congressional relations, are also under the direct control of the comptroller general's office.

The GAO's auditing activities, the bulk of its work, are managed by five audit divisions: General Government; Health, Education, and Human Services; National Security and International Affairs; Resources, Community, and Economic Development; and Accounting and Information Management. Each of these divisions conducts audits and evaluations in its area of expertise and is headed by an assistant comptroller who reports directly to the comptroller general. In 1992 the comptroller general established an external group to advise the agency on its internal financial operations and controls. This group, the Audit Advisory Committee, discusses with and reports to the comptroller general the effectiveness of the GAO's financial reporting and audit processes, internal quality controls, and other processes.

The GAO is also served by assistant comptrollers who are responsible for the agency's own information and communications network and for the agency's own internal policies. Other important GAO officers are the general counsel, who serves as the GAO's legal representative and advises the agency on its decisions, and the chief economist, who is the principal adviser to the comptroller general in matters relating to economic policy. To help the GAO gather data from all parts of the country and distribute information on a wide scale, the agency operates 10 field offices throughout the United States.

PRIMARY FUNCTIONS

The GAO's fundamental activity is supporting Congress—more than 83 percent of the agency's work is done at the specific request of Congress—from studying how well computers could reduce fraud and abuse of the Food Stamp Program, to how prepared the Department of Defense is to deal with a chemical weapons attack, to the challenges of U.S. counternarcotics efforts in Colombia. The GAO is required to do work requested by congressional committees, and as a matter of policy the agency assigns equal status to requests from committee chairs and ranking minority members. To the extent possible, the GAO also responds to requests from individual members of Congress. Although many of its activities are required by law, the GAO also undertakes assignments independently.

In meeting its objective as a congressional support agency, the GAO performs a number of services. Most prominently, the agency audits and evaluates government programs and activities. The issues examined by the GAO cover the entire scope of national concerns, including health care financing, financial management and accountability, law enforcement, banking, information technology, national security, energy and the environment, defense, education and employment, and transportation. If its investigations or audits uncover possible criminal or civil misconduct, the GAO refers the results of its investigations to the Department of Justice or other law enforcement agencies.

The GAO communicates results of its work to Congress and the public; it offers testimony, oral briefings, and written reports regarding virtually every one of its investigations, audits, and legal decisions. GAO findings are used particularly by Congress in making policy decisions. Each month a list of GAO reports released during the previous month is furnished to Congress, its members, and its committees. The reports are also made available to federal, state, and local governments; members of the press; college faculty; students; and nonprofit organizations.

These evaluations, audits, and investigations are the most visible components of the GAO's work and absorb the largest portion of its resources, but the agency has other important functions as well. In conjunction with the Office of Management and Budget (OMB) and the Department of the Treasury, it prescribes accounting standards for the entire federal government and issues generally accepted auditing standards for all levels of government. Likewise, the GAO advises federal agencies on fiscal policies and procedures. The agency also issues legal decisions on subjects involving government revenues and expenditures and on bid protests against the awarding of federal contracts.

PROGRAMS

The GAO generally does not conduct programs or initiatives, as its work is more reactive than proactive in nature. The agency exists to help Congress carry out its agenda, often by assessing how well individual federal offices and agencies are accomplishing their agendas. For example, concerned about the fact that nearly a quarter of aviation accidents in the last ten years have been attributed to weather conditions, Congress asked the GAO to look into the safety inspections conducted by the Federal Aviation Administration (FAA). Specifically, Congress commissioned the GAO to examine the effectiveness of actions the FAA had taken in response to earlier reports by the FAA advisory committee and the National Research Council (NRC) that pointed to problems in FAA management of aviation weather activities. Such findings are available to the public, and the agency's reporting and information management services operate the GAO Research Service, which fields requests for information via fax, E-mail, telephone, and U.S. mail. However, aside from its information distribution activities the GAO has limited contact with the public.

The GAO is more likely to participate in intergovernmental programs like the Joint Financial Management Improvement Program (JFMIP), which is the official

BUDGET:

General Accounting Office

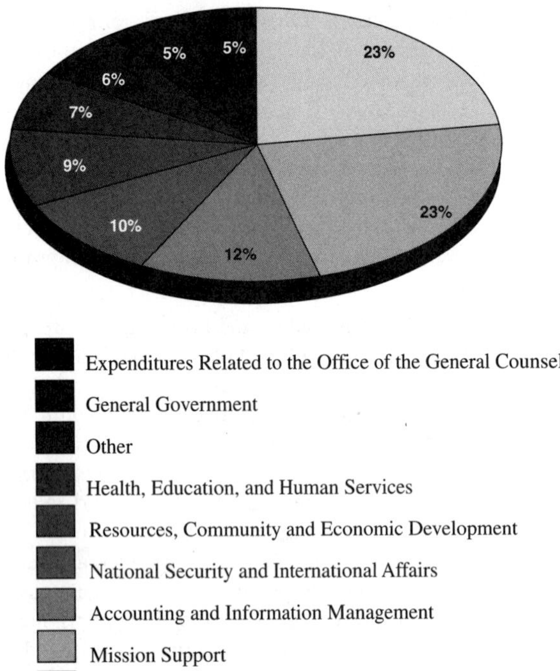

name given to the federal accounting standards that the GAO develops with the OMB and the Department of the Treasury. This program was developed to provide concrete, consistent financial management systems policies and standards for executive agencies to follow in developing, operating, evaluating, and reporting on financial management systems. A series of publications, collectively known as the *Federal Financial Management Systems Requirements,* is a product of this program. These have become the primary source of governmentwide requirements for financial management systems.

Such a system was necessary, according to the National Partnership on Reinventing Government (NPR), because agency financial audits have been subject to varying and conflicting interpretations of accounting standards. Additionally, agency financial systems and processes have been developed by government employees with varying levels of accounting sophistication and expertise, and agencies have sometimes been caught between arguments on standards between the GAO, the OMB, and the Department of the Treasury. Along with the prescribed accounting guidelines, this program incorporates a Federal Accounting Standards Advisory Board, which has representatives from the federal government and private industry and is headed by the GAO's comptroller general, the director of the OMB, and the Secretary of the Treasury.

BUDGET INFORMATION

The GAO budget authority comes almost entirely from congressional appropriations, although it does perform a small amount of work for other agencies for which it is reimbursed. The 1998 GAO annual budget was about $368 million. The two largest areas of expenditure for the agency are the operation of its field offices, and "mission support," a broad designation that includes any work, research, analysis, or reporting done by hired contractors for the agency. Each of these areas accounted for about 23 percent of the agency's budget. Of the five auditing divisions, Accounting and Information Management consumes 12 percent of the budget; National Security and International Affairs, 10 percent; Resources, Community and Economic Development, 9 percent; Health, Education, and Human Services, 7 percent; and General Government, 7 percent. Because of the significant legal implications of the GAO's work, its expenditures related to the Office of the General Counsel are a sizable 5 percent of the budget. Other spending areas are top management, special investigations, and the Office of the Chief Economist.

HISTORY

The GAO has its roots in the U.S. Treasury's Office of the Comptroller and six auditors under the comptroller's authority. The work of these officers was mostly clerical in nature; they verified and checked each government payment, voucher by voucher. In 1921 the Budget and Accounting Act removed these officers from under the authority of the Department of the Treasury and consolidated them under a new chief who would operate independently of the executive departments. The new comptroller general was given the authority to interpret any laws concerning government payments and in addition was assigned the power to investigate "all matters relating to the receipt, disbursement, and application of public funds." The comptroller general's authority was also expanded to include two new and important functions: the submission of reports to Congress that recommended ways to make government expenditures more economical and efficient; and the standardization of accounting systems, forms, and procedures among all government agencies.

The First and Second GAOs

The GAO underwent three distinct changes from 1921 to 1980 that transformed it into an agency virtually unrecognizable from that of its origins. Although certain pieces of legislation were important to this process, it was the influence of individual comptrollers that brought about the greatest alterations. The first comptroller general, J. Raymond McCarl, was an appointee of President Warren Harding and pressed the staff to more vigorously check on the appropriateness of government payments. McCarl also issued advance decisions interpreting the laws governing federal expenditures, but otherwise the first GAO did little else to define accountability among government agencies. McCarl did not appear to think it his agency's place to comment on the wisdom or efficiency of certain types of government expenses or to impose many operational consequences on other agencies with its decisions.

McCarl's interpretations of the laws governing expenditures were generally very restrictive, however, and they often brought him into open conflict with executive agencies. In general the departments believed that the agency had too much central authority. In 1936 President Franklin D. Roosevelt suspended the GAO's authority and attempted to dismantle the organization, distributing its functions among the Department of the Treasury and the Office of the Auditor General. This would have limited the GAO to postaudit reviews and reports to Congress. Roosevelt's redesign was defeated by Congress, and the GAO was reauthorized about four years later.

In 1940 the reinstated GAO began operations under Lindsay Warren, who had accepted the comptroller general position on the condition that Roosevelt and other agencies cease their attacks. Warren believed that to be efficient the centralized voucher-checking system of the GAO should to be distributed among various locations. During World War II (1939–45) GAO operations were divided among offices in Europe, the Far East, and other locations, and Warren began to hire accountants on a large scale, permanently altering the makeup of the GAO staff. The Government Corporation Control Act of 1945 made the GAO a part of the legislative branch, assigning it the status of congressional watchdog.

When Joseph Campbell, a former CPA appointed by President Dwight Eisenhower, took over in 1954, it was the first time a comptroller general's position had been assumed by an accountant. Under Campbell the GAO grew increasingly to resemble, in structure and function, a large accounting firm, concerned primarily with the validity of financial statements.

The Third GAO and Its Contemporary Successor

Further changes in the GAO were largely the work of Elmer Staats, appointed by President Lyndon Johnson in 1966. Staats was a trained public administrator who believed that federal programs should achieve the ends for which they were established. As a result of this philosophy, he greatly diversified the qualifications of his staff. The business of voucher checking was returned to the Treasury Department as Staats and his staff worked to improve the internal financial controls in the departments. Above all, Staats concentrated on making the GAO a useful servant to Congress. Although in any other major government the powers to veto expenditures and establish accounting systems rest with the executive, the GAO under Staats declared them to be legislative authorities. In 1980 the GAO's final break from presidential authority was made official by the GAO Personnel Act, which severed its final ties to the executive branch of government and gave the GAO independent authority over virtually all of its operations.

Throughout the 1980s and into the 1990s, the GAO became increasingly unpopular among certain lawmakers, especially during the conservative administration of President Ronald Reagan, when it was viewed as making unreasonable restrictions on programs that were popular with the president and the congressional majority. From an agency of approximately 5,200 employees in 1980, the GAO saw its budget continually slashed by Congress. Today it is considerably smaller, with about 3,500 employees. In the years since 1980 the Office of the Comptroller General has become a much more politically sensitive position; GAO chiefs do not generally serve as long as they used to, and their appointments are more hotly debated than ever before.

Given the shape and function of today's GAO, it seems likely that Elmer Staats was the official most responsible for altering the course of the agency's work: rather than merely monitoring the amounts of money directed at certain programs to measure their success, the GAO increasingly seeks to verify that taxpayers are receiving clear and measurable benefits from the investment of their money. The contemporary definition of accountability in government has been refined repeatedly by legislation, including the Chief Financial Officers Act of 1990, which required chief financial officers for each of the executive branch agencies; the Government Results and Performance Act of 1993, aimed at improving program performance (in part by developing five-year strategic plans); and the Government Management and Reform Act of 1994, which required that all major government agencies produce annual audited financial statements. Later legislation—the Paperwork Reduction Act of 1995 and the Clinger-Cohen Act of 1996—pushed agencies toward making use of new computer technologies such as the Internet and direct deposit banking in improving their efficiency and performance.

CURRENT POLITICAL ISSUES

Because it is concerned with government efficiency and accountability, virtually every investigation, audit, and report conducted by the GAO involves a political issue, whether the evaluation explores the wisdom of the Pentagon's expenditures on the B-2 bomber or the effi-

FAST FACTS

In fiscal year 1997 the GAO produced 1,337 audit and evaluation products in support of Congress's legislative and oversight needs, including 1,006 reports on Congress and agency officials, 149 informal congressional briefings, and 182 congressional testimony statements delivered by 65 GAO executives.

(Source: General Accounting Office. *Comptroller General's Annual Report*, 1997.)

ciency of penny production at the U.S. Mint. The GAO's methods of inquiry and findings often come under fire, especially when the issue at hand not only concerns financial management, but the efficiency and productivity of an agency as well. In such cases the GAO has been accused of making subjective judgments. An example of such a controversy surfaced in September 1998 when the GAO reported that Congress, in deciding on export policy concerning technology, had relied on a flawed study.

Case Study: Export Controls on High Performance Computers

Trying to gain access to new markets abroad, U.S. computer manufacturers and suppliers lobbied Congress in 1995 to relax the export controls that restricted sales of high performance computers (HPCs) to foreign nations. Such controls had been put into effect in an effort to maintain U.S. superiority in computer technology and to avoid giving other nations, particularly U.S. adversaries, technology such as nuclear weapons programs, cryptology, and other defense programs that could be used against the United States.

In considering a relaxation of export restrictions, the Departments of Commerce and Defense commissioned a study of the likely effects of doing so. The study, conducted by Stanford University, concluded that U.S. computer technology was uncontrollable worldwide and that export restrictions would harm the U.S. computer industry by taking away access to markets that other nations could take advantage of. This report was a major reference source used in considering the relaxation of export controls and President Bill Clinton announced policy changes in 1995. According to a September 17, 1998, *New York Times* article, this fulfilled "a pledge he made early in his administration to computer executives," who argued that restrictions had to be reduced to allow the U.S. products to compete with foreign-made technology that was not controlled and therefore more widely available.

The changes in export policy took effect in 1996. Under the new rules, each foreign nation was classified into one of four categories, based on its level of perceived threat to U. S. national security. Although exports to "category-four" nations remained essentially prohibited, nations classified as one, two, or three could import higher performance units, and in some cases, could acquire them more easily. Civilian end-users in Russia and China, for example, were capable of purchasing computers that were of higher power than their governments without having a license. In addition, the decision of whether or not a license was needed for computer purchasing was transferred from the federal government to the exporters. Exporters also became responsible for screening end-users about how they intended to use the computers and for tracking the exported units.

Within a year after these changes took effect, the Russian and Chinese militaries had acquired several powerful computers from the United States, with 17 computers illegally sent to a Russian nuclear weapons lab. These unintended results led to a GAO investigation into HPC export controls, the foreign availability of HPCs in countries of national security concern, and the validity of the entire Stanford study.

The GAO presented its findings in September 1998. According to the agency, the Stanford report was flawed especially when it concluded that HPCs were already widely available. In addition the GAO discovered that the Stanford researchers "although tasked with doing so, did not assess the capabilities of countries of concern to use HPCs for military and other national security applications" (*Information on the Decision to Revise High Performance Computer Controls*, GAO).

According to the GAO HPCs are not readily available in many countries generally regarded as possible security threats, including China, India, and Pakistan. The GAO report further asserted that the Stanford study lacked evidence to back up its claim that there are insufficient resources to control U.S. technology. Additionally, the agency refuted arguments that export controls needed to be loosened for U.S. products to be competitive, saying U.S. computers dominated overseas markets even before export controls were relaxed.

Stanford rebutted, claiming that the government does not have adequate measures to analyze national security issues; in its report it had focused instead on the availability of U.S.-built computer systems. Under Secretary of Commerce for Export Administration William Reinsch defended the study, saying marketplace realities, not national security, should have been the focus. The computers in question "are becoming less and less controllable because they are becoming smaller, cheaper, more powerful and more reliable, requiring less vendor support," Reinsch told the *Times*.

However, the GAO study continued to plant strong doubts about the validity of the Stanford study. In addition, the number of computer export license applications declined from 459 in 1995 to 125 in 1997. Such statistics show the immediate effect of the relaxed export controls. The executive branch soon recanted and again strengthened computer export controls.

Public Impact

While the United States can do little to inhibit foreign nations from developing their own technologies, it is not compelled to actively assist in the process. By guarding its developments, the United States seeks to stay a step ahead when it comes to military intelligence and capabilities. The GAO helped achieve this through its conclusions that led to change.

The GAO's invalidation of the Stanford study was not the goal of its investigation. Rather the agency had been called upon to evaluate the executive branch's decision and its effects. In doing so the GAO focused heavily on the Stanford study to show how its perceived faults had possibly misled policymakers. The agency made the point that "the study itself identified as a major limitation, its inability to assess capabilities of countries of concern to use HPCs for their military programs or national security applications, and recommended that such an assessment be done. The study noted that trends in HPC technology development could affect U.S. security and the ability to control HPC exports in the future and need to be further studied. Despite the study's limitations, the executive branch decided to relax HPC export controls." While the agency may have offended Stanford, its ultimate purpose was to gauge the soundness of a decision that affects the security of the United States.

SUCCESSES AND FAILURES

The GAO uses two key indicators to determine its own performance. The first is its service to Congress and the results of its work, as indicated by a variety of measures such as financial benefits to the government, improvements in government operations, and the percentage of GAO recommendations implemented. In recent years the GAO has been relatively successful in at least one of these areas: about 70 percent of specific GAO recommendations have been adopted by other federal agencies.

The second measure of the GAO's performance is its own efficiency and effectiveness, measured by job duration, job cost, and timeliness in delivering work results. From 1993 to 1997 the GAO achieved steady improvement in each of these areas: the average duration of each GAO job decreased from 9.5 months to 5.4 months; the average cost of each GAO job decreased from $244,000 to $169,000; and the timeliness of all external products generated by the GAO improved remarkably, from 40 percent on time in 1993 to more than 90 percent in 1997.

FAST FACTS

In fiscal year 1997 the GAO estimated that its work contributed to legislative and executive actions that resulted in $21 billion in savings for American taxpayers.

(Source: General Accounting Office. *Comptroller General's Annual Report*, 1997.)

FUTURE DIRECTIONS

The 1997 Strategic Plan of the GAO outlined a number of broad goals that generally focused on the areas on which the agency had worked for several years: promoting more efficient and cost-effective government; exposing waste, fraud, and abuse in management; targeting spending reductions; and strengthening governmental accountability by focusing on results. Because of dramatic reductions in both staffing and budgeting, however, the GAO will be forced to find new ways of achieving these goals in an era in which measures of effectiveness are becoming highly complex and technical. Among the steps the GAO plans to take to meet this challenge is the evaluation of opportunities for private-sector competition for the delivery of government services—for example, functions such as printing, designing, maintaining computer information networks, and analyzing financial data.

AGENCY RESOURCES

The GAO's Web site at http://www.gao.gov is a vast resource with electronic access to virtually all of its unclassified reports and publications. For help in accessing these resources, refer to the GAO's on-line help desk or call (202) 512-1530. General inquiries about the work of the GAO can be directed to the Office of Public Affairs at (202) 512-4800.

AGENCY PUBLICATIONS

The GAO releases its unclassified reports daily in the *GAO Daybook* and monthly in its catalog "Reports and Testimonies Released in [month/year]." Other publications include complete listings of general comptroller decisions, reference guides such as the *GAO Annual Index*, the *GAO Thesaurus*, and annual abstracts of reports and testimony. The comptroller general's office also issues an annual report to Congress at the end of each fiscal year. Virtually all of these publications are available for viewing or ordering on the GAO's Web site. Printed copies are available from the U.S. General Accounting Office, P.O. Box 6015, Gaithersburg, MD 20884-6015. The first copy of each printed report is free; additional copies are $2 each. Orders must be prepaid by cash or check to the Superintendent of Documents.

BIBLIOGRAPHY

Corn, David. "Muzzling a Watchdog." *Washington Monthly*, January-February 1997, pp. 26–8.

Gerth, Jeff. "U.S. Agency Faults Study on Exports of Computers." *New York Times*, 17 September 1998.

Mosher, Frederick C. *Tale of Two Agencies: A Comparative Analysis of the General Accounting Office and the Office of Management and Budget*. Baton Rouge, La.: Louisiana State University Press, 1986.

Skrzycki, Cindy. "GAO's Rule Sleuths Track Down Agency Compliance." *Washington Post*, 19 September 1997, 1 (G).

———. "What, Business Complain About Governmental Burdens?" *Washington Post*, 10 January 1997, 1 (G).

Smith, Darrell H. *The General Accounting Office: Its History, Activities and Organization*. New York: AMS Press, 1980.

Trask, Roger R. *Defender of the Public Interest: The General Accounting Office, 1921–1966*. Washington, D.C.: U.S. Government Printing Office, 1996.

Walker, Wallace E. *Changing Organizational Culture: Strategy, Structure, and Professionalism in the United States General Accounting Office*. Ann Arbor, Mich.: Books on Demand, 1986.

"The Watchdog Withers." *U.S. News and World Report*, 14 July 1997, p. 15.

General Services Administration (GSA)

PARENT ORGANIZATION: Independent
ESTABLISHED: July 1, 1949
EMPLOYEES: 14,526 (1997)

Contact Information:

ADDRESS: General Services Bldg.
18th & F Sts. NW
Washington, DC 20405
PHONE: (202) 708-5082
TOLL FREE: (800) 688-9889
TDD (HEARING IMPAIRED): (800) 326-2996
E-MAIL: public.affairs@gsa.gov
URL: http://www.gsa.gov
ADMINISTRATOR: David J. Barram

WHAT IS ITS MISSION?

According to the General Service Administration's (GSA) Web site, the mission of the agency is to "provide expertly managed space, supplies, services, and solutions, at the best value, to enable federal employees to accomplish their missions."

HOW IS IT STRUCTURED?

The GSA is one of three management agencies of the federal government that, along with the Office of Personnel Management and the Office of Management and Budget, is independent and falls under the executive branch. The administrator of the agency is appointed by the president and confirmed by Congress. The GSA is organized into four major offices: the Public Buildings Service (PBS), the Federal Supply Service (FSS), the Federal Technology Service (FTS), and the Office of Governmentwide Policy (OGP). In addition to these main offices, the GSA has eight staff offices: chief financial officer, chief information officer, Congressional and Intergovernmental Affairs, Enterprise Development, Equal Employment Opportunity, General Counsel, Management Services and Human Resources, and Public Affairs. Additionally, the Offices of the Inspector General and Board of Contract Appeals, while independent of the agency, work to oversee the agency's functions. The GSA is headquartered in Washington, D.C., and operates 11 regional offices in Boston, Massachusetts, New York City, New York, Philadelphia, Pennsylvania, Atlanta, Georgia, Chicago, Illinois, Kansas City, Missouri, Fort Worth, Texas, Denver, Col-

orado, San Francisco, California, Auburn, Washington, and Washington, DC.

PRIMARY FUNCTIONS

The GSA is responsible for the maintenance of federal workplaces, provides supplies and products to federal employees, and buys goods and services from the private sector for use by the government in all its agencies. The agency performs its functions primarily through its four major offices: the Public Buildings Service (PBS), the Federal Supply Service (FSS), the Federal Technology Service (FTS), and Office of Governmentwide Policy (OGP).

The PBS provides many vital services related to federal buildings throughout the United States. It leases and buys buildings for government use and leases and sells property to the public that the government does not need. The PBS has a design and construction division that hires architects to design structures and contracts construction firms to erect them for federal use. Procuring utilities such as gas, electricity, and water from nongovernment vendors is also one of the PBS's many responsibilities. Finally the PBS operates security for many of the federal agencies and their buildings primarily through the Federal Protection Service (FPS). This organization helps to protect federal employees and property by providing FPS Officers and safety information at all federal sites.

The FSS uses government purchasing power to acquire the materials necessary for all federal agencies to function throughout the world. These agencies include federal office buildings, offices for specific agencies such as the Social Security Office, embassies, the U.S. Capitol, and all other federal sites. The FSS assists federal agencies in purchasing supplies, furniture, computers, tools, and equipment. It is also in charge of arranging for federal travel and transportation needs, managing the fleet of 157,000 federal vehicles and assisting agencies to dispose of items they don't want or need. These surplus items are either sold to the public (usually through government auctions) or transferred to other agencies or nonprofit organizations; there is a Web page on the FSS Internet site called GSA Advantage Online Shopping (http://www.gsa.gov/advantage) devoted to such items.

The FTS contracts for and delivers high-quality telecommunications systems, computer networks, software, hardware, security, and integrated technology services to federal agencies. The FTS also provides citizens with access to government agencies via the Federal Information Center (FIC), the blue pages of local phone books, Federal Information Relay Service, and the on-line Government Information Xchange. The FTS and its vendor partners who supply the equipment and expertise provide government agencies with a wide array of technology to meet their equipment needs.

PROGRAMS

The GSA provides an extensive network of programs that are public-oriented as well as programs connected with the services that it provides to the federal government. These programs are part of a system to make government more accessible and responsive to the concerns and needs of the American people. Several representative examples of these programs include the Consumer Information Center (CIC), Missing Child Poster Program, and the Good Neighbor Program (GNP).

The CIC is the GSA's publications outlet. Consumers can order books and pamphlets on a wide variety of topics. These publications can be viewed on-line free of charge at the CIC site at http://www.pueblo.gsa.gov or ordered for a small fee from the CIC. Typical topics include information on the American Civil War (1860–65), job hunting, and the anatomy of a car's engine. The CIC gathers information booklets, pamphlets, books, and monographs from many government agencies and offers them to the public at a nominal fee. Many of the documents are available at government bookstores, or by writing the Consumer Information Center, Pueblo, CO 81009 for a catalog.

Missing Child Poster Program

As the "landlord for the federal government," the GSA operates all federal buildings and offices in the United States. Millions of people pass through these buildings each year making them good sites to post important notices. Therefore, acting on an order from President Bill Clinton, GSA joined the efforts of the National Center for Missing and Exploited Children (NCMEC) and the Department of Justice to post notices of missing children. Each month the GSA creates ten missing child notices and disseminates them to all federal locations in two different media. Hard-copy notices are displayed on wall bulletin boards; these same notices also run on automated computer displays in the lobbies of the largest federal buildings. The program also operates a Web site with all of the missing children posters available for viewing at http://www.r6.gsa.gov/kids.

Good Neighbor Program

The GNP is dedicated to assisting the communities and downtown urban areas where federal offices and property are located. As a Good Neighbor the federal government provides safe public environments in federal buildings and the neighborhoods around them. The GNP participates in special districts, including Business Improvement Districts, to provide services that physically improve neighborhoods. The GNP also sells federal property for public use and helps raise public awareness of the nation's historic building heritage, making certain these facilities are well maintained and open to the public. The GNP's goal is to become an integral part of any community's redevelopment and resurgence. Program officials sit upon advisory boards, enter into public-private partnerships and participate in one-on-one activities to bring out the "best instincts of government" (*GSA Public Affairs News Release*).

BUDGET INFORMATION

Approximately $13.5 billion was appropriated by Congress to the annual budget for the operations and programs of the GSA. The largest portion of this money (42 percent) was spent on the Federal Buildings Fund. Of the money spent on the Federal Buildings Fund, rental space was the most substantial component, consuming 19 percent of the total GSA budget. Other portions of the budget were allocated to the Information Technology Fund (25 percent), the General Supply Fund (24 percent), reimbursable programs (5 percent) and the Working Capital Fund (2 percent). The remaining 2 percent was spent on other activities such as the Land Acquisition and Development Fund and operating appropriations.

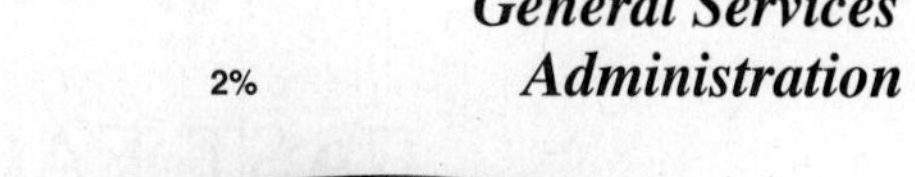

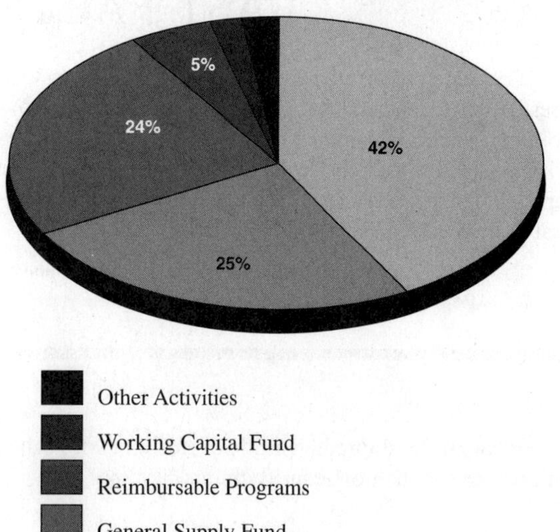

HISTORY

During the 1930s and 1940s, there were many different departments and agencies doing the job of purchasing. President Harry Truman appointed former president Herbert Hoover—an engineer before he entered politics—to head a presidential commission to study federal agencies, streamline them, and examine what savings could be gained by restructuring them. The commission recommended that four small agencies that handled purchasing tasks could be consolidated into one agency to "avoid senseless duplication, excess costs, and confusion in handling supplies" (GSA Web site). The newly formed GSA was given responsibility for all of the federal government's purchases and agencies had to use the GSA to procure supplies, vehicles, and travel. The purchasing system became cumbersome and there were stipulations on everything, even including cleaning supplies, one such restriction was a 1930s rule requiring long distance calls to be monitored and approved by a supervisor. Rules such as this often made the GSA appear slow or unresponsive to customers.

This situation changed in the 1990s. Vice President Albert Gore, under the instruction of President Clinton, undertook efforts to streamline government and make it more "user-friendly." One of the areas where he concentrated his attention was the GSA. In the first Clinton administration, the GSA opened itself up to competition from the private sector. This allowed agencies to make their own purchasing decisions. The FSS had begun already in the late 1980s to open up competition by the private sector to supply items to government agencies. The PBS continued this trend by delegating its leasing authority to agencies, which may choose between the GSA and commercial brokers for leasing services. The policy-making arm of the FSA was separated from its supply duties thus allowing for changes in the way the government buys and leases its products. By 1996 the GSA had redefined itself and was operating as a commercial enterprise and trying to prove itself as better, cheaper, faster and smarter than its private sector competitors. It adopted the theme "Can't Beat GSA Results" and was becoming a market-driven, instead of process-driven, organization. The only GSA service that is still mandatory for federal agencies is its FTS2000 long-distance telephone service.

CURRENT POLITICAL ISSUES

Among duties that the GSA is responsible for, but not well-known for, is the maintenance of federal building security through the PBS department. The Federal Protection Service (FPS) is the unit within the PBS that handles the security function of the GSA and it faces a very difficult task. Keeping federal employees and their buildings free from harm is not easy; the FPS has to cover an enormous number of buildings and areas and is con-

FAST FACTS

GSA employees won 23 Hammer Awards from Vice President Albert Gore for improving the way the government works. Hammer Awards are given to agencies who create new and easier ways to cut bureaucratic red tape and make interactions between citizens and the federal system easier.

(Source: "General Services Administration Annual Report." June 23, 1998.)

---

fronted with the unpredictability of not knowing when and where a breach of security might take place.

Case Study: The Oklahoma City Bombing

On April 19, 1995, a bomb was placed into the Murrah Building in Oklahoma City, Oklahoma. When it exploded, it destroyed a large section of the building and killed 168 people. While extensive rescue and clean-up operations were underway, congressional leaders and the public were unable to understand how this tragedy could have possibly occurred. The PBS and FPS were criticized for not having adequate measures in place to avert the disaster. However, since an act of domestic terrorism on this scale had not been committed before, it would have been difficult to prepare for such an event.

In the wake of the deadly explosion, President Clinton ordered an investigation to assess the security of federal sites throughout the country. The U.S. Marshals Service and its hired security experts classified federal properties and defined the minimum security standards that the FPS needed to implement. They proceeded to inspect all federal facilities and analyzed the security conditions in each. The Marshals Service published its report, *Vulnerability Assessment of Federal Facilities*, in June 1995 and recommended a number of improvements to various federal sites and new constructions based on their findings. The GSA was given the responsibility for upgrading security countermeasures for over 5,000 federal facilities. Congress authorized the GSA to spend $240 million to acquire and install x-ray screening devices, closed-circuit television systems, lighting systems, protective barriers and other devices, as well as significantly increase the number of security guards at many federal facilities.

With these safeguards being put into place, the GSA hopes this type of catastrophe will never occur again. In a statement before the House of Representatives in June 1998, PBS Commissioner Robert Peck stated that numerous security enhancements had been made since the Marshal Service's report. These included a doubling of the number of FPS officers and contracted guards at federal locations and efforts to share more information with other law enforcement agencies in order to be better prepared for any situation that might arise.

FUTURE DIRECTIONS

The GSA plans to help preserve the environment with its newly initiated Planet GSA program. While the GSA has been operating recycling programs and purchasing electric vehicles for its interagency fleet, Planet GSA will step up the GSA's efforts to manage its business of procuring materials and services more responsibly. One of the major innovations of Planet GSA is a new emphasis on constructing buildings that are more environmentally friendly: some of the materials used in construction will be made from recycled substances; buildings will be accessible to mass transit, pedestrians, and bicycles; and the landscape around buildings will have more native plants that should reduce the need for chemical treatment. In addition, Planet GSA will educate federal employees about ways to decrease energy use in buildings and to recycle more waste.

AGENCY RESOURCES

For more information on the GSA, visit its Web site at http://www.gsa.gov, or write to the Office of Public Affairs, General Services Administration, Washington, DC 20405, or phone (202) 501-0705.

In addition, the GSA operates the Federal Information Center (FIC), a single point of contact for people who have questions about federal agencies, programs, and services. If you cannot find what you are looking for, you can call the FIC toll-free number at 1-800-688-9889 (800-326-2996 for TTY users) and ask a FIC information specialist for assistance. The FIC is open for public inquiries from 9:00 A.M. to 8:00 P.M., eastern standard time, Monday through Friday, except federal holidays. The specialists at the FIC can direct you to all GSA programs as well as to those of other federal agencies.

AGENCY PUBLICATIONS

The Consumer Information Center (CIC) provides many publications for the public. In its bimonthly catalog the CIC offers documents from every government agency, some free while others are available at a nominal fee. Some of the published titles include: *1997 Consumer's Resource Handbook, Action Guide for Healthy Eating*, and *Discover America: A Listing of State Tourism Offices of the U.S.*. The GSA offers the following titles through the CIC: *U.S. Real Property Sales List*, *Your Right to Federal Records*, and the *Federal Information Center*. These publications, catalogs, and other documents can be obtained by writing the Consumer Information Center, Pueblo, CO, 81009. Catalogs and publications are also available on-line at http://www.pueblo.gsa.gov.

BIBLIOGRAPHY

"General Services Administration 1996 Annual Report." Washington, D.C.: Government Printing Office, 1997.

"Gore Didn't Open Any Doors." *Business Week*, 27 October 1997, p. 12.

GSA Strategic Plan 1997–2002. Washington, D.C.: Government Printing Office, 1997.

Peck, Robert. "Security In Federal Buildings." *Congressional Testimony*, 4 June 1998.

Shaw, Gaylord. "A Year After Oklahoma City: Lag on Precautions/U.S. Slow To Move on Security Steps." *Newsday*, 16 April 1996, p. A07.

Waszily, Eugene L. "Security In Federal Buildings." *Congressional Testimony*, 4 June 1998.

Government Printing Office (GPO)

PARENT ORGANIZATION: Independent
ESTABLISHED: June 23, 1860
EMPLOYEES: 3,700

Contact Information:

ADDRESS: North Capitol and H Sts. NW
Washington, DC 20401
PHONE: (202) 512-0000
TOLL FREE: (888) 293-6498
FAX: (202) 512-1262
E-MAIL: gpo5@access.digex.net
URL: http://www.access.gpo.gov
PUBLIC PRINTER: Michael F. DiMario

WHAT IS ITS MISSION?

The mission of the Government Printing Office (GPO) is "to fulfill the printing needs of the federal government and distribute government publications to the public." The GPO's responsibilities are outlined in Title 44 of the United States Code. A 1993 amendment to Title 44, the GPO Electronic Information Access Enhancement Act, expanded the GPO's mandate to include the dissemination of government information products online. In effect, the GPO is the largest publisher in the world.

HOW IS IT STRUCTURED?

The GPO is an independent agency under the legislative branch of the federal government. The head of the GPO, the public printer, is appointed by the president with the advice and consent of the Senate. The public printer is required by law to be a practical printer versed in the art of bookbinding. Directly assisting the public printer is the deputy public printer. The GPO has six administrative offices: administrative law judge; general counsel; inspector general; budget; congressional, legislative, and public affairs; and policy coordination. These offices monitor the financial and legal management of the GPO as well as help to direct GPO policy.

The GPO has four functional divisions that are responsible for the day-to-day running of the agency. Customer Services serves as the liaison between government bodies with printing needs and the GPO. Production Services prints and binds GPO publications. The

Office of the Superintendent of Documents disseminates government publications through electronic publishing, sales at its 24 regional bookstores, and placement of materials in more than 1,400 depository libraries nationwide. Finally, the Office of Administration helps manage GPO staff and supplies.

PRIMARY FUNCTIONS

The GPO processes orders for printing and binding made by Congress and the departments, offices, and agencies of the federal government. It procures and provides paper, ink, and other publishing supplies for printing ordered through the GPO. However, the GPO does not publish all government materials.

Another major function of the GPO is to make materials widely and readily available to the public. The GPO prepares and distributes catalogs of government publications and disseminates materials through bookstore sales, library depositories, and electronic products and services. One of the most popular forms of publication for the GPO is GPO Access, an on-line service that provides more than 70 databases for locating government publications and ordering publications via the Internet. Documents such as the federal budget and the *United States Government Manual* may be searched and viewed via the Internet as well. In addition to congressional information, GPO Access includes a wide variety of important executive and judicial information such as the *Federal Register,* the *Code of Federal Regulations, Commerce Business Daily,* Supreme Court opinions, and records for a growing number of federal agencies.

PROGRAMS

While the GPO does not run any programs for the public or other federal agencies per se, its Federal Depository Library Program (FDLP) fills a vital need by placing government publications in libraries across the country. The FDLP provides some communities with access to government information that would otherwise be unavailable to them because of the lack of necessary technology to use GPO Access. Contained within the FDLP are a wide variety of government documents as well as experts on government information to assist those with questions. Nationwide, 1,400 libraries participate in this program—one library for almost every congressional district in the United States.

BUDGET INFORMATION

The projected 1999 budget for the GPO is the same as its 1998 budget, approximately $820 million. Congress appropriates about 14 percent of GPO funds. Two-thirds of these federal funds go toward congressional printing and binding and the remaining one-third covers the salaries and expenses for the Office of the Superintendent of Documents. All other GPO activities are financed through a revolving fund which is reimbursed by payments from customer agencies, sales to the public, and transfers from appropriated funds.

BUDGET:

Government Printing Office

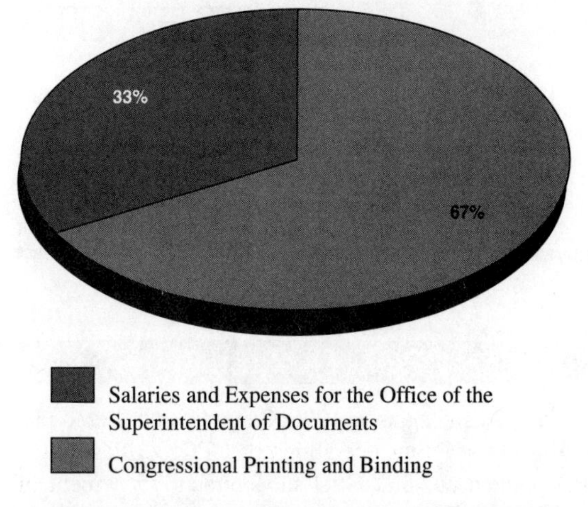

Salaries and Expenses for the Office of the Superintendent of Documents

Congressional Printing and Binding

HISTORY

Before 1860 Congress used systems of contract printing that proved to be inefficient, unreliable, and vulnerable to corruption. To replace these systems, Congress passed Joint Resolution 25 on June 25, 1860, which created the GPO. In 1890 Congress placed the publications distribution activities of the Superintendent of Documents in the GPO to create a link between production and dissemination operations. Title 44 of the United States Code, passed in 1968, outlined and defined GPO operations as they exist today, and the Institute for Federal Printing and Electronic Publishing was established in 1989 to provide training and seminars on various aspects of printing.

In an effort to make government documents more widely available to the public, in 1993 Congress directed the GPO to distribute publications via an increased use of electronic media. The GPO responded by bringing publications such as the federal budget, the *United States Government Manual* and *Congressional Record* on-line by means of GPO Access.

FAST FACTS

The Government Printing Office produces more than 430,000 publications every year.

(Source: Debra Hernandez. "Government Documents Online." *Editor & Publisher,* November 1996.)

CURRENT POLITICAL ISSUES

In 1994 and again in 1996, Congress considered privatizing the printing operations of GPO. Critics of the GPO pointed out that GPO subcontracts 75 percent of government requests to private, or independent, contractors. These orders are paid for by the requesting agency and because the GPO tacks on a six percent surcharge, the government may be paying more for printing costs through the GPO than it would by going directly to independent printing contractors. This surcharge could add as much as $30 million to government printing costs each year. Suggestions for privatizing the GPO included ending its role as a contractor and allowing government agencies to arrange direct printing contracts, creating a system wherein the GPO would contract all printing requests and close its in-house printing facilities.

The GPO and its supporters argued that no private company would want to print an item like the *Congressional Record*, which must be produced overnight and constantly varies in length. GPO supporters also cited the office's improving technological capabilities for immediate reception, printing, and dissemination of the *Congressional Record* and the *Federal Register.* Another argument in favor of maintaining the current GPO structure is the close relationship between the printing and dissemination of government publications. Through the FDLP, the GPO could move in-house publications from its regional plants and contractors to libraries more efficiently than could independent printers that would not have an adequate distribution system.

A 1997 audit by the General Accounting Office (GAO) exonerated the GPO, praising the agency's performance in providing printing services. The GAO also complimented GPO Access, noting it is one of the busiest and most useful Web sites operated by the federal government. Despite these endorsements, however, privatization of the GPO will continue to be debated periodically in congressional efforts to eliminate waste in the federal budget.

SUCCESSES AND FAILURES

The GPO used electronic technology with great success to streamline its prepress systems. CAPNET, a network to a variety of congressional offices, transmits Senate and House proceedings, votes, and bills for the *Congressional Record* directly to the GPO. Drafts of proposed legislation are received electronically from the Senate and House Offices of Legislative Counsel, stored at the GPO, and then accessed on Capitol Hill for revision.

GPO Access has won many awards for the service it provides to the public and other government agencies. In 1995 it won the Madison Award, presented in celebration of Freedom of Information Day (March 16), the birth date of James Madison, who championed the public's right to know. "Once again, it is particularly gratifying to see GPO recognized for its efforts to serve the American public. Our employees have great pride in the role they play in helping to keep their fellow citizens informed," said Public Printer Michael F. DiMario, acknowledging the GPO's selection for the award, according to the GPO Web site (1998).

GPO Access was also named one of the "Best Feds on the Web" in 1997 by *Government Executive* magazine. Criteria for this award include "provid[ing] excellent customer service to the public by having a well-designed site that includes a large amount of useful information; us[ing] the Web to improve business practices in their agencies or across Government; and mak[ing] use of new technologies that other Federal sites should consider emulating." *Government Executive* said GPO Access "provides free electronic access to a wealth of important information published by the Government. The site offers Government information databases for online use, individual federal agency files available for downloading, and tools to assist in finding federal information and user support. Through just this one site, you can access the *Federal Register*, the *Congressional Record*, the *Commerce Business Daily*, and many more publications. It doesn't get more convenient than that."

FUTURE DIRECTIONS

The GPO will further expand its electronic capabilities by exploring plans to convert FDLP to a predominantly electronic system similar to GPO Access. The GPO has planned feasibility studies to include a broad range of participants from both the government and library and information communities. The agency may find that it will have to do this more slowly than it wishes to though, so that smaller public and university libraries can catch up with the technology needed to access such a system. On the other hand the GPO could make the conversion but continue to offer its materials in the more-accessible forms until all libraries have adequate technological capabilities to facilitate an almost totally electronic supply of its materials, so that the GPO does not create barriers to access.

AGENCY RESOURCES

For information about the GPO, access its Web site at http://www.gpo.gov or send a written request to the Office of Congressional, Legislative, and Public Affairs, Government Printing Office, 732 N. Capitol St. NW, Washington, DC 20401. Or phone (202) 512-1991 or send E-mail to gpo5@access.digex.net.

The GPO operates GPO Access, an on-line directory of government publications and documents from the executive, legislative, and judicial branches. Documents that can be viewed and ordered on-line include the *Budget of the United States Government,* congressional bills, economic reports of the president, the *Congressional Record,* and the *Federal Register.* GPO Access is on-line at http://www.access.gpo.gov. Materials available through GPO Access can also be obtained at more than 1,400 libraries nationwide. Contact the FDLP at (202) 512-1119 for information on the depository libraries near you.

AGENCY PUBLICATIONS

GPO publications are available at GPO bookstores, depository libraries, and on-line. Among the tens of thousands of titles available are the *United States Government Manual,* the *Congressional Record, Commerce Business Daily,* and the *Code of Federal Regulations.* The GPO Sales Publications Reference File provides author, title, and subject information on government publications available for sale. The *Monthly Catalog of U.S. Government Publications* is the most comprehensive listing of government publications from federal departments and agencies. These catalogs and all other publications may be ordered by calling the superintendent of documents at (202) 512-1800 or accessed on-line at http://www.access.gpo.gov.

BIBLIOGRAPHY

Gindlesperger, William. "Government Increases Bids: A New Definition of Whether Duplicating is Printing Opens Up Many More Job Bids for the Printer." *Graphic Arts Monthly,* November 1994.

———. "Plugging into the GPO." *American Printer,* June 1996.

Heanue, Anne. "Whither the Depository Library Program?" *American Libraries,* January 1994.

Hernandez, Debra. "Government Documents Online." *Editor & Publisher,* November 1996.

Kranich, Nancy. "Senate to Decide on Fate of GPO." *Library Journal,* March 1994.

Rogers, Michael. "Federal Depository Libraries. Online Via GPO Access Program." *Library Journal,* October 1995.

Health Care Financing Administration (HCFA)

PARENT ORGANIZATION: Department of Health and Human Services
ESTABLISHED: March 9, 1977
EMPLOYEES: 4,000

Contact Information:

ADDRESS: 7500 Security Blvd.
Baltimore, MD 21244
PHONE: (410) 786-3000
FAX: (202) 690-7675
E-MAIL: question@hcfa.gov
URL: http://www.hcfa.gov
ADMINISTRATOR: Nancy-Ann Min DeParle

WHAT IS ITS MISSION?

The Health Care Financing Administration (HCFA) administers the federal Medicare, Medicaid, and child health insurance programs and states its mission as "assuring health care security for beneficiaries through access to affordable and quality health services, protection of beneficiaries' rights, and providing clear and useful information to beneficiaries and providers to assist them in making health care decisions." Since its creation in 1977 the HCFA has worked to remember the needs of the beneficiaries it serves while struggling to control the agency's bureaucracy. As part of a structural reorganization in July 1997, the HCFA restated its mission as written above to reemphasize its dedication to beneficiary service.

HOW IS IT STRUCTURED?

The HCFA is an operating division of the U.S. Department of Health and Human Services (HHS), a cabinet-level department in the executive branch of the federal government. The president, with the advice and consent of the Senate, appoints the administrator of the HCFA. The HCFA headquarters are in Baltimore, Maryland, where staff are responsible for the national direction of the Medicare and Medicaid programs. Regional office staff at 10 locations throughout the country provide oversight of these programs and customer service for their geographic areas.

To support its evolving mission of responsiveness to the needs of beneficiaries, the HCFA established a new internal organizational structure in July 1997. The new structure is built around three large centers, one for each of the agency's customer groups. The Center for Beneficiary Services, the Center for Health Plans and Providers, and the Center for Medicaid and State Operations are assisted and supported by 11 administrative offices that provide support, including financial, clinical, legislative, and information services. Offices of four field executives, called consortiums, were created to represent four geographic areas of the nation: the Northeast, the South, the Midwest, and the West. These consortium offices are to provide oversight of the regional offices and bring local perspectives to decisions made at the top level of the administration.

PRIMARY FUNCTIONS

The HCFA was created to administer the Medicare and Medicaid programs, which finance health care services for more than 72 million elderly, disabled, and poor Americans. The HCFA ensures that state agencies and the health care providers and systems with which it contracts to provide services properly administer Medicaid and Medicare. The agency also assesses the quality of health care facilities and services interacting with its programs and conducts research on the effectiveness of various methods of health care management and financing.

Each of the three large centers within the HCFA are responsible for specific aspects of these functions. As described by the HCFA on its Web site, the Center for Beneficiary Services "serves as the focal point for all of HCFA's interactions with beneficiaries, their families, care givers, and other representatives." Its primary duties are to provide information to beneficiaries (people who receive health care from HCFA programs such as Medicare and Medicaid) about their health care, to provide information to other sections of the HCFA about beneficiaries, and to manage Medicare enrollment and eligibility throughout the HCFA.

The Center for Health Plans and Providers performs the vital function of procuring health care for those who need it through the Medicare program. It handles all issues relating to managed care and fee-for-service care in the health care plan and provider communities. It also decides what benefits Medicare recipients receive and how much these services will cost.

The Center for Medicaid and State Operations facilitates the interactions between the HCFA and all other governments, including those of states, territories, and American Indian and Alaskan Native tribes. It also handles connections with other federal agencies. Most important, it is responsible for all aspects of the Medicaid program.

PROGRAMS

The HCFA administers two major programs, Medicare and Medicaid. Medicare provides health insurance coverage for people age 65 and above, for younger people who are receiving Social Security disability benefits, and for people who need dialysis or kidney transplants for treatment of end-stage kidney disease. In 1996 Medicare provided health care coverage for more than 38 million Americans at an estimated cost of $197 billion. Medicare Part A covers inpatient hospital services, skilled nursing facilities, home health services, and hospice care. Part B helps pay for the cost of physician services, outpatient hospital services, medical equipment and supplies, and other health services and supplies. For persons age 65 and above who are eligible for Social Security, Part A coverage is guaranteed. Coverage under Part B requires payment of a monthly premium.

Medicaid is a jointly funded, federal-state health insurance program for certain low-income people. In 1996 Medicaid provided coverage for more than 36 million people at a cost of almost $100 billion. Within broad federal guidelines, each state establishes its own eligibility requirement for the Medicaid program; determines the type, amount, duration, and scope of services; sets the rate of payments for services; and administers its own program. Thus, the Medicaid program varies from state to state, as well as within each state, over time. To be eligible for federal funds, states are required to provide coverage for most individuals who receive federal income assistance payments. Medicare recipients whose income is so low they cannot afford the monthly premium for Part B coverage may also be covered by Medicaid.

States also have the option to provide Medicaid to other needy populations and receive federal matching funds to provide coverage. Examples of optional groups include infants up to age one and pregnant women whose family income is at or below 185 percent of the federal poverty guidelines, institutionalized individuals whose income and resources are below specified limits, and persons who would be eligible if institutionalized but are receiving care under home-services waivers. Federal guidelines also determine the basic services that each state Medicaid program must provide to receive federal funds. States may also receive federal funds if they choose to provide optional services such as optometrist services and eyeglasses, prescribed drugs, dental services, or services for the mentally retarded.

BUDGET INFORMATION

The HCFA's budget as appropriated by Congress was approximately $170 billion in 1998. The largest chunk of these funds, $99.59 billion or 59 percent, went toward grants to states for Medicaid. Payments to health

BUDGET:
Health Care Financing Administration

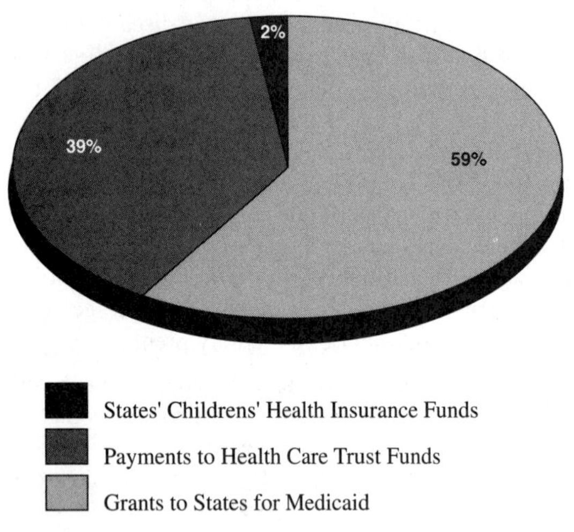

care trust funds were alloted $66.17 billion or 39 percent of the total HCFA congressional appropriation. The final 2 percent was spent on health insurance funds for children in individual states.

The HCFA's budget also includes money dedicated to trust funds. This money in 1998 was approximately $219 billion. The federal hospital insurance trust fund received $140.62 billion or 64 percent of the total trust funds. The federal supplementary medical insurance fund was allotted $77.25 billion (35 percent) of the trust fund money. Health care fraud and abuse control received the final fraction of the HCFA trust fund allowance.

HISTORY

Medicare and Medicaid were created by federal legislation in 1965. The programs were part of President Lyndon Johnson's War on Poverty, an attempt by the federal government to improve the quality of life for Americans living in poverty, especially children and the elderly, through federal assistance programs. Medicare was originally a responsibility of the Social Security Administration, whereas the Social and Rehabilitation Services Administration provided federal assistance to the state Medicaid programs. In 1977 the HCFA was created to more effectively coordinate the two programs and address the issues created by escalating health care costs and the growing number of beneficiaries. Since its creation in 1977 the HCFA has become more involved in investigating and preventing Medicaid and Medicare fraud and abuse, researching and implementing new health care financing policies, and evaluating the impact of the Medicaid and Medicare programs.

CURRENT POLITICAL ISSUES

In 1995 the Medicare Board of Trustees issued a report stating that Medicare funding was in such desperate trouble that the program could remain solvent only until 2001. The reasons for the funding crises are the growing number of beneficiaries—which will soon double, causing skyrocketing health care costs—and the way Medicare is funded.

Part A is funded by a trust fund created by payroll taxes paid by employers and employees. In 1997 the ratio of workers paying Medicare taxes to each Medicare beneficiary was six to one. By the time the first wave of the baby boom generation reaches retirement age, the ratio will dwindle to only two workers to every one beneficiary. Some observers believe the trust fund will gradually be depleted to cover the funding gap and that revenues will fall far short of the program's expenditures.

General taxes cover 75 percent of Part B; the other 25 percent comes from the premiums paid by Medicare beneficiaries. In 1997 beneficiaries each paid $43 per month for Medicare coverage, regardless of income or financial resources, except for the six million seniors covered by both Medicare and Medicaid, who paid no premium. As the number of citizens eligible for Medicare rapidly increases, the amount of general taxes funding the program will not be sufficient to meet the growing expenses. The number of low-income beneficiaries who pay no premium will also increase and add costs. If premiums are not raised for all beneficiaries or are raised according to a beneficiary's ability to pay, funds from premiums will not increase significantly in relation to rising costs.

Economists and some government officials have made it clear that if Medicare funding problems are not resolved, workers who currently pay into the program will never be eligible for benefits because Medicare will be bankrupt. Yet despite the many subsequent reports that confirm the 1995 findings, plans to remedy Medicare's problems have not been forthcoming. Seniors who are receiving benefits or will soon be eligible are unwilling to give up benefits they feel they have earned. Powerful lobbying organizations that represent seniors, such as the American Association of Retired Persons (AARP) and the retiree councils of labor unions, have fought suggested remedies that would result in reduced benefits or higher or income-based premiums. Today's workers resist suggestions that would raise either general or payroll taxes. Middle-age and younger voters refuse to increase their support of a program they might never benefit from. And most politicians are unwilling to make hard decisions affecting benefits, premiums, or increased taxes for Medicare for fear they will lose the support of any segment of voters, especially seniors who represent the largest voting population.

Case Study: 1997 Medicare Reforms

In June 1997 a majority of the Senate voted to approve a bill containing several controversial reforms of the Medicare program in an effort to extend the solvency of the program beyond 2001. The reforms included raising the Medicare eligibility age from 65 to 67, requiring wealthier retirees to pay higher premiums, and requiring nursing home residents to make small copayments. The bill was then sent to the House of Representatives, where it was coolly received.

House Republicans were reluctant to support the unpopular reforms without being sure the bill would also be supported by Democrats. They did not want to be attacked by Democrats as the party at fault if voters and organizations became angry. House Democrats also stalled their response to the bill, waiting to determine whether Clinton would support the proposed Medicare reforms. When it became clear Clinton would not support the bill, House Democrats, and in turn House Republicans, rejected the proposed reforms. Neither the House nor Clinton initiated alternative reform proposals.

During August Congress and Clinton agreed to the Balanced Budget Act of 1997, which included some limited cuts in the Medicare budget. These cuts took the form of limited payments for some physician costs and reduced assistance payments to hospitals that serve high numbers of Medicare patients. These budget cuts were projected to ensure Medicare's stability to 2007, and the president announced that an independent commission would be appointed to investigate and make recommendations on Medicare's long-range future. Thus, the Medicare problem was temporarily solved, although this short-term fix almost certainly guarantees the government will have to address the issue again.

SUCCESSES AND FAILURES

In addition to providing health care insurance to more than 74 million Americans, the HCFA has had success in its efforts to streamline some of the procedures by which health care providers are paid for services. The National Provider Identifier and the PAYERID initiatives have created electronic systems for providers to exchange information with the HCFA and streamline administrative operations. The systems created through these initiatives also facilitate more rapid claims submissions and payments.

FAST FACTS

The 18.7 million children served by Medicaid in 1996 represented one out of every five children in the nation.

(Source: Health Care Financing Administration, 1997.)

FUTURE DIRECTIONS

The HCFA is developing and implementing the Medicare Transaction System (MTS), a state-of-the-art information management system. The MTS will consolidate the multiple systems being used by Medicare providers into one integrated operating system using standardized language, forms, and data. The HCFA estimates the MTS could achieve more than $200 million in annual administrative savings and $500 million in program savings once it is fully implemented.

The agency has also proposed a Healthy Working Families initiative to help more than three million people in unemployed families keep their health insurance for up to six months after a job loss. The new program would provide annual grants to states to finance up to six months of coverage for workers who become unemployed and for their families. The program would be available to people who had employer-based coverage, were laid off, and were below a designated income level. The proposed cost for the program from 1998 to 2002 is $9.8 billion.

AGENCY RESOURCES

Information on the Medicaid and Medicare programs, including eligibility requirements and application information, can be obtained on-line at http://www.hcfa.gov or by calling the HCFA at (410) 786-3000. Information on Medicare is also available at any Social Security branch office.

AGENCY PUBLICATIONS

Medicare has several publications available to the public free of charge on the Medicare program, health care services, and supplemental health insurance programs. Publication titles include *The Medicare Handbook, Guide to Choosing a Nursing Home,* and *Medicare Hospice Benefits.* These titles and many others can be viewed on-line at http://www.hcfa.gov or by calling the HCFA at (410) 786-3000.

BIBLIOGRAPHY

Aston, Geri. "New Medicare Appeal Rules; Federal Court Ruling May Force Even More Revisions." *American Medical News,* 26 May 1997.

Fenninger, Randy. "HCFA's Folly: Effort to Revise Doc's Overhead Expense Pay Is a Failure and Should Be Scrapped." *Modern Healthcare,* 26 May 1997.

Gardner, Jonathan. "Docs Hire Lobbying Guns: Surgeons, Specialists Try to Stall Medicare Fee Change." *Modern Healthcare,* 31 March 1997.

———. "Managed Care Helps Trim Health Cost Hikes." *Modern Healthcare,* 3 February 1997.

———. "Surgeons Face Big Cuts: Budget Deal Assumes 10% Drop in Medicare Fees, But Hospital Freeze Gets Attention." *Modern Healthcare,* 19 May 1997.

Jaklevic, Mary Chris. "Disclosing Doc Incentives: New Rules Force HMOs to Tell How Physicians Are Paid; Consumer Groups Dissatisfied." *Modern Healthcare,* 6 January 1997.

Jeffrey, Nancy Ann. "How to Tell If an HMO's 'Quality' Promise Is Real." *Wall Street Journal,* 13 June 1997.

McIlrath, Sharon. "AMA Hits Medicare Numbers." *American Medical News,* 17 February 1997.

Stephenson, Joan. "Health Agencies Update." *American Medical Association,* 15 January 1997.

Weissenstein, Eric. "HCFA Computer Quandary: Medicare Claims System Won't Do the Job, Detractors Claim." *Modern Healthcare,* 5 May 1997.

Health Resources and Services Administration (HRSA)

PARENT ORGANIZATION: Department of Health and Human Services
ESTABLISHED: September 1, 1982
EMPLOYEES: 2,000

Contact Information:

ADDRESS: 5600 Fishers Lane
Rockville, MD 20857
PHONE: (301) 443-2086 or 443-3376
E-MAIL: comments@hrsa.dhhs.gov
URL: http://www.hrsa.dhhs.gov
ADMINISTRATOR: Claude Earl Fox, M.D., M.P.H.

WHAT IS ITS MISSION?

According to the agency, the mission of the Health Resources and Services Administration (HRSA) is to direct "national health programs which improve the health of the Nation by assuring quality health care to underserved, vulnerable and special-need populations and by promoting appropriate health professions workforce capacity and practice, particularly in primary care and public health." The HRSA focuses on population groups such as migrant workers, the homeless, the uninsured, and rural dwellers. HRSA seeks to improve the availability and quality of primary health services to these populations. "Primary health services" includes more than just basic medical needs such as vaccinations and disease-prevention education. Rather, the HRSA maintains that every person is entitled to more extensive medical services such as prenatal care or an HIV/AIDS treatment program.

HOW IS IT STRUCTURED?

HRSA is an operating division within the United States Department of Health and Human Services (HHS), which is a cabinet-level department in the executive branch of the federal government. HRSA is headed by an administrator who is selected by the secretary of HHS. The administrator reports directly to the secretary. The Office of the Administrator has six divisions: the Office of Equal Opportunity and Civil Rights, the Office of Planning, Evaluation and Legislation, the Office of Communications, the Office of Minority Health, the Office of Management and Program Support, and the Office of Field Coordination.

Reporting to the Office of the Administrator are several offices that support program activities and oversee policy, planning, and operations. HRSA's four program components are the Bureau of Primary Health Care, the Bureau of Health Professions, the Bureau of Health Resources Development, and the Maternal and Child Health Bureau. Additionally, an Office of Special Programs includes a Division of Transplantation, which manages the Organ Procurement and Transplantation Network, the Scientific Registry of Transplant Recipients, and National Marrow Donor Program contracts; the Division of Facilities and Loans, which administers Department of Health and Human Services loans and assists the Department of Housing and Urban Development in operating hospital mortgage insurance programs; and the Division of Facilities Compliance and Recovery, which assures that obligated health facilities provide free or reduced-cost services to those who are eligible. An HIV/AIDS Bureau administers the Ryan White Comprehensive AIDS Resources Emergency (CARE) Act.

PRIMARY FUNCTIONS

The agency seeks to identify the specific needs of populations in order to develop specialized services to address them. For instance, HRSA's Office of Minority Health specifically handles programs and activities that "address the special health needs of racial/ethnic minorities to eliminate disparities, while improving health status." The HRSA determined that racial and ethnic minorities need health care and health promotion systems that take into consideration linguistic barriers and are culturally compatible. Also, adolescents with special health needs are considered underserved because they often lack adequate access to health insurance. The HRSA researches each underserved population so that it can attempt to alleviate the groups chronic health issues. Once a problem is isolated, the agency develops a strategy and goals aimed at addressing it. Sometimes the agency develops programs that it will carry out itself, and other times the HRSA will grant funding to state or local governments to help them expand a program that already addresses a problem.

Programs the HRSA carries out are as diverse as the populations the agency serves. For example, the Bureau of Public Health runs the Community Health Center (CHC) program and the National Health Service Corps (NHSC) program, which provide primary health services in medically underserved areas. The NHSC recruits medical professionals and places them in areas the HRSA has designated as health professional shortage areas. Services at CHC facilities include dental care, acute and chronic care, hospitalization and specialty referrals, immunizations, laboratory tests, pharmacy, and basic health care. In addition, many centers provide transportation, translation, health education, nutrition, and counseling services. CHC provides programs for specific populations including the homeless, migrant and seasonal farm workers, HIV/AIDS carriers, the elderly, and substance abusers. CHC operates programs in over 3,000 communities, serving more than 8 million Americans a year who would otherwise have no primary health care.

HRSA's Bureau of Health Professions (BHP) monitors and guides the development of health resources by providing programs that improve the educational training, distribution, utilization, and quality of the nation's health personnel. BHP programs include the Council on Graduated Medical Education and the National Advisory Council on Nurse Education and Practice. Both of these BHP programs advise the secretary for health and human services and Congress on matters related to the education and practice of nurses and graduate medical students. BHP has also created 26 geriatric education centers (GECs) to prepare for the increasing elderly population. GEC trains health profession faculty, students, and practitioners on the health and treatment needs of older citizens and develops and implements new curricula and training materials on these issues.

PROGRAMS

Though diverse, the HRSA's programs have one objective: to provide medically underserved populations the specific medical attention they need. The agency's Bureau of Primary Health Care serves a broad base of underserved and vulnerable populations that experience financial, geographic, and cultural barriers to care. The bureau targets the needs of groups that include native Hawaiians and Pacific Islanders, school children in poor communities, and substance abusers. For example, this bureau runs the Lower Extremity Amputation Prevention (LEAP) program, for people with Hansen's disease, diabetes mellitus, or any condition that results in loss of protective sensation in the feet. According to the bureau, "the LEAP Program consists of five relatively simple activities: annual foot screening, patient education, daily self inspection of the foot, appropriate footwear selection, and management of simple foot problems."

The HIV/AIDS Bureau runs programs aimed at low-income, uninsured and underinsured people affected by HIV/AIDS. This bureau's programs correlate directly to four titles and Part F of the CARE Act; programs include an HIV emergency relief grant program for eligible metropolitan areas; HIV care grants to states; HIV early intervention services; coordinated HIV services and access to research for children, youth, women, and families; the Special Projects of National Significance program; the HIV/AIDS dental reimbursement program; and AIDS education and training centers. These CARE Act programs, from 1991 to 1998, have cost $4.96 billion.

The Bureau of Health Professions provides leadership in educating and training medical professionals.

These programs are designed to "promote a health care workforce with a mix of the competencies and skills needed to deliver cost-effective quality care; support educational programs' ability to meet the needs of vulnerable populations; improve cultural diversity in the health professions; and stimulate and monitor relevant systems of health profession education in response to changing demands of the health care marketplace." This bureau also runs a consumer-based program, the National Vaccine Injury Compensation Program (VICP), which handles claims of adverse reactions to mandated childhood vaccines, such as diphtheria, tetanus, and pertussis DTP. The VICP received more than 5,000 claims in its first eight years of existence.

HRSA's Maternal and Child Health Bureau administers four major programs: the Maternal and Child Health Services Block Grant, the Healthy Start Initiative, the Emergency Medical Services for Children Program, and grants for HIV Coordinated Services and Access to Research for Women, Infants, Children and Youth. In 1997 the bureau spent $825 million on these programs. This bureau runs additional programs such as the Minority Adolescent Health Program and a hemophelia prevention and treatment program.

The Office of Rural Health Policy (ORHP) runs rural health outreach and rural network development grant programs as well as a National Advisory Committee on Rural Health, which addresses rural issues in medicine, nursing, administration, finance, law, research, business, and public health. The office also oversees Rural Health Research Center programs that focus on areas such as rural mental health services and the impact Medicare reforms will have on the rural community.

The Office of Minority Health deals with the special health needs of racial and ethnic minorities. One major focus of this division is the need for medical care to be "culturally competent," or compatible with the customs and characteristics of the populations it serves. Programs such as the National Hispanic Religious Partnership for Community Health Project and the Minority Management Development Program seek to get minority persons directly involved in helping to solve their communities health and health care issues.

National Hispanic Religious Partnership for Community Health Project

According to HRSA, there is a shortage of bilingual/bicultural Hispanic health providers, Hispanics often lack a regular source of health care, and almost one-third of Hispanics don't have health insurance. The National Hispanic Religious Partnership for Community Health Project, begun in 1996, seeks to overcome such barriers through churches in the Hispanic communities.

The program helps these churches develop a network of comprehensive health services, including AIDS programs, women's centers, youth projects, child abuse prevention, health education, mental health services, rehabilitation programs, and community centers.

BUDGET:

Health Resources and Services Administration

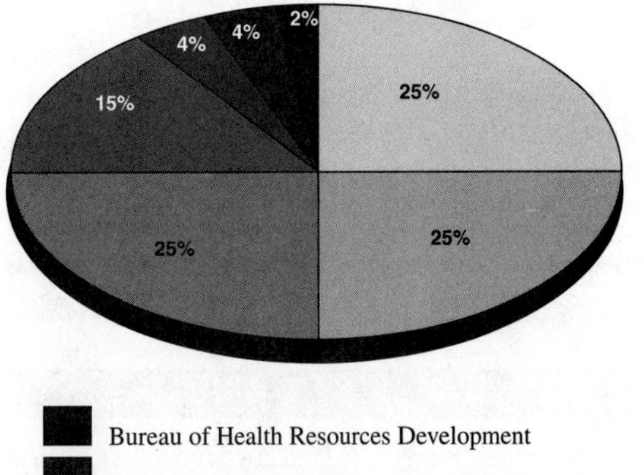

- Bureau of Health Resources Development
- Special Initiatives and the Health Education Assistance Loan Program
- Administrative Costs
- Bureau of Health Professionals
- Activities Related to HIV/AIDS
- Maternal and Child Health Bureau Activities
- Bureau of Primary Health Care Activities

BUDGET INFORMATION

In 1997 the HRSA operated on a budget of approximately $3.6 billion, appropriated entirely by Congress. Approximately 25 percent of the HRSA budget is allocated to the Bureau of Primary Health Care activities, 25 percent to Maternal and Child Health Bureau activities, and 25 percent for activities related to HIV/AIDS that are administered by HRSA's program bureaus. The Bureau of Health Professional receives 15 percent of the budget for its work and the Bureau of Health Resources Development receives about 2 percent. Administrative costs are about 4 percent of the total budget and the remaining funds are spent on special initiatives and the Health Education Assistance Loan Program.

FAST FACTS

Over 43 million people in the United States lack access to primary health care.

(Source: "HRSA Report Shows Primary Care Shortage Continues." *Public Health Reports*, January–February 1996.)

HISTORY

During the 1960s, the federal government established several health services programs to meet the needs of minority and low-income Americans. These programs were part of the Johnson administration's War on Poverty, a comprehensive legislative effort to eradicate the effects of poverty in the United States and provide programs to enhance the quality of life for low-income citizens. In 1968 many of these health programs were brought together under the new Health Services and Mental Health Administration (HSMHA). In 1973 two new public health service agencies were created when HSMHA was dismantled. The Health Resources Administration was comprised of training and construction programs and the Health Services Administration oversaw health delivery activities. In 1982 the two agencies were merged to form the Health Resources and Services Administration and assigned the functions it performs today.

In the political arena of the 1990s, HRSA has enjoyed a relatively secure position. Continued funding, with occasional increases, for HRSA programs has received support from Republicans and Democrats alike. HRSA offers programs and services that are too costly for existing health systems to provide.

CURRENT POLITICAL ISSUES

Because the United States does not have a socialized medicine system, Americans primarily receive health care through private practitioners, whose fees are usually paid by private insurance companies. It is only when such services are inaccessible that the government assumes the health care needs of people. This means the level of care that each person receives varies greatly. The HRSA is responsible for identifying and eliminating the factors that result in low levels of health care and health care quality to specific populations. One of HRSA's objectives is to understand how race or ethnicity can be a barrier to medical attention.

Case Study: HIV/AIDS Treatment in American Indian and Alaskan Native Communities

In its mission of ensuring equal access to health care, the HRSA emphasizes HIV/AIDS treatment programs. Two groups that the HRSA serves, American Indians and Alaska Natives, became the focus of a 1992 HRSA study to determine the barriers or problems that might prevent these people from getting adequate HIV/AIDS treatment.

To make this determination, in April 1992 the HRSA brought together 21 American Indians and Alaska Natives. This sample group was intended to represent "a diverse spectrum of American Indian traditions," according to the resulting HRSA summary report titled *HIV/AIDS Work Group on Health Care Access Issues for American Indians/Alaska Natives.* The group's goal was to identify specific treatment access problems and develop programs to solve them. Over a day and a half, the group identified physical barriers to HIV/AIDS treatment programs, cultural and behavioral barriers, and cultural factors that should be taken into consideration when designing an HIV/AIDS treatment program for American Indians and Alaska Natives.

One major barrier identified was the lack of a stable, equal AIDS/HIV system from Indian Health Service (IHS), an agency of the U.S Public Health Service that provides free health services to American Indians from federally recognized tribes. IHS facility locations are based on the American Indian population distribution of 1955, when few Indians lived in urban areas. While IHS clinics primarily operate in rural communities, many American Indians with HIV live urban areas. "If the services do not exist at a close-by urban clinic the only option is an IHS hospital or contract care service which require one to reside within service boundaries and be a member of the tribe for whom that particular facility or service was established. There are only two IHS health units east of the Mississippi River and only one hospital providing comprehensive care," according to the report. "The American Indians and Alaska Natives live in every State of the United States, making a centralized system of health care delivery difficult."

Additional barriers included the reliance on a seasonal fishing economy, which makes it difficult for inhabitants to leave during peak fishing season to go far for health care; lack of transportation; and limited telephone communications, which makes it difficult to schedule appointments, report laboratory results, and maintain confidentiality.

American Indian citizenship and sovereignty creates funding difficulties because of government-to-government problems, and patients sometimes fall between the cracks. The many levels of bureaucracy—the Bureau of Indian Affairs (BIA), the IHS, state and local governments, and the tribes—reinforce and contribute to health care barriers. An American Indian seeking health care may be bounced between these entities, as there is not a clear-cut system.

Lack of HIV/AIDS prevention education was also cited, with one participant relating the example of a woman who learned that she should be tested every six months. "She did just that, but nowhere along the line did anyone teach her how to keep from getting HIV infection," the report said. Additionally, an American Indian spokesperson has not been identified to make AIDS real for American Indian communities, as Magic Johnson has done for young people and African Americans. AIDS hysteria is high, in part because "American Indians, like many others, do not understand how it is transmitted," says the report. Other cultural barriers that government programs need to address include: confidentiality; the importance of family and traditions; and the lack of knowledge about specific provisions/of the CARE Act, resulting in missed opportunities for services or funding.

Findings such as these will help HRSA and other government agencies better address their clients. Because this particular HIV/AIDS focus group targeted how to improve services to American Indians and Alaska Natives, it illustrates how the culture of a specific community can affect access to health care and therefore how those factors should shape the services offered them.

FUTURE DIRECTIONS

In the future, HRSA will proceed with its multiyear Women's Initiative for HIV Care and Reduction of Perinatal HIV Transmission. This initiative seeks to support innovative programs that will identify women needing services, provide access to care and medication, and promote community awareness programs. Model programs will then be evaluated to determine if they can be established in other communities.

In 1996, HRSA completed a strategic planning process that resulted in priority committees being formed in 1997 for a multiyear process of investigating and making recommendations for action in key service areas. The eight priority areas are: academic and community education partnerships, managed care, state-based initiatives, community infrastructure building, telecommunications and advanced information systems, health in southern border areas, integrated HIV/AIDS programs, and school health and adolescents. Data and recommendations from these committees will guide HRSA's activities in the 21st century as it works to continue to fulfill its mission.

AGENCY RESOURCES

The Bureau of Primary Health Care provides an online database with information on health professional shortage areas, model programs, training for health professionals, state primary-care profiles, drug pricing, and BPHC health centers. The database is accessible by going to the BPHC Web site at http://www.bphc.hrsa.dhhs.gov.

The Bureau of Maternal and Child Health operates the National Maternal and Child Health Clearinghouse (NMCHC) which provides databases, reports, videos, educational materials, and other products related to women's, adolescent's, and children's physical and mental health. The Clearinghouse can be visited on-line at http://www.circsol.com/mch/html/cf/catalog. Information on the Clearinghouse resources can be obtained by writing the NMCHC at 2070 Chain Bridge Road, Suite 450, Vienna, VA 22182-2536 or by calling (703) 356-1964.

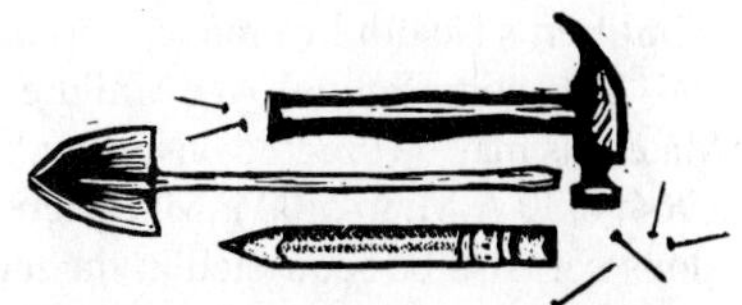

GET INVOLVED:

If you are interested in pursuing a career in any of the health professions as well as providing public service, contact HRSA's National Health Service Corp. for information on obtaining educational grants and scholarships in exchange for future service. Primary care fellowships before and after graduation are also available. NHSC can be contacted at 1-800-221-9393 and information about NHSC programs can be viewed on-line at http://www.bphc.hrsa.dhhs.gov/nhsc/nhsc.html-ssi.

AGENCY PUBLICATIONS

The Bureau of Health Resources Development (BHRD) offers publications on HIV/AIDS, facilities, and organ transplantation. Publications lists can be viewed on-line at http://www.hrsa.dhhs.gov/bhrd/od/pub.htm or ordered by contacting the communications office at (301) 443-6846. Titles of available reports and pamphlets include: "Questions and Answers About Organ Transplantation," "Directory of Facilities Obligated to Provide Hill-Burton Uncompensated Services by State and City," and "Progress and Challenges in Linking Incarcerated Individuals with HIV/AIDS to Community Services."

The Maternal and Child Health Bureau has an extensive catalog of publications available from the National Maternal and Child Health Clearinghouse. Hundreds of pamphlets and reports are available for online viewing at http://www.circsol.com/mch/html/cf/catalog.cfm, including, "Adolescent Health Programs,"

"Children's Health Insurance," "Maternal Weight Gain," and "Parenting School Age Children and Adolescents." Materials may be ordered on-line or by calling (703) 356-1964, 8:30 A.M. to 5:00 P.M. eastern standard time. Catalogs can also be requested at the number above and up to 15 items a month can be ordered free of charge.

BIBLIOGRAPHY

Culhane, Charles. "Budget Raises Community Program Funds, Cuts Education." *American Medical News*, 27 February 1995.

Greenberg, Leonard. "Forecasting The Need For Physicians In The United States." *Health Services Research*, February 1997.

Herbert, Bob. "In America: Health-Care Road Trip." *New York Times*, 31 August, 1998.

"HRSA Report Shows Primary Care Shortage Continues." *Public Health Reports*, January–February 1996.

Jones, Laurie. "HIV: More Research, More Treatment—Still More To Be Done." *American Medical News*, 7 February 1994.

Page, Leigh. "Feds Try To Embarrass Defaulters Into Repaying Loans." *American Medical News*, 3 April 1995.

U.S. Department of Health and Human Services. "HIV/AIDS: Work Group on Health Care Access Issues for American Indians/Alska Natives." Crystal City, Virginia, 1992.

U.S. Department of Health and Human Services. "HRSA Profile 1996." Washington, D.C., 1996.

House of Representatives

WHAT IS ITS MISSION?

The House of Representatives is the lower house of the bicameral (two-chambered) U.S. Congress. The House was intended to be the lawmaking body that links the federal government and private citizens. To fulfill this purpose, the House is designed to be large and responsive to public needs.

HOW IS IT STRUCTURED?

The House of Representatives is composed of 435 representatives. The number of representatives serving each state is determined by the census conducted every 10 years. Each state is entitled to at least one representative, no matter how small its population. Each member of the House, with the growth of the U.S. population over time, has come to serve more than 500,000 constituents.

Members of the House are elected for two-year terms by the people of their states, and all terms run concurrently. There is no limit on the number of terms a representative may serve. To qualify for membership in the House, one must be at least twenty-five years of age and must have been a citizen of the United States for at least seven years prior to election.

The House is required by the Constitution to meet once a year. The Twentieth Amendment established January 3 of the year immediately following elections as the beginning of each session. Each congressional term is usually composed of two annual sessions, excluding special sessions, which may be ordered by the president. It

PARENT ORGANIZATION: Congress
ESTABLISHED: September 17, 1787
EMPLOYEES: 435 representatives plus support staff

Contact Information:

ADDRESS: The Capitol
Washington, DC 20505
PHONE: (202) 224-4121
E-MAIL: LRC@clerk.house.gov
URL: http://www.house.gov
SPEAKER OF THE HOUSE: Robert L. Livingston
HOUSE MAJORITY LEADER: Richard Armey
HOUSE MINORITY LEADER: Richard Gephardt
HOUSE MAJORITY WHIP: Tom DeLay
HOUSE MINORITY WHIP: David Bonior

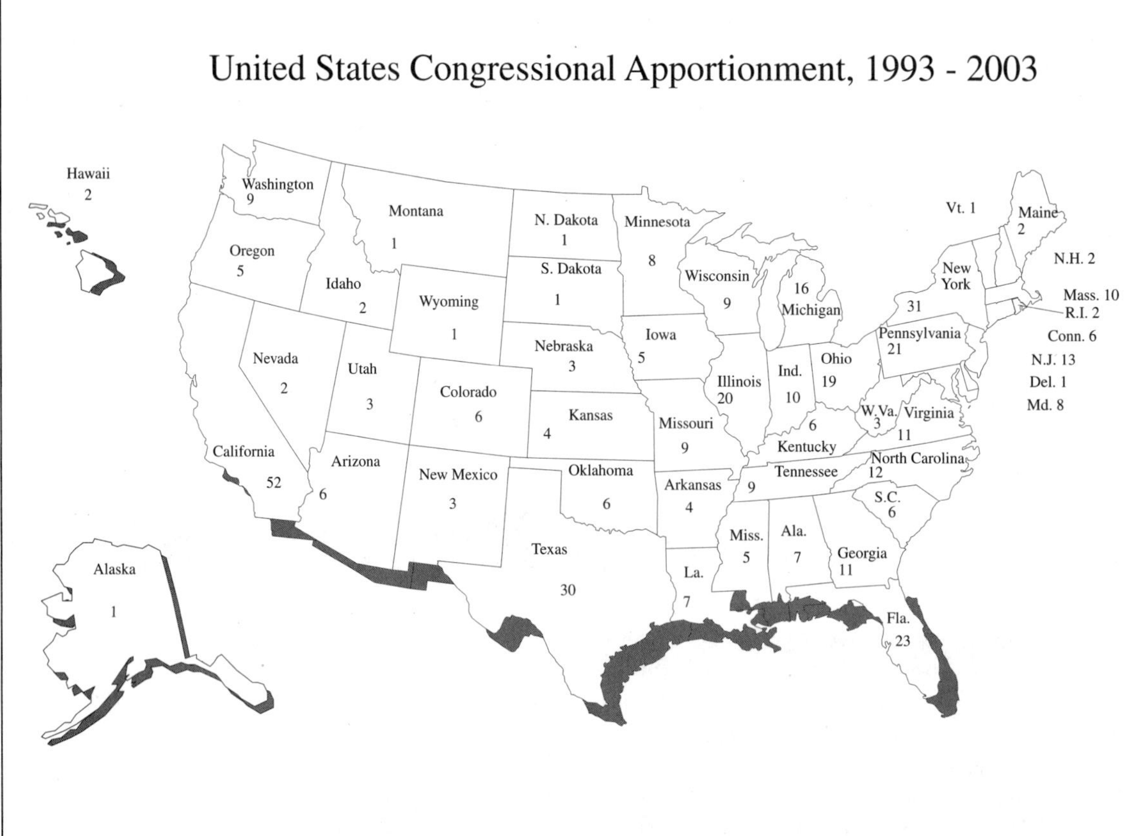

The House of Representatives has a total of 435 full members. The number of representatives serving each state is determined by the census conducted every 10 years. Figures are based on data from the 1990 census. There are also five delegates, who represent the District of Columbia and four islands closely linked to the United States: Puerto Rico, Guam, the Virgin Islands, and American Samoa.

has become tradition to refer to each congressional term by number; the term that began after the 1996 congressional elections was designated the 105th Congress.

House Leadership and Power Structure

The Speaker of the House. The presiding officer of the House of Representatives is the Speaker of the House. Although the Speaker is elected by the House, this election is a matter of form; he or she is always elected by a straight party vote. That is, all members from the same party vote for the same person, so the Speaker always represents the majority party. The Speaker's tenure is limited to four consecutive congressional terms. The Speaker of the House is second in line, behind the vice president, to succeed to the presidency in the event of an emergency.

The Speaker is widely regarded as the most powerful person in Congress. In presiding over the sessions of the House, he or she puts questions to vote and announces the vote, appoints chairpersons for the Committee of the Whole, chooses Speakers *pro tempore*, and exercises control of the floor through his or her power to grant or deny recognition to members who ask to address the chamber. Assisted by the parliamentarian, the Speaker interprets and applies all rules of the House and is the final authority on every House action.

The Speaker also exercises considerable influence over the fate of proposed legislation. The Speaker alone has the power to refer bills or reports to a committee or sidetrack legislation through the various scheduling authorities at his or her disposal. Although a majority of House members may overrule the Speaker's interpretations or applications of the House rules, this rarely happens since the Speaker himself represents the majority.

The Speaker *pro tempore* is appointed by the Speaker to preside over the House in his or her absence and is almost always a member of the majority party. The Speaker may appoint the Speaker *pro tempore* to preside up to three legislative days without approval by the House.

The Majority and Minority Leaders. The majority leader in the House is second in command to the Speaker and is selected by secret party caucus (a closed meeting of party members) He or she is the floor leader and chief party strategist for the majority party in the House, and in this role helps design, promote, negotiate, and defend the majority party's agenda. One of the main ways he or she does so is coordinating with party members and bringing them together as a unified, voting force, for or against proposed legislation. The majority leader consults with the president about the administration's proposals.

The House minority leader guides opposition in the House; the post is always assumed by the minority party's candidate for Speaker. As spokesperson for his or her party, the minority leader defends the rights of the minority party, especially in respect to committee membership. The minority leader analyzes and criticizes the policies and programs of the majority. The minority leader rarely offers a legislative program; if the president is of the minority party, however, the minority leader promotes the president's proposals.

Party Whips. The majority and minority whips are elected by party caucus to serve as assistant party leaders. The whip helps to solidify support of the party agenda by encouraging unity and discipline among the party membership, as well as by ensuring that members are present for votes and quorum calls—calls by the Speaker to see whether a quorum, or majority of the House membership, is present. The whips also survey individual members on pending issues, in order to inform the party leader of the membership's stance on proposed measures. Because much of the party leader's time is spent on scheduling, strategy sessions, and conferences, the whips serve as the link between them and individual members.

The Committee System

In the House of Representatives, most work, especially the drafting and revision of bills, is performed in committees. Although not mentioned in the Constitution, the committee system is an intricate hierarchy of power that has evolved over time in response to the growing complexity of the House's work. A committee's work—and its relative power in the House—is decided by the committee's jurisdiction and by its status (standing, select, joint; and legislative or nonlegislative). Ultimately it is committees that sift through the thousands of proposed measures that are referred to them and decide which measures are important enough or promising enough to send to the floor for House debate.

Standing committees have a permanent staff and broadly defined duties that are mandated by law. These committees have been established either by public law or by permanent amendment to the House rules. The legislative committees (including Agriculture, Commerce, and International Relations) generally correspond to the organizational divisions of the executive branch. Important standing committees in the House include those assigned to review the budget requests of the federal departments. Non-legislative committees include those charged with overseeing the spending habits of the federal bureaucracy (the Committee on Government Reform and Oversight). Other committees such as Rules or House Oversight are responsible for overseeing the internal workings of the House itself.

Most standing committees have a number of subcommittees. In general, the broader the committee's jurisdiction the greater the number of its subcommittees—the Appropriations Committee, for example, is currently composed of thirteen subcommittees. House subcommittees are usually responsible for the first markup session of a bill—the session in which the content and language of the bill are revised and agreed upon.

Select or special committees are established periodically to study special problems or concerns—such as drug abuse or violent crime. Usually—but not always—the work of these committees is investigative in nature, rather than legislative. A significant example is the joint House and Senate panel that investigated the Iran-contra affair in 1987 which involved key government figures in a plot to sell arms to Iran. The duration of select committees is determined by the House resolutions that create them. Most last for only one or two terms, although a few are actually permanent.

Joint committees are panels, typically permanent, that are created by law or resolution. They consist of members from both the House and the Senate and do not have legislative authority. For example, the Joint Economic Committee is a permanent committee which examines national economic problems and reviews the execution of economic and budgetary programs.

Negotiations between majority and minority party leadership, who act on votes and recommendations of their prospective caucuses, determine the size and membership of the committees. While House standing rules do not stipulate how many members from each party must be in a committee, the caucuses usually arrive at a concensus proportional to the parties' strength in the House. The chairman of each committee is a member of the House majority who is elected by the majority caucus. The chairman calls meetings and establishes agendas, schedules hearings, chairs markup sessions, recommends participants to committee discussions (conferees), controls the budget of his or her committee, and serves as the spokesperson for the committee—as well as spokesperson of the party, in his or her area of expertise.

BIOGRAPHY:
Jeannette Rankin

Congresswoman and Reformer (1880–1973) Jeannette Rankin was a social activist, a suffragist, the first woman elected to the U.S. House of Representatives, and the only member of Congress to vote against U.S. entry into both world wars. When Rankin secured her seat in the House in 1916, she became not only the first woman ever elected to Congress, but also the first woman elected to any national legislature in a Western democracy. When the House voted on U.S. entrance into World War I, Rankin was advised by many to approve the resolution. But she broke congressional precedent by rising to her feet and commenting, "I want to stand by my country, but I cannot vote for war. I vote no." During the war Rankin concentrated on civil liberties. She helped secure equal employment for women, exposed illegal working conditions, and introduced a bill that called for government-sponsored instruction in maternity, child care, and birth control. When Rankin's term in the House ended in March 1919, her legislative career only came to a temporary halt. Rankin was active as a social worker and peace advocate until 1939 when she was reelected to Congress. She again took an antiwar stance, introducing bills to slow U.S. entrance into World War II. On December 8, 1941, Rankin cast the only vote in Congress against declaration of war on Japan. In the next election Rankin was not reelected, but she continued to work for the pacifist cause into her nineties, opposing the Cold War and U.S. involvement in the Korean and Vietnam wars.

The only committee chairman who is not elected by party caucus is the Chairman of the Committee of the Whole. The Committee of the Whole comprises the House's entire membership. Bills that raise or disburse money must be considered by the Committee of the Whole. During the House's regular session, the Speaker of the House can turn the House into the Committee of the Whole without a vote. After doing so, he names a member of the majority party as chairman to preside over the work of the committee. When the committee's work is finished, it returns to regular session (resolves itself) by rising. Then the Speaker returns to his platform and delivers the committee's recommendation on passage or rejection of a measure.

Other Important Officers

Clerk of the House. The clerk is the House's chief administrative officer. He is nominated by the Speaker and elected by the majority caucus. The clerk is responsible for most House operations—taking votes, certifying bills, processing legislation, and keeping daily records of all debates and proceedings. The Office of the Clerk is the official repository of all published documents produced by the House and its committees.

Sergeant-at-Arms. The sergeant-at-arms, under the direction of the Speaker, maintains order and civility in the House, and enforces its rules. The sergeant-at-arms has the power to "arrest" absent members and bring them into the chamber during sessions. This office is also the keeper of the mace—a sizeable silver-tipped staff that is the symbol of parliamentary authority in the House.

Parliamentarian. The parliamentarian administers the procedural rules of the House, which are numerous and complex. The Speaker customarily consults the parliamentarian for procedural advice before making a ruling. Although the parliamentarian is usually appointed by the Speaker, this office is considered a nonpartisan position, and typically is held regardless of changes in the House's political control.

PRIMARY FUNCTIONS

Together, the House of Representatives and the Senate form the U.S. Congress, which is responsible for raising taxes, coining money, declaring war, and raising an armed force. The broad function of Congress is to "make all laws which shall be necessary and proper for carrying into Execution the foregoing powers, and all other powers vested by this Constitution in the Government of the United States" (Article I, Section VIII of the Constitution). The passage of these laws involves a complex interplay among the House of Representatives, the Senate, and the president. Because there are two senators from each state, the Senate represents areas, whereas representation in the House is based on population and represents numbers. The Founding Fathers intended that this balance should exist.

In addition, the House and Senate share the right to propose amendments to the Constitution whenever two-thirds of both houses consider it necessary. If two-thirds of the state legislatures demand changes to the Constitution, it is Congress's duty to call a constitutional convention. Proposed amendments may only be ratified if three-fourths of the state legislatures agree.

In an effort to keep one house of Congress from dominating the other, the Constitution provides each house with special powers that are not shared. The House of Representatives alone is granted the power to originate all appropriations bills, or bills for the raising of revenue. The House is also the sole body within the U.S. government that can bring charges of impeachment against federal officials who are suspected of misconduct. After such charges are made by the House, impeachment proceedings are referred to the Senate, where the charges are tried.

The House of Representatives has three primary responsibilities: it makes laws, serves the U.S. public as a representative assembly, and oversees the administration of public policy by the federal government. Legislative duties are shared with the president and the Senate; all bills passed by the House must also be passed by the Senate and signed by the president. If the president refuses to sign the bill, or vetoes it, the veto may be overridden by a two-thirds majority in Congress before becoming law. If Congress is not in session and the president has a bill for more than 10 days it is automatically killed. This is a pocket veto.

Because of the size of the House's membership (435), voting is more complex than in the 100-member Senate. Occasionally the House will take several votes on the same proposition. Most decisions in the House are reached when the chamber is sitting as the Committee of the Whole. A voice vote is the simplest method of voting and is usually used when a measure first comes before the House. The Speaker asks the membership in favor of a measure to shout, "aye," and then those opposed to shout, "no." The committee chair then determines the results. If the results of a voice vote are unclear, or if a single House member calls for a further test, a standing vote may be demanded—first members for the measure stand up; then those against stand up to be counted by the chair. Only vote totals are recorded; there is no record of how individual members voted.

Most House votes are recorded votes, which show how each member voted on a bill or amendment. The House uses an electronic voting system in which a member's "yes" or "no" vote appears next to the member's name on a huge electronic board that is mounted behind the Speaker's desk. The traditional "roll call," when the Speaker calls upon each member to announce his or her vote, is rarely used because of the time it takes to record the votes of all 435 members.

House members spend a large amount of time attending to duties related to their districts. They often travel from the Capitol in Washington, D.C., to their districts, and frequently meet with constituents who visit Washington. Each representative has a personal staff

HOUSE COMMITTEES

Standing Committees

- Agriculture
- Appropriations
- Banking and Financial Services
- Budget
- Commerce
- Education and the Workforce
- Government Reform and Oversight
- House Oversight
- International Relations
- Judiciary
- National Security
- Resources
- Rules
- Science
- Small Business
- Standards of Official Conduct
- Transportation and Infrastructure
- Veterans Affairs
- Ways and Means

Select Committees

- Permanent Select Committee on Intelligence
- Select Committee on U.S. National Security and Military/Commercial Concerns with the People's Republic of China

Joint Committees of Congress

- Joint Economic Committee
- Joint Committee on the Library
- Joint Committee on Printing
- Joint Committee on Taxation

FAST FACTS

The term whip was first used in the British Parliament in 1769; it comes from the whipper-in of British fox-hunting, who was responsible for keeping the fox-hounds from leaving the pack.

(Source: *How Congress Works*. Congressional Quarterly Publications, 1991.)

which answers correspondence, attends to constituent concerns, and develops legislative proposals beneficial to the people of the district.

The federal government has grown substantially during the twentieth century, and the House has had to devote increasing amounts of time to overseeing federal policies and programs. Despite the size of the federal government, and the reluctance of many agencies to be examined by Congress, the House has risen to the challenge by appointing new oversight subcommittees and by expanding its support staff.

BUDGET INFORMATION

Unlike most government departments and agencies, the House does not operate programs; therefore, approximately 90 percent of its annual budget, which totaled about $1.4 billion in 1998, is devoted to the salaries and expense accounts of individual representatives and their staffs. Members of the U.S. Congress are among the most highly paid officials in the federal government, earning $136,673 each year. Members holding leadership positions, such as the Speaker of the House ($175,400) and the House Majority and Minority Leaders and Whips ($151,800), are paid considerably more. The remainder of the House budget is consumed by allowances and expenses including official mail, administrative costs, federal tort claims, and employee benefit programs.

HISTORY

The basic structure of Congress was decided at a very early stage of the Constitutional Convention of 1787. From the beginning it was agreed that the national legislature should be bicameral—composed of both a House and a Senate—in order to ensure that one body could check or restrain the other and guard against abuses of power. During the convention, the method of electing the first branch of the legislature, the House of Representatives, was heatedly debated. Some believed that most Americans lacked the knowledge to make informed decisions about representation, and were likely to be misled by deceitful politicians; the membership of the House, they believed, should be decided by the state legislatures. George Mason and James Madison, however, were among those who believed that the House should reflect as much as possible the democratic principles of the newly formed United States. Eventually, this argument won out, and it was decided that the House of Representatives would be selected through direct popular elections. In order to ensure that the populace was being fully represented, it was decided that their representatives would stand for re-election frequently: every two years.

The first Congress that met in 1789 was composed of 59 representatives. Its first task was to elect a Speaker of the House (Frederick A. Muhlenburg of Pennsylvania) and to determine its rules of procedure, which were largely modeled after English parliamentary practice. These early procedural rules quickly proved cumbersome, even for such a small membership. There were no time limits placed on the right of members to speak. To save time the Speaker was given the right to appoint all committees unless otherwise directed by the House. Because the number of select committees chosen to draft and propose individual measures increased beyond control (and then ceased to exist once their measures had been decided), the first standing committees to consider related measures began to emerge in the House.

During these formative years, the House began to experience the powerful influence of political parties, an issue that had not been addressed by either the Constitution or the early House rules. The aristocratic Federalists, led by Alexander Hamilton, and the Democratic-Republican followers of Thomas Jefferson and James Madison, engaged in the first partisan power struggles within the House. When Jefferson became president in 1801 and his party enjoyed a House majority, the House of Representatives operated in the shadow of the executive; for the most part, the legislative process was dominated by the president and the Democratic-Republican caucus.

The Nineteenth-Century Rise and Fall of Congressional Power

The president's dominance of Congress came to an end with the election of James Madison to the presidency in 1809. Madison quickly lost control of his party to a group of young congressional "war hawks" who pressured him into declaring war on England, which resulted in the War of 1812. Led in the House by Henry Clay of Kentucky, these young radicals resisted presidential control and marked a shift of power to Congress that was to last for twenty years. Though only 34 when he entered the house in 1811, Henry Clay was promptly elected to the Speakership by the Democratic-Republicans. He was a charismatic and tactful politician who greatly enhanced the power and prestige of the Speaker, and who used his position to pack House committees with his fellow war hawks.

Several conditions soon arose that threatened the Speaker's power, as well as party unity within the House. The size of the House was increasing rapidly in proportion with the population; by 1820 Congress had nearly quadrupled in size, to 213 members. With the right of floor debates still essentially unlimited, the House attempted to refine its procedures. In order to relieve the entire chamber of endless debate and delay tactics, the standing committee was established as the principal forum for the first and most detailed consideration of proposed legislation. The rapid growth in membership also gave rise to differing opinions within parties, and as a result the party caucuses were no longer as powerful. Electors to the electoral college were increasingly chosen by popular vote in the states, rather than by the caucus. The emergence of this mass electorate brought Democrat Andrew Jackson to the White House in 1828, and he dominated Congress throughout his entire presidency.

Under Jackson, congressional power was further weakened by partisan infighting. The issue of slavery was growing as a national concern, and as the United States began to expand beyond the Mississippi River, the debate over whether to assign "free" or "slave" status to new states and territories infiltrated every aspect of House politics. Contests for the Speakership created bitter rivalries within majority parties that lasted until the American Civil War (1860–65), when the Democratic and Republican wings of the majority party split permanently.

FAST FACTS

The record for longest service as Speaker of the House is held by Texas Democrat Sam Rayburn. Rayburn continuously held the post from 1940 until his death in 1961, except for two stints as minority leader from 1947 to 1949 and 1953 to 1955.

(Source: *Guide to Congress*. Congressional Quarterly, Washington, 1993.)

The Civil War and Political Turmoil

The South was all but eliminated from national politics by the Civil War, and the region's dominant political party, the Democrats, also suffered as the nation attempted to rebuild itself after the war—a period that came to be known as Reconstruction. While the Republican president, Abraham Lincoln, attempted to steer a moderate course in rebuilding the South, the radical wing of his party in Congress, working virtually unopposed, wanted a more aggressive approach that would exact greater punishment from the defeated Confederate enemy. The radicals passed a bill placing all reconstruction authority under direct congressional control, but Lincoln effectively vetoed the bill by refusing to sign it before the congressional session expired (pocket veto).

The radical Republicans in the House struggled even more forcefully with Lincoln's successor, Andrew Johnson. The bill giving reconstruction authority to Congress was passed over Johnson's veto, and the continued friction between the executive and the legislature led to the House's impeachment of Johnson in 1867. Although Johnson was later acquitted by the Senate, he had been effectively stripped of power by the House's political maneuvering.

The Civil War had produced an unchecked surge in government spending, and this became an overriding concern in the House until the turn of the nineteenth century. Much of the problem, most congressmen believed, was that too much power was held in committees such as Appropriations, which controlled virtually all of the spending bills. Over the next few decades, the House revised its rules to distribute legislative power among the various standing committees. In order to further address its continuing procedural problems, the House made the Rules Committee—which governed the amount of time to be allowed for discussion of major bills—into a permanent standing committee as well.

This intended reform created more problems than it solved, because the Speaker of the House was considered to be the chairman of the Rules Committee. Two Republican Speakers—Thomas Brackett Reed (1889–91) and Joseph Cannon (1903–10) used the Rules Committee to exercise virtually dictatorial powers over the proceedings of the House, and were able for some time to defeat any attempts at further reform by using the House rules to deny discussion of these measures. The Speaker's power was finally curbed by a House resolution known as the Norris Resolution, authored by a coalition of Democrats and moderate Republicans. The Norris Resolution stripped the Speaker of all authority to appoint committee members and their chairmen and removed him from the Rules Committee. The House committees were thereafter to be selected by party caucuses.

The Beginning of the Modern House

The Norris Resolution marked a resurgence in the power of the party caucuses, which now followed party leadership in determining the members and chairs of all House committees. The method of reaching consensus as to the composition and leadership of the committees was increasingly decided upon the seniority system, with key chairmanships and ranking minority positions going to those who had served the longest in Congress. The seniority system is still in force today, though to a much lesser degree as reforms have been undertaken to open up leadership positions to newer members with fresh ideas.

The early twentieth century ushered in several important changes in both the role and structure of the House of Representatives. Until 1920 there was no centralized system or single congressional procedure for drawing up the federal budget. When President Woodrow Wilson wanted to increase executive control over expenditures within the executive branch, a new budget system was proposed and passed into law as the Budget and Accounting Act of 1921. With the House now responsible for reviewing the entire federal budget in a single package endorsed by the president, responsibility for reviewing budget estimates again rested almost entirely within the subcommittees of the House Appropriations Committee.

One of the most significant issues to arise during the early twentieth century was the question of reapportioning congressional members to match the state populations. It was becoming clear that simply increasing the House membership to correspond to increases in population was no longer workable; the House had already swelled to 435 members by 1910. In 1929 a permanent method for reapportionment, based on state populations, was made into law.

From 1919 to 1933, the House was dominated by Republicans who were able to significantly stall reform in the conduct of House sessions. Since the House's earliest days, the tradition of the "short session" had been held; the terminating date of the first session of Congress was extended from March to January 3 of the following year, leaving a short two-month session that had to be ended in March, upon the expiration of the congressional term. House leaders liked the short session because it helped them to control legislative output; the goal was nearly always to delay rather than advance measures. This short session became known as the lame duck session because from January to March, many congressional members who had been voted out of office were still allowed two months to exercise their influence over the legislative process. This was intolerable to most citizens, as well as to most Progressive House members. A constitutional change was proposed in 1931 by George W. Norris of Nebraska, the same Progressive who had helped check the Speaker's power more than twenty years earlier, and within a year was made into law. The Twentieth Amendment to the Constitution (known as the Lame Duck Amendment) required each congressional session to expire on January 3 of the year following elections.

From the New Deal to the Post-War Era

The Great Depression that began in 1929 foretold an end to Republican dominance in the House; with 12 million Americans unemployed by 1932, Franklin Roosevelt was elected president along with a commanding Democratic majority in both chambers of Congress. Throughout much of his administration, which lasted an unprecedented four presidential terms, Roosevelt and his congressional counterparts put the president's New Deal programs into action. His dominance of House Democrats was finally challenged by a conservative coalition of Republicans and southern Democrats who were opposed to the president's levels of federal spending, and who managed to control the Rules Committee with an iron hand. Many later New Deal programs were blocked by this committee.

The demands of World War II (1939–45) on the United States vastly expanded the powers of the president and the executive branch, which, unlike Congress, could take swift action in response to national concerns. A need to keep pace with the executive branch, and to be more responsive to the needs of the people, quickly became a congressional priority in the aftermath of World War II. Working jointly, the House and the Senate composed and passed the Legislative Reorganization Act of 1946, which cut down on the number of standing committees in both houses; limited House members to serving on only one committee at a time; established a joint budget committee for estimating annual federal receipts and expenditures; and attempted to cut the workloads of congressional members by allowing them to hire more professional and clerical staff members.

The Legislative Reorganization Act of 1946, however, is historically considered to be a failure. Its few reforms at making congressmen more efficient were soon dropped as unrealistic, and it did nothing to address what had been, and would remain, two of the most crucial issues facing Congress: the balance of power between the executive and legislative branches of government, and the distribution of power within the Congress itself.

The most troublesome obstacle to a balance of power within the House remained the ability of the Rules Committee to effectively censor the legislative agenda, even one belonging to a congressional majority. Partisan and unproductive infighting stigmatized House sessions for over two decades, until the House was able to force changes in the powers of the committee and its chairman in 1967.

Additional pressures for reform were beginning to mount from both within and without the House regarding both the conduct of congressional investigative committees (such as the House Un-American Activities Committee, which played a prominent role in the Communist "witch hunts" of the 1950s) and the scandalous abuses of congressional privilege committed by a few members. One congressman in particular, Adam Clayton Powell (D-N.Y.), perpetrated a number of offenses, some as brazen as keeping his wife on his congressional payroll at a salary of $20,000 although she lived in Puerto Rico. In 1967 the Democratic Caucus removed Powell from his chairmanship of the Education and Labor Committee, but was unable to remove him permanently from the house—that task fell to voters in his district, who refused in 1970 to nominate him for another term.

The Powell case helped persuade the House to adopt its own Code of Official Conduct, which spelled out in detail the guidelines all House members must follow. Along with the continued perception of Congressional inefficiency, it also inspired the second major legislative reorganization of the century, the Legislative Reorganization Act of 1970. The bill attempted to shed some light on the secret dealings of congressional committees; for the first time, members were forced to disclose their positions on all major legislative issues. The House also made its proceedings more accessible to the public. By the mid-1970s, all markup sessions were declared open to the public unless a majority voted in open session to close them. The televised impeachment proceedings of President Nixon in 1974 led to increased public interest in the daily operations of the House. In 1979 a permanent, high-quality television broadcast system, the Cable Satellite Public Affairs Network (C-SPAN) operated by House employees, began providing full coverage.

An Era of Partisan Warfare

The House passed campaign finance laws in 1972, 1974, and 1976, which brought about major changes in the way House members ran for office. The election measures did much to open the election process to the press and the public, but many critics believed it increased the reliance of members on funding from political action committees (PACs) and other big-money interest groups. Several separate pieces of legislation were proposed during the 1990s to address this issue, but all were defeated in either the House or the Senate—as incumbent politicians, representatives are understandably reluctant to pass a law that would make it easier for a less well-funded or well-connected challenger to defeat them.

When Ronald Reagan, a Republican, was elected president in 1980, the House remained under Democratic control, and party differences became more antagonistic. Throughout the mid-1980s, Republicans used outdated House rules to disrupt floor proceedings, frustrate Democratic leaders, and advance the legislative agenda of the president. The partisan unpleasantness seemed to reach a boiling point in 1984, when Newt Gingrich, a representative from Georgia, gave a speech that attacked the foreign policy views of the Democrats in an unusually harsh manner. When Speaker Tip O'Neill (Thomas P. O'Neill) called Gingrich's speech "the lowest thing I have ever seen in my thirty-two years in Congress," the House had no choice but to reprimand O'Neill for his lack of decorum.

The hostile partisan atmosphere in the House continued throughout the administrations of Presidents George Bush and Bill Clinton, and during these administrations congressional elections often produced dramatic turnarounds in House membership and leadership. While some analysts claim these elections—such as the elections of 1994, in which the Democrats lost control of the House and Democratic Speaker Thomas Foley was voted out of office—indicated a shift in voters' party affiliations, others have interpreted them as a product of the electorate's disenchantment with the continued power struggles of incumbent representatives and their congressional factions. The increasingly bitter partisanship in the House is commonly mentioned as a prime reason to consider contemporary reforms—but given the obstructive political atmosphere of the House, little has been done to address the issue.

CURRENT POLITICAL ISSUES

Arguably the most political of all U.S. government organizations, the House of Representatives is involved in practically every issue that affects the American society. Because the House is intended to be the most intimate link between U.S. citizens and the federal government, however, there is at least one issue that historically has been identified exclusively with the House: the defining and redefining of congressional districts for the purpose of popular elections.

Article I, Section II of the Constitution set forth the guidelines for congressional elections as follows: every two years, members are to be chosen by the people of the states, and the number of representatives will be apportioned among the states according to their populations, which will be determined in a decennial (every ten years) census conducted by the federal government. Aside from these requirements, the Constitution leaves how to divide or apportion the state districts up to individual state legislatures.

Political scientists and historians have often remarked that in outlining the nation's legislature, the framers of the Constitution failed to anticipate the powerful influence that would be exerted by political parties in Congress. Nowhere is this influence more apparent than in the reapportionment process that has been used to divide the states into districts. In fact, it took less than two decades after the ratification of the Constitution for politics to infiltrate the redistricting process; in 1812, Massachusetts governor Elbridge Gerry signed into law a redistricting bill that was designed to ensure continued majorities for his party, the Democratic-Republicans. For the first time, congressional districts in a state were drawn not according to boundaries that defined discrete communities within the state, but according to the voting trends of the population. To this day, this sort of redistricting is known as "gerrymandering."

After the number of representatives in the House was fixed at 435 in 1910 and the U.S. population continued to grow, the gerrymander began to be refined as a political tool. Following each ten-year census, Democrat and Republican representatives in each state gather to carve up the landscape into gerrymandered districts. Incumbents use increasingly sophisticated computer software, demographic data, and professional statisticians to determine the boundaries of their districts. According to critics of this process, the politicians are in effect choosing their voters before their voters have a chance to choose them. Most voters are locked into one-party districts by this process, and are left with only one real choice—to ratify the incumbent of the party controlling their district. In recent elections, there have been few close decisions: two-thirds of the 1996 congressional elections, for example, were decided by landslides of 20 percentage points or more. Detractors of the redistricting process allege that low voter turnout in the United States, among the poorest of contemporary democracies, is caused by the fact that American voters do not feel their vote will make a difference.

Redistricting has become a reform objective in the American political process. Despite several high-profile court cases in the 1990s, the issue has yet to be definitively resolved. Critics present several arguments for reform: first, the redistricting process should be made as public as possible, to make obvious "power grabs" by politicians more open to media attention and public input. Second, the process should be taken out of the hands of incumbent politicians and turned over to an independent, nonpartisan commission. This process has been used by the state of Iowa since 1981, and in the opinion of many has produced more competitive elections. Finally, instead of the "winner take all" form of democracy, where it is possible for a Democratic representative to serve a district that is 49.9 percent Republican, the states should try a "proportional representation" system, in which most voters would be able to win at least some representation in Congress. Though proportional voting is used in many strong democracies throughout the world, it is seen as a radical idea in the United States, and it is not viewed by many as a likely solution to the problems facing the redistricting process.

In the United States racial politics influence the political process. The primary tool used to perpetuate this influence is gerrymandering.

Case Study: The Voting Rights Act and Racial Gerrymandering

Gerrymandering took a new direction when African American citizens were granted the right to vote following the Civil War. By drawing districts not along geographical lines but according to demographics, states created voting districts dominated by large blocs of white voters who would essentially cancel out the votes of African Americans and other minorities. The right to vote by African Americans, especially in the South, was also restricted by state poll taxes and literacy tests, which effectively barred many poor blacks from even registering to vote. The Voting Rights Act of 1965, a product of the civil rights movement led by Martin Luther King, Jr., struck down many of these barriers to the African American vote.

As amended, the legislation also addressed gerrymandering. Under the Voting Rights Act, a state wishing to redraw its districts must submit its plan to the Justice Department or a three-judge panel of the Federal District Court. The panel must be convinced that the change does not undermine minority voters. For the better part of the 1990s, beginning with the administration of President George Bush, the Justice Department has taken the view that it can not only fail to approve redistricting plans that weaken the position of minority voters, but also plans that do not improve these voters' positions as much as possible.

The practice of racial gerrymandering had been challenged in several Supreme Court cases since 1965, but one of the most interesting cases concerned the 1994 congressional elections in the state of Georgia. The case, *Johnson v. Miller*, challenged the districts that had been drawn up in Georgia for the 1990s. The 1992 congressional elections had produced two African American members of Congress, Cynthia McKinney and Sanford Bishop, representing districts that had taken on peculiar geographic shapes in order to achieve African American dominance. Representative McKinney's district stretched from urban Atlanta (skirting the mostly-white suburbs) to reach out to black voters in Augusta, and continued all the way to the city of Savannah, on Georgia's Atlantic coast.

In 1996 the Supreme Court decided that while race could not be discounted as an influence in drawing congressional districts, the use of race as a predominant factor was discriminatory and unconstitutional. While the decision was clearly vague and open to interpretation, the Georgia legislature promptly redrew its districts in time for the 1996 congressional elections. McKinney and Bishop found themselves running for reelection in very different districts: the percentage of African Americans in McKinney's district dropped from 60 percent to 32 percent, and Bishop's dropped from 52 percent to 35 percent.

But since 1992, McKinney and Bishop had proven themselves to be skillful legislators, attentive to the needs of their constituents, and each was reelected by a comfortable margin in the 1996 elections. After his primary victory, Bishop told supporters, "It's not about where the lines are drawn, its about the quality of service rendered (*Washington Post,* July 11, 1996).

Supporters of the Supreme Court decision claimed that the elections of 1996 proved that white voters were increasingly able to transcend race and make rational voting decisions without being strong-armed by gerrymandering. However, both McKinney and Bishop pointed out that while they had won their elections based on the strength of their previous service, they might not have earned the right to serve at all without the support of their earlier black-majority districts. The elections were proof not of decreasing discrimination in electoral politics, McKinney claimed, but of the power of incumbency—a problem that has still not been addressed in the redistricting process. While an additional Supreme Court decision in 1997 further curbed the Justice Department's ability to approve or disapprove of redistricting plans on the basis of race, the powerful influence of political parties on congressional reapportionment remained to be addressed in a substantial way.

FUTURE DIRECTIONS

For the foreseeable future, the House will most likely be involved in expanding its government oversight duties in response to recent legislation. At least two important pieces of legislation now being implemented by the federal government will ensure this: the Government Performance and Results Act (GPRA) of 1993, which requires greater agency accountability and preparation in reaching goals, and the Balanced Budget Act of 1997, which sets a target date of 2002 as the year in which the federal government is slated to earn at least as much in revenue as it spends. In addition to ensuring compliance in federal expenditures, the House must make sure that every piece of taxation or appropriations legislation passed until the year 2002 is consistent with the terms of the Balanced Budget Act.

AGENCY RESOURCES

One of the most helpful resources concerning both the House and Senate is the *Weekly Report*, published by Congressional Quarterly, Inc. (a private, non-partisan research organization), which provides updates about members and legislation. The Clerk of the House is also a valuable resource for the House records and disclosure documents. General requests for information can be directed to the Clerk of the House, Legislative Resource Center, B106 Cannon House Office Building, Washington, DC 20515, (202) 225-1300 or by e-mail at LRC @clerk.house.gov.

The Library of Congress also offers a number of resources on its home page on the World Wide Web (http://www.loc.gov). Probably the most helpful of these resources to the average citizen is the THOMAS site, named for Thomas Jefferson. THOMAS provides on-line public access to legislative and congressional information, the full text of laws and the *Congressional Record*, summaries and status reports on bills, E-mail addresses for members and committees of both the House and the Senate, and the Constitution of the United States. The THOMAS site can be reached directly at http://www.thomas.loc.gov.

If your television is wired for C-SPAN, listings for televised House proceedings are posted on the World Wide Web at http://www.c-span.org.

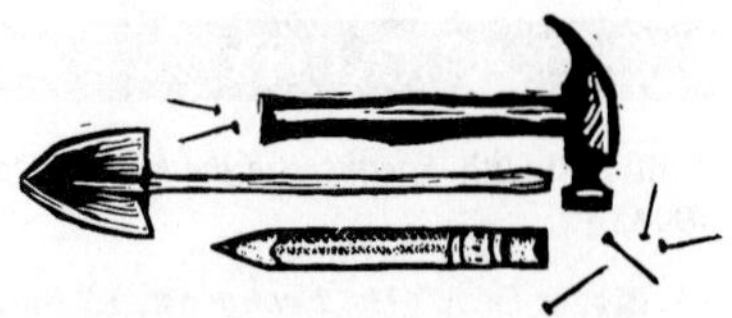

GET INVOLVED:

House representatives encourage and depend upon the political participation of all constituents. The easiest way to find out who represents you in Congress is to click on the Write Your Representative section in the lower left-hand corner of the House's home page on the World Wide Web at http://www.house.gov. After entering your nine-digit zip code, you'll be told who your representative is and given a mailing address to your representative's office. In most cases there is a hypertext link to the representative's home page. If you want to express an opinion to your representative or ask a question about pending measures, you may do so either through direct mail, or by E-mail from this site. All representatives have staffs that assist them in responding to inquiries.

AGENCY PUBLICATIONS

Among the most important House publications are its complex *Rules* and its *Ethics Manual*, which are available for viewing or downloading at the House Web site (http://www.house.gov). An important congressional publication is the *Congressional Directory*, edited by the Joint Committee on Printing, which lists member biographies, committee assignments, and seniority rankings. Also available is the *Congressional Record*, the daily word-for-word account of congressional proceedings. The first section of the *Congressional Record* is always devoted to the proceedings of the House. Printed copies of the *Congressional Record*, the *Congressional Directory*, the *Rules*, or the *Ethics Manual* can also be obtained from the Superintendent of Documents, Government Printing Office, Washington, DC 20402.

Historical information about the House, or copies of documents that cannot be located at the THOMAS Web site, can often be obtained from the Legislative Resource Center, which is maintained by the Clerk of the House. The mailing address of the Legislative Resource Center is B106 Cannon House Office Building, Washington, D.C. 20515.

BIBLIOGRAPHY

Bentley, Judith. *Speakers of the House*. Danbury: Franklin Watts, 1994.

"A Bigger Deal." *The Economist*, 13 June 1998, p. 4.

Clymer, Adam. "Leaders Aim for a House No Longer So Divided." *New York Times*, 27 January 1997, p. A10(N); p. A15(L).

Deering, Christopher J., and Steven S. Smith. *Committees in Congress*. Washington, D.C.: Congressional Quarterly, 1997.

DeGregorio, Christine A. *Networks of Champions: Leadership, Access and Advisory in the U. S. House of Representatives*. Ann Arbor: University of Michigan Press, 1997.

Duvall, Jill. *Congressional Committees*. New York: Franklin Watts, 1997.

Gingrich, Newt. "The Agenda for the House of Representatives." *Vital Speeches*, 1 February 1997, pp. 231–33.

Grann, David. "Broken Rules." *New Republic*, 6 April 1998, pp. 12–13.

Greenberg, Ellen. *The House and Senate Explained*. New York: W. W. Norton, 1996.

Guide to Congress. Washington, D.C.: Congressional Quarterly, 1993.

How Congress Works. Washington, D.C.: Congressional Quarterly, 1991.

Kaptur, Marcy. *Women of Congress: A Twentieth-Century Odyssey*. Washington: Congressional Quarterly, 1996.

Maltzman, Forrest, and Lee Sigelman. "The Politics of Talk: Unconstrained Floor Time in the U.S. House of Representatives." *The Journal of Politics*, August 1996, pp. 819–30.

Ragsdale, Bruce A., and Joel D. Treese. *Black Americans in Congress, 1870–1989*. Washington, D.C.: U.S. Government Printing Office, 1990.

Seib, Gerald F. "House Races: Open and Shut?" *Wall Street Journal*, 8 April 1998, p. A24.

Seelye, Katharine Q. "After Months Without Ethics Committee House May Resurrect It This Week." *New York Times*, 10 April 1997, p. 17 (N); p. 28(L).

Immigration and Naturalization Service (INS)

PARENT ORGANIZATION: Department of Justice
ESTABLISHED: March 3, 1891
EMPLOYEES: 28,000

Contact Information:

ADDRESS: 425 I St. NW
Washington, DC 20536
PHONE: (202) 514-4316
TOLL FREE: (800) 755-0777
FAX: (202) 514-3296
URL: http://www.ins.usdoj.gov
COMMISSIONER: Doris Meissner

WHAT IS ITS MISSION?

The U.S. Immigration and Naturalization Service (INS) oversees and enforces the laws that apply to the entry of non-U.S. citizens, referred to as "aliens" or foreign nationals, into the United States. The INS oversees the legal entry of non-U.S. citizens who are temporarily or permanently settling in the United States, and enforces the laws of naturalization, the process by which a foreign-born person becomes a citizen. The INS also tackles illegal entrance into the United States, preventing receipt of benefits such as social security or unemployment by those ineligible to receive them and investigating, detaining, and deporting those illegally living in the United States.

HOW IS IT STRUCTURED?

At the head of the INS is a commissioner appointed by the president who reports to the Attorney General in the Department of Justice. INS works closely with the United Nations, the Department of State, and the Department of Health and Human Services. The INS is a very large and complex organization that has four main divisions—Programs, Field Operations, Policy and Planning, and Management—that are responsible for operations and management.

The operational functions of the INS include the Programs and Field Operations divisions. The Programs division is responsible for handling all the functions involved with enforcement and examinations, including the arrest, detaining, and deportation of illegal immigrants as well as controlling illegal and legal entry. The

BUDGET:

Immigration and Naturalization Service

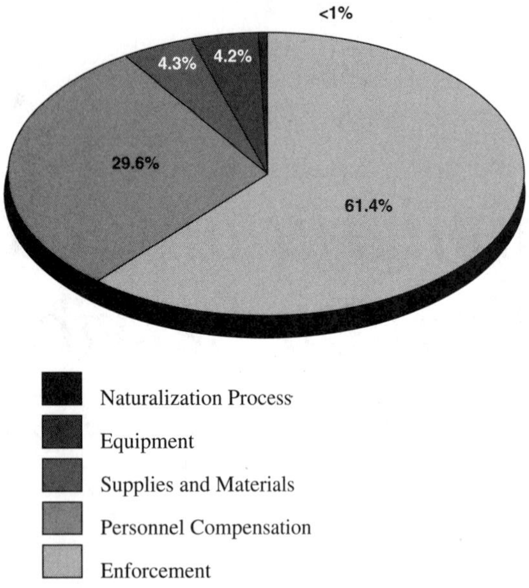

Field Operations division is responsible for overseeing INS's many offices operating throughout the country and the world. The Field Operations division implements policies and handles tasks for its three regional offices, which in turn oversee 33 districts and 21 border areas throughout the country. Internationally, the Field Operations division oversees the Headquarters Office of International Affairs which in turn oversees 16 offices outside the country.

The managerial functions of the INS include the Policy and Planning and Management divisions. The Office of Policy and Planning coordinates all information for the INS and communicates with other cooperating government agencies and the public. The office is divided into three areas: the Policy Division; the Planning Division; and the Evaluation and Research Center. The second managerial division, called the Management division, is responsible for maintaining the overall mission of the INS throughout its many offices and providing administrative services to these offices. These duties are handled by the offices of Information Resources Management, Finance, Human Resources and Administration, and Equal Employment Opportunity.

PRIMARY FUNCTIONS

In its effort to control immigration, the INS actively patrols the 8,000-mile border of the United States with an armed presence using automobiles, airplanes, boats, and even horses. The INS also polices all other entry points into the country such as airports and harbors. In addition officers of the INS investigate many violations of the laws within the U.S. and aid other agencies in the prevention of drug smuggling, fraud, and other violent crimes. They investigate places of employment for the presence of illegal workers and are responsible for holding illegal immigrants until they are tried and then deporting them if they are found guilty of being in the country illegally.

The INS also is responsible for allowing and monitoring legal immigration. They screen people and documents at approximately 250 ports of entry, such as airports, harbors, and highways. They also screen applications for people desiring to enter the country temporarily or permanently and administer the test to foreign nationals to become permanent citizens.

PROGRAMS

Most INS programs involve either enforcement or examinations. The four main enforcement programs are Border Patrol, Investigations, Intelligence, and Detention and Deportation. The goal of the enforcement programs is to keep people from illegally entering the country and to find and deport those who are already living illegally in the country. The four main examinations programs are Adjudication and Nationality, Inspections, Service Center Operations, and Administrative Appeals. Their goal is to determine applicants' eligibility for temporary or permanent visas or for U.S. citizenship.

BUDGET INFORMATION

In 1997 the estimated amount of money appropriated by Congress from the overall budget of the United States for the operation of the INS was $1.684 billion, with an additional $430 million in fees collected, for a total budget of $2.114 billion. By far, the largest portion of this total (62 percent) went toward enforcement, $1.299 billion. This included the costs of inspecting 475 million people; deporting 1 million illegal aliens; apprehending 13,600 smugglers; and seizing 9,600 vehicles.

Other significant allotments include: $626 million (30 percent) directed toward personnel compensation; supplies and materials, $91 million (4 percent); and equipment, $89 million (4 percent). The smallest portion of the budget goes toward the naturalization process, $9 million (less than 1 percent).

HISTORY

In 1864 a federal office was established to encourage immigration into the U.S. at a time when the popu-

The INS screens applicants for entry into the United States and administers the test foreign nationals must pass to become U.S. citizens. Pictured are people waiting outside an INS office. (UPI/Corbis-Bettmann)

lation was sparse and skilled workers were needed to fuel the second Industrial Revolution. At the time, however, each state handled immigration into its own territory as its own laws dictated, so the new federal office lacked any real legal authority over the states and was largely ineffective. Four years after this office was established, Congress abolished it. For the next several decades various laws were passed to deal with the rising number of "undesirable" aliens who were entering the country, such as criminals, the ill, or those of certain ethnic backgrounds; but immigration was still governed by individual states.

The situation grew more unwieldy as the population grew, and the individual states and members of the Congress felt pressure to control the influx. In 1882, under the Chinese Exclusion Act, the Treasury Secretary was put in charge of implementing new restrictions on immigration and worked closely with the states to devise an efficient way to enforce the new standards. These restrictions primarily applied to Chinese, contract laborers, prostitutes, and criminals.

However, the crush of immigrants continued until the problem grew too big for individual states. As a result Congress enacted the Immigration Act in 1891 which created the first federal agency, the Bureau of Immigration. Standards for entrance were broadened to exclude more categories of people, such as the insane, paupers, and those with diseases. Also contract labor was defined more specifically. Many businesses, such as the railroads, depended on cheap contract labor from other countries to operate profitably. Inspection stations were opened, such as Ellis Island in New York, and medical examinations of new arrivals were initiated.

In 1903 the Bureau of Immigration was reorganized and transferred to the Department of Commerce and Labor. The naturalization division of the INS didn't become a part of the organization until 1906, when Congress passed the Naturalization Act. Formerly, examinations for citizenship and visa status were conducted within the Department of Justice by the courts. For a brief period following the Naturalization Act both the duties of naturalization and immigration were combined under one agency. As their parent organizations evolved, and the political climate and the types of issues around immigration changed, they were once again separated in 1913 only to then be finally consolidated into one agency in 1933. By that time the Department of Commerce and Labor had become the Department of Labor, and the Bureau of Immigration and Naturalization was firmly established as a single organization. In 1940, as more and more of its work involved legal issues, it was moved to the Department of Justice where it remains today.

In the 1990s the administration of President Bill Clinton responded to the country's changing political cli-

FAST FACTS

In 1996 1.1 million people became naturalized citizens of the United States.

(Source: Eric Schmitt. "Milestones and Missteps on Immigration." *New York Times*, October 26, 1996.)

mate by taking a variety of positions on immigration, trying to satisfy various segments of society. For example, in 1992 the Clinton administration and the INS offered an "open arms" policy to political refugees from Cuba and Haiti who were arriving daily by boat. By 1994, however, the influx had become great and many refugees were being lost at sea. The administration and the INS responded by closing that means of entrance and sending the refugees back to camps at the U.S. military base at Guantanamo, Cuba. Cuba agreed to limit the number of refugees and the INS agreed to allow 20,000 refugees from the camps to immigrate per year.

CURRENT POLITICAL ISSUES

The INS handles a great number of immigrants into the United States every year. For example, in 1995 484 million travelers passed through inspection stations at the country's approximately 250 ports of entry. In that same year, the INS naturalized 500,000 new citizens, allowed more than 100,000 refugees to enter, granted asylum to more than 12,000 people fleeing from persecution in their own countries, and permitted 18 million tourists, students, and business people into the United States under different types of visas. In addition to these numbers, the INS is responsible for policing nearly 8,000 miles of borders, an enormous task that generates controversy over who should be admitted under what circumstances and whether the agency is effective in applying these policies.

Case Study: Border Patrol

For many years, thousands of illegal immigrants have been known to cross the border daily in order to seek work and better financial conditions in the north. They cross at well-known entry points in urban areas, such as San Diego, where it is easier for them to escape in the urban landscape of streets and neighborhoods. Under political pressure, the INS began a series of crackdowns beginning in 1994 against illegal immigrants entering the country across the Mexican border. Local residents had long complained of property damage and danger to the residents, and that illegal immigrants were using their schools, public facilities, and welfare benefits but paying no taxes and that the expense was threatening to bankrupt local governments. Resentment had been growing on the part of taxpayers for many years. With the inauguration of the Clinton administration in 1992 and the subsequent appointment of Attorney General Janet Reno, new attention was brought to the issue.

In 1993 Reno toured the border areas and saw how weak enforcement was. In response to her inspection and growing protests by local citizens, the Department of Justice initiated a new program in San Diego County, California, called Operation Gatekeeper. Similar programs were later begun in other areas, such as in Arizona (where it is called Safeguard), and in Texas and New Mexico (where it is called Rio Grande). The strategy of these operations is to put a huge amount of manpower at these urban points and force the illegal immigrants to enter from the open countryside, where the Border Patrol can more easily catch them. The effectiveness of these operations is the focus of much controversy.

According to the Border Patrol, the number of arrests at these targeted, well-known entry points has fallen while the number of overall arrests has risen and therefore it considers the operations successful. For example, in one area of the San Diego County border, arrests went from 18,847 to 9,130. They also claim that, as planned, the arrests and illegal crossings have risen in the nonurban areas.

Opponents, however, cite the high total number of illegal immigrants still getting across and the deteriorating quality of life for many residents in nonurban areas. They say that thousands of people are crossing their property and moving into their towns at these new focal points at an alarming rate, so the Border Patrol operations have shifted the problem from one place to another. Arrests at one California border station, for example, jumped from 2,500 in 1994 to more than 51,000 in 1996.

Contributing to the problem is the uncertainty about the true number of immigrants who cross the border illegally each year. The Border Patrol says that the overall number of arrests along the San Diego/Imperial County border for 1996 was 85,000, representing 50 percent of the total number of illegal crossings in a year. Opponents claim that this number represents only one-tenth of the total number of illegal crossings at that location. Estimates, in their opinion, of the number of all illegal crossings along the entire border run as high as 850,000 per year.

As a result of this controversy, more agents have been put along the border. For example, since 1994, the number of border patrol agents in California alone went from 100 to 500. These agents are being given more sophisticated and more expensive equipment, such as night vision goggles and four-wheel-drive vehicles. In addition, plans are in effect to build a 10-foot-high fence along the entire border, an enormously expensive project that opponents doubt will ever be finished.

SUCCESSES AND FAILURES

In 1996 the INS instituted the Machine Readable Data (MRD) program, which involves the computerization of fingerprints so that they can be better tracked throughout the nation. They have also reduced the average time it takes to process fingerprints on naturalization applications. In New York City, the INS completed a successful, extensive, antismuggling investigation involving deaf Mexican aliens who were brought illegally into the country and put to work at slave wages. On an international level, the INS instituted a program called Operation Global Reach, which involved the opening of 13 new overseas offices to help prevent smuggling and illegal entry before they reach U.S. borders. In 1996 in the United States, the INS identified more than 33,000 jobs being held by illegal aliens and took action to enforce the relevant immigration laws.

FUTURE DIRECTIONS

The INS plans to further increase the number of Border Patrol agents along the Mexican-U.S. border and to supply them with the most up-to-date equipment. The agency has also created a group to work directly with the Mexican government to find better ways to decrease immigration and ensure the public safety. The INS also has formed a closer working partnership with the FBI in order to combat alien smuggling along the borders.

AGENCY RESOURCES

Information can be obtained from the INS by writing to the Office of Information, Immigration and Naturalization Service, Department of Justice, 425 I St. NW, Washington, DC 20536 or by calling (202) 514-4316. The INS Web page can be reached on the World Wide Web at http://www.ins.usdoj.gov. The INS recommends locating the INS regional office in the telephone directory for more information. The *Federal Yellow Book,* found in public libraries, contains a more detailed listing of all the offices under "Immigration and Naturalization Service."

AGENCY PUBLICATIONS

Publications are available on the INS's home page at http://www.ins.usdoj.gov. Many INS publications are available in their Electronic Reading Room at http://www.ins.usdoj.gov/inserr/default.htm. These include INS *Handbooks and Guides*, *Foreign Affairs Manual*, *INS Guides to the Public*, and the *Employee Sanctions Litigation Manual*. Also available on the Web are various INS forms which can be downloaded from the site or received by mail by contacting Office of Information, Immigration and Naturalization Service, Department of Justice, 425 I St. NW, Washington, DC 20536 or by calling (202) 514-4316.

BIBLIOGRAPHY

Bhabha, Homi K. "Halfway House." *Artforum*, May 1997.

Carroll, Mary. "Multicultural U.S.A." *Booklist*, August 1997.

Emsden, Katharine. *Coming to America: A New Life in a New Land.* Lowell, Mass.: Discovery Enterprises, 1993.

Glass, Stephen. "Kicked Out." *New Republic*, 20 October 1997, pp. 13–14.

Harris, Nigel. *The New Untouchables: Immigration and the New World.* London: I. B. Tauris, 1995.

Holden, Constance. "Pay Before You Go." *Science*, 22 August 1997.

"Overload at the INS." *Christian Science Monitor*, 18 July 1997.

Schmitt, Eric. "Milestones and Missteps on Immigration." *New York Times*, 26 October 1996.

Talbot, Margaret. "Baghdad on the Plains." *New Republic*. 11–18 August 1997.

Zengerle, Jason. "Exhibiting Bias." *New Republic*, 20 October 1997.

Indian Health Service (IHS)

PARENT ORGANIZATION: Department of Health and Human Services
ESTABLISHED: 1955
EMPLOYEES: 15,800 (1996)

Contact Information:

ADDRESS: 5600 Fishers Lane
Rockville, MD 20857
PHONE: (301) 443-3593
FAX: (301) 443-0507
E-MAIL: feedback@ihs.gov
URL: http://www.tucson.ihs.gov
DIRECTOR: Michael H. Trujillo, M.D.

WHAT IS ITS MISSION?

The Indian Health Service (IHS) is the division of the Department of Health and Human Services responsible for the health care of American and Alaskan Indians. According to Dr. Michael H. Trujillo, the 1998 director of the IHS, this agency "is the principal federal health care provider and health advocate for Indian people, and its goal is to raise their health status to the highest possible level." The IHS builds partnerships with tribes and assists them in planning and managing their health services. It also aims to be a voice for the Indian people and represent their health interests at the federal level.

HOW IS IT STRUCTURED?

The IHS grew out of a unique government-to-government relationship between the federal government and Indian tribes. This relationship was established in 1787 and is based on Article I, Section 8, of the U.S. Constitution. It provides federal aid for American and Alaskan Indians for such services as health care but also allows tribal leaders direct involvement in managing these services for their people.

This dual governance system became a dual management system when the Indian Health Care Improvement Act (Public Law 94-437) was passed in 1994, giving tribes the choice between IHS health services and tribal-operated health care. Since this 1994 law was passed, a growing number of tribes have taken over responsibility for their health care services. This led the IHS to streamline its Maryland headquarters in 1997 and delegate more operational activities to the field. Before the reorganization, the IHS was composed of nine major offices and 154 organizational units. After the reorganization, there were three major offices and fewer than 40 organizational units.

The director of the IHS is a presidential appointee who serves for a four-year term. IHS headquarters consists of three major offices: the Office of the Director, the Office of Public Health, and the Office of Management Support. They are responsible for the planning, management, and finances of the IHS. They are also the primary advocate for American and Alaskan Indian health issues in the federal government. Specific programs and daily activities are the primary responsibility of 12 area offices located in reservation states, because these offices are closer to the people they serve. This means that the IHS employs approximately 840 doctors, 380 dentists, 100 physical assistants, and 2,580 nurses. The agency also oversees 37 hospitals, 64 health centers, 50 health stations, and five school health centers. In addition, tribal health programs administer 12 hospitals, 116 health centers, three school health centers, 56 health stations, and 167 Alaska village clinics.

The IHS provides a wide range of medical services for tribal communities. However, in places where the IHS does not have the facilities or equipment for a particular service, the agency contracts with local hospitals, state and local health agencies, tribal health institutions, and individual health care providers. As a division of the Public Health Service of the Department of Health and Human Services, the IHS also works with other agencies in this department. For example, the Health Care Financing Administration and the Administration on Children and Families work with the IHS to ensure that federal funds are divided fairly between tribes and states.

PRIMARY FUNCTIONS

The IHS was established to provide comprehensive health service for members of federally recognized American Indian tribes and their descendants. This means that the IHS serves approximately 1.4 million Americans from about 550 federally recognized tribes in 34 states.

The IHS strives to improve tribal health through programs such as health management training, technical assistance, and human resource development. It assists tribes in coordinating health planning and evaluating health programs. It provides comprehensive health care services, such as hospital care, ambulatory medical services, and preventative (for example, community sanitation facilities) and rehabilitative services. The IHS also documents Indian health needs, supports a nationwide Indian health network, and maintains an Indian health data bank.

In addition the IHS is the main federal health advocate for American and Alaskan Indians. It encourages them to participate in health issues both inside and outside the organization. For example, the IHS sponsors the Public Health Service Commissioned Officer Student Training and Extern Program and the Indian Health Profession Program to encourage career development in the health professions. More than 62 percent of all IHS employees are of American or Alaskan Indian descent.

PROGRAMS

The IHS administers a variety of programs to provide basic health services to its constituency. For example, IHS Preventative Health Services sponsor treatment and educational programs that prevent medical problems, covering such areas as baby care, family planning, dental health, nutrition, and health education. The Emergency Medical Services (EMS) program is organized around the living conditions of most Indians. Because many of these people live on reservations in remote locations, ambulance response to medical emergencies may be slow. To adjust for this, the EMS program has created a "first responder" system, whereby trained community members can respond to a crisis within 15 minutes and communicate with radio to the next level of medical care. Other basic health program areas include environmental health and engineering services, pharmacy services, contract health services, health education, community-based programs, school-based programs, mental health services, a dental program, and a nutrition program.

Special Health Concerns

In addition to providing comprehensive health services to American and Alaskan Indians, the IHS also coordinates programs that address special health concerns within the community. Such health concerns include acquired immunodeficiency syndrome (AIDS), maternal and child care, diabetes, otitis media (a middle-ear disease), and aging.

One of the largest of these IHS special programs is the Alcoholism and Substance Abuse Program, established because the IHS recognized alcohol and substance abuse as the most significant problem facing American and Alaskan Indian communities. The IHS funds more than 200 programs to provide treatment and prevention services on reservations and in urban communities. In addition it has established a youth regional treatment center within each IHS area to help youth in need. The IHS explains the vision of this program as follows: "So that the unique balance, resiliency, and strength of our American Indian and Alaska Native cultures are supported and enriched, we at the Indian Health Service Alcoholism and Substance Abuse Program strive to eliminate the disease of alcoholism and other drug dependencies and the associated pain it brings to individuals of all ages, families, villages, communities, and tribes."

BUDGET:

Indian Health Service

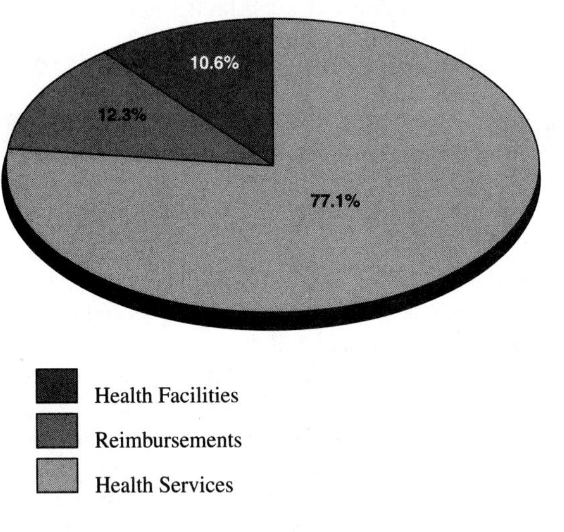

Another special health program of the IHS is the Injury Prevention Program. According to the IHS, "more than 1,000 Native Americans die and 10,000 more are hospitalized for injuries each year." The age-adjusted death rates from injury are three times greater for Native Americans than for all other Americans. Some factors contributing to these higher rates are rural or isolated living poor, working environments, minimal emergency medical services, and long distances from sophisticated trauma care facilities.

In response to this situation, the IHS has initiated a public health attack on traumatic injury. For example, through its Injury Prevention Program it has instituted community-based injury prevention programs. In addition, it convened the first Native American Lifesavers Conference in 1996 to exchange information on injury prevention. The most common cause of injury is motor vehicle crashes; therefore, highway safety is a major part of this program. Other projects focus on preventing falls among the elderly, encouraging the use of helmets to prevent brain injury, preventing burn and fire injuries at home, and preventing drowning.

BUDGET INFORMATION

The 1997 IHS budget was $2.342 billion. Of this total amount, 77.1 percent was spent on health services, 10.6 percent on health facilities, and 12.3 percent on reimbursements. Of the portion that was allocated to health services, 62 percent went to clinical services, 3.5 percent to preventive health, 1.1 percent to urban health, 2.1 percent to direct operations, 6.9 percent to contract support costs, and 1.6 percent to other health services. The 1998 budget request was $2.4 billion, almost $70 million more than the 1997 budget. The additional money will mostly be spent on replacing two old and overcrowded health care facilities in Arizona.

HISTORY

The U.S. government began to offer health services to Indians in the early 1800s. These were localized efforts to contain contagious diseases among tribes living near military posts. It was not until 1849 when the Bureau of Indian Affairs (BIA) was transferred from the War Department to the Department of the Interior that physician services were extended to Indians with the creation of a corps of civilian field employees called the Indian Medical Services. By 1900 the Indian Medical Services employed 83 physicians and 25 nurses. The first hospital for American Indians was built in Oklahoma in the 1880s.

The government became more involved in Indian health care in the early 1900s. The position of chief medical supervisor was created in 1908 to oversee Indian health care. In 1911 Congress made the first federal appropriation for Indian health care. Gradually, disease control, health education, and dental services were also added to the health care program.

Two congressional acts greatly changed the direction of the IHS. In 1921 the Snyder Act was passed, guaranteeing regular federal appropriations of funds for American and Alaskan Indian health care and creating the BIA Health Division. The second important congressional act was the 1954 Transfer Act, which transferred responsibility for Indian care from the Department of Interior's BIA to the Department of Health and Human Services' Public Health Service. This transfer agreement created the Indian Health Service in 1955. It created the staff, facilities, and programs necessary to provide treatment and preventative care for Indians.

The organization significantly changed again in the 1990s with the 1994 Indian Health Care Improvement Act, which allowed tribes to choose between IHS and tribal-operated health care. This led to a reorganization of the IHS headquarters to streamline operations there and increase field activities. This change allowed the IHS to focus on assisting tribes in providing health care in their own communities and serving as advocates for Indians at the national level.

CURRENT POLITICAL ISSUES

Many health statistics show a significant improvement in Indian health over the last few decades. For example, the life expectancy of Indians has risen 19 percent since 1955 to an average life expectancy of 67.9 years for males and 75.1 years for females. In addition, according to the IHS, infant mortality has decreased by 54 percent, maternal mortality by 65 percent, and pneumonia and influenza mortality by 50 percent since 1973. Many of these improvements are the direct result of IHS initiatives, especially the increase in emergency medical services, the construction of sanitation facilities, and the development of community-based health care programs.

Despite these successes the state of American and Alaskan Indian health is still worse than that of most Americans. This is apparent in the higher mortality rates of Indians in comparison with the U.S. population as a whole. According to the IHS, "the age-adjusted alcoholism death rate for Indians is 400 percent higher than for the general U.S. population; accidents, 165 percent higher; diabetes mellitus, 154 percent higher; homicide, 50 percent higher; and suicide 43 percent higher."

These mortality rates are closely linked to behavioral and social conditions among American and Alaskan Indians. According to the 1990 census, populations living on reservations have fewer economic and educational opportunities than other Americans. The median annual family income for Indians on reservations in 1990 was only $13,700, which was $5,300 lower than for the general population. Poverty, and the social and environmental conditions associated with it, take their toll on the health of Indians. It is a serious challenge to the IHS to provide the necessary medical care to these communities given these poor conditions.

FAST FACTS

Since 1972 the IHS has helped to reduce the mortality rate of American Indians and Alaska Natives by 42 percent.

(Source: IHS Fiscal Year 1999 Performance Plan, September 1998.)

Case Study: The Pine Ridge Reservation

The Pine Ridge Reservation in South Dakota is a two-million-acre reservation that is home to the Oglala Sioux. The area is famous as the site of the 1890 Wounded Knee massacre, and the Oglala are the tribe of the great Indian chiefs Red Cloud and Crazy Horse. Unfortunately, in the late 1990s, the Oglala Sioux became famous for another reason. According to a *Washington Post* report of findings by the Harvard School of Public Health, "the 26,000 men and women living in this storied warrior tribe die younger than any other group in the nation." The average life expectancy of the Oglala Sioux is 56.5 years for men and 66 years for women. This is much lower than the average for Indians as a whole, and comparable to that of sub-Saharan African countries.

The low life expectancy of the Oglala is related to the high poverty level at Pine Ridge. The reservation is extremely isolated, being 80 miles from the nearest city, and has no natural resources to generate income or attract businesses. The tribal government is the largest employer on the reservation, and almost 75 percent of adults are unemployed and depend on some sort of government or tribal assistance. The tribe even built a casino to try to boost the local economy but the isolation of the reservation and the poor quality of the casino have not made this venture as successful for the Oglala as it has been for other tribes.

The lack of money creates poor living conditions which result in poor health. Health problems among the general American Indian and Alaska Native population, such as alcoholism, diabetes, suicide, and traumatic injuries, are especially problematic at Pine Ridge. Northern Plains Indians have a genetic predisposition to diabetes, and the poor diet of the Oglala compounds this problem. A very large proportion of the population suffers from this disease. In addition, the infant mortality rate on the reservation is almost three times higher than the national average, and motorists are four times more likely to die there in a fatal car accident than anywhere else.

The health problems at Pine Ridge highlight the challenges that poverty poses for the health and quality of life of American Indians. It is the responsibility of the IHS to respond to these challenges and improve the health conditions of all American Indians regardless of their economic standing. The case of the Oglala Sioux illustrates the health disparities within the American and Alaskan Indian community. These geographic differences in health care are a major concern of the IHS and the subject of an annual publication called *Regional Differences in Indian Health*. Through the study of regional differences the IHS can identify the communities most in need and devote more resources to improving health conditions in these areas.

For example, the Oglala live in the IHS area office of Aberdeen, which serves North Dakota, South Dakota, Nebraska, and Iowa. The IHS has recently made two large investments in the Aberdeen area, specifically on the Pine Ridge Reservation. The first improvement is the construction of the Pine Ridge Hospital, which has 46 beds, 16 physicians, and serves a population of 17,000. It is the largest hospital in the Aberdeen area. The second improvement is the Kyle Health Center, also in Pine Ridge, which is an ambulatory care facility with outpatient services. It staffs one physician, four nurses, a phar-

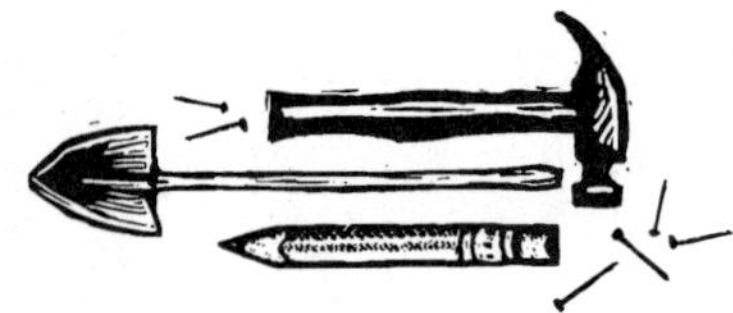

GET INVOLVED:

The IHS Injury Prevention Program sponsors the Safe Tribal Communities Campaign for American Indian and Alaska Native Youth. This campaign includes a competition for American Indian high school students to develop a community service project to reduce injury risks in their community. Each area awards cash prizes to the best projects, with regional winners competing at the national level. The top three national project winners win a trip to Washington, D.C., as well as $1,000 for their school or community organization. For more information, call the local area office or the IHS National Headquarters at (301) 443-3593 or visit the Web site at http://www.tucson.ihs.gov/Healthcare/Professions/injprev/announce.asp.

The Indian Health Professions program provides scholarships, loans, and summer employment in return for service in IHS, tribal, or rural Indian programs. Information about the scholarship program can be obtained from the Scholarship Program, Twinbrook Metro Plaza, Ste. 100A, 12300 Twinbrook Pkwy., Rockville, MD 20852; phone (301) 443-6197, or fax (301) 443-6048. Information about other Indian Health Professions programs can be obtained from the IHS, Indian Health Professions Support Branch, Rm. 6-39, Parklawn Bldg., 5600 Fishers Lane, Rockville, MD 20857; phone (301) 443-4242; fax (301) 443-1071.

macist, an optometrist, and several technicians. It also offers dental, mental health, public health, and environmental health services to the area residents. These two new facilities are significant improvements to this community and will hopefully improve health care on the reservation.

FUTURE DIRECTIONS

While outlining his vision for the IHS, Director Michael H. Trujillo emphasized the need of the organization to pursue "increased efficiency, effectiveness, accountability, and integrity while maintaining our customer focus." He also stressed the importance of expanding tribal participation within the agency. Other goals for the next 10 years include strengthening the Prevention and Environmental Health Services with the development of a new National Indian Health database, which will assist tribal communities with local health planning. In addition, the IHS has declared new "IHS Initiatives," programs that focus on special health problems in the American and Alaskan Indian communities, including AIDS, maternal and child health, otitis media, aging, and nursing.

AGENCY RESOURCES

One of the best sources of information about the IHS and its programs is its Web site at http://www.tucson.ihs.gov, particularly in the *Comprehensive Health Care Program for American Indians and Alaska Natives* publication, available at http://www.tucson.ihs.gov/healthcare/Programs/Profiles/profileTOC.asp. The Web site also has information about area offices at http://www.tucson.ihs.gov/AboutIHS/AreaOffices/index.asp, an IHS Interactive Recruitment database at http://www.tucson.ihs.gov/recruitment/General/career.asp, and an on-line customer service center at http://www.tucson.ihs.gov/Recruitment/Help_Center, which includes frequently asked questions about the IHS and contact information. The IHS is also developing a National Indian Health database.

The IHS communications office distributes a general information packet about the IHS free of charge to those who contact the office at (301) 443-3593. The staff will also answer other questions about IHS activities and distribute area office phone numbers. Information about the IHS can also be obtained by writing the Customer Service Workgroup, 12300 Twinbrook Pkwy., Ste. 450, Rockville, MD 20852.

AGENCY PUBLICATIONS

The IHS offers several publications about Indian health care, as well as about the organization and administration of the IHS. The most important publications are *Indian Health Manual*, *Trends in Indian Health, 1996*, *Regional Differences in Indian Health*, *Indian Health Service Directory*, *State of the Indian Health Service: Challenges and Change*, and *The Adventures of McGruff and Scruff in Indian Country*. All of these publications, as well as director's statements and IHS archives can be found at http://www.tucson.ihs.gov/Publicinfo/General/pubs.asp.

BIBLIOGRAPHY

Chase, JoAnn K. "Sen. Gorton and the Indian Treaties." *Washington Post,* 20 September 1995, p. A18.

Comprehensive Health Care Program for American Indians and Alaska Natives. Washington, D.C.: Indian Health Service, 1996.

"It's the Government Way." *New York Times,* 10 August 1997.

Jeter, Jon. "Reservation's Despair Takes Greatest Toll; Oglala Sioux Face Shortest Life Spans." *Washington Post,* 16 December 1997, p. A01.

Kilborn, Peter T. "For Poorest Indians, Casinos Aren't Enough." *New York Times,* 11 June 1997.

Romano, Lois. "Urban Indians Squeezed Out of Health Care; Federal Services Scarce Away from Reservations." *Washington Post,* 17 December 1996, p. A3.

Schneider, Carol. "Letter to the Editor: Pine Ridge Indians Have Untold Riches." *New York Times,* 13 June 1997.

Serrano, Richard A. "Budget Cuts Pose Dilemma Among Native Americans." *Los Angeles Times,* 8 May 1995, p. A1.

Sternberg, Steve. "Study Shows Yawning Gaps in U.S. Health Care: Longevity Affected by Environment." *USA Today,* 4 December 1997, p. 11A.

Trends in Indian Health. Washington, D.C.: Indian Health Service, 1996.

Inter-American Foundation (IAF)

PARENT ORGANIZATION: Independent
ESTABLISHED: 1969
EMPLOYEES: 70

Contact Information:

ADDRESS: 901 N. Stuart St., 10th Fl.
Arlington, Virginia 22203
PHONE: (703) 841-3800
FAX: (703) 841-0973
URL: http://www.iaf.gov
CHAIRMAN: Maria Otero

WHAT IS ITS MISSION?

The primary focus of the Inter-American Foundation (IAF) is to improve the quality of life for the inhabitants of Latin America and the Caribbean. In the course of fulfilling this mission the IAF sponsors outreach and self-help programs among the underdeveloped and emerging nations of Latin America and the Caribbean. The IAF channels a significant portion of its resources into monetary grants and fellowships "to support innovative, experimental programs that promote the participation of groups and persons in solving development problems." IAF is somewhat unique among government enterprises in that it responds to a "value-driven mandate" that entails the principles of democracy, self-help, self-reliance, and self- esteem for all people.

HOW IS IT STRUCTURED?

IAF operates as an autonomous, bipartisan public corporation. IAF's nine-member board of directors includes three representatives from the federal government and six members from the private sector. Panel members are appointed by the president of the United States with Senate approval. The IAF Board of Directors is headed by a chairperson.

IAF board members in turn appoint the president of IAF, who is also its chief executive officer and is assisted by a senior vice president and general counsel, a vice president for external affairs, vice president for financial management and systems, vice president for learning and dissemination, and vice president for programs.

IAF is supported and operated by a staff of approximately 70 employees headquartered in Arlington, Virginia. In order to promote principles of self-help, the corporation does not locate its staff members in its beneficiary countries of Latin America or in the Caribbean.

PRIMARY FUNCTIONS

The main function of the IAF administration is to make grants directly to regional and local organizations of indigenous peoples in the Western Hemisphere. IAF grant money is specifically designated to assist grassroots organizations in implementing those self-help programs that will benefit the local populace. IAF grants are distributed by means of an application process which is administered through the graduate studies or financial aid offices of many universities. IAF maintains formal links with designated offices at major universities throughout the United States, but any university is eligible to apply for grant money to support a proposed project under IAF guidance. IAF specifically avoids dispensing grants and other financial assistance directly to the national governments of beneficiary countries in order is to bypass the persistent upheavals in leadership that characterize the politics of underdeveloped and emerging nations.

Members of the IAF staff and administration are also involved in disseminating information directly to beneficiaries in the form of educational publications and monologues. It also develops seminars and other educational or self help programs.

IAF Menu of Indicators

IAF reserves a portion of its yearly stipends for the Grassroots Development Framework (GDF) program, a system of criteria conceived by IAF to assess the developmental progress of its beneficiary nations. The IAF employs researchers in its fellowship programs to conduct GDF studies and to collect information based on predefined indicators. The IAF staff then analyzes and applies the results toward the optimization of IAF operations.

PROGRAMS

IAF contributes to the support of hundreds of programs throughout Latin America and the Caribbean each year. Grant contributions to individual projects may range from a few hundred dollars, to hundreds of thousands of dollars. Although the IAF encourages self-reliance and community involvement, it also aims to foster social investment partnerships to mobilize existing resources to the fullest extent possible. The IAF expects local civic organizations and businesses as well as individuals to contribute financial and other resources to every project funded. In most cases the IAF provides less than one-half of the monetary resources necessary for each project.

In Bolivia in 1997, for example, IAF grant contributions supported 35 programs, including those for civic training, forestry, agriculture, and more; yet the IAF expenditure for all programs combined totaled less than one million dollars. In Costa Rica that same year, an IAF contribution of less than $216,000 provided partial funding for what would normally be a costly venture in neighborhood development, yet the IAF grant was effectively allocated for three purposes: operational expenses, the establishment of a development trust fund, and contributions to investment capital. Few U.S. corporations are capable of subsidizing so many effective programs for so few dollars.

Social Investment Program

The IAF social investment program is a predefined set of objectives and criteria for building partnerships with local governments and organizations in beneficiary regions. Through the social investment program the IAF seeks to improve quality of life through grassroots development. Each candidate must present a work plan that, like any standard business plan, must include a detailed budget and descriptions and explanations of how resources will be acquired, including raw materials, technology, labor, and funds. In addition, prospective partners are required to define long-range goals and benefits and to demonstrate commitment by the beneficiary community.

Grassroots Development Framework (GDF)

In 1992 the IAF expanded its research activities in response to a bipartisan initiative known as the Government Performance and Results Act. Enacted in 1993 it required federal agencies to justify their respective programs by establishing clearly defined goals. Each agency is further required to devise a means of measuring its performance in relation to those goals and provide reports of its accomplishments.

In order to investigate, evaluate, and assess the accomplishments of grassroots development efforts in tangible ways, the IAF implemented the Grassroots Development Framework (GDF), a comprehensive menu of indicators and variables. For example, the standard of living indicator is subdivided into satisfaction of basic needs, changes in knowledge skills, changes in employment and income levels, and changes in assets and savings levels. Other measured indicators include personal capacity traits such as self-esteem and cultural identity; changes in organizational capacities including planning and administrative skills; and community norms such as values, attitudes, and behavior.

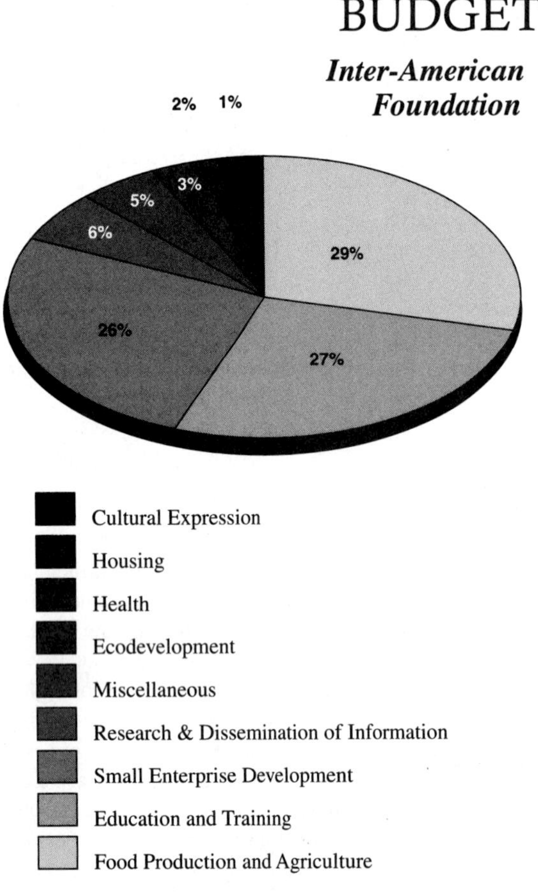

While GDF to a large extent satisfies the requirements of the Government Performance and Results Act, the program since its inception has evolved into an important gauge for self-evaluation by the IAF.

Fellowships

IAF-sponsored fellowships target U.S. students, foreign students, and foreign leaders. Postgraduate awards are given to U.S. students and universities that can devise blueprints for programs that demonstrate reasonable potential for promoting self-help. Fellowship money is also designated to bring students from developing nations to U.S. institutions so that they can return to their respective countries with the appropriate education and necessary skills to become leaders in the grassroots development effort. In addition to other fellowships and grants, the Dante B. Fascell Inter-American Fellowship helps promising leaders of emerging nations to promote self-help within their own countries.

BUDGET INFORMATION

The IAF budget consists of congressional appropriations (tax dollars), plus additional funding from the Social Progress Trust Fund, which is under the control of the Inter-American Development Bank. The total 1995 IAF budget was $39.1 million. Two-thirds of the funds, $26.6 million, were assigned to finance grants that were distributed between 22 countries. Of the total grant money 68 percent was assigned to grassroots development projects. In addition to the funding of IAF grants, In-Country Support (ICS) accounted for $3.7 million of the IAF budget. ICS allotments are used to procure services contracted through local development professionals in beneficiary countries. Most of the remaining $8.8 million went to programs funded through the Social Progress Trust Fund of the Inter-American Development bank. These funds were distributed among 15 countries according to congressional specifications enacted in 1973. The funds are issued in the currency of the respective nations receiving assistance and are designated for the following purposes: agriculture, education, health, housing, land use, business enterprise, and technical assistance.

A breakdown of IAF spending shows the nature of IAF allocations: food production and agriculture: 29 percent; health: 2 percent; education and training, 27 percent; cultural expression, 1 percent; small enterprise development, 26 percent; housing, 1 percent; research and dissemination of information, 6 percent; ecodevelopment, 3 percent; miscellaneous, 5 percent.

HISTORY

General Simon Bolivar may be credited with the first attempt to establish a mutually beneficial alliance between the Americas in 1826 at the Congress of Panama. At the First International Conference of American States in 1890 in Washington, DC, the International Union of American Republics was successfully approved by 18 nations. In 1910 a part of that agreement was renamed the Pan American Union. In the late 1940s, after World War II, the American nations adopted the Inter-American Treaty of Reciprocal Assistance to provide for mutual security in the Western Hemisphere.

By 1948 a new, more comprehensive charter was drafted, accepted, and signed, establishing the Organization of American States (OAS). Through the OAS the countries of the Western Hemisphere reaffirmed a commitment to foster social and economic development in the underdeveloped regions of Latin America.

Alliance for Progress

Through its OAS commitment, the United States initiated the Alliance for Progress in 1961. The alliance for the most part involved a series of agreements between the United States and individual Latin American nations in which the United States agreed to furnish $1 billion annually to spur the economies of the emerging regions of South and Central America and to mobilize local investment in those countries.

The alliance faltered and failed almost immediately, to a large extent because of the Latin American political climate, which was plagued by civil war and communist-backed uprisings. President Lyndon B. Johnson attempted to rekindle the alliance through support of the Central American Common Market (CACM), but U.S. contributions of monetary aid served only to finance the persistent revolutions, which in turn resulted in further economic deterioration. By the end of the decade the Alliance for Progress was essentially defunct, and CACM had collapsed as well.

In a renewed attempt to improve conditions in Latin America and the Caribbean, IAF was established as an independent corporation in 1969 under the provisions of the Foreign Assistance Act of 1969. Although the foundation received little fanfare during its initial years, it established a reputation as a cost-effective, apolitical operation and an innovative resource.

In 1981 during the administration of President Ronald Reagan, an independent conservative policy organization conducted an assessment of IAF and issued a report praising the IAF's ability to operate effectively with limited financial resources. It criticized the IAF, however, for placing unwarranted trust in the naive communities of underdeveloped countries and for providing economic assistance to groups and organization believed to be affiliated with the Communist Party. The IAF was criticized for giving its beneficiaries too much autonomy, for its non-partisan philosophy, and for failing to support a conservative political agenda in Latin America.

Politics notwithstanding, the IAF continues to perform its vital function in relative obscurity; to this day the corporation remains widely unknown to many Americans.

CURRENT POLITICAL ISSUES

IAF grants for the development of Latin American countries can be an important step in improving the situations there. Even with relatively small amounts of funding, the IAF has been able to accomplish a great deal; however, it wishes to gain a firm understanding of the various ways in which its efforts make a difference. The agency employs the Grassroots Development Framework (GDF) to measure 22 variables which contribute intrinsically to grassroots development. Although the nature of GDF indicators varies—some are based on opinion or estimates—others are accumulated from quantitative measurements. Ecuador was one of the first IAF-assisted countries to be measured through the GDF.

FAST FACTS

Between 1969 and 1996 the IAF awarded $447 million in grants to 36 countries throughout Latin America and the Caribbean.

(Source: *The United States Government Manual 1997/98.*)

Case Study: IAF Assistance in Ecuador

The IAF focused on many areas of Ecuadorian development including food production/agriculture, health, education and training, cultural expression, small enterprise development, housing research and dissemination, and ecodevelopment. Most of the agency's monetary resources, however, were directed toward advancements in agriculture. One of the nongovernmental organizations that IAF supported in Ecuador was the Fundacion Natura, which focused on making the public aware of various contributors to deforestation and erosion of farmland. Funded both by the IAF and its membership of 800, this organization was able to make farmers aware of techniques for maintaining soil integrity. It also established networks with other Ecuadorian and worldwide organizations for communicating about important agricultural issues.

Due to IAF contributions and assistance to organizations such as the Fundacion Natura, Ecuador experienced remarkable improvements, and the Ecuadorian GDF pilot assessment program revealed a dramatic mobilization of resources: 80 percent of those who benefited from IAF's presence were identified as contributors to the projects in which they were involved; 72 percent of beneficiaries in this GDF pilot received new skills or other significant knowledge; and 74 percent successfully expanded their socioeconomic linkage (connections to people and organizations that can offer help). In addition 80 percent of Ecuadorian beneficiaries agreed that tolerance and synergy among the local population was improved.

SUCCESSES AND FAILURES

Francis Adams stated in the *Christian Science Monitor* that ". . .[t]he little-known IAF is a remarkable success . . . they have often had a very large impact on the lives of Latin America's poor." IAF success can be expressed in more precise terms by means of the GDF. Preliminary GDF findings, from four pilot programs reveal that the IAF investment return in the pilot nations was $3.25 for each dollar expended.

A 20-year retrospective of IAF involvement in Costa Rica, based on GDF indicators, further showed that IAF directly reached a total of 51,000 beneficiaries. Entrepreneurial assistance was provided to 3,400 microenterprises, and 40,000 new jobs were created, including 25,000 permanent positions.

The IAF has also established programs for Latin American and Caribbean studies at more than 20 U.S. universities, and the foundation has contributed to existing programs at hundreds of other institutions.

FUTURE DIRECTIONS

As IAF beneficiaries in emerging nations develop the skills necessary to support their own needs, IAF will shift the focus of its programs to limit the injection of foreign investment dollars into developing economies. Instead foreign resources will be spent on resource mobilization, the encouragement and support grassroots development from within each respective country. This tactic will reduce the amount of money that is "funneled down" to beneficiary organizations and individuals for particular industries or specific projects, and increase the amount "bumped up" to civic organizations, regional government divisions, and local business leaders for education, training, and seminars. The IAF hopes that this type of resource mobilization will provide long–range solutions which will truly prepare the emerging peoples to successfully confront future challenges.

AGENCY RESOURCES

IAF acknowledges and regrets the general lack of resources on grassroots development programs, a comparatively recent innovation in the field of foreign aid and economic development, but expects the scarcity will improve as the grassroots movement gains momentum worldwide. Sources of further information on economic growth include the U.S. Agency for International Development at 320 Twenty-first St. NW, Washington, DC 20523-0001; phone (202) 647-1850. Information is also available from the Interamerican Development Bank at 1300 New York Ave. NW, Washington, DC 20577; phone (202) 623-1000. The World Bank also provides information on local development and specific projects via a searchable page on the World Wide Web at http://www.worldbank.org. Also see the United Nations (UN) Internet site, which provides a large quantity of information on a variety of assorted topics at http://www.un.org.

AGENCY PUBLICATIONS

Grassroots Development Journal, the IAF biannual publication, includes feature articles, financial statements, project details, country reports, and general information about IAF. It is available from the IAF Publications Office. Also available are *Year in Review*, an annual report, miscellaneous videos, and a variety of informative books. To receive a copy of the journal or the report contact the Inter-American Foundation, Publications Office, 901 N. Stuart St., 10th Fl., Arlington, VA 22203. For a list of published books and videos write the Publications Office or visit the IAF home page on the World Wide Web at http://www.iaf.gov. Most publications, including journals and reports, are available in English, Spanish, and Portuguese.

BIBLIOGRAPHY

Bergsman, Steve. "A Foundation for Disaster." *Hispanic Business,* April 1994, p. 34.

Hirschman, Albert O. "Grassroots Development in Latin America." *Challenge,* September–October 1984, p. 4.

Kleymeyer, Charles David, ed. *Cultural Expression and Grassroots Development: Cases from Latin America and the Caribbean.* Boulder, Colo.: Lynne Rienner Publishers, 1994.

LaFeber, Walter. "Inevitable Revolutions." *Atlantic,* June 1982, p. 74.

Levinson, Jerome. *The Alliance that Lost its Way.* Chicago: Quadrangle Books, 1970.

Mesa-Lago, Carmelo. *Health Care for the Poor in Latin America and the Caribbean.* Inter-American Foundation, 1992.

Murphy, Ellen C. "Development and Use of Outcome Information in Government." Congressional Institute: Office of Learning and Dissemination, 1998.

Reilly, Charles A., ed. *New Paths to Democratic Development in Latin America: The Rise of NGO-Municipal Collaboration,* Boulder, Colo.: Lynne Rienner Publishers, 1995.

Vilas, Carlos. "Prospects for Democratization in a Post-Revolutionary Setting: Central America." *Journal of Latin American Studies,* May 1996.

Wilde, Alexander. "Ideology vs. the IAF, an Omen for Future Aid." *Commonweal,* 10 February 1984, p. 72.

Internal Revenue Service (IRS)

WHAT IS ITS MISSION?

The stated mission of the Internal Revenue Service is "to collect the proper amount of tax revenue at the least cost to the public, and in a manner that warrants the highest degree of public confidence in the Service's integrity, efficiency, and fairness."

HOW IS IT STRUCTURED?

The Internal Revenue Service (IRS) is headed by a commissioner who is responsible for the administration of the agency. The commissioner is under the guidance of the secretary and deputy secretary of the Department of the Treasury. There are three organizational levels within the IRS: the national office, which is its headquarters; seven regional offices; and sixty-four district offices, service centers, and the Austin Compliance Center. The national office, located in Washington, DC, develops nationwide policies and programs for the administration of the internal revenue laws and provides overall direction to the field organizations. The national office also administers the Martinsburg Computing Center in Martinsburg, West Virginia; the Detroit Computing Center in Detroit, Michigan; and 10 service centers in various states across the country. The regional offices are each headed by a regional commissioner and supervise and evaluate the operations of district offices.

This organizational structure is designed to offer centralized and widespread access to tax information and laws as well as to use of resources effectively. To further this end, the IRS is developing and implementing strate-

PARENT ORGANIZATION: Department of the Treasury
ESTABLISHED: July 1, 1862
EMPLOYEES: 106,000

Contact Information:

ADDRESS: 1111 Constitution Ave. NW
Washington, DC 20224
PHONE: (202) 622-5000
TOLL FREE: (800) 829-1040
URL: http://www.irs.treas.gov
COMMISSIONER: Margaret Milner Richardson

BUDGET:

Internal Revenue Service

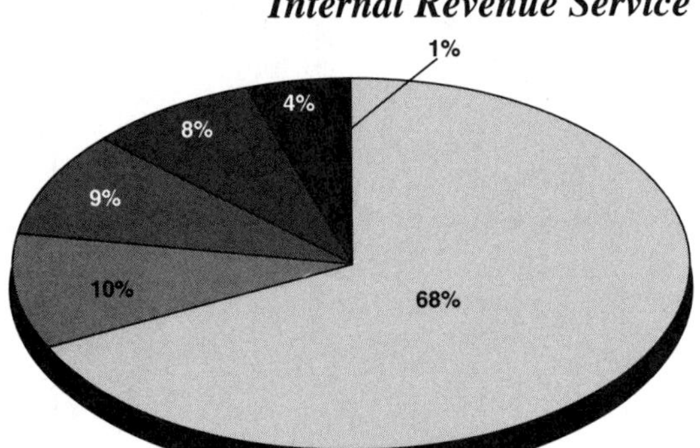

Information Technology Investments

Information Systems

Interest on Refunding Internal Revenue Collections

Processing, Assistance, and Management

Tax Law Enforcement

Earned Income Tax Credit

gies to specifically deal with severe internal problems. Oversight of the IRS has taken on new stamina, and typically the deputy secretary of the treasury oversees the IRS. The Clinton administration's deputy secretary Larry Summers became increasingly involved in the IRS as it struggled to modernize and improve its systems. In addition, the Government Accounting Office and the House Ways and Means Committee are external federal government entities which are responsible for oversight of the IRS. Finally, the National Performance Review program of the Clinton Administration is working closely with the IRS to bring about positive changes in the agency.

PRIMARY FUNCTIONS

The most important assignment of the IRS is to collect personal and corporate income taxes. All eligible citizens are expected to voluntarily comply with the tax laws, and to that end the IRS works to advise the public of their rights and responsibilities. Once a citizen or corporation has filed a tax statement with the IRS, the agency must determine the accuracy of the document. If the filer does not comply or submits inaccurate or fraudulent information, the IRS administers and enforces tax laws. Enforcement usually imposes penalty fees, but legal disputes in the case of extreme tax fraud can also result in prison sentences.

A primary document of the IRS is the *Internal Revenue Code*, which explains regulations and supplements tax forms created for the public. In addition, IRS personnel are constantly engaged in preparing and issuing rulings and regulations to supplement the provisions of the *Internal Revenue Code*.

By April 15 of every year, citizens mail in approximately 200 million claims of taxes from the previous year to the IRS. Throughout the year, the IRS is busy resolving taxpayer complaints and providing taxpayer service and education. Among its basic services are the description of pension plan qualifications and granting tax-exempt organization status, to religious or nonprofit organizations.

PROGRAMS

Each IRS service center processes tax returns and related documents and maintains records of taxes collected. Programs include the processing, verification, and accounting control of tax returns; the assessment and certification of tax refunds; and administering assigned examination, criminal investigation, and collection functions.

Other programs include Taxpayer Help and Assistance, which supplies information and answers questions on such topics as exemptions, small business, filling out forms and understanding schedules. Specific education programs focus on a particular segment of the population who may be eligible for a tax credit such as the Earned Income Tax Credit program, which offers tax credits to lower income citizens.

BUDGET INFORMATION

The budget of the IRS is allocated by Congress. In 1998 it totaled approximately $32.75 billion. By far the largest portion of the IRS budget goes to payment where earned income credit exceeds liability for tax. This money, $22.3 billion or nearly 68 percent of the IRS budget, was given to those tax filers whose earned income credit (a special tax credit, for certain persons who work, intended to offset some of the increases in living expenses and social security taxes) is larger than the amount that they owed to the federal government in taxes.

Tax law enforcement accounted for $3.2 billion or 10 percent of the IRS budget; processing, assistance, and management, $3.0 billion or 9 percent; interest on refunding internal revenue collections, $2.5 billion or 8 percent, information systems, $1.4 billion or 4 percent; and information technology investments, $325 million or 1 percent. The fraction of the remaining IRS budget funds was spent on the earned income tax credit compliance initiative and informant payments.

Staff at the IRS service center in San Francisco, California, are busy helping people fill out their tax forms on April 15, 1998. Midnight on April 15 is the customary deadline for filing tax returns for the previous year. (AP/Wide World Photos)

HISTORY

The IRS, initially named the Bureau of Internal Revenue, was created in 1862 in response to the need for increased revenue for the War Department during the Civil War. During the early years of independence, taxation was a very sensitive issue and did not have strong constitutional support. The original states were reluctant to give the federal government the power to tax, and the taxation debate put the states and the federal government at odds. From the moment of U.S. independence, states wanted the right to determine taxation without the burden of a federal system. Initially fees were assessed for government operating costs but many states paid late or not at all. A tariff system of fees on imported goods was used to raise the necessary revenues for federal government expenses, and tariffs were raised when more funds were needed. In some cases, as in the War of 1812, taxes were imposed to fund a war, then quickly repealed at the war's end. The tariff system was also controversial, however, as it affected regions of the United States differently. In fact, the tariff system became a major component of the North-South conflict, erupting later into the Civil War.

Just one year after the start of the Civil War, support for the Bureau of Internal Revenue was sufficient to impose a series of taxes including excise taxes, stamp taxes, commodities taxes, and license and legal document taxes.

The legislative branch was then responsible for determining the type and amount of tax Americans would pay. Taxation was termed progressive, regressive, or proportional. Progressive taxation collects a progressively higher percentage rate from higher income. Regressive taxes collect a larger percentage of taxes from citizens with middle income. Proportional taxes collect the same percentage rate of all incomes. The earliest income tax levied by the federal government exempted the first $600 dollars of income. Income between $600 and $10,000 was taxed at three percent and income over $10,000 was taxed at five percent. While these figures have changed over time, the basic structure of income taxes in the U.S. remains progressive.

As tax law grew more complex, the impact of taxation on the economy became evident in the way it promoted or retarded certain kinds of investment, spending, and corporate fiscal management. Economists and politicians began to formulate tax policy as a way of manipulating the economy. Especially during the nineteenth century, tax policy became a method of social and economic engineering. Tax policy was debated and implemented as a mechanism for ensuring the well-being of the wealthy and middle classes and ultimately for improving the distribution of wealth. In times of prosperity the income tax was quickly reduced or eliminated but it would be revived during economic depression.

FAST FACTS

Every year the IRS sends out more than 8 billion pages of forms and instructions to American citizens.

(Source: John Steele Gordon. "American Taxation." *American Heritage*, May–June 1996.)

World War II also had an important impact on taxation. At the close of the war, when Allied nations were unable to produce the goods for import from which tariff revenues were derived, legislators increase reliance on the income tax to fund the growing federal government. During this period Congress passed the Revenue Act of 1942, which contained 208 pages of tax law and was 15 times as long as a previous act passed in 1913. The majority of the 1942 act was written to deal with the fiscal and economic consequences of earlier tax legislation. Corporations and individuals unhappy with income tax laws were devoting more resources to finding loopholes, working political favors into tax law, and increasing the number and kinds of deductions to provide savings. Lists of tax codes, meaningless to the uninitiated could reduce the impact of income tax for those who could manipulate the system to their advantage.

Modernization and Reform

Throughout the 1990s, the IRS became the focus of intense criticism and scrutiny. The dizzying complexity of the tax code, lack of coherent service delivery to the taxpayer, and the failure of multimillion-dollar programs meant to upgrade IRS capabilities were recognized by citizens and politicians alike. The public's loss of confidence in this most critical federal government function has led directly to political movements such as the National Performance Review, a Clinton administration reform program aimed at providing government services that cost less and do more. Under pressure to improve services, the IRS signed on as a pilot program of the Government Performance and Results Act of 1993. A separate government agency, the National Commission on Restructuring the IRS, was also formed to provide specific direction in modernizing the IRS.

CURRENT POLITICAL ISSUES

The IRS is the primary revenue collector for the federal government. If the system of revenue collection is flawed, as critics assert, then not only does the issue of how much to tax becomes politically controversial, but so do the acts of collection and enforcement. Representative Bill Archer, Chairman of the House Ways and Means Committee overseeing the IRS, has commented: "We eat $200 billion a year in unpaid taxes. All of that is fraud. The IRS's computer problems open the door to more and more fraud." Shortfalls of this size are a major concern for Congress, and as a result, at least three government bodies are involved in IRS oversight. Congress, treasury officials, and the White House are involved in the debate over how much it will cost to fix these problems.

Case Study: The Cost of Modernization

The Tax System Modernization program was implemented by the Department of Treasury to bring needed technical solutions to the IRS by developing new methods that would increase administrative efficiency, save taxpayers money, and eliminate fraud. One example of such modernization was the Service Center Recognition/Image Processing System, a new tax return reading technology which promised to save taxpayers $17 billion. Instead the program lost $209 million in cost overruns. It was one of ten high-cost modernization programs implemented within the IRS that not only failed to achieve its goals but also lost millions of dollars during implementation. Deputy Secretary of Treasury Lawrence Summers, head of the IRS admitted, "I think modernization has gone way off track."

While the $1 billion spent so far on modernization has produced few results, the cost of not reforming the IRS is even greater. The National Commission on Restructuring estimates that $25 billion in refunds have gone to ineligible recipients. In order to address such problems, the IRS uses emergency computer filters in order to screen returns; but such short-term solutions continue to cost money not currently in the IRS budget, and Congress is increasingly unwilling to provide more funding. The IRS and its oversight bodies must determine other ways for the agency to solve its problems during a time of budget reductions.

The IRS will spend an estimated $8 billion over six years on its modernization programs. The continued goals of the program will be to correctly process returns, catching fraud and other tax crimes, and reduce the cost of revenue collection in general.

SUCCESSES AND FAILURES

During her first year in office, Commissioner Margaret Richardson worked to provide taxpayers with better service, making it easier for them to obtain information and file tax returns. In 1996 the IRS offered the TeleFile system nationwide, and almost three million taxpayers filed their tax returns by telephone. In January

1996 the IRS launched its own homepage on the Internet, receiving over 100 million hits in its first 10 months of operation. In 1996, the IRS also unveiled the Electronic Federal Tax Payment System, which will enable millions of business and individual taxpayers to make their federal tax deposits quickly and easily using a telephone or a personal computer.

One element of the IRS modernization system that has shown positive results is electronic filing and significant increases in this service have been reported by the IRS. For the tax year 1996, 15.9 million electronic returns were filed with the IRS, up three million from the previous year. This program is evidence that the IRS is making progress in providing cost-saving measures to the public and increasing its technological capabilities.

FUTURE DIRECTIONS

The IRS is under tremendous pressure from government bodies, business interests, and private citizens to upgrade its computer and information technologies and implement customer service enhancements that allow citizen access to accurate information and assistance on request. The failures of the IRS to accurately collect taxes, or enforce the tax law have been the source of much debate. The National Performance Review, the National Commission on Restructuring the IRS, the secretary and deputy secretary of the Treasury, and Congress are all looking for ways to improve the IRS. The political impact of IRS problems are enormous. The IRS is one of the few federal government agencies that directly impacts every working American and every business.

In response, the IRS has hired a new chief information officer whose primary responsibility is to review the technical capabilities of the IRS and insure that systems are developed which equal or exceed the capabilities of systems already employed in the private sector. The new chief information officer has already collapsed 26 IRS programs into nine as restructuring gets under way.

In addition, the IRS will begin to change the way it seeks to develop new programs and methodologies by using outside contractors. Sixty percent of new programs are being developed outside the IRS in the hope of shifting the agency's perspective and ultimately successfully reforming it. Finally, a Five Point Plan is being implemented within the IRS which stresses oversight, flexibility, budgeting, tax simplification and leadership. Oversight will be the role of high-ranking Treasury officials and other government bodies. Flexibility is required to reduce administrative restrictions on the agencies ability to hire, train, and retain skilled professionals. Budgeting reform will require working with Congress to secure budget appropriations which promote long-range planning. Tax simplification will require legislative and IRS action to reduce confusion, litigation, and inaccurate returns, thus saving both the agency and citizens time and money. Introduction and retention of skilled high-ranking leadership that can put IRS operations on a par with major private corporations are a critical part of this plan. If the IRS is able to restructure and reform with the guidance of multiple government bodies, it may become the best example of, in Vice President Al Gore's words, "creating a government that costs less, and does more."

AGENCY RESOURCES

The IRS provides information to the public in a variety of formats. Tax forms used in filing a return with the IRS are available at most U.S. Post Offices and at some public libraries. The IRS also operates a toll-free Helpline, 1–800–829-1040 to answer questions about tax code. The IRS's award-winning Web site is located at http://www.irs.ustreas.gov, called *The Daily Bulletin.* The site is easy to use and provides advice and answers to tax questions. Downloadable forms are also available and links provide detailed information on the tax code and its application.

AGENCY PUBLICATIONS

The IRS publishes hundreds of documents which provide specific information on the tax system and guide the taxpayer through the process of filing a tax return. Among them are: *Your Rights as a Taxpayer, Students Guide to Income Tax, Farms Tax Guide,* and *Quick and Easy Access to Tax Help and Forms.*

BIBLIOGRAPHY

Gleckman, Howard. "IRS Reforms Are Only A Good Start." *Business Week*, 31 March 1997 p. 47.

Herman, Tom. "IRS Computer Security Needs Major Improvement, a New Report Warns." *Wall Street Journal*, 9 April 1997 p. A1.

Johnston, David Cay. "IRS Appears to Be Focusing on the Poor." *New York Times*, 13 April 1997 p. 13.

McNamee, Mike. "Dr. Elbows Gets More Room. (Department of Treasury Secretary Larry Summers)." *Business Week*, 14 April 1997 p. 78.

Schlesinger, Jacob M. and Greg Hitt. "Plans to Give IRS More Independence from Treasury Get Capitol Hill Support." *Wall Street Journal*, 16 April 1997 p. A2.

Stevenson, Richard W. "Congress Plans to Investigate Audits of Tax Exempt Groups." *Wall Street Journal*, 25 March 1997 p. A11.

International Trade Administration (ITA)

PARENT ORGANIZATION: Department of Commerce
ESTABLISHED: January 1, 1980
EMPLOYEES: 2,500

Contact Information:

ADDRESS: U.S. Department of Commerce
1401 Constitution Ave. SW
Washington, DC 20230
PHONE: (202) 482-3809
FAX: (202) 482-5819
URL: http://www.ita.doc.gov
UNDER SECRETARY OF COMMERCE FOR INTERNATIONAL TRADE: Aaron L. Davis

WHAT IS ITS MISSION?

The International Trade Administration (ITA) is the agency within the Department of Commerce whose mission is most closely identified with the department's primary purpose. The ITA's mission is generally to promote world trade and to strengthen the international trade and investment position of the United States by encouraging, assisting, and advocating U.S. exports; by ensuring that U.S. businesses have equal access to foreign markets; by enabling businesses to compete against unfair trade imports; and by safeguarding jobs and the competitive strength of U.S. industry.

HOW IS IT STRUCTURED?

The ITA is one of 14 bureaus within the Department of Commerce, a cabinet-level agency that is part of the executive branch. Its administrator holds the title of under secretary for International Trade. The administration, legal affairs, and community relations of the ITA are the responsibility of several offices associated with the under secretary's office, including the Office of Administration, the Office of Public Affairs, and the Office of Legislative and Intergovernmental Affairs.

The program work of the ITA is carried out through its four operating units: Trade Development, Market Access and Compliance, Import Administration, and the Commercial Service. Each is led by an assistant secretary who reports to the under secretary. Trade Development houses the ITA's Advocacy Center, which acts on behalf of U.S. industry in the competition for overseas contracts and runs the Trade Information Center to counsel American businesses and promote trade. Market Access and Compliance uses the knowledge of country experts to provide market analysis to U.S. companies, identifying trade barriers and the means to overcome them.

Import Administration protects U.S. companies from unfair trade practices by administering antidumping and duty laws, together with agreements with Japan and Canada. The Commercial Service, the largest of ITA's operating units, provides export counseling and export promotion services through a network of 85 district offices and 134 overseas offices in 69 countries. The Commercial Service also develops and distributes information products and conducts overseas trade shows and fairs.

BUDGET:

International Trade Administration

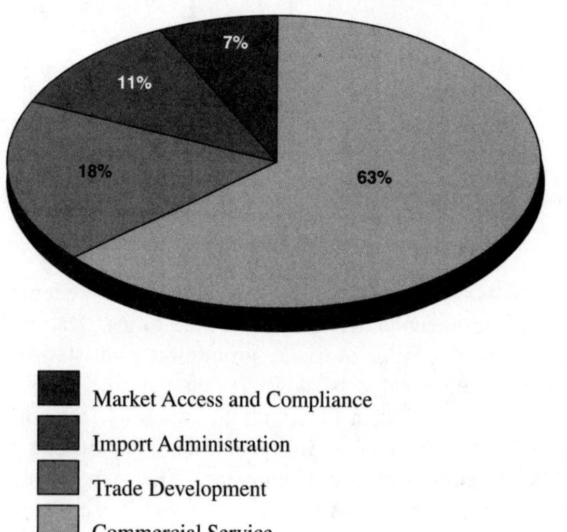

Market Access and Compliance
Import Administration
Trade Development
Commercial Service

PRIMARY FUNCTIONS

The ITA's scope of activities is broad and complex. It advises on the analysis, formulation, and implementation of international economic policies and coordinates the discussion of trade issues with other countries. Through Import Administration, it defends U.S. industry against unfair trade practices, ensures the proper administration of foreign trade zones, and administers statutory import programs, such as those governing watch assemblies.

Through Trade Development, the ITA conducts programs to increase domestic export competitiveness, promotes increased U.S. industrial participation in international markets, and conducts analyses of specific industrial sectors. The Commercial Service produces, markets, and manages a line of products and services to satisfy the marketing information needs of the U.S. exporting and international communities, manages the delivery of ITA programs through its district offices and international posts, supports overseas trade events, promotes U.S. products and services throughout the world, and assists state and private organizations in export financing.

PROGRAMS

The ITA administrates numerous programs designed to promote U.S. trade in international markets, but perhaps two of the best known are operated through Trade Development. The Advocacy Program is a government-wide effort to counter the unfair trade practices of foreign governments. Through the ITA's Advocacy Center, the government fights for a level playing field in international trade, supporting U.S. companies' bids abroad with the full resources of the government.

The Trade Information Center, another ITA program, is often referred to as the nerve center for information for small and midsized businesses who want to export products abroad. The Trade Information Center provides a single point of contact in the government for counseling and assistance; it counsels more than 60,000 companies and individuals each year.

BUDGET INFORMATION

The ITA's budget authority is granted almost entirely through congressional appropriations, with a small amount coming from revenue generated through the sale of ITA products and services. The 1997 ITA budget was slightly over $270 million. With its large network of international and domestic offices, the Commercial Service accounts for more than half—63 percent—of the ITA's expenditures. Approximately 18 percent of the ITA budget is spent on Trade Development, 11 percent on Import Administration, and 7 percent on Market Access and Compliance.

HISTORY

The history of government agencies assigned the task of promoting and developing commerce and industry in the United States is a long, complex chronicle of

FAST FACTS

In 1997 U.S. total trade in goods and services reached $937 billion.

(Source: International Trade Administration, 1998.)

agencies created, transferred, abolished, or renamed according to economic demands of the times. Scattered government efforts at trade promotion and statistic-keeping began as early as 1820, but the first focused effort was launched in 1912 with the creation of the combined U.S. Chamber of Commerce and the Bureau of Foreign and Domestic Commerce. The new bureau placed commercial associates in 14 foreign countries together with many agents who specialized in promoting specific products in appropriate countries. Shortly before World War I (1914–18), the Bureau of Foreign and Domestic Commerce began to create a network of district offices that still exists today.

During World War I, the bureau continued to seek new outlets for U.S. trade products, but the needs of the war economy took highest priority; the bureau licensed exports of strategic materials, drafted legislation dealing with enemy trade, and audited the costs of government contracts. High worldwide demands and disrupted foreign production increased the demand for U.S. products, and trade reached unprecedented levels after the war. To meet the growing demands, the bureau formed separate divisions for the Far East, South America, and Europe.

Changing Market Forces

The stock market crash of 1929 and the ensuing Great Depression changed the economic picture considerably for the United States, providing the Bureau of Foreign and Domestic Commerce with three important challenges: find and develop trade opportunities in a depressed world economy, deal with increasing numbers of tariffs and other protectionist trade barriers, and slow the transport of U.S. production facilities to foreign countries. The difficulty of these challenges was compounded by the Roosevelt Administration's Department of Commerce budget cuts, which reduced bureau funds by 62 percent.

One method for dealing with the Depression was to transfer the bureau's foreign offices to the Department of State, a move which lasted 40 years. The move signaled the first recognition by the U.S. government that trade was becoming tied more and more to foreign policy, with nations protecting and developing their own national interests.

The Post-War Economy

World War II (1939–45) and the following decade marked a period of intense industrial activity and general prosperity. The Bureau of Foreign and Domestic Commerce responded to the total war effort, the following peacetime conversion, and the limited Korean conflict by undergoing a series of restructurings. In 1953, the bureau was abolished and replaced by two new agencies, the Business and Defense Services and the Bureau of Foreign Commerce. The Bureau of Foreign Commerce became an agency that stressed new services, including trade promotion, intended to capture international markets.

Despite this period of prosperity, the United States began to experience some balance of payments problems, caused primarily by the practices of extending credit to countries short of foreign funds and trading with protectionist countries in the Communist bloc. In spite of efforts by the Johnson administration, the balance of trade continued to decline, resulting in the first U.S. trade deficit (in 1971) since statistics had been kept. Gradually, U.S. trade with the growing Eastern bloc countries expanded, alleviating some of the problem; but in order to deal with isolated powers such as China and the Soviet Union, another reorganization took place in 1972.

By the late 1970s the U.S. merchandise trade deficit had skyrocketed, and in 1980 Congress passed the Trade Reorganization Act, effectively establishing a new national export policy. The International Trade Administration was created from this act, and supervision of unfair trade practices was transferred to the ITA from the Department of the Treasury.

Japan and the End of the Cold War

One nation whose trade practices were most troubling to the United States was Japan. The country was clearly a rising economic power and was generally allowed free access to U.S. markets, but it had established many trade barriers to prevent U.S. goods from reaching its markets. In 1986 President Ronald Reagan pronounced the formation of a new cabinet-level Trade Strike Force to identify unfair foreign trade practices and propose ways to eliminate them. Based on Strike Force recommendations, a strategy for dealing with Japanese trade barriers was developed, elements of which are still being negotiated today between the two nations. Very gradually, Japanese markets are opening up to free trade.

In 1988 the ITA's export control functions were transferred to a new agency, making trade promotion the ITA's primary mission. The fall of the Soviet Union in December 1991 and the resulting democratization of many of its former satellite countries created a new dynamic in the world of international commerce, giving the ITA mission plenty of new opportunities for development. The Newly Independent States, former republics of the Soviet Union, were ready to try free market economies and were suddenly wide open to U.S. goods and services. The ITA's efforts to penetrate these new markets is ongoing.

CURRENT POLITICAL ISSUES

International trade promotion by the government has long been a common practice, but in recent years it has acquired an unprecedented position in the federal government, where trade promotion now involves approximately 19 different agencies. In 1992 President Bill Clinton promised to focus the nation's foreign policy on its trading interests—pushing for more trade, more jobs, and more investment. Critics of government trade promotion argue that promotion, if it is encouraged at all, should be handled by individual companies in the traditional form of advertising or trade shows. In both principle and practice, these critics argue, government involvement in promoting exports is a waste of taxpayers' money, a form of "corporate welfare," and at its worst creates circumstances that breed corruption and influence-buying.

Case Study: U.S. Taxpayers and "Corporate Welfare"

Critics argue that the principle of export promotion is flawed simply because nothing is free, especially in international trade. If a representative of the U.S. government goes abroad to help secure a deal for goods or services, the buyers of these exports rarely profit in terms of jobs created or income earned. The deal is usually more complicated; the export buyer must deal with many more government ministers, and if the U.S. minister cannot offer an attractive incentive, the buyer will deal with someone else. Frequently an indirect subsidy is offered—cash to cover a discount rate offered the buyer, or a generous deal for establishing export credit, or government aid contingent on the purchase of the goods or service. In most cases, these deals end up costing taxpayers—they are in effect subsidizing exporters to produce goods and then paying foreigners to take the goods away.

In the U.S. political culture, many find such government subsidies indefensible. Passage of the Welfare Reform Act under the Clinton administration discontinued a large portion of federal aid to poor Americans and the government's intention to continue to spend increasingly large amounts of tax revenue on "corporate welfare" outrages many. Such services as trade assistance, advice hot lines for exporters, and government-hosted international trade shows are all seen as forms of corporate welfare, for they constitute the kind of assistance that the U.S. government has become unwilling to offer the poor.

Opponents of corporate welfare are not merely defenders of the poor, however; they include congressional conservatives and members of the business community who want government to stay out of American business interests altogether. In September 1996, a large majority in the House of Representatives, liberals and conservatives alike, soundly rejected legislation (H.R. 3759) that would reauthorize expenditures for three trade promotion agencies—the ITA, the Trade and Development Agency (TDA), and the Overseas Private Investment Corporation (OPIC). Though the bill's defeat (by a 260–157 vote) will most likely not mean the end of any of these agencies, it indicates that trade promotion activities will be closely monitored in the immediate future.

Corrupt Practices?

Other important questions to be asked of government trade promotion are whose products or services are being promoted and why. During the administration of Ronald Brown, secretary of commerce from 1992 to 1996, critics charged that many of the most sought-after places on trade missions abroad went to donors to the Democratic Party. In a lawsuit brought by the conservative group Judicial Watch, the Commerce secretary was accused of "selling" seats, using trade missions to reward party donors. Commerce Department papers turned over to the group clearly indicate that many corporate contributors to the president's campaign expected their money to earn them special consideration—in fact, some contributors stated this expectation explicitly. In addition, some of these donors were eventually selected to accompany the secretary on trade missions.

Though it has not yet been proven whether donors were given preference—non-donors are said to have outnumbered donors 2 to 1 on trade missions under Secretary Brown—the scandal caused the Commerce Department some embarrassment. In 1996 at the beginning of his administration (Secretary Brown was killed in a plane crash while on a trade mission in Europe), Commerce Secretary William Daley suspended all overseas trade missions for 30 days until new selection guidelines could be formulated.

SUCCESSES AND FAILURES

The ITA's Advocacy Center, created to combat the increasing problems related to the competitive nature of the international private sector and government trade practices, has become one of the ITA's most successful enterprises. The Advocacy Center's sole mission is to mobilize the resources of the entire government in support of U.S. firms competing against aggressive competition on overseas projects. The center's pursuit of this mission in 1995 and 1996 resulted in 230 successful projects, with an estimated U.S. export content of $38 billion—an amount that will support more than 500,000 jobs across the country.

Other ITA successes include negotiations by the offices of Market Access and Compliance, which in 1994 successfully negotiated a framework agreement with Japan to open its multibillion-dollar public works market and its $2.6 billion government medical technology market.

To access the trade information available through the Trade Information Center, information seekers can call 1-800-872-8723. Trade specialists are available to provide export assistance weekdays from 8:30 A.M. to 5:30 P.M. The Trade Information Center is also available on-line at http://www.ita.doc.gov/tic.

FUTURE DIRECTIONS

The ITA's plans for responding to the increasing globalization of the U.S. economy involve a general strengthening of the ITA's promotion policies and functions. One of the most interesting elements of the ITA's future plans is the Big Emerging Markets (BEMs) Strategy. The BEMs strategy focuses on ten countries—Argentina, Brazil, China, India, Indonesia, Mexico, Poland, South Africa, South Korea, and Turkey—which are expected to account for more than 40 percent of total global imports over the next 20 years. The BEMs strategy aims to secure and maintain access to these markets for U.S. companies.

The administration's future developments will also tend to focus on trade assistance to small-to-midsize businesses. Small businesses are the fastest growing part of the U.S. economy, employing 54 percent of the private workforce and accounting for half of the Gross Domestic Product. The Small Business Administration estimates that companies with fewer than 100 employees account for 60 percent of American exporting firms. The ITA hopes to strengthen the market-access power of these smaller companies in a variety of ways, including by an expansion of the trade information infrastructure. Updates and enhancements of the Trade Information Center, the Commercial Information Management System, and the National Trade Data Bank are under way.

AGENCY RESOURCES

General inquiries about the work of the ITA should be directed to the Office of Public Affairs, ITA, U.S. Department of Commerce, HCHB, 1401 Constitution Ave. SW, Washington, DC 20230; phone (202) 482-3809. Much information about past and current ITA activities can be located on-line through the ITA's Pressroom Reference library at http://www.ita.doc.gov/media.

AGENCY PUBLICATIONS

One of the ITA's most popular publications is *Business America,* the Department of Commerce's magazine of international trade. A free issue is available on the ITA's Web site, and subscriptions are available through the Public Affairs Office. Other popular ITA publications are the *Metropolitan Area Exports* series, the *Big Emerging Markets,* and the *National Export Strategy 1996.* All are available through the Public Affairs Office.

BIBLIOGRAPHY

Corson, Richard and Camille Richardson. "ITA's Model Approach Arms U.S. Environmental Technologies Exporters for International Competition." *Business America*, April 1996, pp. 53-54.

"Don't be Salesmen (Governments Should not Promote Private Export Deals)." *The Economist*, 1 February 1997, p. 34.

El-Agra, Ali M. *International Trade*. New York: St. Martin's Press, 1989.

Gowa, Joanne. *Alliances, Adversaries, and International Trade*. Princeton, N.J.: Princeton University Press, 1993.

Kelly, Nancy E. "ITA Overhaul May Speed Relief." *American Metal Market*, 10 May 1996, p. 92.

Kullman, Paul J. "The Commerce Department's Trade Compliance Center Gears Up." *Business America*, May 1997, pp. 28–31.

Lenz, Allen J. *Beyond Blue Horizons: U.S. Trade Performance and International Competitiveness in the 1990s*. Westport, Conn: Greenwood Publishing Group, Inc., 1990.

Summers, Lawrence. "The Clinton Administration's International Economic Policy." *Challenge*, March–April 1994, pp. 24–27.

"Trade Promotion." *Business America*, September 1996, pp. 30–61.

Winham, Gilbert R. *The Evolution of International Trade Agreements*. Toronto: University of Toronto Press, 1992.

Joint Chiefs of Staff (JCS)

PARENT ORGANIZATION: Department of Defense
ESTABLISHED: 1947
EMPLOYEES: 1,400

Contact Information:

ADDRESS: The Pentagon
Washington, DC 20318
PHONE: (703) 697-4272
FAX: (703) 697-8758
E-MAIL: publicaffairs@js.pentagon.mil
URL: http://www.dtic.mil/jcs
CHAIRMAN: Gen. Henry S. Shelton
VICE CHAIRMAN: Gen. Joseph W. Ralston

WHAT IS ITS MISSION?

The mission of the Joint Chiefs of Staff (JCS), one of the most important command elements in the military establishment of the United States, is to serve as the chief military planning and advisory committee to the commander in chief of the U.S. armed forces—the president of the United States—and to the secretary of defense. As the highest-ranking military officers in the nation, the Joint Chiefs of Staff are responsible for designing and directing strategic military policy, coordinating joint operations, and evaluating the strength and readiness of the armed forces.

HOW IS IT STRUCTURED?

The chairman of the Joint Chiefs of Staff and the Joint Staff are part of the U.S. Department of Defense, a large and complex government agency that also includes the secretary of defense; the military departments and services within the departments; the unified combatant commands; the defense agencies; department field activities; and other agencies, offices, and activities established by law or executive order. Within this structure the Joint Chiefs of Staff assist in providing for the strategic direction and planning of the armed forces but have no executive authority to command combatant forces. The chairman of the JCS functions in the military chain of command by passing on orders from the president or defense secretary to the unified combatant commands.

A U.S. Marine trains in the use of a metal detector for locating buried anti-tank mines. Due to the insistence of the Joint Chiefs of Staff, the United States refused to endorse a proposed moratorium on land mines. (Courtesy of the United States Defense Department)

The Joint Chiefs

The Joint Chiefs of Staff consist of the chairman; the vice chairman; the chief of staff of the army; the chief of naval operations; the chief of staff of the air force; and the commandant of the marine corps. The label "Joint Chiefs of Staff" is often confusing because it is used not only to name these military leaders but the entire agency and the support structure serving them, including the Joint Staff.

The chairman of the Joint Chiefs of Staff is the senior ranking member of the armed forces and the principal military adviser to the president, the secretary of defense, and the National Security Council. He or she is appointed by the president, with the advice and consent of the Senate, and serves a two-year term. Subject to the authority of the president and the secretary of defense, the chairman is responsible for assisting them in the strategic direction and planning of the armed forces; allocating resources to fulfill these plans, and making specific recommendations for the assignment of responsibilities within these plans. The chairman establishes and maintains a system for evaluating the preparedness of each of the unified combatant commands and advises the defense secretary of the critical deficiencies and strengths of these forces. The chairman also advises the secretary on budgetary and manpower priorities and coordinates the education and training of personnel.

In addition to these responsibilities, the chairman of the Joint Chiefs of Staff calls and presides over meetings of the Joint Chiefs of Staff, schedules issues for consideration by the Joint Chiefs, and assists the Joint Chiefs in carrying on their business as promptly as possible. The chairman represents the United States on the Military Staff Committee of the United Nations.

The vice chairman of the JCS performs duties assigned by the chairman and acts as chairman in the absence or disability of the chairman. While serving in the capacity of vice chairman, he or she outranks all other officers of the armed forces except for the Joint Chiefs of Staff. The other members of the JCS, the Service Chiefs, are military advisers who provide additional information on request and who may submit their advice when it does not agree with that of the chairman. These officers serve two functions; first and most important, they are members of the Joint Chiefs of Staff, and second, they are the chief military officers of their respective military departments, and as such they are responsible to their departmental secretaries for management of their services.

The Joint Staff

The chairman is assisted in accomplishing his responsibilities by the Joint Staff. Specifically, the Joint Staff helps create a unified strategy for directing the combatant forces, oversees operation of the forces under unified command, and integrates the forces into an efficient team. The Joint Staff is composed of approximately equal numbers of officers from the army, the navy and marine corps, and the air force. Marine officers make up about 20 percent of the navy's contingent. Although the final authority for managing the Joint Staff rests with the chairman of the Joint Chiefs, the chairman and the other chiefs appoint a director for the Joint Staff who serves to assist in this capacity and who is the primary go-between for the Joint Chiefs and the Joint Staff. Officers who serve on the Joint Staff have no command authority over combat forces.

The Joint Staff is divided into nine directorates. One of these, the directorate of Management, is primarily administrative in nature and provides assistance through management, planning, and direction of support activities. These activities include correspondence administration, budget and finance, action management and archiving, information technology, services, resources, and all aspects of staff and information security.

The other directorates are military in nature and are designated by the acronyms J-1 through J-8. They are: Manpower and Personnel (J-1); Intelligence (J-2); Operations (J-3); Logistics (J-4); Strategic Plans and Policy (J-5); Command, Control, Communications, and Computer Systems (J-6); Operational Plans and Interoperability (J-7); and Force Structure Resources and Assessment (J-8). When referred to by name, the J-6 directorate is sometimes referred to as C4 Systems.

PRIMARY FUNCTIONS

The Joint Chiefs submit to the secretary of defense alternative program recommendations and budget proposals; prepare plans for logistics, mobility, and field strength; and, in times of conflict, advise the president and the defense secretary on the strategic direction of the armed forces. These functions include a broad range of support activities on the part of the Joint Staff, carried out through the directorates.

The directorate for Manpower and Personnel, J-1, provides the Joint Chiefs with manpower and personnel advice support in order to ensure maximum readiness of the total force. The directorate for Intelligence, J-2, provides intelligence to the Joint Chiefs, the secretary of defense, and the unified commands. J-2 is unusual in the Joint Staff structure in that it is also a part of another agency, the Defense Intelligence Agency (DIA). The directorate that effects the movement of military forces, conducts operational briefings to the national leadership, and serves as the operational link within the national command authority is J-3, Operations. Logistics—the procurement and transport of the materials needed for proper execution of warfighting—are planned through J-4.

The J-5 directorate, Strategic Plans and Policy, helps the Joint Chiefs to shape the long-term plans for the implementation of U.S. forces. Part of this directorate's responsibility is to periodically evaluate how changes in the global environment might alter deployment and planning for the military. The directorate for C4 Systems, J-6, takes the lead in identifying and resolving military aspects of information-based issues. Part of the C4 directive is to anticipate and develop new "information warfare" technologies. The coordination of joint operations and command structures is accomplished through the work and advice of the J-7 directorate. J-7 helps establish the overarching theories of joint warfare and arranges joint and multinational training exercises. Finally, the J-8 directorate assists the chairman in handling his broad range of responsibilities by developing requirements and options for military forces and systems and by conducting studies, analyses, and assessments of different aspects of the military.

FAST FACTS

The chairman of the Joint Chiefs of Staff holds the rank of five-star general (or admiral if he is a naval officer) and outranks all other officers of the armed forces. However, the chairman may not exercise military command over the Joint Chiefs of Staff or any of the armed forces.

(Source: "Goldwater-Nichols Act of 1986," JCSLink.)

PROGRAMS

Because the Joint Chiefs of Staff and the Joint Staff have no direct command authority over combat troops, their initiatives rarely take the form of direct action. Joint Chiefs of Staff programs are typically initiatives that involve gathering and analyzing information. This information is then reported to the appropriate command operatives. An example of this type of program is the Joint Warfighting Capabilities Assessment/Joint Monthly Readiness Review (JWCA/JMRR). This evaluation, carried out largely by the J-1, J-7, and J-8 directorates, is a report that is ultimately intended to improve total force readiness by identifying, analyzing and acting on issues of manpower and personnel, interoperability, and force structure.

HISTORY

The concept of joint operations among the nation's military branches began during the War of 1812, when the naval operations of Captain Thomas McDonough on Lake Champlain gave vital support to the ground campaigns of the U.S. Army. During the Civil War, the collaboration between General Ulysses S. Grant and Admiral David D. Porter in the Vicksburg campaign of 1863 served as a prime example of joint military planning and execution. By the turn of the century, war had become too complex for joint planning to occur merely in response to present threats. Joint military actions during the Cuban campaign of the Spanish-American War (1898) were often confused and poorly coordinated and drew criticism from both Congress and the public.

The U.S. military establishment attempted to address these problems in 1903 with the formation of a joint board composed of the military heads of the army and navy, and the chief planner for each service. The army-navy board was meant to plan for joint operations and to address concerns that were common to the two service branches. The board's charter, however, gave it no actual authority to enforce its decisions, and the board was limited to commentary on problems submitted by the secretaries of the two military departments. As a result the board had little impact on the conduct of American armed forces during World War I (1914–1918). Subsequent attempts at revitalizing the board also proved too weak to give it much central decision-making power.

World War II and the Origins of the Joint Chiefs of Staff

Despite some similarities between these early joint boards and the present-day Joint Chiefs of Staff, it was not the joint board that evolved into the JCS; it was rather a body of military authority that was composed for the purpose of British-American cooperation during World War II (1939–1945). Soon after the Japanese bombing of Pearl Harbor and the American entry into the war, President Franklin Roosevelt and British Prime Minister Winston Churchill established the Combined Chiefs of Staff as the supreme military body for strategic direction of the British-American war effort.

Unlike Great Britain, the United States did not have an established agency for furnishing input to such a committee. The British Chiefs of Staff, however, had for many years been assigned the administration, tactical coordination, and strategic direction for British forces. This committee also used planning and intelligence personnel who helped provide the war cabinet and the prime minister with military advice. To coordinate staff work for fighting the war in Europe, the United States needed a body similar to this that could meet and plan with its British counterparts.

The concept first described as a "unified high command" was adopted by the United States in 1942 and came to be known as the U.S. Joint Chiefs of Staff. These first Joint Chiefs of Staff worked throughout the war without any legislative authorization or even formal presidential definition—President Roosevelt preferred it that way for the time being in order to grant the Joint Chiefs the flexibility to meet the needs of the war. The first members of the Joint Chiefs of Staff were simply the corresponding leaders to the British Chiefs of the Army, the Navy, and the Royal Air Force (RAF). Following the model of the RAF as a coequal and autonomous branch of the military, the U.S. Army Air Corps later became a separate branch as well: the United States Air Force.

Legislative Authority for the Joint Chiefs

Under the leadership of President Roosevelt, the JCS gradually grew in influence and became the primary agent in coordinating and giving strategic direction to the army and navy. In collaboration with the British Chiefs of Staff, the Joint Chiefs mapped and issued broad strategic direction for both countries during World War II.

Immediately after the war, the need for a formal structure of joint command among U.S. armed forces was apparent. Without the backing of Congress and the American public, the Joint Chiefs could not hope to continue in their role with much authority. The first legislative step was the landmark National Security Act of 1947, which effectively established the three military departments that exist today—the U.S. Army, Navy, and Air Force—and used the wartime Joint Chiefs of Staff as its model for the armed forces' central planning body. The older joint board, considered the remnant of an ineffective past, was disbanded by the new law, and a 1949 amendment established the Department of Defense and gave more centralized powers to the secretary of defense and the Joint Chiefs.

The newly created department was at first a confederation of armed forces that acted as budgetary rivals. Interservice rivalry had always been considered a means of healthy competition among American soldiers, sailors, and airmen, but continued squabbling over roles, missions, weapons, and money made clear the need for further strengthening of a central military authority. Since then, a series of legislative and executive changes have produced today's defense organization. The most recent major congressional action was the 1986 Department of Defense Reorganization Act, or the Goldwater-Nichols Act, which enhanced the legal authority of the chairman of the Joint Chiefs of Staff and the unified commanders.

CURRENT POLITICAL ISSUES

Sometimes a political problem arises for presidents who differ with the nation's highest military leaders, the Joint Chiefs of Staff, on proper actions or policies. In 1993, for example, the Joint Chiefs wanted the United States to resume testing nuclear weapons—a practice that was in clear violation of international nuclear test-ban treaties that had been signed by the United States. President Bill Clinton at first adopted the Joint Chiefs' recommendation as U.S. policy; then a storm of criticism from Congress, the media, and the public forced him to reject it. It was not the last time, however, that the president and the Joint Chiefs would differ on an issue.

Case Study: The International Effort to Ban Land Mines

At the start of the 1990s, an international campaign to ban land mines was gathering momentum. As inexpensive "antipersonnel" weapons that were buried just below the ground and then detonated on contact, land mines had always played an important role in ground warfare. Their increased use in the conflicts of lesser-developed countries had made them, in the words of former U.S. secretary of state Warren Christopher, "the smallest weapon(s) of mass destruction." It is now estimated that each year land mines kill or maim 10,000 to 25,000 people, often innocent civilians. In the war-torn country of Cambodia it has been estimated that about 80,000 have been killed by land mines since 1970 and that one in every 236 Cambodians has lost a limb because of the devices. As a military weapon, the land mine is unique in its ability to cause death and destruction long after armies have left the battlefield.

By 1997 the call for a total ban on the production and use of land mines was endorsed by nearly 90 countries, and it seemed that the United States, one of the most technologically advanced nations in the world, would take the lead in this initiative. But when these countries gathered at an international conference in Oslo, Norway, to discuss the issue, they were surprised to find that the United States would not approve an outright moratorium. Rather, the United States wanted to reserve the right to use land mines in Korea and in other special circumstances.

As one of the primary military defenders of South Korea, the United States had more than 37,000 troops stationed at the demilitarized zone (DMZ) marking the boundary between South Korea and its communist neighbor, North Korea. In defending his country's refusal to agree to a moratorium, President Clinton explained that the U.S. troops stationed in South Korea were protected by antipersonnel and antitank mines in the DMZ that deterred an invasion from the north and that he could not in good conscience endanger these troops by removing the mines.

Although the U.S. military used only "smart" mines, which disarmed after a typical period of 48 hours, and spent $150 million on demining and training deminers worldwide, other countries wanted the United States to demonstrate the leadership that would lead countries such as Russia, Iran, India, and Vietnam to join in the agreement. Without U.S. participation, the participation of these countries seemed unlikely.

At the time President Clinton made his announcement it was clear that his conscience and his public statements were not in agreement. In fact, a year earlier he had announced that he was launching an international effort to ban antipersonnel land mines. It was the Joint Chiefs of Staff, and not the president, who wanted the land mines to remain in Korea and who wanted to reserve the right to use them in the Persian Gulf if Iraq renewed the aggressive posture that had led to the Persian Gulf War (1991). The Chiefs of Staff were strongly opposed to any international effort to curb U.S. applications of land mines. President Clinton often found himself under attack from political opponents when he disagreed with the country's military leadership. In this case, the president abandoned his firm support of the ban on land mines in order to preserve his relationship with the Joint Chiefs.

The public, the media, and many members of the international community viewed this as a moral failure on the part of the president. As commander-in-chief, they argued, the president had every right to insist on what he believed was right. To many, the land mine moratorium was an issue on which the president had shown lack of leadership.

FUTURE DIRECTIONS

In November 1997, Secretary of Defense William Cohen announced a large-scale program to reform the way in which the Department of Defense does business. The secretary's plan, the Defense Reform Initiative, was designed to apply to the department business practices that American industry had successfully used to become leaner and more flexible in order to remain competitive.

The secretary's initiative had a profound effect on the structure of the Joint Staff. Command and control of five Joint Staff organizations—the Joint Warfighting Center, Fort Monroe, Virginia; the Joint Communications support element, MacDill Air Force Base, Florida; the Joint Command and Control Warfare Center, Kelly Air Force Base, Texas; the Joint Battle Center, Suffolk, Virginia; and the Joint Warfighting Analysis Center, Dahlgren, Virginia—were transferred to the authority of the United States Atlantic Command, one of nine unified combatant commands. The command and control of these activities became effective October 1, 1998. Although no relocation or name changes were planned, the transfer created some changes for the Joint Staff. It is hoped that these transfers will help the Joint Staff focus on its policy, direction, and oversight duties, in effect moving the Joint Staff one step further away from becoming involved in the implementation of policies and recommendations developed by the Joint Chiefs.

AGENCY RESOURCES

Information about the Joint Chiefs of Staff is available from their Web site at http://www.dtic.mil/jcs. General inquiries about the Joint Chiefs of Staff should be directed to the Public Affairs Office, OCJCS-PA, The Pentagon, Rm. 2D844, Washington, DC 20318-9999;

phone (703)-697-4272. For information on the Department of Defense, visit its Web site at http://www.defenselink.mil/ or contact the Office of the Assistant Secretary of Defense for Public Affairs, The Pentagon, Washington, DC 20201; phone (703)-697-5737.

AGENCY PUBLICATIONS

Publications of the Joint Chiefs of Staff include two periodicals; the *J-Scope*, a weekly newspaper for Defense Department employees, and the *Joint Force Quarterly*, which focuses on larger questions of joint doctrine, coalition warfare, and contingency planning. Other publications include the *Joint Doctrine Capstone and Keystone Primer*, *Joint Warfare of the Armed Forces of the United States*, and *Joint Intelligence Support to Military Operations*. Many publications are available on the Joint Staff Web site (JCSLink) in the Joint Electronic Library at (http://www.dtic.mil/doctrine/jel). For further information about JCS publications, contact the Joint Staff Information Management Division at (703) 697-9127. For Defense Department publications, contact the Public Affairs Directorate at (703) 697-5737.

BIBLIOGRAPHY

Auster, Bruce B. "America as Supercop." *U.S. News and World Report*, 24 Oct 1997, pp. 30–36.

Glazier, Michael. *The History of the Joint Chiefs of Staff: The Joint Chiefs of Staff and National Policy*. Wilmington, Va.: M. Glazier, 1979.

JCS Reform: Proceedings of the Newport Conference on JCS Reform. Newport, R.I.: Naval War College, 1985.

"The Joint Chiefs of Staff." *Defense*, 96 (2): 1996, pp. 6–7.

Korb, Lawrence. *The Joint Chiefs of Staff: The First Twenty-Five Years*. Bloomington, Ind.: Indiana University Press, 1976.

Luttwak, Edward N. "Washington's Biggest Scandal." *Commentary*, May 1994, pp. 29–33.

Nelan, Bruce W. "No Clean Sweep for Mines." *Time*, 19 September 1997, p. 38.

Shalikashvili, John. "The United States Armed Forces: A Prospectus." *Vital Speeches*, 1 January 1997, pp. 165–8.

Shenon, Philip. "Joint Chiefs Weaken Proposal for Land-Mine Moratorium." *New York Times*, 11 May 1996, p. 4.

Stout, David. "General Who Sets Pace: Henry Hugh Shelton." *New York Times*, 17 September 1997, pp. A12 (N), A20(L).

Legal Services Corporation (LSC)

PARENT ORGANIZATION: Independent
ESTABLISHED: 1974
EMPLOYEES: 81

Contact Information:

ADDRESS: 750 First St. NE
Washington, DC 20002-4250
PHONE: (202) 336-8800
FAX: (202) 336-8959
E-MAIL: info@smtp.lsc.gov
URL: http://ltsi.net/lsc
PRESIDENT: John McKay

WHAT IS ITS MISSION?

As defined by the Legal Services Corporation Act, the Legal Services Corporation's (LSC) mission is to promote equal access to the system of justice and improve opportunities for low-income people throughout the United States by making grants for the provision of high-quality civil legal assistance to those who would be otherwise unable to afford legal counsel.

HOW IS IT STRUCTURED?

The LSC is a private, nonprofit organization that is funded by Congress. It is governed by an 11-member board of directors who are appointed by the president and confirmed by the Senate. Each member of the board serves for a term of three years, with the exception of five members first appointed to serve two-year terms (as designated by the president at the time of the appointment). No more than six board members can be of the same political party. Board membership is generally representative of the organized bar, attorneys providing legal assistance to eligible clients, and the general public. The president of the corporation, appointed by the board of directors, is the chief executive officer and serves as an *ex officio* (non-voting) board member. Under the executive office, the LSC is divided into five offices: General Counsel/Corporate Secretary, Administration and Human Resources, Program Operations, Comptroller/Treasurer, and Information and Technology. A sixth office, Office of the Inspector General, reports directly to the board and audits the LSC, ensuring proper compliance with its mandates.

PRIMARY FUNCTIONS

According to *The U.S. Government Manual 1997/98*, the primary function of the LSC is to "provide quality legal assistance for non-criminal proceedings to those who would otherwise be unable to afford such assistance." The LSC is not actively involved in providing legal services to clients but awards grant money to organizations that do provide these services. The corporation establishes maximum income levels for prospective clients based on family size, urban and rural differences, and cost-of-living variations.

The primary purpose of the LSC is to award grants to organizations and applicants who, in return, provide legal assistance and representation to low-income clients. Applicants for LSC grants include nonprofit organizations that provide legal assistance to eligible clients, private attorneys, law firms, state or local governments, and regional planning and coordination agencies.

The LSC awards its grants through a system of competition and grant renewals. The application review process evaluates the legal services to be provided by each applicant by measuring it against widely recognized quality standards, such as the American Bar Association (ABA) Standards for the providers of civil legal services to the poor, and the LSC's own performance criteria. The LSC's competitive review process prohibits preference for current or previous recipients of LSC funds. Applicants who have demonstrated that they can provide the best legal help are awarded grants.

Notice of the availability of LSC funds is published in the *Federal Register* and sent to state bar associations, newspapers, law schools, recipients of LSC funding, state and local governments, and sub-state regional planning and coordination agencies. The LSC publishes and circulates a Request for Proposals (RFP) which is provided to all persons and organizations requesting a copy. To apply for funding, applicants must request an RFP, submit a Notice of Intent to Compete, and submit a complete application responsive to the RFP. The LSC reviews the applications and the proposals with the most merit are awarded funds so they can provide services to the poor and needy under the LSC authority.

PROGRAMS

The LSC funds more than 260 local programs throughout the United States. Although operating under its guidelines, the local programs are not actually a part of the corporation, and each program is tailored to local needs. The most common categories of cases handled by LSC grant recipients are family, housing, income maintenance, consumer, and employment. Specific cases often involve evictions, foreclosures, divorces, child custody and support, spousal abuse, child abuse or neglect, wage claims, access to health care, and unemployment or disability claims.

BUDGET INFORMATION

Approximately $283 million was appropriated by Congress to the LSC in 1998. Almost all of this budget is directed toward grants that go directly to independent local programs that provide civil legal assistance to those who otherwise would be unable to afford it.

HISTORY

The LSC was founded by Congress in 1974 under the Nixon administration as a bipartisan nonprofit federal corporation to ensure equal access to legal services under the law for all Americans. The agenda of the president and Congress was to provide for the segments of society that had been neglected or abused; the American people at this time favored providing a safety net for those who could not afford legal services.

The LSC provided much-needed legal funding to small firms and agencies who assisted the poor and needy in their quest for equal justice under the law. Since its inception, LSC grantees have handled well over 30 million cases. The vast majority of them were individual matters and not part of a social or political agenda—except that these services were provided to the poor and financed by government grants.

During the Reagan administration (1981–89), however, the LSC came under attack. Only eight years after the LSC's creation, the atmosphere of social conscience had changed, and the new president vowed to eliminate the corporation altogether in the belief that legal assistance was not a federal concern. Congress did not eliminate the agency and even its Reagan-appointed board balked at the idea; they did, however, campaign and hire lobbyists to reduce congressional funding for the LSC (*Time*, June 20, 1988).

Meanwhile, the LSC concentrated its efforts on cases that involved individual concerns such as spousal abuse, child endangerment, advocacy issues over health care, and other *pro bono* (Latin for "the public good") activities. Some cases were class action lawsuits, those in which a group of people with similar complaints join together in one large lawsuit, pooling their resources to get better legal representation and bargaining power. Many of these class actions were high-profile cases dealing with socially and politically charged issues, and as a representative for the poor the LCS was often seen as attacking established interests.

In 1995 and 1996 Congress reaffirmed the federal government's interest in providing representation for individuals facing legal problems who would otherwise be unable to afford assistance. However, it was determined that federal funds should go to programs that handle individual cases, while broader efforts to address the problems of the client community should be left to organizations and law firms that did not receive federal funds. The LSC was no longer allowed to become involved in class action lawsuits, and new restrictions were placed on activities in which LSC-funded programs could engage on behalf of their clients.

Congress substantially reduced funding for the program, cutting it by roughly one-third. As a result of these cuts, 300,000 fewer cases were handled in 1996 than in 1995. Because most cases benefit family members in addition to the named client, almost one million fewer Americans benefited from legal services as a result of these new restrictions.

CURRENT POLITICAL ISSUES

Since the Reagan administration, the LSC has often been the subject of fierce debate. In representing the poor, LSC attorneys sometimes challenge powerful businesses, and even the government itself, in court. Operating without strict guidelines on how its grants can be used—other than that to help poor clients—the LSC has frequently been criticized as going far beyond its mandated role of assisting low-income individuals. Conservative politicians, in particular, have attacked the LSC for what they see as a diversion of federal funds toward political lawsuits and promotion of social change. Powerful business organizations such as the American Farm Bureau Federation (AFBF) accused the LSC of persecuting its member businesses with groundless lawsuits that were costly to defeat.

Case Study: Class Action Lawsuits

In the 1990s class action lawsuits became the focal point for criticism of the LSC. The LSC had paid for many such suits over the years and maintained that class action lawsuits were a powerful and effective way for those with limited resources to achieve justice.

The LSC's opponents did not deny that class action suits could be of great use, but some considered them too far outside the corporation's purpose of defending the rights of poor individuals. Critics claimed that the LSC had strayed from its stated mission by getting involved in large-scale cases that represented the interests of many individuals at once. Although class actions were the best method to redress the grievances of groups, critics countered that individuals were being shortchanged as the class action suits sought to get something for everyone. Furthermore, critics claimed, some lawyers were using LSC-funded lawsuits as a tool to further their own social and political views rather than serve their clients.

In 1995 Congress decided to restrict the uses of LSC grant money even further. Under the new guidelines the LSC could not provide funding for class action lawsuits, and organizations which wanted LSC grant money could not get involved in class action lawsuits of any kind, even using other sources of funding.

FAST FACTS

One in every five Americans (or about 50 million people) is potentially eligible for assistance from the Legal Services Corporation in noncriminal matters.

(Source: Legal Services Corporation, 1998.)

FUTURE DIRECTIONS

If the LSC succeeds in defeating congressional attempts to eliminate it, the agency will have to retrench and reorganize its priorities. The goals it has set for itself in its "Strategic Plan 1997–2003" reflect a redefinition of its mandate and a compliance with the new restrictions placed upon it by Congress. These goals are: "(1) to preserve and strengthen a legal services delivery system that provides a foundation for meeting the critical legal needs of low-income people throughout the nation; (2) ensure compliance by grantees with legal requirements and restrictions; (3) enhance the effectiveness and quality of services to clients; (4) expand the delivery of legal services to clients through partnerships and initiatives that build upon federal funding; and (5) preserve and strengthen our national commitment to equal access to justice."

AGENCY RESOURCES

The LSC maintains an extensive on-line Web site at http://ltsi.net/lsc that provides the researcher with details about every aspect of its services. More information can also be obtained by either calling the LSC at (202) 336-8800 or writing to the Legal Services Corporation, 750 First St. NE, Washington DC 20002-4250.

AGENCY PUBLICATIONS

In addition to publishing grant applications and compliance rules, the LSC also publishes testimony and speeches, the *LSC Annual Performance Plan*, the strategic plan, and congressional reports. To obtain these and other materials call the LSC at (202) 336-8800 or write to the Legal Services Corporation, 750 First St. NE, Washington, DC 20002-4250. Another source for publications is the LSC Web site at http://ltsi.net/lsc.

BIBLIOGRAPHY

Brogan, Pamela. "Ross County Judges Want Legal Services Saved." *Gannett News Service*, 8 June 1995.

"Head Of N.Y. State Bar Association Calls On Congress To Adequately Fund Legal Services Corp." *US Newswire*, 16 April 1997.

Isaac, Rael Jean. "Illegal Services: When Congress Passed Restrictions on the Legal Services Corporation, the LSC Called in its Lawyers." *National Review*, 24 March 1997, pp. 42–6.

———. "War on the Poor." *National Review*, 15 May 1995, pp. 32–8.

Lacayo, Richard. "The Sad Fate of Legal Aid." *Time*, 20 June 1988, p. 59.

"The LSC Strikes a Blow for Freedom." *Washington Times*, 12 January 1997, p. 36.

Stycos, Steven. "Revoking Legal Services: Republicans Want to Keep Lawyers from the Poor." *Progressive*, 1 April 1996, pp. 29–33.

"U.S. Representative Harold Rogers (R-Ky) Chairman Holds Hearing On FY 1999 Appropriations for the Departments Of Commerce, State, and Justice. *Washington Transcript Service*, 25 February 1998.

Vickery, Jonathan. "Legal Services: Work is Vital, but Funding has Dangerously Declined." *Dallas Morning News*, 21 September 1997, p. 6J.

Library of Congress (LOC; LC; The Library)

WHAT IS ITS MISSION?

The United States Library of Congress (LOC or LC) is charged with maintaining a "universal collection of knowledge." In "The Mission and Strategic Priorities of the Library of Congress," James H. Billington states that the Library must ". . . make its resources available and useful to the Congress and the American people and . . . sustain and preserve a universal collection of knowledge and creativity for future generations."

The Library's mission is similar in some ways to that of the National Archives and Records Administration (NARA). The Library's scope, however, is much larger: "universal knowledge" versus materials specific to the operations of the U.S. government. The Library further accepts the mission "to add interpretive and educational value to the basic resources of the Library in order to enhance the quality of the creative work and intellectual activity derived from these resources, and to highlight the importance of the Library to the nation's well-being and future progress."

The priorities of the Library of Congress are to serve as a resource to the U.S. Congress and to maintain and dispense these resources for the people and for future generations. The knowledge base of the Library excludes only two disciplines—agriculture and clinical medicine, which are addressed by the resources of the National Agricultural Library and the National Library of Medicine.

HOW IS IT STRUCTURED?

The librarian of Congress, who directs the Library, is appointed by the president with approval of the Sen-

ESTABLISHED: April 24, 1800
EMPLOYEES: 3,771

Contact Information:

ADDRESS: 101 Independence Ave. SE
Washington, DC 20540
PHONE: (202) 707-5000
TDD (HEARING IMPAIRED): (202) 707-6200
FAX: (202) 707-9199
URL: http://www.loc.gov
LIBRARIAN OF CONGRESS: James H. Billington

FAST FACTS

Library of Congress holdings are estimated as follows: "materials in more than 450 languages; approximately 110 million items; more than 16 million books; 2 million recordings; 4 million maps; 46 million manuscripts; nearly 4 million pieces of music; more than 12 million photographs; and more than 700,000 motion pictures."

(Source: *Collier's Encyclopedia.* s.v. "Library of Congress," 1997.)

ate and is assisted by the deputy librarian. Supporting the librarian and his deputy is the Office of the Librarian Chief of Staff. This office contains most of the administrative offices of the Library, including the Congressional Relations Office, Diversity Office, and Office of the General Counsel. The Office of the Inspector General is an independent office that reports to the librarian. The Infrastructure Division handles the remaining administrative and support tasks of the Library, including financial services, human resources, the National Digital Library, information technology services, and integrated support services.

The Library has many specialized branches and collections. A few of the most important are the Congressional Research Service, devoted to meeting the needs of Congress; the Copyright Office, which handles copyright protections in the United States; and the National Film Preservation Board (NFPB), a diverse advisory council dedicated to the preservation of the nation's valuable motion picture archives.

PRIMARY FUNCTIONS

The primary function of the LOC is to amass as much material on as many different subjects as possible and make this material readily available to all who wish to use it. However, assisting Congress with research and issuing copyrights are two particularly important duties of the Library.

Copyrights and Aquisitions

Due to the exceptionally large volume of materials it handles, the Library publishes specific collection policy guidelines to insure the acquisition and maintenance of bona fide materials that fall within the scope of its mission. In order to qualify for acquisition, materials must meet standards based on subject, format, and publication type. Standards are also defined for library catalogs and access procedures. Many libraries throughout the country use these standards in developing their own collections and catalogs.

The Copyright Office handles copyright protections in the United States and, by law, provides the librarian of Congress with two copies of every manuscript copyrighted in the United States. These manuscripts are then cataloged and included in the Library's collection. The Copyright Office also works with the World Intellectual Property Organization (WIPO) to create international treaties and policies for protection of copyrighted materials.

The Library Services division of the LOC acquires materials from dozens of foreign countries worldwide through a network of remote offices in Brazil, Egypt, India, Indonesia, Kenya, and Pakistan. These too are cataloged and placed in the Library's collection.

Research Support

The Library develops and maintains electronic catalogs and other database systems to facilitate access to library materials. Many of the Library's catalogs are published on the Internet for easy access through its home page on the World Wide Web. Bibliographic services and card catalog services are extended to other libraries for a nominal fee.

The Congressional Research Service is staffed by experts in law, public policy, and political science. The service supports the U.S. Congress with timely, nonpartisan response and analysis to legislators' requests. The Research Service Office develops seminars, generates enrichment materials, provides translation services to the members of Congress and also maintains information services on legislative matters including daily updates of pending bills.

PROGRAMS

The LOC operates a number of special programs in pursuit of its mission to make its resources available to Congress and the American people. While the CRS is exclusively for the use of Congress, many other tools are available for accessing the Library's vast store of information.

Thomas: Legislative Information Program

"Thomas—U.S. Congress on the Internet," a Web site located at http://thomas.loc.gov, provides ready access to current information about congressional activities. The Thomas Web site brings the daily workings of

Congress into homes and workplaces around the nation, providing access to the *Congressional Record* and congressional directories, resumes of congressional activities, legislative updates, Senate and House roll calls, bill summaries, and bill status reports. Thomas also features a search program to locate congressional bills by topic and offers detailed historical documentation for compiling legislative histories.

National Library Service for the Blind and Physically Handicapped (NLS)

NLS evolved from the talking-book program established in 1931. The original program was geared to blind adults but has since grown to include otherwise visually impaired adults as well as children. The program was further enhanced in 1962 to provide music materials as well as talking books.

Talking books and the special talking-book player machines are available from libraries within the NLS network. This program is supported by tax dollars and participants pay nothing. Enhanced reading machines are available for the hearing-impaired. A doctor's certification is required to establish eligibility for the program. Details about NLS and its services are available on the Internet at http://lcweb.loc.gov/nls/nls.html.

BUDGET:

Library of Congress

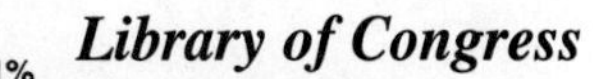

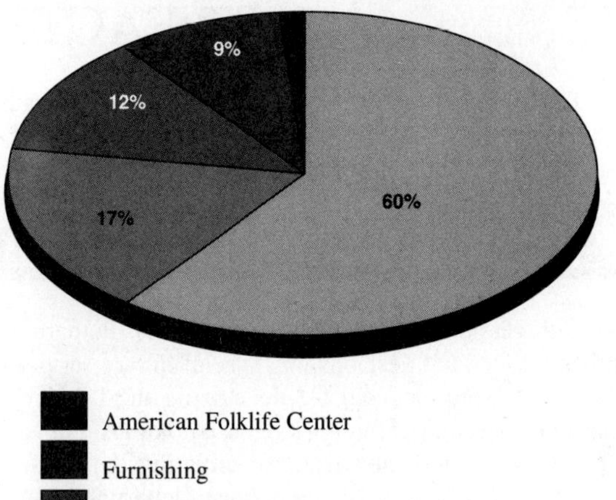

BUDGET INFORMATION

The LOC operates on a combination of congressional appropriations, receipts from its Copyright Office and Cataloging Distribution Service, and private donations. In 1998 the LOC operated on a budget of $377 million. By far the largest portion of this budget, $227 million (60 percent), paid for the salaries and expenses of running the library. This includes funding for the acquisition of new materials, as well as the cost of maintaining the law library. The Congressional Research Service was allotted 17 percent of the LOC's budget, $64.6 million. The National Library Service for the Blind and Physically Handicapped received $46.56 million (12 percent). The Copyright Office accounted for $34.36 million, or 9 percent of the total budget. The American Folklife Center received less than one percent of the LOC's budget, $956,500. The remaining $4 million, 1 percent of the budget for 1998, was spent on furnishing the Library itself.

HISTORY

The Library of Congress was established during the presidency of John Adams, on April 24, 1800, by the "Act to Make Provision for the Removal and Accommodation of the Government of the U.S.," which allocated $5,000 for the purchase of books.

The original library in the Capitol was burned by the British during the War of 1812. Blodget's Hotel temporarily served as the Capitol and library facilities. A second accidental fire in 1851 burned over half of the Library's holdings, but it quickly recovered from the loss and began an era of rapid expansion under the leadership of Librarian of Congress Ainsworth Rand Spofford in 1864.

Under Spofford, Congress expanded the Library's mission and opened the facility to the public. Previously only members of Congress and other government officials were allowed to use the Library. Once the public was welcomed, the Library facilities grew rapidly. Spofford also centralized U.S. copyright operations under the Library of Congress in 1870. As a result, the Library collection includes at least one copy of every item that has received a copyright in the United States since that time.

In 1897 the library opened in a new facility, the Jefferson Building, which still serves as the main building of the library complex.

Herbert Putnam became the Librarian of Congress in 1899 and held the position for 40 years. In 1915 Putnam created a new division of library services expressly to serve the U.S. Congress. Putnam's innovation, the Legislative Reference Service, was the forerunner of the pre-

FAST FACTS

The Library of Congress collection grows at a rate of 7,000 items per day.

(Source: Library of Congress. "25 Questions Most Frequently Asked," 1998.)

sent Congressional Research Service (CRS). Putnam is further credited with establishing special library services to outside institutions and for developing the Library's extensive collection of foreign language holdings. Putnam is best remembered, however, for initiating the Dewey Decimal System, a coded combination of letters and numbers for organizing library books. The "alphanumeric" code of the Dewey Decimal System indicates the subject matter contained in each book and defines the exact location where each book belongs on the library shelf.

In 1939 the library expanded into the John Adams Building. That same year Putnam was succeeded as Librarian of Congress by Pulitzer Prize-winning poet Archibald MacLeish, who held the post until he was named assistant secretary of state in 1944.

By 1954 the Library of Congress collection had surpassed 10 million books. The diverse collections had grown to encompass the humanities, law and government, science and technology, American studies, area (international) studies, and the social sciences. Over the years the special collections grew to include non-textual matter such as photographs, motion pictures, priceless maps, computer files, sound recordings, and videotapes. Foreign language materials alone now account for approximately 50 percent of the Library's holdings. Children's books, doctoral dissertations, government documents, and books of magnificent historical significance are also among its holdings. Eventually a third building was needed to house the continually expanding facilities. The James Madison Building, the largest of the three buildings, was added to the Capitol Hill complex in 1980.

In 1987 James H. Billington was appointed the thirteenth Librarian of Congress. In the mid-1990s, as the library acquired its 100 millionth title, Billington began preparations for the Library of Congress to host its own bicentennial celebration in 2000.

CURRENT POLITICAL ISSUES

With its majestic buildings, impressive holdings, and dedication to knowledge and culture, the Library of Congress is not a likely target of controversy. Differences of public opinion that erupt from time to time are generally low-keyed and attract very little attention from the media.

Case Study: Political Correctness in the 1990s

A movement toward political correctness, or the etiquette of cultural awareness, gained popularity during the 1990s, giving rise to new thinking not only about the day-to-day interactions between Americans but also about history and government. In keeping with the sensitivities of political correctness, the Library elected on more than one occasion to abandon a historical exhibit rather than invite public controversy.

"Back of the Big House: The Cultural Landscape of the Plantation," by Professor John Michael Vlach, was taken largely from the Library's photographic archives and depicted actual plantation houses and slave quarters from early Americana. Ordinarily the Library does its utmost to allow access to all information, but because of outspoken protests by many of the Library's African American employees the exhibit was canceled before it opened.

Billington defended the Library's position when it canceled the exhibit, indicating a reluctance to antagonize African American library employees. At least one other library exhibit was eliminated at that time for its harsh graphical depictions of lynching practices in the South. The mood of the employees, who complained of being offended, was summed up by the Daniel A. P. Murray African American Cultural Association President Allene Hayes, quoted in the *New Republic:* "An exhibit is supposed to celebrate something positive."

Museum curator Barbara Clark Smith further clarified his sentiment in the *New Republic*: "There is anxiety about anything that suggests conflict along lines of class. . . . But we don't know how to talk with each other about why things offend us. We only known how to say, 'Don't do it.'" Many critics came forward to publicly assess the situation and to pass judgment on the actions of the library administration. Todd Gitlin of *New Republic* summed up the situation from all angles saying, "Censors of left, right and center agree on one thing: the virtue of amnesia."

SUCCESSES AND FAILURES

In 1985 the Library of Congress Center for the Book gave public endorsement to Project Literacy United States (PLUS) as a public effort to combat the problems of functional illiteracy among an estimated 23 million adults in the United States. Librarian of Congress Daniel J. Boorstin read a public statement from President Ronald Reagan that applauded the founders of PLUS: "I'm delighted to see organizations . . . rolling up their sleeves and getting to work on this dangerous and already tragic problem."

Checks and Checkbook Balances at the Library

The Library's political reputation was in question after it was audited by the General Accounting Office (GAO). The GAO expressed complaints about the Library's catalog after performing an audit for fiscal year 1988, the first ever in the Library's 200-year history. Harsh criticisms were leveled at LOC management for substandard accounting and cataloging practices.

The overall reliability of the Library's financial reporting methods were questioned when the GAO uncovered millions of uncataloged items among the Library's assets. The irregularity, traced to a backlog in work flow, led Frankie Pelzman of *Wilson Library Bulletin* to comment, "It's discouraging to learn that within that amazing place [the Library of Congress], they're as disorganized about their checkbook as I am."

FUTURE DIRECTIONS

There is little question that the future of the Library of Congress, and libraries in general, lies in digital information retrieval. The Library has been a pioneer in applying computer technologies to the challenges of digitizing and organizing information and materials. It continues to expand its technology resources whenever appropriate and to share this technology with libraries around the country and around the world. Typical innovations include an optical disk program for viewing non-print materials via microcomputer that has served as a base for the Library's on-line Internet museums.

As an active participant in the Digital Library Federation, the Library contributes to a consortium of 15 large research libraries and archives that are engaged in a wide range of cooperative effort to assemble digitized materials from every possible source for access by all.

FAST FACTS

The Thomas Jefferson Building, the first permanent building of the Library of Congress complex, was designed by John L. Smithmeyer and Paul J. Pelz at a cost of nearly $6.5 million. More than 50 American artists, including sculptors, contributed works to decorate the Jefferson Building.

(Source: Library of Congress. "25 Questions Most Frequently Asked," 1998.)

AGENCY RESOURCES

For general information about the Library, contact the Public Affairs Office at the Library of Congress, 101 Independence Ave. SE, Washington, DC 20540-8610; phone: (202) 707-2905; fax: (202) 707-9199.

Visitors to the library may take a free guided tour, rent an audio tour, or follow the self-guided brochure. Visitor highlights include the Great Hall in the Thomas Jefferson Building and the Main Reading Room. Recorded visitor information and information about public events and special exhibitions is available by calling (202) 707-8000. The library attempts to maintain full compliance with the Americans with Disabilities Act.

The main reading room in the Thomas Jefferson Building is open on Monday, Wednesday, and Thursday from 8:30 A.M. until 9:30 P.M.; and on Tuesday, Friday, and Saturday from 8:30 A.M. until 5:00 P.M. The library is closed on Sunday. Visitors must obtain a reader registration permit, or library card, in order to use materials. Reader registration is available at Room G-40 of the Jefferson Building on Capitol Hill in Washington, DC A passport or driver's license and registration must be presented for identification.

For the monthly calendar of events (free of charge to Washington area residents) contact: Library of Congress, Office Systems Services, Mail and Distribution Management Section, 101 Independence Ave. SE, Washington, DC 20549-9441.

Contact the National Library Service for the Blind and Physically Handicapped at 1291 Taylor St. NW, Washington, DC 20542 or call (202) 707-5100; TDD: (202) 707-0744; fax: (202) 707-0712; e-mail: nls@loc.gov; website: http://www.loc.gov/nls.

The foreign acquisition divisions handle the sale and exchange of library materials from outside of the United States. These are listed according to geographic region on the World Wide Web at http://lcweb.loc.gov/acq/acquire.html.

For out-of-print documents contact the Documents Expediting Project in care of Joseph Mahar (Documents Expediting Project, Anglo/American Acquisitions Division, LS/ACQ/ANAD) at e-mail: jmah@loc.gov or fax: (202) 707-0380.

Contact the Surplus Books Program in care of Robert Overmiller (Government Documents Section, Anglo-American Acquisitions Division, LS/ACQ/ANAD) at e-mail: rove@loc.gov or fax: (202) 707-0380.

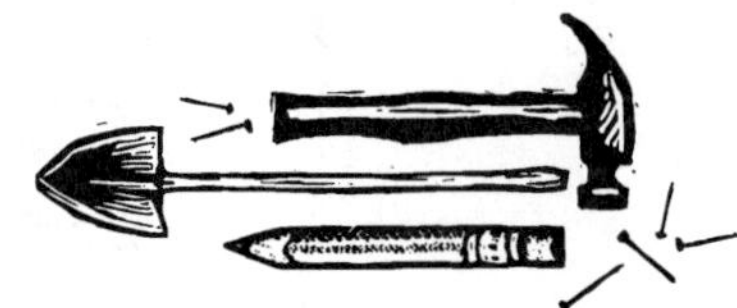

GET INVOLVED:

The Library of Congress sponsors the Junior Fellows Program for college and university students at the junior level and higher. The purpose of the Junior Fellows Program is to foster greater knowledge and awareness of the Library and its extensive collections. Fellows receive a weekly stipend in return for organizing and documenting collections, researching and creating bibliographic listings, preparing new library materials, and digitizing information. For further information contact the Junior Fellows Program Coordinator, Library Services, Library of Congress, LM-642, Washington, DC, 20540-4600.

For information on employment opportunities, classes, grant information, and conference and seminar schedules, request the *American Folklife Center News* from Folklife Center News, American Folklife Center, Library of Congress, Washington, DC 20540-4610, or visit the Library's home page on the Internet at http://www.loc.gov.

The Library of Congress Web site home page at http://www.loc.gov includes links to library catalogs, information, text, and graphical images from LOC exhibitions plus the Thomas legislative information service and the Learning Page for elementary and high school students. See the Library home page for Research Tools, Books for the Blind and Physically Handicapped, Cataloging Data Distribution, Contracts, Copyright Services, Employment, Photoduplication Service, Publications, and Reference and Bibliographic Services.

AGENCY PUBLICATIONS

The Library of Congress Publishing Office creates and sells calendars, posters, illustrated guides, and other memorabilia of the Library of Congress collection. An on-line catalog is published at http://lcweb.loc.gov/loc/pub/cal, or contact the Sales Office, Library of Congress, Washington, DC 20540-4985, phone: (202) 707-0204. The library also publishes and distributes informational materials including press releases.

The *Library of Congress Information Bulletin* is available free of charge from the Public Affairs Office, Library of Congress,

101 Independence Ave., SE, Washington, DC 20540-1610, e-mail: lcib@loc.gov. Back copies (text only) are available on the World Wide Web at http://lcweb.loc.gov/loc/lcib.

Civilization Magazine, a bimonthly cultural publication, is available as a benefit to Library of Congress Associates. Subscription information is available on the World Wide Web at http://www.civmag.com/articles/abtloc.html.

The American Folklife Center publishes *Folkline Script* each week on the Internet at gopher://marvel.loc.gov:70/00/.ftppub/folklife/folkline, or write to Folklife Center News, American Folklife Center, Library of Congress, Washington, DC 20540-4610 to receive the American Folklife Center News. Folklife publications feature announcements concerning employment opportunities, training, grants, and conferences.

Library of Congress Cataloging Newsline, a newsletter from the Cataloging Directorate, is published online via links at http://lcweb.loc.gov/loc/pub/index.html. This link may also be used to access *A Periodic Report from the National Digital Library Program* as well as area studies handbooks, conference and seminar papers, technical publications, special program publications, and *Library of Congress Brief Guides to the Internet.*

BIBLIOGRAPHY

Berry III, John N. "It's a Question of Open Government." *Library Journal*, 15 June 1993, p. 8.

Billington, James H. "The Mission and Strategic Priorities of the Library of Congress." 20 January 1996.

Clement, Richard W. *The Book in America.* Golden, Colo.: Fulcrum Publishing, 1996.

Cole, John Y. *Jefferson's Legacy: A Brief History of the Library of Congress.* Library of Congress, 1993.

Gurney, Gene. *The Library of Congress: A Picture Story of the World's Largest Library.* New York: Crown Publishers, 1981.

Karp, Abraham J. *From the Ends of the Earth: Judaic Treasures of the Library of Congress.* Library of Congress, 1991.

Parker, Elisabeth Betz. "The Library of Congress Non-Print Optical Disk Pilot Program." *Library of Congress*, December 1985, pp. 289–299.

Pelzman, Frankie. "Washington Observer." *Wilson Library Bulletin*, November 1991, pp. 18, 20.

Maritime Administration (MARAD)

PARENT ORGANIZATION: Department of Transportation
ESTABLISHED: May 24, 1950
EMPLOYEES: 969

Contact Information:

ADDRESS: 400 7th St. SW
Washington, DC 20590
PHONE: (202) 366-5807
FAX: (202) 366-3889
E-MAIL: pao.marad@marad.dot.gov
URL: http://marad.dot.gov
MARITIME ADMINISTRATOR: Clyde J. Hart, Jr.

WHAT IS ITS MISSION?

The Maritime Administration's (MARAD) mission "is to promote the development and maintenance of an adequate, well-balanced, United States merchant marine, sufficient to carry the nation's domestic waterborne commerce and a substantial portion of its waterborne foreign commerce, and capable of serving as a naval and military auxiliary in time of war or national emergency. MARAD also ensures that the United States enjoys adequate shipbuilding and repair service, efficient ports, effective intermodal water and land transportation systems, and reserve shipping capacity in time of national emergency." MARAD's mission is based on the long-standing maritime policy of the U. S. government to support with federal subsidies a privately owned and operated U.S. merchant fleet.

HOW IS IT STRUCTURED?

The Maritime Administration is a regulatory agency in the executive branch of the federal government. It is part of the Department of Transportation (DOT). MARAD is headed by an administrator who is appointed by the president and confirmed by the Senate; the administrator serves a term of office at the pleasure of the president. The Maritime Subsidy Board is an adjunct to the administrator's office and administers MARAD's various subsidy programs. The Subsidy Board is chaired by the maritime administrator. There are five additional administrative offices. The deputy administrator of inland waterways and Great Lakes administers programs and policies related to the inland waterways and is

responsible for implementing President Bill Clinton's National Shipbuilding Initiative as well. The chief counsel is the agency's chief legal adviser. The coordinator of research and development administers agency research programs and manages MARAD's research budget. The Office of Labor, Training and Safety Functions performs functions related to the training and licensing of maritime workers. The Office of Congressional and Public Affairs is the liaison office with Congress. It also manages MARAD public affairs programs.

The administrator is assisted by six associate administrators, each responsible for a particular agency activity or policy area. The associate administrator for policy and international trade formulates and coordinates agency policy and administers its various international activities. The associate administrator for port, intermodal, and environmental activities develops policies to encourage the use of U.S.-flag ships in foreign commerce, promotes American ports, and develops programs to promote domestic maritime commerce. The associate administrator for shipbuilding and technology development administers national shipbuilding policies and programs. The associate administrator for ship financial assistance and cargo preference oversees individual agency subsidy programs as well as the agency's marine and war-risk insurance programs. The associate administrator for national security is responsible for the Maritime Security Program (MSP) and maintains liaison with the Department of Defense (DoD). The associate administrator for administration is responsible for agency administration, which includes administrative services, acquisitions, budgets, accounts, automated information management, management analysis, personnel, security, equal employment opportunity, and affirmative action.

Five regional offices are responsible for field operations and administering MARAD programs on the local level. The regional offices are located on the Atlantic, Pacific, and Gulf Coasts and on the Great Lakes. MARAD also operates the U.S. Merchant Marine Academy in Kings Point, New York, which trains men and women to become officers in the American Merchant Marine.

PRIMARY FUNCTIONS

MARAD functions fall into three broad areas: federal maritime subsidies and preference programs, maritime system development, and defense and national security. Its most important function is to provide financial assistance to the U.S. maritime industry. MARAD guarantees loans made by private institutions to finance the construction of ships in the United States and for the improvement of shipbuilding facilities. The administration subsidizes American shipping companies in order to offset the costs of operating U.S.-flag ships for foreign trade. As an additional aid to American shipping companies, the government is required to use U.S.-flag vessels to ship at least 50 percent of its cargo, and 75 percent of certain agricultural cargoes (administered in cooperation with the Department of Agriculture). MARAD oversees these preference programs. MARAD also regulates the purchase of foreign ships and the transfer to foreign registry of ships owned by U.S. citizens.

MARAD administers federal policies and programs for the design of U.S. ports in order to improve domestic shipping facilities. Developing strategies for using advanced ship design and new technologies to help the U.S. shipbuilding industry compete throughout the world is another primary function of MARAD, as well as devising and administering programs to sell U.S.-flag shippers in the world market.

All U.S.-flag vessels (vessels registered in the United States) can be called into national service in the event of a national emergency. The Maritime Administration and the U.S. Coast Guard are primarily responsible for national security within DOT. The National Defense Reserve Fleet (NDRF) is comprised of vessels which can be called into shipping service in an emergency and is maintained by MARAD. The Ready Reserve Fleet (RRF) comprises that portion of NDRF that can be called into service on very short notice—in four to thirty days.

PROGRAMS

MARAD programs support the U.S. shipbuilding industry, the growth and prosperity of the U.S. maritime fleet, the development of ports, the security of U.S. merchant vessels, research programs, and the promotion of maritime commerce.

Title XI of the Merchant Marine Act of 1936 created the Federal Ship Financing Program, which provides credit guarantees for shipbuilders. The program is intended to promote the growth and modernization of the U.S. merchant marine and U.S. shipyards. The loans originate in the private sector. Once a lender is found—a bank for instance—MARAD guarantees that the loan will be repaid. The government guarantee provides a fixed interest rate for up to 87 percent of project financing. Projects that qualify include construction and reconstruction of ships in U.S. shipyards and shipyard modernization. Foreign as well as American shipowners may qualify for funds.

The MARITECH program, which is administered by MARAD and the Defense Advanced Research Projects Agency (DARPA), an agency within the Department of Defense (DoD), was created to advance shipbuilding technology. It is a joint government-industry project in which the two partners put up matching funds for shipbuilding research and development projects. Since 1993 more than two hundred companies in the private sector have participated in the program; a total of 36 commercial ship designs, as well as new commercial shipbuilding processes and procedures, have been developed with MARITECH funding.

The Port Facility Conveyance Program enables communities to acquire surplus federal land to use as port facilities. Under the program, for example, a city could obtain land that was part of a closed naval base and convert it into a port. The program is also intended to create jobs in order to offset unemployment caused by base closures or other federal actions. Five applications were under review at the start of fiscal year 1997.

The Maritime Security Program (MSP) was created by the Maritime Security Act of 1996 and replaced the Operating-Differential Subsidy Program (ODS) which had subsidized the costs of U.S. merchant ships engaged in foreign trade. Under MSP the government provides the owners of U.S.-flag commercial ships with a subsidy of $2.1 million per vessel. In exchange the shipowner agrees to make the vessel available for service in war or other national emergencies. The arrangement enables the government to avoid spending billions of dollars on cargo ships dedicated solely to carrying military cargoes and millions of additional dollars to maintain more standby vessels. In the spring of 1998 a total of 47 vessels participated in the program.

BUDGET:

Maritime Administration

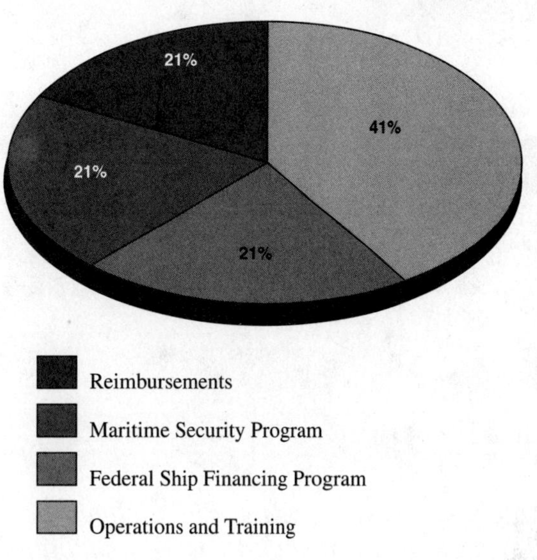

Reimbursements

Maritime Security Program

Federal Ship Financing Program

Operations and Training

BUDGET INFORMATION

The total budget enacted for the Maritime Administration for fiscal year 1998 was $167 million. That represented approximately 3 percent of the 1998 DOT budget. About $36 million (21 percent) went to the Federal Ship Financing Program, while another $36 million (21 percent) was used for the Maritime Security program. Another $28 million (17 percent) was spent to reimburse the Department of Agriculture for the cost of obeying MARAD regulations and shipping grain on expensive U.S. ships. The remaining $68 million (41 percent) of MARAD's budget went to pay for operations and training. The Ready Reserve Force, the reserve transport fleet kept for national emergencies, is managed by MARAD but paid for by Department of Defense funds.

HISTORY

In 1914 a shortage of commercial ships caused the wheat harvest to back up at port cities. The problem was so critical that the railroads finally refused to carry any more grain from the plains. In response to the problem, the creation of a government body was proposed which would have authority to buy and operate ships. Congress defeated the measure but two years later enacted a similar bill, the Shipping Bill of 1916. The Shipping Board created by the bill was not empowered to own ships—private shipping companies opposed government competition in their business—but it was authorized to build and charter merchant ships. The Shipping Board would evolve into today's MARAD.

After an accelerated shipbuilding program fueled by the demands of World War I (1914–18), the American Merchant Marine fell into gradual decline. By 1935 the fleet was in such serious disrepair that President Franklin Roosevelt asked Congress to address the problem. On June 29, 1936, the Merchant Marine Act of 1936 was signed into law. The act called for the maintenance of U.S.-owned and operated merchant marine fleet that could carry the waterborne commerce of the nation and that would be available as a naval auxiliary in times of war or national emergency. The act still forms the statutory basis for many of the Maritime Administration's activities; Title XI loan guarantees were provided for in Title XI of that Merchant Marine Act.

The law also created the Maritime Commission, a five-man body that replaced the Shipping Board. The commission was empowered to subsidize the U.S. shipbuilding and merchant shipping industry in a variety of ways: mail had to be shipped in U.S.-flag vessels; the Maritime Commission was authorized to pay shippers the difference—up to half the cost of the ship—between building a ship in the United States and a foreign yard; and the commission extended low-interest shipbuilding

An empty dry-dock at the Philadelphia Naval Shipyard behind a row of mothballed Navy ships. Once one of the U.S. Navy's major shipbuilding centers, the shipyard was closed in 1995. Renovations began in 1997 that will modernize the facility and convert it for the construction of merchant ships. (AP/Wide World Photos)

loans. Subsidized ships were required to employ American crews.

The Maritime Commission's first chairman was Joseph P. Kennedy, the father of the future president John F. Kennedy. During his short tenure, Kennedy attempted to obtain new ships and to make domestic water freight transit as efficient as possible. His successor, Rear Admiral Emory Scott Lane, introduced an ambitious program of shipbuilding to replace the nation's aging commercial fleet.

Shipbuilding procedures had to be greatly streamlined after the outbreak of World War II (1939–45). Because of the introduction of mass production techniques in American shipyards, by the time hostilities had reached their height, ships were being produced faster than the enemy could sink them. The most efficient yards could manufacture a ship in as few as sixteen days. In all, 5,592 merchant ships were built between 1942 and 1945. The government took over ship operations during the war with the creation of the War Shipping Administration (WSA), which was headed by the chairman of the Maritime Commission. The two organizations worked together closely, transporting men and raw materials wherever necessary during the war.

After the war the Maritime Commission took over the remaining duties of the WSA. By 1948 all private vessels that had been requisitioned into war service had been returned to their owners; ships built specifically for war service were auctioned off. Government ships were also chartered for the transport of relief supplies to Europe and Asia.

In 1950, during the administration of President Harry S Truman, the Maritime Commission was abolished by Presidential Reorganization Plan 21. The commission, it was felt, was not flexible enough to carry out its many regulatory and administrative duties. In its place, the Reorganization Plan created two bodies: the Federal Maritime Board, which was given responsibility for regulating the maritime industry and determining subsidies, and the MARAD, which oversaw federal Merchant Marine programs associated with the Department of Commerce. In 1961 MARAD took over subsidy programs as well.

MARAD was a component of the Department of Commerce. The original draft of the Department of Transportation Act developed by the administration of Lyndon Johnson, however, would have transferred it to the newly created Department of Transportation (DOT). Congressional opposition blocked the move for fifteen years. The MARAD was eventually moved to DOT on August 6, 1981, when Public Law 97-31 was signed by President Ronald Reagan.

On March 20, 1984, Reagan signed the Shipping Act of 1984. The act was the result of several years of effort on the parts of various members of the government, ship operators, and shippers to modernize and streamline regulations based on the Shipping Act of 1916 that were still in force. The new law, which covered ocean lines shipping in U.S. trade, substantially deregulated the industry and removed many administrative requirements that U.S. shippers considered burdensome.

In 1981 Congress ended all Title XI funding, a reaction to years of mixed feelings in government and industry to the huge subsidization of the shipbuilding industry. Once loan guarantees stopped, U.S. shipbuilding fell by more than 50 percent. Construction of merchant ships virtually ground to a halt as yards concentrated on building for the Navy. In the late 1980s the shipbuilding industry began complaining about its inability to compete with foreign companies. Shortly after Bill Clinton's election in 1993, the loan guarantees were reestablished.

Operation Desert Storm (1990-91) illustrated how MARAD functions in times of emergency. The MARAD's principle focus during the Gulf War (1991) was the activation of most of the RRF ships. Shipments began within ten days of the Iraqi invasion of Kuwait. Altogether 3.2 million tons of dry cargo and over 6 million tons of petroleum were delivered by ship until March

10, 1991, when the resupply effort officially ended. Of the total supplies 95 percent went by sea, 80 percent of which was transported by U.S.-flag ships.

The Clinton administration focused MARAD activities on three areas. MARAD began to carry out Clinton's National Shipbuilding Initiative (NSI), a five-part plan designed to revitalize shipbuilding in the United States. It also worked with the DoD, the U.S. Transportation Command (TRANSCOM), and the Joint Chiefs of Staff to strengthen its role in national security. Finally MARAD was instructed to work on integrating the nation's waterways into the intermodal transportation system that the DOT was committed to creating.

CURRENT POLITICAL ISSUES

International shipbuilding is an industry characterized by intense competition. One way nations have supported their shipbuilders over the years is through subsidies, similar to those outlined in Title XI administered by MARAD. The United States unilaterally ended its subsidies in 1981 when Congress stopped Title XI funding, which resulted in a 50 percent drop in American shipbuilding over the rest of the decade. This drop was accompanied by protests from the shipbuilding industry that it was no longer able to compete with heavily subsidized foreign shipyards. At that time the Organization for Economic Cooperation and Development (OECD), a multinational organization devoted to increasing economic cooperation and standards of living, began a study of shipbuilding subsidies.

Case Study: The OECD Shipbuilding Agreement

The result of the OECD's interest was "The Agreement Respecting Normal Competitive Conditions in the Commercial Shipbuilding and Repair Industry," a treaty that drastically limited national subsidies to shipbuilders and provided mechanisms for dealing with injurious pricing practices and settling disputes among member nations. Negotiated for more than five years, the major shipbuilding nations of the world—the European Union, Norway, Japan, Korea, and the United States—signed the treaty in early 1995. U.S. shipbuilders were expected to benefit; they had less than 0.5 percent of the total global shipbuilding market and received only $50 million per year. By comparison foreign shipbuilders received billions in state aid. The agreement was supposed to open U.S. shipyards to foreign customers.

The agreement hit snags, however, when it went to Congress for ratification. It bounced around committees in both houses and came to the floor of the House of Representatives for a vote where a number of amendments inconsistent with its intent were attached. It eventually went back to committee for further consideration. Efforts in the Senate were also unsuccessful. The agreement was originally scheduled to go into effect on January 1, 1996; it was extended to July 15, 1996. By then it had been ratified by all the other signatory nations. Attempts at ratification by the Senate in 1996 and 1997 both failed, leaving the fate of the treaty uncertain.

The failure pointed to a deep split in the U.S. shipbuilding industry that began when the Clinton administration reinstated Title XI monies in 1993. Before those subsidies were restored, while the OECD plan was being negotiated, most U.S. shipyards agreed their best chance to compete in the international market was through a multilateral agreement that did away with subsidies. Afterward, however, the big shipbuilders began lobbying against the bill. They argued that the elimination of their subsidies would set back their economic recovery. They also maintained that the agreement would open up production of so-called "Jones Act" vessels—ships used in American domestic maritime trade which, by current law, must be manufactured, owned, and crewed by Americans—to foreign competitors. (Jones Act regulations are also overseen by MARAD.)

On the other hand 37 smaller shipbuilders favored ratification. They argued that foreign subsidies were responsible for the decline in the U.S. market share and led to continuing job losses in the U.S. shipbuilding and ship repair industry. The agreement, as they saw it, would enable the domestic industry to regain some competitiveness. If foreign subsidies continued, the American decline would also. Coincidentally proponents of the agreement receive a very small percentage of the total annual Title XI monies.

Title XI favored shipbuilding for the domestic rather than the export market. Of new Title XI loan guarantees, 79 percent went toward building tankers for domestic trade despite MARAD statistics that show that under present rates a new double hull tanker cannot be operated profitably. Opposition led to unsatisfactory ratification legislation and two years of delays. In the meantime, foreign nations began implementing new subsidy programs—programs that would not have been possible if Congress had ratified the agreement in a timely fashion.

SUCCESSES AND FAILURES

The Maritime Security Program (MSP) is considered a major success within MARAD. The culmination of a 15-year reform effort, the program replaced the old operational differential subsidy program, which was based on a complicated calculation of foreign versus domestic costs. The new program pays out a flat rate subsidy that is expected to cut costs in half. The MSP also relaxed restrictions thereby opening opportunities to obtain subsidies to a broader range of companies.

The RRF of MARAD has improved MARAD's emergency response capabilities. RRF is crucial for the transport of military equipment and supplies to U.S. forces anywhere in the world during the early critical period before commercial ships can be marshaled. RRF was rapidly deployed at the outset of Desert Storm, and during the Bosnian peacekeeping effort (1995–present) its response time averaged only two days.

FUTURE DIRECTIONS

MARAD expects that in the future most U.S. ship companies will continue to operate both U.S.- and foreign-flag ships in international trade. U.S.-flag ships will continue to be at a cost disadvantage in comparison to foreign-based competitors who enjoy significantly lower costs due to simpler registration procedures, lower taxes, and less costly crews employed from lesser developed countries. The U.S. Coast Guard (USCG) and MARAD are working with industry to relax regulations that impose unnecessary burdens on U.S.-based carriers.

MARAD predicts that waterborne commerce will increase in the coming years and ships are expected to grow in size in order to keep up with this increased commerce. Domestic freight movement along the American seaboard should grow as well. That business is restricted by law to U.S.-flag vessels, so that increase should lead to an increased need for construction and repair of ships for the coast, which will benefit U.S. shipyards.

AGENCY RESOURCES

General information about the Maritime Administration and the maritime industry can be obtained from MARAD's Office of Congressional and Public Affairs.

Their telephone number is (202) 366-5807; the E-mail address is pao.marad@marad.dot.gov. MARAD news, history, and congressional testimony is available at its Web site at http://marad.dot.gov/. MARAD rules are published in Code of Federal Regulations Title 32a, Chapter 18, and Title 46, parts 201-391. They can also be found at the agency Web site: http://marad.dot.gov/Regulation/cfr.html. Dockets are maintained at the Office of the Chief Counsel of MARAD. Dockets can be viewed between 9:00 A.M. and 4:00 P.M. Monday through Friday in Room 2200 of the Department of Transportation Building, 400 7th St. SW, Washington, D.C. The Dockets Room can be reached by telephone at (202) 366-9322.

AGENCY PUBLICATIONS

Publications of the Maritime Administration is published regularly and is available from the MARAD Office of Congressional and Public Affairs. Copies can be ordered by writing the office at 400 7th St. SW, Washington, DC 20590. Many MARAD publications are available on-line as well, usually in PDF format. They can be accessed at http://marad.dot.gov/publications/index.html. The MARAD Statistical and Economic Analysis Office issues statistics and reports on the U.S. Merchant Marine. Reports can be requested by calling (202) 366-2400

BIBLIOGRAPHY

Beargie, Tony. "Revamping Marad." *American Shipper*, February 1994.

"Competition, Cost Challenge U.S. Shipping." *Christian Science Monitor,* 4 September 1984.

Cottrill, Ken. "Carriers Campaign to Sink Title XI Subsidy Program." *Chemical Week,* 20 September 1995.

Healey, Jon. "Legislators Fear U.S. Shipping May Sink with Subsidies Bill." *Congressional Quarterly Weekly Report*, 8 October 1994.

Jantscher, Gerald R. *Bread Upon the Waters: Federal Aids to the Maritime Industries.* Washington, D.C.: Brookings Institution, 1975.

"MARAD to Test New Preference Rules." *American Shipper*, February 1997.

Maritime Administration: Stronger Management Controls Needed Over Vessels in Title XI Custody. Washington, D.C.: United State General Accounting Office, 1992.

U.S. Merchant Marine: A Brief History. Washington, D.C.: Department of Commerce, 1976.

Victor, Kirk. "Anchors Away: Can Anything Be Done to Save the Nation's Shrinking Merchant Marine? Should Anything Be Done?" *National Journal*, 11 September 1993.

Wines, Michael. "Reagan's Cure for Maritime Industry—Fewer Subsidies and More Protection." *National Journal*, 24 April 1982.

Mine Safety and Health Administration (MSHA)

PARENT ORGANIZATION: Department of Labor
ESTABLISHED: 1977
EMPLOYEES: 2,186

Contact Information:

ADDRESS: 4015 Wilson Blvd.
Arlington, VA 22203
PHONE: (703) 235-1452
TOLL FREE: (800) 746-1553
URL: http://www.msha.gov
ASSISTANT SECRETARY OF LABOR: J. David McAteer

WHAT IS ITS MISSION?

The stated mission of the Mine Safety and Health Administration (MSHA) is "to administer the provisions of the Federal Mine Safety and Health Act of 1977." The purpose of the Mine Act, as it is called, is to ensure that all U. S. mining and mineral processing operations are in compliance with government standards of health and safety. MSHA is dedicated to preventing fatal mining accidents, reducing the number and the seriousness of all accidents, and improving the overall working conditions of mining operations throughout the United States, regardless of their size or type.

HOW IS IT STRUCTURED?

The MSHA falls under the U.S. Department of Labor (DOL), a cabinet-level agency that is part of the executive branch. MSHA is responsible for carrying out the goals of the DOL, which are to prepare the country's workers for new and better jobs and to ensure acceptable standards of operation in the workplace, in its specific area of expertise—mines and mineral processing operations.

MSHA is led by the assistant secretary of labor for mine safety and health, whose office has eight major divisions: the Directorate of Administration and Management; Metal and Nonmetal Mine Safety and Health ; Coal Mine Safety and Health; The Office of Standards, Regulations, and Variances (OSRV); the Directorate of Technical Support; Directorate of Educational Policy and Development; Office of Assessments; and the Directorate

FAST FACTS

There are approximately 3,500 coal mines in 27 states.

(Source: Mine Safety and Health Administration. "Coal Mine Safety and Health," 1998.)

of Program Evaluation and Information Resources. Each of these offices plays a significant role in MSHA's implementation and enforcement of the Federal Mine Safety and Health Act of 1977.

MSHA has 17 district offices and 115 field offices widely dispersed throughout the country that oversee variously located mining and mineral processing operations.

In addition, the Office of the Assistant Secretary also includes two deputy assistant secretaries and three offices which aid in implementing MSHA's stated missions—the Office of Congressional and Legislative Affairs, the Office of Equal Opportunity, and the Office of Information and Public Affairs.

PRIMARY FUNCTIONS

The MSHA works to maintain safe conditions in mining operations in the United States as mandated by the Mine Act of 1977. The Mine Act provides that the MSHA will inspect each surface mine at least twice a year and underground mines at least four times a year in order to monitor their safety. Among other responsibilities, inspectors commonly check on the levels of silica dust and the concentration of methane gas in the air. Methane gas emanates from coal in the ground and can accumulate to hazardous levels. The MSHA also investigates accidents, and miner's complaints of discrimination. The MSHA determines penalties and collects fines for violations of safety and health standards and reviews mine operators' mining plans before they are put into practice. The MSHA also maintains a school to educate and train inspectors and provide technical support for mining operators in their efforts to comply with the Mine Act and provides grants to mining states.

PROGRAMS

The many programs of the MSHA are primarily concerned with raising and maintaining standards of safety and health in mining operations through education and training operations and technical assistance to mining operators. Each division of the MSHA operates programs specific to its responsibilities. For example, the Roof Evaluation Accident Prevention Program (REAP) under Coal Mine Safety and Health is used to improve roof support practices in mines through training, analysis, enforcement of regulations, and the introduction of new technologies.

The Office of Educational Policy and Development promotes most of MSHA's educational and training programs through the Policy and Program Coordination Division; and the National Mine Health and Safety Academy in Beckley, West Virginia. It also offers a State grants program to help state mining agencies fund their own additional mining health and safety programs.

The most significant program is Program Evaluation Information Resources (PEIR) under the Directorate of Program Evaluation and Information Resources, which analyzes the effectiveness of MSHA's programs to make sure that problems, once diagnosed, have been effectively corrected. PEIR also makes various data available to mine operators on workplace injuries and provides training in the use of new technologies.

BUDGET INFORMATION

The MSHA budget is divided into five program areas: enforcement, assessment, educational policy and development, technical support, and program administration. Out of an estimated 1998 budget totaling $206 million, approximately $153 million went toward enforcement (divided among three subdivisions: $108 million to coal; $44 million to metal/non-metal; $1 million to standards development); $4 million to assessments; $15 million to educational policy and development; $25 million to technical support; and $9 million to program administration.

HISTORY

Federal legislation and concern for setting and maintaining safety standards in mining operations began in 1891 with minimum requirements for ventilation in underground coal mines and a minimum employee age of twelve years. No consideration had previously been given to the substances in underground mines, such as dust from earth and rock and methane gas from explosions used to loosen the rock, that miners were forced to breathe. Miners simply tied handkerchiefs or rags over their mouths. Prior to this legislation, most children began to work at the age of ten. Legislation and concern for health and safety has continued to evolve with ever-increasing comprehensiveness and complexity until the present day.

BUDGET:

Mine Safety and Health Administration

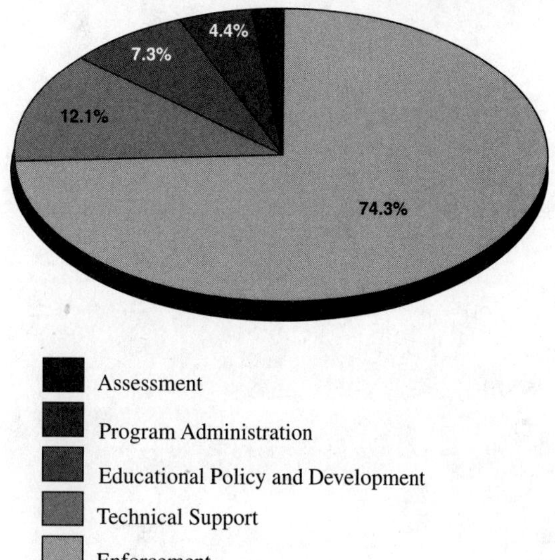

In 1910, Congress established the Bureau of Mines in order to reduce the number of fatal mine accidents, which exceeded 2,000 annually. The bureau, however, was not given the power to inspect mines until 1941, and the first code of federal regulations specifically for mine safety was not initiated until 1947.

In following years, the Bureau of Mines was granted increasing powers of inspection and enforcement. The Federal Coal Mine Safety Act of 1952 allowed it to make annual inspections of certain mines and to issue notices of violations or orders to withdraw from mines and to assess violations and penalties for noncompliance. No authority was provided to assess financial penalties, however, until the Federal Coal Mine Health and Safety Act of 1969 (The Coal Act), which provided the bureau with greater powers of inspection and enforcement of standards in all mines and established financial and criminal penalties for violation.

The Modern Era

In 1973, a new independent agency was created, the Mining Enforcement and Safety Administration (MESA), whose purpose was to carry out the enforcement of safety and health standards, perceived at that time to be in conflict with the bureau's other goals of encouraging the development of mineral resources and the mining industries. The government wanted to promote the mining industry in order to provide jobs and tax revenue and economic growth while protecting workers from mine operators who cared more for profits and protecting their businesses than for workers' health and safety. The two goals were believed to be served best by the creation of two separate agencies.

The Federal Mine Safety and Health Act of 1977 (the Mine Act) created the Mine Safety and Health Administration (MSHA) and placed it under the U.S. Department of Labor to prevent any possible conflicts of interest between enforcement of standards and the development of resources. The MSHA was a consolidation of all federal mine health and safety regulations to date under one statute.

CURRENT POLITICAL ISSUES

One of the most persistent problems in the mining industry is "black lung," or pneumoconiosis, a disabling disease that miners contract from breathing dust in both underground and surface mines. It has plagued the mining industry since its very beginnings, and the industry has yet to satisfactorily eliminate it.

Case Study: Black Lung

The prevalence of black lung disease is hotly debated. In 1969, the U.S. Surgeon General estimated that 100,000 miners had the illness, and in 1972, 150,000 miners received disability benefits for the disease. It has been estimated that 10 to 30 percent of miners suffer from black lung disease.

Authorities disagree on the definition of black lung, and the federal government's interpretations of the Black Lung Benefits Act of 1969 have changed over the years in response to pressures from either representatives of miners or industry owners. The Black Lung Benefits Act of 1969 recognized the condition as a disability, but in succeeding years the battle between industry and workers has focused on the system used to award benefits. Activists for the miners such as the Black Lung Association and the United Mine Workers claim that industry and government both have made the standards for determining what is or is not black lung so difficult to understand and apply that most applicants cannot manage to prove they have the disease or even get through the application process in order to qualify and actually receive benefits. These activists claim that industry and government have long used these tactics to avoid paying benefits and to avoid the responsibility for better safety and health measures. In response, mining operators claim that standards are strict because of rampant abuse. During the mid-1970s in states such as Kentucky, operators claim that the vast majority of claimants showed no sign of the disease but were merely seeking to profit from the receipt of benefits.

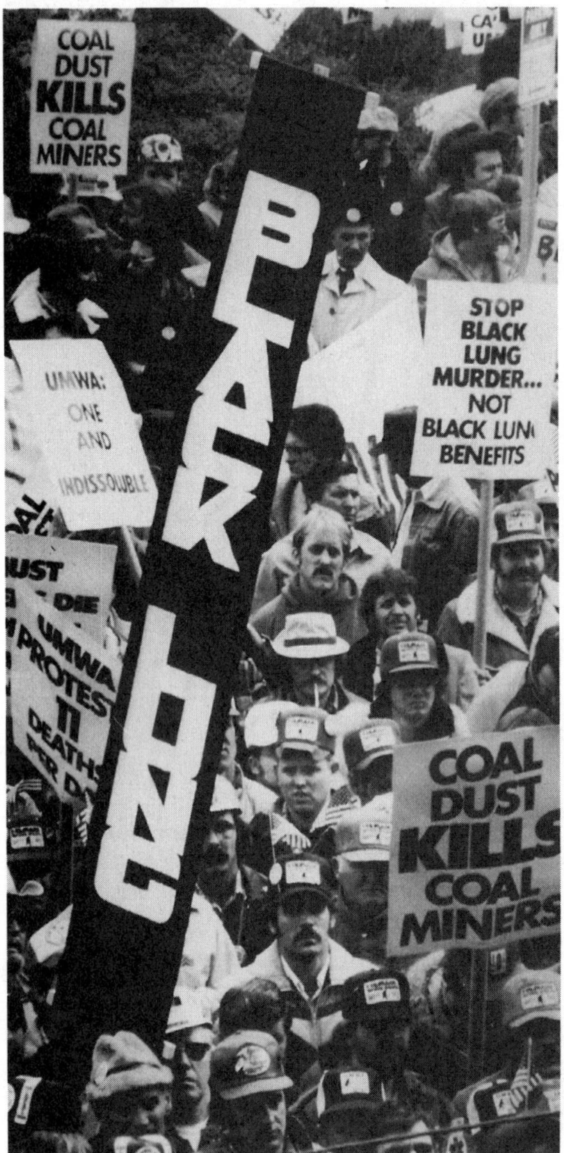

Miners rally near the White House to demonstrate against proposed government cuts in disability to miners with black lung disease. As many as 30 percent of all miners in the United States suffer from black lung. (Photograph by Larry Rubenstein. UPI/Corbis-Bettmann)

Public Impact

Federal legislation has been passed to deal with the problem of black lung benefits. In 1978 the Black Lung Reform Act made it easier to qualify for benefits, but in 1981 President Ronald Reagan changed many of its provisions to make qualification more difficult. Today, the controversy is still a primary issue in the mining industry. In the meantime, the industry continues to employ people in conditions that present an identifiable risk, but, according to Government Accounting Office (GAO) figures, approximately 94 percent of black lung claims are denied.

SUCCESSES AND FAILURES

Since the inception of the MSHA, the rights of miners have been strengthened. Through such programs as the Special Accident and Illness Reduction Programs, the rights of miners to a healthy and safe workplace have been recognized and promoted, largely by educating mining operators and by encouraging them to enact better health measures. This program has studied and made recommendations concerning the dangers associated with excessive noise and exposure to diesel exhaust.

According to the *MSHA Informational Reports 1930–1977* and *Mine Injury and Work Time Quarterly Reports 1978–1991*, mining fatalities have declined from an average of 260 a year in the 1960s to 55 in the 1990s, and the decline continues to the present.

Another of MSHA's successes is the Alternate Case Resolution Initiative (ACRI), created as a less expensive and cumbersome way for mine operators to contest citations they have received and to settle disputes before they escalate to the court system. Since its inception, the ACRI has saved money and time for both sides in disputes, easing the financial burdens on both the MSHA and the federal judicial system. It has also given mine operators a better understanding of MSHA's interpretation of the required safety and health standards.

FUTURE DIRECTIONS

One of the MSHA's goals is to encourage more voluntary participation and compliance with the Mine Act by offering training to mine operators and making available MSHA's continued research into new technologies and safety methods. Through an instruction package of videotapes and guidebooks, the Job Safety Analysis program shows mine operators proven safety measures and then provides training on how to implement those changes. The MSHA also works closely with the National Institute for Occupational Safety and Health (NIOSH) on studying the dust or ground silica levels in mines, a cause of "black lung", in order to recommend dust control methods.

The agency hopes to find more methods to educate and raise the industry's standards of safety and health in ways that prevent problems long before violations occur and penalties must be assessed and collected.

AGENCY RESOURCES

The MSHA offers a variety of training courses and publications and videos and other tools to educate mining operators through the National Mine Health and Safety Academy in Beckley, West Virginia. For information about the academy, contact the National Mine Health and Safety Academy, Office of Academy Services, 1301 Airport Road, Beaver, West Virginia 25813-9426 or phone (304) 256-3257. Information is also available from the Office of Information and Public Affairs, Mine Safety and Health Administration, Department of Labor, Room 601, 4015 Wilson Boulevard, Arlington, VA 22203; phone (703) 235-1452. In many areas, a local MSHA office will be listed in the phone book under "U.S. Government." The MSHA home page on the World Wide Web is at http://www.msha.gov/WELCOME.HTML-SSI.

AGENCY PUBLICATIONS

MSHA publications include a variety of training courses and publications and videos and other tools aimed at educating those in the industry. These include "Job Safety Analysis" instructional materials prepared by MSHA and videotapes and brochures about such subjects as substance abuse or setting up employee assistance programs (EAPs), available by mail from the National Mine Health and Safety Academy, Office of Academy Services, 1301 Airport Road, Beaver, West Virginia 25813-9426 and by phone from (304) 256-3257. For further information about MSHA publications, contact the Office of Information and Public Affairs, Mine Safety and Health Administration, Department of Labor, Room 601, 4015 Wilson Boulevard, Arlington, VA 22203 or phone (703) 235-1452.

BIBLIOGRAPHY

Berss, Marcia. "Against the Wall." *Forbes*, 5 July 1993, p. 43.

Johnson, Robert, and Solomon, Caleb. "Coal Quietly Regains a Dominant Chunk of Generating Market." *Wall Street Journal*, 20 August 1992, p. A1, A4.

Kilborn, Peter T. "Saving Money or Saving Lives?" *New York Times*, 19 September 1995, p. A8(N), A14(L).

McAteer, J. David. "Let's Not Abandon Safety For Our Nation's Miners." *Christian Science Monitor*, Vol. 88, no. 49, p. 19.

McCarthy, Colman. "His Whistle Keeps on Sounding." *Washington Post*, 9 December 1995, p. A24.

———. "Lifeline For the Miners." *Washington Post*, 12 August 1995, p. A21.

Reardon, Jack. "Injuries and Illnesses Among Bituminous and Lignite Coal Miners." *Monthly Labor Review*, Vol. 116, no. 10, p. 49.

Southmountain Coal, Co. "Southmountain, 2 Officials indicted in 92 Mine Blast." *Wall Street Journal*, 17 January 1994, p. A5(W), B2(E).

Thompson, Alexander M. *Technology, Labor and Industrial Structure of the U.S. Coal Industry*. New York: Garland Publishing, 1979.

Minerals Management Service (MMS)

PARENT ORGANIZATION: Department of the Interior
ESTABLISHED: January 19, 1982
EMPLOYEES: 1,825

Contact Information:

ADDRESS: 1849 C St. NW
Washington, DC 20240
PHONE: (202) 208-3985
FAX: (202) 219-1703
URL: http://www.mms.gov
DIRECTOR: Cynthia L. Quarterman

WHAT IS ITS MISSION?

The stated mission of the Minerals Management Service (MMS) is "to efficiently and effectively provide for the transfer of royalty and mineral revenue management functions for the United States federal government." In effect, the MMS manages and regulates the nation's natural gas, oil, and other mineral resources on the Outer Continental Shelf and collects, accounts for, and disburses revenues from offshore mineral leases and from onshore mineral leases on federal and American Indian lands.

HOW IS IT STRUCTURED?

The MMS, headquartered in Washington, D.C., is a branch of the Department of the Interior (DOI), a cabinet-level agency. The MMS is administered by a director who is nominated by the president and confirmed by the Senate. The director works closely with the DOI's assistant secretary of land and minerals management in developing policy and administering MMS programs.

The MMS has two primary programs, the Royalty Management Program (RMP), headquartered in Lakewood, Colorado, and the Offshore Minerals Management (OMM) Program headquartered in Washington, D.C. The RMP processes and manages the money collected from all federal mineral leases. The OMM is responsible for assessing and leasing offshore mineral rights.

PRIMARY FUNCTIONS

The MMS has two primary functions. It is responsible for managing all aspects of the federal government's undersea mineral claims. This includes assessing the value of mineral deposits, leasing the rights to these deposits to private industry, regulating the use of these deposits for the safety of the environment and workers, and collecting lease payments, including royalties, for any minerals extracted from the deposits it has leased. The MMS is also responsible for managing the money collected from all mineral leases on federal or American Indian land. Other agencies, including the Bureau of Land Management and the Bureau of Indian Affairs, lease lands under their control and collect royalties in a manner similar to the way the MMS manages offshore resources. The money these agencies collect is then given to the MMS, which sees that it is distributed among the state, federal, and tribal governments as directed by law.

FAST FACTS

The revenues generated by mineral leases are one of the largest nontax sources of income to the federal government.

(Source: *The United States Government Manual 1997/98.)*

PROGRAMS

All mineral revenue management functions are centralized in the MMS within the Royalty Management Program, which administers and distributes revenues generated from federal and American Indian lands. With its computerized accounting systems—RMP processes more than 200,000 transactions each month—totaling about $300 million per month from nearly 100,000 federal and Indian land leases.

Money collected from offshore leases goes primarily to the U.S. Treasury, with some money also going to the coastal states nearest the deposits. Money from onshore leases on federal land is split 50-40-10: 50 percent goes to the states in which the minerals were recovered, 40 percent goes to the Reclamation Fund in the U.S. Treasury and 10 percent goes to the U.S. Treasury's general fund. The Reclamation Fund is a special fund that finances the Bureau of Reclamation's water projects in the western United States. One exception to this rule is money from Alaskan leases, 90 percent of which goes to that state. All of the proceeds from leases on American Indian lands is given to the tribes.

The leasing and oversight of mineral operations on North America's Outer Continental Shelf (OCS) is centralized in the MMS within the Offshore Minerals Management (OMM) Program. The OMM has regional offices located in Alaska, California, and Louisiana. This program is responsible for all phases of OCS mineral resource management, from the initial offering of OCS lands for lease through the regulation of mineral development and lease abandonment activities. To manage OCS mineral resources (natural gas, oil, and hard minerals such as sand and gravel), the OMM carries out a wide array of functions, such as analyzing geological, geophysical, and other geoscientific data to support OCS program decisions. The OMM also periodically assesses the nature and extent of undiscovered OCS natural gas and oil resources, estimates current discovered natural gas and oil reserves by fields, and develops overall resource estimates for proposed OCS lease sales. The OMM determines the prices at which federal mineral deposits will be leased, ensuring that the government receives the fair market value for its resources. The OMM is also responsible for regulating the offshore mining industry, ensuring that it protects both its workers and the undersea environment.

BUDGET INFORMATION

In 1998 Congress appropriated a budget of approximately $205 million for the administration of MMS. This is not to be confused with the money MMS collects and redistributes to state governments, American Indian tribes, and the federal government, which is usually about $4 billion annually.

HISTORY

The federal Outer Continental Shelf program has been active since 1953. Since that time the program has changed dramatically in response to changing technology, national energy priorities, and environmental considerations. In 1982 congressional legislation created the Minerals Management Service which took responsibility for managing the leases on North America's Outer Continental Shelf and on American Indian tribal lands. During its short existence the agency has improved its programs in financial management and environmental science to keep pace with the complex energy needs of the nation. The MMS has developed its programs to support the leasing of mineral rights to the energy industry while overseeing the industry's accountability for its financial and environmental activities. The agency's numerous governmental awards attest to its ability to manage complex energy issues.

CURRENT POLITICAL ISSUES

Nationwide the MMS collects and disburses approximately $4 billion to states and Indian tribes in revenues from mineral leases on federal lands. Collecting accurate revenues on the approximately 6,500 active leases has proved to be a challenge in some states.

Case Study: Investigation of California Leasing Royalties

In 1997 the U.S. Justice Department was called on by the DOI and the MMS to assist in a probe of oil companies in California. A DOI economist revealed in a congressional hearing that oil companies paid artificially low royalty fees because they undervalued the price of crude oil. Some companies sought to cooperate with the investigation but others refused to reopen their financial books saying they had already been audited and thought the issue was closed. Many disputes over final royalty charges were resolved through the MMS alternative dispute resolution process, which utilizes mediation before legal action is taken.

The resulting loss of revenues to California government, where much of the money goes to the school system, makes some politicians in that state very supportive of actions by the OMM to seek reimbursement. Estimates were that as much as $165 million in revenues was not paid by oil companies, representing a substantial loss of funding for California schools.

SUCCESSES AND FAILURES

MMS employees worked closely with mining industry representatives to focus on a solution to a longstanding data management problem in the Gulf of Mexico region and on the Outer Continental Shelf. The standard government naming and numbering system for well site identification had become outdated over the years. Technological advances in mining practices increased the types and number of mines, which over time caused inconsistent identification numbers to be used. A draft plan for a new set of standards was developed and provided to industry representatives for a period of cooperative comment and review. The new system of well identification is designed to increase the ability of inspectors, regulatory officials, and mine operators to efficiently manage the additional numbers of boreholes and well types.

The National Association of Environmental Professionals awarded the MMS its Federal Environmental Quality Award for successfully integrating environmental values into its agency mission and decision-making process in 1994 and again in 1996. The awards demonstrate that the MMS has accomplished its goal of enhancing and protecting the marine environment.

FUTURE DIRECTIONS

The MMS is focusing more of its resources on its leasing and environmental divisions by performing additional environmental studies on the risks associated with deep-water drilling operations. Increased interest in exploration and development of deep-water drilling sites has encouraged the MMS to collect environmental data that will allow it to more effectively and accurately gauge the operating plans and permit process for deep-water facilities. The MMS data is used to support increased work flow in the permitting process so industry can be spared financial losses caused by unreasonable delays. The agency is working to improve the regulatory framework to address the many technical, safety, and environmental challenges associated with complex deep water developments.

AGENCY RESOURCES

The MMS provides a wide range of information related to mining regulation and science at its Web site, http://www.mms.gov. For example, the MMS makes more than 20 years of scientific research available through the site in its Environmental Studies Program Information System. More than two hundred abstracts of offshore engineering and safety-related research, as well as oil spill research, is available on-line.

AGENCY PUBLICATIONS

MMS publications are largely industry-specific scientific data, proposed and draft rulings for industry application, and other regulatory documents. Publications can be requested by calling the Office of Communications at (202) 208-3985 or by accessing the MMS Web site at http://www.mms.gov.

The MMS has taken advantage of digital technology by publishing 50 years of paleontological data on CD-ROM. The CD contains 14,000 reports spanning 50 years of data collection from the Outer Continental Shelf of the Gulf of Mexico. The information is used in the exploration and development of petroleum reserves on federal lands. The CD can be purchased for $10 by calling 1-800-200-GULF.

BIBLIOGRAPHY

Eisler, Peter. "Shaky Alliance Should Limit Acreage for Coastal Drilling." Gannett News Service, 12 May 1994.

Rosenblatt, Robert A. "U.S. Scrutinizes Oil Industry's Royalty System. *Los Angeles Times*, 18 June 1996, p. D1.

Sonali, Paul. "Five Oil Companies Fight Federal Subpoenas." *Reuters Business Report*, 30 January 1997.

Minority Business Development Agency (MBDA)

PARENT ORGANIZATION: Department of Commerce
ESTABLISHED: March 5, 1969
EMPLOYEES: 133

Contact Information:

ADDRESS: 14th St. & Constitution Ave. NW
Room 5053
Washington, DC 20230
PHONE: (202) 482-2678
E-MAIL: mbda@doc.gov
URL: http://www.mbda.gov
DIRECTOR: Courtland Cox
ASSISTANT DIRECTOR: Paul R. Webber, IV

WHAT IS ITS MISSION?

The Minority Business Development Agency (MBDA) describes itself as the only federal agency specifically created to encourage the growth of minority-owned businesses in the United States. To fulfill this core mission, the agency seeks to coordinate federal government plans and programs that affect minority enterprises and to promote and coordinate government and private enterprise activities that will help minority businesses grow.

HOW IS IT STRUCTURED?

The MBDA is a bureau of the Department of Commerce. It is unusual in that the agency's director does not report to an intermediary under secretary but directly to the secretary of commerce. All MBDA activities are planned, developed, coordinated, and evaluated at the MBDA headquarters in Washington, D.C. A significant office at MBDA headquarters is the International Trade Office, which works closely with Commerce's International Trade Administration (ITA) to help minority-owned businesses expand abroad by facilitating international trade missions. The very small MBDA staff (just over 100) is concentrated in Washington and serves a primarily administrative function; the five MBDA regional offices and four district offices, which oversee the work of MBDA's national network of business development centers, are also administered by MBDA staff.

Program work of the MBDA is carried out in agency-funded centers that are operated and staffed by

private firms, non-profit organizations, state and local government agencies, American Indian tribes, and educational institutions. Centers are designated as Minority Business Development Centers (MBDCs), Native American Business Development Centers (NABDCs), or Business Resource Centers (BRCs). The centers provide assistance for bonding, bidding, estimating, financing, procurement, international trade, franchising, acquisitions, mergers, and joint ventures to increase opportunities for minority entrepreneurs. People eligible for the center's business assistance include Spanish-speaking Americans, African Americans, Asian Pacific Americans, American Indians, and Hasidic Jews.

Each MBDA region also contains at least one Minority Business Opportunity Committee (MBOC), an office designed to coordinate federal, state, and local business resources to benefit minority business development. MBOCs also identify education programs and capital opportunities in the community and attempt to bring those opportunities to minority business entrepreneurs.

PRIMARY FUNCTIONS

The MBDA collects and disseminates information that will help those interested in establishing or expanding a successful minority-owned business and it offers assistance in identifying sources of financing and in the preparation of financial and bonding proposals. The agency itself, however, has no authority to make grants, loans, or loan guarantees. The MBDA also funds the entire national network of MBDCs, NABDCs, BRCs, and MBOCs, which provide management and technical assistance to minority entrepreneurs. These centers provide minority entrepreneurs with individual assistance in writing business plans, marketing, management, technical assistance, and financial planning to assure sufficient financing for business ventures. The centers are staffed by business specialists with practical experience in the working world.

PROGRAMS

Each local or regional business center within the MBDA structure runs its own programs, tailored to meet the needs of its community. The MBDA works on a national level to coordinate these programs, and does not initiate many activities of its own, but it does cosponsor a few programs with other agencies.

Together with the U.S. Small Business Administration, the MBDA sponsors Minority Enterprise Development Week, or MED Week. This annual celebration features a conference, where the contributions of America's minority entrepreneurs are recognized, a marketplace where the government and major corporations provide contract information, and many other presentations. MED Week is typically observed during the first full week of October. Other MBDA initiatives include the Minority Business Matchmaker (MBM) and Minority Export Initiative (MEI) programs, which are conducted in partnership with the International Trade Administration, another Commerce agency. Since their formation in 1993, these programs have enabled hundreds of minority companies to travel abroad and penetrate new markets. The primary mission of these programs is simply to allow small- or medium-sized minority-owned firms to introduce their company and products or services to overseas markets. American minority-owned businesses that are considered "ready to export" can use MBDA's staff and resources to obtain marketing advice, international contacts, and other administrative support.

BUDGET INFORMATION

The MBDA budget is part of the Department of Commerce budget, and the agency's spending authority is granted largely through congressional appropriation of tax revenues. A small portion, however, is covered by service fees that are charged for specific services at MBDA centers around the country. In 1998 the MBDA budget was about $27.8 million.

HISTORY

The MBDA's predecessor agency, the Office of Minority Business Enterprise, was created by executive order on March 5, 1969, by President Richard Nixon. Nixon's purpose for the order was to recognize the "additional need to stimulate those enterprises that can give members of minority groups confidence that avenues of opportunity are neither closed nor limited."

The office's early operating philosophy was driven by the assumption that four ingredients were essential to successful business ownership: a qualified and qualifiable entrepreneur, a sound business idea or opportunity, adequate financing through a reasonable mix of equity and debt capital, and managerial and technical knowledge. One of the office's first projects was to compile a list of directories of federal and private assistance programs for minority businesses. The office also created an information clearinghouse.

The new office also began to turn its attention toward increasing government purchases from minority businesses. Along with the Small Business Administration and the General Services Administration, the office implemented programs which, by the mid-1970s, placed minority-owned concessions in 140 federal installations.

Expanding Opportunities

To many people within the organization, the early work of the Office of Minority Business Enterprise was not living up to the agency's potential, because it was unable to finance projects and organizations which could more directly benefit minority businesses. In late 1971, Congress authorized $40 million for federal contracts and grants to nonprofit development organizations and trade associations to assist minority entrepreneurs. By 1972, federal contracts, loans and loan guarantees, and grants to minority businesses tripled what they had been in 1969.

In 1976, the office launched a program to increase minority involvement in telecommunications, computers, manufacturing, construction, and energy-related enterprises. Regional "technology commercialization" centers—predecessors of the MBDA's regional offices—were established in five locations. The Office of Minority Business Enterprise was renamed the Minority Business Development Agency in 1979.

The MBDA began the 1980s with a mandate to join the Small Business Administration in facilitating the formation of 60,000 new minority businesses and expanding an additional 60,000 by 1990. To help reach this goal, the agencies began a national campaign to increase the involvement of private industry and educational institutions in minority business development. During the 1980s, the international trade programs of the agency began to achieve success and minority business owners were invited to participate in trade missions to Mexico and the Caribbean. By the late 1980s, there were more than 800,000 minority-owned businesses in the United States, up from an estimated 100,000 in 1969.

At the beginning of the Clinton administration in 1992, a presidential commission (the Commission on Minority Business Development) criticized federal aid to minority businesses for limiting funding and access to more profitable areas of business. New avenues of funding were explored, but these avenues were cut off in 1994 with the election of a Republican-led Congress. The MBDA was forced to revise its role in the development of minority businesses to emphasize an ever-increasing reliance on assistance from private companies, nonprofit organizations, and universities.

CURRENT POLITICAL ISSUES

With the election of a Republican-controlled Congress in 1994, the MBDA had to fight for its very survival. In 1995, the Senate Appropriations Committee began considering a bill that would eliminate the MBDA entirely, but minority small-business groups and other supporters of the agency argued strenuously against the bill, and it did not come to a vote. The funding for MBDA did suffer some drastic cuts, however. The agency's current $27.8 million budget is a sharp reduction from its $44 million budget in 1994, and the MBDA is struggling to make its limited resources effective.

FAST FACTS

As a result of the MBDA's international trade programs, 325 minority firms have participated in 18 trade missions, producing an estimated $295 million in new gross sales.

(Source: Minority Business Development Administration. "International Trade, 1998.")

Critics of the MBDA argue against its existence on two fronts. The first is that the MBDA is yet another "corporate welfare" program, channeling tax dollars into business enterprise. While the MBDA does offer assistance to business owners, that assistance is not financial; the agency does not offer loans, loan guarantees, or grants. Many of its programs are fee-for-service, and in light of the "corporate welfare" criticisms, the MBDA is turning increasingly to the private sector for help. The MBDA does not provide the kind of direct subsidies and financing offered to large corporations by the Export-Import Bank, for example. These kinds of large corporate welfare programs are increasingly unpopular with the public, but very few Republicans, who profess a desire to cut the federal budget, have attacked them; instead, they focus on much smaller programs such as those offered by the MBDA. Supporters of the agency point out that it generates much more than it costs—in 1994, $400 million in tax revenue at a cost of only $40 million. MBDA supporters also emphasize the agency's growing international trade benefits.

MBDA critics also argue that its responsibilities overlap those of the Small Business Administration (SBA) and that it should be absorbed into that agency in order to increase the efficiency of the government and eliminate wasteful spending. The Small Business Administration is an independent federal agency created in 1953 to aid, counsel, assist, and protect the interest of the entire small business community. It administers a $29 billion loan portfolio. The MBDA and its supporters deny any program duplication; both agencies do serve minority businesses, they say, and many of these businesses fall into the small business category, but each agency has a unique mission and range of services. The MBDA has been struggling, however, to reinvent itself to give the appearance of distinctness and independence. Though the MBDA will continue to collaborate with the SBA on programs such as Business Resource Centers and Empowerment Zones, it will fight hard to remain an independent agency with its own self-determined mission and programs.

SUCCESSES AND FAILURES

The success of MBDA programs is measured by the success of minority businesses. The MBDA is proud of the role minority companies played in the 1997 mission of the Mars Pathfinder. Minority businesses made products that were included in all of the spacecraft's subsystems: the Attitude Information Management (AIM) system of the spacecraft—its avionics or "brains"—was designed with the assistance of two California minority firms, Falcon Design and R.C. Kawaya Engineering. Midcom Corporation, a woman-owned firm, provided the engineers who helped develop the flight software, and an Asian-owned company, Pioneer Circuits, provided the technology for Pathfinder's roving robot, Sojourner. Falcon Design, an African American-owned business, also provided other services to the Pathfinder mission, together with the Hispanic-owned BST Systems and the Asian-owned U Research.

FUTURE DIRECTIONS

Under increasing congressional pressures, the MBDA conducted a series of "supply and demand" studies to determine where the agency could most help minority entrepreneurs. Most of the agency's "reinvention" activities are based on the results of these studies. The MBDC program, in particular, has been seriously revised under the new budget restrictions; in the past, the agency required a 15 percent cost share for organizations who wanted to start up a center, but the cost share requirements are being raised to as much as 40 percent.

In general, the MBDA will shift its focus in the future from one-on-one counseling and technical assistance to a more balanced approach that includes other needs, such as access to capital and markets (as in the international trade programs). The agency will also target resources to existing public and private institutions that are already involved in business and economic development in order to avoid duplication and start-up costs. The MBDA will also take a more visible role in helping minority firms gain access to specialized markets offering high growth potential and coordinating the often disconnected and overlapping efforts of private and public institutions at the state and local levels.

AGENCY RESOURCES

General inquiries about the work of the MBDA should be directed to the Public Affairs Office at (202) 482-4547. The nearest Minority Business Development Center is typically the best information resource for general information about the development of minority enterprise; the Public Affairs Office can suggest the MBDC nearest you.

The MBDA's Web site offers a number of resources for those seeking information about minority business development. For example, there is a page of electronic links to government and private organizations that might offer further information and a set of databases offering statistics and information about minority businesses in America. The Web site can be accessed at http://www.mbda.gov.

AGENCY PUBLICATIONS

The MBDA focuses its efforts on making information and publications available to the public through its business centers rather than through its own publishing endeavors. The agency does, however, release some brochures and an occasional study or position paper. The Electronic Reading Room on the MBDA Web site offers a few publications for downloading, such as "Minority Business and Entrepreneurship" and "Entrepreneurship Programs that Reach Minority Youth." The site also offers links to other research reports and documents and can be accessed at http://www.mbda.gov/rroom.html. For further information about MBDA publications, contact the Public Affairs Office at (202) 482-4547.

BIBLIOGRAPHY

Brown, Carolyn, and Tonia L. Shakespeare. "A Call to Arms for Black Business." *Black Enterprise*, November 1996, pp. 79–84.

"Commission Calls for Revamp of Federal Minority Business Plan." *Jet*, 6 July 1992, p. 8.

Guadalupe, Patricia. "Corporate Welfare or 'Good Business Sense?'" *Hispanic Business*, October 1995, p. 14.

Jones, Joyce. "Second Time Around." *Black Enterprise*, September 1995, p. 29.

———. "What's Up at the MBDA?" *Black Enterprise*, June 1994, pp. 43–5

Mackowski, Maura. "Can the MBDA Find a Focus?" *Hispanic Business*, June 1994, pp. 124–25.

Mehta, Stephanie N. "Groups to Fight Bid to Eliminate Minority Program." *Wall Street Journal*, 15 September 1995, p. A9.

Richardson, Linda L. "Minority Business Development Agency Helps Minority-Owned Firms Overcome Export Hurdles and Compete in the International Marketplace." *Business America*, September 1995, pp. 25–27.

Rosenstein, Carolyn. *Race, Ethnicity, & Entrepreneurship in Urban America*. Hawthorne: Aldine de Gruyter, 1995.

Russell, Joel. "Reinventing Commerce." *Hispanic Business*, August 1995, pp. 8–9.

National Aeronautics and Space Administration (NASA)

PARENT ORGANIZATION: Independent
ESTABLISHED: April 1958
EMPLOYEES: 19,500

Contact Information:

ADDRESS: 300 E St. SW
Washington, DC 20546
PHONE: (202) 358-0000
TDD (HEARING IMPAIRED): (202) 358-2947
FAX: (202) 358-3010
URL: http://www.nasa.gov
ADMINISTRATOR: Daniel S. Goldin
ACTING DEPUTY ADMINISTRATOR: John R. Dailey

WHAT IS ITS MISSION?

The mission of the National Aeronautics and Space Administration (NASA) contains three basic elements. As a research and development agency, it seeks to advance and communicate scientific knowledge of the earth, the solar system, and the universe, and it aims to use the environment of space as much as possible for its research activities. The agency also seeks to explore, use, and enable the development of space for human enterprise. For strictly practical purposes, NASA attempts to research, develop, verify, and transfer advanced aeronautics, space, and related technologies to industry and the public.

HOW IS IT STRUCTURED?

The planning, coordination, and control of NASA programs are established at NASA's headquarters, where the Office of the Administrator, the NASA Advisory Council, the Aerospace Safety Council, and the staff offices are located. More than a dozen staff offices each carry out a specific headquarters function. These staff offices include the Office of Public Affairs, the Office of Procurement, and the Office of Headquarters Operations.

The direction and management of NASA's programs are the responsibility of seven different program offices, all reporting to the Office of the Administrator. The Office of Aeronautics is responsible for conducting programs that develop and commercialize high-payoff aeronautics technologies; similarly, the Office of Space Access and Technology takes the lead in developing innovative space technologies and transferring them to aerospace and nonaerospace applications. NASA's pro-

BUDGET:

National Aeronautics and Space Administration

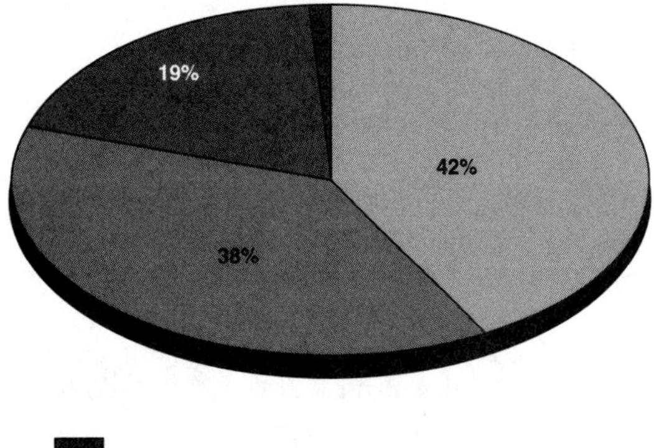

grams concerning human interaction with the microgravity environment of space, including research into aerospace medicine and life support, are the responsibility of the Office of Life and Microgravity Sciences and Applications.

The Office of Mission to Planet Earth is responsible for studying global climate changes and the integrated function of the earth as a system. This office is also responsible for managing NASA's remote satellites and instruments. The Office of Space Science conducts programs and research designed to understand the origin, evolution, and structure of the universe and the solar system.

Two NASA program offices are devoted specifically to NASA's space flight programs. The Office of Space Flight is responsible for some of NASA's most glamorous work, including the Space Shuttle program. The Office of Space Communications supports NASA's aeronautic and space flight missions. Its responsibilities include spacecraft operations and control centers, ground and space communications, and flight dynamics and trajectories.

The majority of NASA's program work is carried out at the 10 NASA centers, located from coast to coast. Each of the centers is the direct responsibility of a certain program office—for example, the Kennedy Space Center in Florida is managed by the Office of Space Flight, and the Langley Research Center is managed by the Office of Aeronautics.

PRIMARY FUNCTIONS

Through its five strategic enterprises, NASA conducts research for the solution of problems of flight, both within and beyond the earth's atmosphere, and it develops, constructs, operates, and evaluates aeronautical and space vehicles. It conducts the missions and support activities involved in exploring space with both manned and unmanned vehicles. The agency also arranges for the most efficient use of American scientific and engineering resources to assist other countries engaged in aeronautical and space activities for peaceful purposes. As a government agency whose basic product is the advancement of human knowledge, NASA conducts an extensive education program to promote excellence in America's education systems by providing access and engagement in NASA's missions.

PROGRAMS

In addition to glamorous programs such as Apollo and the space shuttle, NASA operates a wide array of other programs, usually in conjunction with military or industrial organizations. One of NASA's most important programs is the Technology Transfer Program, which seeks to contribute to the U.S. economy by passing on technology in the form of processes, products, or programs to fulfill the technical and business needs of the public. Similarly, the agency's Education Program's mission is to promote excellence in America's education system by providing access to NASA's work and by increasing awareness of the impact that science, math, and technology will have on the quality of life in the twenty-first century. The Origins Program, an astronomical search for the origins of the earth system, seeks concrete evidence about the formation of stars and galaxies, the conditions necessary for the existence of life, and the possibility that other planets in the universe are able to support life.

More specialized programs include the High Speed Research Project, whose goal is to enable the U.S. transport industry to produce an environmentally acceptable, economical 300-passenger aircraft that will have a range of five thousand miles and fly at a speed of Mach 2.4. NASA's Research Airplane Program, which it operates in conjunction with the military services, studies the performance of military aircraft in all imaginable flight conditions.

BUDGET INFORMATION

NASA's 1997 budget of approximately $13.8 billion accounted for less than 1 percent of the total federal budget. It considers itself to have the "smallest budget of the major federal agencies." The largest portion of NASA's budget, about 42 percent or $5.8 billion, is spent in the area of Science, Aeronautics and Technology, including the Space Science and Mission to Planet Earth Enterprises. The Human Space Flight area, including the space shuttle and space station programs, accounts for slightly less, about 38 percent or $5.3 billion. To meet its goal of greater quality assurance, 19 percent of NASA's budget, about $2.6 billion, is spent in the area of Mission Support, which includes safety and communications services. The remainder of the budget, about $18.3 million, is set aside for the Office of the Inspector General.

FAST FACTS

As of 1997 space shuttle personnel had spent a total of over 11 years in space.

(Source: NASA Headquarters Public Affairs Office. "Space Shuttle: Operating the World's Most Versatile Launch System," 1998.)

HISTORY

NASA is unusual among government agencies in that it originated in response to a single event—the launch of *Sputnik*, the first man-made satellite by the Soviet Union on October 4, 1957. *Sputnik* teed off a national debate that concluded in the admission that American military preparations for space activity must be supplemented by a new program to demonstrate technological superiority over the Cold War enemies of the United States, the Soviets.

In April 1958 President Dwight D. Eisenhower sent Congress a bill providing for a civilian space program run by the National Aeronautics and Space Agency, to be formed around the existing National Advisory Committee for Aeronautics (NACA). Over the next few years, NASA's responsibilities and authorities were laid out, and its staff and facilities began to expand from the nucleus of the NACA—largely through transfers from other government agencies, including the air force's transfer of two lunar probes and several engine-development projects. By the end of Eisenhower's administration, NASA had become the principal operating agency for manned space flight, space science, and launch-vehicle development, as well as a significant research-and-development source for space flight technology and aeronautics.

The Apollo Years

NASA's growth during the last years of the Eisenhower administration was remarkable, but it was nothing compared to the activities undertaken during the administration of President John F. Kennedy. Spurred by the Soviet launching of the first man into space, Kennedy proposed a national commitment to land an American on the moon in the 1960s. Congress quickly appropriated the first portion of the $25 billion that would finance the mission.

In the 1960s the U.S. civilian space program was dominated by Apollo, the moon mission. During this time NASA was pursuing a broad range of activities that included significant advances in weather and communications satellites, but these programs were carried out in the shadow of Apollo. The moon mission captured most of NASA's budget, along with the public's attention. When the program mission was accomplished by *Apollo 11* in July 1969, NASA gained a reputation for competence and technological excellence that it was to enjoy for many years.

The Space Program Cools Off

Public and congressional sentiment for the space program became more reserved even before the Apollo landing, largely because of the expense of manned space flight. Various domestic problems—from the Vietnam War (1959–75) and the protests of the 1960s to the increasingly expensive War on Poverty—made many Americans skeptical of such grandiose projects. By 1980 NASA personnel had declined from a 1967 high of nearly 37,000 to fewer than 25,000.

As a result, the emphasis of NASA programs turned primarily to space science and earth applications during the 1970s. The most spectacular mission of the decade was the Viking mission to Mars, which sent close-up pictures of the planet back to earth. Other advances were made in the development of communications and weather satellites. Through its Technology Transfer Program, NASA ensured that its scientific and technological discoveries were widely distributed, not only in the United States but throughout the world.

The Challenger Disaster and Beyond

After a remarkable 20-year record of successes, NASA's operations began to be questioned in the 1980s, as the space shuttle program began to unfold. Originally named the Space Transportation System, the program had originated in the late 1960s but did not begin to gather steam until the 1980s. Its goal was to replace expensive launch vehicles with a versatile, economical vehicle that could be launched aboard a rocket and fly back to land on the earth, eventually to be launched again. Unfortunately, budget constraints forced NASA to scale back and accept a more limited version of the shuttle than had originally been planned. The resulting development program was plagued by delays and cost overruns, which conflicted with NASA's Apollo reputation.

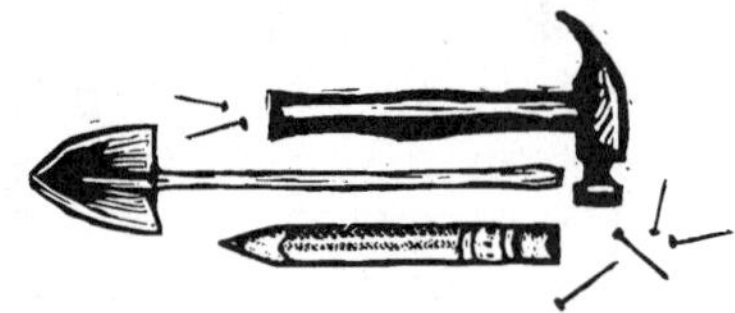

GET INVOLVED:

NASA maintains an extensive education program for people of all ages and backgrounds, with a particular emphasis on science and technology. Information on these programs is available on-line at http://www.hq.nasa.gov/office/codef/education/fieldcenterdetails.html, or from the Education Division, Mail Code FE, NASA Headquarters, Washington, DC 20546-0001; phone (202) 358-1110. NASA also maintains a number of on-line educational resources, including Quest, for children in grades K-12 and Spacelink available at http://www.hq.nasa.gov/office/codef/education/online.html.

Space Camp

The U.S. Space Camp, where children and adults can learn about the space program and NASA by experiencing astronaut "training," including hands-on experience with equipment used to prepare astronauts for space, is perhaps NASA's most famous program for the public. U.S. Space Camp has its own Web site at http://www.spacecamp.com where information on programs and an on-line application are available. Call 1-800-63SPACE for more information and an application.

NASA's problems were exposed tragically on January 28, 1986, when the space shuttle *Challenger* exploded a little more than a minute after takeoff. All seven aboard the shuttle were killed, including a schoolteacher named Christa McAuliffe, the shuttle program's first civilian passenger. The public was saddened by this tragedy, and the sadness turned to anger when it was revealed that the explosion was the result of a minor technical flaw in the shuttle's construction. An official investigation of the *Challenger* accident resulted in comments that the pressure to maintain 24 shuttle launches a year, encouraged by Congress and the administration, had prompted NASA to cut corners. The report also noted that over the years NASA had drifted in its mission focus from a primarily research and development orientation and had evolved into an agency that indulged in showy and expensive operations.

The years following the *Challenger* disaster were difficult for NASA as it attempted to rebuild its space program and refocus its efforts. The space shuttle program was grounded for two and one-half years while NASA reassessed its program and the makers of military and commercial satellites sought alternative ways to get them into orbit. The agency's current strategic plan emphasizes the need to transfer more of its operations to private institutions, and NASA has begun to devise programs that will supplement the costly space shuttle. The agency's goal is to become safer for its space flight personnel while growing more streamlined and efficient in its operations.

CURRENT POLITICAL ISSUES

NASA's primary political issue has always been, and remains, the overwhelming costs of its high-tech space programs. Public support for the cost of NASA missions began to fade even before the *Apollo 11* landing was achieved, and as a result the final two flights of NASA's most popular program were scrapped. Critics of NASA say that despite its current efforts at faster, better, cheaper ways of achieving its missions, most of its programs are trapped by a bureaucratic tendency toward planning missions that are big, slow, and expensive. They point out that many of the agency's space programs are sold to the public and to Congress by understating their costs and overstating their usefulness. The space shuttle program is a prime example: proposed in 1972 at a cost of $88 million per launch, the shuttle actually costs about $1.8 billion per launch—about 20 times the original estimate.

Case Study: The X-33

Just before the 1996 election, Vice President Al Gore and NASA Administrator Dan Goldin, at a highly publicized visit to the Jet Propulsion Laboratory in Pasadena, California, praised the proposed *X-33*, a reusable launch vehicle (RLV) that would, after an initial $941 million investment by taxpayers, evolve into an entirely privately financed launch vehicle that would slash the cost of getting to space by 10 times, replace the aging shuttle fleet, and create an array of new space industries. Even people within the administration believed the estimates of the *X-33*'s costs, and its effect on the space industry, were outrageously embellished. This opinion has been borne out to some degree by the fact that no private company—not even Lockheed Martin, who is teamed with NASA to develop the *X-33*—has yet stepped up to assume responsibility for the *X-33* once a prototype has been constructed. The financial risks are simply too great for a private company.

Another point of contention regarding NASA is the agency's entrenched system of doing business. Decisions are made through an extensive hierarchy of NASA officials, most of whom are unfamiliar with the technical details of a given mission. As a result, the cost of a NASA mission is mainly driven by the salaries of the many people involved rather than by the costs of materials. This problem is perhaps best illustrated by a recent international effort at measuring the effects of solar wind—the particles and fields expelled by the sun—with a pair of satellites, one built by NASA and the other by the Swedish space program, which employs about 230 people.

Although the two satellites were nearly identical, NASA's satellite cost 10 times more than its Swedish counterpart.

SUCCESSES AND FAILURES

High-profile NASA successes such as the *Apollo 11* moon landing tend to lure much of the public's attention away from other important NASA programs, but nevertheless the agency quietly contributes much to space and aeronautics research and industry. NASA's recent contributions to the aeronautics industry include the conclusion of the Laminar Flow Control Program, which achieved smooth air flow over the wings of an aircraft at supersonic speed, and the development of the Crack Finder, a handheld device that can scan the exterior surfaces of older aircraft for structural weaknesses. Continental Airlines recently became the first commercial air carrier to use the NASA-developed wind-shear detection system. NASA has even shared technology with the Ford Motor Company to help improve the design and engineering of Ford vehicles.

FUTURE DIRECTIONS

According to the "Strategies to Revolutionize NASA" section of the agency's *Strategic Plan*, NASA intends to consolidate and streamline the organization in several ways to cut costs and increase efficiency. The main element of the plan involves increasing emphasis on NASA as a research and development agency and transferring operational activities to commercial operators or other federal agencies. The ultimate result will be a reduction in the number of employees and support contractors who perform operational functions.

NASA's *Strategic Plan* also outlines some exciting long-term goals for the agency. It intends to conduct international missions to planetary bodies in the solar system, enable air and space system advances to support the development of "smart aircraft," and establish a tangible presence—through space stations, satellites, and probes—throughout the solar system.

Other long-term goals of the agency include supporting the ongoing maturation of established private aeronautics and space industries, as well as the development of new high-tech industries, and enabling humans to forecast and assess the health of the earth system.

AGENCY RESOURCES

The NASA Headquarters Information Center is the main outlet for NASA information, but interested parties may also want to look into Spacelink, NASA's electronic aeronautics and space resource, designed to provide current and historical educational information. Spacelink is on the World Wide Web at http://spacelink.msfc.nasa.gov.

For general information about how to obtain services or educational materials, the agency distributes several publications, including the *NASA Educational Publications List, NASA Film List*, and *NASA Directory of Services for the Public*. These may be obtained by contacting the Public Affairs Office of the nearest NASA center.

AGENCY PUBLICATIONS

NASA publishes a variety of historical works about its missions and research, including general histories such as *Orders of Magnitude, A History of the NACA and NASA*; center histories such as *On the Frontier: Flight Research at Dryden, 1946–1981*; and program histories such as *Moonport: A History of Apollo Launch Facilities and Operations*. Information about these books can be obtained through either the NASA History Office or the Information Center, NASA Headquarters, 300 E St. SW, Washington, DC 20546. The headquarters telephone directory and certain publications and picture sets are available for sale from the U.S. Government Printing Office, 732 N. Capitol St. NW, Washington, DC 20401.

BIBLIOGRAPHY

Agres, Ted. "NASA at the Crossroads." *R and D*, January 1996, p. 33.

Air and Space Library. Rapid City, S. Dak.: Spizziri Publishing, 1993.

Anselmo, Joseph. "NASA Picks Low-Cost Earth Study Missions." *Aviation Week and Space Technology*, 146, No. 12, p. 26.

Benedict, Howard. *NASA: The Endless Journey*. Orlando, Fla.: Graphic House, 1992.

Chang, Maria L. "Radical New Rocket" *Science World*, 18 October 1996, p. 6.

Lawler, Andrew. "NASA Mission Gets Down to Earth." *Science*, 1 September 1995, pp. 1208–11.

Lovell, James A., Jr. "Life After Apollo 13." *Wall Street Journal*, 22 March 1996, p. A12.

McCurdy, Howard E. *Inside NASA: High Technology & Organizational Change in the American Space Program*. Baltimore: Johns Hopkins University Press, 1993.

Moore, David. *Reinventing NASA*. Upland: Diane Publishing, 1994.

"Space Race." *Industry Week*, 17 June 1996, p. 72.

Walker, Peter M., ed. *The Cambridge Air and Space Dictionary*. New York: Cambridge University Press, 1990.

National Archives and Records Administration (NARA)

PARENT ORGANIZATION: Independent
ESTABLISHED: April 1, 1985
EMPLOYEES: 2,514

Contact Information:

ADDRESS: 8601 Adelphi Rd.
College Park, Maryland 20740-6001
PHONE: (301) 713-6800
TDD (HEARING IMPAIRED): (202) 501-5404
FAX: (301) 713-6497
E-MAIL: inquire@nara.gov
URL: http://www.nara.gov
ARCHIVIST OF THE UNITED STATES: John W. Carlin
DEPUTY ARCHIVIST OF THE UNITED STATES: Lewis J. Bellardo

WHAT IS ITS MISSION?

The National Archives and Records Administration (NARA) is the legal guardian of all of the information of the nation. Its stated mission is "to ensure ready access to essential evidence . . . that documents the rights of American citizens, the actions of federal officials, and the national experience."

HOW IS IT STRUCTURED?

NARA exists as an independent agency within the executive branch of the federal government. The archivist of the United States, is the head of NARA. The archivist is appointed at the discretion of the president, with the approval of Congress, but is not a member of the presidential cabinet.

The deputy archivist is the NARA chief of staff. The Office of the Deputy Archivist includes the general counsel, the policy and communications staff, and the development staff. Congressional affairs and equal employment opportunity and diversity programs are also handled by the Office of the Deputy Archivist.

The internal administration of NARA is divided between the Office of Administrative Services and the Office of Human Resources and Information Services.

Program Offices

The Office of the Federal Register (OFR) is responsible for the Federal Register system, a massive clearinghouse for filing and publishing laws and executive

The Declaration of Independence and the Constitution of the United States of America are displayed in the rotunda of the National Archives in Washington, D.C. NARA is responsible for maintaining all government documents and making their information available to the public. (National Archives and Records Administration)

documents. The CFR also coordinates the activities of the U.S. Electoral College and the U.S. constitutional amendment processes.

The Office of Records Services in Washington, D.C., distributes records to the public and administers the Washington National Records Center in Suitland, Maryland. The Office of Regional Records Services maintains field branches in 16 cities across the United States and at the National Personnel Records Center in St. Louis, Missouri.

The administration of the Presidential Library System belongs to the Office of Presidential Libraries. The activities of this office are defined by the Presidential Records Act of 1978 and the Presidential Libraries Act of 1986.

Independent Offices (Arms)

NARA is closely associated with three affiliate offices called "arms." Each arm operates independently to provide services that enhance the function of NARA. The Information Security Oversight Office oversees the declassification of documents. The National Historical Publications and Records Commission (NHPRC) funds grants to independent projects for the preservation of historical documents and relics. The Office of the Inspector General (OIG) conducts internal audits of NARA and makes recommendations for improving NARA operations. The appointed head of the OIG is accountable to the U.S. Congress as well as to the archivist.

PRIMARY FUNCTIONS

NARA is an independent operation serving all three branches of the U.S. government: the executive branch, the legislature, and the judiciary. NARA holds records from the Internal Revenue Service, U.S. Military, Bureau of Immigration and Naturalization, Federal Aviation Administration—virtually every department, agency, bureau, and compartment of the federal government.

NARA receives old records from agencies and departments of the federal government after the records are no longer needed. NARA sorts, catalogs, files or publishes, and maintains this information as part of the permanent archives of the United States. Some archived records are permanently transferred to NARA field offices throughout the United States; others are eventually retained by the agency that created them. NARA is additionally entrusted with the task of preserving the nation's priceless artifacts. NARA, in fact, concerns itself with virtually every medium in existence: microfiche and microfilm, drawings, artifacts, videotape, magnetic

FAST FACTS

NARA facilities house more than 20 million cubic feet of original archival materials, or the equivalent of more than 4 billion pieces of paper.

(Source: John W. Carlin. *Ready Access to Essential Evidence.* National Archives, 1997.)

media, and others. Authors Loretto Szucs and Sandra Luebking write in *The Archives: A Guide to the National Archives Field Branches*(1988), "The National Archives . . . [are] the nation's memory."

NARA is responsible for saving, organizing, and making public every relevant document involved in the operations of the U.S. government. The function of NARA differs from that of historical agencies and organizations such as the Smithsonian Institution because NARA exclusively is charged with the mandate to "provide ready access" to the information of the government. NARA also takes an active role in the preservation of nonarchival historical memorabilia.

PROGRAMS

NARA serves the people of the United States through many avenues. It preserves the history of the nation through archives and museums and keeps the public informed through the publication of voluminous chronicles of day-to-day government activities. NARA organizes legislative paperwork and provides public access to the workings of the government through records management services and cataloging operations.

National Historical Publications and Records Commission

NARA's National Historical Publications and Records Commission (NHPRC) affiliate sponsors educational programs on the preservation of historical documents and artifacts and offers financial assistance in the form of grants for projects of this nature. The grants go to state and local archives, colleges and universities, historical societies, libraries, and other nonprofit organizations. Recent ongoing projects include archival collections and the collected papers of such historical figures as George Washington, Jefferson Davis, and Martin Luther King, Jr.

Genealogical Services

The Washington National Records Center in Washington, D.C., houses millions of cubic feet of archival records. These are available to the government and to the public at large through a variety of programs. Genealogists are among the most frequent public users of the information in the National Archives. At NARA records centers in Washington, D.C., Maryland, and throughout the country, researchers have access to a variety of data, including Civil War records, post office files, census reports, and naturalization records.

In an effort to accommodate genealogical research, NARA offers workshops and other instructional programs to assist researchers. "Quick Guides" and "General Information Leaflets" are also available from NARA by mail and through the Internet. NARA publications provide guidance to the beginning genealogist plus instructions for using the microfilm catalogs, index systems, and other record banks. NARA's bookstore also stocks and sells assorted books on genealogy.

NARA sponsors "The Genealogy Page" on the Internet to post announcements, provide assistance, and publicize news and information concerning its genealogical research tools and data stores. "The Genealogy Page" features electronic links to nongovernmental genealogical resources, including search engines and genealogical societies. NARA is deeply committed to expanding public access to its on-line resources, and efforts in this area are continually in progress.

Presidential Libraries

The Presidential Library System was officially authorized in 1955, and a presidential library exists for every modern president since Herbert Hoover. Each library is a museum, established independently by the respective president through a combination of private and public funding. Under the provisions of law, the contents of each library may be donated to the American people. NARA takes responsibility for the administration of the system. Collectively the libraries house hundreds of millions of artifacts, including more than 250 million pages of text and millions of photographs, audio- and videotapes, and motion picture footage. The libraries offer tours, lectures, and other programs. They are valuable educational resources.

BUDGET INFORMATION

As a federal agency, NARA receives congressional appropriations from federal tax dollars each year. In 1998 NARA received $206.5 million. The requested budget for 1999 reached $241.3 million with the following allocations: $224.9 million for operating expenses; $10.5 million for repairs and restoration; and $6 million toward grants.

NARA funding supports critical records management functions: accessioning, declassification, and publication. The *Federal Register*, *Code of Federal Regulations*, and *U.S. Statutes-at-Large*, all are funded through NARA. Over $6 million is earmarked for storage and maintenance costs of the nation's archival facilities, and NARA receives a Federally guaranteed loan in the amount of $301.7 million annually, toward the development of the new Archives II Facility in Washington, DC.

Funding for NHPRC grants totals $4 million to $10 million annually. The NHPRC account is allocated separately, and the funds are supplemented by revenues from NARA museums and libraries and other public services.

FAST FACTS

In 1997 NARA received 18.5 million requests for information, its facilities hosted more than 2.3 million visitors, and its Web and gopher sites recorded 4.1 million hits on average each month.

(Source: National Archives and Records Administration, 1998.)

HISTORY

The first committee to study records management in the U.S. government was formed in 1810. The earliest discussions focused on the need for efficiency in document retrieval, but over time other issues came to light.

During the War of 1812 a devastating fire (set by British soldiers) in the U.S. Capitol destroyed many valuable books and records, including the holdings of the newly formed Library of Congress. In addition to the problems of vandalism and natural disasters, government records, printed on brittle parchment and other nondurable papers, crumbled with the passage of time. Also, inadequate storage facilities failed to protect the materials, and soluble inks faded as the years took their toll on the invaluable documents.

It would seem that practicality should have impelled the government to address these circumstances of document maintenance in a more timely fashion. In reality it was persistent political pressure on the part of scholars and historians that ultimately brought about the institution of the National Archives more than 150 years after the nation was founded.

National Archives Established

Little was accomplished to centralize the recordkeeping process of the government until the National Archives Establishment of 1934 under President Franklin Delano Roosevelt. Prior to that each office of the government was responsible for maintaining its own records. The National Archives began formal operations in 1935, and by the end of World War II (1939–45) it had succeeded in developing effective procedures for the systematic maintenance of public records.

National Archives and Records Service

The role of the National Archives was expanded during the postwar years. On June 30, 1949, the National Archives and Records Service was created under the Federal Property and Administrative Services Act as a branch of the General Services Administration.

The reorganized agency focused its attention on developing new systems to handle the increasing volume of official records. The National Archives field branches were first established in 1969. The remote facilities brought new innovations and set the precedent of documenting for posterity federal activities outside of Washington, D.C. Duplicate archives were also stored at the field branches for greater public access.

National Archives and Records Administration

On April 1, 1985, NARA regained its status as an independent agency under the National Archives and Records Administration Act, which was enacted following several years of pressure from lobbyists and other groups. In this capacity NARA operates independently within the executive branch of government.

CURRENT POLITICAL ISSUES

The mission of NARA is rooted in the principle that the people of the United States have the right to know about their government. This issue serves to ignite many political controversies. Indeed, NARA's very existence causes controversy between those who support paperwork reduction and those who favor the public's right to know. Lawmakers and lobbyists persist in debate over notions of confidentiality versus efficiency. This "right to know" argument raises concerns about personal privacy and further concerns about executive privilege. NARA, the legal custodian of the information of the country, must resolve these issues to the satisfaction of both sides.

Case Study: The Nixon Papers

The years of Richard Nixon's presidency were among the most controversial in the history of the United

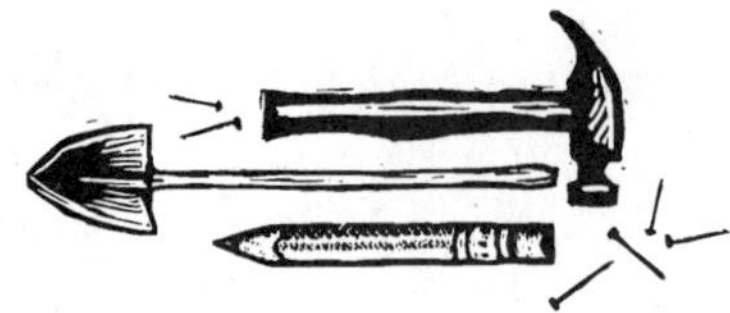

GET INVOLVED:

NARA actively solicits volunteers to assist with the preservation of archives and to develop educational programs and other public services. Positions are available at the Washington, D.C., facility, at the presidential libraries, and at regional facilities around the country. Volunteers work as research assistants, staff aides, docents, and information specialists. Information about these positions is available on the Internet at http://www.nara.gov/professional/volunteer/naravol.html or by calling NARA Volunteer and Visitor Services at (202) 502-5205.

States. In 1973 explosive disclosures made by the television and newspaper media implicated President Nixon in the burglary and wiretapping—among other crimes—of the Democratic National Committee headquarters during the 1972 presidential campaign. The affair came to be known as the Watergate scandal, named for the apartment and office complex where the break-in occurred. Nixon resigned from office when his presidential documents and tapes were subpoenaed as a probable basis for impeachment proceedings. The federal government then seized Nixon's presidential records. They were entrusted to NARA for holding.

The Presidential Recordings and Materials Preservation Act of 1974 authorized NARA to keep the Nixon papers and to make them available to the public. The former president filed a lawsuit, objecting that executive privilege would override the public's right to view the material. Citizens' groups meanwhile filed lawsuits defending the public's right to know.

The ownership of the Nixon papers was never resolved. The matter was pursued by Nixon's heirs after his death. They offered to sell the Nixon papers back to the government in order to raise money to rebuild the privately held Nixon Library in Yerba Buena, California. The government maintains that the Nixon papers belong to the United States and cannot be sold. Public access to the papers and tapes was severely restricted by NARA pending the outcome of the complex legal issues.

Public Impact

Despite a congressional mandate to declassify the documents, NARA implemented complex access restrictions that undermine the public's right to examine the materials. *The Nation* quoted an alliance of historical societies that maintain that suppression of the documents gives a license to the Nixon estate "[to be] in control of United States history between 1968 and 1974." Unanswered questions remain regarding the full extent to which the Watergate affair might have jeopardized the integrity of the presidency and the democratic process in general.

FUTURE DIRECTIONS

According to a strategic plan outlined by U.S. Archivist John Carlin in 1997, NARA looks to technology as the key to improving its operations. Key points of the strategy involve extensive implementation of information technology combined with human resource development, innovation, and streamlined operations. Specific goals are defined, with emphasis on providing access to records through on-line media, especially the Internet.

Improved Record Maintenance

Another of NARA's goals is to improve federal record keeping. It aims to keep public officials and agencies apprised of the most efficient means of recording information so as to expedite the cataloging and appraisal processes, which in turn will speed access of information to the public. The strategic plan addresses the need to further public access to information through expanded use of the Internet as well as through mounted exhibits that can be transported throughout the country. NARA also intends to expand its technology infrastructure to better integrate the automated storage and retrieval of information. This will further facilitate remote access, which will permit greater consolidation of archival repositories and reduce space requirements in the process.

NARA Archival Information Locator (NAIL)

In keeping with future goals and strategies, the archives administration hosts the NARA Archival Information Locator (NAIL) on the Internet. NAIL is a comprehensive on-line catalog system for information retrieval. More than 307,000 documents and other materials are cataloged through NAIL. Digital facsimiles of many items are also available on-line through NAIL. NARA encourages the public to access and utilize NAIL, available at http://www.nara.gov/nara/nail.html.

AGENCY RESOURCES

The National Archives in Washington, D.C., offers public information assistance through many avenues. Access the public reference information line at (202)

502-5400, the genealogy staff at (202) 501-5410, and the Center for Legislative Archives at (202) 501-5350. E-mail inquiries can be made at inquire@arch2.nara.gov. The National Archives in Maryland provides fax-on-demand services at (301) 713–6905. The office of the Inspector General maintains a telephone hot line at 1-800-786-2551 and an E-mail hot line at oig.hotline@ arch2.nara.gov.

NARA features an extensive Internet site on the World Wide Web. It is easy to navigate via links on the NARA home page at http://www.nara.gov. Web sites include access to NARA catalogs, files, features, and comprehensive search tools.

The National Archives Library and the Archives Library Information Center are on-line at http://www. nara.gov/nara/naralibrary/refmenu.html. "The Genealogy Page" is at http://www.nara.gov/genealogy/genindex. html. Information about the presidential libraries, including location, tour times, and programs, is published at http://www.nara.gov/nara/president/overview.html. NHPRC information, including workshop announcements and grant applications, can be found at http://www. nara.gov/nara/nhprc/#directory.

AGENCY PUBLICATIONS

NARA's Office of the Federal Register publishes official government documents, all of which are available on the Internet through the NARA home page at http://www.nara.gov. These include the *Federal Register*, the *U.S. Government Manual*, *Public Laws,* and the *Code of Federal Regulations*. *Prologue*, NARA's scholarly journal, is published quarterly and is available in print by calling the Product Sales Section at 1-800-234-8861. Informational pamphlets on record management and genealogy are available at the same number.

BIBLIOGRAPHY

Hersh, Seymour. "A Reporter at Large: Nixon's Last Cover-Up: The Tapes He Wants the Archives to Suppress." *New Yorker*, 14 December 1992, p. 76(18).

Klaw, Barbara. "In Safekeeping: The National Archives, America's Official Safe-Deposit Box is Only Fifty Years Old—But It is Already Bulging with Our Treasures and Souvenirs." *American Heritage*, August–September 1984, p. 89 (7).

Linder, Bill R. "An Overview of Genealogical Research in the National Archives." *Library Trends*, Summer 1983, p. 25(14).

Parshall, Gerald. "The Secrets of the Oval Office." *U.S. News and World Report*, 15 December 1986.

Penn, Ira A. "Information Management Legislation in the Last Quarter of the 20th Century: A Records Management Disaster." *Records Management Quarterly*, January 1997, p. 3(6).

Pepper, Ann, and Marilyn Kalfus. "Nixon Library May Be Turned Over to the National Archives." Knight-Ridder/Tribune News Service, 5 April 1997.

Ready Access to Essential Evidence: The Strategic Plan of the National Archives and Records Administration 1997–2007. National Archives and Records Administration, 30 September 1997.

Szucs, Loretto Dennis, and Sandra Hargreaves Luebking. *The Archives: A Guide to the National Archives Field Branches.* Salt Lake City, Utah: Ancestry Publishing, 1988.

United States National Archives and Records Administration. *Guide to Federal Records in the National Archives of the United States.* National Archives and Record Service, 1996.

Walch, Timothy, ed. *Guardian of Heritage: Essays on the History of the National Archives.* National Archives and Records Administration, 1985.

Warner, Robert M. *Diary of a Dream: A History of the National Archives Independence Movement, 1980–1985.* Metuchen, N.J.: Scarecrow Press, 1995.

Webb, Tom. "National Archives Facing a New Challenge in the Electronic Age: How to Protect Records." Knight-Ridder/Tribune News Service, 1 June 1995.

National Cancer Institute (NCI)

PARENT ORGANIZATION: Department of Health and Human Services
ESTABLISHED: August 5, 1937
EMPLOYEES: 2,458

Contact Information:

ADDRESS: Bldg. 31, Rm. 10A16
31 Center Dr.
Bethesda, MD 20892-6200
PHONE: (301) 496-5585
TOLL FREE: (800) 422-6237
TDD (HEARING IMPAIRED): (800) 332-8615
FAX: (301) 402-5874
E-MAIL: cancernet@icicc.nic.nih.gov
URL: http://www.nci.nih.gov
DIRECTOR: Richard D. Klausner, M.D.

WHAT IS ITS MISSION?

The National Cancer Institute (NCI) is the government's primary agency for cancer research. Its ultimate goal is to find a cure for cancer. Until that happens, the NCI aims to improve the quality of life of those suffering from cancer and keep the general public informed of the progress the institute is making in the fight against the disease. According to Richard Klausner, M.D., the director of the NCI, the institute supports research, training, and education initiatives related to "the cause, diagnosis, prevention, and treatment of cancer, rehabilitation from cancer, and the continuing care of cancer patients and the families of cancer patients."

HOW IS IT STRUCTURED?

The NCI is the largest of the 24 branches of the National Institutes of Health (NIH). In turn, the NIH is one of eight agencies that make up the Public Health Service branch of the Department of Health and Human Services (DHHS). The NCI is composed of nine offices and eight divisions.

The Offices of the NCI

The Office of the Director oversees all of the institute's programs and activities. It is headed by the director, who is appointed by the president. The director determines the cancer program and priorities of the institute and its related agencies. The Office of Intramural Management is responsible for directing the institute's intramural programs, managing information resources, and all of the administrative activities of the director's office, including budgets, grants, contracts, and personnel. The Office of Cancer Communications relays institute news and activities to the media and the public, responds to media and public inquiries, and prepares congressional testimony and special reports. As the liaison between the NCI and the international cancer research community, the Office of International Affairs plans, manages, and evaluates international research and information activities and facilitates the international exchange of scientists. The Office of Science Policy is in charge of all policy decisions for the institute as a whole and for specific programs. The Office of Centers, Training, and Resources coordinates the scientific extramural programs that focus on cancer research in academic and research institutions and provides training programs for health professionals. The Office of Special Populations Research directs research concerning special populations such as ethnic groups and the elderly. The Office of Cancer Information, Communication, and Education oversees the dissemination of information about cancer to the public, patients, health professionals, and the media. It is responsible for such information services as the Physician Data Query (PDQ), CancerNet, the NCI Web site, the Cancer Information Service, and the institute's publications.

Intramural Divisions of the NCI

The eight divisions of the NCI are either intramural divisions, which focus on the internal activities of the institute, or extramural divisions, which are concerned primarily with organizations and activities outside the institute. The three intramural divisions are the Division of Basic Sciences, the Division of Clinical Sciences, and the Division of Cancer Epidemiology and Genetics. The Division of Basic Sciences is responsible for basic research within the NCI, including the cellular, molecular, genetic, biochemical, and immunological aspects of cancer. The Division of Clinical Sciences focuses on the cancer patient. It oversees applied research programs and examines the results and implications of research studies. The Division of Cancer Epidemiology and Genetics aims to understand the causes, distribution, and natural history of cancer. It provides epidemiological, demographic, and bio-statistical research on the disease.

Extramural Divisions of the NCI

The remaining five divisions of the NCI focus on extramural activities. The Division of Extramural Activities administers research grants and contracts to universities and organizations outside the NCI. The Division of Cancer Treatment and Diagnosis is responsible for drug development, diagnosis, and radiotherapy development and coordinates experimental and clinical studies of cancer treatment. It also oversees 27 Comprehensive Cancer Centers nationwide, which bring cancer research and care directly to the American public. The Division of Cancer Biology directs extramural research in cancer cell biology and cancer immunology. One of its main responsibilities is to coordinate activities at the Frederick Cancer Research and Development Center in Fort Detrick, Maryland. The Division of Cancer Control and Population Sciences supports research and career development in cancer control. It oversees extramural research in epidemiology, cancer genetics, the behavioral sciences, and cancer surveillance.

FAST FACTS

In the United States more than 70 percent of children with cancer are now alive five years after diagnosis, compared with only 55 percent in the mid-1970s.

(Source: National Cancer Institute. "Q & A: Cancer Centers for Children and Adolescents," June 26, 1997.)

PRIMARY FUNCTIONS

The National Cancer Institute coordinates the National Cancer Program, which conducts and supports research, training, and health information dissemination, and other programs related to cancer. Specifically the NCI awards grants to universities, hospitals, research foundations, and businesses to support cancer research, and it conducts research of its own at the institute. It supports cancer centers nationwide to maximize the number of people who can benefit from its services. In addition to research, the NCI encourages the free flow of information about cancer. It invests heavily in programs and publications to educate the general public. It also works with voluntary organizations and international institutes to share information and coordinate activities. The NCI works closely with the other institutes of the NIH and with the DHHS. For example, the NCI coordinates cancer research efforts with the Centers for Disease Control and works with the National Institute on Aging to see how cancer affects the elderly. It advises the Food and Drug Administration on cancer-causing agents found in food and drugs. It also helps the Indian Health Services set up mobile mammogram services for American Indian reservations.

PROGRAMS

The NCI has two main objectives: research and education. It sponsors various types of funding for individuals and organizations to encourage research on cancer. In

BUDGET:

National Cancer Institute

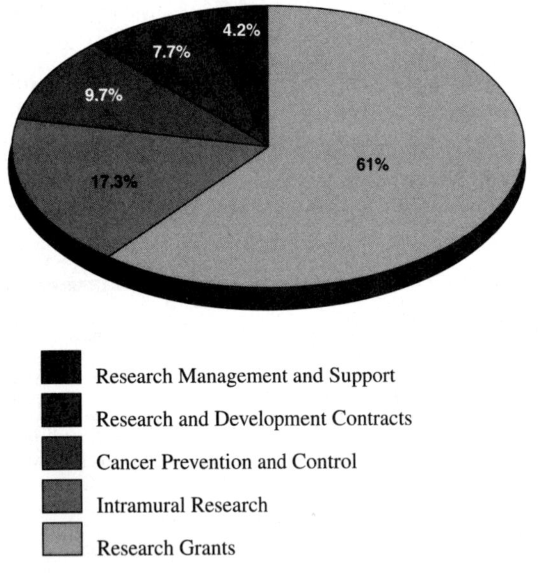

addition, the NCI has established a wide variety of programs to facilitate communication among researchers, physicians, educators, the media, and the public to fulfill its education objective. The most widely known programs include the Physician Data Query database, which allows doctors across the country to access the most recent research findings of the NCI, and the Cancer Information Service, a toll-free telephone service that lets Americans across the country get free information about cancer.

Another NCI program is the Director's Consumer Liaison Group (DCLG). This group is made up of 15 consumers who meet with researchers to discuss key issues in cancer research. It was developed to allow people who directly experience the problems of cancer to shape the focus of research on the disease. The group discusses such issues as clinical trials, cancer genetics, early detection, and public information.

In addition to these programs, the NCI has created two key education programs on its Web site at http://www.nci.nih.gov. The first is the Cancer Research Program, which provides basic information to the public. The NCI was concerned that much of the research done on cancer was so technical that the average person would not be able to understand it. This program was designed to minimize confusion about cancer research. It provides information on how cancer research has saved lives and greatly improved the quality of life of those suffering from the disease. It aims to inform the public about progress in cancer research, new opportunities in cancer research, and the way in which cancer priorities are set.

The other education program is "About Mammograms." This program serves to educate women, doctors, health educators, and the media about the importance of regular screening mammograms for early detection of breast cancer for women over 40 years old. The Web site has an on-line program to answer questions about mammograms. It also provides fact sheets and statistics about breast cancer and mammography and offers a list of publications on the subject.

BUDGET INFORMATION

Since the National Cancer Act was passed in 1971, the NCI budget has been approved directly by the president. The continuing commitment to fighting cancer is demonstrated by the fact that the budget has increased annually since 1984. The 1997 total budget of $2.4 million was a 12.2 percent increase over the funds NCI received in 1996. Of this amount 61 percent was allocated to various research grants, 7.7 percent went to research and development contracts, 17.3 percent was invested in intramural research, 4.2 percent was spent on research management and support, and 9.7 percent was used for cancer prevention and control. These budgetary allocations illustrate the strong research focus of the NCI.

HISTORY

In the early twentieth century, cancer was so greatly feared by people that it was rarely discussed in public. It was not until 1913 that the first organization dedicated to educating the public about cancer—the American Society for the Control of Cancer—was founded.

The federal government began to fund cancer studies in 1922 at the Division of Pharmacology of the Hygienic Laboratories in Washington, D.C., a branch of the Public Health Service. In 1927 the Public Health Service established the Office of Cancer Investigations at Harvard University. Despite these research initiatives by the government, the general public was still terrified of the disease. Politicians responded to the public fear with legislation for federal involvement in the prevention and control of cancer. The National Cancer Institute Act was signed into law by President Franklin D. Roosevelt on August 5, 1937.

This bill created a division of the Public Health Service called the National Cancer Institute. It would be run by a director, who would report directly to the U.S. surgeon general, and a six-member National Advisory Cancer Council, made up of leading cancer researchers. The first director of the NCI was Carl Voegtlin, former head of the Division of Pharmacology. A new building was

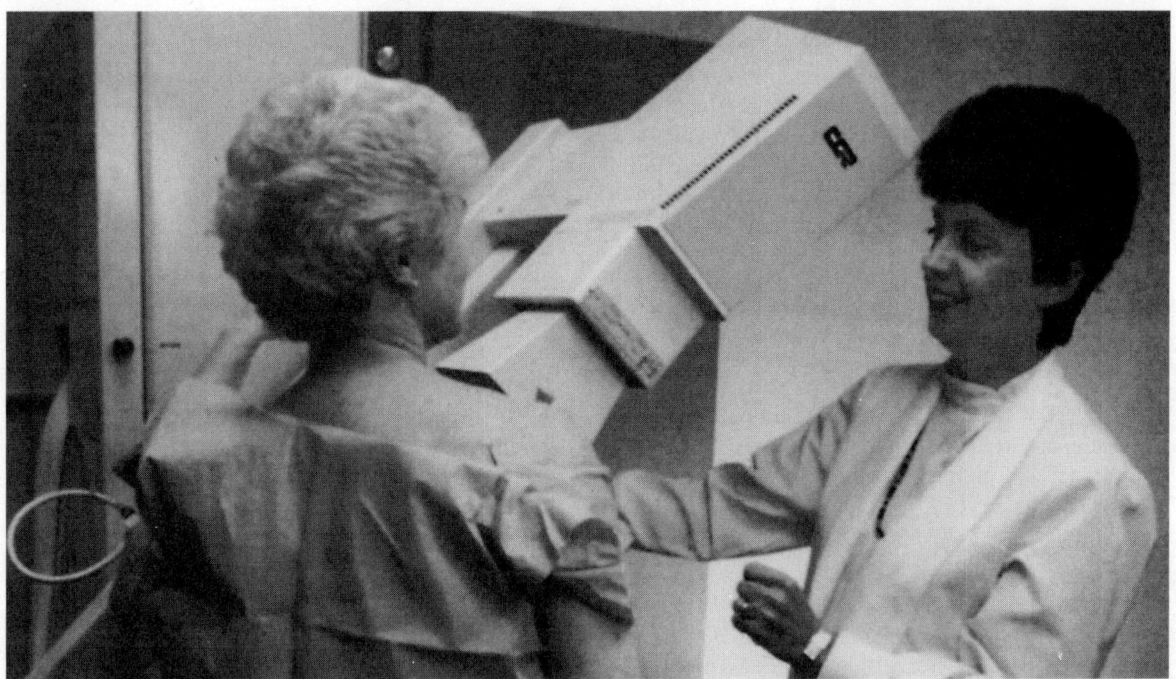

Breast cancer is the most common type of cancer among women in the United States. A mammography is the most reliable method of early breast cancer detection, especially in women ages 40 and up. (AP/Wide World Photos)

built on the campus of the National Institutes of Health in Bethesda, Maryland, to house the new institute. By 1940 the NCI was publishing its own journal.

In 1944 the Public Health Service Act made the NCI a division of the National Institutes of Health (NIH), and in 1950 the National Advisory Cancer Council was reorganized. The number of members was increased from six to 12, the terms of the members were lengthened, and people from outside the research community were allowed to sit on the council.

The NCI faced new debates in the 1960s and early 1970s regarding how to best use government funds to fight cancer. Some people felt that it would be best to establish a research program separate from the government bureaucracy that would be solely dedicated to the fight against cancer. In 1971 President Richard Nixon responded to this public pressure. First he converted a biological warfare facility in Fort Detrick, Maryland, into a cancer research center. This facility, named the Frederick Cancer Research and Development Center, soon became a world leader in cancer and acquired immunodeficiency syndrome (AIDS) research. On December 23, 1971, President Nixon signed the National Cancer Act, which created the National Cancer Program, designed to provide more resources for the search for a cure and to protect the NCI from bureaucratic problems that might slow their search.

The National Cancer Act stipulated that the NCI budget go directly to the president for approval and the director of the NCI be appointed by the president as well. The 18–member National Cancer Advisory Board replaced the National Advisory Cancer Council. In addition, the President's Cancer Panel, composed of two scientists and one management specialist, was created to provide the president with progress reports on the NCI.

In 1973 the NCI expanded its operations nationwide. It designated eight medical institutions across the country as Comprehensive Cancer Centers to make quality cancer care available to as many people as possible. By 1996 the number of such centers increased to 27. Also in 1973, the Surveillance, Epidemiology, and End Results (SEER) program was developed to provide the most accurate cancer statistics about the U.S. population.

To pass along important cancer information to the general public, the Cancer Information Service (CIS) was established in 1976. Through a toll-free telephone number, Americans throughout the country are able to find answers to their questions about cancer. By 1996 the CIS was answering about 600,000 calls per year.

In 1982 the NCI created a new program to increase communication between researchers and practicing doctors. The Physician Data Query (PDQ) database was designed so that doctors could find the latest information on research findings at the NCI. Such information includes clinical trials, cancer screening, prevention, and treatment. Another program was created in 1983 to continue to foster this link between researchers and clinicians. The Community Clinical Oncology Program was created to involve more hospitals nationwide in clinical trials so that a wider range of patients could benefit from such treatments. It also allowed community physicians more opportunities to work with researchers on developing treatments.

In the mid-1980s the NCI became more concerned about meeting the needs of at-risk populations. For example, in 1985 the Cancer Prevention Awareness Program for Black Americans was developed, and two years later the National Black Leadership Initiative on Cancer was formed out of a partnership among business, religious, and government leaders. These programs sought to bring attention to the high incidence of cancer in the African American community.

In the 1990s the NCI worked with many other branches of the Department of Health and Human Services in the fight against smoking. In 1991 the NCI joined with the American Cancer Society to start the American Stop Smoking Intervention Study for Cancer Prevention (ASSIST) program. It also became involved in the major government campaign to prevent children from smoking.

CURRENT POLITICAL ISSUES

Since the National Cancer Act was signed into law in 1971, the NCI has made great strides in medical discoveries related to understanding cancer and ways to treat it. It has also been very successful in creating a nationwide network of cancer centers, training cancer experts, and developing community outreach and cancer prevention programs. Despite this progress, a cure for the disease still proves elusive. In 1997 media criticism of the government's efforts in fighting cancer reached a high point. Articles in the *Washington Post*, *USA Today*, and *Healthfacts* assessed the progress made in cancer research since 1971 and concluded that cancer was still a deadly and terrifying disease. In essence, they argued that the NCI was not winning the war on cancer. The authors criticized the NCI for focusing too much attention on treating cancer and not enough attention on prevention. The NCI faces a difficult challenge in admitting its limitations and yet convincing the American people that it still provides valuable services.

Case Study: Mammograms for Forty-Year-Olds

According to the NCI about 180,000 new cases of breast cancer were estimated for 1997. The best method known for early detection of breast cancer is a mammogram, an x-ray of the breast. The NCI has been a leader in the fight against breast cancer and a strong supporter of the benefits of mammography. It supported the 1992 Food and Drug Administration Mammography Quality Standards Act, which required mammography centers to be federally certified. It also established an "About Mammography" center on the NCI Web site to provide the public with easy access to information about breast cancer and mammography.

However, in 1997 the NCI stance toward the recommended age for mammograms changed slightly, and its new position came under attack by the public and the media. In February 1997 a 13–member National Institutes of Health panel heard 32 expert presentations on the usefulness of regular mammograms for women in their forties as a means of breast cancer prevention. The panel concluded that it was best not to recommend regular mammograms for these women. They based their decision on studies indicating that deaths from breast cancer are not lower for women who have mammograms in their forties than for women who do not. In addition, the panel argued that because the breast tissue in younger women is dense and mammograms cannot always see through it well, mammograms fail to detect as many as 25 percent of invasive cancers in women in their forties. Therefore, mammography is a more effective detection method for older, post-menopausal women, and it may give younger women a false sense of security.

Although there might have been medical support for the NIH decision, there were mixed reactions among the public. *Newsweek* magazine reported a great deal of public concern over the announcement, in a 1997 article by Todd Oppenheimer, "My Turn On-line: That Mammogram Decision." Even NCI Director Richard Klausner, who had convened the NIH panel, was surprised by the decision. The U.S. Senate decided to disregard the NIH panel and unanimously passed a nonbinding resolution supporting the use of mammograms for women in their forties.

In the end the NIH panel advised women in their forties to make up their own minds about regular mammogram screenings. Their decision served to inform women of the limitations of mammography so that these women could discuss these concerns with their doctors. In addition, the decision emphasized the importance of self-examinations, which detect about three-fourths of the tumors in the breasts of women in their forties.

FUTURE DIRECTIONS

The ultimate goal of the NCI is to find a cure for cancer. To that end, the institute will continue to devote resources to cancer research. The NCI has five main goals for the future. First, the institute is dedicated to developing new technologies, such as the Cancer Genome Anatomy Project, designed to identify the genetic changes that result in cancer for each individual. This information could lead to better methods of early detection, more accurate diagnoses, and better treatment. Second, the NCI is focusing resources on better treatments, such as developing new drugs that can treat cancer without causing damage to healthy cells. Third, the NCI aims to improve patients' access to the benefits of cancer research, especially those patients with managed-care health insurance. Fourth, the NCI plans to improve access to information about cancer through the Cancer Information Service and the Physician Data Query (PDQ) database. In a new initiative, the NCI is joining patient groups to make PDQ descriptions of cancer studies more easily understandable to nonresearchers. Last, the NCI seeks to forge new working relationships with various segments of society to address the problem of cancer. To this end, the NCI is forming a National Cancer Policy Board, on which representatives from diverse groups participate in the nation's policy debate regarding cancer.

AGENCY RESOURCES

The NCI Web site (http://www.nci.nih.gov) provides a wealth of information on the institute itself, the current state of cancer research, and various aspects of cancer. The information is well organized to suit the reader, whether it be the general public, patients of cancer, doctors, educators, or the media. Two special programs that are available through the Web site are the "About Mammography" program and the "Cancer Research" program. There is a special NCI Web site for children called Kids' Home at http://cancernet.nci.nih.gov/occdocs/KidsHome.html. Specific questions about cancer can be directed to the information specialists of the Cancer Information Service. Their toll free number is 1-800-4-CANCER, and they are available Monday through Friday, 9:00 A.M. to 4:30 P.M. EST. The NCI also supports two searchable databases. CancerNet offers cancer information for patients, health professionals, and researchers. It can be accessed at http://cancernet.nci.nih.gov. CancerLit is a branch of CancerNet that contains bibliographic information on numerous publications related to cancer, and is available at http://cancernet.nci.nih.gov/cancerlit.html.

AGENCY PUBLICATIONS

The official publication of the NCI is the *Journal of the National Cancer Institute,* which contains scientific reports on cancer research. For the general public, the NCI has publications on a wide variety of topics, including children, pain, prevention, types of cancers, treatment, help for those living with cancer, help for survivors of cancer, and Spanish-language publications. For instance, the *Action Guide for Healthy Eating* shows how changing diet can reduce the risk of cancer. Other important publications include: "What You Need to Know About Cancer," "When Someone in Your Family Has Cancer," "Cancer Rates and Risks." A complete list of all NCI publications can be found at their Web site at http://www.nci.nih.gov/NCI_PUB_INDEX/PUB_INDEX_DOC.html. Many of these publications are available on-line and all are available through the toll-free number of the Cancer Information Service 1-800-4-CANCER.

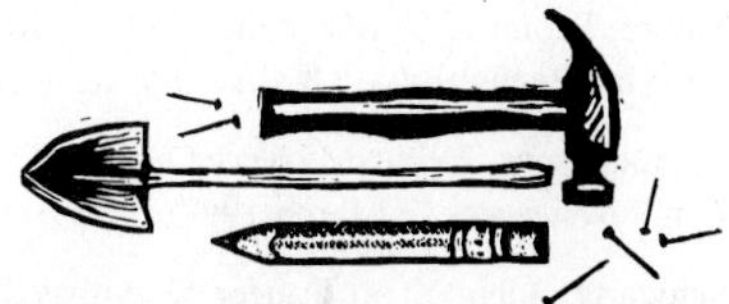

GET INVOLVED:

The NCI is a cosponsor, along with the Centers for Disease Control and Prevention, the President's Council on Physical Fitness and Sports, and the U.S. Women's National Soccer Team, of the Smoke-Free Kids and Soccer program. Television and radio advertisements encourage children to "Smoke defenders, not cigarettes." The program also has its own Web site at http://www.smokefree.gov. The Web site offers free posters and screensavers to children who can pass a quiz about the effects of smoking, and will pledge not to smoke themselves. For educators and coaches, the Web site offers many recommendations on how to teach children about the dangers of smoking. For example, have 6 or 7 children out of a group of 20 stand up, and explain how this is the percentage of young smokers who die prematurely from tobacco-related disorders each year. Athletics and exercise are presented as alternatives to smoking; activities that parents can encourage their children to pursue through example and encouragement.

BIBLIOGRAPHY

Cancer Rates and Risks, 4th Edition. Bethesda, MD.: National Cancer Institute, 1996.

"Cancer Research in Brief: Where It Stands, Where It Is Headed." Bethesda, MD.: National Cancer Institute, 1997.

Carper, Jean. "How to Help Prevent Cancer." *USA Weekend,* 7 December 1997, p. 12.

Cowley, Geoffrey, et al. "Can Marijuana Be Medicine?" *Newsweek,* 3 February 1997.

Dickson, Ben. "What If Weed Is Exactly What You Need?" *Esquire,* 1 October 1997, p. 134.

Kolata, Gina. "Fortysomething Mammograms: Still More Advice." *New York Times,* 30 March 1997, p. E2.

McCaffrey, Barry R. "We're on a Perilous Path." *Newsweek,* 3 February 1997.

Moore, Thomas J. "Look at the Mortality Rates; The 'War on Cancer' Has Been a Bust." *Washington Post*, 23 July 1997, p. A23.

Oppenheimer, Todd. "My Turn On-line: That Mammogram Decision." *Newsweek*, 3 March 1997.

Schwartz, John. "Top Cancer Scientists Join Crusade on Teen Smoking." *Washington Post*, 16 August 1995, p. A17.

Sternberg, Steve. "Breast Cancer Gamble: Not Every Cancer-Prone Woman Will Actually Get It." *USA Today*, 15 May 1997, p. 1A.

———. "$30 Billion 'War on Cancer' a Bust? Researchers Suggest Putting an Emphasis on Prevention." *USA Today*, 29 May 1997, p. 1A.

"Update on the War on Cancer: The Disease Is 'Undefeated.'" *Healthfacts*, 1 June 1997, p. 3.

Wallis, Claudia. "Medicine Cover Stories: A Puzzling Plague. What Is It About the American Way of Life that Causes Breast Cancer?" *Time*, 14 January 1991, p. 48.

National Center for Atmospheric Research (NCAR)

PARENT ORGANIZATION: Independent
ESTABLISHED: June 1960
EMPLOYEES: 900

Contact Information:

ADDRESS: 1850 Table Mesa Dr.
Boulder, CO 80307
PHONE: (303) 497-1000
FAX: (303) 497-1172
E-MAIL: munoz@ucar.edu
URL: http://www.ncar.ucar.edu
DIRECTOR: Dr. Robert J. Serafin
ASSOCIATE DIRECTOR: Walt Dabberdt

WHAT IS ITS MISSION?

The National Center for Atmospheric Research, or NCAR, is a nonprofit, privately managed scientific research institute that operates largely through U.S. government funding. According to its Web site, the "NCAR's mission is to plan, organize, and conduct atmospheric and related research programs in collaboration with universities, to provide state-of-the-art research tools and facilities to the entire atmospheric sciences community, to support and enhance university atmospheric research education, and to facilitate the transfer of technology to both the public and private sectors."

HOW IS IT STRUCTURED?

Because the oversight and funding of NCAR activities are the function of many separate agencies and private organizations, the center's organizational structure is complex. The NCAR itself is not a true agency; it merely comprises the facilities to carry out the mission of its parent organization, the University Corporation for Atmospheric Research (UCAR). UCAR is composed of over 60 North American universities, and is the NCAR's managing entity. Research priorities and new program development at the NCAR are decided through UCAR's Office of Programs (UOP).

UCAR's responsibility for managing the National Center for Atmospheric Research was originally assigned under contract with the National Science Foundation (NSF), an independent U.S. government agency that funded the establishment and maintenance of the center.

FAST FACTS

The list of international affiliates involved in UCAR has grown to more than 35 and includes the Hong Kong Royal Observatory; the Russian Academy of Sciences; the International Meteorological Institute in Stockholm, Sweden; and the University of Nairobi, Kenya.

(Source: University Corporation for Atmospheric Research, 1998.)

The NSF is still the NCAR's primary sponsor, but today only 60 percent of the NCAR's funding comes from this agency; additional financing comes from other government agencies and various private sources. Because the NCAR is privately managed by universities, but largely funded by the federal government, it considers itself a "quasi-government" organization.

Direct responsibility for the NCAR's divisions and programs belongs to the director of the National Center for Atmospheric Research. The director is appointed by and reports directly to UCAR—although the NSF, as the center's funding agency does have some input into the selection of a director. As the administrator with direct oversight of the NCAR's scientific programs, the director provides scientific and technical leadership; plans NCAR's programs with guidance from the NCAR senior scientists, UCAR management, and officers from the NSF; and also manages any activities necessary to implement NCAR's worldwide research programs. Day-to-day management of the center, including budgeting and planning, support for NCAR's computer information network, and support services for NCAR facilities are typically handled by departments under the direct control of the associate director.

The center is divided into scientific divisions that carry out the center's research according to discipline: atmospheric chemistry, climate and global dynamics (large-scale climatic changes), solar physics and solar-terrestrial (sun and earth) interactions, and mesoscale and microscale meteorology (the basic physical processes that govern weather).

The center also includes three technology divisions. The Atmospheric Technology Division (ATD) provides facilities such as research aircraft, advanced radars, weather stations, and sounding systems to researchers, together with observing facilities. Research and the development of products for the aviation industry is conducted under the Research Applications Program (RAP) of NCAR. The Scientific Computing Division (SCD) provides high-performance computers, data archives, and high-quality computing support services to researchers in atmospheric and related sciences.

The NCAR also conducts two other programs with broad educational goals. The interaction between human societies and the atmospheric sciences is the focus of the Environmental and Societal Impacts Group (ESIG), a group devoted to learning how communities can better understand and cope with severe weather events and climate shifts. The center also conducts the Advanced Study Program (ASP), which sponsors young scientists—graduate students or recent Ph.Ds—to conduct research at the NCAR.

Most of the NCAR's work is performed at the Mesa Laboratory and the Foothills Laboratory in Boulder, Colorado, although the center maintains other facilities such as remote observation stations.

PRIMARY FUNCTIONS

As a national center for the development of a scientific field, the NCAR invests much of its resources in basic research, or a fundamental understanding of the processes that drive the weather and climate. These processes are extremely complex, and to understand them NCAR scientists must look at everything from the center of the sun to the bottom of the oceans. The NCAR also seeks to develop practical uses for emerging technologies in computing, aeronautics, and advanced weather detection, among other applications. The plan for the center's research is composed by the Office of the Director, the leaders of each scientific division, and the center's supervisory agencies—NSF and UCAR. Each scientific division provides an accounting of its activities in an Annual Scientific Report which is made available to the NCAR's sponsors and the general public.

The center also serves a vital role with its various programs in education, training, and knowledge transfer. The center's original focus on teaching and training graduate students and Ph.Ds in scientific research has expanded, and it now reaches out to students at the secondary and elementary levels, as well as the general population. Through its educational programs, the NCAR promotes the importance of atmospheric sciences to the public and increases awareness of the center's activities.

PROGRAMS

Scientists and educators at NCAR conduct numerous research, technology, and teaching programs. Some, like the U.S. Global Change Research Program

(USGCRP), are high-priority projects that receive year-round attention from NCAR scientists and other government agencies, while other projects rotate in and out with visiting scientists. Many NCAR projects involve scientists and funds from other government agencies.

NCAR is only one of many organizations involved in the U.S. Global Change Research Program (USGCRP), a huge program involving research institutions in the United States and abroad. USGCRP research provides a foundation for improving predictions of seasonal-to-interannual climate fluctuations (which can bring excessively wet and dry periods) and long-term climate change. The USGCRP also sponsors research to understand exposures to changes in important environmental factors, including changes in climate, ultraviolet (UV) radiation at the earth's surface, and land cover.

The center also conducts a number of educational programs. One the most noteworthy is Project LEARN (Laboratory Experience in Atmospheric Research at NCAR), an NSF-funded program designed to benefit teachers of K-12 students. During summer workshops, teachers work with more than 60 NCAR scientists to increase their understanding of atmospheric sciences, to improve their teaching methods, and to develop curricular materials for teaching related to NCAR research.

BUDGET INFORMATION

In 1997 the NCAR spent about $98 million on its research and educational programs. Funding from its primary sponsor, the National Science Foundation, accounted for about 60 percent, or $63 million, of these 1997 expenditures. Because the NCAR is also involved in research that is pioneered by other government agencies, about 40 percent of its funding comes from these agencies, along with certain members of the private sector (usually members of the aeronautics, aerospace, or navigation industries). Agencies involved in and contributing to NCAR research include the National Aeronautics and Space Administration (NASA); the Department of Energy, the National Oceanic and Atmospheric Administration (NOAA), the Environmental Protection Agency (EPA), and the Federal Aviation Administration (FAA).

NSF funding is divided into three categories. The first is base funds, which provide the center with the greatest discretion and flexibility (the center may allocate funds as it deems necessary). About $41.2 million of NSF support was allocated to base funding. Funding for focused or named programs is restricted to spending on specific programs ($17.3 million in 1997) and special funds ($4.5 million), which provide support for the center's field activities and research grants for special programs.

HISTORY

Just after World War II (1939–45), the young science of meteorology—the study of weather and climate—began to grow and offer promising applications to the U.S. scientific and business communities. Meteorology as a science began to develop during the 1950s, and it continued to gain importance as the decade progressed. Because the field was so new, however, there was a shortage of scientists and a vague idea of what meteorological research should involve. The promise of meteorology, along with the need for more researchers and facilities, inspired the creation of a national center devoted entirely to the study of weather and climate.

In 1956, the president of the National Academy of Sciences appointed a committee on meteorology, to examine the status of meteorological research in America. The nine scientist members—six of whom were not meteorologists and were therefore considered unbiased—recommended to the academy in 1958 that basic research at American universities should be increased and that a National Institute for Atmospheric Research should be established.

The university community responded quickly. Within a month of the committee's report, the University Committee on Atmospheric Research had been established to study the issue, and soon the idea of a new research institute was endorsed by representatives from 14 American universities. These representatives made plans to establish a nonprofit corporation to sponsor support of meteorological research at the universities; to organize and maintain a National Institute for Atmospheric Research; and to support the education and training required to carry on an expanded program of atmospheric research. The committee envisioned an institute working in conjunction with U.S. universities, in which scientists could meet and exchange ideas and be given access to advanced tools—instruments and observing platforms, computers, scientific reference collections, and facilities for conferences and seminars.

Twelve of these 14 universities announced later that year their decision to band together and assume the responsibility for organizing and operating the new institute. In March 1959, the University Corporation for Atmospheric Research, or UCAR, was formally established as a nonprofit Colorado corporation.

While UCAR was planning its new institute, now renamed the National Center for Atmospheric Research, (NCAR), the corporation signed a contract with the National Science Foundation (NSF), an independent federal agency, stating that UCAR would organize and manage the center, while funding would come from NSF. The UCAR trustees named Dr. Walter Orr Roberts as the first director of NCAR, and in June 1960 both UCAR and NCAR were formally established in Boulder, Colorado. After interviewing six nationally known architects, the committee selected I. M. Pei, who worked closely with

Roberts on the design of the Mesa Laboratory to fashion the center's permanent home. The building is considered an architectural wonder and is one of the most acclaimed structures in the United States.

Since its establishment, UCAR and NCAR have both grown to include 63 universities. The original NCAR staff of five scientists has expanded to more than 120 Ph.D. researchers. In 1990, the center's growth and increased needs led NCAR to relocate half its staff to another nearby facility, the Foothills Laboratory.

CURRENT POLITICAL ISSUES

As a scientific institute focused on learning and disseminating knowledge, the NCAR is relatively isolated from federal politics; but as an agency primarily funded by the U.S. government, the center sometimes finds itself entangled in the politics involved in congressional appropriations of agency budgets.

Case Study: Climate Modeling Computers

In 1995, the NCAR asked 12 U.S. and two Japanese computer companies to submit bids for advanced computing systems that would perform climate modeling as part of the institute's Climate and Global Dynamics Division. Each of the proposed computers would run global circulation models for the institute, which needed machines capable of conducting between 20 and 80 billion mathematical operations per second. The winner would ultimately sell more than $35 million in computer equipment to the NCAR.

When NCAR computer experts selected their finalists in early 1996, proposals from all but one of the American companies had been rejected. The finalists were Cray Research, a Minnesota-based company, and the Japanese firms NEC and Fujitsu. Immediately upon learning of NCAR's selections, at least two members of Congress—David Obey, a Wisconsin representative, and Martin Sabo from Cray's home state of Minnesota—urged the NCAR to buy a U.S. computer to help maintain the U.S. computer industry.

The NCAR was not worried about the U.S. computer industry, however; it simply wanted the best research tool available for its global climate modeling project. In May 1996, the center chose NEC's proposed machine, the SX-4, as its next generation of climate modeling computer.

The idea of a federally funded organization spending $35 million on a foreign-manufactured machine produced a swift reaction from both Cray, the losing competitor, and congressional representatives. Cray complained that NEC, hoping to carve out a portion of U.S. supercomputer sales, was "dumping" its machine in the United States at far below its actual production cost—a practice which violates international trade laws. Cray promptly filed a complaint against NEC with the U.S. International Trade Commission. Meanwhile, members of the House of Representatives did their part in holding up the sale by tinkering with the appropriations bill for the National Science Foundation (NSF), the NCAR's primary funding agency. The new bill added language that effectively barred the NCAR from purchasing its equipment from NEC.

Before long, the Commerce Department was involved and conducted an investigation of the charges against NEC. Comparing the costs of the NEC and the Cray machine, the Commerce Department made a preliminary finding that NEC had in fact violated antidumping laws. NEC's American representatives claimed the finding was unfair, because the investigation had compared Cray's less advanced, costlier technology to NEC's cheaper and more sophisticated system. The Commerce Department proposed and undertook further investigation which resulted in the NCAR terminating negotiations for the SX-4 on August 28, 1998, nearly two years after it originally awarded its contract to NEC.

SUCCESSES AND FAILURES

Each year NCAR scientists announce several significant scientific breakthroughs, but some discoveries have a more direct impact on everyday life than others. The Research Applications Program (RAP), for example, exists largely for the advancement of aircraft technology and safety. One of RAP's successes has been the development of an in-flight icing algorithm that can predict where and when aircraft are likely to encounter the freezing drizzle that produces a dangerous layer of ice on an aircraft's wings. The probability of icing is calculated using a complex set of data—including cloud temperature, water droplet and ice crystal size, and relative humidity—gathered by sophisticated NCAR-developed radar. The algorithm was recently transferred to the National Weather Service's Aviation Weather Center, where it is used in daily operations to direct aircraft safely around icing hazard areas.

One well-known technological initiative is NCAR's development of the Electric Doppler Radar (ELDORA), a project which involved two of France's top research institutions. One of the most advanced Doppler radar systems for meteorological studies, ELDORA is capable of scanning rapidly to produce three-dimensional depictions of precipitation systems. ELDORA allows observations of clouds and storms over remote regions of the globe, particularly over the oceans.

FUTURE DIRECTIONS

In 1991, UCAR developed its strategic plan for the last decade of the 1900s, UCAR 2001. The document outlines a number of specific goals for the NCAR in each area of its research and tries to anticipate changes in the sources of NCAR funding and the growth of information technology. Although the NCAR has gradually come to rely on diverse funding sources, the growing importance of atmospheric science will require the center to broaden further its base of financial support, and in the future NCAR funding will come increasingly from the private sector. The NCAR also plans to develop more sophisticated and extensive on-line information systems for the dissemination of data and information to the scientific community and the general public.

AGENCY RESOURCES

Further information about the NCAR can be obtained from the center's Office of Education, which can be reached by telephone at (303) 497-1174. The general information area of UCAR's Web site at http://www.ucar.edu/cc_new.html also contains links to other information resources, including scientific libraries and specific NCAR programs. For more information about UCAR, contact UCAR Communications, PO Box 3000, Boulder, CO 80307; phone (303) 497-8600.

AGENCY PUBLICATIONS

NCAR's scientists publish hundreds of research findings each year, but most publications of general interest are released by UCAR. They include annual reports and planning documents such as "UCAR 2001," the *UCAR Quarterly* newsletter, and scientific and technical publications such as *NCAR Annual Scientific Report*. Many of these publications can be viewed online from UCAR's general information page. For further information about NCAR publications, contact the Office of Education.

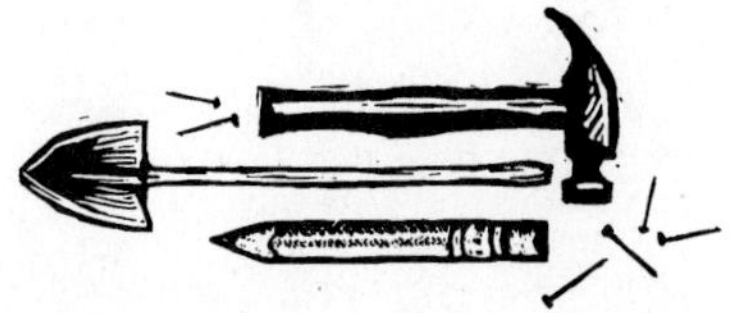

GET INVOLVED:

The Mesa Laboratory at Boulder, Colorado, is visited by thousands each year. Individuals and families are invited to take self-guided tours that include hands-on displays of weather-related phenomena such as a model tornado or an electrical storm. To arrange for a guided tour please call ahead at (303) 497-1000. Tours can be tailored for small and large groups of students ranging from preschoolers through college age and for adult groups. The Mesa Laboratory is open weekdays to the public from 8:00 A.M. to 5:00 P.M. It is also open from 9 A.M. to 3 P.M. on weekends and on holidays.

BIBLIOGRAPHY

Cohn, Stephen A., John Hallet, and Darko Koracin. "Blending Education and Research in Atmospheric Science—A Case Study." *Physics Today*, May 1997, pp. 34–39.

Fields, Scott. "Weather Radar Starts to Shape Up." *Earth*, 1 April 1997, pp. 16–7.

Henson, Bob. "What Next For SCD?" *UCAR Newsbrief*, September 1997.

Holden, Constance. "Trade Skirmish Hobbles Modelers." *Science*, 30 August 1996, p. 1177.

Kerr, Richard A. "Greenhouse Forecasting Still Cloudy." *Science*, 16 May 1997, pp. 1040–2.

———. "NCAR: Doing Quality Science in 'Garage for Planes.'" *Science*, 28 May 1993, pp. 1236–7.

Wheeler, Paul. "Spying on the Stratosphere." *Geographical Magazine*, December 1994, p. 8.

National Council on Disability (NCD)

PARENT ORGANIZATION: Independent
ESTABLISHED: 1978
EMPLOYEES: 8 full-time employees; 15 board members

Contact Information:

ADDRESS: 1331 F St. NW, Ste. 1050
Washington, DC 20004
PHONE: (202) 272-2004
TDD (HEARING IMPAIRED): (202) 272-2074
FAX: (202) 272-2022
URL: http://www.ncd.gov
CHAIRPERSON: Marca Bristo

WHAT IS ITS MISSION?

According to the agency, the mission of the National Council on Disability (NCD) is "to promote policies, programs, practices, and procedures that guarantee equal opportunity for all individuals with disabilities, regardless of the nature of or the severity of the disability; and to empower individuals with disabilities to achieve economic self-sufficiency, independent living, and inclusion and integration into all aspects of society."

HOW IS IT STRUCTURED?

The NCD is composed of a chairperson and 15 board members who are appointed by the president and approved by the Senate. Board members are directly involved in organizations concerned with the disabled, such as Access Living in Metropolitan Chicago, Illinois, Very Special Arts, and the Steelcase Foundation. Eight full-time employees administer the projects that are initiated by the NCD board. They conduct studies, issue reports, and organize surveys. The NCD meets in Washington, D.C., and other parts of the country as needed, where they hold public hearings concerning the equitable treatment of the disabled.

PRIMARY FUNCTIONS

The NCD is the official contact point within the U.S. government for disability issues. Its primary function is to provide guidance to the federal government on issues

*Carol Smith, (*left*), with the help of her mother Jean, uses a computer to testify before the Senate Labor Committee hearing on disability technology.* (AP/Wide World Photos)

affecting the 54 million Americans with disabilities. Of particular concern to the NCD is the proper implementation and enforcement of the Americans with Disabilities Act of 1990 (ADA). This act outlaws discrimination against disabled individuals and defines the federal government's role in preventing such discrimination. The NCD advises the Department of Justice (DOJ) and the U.S. Equal Employment Opportunity Commission (EEOC) on how to best enforce the ADA. Other major goals of the NCD include: developing a coherent national disability policy; enhancing communication with the disabled; ensuring that programs and services are available to minorities with disabilities; identifying issues or policy that may affect the disabled; and identifying emerging technologies that can aid the disabled, such as closed-captioned television.

The NCD issues position papers on disability issues to the executive and legislative branches of government. Other departments that work closely with the NCD and enforce applicable laws include the Administration on Development Disabilities, the National Institute on Disability and Rehabilitation Research, the Office of Special Education Programs, the Office of Special Education and Rehabilitation Services, the President's Committee on the Employment of People with Disabilities, and the President's Committee on Mental Retardation. These agencies depend on NCD reports and studies to guide their organizational goals. Such papers as the "Disability Perspectives and Recommendations on Proposals to Reform the Medicaid and Medicare Programs" (1995) propose changes and suggest methods to achieve adequate service for the disabled.

PROGRAMS

The NCD Web page links directly to a service developed by and available through the Center for Applied Special Technology (CAST). Playing on the term "bobby," a nickname for English police officers, CAST's Bobby Service polices the Internet and for no charge analyzes the accessibility of individual Web pages. Pages that are formatted and contain coding compatible with various devices the disabled use to browse the Web receive a Bobby-approved rating and may display a "Bobby Approved" icon—an English-style police officer with a handicap symbol displayed on his round-topped hat.

As Web master and site designer Gregory Rosmiata said in the July 3, 1997, issue of *Wired* magazine, "the problem with the Web is that it's point and shoot, but if you're blind, you can't see the target." Various devices allow the blind to see the target in a different way, but only if the site is designed to be compatible with these devices. Web site developers are encouraged to run Bobby on their own pages to see them as they would seem to a blind person. A new version of Bobby will provide programming suggestions so developers can make pages more accessible.

FAST FACTS

Businesses are beginning to recognize the fact that persons with disabilities make up a vast consumer market. There are approximately 54 million individuals with $800 billion in spending power. It is projected that the targeted market will have over $1 trillion in disposable income by 2001.

(Source: *American Demographics,* February 1, 1998.)

Youth Leadership Conference

The NCD Youth Leadership Development Conference, held each summer, provides a forum for youth with disabilities to learn about assistive technologies, work opportunities, employment-related programs, their legal rights, and how to advocate for their rights. Participants hear from keynote speakers, tour government buildings in Washington, D.C., and talk directly with participating congressmen and government officials. The underlying purpose of the conference is to help disabled youth become pro-active leaders in their communities.

BUDGET INFORMATION

In 1998 $1.8 million was appropriated by Congress to fund the NCD. The majority of this money was directed toward staff salaries.

HISTORY

In 1978 Congress established the NCD as an advisory board within the Department of Education to address educational issues affecting the disabled. The Rehabilitation Act Amendments of 1984 transformed the NCD into an independent federal agency, charged to address, analyze, and make recommendations on issues of public policy that affect the disabled regardless of individual circumstances, such as age, disability type, perceived employment potential, economic need, specific functional ability, or status as a veteran.

In 1986 the NCD proposed that Congress enact a civil rights law specifically designed to protect the rights of the disabled. The goal of such legislation was to ensure an informed and coordinated approach to the concerns of individuals with disabilities and the elimination of barriers to disabled individuals active in work, community, and family life. After several years of debate President George Bush signed the Americans With Disabilities Act into law in 1990. The NCD's mandate became to ensure that the provisions of the ADA were followed.

The ADA forbids discrimination against the disabled in hiring, wages, or benefits. The act requires that public services, including public transportation and government services, be made readily accessible to the disabled. Newly constructed buildings are required to be fully accessible to the disabled, and older buildings were required to remove barriers to access if possible. Provisions of the ADA deemed crimes against the disabled "hate crimes," which carry the same penalties and attention by the law as those that are racially motivated. After a time the NCD polled and studied the impact of the ADA on the workplace. They found that 90 percent of those surveyed supported the antidiscrimination provisions of the ADA and were making the appropriate adjustments.

In 1996, after conducting a National Summit on Disability Policy and presenting the president and Congress with its results, the NCD lobbied to form a presidential committee comprised of people with disabilities to work cohesively on issues affecting the disabled. The NCD recommended that a study be conducted to find ways to increase employment opportunities for adults with disabilities. In March, 1998, President Bill Clinton created a task force composed of the chairperson of the NCD, the secretaries of labor, health and human services, Treasury, and commerce, and others who are involved with employment and civil rights.

CURRENT POLITICAL ISSUES

While the ADA was widely hailed as an important victory for civil rights in the United States, many people continue to disregard its mandates. Like other civil rights acts, such as the Civil Rights Act of 1964, the ADA is still often met with hostility. The discrimination that prompted the passage of the ADA still remains, and resentment over the new laws and protections for the disabled has led to some negative reactions.

Case Study: Hate Crimes and the Disabled

"We shouldn't be surprised by the backlash," said Marcia Bristo, chairperson of the NCD, to *The Progressive*. "It happens in our society whenever a constituency fights for its civil rights. The ADA gave us our rights; we can't be turned away from jobs or public accommodations because of our disability. So now we're feeling the effects of this not-unexpected backlash."

There have been many documented cases of hostility against persons with disabilities both in public and private sectors. One incident surrounded Jean Parker,

Director of the Colorado Cross-Disability Coalition. While Parker was waiting for a bus, her seeing eye dog was kicked. Because she was blind, Parker could not identify the dog's attacker and no one else at the bus stop was willing to make a statement to the police because they feared retribution from the criminal. In another case, a couple, both wheelchair users, bought a house in a Chicago suburb. A wheelchair ramp needed to be installed to make their home accessible. The neighbors were against the construction of the ramp, because they said that it would ruin the aesthetics of their community. Rocks were thrown at the couple's home and threatening letters were mailed to them. The couple eventually moved away from the area.

In response to NCD studies and reports on cases of abuse and harassment against disabled persons, the Hate Crimes Statistics Act was amended to include bias based on disability. It stipulates that the FBI will collect data about hate crimes against the disabled as it does for crimes based on race, ethnicity, sexual orientation, and religion. These new statistics will enable disability groups to understand and identify hate crimes and will enable police and local communities to become more aware and sensitive to the needs and rights of the disabled. Through the efforts of the NCD the disabled have new opportunities to work, succeed, live independently, exercise new rights, and defend themselves when those rights are infringed upon.

FUTURE DIRECTIONS

The road ahead for the NCD is one of ongoing implementation and monitoring of the ADA and its related legislation. Recently the NCD tackled the issue of assisted suicide in a position paper, which was presented to the president and Congress. Other positions will be studied as the need arises. The NCD is determined to ensure that individuals with disabilities have an equal opportunity to participate fully in American society.

AGENCY RESOURCES

Information about the NCD can be obtained on-line at http://www.ncd.gov or by writing the Public Affairs Office, 1331 F St. NW, Ste. 1050, Washington, DC 20004. The NCD Web site contains a calendar of upcoming events, an archive of NCD Bulletins, a publications list, and information about the NCD staff.

AGENCY PUBLICATIONS

The NCD publishes a monthly bulletin, available on-line, that focuses on legislative issues pertinent to the disabled. It also publishes the quarterly newsletter *FOCUS*, an annual report and reports and studies, such as "ADA Watch-Year One: A Report to the President and the Congress on Progress in Implementing the Americans with Disabilities Act," "Access to Multimedia Technology by People with Sensory Disabilities," and "Achieving Independence: The Challenge for the Twenty—first Century." "A Decade of Progress in Disability Policy," "Education of Students with Disabilities: Where Do We Stand?" and "Assisted Suicide: A Disability Perspective Position Paper," are available on-line at http://www.ncd.gov; by calling the NCD Public Affairs Office at (202) 272-2004; or by writing the National Council on Disability, 1331 F St. NW, Ste. 1050, Washington, DC 20004.

BIBLIOGRAPHY

Alston, Reginald J., Tyronn Bell, and Paul Leung. "Reform Laws and Health Care Coverage: Combating Exclusion of Persons with Disabilities." *Journal of Rehabilitation,* 18 July 1997, pp. 15(5).

Gleick, Elizabeth. "Society: Mental Adjustment How Far Should Employers Go to Help Someone with a Psychiatric Illness Stay on the Job?" *Time,* 19 May 1997, p. 62.

Hansen, Louis S. "Quest for a Typical Education Change Wanted in Disability Education." *Newsday,* 17 November 1994, p. B7.

Houck, Cherry K., and Catherine J. Rogers. "The Special/General Education Integration Initiative for Students with Specific Learning." *Journal of Learning Disabilities,* 1 September 1994, p. 435.

Pelka, Fred. "Bashing the Disabled: The Right-Wing Attack on the ADA." *Humanist,* 21 November 1996, pp. 26(5).

Raasch, Chuck. "Dole Portrait: What Would he Bring to the Presidency?" *Gannett News Service,* 22 March 1996.

Reynolds, Larry. "ADA is Still Confusing After All These Years." *HR Focus,* 11 January 1994, pp. 1(2).

"Text of Executive Order on Increasing Employment of Adults with Disabilities." *U.S. Newswire,* 13 March 1998.

Traver, Nancy. "Nation: Opening Doors for the Disabled But the Handicapped-Rights Law May Harm Those it Aims to Help." *Time,* 4 June 1990, p. 54.

Wolfe, Kathi. "Bashing the Disabled: The New Hate Crime." *The Progressive,* 1 November 1995, pp. 24(4).

National Credit Union Administration (NCUA)

PARENT ORGANIZATION: Independent
ESTABLISHED: 1970
EMPLOYEES: 950

Contact Information:

ADDRESS: 1775 Duke St.
Alexandria, VA 22314-3428
PHONE: (703) 518-6300
TOLL FREE: (800) 755-1030
FAX: (703) 518-6319
E-MAIL: csdesk@ncua.gov
URL: http://www.ncua.gov
CHAIRMAN: Norman E. D'Amours
EXECUTIVE DIRECTOR: Karl Hoyle

WHAT IS ITS MISSION?

According to the agency, the mission of the National Credit Union Administration (NCUA) is "to monitor and promote safe and sound Credit Unions; responsibly administer the share insurance fund; and encourage service to the American consumers, particularly to people of small means; while providing a flexible regulatory environment and carefully managing the agency's resources."

HOW IS IT STRUCTURED?

The NCUA is an independent agency that was founded in 1970. At the head of the NCUA are three board members and a chairperson, all of whom are appointed by the president and approved by the Senate. This nucleus provides agency oversight. No more than two board members may be from the same political party, and each member, including the chairman, serves a staggered six-year term. The NCUA board regularly meets in open session each month, except August, at the administration's headquarters in Alexandria, Virginia.

Under the auspices of the NCUA board, the administration is divided into four offices: the Office of Inspector General, the Office of Community Development Credit Unions, the Board Staff, and the Office of the Executive Director.

The Executive Director's Office is responsible for the administration's daily operations, and the director reports directly to the NCUA chairman. All central and regional offices also report to this office. Regional offices, where the credit union examiners are based, are located in Albany, New York; Alexandria, Virginia; Atlanta, Georgia; Lisle, Illinois; Austin, Texas; and Concord, California. The regional office in Austin is also home to the NCUA's Asset Liquidation Management Center. The central offices under the Office of the Executive Director are: Equal Opportunity Programs, Public and Congressional Affairs, General Counsel, Examination and Insurance, Administration, Publications, Human Resources, Chief Financial Officer, Investment Services, Corporate Credit Unions, Technology and Information Services, and Training and Development.

PRIMARY FUNCTIONS

A credit union is a nonprofit, cooperative financial institution that is owned and run by its members, who pool their funds to make loans to each other. The NCUA charters and regulates such credit unions, in accordance with the Federal Credit Union Act, and oversees their fiscal health, safety, and soundness through its regional offices. Additionally, just as the Federal Deposit Insurance Corporation (FDIC) backs money deposited in banks, the NCUA insures accounts in approximately 7,200 federal credit unions and 4,200 state-chartered credit unions. The NCUA board manages the National Credit Union Share Insurance Fund (NCUSIF)—the fund that serves to insure approximately $275 billion in member share deposits. The NCUSIF is funded solely by credit union contributions.

In the interest of credit unions, the NCUA works with many interested parties including credit unions, their members, Congress, trade organizations, state credit union leagues, state supervisory authorities, and interagency departmental staff. The NCUA advises Congress and the courts on issues that affect credit unions, such as changes to the Federal Credit Union Act. The Administration also acts as a liaison, keeping credit unions apprised of new or altered government policy that affects them.

PROGRAMS

The programs of the NCUA have the common goal of ensuring that funds in credit unions are secure. For example, the Federal Credit Union Program promotes financially-sound management of federal credit unions; the Liquidity Management Program assists member credit unions in need of funding; the Community Development Program promotes credit unions to the public in order to build and strengthen them; and the Consumer Compliance and Resource Management Programs ensure that staff are trained and ready to focus on NCUA programs.

FAST FACTS

Credit union membership grew from 24.5 million members in 1980 to 43.5 million members in 1997.

(Source: *Atlanta Journal and Constitution.* March 1, 1998.)

Asset Liquidation Management Center

When a credit union fails, the NCUA steps in and takes over its assets including property, money, and computers. The Asset Liquidation Management Center began in 1988 as an assets management service and added liquidation activities in 1990. (Liquidation is the process of selling assets, generally with the intent of using it to clear debt.) The purpose of the Asset Liquidation Management Center then, is to recover costs from involuntary and voluntary liquidation, assumptions, and asset purchases. To do this the Asset Liquidation Management Center conducts bulk sales of assets and properties. Ultimately, it attempts to recover the costs of these assets to the benefit of the shareholders of the failed credit union.

Since 1991 the Asset Liquidation Management Center has handled more than $200 million in assets. Its size and operations expand and contract based on the number of liquidations that are occurring at a given time. At its peak in 1993 the center managed 1,243 assets and properties.

Office of Community Development Credit Unions

The Office of Community Development Credit Unions addresses the special needs and problems of smaller or weaker credit unions so that, in turn, they may deliver financial services to low-income individuals and communities. Such "low-income" credit unions may take advantage of special provisions that are not available to all federal credit unions, like accepting non-member deposits and participating in the Community Development Revolving Loan Program.

The Revolving Loan Program offers low-interest loans and deposits to assist low-income credit unions deliver financial services and improve their long-term growth and stability. These credit unions in need of assistance may apply for a grant to improve the operations or soundness of the credit union, provide training, or, in some cases, help pay salaries so that the credit union may remain open.

The Office of Community Development Credit Unions also offers an internship in which college juniors and seniors work for a low-income credit union. The purpose of the internship program is to build a workforce that is not only qualified to work in the various areas of credit union operation, but that is also familiar with the special needs of low-income credit unions.

BUDGET INFORMATION

The NCUA is entirely funded by fees paid by the credit unions it insures and regulates. The NCUA receives no taxpayer dollars. In 1998, the NCUA operated with a budget of $109.3 million. The majority of these funds were spent on the examination and supervision of credit unions, while the rest was spent on administration and staff salaries.

HISTORY

At the beginning of the 20th century, American workers imported a new idea from Europe that enabled them to bypass a banking industry that, to a large degree, charged high fees and most importantly, refused to loan working class people money. The new concept of the credit union provided lower income peoples with a place to safely keep money that could, in turn, be lent to other members for a modest fee.

By 1908 New Hampshire had its first legally chartered credit union and within a year, Massachusetts established state regulations and charter requirements. These credit unions became so popular that in 1934 President Franklin Roosevelt signed the Federal Credit Union Act.

The prosperity brought on by the post-World War II era had Americans desiring consumer goods like never before, a desire that brought with it an increased need for credit to buy with. As the traditional banking system maintained strict credit requirements, working class people continued to turn to credit unions. By 1960 six million members were doing their banking through more than 10,000 federal credit unions.

The regulatory responsibility for credit unions was shared among the different agencies responsible for other financial operations until 1970, when Congress decided to create a unique agency to oversee credit unions, the NCUA. This new agency was responsible for the administration of the National Credit Union Insurance Fund (NCUIF) and the regulation of the credit unions.

Congress allowed credit unions to expand their services during the 1970s, permitting them to issue share certificates and participate in mortgage lending. The NCUA was restructured to report to a three-member board rather than an administrator, and the continued growth of credit unions seemed assured. By the end of the 1980s, however, the economy went into a recession with high unemployment. As the economy declined into a near depression many credit unions failed, which nearly bankrupted the insurance fund. The NCUA, on behalf of its member credit unions, requested that Congress make the fund sound.

Within a year the request was granted and credit unions began a new period of growth. The NCUA expanded its services to checking and mortgages. By 1995 more than 57 million members were doing their banking through credit unions, and along with the industry, the role of the NCUA expanded beyond its traditional regulatory duties. The NCUA started charging fees, or premiums, to insure their clients' accounts, and the NCUA also examined the credit unions for financial viability. Additionally, the agency began to take over assets of failed credit unions. Along the way, the NCUA became an advocate for credit unions. As the power and advantages available through credit unions have grown, the NCUA has found itself in legal battles with the banking industry, which seeks to curtail the membership and scope of what credit unions can offer.

CURRENT POLITICAL ISSUES

At the heart of many NCUA issues is the growing competition between credit unions and traditional banking institutions. Banks tend to see credit unions as a threat to their existence, because they attract traditional bank customers with lower interest loans and more affordable services. While the Federal Credit Union Act of 1934 gives credit unions some clear advantages, such as tax-exempt status, which allows them to offer more competitively-priced services, other portions of the act had been misinterpreted and inappropriately used to credit unions' advantage, according to the First National Bank and Trust Company, the American Bankers Association (ABA)—and the U.S. Supreme Court.

Case Study: Interpreting the Federal Credit Union Act

The Federal Credit Union Act, passed in 1934, brought credit unions under federal regulation. Its declaration that "federal credit union membership shall be limited to groups having a common bond" had been interpreted to mean that members of a credit union must share the same single common bond, for example an employer. However, the NCUA changed that interpretation in 1982 in response to a wave of failed credit unions.

According to NCUA chairman Norman E. D'Amours, it became apparent during the recession in the early 1980s that it was necessary to diversify credit unions' membership. As companies grappled with the failing economy, they were forced to downsize. There were many closures and large numbers of employees were laid off or fired. Because credit unions did not have a diverse membership base, when an affiliated company let employees go and the out-of-work employees could not repay their loans on time, the credit union would almost immediately experience financial difficulties.

As a result of the large number of failures, the NCUA shifted its interpretation of the "common bond" clause and adopted a "multiple field of membership" policy which allowed credit unions to service several groups, each having its own common bond. This change enabled the NCUA to merge and transfer assets of failed or failing credit unions into larger, stronger, more viable credit unions. In 1981, before the new interpretation was implemented, 222 federal credit unions had failed. After the shift, in 1982, 112 of them failed, and only 40 failed in 1983. The revised policy also fulfilled part of the mission of the NCUA because it allowed employees of small businesses—too small to sponsor federal credit unions on their own—to join with other small groups and achieve the critical mass needed to establish a viable credit union. With newfound strength credit unions took off, expanding "far beyond their traditional base among employees of a single company or members of a single occupation," wrote Linda Greenhouse in the *New York Times* (October 7, 1997).

This put the credit unions into a more directly competitive position with banks and led to a legal dispute over the change in policy. North Carolina's First National Bank and Trust Company (FNBT) and several supporting banks, took the NCUA to court over the policy in 1990. The NCUA had approved the applications filed by the AT & T Family Federal Credit Union (ATTF) to extend its membership base to include otherwise unaffiliated employees of various small businesses in North Carolina and Virginia. Before this the ATTF had already used the multiple field of membership policy to grow its membership to 112,000 from more than 150 disparate occupations in all 50 states. At the base of the FNBT's argument was the premise that, by allowing ATTF to accept members from among the employees of any number of employers, membership is virtually open to anyone with a job.

The U.S. District Court for the District of Columbia dismissed the case for "lack of standing," which means that the plaintiffs, those that filed the lawsuit, were not seen as suitable challengers to a statute that did not directly address them. However, the U.S. Court of Appeals for the District of Columbia Circuit voided this decision and sent the case back to the district court, which heard the case and ruled in favor of the NCUA. FNBT appealed the decision.

The appeals court ruled in favor of the FNBT, and in doing so made two main points. First, the court decided, the Federal Credit Union Act was not ambiguous in language or intent—Congress expressly stated that all members of a federal credit union are to share the same single common bond. Further, the court's written opinion says, FNBT "makes a more persuasive argument based upon the purpose of the common bond requirement. The Congress intended that each FCU [federal credit union] be a cohesive association in which the members are known by the officers and by each other in order to 'ensure both that those making lending decisions would know more about applicants and that borrowers would be more reluctant to default. That is surely why it was thought that credit unions, unlike banks, could loan on character.' There can be little doubt that growth on the scale achieved by ATTF is inconsistent with that purpose."

The NCUA appealed its case to the U.S. Supreme Court, but lost on the same basic grounds. "Because we conclude that Congress has made it clear that the same common bond of occupation must unite each member of an occupationally defined federal credit union, we hold that the NCUA's contrary interpretation is impermissible," wrote Supreme Court Justice Clarence Thomas for the Court.

Throughout these years of legal proceedings the NCUA played an important role for credit unions. In addition to representing them, the agency was constantly updating the credit unions on the status of its case. More importantly, the credit unions constantly looked to the NCUA for guidance regarding permissible and prohibited actions. For example, as part of the lower court's decisions against the NCUA, federal credit unions were ordered to stop admitting new membership groups that do not have the same common bond as the union's original, or core, group. However, some provisions and exceptions were made so that existing unions would not collapse. For example, unions that had already added groups, those in the process of doing so, and designated low-income credit unions were in very different situations and looked to the NCUA for answers.

Additionally, since court decisions in the case could potentially be narrow enough as to affect only the parties involved in the case—the ATTF and its members—a second, more threatening suit was filed against the NCUA by the American Bankers Association (ABA). This suit was based on the same argument but was more broadly aimed at all federal credit unions. If the ABA succeeded in its suit, all credit unions could have been forced to evict members that were not part of the core membership.

Having anticipated defeat at the Supreme Court level, the NCUA pursued another avenue and asked Congress to change the wording of the National Credit Union Act. NCUA Chairman D'Amours testified before the House Subcommittee on Financial Institutions and Consumer Credit of the Committee on Banking and Financial Services that credit unions were in sound financial health but that health would be threatened if federally chartered credit unions were forced to abandon the strategy of diversification that was adopted in 1982 to strengthen their operations. Among others, the NCUA had the powerful support of House Speaker Newt Gingrich, Senator Alfonse D'Amato (chairman of the Senate Banking Committee), and 100 sponsors, according to the *New York Times* (March 8, 1998).

Congress voted overwhelmingly in favor of allowing credit unions to diversify their membership bases. The strong banking lobby, nevertheless challenged the wording of the Federal Credit Union Act and the proposed single-page piece of legislation, H.R. 1151, became a 30-page document before it was finally passed by both houses of Congress. While the final document was somewhat of a compromise between the federal credit unions and the banking industry, overall the bill was favorable to credit unions.

The Credit Union Membership Access Act, H.R.1151, was signed into law by President Clinton on August 7, 1998. The four titles to the act address the following areas: credit union membership, regulation of credit unions, capitalization and net worth of credit unions, and miscellaneous provisions.

Public Impact

Once the Credit Union Membership Access Act passed, the Credit Union National Association (CUNA) published a "statement stuffer" titled "What You Won In Congress." The document was made available for credit unions to purchase, so it could be included in their members' statements. The stuffer claimed: "63 million working Americans will no longer be denied access to affordable financial services through credit unions. Employees of companies too small to start their own credit unions now have the opportunity to join. Credit unions will continue to offer affordable financial services and can grow to support their operations," and "even bank customers benefit, because credit union competition will keep interest on savings higher and bank fees and loan rates lower."

FUTURE DIRECTIONS

The Credit Union Membership Access Act (H.R.1151) included provisions that alter the way federal credit unions must operate. Thus the NCUA will focus on helping its credit unions implement and adapt to the mandated changes. Additionally, as the NCUA informed its credit unions, certain provisions are not self-implementing, therefore the NCUA must issue implementing rules. The agency will also be working closely with its credit unions in developing those rules.

All of the changes mandated by the act were put on a schedule, allowing for new policies and rules to be implemented gradually, in order to minimize confusion and problems. The first schedule extends into 2001. This means the NCUA will keep its clients apprised of deadlines by which changes must be made to meet the schedule, as well as, coach its credit unions through those changes. The agency will also need to monitor and analyze the effects of each change, as its ultimate mission is the promotion of sound credit unions. If mandated changes appear to be having a negative or destabilizing effect on federal credit unions, the NCUA may need to step in on behalf of its credit unions to persuade Congress to alter the changes or the schedule.

AGENCY RESOURCES

Information about the scope and policies governing credit unions can be obtained by writing the NCUA at 1775 Duke Street, Alexandria, VA 22314-3428 or contacting the regional office in your area.

AGENCY PUBLICATIONS

The NCUA publishes handbooks, monthly newsletters, guidelines, policies, reports and other materials for the member credit unions. Some of the titles that are produced include "Federal Credit Union Bylaws," "Federal Credit Union Standard Bylaw Amendments and Guidelines," "Federal Credit Union Act," and "The Federal Credit Union Handbook." These can be ordered by using the order form found on-line at http://www.ncua.gov/ref/Pub_avail/pub_avail.html or by calling the NCUA at (703) 518-6304 and requesting a price list. Other publications can be found on-line at http://www.ncua.gov/indexref.html.

BIBLIOGRAPHY

"Bankers File New Suit Against N.C.U.A. in Credit Union Fight." *Business Newswire*, 6 October 1997.

"Banking Industry Wins Court Battle vs Credit Unions." *Reuters Business Reports*, 28 October 1996.

"Banks Win, Consumers Lose." *Business Wire* , 26 March 1998.

Chambers, Rob. "Credit Union Issue Still Open: High Court Ruling Could Lead to Expulsion of Some Members." *Atlanta Journal and Constitution*, 1 March 1998, p. D04.

Childears, Don A. "Banks Want Credit Unions To Play Fair." *Rocky Mountain News*, 27 March 1998, p. 49A.

Dugas, Christine. "Crunching Credit Unions Banks Battle Back Against a Growing Rival." *USA Today*, 19 December 1996.

Kaushik, Surendra K., Raymond H. Lopez, "Profitability of Credit Unions, Commercial Banks and Savings Banks: A Comparative Analysis." *American Economist*, 22 March 1996, p. 66(13).

Morehouse, Macon. "Credit Union Battle Shifts to Capitol Hill." *Atlanta Journal and Constitution*, 26 February 1998, p. G01.

Shuler, Deardra. "Credit Unions vs Banks: In A Battle Of Survival." *New York Beacon*, 4 December 1996, p. PG.

National Economic Council (NEC)

WHAT IS ITS MISSION?

The mission of the National Economic Council (NEC) is to give economic issues coordinated and focused attention by the president of the United States. The NEC's purpose is to eliminate bureaucratic rivalries, miscommunications, and overlapping goals among various agencies in the government regarding the nation's economy. This focused voice from the presidency is expected to promote U.S. international interests. The NEC aims to achieve this focus by providing a group of advisers to the president that will decide upon and present a cohesive set of goals.

HOW IS IT STRUCTURED?

The National Economic Council is part of the Office of Policy Development (along with the Domestic Policy Council) and falls under the Executive Office of the President of the United States. It is made up of the heads of various departments and agencies of the U.S. government including the president and vice president of the United States, secretary of state, secretary of the Treasury, secretary of agriculture, secretary of commerce, secretary of labor, secretary of housing and urban development, secretary of transportation, secretary of energy, the administrator of the Environmental Protection Agency, the chair of the Council of Economic Advisers, the director of the Office of Management and Budget; the Office of the United States Trade Representative, the assistant to the president for economic policy, the assistant to the president for domestic policy, the national security adviser, and the assistant to the president for science and

PARENT ORGANIZATION: Executive Office of the President
ESTABLISHED: January 25, 1993
EMPLOYEES: The exact number varies. Normally, the NEC has approximately 24 members.

Contact Information:

ADDRESS: Room 235, Old Executive Office Bldg.
Washington, DC 20502
PHONE: (202) 456-6630
FAX: (202) 456-2223
URL: http://www.whitehouse.gov/WH/EOP/nec/html
CHAIRMAN: William Jefferson Clinton
DIRECTOR: Gene B. Sperling
ASSISTANT TO THE PRESIDENT FOR INTERNATIONAL ECONOMIC AFFAIRS: Lael Brainard

FAST FACTS

In the 1997 budget, funding for student financial-assistance programs increased by enough money to assist 8.2 million students.

(Source: Lewis Kamb. "Congress Increases Student Aid by More Than $1.3 Billion." Knight-Ridder/ Tribune News Service, October 7, 1998.)

technology policy. Each of these advisers has many other complex responsibilities within their own agency. They oversee vast organizations within the government and are involved with implementing the goals specific to their particular areas.

The assistant to the president for economic policy is the director of the NEC and functions as an economic adviser to the president of the United States. It is the director's job to coordinate the presidential administration's economic policy and see that it is implemented throughout the various areas of government and the economy.

Operating alongside the director is the assistant to the president for international economic policy, who also functions as an adviser but focuses on international issues. The assistant to the president for international economic policy aids in creating international economic policy and participates in both the National Security Council and the NEC.

Whenever issues are so broad as to involve military affairs or other noneconomic problems, two other agencies are brought in to work with the NEC: the National Security Council (NSC) and the Domestic Policy Council. The NSC is an advisory group similar in structure to the NEC that aids the president in making and implementing policy concerning national security. The Domestic Policy Council is also similar to the NEC in structure but is responsible for noneconomic issues.

The responsibilities of the NEC include supporting all presidential goals and initiatives, helping these policies pass in Congress, and then advising the president during their implementation.

PROGRAMS

The programs of the NEC by their very nature are broad and comprehensive and affect wide segments of the population. The NEC's programs are the direct result of presidential policies. An important program undertaken by the NEC was the development and passage of the 1993 deficit reduction plan, a budget plan to reduce the nation's overall deficit. The projected deficit was reduced from $239 billion in 1994 to $190 billion in 1997.

The NEC achieved this primarily by setting out to create a perception that the government was serious about cutting spending, which calmed investors' worries over inflation (thought to be a primary cause of the increasing deficit). As a result of this confidence, long-term bond prices rose and interest rates fell, which inspired people to take their money out of safe, low-interest investments such as bank accounts and move it out into the economy, taking risks, investing, and thus spurring growth.

In addition the administration aggressively supported pro-U.S. business efforts throughout the globe, which brought into the country increased profits from export-import activities. This was done through such programs as the North American Free Trade Agreement (NAFTA) and the most-favored-nation trading status afforded China, and through hands-on diplomacy by senior NEC officials when appropriate.

Although the effort to cut expenditures also led to reducing the amount of spending on public programs, the NEC was responsible for a number of public spending programs being initiated. These include the Earned Income Tax Credit, the initiation of the Direct Student Loan Program, and the President's Empowerment Zones initiative. Other programs include new policy initiatives such as America Reads, in conjunction with the Department of Education, which is a move to increase the level of literacy in children; the Welfare-to-Work initiative; school construction; education technology; and the HOPE Scholarships college tuition tax cuts.

PRIMARY FUNCTIONS

The NEC aids the president in analyzing and understanding current economic trends, offers advice on policies that will ensure a healthy U.S. economy and aids in the implementation of economic policies. Meetings are a forum for debate in which ideas are discussed and analyzed to help the president formulate his economic policies.

BUDGET INFORMATION

The budget of the NEC is incorporated into the overall budget of its parent organization, the Office of Policy Development, which oversees both the NEC and the Domestic Policy Council (DPC). This amount is appropriated by Congress from the overall budget of the United States. The budget for the Office of Policy Development was an estimated $3.98 million in 1998.

HISTORY

The NEC was created on January 25, 1993, by President Bill Clinton as an advisory council that would meet in order to help him formulate and then coordinate economic policy throughout the government in both the domestic and the international arenas. It was the fulfillment of a campaign promise to make economic policy a foremost concern of his presidency. Previous bureaucratic disputes over economic issues and policies indicated a need for one body that could organize many opinions into a collective voice. Clinton believed this was especially necessary in complex international economic issues.

Clinton's goal was to make the economy as important to the presidency and the country as military and national security concerns had been to past administrations. His model for the NEC was the National Security Council (NSC), which is concerned with the U.S. military and national security of the country. Clinton admired the effectiveness of the NSC and wanted to create a similar council for the economy.

To do this, the Clinton administration sought out the NEC's first directors from leaders in the financial world, rather than the political arena, starting with Robert Rubin, a successful cochairman of a Wall Street investment bank. Rubin served on the NEC from 1993 to 1995 and was succeeded as director by Dr. Laura D'Andrea Tyson, a well-known economist from California who served from 1995 to 1996.

CURRENT POLITICAL ISSUES

One of the biggest problems facing the NEC is the question of how to reduce the national deficit and find a way to balance the nation's budget. One of the ways to achieve this is for the NEC to help agencies and departments cut spending and operate more efficiently. In a country as large as the United States, any attempts are sure to be met with opposition, and their implementation can be extremely complex.

Case Study: Medicare Reform

One of the largest expenditures of the federal government is on Medicare benefits. Medicare falls under the Department of Health and Human Services and is administered by the Health Care Financing Administration (HCFA). The system is considered by many to be wasteful and poorly managed, and the costs of implementing it have been steadily increasing for many years. This means that health care for the elderly is at risk of both weakening the nation's economy if left unchecked and of leaving the elderly with poor medical care. This also jeopardizes health care for future generations as they age.

The budget President Clinton signed into law in 1997 included significant changes to the Medicare program. As part of this approach the president and his NEC advisers sought to try and provide more choice and competition within the program. Advocates of the plan claimed that the increase in competition would force efficiency upon the system, because in order for providers to stay in business they will have to keep their costs down, and beneficiaries will be able to decide from whom they want to purchase medical treatment. The NEC claimed that the result of this change in approach will be nearly $100 billion (1997) in savings over a five-year period that places no undue burdens on beneficiaries, modernizes the program, and extends the life of the Medicare Trust Fund to the year 2007.

Also included in the plan is an increase in the cost of premiums that beneficiaries pay. The NEC said that such increases will provide more money to offset the expense of running the program, which has never paid for itself. Advocates also claimed that premiums would have increased anyway, therefore it was better to schedule in the costs in a controlled and gradual manner. Opponents, however, said that the elderly are already spending an average of $2,600 per year (1997), nearly 21 percent of their incomes, on health care, and that new increases would be impossible for many to afford. It would leave these elderly without available medical treatment. Opponents also claimed that the array of choices the new plan allowed were too complicated. Opponents were not convinced that a market-driven program would work, because the market would be stifled by strict government controls.

Public Impact

Beginning in 2002, all Medicare recipients will have to choose between traditional Medicare and a "Medicare+Choice" plan. The traditional plan pays medical bills as they occur and allows beneficiaries to choose whatever doctors or hospitals they wish. The new Medicare+Choice plan will offer a variety of choices which, once committed to by a beneficiary, will place limits on the type of treatment they will have available. The government will send out information packets at the beginning of each year describing these various choices. They will include HMOs, provider-sponsored organizations, medical savings accounts, and private fee-for-service plans. Beneficiaries will have to commit to the plan they want, even though it will be possible to switch plans. Under the new laws, beneficiaries who lose their policy coverage through no fault of their own will be able to get new coverage without new restrictions being applied because of the lapse. Doctors also will be allowed to quit Medicare and negotiate private contracts with elderly patients, which could benefit wealthier patients, who can afford to buy whatever supplement to Medicare that they require. Poorer beneficiaries, of course, would not have this option.

SUCCESSES AND FAILURES

The effects of the NEC on the economy are complex. They begin with certain policy decisions and then take shape in the form of a program, initiative, or bill. Once they are implemented the results reverberate through society. Some of the initiatives that the NEC points to as successes are the initial budget reduction plan of 1993, the Earned Income Tax Credit, the establishment of the Direct Student Loan Program, and the President's Empowerment Zones initiative. The Clinton administration also participates in the annual summit meetings of the leaders of the G-7 group of industrialized nations. In the end, the best evidence of the NEC's effectiveness is to judge the health of the present-day economy.

FUTURE DIRECTIONS

The NEC is an organization created to meet the administrative style of a particular presidency and the style of that president's decision-making process. Although it has been an effective means of formulating administrative policy, whether or not it will continue to be utilized with succeeding administrations is undecided. Its survival depends on whether later presidencies find it useful. Not all leaders will rely on the process of group decision making. This, combined with one of the NEC's primary failures so far, formulating more ideas than it can successfully implement, will play a large role in deciding whether or not the agency survives.

AGENCY RESOURCES

Further information about the policies and activities of the NEC can be obtained by contacting Room 235, Old Executive Office Building, Washington, DC 20502 or by calling that office at (202) 456-6630. Information can also be found on the World Wide Web at http://www.whitehouse.gov/WH/EOP/nec/html/main.

AGENCY PUBLICATIONS

Documents published by the NEC include *President Clinton's Fiscal Year 1998 Balanced Budget Summary Documents* and others about the NEC's specific policy proposals. They are available by writing the NEC at Room 235, Old Executive Office Building, Washington, DC 20502 or by calling (202) 456-6630.

BIBLIOGRAPHY

Borrus, Amy. "Bad Counsel at the Economic Council?" *Business Week* (Industrial/Technology edition), 26 February 1996, p. 34.

Clinton, William J. Executive Order 12835—Establishment of the National Economic Council. "Weekly Compilation of Presidential Documents," 1 February 1993, pp. 95–96.

———. Remarks on the Establishment of the National Economic Council and an Exchange with Reporters. "Weekly Compilation of Presidential Documents," 1 February 1993, p. 94.

Donlan, Thomas G. "Editorial Commentary: Shrinking Government." *Barron's,* 18 November 1996, p. 74.

Dowd, Ann Reilly. "Clinton's Point Man on the Economy." *Fortune,* 3 May 1993, pp. 75–79.

Goode, Stephen. "Too Early to Grade Clinton's Student-Loan Reform Plan." *Insight on the News,* 3 July 1995, p. 18–19.

Judis, John B. "Old Master." *New Republic,* 13 December 1993, pp. 21–28.

Kamb, Lewis. "Congress Increases Student Aid by More Than $1.3 Billion." Knight-Ridder/Tribune News Service, 7 October 1996.

Kosterlitz, Julie. "Fiscal and Economic Policy: Making Ends Meet Won't Be Easy." *National Journal,* 16 November 1996, pp. 2487–88.

Risen, James. "Honest Broker." *Financial World,* 11 May 1993, pp. 24–25.

Stokes, Bruce. "Where Now for Trade Talks with Japan?" *National Journal,* 11 June 1994, pp. 1354–55.

Tyson, Laura D'Andrea. *Current Biography,* September 1996, pp. 48–52.

National Endowment for the Arts (NEA)

PARENT ORGANIZATION: Independent
ESTABLISHED: September 29, 1965
EMPLOYEES: 140

Contact Information:

ADDRESS: 1100 Pennsylvania Avenue, NW
Washington, DC 20506-0001
PHONE: (202) 606-8400
TDD (HEARING IMPAIRED): (202) 682-5496
FAX: (202) 682-5611
URL: http://arts.endow.gov
CHAIRMAN: Jane Alexander

WHAT IS ITS MISSION?

The published mission of the National Endowment for the Arts (NEA) is "to foster the excellence, diversity and vitality of the arts in the United States and to broaden public access to the arts." The NEA supports the visual, literary, and performing arts to benefit all Americans by developing creative talent, preserving and transmitting our diverse cultural heritage, and by making the arts an integral part of education.

HOW IS IT STRUCTURED?

The NEA is a division of the National Foundation on the Arts and Humanities, an independent agency in the executive branch of the federal government; the National Endowment for the Humanities (NEH) makes up the other part of the Foundation. The chairman of the NEA is appointed for a four-year term by the president of the United States with the advice and consent of the Senate. The National Council of the Arts, made up of 26 private citizens, who are appointed by the president and confirmed by the Senate, advises the chairman on policies, programs, grants, and procedures. Council members usually serve six-year terms, staggered so that roughly one-third of the membership rotates every two years.

PRIMARY FUNCTIONS

The NEA provides grants to nonprofit arts organizations in support of outstanding performances, projects,

FAST FACTS

Since the NEA was established, the number of nonprofit theaters has grown from 56 to 427, the number of large orchestras has grown from 100 to 238, and the number of dance companies has grown from 37 to over 400.

(Source: The National Endowment for the Arts home page. http://arts.endow.gov/.)

and exhibitions and fellowships to creative writers. The NEA also funds projects that preserve and share the nation's cultural heritage through music, dance, theater, writing, and the visual arts. The primary functions of the NEA are to design and fund programs that educate Americans, especially schoolchildren, about the arts. The NEA also disburses funds to and establishes partnerships with state, regional, and local agencies involved in arts education and presentation in an effort to make the arts accessible to all Americans.

The NEA maintains 25 formal interagency agreements with other federal agencies. The purpose of these partnerships is to increase support for artists and arts organizations through more direct involvement in the programs and policies of other federal agencies. An example of these partnerships is the Pathways to Success Program, which began in 1996 and is jointly funded by the NEA and the Department of Justice, and provides after school, weekend, and summer programs for at-risk youth.

PROGRAMS

The NEA considers applications and proposals from eligible individuals and organizations in four ways: grants to organizations, grants to individuals, partnership agreements, and leadership initiatives.

Funding opportunities for organizations are available in four categories: Heritage and Preservation, Education and Access, Creation and Presentation, and Planning and Stabilization. NEA grants are available to projects in dance, design, folk and traditional arts, literature, media arts (film, television, radio, and audio), music, musical theater, opera, theater, visual arts (painting, photography, sculpture, crafts, works on paper, and other genres), and multidisciplinary works.

Heritage and Preservation works should reflect artistic expressions rooted in the varied cultures of the nation, preserve artistic accomplishments for future generations, or conserve important works of art. For example, the Mad River Theater Works in Logan County, Ohio, received NEA funds to present and tour plays that depicted events from the history of the region.

Education and Access project goals are to broaden the arts experiences for Americans of all ages. Programs that fall into the Education and Access area include: touring performances; curriculum-based arts instruction in schools; activities that extend the work of older, disabled and/or ethnically diverse artists; and outreach projects that engage communities in arts activities. As part of the NEA-sponsored Rural Residency Initiative, the Ying Quartet spent two years in Jesup, Iowa, performing chamber music concerts at schools, churches, nursing homes, and social clubs in the area.

Creation and Presentation projects provide resources for artists to create a specific work or body of work or present art from any era or discipline to diverse audiences. Such projects include, but are not limited to: commissions, residencies, workshops, exhibitions, performances, literary publishing, broadcasts, and festivals. In one example of such a program, the Yale Repertory Theater presented a series of plays written by local, minority playwrights funded in part by the NEA.

Planning and Stabilization projects help organizations develop structures that will enable them to carry on their work in the arts effectively and creatively. Projects funded under this program might include: technical assistance, income enhancement planning, community planning, resource development, or partnership creation.

Individuals receive grants in the form of fellowships. These fellowships are given to creative writers in the areas of poetry and prose. Each fellowship area is offered every other year. For many years, NEA offered fellowships to individual artists in other disciplines, but due to legislation in 1995, only the category of creative writing remains open for applications.

The NEA Partnership Agreements program supports state arts agencies by providing funds, helping develop plans that address arts education, and helping develop plans to foster the arts in underserved communities.

Leadership Initiatives at the NEA include research, outreach to corporate and individual sponsors and donors, and advising other federal and state agencies involved in the creation, presentation, and preservation of the arts.

BUDGET INFORMATION

In 1997 the NEA received a budget from Congress of $99.5 million, the same amount that was awarded in 1996. Contributions from industries, organizations, and individuals which vary from year to year, supplement the NEA budget. Approximately 85 percent of the NEA budget is awarded in grants. Fifteen percent is allocated to administrative costs. Of the grants awarded yearly, approximately 25 percent fund new works, 30 percent are distributed to communities through the Partnership Agreements Program, and the remaining 45 percent are for continuing and national projects.

Debate over funding for the NEA centers around a 1995 House of Representatives agreement that the NEA would receive $99.5 million in 1996 and 1997 and then receive no funding beyond 1997. This agreement was never finalized, however, and was not supported by the Senate or President Clinton. In 1997 the Senate Interior Appropriations Subcommittee stated that the subcommittee would support continued funding at the $99.5 million level, but felt that any increases were unlikely.

BUDGET:

National Endowment for the Arts

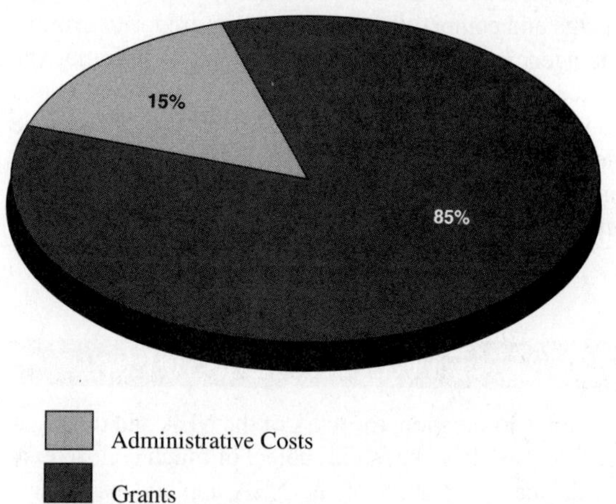

Administrative Costs

Grants

HISTORY

Though the National Foundation on the Arts and Humanities was not established until 1965, the federal government has a long history of interest in and support of the arts in the United States. Presidents George Washington, Thomas Jefferson, and John Adams believed that appreciation of and accessibility to the arts were hallmarks of a democratic society, but none established a formal relationship between the federal government and the arts. For many years, the government supported the arts primarily through commissions and support for individual projects. In 1790, the United States Marine Corps Band became the first federally supported musical ensemble. John Trumbull's commission for four paintings to hang in the Capitol Rotunda in 1817, was the first federal support of the visual arts.

In 1839, President James Buchanan appointed a National Arts Commission, but it was disbanded two years later due to a lack of congressional appropriations. Proposals to establish a national fine arts council were introduced in Congress in 1879 and again in 1897, but no action was taken. Theodore Roosevelt appointed a thirty-member Council of Fine Arts in 1909, but they too disbanded because of a lack of funds. By this time the federal government had become responsible for several permanent arts institutions including the Library of Congress, the Smithsonian Institution, and the National Conservatory of Music.

The 1930s brought a new measure of respect for artists as workers and the importance of their work to U.S. culture and heritage. The Federal Writers Program, the Federal Theater Project, the Federal Art Project, and the Federal Music Project were established in 1935 under the Works Project Administration (WPA) as public service employment programs. Artists working for the WPA wrote, painted, photographed, and presented works that explored the nation's history and the hard times of the Great Depression.

For the next 25 years, several more proposals were made in Congress to establish national arts offices and several arts councils were organized, but lack of broad-based political support stalled these efforts. In the early 1960s, President John F. Kennedy expressed support for the arts by establishing the President's Advisory Council on the Arts and appointing a special consultant on the arts. But it was not until 1964 that Congress voted to establish a National Council on the Arts (NCA).

On March 10, 1965, President Lyndon Johnson, asked the 89th Congress to establish the National Foundation on the Arts and Humanities (NFAH). By September, both houses of Congress approved the request, and on September 29, the NFAH was officially created, composed of the National Endowment for the Arts and the National Endowment for the Humanities.

Since its creation, the NEA has sponsored thousands of individual and organizational arts projects, supported the establishment of an arts council in every state, and worked to make the arts in the United States excellent and accessible. During the early years, the NEA provided grants mainly for pilot projects, as funds were limited and the possibilities of long-term project development were unclear. Heavy emphasis was given to the support of theaters such as the American Ballet Theater. Additionally, the American Film Institute was established.

Nancy Hanks was appointed chairman in 1969 and oversaw the development of the NEA through 1977. She brought about cooperation between the NEA and the American Symphony Orchestra League, which led to increased funding for musical projects. Funds also became available for touring programs and dance projects. The Challenge Grants Program was created to encourage donations from large-budget organizations and industries as grants awarded by the program required artists to secure three dollars of funding from sources other than the NEA for every dollar granted by the NEA.

In the 1980s, the NEA struggled with drastic budget cuts and competition for funds from minority groups, state agencies, and artist's unions. Leadership initiatives to encourage the growth of community arts foundations and increase private donations to support the arts became priorities for the NEA. In 1994, a major controversy erupted over federal funding for the NEA, and the projects the NEA decides to fund.

CURRENT POLITICAL ISSUES

Since its creation, the work of the NEA and the organization itself have been the subject of much controversy and debate. Supporters of the NEA applaud its leadership in making the arts more respected and more accessible. As measures of the NEA's success, they point to the thousands of arts projects that would not have existed without NEA support and the development of regional and state arts councils that relied on the NEA for initial support and guidance. Those who advocate for the continued existence of the NEA feel that the federal government has a responsibility to foster the arts in the United States, so that Americans are assured of having the opportunity to participate in and enjoy all kinds of artistic experiences.

Opponents of the NEA question the role of the federal government in promoting the arts and feel that the arts should be addressed at state and local levels and by the private sector. Many groups feel that the NEA is an elite resource, supplying too many funds to projects in New York and Boston that are not accessible or appreciated by most Americans. Opponents of the NEA also charge that the NEA fosters the political agendas of minorities and special-interest groups by overfunding nonmainstream projects.

At the heart of the debate over the NEA is the question of what is art, and what role does the government play in determining the answer. The NEA has maintained that art must be defined by the artists that create it and audiences that view it, and to limit either group's opportunity to decide, would be censorship and undemocratic. But with tax dollars at issue, politicians want to have influence over the choices.

Case Study: The Maplethorpe Exhibit and the 104th Congress

A major battle over the NEA began with the 1994 midterm elections when the Republicans seized control of Congress. Newly elected Republican representatives had campaigned on pledges to reduce the cost and influence of the federal government and to promote a return to "family values." Among hundreds of other choices for budget cutting, the NEA became a primary target, not only as an example of federal spending that could be eliminated for financial reasons, but one that should be eliminated for moral reasons.

The Republican candidates had researched past NEA grants and began to publicize projects that they felt were particularly offensive. The example that garnered the most attention was a 1988 grant to the Institute of Contemporary Art. The grant was awarded to the Institute for a retrospective show of photographs by Robert Maplethorpe. The show moved to the Corcoran Gallery of Art in Washington, D.C., where its homoerotic themes aroused the anger of many members of Congress. The NEA was accused of spending taxpayers' money on pornography posing as art. The Corcoran exhibit was closed.

In response to the furor over the Maplethorpe exhibit, NEA Chairman Jane Alexander, began touring the country in 1994 to defend the NEA. In lectures and project inspections, she de-emphasized avant-garde art and stressed the NEA's support of regional U.S. arts, crafts, and performances. Alexander said that only a minute portion of the federal budget (less than a hundredth of one percent) is allocated to the NEA. She also stated that the NEA required grant applicants to obtain the majority of project funds from sources other than the NEA.

Despite the fact that the majority of NEA grants were not made to controversial projects and that 79 percent of Americans in 1994 not only supported funding for the NEA, but supported increased funding, congressional Republicans continued to press for elimination of the NEA. In 1995, House of Representative leaders made an agreement with conservative members that NEA funding would be reduced in 1996 and 1997 and eliminated in 1998. Though the Senate did not agree to eliminating the NEA, funding leveled off in 1996.

Public Impact

The NEA emerged from this battle with new restrictions and priorities. Under changes dictated by Congress or instituted by the chairman, the NEA no longer endows institutions. Instead, it funds individual programs, such as special exhibitions or performances that an institution develops. The NEA has also eliminated funding for individual arts, except for creative writers, per congressional dictates. However, the NEA redoubled its efforts to promote arts education, a relatively neutral political issue.

SUCCESSES AND FAILURES

In an effort to fulfill its mission of making the arts accessible, the NEA has taken full advantage of reaching Americans through technology. The NEA's on-line magazine, *arts.community* at http://arts.endow.gov/ provides information, news, ideas, and feature articles on the arts. Users can view paintings and photographs, read the works of featured writers, and participate in interactive arts forums. Detailed information on regional, state, and local arts exhibitions, presentations, festivals, and programs is also provided. Comprehensive directions for applying for NEA grants are available and links to other federal and private funding sources are continuously updated and expanded.

FUTURE DIRECTIONS

The NEA continues to provide leadership to arts organizations while adapting to an environment with fewer public dollars and increased competition for private sector funding. With scarce public dollars, the NEA plans to fulfill its commitment to arts education for Americans of all ages and backgrounds by encouraging art organizations and their communities to share resources.

The NEA plans to expand projects such as the Creative Writers on the Net, a high school course in creative writing conducted completely on-line using virtual conferences, libraries, and multimedia resources. The on-line campus includes sites for student authors to talk with each other, consult mentors, create collaborative projects, and share their work.

AGENCY RESOURCES

Information on NEA grants is available on their Web site at http//arts.endow.gov/Guide/Guidelines_List.html. Detailed descriptions of their selection guidelines are available as well as information on deadlines and applications materials.

The NEA's Arts Resource Center (ARC) provides research from studies of artists and arts organizations, statistics, arts education materials, and general interest materials. ARC can be accessed on-line at http://arts.endow.gov/resource/catelogue.

AGENCY PUBLICATIONS

NEA publications can be requested by mail from the NEA Office of Communications, 1100 Pennsylvania Avenue NW, Washington, DC 20506, or by E-mail at webmgr@arts.endow.gov. Catalogues can also be requested or viewed on-line at http://arts.endow.gov/pub/. Publications include: "Arts in Schools: Perspectives from Four Nations," "Understanding How the Arts Contribute to Excellent Education," "Part of the Solution: Creative Alternatives for Youth," and "The Accessible Museum: Model Programs of Accessibility for Disabled People."

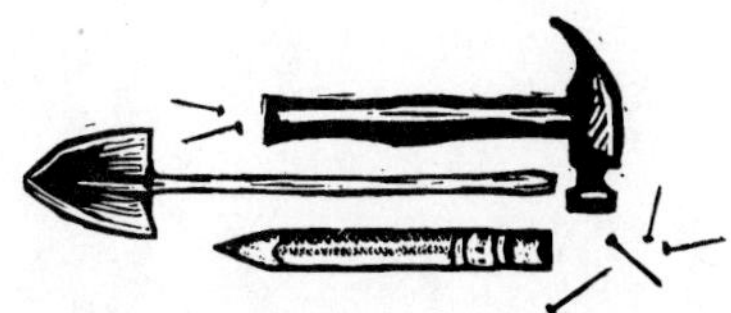

GET INVOLVED:

- For those interested in obtaining grants from the NEA, their Web site at http//arts.endow.gov/Guide/Guidelines_List.html provides detailed descriptions of selection guidelines. Application materials are also available at this site, or you can contact the NEA Web manager at webmgr@arts.endow.gov; or write to The Office of Public Information, National Endowment for the Arts, Nancy Hanks Center, 1100 Pennsylvania Ave. NW, Washington, DC 20506-0001.
- State arts councils, in partnership with the NEA, sponsor yearly Conferences for Artists where students can submit their work for critique by established artists. Discussions and panel presentations are held on techniques, use of media, grant opportunities, and exhibition planning. Contact the NEA at (202) 682-5496 for information on the arts council nearest you.

BIBLIOGRAPHY

Bozell III, L. "Circling the Arts Welfare Wagons." *Indianapolis Business Journal*, 20 March 1995.

Hughes, Robert. "Pulling the Fuse on Culture." *Time*, 7 August 1995.

Hulbert, Dan. "Warming Trend: The NEA Enters Calmer Waters After Weathering Political Storms; Arts: Advocates Say it's About Time." *Atlanta Journal and Constitution*, 2 March 1997, p. L1.

Jensen, Richard. "The Culture Wars, 1965 to 1995: A Historian's Map." *Journal of Social History*, 5 February 1996, p. 17.

Lambro, Donald. "House Refuses to Kill NEA." *Human Events*, 8 July 1994.

MacLeish, Rod. "Gingrich & Company Keep Bead on Arts Endowment." *Christian Science Monitor*, 22 April 1997, p. 10.

Meroney, John. "House Panel Slashes NEA Funding." *Human Events*, 30 June 1995.

Streisand, Barbra. "The Artist as Citizen." *New Perspectives Quarterly*, 1 April 1995.

Strong, Catherine. "GOP Pushes Federal Arts Elimination." *Washington Post*, 13 May 1997.

Williams, Dick. "Nothing for Individuals: Revisions Would Slow NEA's Smear Campaign." *Atlanta Journal*, 15 April 1997, p. A16.

National Endowment for the Humanities (NEH)

PARENT ORGANIZATION: Independent
ESTABLISHED: September 25, 1965
EMPLOYEES: 170

Contact Information:

ADDRESS: 1100 Pennsylvania Ave. NW
Washington, DC 20506
PHONE: (202) 606-8400
TOLL FREE: (800) 634-1121
TDD (HEARING IMPAIRED): (202) 606-8282
FAX: (202) 606-8240
E-MAIL: info@neh.fed.us
URL: http://www.neh.fed.us
CHAIRMAN: Sheldon Hackney
DEPUTY CHAIRMAN: Juan Mestas

WHAT IS ITS MISSION?

The published mission of the National Endowment for the Humanities (NEH) is "to promote progress and scholarship in the humanities in the United States." The humanities include the study of literature, history, philosophy, languages, archaeology, religion, and ethics. Over the years, the NEH's mission has expanded to emphasize education in and creating access to the humanities.

HOW IS IT STRUCTURED?

The NEH, along with the National Endowment for the Arts (NEA), is a division of the National Foundation on the Arts and Humanities, an independent agency within the executive branch of the federal government. The NEH is directed by the chairman, who is appointed by the president and confirmed by the Senate for a four-year term. Advising the chairman is the National Council on Humanities, which is made up of 26 private citizens involved in the humanities. Council members serve staggered six-year terms and are also appointed by the president and confirmed by the Senate.

The NEH is organized into three divisions: Research and Education, Preservation and Access, and Public Programs. Two offices, Challenge Grants and Federal/State Partnerships, are also administered by NEH.

PRIMARY FUNCTIONS

NEH provides grants to individuals and organizations such as museums, libraries, universities, and private nonprofit groups that conduct research, education, creation, preservation, study, and public exhibition projects in the humanities. The NEH strives to make experiences in the humanities accessible and available to all Americans and supports excellence in all the disciplines of the humanities. Encouraging private support of the humanities is also a NEH function and many NEH-funded projects are required to raise additional funds from private sources. For most grants, a request is made by an individual or group, which is then reviewed by a panel of experts. The experts then pass their recommendations on to the National Council on the Humanities who make their own recommendation to the director of the NEH. The director then makes the final decision on what to fund; approximately one-sixth of all applications are approved in any given year.

BUDGET:

National Endowment for the Humanities

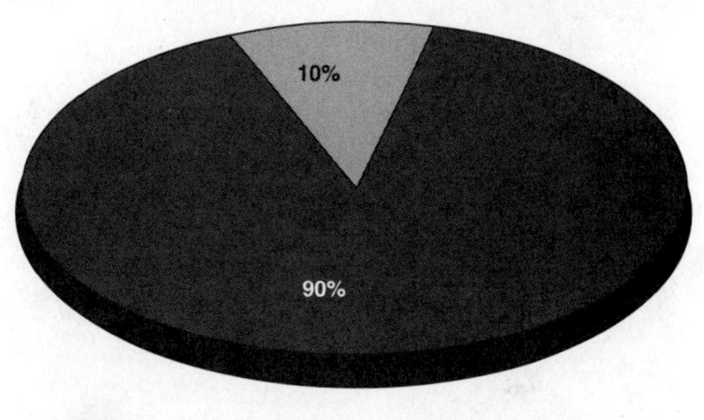

Administrative and Processing Costs

Grants to Individuals and Organizations

PROGRAMS

The NEH has five general categories of grants and programs, each with its own special focus or source of funding. They are: Research and Education, Preservation and Access, Public Programs, Challenge Grants, and Federal/State Partnerships. All the NEH's programs channel funds to the scholars and artists who are doing the work, which can vary from one grant to another even within the same NEH program.

Programs and projects sponsored through the NEH Research and Education division target curriculum development, faculty training, and educational conferences through fellowships, seminars, and independent study. Some examples of these types of projects include the documentary film series *The Civil War* and Northwestern University's multimedia project *Oyez, Oyez; the History of the United States Supreme Court*, available on the World Wide Web at http://oyez.nwu.edu.

Preservation and Access projects target preserving and increasing the availability of materials such as books, newspapers, journals, still and moving images, maps, and sound recordings. The United States Newspaper Project has transferred 54 million pages of newspapers from all 50 states and two territories to microfilm and created a national database to make them available to the public.

Public Programs support projects that bring the humanities to audiences of all ages through exhibitions, radio and television programs, lectures, and printed materials. In Montana, literature by local authors reaches the scattered population on the "Big Sky Radio" program. The "Age of Rubens" exhibit in Toledo, Ohio, allowed record-attendance crowds to view paintings that had never been displayed in the United States.

Challenge Grants are available to nonprofit institutions to help develop sources of long-term support for education, preservation, and public programs. To do this, Challenge Grants are awarded in the form of matching funds; grantees must raise three or four dollars in new or increased donations for every federal dollar awarded. This helps the grant recipient by providing them with federal funding and by encouraging other organizations to assist the grantee as well. Challenge Grants are typically used to develop endowments (money which is not spent, but rather used to generate interest, which is spent instead) that will provide a steady source of income for programs that would otherwise need to seek new funding every year. One example is the grant awarded to the University of California, Berkeley, to enrich and support its library's humanities collections.

Federal/State Partnerships exist in all 50 states and link state and local humanities councils to the NEH through jointly funded programs, guidance, materials, and research.

BUDGET INFORMATION

The 1998 NEH budget of approximately $122 million was appropriated by Congress. Donations from private resources vary from year to year and generally target specific projects rather than supplying the NEH with funds to distribute as it chooses. Of the budgeted amount, 90 percent of NEH funds are awarded as grants to individuals and organizations with the remaining 10 percent covering administrative and processing costs.

The Golden Age, *a painting by Peter Paul Rubens, on display in Toledo, Ohio. The NEH-sponsored "Age of Rubens" exhibit in Toledo featured many works of art never before displayed in the United States.* *(Corbis-Bettmann)*

HISTORY

Prior to the establishment of the NEH in 1965, the role of the federal government in the humanities was primarily to support educational programs and specific institutions, such as the Library of Congress and the Smithsonian Institution. In the 1930s the federal government recognized the role of scholars as workers and created employment projects through the Works Progress Administration (WPA) for artists and writers.

In the 1960s the federal government became concerned about the quality of U.S. education in math and science as the Soviet Union claimed several technological firsts. When advocates of the humanities in the United States saw the large investments being made for improvements in the sciences, they organized themselves and argued that improving the disciplines of the humanities was equally important to the country's interests. Joined by supporters of the arts, proponents of a national foundation for the humanities lobbied for the creation of such an organization. In 1965 their efforts were successful and the National Foundation on the Arts and Humanities was created with its equal endowments, the National Endowment for the Arts and the National Endowment for the Humanities.

The early years of NEH were characterized by modest budgets and low visibility. In 1969 the Public Programs division was created to bring the humanities to a nonacademic audience on a wide scale. Amidst the turbulent social issues of the 1960s and the 1970s, the NEH explored ways the humanities could be of service to society. Research and presentation projects that increased communication and cultural understanding became priorities. These activities brought the NEH more attention and more criticism as its activities were portrayed as promoting the agendas of special-interest groups and wasting taxpayer dollars on programs of little value to average Americans.

In response to such criticism, the NEH in the 1980s and 1990s returned to funding more traditional projects, such as the collection and preservation of the papers of influential Americans, such as Dr. Martin Luther King Jr. The NEH has also made improving the quality of humanities education in primary and secondary schools a major goal.

CURRENT POLITICAL ISSUES

For many years, the NEH went quietly about its work, sparking little controversy except among academics who debated whether the NEH should emphasize traditional scholarly projects or a more broad-based approach to the humanities. Then, in the mid-1990s, the

NEH became a symbolic and specific target of conservative Republicans in Congress. The newly elected Republican majority argued that the federal government should be downsized and streamlined, and that involvement in supporting humanities programs should be left to states and private sector institutions, not the federal government. Despite the small budget of the NEH (less than one-half of one percent of government expenditures), it was held up as an example of wasting taxpayer dollars on projects that were of little use to most Americans and that funding for its programs should come from other sources.

Supporters of the NEH countered that it was necessary to maintain a national organization to ensure high standards in the humanities and increase accessibility to historical and scholarly materials. They provided figures showing that private support of humanities projects would not fill the gaps left if federal support were eliminated.

Also at issue was the role of the NEH in supporting the traditional "family values" of the conservative Republicans and their supporters. These groups charged that the NEH had funded too many projects that appealed to audiences that were critical of the U.S.'s history and that the projects supported revisionary works that promoted the roles and interests of minority and special-interest groups. Other groups argued that humanities projects must be given the resources to pursue a variety of interpretations and that only government involvement could ensure those freedoms.

An uneasy compromise was struck in 1995 when Congress agreed to continue funding for the NEH with no increases. Hearings on the continued reauthorization of the NEH, begun in 1997, insure that the role of the NEH, in fact its very existence, will continue to be a political issue for many years.

Case Study: The National History Standards

In the early 1990s conservative intellectuals were increasingly troubled by the decline of intellectual skills in elementary and secondary schools, especially in history. They promoted a plan for national education standards to be established in schools and worked with the Department of Education and NEH to develop a model curricula in history and other fields. In 1991 the NEH awarded a $1.6 million grant to the University of California, Los Angeles (UCLA), to create comprehensive national history standards that would be available to textbook publishers, high schools, and elementary schools.

When the standards were published, conservatives rejected them as biased and revisionist. They charged that the standards used for world history denigrated the role of Western civilization while exaggerating the achievements of nonwestern cultures. They also said that the standards for U.S. history were distorted because they depicted heroic women and minorities resisting oppressive white males. Critics further alleged that the man who supervised the creation of the standards, Gary Nash, had misrepresented the story of U.S. history by emphasizing the disreputable actions of historical figures such as Senator Joseph McCarthy and the Ku Klux Klan while downplaying the contributions of notable people such as George Washington, Abraham Lincoln, and Franklin Roosevelt.

Supporters of the standards argued that they were meant to be guides and to lay out themes and issues for students to explore further. Properly used, they would invite inquiry and discussion, a departure from traditional rote learning. These supporters also argued that the standards presented a more balanced view of world and U.S. history, precisely because they included the study of cultures outside of Europe and North America and asked students to think seriously about issues of race, class, and gender that are crucial to understanding history.

Ultimately, the Senate settled the issue by voting 99 to 1 in 1994 to reject the standards. It was not until President Bill Clinton's 1997 State of the Union address that the issues of national education standards was seriously raised again. The shape and content of such standards remains an ongoing debate.

SUCCESSES AND FAILURES

Perhaps the most universally praised of all of the NEH's projects is the study of the personal documents from some of the most influential people from the history of the United States. The NEH has funded the study, preservation, and publication of the papers of George Washington, Thomas Jefferson, Frederick Douglass, Ulysses S. Grant, Mark Twain, and Dr. Martin Luther King Jr. The NEH also sponsored the first printed version of the journals of Lewis and Clark on their epic trek across the nation. By funding these programs, the NEH has helped to preserve the heritage of some of the greatest heroes of the United States.

FUTURE DIRECTIONS

In an era of shrinking federal dollars to support humanities projects, the NEH will make developing partnerships with corporations and foundations a top priority. EDSITEment, a new Web site that serves as a gateway to the best humanities-related educational sites on the Internet, is an example of just such a partnership. The NEH is working in conjunction with MCI Communications and The Council of the Great City Schools to operate the site, which is located at http://edsitement.neh.gov. In addition to links to 49 humanities Web sites, EDSITEment provides on-line lesson plans and informational E-mail lists. On-line projects like EDSITEment, as well as corporate partnerships, are a major part of the NEH's future.

AGENCY RESOURCES

To request information on NEH grants, grant applications, or annual reports, contact the NEH by phone at 1-800-634-1121 or by E-mail at info@neh.fed.us.

AGENCY PUBLICATIONS

The two major publications produced by the NEH are *Humanities* and *NEH Media Log* magazines. Also available on the NEH Web site are the NEH's annual reports and other internal publications, at http://www.neh.fed.us/html/publicat.html.

Humanities is published six times a year by NEH and includes articles on humanities, essays, listings of exhibitions, conferences, films and funding opportunities, and pictorial essays. Annual subscriptions are $16 and can be requested by calling NEH at 1-800-634-1121 or ordering via the Internet at http://www.neh.fed.us/html/publicat.html.

The *NEH Media Log* is a guide to film, television, and radio programs supported by the NEH. The *NEH Media Log* can be viewed on-line at http://www.neh.fed.us./html/media, or ordered by calling NEH at 1-800-634-1121.

BIBLIOGRAPHY

Bertman, Stephen. "Cultural Amnesia." *Vital Speeches*, 15 July 1995.

Casement, William. "The Great Books and Politics." *Perspectives on Political Science*, 1 June 1991.

Cass, Connie. "African Burial Ground Part of Map Exhibit." *New York Beacon*, 5 October 1995.

De La Torre, William. "Multiculturalism." *Urban Education*, 1 September 1996.

Hughes, Robert. "Pulling the Fuse on Culture." *Time*, 7 August 1995.

Jensen, Richard. "The Culture Wars." *Journal of Social History*, 5 February 1996, p. 17.

Kaye, Harvey. "Whose History Is It?" *Monthly Review: An Independent Socialist Magazine*, 1 November 1996.

MacLeish, Rod. "Keep Bead on Arts Endowment." *Christian Science Monitor*, 22 April 1997.

National Highway Traffic Safety Administration (NHTSA)

PARENT ORGANIZATION: Department of Transportation
ESTABLISHED: March 19, 1970
EMPLOYEES: 632

Contact Information:

ADDRESS: 400 Seventh St. SW
Washington, DC 20590
PHONE: (202) 366-9550
TOLL FREE: (800) 424-9393
FAX: (202) 366-2106
URL: http://www.nhtsa.dot.gov
ADMINISTRATOR: Ricardo Martinez, M.D.

WHAT IS ITS MISSION?

The mission of the National Highway Traffic Safety Administration (NHTSA) is "to save lives, prevent injuries and reduce traffic-related health care and other economic costs." According to the NHTSA, this is accomplished by "setting and enforcing safety performance standards for motor vehicles and items of motor vehicle equipment, and through grants to state and local governments." Toward this end, the NHTSA administers educational, engineering, and enforcement programs aimed at reducing both economic losses and loss of human lives caused by highway accidents.

HOW IS IT STRUCTURED?

The NHTSA is a federal regulatory agency in the Department of Transportation (DOT). It is headed by an administrator who is nominated by the president and confirmed by the Senate. The administrator is responsible for determining and establishing national safety priorities as they relate to the nation's highways and motor vehicle traffic. As the agency's liaison with the public and other federal bodies, the administrator presents the NHTSA's perspective on issues in testimony before members of Congress. The administrator is supported in these duties by a deputy administrator and seven associate administrators, each of whom is responsible for an area of agency activity.

The associate director for State and Community Services administers the NHTSA's various state grant programs and its 10 regional offices, which deal with vari-

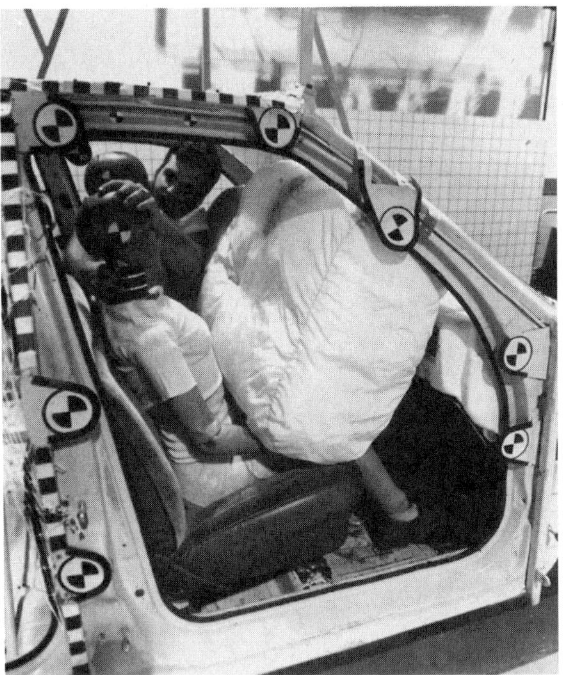

A test technician positions a crash dummy in front of an inflated air bag. NHTSA guidelines call for all automobiles manufactured after 1996 to be equipped with air bags. (AP/Wide World Photos)

ous highway and vehicle issues in the 50 states, Puerto Rico, the Virgin Islands, Guam, American Samoa, and the Mariana Islands. An important responsibility of the regional offices is their work with local authorities in investigating cases of odometer fraud, which are referred to the Department of Justice for prosecution.

The associate administrator for Safety Performance Standards oversees the Office of Crashworthiness Standards, the Office of Crash Avoidance Standards, and the Office of Planning and Consumer Programs. The associate administrator for Safety Assurance oversees the Office of Defects Investigation and the Office of Vehicle Safety Compliance. The associate administrator for Traffic Safety Programs administers NHTSA programs that target special problems, like drunk and drugged driving, motorcycle safety, and pedestrian and bicycle safety; the Office of Traffic Injury Control Programs, the Office of Communication and Outreach, and the office of Research and Traffic Records are under this associate administrator. The associate administrator for Research and Development maintains the NHTSA's Vehicle Research Test Center in East Liberty, Ohio, where various crash tests are conducted. Also under this associate administrator's oversight are the Office of Crashworthiness Research, the National Center for Statistics and Analysis, the NHTSA's data-collection program, and the Office of Crash Avoidance Research. The associate administrator for Administration oversees the Office of Human Resources, the Office of Contracts and Procurements, and the Office of Information Resource Management. The associate administrator for Plans and Policy oversees the Office of Strategic and Program Planning, the Office of Regulatory Analysis and Evaluation and the Office of Fiscal Services.

PRIMARY FUNCTIONS

The NHTSA's functions can be divided into four broad, overlapping areas: regulation, testing and investigation, public information, and administration. The combined efforts of all areas help accomplish the agency's primary goal: to reduce accidents and deaths on the nation's highways.

Regulation

The NHTSA establishes and enforces a myriad of vehicle standards. The agency develops mandatory minimum safety standards for all automobiles, vans, pickup trucks, utility vehicles, and school buses sold in the United States. The standards encompass special safety equipment like seat belts and air bags, vehicle parts like glass and tires, and structural elements like bumpers and side panels. The NHTSA also sets fuel economy standards like the Corporate Average Fuel Economy (CAFE) standards, which determine average levels of fuel economy for each manufacturer. However, this is one area in which the NHTSA is responsible only for establishing the standards. Compliance testing is carried out by the Environmental Protection Agency (EPA), and enforcement is handled by the Department of Justice and the Federal Trade Commission (FTC).

Testing and Investigation

The NHTSA sets its safety standards by testing new cars. One of the most well known tests is one in which cars crash against stationary barriers at 30 miles per hour to test the effects of occupant restraint equipment. Another test measures the protection provided by a given vehicle in a head-on crash at 75 miles per hour. The NHTSA also tests for safety defects in vehicles. Test data and data obtained from actual traffic accident investigations are collected and analyzed. Findings are distributed to state and local government agencies, law enforcement bodies, industry, and the public.

The agency is empowered to order recalls of defective products that affect vehicle safety. Defect investigations, in principle, go through three stages. The first step is gathering information about the alleged defect, primarily from consumers who E-mail, send letters of complaint, or call the agency's Auto Safety Hotline. The information is collected in a data bank, where it is analyzed for patterns that indicate a possible defect. If the data indicate that a defect exists, the second stage begins—NHTSA engineers gather technical information from the vehicle's manufacturer. The information is examined, and vehicles are tested. By the time an investigation reaches this point, manufacturers generally issue a voluntary recall; it is rare for the NHTSA to order a manufacturer's recall.

If a voluntary recall is not issued, however, a formal defect hearing is called—the third stage in an investigation. When the hearing is complete, the NHTSA administrator examines the findings and decides whether or not to order a recall. The NHTSA's safety assurance division monitors the scope and effectiveness of any such recall, and manufacturers that refuse to comply with a recall order can be taken to federal court.

Public Information

An important part of the NHTSA's mission is informing the public about highway safety. Agency information campaigns take many forms, the most visible of which are public service advertisements on television—for example, the seat belt spots featuring Vince and Larry, the crash-test dummies. The agency also produces some hard-hitting ads against drunk and drugged driving. Additionally, the agency regularly informs the media of its research findings. One high-profile example of this is its studies regarding the use of air bags. The NHTSA established who is at risk when using them, why certain individuals have been injured by them, and what can be done to avoid injury or death. These findings made their way into newspaper, television, and radio news stories as the public debate went on over whether air bags do more harm than good. The Office of Safety Programs also issues numerous fact sheets, booklets, manuals, reports, posters, videos, and other materials every year on every aspect of traffic safety.

Administration

The agency believes that localities are best able to cope with and respond to their own specific safety problems. It works closely with the states in implementing programs funded through highway safety grants. Money is made available to the states, Puerto Rico, the Trust Territories, and the Indian nations. Grant programs cover issues like drunk driving and occupant protection, and they enable the states to develop their own programs in areas of high national priority. The NHTSA works closely with other federal agencies, in particular the Federal Highway Administration, with which it coadministers some programs. It also receives recommendations from the National Transportation Safety Board (NTSB) on improving highway safety, and works with the EPA, the FTC, and the Department of Justice on enforcement issues.

PROGRAMS

The NHTSA is a program-based agency; that is, the vast majority of its activities are carried out through special programs. Because there are so many, those mentioned here are but a sampling; current information about the full spectrum of programs is available on the agency's Web site.

The Auto Safety Hotline is a major NHTSA program and has been designed as its "single point of contact" with the public. It is the agency's primary channel for disseminating information. The public can call and request information from operators who speak English or Spanish, or material can be ordered through the hot line's automated system. The hot line also takes complaints about vehicle safety and therefore serves as an important resource in enabling the NHTSA to pinpoint defects and initiate investigations.

The Buckle Up America program is the result of a presidential initiative to bring American seat belt use up to the level of other nations, especially those in Europe. Its primary goals are to increase national seat belt use to 85 percent by 2000 and to 90 percent by 2005 (from 68 percent in 1996) and to reduce occupant fatalities among children four years old and younger by 15 percent by 2000 and 25 percent by 2005. Materials for individuals interested in participating at the local level are available on-line from the NHTSA.

A four-point plan has been developed to achieve these goals, including building partnerships in the public and private sectors, enacting strict legislation in the states, high-visibility enforcement of seat belt laws, and expansion of public education efforts about seat belt and child seat use. Step two is considered an especially high priority; it calls for all states to enact primary seat belt laws. In states with primary seat belt laws, police can stop and ticket motorists for not wearing seat belts, whereas motorists in states with secondary laws can be cited for failing to wear seat belts only if they were stopped for another offense. In early 1998, 12 states and the District of Columbia had primary seat belt laws, 37 had secondary laws, and New Hampshire did not require seat belt use.

The Special Crash Investigation (SCI) program has been in effect since 1972 and provides the agency with its most in-depth information about crashes. Data are collected on 50–75 key crashes annually from routine police and insurance reports and from detailed reports produced by special investigation teams. Historically, key crashes have primarily been those involving school buses and occupant restraint systems, like seat belts or air bags. The data analyzed include information on occupants, their injuries, road conditions, and safety equipment. By their nature, SCI studies provide engineers with anecdotal rather than statistical information.

BUDGET:

National Highway Traffic Safety Administration

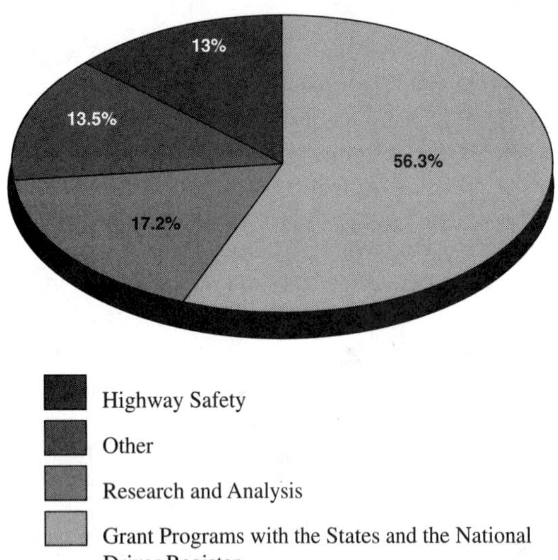

Highway Safety

Other

Research and Analysis

Grant Programs with the States and the National Driver Register

BUDGET INFORMATION

The NHTSA budget for 1998 totaled $333.28 million, just under one percent of the Department of Transportation's budget for that year. About half of NHTSA funding, $187.5 million, went toward its grant programs with the states and the National Driver Register. The next-largest amount was allocated to research and analysis, which received $57.35 million, followed by highway safety with $43.3 million. The budget proposed for 1999 would increase funding for the NHTSA by a little more than 21 percent.

HISTORY

Until the 1920s, most automobile safety initiatives originated with private industry and local government. For example, the City of Detroit introduced the first center lines on streets in 1911, the first stop sign in 1914, and the first green-yellow-red timed electric traffic light in 1919. The federal government's first involvement came in 1924 when Secretary of Commerce Herbert Hoover convened the first National Conference on Street and Highway Safety. Two years later it met again to assess its committees' work, and it issued the Uniform Vehicle Code, the first guidelines for road and vehicle safety. Similar national conferences were held during the administrations of Presidents Franklin Roosevelt, Harry Truman, and Dwight Eisenhower.

Increased attention was paid to highway safety in the 1950s, reflecting the growing fascination with automobiles, the gradual move from cities to suburbs, and increased automobile sales. In 1954 the President's Committee for Traffic Safety adopted an action program aimed at reducing accidents. Two years later, the House of Representatives held the first congressional hearings on safety. In 1959 the secretary of commerce presented a report to Congress detailing traffic safety problems and proposing an enlarged role for the federal government in dealing with them. The same year, Congress passed the first law aimed at controlling motor vehicle emissions.

Between 1925 and 1960 traffic fatalities rose steadily, matching the growth of the population: they increased from 25,000 in 1925 to 35,000 in 1960. They jumped dramatically after 1960 to 50,000 in 1966. By this time Congress was alarmed at the rise in highway fatalities. Senator Abraham Ribicoff of Connecticut used his Subcommittee on the Reorganization of Government Operations to marshal public support for federal government involvement in safety issues. Aided by the media and a dynamic aide named Ralph Nader (who would later write *Unsafe At Any Speed,* a best-selling book documenting the auto industry's perceived neglect of safety), the Ribicoff hearings resulted in the National Traffic and Motor Vehicles Act of 1966.

The act made auto design and manufacture subject to federal regulation and created an agency in the Department of Commerce—the National Highway Safety Bureau—to do the regulating. Under its first head, William Haddon, the bureau issued twenty new-vehicle safety standards by the beginning of 1967. In 1967 the bureau was transferred out of the Commerce Department and into the newly crated Department of Transportation, a move intended to give the bureau greater independence from business interests. Later, the bureau was made an independent agency within the Department of Transportation, and its name was changed to the National Highway Traffic Safety Administration.

Air Bags and Seat Belts

John Volpe, Secretary of Transportation under President Richard Nixon, was interested in air bags as a vehicle safety device and ordered the NHTSA to study the feasibility of making them mandatory on all cars beginning in 1972. Concern over a range of issues—reliability, cost, and the state of development of air bag technology—caused the NHTSA to repeatedly push back the deadline for implementation. In 1976 a test program was initiated in which 500,000 vehicles during 1979 and 1980 were to be equipped with air bags. In 1977 President Jimmy Carter's transportation secretary, Brock Adams, announced that air bags would have to be built into all American cars over the next three years. Neither of these programs came to pass.

In the 1970s the NHTSA had issued seat belt standards and in 1973 the agency required car makers to begin equipping vehicles with the seat-and-shoulder-harness style belts rather than the airline-style seat belts that were standard at that time.

In July 1984 Transportation Secretary Elizabeth Dole issued new goals for the implementation of air bags in vehicles—10 percent in 1987 and 100 percent by 1990—but those deadlines were also eventually pushed back. One hundred percent implementation did not happen until 1997.

FAST FACTS

More than 60 percent of people killed in automobile crashes were not wearing seat belts.

(Source: Joan Claybrook. "Congressional testimony," October 29, 1997.)

CURRENT POLITICAL ISSUES

The NHTSA is concerned with a broad range of traffic safety issues. It is an outspoken advocate of strict drunk-driving laws and strict enforcement of those laws. The agency has been active in promoting public awareness of the dangers of substance abuse on the nation's roads and highways. The NHTSA has worked toward higher standards of safety for school buses. It plays an important role in gathering information on vehicle defects and enforcing manufacturer recalls. But one of the most visible and controversial issues it has been involved in is the use of air bags.

Case Study: Deadly Air Bags

In 1991 Congress passed a bill that instructed the NHTSA to require that 95 percent of all passenger cars and light trucks manufactured after August 31, 1996, be equipped with driver and passenger air bags, and 100 percent as of September 1997. Since their introduction air bags have saved an estimated 1,600 lives, but in 1996, around the time laws mandating air bags went into effect for the first time, it was reported that at least 34 children and 20 adults had been killed when their air bags deployed, often in low-speed accidents. Most of the adults, it was later established, were of small stature, and air bags that would normally strike a man in the chest were striking small children and women in the neck, particularly if they were too close to the dashboard.

The NHTSA suggested two responses to the problem: air bags could be designed to deploy with 20 to 35 percent less explosive impact, or switches could be installed to enable drivers to turn off an air bag for someone at risk. Automakers agreed that some bags needed to be less forceful but maintained that they were blocked from producing such air bags because laws required all air bags to be able to catch a 170-pound male dummy not wearing a seat belt when a car crashes into a wall at 30 miles per hour. Automakers urged the government to legalize the slower bags instead of on-off switches. Widespread use of the switches would result in more deaths than lives saved, they argued, and automakers and dealers feared they might be the target of lawsuits if people were killed because of disabled air bags. The NHTSA aggressively advocated switches, saying they would be an interim measure until "smart" air bags could be developed. Such bags would have sensor/actuator systems to register the height, weight, and position of the occupant as well as whether or not the occupant's seat belt is fastened. In an accident smart air bags would modify deployment accordingly. But manufacturers argued convincingly that smart air bags were an unproved technology as well as an expensive one and would result in more expensive automobiles, a prospect unwelcome to carmakers.

In summer 1997, with the support of President Bill Clinton, the NHTSA prepared to make public a plan that would allow drivers to deactivate air bags. The plan drew criticism from an unlikely coalition of allies—the auto industry and consumer activists, who in August 1997 sent a letter to Transportation Secretary Rodney Slater citing a study showing that, during the previous year, deactivated air bags would have resulted in the death of 82 people who survived crashes.

In the first nine months of 1997, automakers, air bag suppliers, insurers, and safety advocates put pressure on NHTSA Administrator Ricardo Martinez by appealing to Secretary Slater and Congress and taking out newspaper ads. Martinez had the president's support however, with Clinton on record supporting the air bag switch plan as early as December 1996.

Then in September 1997 a 12-year-old boy, properly restrained with a seat belt in the front seat of his parents' minivan, was killed when a deploying air bag broke his neck as he reached for a tissue on the floor. The fluke death seemed to show, contrary to auto industry claims, that even a properly belted occupant could be seriously injured by air bags. In its wake, the NHTSA notified state agencies to expect rules on "temporary disconnections" of air bags. The agency assured manufacturers that the plan would be accompanied by a vigorous publicity campaign to educate motorists on the use of air bags and the circumstances under which they should be deactivated.

In November 1997, the DOT and the NHTSA announced that switches would be permitted in certain limited circumstances. They would be allowed for adults who must put children in the front seat because they are in a carpool and require the use of all front and back seats; for drivers who cannot sit far enough from the air bag, generally because of height; for children or adults with medical problems that require monitoring in the front seat; and for vehicles with no back seat. This seemed to cover the situations in which people would need an air bag cutoff switch; others are at maximum protection by buckling seat belts, keeping about ten inches between the breastbone and the air bag, never placing a rearfacing infant seat in the front seat, and seating and seat belting children in the back seat. The next day, the department presented an educational advertising campaign on the switches.

The switch first became available in January 1998. In the first two months about seven thousand people applied for the switches. That was far less than the nine million that had been predicted by the auto industry during debate over the issue but also much more than the NHTSA's prediction of one thousand. The NHTSA continued to lead an aggressive research effort aimed at developing advanced air bags that will have improved performance and will eliminate risks from air bags to all vehicle passengers.

FUTURE DIRECTIONS

The NHTSA is contributing both expertise and leadership to the Department of Transportation's Intelligent Transportation System (ITS) Project, aimed at developing an advanced highway system with intelligent transportation system technologies, including automated toll collection systems to eliminate the need for vehicles to stop at toll booths, real-time information on traffic conditions and transit schedules for travelers, and automated traffic management systems that can adjust traffic signals to respond to real-time traffic conditions. Further in the future the project aims at a vehicle/highway system equipped with sensors, actuators, and computer technology that will enable vehicles to sense and react to other vehicles on the road. Cars would then automatically maintain a safe speed and distance from other vehicles, depending on road conditions and traffic, and driving would become proportionately safer. The project, which has already received more than $1.3 billion in funding, is intended to relieve traffic gridlock and increase safety. Its first phase was completed in October 1996, and the second phase was scheduled for completion in early 1999.

The NHTSA and the Federal Highway Administration are working together to establish a uniform, nationwide cellular phone access number that motorists could call to report accidents, summon emergency medical help, or report incidents of aggressive driving. The program would be organized in conjunction with state governments and local law enforcement agencies. The NHTSA is also planning to include a flyer in the phone bills of some 20 million cell phone users to present tips on avoiding conflict with aggressive drivers.

AGENCY RESOURCES

The toll-free Auto Safety Hotline is the most important NHTSA information resource. Callers can request information on subjects like infant and child seats, tires, the safety of new car models, seat belts, and air bags. Agency publications can be obtained through the hot line as well. The hot line also takes public complaints about vehicle safety and about their general highway safety suggestions. English-speaking operators take calls from 8 A.M. to 10 P.M. Eastern Standard Time, Monday through Friday. A Spanish-speaking operator is available from 8 A.M. to 4 P.M. Outside normal business hours, an automated system takes calls and facilitates information distribution. The nationwide toll-free number is 1-888-327-4236; in the Washington, D.C., metropolitan area call (202) 366-0123. The TTY numbers for the hearing impaired are 1-800-424-9153 and (202) 366-7800 in the District of Columbia.

The NHTSA Web site is comprehensive and easy to use, with a wealth of information on vehicle and highway safety, including NHTSA reports, news, upcoming events, and databases. Complaints and recommendations can be made to the agency through the Web site as well. It can be accessed at http://www.nhtsa.dot.gov.

The NHTSA Technical Reference Division maintains a small technical library with materials on vehicle and highway safety, although there is a fee for database searches. NHTSA dockets are also maintained by the Technical Reference Division and can be examined there. The library is open from 9:30 A.M. to 4 P.M., Monday through Friday. It can be contacted at 400 7th St. SW, Room 5111, Washington, DC, 20590; Telephone (202) 366-2768; fax (202) 493-2833.

Freedom of Information requests should be filed with the NHTSA Office of the Chief Counsel at NHTSA headquarters. The telephone number is (202) 366-9511.

AGENCY PUBLICATIONS

The NHTSA produces pamphlets, manuals, information sheets, reports, videos, and posters on safety issues, including emergency medical services (EMS), impaired driving, seat belts, air bags, child passenger safety, and school bus and pedestrian safety, to name a few. It has material for all audiences as well, including elementary school students, community activists, and law enforcement personnel. A 75-page catalog of agency publications can be obtained by calling the Auto Safety Hotline at 1-800-424-9393; writing to U.S. DOT/

NHTSA, Rm. 5118, NTS-13, 400 7th St. SW, Washington, DC, 20590; or faxing NHTSA, Attn.: TSP Resource Center Orders, (202) 493-2062. Many agency publications, including technical reports issued by the Center for Statistics and Analysis, are available at the agency Web site, http://www.nhtsa.dot.gov.

BIBLIOGRAPHY

Claybrook, Joan. "Congressional testimony." House Committee on Commerce, Subcommittee on Telecommunications, Trade and Consumer Protection. 22 October 1997.

Crandall, Robert W. *Regulating the Automobile*. Washington, D.C.: Brookings Institution, 1986.

Jewett, Dale. "GM, NHTSA Battle Over Brakes," Gannett News Service, 14 January 1998.

Martinez, Ricardo. "Congressional testimony." House Committee on Commerce, Subcommittee on Telecommunications, Trade and Consumer Protection, 22 May 1997.

———. "Congressional testimony." House Committee on Transportation and Infrastructure, Subcommittee on Surface Transportation, 17 July 1997.

Nader, Ralph. *Unsafe At Any Speed: The Designed-in Dangers of the American Automobile*. New York: Grossman, 1965.

National Highway Transportation Safety Administration. *This is the NHTSA*. Washington, D.C., December 1991.

———. *Twenty-Five Years of Highway Safety*. Washington, D.C., 1991.

Recht, Philip R. "Congressional testimony." House Committee on Commerce, Subcommittee on Telecommunications, Trade and Consumer Protection, 29 October 1997.

SAE International Congress and Exposition. *Passenger Comfort, Convenience, and Safety: Test Tools and Procedures*. Detroit, Mich.: Society of Automotive Engineers, 1986.

Yanik, Anthony J. "The First 100 Years of Transportation Safety: Part 1." *Automotive Engineering*. January 1996.

———. "The First 100 Years of Transportation Safety: Part 2," *Automotive Engineering*. February 1996.

National Institute for Literacy (NIFL)

PARENT ORGANIZATION: Department of Education
ESTABLISHED: 1991
EMPLOYEES: 13

Contact Information:

ADDRESS: 800 Connecticut Ave. NW, Suite 200
Washington, DC 20006
PHONE: (202) 632-1500
TOLL FREE: (800) 228-8813
TDD (HEARING IMPAIRED): (800) 552-9097
FAX: (202) 632-1512
E-MAIL: staffasst@nifl.gov
URL: http://www.nifl.gov
DIRECTOR: Andrew Hartman
DEPUTY DIRECTOR: Carolyn Staley

WHAT IS ITS MISSION?

The National Institute for Literacy (NIFL) was created to implement the goals of the National Literacy Act of 1991 as part of the National Education Goals established in a 1990 accord between President George Bush and a conference of U.S. governors. The institute aims to provide necessary services and support to enable all adults in the United States to achieve full literacy by the year 2000. According to its mission statement, the NIFL "will advance the nation's agenda with special emphasis given to building public consensus and policy, monitoring programs, sponsoring promising initiatives, disseminating valid information on programs and research pertinent to literacy, and building interagency collaboration at the federal and state levels."

HOW IS IT STRUCTURED?

The National Institute for Literacy is a unique government body that is independent yet is closely allied with three separate cabinet departments in the executive branch: the Department of Labor, the Department of Education, and the Department of Health and Human Services. There are three components to its internal organization as mandated by Congress: the National Literacy Board, the Interagency Group, and the Director of NIFL.

The National Literacy Board is a decision-making body of ten presidential appointees, subject to Senate confirmation, who represent a cross-section of literacy activism in the United States. Some appointees are academics who specialize in adult learning issues; others are activists in national or regional literacy organizations; and still others are business or labor leaders with a particular interest in national literacy goals. They serve three-year terms, which may be extended once. Board members since 1996 have included Marciene Mattleman, former English professor and head of Philadelphia Futures, a community program for that city's youth; Toni Fay, an executive at Time-Warner, Inc. and founder of its privately funded national literacy program, "Time to Read;" and Mark E. Emblidge, executive director of the Virginia Literacy Foundation and a college administrator.

The board gives directives concerning the goals and operations of the NIFL and receives the reports submitted by the director and the Interagency Group. The board is also charged with providing guidance for NIFL staffing. They do not appoint the institute's executive and deputy directors, program staff, and administrative support but merely review names and submit recommendations.

The Interagency Group is the NIFL's second component. It is composed of the Secretary of Labor, the Secretary of Education, and the Secretary of Health and Human Services. The Interagency Group works with the Board and the director of NIFL to plan and implement the agency's literacy goals. It is also responsible for selecting the NIFL director, based on the recommendations of the board.

The director is the third and final element of NIFL's organizational structure. The director works with the Interagency Management Group, representatives of each cabinet department who help the Institute accomplish its objectives on a daily basis. They are usually deputy assistant secretaries, but they may also be planning or policy development executives.

In addition to creating the NIFL, the National Literacy Act also established State Literacy Resource Centers under the umbrella of the NIFL that provide a link between national literacy policy coordinating efforts and the organizations and individuals heading or actively working in literacy programs.

PRIMARY FUNCTIONS

The NIFL serves as a governmental nucleus for literacy efforts. Its functions were outlined in the National Literacy Act of 1991 and reflect a strong interdepartmental focus. The NIFL works with and provides guidelines to federal, state, and local agencies in coordinating various literacy efforts, policies, and specific programs. The NIFL was involved, for example, with the Department of Education's National Service project, a program initiated during the Clinton administration that used the skills of young adult volunteers in community-service projects. Welfare reform efforts within the Department of Health and Human Services were also connected with NIFL goals for full literacy.

Developing methods of tracking progress in various literacy programs is also one of the Institute's main responsibilities. Instituting and overseeing research efforts on literacy and adult-learning issues is another important task. Through its publications and standards practices, it gives assistance and training to literacy volunteers throughout the country and also tracks and promotes specific literacy programs or methods that have proven successful.

On a more interactive level, NIFL provides a toll-free telephone number, the National Literacy Hotline, for information on literacy and also grants literacy fellowships to individuals who are active in the literacy or adult-learning fields. The agency promotes literacy awareness needs in the United States to attract more adults to local literacy programs both as volunteer tutors or as potential students through public-awareness campaigns. In 1996 NIFL launched a media campaign whose slogan was "Literacy: It's a Whole New World."

PROGRAMS

The NIFL is involved with a number of programs to fight illiteracy, but as a national clearinghouse its primary focus has been the creation of an infrastructure to help fulfill the stated National Education Goal. The NIFL staff has created a national database to coordinate regional efforts with this national policy goal. Known as LINCS (Literacy Information and Communication System), it is a comprehensive on-line database primarily aimed at adult-learning professionals. Accessed at the NIFL Internet site, LINCS provides a wealth of information that includes names of literacy organizations, links to regional sites, and full-text training materials for literacy volunteers.

Literacy Leader Fellowships

NIFL provides annual grants to literacy professionals. Its Literacy Leader Fellowships are stipends awarded for a one-year period to individuals working on adult literacy projects. The fellowships recognize and fund innovative ideas that are created and carried out by literacy volunteers, adult-learning specialists, and community activists. Fellowships are reviewed and awarded by a committee of representatives of the literacy community.

Past recipients of Literacy Leader Fellowships include Leslie Shelton (1995), who directed Project Read at the South San Francisco (California) Public Library. Her project, "Focusing on Learning Strengths: The Excellence for All Model," used the theory of multiple intelligence—the recognition that intelligence can be measured in many different ways besides with traditional standardized testing—to help students determine their particular intellectual strengths. Her Literacy Leader Fellowship allowed Shelton to share, through workshops and the development of written guidelines, this diversity-focused literacy program with others in the adult-learning community.

Laura Chenven, a Literacy Leader from 1997, used her grant to investigate workplace literacy programs. The effectiveness of "learner-leaders" was the focal point of Chenven's study. She tracked the work of literacy volunteers in the Baltimore/Washington area.

National Adult Literacy and Learning Disabilities Center

Another NIFL program is an on-line help center for teachers and adults who have an interest in adult-learning difficulties such as dyslexia. The National Adult Literacy and Learning Disabilities Center provides a list of contacts, on-line discussion forums, and a look at various computer software programs aimed at such learners. It also lists regional resources for all aspects of literacy awareness.

BUDGET INFORMATION

The National Institute for Literacy receives its funding at the federal level from congressional allocations to the Department of Education. Its budget for the 1998 fiscal year was $5.5 million, up from $5 million from 1997. The increase was used to expand the LINCS computer network and to focus on reaching out to adults in literacy programs with learning disabilities. The increase was part of a greater commitment to education initiatives on the part of the Clinton administration; several million dollars were allocated to children's literacy programs as well for the same fiscal year.

HISTORY

NIFL was created in 1991 as part of the National Literacy Act passed that year. The goal of this legislative initiative was to ensure 100 percent literacy for all adults in the United States by the year 2000. The NIFL was set up to implement this goal by using the resources of the Departments of Education, Labor, and Health and Human Services. Some of the impetus for passage of the act resulted from a prior public-awareness campaign launched in 1985, Project Literacy United States (PLUS), and the efforts of Barbara Bush to publicize literacy issues during her husband's tenure as vice-president (1981–89) and president (1989–93).

A Political Football

The Bush administration opposed the 1991 National Literacy Act and its provision for the funding of the NIFL on the grounds that it would duplicate some federally-funded literacy projects already in place or scheduled to be implemented that year. Supporters of the NIFL countered by pointing out that a much wider national literacy infrastructure was needed and that existing or planned programs were not reaching enough adults with literacy needs. Furthermore, lack of any national center for literacy goals made collection of research and effectiveness data difficult.

What Is Illiteracy?

The National Literacy Act specifically defined "literacy" as part of its strategy: "an individual's ability to read, write and speak in English, and compute and solve problems at levels of proficiency necessary to function on the job and in society, to achieve one's goals, and develop one's knowledge and potential." These aims were also part of the wording for one of the National Education Goals, a set of standards created in the early 1990s to help adults in the United States meet the levels of other industrialized nations such as Germany and Japan.

CURRENT POLITICAL ISSUES

Much of the difficulty in achieving full national literacy by 2000 is related to the various federal, state, and local forces all working concurrently toward this goal, and their competition for funding. Traditionally, literacy efforts have been based in public libraries—librarians were intensely involved in program coordination efforts—but new attitudes encouraged different, nonlibrary-focused literacy efforts. The political issues surrounding NIFL and its aims reflect this change.

Case Study: NIFL and the American Library Association

One of the most pressing issues in literacy programs for adults is their low rate of effectiveness. Although libraries had been the focal point of such programs coordinated by Literacy Volunteers of America tutors and other groups, 1970s-era research determined that such programs had dropout rates as high as 70 percent. Furthermore, library-based programs failed to attract those in the community who needed literacy programs the most—those whom journalist and literacy consultant Carolyn Ebel Chandler called "the stationary poor . . . the unemployed and unemployable"—because the programs were located in libraries. As she pointed out in her article in *Editor and Publisher,* far greater progress was found in two other types of literacy programs: "participatory education" and "captive audience" literacy efforts. Participatory literacy programs used recent learners as tutors and were more often located in low-income communities, and the captive-audience classes were generally workplace literacy programs or were connected to welfare-reform programs or located within homeless shelters, prisons, or churches.

When high-ranking literacy professionals were nominated for seats on the National Literacy Board in the early 1990s, no librarians were among the nominees. In a December 1992 article in *Library Journal,* it was hinted that the ten ultimately selected were political appointees and that library professionals and the American Library Association had long campaigned for increased funding for literacy outreach programs and were now being slighted.

The 1996 National Literacy Board nominations again failed to seat a library professional, perhaps in an attempt to focus on other types of literacy programs—and especially in view of the 1998 increased budget for "captive audience" literacy efforts in prisons and in the workplace. Furthermore, the 1998 federal allocation for literacy included no funds at all under the "libraries" category. Instead, state legislatures were instructed to fund literacy programs at libraries from specific state library budgets.

SUCCESSES AND FAILURES

According to *NIFL News,* the agency's newsletter, by 1996 more than 2,200 literacy professionals had been trained in using LINCS, which allowed them electronic access to distant colleagues and increased the number of published resources available on LINCS for others to access. There are 37 individual LINCS pages at the state level, and about 120 community literacy programs coordinate their efforts and training with regional LINCS sites. These achievements dovetail with NIFL's original goal: to create the national infrastructure for full literacy.

FUTURE DIRECTIONS

Achieving full adult literacy in the United States by the year 2000 may prove to be a lofty goal, but NIFL has begun the process by which it may be accomplished. It has constructed an information superhighway with LINCS, and it continues to work on methods to track literacy program effectiveness at all levels and incorporates those findings into new policies. It also enlists help from the literacy community itself by holding focus groups and workshops at state and local levels for the tutors and learners.

One new NIFL initiative is "Equipped for the Future" (EFF). As discussed in the Spring 1997 issue of *NIFL News*, EFF-based literacy programs do not instruct from a specific curriculum, but instead attempt to integrate the individual student's abilities and needs into the learning process.

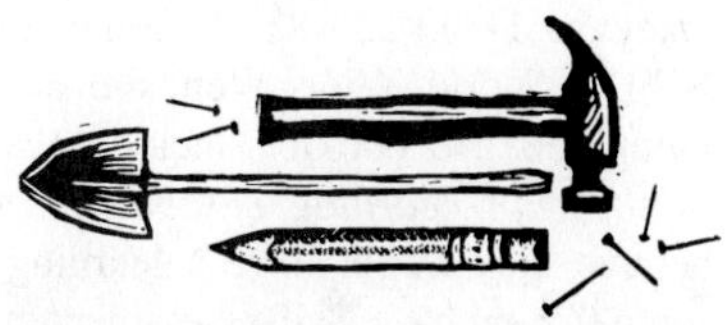

GET INVOLVED:

Top Ten Things YOU Can Do to Support Literacy: An NIFL Fact Sheet

1. Be a Lifelong Learner.
2. Encourage Others to Be Lifelong Learners.
3. Read With Your Child.
4. Volunteer to Tutor. There is a significant shortage of tutors to help adults with literacy needs. Volunteers are needed in every community and can be put in touch with local organizations by calling the National Literacy Hotline at 1-800-228-8813.
5. Volunteer to Support an Education Program in Other Ways. Literacy programs also need volunteer support staff to handle such administrative work as answering telephones.
6. Support Friends Who Want to Participate in a Literacy Program.
7. Donate Equipment or Other Materials.
8. Donate Money.
9. Start a Literacy Program.
10. Strengthen the Links Between Literacy Programs and Other Community Groups.

NIFL accepts applications for internships from eligible college students. Interns generally work with a program officer at the NIFL and can undertake a variety of projects according to individual interests. Time commitments range from 20 to 40 hours a week, and although they are unpaid internships, college credit is possible. For more information contact the NIFL at (202) 632-1515.

AGENCY RESOURCES

The National Institute for Literacy can be contacted through its toll-free National Literacy Hotline at 1-800-228-8813. Its Web site at http://www.nifl.gov provides users with access to a wealth of literacy information sources, including volunteer organizations, educational associations, directories of literacy professionals, and its own publications. Inquiries directed to NIFL staff can be E-mailed to staffasst@nifl.gov.

AGENCY PUBLICATIONS

NIFL has issued a number of publications aimed at a wide audience. All are free and can be obtained at public libraries or by contacting the National Institute for Literacy at 1-800-228-8813. Some are also available on NIFL's World Wide Web site at http://www.nifl.gov. Pamphlets and booklets include *National Resources for Adults with Learning Disabilities,* aimed at those who believe they might have a learning disability. It offers some tips on basic self-assessment, a learning disabilities checklist, and information about community educational resources that can provide further assistance. *Equipped for the Future: A Customer-Driven Vision for Adult Literacy and Lifelong Learning* gives first-person accounts of how literacy changed the lives of several individuals.

BIBLIOGRAPHY

Adult Learner Perspectives on National Education Goal #5 Guidelines. Washington, D.C.: The Institute, 1993.

Chandler, Carolyn Ebel. "In Search of a Literate America." *Editor and Publisher*, 1 September 1990.

Davis, Nancy Harvey, and Pam Fitzgerald. "Libraries and the 1991 Literacy Act." *Library Journal*, December 1992.

Equipped for the Future: A Customer-Driven Vision for Adult Literacy and Lifelong Learning. Washington, D.C.: The National Institute for Literacy, 1995.

Galvin, Thomas. "Adult Literacy Legislation on Fast Track in House." *Congressional Quarterly*, 9 March 1991.

Graff, Harvey J. *The Labyrinths of Literacy: Reflections on Literacy Past and Present.* Pittsburgh: University of Pittsburgh Press, 1995.

Johnson, James N. *Adults in Crisis: Illiteracy in America.* San Francisco: Far West Laboratory for Educational Research and Development; Andover, Mass: Network of Innovative Schools, 1985.

Kaestle, Carl F. *Literacy in the United States: Readers and Reading since 1880.* New Haven, Conn.: Yale University Press, 1991.

Literacy of Older Adults in America: Results from the National Adult Literacy Survey. Washington, D.C.: Office of Educational Research and Improvement/U.S. Department of Education, 1996.

Macedo, Donaldo P. *Literacies of Power: What Americans Are Not Allowed to Know.* Boulder, Colo.: Westview Press, 1994.

Morris, Paul M. *The New Literacy: Moving Beyond the 3 Rs.* San Francisco: Jossey-Bass, 1996.

Stuckey, J. Elspeth. *The Violence of Literacy.* Portsmouth, N.H.: Boynton/Cook Publishers, 1991.

What Other Communities Are Doing: National Education Goal #5. Washington, D.C.: U. S. Department of Education, 1992.

National Institute of Allergy and Infectious Diseases (NIAID)

PARENT ORGANIZATION: Department of Health and Human Services
ESTABLISHED: November 1, 1948
EMPLOYEES: 1,029

Contact Information:

ADDRESS: 31 Center Dr., MSC 2520
Bethesda, MD 20892-2520
PHONE: (301) 496-5717
E-MAIL: ocpostoffice@flash.niaid.nih.gov
URL: http://www.niaid.nih.gov
DIRECTOR: Anthony S. Fauci, M.D.

WHAT IS ITS MISSION?

According to the agency, the National Institute of Allergy and Infectious Diseases (NIAID) "provides the major support for scientists conducting research aimed at developing better ways to diagnose, treat and prevent the many infectious, immunologic and allergic diseases that afflict people worldwide." According to Dr. Anthony Fauci, director of the institute, NIAID strives to "further reduce the burden of disease in this country and around the world" through its commitment to "fight against infectious microbes and diseases of the immune system."

HOW IS IT STRUCTURED?

NIAID is one of the 24 branches of the National Institutes of Health (NIH), which is a branch of the U.S. Department of Health and Human Services. It consists of 10 administrative offices and five research divisions. In addition, a NIAID Council consisting of academics, researchers, practitioners, and government officials oversees the activities of the institute and shapes its overall agenda.

Administrative Offices

Ten main offices of NIAID handle the administrative duties of the institute. The Office of the Director is responsible for setting the research goals and priorities for the entire institute. It works closely with the NIAID Council, other government agencies, and private organizations to advance the state of research in this field. The Office of Clinical Research oversees the applied research

projects of the institute. The Office of Communications handles public relations and disseminates research information to the public, media, research community, and health professionals. The Office of Policy Analysis follows congressional decisions related to the institute and studies the policy implications of NIAID-sponsored research. The Office of Research on Minority and Women's Health is specially dedicated to promoting research in areas that were traditionally underrepresented. Additional offices include the Office of Administrative Services, Office of Financial Management, Office of Technology Development, Office of Human Resources Management, and Office of Technology and Information Systems, which provide the personnel, financial management, information resources, and technical support for the research programs.

Research Divisions

There are five research divisions of NIAID. First, the Division of Intramural Research is responsible for research that is conducted at NIAID. The institute runs 13 laboratories in Bethesda, Maryland, and three at the Rocky Mountain Laboratories in Hamilton, Montana. At these laboratories scientists conduct basic and applied research in immunologic, allergic, and infectious diseases. Specific areas of study include virology, parasitology, mycology, microbiology, biochemistry, and immunology. The division also conducts various clinical trials at the NIH Clinical Center.

The other NIAID divisions are dedicated to extramural research. The Division of Extramural Activities sets the guidelines and research priorities for NIAID extramural programs and oversees the grant application and funding processes. The other three divisions support specific types of extramural research.

The Division of Microbiology and Infectious Diseases supports research in eight major areas. One of these areas is the study of viral diseases, such as respiratory infections, hepatitis, and diarrheal diseases, and the development of antiviral drugs to combat such diseases. Other areas include bacterial diseases, such as Lyme disease, tuberculosis (TB), leprosy, cholera, and fungal diseases, as well as antimicrobial drug development to fight such diseases. Sexually transmitted diseases (STDs) such as gonorrhea, syphilis, genital herpes, and chlamydia constitute another major research area. In addition, the division studies parasitic diseases, such as malaria. Finally, the division also supports research in vaccine development. As part of its research agenda, this division supports the Tropical Disease Research Units and Vaccine Treatment and Evaluation Units at institutions across the country.

The Division of Allergy, Immunology, and Transplantation supports basic and clinical research on the biology, chemistry, and genetics of the immune system. It also supports transplant centers nationwide to study organ availability and preservation, as well as organ rejection. In addition, it funds research on the cause, prevention, and treatment of allergic diseases. As part of this effort, this division supports Asthma, Allergic, and Immunologic Disease Cooperative Research Centers across the country and also funds the National Cooperative Inner-City Asthma Study in six U.S. cities. Last, the division supports work in clinical immunology in order to apply basic scientific knowledge to real patients.

The Division of Acquired Immunodeficiency Syndrome (DAIDS) was established in 1986 to organize the nation's research efforts on the human immunodeficiency virus (HIV) and acquired immunodeficiency syndrome (AIDS). It supports five broad research areas. The first is HIV pathogenesis, or the biological causes of HIV-related disease. The second area is epidemiology and natural history, which seek to understand the prevalence, transmission, and clinical course of HIV. Third, the division supports vaccine and prevention research and development. The fourth area is therapeutics research and development, which aims to develop mechanisms to improve the quality and length of life of HIV-infected patients. Last, this division is dedicated to pediatric disease and studies the prevention and treatment of HIV in infants, children, and adolescents. This division supports the Centers for AIDS Research, which conduct AIDS research at academic and research institutes.

PRIMARY FUNCTIONS

The NIAID is primarily a research institute. It conducts both basic and applied research on allergic, immunologic, and infectious diseases. Some of this research is done at the institute through the Division of Intramural Research. In addition, NIAID funds extramural research at universities and research institutes across the country. This research aims to understand the immune system and related disorders. In addition to gathering knowledge, NIAID serves to translate the scientific information into clinical applications through treatment and prevention programs. To carry out its work, NIAID works closely with other NIH organizations, as well as with other research institutes, professional associations, and voluntary organizations. In addition, NIAID collaborates with many international researchers to combat diseases that span geographic boundaries.

PROGRAMS

NIAID dedicates many of its resources to the DAIDS for AIDS-related research. One of the many programs on AIDS is the AIDS Clinical Trials Information Service (ACTIS), which is cosponsored by NIAID, the Centers for Disease Control and Prevention, the Food and Drug Administration, and the National Library of Medicine. This service provides information on federally and privately sponsored clinical trials for patients with HIV and AIDS. Patients can speak with health information specialists in English or Spanish about the types of studies being conducted and how to participate. They even offer a video about clinical trials, as well as other patient information. In addition, ACTIS maintains a Web site at http://www.actis.org with links to other information resources, including two AIDS databases called AIDS-TRIALS and AIDSDRUGS.

Another DAIDS program is the HIV/AIDS Treatment Information Service, which disseminates information about federally approved guidelines for HIV and AIDS treatment. This service also has health information specialists to answer questions in English and Spanish. In addition, there is a Web site at http://www.hivatis.org that provides general treatment information, as well as treatment guidelines. This service is also cosponsored by NIAID and a variety of other health-related government agencies.

The Division of Microbiology and Infectious Diseases coordinates many research programs, such as the International Centers for Tropical Disease Research (ICTDR) Network. This program brings U.S. and foreign researchers together to share knowledge and technology to combat infectious tropical diseases. In addition, the institute fosters partnerships with private and international agencies to facilitate scholarly exchanges. The program was started in 1991, and as of 1997 it included 22 research centers around the world.

Many other institute programs are coordinated by the Office of Research on Minority and Women's Health, which was established in 1994 to improve research on diseases that disproportionately affect the health of minorities and women. The Office of Research has initiated various programs in this area, which are summarized in an on-line document called "Minority Programs and Initiatives" at http://www.niaid.nih.gov/facts/mwhhp0.htm. For example, NIAID has supported outreach activities to disseminate research results to minority communities. HIV informational booklets have been translated into Spanish, Tagalog, Korean, and Hindi and distributed to inner-city clinics, community health centers, and community-based organizations. NIAID has also created an "Asthma Awareness Day Planning Guide" for local communities and an asthma video for health care professionals describing the results of NIAID inner-city asthma studies. NIAID also promotes diabetes information because African Americans and American Indians have higher rates of diabetes than do other American populations.

BUDGET:

National Institute of Allergy and Infectious Diseases

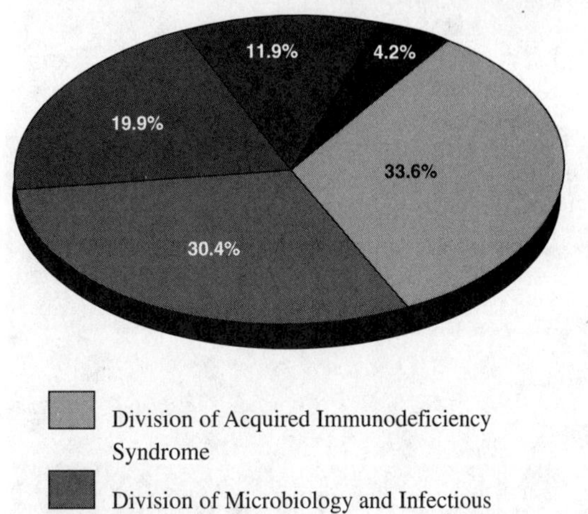

- Division of Acquired Immunodeficiency Syndrome
- Division of Microbiology and Infectious Diseases
- Division of Allergy, Immunology, and Transplantation
- Division of Intramural Research
- Research Management and Support

BUDGET INFORMATION

The NIAID budget for fiscal year 1997 was $1.258 billion. The largest share of this budget, 33.6 percent, was allocated to the Division of Acquired Immunodeficiency Syndrome. The second largest share, 30.4 percent, was given to the Division of Microbiology and Infectious Diseases. The Division of Allergy, Immunology, and Transplantation spent 19.9 percent of the total budget and the Division of Intramural Research received 11.9 percent. The remaining 4.2 percent was allocated to Research Management and Support.

HISTORY

Federal research in the areas of allergy and infectious diseases dates back to 1902 to the founding of the Rocky Mountain Laboratory and the Biologics Control Laboratory. These two facilities became part of the National Microbiological Institute on November 1, 1948, along with the Division of Infectious Diseases and the Division of Tropical Diseases of the NIH. On December 29, 1955, the National Microbiological Institute became the National Institute of Allergy and Infectious Diseases, and the Biologics Control Laboratory was separated from this institute to become a division within the NIH.

Since that time, NIAID has continued to grow to meet research demands. The institute created the Labo-

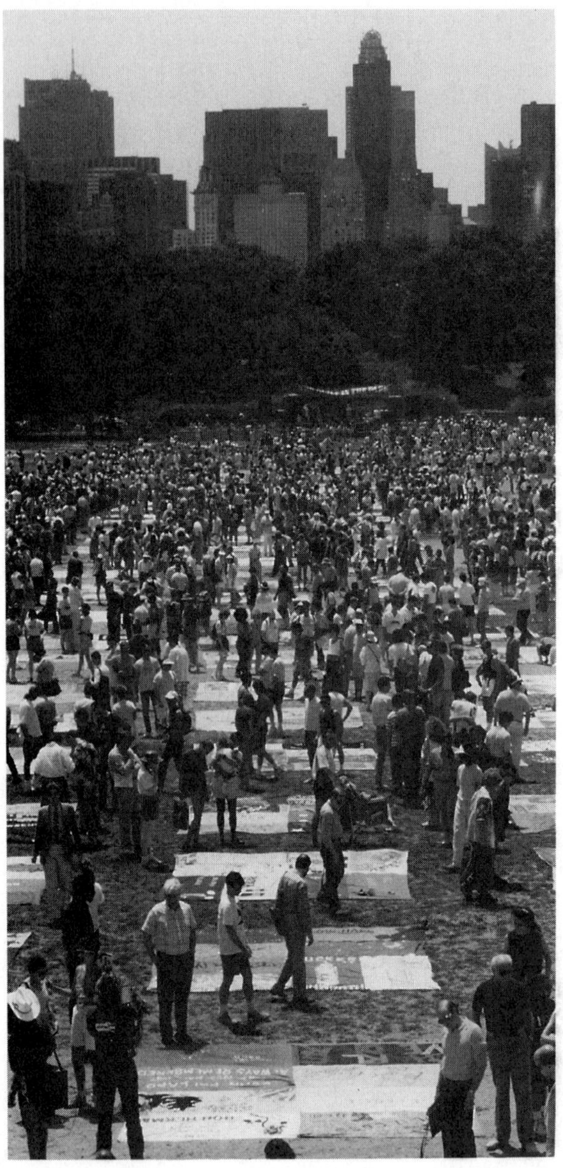

A crowd examines the New York Memorial Quilt in New York City's Central Park. The quilt's 1,500 panels bear the names and images of people who have died of AIDS. The NIAID's Division of AIDS is a leader in the federal government's efforts to find a cure for HIV. (UPI/Corbis-Bettmann)

ratory of Immunology in 1957, the Laboratory of Parasitic Diseases in 1959, and the Laboratory of Viral Diseases in 1967. In the 1970s research centers across the country were established to apply scientific research in clinical settings. In 1971 the first seven Allergic Disease Centers were founded, and in 1974 the first centers for the study of sexually transmitted diseases and of influenza were created.

Several more laboratories were founded in the 1980s, including the Laboratory of Immunoregulation in 1980, the Laboratory of Molecular Microbiology in 1981, the Laboratory of Immunopathology in 1985, and the Laboratory of Cellular and Molecular Immunology in 1987. In 1986 NIAID established its first AIDS program, which became a division in 1989.

In 1989 NIAID reorganized its programs into five major research divisions: Intramural Research; Microbiology and Infectious Diseases; Allergy, Immunology, and Transplantation; AIDS; and Extramural Activities. In the early 1990s two new laboratories were added, the Laboratory of Host Defenses in 1991 and the Laboratory of Allergic Diseases in 1994. In 1998 NIAID celebrated its fiftieth anniversary.

CURRENT POLITICAL ISSUES

NIAID studies a variety of diseases, from the common cold to long-standing life-threatening diseases such as tuberculosis to exotic tropical diseases. However, for the last decade the institute has dedicated a considerable amount of its resources to controlling the AIDS epidemic and searching for a cure. The sudden appearance of the disease, its rapid spread across the world, and the high mortality rate associated with the disease have made HIV and AIDS research a top priority for U.S. health officials and researchers.

Case Study: The Politics of AIDS

Acquired immunodeficiency syndrome (AIDS) is caused by the human immunodeficiency virus (HIV), which attacks the cells of the immune system and destroys the body's ability to fight diseases. It was first reported in the United States in 1981, and more than 500,000 cases of AIDS have since been reported. In fact, AIDS has become a major worldwide epidemic.

In response to this crisis, NIAID created the Division of Acquired Immunodeficiency Syndrome (DAIDS) in 1986. DAIDS aims to understand the biology of the disease, its life cycle, and how it is transmitted. With this knowledge, researchers can work to develop therapies and preventions, such as vaccines. Because of such research efforts, scientists now know how HIV is transmitted, what the early symptoms are, and how to diagnose the disease. In addition, great progress has been made in the area of treatments, as there are now several federally approved drugs to treat HIV infection. Researchers are currently developing and testing HIV vaccines, but until these are available, the only sure prevention against the virus is to avoid risky behaviors, such as sharing needles and having unprotected sex.

Despite the progress being made in this field, there is still no cure for the disease and it has become a worldwide problem. AIDS is such a frightening and deadly disease that there is strong public and political pressure to control it and eventually to cure it. Amidst the diverse opinions about how to deal with AIDS, NIAID has had to forge a national agenda. In doing so, the institute has been subject to criticism, both nationally and internationally.

For example, an article in the October 1994 issue of *Health Quest: The Publication of Black Wellness*, called "Race, AIDS & Economics," criticized the NIAID's funding priorities. The article reported that African Americans had been underrepresented as participants and researchers in NIAID-funded clinical trials. When the trials began in 1987, 18.7 percent of the participants were minorities. This figure rose by 1993, when 42 percent of the patients for new AIDS drugs were African Americans and Hispanics. The lack of minority participation in trials stands in sharp contrast to the overrepresentation of minorities as victims of AIDS. According to NIAID, the prevalence of AIDS in the United States is six times higher among African Americans and three times greater among Hispanics than among white Americans.

NIAID has since tried to rectify this problem by including more minorities in clinical trials. In addition, it awarded grants to Howard University, the University of Hawaii, and the University of Puerto Rico to improve the infrastructure of these minority-populated universities so that they could successfully compete for federal research money. More important, in 1994 NIAID established the Office of Research on Minority and Women's Health to improve the institute's research efforts on diseases, including AIDS, which disproportionately affect minorities or women.

SUCCESSES AND FAILURES

According to Anthony Fauci, director of NIAID, five decades of "NIAID-supported research in fields such as microbiology and immunology has led to new therapies, vaccines, and diagnostic tools that have profoundly benefited global health." For example, NIAID researchers are currently developing new approaches to prevent the rejection of transplanted organs and tissue grafts by the recipient's immune system. In the area of AIDS, HIV research has led to the development of 12 licensed antiretroviral drugs and several others are currently being tested. In addition, researchers now better understand the pathogens that attack immune systems that have been weakened by HIV. By studying the new hepatitis C virus (HCV), NIAID-supported researchers have successfully used genetic engineering to clone the virus. In the area of malaria research, NIAID has begun a new repository of malaria research materials that are available to researchers around the world. Last, NIAID scientists have made great strides in the area of vaccine research. They have developed an oral vaccine for diarrheal diseases that is expected to be licensed soon in the United States. In addition, they have had early success in the development of a nasal spray vaccine to prevent the flu.

FUTURE DIRECTIONS

In a 1998 speech to Congress, Director Fauci outlined the future directions of the institute. The three key priorities are: to expand basic and applied research of infectious diseases, the immune system, and environmental factors related to diseases; to develop new tools to prevent and control infectious diseases, including therapies, diagnostics, and vaccines; and to build the scientific expertise and resources within the United States and abroad needed to control infectious diseases. Specific examples of new directions include tackling the problem of drug resistance and keeping up with the emergence of new diseases. For example, more than three dozen new diseases have been discovered since the mid-1970s. In addition, NIAID has joined forces with the National Cancer Institute to explore the relationship between infectious diseases and certain forms of cancer. NIAID is committed to advancing vaccine development. This means improving the safety and effectiveness of current vaccines, as well as developing new ones. As part of this effort, NIAID awarded 58 grants for HIV vaccines alone and is developing a vaccine research center as part of the institute's intramural program.

AGENCY RESOURCES

General information about NIAID and its research is available through the institute's Web site at http://www.niaid.nih.gov or by contacting the Office of Communications at (301) 496-5717. Special information from the Division of Acquired Immunodeficiency Syndrome can be found at http://www.niaid.nih.gov/research/Daids.htm. This Web site includes news, conference proceedings, publications, databases, and links to related AIDS sites.

The HIV/AIDS Treatment Information Service provides information about federally approved guidelines for HIV and AIDS treatments. It can be reached by mail at PO Box 6303, Rockville, MD 20849-6303; phone 1-800-448-0440; fax (301) 519-6616; or through E-mail to atis@hivatis.org.

The AIDS Clinical Trials Information Service (ACTIS) provides information on federally funded and privately supported clinical trials for patients with AIDS and HIV infection. It maintains a Web site at http://www.actis.org or can by reached at PO Box 6421, Rockville, MD 20849-6421; phone 1-800-874-2572; fax (301) 519-6616; or E-mail actis@actis.org. For information on other NIAID clinical trials contact the NIH Patient Recruitment and Referral Service at Quarters 15D-2, 4

West Dr., MSC 2655, Bethesda, MD 20892-2655; phone 1-800-411-1222; or fax (301) 480-9793.

AGENCY PUBLICATIONS

NIAID produces newsletters, fact sheets, and other publications on a variety of topics that are freely available to the public. The three newsletters are "NIAID Council News," "Dateline: NIAID," and "AIDS Agenda." They provide thorough information about the most recent NIAID activities and AIDS research. Fact sheets and other publications cover a variety of specific diseases. Examples include "Allergies: Living with Allergies," "Chronic Fatigue Syndrome," "Malaria Research," "Sexually Transmitted Diseases: An Introduction," "Common Cold," and "Foodborne Diseases." There are a lot of publications about AIDS, such as "How to Help Yourself," "HIV/AIDS Statistics," "HIV and Adolescents," and "Women and HIV Infection." All NIAID publications are available on-line at http://www.niaid.nih.gov/publications/publications.htm or can be ordered through the NIAID Office of Communications, Bldg. 31, Rm. 7A-50, 31 Center Dr. MSC 2520, Bethesda, MD 20892-2520, phone (301) 496-5717.

BIBLIOGRAPHY

Cohen, Jon. "AIDS Research: The Rise and Fall of Project SIDA." *Science*, 28 November 1997.

Fauci, Anthony. "Global Health: The United States Response to Infectious Diseases." Bethesda, Md.: National Institute of Allergy and Infectious Diseases, 1998.

National Institutes of Health. *NIH Almanac 1997*. Publication no. 97-5. Rockville, Md., 1998.

"NIAID News: First Human Trial Shows that an Edible Vaccine is Feasible." Bethesda, Md.: National Institute of Allergy and Infectious Diseases, 1998.

"NIAID News: Nasal Spray Vaccine Prevents Both the Flu and Flu-Related Earaches." Bethesda, Md.: National Institute of Allergy and Infectious Diseases, 1998.

"Sexually Transmitted Diseases: An Introduction." Bethesda, Md.: National Institute of Allergy and Infectious Diseases, June 1998.

Smith, Shirley L. "Race, AIDS & Economics." *Health Quest: The Publication of Black Wellness*, 31 October 1994.

Stolberg, Sheryl Gay. "A Revolution in AIDS Drugs Excludes the Tiniest Patients." *New York Times*, 8 September 1997.

National Institute of Child Health and Human Development (NICHD)

PARENT ORGANIZATION: Department of Health and Human Services
ESTABLISHED: October 17, 1962
EMPLOYEES: 504

Contact Information:

ADDRESS: 31 Center Dr., Rm. 2A32
Bethesda, MD 20892-2425
PHONE: (301) 496-5133
FAX: (301) 496-7101
URL: http://www.nih.gov/nichd
DIRECTOR: Duane Alexander, M.D.

WHAT IS ITS MISSION?

The National Institute of Child Health and Human Development (NICHD) is dedicated to the health concerns of children, from the mother's pregnancy through adulthood. The mission of the institute is to ensure that "every individual is born healthy, is born wanted, and has the opportunity to fulfill his or her potential for a healthy and productive life unhampered by disease or disability." To meet this goal, the NICHD administers research, training, and information dissemination programs. According to the institute, these programs are based on "the concepts that adult health and well-being are determined in large part by episodes early in life, that human development is continuous throughout life, and that the reproductive processes and the management of fertility are of major concern, not only to the individual, but to society."

HOW IS IT STRUCTURED?

The NICHD is one of 24 branches of the National Institutes of Health (NIH), which is part of the U.S. Department of Health and Human Services (HHS). The NICHD is composed of six major divisions: the Center for Research for Mothers and Children (CRMC); the Center for Population Research (CPR); the National Center for Medical Rehabilitation Research (NCMRR); the Division of Intramural Research; the Division of Epidemiology, Statistics, and Prevention Research; and the Division of Scientific Review.

The CRMC supports biomedical and behavioral research that promotes healthy pregnancies and births. It

is composed of six branches. The Endocrinology, Nutrition, and Growth branch focuses on the nutritional and hormonal needs of pregnant women, fetuses, and children. The Human Learning and Behavior branch supports research in developmental psychobiology, behavioral pediatrics, cognitive processes, communication, social and emotional development, and health-related behaviors. The Mental Retardation and Developmental Disabilities branch concentrates on the diagnosis, treatment, and prevention of mental retardation and other disabilities. The Developmental Biology, Genetics, and Teratology branch studies congenital malformations, genetics, and the development of the immune system. The Pregnancy and Perinatology branch is concerned with pregnancy, maternal health, embryonic development, fetal growth, and infant health. The Pediatric, Adolescent, and Maternal AIDS branch supports research on acquired immunodeficiency syndrome (AIDS), particularly its effects on pregnant women, fetuses, and children.

The CPR conducts research in reproductive biology and family planning. It consists of four branches. The Reproductive Sciences branch studies reproductive biology and medicine related to fertility. The Contraceptive Development branch develops safe and effective means to control fertility. The Contraceptive and Reproductive Evaluation branch studies and reviews contraceptives, gynecological products, medical devices, and surgical procedures. The Demographic and Behavioral Sciences branch focuses on the social, psychological, economic, and environmental factors related to population change.

The NCMRR is concerned with the health care of people with disabilities. It aims to restore or improve abilities lost because of injury, disease, or medical disorder. This center consists of two branches: the Applied Rehabilitation Medicine Research branch and the Basic Rehabilitation Medicine Research branch.

The Division of Intramural Research conducts basic science and clinical research at the NICHD. The division sponsors six major clinical research and training programs in the areas of genetics, endocrinology, maternal-fetal medicine, vaccine development, and behavioral development, and also sponsors eleven fundamental research laboratories.

The Division of Epidemiology, Statistics, and Prevention Research conducts epidemiological work in areas such as infant mortality, childhood injuries, pediatric diseases, and community-based interventions. It consists of four branches: Biometry and Mathematical Statistics, Epidemiology, Computer Sciences, and Prevention Research.

The final component of the NICHD is the Division of Scientific Review. It develops the policy guidelines for the institute and coordinates the overall direction of research. In addition, it is responsible for grant applications and contract proposals.

PRIMARY FUNCTIONS

The NICHD addresses issues of child health and human development through research, training, and public information dissemination. In particular, according to the institute, the "NICHD supports and conducts basic, clinical, and epidemiological research on the reproductive, neurobiological, developmental, and behavioral processes that determine and maintain the health of children, adults, families, and populations." The institute conducts its own research on the campus of the NIH, and it also supports research at universities, hospitals, and research institutes throughout the United States through grants and contracts. The NICHD is also committed to training public health professionals and informing researchers, practitioners, and the public of particular health concerns and developments in the field.

PROGRAMS

The NICHD sponsors two major educational programs. One is the "Milk Matters" campaign, designed to warn teens of the dangers of low calcium consumption and encourage them to drink more milk. A significant part of this long-term education campaign is the "Crash Course on Calcium," designed by a coalition of the federal government, the private sector, and medical organizations. This campaign seeks to educate teens and parents through videos, print advertisements, brochures, teacher's guides, and a special Web site.

The second educational program is the "Back to Sleep" campaign, which was started in 1994 to inform the public about sudden infant death syndrome (SIDS). Popularly known as crib death, SIDS is the sudden and inexplicable death of an apparently healthy infant typically occurring between the ages of three weeks and five months. Although the causes and cure of the disease are unknown, there are certain things that can be done to reduce the risk of SIDS. The "Back to Sleep" campaign was designed to inform the general public of these risk-reducing methods. Educational materials are available through the Internet and in print form from the NICHD.

In addition to these educational programs, the NICHD also sponsors the Pediatric Pharmacology Research Network Unit to study drug action in children. It conducts research on pediatric drugs and informs the public of its findings through publications such as *A Child is Not Just a Miniature Adult.*

The NICHD also sponsors clinical trials relating to glandular, reproductive, and genetic problems in children and adults. These trials allow researchers to better understand these diseases and develop new diagnostic tests and treatments.

BUDGET INFORMATION

The NICHD budget for 1997 was $631.3 million. Of this amount, 83.1 percent was spent on extramural research, 12.6 percent on intramural research, and 4.3 percent on research management and support. The extramural research appropriation was divided among three major research areas. Population research received 26.6 percent of the total NICHD budget, Research for Mothers and Children received 52.9 percent, and Medical Rehabilitation Research was allocated 3.5 percent. The estimated 1998 NICHD budget of $674.8 million is almost a 7 percent increase over 1997.

BUDGET:

National Institute of Child Health and Human Development

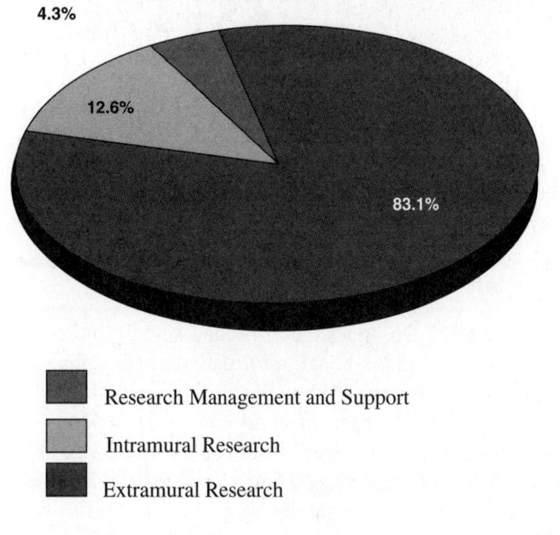

Research Management and Support

Intramural Research

Extramural Research

HISTORY

In 1961 the Task Force on Health and Social Security recognized the need for an institute dedicated to children's health. However, the law at that time only allowed for the creation of institutes that focused on a particular disease. That was changed on October 17, 1962, with Public Law 87-838, which allowed for the establishment of an institute committed to maternal health, child health, and human development. In January 1963 the secretary of health, education, and welfare approved the establishment of the NICHD, and five months later the surgeon general appointed the first members of the National Advisory of Child Health and Human Development Council.

In 1965 a major reorganization of the NICHD established four key program areas: reproduction, growth and development, aging, and mental retardation. Two years later another reorganization separated intramural and extramural research and created seven intramural research laboratories. In 1968 the Center for Population Research was founded, and in 1975 the Center for the Research for Mothers and Children was established. In 1985 the NICHD formed research networks of neonatal intensive care units and maternal-fetal medicine units to provide faster and more effective systems of neonatal and maternal-fetal care. Four years later the institute established the first American research center focused on learning disabilities. In 1990 the National Center for Medical Rehabilitation Research was established, and it awarded its first research grants in 1992. In 1997 the NICHD celebrated its 35th anniversary.

CURRENT POLITICAL ISSUES

Research at the NICHD directly affects social policy in many ways. The health and care of children is a subject of great importance to most Americans, and the NICHD is the source of much of the research into factors affecting a child's health. For example, NICHD research is shaping the debate around the politically hot topic of child care.

Case Study: The Consequences of Child Care

In 1980, according to the U.S. Bureau of the Census, 38 percent of mothers ages 18 to 44 who had infants less than one year old worked outside the home. This number increased to 50 percent by 1990, according to a 1997 NICHD report. Given that so many mothers now return to work soon after childbirth, early childhood care has become an important social and political issue. Parents and politicians alike are struggling to find quality child care that is affordable and easily accessible for all Americans. Various media reports, however, illustrate the difficulties that many American families are having. For example, *Money* magazine reported in January 1998 that "middle-class kids are at greater risk of receiving care that is unsafe and inappropriate for their age in daycare centers than are lower-income and upper-income children." This situation exists because upper-income families can pay more to ensure better care, and lower-income families qualify for day care that is subsidized by the federal government and therefore meets strict federal standards. To date there are no national standards for private child care.

As one means of addressing the child care problem, President Bill Clinton announced a child care package in

FAST FACTS

The Census Bureau estimates that in 1996, 10.6 million children were not covered by health insurance for the full year.

(Source: Anamaria Wilson. "Features/Investing in Children." *Money*, January 1, 1998.)

January 1998. This package consisted of $21 billion in federal grants and tax benefits for parents and businesses to pay for child care. Although this plan sounds like it could reduce the burden of child care, it is opposed by many politicians and other Americans who do not support subsidized child care. They worry that nonparental child care in general might not be best for a child's emotional, social, and cognitive development, and is only made worse by low-quality child care. According to a January 1998 article in the *National Review*, "a growing number of child development experts have joined the ranks of parents who worry that extensive day care is not good for young children." The article supports this claim with evidence that child care has negative consequences on children's well-being. These negative effects are both physical (such as increased risk of infections) and behavioral (such as producing increased signs of aggression and disobedience and decreased security and attachment).

However, not all researchers agree that child care is bad for children. As part of an effort to increase knowledge about the consequences of child care, the NICHD launched the Study of Early Child Care in 1991 in conjunction with fourteen universities. This longitudinal study enrolled more than 1,300 families with children less than one month old from ten areas throughout the United States. The plan was to follow these families and their child-care arrangements until the children reached age seven. According to the NICHD, "the study was spurred by the many questions from parents, developmental psychologists, and policymakers about the effects of early child care on children's development."

The first report from this study was released in April 1996. It analyzed the effects of child care on children's attachment to mothers at age fifteen months and found neither positive nor negative effects. In April 1997 the second report from this study claimed that "the quality of child care for very young children does not matter for their cognitive development and their use of language." The criteria used to measure quality child care were the level of positive caregiving and the degree of language stimulation, particularly how much caregivers talked to the children. The effect of quality child care on children's performance on cognitive and language tests was positive but small. A combination of other factors, such as family income and home environment, was stronger than the quality of child care in predicting performance on these tests.

This well-developed, comprehensive NICHD study may help researchers answer many of the questions surrounding the issue of child care, and the preliminary results seem to indicate that child care is not necessarily bad for children. However, not everyone has interpreted the NICHD results in a positive light. One observer, writing in the *National Review* in January 1998, interpreted the findings as suggesting that "most children now placed in early day care are at intellectual risk." The study has been criticized for its definition of child care, and questions have been raised regarding how well the families studied represent most American families. Although the NICHD study increased knowledge of the consequences of child care, many questions remain unanswered. Given the gaps in knowledge on the subject, some observers have questioned the wisdom of using government subsidies to coerce parents into using day care, saying it might worsen any negative effects of child care. Opponents of federal funding for child care support tax breaks and other incentives for a parent to stay home and care for the family's children, rather than placing the child in the care of another.

Public Impact

The NICHD Study of Early Child Care shows how federally funded research shapes social policies that directly affect the lives of American families. The research generated from this study has been central to the debate about child care in the media and has influenced parents and politicians alike. Parents who must make the best child-care provisions for their own families can use the information from the NICHD to weigh the pros and cons of their decisions. In addition, politicians use such studies to support their cases for or against particular child-care policies. The results of the Study of Early Child Care have been mostly encouraging to those who want to see the availability of child care expanded. Democrats in Congress introduced a plan very similar to President Clinton's in June of 1998.

SUCCESSES AND FAILURES

In the 35 years of its existence, the NICHD has made many significant research discoveries to improve knowledge of child health and human development. For example, NICHD scientists developed screening tests for mental retardation in newborns. The institute also led the Diabetes in Early Pregnancy Study which showed how to control a diabetic mother's blood sugar to reduce the risks of giving birth to a stillborn or malformed infant. NICHD scientists also discovered a vaccine to prevent type B meningitis, which was once the leading cause of acquired mental retardation in the United States. In addition, NICHD research has improved care for premature infants and thereby reduced infant mortality. Another significant contribution to the reduction of infant mortality by the institute is the SIDS campaign, which has helped reduce the number of SIDS cases by two-thirds since 1994.

FUTURE DIRECTIONS

In a 1998 speech to Congress regarding the NICHD fiscal year 1999 budget request, Dr. Duane Alexander, director of the NICHD, outlined the major areas of research on which the institute will focus future efforts. One of these areas is birth defects, the leading cause of infant mortality in the United States. Another area is vaccine research, particularly for *E. coli*, typhoid fever, and dysentery. Also important is gene research into the cause of premature labor. In addition, the NICHD is committed to further work in the social and developmental sciences. For example, it will continue its research into reading development and disability as well as early child care. The NICHD also plans to launch two women's health initiatives. The first will establish a group of Women's Reproductive Health Research Career Development Centers to encourage clinicians and researchers to work together. The second is a commitment to expand the knowledge of the long-term consequences of childbearing on women. The NICHD will continue its support of the Pediatric Pharmacology Research Unit Network to facilitate drug testing in children; it plans to expand its seven test sites to ten.

AGENCY RESOURCES

Most information about the NICHD, including research reports, press releases, fact sheets, and numerous other publications, can be obtained through the Public Information and Communications Branch, 31 Center Dr., Bldg. 31, Rm. 2A32, MSC 2425, Bethesda, MD 20892-2425; phone (301) 496-5133; fax (301) 496-7101.

Specific information about clinical studies can be directed to the Patient Recruitment and Referral Service at (301) 496-4891. The Office of the Scientific Director handles information requests regarding research opportunities. The phone number for this office is (301) 496-2133; the fax number is (301) 401-0105.

Information and published materials on the "Back to Sleep" campaign against SIDS can be found on the Internet at http://www.nih.gov/nichd/news/html/patients.html or by calling 1-800-505-CRIB. Requests for materials and questions about the "Milk Matters" campaign can be directed to 1-800-WHY-MILK or http://www.whymilk.com. Teachers and students can request educational materials, such as a video featuring Olympic gold medalists, a poster, a "Clueless About Calcium" brochure, and a teacher's guide.

AGENCY PUBLICATIONS

The Public Information and Communications Branch of the NICHD publishes and freely distributes materials for the general public on a wide variety of child and developmental health issues. Many of these are available on-line; some are also available in Spanish. Examples of general publications include *Facts about Dyslexia*, *Pituitary Tumors in Children*, and *Understanding Gestational Diabetes*. Publications are available on-line at http://www.nih.gov/nichd/html/lay_pubs.html or through the Public Information and Communications branch at 31 Center Dr., Rm. 2A32, MSC 2425, Bethesda, MD 20892-2425; by phone (301) 496-5133; or fax (301) 496-7101.

The NICHD also produces a number of scientific publications, including research program reports, evaluation and assessment reports on the state of science at the NICHD, conference proceedings, and grants and contracts information. Many of these reports are available on-line at http://www.nih.gov/nichd/html/scient_pubs.html or can be obtained from the Public Information and Communications branch.

Select technical publications are also available online at http://www.nih.gov/nichd/html/publications.html or through the Public Information and Communications branch. These include the *Current NICHD Intramural Report*, *Town Meeting on Fatherhood and Fertility*, and *Public and Panel Meeting on the Reproductive Health of Gulf War Veterans*.

BIBLIOGRAPHY

"Dubious Data in 1996's News." *Washington Post*, 8 January 1997, p. H03.

Evans, V. Jeffery. "The NICHD Family and Child Well-Being Research Network." *Journal of Family Issues*, 16 September 1995, pp. 517–8.

Gallagher, Maggie. "Day Careless (Dangers of Day Care to Children)." *National Review*, 26 January 1998.

National Institute of Child Health and Human Development. "The Effects of Infant Child Care on Infant-Mother Attachment Security: Results of the NICHD Study of Early Child Care." *Child Development*, October 1997, pp. 860–79.

National Institutes of Health. *NIH Almanac 1997*. Publication no. 97-5. Bethesda, Md.: National Institutes of Health.

"Secretary Shalala Announces Partnership to Increase Teen Calcium Consumption." *NIH/NICHD News Alert*, 12 November 1997.

Wilson, Anamaria. "Investing in Children: Why Middle-Class Kids Are Losing Out." *Money*, 1 January 1998.

National Institute of Environmental Health Sciences (NIEHS)

PARENT ORGANIZATION: Department of Health and Human Services
ESTABLISHED: November 1, 1966
EMPLOYEES: 669

Contact Information:

ADDRESS: PO Box 12233
Research Triangle Park, NC 27709
PHONE: (919) 541-3345
TOLL FREE: (800) 643-4794
E-MAIL: Envirohealth@niehs.nih.gov
URL: http://www.niehs.nih.gov
DIRECTOR: Kenneth Olden, Ph.D.

WHAT IS ITS MISSION?

The National Institute of Environmental Health Sciences (NIEHS) is dedicated to studying the mechanisms and effects of environmental factors on human health. According to the institute, "Human health and human disease result from three interactive elements: environmental factors, individual susceptibility and age. The mission of the National Institute of Environmental Health Sciences (NIEHS) is to reduce the burden of human illness and dysfunction from environmental causes by understanding each of these elements and how they interrelate." To achieve this mission, the NIEHS supports biomedical research, prevention, intervention, education, and community outreach programs.

HOW IS IT STRUCTURED?

The NIEHS is one of 24 branches of the National Institutes of Health, which is a part of the U.S. Department of Health and Human Services (HHS). The director of the NIEHS is appointed by the secretary of the HHS. The institute is made up of six administrative offices and two major research divisions. The administrative offices are the Office of the Director, the Office of Communications, the Office of Equal Employment Opportunity, the Office of Institutional Development, the Office of Management, and the Office of Policy, Planning, and Evaluation.

The Division of Intramural Research is responsible for the research conducted by the institute itself. It oversees research in the basic, applied, and clinical sciences. Examples of intramural research at the institute include environmental effects on aging, respiratory disease, reproductive disorders, and cancer. The Division of Intramural Research is divided into the Environmental Biology Program, the Environmental Diseases and Medicine Program, and the Environmental Toxicology Program.

The Division of Extramural Research and Training supports environmental research outside of the institute. It provides universities, colleges, and research foundations with financial and administrative support for environmental research programs. It works through its Center Program to establish Environmental Health Sciences Centers and Marine and Freshwater Biomedical Sciences Centers at educational institutions across the country. This brings the research and applications of the institute closer to the people who benefit most from them. The two main offices of the Division of Extramural Research and Training are the Office of Program Development and the Office of Program Operations.

PRIMARY FUNCTIONS

The NIEHS is primarily a research institute. It conducts and supports research on ways the environment affects human health. These research efforts focus on both basic biomedical science and applied prevention and intervention strategies. The institute also supports programs that make this research and its benefits accessible to the general public. This includes supporting outreach programs as well as education and training programs. The NIEHS works closely with other federal agencies such as the National Institute of Cancer and the Centers for Disease Control and with other public and private universities and organizations toward the common goal of reducing the harmful effects of environmental agents.

PROGRAMS

Most NIEHS programs fall into one of several areas. Outreach programs include educational programs for parents, teachers, and students of elementary schools. Career training and education programs target institutions and individuals with projects that promote minority recruitment to the environmental health field, and training for new environmental health scientists. Intramural Research is carried out by NIEHS scientists within NIEHS labs on the subjects of environmental diseases and medicine, environmental toxicology, and environmental biology. Extramural research, to which the NIEHS lends financial support through grants, is extremely broad and includes some collaborative efforts with other agencies.

The National Toxicology Program is an example of a collaborative extramural research program. The NIEHS coordinates the National Toxicology Program, which is a joint project of the NIEHS, the Centers for Disease Control and Prevention's National Institute for Occupational Safety and Health (CDC/NIOSH), and the Food and Drug Administration's National Center for Toxicological Research (FDA/NCTR). This program coordinates toxicology research and testing activities within the Department of Health and Human Services. In particular it aims to strengthen basic scientific research in toxicology and provide regulatory and research agencies and the public with important and timely information about toxic chemicals.

The main program of the NIEHS is also an external research program, the Center Program. The institute awards grants to universities to develop Environmental Health Science Centers. These centers serve to strengthen the research focus of the host university, provide the technology needed for effective research, encourage interdisciplinary collaboration, provide administrative assistance, and promote community outreach and education activities. As of 1998 the NIEHS was supporting 18 Environmental Health Science Centers at such universities as Harvard, Johns Hopkins, Massachusetts Institute of Technology, Vanderbilt, and Wayne State University. In addition, the NIEHS supports developmental centers at Columbia University, Tulane University, and the University of Louisville that focus on the health problems of underserved populations, as well as Marine and Freshwater Biomedical Sciences Centers at Duke University, Mount Desert Island Biological Laboratory, Oregon State University, the University of Miami, and the University of Wisconsin-Milwaukee.

As a requirement of the NIEHS Center Program, participants must develop and implement Community Outreach and Education Programs (COEP). These programs are specifically designed around the environmental health issues that are most important to each community. The centers work closely with other community organizations, as well as with state and local government agencies and health departments, to develop successful programs. Examples of COEP activities include a public forum on diet and cancer prevention sponsored by Oregon State University, a recycling campaign by Tulane University, and a summer intern program run by New York University.

Another major research program of the NIEHS is the Superfund Basic Research Program. This program is funded by the U.S. Environmental Protection Agency (EPA) through an interagency agreement with the NIEHS. It supports basic research efforts at universities across the country to study the health effects of hazardous substances in the environment, especially those found at uncontrolled waste disposal sites.

BUDGET:

National Institute of Environmental Health Sciences

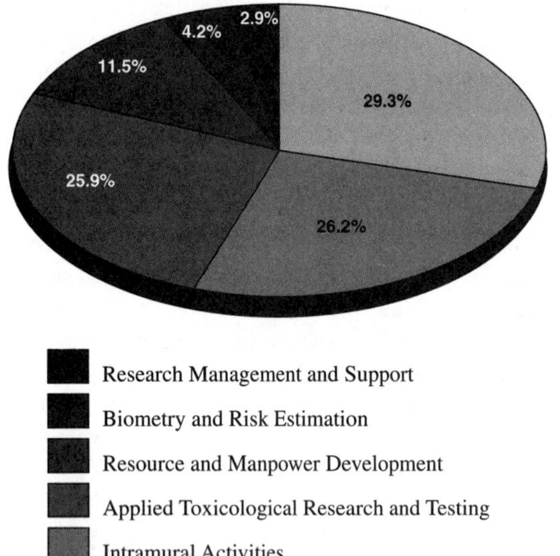

Research Management and Support
Biometry and Risk Estimation
Resource and Manpower Development
Applied Toxicological Research and Testing
Intramural Activities
Studying Biological Responses to Environmental Agents

BUDGET INFORMATION

The budget for the NIEHS must be approved yearly by Congress. The 1997 NIEHS budget was $307.6 million, an increase of almost $20 million over the 1996 budget. Of the total budget, 29.3 percent was allocated to studying biological responses to environmental agents, 26.2 percent went to intramural activities, 25.9 percent was given to applied toxicological research and testing, 11.5 percent was spent on resource and manpower development, 4.2 percent went to biometry and risk estimation, and 2.9 percent was allocated to research management and support. In 1998 the director of the NIEHS requested $313.6 million from Congress.

HISTORY

In 1961 the Public Health Service proposed the development of a national center dedicated to environmental health problems. Five years later, on November 1, 1966, the U.S. surgeon general announced the establishment of the Division of Environmental Health Sciences as part of the National Institutes of Health (NIH), and the first director, Dr. Paul Kotin, was appointed. In 1967 Research Triangle Park in North Carolina became the home of the new division. The division gained institute status in 1969, only three years after its creation. In 1971 Kotin was succeeded as the director of the institute by Dr. David P. Rall. In 1978 the National Toxicology Program was created by the secretary of Health and Human Services, and it became a permanent activity of the NIEHS in 1981. In 1990 Rall retired as director and was replaced by Dr. Kenneth Olden. The NIEHS celebrated its thirtieth anniversary in 1996 and opened a four-story laboratory addition to its research campus.

CURRENT POLITICAL ISSUES

To stay on the cutting edge of environmental health research, the NIEHS must be able to address a wide range of environmental health problems. For example, current NIEHS research projects include breast and testicular cancers, women's health issues such as osteoporosis, neurologic disorders such as Alzheimer's and Parkinson's diseases, lead poisoning, agricultural pollution, and biomarkers. In addition, the institute must keep up with a changing environment. Environmental changes can result from a number of factors, such as nature, technological advances, or social upheavals such as war.

Case Study: Gulf War Syndrome

The Persian Gulf War, in which the United States led a multinational team against Iraq to protect Kuwait, lasted from January 16 to February 27, 1991. During this brief period, 700,000 U.S. troops were sent to the Persian Gulf. Of this number, there were approximately 300 deaths and 400 injuries. Compared to the losses suffered by the Iraqis—and compared to other U.S. armed conflicts—this battle was a tremendous military success for the United States.

After troops returned from the region, however, a number of veterans reported health problems. Symptoms included "fatigue, diarrhea, skin rashes, muscle and joint pain, headaches, loss of memory, difficulty breathing, gastrointestinal and respiratory problems, and worse," according to Peter Radetsky in a 1997 article in *Discover Magazine*. As of August 1997 more than 110,000 veterans had registered with federal agencies as having what has become known as Gulf War syndrome. In addition, 1,100 of 51,000 British troops complained of similar symptoms.

The exact nature of this ailment is hard to determine because veterans have reported such varied health problems. Even more difficult to determine is the cause of the syndrome. Some investigators propose that the Gulf War syndrome is a psychological condition. For instance, several of the symptoms such as sleep disorders, memory problems, and depression, could be a result of stress. Other experts who have studied Gulf War syndrome argue that it is simply a form of post-traumatic stress dis-

BIOGRAPHY:
Martin Rodbell

Biochemist (b. 1925) Known for his discovery of G-proteins, Martin Rodbell has performed ground-breaking work in cell biology. Specifically, he helped determine how cells communicate. Until Rodbell's breakthrough, scientists strongly supported a three-step message-receptor-response communication model. But Rodbell introduced a four-step model that implied the existence of a special type of molecule, the G-protein. According to Rodbell, when adrenaline (message) reaches the receptors of a liver cell, the G-proteins enable the cell to produce an enzyme response. The activated enzymes allow the liver cells to release glucose, which increases an organism's ability to deal with stress. However, since Rodbell had not empirically proved the existence of G-proteins, the scientific community was resistant to his hypothesis. It was not until Alfred Gilman isolated these proteins that Rodbell's model became an accepted scientific paradigm. In addition, research has established that G-proteins play an important role in various cellular functions and that G-protein malfunctions underlie a number of diseases including cancer and cholera. In 1994 Rodbell received overdue international recognition when he shared the Nobel Award in Physiology or Medicine with Gilman. Rodbell worked at the National Institutes of Health (NIH) from 1956 until 1985, when he was appointed director of the National Institute of Environmental Health Sciences. He retired in 1994 as scientist emeritus at NIH. Ironically, only a few months before receiving the Nobel Award, Rodbell opted for early retirement because his institute was suffering from insufficient funding. Rodbell's other awards include the NIH Distinguished Service Award (1973) and the Gairdner Award (1984).

---

order, a problem fairly common among veterans returning from combat.

Other researchers, however, argue that Gulf War syndrome is a result of environmental, especially chemical, factors. Troops in the Gulf were exposed to large doses of a variety of chemicals. Petroleum was used for fuel and heating; it was also expelled from large oil-well fires in Kuwait. Pesticides and insect repellents were used generously by troops to protect themselves against desert insects. Troops were also exposed to vaccinations against common infectious diseases as well as against two biological warfare agents: anthrax and botulism toxins. Finally, there were biological and chemical weapons. It was suspected that the Iraqis possessed four different chemical weapons: mustard gas, sarin, soman, and tabun. Whether these were used, or to what extent they were used, has not yet been determined. However, the U.S. government has reluctantly admitted that thousands, and possibly hundreds of thousands of American troops might have been exposed to chemical weapons, including deadly nerve gases, when they bombed an Iraqi ammunitions building after the war. Although it is difficult to isolate the exact cause of Gulf War syndrome, some researchers argue that it is likely the result of a mixture of the various chemicals to which these troops were exposed.

Because of the inconclusive findings, many government officials refused to acknowledge that the syndrome is a true medical problem. After several years of relatively little activity, the federal government began to systematically study the Gulf War syndrome. This was in large part due to pressure from veterans' organizations. Many in the Defense Department still insist that the syndrome is at most a psychological reaction to the stress of battle. Some studies conducted in the years immediately following the Gulf War support this position, as they found that the Gulf War soldiers as a group were just as healthy as soldiers who did not serve in the war, and healthier than the general population. Other studies support the hypothesis that exposure to toxic chemicals, especially nerve gas and chemical weapons, whose ingredients can also be found in much smaller amounts in many pesticides, may be responsible for the syndrome. One study conducted on animals found that exposure to a combination of chemicals present in the Gulf leads to symptoms resembling the Gulf War syndrome, even when exposure to the individual chemicals had no negative effects.

Based on these results, and others like them, the federal government began to take the possibility of a chemical cause to the Gulf War syndrome much more seriously. Further research was necessary, however, to truly determine the causes of the syndrome and develop methods of treatment. The NIEHS was called upon in 1998 to lead the investigations into the effects of chemical exposure during the Gulf War. Having determined which areas of research are most promising, it is hoped that the

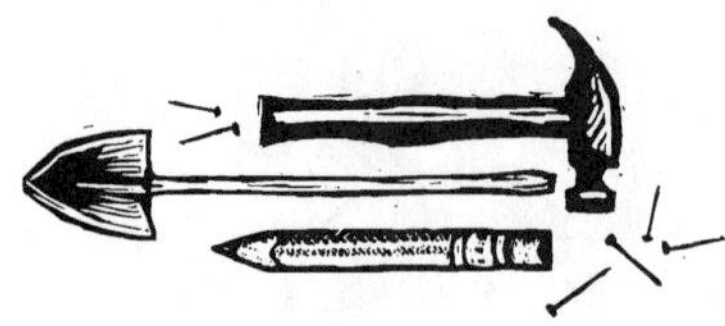

GET INVOLVED:

- The NIEHS sponsors many community outreach and education programs that involve public participation. For example, it sponsors the Summers of Discovery Program for students and teachers at high school and college levels to improve their science skills by working in an NIEHS research laboratory for two or three months during the summer. More information on the program can be obtained by calling (919) 541-3433. The program also has a Web page at http://www.niehs.nih.gov/od/k-12/discovery.htm.
- Each of the NIEHS centers conducts Community Outreach and Education Programs (COEPs) that encourage public participation. For example, the Harvard School of Public Health provides classroom education programs on lead exposure, asthma, and air pollution for fourth and fifth graders, their parents, and teachers. In addition, the centers publish the *Asthma Warriors* comic book. The NIEHS Center at Wayne State University also introduced lessons to Detroit area grade schools on environmental health issues. They sponsored a community presentation about lead poisoning called "Get the Lead Out" and organized a science summer camp called "Lab Coats and Microscopes" for young members of the community. For more information about NIEHS center COEP activities in individual communities, see the list of activities for each center on the Internet at http://www.niehs.nih.gov/centers/coep/coepcur.htm or call NIEHS at (919) 541-3345.

grants provided by NIEHS to private investigators will someday find a cure to this mysterious disorder.

SUCCESSES AND FAILURES

Throughout its brief history, the NIEHS has made great strides in understanding how the environment affects human health. For example, in 1979 NIEHS supported researchers who discovered that exposure to low levels of lead during early childhood could delay cognitive and behavioral development. Ten years later, NIEHS-funded studies showed how asbestos can damage lung tissue. In 1994 NIEHS scientists were part of the team that discovered the first breast cancer susceptibility gene. NIEHS-sponsored research led to the awarding of a Nobel Prize in 1994. Dr. Martin Rodbell, an NIEHS scientist, was the corecipient of the 1994 Nobel Prize in physiology and medicine for his work on the communication system that regulates cellular activity. In 1997 the NIEHS continued to enjoy many research successes, including cloning the breast cancer gene and identifying enzymes related to leukemia.

FUTURE DIRECTIONS

At the first National Children's Environmental Health Conference, Dr. Kenneth Olden, the director of the NIEHS, outlined the future directions of the institute. He announced a "vision for environmental health research that will transform the environmental health decision making process, a vision based on investment in four critical areas of science where major information gaps exist."

The first of these areas is genome research, which can identify which genes are susceptible to environmentally induced diseases. The NIEHS has begun a new Environmental Genome Project to learn more about DNA diversity among Americans and try to understand why there is so much individual variation in response to environmental factors. The second information gap Olden plans to address concerns the ways to determine what kinds of chemicals people are exposed to and in what amounts. He proposes developing new screening strategies to improve information in this area. The third focus is on chemical combinations. Most toxicology research studies the effects of a single chemical, whereas future research will be devoted to understanding how chemicals interact with one another in mixtures. The final area of improvement for the NIEHS is the monitoring of human exposure to specific chemicals. The goal is to use new survey technology, such as the National Center for Health Statistics' National Health and Nutrition Examination Survey, to measure "real world" exposure to dangerous chemicals.

AGENCY RESOURCES

The NIEHS environmental health information service (NIEHS.ehis) is the main information dissemination program of the institute. It provides access to information about the environment, toxicity, and cancer through publications and electronic databases. Some services are freely available to the public, but others are reserved for subscribers. More information about the services available and their cost can be obtained from NIEHS.ehis by phone, (919) 541-3841; fax, (919) 541-0273; or E-mail, ehis@niehs.nih.gov. The service is available on-line at http://www.niehs.nih.gov/docs/admin/statement.html.

The NIEHS also maintains an on-line library at http://library.niehs.nih.gov/home.htm. This Web site provides links to electronic journals, reference resources, database search engines, photocopy requests, and NIEHS publications.

NIEHS also sponsors the Environmental Health Clearinghouse of information on electric and magnetic fields. The clearinghouse provides publications and answers questions through the EMF Infoline at 1-800-643-4794, or 1-800-363-2383, or envirohealth@infoventures.com.

AGENCY PUBLICATIONS

The official publication of the NIEHS is the journal called *Environmental Health Perspectives*, which largely publishes technical articles about advances in research. It is available through the Environmental Health Information Service (NIEHS.ehis) by phone, (919) 541-3841; fax, (919) 541-0273; or E-mail, ehis@niehs.nih.gov. The service is also available on-line at http://www.niehs.nih.gov/docs/admin/statement.html.

For the general public NIEHS publishes environmental fact sheets and pamphlets, such as "Lead and Your Life," "Medicine for the Layman—Environment and Disease," and "Reaching Out to Help Our Communities." A list of publications, as well as full-text documents of many of the fact sheets and pamphlets, are available on-line at http://www.niehs.nih.gov/oc/factsheets/fsmenu.htm or by calling the Office of Communications at (919) 541-3345.

NIEHS press releases and news updates, as well as National Toxicology Program updates, are available on-line at http://www.niehs.nih.gov/oc/news.home.htm or by calling the Office of Communications at (919) 541-3345.

BIBLIOGRAPHY

Cook, Allan R. *Environmentally Induced Disorders Sourcebook.* Detroit: Omnigraphics, 1997.

"Darkness at Noon." *The Economist*, 11 January 1997.

Getler, Warren. "Scrutiny of Pesticides Comes None Too Soon." *USA Today*, 24 March 1998, p. 13A.

"How Do You Study Environmental Health?" NIEHS fact sheet no. 2, August 1996.

National Institute of Environmental Health Sciences. "Lead—The No. 1 Environmental Hazard to Many Children." NIEHS fact sheet no. 8, March 1997.

National Institute of Environmental Health Sciences. "Reaching Out to Help Our Communities." NIEHS fact sheet no. 25, March 1997.

National Institutes of Health. *NIH Almanac 1997.* Publication no. 97-5. Rockville, Md., 1997.

Odum, Eugene Pleasants. *Ecology: A Bridge Between Science and Society.* Sunderland, Mass: Sinaeur Associates, 1997.

Radetsky, Peter. "The Gulf War Within (Gulf War Syndrome)." *Discover Magazine*, August 1997, p. 68.

Romano, Jay. "Taking the Measure of Lead-Paint Hazards." *New York Times*, 15 June 1997.

"U.S. HHS: NIEHS Establishes Environmental Health Information Service on the Internet." *M2 PressWIRE*, 16 December 1997.

U.S. House of Representatives. Appropriations Subcommittee Hearings. "Statement of Kenneth Olden, Director," NIEHS. 1998.

National Institute of Mental Health (NIMH)

PARENT ORGANIZATION: Department of Health and Human Services
ESTABLISHED: April 15, 1949
EMPLOYEES: 833

Contact Information:

ADDRESS: 5600 Fishers Lane
Bethesda, MD 20892-8030
PHONE: (301) 443-3673
FAX: (301) 443-0008
E-MAIL: nimhinfo@nih.gov
URL: http://www.nimh.nih.gov
DIRECTOR: Steven E. Hyman, M.D.

WHAT IS ITS MISSION?

The National Institute of Mental Health (NIMH) is the federal government's primary research agency investigating the brain and mental health. It is dedicated to understanding, treating, and preventing mental and brain disorders. According to the director of the institute, Dr. Steven Hyman, the "NIMH is the foremost mental health research organization in the world, with a mission of improving the treatment, diagnosis, and prevention of mental disorders such as schizophrenia and depressive illnesses, and other conditions that affect millions of Americans, including children and adolescents."

HOW IS IT STRUCTURED?

The NIMH is one of the 24 branches of the National Institutes of Health (NIH), which is part of the U.S. Department of Health and Human Services (HHS). The NIMH consists of five administrative offices and five research divisions. The institute's activities are overseen by the National Advisory Mental Health Council, which is composed of educators, researchers, and government officials interested in the direction of mental health care and research in the United States.

Administrative Offices

There are five main administrative offices of the NIMH that coordinate the institute's activities. The Office of the Director sets the overall goals and research priorities for the institute and develops the institute's policies. The Office of Legislative Analysis and Coordination monitors legislative action related to mental health and works with Congress to develop mental health policies. The Office of Scientific Information makes sure that new and accurate research information is disseminated to the public, the media, the research community, and health care workers. The Office of Resource Management oversees financial and personnel management and provides information resources and technical assistance to other NIMH departments. The Office of Science Policy and Program Planning develops mental health research policies and programs.

In addition to these main offices, the Office of the Director is further divided into five offices that focus on special areas. The Office of Prevention directs research and communication solely on mental illness prevention. The Office of Equal Employment Opportunity is responsible for ensuring that NIMH employment policies and practices follow equal employment opportunity guidelines. The Office of Rural Mental Health Research ensures that important information and mental health services reach people living in rural areas. A fourth division, the Office on Acquired Immunodeficiency Syndrome (AIDS) places special emphasis on studying the relationship between AIDS and central nervous system disorders and helping mentally ill patients who suffer from AIDS. The fifth office is the Office for Special Populations.

Research Divisions

The NIMH also maintains five research divisions. The Division of Extramural Activities funds mental health research conducted at universities and other research organizations. It issues program announcements to let the research community know the kinds of studies the NIMH would like to fund. It also oversees the grant review process. The Division of Intramural Research Programs directs the research activities carried out at the NIMH. The institute's research is conducted at three main facilities located on the NIH campus in Bethesda, Maryland, at St. Elizabeth's Hospital in Washington, D.C., and at the NIH Animal Center in Poolesville, Maryland. Research is conducted in such areas as socioenvironmental studies, genetics, pharmacology, preclinical neuroscience, and cognitive neuroscience. The Division of Basic and Clinical Neuroscience Research aims to better understand the causes, treatment, and prevention of brain disorders. Its four main areas of research are behavioral and integrative neuroscience, molecular and cellular neuroscience, genetics, and therapeutics. The Division of Services and Intervention Research focuses on prevention and treatment interventions, services research, and diagnostics. It assesses how well services work in practice and develops more effective and efficient means of treating mentally ill patients. The Division of Mental Disorders, Behavioral Research, and AIDS is concerned with the relationship between AIDS and mental disorders as well as how AIDS affects mentally ill patients. It conducts research in behavioral science, developmental psychopathology, prevention, and early intervention.

FAST FACTS

In developed countries such as the United States, four of the ten leading causes of disability are mental disorders.

(Source: National Institute of Mental Health. "Fiscal Year 1999 President's Budget Request.")

PRIMARY FUNCTIONS

The NIMH is primarily a research institute. It conducts both intramural and extramural research on mental disorders, neuroscience, and behavior. The intramural program employs scientists from around the world to conduct research at NIMH facilities. These scientists conduct basic and clinical studies on the causes and treatments of mental illness. The NIMH also supports the work of scientists at universities and other research facilities across the United States and abroad who are conducting biological, behavioral, clinical, economic, and social research on mental illness. The extramural program provides funding for research through individual research grants, cooperative grants, research center development grants, and fellowship and career development awards. In addition to these research activities, the NIMH collects, analyzes, and distributes statistical information on the occurrence of mental illness and its causes. It is also dedicated to training scientists in the mental health field, especially in areas experiencing staffing shortages. The NIMH disseminates information on mental health, mental illness, and the brain to the public, the media, researchers, and health care workers. This involves producing print materials, videos, films, and radio and television public service announcements. In addition, the NIMH responds to information requests from the public and works with other government agencies and private organizations in the mental health field.

PROGRAMS

Aside from the research activities conducted by the various branches of the NIMH, the institute sponsors three major educational programs. In 1985 the NIMH established a program, Depression: Awareness, Recognition, and Treatment (D/ART), to educate the public, health care providers, and mental health specialists about

BUDGET:
National Institute of Mental Health

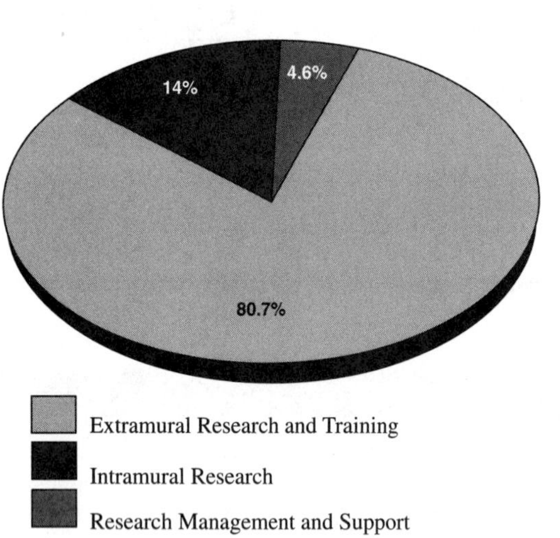

depressive illnesses. This is a cooperative public and private initiative that has brought together more than 150 professional, business, community, government, media, and private organizations to participate in the education campaign.

The D/ART program has three main components. The first is a public education campaign, which has produced a variety of publications, television and radio public service announcements, and an educational video package in several languages. This campaign also organizes educational programs with advocacy and support groups and promotes networks across state boundaries through the Community Partnership Program. The second main component of D/ART is a professional training program that provides funds to universities and professional associations to train physicians and mental health professionals to better diagnose and treat mental illness. The third component is the National Worksite Program, which educates businesses on how to manage depression in the workplace.

The second major educational program focuses on brain research. In 1990 President George Bush declared the 1990s the "Decade of the Brain" to increase public awareness about brain research. The NIMH responded by joining the Library of Congress to launch the Project on the Decade of the Brain to educate the public about how the brain works and what research is being conducted to learn more about this complex organ. The project maintains a Web site at http://lcweb.loc.gov/loc/brain. In addition, it sponsors a variety of educational activities, such as a public conference on the science of emotion, congressional breakfasts to update members of Congress about current mental health issues, and a special program series celebrating the fiftieth anniversary of the National Mental Health Act.

The third educational project sponsored by the NIMH is the Anxiety Disorders Education Program. It was developed to improve the public's understanding of anxiety disorders, reinforce the idea that anxiety disorders are real medical problems, and reduce the social stigma associated with these disorders. Many anxiety disorders have effective treatments, but they often go untreated because patients are too ashamed to seek help or because they are not properly diagnosed. The Anxiety Disorders Education Program provides information for professionals and the public so that patients with anxiety disorders can be treated and resume healthy lives. This information includes pamphlets and brochures on how to find help for anxiety disorders and information in both English and Spanish on specific disorders, as well as a list of books and videotapes and contact information for other organizations that work with anxiety disorders.

BUDGET INFORMATION

The 1997 budget for the NIMH was $603.8 million. Of this total amount, 80.7 percent was spent on extramural research and training, 14 percent was allocated to intramural research, and the remaining 4.6 percent went to research management and support. The 1998 budget estimate was $649.4 million, a 7.6 percent increase over 1997. The 1999 fiscal year estimate rose to $701.8 million, a 16.2 percent increase over the 1997 budget.

HISTORY

Mental illness became recognized as a social and medical problem in the late 1700s. Even before the United States became an independent nation, the first hospital for the mentally ill was established in Virginia in 1773. A Pennsylvania doctor, Benjamin Rush, was a leader in the mental health field around this time. He is remembered as "the Father of American Psychiatry" for his crusade against the ignorance surrounding mental illness at that time and for his efforts to improve the living conditions of patients. His crusade for the mentally ill was continued by Dorothea Dix, who led a movement in the 1800s to increase the number of insane asylums from eight to 32 to house patients who were being kept in jails and poorhouses.

Government involvement in the field of mental illness began in 1840, when the U.S. Census first tried to measure the extent of mental illness and mental retardation. In 1855 the government opened the first Government Hospital for the Insane. The government's commitment to mental health was institutionalized in 1930 with the establishment of the Narcotics Division of the Public Health Service (PHS), which later became the Division of Mental Hygiene (DMH). This was the first time that drug addiction and mental illnesses were treated as part of an overall mental health movement.

World War II (1939–45) brought public attention to mental illness as numerous men were either rejected for military service or medically discharged for neuropsychiatric disorders. After the war it became apparent that there was a critical lack of knowledge about mental illness and subsequently a severe shortage of mental health professionals. In response to this dilemma, the director of the Division of Mental Hygiene, Dr. Robert H. Felix, proposed a national mental health program to the U.S. surgeon general. This proposal was the basis of the National Mental Health Act, which was signed into law on July 3, 1946 by President Harry S Truman. The act called for the founding of the National Institute of Mental Health. However, Congress did not appropriate funds for the institute until 1948. On April 15, 1949, the DMH was formally replaced with the NIMH, one of the first four institutes of the NIH.

During the 1950s psychopharmacology was introduced as a treatment for mental illness and successfully reduced the number of patients in mental hospitals. In 1955 the Mental Health Study began to analyze the human and economic problems caused by mental illness. It resulted in a ten volume publication about mental health conditions in the United States, which was released in 1961. *Action for Mental Health* outlined a national program to address the needs of the mentally ill. In response to the information in this report, President John F. Kennedy made a special address to Congress to garner support for mental health programs. His efforts resulted in passage of the Mental Retardation Facilities and Community Mental Health Centers Construction Act, which provided government support for mental health services.

During the mid-1960s alcoholism and alcohol abuse gained public attention as a serious health problem. In 1966 the NIMH established the National Center for Prevention and Control of Alcoholism to address these problems. At the same time, the NIMH also established the Center for Studies of Narcotic and Drug Abuse to support research in this area.

The NIMH's locus within the government's structure has changed several times. In 1967 the NIMH was moved from the NIH to become a bureau of the Public Health Service (PHS). The following year it became part of the Health Services and Mental Health Administration (HSMHA) of the PHS. In 1973 the HSMHA was abolished and replaced by the Alcohol, Drug Abuse, and Mental Health Administration (ADAMHA), which contained the National Institute on Alcohol Abuse and Alcoholism (NIAAA), the National Institute on Drug Abuse (NIDA), and the NIMH.

For nearly 20 years, the NIMH operated as part of the ADAMHA. Then, in 1992, the ADAMHA Reorganization Act abolished that agency to separate research and service activities. The three institutes—the NIAAA, the NIDA, and the NIMH—rejoined the NIH in order to focus more on research. In addition, the Substance Abuse and Mental Health Services Administration (SAMHSA) was created to coordinate services for the public in the areas of alcohol abuse, drug abuse, and mental health. The NIMH has since remained a part of the NIH. In 1996 the NIMH celebrated the fiftieth anniversary of the National Mental Health Act.

CURRENT POLITICAL ISSUES

The NIMH has devoted many resources to educating the public about mental illnesses, to reduce the social stigma associated with these diseases, and to encourage patients to seek professional help. This effort has increased public awareness of many mental health problems, such as eating disorders, attention deficit disorder, and Alzheimer's disease. One disease in particular, depression, grabbed the public's attention and saturated the media during the 1990s. Improved treatments for depression have revolutionized Americans' attitudes toward this disease and toward mental illness in general.

Case Study: Finding a Cure for the Blues

According to the NIMH, depression is an illness that affects about 18.4 million Americans each year. It is a mood disorder caused by a biochemical imbalance in the brain. Its symptoms include loss of interest and pleasure in most activities, feelings of emptiness or sadness, feelings of worthlessness or guilt, fatigue, difficulty concentrating or remembering, and changes in eating or sleeping patterns. Many American still view depression as a weakness, but it is a physical disorder that can be treated.

Depression tends to occur when serotonin levels in the brain are too low (serotonin is a neurotransmitter, a chemical that carries messages within the brain). If depression occurs as a result of chemical imbalance, the treatment is to bring those chemicals back into balance by raising the serotonin level. Early research in this area led to two classes of antidepressant drugs: monoamine oxidase (MAO) inhibitors and tricyclics. Both drugs seemed to be successful in treating depression, but they had major side effects, such as extreme drowsiness and heart palpitations. Researchers learned that these side effects occurred because these antidepressants affected other neurotransmitters as well. They then began to focus on how to control serotonin alone. The result was a class of antidepressant drugs known as selective serotonin reuptake inhibitors (SSRIs).

Prozac was the first SSRI, developed in 1974 by the Eli Lilly pharmaceutical company. It was approved by the Food and Drug Administration (FDA) in 1987 and has since become one of the most widely used treatments for depression in the United States. According to a September 1997 article in the *St. Louis Post-Dispatch*, "more than 17 million Americans have used Prozac since it was first approved in 1987." Prozac's appeal has increased because scientists have realized that Prozac helps patients suffering from obsessive-compulsive disorder, panic disorders, and social phobias as well as depression.

Although the public and the media have readily embraced Prozac and the other SSRIs that have since become available, some experts are warning people to be cautious about these antidepressants and about any drug that seems to be a "cure-all" for life's problems. They worry that doctors are prescribing drugs over other treatments because they are quick and easy to administer and can be cheaper than other alternatives. They point out that researchers have shown that certain forms of psychotherapy can adjust brain chemistry as well as antidepressants can and that the long-term effects of Prozac are still unknown. In fact, researchers still have much to learn about serotonin in general.

For example, another drug that acts on serotonin and other neurotransmitters to aid in weight loss recently lost FDA approval and was pulled off the market because it led to serious heart problems in some patients. This drug, popularly known as Fen/Phen or Redux, had been used in Europe for more than 20 years before these heart problems were noticed.

The questions surrounding serotonin in general, and Prozac in particular, are grounds for further research. As NIMH Director Steven Hyman noted in a 1998 speech to Congress, the widespread use of antidepressants should not be interpreted to mean that all cases of major depression are being accurately identified and correctly treated. In fact, despite the progress made in the treatment of depression, many patients suffer recurrences or cannot achieve full remission.

SUCCESSES AND FAILURES

NIMH research has increased understanding of many different types of mental illnesses. For example, NIMH-funded scientists have found small abnormalities in the brains of patients suffering from schizophrenia. Because of these findings, developmental neurobiologists are exploring the possibility that this disease occurs during fetal development, even though the symptoms do not appear until later in life. In the area of mood disorders, NIMH researchers have begun to understand how the commonly prescribed drug lithium actually works to control moods. They plan to use this knowledge to develop new medications for patients who do not respond to lithium. In addition, research on anxiety disorders has led to new, effective therapies that combine medications with behavioral therapy to reduce symptoms of patients suffering from obsessive-compulsive disorder.

Aside from these advances in basic science, the NIMH has also been successful in developing clinical treatments. Research on the neurochemistry of the brain has led to new psychotherapeutic drugs for schizophrenia, as well as SSRIs such as Prozac, which help treat depression, panic disorder, and obsessive-compulsive disorder. The NIMH has also invested in behavioral therapies, especially for the treatment of anxiety disorders. In addition, the NIMH has collaborated with employers, insurers, and managed-care specialists to design new methods of treatment that both lower the costs of health care and improve patients' health. NIMH research shows that mental illnesses are definable, treatable, and, to some extent, preventable.

FUTURE DIRECTIONS

In a 1998 report to Congress, the NIMH Director Steven Hyman outlined the research priorities of the institute for the near future. One of these is to improve research in the area of childhood mental disorders, including supporting clinical trials for children. Another important priority is to develop underresearched fields, such as suicide prevention. In addition, the NIMH is committed to continuing gene research on mental disorders, particularly analyzing clinical data from families with high rates of certain illnesses. Brain research continues to be an important field for the NIMH. The institute has joined the National Institute of Neurological Disorders and Stroke and other NIH institutes in the collaborative Brain Molecular Anatomy Project to better understand how the brain works. The NIMH is also committed to behavioral research, particularly on how to treat mental disorders with such tools as psychotherapy.

AGENCY RESOURCES

General information about the NIMH and mental health research is available through the institute's Web site at http://www.nimh.nih.gov. This Web site has a reading room with information about specific mental disorders and their treatments in English and Spanish. In addition, there are full-text documents of conference proceedings and technological assessments. The site provides a list of NIMH publications in English and Spanish, as well as research reports from the institute and links to NIMH education programs. The Office on AIDS has a special Web page with news and research updates on AIDS and mental illness at http://www.nimh.nih.gov/oa/index.htm. General information about the NIMH can also be obtained by sending E-mail to nimhinfo@nih.gov or calling (301) 443-3673.

Information about depression, including its symptoms and treatments, or about the educational campaign on depression sponsored by the NIMH, can be found on-line at http://www.nimh.nih.gov/dart; or by phone at 1-800-421-4211; or by writing to D/ART, 5600 Fishers Lane, Rockville, MD 20857.

Information about anxiety disorders can be obtained through the Anxiety Disorders Education Program at http://www.nimh.nih.gov/anxiety. This Web site contains news, publications, and other information for the public and professionals. The program can also be reached by calling 1-888-269-4389; or by writing Anxiety Disorders, NIMH, 5600 Fishers Lane, Rm. 7C-02, MSC 8030, Bethesda, MD 20892-8030.

AGENCY PUBLICATIONS

The NIMH distributes publications to the general public and to patients on a variety of topics related to mental illness. Examples include *A Consumer's Guide to Mental Health Services*, *Eating Disorders*, *Plain Talk About Handling Stress*, and *Understanding Panic Disorder*. A complete list of publications can be found on-line at http://www.nimh.nih.gov/publist/puborder.htm. These publications can be ordered by completing the on-line order form at this Web site; by writing NIMH Public Inquiries, 5600 Fishers Lane, Rm. 7C-02, MSC 8030, Bethesda, MD 20892-8030; or by faxing (301) 443-4279.

The program Depression: Awareness, Recognition, and Treatment offers a variety of free print materials about depression. Examples include *Depression—Effective Treatments Are Available* and *Helping the Depressed Person Get Treatment*. An order form is available on-line at http://www.nimh.nih.gov/dart/order.htm. Publications can also be ordered by calling 1-800-421-4211; or by writing to D/ART Public Inquiries, NIMH, 5600 Fishers Lane, Rm. 7C-02, Rockville, MD 20857.

The first volume in the Decade of the Brain series, called *Neuroscience, Memory, and Language*, is available for purchase. Orders can be placed with the Superintendent of Documents, P.O. Box 371954, Pittsburgh, PA 15250-7954; telephone (202) 512-1800; fax (202) 512-2250.

Publications about anxiety disorders can be obtained through the Anxiety Disorders Education Program at http://www.nimh.nih.gov/anxiety/library/edu_res.htm. Some brochures, such as "Anxiety Disorders, Getting Treatment for Panic Disorder," are available on-line at http://www.nimh.nih.gov/anxiety/library/brochure/pubs.htm. Information about other publications, books, and videotapes can be obtained from the Anxiety Disorders Education Program Web site by calling 1-888-269-4389; or by writing Anxiety Disorders, NIMH, 5600 Fishers Lane, Rm. 7C-02, MSC 8030, Bethesda, MD 20892.

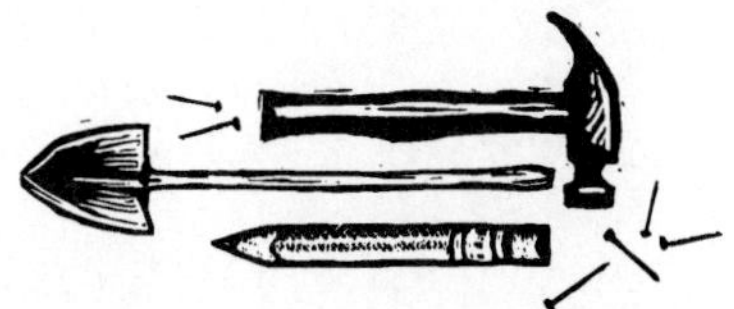

GET INVOLVED:

The NIMH encourages the public to participate in its educational programs. The program Depression: Awareness, Recognition, and Treatment (D/ART) offers a variety of campaign materials in several languages that can be used in school or community awareness programs. In addition, D/ART coordinates the Community Partnership Program in 28 states plus the District of Columbia. The organizations that participate in this partnership organize state and local educational activities. To find out more about the organizations in this program or to order educational campaign materials, contact D/ART at 1-800-421-4211 or write to D/ART, 5600 Fishers Lane, Rockville, MD 20857.

BIBLIOGRAPHY

Begley, Sharon. "Is Everybody Crazy?" *Newsweek*, 26 January 1998.

Broadwell, Richard D., ed. *Neuroscience, Memory, and Language*. Washington D.C.: Library of Congress, 1995.

Department of Health and Human Services. *Department of Health and Human Services Fiscal Year 1999: National Institutes of Health Volume IV: National Institute of Mental Health*. Washington, D.C., 1998.

Johnston, H. F. *Obsessive Compulsive Disorder in Children and Adolescents: A Guide*. Madison, Wis.: Child Psychopharmacology Information Center, 1993.

Lemonick, Michael D. "The Mood Molecule Serotonin Drugs Treat Everything from Depression to Overeating, But as We Learned Last Week, Altering the Brain Can Be Risky." *Time*, 29 September 1997.

National Institutes of Health. *NIH Almanac 1997*. No. 97-5. Rockville, Md., 1997.

———. *Mental Illness in America: The NIMH Agenda*. Rockville, Md., 1997.

Swedo, S. B. and H. L. Leonard. *It's Not All in Your Head*. New York: Harper Collins, 1996.

Talan, Jamie. "A Decade on Prozac: Much Still Unknown but the Drug Has Become First Choice for Depression." *St. Louis Post-Dispatch*, 1 September 1997.

National Institute of Standards and Technology (NIST)

PARENT ORGANIZATION: Department of Commerce
ESTABLISHED: March 3, 1901
EMPLOYEES: 3,300

Contact Information:

ADDRESS: National Institute of Standards and Technology
Gaithersburg, MD 20899
PHONE: (301) 975-3058
TDD (HEARING IMPAIRED): (800) 735-2258
FAX: (301) 926-1630
E-MAIL: inquiries@nist.gov
URL: http://www.nist.gov
DIRECTOR: Raymond Kammer

WHAT IS ITS MISSION?

The National Institute of Standards and Technology's (NIST) mission statement is "to promote U.S. economic growth by working with industry to develop and apply technology, measurements, and standards." The institute does this by attempting to build the basic infrastructure needed for U.S. industry and commerce and providing the technical capabilities necessary for developing successful products, services, and processes. It aims to maintain a direct connection to private industry, a partnership for the development of technology and standards.

HOW IS IT STRUCTURED?

The NIST is an agency of the Technology Administration within the Department of Commerce (DOC). The under secretary for technology administration directly supervises the director of the NIST.

Aside from the Office of the Director, the NIST has two other officers who supervise its internal workings: the director of administration and the chief financial officer. Matters such as budgeting, personnel management, and communications are handled through these two offices.

Three of the four program areas of the NIST—the Advanced Technology Program (ATP), the Manufacturing Extension Partnership Program (MEP), and the National Quality Program (NQP)—are each structured around a single administrative office that is responsible for planning, executing, and participating in program evaluation by an outside visiting committee of representatives of science and industry. The fourth program area—the Laboratory Program—is carried out through eight separate research areas, each with a specific directive. Research areas include chemical science and technology, physics, building and fire research, and electronics and electrical engineering. Laboratory facilities are located in both Gaithersburg, Maryland, and Boulder, Colorado.

PRIMARY FUNCTIONS

The ATP provides financial aid to private industry for the development of high-risk technologies with economic potential. To provide technical and business assistance to small manufacturers in adapting new technologies, the NIST administers the MEP. Through its laboratory and research efforts, the NIST joins private industry in investigating "infrastructural technologies" such as measurements, standards, data evaluation, and test methods. The NIST also directs the NQP (established with the signing of the National Quality Improvement Act of 1987 by President Ronald Reagan) that awards the Malcolm Baldridge National Quality Award recognizing quality achievements in manufacturing, service, and small business. The NIST not only judges the winner of the award but also is instrumental in establishing the quality criteria that all industry members must use in measuring their own performance.

PROGRAMS

The NIST and industry are involved in literally hundreds of individual programs and projects. The ATP alone conducts nearly 300 development projects in key technologies with concentrations in information technology, electronics, biotechnology, and advanced materials. For example, an innovative technique to create prosthetic tissue from animal by-products is an ATP project under development by Tissue Engineering, Inc., a small biotechnology company in Massachusetts. The tissue substitute would be processed and woven like a cloth to make biodegradable implants that would serve as a matrix where the body's own cells could grow and replace damaged tissues.

The NIST also offers traditional services which, although they evolve with technology, do not change over time. The Weights and Measures Program (WMP), the oldest of NIST programs (dating to the Office of Weights and Measures, created in 1837), still serves its original function: promoting uniformity among the states in weights and measures standards, laws, and practices. The WMP facilitates trade and protects U.S. businesses and citizens, whose sales and purchases by weight or measure total more than $2 trillion each year.

BUDGET:

National Institute of Standards and Technology

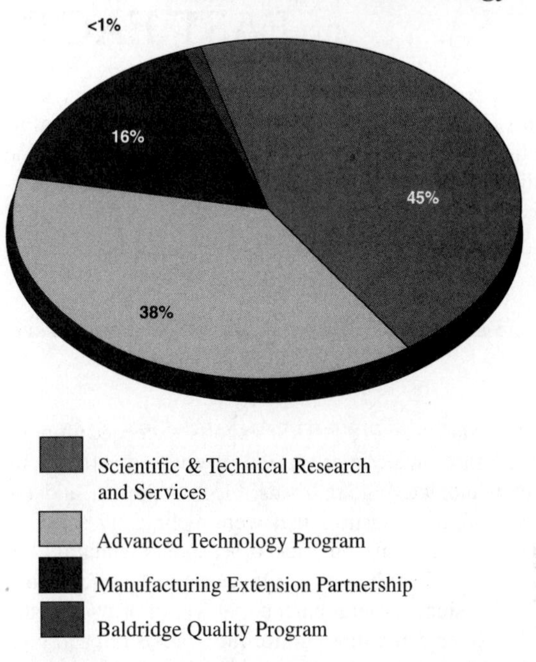

Scientific & Technical Research and Services
Advanced Technology Program
Manufacturing Extension Partnership
Baldridge Quality Program

BUDGET INFORMATION

Because NIST's expenses in the running of its programs are generally matched by its partners in private industry, the agency's budget is relatively small, considering the amount of work it accomplishes. The 1997 NIST budget was $588 million. Most of NIST's expenditures are associated with its Industrial Technology Services, including the Advanced Technology Program with $225 million, 38 percent of the NIST budget, and the Manufacturing Extension Partnership with $95 million, 16 percent of the total budget.

The Scientific and Technical Research and Services of NIST account for nearly all of the remainder of the budget. The laboratory program, through which NIST conducts its research, accounts for nearly 45 percent of the budget with $265.1 million, while the Baldridge Quality Program spends $2.9 million—less than 1 percent of the agency's funds.

HISTORY

The end of the nineteenth century was a time of enormous industrial development and economic growth in the

FAST FACTS

In response to increased emphasis on quality standards in international markets, the NIST provides information and assistance to about 20,000 organizations and individuals every year concerning voluntary and regulatory product standards and certification systems.

(Source: National Institute of Standards and Technology. "Guide to NIST," 1997.)

United States—in 1899 U.S. exports exceeded imports for the first time. American industry was dominated by steel manufacturing, railroads, electric power, and the telephone, all industries that were technically sophisticated for their time but lacked accepted standards. For many years there had been advocates in American politics for a single federal bureau that would provide better measurements and more uniformity, precision, and control in laboratory and factory activities.

Such an agency was created on March 3, 1901, with the passage of the Organic Act of the NBS. The agency was and still is distinct in at least two ways: it had no regulatory or enforcement power but left enforcement to the states, and it was to be consulted periodically by a visiting committee of leaders in science and industry who would review the work of the new bureau and make recommendations concerning current and proposed programs.

Successes in the early years of the NBS laid the foundation for advances and improvements in lighting, electric power usage, corrosion of metals, and metallurgy. The agency won international recognition for its achievements in physical measurements, development of standards, and test methods. It was also helpful in resolving the problem of how and on what basis electrical utilities would be regulated. During the two World Wars the agency was involved in urgent weapons and war material problems, and little progress was made in specific industrial research.

A Shift in Focus

The period immediately following World War II (1939–45) brought rapid and far-reaching changes for the NBS. Private industry was forced to become more self-reliant during World War II, and many private laboratories were established to serve the purpose that had been formerly fulfilled by the NBS. The agency's focus turned to more basic technological research in areas such as nuclear physics, computers, and polymers rather than work centered on the needs of industry. One of the most historically significant achievements during this period was the construction of SEAC (Standards Eastern Automatic Computer), the fastest general-purpose digital computer in the world. Beginning with its dedication on June 20, 1950, SEAC operated for 4,000 hours in its first nine months without a malfunction. It is widely considered the forerunner of the modern computer.

Under the leadership of Director Alan Astin, who was named in 1951, the NBS underwent two significant geographic changes: its main headquarters moved from the crowded offices in downtown Washington, D.C. to a 640-acre permanent home in Gaithersburg, Maryland; and the agency built radio and cryogenic (a branch of physics that deals with the production and effects of very low temperatures) laboratories in Boulder, Colorado.

In the 1950s and 1960s the NBS became involved in the space race. Later, as the social concerns of the 1960s and 1970s took on public prominence, NBS assignments became more concerned with the environment, health, and safety. In the 1970s and 1980s the agency's emphasis began to turn once again to its original mission—support of American private industry. NBS efforts became increasingly coordinated with private commerce.

In 1988, with the passage of the Omnibus Trade and Competitiveness Act, the agency was reorganized to add another mission its support of industry—the speedy acquisition of rapidly growing technology. In order to better reflect its new, broader mission, the agency's name was changed to the National Institute of Standards and Technology. Within a year, further structural changes took place in the Department of Commerce, creating the Technology Administration and transferring the NIST to its control (previously, the director of the bureau had reported directly to the secretary of commerce). Though it still retains many of the characteristics of the NBS, including its cooperative support role and its quarterly meetings with the visiting committee, the NIST has become an agency designed to handle the technological explosion of the late twentieth century.

CURRENT POLITICAL ISSUES

Still a young and developing government agency, the NIST is a common target of members of Congress and the public who want to trim the nation's budget by cutting certain programs. In fact, the NIST's parent agency, the DOC, is often a particular point of contention for congressional conservatives who see its programs as an indirect means of regulating U.S. business enterprise. In the 1990s it was not unusual to hear conservative arguments for the "zeroing out" of the DOC's budget—essentially eliminating the entire department.

The NIST has its defenders, however. When congressional threats were made against the funding of NIST projects in 1995, 25 Nobel Prize-winning physicists and the presidents of 18 research societies petitioned Congress to preserve the NIST as a critical component of the nation's long-term basic research. At a later press conference, research leaders pointed out the NIST's leading position in developing precise measurements and noted that the compatibility of U.S. computer systems could be traced to standards developed by the NIST. Furthermore, they noted, the NIST was the only civilian agency working on increasingly important solutions to computer security.

Case Study: The Advanced Technology Program

The example of the ATP illustrates the arguments surrounding the NIST. The ATP awards grants to private companies who want to research and develop particular technological solutions to industry problems. The NIST also provides grant applicants with a preconference coaching service, advising them on the requirements that a successful ATP project must meet.

Opponents argue that this is an indirect way for the government to manage industry from Washington. By deciding what types of technologies to fund and by coaching companies on the content of their proposals, the ATP determines the future of U.S. industry rather than facilitates it—an important distinction among members of Congress who believe that the federal government has too much control over business. In the congressional budget fights of the mid-1990s, the ATP was a marked target, but with its defenders from science and industry it managed to survive.

The NIST and other government officials argue that coaching addresses formal and stylistic questions—how to word and structure a proposal, for example—and does not question or endorse the suitability of certain types of research. In fact, they say, the program's structure is designed to ensure that each project's leadership comes from industry; not until an ATP award is made does the NIST offer its scientific and technical expertise to make the industry-led project a success.

SUCCESSES AND FAILURES

The measure of the NIST's success is often the testimony of its partners in private industry and many credit remarkable accomplishments to the NIST. U.S. makers of coordinate measuring machines, for example, assert that the NIST's laboratory assistance has saved them five to ten years in early stage research, and an independent study sponsored by the NIST showed that participating companies gained 10 to 30 percent in production efficiency between 1985 and 1988.

Many of the gains of the NIST laboratory program, however, are more immediately useful. A recently constructed NIST calibration facility enables more than 10,000 mammography centers nationwide to trace the accuracy of their x-ray exposure measurements to national standards, reducing the risk that women undergoing breast exams will be exposed to inappropriate radiation levels.

FUTURE DIRECTIONS

The NIST's most urgent concerns for the future involve its laboratory program and the Baldridge National Quality Program. The laboratory facilities in Gaithersburg and Boulder were built 30 to 40 years ago and conduct advanced research in areas such as semiconductor electronics, biotechnology, manufacturing engineering, atomic scale physics, computer science, and advanced materials. Some of the NIST's research areas (microprocessors, lasers, and biotechnology) did not exist when the NIST facilities were built, and the laboratories lack the environmental system controls needed to make precise measurements under stable conditions. The decay and outdated condition of the NIST laboratories is a critical issue that the institute will address in the future.

The NIST also recognizes that education and health care lag behind the nation's top businesses in performance. Because this situation affects businesses directly through rising employee health care costs and increasing needs for multidisciplinary and technological skills, the NIST intends to focus the efforts of its Baldridge program on these two areas. As a vehicle for education and self-assessment, the Baldridge program's quality criteria can help both the health care and educational systems build foundations for the future.

AGENCY RESOURCES

The NIST has a well-staffed public inquiries unit for handling general information requests. The mailing address is: NIST Public Inquiries, Administration Building A903, NIST, Gaithersburg, MD 20899-0001; phone: (301) 975-3058. For browsing technical information and results of the NIST's research and development, the NIST Virtual Library is available on the Internet at http://nvl.nist.gov.

AGENCY PUBLICATIONS

The NIST releases more than 480 publications each year, including reports on research results and standards, catalogs of products and services, and technical handbooks. The staff of NIST also write about 1,700 technical and professional papers. Publications of general interest include "Setting Priorities and Measuring Results at the National Institute of Standards and Technology," and "The Advanced Technology Program: A Progress Report on the Impacts of an Industry-Government Technology Partnership."

The institute also publishes periodicals, such as *The Journal of Research of the National Institute of Standards and Technology*, which reports the results of current research and development, and *Technology at a Glance*, a four-page newsletter designed for a general audience that is written in plain language and provides brief updates on research, grants, and other program activities. A subscription to *Technology at a Glance* is free and can be obtained by calling (301) 975-3392.

Other NIST (or older NBS) publications are sold by both the National Technical Information Service (NTIS, Springfield, VA 22161) and the Government Printing Office (Government Printing Office, Washington, DC 20402). Order numbers can be obtained from the NIST public inquiries unit.

BIBLIOGRAPHY

Abelson, Philip H. "National Institute for Science and Technology." *Science,* 20 May 1994, p. 1063.

Cioffi, Denis F. "Clinton Philosophy Transforms NIST into 'Partner for Industry.'" *Physics Today,* November 1994, pp. 75–7.

Cochrane, Rexmond C. *Measures for Progress: A History of the National Bureau of Standards.* New York: Arno Press, 1976.

Cramer, Jerome. "NIST: Measuring Up to a New Task." *Science,* 26 March 1993, pp. 1818–9.

Kammer, Raymond G. "NIST: Helping Industry to Compete." *NIST Research Reports,* June 1989, pp. 16–19.

Litsikas, Mary. "NIST Helps U.S. Manufacturers Build Communication Bridges." *Quality,* April 1996, pp. 34–38.

Teresko, John. "NIST: More than Weights and Measures." *Industry Week,* 19 Dec 1994, pp. 75–8.

Weber, Gustavus A. *The Bureau of Standards: Its History, Activities & Organization.* New York: AMS Press, Inc., 1980.

National Institute on Aging (NIA)

PARENT ORGANIZATION: Department of Health and Human Services
ESTABLISHED: May 31, 1974
EMPLOYEES: 399

Contact Information:

ADDRESS: Building 31, 31 Center Dr., MSC 2292
Bethesda, MD 20892-2292
PHONE: (301) 496-1752
TOLL FREE: (800) 222-2225
TDD (HEARING IMPAIRED): (800) 222-4225
E-MAIL: niainfo@access.digex.net
URL: http://www.nih.gov/nia
DIRECTOR: Richard J. Hodes, M.D.

WHAT IS ITS MISSION?

For nearly 25 years the National Institute on Aging (NIA) has been the federal government's leading agency for aging research. According to the institute, the NIA aims to "conduct and support biomedical, social, and behavioral research, training, health information dissemination, and other programs with respect to the aging process and diseases and other special problems and the needs of the aged." It strives to understand the aging process and develop the means for aging Americans to live healthy and active lives.

HOW IS IT STRUCTURED?

The NIA is one of 24 institutes, centers, and divisions of the National Institutes of Health (NIH), which is a branch of the Department of Health and Human Services. The NIA consists of six administrative offices and extramural, intramural, and international programs.

The Administrative Offices

The administrative offices are headed by the Office of the Director and Deputy Director. It is responsible for the overall functioning of the institute, and its sets the goals and priorities for NIA aging research. The director and deputy director also work closely with the National Advisory Council on Aging. The council consists of educators, researchers, and government officials who help set the research agenda for the NIA. There are three other offices that assist with the administrative duties of the institute. These are the Office of Administrative Man-

FAST FACTS

Men and women with higher levels of education—regardless of race—can expect to stay healthier 2.5 to 4 years longer than people with less schooling.

(Source: National Institute on Aging. *Aging Research: Practice, Promise, and Priorities*, March 1994.)

agement; the Office of Extramural Affairs; and the Office of Planning, Analysis, and International Activities. These offices provide the personnel, financial management, information resources, and public relations support for the research programs. In addition, the Office of Alzheimer's Disease leads the nation's efforts against this disease and works with outside agencies and the international community on issues related to Alzheimer's. The Public Information Office disseminates information and educates the public, media, health care providers, and other government agencies about aging issues.

The Extramural Research Program

The extramural program of the NIA provides financial support to universities, medical centers, and public and private organizations across the country to conduct aging research. The extramural programs are divided into four research areas. The Biology of Aging program funds research in biochemistry, molecular biology, cellular biology, genetics, immunology, nutrition, endocrinology, and pathobiology to study the basic aging process and the onset of age-related disease. Other areas of support include animal models, biomarkers, physiology, and protein structure.

The Behavioral and Social Research program supports research on the psychological and social aspects of aging, particularly how older people relate to social institutions, as well as the causes and consequences of changes in the age composition of the population. The three branches of this program are Adult Psychological Development, Social Science Research on Aging, and Demography and Population Epidemiology.

The third extramural program, the Neuroscience and Neuropsychology of Aging program, researches the aging of the nervous system and the brain. It consists of three primary research areas: neurobiology of aging, dementias of aging, and neuropsychology of aging. The dementias of aging branch dedicates much of its resources to understanding Alzheimer's disease. It supports the Alzheimer's Disease Research Centers across the country and manages the Alzheimer's Disease Center Core Grants programs.

The last division of the extramural programs, the Geriatrics Program, sponsors research on the causes, prevention, and treatment of health problems of the elderly, such as frailty, menopause, and osteoporosis. It oversees the Claude D. Pepper Older American Research Centers located throughout the country, which promote independent living among the elderly. In addition, it has begun a new initiative, the Integration of Aging and Cancer Research, to understand the relationship between age and cancer.

The Intramural Program

The intramural program of the NIA conducts its own basic and clinical research. Much of the intramural program research is conducted at the Gerontology Research Center (GRC) located at Johns Hopkins Bayview Medical Center in Baltimore, Maryland. The GRC conducts research in eight key areas: longitudinal studies, clinical physiology, behavioral sciences, personality and cognition, cellular and molecular biology, biological chemistry, molecular genetics, and cardiovascular science. These studies aim to understand aging and age-related diseases. One branch of the GRC, the Laboratory of Neurosciences, is located in the NIH Clinical Center in Bethesda, Maryland.

The NIA intramural program also runs the Epidemiology, Demography, and Biometry program located in the Gateway Building in Bethesda, Maryland. This program analyzes the demographic, social, and genetic factors influencing the health of older Americans. For example, a special project of this program studies women's health and aging.

PRIMARY FUNCTIONS

The NIA is primarily a research institute. It conducts both biomedical and behavioral research on the aging process. Some of this research is done at the institute through its intramural research program. However, the NIA also supports extramural research at universities and medical centers throughout the country through grants and contracts. Both types of research cover a broad range of scientific areas, such as genetics, neuroscience, biology, geriatrics, and demography. To carry out its work, the NIA works closely with other federal programs, especially other institutes of the NIH, as well as research institutes, professional associations, and voluntary organizations, that are also involved in age-related research. These collaborations span local, state, national, and international boundaries. In addition to conducting research, the NIA serves to disseminate this research knowledge and educate health care providers, researchers, policymakers, and the general public about age-related issues through publications, a Web site, and a special reference service for Alzheimer's disease.

PROGRAMS

The NIA emphasizes the variety of research programs it sponsors under the extramural, intramural, and international program divisions. One unique intramural program is the Baltimore Longitudinal Study of Aging (BLSA). In this study researchers have been following a group of more than 1,100 Baltimore residents between the ages of 20 and 96 to examine physiological and behavioral changes throughout the adult life span. Participants return to the NIA every two years for intensive biological and psychological testing. The study is unique because of its duration. It has examined men for nearly 40 years and women for 20 years.

Aside from research programs, the NIA is also committed to education and information dissemination. For example, the Alzheimer's Disease Education and Referral (ADEAR) Center is a service of the NIA established in 1990. It provides information on Alzheimer's disease for the general public, patients with Alzheimer's and their families, and health professionals. The center distributes publications about the disease, maintains a special Web site at http://www.alzheimers.org, and also provides information and referral services through a toll-free number, 1-800-438-4380.

The NIA also supports the training of experts in the field of aging. For example, each year it sponsors the Summer Institute on Aging Research. Researchers new to the field of aging participate in a week-long workshop to learn about current issues in aging research, research methodologies, and funding opportunities. More information about this program can be found at the NIA Web site at http://www.nih.gov/nia/new/summer/sum98.htm or by contacting the NIA at (301) 496-0765 or fax (301) 496-2525.

The NIA also supports an international program to increase communication and collaboration with international aging researchers. Through the NIH's Fogarty International Visiting Program, the NIA hosts foreign researchers to work with the NIA intramural program. The institute also supports and participates in international conferences on aging. In addition, it is a World Health Organization Collaborating Center for Research on the Health of the Elderly.

BUDGET INFORMATION

The total budget appropriated by Congress to the NIA in 1998 was $519.3 million. Of this amount 64.9 percent was allocated to research project grants, 12.3 percent was given to research centers, 8.8 percent was allocated to intramural research programs, 4.5 percent was spent on research and development contracts, 3.8 percent went to research management and support, and 2.9 percent was spent on other research expenses. The final 2.7 percent of the NIA budget went to training. The 1999 estimated budget is $558 million, which is an increase of 7.5 percent over the 1998 budget.

BUDGET:

National Institute on Aging

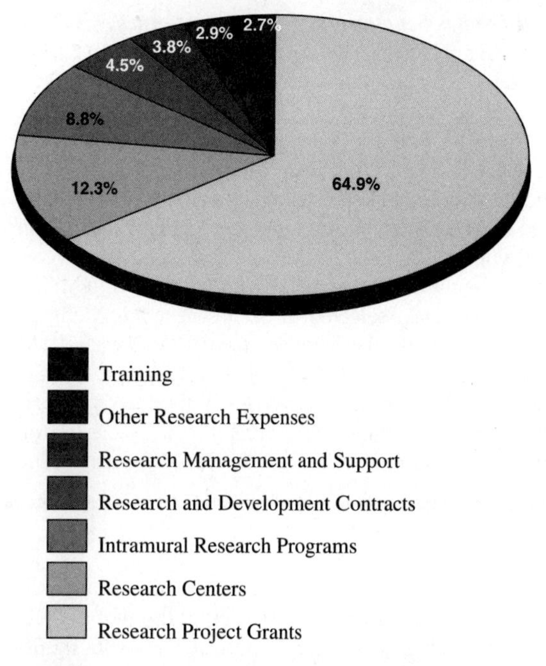

Training
Other Research Expenses
Research Management and Support
Research and Development Contracts
Intramural Research Programs
Research Centers
Research Project Grants

HISTORY

The federal government recognized the need for a separate institute on aging at a 1971 White House Conference on Aging. On May 31, 1974, the institute was authorized by Public Law 93-296, and it came into existence on October 7, 1974. The first meeting of the National Advisory Council on Aging took place six months later on April 23, 1975.

During the 1980s, the NIA increased its focus on Alzheimer's disease. In 1984 the NIA funded the first Alzheimer's Disease Centers at medical institutions nationwide to dedicate the time and money needed to understand this disease. The Alzheimer's Disease Education and Referral (ADEAR) Center was approved by Con-

BIOGRAPHY:
Claude D. Pepper

United States Senator (1900–1989) Attorney, state representative, U.S. senator, and U.S. representative, Claude Denson Pepper was known for championing the working class, the poor, and especially, the elderly. In the U.S. Senate, from 1936 to 1950, the avid New Dealer supported President Franklin D. Roosevelt's views on the need for labor laws, minimum wage, a national health care system, and Social Security. Pepper continued to practice law from 1950 until 1962, when he was elected to the U.S. House of Representatives from a newly-created district in Miami, Florida. He was reelected to each succeeding Congress into the mid-1980s. During the late 1970s and early 1980s he chaired the Select Committee on Aging, gaining national prominence as an advocate for the elderly. Specifically, he was instrumental in saving Social Security from bankruptcy and preventing cuts to Social Security benefits when the program met with financial problems in the 1980s. In 1983 Pepper was appointed chairman of the Rules Committee. He served in office until his death on May 30, 1989, in Washington, D.C. His remains were lain in state at the Rotunda of the U.S. Capitol as a final tribute to one of the country's most eminent citizens. As a lasting tribute his name has been given to Claude D. Pepper Older American Research Centers located throughout the country. These centers focus on diseases that threaten independent living among the elderly.

gress on November 14, 1986, to better educate the public and professionals about the disease. In 1988 the NIA began to distribute awards to researchers who significantly advanced understanding of Alzheimer's disease.

Aside from Alzheimer's disease, the NIA has expanded other research areas as well. In 1988 the first Geriatric Research and Training Centers were created nationwide. In 1990 these were renamed Claude D. Pepper Older American Independence Centers, and they began to focus on diseases that threatened independent living among the elderly. In 1993 six Edward R. Roybal Centers for Research on Applied Gerontology were created to turn research findings into practical programs. In 1994 the NIA created nine Demography of Aging Centers and in 1995 it funded three Nathan Shock Centers of Excellence in Basic Biology of Aging.

CURRENT POLITICAL ISSUES

Although the NIA is primarily a research institute, it strives to turn research into practice and to show how science can impact people's lives. For example, in April 1998 NIA-funded researchers announced a new test that can predict the risk of car accidents among older drivers, who are involved in more car accidents than most other age groups. However, it has been difficult for safety officials to regulate driving by the elderly. Setting an age at which drivers must give up their licenses would be age discrimination, and it would limit the independence of elderly Americans. Researchers at the University of Alabama at Birmingham, who are part of an NIA Edward R. Roybal Center for Research on Applied Gerontology, have created a test that can determine which older drivers are more likely to be involved in car accidents. The "useful field of view" test measures how well people process visual information. Although more research is needed to determine its effectiveness, this test may become a practical and fair way for licensing agencies to determine an older person's ability to drive.

The institute's longest and most publicly recognized effort to use research to improve the quality of life has been in the area of Alzheimer's disease. For over a decade, the NIA has led the nation's fight against the disease and has made significant efforts to educate the public about its research findings.

Case Study: Alzheimer's Disease

Alzheimer's disease (AD) is a type of dementia found most often in people over age 65. AD affects thought, memory, and language. Symptoms usually start with mild forgetfulness but then progress to serious memory loss and language problems. AD afflicts about four million Americans and, to date, there is no cure for this disease. However, research advances over the past decade have improved understanding of the disease and ways to ease the suffering of patients and their families. For example, doctors now know how to better diagnose the disease through a combination of medical history, basic medical tests, neuropsychological tests, and brain scans. There are also new treatments for symptoms of AD, such as sleeplessness, depression, and anxiety. There is also one federally approved drug, called tacrine, which can alleviate some of the cognitive symptoms in the early stages of the disease. Scientists are also making advances in understanding the genetic, environmental, and viral factors that are related to AD.

The NIA has been the government's leading agency in the fight against this disease. Not only has the institute faced the medical challenges of AD, it has also had to educate politicians and the public about the importance of research in this field. For example, in 1976 the NIA had less than $1 million a year to spend on AD research. By 1994, that amount had increased to $213 million annually. This increased support is largely due to the NIA's educational efforts, such as the creation of Alzheimer's Disease Centers across the country and the establishment of the Alzheimer's Disease Education and Referral (ADEAR) Center. In addition, private organizations such as the Alzheimer's Association have lobbied for political and financial support.

This awareness campaign received a major boost in 1994 when former president Ronald Reagan, then 83, publicly announced that he has AD. By making his illness public, Reagan sought to reduce the social stigma associated with the disease and shed light on the difficulties that family members and caregivers of patients face. But while public awareness and political support are needed to raise research money, the cure for AD ultimately lies in science. NIA researchers have made great strides in this area. For example, scientists now know that certain common medications, such as nonsteroidal anti-inflammatory drugs like ibuprofen, may slow the progression of AD.

Many of the AD research advances have come in the area of genetics. In the early 1990s a major breakthrough occurred with the discovery of an Alzheimer's-related gene called apoliprotein E, or ApoE. Since then, NIA researchers have been trying to put this knowledge to good use. For example, 26 national Alzheimer's Disease Centers collaborated on a study of genetic testing for AD based on the presence of ApoE. They found that testing for a certain form of ApoE, known as E4, alone was not enough to successfully diagnose AD. However, genetic testing used with other clinical criteria could successfully reduce the number of people incorrectly diagnosed as having AD. In early 1998 NIA researchers discovered yet another gene, bleomycin hydrolase (BH), associated with AD.

FUTURE DIRECTIONS

The scientific successes of the NIA in the areas of Alzheimer's disease, the biology of aging, and disease and disability have laid the groundwork for future advances in these areas. For example, recent progress made in the area of Alzheimer's disease, such as the discovery of important risk factors and the identification of possible interventions, has meant that these new discoveries can be turned into therapies. The NIA plans to launch new clinical trials to test the possibilities of such treatments as vitamin E, ibuprofen, and hormonal replacement on Alzheimer's disease and cognitive impairment. In addition to these scientific plans, the NIA is also planning a new initiative to help families and friends manage the caring for a patient with Alzheimer's disease.

In the area of the biology of aging, the NIA is committed to finding the genes that influence human longevity. In addition, it is collaborating with the National Institute of Allergies and Infectious Diseases to understand how the immune system declines with age. In the field of disease and disability, the NIA is working with the National Cancer Institute to identify the factors related to tumor development and the effects of anti-cancer drugs on older patients. The NIA is also joining the National Institute on Arthritis and Musculoskeletal and Skin Diseases to understand the age-related loss of muscle mass.

In addition to these scientific advances, the NIA is committed to developing a scientific infrastructure for aging research. This includes training new clinical geriatric investigators, especially those interested in the growing populations of older minority Americans. The NIA is also dedicated to improving information technology, especially access to computerized aging data to make research easier and more efficient. Last, the NIA plans to improve its animal models. Large colonies of aging mice and rats have been used for aging research for more than two decades. For future research, more specialized colonies for genetically-engineered animals will need to be developed to further research advancements.

AGENCY RESOURCES

General information about the NIA and aging research is available through the institute's Web site at http://www.nih.gov/nia. In addition, the NIA Information Center has brochures, booklets, press releases, and public service advertisements for the public and health professionals. It can be reached by calling 1-800-222-2225, by sending E-mail to niainfo@access.digex.net, or by writing PO Box 8057, Gaithersburg, MD 20898-8057.

People interested in conducting their own research on aging can look for data at the National Archive of Computerized Data on Aging (NACDA), which is a branch of the Inter-University Consortium for Political and Social Research at the University of Michigan. This NIA-sponsored project is the largest U.S. library of electronic data on aging, containing demographic, social, economic, psychological, and health information. The NIA has made these data available to encourage analyses for scientific and policy purposes. More information is available at the NACDA Web site at http://www.icpsr.umich.edu/NACDA.

The Alzheimer's Disease Education and Referral (ADEAR) Center provides information about Alzheimer's disease through its Web site at http://www.alzheimers.org or through a toll-free number at 1-800-438-4380. The phone service is available from 8:30 A.M. to 5:00 P.M. EST Monday through Friday. The ADEAR service can also be reached by fax at (301) 495-3334, by E-mail at adear@alzheimers.org, or by writing ADEAR Center, PO Box 8250, Silver Spring, MD 20907-8250.

AGENCY PUBLICATIONS

The NIA Information Center distributes NIA publications for the public and health professionals. These include easy-to-read brochures and fact sheets on a variety of aging topics, including diseases, medical care, nutrition, and safety. Examples of these publications include "Aging and Your Eyes," "Osteoporosis: The Bone Thinner," "Arthritis Advice," and "Finding Good Medical Care for Older Americans." In addition, the NIA has more detailed books, such as *The Resource Directory for Older People*, *Talking with Your Doctor: A Guide for Older People*, and *The NIA: Research for a New Age*. Most of these publications are free of charge and many are available on-line at http://www.nih.gov/nia/health/health.htm. Requests can also be directed to the NIA Information Center by calling 1-800-222-2225, by sending E-mail to niainfo@access.digex.net, or by writing PO Box 8057, Gaithersburg, MD 20898-8057.

Publications on Alzheimer's disease can be obtained through the Alzheimer's Disease Education and Referral (ADEAR) Center. Publications include general information for the public, as well as research updates. Examples include the "Alzheimer's Disease Fact Sheet," "Alzheimer's Disease Centers Program Directory," and the "Progress Report on Alzheimer's Disease, 1996." Many of these publications are available in full-text format on-line at http://www.alzheimers.org/pubsonln.html. Print copies can be ordered through ADEAR by calling 1-800-438-4380.

BIBLIOGRAPHY

Altman, Lawrence K. "Studying Aging in Space? Send an Aging Astronaut." *New York Times*, 27 January 1998.

American Federation of Aging Research and the Alliance for Aging Research. *Putting Age on Hold: Delaying the Disease of Old Age*. Official Report to the White House Conference on Aging. 1995.

Cowley, Geoffrey. "How to Live to 100." *Newsweek*, 30 June 1997.

Friend, Tim. "Reagan Puts Spotlight on Alzheimer's." *USA Today*, 7 November 1994.

Morrow, David J. "Stumble on Road to Market; Haste Makes Problems for Creator of Alzheimer's Test." *New York Times*, 5 March 1998.

National Institutes of Health, National Institute on Aging. *Aging Research: Practice, Promise, and Priorities*. Publication no. 96-3696. Baltimore, March 1994.

———. *In Search of the Secrets of Aging*. 2nd ed. Baltimore, 1996.

———. "New Test Predicts Crash Risk of Older Drivers." Press release. 7 April 1998.

———. "Osteoporosis: The Silent Bone Thinner," 1997.

National Institutes of Health, National Institute on Aging, and the Administration on Aging. *The Resource Directory for Older People*. Baltimore, 1997.

National Institute on Alcohol Abuse and Alcoholism (NIAAA)

PARENT ORGANIZATION: Department of Health and Human Services
ESTABLISHED: December 31, 1970
EMPLOYEES: 219 (1997)

Contact Information:

ADDRESS: Willco Bldg., Ste. 409
6000 Executive Blvd.
Bethesda, MD 20892-7003
PHONE: (301) 443-3885
URL: http://www.niaaa.nih.gov
DIRECTOR: Enoch Gordis, M.D.

WHAT IS ITS MISSION?

The National Institute on Alcohol Abuse and Alcoholism (NIAAA) is the nation's primary research center for alcohol-related problems. According to the *1997 NIH Almanac*, "the National Institute on Alcohol Abuse and Alcoholism (NIAAA) is responsible for research on the causes, consequences, treatment, and prevention of alcohol-related problems." Its goal is to conduct biomedical and behavioral research on alcohol abuse and alcoholism, to work with practitioners and policymakers to apply this knowledge to treatment and prevention programs, and to inform the general public about this disease. Through these efforts, the institute hopes to reduce the health, economic, and social consequences of alcohol abuse.

HOW IS IT STRUCTURED?

The NIAAA is one of the National Institutes of Health (NIH), which is part of the U.S. Department of Health and Human Services (DHHS). It consists of five administrative offices and four research divisions. The five offices of the NIAAA are responsible for the administration of the institute.

The Office of the Director provides the leadership for the institute. It establishes the overall research agenda and develops the institute's policies and programs. It is also responsible for maintaining communication between the NIAAA and the rest of the NIH, as well as other government agencies, professionals outside of the government, and the general public. The director reports periodically to the National Advisory Council on Alcohol

FAST FACTS

The risk of a car accident for a driver with a blood alcohol content of .08 percent or higher is 11 times greater than for a driver with no blood alcohol.

(Source: Matthew L. Wald. "Drunken-Driving Standard May Shift." *New York Times*, January 30, 1998.)

Abuse and Alcoholism, which is composed of researchers, educators, and government officials who oversee the institute's activities.

The Office of Collaborative Research Activities works with other government agencies and organizations interested in alcohol-related problems, as well as international researchers, to develop joint programs and offer mutual support and assistance in the pursuit of a common goal. For example, the NIAAA works with the Department of Transportation on drunk-driving regulations and collaborates with the Department of Education on college alcohol problems. It also works with special interest groups such as Mothers Against Drunk Driving (MADD).

The Office of Scientific Affairs is responsible for the Extramural Research Program. It establishes the research policies and programs and reviews grant applications and contract proposals. It is also responsible for the public information and scientific communications program.

The Office of Policy Analysis conducts and sponsors research on the policies related to alcohol abuse and alcoholism. It monitors alcohol-related legislation and makes policy recommendations to the Secretary of Health and Human Services and Congress.

The Office of Planning and Resource Management provides the administrative support for the institute, including financial, personnel, and information resources management.

The four divisions of the NIAAA specialize in different types of research activities. The Division of Clinical and Prevention Research focuses on the development of treatment and prevention procedures for alcohol-related problems, such as the development of new medications and intervention programs. The Division of Basic Research aims to understand the scientific mechanisms of alcohol addiction and injury through basic sciences such as genetics, neuroscience, and molecular biology. This division also oversees the National Alcohol Research Centers Program, which funds 14 research centers nationwide to study alcohol-related problems. The Division of Biometry and Epidemiology studies the incidence and prevalence of alcohol-related problems, particularly the types of people most affected by this disease. The Division of Intramural Clinical and Biological Research aims to understand how alcohol causes intoxication and chemical dependence and the damage that it does to the body.

PRIMARY FUNCTIONS

The NIAAA is primarily a research institute. It conducts both biomedical and behavioral research on the causes of alcoholism, the damage that alcohol does to the body, and the methods to prevent and treat the disease. Much of this research is done at the institute itself through the intramural research program. However, the NIAAA also supports extramural research outside of the institute through grants and contracts. Both types of research cover a broad range of scientific areas, such as genetics, neuroscience, medical consequences, medication development, policy studies, and epidemiology.

To carry out its work, the NIAAA works closely with other federal programs, research institutes, professional associations, and voluntary organizations, which are also involved in alcohol-related research. These collaborations span international, national, state, and local boundaries. In addition to conducting research, the NIAAA seeks to disseminate this knowledge and educate health care providers, researchers, policymakers, and the general public about alcohol-related issues.

PROGRAMS

NIAAA's research programs consist of extramural research conducted outside of the institute, primarily at the National Alcohol Research Centers, as well as intramural programs of research within the institute and programs involving collaboration with the international community.

Extramural Program

The NIAAA Extramural Program supports research at universities and research institutes across the country on alcohol-related problems. Examples of extramural research efforts include genetic research on how the vulnerability to alcoholism is transmitted genetically through families. Research on alcohol and pregnancy studies the ways in which alcohol affects fetal development. Extramural programs also support the development of medications to reduce the craving for alcohol and the risk of relapse, and neuroscience research explores how alcohol interacts with the brain. In addition, the extramural program focuses on treatment, especially on ways to best match patients with treatments that would be most effective for their particular circumstances. Prevention research focuses on community prevention trials for alcohol-related trauma, underage drinking, and drunk driving. These programs test school, parental, and media intervention.

A key part of the extramural program is the National Alcohol Research Centers Program. The NIAAA provides long-term support for 14 centers nationwide to conduct interdisciplinary research on particular problems related to alcohol. In addition, the centers provide training opportunities and serve as a regional resource on alcohol-related problems.

Intramural Programs

According to the *1997 NIH Almanac*, the goal of the Intramural Research Program is "to understand the mechanisms by which alcohol produces intoxication, dependence, and damage to vital body organs, and to develop tools to prevent and treat those biochemical and behavioral processes." The program accomplishes this through a combination of basic scientific research and clinical applications. Key areas of intramural research are the genetics of alcoholism, essential fatty acids and alcohol, and the molecular effects of alcohol in the brain.

International Activities

The Office of Collaborative Research works to foster research ties with other countries and international organizations. The NIAAA exchanges research information with more than 30 countries on a regular basis. It has developed collaborative projects or supported grantees to work with scientists in such countries as Finland, Poland, Mexico, Russia, the Czech Republic, Canada, and Spain, as well as many others. Cosponsored projects have been conducted on birth defects, liver disease, acquired immunodeficiency syndrome (AIDS), women's health, minority health, and aging.

BUDGET INFORMATION

The 1997 budget for the NIAAA was $222.3 million. Of this total amount, 77.5 percent went to extramural grants and contracts and 2.6 percent was allocated to extramural research training. Intramural research received 9.4 percent of the 1997 budget, while 5.5 percent was spent on research management and support and 5 percent on research related to AIDS. The 1998 budget request was $230.6 million, which included a 21 percent increase for AIDS research and a 6.3 percent increase for non-AIDS research over the 1997 budget.

BUDGET:

National Institute on Alcohol Abuse and Alcoholism

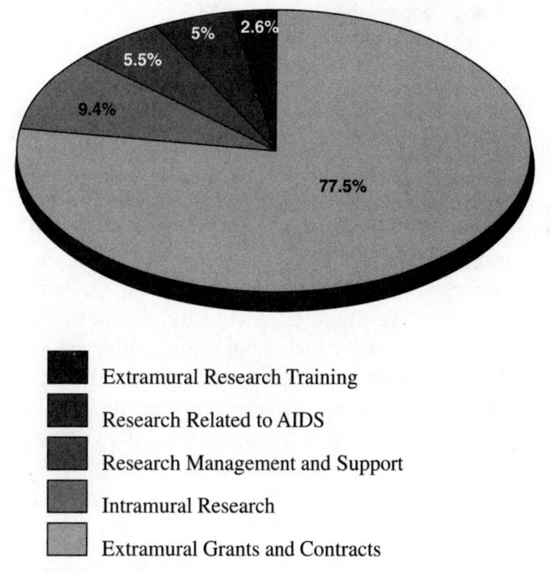

- Extramural Research Training
- Research Related to AIDS
- Research Management and Support
- Intramural Research
- Extramural Grants and Contracts

HISTORY

The comprehensive Alcohol Abuse and Alcoholism Prevention, Treatment, and Rehabilitation Act of 1970 (Public Law 91-616) created the NIAAA to develop health, education, training, research, and planning programs for alcohol-related problems. In 1974 the NIAAA became part of the Alcohol, Drug Abuse, and Mental Health Administration (ADAMHA), along with the National Institute of Mental Health and the National Institute of Drug Abuse. In 1976 Public Law 91-616 was amended to expand the NIAAA's research mission to include the social and economic consequences of alcohol abuse and alcoholism. Ten years later the NIAAA's nonresearch activities were transferred to the newly created Substance Abuse Prevention division of ADAMHA, allowing the NIAAA to focus almost exclusively on research activities.

On July 10, 1992, the ADAMHA Reorganization Act clearly separated alcohol and substance abuse service programs from research activities. All services were transferred to the newly created Substance Abuse and Mental Health Services Administration (SAMHSA), and the NIAAA became a new research institute of the National Institutes of Health.

CURRENT POLITICAL ISSUES

In the late 1990s the Clinton administration, along with the secretary of health and human services, Donna Shalala, launched political, legal, social, and media campaigns about the tobacco industry. They sought to educate the public against the dangers of smoking and to hold tobacco companies legally and financially responsible for the health hazards that smoking has caused Americans.

The success of this public attack against the tobacco industry has led many politicians and business leaders to wonder whether the alcohol industry would be next. After all, according to the NIAAA, alcohol abuse affects nearly 10 percent of American adults and is responsible for 44 percent of all traffic fatalities each year, not to mention the deaths caused by cirrhosis of the liver and fetal alcohol syndrome. Like the tobacco industry, alcohol is big business, which means that money and influence are needed to protect its financial interests. Given this, it is no wonder that numerous groups, both for and against alcohol, lobby in Congress regarding the extent of government regulation needed to protect the health of Americans. The NIAAA plays a crucial role in this debate by providing scientific facts to fuel the arguments.

Case Study: Alcohol Advertisements

One main issue of the tobacco debate was whether cigarette advertisements, such as those featuring "Joe Camel" and "the Marlboro Man," were targeting youth. As part of a settlement with the federal government, the tobacco industry agreed to stop this type of advertising. A similar debate has arisen with the alcohol industry, which often uses endearing animals—such as dogs and frogs—to sell its products.

Some politicians and special-interest groups argue that alcohol advertising, especially when it is appealing to minors, should be regulated. Much of the controversy began in 1996 when the Seagram company decided to end a 48-year-old voluntary ban on hard-liquor television ads and began advertising its products with television commercials. The public outcry from this decision motivated politicians to address the issue of alcohol advertising. Congressman Joseph Kennedy (D-Mass.) introduced several bills in 1997 that would regulate alcohol advertisements. The proposals included restrictions on the content, frequency, and timing of television and radio commercials for alcohol, as well as the type and location of print advertisements, particularly in relation to schools and college campuses. In addition to these bills, Senator Robert Byrd (D-W.V.) introduced a bill to tax the money spent on alcohol advertising, and the chairman of the Federal Communications Commission (FCC), William Kennard, announced plans to launch a study of liquor advertising on television.

However, the powerful alcohol lobby has managed to quell this debate. The beer industry in particular exercised considerable influence to postpone congressional subcommittee hearings on the issue of alcohol advertising on television. In addition, Senator Byrd's bill was defeated by a vote of 86 to 12, and Congressman Kennedy was unable to gain many supporters for his proposals.

Although the issue lingers in the media and in certain political circles, those against alcohol advertising lack substantial evidence of the effects of such ads on the public, especially on youth. In response to the public and political interest in this subject, in 1998 the NIAAA announced plans for research studies on the effects of alcohol advertising on underage drinking. According to the institute, this research plan aims "to explore the role of alcohol advertising in the initiation of drinking."

Case Study: Drunk Driving

Another topic that has created a debate over the federal regulation of alcohol is drunk driving. After a decade of decline in the number of deaths caused by drunk driving, the death toll has been rising since 1994. This alarming trend has caused Mothers Against Drunk Driving (MADD) and federal safety officials to lobby for a stricter definition of drunk driving that would apply to all states.

This debate was outlined in a *New York Times* article by Matthew L. Wald called "Drunken-Driving Standard May Shift." Each state sets its own drunk-driving standards based on a measure of blood alcohol content. Most states—33 plus the District of Columbia—set the definition of drunkenness at .10 percent blood alcohol content or higher. Fifteen other states set the limit at .08 percent. The remaining two states have no official blood alcohol content limit but instead rely on officers' observations. MADD is fighting for a national standard of .08 percent and is asking Congress to deny highway money to states that do not comply.

The alcohol industry and the hospitality industry, especially restaurant owners, have joined forces to oppose this legislation because of the financial consequences it will have on their businesses. They argue that blood alcohol content varies depending on how much people weigh, how much they have eaten, how fast their metabolism works, as well as how much they have had to drink. Given this variability, they argue it is too difficult for a person to know when they have reached the .08 percent level. In addition, this lower level would affect social drinkers who are not necessarily alcohol abusers.

Advocates of the legislation are not convinced by these arguments. The National Highway Traffic Safety Administration, for example, argues that people become impaired before they even reach the .08 percent level. Therefore, drinkers should be able to recognize their condition without actually knowing their blood alcohol level and should not be driving. Early support for the legislation has come from President Clinton, and from the Senate, which passed the bill to cut federal highway funds to states that do not adopt the .08 percent standard. By mid-1998, 25 states were considering legislation to adopt a .08 percent level; the U.S. House of Representatives was also considering a bill, one similar to that already passed by the Senate.

Scientific research helped decide a similar debate in 1995, when Congress passed the National Highway System Designation Act. This is a national "zero tolerance" policy that considers a driver under 21 years old with a blood alcohol content of .02 percent or higher to be legally drunk. States that do not comply with this act by 1999 will lose federal highway funds. According to Dr. Enoch Gordis, director of the NIAAA, research showed that zero-tolerance laws resulted in an average of 20 percent fewer fatal single-vehicle nighttime accidents than for states that did not adopt these laws. This evidence helped persuade Congress to pass this act.

MADD is now looking for similar support from the scientific community regarding the .08 percent standard. The organization approached the National Advisory Council on Alcohol Abuse and Alcoholism in February 1998 to ask for assistance in educating Congress about drunk driving and blood alcohol content to gather support for the passage of this federal law.

SUCCESSES AND FAILURES

As the federal government's primary agency for alcohol-related research, the NIAAA has made much progress in understanding alcohol abuse and alcoholism during its short existence. For example, NIAAA-supported clinical trials led to the Food and Drug Administration's approval of naltrexone in the 1970s; it was the first medication developed to help maintain sobriety since 1949.

In the area of neuroscience, the NIAAA has made great strides in understanding the mental processes that govern drinking. The institute has identified the different neural systems that guide positive and negative responses to alcohol, and researchers are trying to understand how different medications affect these processes. The NIAAA grantees' discovery of the crystal structure of the alcohol-metabolizing enzyme called aldehyde dehydrogenase is now allowing researchers to develop new medications tailored to known biological structures.

The Cooperative Study on the Genetics of Alcoholism (COGA), an NIAAA study conducted at six research centers, has been producing informative new findings on how alcoholism is inherited. For example, scientists have located chromosomal "hot spots," or certain chromosomes that could be linked to either alcohol dependence or resistance.

The NIAAA has also increased its efforts to pass on these important research findings. Its Web site includes many full-text publications and press releases, as well as funding information. The official publication of the NIAAA, *Alcohol, Health, and Research World*, is an award-winning journal. In addition, in 1997 alone the NIAAA distributed 75,000 copies of *The Physicians' Guide to Helping Patients with Alcohol Problems*.

Despite these research successes and increased information dissemination techniques, the NIAAA still faces many challenges. As stated by Dr. Enoch Gordis, director of the institute, in a speech to Congress, "Alcoholism is one of our country's most serious and persistent health problems." Therefore, turning scientific research into applied programs that will actually change people's behaviors is still a challenge to the institute. In addition, the NIAAA must continuously remind the public and policymakers that alcoholism is a medical condition whose cure lies in scientific research.

FUTURE DIRECTIONS

Despite the many research successes of the NIAAA, much is still unknown about the causes and consequences of alcohol abuse and alcoholism. According to Gordis, the NIAAA plans to continue the progress that has been made "by focusing on research to determine which aspects of the vulnerability to alcoholism are inherited; how genetic and non-genetic factors interact in the development of alcoholism; how biology and behavior interact in the development of alcohol use disorders; and by developing and testing new prevention and treatment methods to reduce the risk for alcoholism, improve the chance for recovery, and reduce the risk of relapse." In addition, the NIAAA will continue its research efforts in the areas of fetal alcohol syndrome, drunk driving, alcohol advertising, and the health effects of moderate drinking.

AGENCY RESOURCES

Information about the NIAAA and its research is available through its Web site at http://www.niaaa.nih.gov, in print form from the Publication Distribution Center at PO Box 10686, Rockville, MD 20849-0686, or fax (202) 842-0418.

The NIAAA supports an electronic bulletin board system called Quick Facts, which contains up-to-date information on important alcohol-related topics. It can be reached by calling (202) 289-4122 or at the Internet site http://www.fedworld.gov.

The NIAAA also maintains two electronic databases. The Alcohol Epidemiologic Data System (AEDS) is a national repository of alcohol-related data sets. More information can be found on-line at http://silk.nih.gov/silk/niaaa1/publication/DATADIR.pdf. The second data-

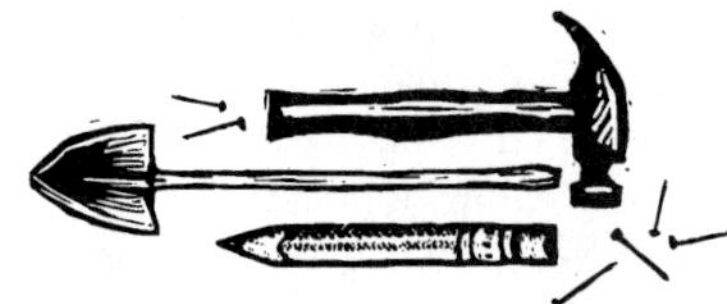

GET INVOLVED:

The NIAAA participates in the NIH Summer Intern Program in Biomedical Research. This program gives students in high school, college, and graduate school an opportunity to participate in ongoing biomedical research projects. Examples of NIAAA projects include clinical research on how the body is altered by alcohol use, biochemical research on plasma membrane, neurobiological research on the neurons and synapses of the nervous system, and neurogenetic research on the genetic determinants of alcoholism. A complete guide and application for this program are available on-line at http://www.training.nih.gov/student/sip/catalog/index.htm; or by writing NIAAA, Bldg. 31, Rm. 1B58, 31 Center Dr., MSC 2088, Bethesda, MD 20892-2088; fax (301) 402-0016; phone (301) 402-6342.

base is the Alcohol and Alcohol Problems Science Database called ETOH for the chemical name for ethyl alcohol. It contains more than 93,000 bibliographic references in medical and social fields related to alcohol research. It is located at http://etoh.niaaa.nih.gov.

AGENCY PUBLICATIONS

The NIAAA publishes a wide variety of materials for health professionals and the general public. The official publication of the institute is *Alcohol, Health, and Research World*, which publishes scientific findings from the latest research at the NIAAA. *Alcohol Alerts* is another quarterly bulletin that prints key research findings on a particular subject. The NIAAA also produces a report to Congress outlining the current state of research on alcohol abuse and alcoholism. The latest version, the *Ninth Special Report to the U.S. Congress on Alcohol and Health*, was published in 1996.

For the general public, the NIAAA publishes and distributes easy-to-read pamphlets and brochures on a variety of topics. Many of these are also available in Spanish. Examples of these publications include "Alcoholism: Getting the Facts," "Drinking and Your Pregnancy," and "How to Cut Down on Your Drinking."

The NIAAA also produces technical reports, manuals, and guides for health professionals. Examples of these publications include *Training Physicians in Techniques for Alcohol Screening and Brief Intervention* and *The Physicians' Guide to Helping Patients with Alcohol Problems*.

All publications can be obtained from the NIAAA Publication Distribution Center at PO Box 10686, Rockville, MD 20849-0686; fax (202) 842-0418. Many of these are available in full text from the Internet at http://silk.nih.gov/silk/niaaa1/publication/publication.htm.

BIBLIOGRAPHY

Gordis, Enoch. "Alcohol Research and Social Policy: An Overview." *Alcohol, Health, and Research World*, September 1996, p. 208.

Massing, Michael. "Strong Stuff." *New York Times*, 22 March 1998.

National Institutes of Health. "Age of Drinking Onset Predicts Future Alcohol Abuse and Dependence." News release. Bethesda, Md., 14 January 1998.

———. *NIH Almanac 1997. [Publication no. 97-5]* Rockville, Md.

———. *Ninth Special Report on Alcohol and Health Marks Research Gains*. Bethesda, Md., 1997.

"Out in the Open: Changing Attitudes and New Research Give Fresh Hope to Alcoholics." *Time*, 1997.

Rice, D. P. "The Economic Cost of Alcohol Abuse and Alcohol Dependence: 1990." *Alcohol Health and Research World* 1993, p. 10–11.

Wagenaar, A. C. "Research Affects Public Policy: The Case of the Legal Drinking Age in the United States." *Addiction* 88 (suppl): 75S-81S, 1993.

Wald, Matthew L. "Drunken-Driving Standard May Shift." *New York Times*, 30 January 1998.

National Institute on Drug Abuse (NIDA)

PARENT ORGANIZATION: Department of Health and Human Services
ESTABLISHED: 1974
EMPLOYEES: 353

Contact Information:

ADDRESS: Rm. 10A-39
5600 Fishers Ln.
Rockville, MD 20857
PHONE: (301) 443-6480
E-MAIL: information@lists.nida.nih.gov
URL: http://www.nida.nih.gov
DIRECTOR: Alan I. Leshner, Ph.D.

WHAT IS ITS MISSION?

The stated mission of the National Institute on Drug Abuse (NIDA) is "to lead the nation in bringing the power of science to bear on drug abuse and addiction." Founded in 1974, NIDA's original mission was to serve as the federal focal point for developing drug abuse treatment and prevention services and to become the premier research institution on drug abuse. NIDA's mission changed during 1981 when states were given more control over treatment and prevention services. All NIDA funds are now devoted to drug abuse research projects and to disseminating the results of research projects.

HOW IS IT STRUCTURED?

NIDA is one of the 24 branches of the National Institutes of Health (NIH). The NIH is an operating division of the U.S. Department of Health and Human Services, a cabinet-level department in the executive branch of the federal government.

The institute is organized into four offices and five divisions and is overseen by a director who is selected by the director of the NIH after a competitive screening process. The Office of Planning and Resource Management provides financial, personnel, information, and management services to NIDA. The Office of Extramural Program Review evaluates research proposals from scientists and institutions outside NIDA who are involved in drug abuse research. The Office of Science Policy and Communications provides scientific advice on drug

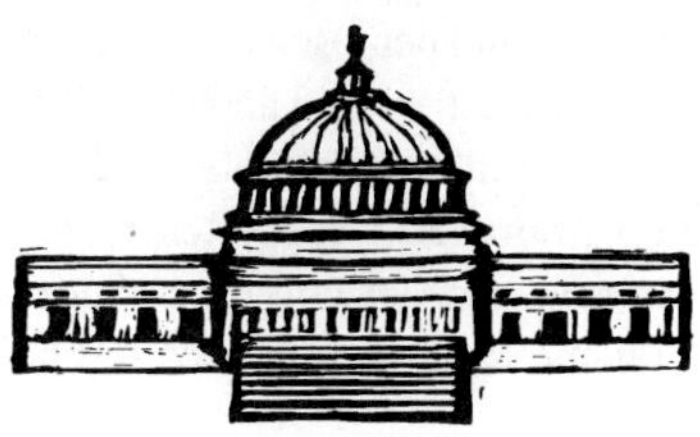

BUDGET:

National Institute on Drug Abuse

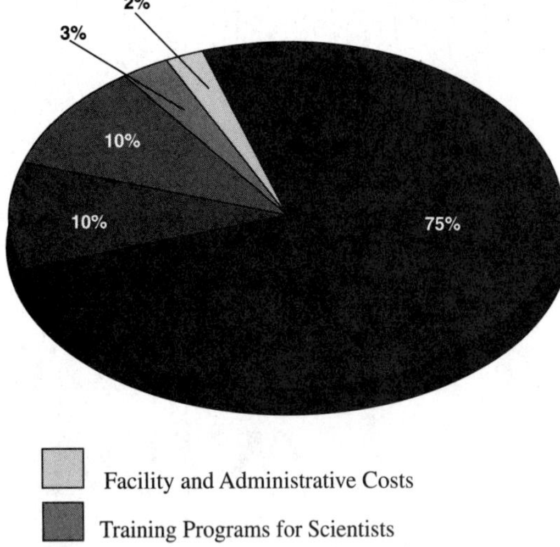

Facility and Administrative Costs

Training Programs for Scientists Interested in Drug Abuse Research

NIDA Information Dissemination

Intramural Research Projects

Extramural Research Grants

abuse policy issues and carries out NIDA information dissemination activities. The Office on Acquired Immunodeficiency Syndrome (AIDS) at NIDA coordinates a multidisciplinary research program aimed at improving the knowledge base on drug abuse and human immunodeficiency virus (HIV). The five divisions within NIDA—basic research, clinical and services research, epidemiology and prevention, medications development, and intramural research—conduct research in their specific areas.

PRIMARY FUNCTIONS

NIDA performs two major functions. The first is to support and conduct drug abuse research across a broad range of disciplines, including genetics, psychology, biology, and neuroscience. The second function of NIDA is to ensure the rapid and effective dissemination and use of the results of drug abuse research findings. Information from NIDA-supported research projects is used to improve and develop drug abuse and addiction prevention and treatment services and policies.

PROGRAMS

NIDA supports more than 85 percent of the world's research on the health aspects of drug abuse and addiction. The Extramural Research Program supplies grants to scientists and institutions involved in research projects outside NIDA. The research divisions within NIDA conduct research in specific areas of drug abuse and addiction through the Intramural Research Program.

In addition to its research programs, NIDA supports a number of programs intended to disseminate the results of drug abuse research and use these findings to educate the public. An example of this type of program is the drug abuse and AIDS prevention campaign for teens "AIDS: Another Way Drugs Can Kill." NIDA developed a campaign of broadcast and print public service announcements (PSAs) in its first effort to motivate teenagers away from drug use because of the connection between "getting high" and risky behaviors that can result in HIV infection. PSAs for television and movie trailers were directed by well-known film director Martin Scorcese and narrated by actor/director Spike Lee. After a dramatic scene, the narrator tells the brief story of a young girl, and others like her, who used drugs, forgot about AIDS prevention, and became infected with HIV. Print PSAs present the same scenario in photographs or feature statistics on HIV-infected teens in comparison with the number of teens who die in car accidents.

NIDA also supports the development and training of scientists interested in pursuing drug abuse research. As part of its research training program, NIDA funds more than 40 training sites for predoctoral and postdoctoral fellows and awards several training grants to individuals.

BUDGET INFORMATION

In 1996 NIDA's operating budget was approximately $458 million. This figure represented about 4 percent of the NIH budget, which is allocated entirely by Congress. Approximately 75 percent of NIDA's funds were spent on extramural research grants and 10 percent on intramural research projects. Another 10 percent of budget funds supported NIDA information dissemination activities. About 3 percent of NIDA funds were allocated to training programs for scientists interested in drug abuse research and the remaining 2 percent of the NIDA budget covered facility and administrative costs.

HISTORY

NIDA was established in 1974 in response to the growing national concern over the rapid rise of casual drug use and the abuse of some prescription medications. NIDA was originally the primary federal agency responsible not only for drug abuse research but also for developing prevention and treatment services and collecting data on the nature and extent of drug abuse in the United States. In 1981, when states began receiving federal block grants for their own treatment and prevention services, NIDA's mission became more focused on drug abuse research, data collection, and disseminating research results. When the epidemic nature of drug abuse and drug abuse-related HIV infection became increasingly apparent in 1986, Congress responded by quadrupling NIDA's budget for research in these areas. NIDA's budget received a large increase again in 1988 to expand research on the maternal and fetal effects of drug use and for medication development. The new Medications Development program was created by NIDA in 1990 to focus research efforts on developing new pharmacological therapies for drug addiction. In 1992 NIDA officially became part of the National Institutes of Health, the world's premier biomedical and behavioral research organization.

FAST FACTS

NIDA commits more than one-third of its total budget to funding research projects to prevent HIV infection and reduce the consequences of HIV/AIDS that are related to drug abuse.

(Source: National Institute on Drug Abuse, 1998.)

CURRENT POLITICAL ISSUES

Drugs and drug abuse are topics that lead to controversy in which NIDA often becomes included. There is constant debate over the proper status of the more socially accepted drugs, and those on both sides of the debate are often displeased with NIDA's actions.

Case Study: Marijuana

For decades, the debate over marijuana's role in medicine has created strong feelings on both sides of the issue. In 1997 the debate intensified in light of two new factors; voters in Arizona and California passed measures in November 1996 allowing seriously ill patients to obtain marijuana for medical purposes, and researchers discovered that marijuana triggers the same addiction-producing chemical reactions in the brain as "hard core" drugs such as cocaine and heroin.

On one side of the debate are federal officials and others who believe that marijuana is, first and foremost, a hazardous and illegal substance. Under the Controlled Substance Act, marijuana is classified as a Schedule I drug, one that has no medicinal value and may prove addictive. Physicians who prescribe marijuana could be prosecuted under federal law. Those who believe marijuana has no value in medicine are deeply concerned that publicizing marijuana's use as a medical treatment will send a message to young people that smoking marijuana is not harmful.

Advocates of using marijuana to treat some illnesses include many scientists, physicians, and patients who have firsthand knowledge of the benefits of medical marijuana. They claim that marijuana reduces the nausea experienced by cancer patients receiving chemotherapy, staves off blindness in people who suffer from glaucoma, and reduces intense pain in people with AIDS. These groups want marijuana reclassified as a Schedule II drug, one that physicians can legally prescribe, despite its potential for addiction (morphine is an example of a Schedule II drug). This change would encourage more research into the medical benefits of marijuana.

The debate places NIDA squarely in the middle of the opposing sides. As a federal agency, NIDA must be careful not to encourage activities that are against federal law by providing research findings that support such activities. Yet NIDA oversees the Investigational New Drug (IND) program, which has been growing marijuana and distributing it to seriously ill patients since the 1960s. The program, established for research purposes only, was seen as giving tacit approval for medicinal use of marijuana and was not allowed to accept new applicants after 1992. NIDA has the obligation to pursue research on medications that can be beneficial in treating disease but must not support public practices that violate federal law.

In response to the growing debate, leaders from NIDA and other NIH institutes organized a workshop to study the issue during March 1997. NIDA issued statements in which the agency committed to supporting further research on medical marijuana and fulfilling its obligation to provide scientific information on the issue to the public. Formal committees were established to develop long-term research projects and reports addressing medical conditions that marijuana may be useful in treating and special issues in designing appropriate and effective clinical trials. The debate over the medical uses of marijuana could continue for decades.

SUCCESSES AND FAILURES

For more than 20 years, NIDA-supported research has led to information that has increased knowledge about drug abuse and addiction and aided the development of effective prevention and treatment programs. NIDA research projects defined nicotine addiction and provided the scientific basis for smoking-cessation therapy using nicotine gum and skin patches. Pharmacological treatments were developed based on NIDA research to treat newborns suffering from withdrawal from exposure to narcotics. NIDA-supported research has also demonstrated that successful drug abuse treatment reduces future criminal behavior, as well as relapse to addiction, and that treating drug abusers' depression and other mental disorders improves the success rate of addiction therapy. These two findings have helped create more effective treatment programs and have encouraged continued public funding for such programs.

FUTURE DIRECTIONS

NIDA-supported research has identified the molecular sites in the brain where every major drug of abuse has its initial effect. These discoveries have created the basis for future priority research projects at NIDA that involve the design and development of medications to successfully treat addiction, especially during pregnancy.

In addition to treating neonatal drug addiction, NIDA will focus additional future research on improving the health of infants and children affected by drug abuse. NIDA has begun to develop techniques to detect the subtle effects of drug exposure in children of drug-using parents to provide opportunities for early preventative or treatment services.

AGENCY RESOURCES

NIDA provides resource capsules to the press and the public that provide concise summaries of drug abuse issue areas. The topics of these fact sheets range from drug abuse statistics to public education campaigns. Capsules can be accessed on-line at http://www.nida.nih.gov/drugabuse.html.

The NIDA *Director's Report* is issued three times a year and contains detailed information on NIDA activities and research findings. Director's reports are available on-line at http://www.nida.nih.gov/drugabuse.html. For information on receiving printed copies of the *Director's Report*, contact NIDA by phone at (301) 443-6245.

AGENCY PUBLICATIONS

NIDA Notes is a publication produced by NIDA that deals with treatment and prevention research, epidemiology, neuroscience, behavioral research, health services research, and AIDS. The journal reports on advances in the drug research field, identifies resources, and improves communication between researchers, administrators, and policymakers. Subscriptions to *NIDA Notes* are free and can be ordered on-line at http://www.nida.nih.gov/nidanotes/nnindex.html#about, by fax at (301) 294-5401, by E-mail at nidanotes@hq.row.com, or by writing *NIDA Notes* Subscription Department at R.O.W. Sciences, Inc., Ste. 400, 1700 Research Blvd., Rockville, MD 20850-3142.

NIDA also publishes several pamphlets, monographs, and research reports that are available to the public free of charge. Titles include "Facts About Marijuana," "Women and Drug Abuse," "Anabolic Steroids—A Threat to Body and Mind," and "Behavioral Studies of Drug-Exposed Offspring." These publications can be viewed on-line at http://www.nida.nih.gov/publicationsindex or ordered via E-mail at information@lists.nida.nih.gov.

NIDA has established an on-line series called Mind Over Matter, which is designed to explain the effects of drugs on the brain to schoolchildren in grades 5 through 9. This Web site can be accessed at http://www.nida.nih.gov/MOM/MOMIndex.html.

Additional publications are available in a wide range of prices. A complete NIDA publications catalog can be viewed on-line at http://www.nida.nih.gov/publicationsindex. Publications can be ordered through the National Technical Information Service at 1-800-553-NTIS. Videos and training manuals are also available.

BIBLIOGRAPHY

Bower, B. "Marijuana's Effects Tracked in Rat Brains." *Science News*, 28 June 1997.

Fackelmann, Kathleen. "Marijuana on Trial: Is Marijuana a Dangerous Drug or a Valuable Medicine?" *Science News*, 22 March 1997.

Saltonstall, David. "Uncle Sam's Pot Farm: Ten Joints a Day Keeps Your Illness at Bay, Thanks to a Government Stash in Mississippi's Highlands." *George*, July 1997.

Schlosser, Eric. "More Reefer Madness." *Atlantic Monthly*, April 1997.

Stapleton, Stephanie. "Medical Pot: Feds Say Talk Is OK, Just Don't Recommend It." *American Medical News*, 17 March 1997.

———. "NIH Advisory Panel to Delineate Research on Medical Marijuana." *American Medical News*, 10 March 1997.

Storey, David. "Smoking Marijuana Can Fight Illnesses, Study Says." *Detroit News*, 11 August 1997.

Voelker, Rebecca. "NIH Panel Says More Study Is Needed to Assess Marijuana's Medicinal Use." *JAMA*, 19 March 1997.

National Institutes of Health (NIH)

PARENT ORGANIZATION: Department of Health and Human Services
ESTABLISHED: May 26, 1930
EMPLOYEES: 16,680 (1997)

Contact Information:

ADDRESS: 9000 Rockville Pike
Bethesda, MD 20892
PHONE: (301) 496-4000
E-MAIL: nihinfo@od31tm1.od.nih.gov
URL: http://www.nih.gov
DIRECTOR: Harold E. Varmus, M.D.
DEPUTY DIRECTOR: Ruth L. Kirschstein, M.D.

WHAT IS ITS MISSION?

The published mission of the National Institutes of Health (NIH) is "to employ science in the pursuit of knowledge to improve human health conditions." From its roots in a one-room laboratory for research on cholera to its present sprawling campus and 24 separate branches, the NIH has retained its core mission. All of the NIH's research projects have been focused on the goal of acquiring new knowledge to help prevent, detect, diagnose, and treat disease and disability, from the rarest genetic disorder to the common cold. Today the NIH is one of the world's foremost biomedical research centers and the federal focal point for biomedical research in the United States.

HOW IS IT STRUCTURED?

The NIH is one of eight agencies making up the Public Health Service, which is itself a part of the Department of Health and Human Services, a cabinet-level department in the executive branch of the federal government. The NIH is headed by a director who is appointed by the president with the advice and consent of the Senate. The NIH is headquartered in Bethesda, Maryland, where 75 buildings on more than 300 acres house the administration of the NIH and many of its distinct divisions. The Office of the Director and numerous other administrative offices provide direction and financial, legal, communications, and legislative support to the centers and institutes under the NIH umbrella.

The NIH is made up of 24 separate institutes and centers. These include many large institutes that conduct

BUDGET:
National Institutes of Health

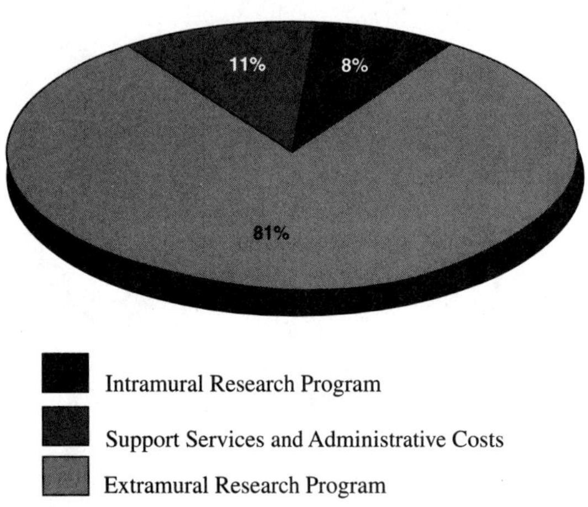

Intramural Research Program
Support Services and Administrative Costs
Extramural Research Program

research in specialized areas, including cancer; heart, lung, and blood diseases; diabetes and digestive and kidney disease; allergy and infectious diseases; child health and human development; deafness; dental diseases; environmental health; general medical studies; neurological disorders and strokes; eye disorders; alcohol abuse and alcoholism; arthritis and musculoskeletal and skin disorders; drug abuse; mental health; aging; genetics; and nursing. Also included in the NIH's 24 divisions are its administrative branches, a research hospital, an international center, and the National Library of Medicine.

PRIMARY FUNCTIONS

The NIH works toward its mission by conducting research in its own laboratories and supporting the research of scientists in universities, medical schools, hospitals, and research institutions throughout the United States and overseas. The NIH provides grants for biomedical and behavioral research to discover knowledge that will extend and improve human health. It also assists in training young researchers and disseminating medical information that emerges from its research projects.

PROGRAMS

The Extramural Research Program of the NIH provides grants to support medical research and training in more than 1,700 institutions throughout the country. Individual scientists submit written applications for grants that are reviewed by a committee of their scientific peers. A panel of scientific experts, primarily from outside the government, evaluates the scientific merit of each application. Then a national advisory council, composed of noted scientists and members from public health fields, determines the project's overall merit. The council also determines the project's priority on the research agenda of the particular NIH funding institute. Final decisions about funding extramural research projects are made at the NIH headquarters.

Extramural research grants can be small or involve millions of dollars. Project results may become useful immediately as diagnostic tests or new treatments or may lead to further research or basic information and take years to be put to practical value. About 36,000 research grant applications are reviewed annually by the NIH, and at any given time the NIH supports 35,000 grants in universities, medical schools, and other research institutions.

The Intramural Research Program is the other primary program administered by the NIH. Through this program, NIH scientists pursue research in areas of national health concerns. These scientists work in the laboratories of the various NIH institutes and collaborate with each other on comprehensive projects. Their explorations range from basic biology to behavioral research to studies on treatments for major diseases. About two thousand projects are being conducted through the program at any given time.

BUDGET INFORMATION

The 1997 budget of NIH was approximately $12.7 billion and is appropriated entirely by Congress. The majority of the NIH budget, 81 percent, funded the Extramural Research Program. Approximately 11 percent of total funds were allocated to the Intramural Research Program. The remaining 8 percent of NIH funds were spent on support services to the two major programs and administrative costs. Research projects and activities conducted through the National Cancer Institute accounted for approximately 20 percent of the NIH budget, the largest amount allocated to any of the individual institutes.The proposed budget for 1998 was $13.5 billion.

HISTORY

In 1798 the Marine Hospital Service was established by President John Adams to treat sick and disabled seamen. Over the years the services and personnel of the Marine Hospital were expanded at the direction of the federal government. A bacteriological laboratory was established at the Marine Hospital to research cholera and other infectious diseases. This laboratory was moved to

Washington, D.C., in 1891 and expanded its research to other diseases, navigable stream pollution, and information dissemination by 1912.

In 1930 the original laboratory was redesignated by Congress as the National Institute of Health, and building funds were allocated to expand its facilities. The National Cancer Institute was created in 1937 and became a division of the NIH in 1944. With the addition of the National Heart Institute in 1948, the NIH's name was changed again to its present plural form. New institutes and facilities continued to be added to the NIH throughout the 1950s, 60s, and 70s. Grant opportunities also increased, and the NIH expanded its information dissemination efforts. The last institute established in the NIH was the National Institute for Nursing Research in 1986. In 1992 the National Institute on Alcohol Abuse and Alcoholism, the National Institute on Drug Abuse, and the National Institute of Mental Health were transferred from the Alcohol, Drug Abuse, and Mental Health Administration to the NIH.

FAST FACTS

In part because of NIH research, the five-year survival rate for people with cancer has risen 52 percent.

(Source: Paulette V. Walker. "NIH Plans to Use Some Money in Its 1997 Budget for Research in Future Years." *Chronicle of Higher Education*, November 22, 1996.)

CURRENT POLITICAL ISSUES

Until 1997 organizations that supported and advocated research on specific diseases and illnesses banded together to work for the common goal of increased overall funds for the NIH. The idea was that if funding for the NIH was increased, research on these many specific diseases would also be increased through NIH grants. But in 1997 several individual advocacy organizations formed political action committees (PACs). They began to make political and public appeals for increased funds or a reallocation of NIH funds for research into the areas of research they advocated, resulting in a tumultuous debate over the way the NIH determines what research to fund.

Case Study: The Controversy over NIH Research Funding

At the heart of this controversy was NIH funding for research on the human immunodeficiency virus (HIV) and acquired immunodeficiency syndrome (AIDS). Although the leaders of the new PACs denied it, they seemed specifically to want a more "equitable" distribution of the $1.5 billion the NIH had spent on HIV and AIDS research.

For example, the Parkinson's Action Network handed out fact sheets to the public and Congress that claimed that in 1994 the NIH spent more than $1,000 per affected person on HIV/AIDS research but only $93 on heart disease research and $26 on Parkinson's disease research. The American Heart Association publicized statistics that showed the NIH budget rising by 35 percent since 1986, whereas funding for heart disease research had fallen by 5 percent even though heart disease remained the nation's number one killer. The Juvenile Diabetes Foundation (JDF) claimed that funds for diabetes research had increased by only 53 percent since 1987 although the overall NIH budget increased 97 percent. To counteract the NIH funding choices that the JDF believed were unfair, it began looking for congressional sponsors for a bill that would mandate a national diabetes research plan and require a 15 percent increase in NIH funds targeted for diabetes research.

Several members of Congress took note of the organizations' complaints that particular diseases were not receiving their fair share of research funds. NIH director Harold Varmus was called before congressional committees to explain how NIH research priorities are determined. Conservative members of Congress promised to investigate NIH-funded HIV/AIDS research projects to determine whether funds should be redistributed to more "mainstream" disease research. Other congressional representatives used the complaints as a springboard to advocate for increased research funding for diseases that affected large numbers of their constituents.

Varmus responded to the funding debate by saying that the figures being reported were based on different definitions and variables and therefore did not reflect a true or complete picture of NIH funding allocations. He also argued that funding requests must be judged on merit by qualified scientific reviewers, not influenced by political pressure. Varmus initiated a public-education campaign to explain the NIH's method for allocating research funds based on national priorities and the potential benefit of research proposals.

In the 1998 Balanced Budget Act, the NIH's overall budget was increased by 8 percent, and no requirements for specific disease research allocations were included. However, several House and Senate representatives pledged to continue their investigation and review of the NIH's funding policies. As disease lobbies continue to pursue their individual agendas, the NIH's autonomy will continue to be scrutinized.

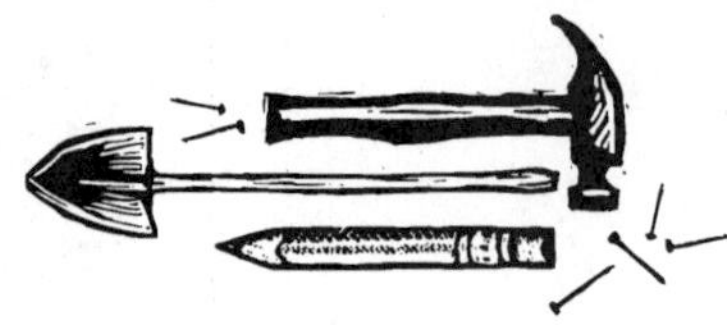

GET INVOLVED:

The NIH is committed to providing summer internships to high school, college, and graduate students who are interested in participating in an NIH research project. The intern experience is intended to expose students to research procedures in an environment devoted totally to biomedical research and training. Students conduct research in selected areas of laboratory investigation under the guidance of project scientists. Lecture series are also open to students. Each institute within the NIH that offers internships has its own volunteer coordinator; they can be contacted by calling the NIH at (301) 496-4000. Students interested in summer internships at the NIH can learn more about, and apply for, available opportunities on-line at http://helix.nih.gov:8001/oe/student/sip/catalog.

Public Impact

The debate over NIH funding will reach the public in a variety of ways. Citizens affected by diseases viewed as underfunded by the NIH might benefit if legislation mandating certain funding levels is enacted. Citizens affected by diseases receiving high percentages of NIH research funds might feel a negative impact if legislation is enacted requiring the reallocation of funds based on specific formulas. The general public could also suffer if disease research funding is determined by legislative dictates rather than by scientific evaluation of public health needs and the validity of individual projects. American citizens will all benefit from increased funds for biomedical research that leads to the prevention of, and improved treatments for, disease. However, the most equitable distribution of limited funds to projects that will do the most good will be the subject of a long-term debate.

SUCCESSES AND FAILURES

NIH research has played a major role in discovering causes and treatments for many diseases that threaten human health. Deaths from heart disease (although still the highest cause of death in the United States) dropped by 41 percent from 1971 to 1991. Death rates from stroke decreased by 59 percent during the same period. The reduction of deaths from heart disease and stroke are results of NIH research that allows doctors and scientists to understand more about preventing, detecting, analyzing, and treating these conditions.

NIH research also led to the discovery of drugs that, when administered within eight hours of injury, significantly reduce paralysis from spinal cord injury. Rapid treatment with high doses of steroids increases recovery in severely injured patients who have lost mobility at or below the point of injury.

FUTURE DIRECTIONS

The goal of NIH research in the twenty-first century is to produce information that will yield the greatest good for the largest number of people. Future research agendas for the NIH will focus on projects that will continue to improve the health of infants, children, women, and minorities. Finding ways to meet the health needs of the nation's aging population will also be a priority for the NIH. NIH grants will continue to support research on the prevention and treatment of cancer, heart disease, AIDS, Alzheimer's disease, mental illness, and other unconquered diseases.

AGENCY RESOURCES

The NIH operates hot lines that provide prevention and treatment information on specific diseases and conditions, for example, the Weight Control Information Network at 1-800-WIN-8098, the AIDS Treatment Information Service at 1-800-HIV-0440, and the Cancer Information Service at 1-800-4-CANCER. For a complete listing of NIH information lines, visit the NIH Web site at http://www.nih.gov/news/infoline.htm or call the NIH at (301) 496-4000.

The NIH also operates the National Library of Medicine (NLM), which is the world's largest medical library. MEDLINE is the NLM's primary database covering the fields of medicine, nursing, dentistry, veterinary medicine, the health care system, and the preclinical sciences. MEDLINE contains about 8.8 million records and can be accessed free of charge on the World Wide Web at http://www.nlm.nlm.gov/databases/medline.html. For more information on MEDLINE, contact the NIH at 1-888-FINDNLM.

AGENCY PUBLICATIONS

The NIH publishes a large number of consumer information pamphlets and reports on topics ranging from cancer to child health to drug abuse. These publications can be viewed on-line at http://www.,nih.gov/health/consumer/concid.htm, or a complete list of available titles can be requested by contacting the NIH at (301) 496-4000. Sample titles include, "The Healthy Heart Handbook for Women," "In Search of the Secrets of

Aging," "Marijuana: Facts for Teens," and "Because You Asked About Smell and Taste Disorders."

BIBLIOGRAPHY

Langdon, Steve. "Senate OKs Reauthorization of Expiring NIH Programs." *Congressional Quarterly Weekly Report*, 28 September 1996.

Lawler, Andrew, and Eliot Marshall. "NIH Up, for Now; Fusion Down." *Science*, 20 September 1996.

Marshall, Eliot. "Too Radical for NIH? Try DARPA." *Science*, 7 February 1997.

Marwick, Charles. "Hepatitis C Is Focus of NIH Consensus Panel." *Journal of the American Medical Association*, 23 April 1997.

———. "Scientists Flock to Hear Cloner Wilmut at the NIH." *Journal of the American Medical Association*, 9 April 1997.

Stix, Gary. "Profile: Wayne B. Jonas, Probing Medicine's Outer Reaches." *Scientific American*, October 1996.

Walker, Paulette V. "Lawmakers Push NIH to Spend More on the Most-Prevalent Diseases." *Chronicle of Higher Education*, 18 April 1997.

———. "NIH Plans to Use Some Money in Its 1997 Budget for Research in Future Years." *Chronicle of Higher Education*, 22 November 1996.

———. "NIH Restructuring Could Weaken Alternative-Medicine Program." *Chronicle of Higher Education*, 9 August 1996.

———. "Scientists and Universities Split on Value of 'Bridge' Grants from NIH Division." *Chronicle of Higher Education*, 6 December 1996.

National Labor Relations Board (NLRB)

PARENT ORGANIZATION: Independent
ESTABLISHED: July 5, 1935
EMPLOYEES: 1,950

Contact Information:

ADDRESS: 1099 14th St.
Washington, DC 20570
PHONE: (202) 273-1790
FAX: (202) 274-4270
E-MAIL: dbparker@nlrb.gov
URL: http://www.nlrb.gov
CHAIRMAN: William J. Gould, IV
GENERAL COUNSEL: Fred Feinstein

WHAT IS ITS MISSION?

The National Labor Relations Board (NLRB) serves as the primary regulatory agency dedicated to monitoring the relationships and interactions between labor unions and employers in the private sector. The NLRB protects the rights of workers to collectively bargain and to seek or decline labor union representation. It also monitors the practices of employers and unions, prohibiting unfair labor practices.

HOW IS IT STRUCTURED?

The NLRB is an independent agency within the executive branch and is made up of two major branches: the Office of the Board and the Office of General Counsel. The Office of the Board consists of five members and is structured to be bipartisan (not dominated by any one political party). Each board member is appointed by the president for a term of five years. The board serves as a decision-making body, ruling on cases in which an original decision has been appealed.

The general counsel is appointed by the president for a four-year term. The office acts independently from the board and is responsible for investigating and prosecuting cases involving unfair labor practices. The general counsel oversees 33 regional offices and sixteen field offices where initial decisions are made about the validity of a case.

Other NLRB departments include the Offices of the Executive Secretary, Solicitor, Inspector General, and Representation Appeals as well as the Divisions of Infor-

The NLRB works to equitably settle differences between management and labor through negotiations and, if necessary, arbitration. Here, striking airline workers at O'Hare International Airport celebrate the news that their dispute will go to binding arbitration. *(Reuters/Corbis-Bettmann)*

mation, Judges, Equal Employment Opportunity, Advice, Operations-Management, and Enforcement Litigation.

PRIMARY FUNCTIONS

The two main functions of the NLRB are to ensure the right of workers to labor representation and to investigate, enforce, and interpret existing labor laws when claims of unfair labor practices are made against employers or labor unions.

The NLRB provides employees with opportunities to determine whether or not they wish to be represented by labor unions during negotiations with their employers. The NLRB conducts polls of all workers involved in the decision by secret ballot to determine which union, if any, they choose to bargain on their behalf.

The second major function of the NLRB is to prevent and correct unfair labor practices (illegal actions) by both employers and unions, placing restrictions on both parties in terms of their interactions with each other and with employees. The statutes that the NLRB monitors cover most employees and employers in the private sector—except for the airline, railroad, and agriculture industries—as well as the federal government and its employees.

With each function the NLRB acts only when its services are specifically requested. For example, it does not initiate investigations but conducts them at the request of interested parties who file a petition at one of the NLRB field offices.

PROGRAMS

Upon receiving a complaint, the local NLRB office investigates to determine whether unfair labor practices may exist. The regional director then either dismisses or proceeds with a case once a charge has been filed based on the initial evidence the field office collects. If the charges are dismissed, the party who first raised the issue can appeal to the general counsel in Washington, D.C. If the charges warrant further investigation, the regional office will first seek a voluntary settlement between the parties before proceeding further. Approximately 35,000 complaints are filed each year, and in 90 percent of the cases, the NLRB is able to reach a settlement.

If a negotiated agreement cannot be reached, the case is then assigned to an administrative law judge who hears evidence from both sides and makes a decision which can be appealed to the board. Finally, any decision by the board is subject to review by a U.S. court of

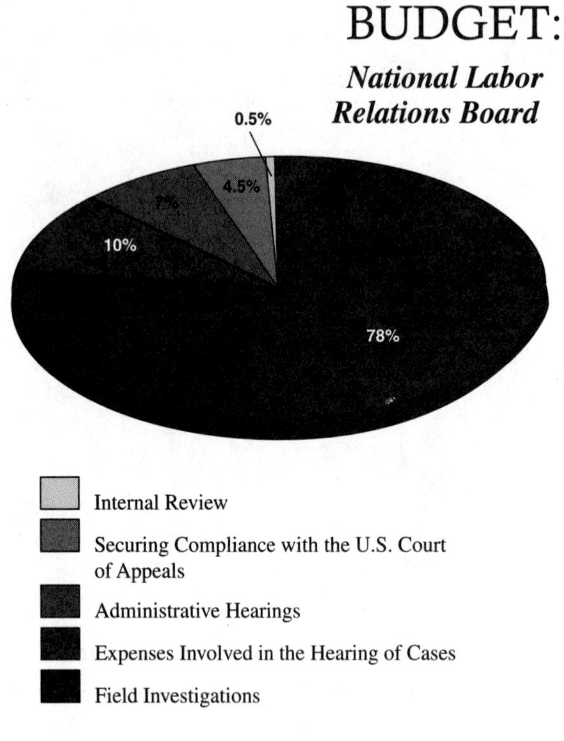

appeals. Based on the final decision, a remedy is then determined to resolve each case.

Two examples of cases that could not be settled before reaching the board involve the Watt Electrical Corporation and Straight Creek Mining, Inc. On May 16, 1997, the board agreed with the administrative law judge assigned to the Watt case that the company had violated the law by firing an employee because of his union activities. Not only was the firing considered unlawful but it also raised a broader issue that employees of the company may not be threatened by the employer for participating in unions, a right protected by the NLRB. In this case, charges were initially filed by the local division of the Electrical Workers Union.

In the Straight Creek Mining, Inc. case, charges arose after a mine was sold by the original owner to a new company. While a complete shutdown due to a change in ownership may have allowed the new owners to avoid negotiating with the workers, the NLRB determined that the mine did remain partially operational and that workers hired by the former employer were still required to perform their duties. As a result, the new company was still responsible for bargaining with workers employed by the original owners. On May 21, 1997, it was determined the new owners had committed unfair labor practices by initially refusing to negotiate employment terms with the employees.

BUDGET INFORMATION

The NLRB has been subject to government downsizing over the years, while its case load has remained relatively the same. The NLRB's total budget for fiscal year 1997 was about $175 million, approximately a third less than its peak in the 1980s.

Of the current budget, nearly 78 percent is allocated for field investigations that include examining charges of unfair labor charges and calls for representation elections. Board expenses involved in the hearing of cases comprise 10 percent of the budget. Administrative law judge hearings make up 7 percent of the budget; securing compliance with Board decisions with the U.S. Court of Appeals equals 4.5 percent; and finally, 0.5 percent of the budget is allocated for internal review of the NLRB.

HISTORY

Labor unions first developed with the rise of the Industrial Revolution in the early nineteenth century in Europe and following the end of the Civil War (1860–65) in the United States. Employees worked grueling hours in order to fuel the post war economy and had little job security or benefits; workers either followed orders or were fired, despite the legitimacy of some of their complaints.

During World War I (1914–18) workers' rights advanced slightly due to the efforts of the National War Labor Board, which established regulations regarding employer-employee relations. By 1918 the first laws protecting the rights of workers to bargain collectively were put in place. Management interference in the organizing process was prohibited but these laws offered only minimal protection for workers and relied on employees and employers themselves to make reasonable efforts to reach agreements with or without representatives.

Early organizers and union representatives were condemned by employers as threats to the U.S. economy. As a result, these first leaders were subject to intimidation and violent attacks, often at the hands of men hired by companies to suppress the formation of unions. By the 1930s federal and state laws favored employers, with strikes considered criminal acts and unions treated as monopolies that were illegal under antitrust laws.

Rising animosity between unions and management coincided with the Great Depression of the 1930s and the subsequent New Deal policies. Under President Theodore Roosevelt, the government began to take a stronger stance in regulating economic and social policy and thus monitoring the interactions between workers, unions, and employers. In 1935 President Roosevelt appealed to Congress for a greater degree of "industrial peace" so that economic recovery from the depression could be achieved. In response, Congress passed a number of laws to better regulate the economy, including the Wagner Act, the law that established the NLRB. The Wagner Act went further in protecting workers' rights than any other laws and specifically named practices that would be considered illegal if attempted by employers. These included interfering in any way with employees who wished to engage in organizing activities, interfering with the formation of labor unions, discriminating against employees or potential employees based on their interest or membership in unions, discriminating against employees who brought charges against employers in violation of the new laws, and refusing to bargain with the chosen union of employees.

Subsequent administrations attempted to weaken the Wagner Act and succeeded by establishing policies that placed restrictions on labor unions during collective bargaining and allowed employers to speak out against unions prior to NLRB elections in order to discourage employees from seeking union representation. Furthermore, during the Reagan administration of the 1980s, the NLRB reversed a number of prior rulings in the favor of management. A report by the AFL-CIO conducted in 1985 demonstrated that in 60 percent of its cases, the NLRB ruled in favor of employers, more than double the promanagement decisions made by the board during other periods.

FAST FACTS

The average annual number of large workplace strikes is down from 300 during the 1970s to approximately 35 in 1996.

(Source: U.S. Labor Department. Bureau of Statistics, 1996.)

CURRENT POLITICAL ISSUES

During the 1980s the NLRB experienced what the House of Representatives called a "crisis in management." Between 1983 and 1984 the Manpower and Housing Subcommittee held hearings on the NLRB's enormous backlog of cases brought by unions and management. The subcommittee found that although the total number of cases brought before the board had significantly decreased, the number of unfair labor practice cases pending decision in 1984 totaled 1,184. At the height of its review in another year, the NLRB only had 310 cases pending; the number of requests for elections regarding union representation was also backlogged in excess of other periods of the board's history with similar case loads.

The board countered that its inability to manage its case load was due to high attrition rates (turnover) of NLRB representatives but the subcommittee believed that the true cause of its inefficiency was due to time spent reexamining and in some cases reversing prior board decisions.

Public Impact

During the 1980s the NLRB was thought to be promanagement and reluctant to hand down decisions that would disrupt the flow of business. The backlog of cases went further than merely postponing difficult decisions—it directly impacted the lives of the complainants, who in most cases represented working people. In the report issued by the Manpower and Housing Subcommittee, the NLRB was charged with forcing workers to "wait years before cases affecting their livelihood and economic well-being of their families are decided."

SUCCESSES AND FAILURES

In order to remedy the NLRB's reputation, Chairman William B. Gould IV launched an aggressive program of reformation and reinvention. To this end, the NLRB was honored with three Hammer Awards as part of Vice President Al Gore's National Performance Review program. The first award was given for the NLRB's new case management system, or Impact Analysis. The new system significantly shortened the time required to investigate and resolve charges and prioritized the order of cases based on their public impact.

The second award acknowledged the efforts of NLRB regional offices to conduct union elections more efficiently. The new procedures put in place by the regional offices reduced the median time for holding elections from 75 days in 1993 to 57 days in 1995 in 87 percent of the cases.

The third award was presented to the NLRB's Office of Appeals for significantly reducing the waiting period between a regional director's rejection of a case to be appealed and decided upon by the Office of Appeals. As a result, most appeals at this level must now be ruled on within 60 days.

In spite of these gains, Chairman Gould continued to be attacked by critics who believed his administration was biased in favor of labor interests. In March 1997 Gould explained that his goal for the NLRB was to find "the middle ground—or vital center, as President William F. Clinton has described it. After all, the NLRB is neither prolabor, nor proemployer, nor should it be." As evidence that the board has remained impartial during his tenure, Chairman Gould also noted that more than 80 percent of the board's decisions were upheld by appeals courts.

FUTURE DIRECTIONS

As part of its efforts to remain effective, balanced, and responsive, Chairman Gould has stated that until his term expires in 1998, the NLRB will continue its program of reform. Specifically, the board will continue with its "super panel" system for hearing cases that can quickly be resolved without extensive briefings prepared by board staff. In a further effort to streamline its procedures, the board created "speed teams" for cases in which it is likely to adopt the recommendations of the administrative law judges.

AGENCY RESOURCES

The NLRB employs information officers at each of its 52 field offices throughout the country. Information officers may be contacted by phone or in person for assistance in preparing an unfair labor practice charge or representation petition or explaining how the NLRB works for the public. The NLRB also prepares pamphlets regarding its information services. For more information contact the NLRB at 1099 14th St. NW, Washington, DC 20570.

AGENCY PUBLICATIONS

The *Weekly Summary of NLRB Cases* is published by the NLRB's Division of Information. Copies can be received by contacting the division at (202) 273-1991 or can be accessed on-line at http://www.nlrb.gov/index.html. Other useful publications include *Decisions and Orders of the NLRB* and *The NLRB: What It Is, What It Does,* both of which can be requested from the Division of Information.

BIBLIOGRAPHY

"After Newspaper Strike, Unions Try New Tactics." *New York Times*, 11 March 1997, p. A13.

DiCesare, Constance B. "Salting: Union Organizers Win Right Not to Be Discriminated Against in Hiring." *Monthly Labor Review,* April 1996, p. 29.

"Joe Hill Takes on Joe College." *Business Week,* 23 December 1996, p. 60.

Tyson, James L. "Chill is Gone, But Labor Still Wary." *Christian Science Monitor,* 19 May 1997, p. 1.

Verespej, Michael A. "The NLRB's Secret War on Small Business." *Wall Street Journal,* 19 March 1997, p. A18.

Weiss, Mike. "The Prey: Torturous U.S. Senate Nomination-Investigation of William Gould." *Mother Jones,* July-August 1994, p. 50.

National Mediation Board (NMB)

WHAT IS ITS MISSION?

The *National Mediation Board 1997–2002 Strategic Plan* and the *Customer Service Plan (1994)* state the mission of the National Mediation Board (NMB) as these three goals: "the prompt and orderly resolution of disputes arising out of the negotiation of new or revised collective bargaining agreements [agreements that are made between management and labor unions that represent an entire group of people]; the effectuation of employee rights of self-organization where a representation dispute exists; and the prompt and orderly resolution of disputes over the interpretation or application of existing agreements." Simply put, the NMB's primary mission is to effectively resolve disputes between the employees and employers of the rail and air industries so that there will be as little interruption in service as possible.

HOW IS IT STRUCTURED?

The NMB, established by 1934 amendments to the Railway Labor Act of 1926, is an independent federal agency that falls under the executive branch. The NMB has five principal officers who are appointed by the president and confirmed by the Senate: a chairman, chief of staff, general counsel, and two members. These officials guide the NMB's actions. A supporting staff of mediators, headquartered in Washington, D.C., provide for and work toward minimizing work stoppages in the transportation industry. In addition to its staff of mediators, the NMB certifies appointments of arbitrators to serve as neutral parties on labor/management boards in the railroad industry. Admission to NMB's roster of arbitrators

PARENT ORGANIZATION: Independent
ESTABLISHED: June 21, 1934
EMPLOYEES: 52

Contact Information:

ADDRESS: 1301 K St.
Washington, DC 20572
PHONE: (202) 523-5290
FAX: (202) 523-1494
E-MAIL: comments@nmb.gov
URL: http://www.nmb.gov
CHAIRMAN: Magdalena G. Jacobsen
CHIEF OF STAFF: Stephen E. Crable
GENERAL COUNSEL: Ronald M. Etters

FAST FACTS

Over 97 percent of the disputes heard by the NMB are settled before they come to a strike or binding arbitration.

(Source: Ernest Dubester. "Congressional testimony," April 28, 1998.)

is based on the "Uniform Guidelines for Placement on NMB's Roster of Arbitrators."

PRIMARY FUNCTIONS

The NMB is actively involved in resolving conflicts that arise between management and labor in the transportation industry. Since its inception the NMB has tried to keep the nation's railroads and airlines in working order by minimizing the number and scope of work stoppages that occur when management and labor disagree. The NMB acts as a go-between when disputes arise that affect the collective bargaining between parties. It mediates, arbitrates, and represents the disputants in their grievances.

Mediation

The Railway Labor Act states that, should labor and management of a particular railway or airline disagree over an issue, they may first meet without a mediator. If this fails to result in satisfaction for either side, one or the other party may call for NMB mediation or the NMB may become involved on its own. The NMB will then assign a mediator (or several if the seriousness of the situation warrants it) that has expertise in bringing labor and management to a compromise solution. Mediation will continue for days, weeks, or even months until an agreement is reached or the NMB deems the situation to be irreconcilable. If the latter is the case, then the NMB asks both sides to submit to NMB-run arbitration. Should either party decide against this option, then the NMB declares a 30-day "cooling-off period"; this is a time when talks between the two sides must continue and neither can take "self-help" options (such as the labor organization striking or the management locking its workers out). The next step for the NMB is to decide if a work stoppage involving the two parties "threatens substantially to interrupt interstate commerce to a degree such as to deprive any section of the country of essential transportation service" (NMB Web site). If the NMB decides that the situation is this serious in nature, it will inform the president. The president then has to decide if an Emergency Board is necessary. An Emergency Board, a group whose members are appointed by the president and usually drawn from the National Academy of Arbitrators, prevents any work stoppages for an additional 60 days. It uses this time to investigate the disputed issue and often recommends possible solutions to the president.

Arbitration

Under NMB arbitration, an arbitrator selected from a roster of neutral arbitrators chosen by the NMB, enters a dispute between labor and management of a railroad or airline. After carefully listening to both sides of the argument, the arbitrator makes an impartial decision that is binding for both parties.

Representation

The final function of the NMB is to monitor representation disputes. Employees are often members of unions or collective bargaining units. Many times disputes erupt over who has the right to represent employees in their ongoing discussions with management over labor issues and other matters. The NMB has the authority to step in and decide who is the right agent to represent the collective bargaining units in disputes. The NMB investigates the various agents claiming the right to represent the bargaining unit. It then determines and certifies employee representatives and ensures that the process proceeds smoothly, without undue interference, influence, or coercion. In essence, the "NMB's determination of collective bargaining representation enhances the stability of the railroad and airline industries' collective bargaining process" (NMB Web site).

PROGRAMS

The NMB's functions are mediation, arbitration, and representation. The NMB maintains an ongoing list of persons who arbitrate and mediate disputes and calls upon them as needed. These professionals often have years of experience in negotiating difficult contract disputes. The NMB's list includes contact information for each expert and is available on-line through the agency's Web site.

BUDGET INFORMATION

The NMB's 1998 budget of approximately $9 million was presented by the president in the annual federal budget and appropriated by Congress. Of these funds, about $6 million went to mediation-related activities while $3 million was spent on arbitration activities.

HISTORY

In 1888 the first federal labor relations law was enacted. It applied to railroads and provided for arbitration and presidential boards of investigation into labor disputes that arose between employers and employees. When railroad workers went on strike, it crippled movement of goods and services to the nation. Since the railroads crossed all state and territory boundaries, the federal government felt it necessary to set up a mechanism to deal with the grievances between railroad management and workers. Ten years later, Congress passed another law regarding railroads and mediation. The Erdman Act provided for mediation and voluntary arbitration on the railroads and superseded the law of 1888. The act also made it a criminal offense for railroads to dismiss employees or to discriminate against prospective employees because of their union membership or activity. This last portion of the act was subsequently declared invalid by the U.S. Supreme Court.

The early twentieth century saw a rise in the number of unions and the subsequent attempts to control or destroy them on the part of business and management. By the 1920s railroad workers and management had gone through an enormous number of disputes that severely affected the shipping of goods and passengers around the nation. Finally, in 1926, the Railway Labor Act required employers to bargain collectively and not discriminate against employees for joining a union. An amendment to the act in 1934 provided for the settlement of railway labor disputes through mediation, voluntary arbitration, and fact-finding boards; this marked the creation of the National Mediation Board (NMB). This time the Supreme Court upheld the provisions of the act and allowed for collective bargaining and the freedom for a railway worker to select a union without fear of intimidation or discrimination.

In the years subsequent to the Railway Labor Act, the National Mediation Board handled disputes that often arose between labor and management. The NMB gained added duties when Congress assigned the budding airline industries under the jurisdiction of the board.

In 1952 a NMB Presidential Emergency Board recommended agreement on the union shop between the railroads and nonoperating railroad unions representing about one million workers. Throughout the 1960s, 1970s, and 1980s the NMB maintained the status quo between labor and management by mediating disputes.

Strong customer support for the NMB's programs continued, as demonstrated in part by the December 1994 Report of the Commission on the Future of Worker-Management Relations, which found that "despite differences of interest and experience, the major representatives of labor and management governed by the Railway Labor Act responded unanimously that this Commission should not recommend any changes to the Act." During the mid and late 1990s, the NMB was involved in numerous airline labor disputes. Major airlines, such as TransWorld Airlines, United, Continental, and Northwest were all involved in drawn out, contentious negotiations with their pilots and support staff.

CURRENT POLITICAL ISSUES

One of the less publicized functions of the NMB is to ensure the smooth proceedings of representation elections. Employees must face a difficult decision regarding unionization; if they do band together, they might gain better wages and benefits but they could face the possibility of losing their jobs during strikes. Once labor decides that it wants to join a union, employees choose which of several different organizations they wish to have represent them in contract negotiations. The organization then submits an application to the NMB to enter into the situation and guarantee that the election process is run without interference. The NMB makes sure that there are no disputes regarding who should represent employees and that management does not attempt to unduly influence its workers to accept or reject unionization.

Case Study: International Associations of Machinists Representation for United Airlines, Inc., Employees

In 1997 the passenger service and reservation agents of United Airlines decided that their wages and benefits were not commensurate with their responsibilities. In addition, these employees felt that certain aspects of the Employee Stock Ownership Plan, the plan into which United and its workers jointly entered in 1994 to save the airline from bankruptcy, seemed unfair. Employees who had been represented by a union at the time of the agreement received more than those who did not belong to a union. Some of these nonunion United workers wanted to gain union representation. They decided upon the International Associations of Machinists (IAM), an organization which already represented many other types of United workers.

By April 1998 the IAM had filed its application with the NMB for a representation election for the United workers. It immediately entered into an enormous campaign to gain the support of all of the passenger service employees that it wished to represent. The IAM covered 113 cities, detailing the advantages of representation through the IAM to employees. On July 11 the NMB distributed ballots for voting to the United workers.

Representatives of the IAM and United Airlines met at the NMB's offices in Washington, D.C., on July 17 to observe the counting of the ballots. The passenger service and reservation agents who asked for union representation through the IAM got their wish. The NMB's mediator assigned to the case, Gale Oppenberg, tallied the votes and more than 99 percent of those United Airlines's employees who voted chose to have the IAM represent them in negotiations. The 18,000 workers who were affected by the election made for the largest NMB-run vote ever. Despite the sometimes rocky relationship between the IAM and United, the airline's management credited the IAM's ability to rally support for its certification. "We applaud the IAM for an effective campaign," said United's President John Edwardson. "We will work with the IAM closely and cooperatively to reach a fair and equitable agreement" (IAM Web site). The NMB had successfully concluded its efforts to ensure that employees of the airline had been able to freely choose how they would interact with management.

FUTURE DIRECTIONS

The NMB hopes to speed the process through which it performs its functions. Often negotiations in a contract dispute can take two years. While part of the reason for the length is due to the nature of mediations, the NMB acknowledges that it could move more quickly. To this end, the agency is instituting measures to try to accomplish its goals swiftly. It has put a number of its important forms, such as those for filing a complaint or a request for mediation, on-line at its Web site and plans to expand these resources in the hope that this will result in speedier processing. The NMB is also using additional mediators on cases in an effort to provide more expertise for each case.

AGENCY RESOURCES

There is a Reading Room located at the NMB's headquarters in Washington, D.C., where copies of collective-bargaining agreements between labor and management of various rail and air carriers are available for public inspection, by appointment, during office hours (1 P.M. to 4 P.M., Monday through Friday). To be able to visit the Reading Room, contact the Chief of Staff, National Mediation Board, 1301 K St. NW, Washington, DC 20572; phone (202) 523-5920; fax (202) 523-1494.

Further information on the NMB can be obtained by accessing the NMB Web site at http://www.nmb.gov, or by written request to Chief of Staff, National Mediation Board, 1301 K St. NW, Washington, DC 20572; phone (202) 523-5920; or fax (202) 523-1494.

AGENCY PUBLICATIONS

The NMB distributes a number of publications to the public including *Determinations of the National Mediation Board* (23 volumes); *Interpretations Pursuant to Section 5, Second of the Act* (2 volumes); *Annual Reports of the National Mediation Board*, *Report of the National Railroad Adjustment Board*, *The Railway Labor Act at Fifty*, and *The National Mediation Board at Fifty—Its Impact on Railroad and Airline Labor Disputes*. For further information on how to obtain copies of these publications, contact the Chief of Staff, National Mediation Board, 1301 K St. NW, Washington, DC 20572; phone (202) 523-5920; or fax (202) 523-1494. Various press releases, dispute determination documents, and the NMB handbook can be accessed on-line at http://www.nmb.gov/docsup.htm.

BIBLIOGRAPHY

Brannigan, Martha. "Effort to Unionize Workers at Delta Air is Blocked by Board." *Wall Street Journal*, 10 December 1997, p. B4.

Dobbyn, Tim. "Pilots Resume Talks With Hope of a Settlement." *Reuters*, 14 January 1998.

Dworkin, Andy. "Pilots Ready to Square Off: Emergency Board Starts 5 Days of Hearings Today." *Dallas Morning News*, 27 February 1997, p. 1D.

Field, David. "Emergency Board May Not Build Bridge in Airline Talks." *USA Today*, 18 February 1997, p. 8B.

"National Mediation Board Reconvenes Negotiations." *US Newswire*, 20 November 1997.

NMB Strategic Plan 1997–2002. Government Printing Office, 1997.

"No Strike Until '98: Board Ruling Keeps UPS Pilots in the Air." *Newsday*, 28 August 1997, p. A66.

Song, Kyung M. "Machinists Seek Contract: Deadlock Ruling TWA Seeks Damages for Wildcat Action." *St. Louis Post-Dispatch*, 5 May 1998, p. C6.

National Oceanic and Atmospheric Administration (NOAA)

PARENT ORGANIZATION: Department of Commerce
ESTABLISHED: October 3, 1970
EMPLOYEES: 12,700

Contact Information:

ADDRESS: U.S. Department of Commerce
Washington, DC 20230
PHONE: (202) 482-2985
TDD (HEARING IMPAIRED): (301) 713-0973
FAX: (202) 482-3154
E-MAIL: opca@esdim.noaa.gov
URL: http://www.noaa.gov
UNDER SECRETARY: D. James Baker
DEPUTY UNDER SECRETARY: Douglas Hall

WHAT IS ITS MISSION?

As stated on its Web site, the mission of the National Oceanic and Atmospheric Administration (NOAA) is to "predict and describe changes in the Earth's environment, and conserve and wisely manage the Nation's coastal and marine resources." NOAA's goals in coastal and marine management are to build sustainable fisheries, to recover protected species, to sustain healthy coasts, and to promote safe navigation. In the area of prediction and description, the goals are to implement seasonal climate forecasts, to predict 10 to 100–year changes in weather, provide advance and short-term warning and forecast services, and to provide extensive environmental information services.

HOW IS IT STRUCTURED?

NOAA is the largest of 14 separate bureaus within the Department of Commerce (DOC). The administrator of NOAA holds the title of undersecretary of oceans and atmosphere. Because of the size of the agency and the scope of its responsibilities, the undersecretary is assisted by a large and diverse group of supporting officers, including a chief scientist, a deputy assistant secretary for international affairs, and a naval deputy. The undersecretary is also supported by ten other administrative offices, including the Office of Finance and Acquisition, the Office of Public and Constituent Affairs, and the Office of Finance and Administration.

The main work of NOAA is carried out through its operational line offices: the National Ocean Service (NOS); the National Weather Service (NWS); the

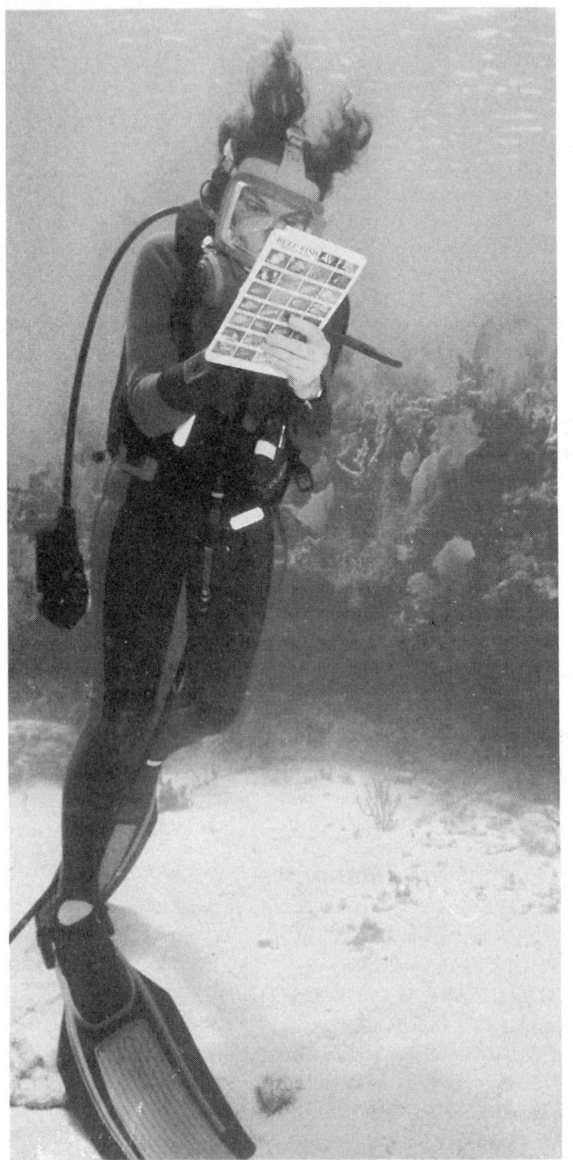

Oceanographer Dr. Sylvia Earle counts fish in the Florida Keys National Marine Sanctuary as part of the two-week long Great American Fish Count in July of 1997. The count was an effort to document fish population and diversity in U.S. waters. The marine sanctuary, one of 12 administered by NOAA, is at risk due to extensive tourism and pollution in the Florida Keys. (AP/Wide World Photos)

National Marine Fisheries Service (NMFS); Ocean and Atmospheric Research (OAR); and the National Environmental Satellite, Data and Information Service (NESDIS). NOS manages ocean and coastal resources, especially within the 200-mile Exclusive Economic Zone (the official coastal territory of the United States), and is responsible for producing nautical and aeronautical charts for sale to the public. The NWS provides weather and flood warnings and forecasts to the general public, and the NMFS manages fisheries within the 200-mile coastal limit to ensure the health of commercial and recreational fish stocks. The research and technology necessary for improving NOAA weather and marine services are provided by OAR, which also provides the scientific basis for national policy concerning climate change, air quality, and stratospheric ozone depletion. NESDIS, one of the youngest NOAA agencies, operates environment observation satellites and manages NOAA's environmental data collections.

Three special program offices also report to the undersecretary. The Office of High Performance Computing and Communications (HPCC) is responsible for developing NOAA's information infrastructure and for its communications to external organizations. The Office of Global Programs sponsors specific scientific research aimed at understanding climate variability and its predictability. To aid policymakers, the Coastal Ocean Program targets critical issues for the nation's coastal waters, estuaries, and the Great Lakes.

The field organization of NOAA and its line offices is vast, with research centers and regional offices located throughout the country.

PRIMARY FUNCTIONS

The activities and responsibilities of NOAA include a broad range of scientific and weather-related tasks. As one of the federal agencies most involved with the study of the environment, NOAA also serves as an important source of information for legislators and policymakers. It conducts an integrated program of managing and researching the use of marine resources and their habitats and protects certain marine species. It also prepares and issues nautical and aeronautical charts, provides geodetic surveys, and leads broad research programs in marine and atmospheric sciences.

NOAA also predicts tides and the weather; provides forecasts to the general public; and provides services in support of aviation, marine activities, agriculture, forestry, and other weather-sensitive activities. The administration conducts research and development to provide alternatives to ocean dumping and develops national policies concerning ocean mining.

NOAA's satellite system also provides satellite observations of the environment. It acquires, stores, and disseminates worldwide environmental data through a system of scientific data centers, and it has a system of marine buoys for automatically obtaining and distributing marine environmental data.

PROGRAMS

The programs of NOAA and its line offices are numerous and varied. Most programs, such as the Fleet Replacement and Modernization Program, which handles the replacement of aging NOAA equipment, carry out necessary everyday tasks within the agency. Other programs are partnerships in which NOAA plays an important role. Its Climate and Global Change Program is an integral part of the U.S. Global Change Research Program which concentrates on understanding the global climate system.

Another NOAA program is the Teacher at Sea Program, which offers K-12 teachers the opportunity to do scientific research at sea under the direction of the chief scientist and other NOAA personnel, and to share the experience with students and colleagues. The National Sea Grant Program, older than NOAA itself, is a partnership between the nation's universities and NOAA that focuses on marine research and the sustainable development of marine resources. The 29 Sea Grant colleges nationwide each produce and make available substantial amounts of information ranging from public school curriculum materials to advanced scientific research. The Sea Grant Program is one of NOAA's most effective means of providing education and technology transfer to the American public.

BUDGET:

National Oceanic and Atmospheric Administration

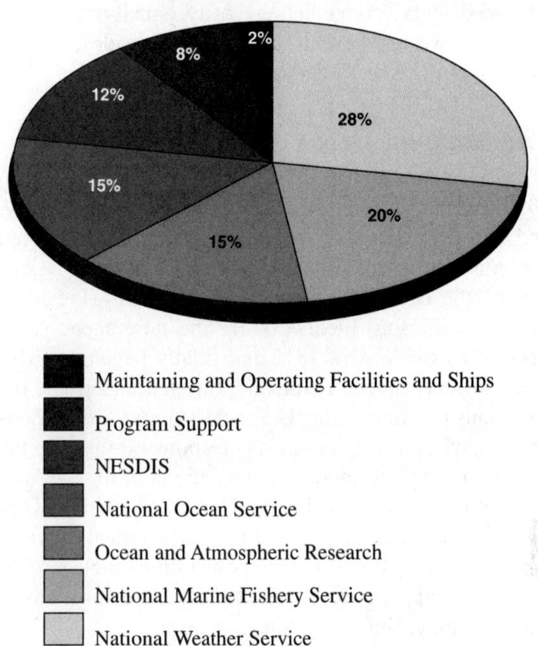

BUDGET INFORMATION

The operations of the NOAA are funded through congressional appropriations, $1.86 billion in 1998, and its own fee collections, $252 million in 1998. Out of its total budget of $2.12 billion, the National Weather Service accounts for the largest portion, about 28 percent, followed the National Marine Fishery Service at 20 percent, Ocean and Atmospheric Research with 15 percent, the National Ocean Service with another 15 percent, and NESDIS with 12 percent. Approximately 8 percent of the NOAA budget is spent on program support, including executive direction and central administrative support, and the remaining 2 percent of the budget is spent maintaining and operating the NOAA's facilities and its fleet of ships.

HISTORY

NOAA was established in 1970 in response to what President Richard Nixon described as an urgent need for better protection of life and property from natural hazards as well as a need for exploration and development leading to the intelligent use of marine resources. The new DOC bureau brought together some of the oldest government agencies from other departments—the NOS, the NWS, and the NMFS—and created two new offices, NESDIS and OAR. NOAA was given responsibility for predicting the weather; charting the seas and skies; protecting ocean resources; and collecting data on the oceans, the sun, and space.

The National Weather Service

The largest scientific agency to become a NOAA unit was the Weather Bureau, now the NWS. Recorded weather observation began not long after the Pilgrims landed at Plymouth Rock, but the first official weather service in the United States was not created until 1870 as a bureau under the secretary of war. The nation's first daily weather maps appeared the following year.

The Weather Bureau became the civilian Weather Service in 1891 when Congress transferred it to the U.S. Department of Agriculture (USDA). It remained there until it was moved to the DOC to permit better coordination of government weather reporting for aviation, commerce, and agriculture.

During the 1950s the Weather Service established a severe storm forecast center and began the National Hurricane Research Project. In cooperation with the National

Aeronautics and Space Administration (NASA), the Department of Defense, and private industry, it undertook the development of a global weather satellite observation system in 1961, a project that by the 1980s had resulted in the only civilian observational satellite system in the United States. The NWS seeks to carry out a modernization program that will provide forecasters with advanced tools for predicting costly, small-scale, fast-breaking, weather events, including tornados, severe thunderstorms, and flash floods.

The National Ocean Service

The oldest agency to be transferred into NOAA in 1970 was the NOS. Initially known as the Coast Survey, and later the Coast and Geodetic Survey, it is considered the nation's first scientific agency. Legislation for a survey of the coast was approved in 1807 by President Thomas Jefferson. Fieldwork for the new agency was delayed by the War of 1812 and finally began in 1816, when superintendent Ferdinand Hassler undertook the enormous task of charting U.S. coasts. Later acts of Congress gave further surveying responsibilities to the agency. In 1871 it undertook geodetic control, or a network of surveyor's baselines and benchmarks in the U.S. interior, and in 1926 it began the aeronautical charting program. Today the NOS's responsibilities include nautical charting, geodesy, seismology, geomagnetism, oceanography, and aeronautical charting.

The National Marine Fisheries Service

Because fish was an important food source, fisheries were the first renewable resource to receive public attention in the United States. A national office in this area was established in 1871 by President Ulysses S. Grant, who created the Office of Commissioner of Fish and Fisheries. Its headquarters was established at Woods Hole, Massachusetts, now an internationally renowned oceanographic and marine research center. The Fish Commission was moved to the Department of Commerce and Labor in 1903 and was renamed the Bureau of Fisheries.

By 1920 the bureau was responsible for fish hatchery maintenance, promoting the preservation of fish, and the conversion of fish waste products into productive commercial uses, such as paint and varnish oil, stock feed meal, and fertilizer. In the early 1970s the NMFS was assigned responsibility for protecting endangered marine species.

Perhaps the most significant piece of fishery legislation in U.S. history was passed in 1976. The Magnuson Act established an exclusive U.S. Fishery Conservation Zone from three to 200 miles off the U.S. coast and charged the DOC with managing the zone's commercial and recreational fish stocks. The bureau did not acquire its present name, the National Marine and Fisheries Service, until it was made a part of NOAA in 1970.

CURRENT POLITICAL ISSUES

NOAA's National Marine Sanctuaries program was established largely in response to a disastrous oil spill off the coast of Santa Barbara, California, in 1969. The sanctuaries are underwater preserves containing significant historical, cultural, ecological, or aesthetic resources. Many of them are still relatively undeveloped and for the most part little known to the American public.

The Marine Sanctuaries program was challenged as soon as it was established in 1972 by both the oil and gas industry and the Department of Defense, all powerful political players. The program has not gained much support since then even within NOAA. Even throughout the Reagan years, however, when Secretaries of the Interior James Watt and Donald Hodel planned to open up one billion acres of the outer continental shelf to offshore oil drilling, the marine sanctuaries survived, largely because of powerful grassroots support from coastal communities who were concerned about deteriorating marine ecosystems and opposed to an explosion of offshore oil leases.

As the administrator of the 12 marine sanctuaries, NOAA has the authority to regulate and restrict virtually all activity within the boundaries of an area designated a sanctuary—swimming, diving, boating, recreational and commercial fishing, waterskiing, whale watching, etc. This control has become unpopular in some communities where local economies rely in part on access to certain marine areas. The marine sanctuaries are again under attack from U.S. citizens who want greater control over their local resources.

Case Study: The Florida Keys National Marine Sanctuary

The Florida Keys National Marine Sanctuary is the largest in the program and covers 220 miles of coastline from Soldier Key to the Dry Tortugas. Even staunch opponents of NOAA acknowledge that the sanctuary is in environmental trouble; declining water quality has affected fish catches and caused coral disease, sponge and seagrass die-offs, and fish kills from fertilizer runoff from sugar fields. Furthermore, Key West has a municipal sewage outfall that dumps right into the sanctuary. Over four million people a year visit the Keys, six times the number of vacationers who visit Australia's Great Barrier Reef, the world's largest reef and ten times the size of the Key reef. NOAA, which oversees the sanctuaries on an annual budget of $12 million, is overworked and understaffed and has been able to do very little to help the marine populations of the Keys to rebound.

Even so, NOAA's meager intervention in the Keys has met with violent protests from members of the local community, especially from the Conch Coalition. The Coalition sees NOAA's protection of the sanctuary as an interference by the federal government in what should be a local affair. The answer to ecological problems, the

Coalition claims, is never supplied by the U.S. government but by local communities.

Members of Reef Relief, a local environmental group that helped to establish the sanctuary in 1990, argue that the area has already reached its carrying capacity, and further tourist development will destroy the very resources that make the Keys so popular. With its small portion of government funding and very little political support NOAA faces an uphill battle in preserving the natural resources of the Florida Keys.

SUCCESSES AND FAILURES

The National Sea Grant Program, established in 1966 by the National Sea Grant College Program Act, has proven very successful. In spite of its relatively small budget appropriation, Sea Grant provides a very high return. For example, the aquaculture of hybrid striped bass was led by the Sea Grant as a small university demonstration project, but within six years it became a $3.75 million fish farming industry and was expected to double its production in the following year.

FUTURE DIRECTIONS

NOAA's Strategic Plan for 1995–2005 outlines several distinct goals in the areas of environmental assessment and stewardship. The NOAA envisions a world in which societal and economic decisions are linked with a comprehensive understanding of the environment and warns that future economic growth must go hand in hand with environmental stewardship.

The plan notes a few current situations that make certain elements of the agency's existing mission more urgent: expanding populations and weather-sensitive commercial ventures are driving the need for a more comprehensive system of environmental observations and information delivery; many marine species are under stress from a combination of habitat degradation, overexploitation, and competing economic concerns; and human populations in coastal counties are growing at a much faster rate than inland counties, contributing to resource degradation and declining environmental quality and economic productivity.

A specific example of NOAA's future implementation strategy is its plan to recover protected marine species. NOAA's objectives are to assess the status of protected species as well as environmental impacts on them in order to focus management actions. After the initial assessment the agency will develop and implement conservation and recovery plans, in part through developing new partnerships with state and private sectors. NOAA plans to develop technologies and measures that will reduce or eliminate harmful interactions between marine species and human activities.

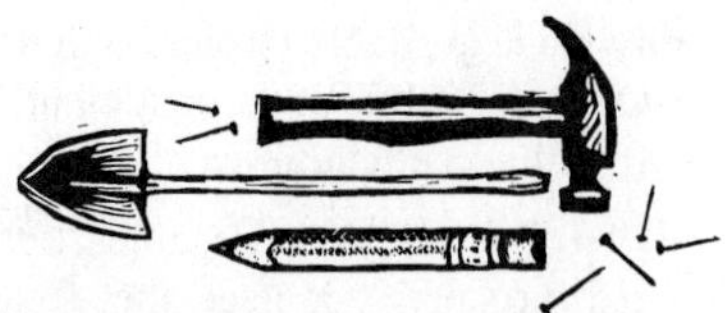

GET INVOLVED:

Through OAR, NOAA encourages involvement in the annual Earth Day celebration, which was created in the 1970s to increase awareness of how people affect the environment. Although not an official NOAA program, Earth Day has become an important event for increasing public awareness of the resources NOAA aims to manage and restore. Public involvement in Earth Day has taken many forms in the past, from activities such as the Groceries Project, in which schoolchildren decorate recyclable grocery bags with environmental Earth Day pictures and messages, to Earth Day's largest national event, the March for Parks, sponsored by the National Parks and Conservation Association (NPCA). The 1996 March for Parks involved more than a million people. Marches were held in over 50 states and nine foreign countries and raised $2 million for community parks. For information on how to organize or participate in a March for Parks near you, call 1-800-628-7275, extension 225. OAR's Earth Day Web page can be accessed at http://www.erl.noaa.gov/EarthDay.

AGENCY RESOURCES

For general information about the work of NOAA, contact NOAA's Correspondence Unit, 1305 East-West Highway, Rm. 8624, Silver Spring, MD 20910. NOAA's Central Library maintains a collection of over one million books, journals, and technical reports on agency-related subjects. The library can be accessed on the Internet at http://www.lib.noaa.gov.

To access the vast store of environmental data provided by NESDIS, a number of options are available, including Environmental Information Services, which can be reached by telephone at (301) 713-3578 or accessed on the Web at http://www.esdim.noaa.gov.

AGENCY PUBLICATIONS

From global sea surface temperature maps and whale song audio recordings to technical reports and informational pamphlets such as "Coastal America" or "A Change in the Weather Service," NOAA and its offices offer a wide selection of publications to the general public. NOAA's publications and products are generally made available through individual line offices, but the Office of Public and Constituent Affairs at (202) 482-6090 will accept enquiries.

To obtain NOAA tide tables, tidal current charts, and related products, contact the Coastal and Estuarine Oceanography Branch at (301) 713-2812. NOS nautical charts and publications may be obtained directly from the NOS Distribution Division, 6501 Lafayette Ave., Riverdale, MD 20737; phone (301) 436-6990.

BIBLIOGRAPHY

"The Blobs." *Discover*, September 1996, pp. 16–17.

Braun, Nina and Nikolas Keresi. "NOAA's Future." *Sail*, February 1997, pp. 94–96.

Caddy, John F., ed. *Marine Invertebrate Fisheries: Their Assessment and Management*. New York: John Wiley and Sons, Inc., 1989.

Cook, William J. "Ahead of the Weather: New Technologies Let Forecasters Make Faster, More Accurate Predictions." *U.S. News and World Report*, April 1996, pp. 55–58.

Coram, Robert. "Water Worlds." *Audubon*, May–June 1995, pp. 38–41.

Gifford, Bill. "Something Fishy in Washington: How the Federal Government Plans to Privatize the Ocean." *Harper's*, June 1996, pp. 54–55.

Helvarg, David. "When Uncle Sam's 'Fish Cops' Reel in a Suspect, He's Usually a Keeper." *Smithsonian*, February 1997, pp. 30–38.

Lawler, Andrew. "Republicans Take Axe to NOAA Research." *Science*, 2 June 1995, p. 1272.

Travis, John. "NOAA's 'Arks' Sail into a Storm." *Science*, 8 July 1994, pp. 177–179.

Weber, Gustavus A. *The Coast and Geodetic Survey: Its History, Activities & Organization*. New York: A.M.S. Press, Inc., 1980.

National Park Service (NPS)

PARENT ORGANIZATION: Department of the Interior
ESTABLISHED: August 25, 1916
EMPLOYEES: 20,342

Contact Information:

ADDRESS: 1100 Ohio Dr. SW
Washington, DC 20242
PHONE: (202) 619-7256
URL: http://www.nps.gov
DIRECTOR: Robert G. Stanton

WHAT IS ITS MISSION?

One of the federal government's leading conservation agencies, the National Park Service (NPS) exists to promote and regulate the use of national parks. Within these federally protected areas the NPS works to conserve scenic beauty, natural and cultural resources, and wildlife, and also to ensure the survival of these sites for use by future generations.

HOW IS IT STRUCTURED?

There are more than 370 sites in the National Park System, including national parks and monuments; scenic parkways, preserves, trails, riverways, seashores, lakeshores, and recreation areas; and historic sites associated with important movements, events, and personalities of the American past. Headquarters for the NPS are located in Washington, D.C., at the National Capitol region offices.

The NPS is administered by a director appointed by the secretary of the interior and confirmed by the Senate. Under the guidance of the Department of the Interior's assistant secretary for Fish, Wildlife, and Parks, the director of the NPS is responsible for planning, developing, administering, and protecting the National Park System and related areas. The director is assisted by two deputy directors who oversee the Equal Opportunity Program, international affairs, and policy management. Supporting these administrators is the assistant director of external affairs, whose responsibilities include oversight of legislative and congres-

The Grand Teton Peak, tallest of the 19 peaks in Grand Teton National Park, Wyoming.
(Courtesy of the Wyoming Division of Tourism)

sional affairs, the Office of Communications, and tourism programs.

Below this top-level administrative team are seven regional directors and five associate directors. Regional directors manage field offices in specific regions of the park system. These include the Alaskan, Intermountain, Midwest, Northeast, Pacific West, National Capitol and Southwest regional offices. Field offices are instrumental in assisting the NPS director in developing and implementing management plans and staffing of sites within the National Park System. Associate directors oversee such program areas as administration, cultural resource stewardship and partnerships, natural resource stewardship and science, park operations and education, and professional services. A superintendent is responsible for each national park, and park rangers and guides help visitors explore and enjoy the areas. National parks also employ naturalists, foresters, biologists, geologists, and historians to study the park areas.

NPS administrators are supported by a service center in Denver, Colorado, which provides planning, architectural, engineering, and other professional services. There are also ten support offices throughout the NPS system providing administrative assistance to the NPS staff. In total, approximately 20,000 permanent and seasonal staff manage the park system.

PRIMARY FUNCTIONS

The NPS works to conserve and protect park sites. It is also responsible for the preservation of national monuments and memorials throughout the United States. Park personnel are responsible for seeing that sites are a safe place to enjoy recreational and educational experiences. Rangers enforce park regulations and strive to provide visitors with information on the unique characteristics of individual sites.

New parks, monuments, and other sites are usually added to the National Park System in response to public support and advocacy. A new site can be created through an act of Congress or a presidential proclamation. Following the establishment of a new site, the NPS engages special resource studies to determine how to best manage the site, what methods of long-term protection to employ, and how to administer the site at a reasonable cost.

Through its park rangers and other on-site staff, the NPS relates the natural values and historical significance of individual areas to the public through talks, tours, films, exhibits, publications, and other interpretive media. The NPS operates campgrounds and other visitor facilities and provides lodging, food, and transportation services at many park sites, usually through concessions.

Additionally, the NPS collects scientific data at appropriate sites, such as information about wildlife populations, habitat, and migration patterns. These statistics are used in conjunction with those of other federal agencies to develop the overall conservation strategies of the Department of the Interior.

PROGRAMS

The NPS administers the following program areas: the state portion of the Land and Water Conservation Fund, coordination and information services for the Nationwide Outdoor Recreation program, state comprehensive outdoor recreation planning, planning and technical assistance for the National Wild and Scenic Rivers System and the National Trails System, natural area programs, the National Register of Historic Places, national historic landmarks, historic preservation, technical preservation services, Historic American Buildings Survey, Historic American Engineering Record, and interagency archaeological services.

Historic preservation functions of the NPS provide for the protection and use by the public of such sites as the homes of George Washington and Thomas Jefferson. Historic memorials such as American Civil War (1860–65) battlefields have been preserved for future generations, as have monuments such as the Statue of Liberty in New York, New York.

However, the NPS is best known for its management of wilderness areas and campsites throughout the United States. Park rangers protect the natural beauty of areas such as the Grand Teton National Park in Wyoming while increasing visitors' awareness of unique wildlife habitats within the parks.

BUDGET INFORMATION

The proposed 1999 budget for the NPS is $1.9 billion, up from $1.86 billion in 1998. NPS staffing is funded at $1.5 million. The majority of the budget is divided among the 374 sites managed by the NPS. For example the operating budget for Yellowstone National Park is approximately $20 million a year. However, cuts in funding to the NPS have directly affected parks such as Yellowstone, resulting in a reduction in funding by approximately $5 million over a two-year period.

Budget shortfalls are a major concern for advocates of the park system, some of whom calculate these shortfalls as high as $9 billion. Congress has compounded the situation by cutting funding while simultaneously adding new sites to the park system, a situation that will demand budget solutions be devised by legislators and Department of Interior leadership in the coming years.

HISTORY

The national park concept is generally attributed to artist George Catlin who, when visiting the Dakota Territories in 1832, worried about the impact of westward expansion on Indian civilization, wildlife, and wilderness. In 1871 the U.S. Geological and Geographical Survey of the Territories undertook to explore lands now in the states of Montana and Wyoming. The survey expedition was accompanied by another painter, Thomas Moran, whose inspiring landscape paintings found their way to Washington, D.C. His paintings captured the startling beauty of the western territories and deeply affected the policymakers of the day. Images of canyons, geysers, and rivers helped convince Congress to pass the Congressional Act of 1872, which established Yellowstone National Park.

In 1890 Congress created Yosemite Valley National Park from lands that had been previously donated to the state of California as a protected area. The uniqueness of this valley was brought to the attention of the American people by naturalist-writer John Muir with the help of a popular magazine, *The Century.* The power of Muir's essays and his tireless advocacy for conservation of the valley had spurred the founding of the Sierra Club, which successfully lobbied Congress for preservation of the valley.

Citing growing interest in the preservation of American Indian civilizations, Congress passed the Antiquities Act in 1906, authorizing presidents to set aside "historic and prehistoric structures, and other objects of historic or scientific interest" in federal custody as national monuments. Theodore Roosevelt used the act to proclaim 18 national monuments, such as California's Muir Woods, before he left the presidency. He is also credited with doubling the number of national parks and with the protection of 125 million acres of forest.

By 1916 the Department of the Interior was responsible for 14 national parks and 21 national monuments but had no internal organization to administer them. Recognizing the need for a new bureau, Congress passed the National Park Service Act, which created the NPS. The first director of the NPS was Stephen T. Mather, who deftly managed the animosity of state representatives who resented the loss of valuable land revenues and resources by promoting a new industry: tourism. Under Mather's guidance the NPS flourished.

Subsequent director Horace M. Albright convinced President Franklin D. Roosevelt to allow the NPS to succeed the War Department and the Forest Department in managing the nation's parks and monuments. Consequently Roosevelt signed the Executive Transfer Order of August 10, 1933, and thereby confirmed the National Park Service as sole caretaker of the country's diverse parks and monuments.

Roosevelt also influenced the future of the NPS by establishing the Civilian Conservation Corps as part of his New Deal Depression-relief program. The corps employed thousands of young men engaged in conservation, rehabilitation, and construction projects in both national and state parks. The program was successful and survives today as part of state park administration.

During World War II (1939–45), NPS Director Newton B. Drury faced enormous pressure to open western parks up to the extraction of resources needed for the war effort. Advocates of utilitarian conservation argued that resources held in protected areas should be available to private interests and can be extracted without damaging the overall value of particular park sites. This conflict over how much protection to apply to a particular region or park site goes to the root of the conservation debate today.

Ecological awareness reached a new level in 1963 when a committee of natural resource management scientists released a report recommending that national parks maintain the environment as closely as possible to what existed when the first Europeans arrived. In 1964 Congress passed the Wilderness Act, which describes wilderness as "a place that is not controlled by humans, where natural ecological processes operate freely and where its primeval character and influences are retained. A place that is not occupied or modified by mankind, where humans are visitors, and the imprint of their activity is largely unnoticeable."

In 1980 Congress passed the Alaska National Interest Lands Conservation Act, which added more than 47 million wilderness acres to the park system. However, under President Ronald Reagan, the NPS underwent a period that focused less on expansion and more on restoration and improvement of existing facilities.

The National Park System has grown to include 374 sites covering more than 80 million acres in 49 states, the District of Columbia, American Samoa, Guam, Puerto Rico, Saipan, and the Virgin Islands, making the United States a world leader in the conservation of public lands. These policies have led to a worldwide national park movement affecting 100 nations and some 1,200 national parks or preserves around the world.

CURRENT POLITICAL ISSUES

The NPS is one of the most publicly recognized and utilized government programs, as evidenced by the approximately 275 million visitors to national parks in 1997. However, financial pressure on Congress to lower federal spending has had an impact on NPS programs. Since 1983, the NPS has seen $200 million in budget cuts even as new parks were being created. Increasingly, budgetary constraint is the issue of greatest concern to park advocates. Ever watchful of deteriorating conditions at national park sites, some advocates describe the future of U.S. parks as uncertain.

Conditions such as overcrowding, increasing pollution, and encroaching commercial development are serious problems for the most-popular park sites. Other sites suffer from an invasion of foreign plant and animal species that have a damaging effect on the food chain in particular environments. Park sites are suffering from deterioration due to the natural aging process and to overuse by visitors. In some cases, parks are understaffed and cannot protect cultural treasures from vandalism.

The National Parks and Conservation Association (NPCA), a private nonprofit citizen organization dedicated to protecting and enhancing the National Park System, carefully monitors legislation that affects the NPS. NPCA leaders support legislation that will change the way new parks are brought into the system, an issue that is especially problematic at a time when the NPS budget is shrinking.

Case Study: Budget Crisis Threatens the Future of the NPS

Despite budget shortfalls, legislators are continuing to add new parks to the overburdened system. Further burdening the NPS is $4 billion in overdue maintenance and repairs needed to keep the park facilities in safe operating condition.

Instead of going to Congress for more money, the NPS is looking elsewhere for financial solutions. Raising park entrance fees is a possible solution pursued by NPS leadership. Yellowstone National Park maintained a $10 per car entrance fee for decades; in 1998 the fee was doubled. A more controversial proposal is to allow businesses and corporations to sponsor park improvements. Critics are leery of private interests so closely involved in the funding of parks when those same companies are often looking to receive benefits from the parks. An example of this kind of conflict is the proposed use of thousands of acres of Yellowstone National Park land for oil and gas exploration.

Public Impact

Throughout the parks system, reduced budgets have led to the steady deterioration of roads, buildings, sewers, and other infrastructure. Campgrounds are being closed, operating hours shortened, interpretive programs trimmed, and seasonal rangers laid off. Priceless natural and historical assets are deteriorating steadily from use and natural aging. Scientific knowledge vital to the parks' long-term protection is lacking, and the shortage of funds has drastically reduced research. Some observers fear that the increase in park entrance fees might render access to public lands unaffordable for many.

SUCCESSES AND FAILURES

Among southern California's Channel Islands, one of 12 national marine sanctuaries, the NPS conducts a program called the Aquatic Count. The program involves a partnership between NPS marine biologists and hundreds of volunteer divers who assess marine life populations. The program represents a creative solution to the serious need for data collection at a time when funding for such endeavors is decreasing. Scientific data collected by volunteers will be used by NPS scientists and other agencies to develop conservation strategies. The partnership has been called "citizen science" and is one example of the ways Americans can show their appreciation for the preservation of wildlife and protected habitats.

FUTURE DIRECTIONS

As one of the chief conservation agencies of the federal government, the NPS has proposed advance funding of approximately $300 million in 1999, 2000, and 2001. In doing so the NPS seeks to ensure the funding for completion of the Everglades Watershed Restoration project in Florida. The funds are to be used to establish the Everglades National Park Fund and to acquire land, build new water delivery systems, and conduct scientific research. The Everglades restoration funds will help to develop and implement a plan to reverse damage caused by years of draining the Everglades through ditch building and river channeling to provide water to the cities and agricultural lands of heavily populated Florida. These practices have resulted in the loss of thousands of acres of wildlife habitat and numerous water shortages in a region that receives one of the highest levels of rainfall in the country.

In addition to appropriations from the federal government the NPS has proposed legislation to create a second source of funding for the project. The Department of the Interior proposes to implement a tax increase of one cent per pound on Florida sugar producers. It is estimated that the tax will generate approximately $35 million per year.

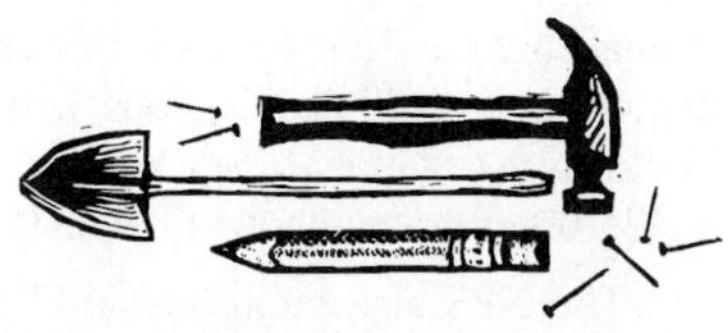

GET INVOLVED:

The Volunteers In Parks Program (VIP), enacted in 1970, strives to utilize volunteers in ways that are mutually beneficial to the park system and the volunteers. More than 85,000 volunteers assisted with NPS projects in 1996. To access the Volunteers Opportunities System, which holds lists of current openings throughout the park system, visit the NPS Web site at http://www.nps.gov. Those interested in the VIP program must complete an application and mail it to a park where volunteers are needed. Local park service sites will also have information about volunteering available to the public.

Student Volunteers

The Student Conservation Association (SCA) is a nonprofit educational organization located in New York. It operates three volunteer programs: the Resource Assistant Program for young adults, the High School Program, and the Conservation Career Development Program. Resource assistants serve as volunteer seasonal staff, working side by side with professional staff. They are not paid but receive funds to cover travel, subsistence for food and housing, and a uniform allowance. High School Program crews consist of six to ten volunteers and their leaders performing conservation maintenance tasks. Leaders are experienced in all aspects of outdoor living and conservation work. Some 2,600 high school students and young adults are placed each year. The Conservation Career Development Program fosters conservation career opportunities for minority youth through service, counseling, and educational grants. For information contact the Student Conservation Association, 1800 N. Kent St., Arlington, VA 22209; telephone (703) 524-2441.

AGENCY RESOURCES

The NPS offers a variety of information and educational resources at its Web site. The "InfoZone" at http://www.nps.gov/pub_aff/index.html provides visitors with information regarding the NPS's mission and history, frequently asked questions, and volunteer opportunities. "Visit Your National Parks," at http://www.nps.gov/parks.html, allows visitors to search for specific parks by name, state, region, or theme. This site provides basic contact information about each park, as well as links to some of the larger parks featuring pictures, maps, and hiking or camping guides. "Links to the Past," located at http://www.cr.nps.gov, provides historical resources, including the *National Register of Historic Places*, *Lighthouses and Ships Within the National Park System*, *Civil War Battlefields*, and *Archeology*, a site devoted to exhibits on the early history and exploration of North America.

The NPS Web site also offers a section for students and teachers titled "Park Smart—The Learning Place."

AGENCY PUBLICATIONS

The NPS produces handbooks, posters, maps, brochures, and charts. A full list of NPS publications is available by viewing the NPS Web site at http://www.nps.gov. Specific publications include American bicentennial charts and cartographic resources. For more information about NPS publications write to the Division of Publications, National Park Service, Harpers Ferry, WV 25425-0050, or telephone (304) 535-6018.

The NPS also publishes an electronic news magazine titled the *Courier On-Line*. The magazine, located at http://www.nps.gov, provides information on events at NPS sites, programs, impending legislation, and business within the NPS.

BIBLIOGRAPHY

Albright, Horace M., and Robert Cahn. *The Birth of the National Park Service: The Founding Years, 1913–33.* Salt Lake City: Howe Brothers, 1985.

"Babbitt Announces Major Land Protection Agreement for Kenai Fjords National Park." US Newswire, 19 May 1997.

Bly, Laura. "Yellowstone at 125: Still an Old Faithful Despite Overcrowding, Nature Springs Eternal." *USA Today,* 1 August 1997, p. 5D.

Butowsky, Dr. Harry A. "The U.S. Constitution: A National Historic Landmark Theme Study: Front Matter, U.S. History." Bureau of Electronic Publishing, 1 September 1990.

Cuneff, Tom. "Environment: Down for the Count, the Newly Popular Annual Fish Census Tells a Troubling Story." *Sports Illustrated,* 30 June 1997, p. R1.

"New Park Legislation Helps Anaktuvuk Residents." *Tundra Times,* 29 January 1997, p. PG.

Satchell, Michael. "Parks in Peril." *U.S. News and World Report,* vol. 123, 21 July 1997, p. 22.

"The White House: President Names Stanton Director of the National Park Service, U.S. Deptartment of the Interior." *Telecomworldwire*, 1 July 1997.

National Partnership for Reinventing Government (NPR)

WHAT IS ITS MISSION?

The National Partnership for Reinventing Government (NPR) is an initiative by the administration of President Bill Clinton and Vice President Al Gore to reform the way the federal government works. Its stated mission is to create a government that works better and costs less and which regulates people and businesses by focusing not on strict rules but on achieving the results that the regulations are intended to produce. Until January of 1998, the organization was known as the National Performance Review; to avoid confusion, the acronym used to identify it has remained NPR.

HOW IS IT STRUCTURED?

Although its activities involve a large number of federal agencies, NPR is considered an operating unit within the Office of the Vice President (OVP). The director of NPR is appointed by the vice president with the informal input of the president. As in White House appointments, there is no set term for the director's service; he or she may be appointed or removed at the discretion of the vice president.

NPR is not generally considered a discrete government agency but describes itself as an "interagency working group." Its 40 staff members are employees of other federal agencies, who work with NPR as part of a "developmental assignment." They work for the Clinton administration's government reform initiative, but their salaries are paid by their respective home agencies.

The staff of NPR is periodically divided into several working teams, which are responsible for creating

PARENT ORGANIZATION: The Office of the Vice President
ESTABLISHED: March 3, 1993
EMPLOYEES: 40

Contact Information:

ADDRESS: 750 17th St. NW, Ste. 200
Washington, DC 20006
PHONE: (202) 632-0150
FAX: (202) 632-0390
E-MAIL: rego.web@npr.gov
URL: http://www.npr.gov
DIRECTOR AND SENIOR POLICY ADVISER: Morley Winograd
PRINCIPAL DEPUTY DIRECTOR: Bob Stone

FAST FACTS

The vice president's Hammer Awards are an ironic reference to former administrations in which outrageous, wasteful items were listed on itemized expenditures. In particular it alludes to a $400 hammer. Today's recipients receive a $6 hammer and a framed note from the vice president.

(Source: National Partnership for Reinventing Government. "PR Press Release," December 17, 1997.)

partnerships among specific types of agencies. Generally, agencies are categorized by the type of services they provide. The most recent NPR teams include safety and health, families and communities, economy, technology, government management, and communication. There is also a service team dealing with federal agencies which interact with citizens the most and an NPR operations team which provides internal operational support for achieving NPR's mission—functions which include budgeting, and equipment and facilities management.

PRIMARY FUNCTIONS

While NPR is ostensibly an agency with the sole purpose of "reinventing" government, its small size and deliberately limited resources make it impossible, in most cases, for the agency to take direct action—in fact, for government to be transformed from the outside would defeat the principles on which NPR was founded. Overall, the organization works as an adviser and facilitator for changes undertaken by agencies themselves. It studies problems associated with government and makes specific recommendations to agencies for how to solve them. It also opens lines of communication across the bureaucracy by arranging numerous partnerships, boards, meetings, and conventions. When NPR recommendations are mandated by law or by a presidential order, NPR advises agencies on how to achieve the required results.

NPR works on several fronts to bring together the various elements of government—federal agencies, state and local governments, and federal employees' unions—to exchange ideas and improve the way these linkages operate. For example, to increase cooperation between federal, state, and local agencies, NPR arranges performance-based partnership grants designed to encourage government at these levels to jointly develop goals and objectives for major program areas such as public assistance or sanitation. The ultimate aim of programs such as these is to allow state and local agencies to use federal funds in a way that is more efficient and flexible. Most recently, NPR has begun to focus on improving the service records of agencies which are most likely to deal directly with the public.

Through its interagency partnerships, NPR works to ease the burden of regulation on the public and business. It arranges partnerships between regulating agencies (such as the Environmental Protection Agency, or EPA) and representatives from the appropriate segment of the population (such as industrial business) in order to make these relationships less coercive and more productive. NPR also works to see that the total volume of federal regulations is streamlined and made more understandable to the public.

NPR also works to communicate its ideas and principles to government employees and contractors through periodical publications, videos, awards programs, and public speeches and appearances (mostly by the vice president).

PROGRAMS

Because NPR is careful not to create a further drain on public funds or resources, most specific programs are carried out with the assistance of other federal, state, or local agencies. For example, a number of government agencies have volunteered to operate national Reinvention Laboratories, units or organizations that are encouraged to test new ways of doing business and to share ideas and successes across the government. The laboratories, while prompted by NPR-inspired ideas, are operated and funded by the agencies that house them. Similarly, NPR's National Benchmarking Consortium, a program funded by an interagency partnership, brings federal agencies together to compare their performance to that of world-class private companies or high-performing government agencies.

Another example of a jointly designed and operated program is the U.S. Business Advisor, one of the many NPR initiatives which has focused on using information technology to link the government and the public. Operated mainly by the National Technical Information Service (NTIS), the U.S. Business Advisor, is a Web site that provides members of the business community with one-stop access to federal government information, services, and transactions.

High-profile NPR programs include several awards programs, such as the Hammer Awards for teams of federal employees who have made significant contributions in support of reinventing government; the President's Quality Awards for federal organizations which have documented high-performance management systems and approaches principles; and the Innovations in Government Awards, Ford Foundation grants for federal agencies that have shown creativity in providing solutions for the public sector.

BUDGET INFORMATION

While most agencies acquire their budgets through congressional appropriations bills, the NPR is funded by other means. The salaries of NPR staffers are paid by their home agencies and its entire operating budget is provided by the Department of Defense, one of the many agencies which sponsors the NPR's efforts. The annual operating budget of about $1.3 million pays for expenses such as rent, telephones, computers, and equipment.

HISTORY

For more than 30 years, public opinion polls have registered the growing public dissatisfaction with the federal government; citizens have generally viewed it as too big, too costly, too intrusive, wasteful, and inefficient. Several major initiatives have been undertaken by presidential administrations in the twentieth century to reform the administrative practices of the federal government. One of the most recent was issued by the Grace Commission, which delivered its recommendations during the Reagan administration. Shortly after taking office in 1993, President Clinton set about designing his own agenda for streamlining and reinventing government. The president's plan borrowed many ideas from these previous reform efforts. Few of these previous efforts had enjoyed much success, largely because the problems were too deep and too entrenched to be repaired within the four-year span of a single administration.

President Clinton's National Performance Review was created on March 3, 1993, when he appointed Vice President Gore as the organization's leader. The vice president was given six months to study the problems associated with the federal government and to then report recommendations for improvement. The review staff of 250 interagency employees began researching problems specific to individual government agencies, while the vice president personally visited several agencies in the next few months in order to learn firsthand what problems they faced.

The vice president's final report was based on a number of accompanying reports prepared by nearly two dozen teams of NPR staffers. It detailed about 1,250 specific actions that could be taken by individual agencies that could save a projected $108 billion, reduce the number of federal employees, and improve government operations. In accord with the president's wishes, these recommendations focused on process, rather than function —the administration had made it clear that the reinvention effort was concerned with how the government operated and not with what the government did. By December 1993, President Clinton had signed sixteen specific directives that implemented NPR's recommendations. Most focused on cutting the workforce, reducing internal rules and regulations, and requiring agencies to set customer (meaning specific users of government services, rather than citizens in the general population) service standards.

REGO I

Shortly after NPR's 1993 report, most of the staff returned to their home agencies, but about 50 staff members remained to begin implementing the organization's initiatives. This first phase of reinvention (REGO I) included activity to lay the groundwork for coming changes: a tracking system was created to monitor the progress of the 1,250 action items, performance agreements were drafted between heads of major agencies and the White House, and a training video was developed that would inform federal employees of the changes ahead. In 1994 NPR helped agencies create their first sets of customer service standards. During the same year Congress enacted about one-fourth of NPR recommendations that required legislative action. The most significant of these included the "buyout" bill, which allowed agencies to offer financial incentives to selected employees to retire from government service, thereby reducing the size of the federal workforce through attrition.

In its first year NPR's formula for reinvention was in place, but many of the specific recommendations had not yet been undertaken, and it was too early to tell whether any changes had produced results. Although Vice President Gore and other NPR officials claimed significant progress, more critical estimates showed that the total savings were roughly half (about $57 billion) of what had been promised. In 1995 Congress asked the General Accounting Office (GAO) to conduct an independent assessment of the NPR's work, and the GAO reported in 1996 that 293 of the 1,250 action items had been completed, while 67 had been partially implemented. According to Congress, NPR still had far to go.

The Midterm Elections of 1994 and REGO II

The 1994 congressional elections were interpreted by many as a resounding rejection of the Clinton administration's agenda. Voters overwhelmingly created a new Congress that would be dominated by many newer members from the Republican Party who were opposed to many of the Democratic president's initiatives. The 1994 elections unseated many powerful Democratic members of Congress, including Speaker of the House Thomas Foley, and the president lost many important congressional allies. The president, however, was convinced that his plan for reforming government did not go far enough.

In response to the 1994 elections, President Clinton asked Vice President Gore to launch a second phase of reinvention (REGO II). Rather than focusing on cutting employees through attrition and streamlining the internal workings of individual agencies, REGO II took a much more aggressive approach. Its four basic goals were to terminate specific programs and agencies; privatize a large number of government functions; devolve funds and responsibilities to state and local governments; and more dramatically consolidate the federal workforce.

The vice president asked NPR to undertake activities in accord with this new, more aggressive approach to identify outdated government regulations that could be eliminated; to create partnerships between regulators and those being regulated; to eliminate "unfunded mandates" on states and localities; and to reduce the number of congressionally mandated reports prepared by federal agencies. REGO II proposals included more than 186 new recommendations for agency actions and 121 reforms aimed at easing government regulations. NPR also continued to implement recommendations from REGO I, such as the Hammer Awards and the expansion of reinvention labs.

By 1996—just prior to a new presidential election—Vice President Gore announced that agencies needed to focus on the ends, not the means, of what government does and should delegate more responsibility to "frontline" managers who deal directly with American citizens. This new concentration changed the original REGO I agenda, in which it was clearly stated that NPR's reinvention efforts would focus on the process rather than on the results of government activity. Gore proposed a new set of initiatives beyond the level of the 1994 REGO II that would more aggressively change the way government operated. He proposed creating single points of contact for larger agencies that would make it easier for Americans to find their way through the bureaucracy and making agencies into performance-based organizations that would deliver measurable benefits and services.

Beginning with President Clinton's second term in 1997, NPR began to target its energies at a lower level in the bureaucracy. Rather than focusing on departments such as Education, Treasury, or Agriculture, NPR turned to the agencies within these departments which dealt most directly with the public, such as the Internal Revenue Service (IRS), the Social Security Administration (SSA), and the National Park Service (NPS). It also created a vast interagency communications network and its own site on the World Wide Web.

In 1998 NPR began to change internally in accord with its evolving mission—most notably by extending its mission statement to include the phrase "to get results Americans care about." It also changed its name to the National Partnership for Reinventing Government to better describe how it intended to accomplish its work.

CURRENT POLITICAL ISSUES

From the start, NPR has been criticized both by political opponents and by proponents of radical government reform on three fronts. Before NPR's proposed reforms were even under way, it was dismissed by critics, especially the Republicans, as a mere political gimmick, a high-profile project that would keep Vice President Al Gore—the Democratic Party's front-runner for its next presidential candidate—in the limelight. Second, while no independent publication or organization has yet undertaken a detailed examination of NPR's claims to success, many opponents describe NPR's periodic progress reports as greatly exaggerated. Some have questioned the accuracy of the NPR's claims of cuts in the federal workforce (a claimed reduction of nearly 350,000 personnel between 1993 and 1997) and overall spending cuts (a claimed savings of $137 billion).

Perhaps the most serious criticism is about the level of real, meaningful changes NPR is prepared to make in the size and efficiency of government. Most analysts, regardless of party affiliation, have regarded the Clinton administration's reform agenda as a mixture of ideas borrowed from various similar reform initiatives during the Eisenhower administration and from current business practices. Advocates of fundamental government reform claim that while the administration commonly uses corporate jargon about "performance-based organizations" and "total quality management," very little is actually being done to change the size of the government in a meaningful way. NPR admitted as much after the midterm elections of 1994, when it was forced to move beyond thinking merely in terms of process. To many critics, NPR was a patch-up job—a small-scale, disorganized battle that was being fought on too many fronts to be effective.

As evidence of the administration's unwillingness to enact real reforms, critics have cited the president's vetoes of congressional efforts to reduce government spending. Rather than working with Congress to eliminate wasteful spending, they claim, the president is actually working to preserve government largely as it is while making highly public claims of radical change. Proponents of more radical reforms, meanwhile, want to see an overhaul of the entire system and some have proposed eliminating entire executive departments such as Commerce and Agriculture. These departments serve a large number of powerful political constituents, however, and given the consequences of such drastic actions, it seems unlikely that any administration would be willing to lead such efforts.

SUCCESSES AND FAILURES

In March 1998, NPR pointed to several statistics that appeared to indicate clear successes in its efforts. The size of the federal workforce had been cut by 348,000 employees since 1993 to become the smallest since President John F. Kennedy's term. Agencies had eliminated about 640,000 pages of internal rules, about 16,000 pages of federal regulations, and were in the process of rewriting 31,000 additional pages in plain language. Over 570 federal government organizations had committed to more than 4,000 customer service standards. In all, NPR estimated the savings to the public had reached $137 billion.

Critics of the NPR's claims were quick to point out these claims had not been independently verified. In particular, some were skeptical of its estimates of the size of the federal workforce and the savings generated by its initiatives. For example, more than 70 percent of the 348,000 government positions "eliminated" since 1993 were defense positions associated with post-Cold War military base closures that had been ordered during the Bush administration.

FUTURE DIRECTIONS

In the immediate future, NPR plans to focus its efforts on what it calls the "High Impact Agencies," government agencies which tend to have the most direct interactions with the American public. These include the IRS, the SSA, the NPS, the FDA, the Patent and Trademark Office (PTO), and the Occupational Safety and Health Administration (OSHA). These agencies have committed to more than 250 specific improvements in service to the public by the year 2000. NPR's role will be to help the agencies integrate their reinvention strategies and overall strategic planning into their daily operations.

AGENCY RESOURCES

The NPR's Web site at http://www.npr.gov is a vast resource of information about the organization and contains links to many other sites, including other government agencies, electronic libraries, and individual NPR-related initiatives. For further information about NPR, contact the Newsroom at (202) 632-0323.

AGENCY PUBLICATIONS

NPR issues a number of periodical publications including *Reinvention Express,* an irregularly released newsletter (about 10 to 20 issues annually); *Reinvention Roundtable*, a quarterly periodical aimed at federal workers, and an annual *Reinvention Calendar* that lists important meeting and conference dates for the coming year. Electronic copies of many of these publications, as well as news releases, speeches, and announcements, can be viewed or downloaded from the NPR's on-line Newsroom at http://www.npr.gov/newsroom. Members of the public may subscribe electronically to *Reinvention Express* and *Reinvention Calendar* by sending an E-mail to Listproc@ect.fed.gov. For printed copies or more information about these publications, contact the NPR Newsroom at (202) 632-0323.

NPR also maintains a vast publications library at http://www.npr.gov/library, which includes numerous reports and background papers. Many can be viewed or downloaded from the site, but some printed copies are available from the NPR; call (202) 632-0150 for information. Documents in the NPR electronic library may also be ordered by stock number from the Superintendent of Documents, Government Printing Office, PO Box 371954, Pittsburgh, PA 15250; phone (202) 512-1800.

BIBLIOGRAPHY

Barr, Stephen. "Experts Give Gore's Plan Mixed Review: Emphasis on Downsizing Called Threat to Success." *Washington Post*, 3 May 1995, p. A19.

———. "Gore's Team Turns to Making Reinvention Deliver." *Washington Post*, 3 March 1998, p. A15.

———. "Marking a Milestone with Testimonials." *Washington Post*, 4 March 1998, p. A19.

Drucker, Peter G. "Really Reinventing Government." *Atlantic Monthly*, February 1995, p. 49.

Glastris, Paul. "Undercovered: Whatever Happened to REGO?" *New Republic*, 2 March 1998, p. 15.

Nesterczuk, George. "Reviewing the National Performance Review." *Regulation*, 1996.

Paige, Sean, and Timothy W. Maier. "Rating the Reinvention." *Insight on the News*, 9 March 1998, p. 8.

Pine, Art. "Early Efforts at 'Reinventing' Agencies May Need Tinkering." *Los Angeles Times*, 1 January 1998, p. A5.

"Twelve Months Wiser: Reinventing Government." *Economist*, September 1994, p. A 26.

York, Byron. "Big Al's Big Scam." *American Spectator*, February 1996, p. 38.

National Resources Conservation Service (NRCS)

PARENT ORGANIZATION: Department of Agriculture
ESTABLISHED: December 7, 1994
EMPLOYEES: 9,500

Contact Information:

ADDRESS: PO Box 2890
Washington, DC 20013
PHONE: (202) 720-3210
FAX: (202) 720-1564
URL: http://www.nrcs.usda.gov
CHIEF: Pearlie S. Reed

WHAT IS ITS MISSION?

The mission of the National Resources Conservation Service (NRCS) is to provide national leadership in a partnership effort to help people conserve, improve, and sustain the national resources and environment of the United States. The NRCS's efforts involve three key elements: identifying the state of existing natural resources and the effect of land uses or management systems on these resources, helping coordinate landowner- or community-initiated conservation planning, and providing voluntary technical or financial assistance to landowners and communities for the application of conservation systems.

HOW IS IT STRUCTURED?

The NRCS is an agency of the Natural Resources and Environment mission area of the U.S. Department of Agriculture (USDA). The head administrator of the NRCS is the chief, who is responsible for guiding the general direction of NRCS programs and policies as well as maintaining communications with the public and the legislature concerning those programs. Three staffs assist the Office of the Chief: the Strategic Natural Resources Issues staff, the Legislative Affairs staff, and the Conservation Communication staff.

The work of the NRCS is divided among four offices, each led by a deputy chief, in each of the following areas: programs, management, soil survey and resource assessment, and science and technology. The Office of Management conducts internal affairs at the NRCS, including administrative support, financial and human resources management, and employee development. The Office of

Programs shares some of these internal responsibilities, such as budget planning, but also coordinates community and international program efforts for the NRCS.

The primary technical arms of the NRCS are the Office of Science and Technology and the Office of Soil Survey and Natural Resource Assessment. The Office of Science and Technology has broad responsibility for researching and implementing the technology needed to carry out the conservation efforts of the NRCS and its partners and also operates the various institutes associated with the NRCS, such as the Soil Quality Institute and the Wetland Science Institute. The responsibilities of the Office of Soil Survey and Natural Resource Assessment are to conduct the National Resources Inventory and the National Cooperative Soil Survey.

In addition to the headquarters, the NRCS has six regional offices responsible for administering the nearly three thousand conservation districts developed by the NRCS and for distributing technical information to partners within each region. Seventeen Major Land Resource offices, located throughout the United States, help conduct the soil survey. The NRCS also works with numerous state and field offices throughout the nation.

FAST FACTS

Every year, over one million land users receive the technical services of the NRCS, which are routed through nearly 3,000 conservation districts throughout the United States and its territories.

(Source: *The United States Government Manual, 1997/98.*)

PRIMARY FUNCTIONS

The NRCS provides technical assistance to land users and government units to uphold agricultural productivity and to protect and improve the natural resource base. The agency is cooperative, rather than regulatory, in nature. Assistance is based on the voluntary cooperation of private landowners and involves comprehensive approaches to reduce soil erosion, improve the quality and quantity of available soil and water, improve air quality, reduce upstream flooding, and enhance wildlife habitat. To generate the information necessary to perform these tasks, the NRCS conducts research at its institutes, plant materials centers, and field offices and distributes the results of its research to private landowners and the public. In some cases the NRCS also provides financial assistance to private landowners, in the form of loans or easement purchases, usually in order to preserve resources.

PROGRAMS

Two of the best-known NRCS programs are the National Cooperative Soil Survey and the National Resources Inventory. The soil survey is conducted on a regional basis, and published copies are distributed to counties or other areas to provide the foundation for farm planning or other land-use decisions. The survey results are also used as a guide for resource planning and policy for federal, state, and local governments. The National Resources Inventory, published every five years, is a detailed technical report on how well the United States is sustaining resources on nonfederal lands. Inventory data and analytical software are available to the public on CD-ROM.

The agency also operates more region-specific programs, such as the Snow Survey and Water Supply Forecasting Program, which collects snowpack moisture data and forecasts seasonal water supplies for streams that derive most of their water from snowmelt.

One of the agency's most significant research programs is the Plant Materials Program, which tests, selects, and ensures the commercial availability of new and improved conservation plants for erosion reduction, wetland restoration, water quality improvement, coastal dune stabilization, and other purposes. Plants are studied at 26 centers across the country.

A few NRCS programs provide financial assistance. The Farms-for-the-Future Program guarantees USDA loans and pays the interest on state loans for agricultural land or development rights purchased to preserve vital farmland resources for the future.

BUDGET INFORMATION

The NRCS budget amounts to approximately $858 million. Most of the agency's budget authority is granted through congressional appropriations, but about 16 percent is funded through fees and receipts collected through various NRCS programs. The NRCS annual budget amounts to approximately $858 million. Most of the agency's budget authority is granted through congressional appropriations; however, approximately 16 percent is funded through fees and receipts collected through various NRCS programs.

The bulk of NRCS funds, about 64 percent, are spent providing technical assistance to private landowners and state and local governments in cooperative conservation

BUDGET:

National Resources Conservation Service

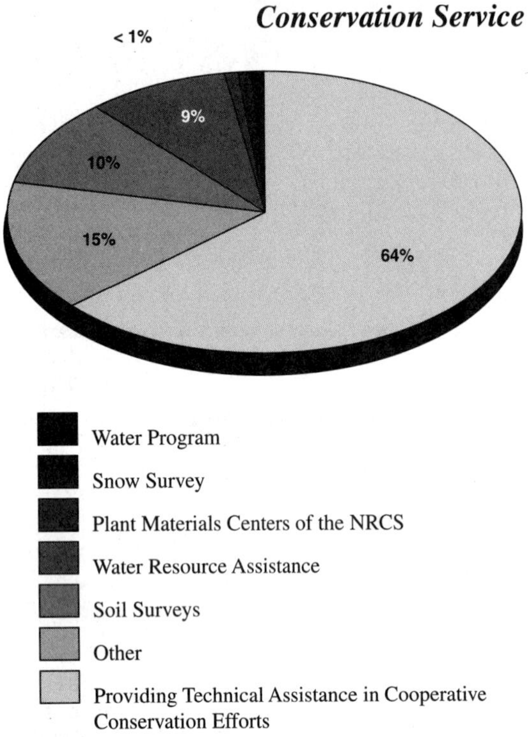

efforts. Another 10 percent of the budget is spent on the organization and conduct of soil surveys, and slightly less, about 9 percent, is spent on the Water Resource Assistance Program. The Plant Materials Centers of the NRCS and the Snow Survey and Water Program each account for a small percentage—less than 1 percent—of the NRCS budget.

HISTORY

When it first became a pressing issue in the United States, soil conservation was far from a new concept. It had its roots in eighteenth-century colonial America and in farming practices of the ancient world. There were a few proponents of such soil conservation practices as terracing and gully planting from the beginnings of American agriculture, but with seemingly unlimited new land available it was difficult to convince American farmers that much time needed to be spent conserving soil. By the time of the American Civil War (1860–65), soil erosion had become a serious problem. Flooding increased throughout the nation's agricultural regions, and rivers were running thick with mud. By the end of the nineteenth century the first government efforts to study and treat this growing problem were under way.

The Dust Bowl and the First National Program

It took several decades, and a national catastrophe, to solidify these scattered government efforts. The Great Depression of the 1930s coincided with several years of drought that were especially severe in the western Great Plains region. Along with crop failures and livestock losses, the drought resulted in "black blizzards" of soil torn loose by prairie winds and lifted into the skies. The Great Plains region quickly became known as the Dust Bowl, and the crisis of American soils was dramatically brought to the attention of the public. The richest agricultural region in the country was literally being blown away.

It was quickly decided that some of the funds that had been set aside for the economic rebuilding of rural America should be used for the control of soil erosion. In 1933 Secretary of the Interior Harold Ickes established what was then called the Soil Erosion Service (SES), the first national action program of soil conservation anywhere in the world. With a staff of 12, agency leader Hugh Bennett, a longtime activist for soil conservation, set out to complete a soil survey of the entire United States. Within two years, the new agency had set up 40 large "demonstration" projects that provided technical design layout, labor, and materials that farmers could not afford. The conservation effort had begun, and after a few years of political squabbling, the agency was transferred to the USDA to avoid duplicating the efforts of other government-sponsored programs.

Bennett was a shrewd spokesperson for soil conservation. He knew that the SES was a temporary government fix to the rural problems caused by drought and the Depression. But he also knew that the problem of soil erosion was not so temporary, and he began to lobby forcefully for a permanent agency. His most notable congressional encounter took place on March 6, 1935, when another big dust storm was blowing into Washington, all the way from the Great Plains. While Bennett presented his argument to a subcommittee of the Senate Committee on Public Lands, the sky darkened and yellow soil from the faraway Dust Bowl rained onto the streets of Washington. In a little more than a month, the Soil Conservation Act of 1935 was passed, creating a permanent agency for soil conservation within the Department of Agriculture. The agency was now called the Soil Conservation Service (SCS).

Reforming the Service

The Depression-era structure of the SCS, with its unwieldy demonstration projects, proved to be too top-heavy for the American economy; it involved huge federal expenditures and relied heavily on a government labor force. With the government doing most of the work, the program was a painfully slow procedure, limited by the available number of government technicians and laborers. It was clear that if the SCS were to be effective, it would have to be carried out through some local administrative body. A model state law was drawn up to enable farmers and ranchers to set up soil conservation districts as local units of government. In 1937, at the urging of President Franklin D. Roosevelt, 22 states passed such a law.

By 1944 all demonstration projects were terminated, and the SCS began to focus its efforts on technical assistance to farmers, ranchers, and other landowners. This has remained the focus of federal soil conservation. The agency has, of course, taken on other responsibilities over the years; it has became involved in soil erosion prevention in suburban real estate developments as well as flood prevention, pollution control, and landscaping. It has expanded its cooperative efforts to governments of other countries. But through all the bureaucratic transfers, abolitions, and reinstatements of programs over the last half century, the technical assistance arm of federal soil conservation has remained intact.

It was not until 1994 that the agency underwent another significant structural change. Under the Reorganization Act of December 7, 1994, the USDA unveiled a dramatic reinvention plan. The SCS was renamed the National Resources Conservation Service, and the agency's conservation operations were transferred to an even more local level; national headquarters operations of the agency were reduced by 50 percent. The proportion of the workforce at the local field level was increased to 80 percent of all NRCS workers, and a number of institutes and centers were established around the country to strengthen the development and transfer of conservation and technology.

CURRENT POLITICAL ISSUES

The conservation programs of the NRCS tend to create some debate around the country for two significant reasons. First, agricultural land that is being conserved is not being used to produce crops that could be sold on the expanding international market, and surrendering this share of the agricultural market to international competitors is unpopular with many U.S. business interests. The second problem is more complex: many federal conservation programs in the United States involve not one but several government agencies, which tends to create both a costly overlap of personnel activity as well as inefficiencies caused by differences of opinion. Sometimes one agency will develop a plan or policy that directly contradicts that of another agency, and it takes time and money for the conflict to be resolved.

Case Study: The Conservation Reserve Program

The purpose of the Conservation Reserve Program (CRP), established by the 1985 Farm Bill, was to have farmers set aside highly erodible or other environmentally sensitive farmland for an extended period of time—10 years under most contracts. During that time, the government would pay farmers an adequate compensation for income that would be lost by not farming the land. The program was a success in many respects; before the passage of the 1985 Farm Bill, farmers lost an estimated average of 7.4 tons of soil per acre to erosion, but by 1994 that figure had been reduced to 5.6 tons per acre.

But the CRP was not without its critics. Some of the most vocal were members of the business community, who claimed that much of the area set aside under the program—36.4 million acres, or an area larger than the state of Iowa—was good agricultural land that could be used by employing basic environmental precautions. At a time when world trade for food was growing, they argued, the program reduced American agricultural production, leaving markets open to competitors, and also inflicted serious social costs on farming communities where many farmers were left with nothing to do.

The program was more popular with farmers, who for the most part considered themselves justly compensated for the loss of production, but many were dissatisfied with what they thought were serious inefficiencies in the way the program was run. In the 1990s, after the program had been under way for several years, many farmers were released from their contracts and allowed to farm their CRP land. However, no research had been conducted on the CRP land to determine whether the restoration efforts had in fact improved the soil. For many years the Agricultural Stabilization and Conservation Service (ASCS; now the Farm Service Agency or FSA), one of the agencies involved in the CRP, would not allow any research on CRP land that dealt with bringing the land back into grain production. The practice of resuming grain production on CRP land without making the effort to determine whether the program was effective in restoring the land made little sense to the farmers involved.

SUCCESSES AND FAILURES

One of the NRCS's most successful efforts has been in the area of wetlands conservation. A joint effort involving four primary government agencies, wetlands conservation was slow to make progress for nearly 20 years, from 1954 to 1974. In the period from 1982 to 1992, however, the loss of wetlands to American agriculture was reduced to about 31,000 acres a year—a 90 percent reduction from the 1954 to 1974 conversion rates.

FUTURE DIRECTIONS

The NRCS has developed a strategic plan based on the passage of the 1996 Federal Agriculture Improvement and Reform Act, informally known as the 1996 Farm

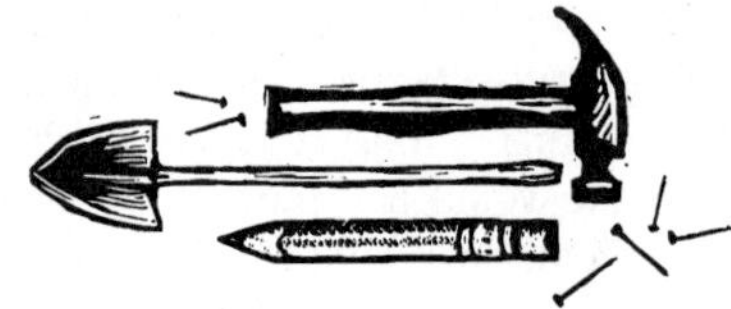

GET INVOLVED:

Earth Team

Earth Team, one of the agency's most recent volunteer programs, has enjoyed success in the states of New Hampshire and Wisconsin, where students, retirees, professionals, and nonprofessionals have teamed with district conservationists, soil engineers, and civil engineering technicians to provide technical assistance to district landowners. In New Hampshire, students worked with NRCS and district employees to install erosion-preventing fiber rolls along the banks of the Connecticut River, took part in water table studies at various sites, staged local soil-judging contests to increase awareness of soil properties and land use; and assisted some county conservation districts with clerical duties. To volunteer for the Earth Team or to get information on organizing a local Earth Team, contact a local NRCS office or call 1-800-743-7645.

Bill. The bill broadened the responsibilities of the NRCS and its partners, calling for a concentration of technical and financial assistance in priority areas—water quality and wildlife habitat—and flexibility in implementing conservation compliance.

The NRCS's efforts to implement the directives of the farm bill will be influenced by several additional trends. The increasing demand for a healthy environment will require the agency to work with a more complex conservation program, requiring a stronger core knowledge and new partnerships. The increasing movement of urban populations to rural areas will require the NRCS to fit modern agriculture into a landscape that is inhabited by people who are not farmers or ranchers. The acceleration of technical innovations in agriculture, including computer applications, has created the need for continual technical improvements in NRCS programs. Also, the changing business of agriculture, shaped as much by social and economic forces as by technology, has created a smaller number of farming units, more often run by conglomerates rather than by individual farmers. The NRCS will have to adapt to this new production environment by providing a more diverse array of conservation services. Finally, the expansion of the agency's responsibilities, combined with a workforce that is shrinking under budget pressures, demands that the agency efficiently allocate scarce program resources and match programs more precisely to natural resource concerns.

AGENCY RESOURCES

General inquiries about the work of the NRCS can be directed to the Office of Public Affairs, Natural Resources Conservation Service, Department of Agriculture, PO Box 2890, Washington, DC 20013; phone (202) 720-3210. For statistical or technical findings of NRCS surveys and inventories, the NRCS Data Clearinghouse offers access to a large volume of agency data, such as information on soils, hydrography, and natural-resource trends. The clearinghouse can be located on the Internet at http://www.ftw.nrcs.usda.gov/nsdi_node.html.

AGENCY PUBLICATIONS

The NRCS offers many publications, including technical references such as *Conservation Practice Standards* and the *Soil Survey Manual*, along with its comprehensive *National Handbook of Conservation Practices*. On its Internet site, the NRCS presents short informational pieces such as "Where the Wetlands Are" and helpful hints on conservation such as "Composting" and "Lawn and Garden Care" for ordinary citizens seeking less technical information. Most NRCS publications can be accessed on-line, but for a full catalog and ordering information contact the Government Printing Office, Superintendent of Documents, by telephoning (202) 512-1800 or visit its Web site at http://www.access.gpo.gov/su_docs/sale/asale001.html.

BIBLIOGRAPHY

De Selincourt, Kate. "Doing Bad by Doing Good." *World Press Review*, February 1997, pp. 34–5.

Lockertz, William. "Soil and Water Quality: An Agenda for Agriculture." *Environment*, June 1994, pp. 28–31.

"NRCS Is Looking for a Few Good Buffers." *Successful Farming*, February 1997, pp. 520–1.

Pimentel, David, et al. "Environmental and Economic Costs of Soil Erosion and Conservation Benefits." *Science*, 24 February 1995, pp. 1117–23.

Simms, D. Harper. *The Soil Conservation Service*. New York: Praeger, 1970.

"Soil." *National Wildlife*, February–March 1995, p. 39.

Steiner, Fredrick R. *Soil Conservation in the United States: Policy and Planning*. Baltimore: Johns Hopkins University Press, 1990.

Williams, Ted. "Invasion of the Aliens: Federally Sanctioned Exotic Plants Are Obliterating the Native American Landscape." *Audubon*, September–October 1994, pp. 24–30.

National Science Foundation (NSF)

PARENT ORGANIZATION: Independent
ESTABLISHED: May 10, 1950
EMPLOYEES: 1,300

Contact Information:

ADDRESS: 4201 Wilson Blvd.
Arlington, VA 22230
PHONE: (703) 306-1234
TDD (HEARING IMPAIRED): (703) 306-0090
E-MAIL: info@nsf.gov
URL: http://www.nsf.gov
DIRECTOR: Dr. Rita R. Colwell

WHAT IS ITS MISSION?

The National Science Foundation Act of 1950 established the mission of the National Science Foundation (NSF) "to promote the progress of science; to advance national health, prosperity and welfare; and to secure the national defense." From this stated mission, the NSF developed a guiding vision that was articulated in its February 1995 publication *NSF in a Changing World: The National Science Foundation's Strategic Plan*: "The National Science Foundation is a catalyst for progress through investment in science, mathematics, and engineering. Guided by its long-standing commitment to the highest standards of excellence in the support of discovery and learning, NSF pledges to provide the stewardship necessary to sustain and strengthen the Nation's science, mathematics, and engineering capabilities and to promote the use of those capabilities in service to society."

HOW IS IT STRUCTURED?

The NSF consists of a 24-member National Science Board (NSB) and a director. The director also serves as a member of the board. The board is appointed by the president and confirmed by the Senate. The criteria for selection to the NSB are eminence in basic science, medicine, social science, engineering, agriculture, education, research management, or public affairs and an ability to represent the scientific and engineering views of leaders in these fields. Board members include professors of science from major universities, science museum directors, and private-sector scientists representing corporate inter-

BIOGRAPHY:
Vannevar Bush

Engineer (1890–1974) Vannevar Bush's most important contribution to engineering was the differential analyzer, a mechanism capable of solving the intricate and lengthy differential equations that have become indispensable to modern engineering. During World War II (1939–45) the differential analyzer was used to solve equations essential to ballistics, acoustics, structures, and atomic physics. Bush also published an influential essay about a hypothetical computing machine called Memex. The essay presented a theoretical prototype for the modern personal computer, and it influenced research in areas such as hypertext, multimedia, and artificial intelligence. However, Bush was best known for his appointment as director of the Office of Scientific Research and Development (OSRD) during World War II. Through this office Bush coordinated a vast network of industrial and academic research geared toward wartime science, including the development of microwave radar, antisubmarine devices, amphibious warfare, and the early stages of the atomic bomb. Many medical advances also resulted from OSRD efforts, including antimalarial drugs, blood substitutes, and the large-scale production of penicillin. After the war Bush established the National Academy of Sciences and made many recommendations on how to transfer wartime research to peaceful efforts. Bush was able to form a consensus of opinion among his fellow scientists that resulted in the report "Science: the Endless Frontier," which called for extensive government support for basic research. As a result, the National Science Foundation was established in 1950.

ests. The NSB term of service is six years, with no member serving more than two consecutive terms.

The chair and vice chair of the NSB serve two-year terms and are elected from the membership. The director and deputy director are appointed by the president and confirmed by the Senate. Eight assistant directors head the directorates and offices that oversee the program areas of the NSF. These are the Directorates for: Biological Sciences; Computer and Information Science and Engineering; Education and Human Resources; Engineering; GeoSciences; Mathematical and Physical Sciences; and Social, Behavioral, and Economic Sciences. The Office of Budget, Finance, and Award Management and the Office of Information and Resource Management provide the administrative services necessary to operate an agency as vast and diverse as the NSF. The Office of the Inspector General oversees the proper distribution and administration of funds. The Office of the Director manages other offices, such the Office of Polar Programs and the Office of Legislative and Public Affairs.

PRIMARY FUNCTIONS

The NSF supports the scientific and research community by funding both institutions of higher learning and individual research in all fields of scientific endeavor. These funds are awarded in the form of either grants or contracts. For instance, the A. T. Waterman Award gives $500,000 grants to young scientists working in their chosen fields. The NSF also bestows several awards that honor high achievement in the sciences. The Presidential Medal of Science, the nation's highest science award, is given to scientists deserving special recognition for their outstanding contributions to knowledge in the physical, biological, mathematical, and engineering sciences and the social and behavioral sciences. The Vannevar Bush Award honors a senior scientist and statesperson who is a distinguished leader in science and technology, demonstrated through years of pioneering discoveries, public service, inspirational leadership, and contributions to the welfare of the nation.

The NSF ensures that all the findings of the scientists it supports are distributed and serves as a link between academia and government. As a clearinghouse for the selection, interpretation, and analysis of scientific and technical data, the NSF is the principal adviser to the president and Congress on science issues.

PROGRAMS

Every directorate of the NSF operates and funds hundreds of programs each year. Nearly 20,000 programs and projects were funded, at a cost of $3.3 billion, in 1997 alone. The NSF sponsors diverse programs, ranging from *Bill Nye, the Science Guy*, a weekly television program dedicated to explaining science to children and teens, to the mapping of human and animal genomes, the source of life.

The Directorate for Education and Human Resources (EHR), through its Learning and Intelligent Systems initiative, has founded three centers for Collaborative Research on Learning Technologies (CRLTs). These centers research and develop projects in urban school settings, train new researchers, and support prototype or model projects, build and test new computer tutoring systems, and help integrate this new technology into existing curriculums.

The NSF' s Office of Polar Research funds the study of the polar ice caps at Antarctica and the Arctic Circle. Since 1956 the U.S. Antarctic Program (USAP) has supported international projects that study the Antarctic and its role in the earth's environment. In February 1998 the NSF announced that a team of Argentinean and U.S. scientists found fossils of a duck-billed dinosaur, an ancient bird, and an array of giant marine reptiles on Vega Island off the eastern side of the Antarctic Peninsula. The find indicates there was once lush vegetation and a complex ecosystem in the land now covered with ice.

The NSF, along with community and corporate assistance, also sponsors National Science and Technology Week (NSTW). NSTW is a week-long event that fosters scientific awareness nationwide and in local schools through family science nights, science and technology fairs, open houses, and hands-on science and technology demonstrations sponsored by the NSF and its community and corporate sponsors. The NSTW also provides free hands-on teaching activities that were developed by the NSF and its partners to stimulate children's imaginations and foster their understanding of science and technology.

BUDGET:

National Science Foundation

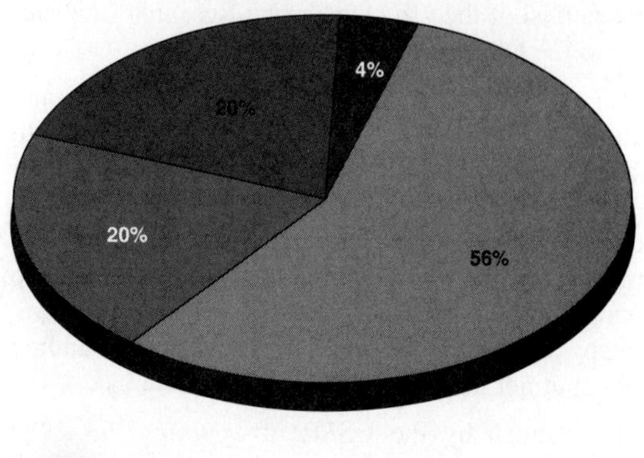

Administration and Management of the NSF and NSB

Education and Training

Support and Maintenance of Research Facilities

Research Projects

BUDGET INFORMATION

The NSF was appropriated $3.4 billion by Congress in 1998. The NSF uses these funds to invest in more than 19,000 research and education projects in science and engineering. Of the total budget $1.88 billion supports research projects; $684 million supports and maintains research facilities; $669 million goes for education and training; and $142 million is used for the administration and management of the NSF and NSB. The NSF budget accounts for only 4 percent of federal research and development spending.

HISTORY

During World War II (1939–45) the U.S. government actively supported scientific and engineering advances to accelerate the war effort through such agencies as the Office of Scientific Research and Development (OSRD). An intensified relationship between the government, the scientific community, and the nation's universities yielded new technology and advances that helped win the war.

Dr. Vannevar Bush, a highly respected engineer who directed the OSRD during the war, wrote *Science: The Endless Frontier*, the 1945 OSRD document that set the stage for a long-term and often heated debate about the government's role in scientific research and support. Bush wrote, "Without scientific progress the national health would deteriorate; without scientific progress we could not hope for improvement in our standard of living or for an increased number of jobs for our citizens; and without scientific progress we could not have maintained our liberties against tyranny."

Senator Harry Kilgore (D-West Virginia) in 1942 introduced the first legislation to create an agency that would encompass all sciences, including the social sciences. For the next several years many forms of this bill were introduced and defeated until one that allowed the president to appoint a director and a board with congressional approval was passed into law. On May 10, 1950, after years of debate over the U.S. government's role in promoting and sponsoring scientific discoveries and projects, President Harry S Truman signed the bill creating the National Science Foundation.

Arguments about the nature of an independent board of scientists to govern the organization, its administration, and the scope of its powers seemed fruitless. The board choice was finally settled by November 1950, and in March 1951 President Truman appointed Alan T. Waterman, a former Yale physics professor who was the chief scientist of the Office of Naval Research (the successor to the OSRD), as the NSF director.

Waterman drew upon his knowledge, expertise, and colleagues at the Office of Naval Research (ONR) to establish the scope and tone of the new foundation for the next 12 years. Waterman's main thrust was to encourage basic scientific research, improve academic-government relations, and provide project grants to encourage a comprehensive national research program. For many years the NSF was a passive partner, funding projects but not initiating them.

The launch by the USSR of *Sputnik 1* in 1957 prompted Congress to allocate more funds to the foundation, create an oversight committee to study scientific events, and create the National Aeronautics and Space Administration (NASA). The NSF played a key role in funding the research that eventually landed Americans on the moon. The National Defense Act of 1958 authorized the creation of the Science Information Service, which became a clearinghouse for statistics, publications, and the collection of foreign scientific information.

The 1960s was a time of tremendous growth for the NSF. During President Lyndon B. Johnson's administration, the NSF was able to share its increased research allocations with both large and small universities and to make grants to improve and even build facilities, hire faculty, and support graduate students.

The NSF's early days were characterized by its independence from the mainstream of government activities. It had no real reporting function until Senators Emilio Q. Daddario and Edward M. Kennedy proposed a modification to the NSF's charter requiring that a report of the foundation's activities be given yearly to the House and Senate Science Subcommittees and that the NSF's allocation be authorized annually instead of in perpetuity as originally stated in its charter. The Daddario-Kennedy amendment gave added emphasis to NSF funding for the social sciences. It also authorized applied scientific research, resulting in a greater focus on engineering.

During the early and middle 1970s funds and focus were shifted from the NSF to the Vietnam War (1959–75) effort and to increased interest in the environment. Presidents Richard M. Nixon and Gerald R. Ford appointed their own science advisers, diminishing the NSF's role as scientific adviser to the president and Congress. Ongoing controversies and a gradual eroding of its authority brought the NSF to its lowest point. President Jimmy Carter restored the NSF's authority during his time in office.

During the late 1970s and early 1980s the NSF initiated, funded, and supported projects with an expanded focus on engineering, the environment, alternative fuel sources, polar research, and oceanographic research. President George Bush's administration was instrumental in increasing the science budget, but leading scientists were concerned that it was not enough to cover all the projects that needed funding.

The 1990s saw the NSF increase funding for Internet research, boosting science and math education, especially in urban areas, and working in partnership with academic institutions to provide a continuous supply of scientists, engineers, and other trained professionals. *Management Review* quoted a letter sent to Congress from a coalition of American corporations in support of the NSF: "The mission of the NSF is to promote and advance scientific, mathematics and engineering research in the United States. Moreover, through its support of science and math education at the K–12 undergraduate and graduate levels, the NSF plays a critical role in educating our nation's future workforce for hi-tech, high wage jobs." The NSF's self-defined role is to ensure scientific advancement in the future by planting the seeds for that advancement in the present.

CURRENT POLITICAL ISSUES

Scientific research is expensive and does not always yield immediate or recognizable results. Perceived abuses of federal funding have made lawmakers hesitant to allocate funds to the research and development agencies without a guarantee that there will be a positive outcome to the research. This has led to fears that innovative research and daring ideas—the hallmark of American scientific research since World War II—would yield to "safe" projects where outcomes are predictable in order to secure funding. Thus far, however, the NSF has been able to continue funding the new and daring, in spite of congressional and public scrutiny and comment.

Another concern for some congressional watchdogs was the perception that the NSF tended to fund only larger institutions and companies. These fears proved unfounded; the NSF focuses not solely on large projects but on smaller, equally significant ones as well.

Case Study: The Tornado Detective

Not all NSF funding is allocated to large research institutions, defense contractors, and universities. There are times when the foundation funds a project taken on by an individual, such as one initiated by Tom Grazulis. Now the head of the Tornado Project, a multimedia firm with more than 10,000 customers that specializes in providing information about tornadoes to the public, Grazulis's success is owed in part to a project funded by the NSF.

Grazulis witnessed the disastrous Worcester, Massachusetts, tornado that passed within one mile of his childhood home in 1953. The experience began a lifelong fascination with these devastating storms. He studied meteorology at Florida State University in the early 1960s, worked as a broadcaster for a time, and then moved to New Jersey, where he taught school. It was there that he first became involved with the NSF, when he worked for the Earth Science Curriculum Project (ESCP). He created a film for the ESCP on the results of storms called *Coastal Erosion, Beach Replenishment* that was still being used in the ESCP curriculum 30 years later.

Grazulis moved to Vermont in the early 1970s where he continued to teach school and make films about tornadoes. He was also gathering thousands of documents, films, posters, and any other information relevant to tornadoes. In 1979 the Nuclear Regulatory Commission (NRC), concerned about the effects of tornadoes on nuclear reactors, contracted with Grazulis to conduct a study on tornado climatology. After three years the NRC contract expired, and the NSF stepped in to ensure that Grazulis could continue his work as a "tornado detective."

Grazulis visited hundreds of small towns and historical societies throughout the country, tracing the history of storms throughout U.S. history. He gathered data on more than 50,000 tornadoes, about 12,000 of which were devastating in terms of loss of human life and property damage. His findings became part of a two-volume 1989 NSF report on the history and nature of tornadoes. After the completion of the project, Grazulis continued the work on his own. The NSF report had focused on the past one hundred years, but Grazulis expanded the study to include facts ranging as far back as colonial times.

From these beginnings, Grazulis began Tornado Project, which produced several successful videos, a Web site, and information for its customers. Pleased with his success, Grazulis's new goal is to study hurricanes.

SUCCESSES AND FAILURES

From its beginnings as a somewhat elitist forum for scientific research through its more broadly based democratic programs in subsequent years, the NSF has proved to be a strong supporter of basic and applied scientific research.

Over the years controversies have arisen about the projects that the NSF funds, but the NSF rarely defends its choices to its critics, who claim some projects are offensive to certain groups' sense of morality, are too difficult to understand, or are a waste of taxpayers' money. The NSF simply explains how the funding was allocated and the results it expects from the various grants. This often-uncomfortable stance has helped the NSF maintain its independence from intrusive government oversight that could stifle creativity and stop the flow of new and innovative applications for science.

Not all NSF programs have met with success, however. Project Mohole, an attempt to gain knowledge of the earth by drilling through its mantle from the ocean floor, was terminated in 1965–66 after it became an enormous financial burden that did not meet its stated expectations. Information learned from Project Mohole did open the way for other deep-ocean sediment investigations, such as the Deep Sea Drilling Project, which began in 1968 and revealed new evidence about the theories of continental drift, sea-floor spreading, and the ocean basins. The program also became a model of international cooperation when several foreign countries joined the operation.

FUTURE DIRECTIONS

According to the NSF Web site, "Today's investments in people, in ideas, and in the exploration of the unknown will help determine the course of the United States in the 21st century." Current projects that will continue to yield new discoveries include the Human Genome Research program, which has the ambition of mapping and understanding the more than 50,000 human genes found on the DNA strand; the study of the polar ice caps; and programs to make the Internet accessible to persons with disabilities.

AGENCY RESOURCES

To obtain information concerning NSF programs, grant applications, and other NSF-related documents, write to the NSF Clearinghouse, PO Box 218, Jessup, MD 20794-0218; call (301) 947-2722; or E-mail pubs@nsf.gov. For information about a particular topic or to be informed about new reports issued by the NSF, sign up for the foundation's Custom News Service at http://www.nsf.gov/home/cns.

When in the Washington area visit the NSF building, where information, publications, and staff information can be obtained from the NSF Information Center. The center is located in Room 215, across from the NSF Library, where all documents are stored. The NSF Information Center and Library are located at 4201 Wilson Blvd., Arlington, VA 22230; (703) 306-1234; or E-mail info@nsf.gov.

AGENCY PUBLICATIONS

The NSF publishes a multitude of reports, statistics, and other documents, which are available through its publications catalog. This catalog is available on-line at http://www.nsf.net. In addition to the catalog and other project-specific documents, the NSF publishes *Frontiers,*

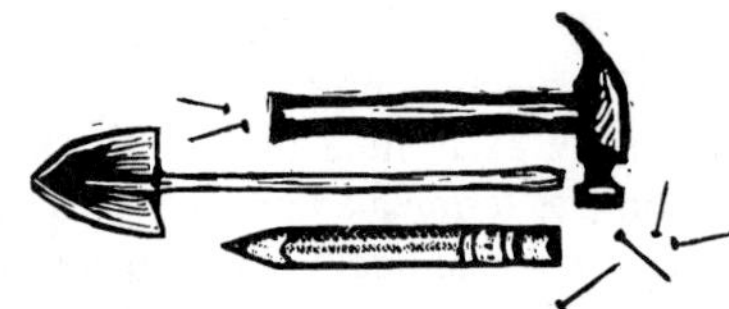

GET INVOLVED:

One of the best ways to get involved with the NSF is to participate in the National Science and Technology Week (NSTW) programs. During the week many NSF partners, including science museums, zoos, arboretums, and health museums, hold interactive science programs for children and adults. In addition to the programs, educators can receive materials free of charge from the NSF and the NSTW program to enhance their classroom activities during the annual event. These materials can be used throughout the year. Kits are available by writing the NSTW at National Science and Technology Week, National Science Foundation, 4201 Wilson Blvd., Rm. 1245, Arlington, VA 22230 or by searching on-line at http://www.nsf.gov/od/lpa/nstw.

a monthly newsletter, both electronically and in print, to profile important projects funded by the NSF. Topics include advances in math and science research, breakthroughs in engineering, and achievements in educational programs. To order the catalog or receive printed copies of these reports and documents or an issue of *Frontiers,* write NSF Clearinghouse, PO Box 218, Jessup, MD 20794-0218; call (301) 947-2722; or E-mail pubs@nsf.gov.

Other publications available from the NSF Clearinghouse include manuals such as *A Guide for Proposal Writing*, scholarly journals such as *Antarctic Journal of the United States*, and field-related newsletters such as *Chemistry Newsletter.*

BIBLIOGRAPHY

Andelman, David A. "Government Money: Seeds for Tomorrow's Technologies." *Management Review,* 1 September 1997.

Bush, Vannevar. *Science: The Endless Frontier.* Washington D.C.: Office of Scientific Research and Development, 1945.

"Crisis in the Labs Beset by a Budget Squeeze." *Time,* 26 August 1991, p. 44.

"Funding the Best of Science," *Los Angeles Times*, 11 January 1998, Opinion, p. 4

Girishankar, Saroja. "News & Analysis: NSF Grants the Web Priority Status." *Internet Week,* 3 November 1997, p. 20.

Henson, Robert. "A Twist of Fate." *Weatherwise*, 16 June 1997 p. 25.

Mazuzan, George T. "A Brief History of the NSF." Washington D.C.: National Science Foundation, 1989.

"National Science Foundation: Science and Technology Pocket Data Book." Arlington, Va.: National Science Foundation, 1996.

Pietrucha, Bill. "Science Foundation Prepares for Internet's Next Generation." *Newsbytes News Network*, 15 August 1996.

National Security Agency (NSA)

WHAT IS ITS MISSION?

The National Security Agency (NSA) describes itself as being responsible for the "centralized coordination, direction, and performance of highly specialized technical functions in support of U.S. government activities to protect U.S. communications and produce foreign intelligence information." In simpler terms, the NSA is the nation's cryptologic organization, charged with both making codes that will protect the transmission (increasingly over computer networks and sophisticated telecommunications networks) of sensitive government information and with breaking such codes to intercept the transmissions of organizations or nations whose activities are considered to be antagonistic to U.S. interests.

PARENT ORGANIZATION: Department of Defense
ESTABLISHED: October 24, 1952
EMPLOYEES: Because of the nature of the NSA's operations, figures on the number of employees working for the agency are not available to the general public.

Contact Information:

ADDRESS: 9800 Savage Rd.
Fort George G. Meade, MD 20755
PHONE: (301) 688-6524
TOLL FREE: (800) 688-6115
URL: http://www.nsa.gov
DIRECTOR: Lt. Gen. Kenneth A. Minahan
DEPUTY DIRECTOR: William P. Crowell

HOW IS IT STRUCTURED?

The NSA is a component of the U.S. intelligence community (IC), a coordinated network of people and organizations. The president has the final authority over all intelligence collection and analysis and is assisted in decision making by the National Security Council (NSC), a group of senior officials who help formulate foreign policy and intelligence priorities. The director of central intelligence, who is both head of the Central Intelligence Agency (CIA) and of the IC, is responsible for directing and coordinating the diverse activities of each of the 13 U.S. intelligence organizations.

Although not a military agency, the NSA is one of several IC elements that is administered by the Department of Defense (DoD). The director of the NSA, a commissioned officer of the military, is appointed by the sec-

FAST FACTS

The NSA/CSS Cryptologic Memorial at Fort Meade honors 152 military and civilian cryptologists who gave their lives in service to their country since World War II (1939–45).

(Source: National Security Agency. "The NSA/CSS Cryptologic Memorial," 1997.)

retary of defense, and approved by the president. The director is the principal signals intelligence (SIGINT) adviser to the secretary of defense, the director of central intelligence, and the Joint Chiefs of Staff. The NSA also controls the activities of the military SIGINT agencies, grouped together into the Central Security Service (CSS); the NSA director serves in a dual role as chief of the CSS. To provide continuity in matters related to signals intelligence, the deputy director of the NSA is a technically expert civilian. The deputy chief of the CSS is a commissioned military officer. The commanders of the CSS cryptological agencies are subordinate to the deputy chief.

The NSA is particularly secretive about its internal organization, and a description can only be based on the most reliable current information. The NSA is organized into five directorates. The Information Systems Security Directorate is responsible for the agency's communications and information security (INFOSEC) mission, the protection of American information through encryption. The Technology and Systems Directorate develops new technologies for signals intelligence SIGINT collection and processing, such as satellites to intercept enemy radio transmissions; the Operations Directorate collects and processes SIGINT and is responsible for breaking their codes. The Plans, Policy, and Programs Directorate provides staff support and general direction for the agency, and the Support Services Directorate provides logistical and administrative support activities. The activities of the NSA are also broken down into groups designated by letter (A Group, B Group, etc.), with each group carrying out a specific function.

The CSS serves within the NSA structure to carry out SIGINT operations as assigned. Its headquarters is jointly staffed by army, navy, marine corps, and air force personnel and other subordinate elements that may be assigned by the secretary of defense. While working for the NSA, the service cryptologic organizations remain technically within their parent services for logistical and administrative support. Other DoD components provide support to the NSA/CSS in the form of personnel, facilities, and funds as the secretary of defense sees necessary.

PRIMARY FUNCTIONS

As the signals intelligence branch of the U.S. intelligence community, the NSA prescribes certain security principles for the government: it organizes, operates, and manages activities and facilities for the production of foreign intelligence information; and it organizes and coordinates the research and engineering activities that support NSA functions.

The NSA also regulates certain communications that support agency missions and operates the National Computer Security Center. The center supports the NSA director's role as national manager for telecommunications security and automated information systems security. The agency also distributes, to authorized members of the intelligence community, a weekly SIGINT digest of the intelligence gathered from all foreign sources.

PROGRAMS

The vast majority of the NSA's work is carried out behind closed doors, and specific NSA programs are not often articulated to the public unless they do not involve information that the IC considers "sensitive." For example, the NSA is proud to publicize its Mathematics Education Partnership Program (MEPP), an NSA outreach program to promote mathematics and science education. Through MEPP hundreds of agency volunteers help local area schools by taking part in interactive math and science discussions and individual tutoring or by providing used computers and laboratory equipment.

Information about other programs, involving spying activities in specific areas, the development of new technology or equipment, or even the development of new intelligence policies, are kept entirely secret by the NSA. A current effort to declassify older, no longer sensitive NSA activities, begun in 1995, is project OPENDOOR. OPENDOOR is an NSA initiative to review for declassification all permanently classified documents that are 25 years old or older. As the documents are declassified, they will be turned over to the National Archives and Records Administration.

So far as the NSA's secretive programs are concerned, little information is available to the public beyond the NSA's purpose and mission. The NSA provides two primary services to the federal government: information systems security (INFOSEC) and foreign signals intelligence (SIGINT). INFOSEC "provides leadership, products, and services to protect classified and unclassified national security systems against exploitation through interception, unauthorized access, or related technical intelligence threats." SIGINT consists of all foreign signals collection and processing. These programs are respectively responsible for the protection of government information systems from spies and for achieving unauthorized access to certain other information.

BUDGET INFORMATION

Budget information about the NSA is hard to determine. The NSA's budget authority is apparently derived from the Central Intelligence Act of 1949, which provides the basis for secret spending—"the black budget"—in which any branch of the government can transfer money to the CIA, which will then confidentially fund the project. Because the NSA budget is classified, it cannot be appropriated through the normal process of congressional procedure; it is instead directly funded through the black budget after the NSA director submits the budget to the secretary of defense.

The process of guessing at the NSA budget is made more difficult by the confusion between the NSA proper and all the military elements of the Central Security Service, which include thousands of personnel at overseas stations. Published reports of the budget vary greatly, with some estimates running as high as $10 billion. The Federation of American Scientists (FAS), a group of scientists and scholars that conducts two large-scale public awareness efforts, the Intelligence Reform Project and the Project on Government Secrecy, has made estimates of the NSA budget based on the following information: the Department of Defense budget documents provide total figures for all defense agencies except for the NSA and Defense Intelligence Agency (DIA). Subtracting the reported components from the total defense budget yields a "missing component" that logically represents NSA and DIA expenditures. The FAS, using a size ratio that compares the NSA to the DIA, comes up with the following estimates: the NSA currently spends about $200 million on military personnel; $2 billion on operations; $2.5 billion on procurement of equipment and technology; and $3.5 billion on research, development, evaluation, and testing. A negligible portion of the budget is spent on construction.

HISTORY

Modern cryptologic communications intelligence activities in the United States date from the advent of radio communications technology used during World War I (1914–18). In 1917 and 1918 the army created a cipher bureau within the Military Intelligence Division (MID). MID assisted the radio intelligence units of American forces in Europe during World War I by attempting to intercept and decode enemy transmissions. Later, the Army Signal Corps assumed responsibility for a small SIGINT service. Navy efforts at cryptology were formally introduced in 1924.

During World War II (1939–45), the army and navy agencies emphasized the security of U.S. military communications, but both developed radio intercept, direction finding, and processing capabilities that helped them to intercept many Japanese diplomatic communications. Toward the end of the war, the services attempted to coordinate their efforts by assigning a governing board.

The passage of the National Security Act of 1947 accelerated the move to a centralized IC. The legislation established the NSC and the CIA, and later directives established the Armed Forces Security Agency (AFSA), with a mission of communications intelligence and security activities with the national military establishment. The AFSA was accountable to the Joint Chiefs of Staff.

During the Korean War (1950–53), the difficulties in having the AFSA report to the Joint Chiefs, each of whom represented a different branch of the military, became obvious. Certain powers and areas of jurisdiction had been vaguely defined, and with each branch of service represented in the leadership, consensus was impossible. The quality of strategic intelligence in the Korean War was not as good as that collected during World War II.

The Secret Formation of the NSA

President Harry Truman, distressed at the obvious weaknesses in the intelligence structure, ordered an analysis in 1951 and acted on the investigation in the following year. A new agency, the NSA, was created by a top secret executive directive on October 24, 1952. The agency assumed the responsibilities of the AFSA but was to be freed from its crippling subordination to the Joint Chiefs of Staff; instead, it was to be directly accountable to the secretary of defense. The policy that directed the agency's actions was to be formulated by a board, to be chaired by the director of central intelligence and including representatives from both military and nonmilitary departments.

The directive (National Security Council Intelligence Directive, or NSCID, #9), also gave the NSA operational control over the SIGINT activities of the three military cryptological agencies: the Army Security Agency, the Naval Security Group Command, and the Air Force Security Service. Over the next two decades, however, the NSA discovered that leading three formerly independent agencies was exceedingly difficult.

To strengthen the NSA's control over their activities, the military cryptological agencies were consolidated in 1971 into the CSS, with the NSA's director serving in a dual role as chief of the CSS. The NSA now had effective control over the SIGINT activities of the military services and assumed the organizational structure it has retained to this day.

During the 1980s the NSA was charged with two additional responsibilities. A 1984 presidential directive assigned the NSA responsibility for computer security, and, in a 1988 directive, responsibility for its own operations security training. Through this career-oriented service, the agency conducts its own recruiting and employment programs to ensure a skilled and sophisticated work force.

CURRENT POLITICAL ISSUES

The NSA's secrecy about its funding, staffing, and missions has often been the subject of serious public attack on an agency whose professed mission is to develop and implement sophisticated methods of electronic and electromagnetic spying. When NSA activities are revealed to the public (almost always after they are well under way), they unfailingly create some controversy, and the debate usually centers on the struggle to ensure public safety, which the NSA is charged to protect, and on protecting individual privacy, which the NSA is charged, at times, to invade for law enforcement purposes.

Case Study: The Clipper Chip

The 1990s saw the issue of encryption become one of the most significant privacy-related issues in American society. Computers and devices such as fax machines and cellular phones communicate by means of digital signals that could be easily intercepted if not for the technology of computer encryption. The military and the government have been using encryption technology for years, but it did not become an issue for private citizens until the 1990s, when they began increasingly to use encryption technology to protect their own privacy. In order to protect the security of computer communications and telecommunications, many consumers use commercially available "scrambling" devices to code information that will later be "unscrambled," or decoded, by a receiving device; as the signal travels through the air or along a cable or optical fiber, it is safe from being decoded. This trend has made federal law enforcement agencies fearful that criminal and terrorist activities in the United States could be more easily concealed through the use of encryption.

In April 1993 President Bill Clinton's administration announced its approval of a directive on "public encryption management." The centerpiece of this plan turned out to be a powerful decoding computer chip—the "Clipper" chip—that would serve as the "brains" in digital scrambling devices. For years, Clipper had been developed in a highly classified environment; the technology upon which Clipper was built had been designed by NSA cryptologists. Implementing the technical specifications of the chip would be the responsibility of another agency, the National Institute of Standards and Technology (NIST). Clipper was to set a new government standard for encryption by being used in all government telephone systems and computer networks. The chip was so powerful, in fact, that private interests such as AT&T were lined up to purchase chips in bulk from the government.

The initiative came with a catch, however, that alarmed many members of the public: the algorithm behind Clipper's operations, known by the code name "Skipjack," was still classified as top secret and therefore immune to public examination; and the "keys" to decoding information scrambled by Clipper would be available only to the government's law enforcement agencies. Accusations of an intelligence conspiracy, of "Big Brother" developing the ultimate totalitarian tool for surveillance and public control, were published and broadcast. Some proclaimed that the implementation of Clipper was like the government demanding to be given sealed copies of all of a person's future telephone conversations and computer communications.

These claims were inaccurate and based largely on misinformation. The administration had been sensitive to these concerns from the start and had attempted to discover a balance between the need for privacy and the need to be assured of safety from crime and terrorism. It had established a "dual-key" system in which two keys would be needed to decode information. To prevent an agency from abusing its power to eavesdrop, each key would be kept with two separate agencies, which would have to cooperate in an investigation. Before tapping telephone or computer communications for the purpose of unscrambling, an appropriate court-authorized warrant would need to be obtained.

Still, the public remained concerned. Two groups, Computer Professionals for Social Responsibility (CPSR) and the Electronic Frontier Foundation (EFF), began to articulate a reasoned argument against the Clipper initiative. Their protests centered on three basic issues: that the administration had undertaken an initiative in total secrecy, without developing inquiry that might have revealed alternative solutions; that the classified Skipjack algorithm could not be trusted unless it could be tested by private companies; and that while the dual-key system might prove to be an effective balance between privacy and security, it was not a solution that should have been adopted without public debate. The government acknowledged these arguments and encouraged ongoing debate while continuing to upgrade its communications to the Clipper standard.

SUCCESSES AND FAILURES

Much is now known about the successful campaign of intercepting Japanese diplomatic communications during World War II. This early SIGINT effort revealed the Japanese plan to invade Midway Island. The resulting intelligence allowed the United States to defeat this attempt, despite a superior Japanese fleet. SIGINT is believed to have contributed to World War II so greatly that it reduced its length by a year.

In 1995, three years after the fall of the Soviet Union, the intelligence community began to declassify documents related to project VENONA. VENONA was the code name used for the U.S. SIGINT effort to collect and decrypt the text of Soviet KGB and GRU messages from the 1940s until the 1991 breakup of the Soviet Union. The VENONA documents provide a startling insight into Soviet attempts to infiltrate the highest levels of the U.S. government.

FUTURE DIRECTIONS

With the collapse of the Soviet Union and the end of the Cold War, the NSA is expected to focus its efforts on its mission of protecting sensitive U.S. information. The NSA sees the Information Age as a time of fundamental change, where control of information technology will be as important as control of industrial technology has been in the past. The NSA therefore sees itself in a key position to protect the interests of the United States and ensure information superiority in the years ahead.

AGENCY RESOURCES

General inquiries can be directed to the NSA's Public Affairs Office at (301) 688-6524. It should be noted, however, that the NSA is a highly secretive agency and is not likely to respond to questions about its current or future operations, its financing, or its organization.

There are many alternative information sources about the NSA, especially on the Internet, but, as is common with matters relating to intelligence, postings about the NSA are frequently unsubstantiated. Perhaps the most reliable source is the Federation of American Scientists (FAS), a privately funded, nonprofit policy organization "engaged in analysis and advocacy on science, technology, and public policy for global security." The FAS's Board of Sponsors includes more than 55 American Nobel Laureates, and its Project on Government Secrecy works to challenge excessive government secrecy and promote public oversight of agencies like the NSA. The FAS maintains an unofficial NSA Web site at http://www.fas.org/irp/nsa that includes carefully researched information that cannot be found on the agency's own official Web site. The Project on Government Secrecy home page is http://www.fas.org/sgp.

Under the Freedom of Information Act and its own OPENDOOR and VENONA projects, much classified NSA information from the 1970s and earlier is now being made available to the public. On the NSA's Web site, http://www.nsa.gov, an index of documents released to the National Archives and Records Administration is available. The NSA also maintains a Web site at http://www.nsa.gov:8080/docs/venona/venona.html, where documents on the NSA's intelligence efforts against the Soviet Union during the 1940s and 1950s are available for viewing on-line.

AGENCY PUBLICATIONS

The NSA does not make its publications available to the public. In recent years, however, an organization calling itself the Institute for the Advanced Study of Information Warfare (IASIW) has obtained and made available an apparently official copy of the NSA handbook for employees. The handbook, given to all new employees of the NSA, includes guidelines as to what may and may not be brought to work; the lifetime requirement that speeches and writings that might contain classified or NSA-derived information, even if unclassified, must be submitted for prepublication review; and discusses regulations regarding amateur radio activities, unofficial foreign travel, and living arrangements. A reading of this document quite effectively demonstrates the operational philosophy—and the preoccupation with secrecy—that characterizes the NSA. The handbook is accessible from the IASIW's home pages at http://www.psycom.net/iwar.1.html.

BIBLIOGRAPHY

"A Baker's Dozen of Spy Agencies." *CQ Researcher*, 2 February 1996, p. 102.

Bamford, James. *The Puzzle Palace: A Report on America's Most Secret Agency.* New York: Viking Penguin, 1983.

Covault, Craig. "Cyber Threat Challenges Intelligence Capability." *Aviation Week and Space Technology*, 10 February 1997, pp. 20–1.

Denning, Dorothy E. "The Case for 'Clipper.'" *Technology Review*, July 1995, pp. 48–55.

Dibbell, Julian. "The Secret Museum." *Village Voice*, 30 August 1994, p. 38.

Haight, Timothy. "NSA Caught NAPing?" *Network Computing*, 1 November 1995, pp. 22–3.

Herman, Michael. *Intelligence Power in Peace & War.* New York: Cambridge University Press, 1996.

Markoff, John. "U.S. Code Agency is Jostling for Civilian Turf." *New York Times*, 24 January 1994, p. D1.

Ra'Anan, Uri, and Warren Milberg. *Intelligence Policy & National Security.* North Haven, Conn.: Shoe String Press, 1981.

Rusbridger, James. *The Intelligence Game: Illusions & Delusions of International Espionage.* Franklin, N.Y.: New Amsterdam Books, 1992.

Weiner, Tim. *Blank Check: The Pentagon's Black Budget.* New York: Warner Books, 1990.

———. "Pentagon Spy Agency Bares Some Dusty Secret Papers." *New York Times*, 5 April 1996, p. A22.

National Security Council (NSC)

PARENT ORGANIZATION: Executive Office of the President
ESTABLISHED: July 26, 1947
EMPLOYEES: 60

Contact Information:

ADDRESS: Old Executive Office Bldg.
Washington, DC 20506
PHONE: (202) 456-1414
FAX: (202) 456-9271
URL: http://www.whitehouse.gov/WH/EOP/NSC/html/nschome.html
ASSISTANT TO THE PRESIDENT: Samuel R. Berger
DEPUTY ASSISTANT TO THE PRESIDENT: Maj. Gen. Donald L. Kerrick
DEPUTY ASSISTANT TO THE PRESIDENT: James B. Steinberg

WHAT IS ITS MISSION?

The primary mission of the National Security Council (NSC) is to coordinate the actions of all federal government agencies into a single cohesive policy for dealing with foreign nations. In working toward this goal, the NSC serves as the president's principal forum for considering and discussing matters of national security with senior national security advisers and officials in the executive cabinet departments.

HOW IS IT STRUCTURED?

In accordance with the National Security Act, the NSC is chaired by the president; its other members include the vice president and the secretaries of state and defense. There are two statutory advisers: the chairman of the Joint Chiefs of Staff is the military adviser, and the director of the Central Intelligence Agency (CIA) is the intelligence adviser. The NSC is itself a support office within the Executive Office of the President, and is responsible to the president alone.

The assistant to the president for national security affairs, the president's national security adviser, is the top administrative official of the NSC, and in recent administrations has played a largely advisory role, coordinating NSC meetings and preparing the president for meetings with foreign leaders in the president's travels. The national security adviser is helped by two deputy assistants to the president for national security affairs. Among them, they share much of the responsibility for articulating the administration's national security policy to the U.S. public and the world. Each of these officials is appointed by the president, and since the positions are not statutory, they are not subject to congressional approval.

The nature of the NSC's supporting staff tends to change dramatically from administration to administration. Typically, the staff is directed by the executive secretary of the NSC, who assists the national security adviser in his or her work and oversees the inner functioning of the staff. Among its many functions, the staff prepares briefing materials for the president and the national security adviser, in order to help them make decisions regarding national security policy and operations. Briefing materials include meeting agendas and decision and discussion papers.

The NSC staff does not work alone. Interagency working groups, which involve NSC members and staff from other federal agencies work together to prepare analysis and recommendations for the national security adviser, the deputy advisers, and the president. These interagency groups vary with the current needs of each administration; many are assigned to analyze security topics related to specific geographical regions such as Africa, Asia, Europe, or Russia. Other groups or offices are assigned to specific topics of particular concern, such as intelligence, international economic affairs, nonproliferation and export controls, and Gulf War illnesses.

Other NSC offices involve mostly NSC personnel and are devoted to the internal workings of the council and the coordination of NSC activities. Such offices include Strategic Planning, Systems and Technical Planning, Legal Affairs, and Legislative Affairs. Committees, offices, and working groups within the NSC have numbered from more than 40 in the Eisenhower administration to fewer than 10 under President Jimmy Carter.

PRIMARY FUNCTIONS

In conjunction with the National Economic Council (NEC), the NSC advises and assists the president in integrating every aspect of national security policy as it affects the United States: domestic, foreign, military, intelligence, and economic. Top NSC officials—the assistant and deputy assistants for national security affairs—help the president to coordinate the advice and positions of the various interested agencies into a single national policy that can be articulated at home and abroad. These officials also help brief the president in connection with his foreign travel and visits with foreign leaders.

The NSC staff assists the overall policy-making effort in a number of ways. Often specialized policy professionals, they participate in presidential briefings, help the president formulate responses to congressional inquiries, and prepare public remarks that are typically presented by the national security adviser or his deputies. The NSC staff serves as an initial point of contact for departments and agencies who want to bring a national security issue to the president's attention.

In order to maintain preparedness, NSC staff participate in interagency working groups, which conduct analyses of particular national security topics, study the national security implications of events in certain geographic areas, and make general recommendations to the deputy assistants to the president for National Security Affairs, the assistant to the president for National Security Affairs, and the president. NSC meetings do not follow a set schedule; they are typically arranged around certain topics or concerns and may or may not be attended by the president.

FAST FACTS

President Eisenhower's commitment to the NSC system was so strong that he chaired every council meeting he could attend—a total of 329 out of 366.

(Source: National Security Council. "NSC History 1947–1997," 1998.)

PROGRAMS

The NSC does not conduct what would generally be considered programs. Acting as an advisory body whose most important members are the heads of other federal agencies, the NSC serves primarily as a forum for the different agencies involved in foreign affairs and as a decision-making team, not as a policy implementing body. This is not to say that the NSC's decisions are not acted upon, but rather that the NSC works to determine what other agencies in the government, such as the State Department and the Department of Defense, should do.

BUDGET INFORMATION

The NSC's budget is set by Congress through the appropriations process, although council officials consistently exceed the established limit by "detailing" or borrowing employees from other agencies who are already paying their salaries. The 1998 NSC budget was

BIOGRAPHY:
Henry Kissinger

Statesman (b. 1923) Henry Kissinger's influence on American foreign policy began when he served as a special consultant to the National Security Council and the Department of State in 1961 and 1962. Kissinger emerged during the 1968 presidential election as the leading Republican foreign policy expert. After his victory in the 1968 presidential election, Nixon named Kissinger his special assistant for national security affairs. His first objective was ending U.S. involvement in the Vietnam War. Kissinger was instrumental in negotiating the peace settlement between the North and South Vietnamese in 1973. During 1972 and 1973, not only was a cease fire negotiated in Vietnam, but the United States initiated diplomatic relations with China and the United States and the Soviet Union signed the Strategic Arms Limitation Treaty (SALT), which established, for the first time, limits on offensive and defensive weapons. For these accomplishments, and also for his role in attempting to bring settlement to the conflicts between Israelis and Palestinians, Kissinger won the Nobel Peace Prize in 1973. With President Gerald Ford's defeat in the 1976 election, Kissinger too left the government. Since then he has written his memoirs, started a private consulting firm, and has continued to serve as a leading commentator on international affairs.

devoted mostly to the compensation and benefits of its staff and totaled about $7 million. Of this amount, $6 million was spent on policy and operations coordination while the other $1 million was spent on the president's advisory boards.

HISTORY

The National Security Act of 1947 was passed to help coordinate the efforts of government foreign affairs and defense agencies; these efforts had been viewed as disjointed during World War II (1939–1945) and in the years immediately following by President Theodore Roosevelt and Congress. The new legislation united the military departments into a single Defense Department, established the Central Intelligence Agency (CIA), and also created a new National Security Council "to advise the president with respect to the integration of domestic, foreign, and military policies relating to the national security." As conceived, the NSC was to play a merely advisory role and was not intended to actively participate in foreign diplomacy or defense decision making. In 1949 the National Security Act was amended to place the NSC permanently within the Executive Office of the President.

In its first years under President Harry Truman, the NSC did not play a significant role in the formation of foreign and domestic policy. The president saw no reason to view the council as anything other than an advisory body and usually did not attend its meetings. President Dwight Eisenhower, however, who came from a military background, made the NSC more institutionalized, creating a strict hierarchy along which policy decisions were made and implemented. One of Eisenhower's most important contributions to the council's development was the appointment of the first assistant to the president for national security affairs—a position that was not mentioned in the 1947 legislation. Eisenhower relied on his NSC staff for advice, and for the first time the possibility for tension between the NSC and the Departments of State and Defense became apparent. Many critics of Eisenhower's reliance on the NSC charged that it had become "overinstitutionalized" and could weaken the images of the secretaries of state and defense.

President John F. Kennedy came to office in 1961 mindful of these criticisms and preferred a more informal style of policy making as well. Although he conferred often with his national security adviser, he dramatically reduced the size and responsibilities of the NSC staff, and relied instead on a smaller group of advisers separate from the NSC bureaucracy. Kennedy's successor, Lyndon Johnson, followed a similar model, but his security adviser, Walt Rostow, was an important influence in Johnson's decision to escalate the U.S. war effort in Vietnam.

The NSC under Nixon and Carter

In the early 1970s the NSC's role underwent a dramatic change in status and authority during the administration of President Richard Nixon, who favored strong executive control over policy and centered his decision-making power in the Executive Office of the President. Under Nixon and his national security adviser, Henry Kissinger, the NSC staff tripled in size and exercised unprecedented influence within the federal bureaucracy. It was Kissinger, not the Secretary of State, who became the primary adviser and diplomat in several key foreign policy moves, including the opening to Communist China, the beginning of detente (relaxation of tensions) with the Soviet Union, and the negotiation of the end of the Vietnam War (1959–75).

Despite apparent diplomatic success, Kissinger's years in the NSC set a dangerous precedent for future presidents, and in later years Kissinger himself would come to believe it was inadvisable for the national security adviser to overshadow the secretary of state's role as the president's principal adviser on matters of foreign policy.

Although President Jimmy Carter came to office determined to place more authority in the cabinet than in executive support agencies such as the NSC, conflicts between his national security adviser, Zbigniew Brzezinski, and Secretary of State Cyrus Vance were obvious from the start. Brzezinski was a hard-line anticommunist who was not content to be a mere facilitator; he insisted on making his views known to Vance, who stressed mutual cooperation and arms control agreements with the Soviet Union. The American public and foreign governments were often confused about which of the two officials truly reflected U.S. foreign policy.

The Iran-Contra Affair

When President Ronald Reagan came to office in 1981, he clearly designated his secretary of state as his principal foreign policy adviser. Although Reagan actively attended NSC meetings, he downplayed the role of the staff and eliminated much of the complex committee system that had been developing for years in the council. Ultimately Reagan's national security advisers were viewed as officials who lacked close ties to the president. It came as a shock then, when it was discovered that two NSC advisers and their staffs secretly directed operations that would prove an enormous embarrassment to the Reagan administration. Throughout their tenures as national security advisers, Robert McFarlane and Vice Admiral John Poindexter orchestrated a secret plan to sell arms to Iran in exchange for the release of American hostages held in Lebanon. In addition, an NSC staffer, Lieutenant Colonel Oliver North, acting on Poindexter's approval, allegedly arranged for the illegal transfer of the arms-sale proceeds to the anticommunist "contra" guerrillas in Nicaragua. Apparently without the knowledge of Reagan or his cabinet advisers, the NSC had become involved in the operational side of foreign policy, even beyond the maneuvers of Henry Kissinger. In the wake of the Iran-Contra affair, Reagan replaced Poindexter with Frank Carlucci, who moved to reduce the power of the NSC staff.

Both presidents who followed the Reagan administration worked to restore trust among the NSC and department heads. Under President George Bush, the NSC helped coordinate U.S. policy through earth-shaking events such as the collapse of the Soviet Union, the unification of Germany, and the Persian Gulf War (1991).

President Bill Clinton, upon taking office in 1992, worked to emphasize the economic aspects of foreign policy in the absence of a Soviet threat to U.S. security. He reorganized the NSC, enlarging its membership to include the secretary of the Treasury, the U.S. ambassador to the United Nations (UN), a newly-created assistant to the president for economic policy, and the president's chief of staff. When appropriate, the attorney general, department and agency heads, or other key officials were to be involved in meetings as well.

The assistant to the president for economic policy was to serve as a senior economic policy adviser to coordinate both foreign and domestic policy through a newly-formed National Economic Council (NEC). The NEC, working closely with the NSC, would assume responsibility for foreign and domestic economic issues in the same way that the NSC coordinated diplomatic and security issues.

CURRENT POLITICAL ISSUES

The effectiveness of the NSC in coordinating the policy of any administration depends on the ability of its staff to remain objective and ever-mindful of the best interests of the United States. This responsibility often includes alerting the administration about apparent conflicts of interest where foreign policy is concerned. During the presidential campaign of 1996, when President Clinton was running for his second term in office, one of his main foreign policy platforms was the development of stronger economic ties to the Asian Pacific nations. The president's eagerness to court Asian-American interest groups became something of a political disaster for the administration, and many of the president's top NSC advisers were unwillingly pulled into the controversy.

Case Study: The 1996 Presidential Campaign

A good deal of the money that was donated to the Democratic National Committee (DNC)—the formal organization of President Clinton's political party—to help with the president's campaign came from wealthy Asian Americans. One supporter, Johnny Chung, donated a total of $366,000 to the DNC; in return for his generous assistance he was granted 49 separate visits to the White House. The NSC's expert on China was suspicious of Chung, and warned White House staffers against excessive relations. As it turned out, Chung did use his audience with the president—along with a photograph that had been taken of him and the president together—to enhance his prestige and influence in Chinese business deals. Chung also began to press for a letter from Clinton that would help him to negotiate the release of

Harry Wu, a Chinese political prisoner. While his request was not granted, his multiple visits to the White House made it look as if foreign policy decisions were for sale.

More serious charges prompted an investigation by the Federal Bureau of Investigation (FBI) into the donations of two other prominent Asian American donors, Charlie Trie and Johnny Huang. After donating about $300,000 to the DNC, Trie requested an assurance from President Clinton that he would not pressure China on the issue of Taiwan, the democratic island off the Chinese coast which the Chinese government wanted to submit to Chinese rule. Trie's request was denied, but the FBI began looking into the possibility that the Chinese government was funneling campaign money, through Trie and Huang, into President Clinton's campaign in order to influence his foreign policy decisions.

In each of these cases, National Security Adviser Anthony Lake and his staff issued repeated warnings against granting political donors with foreign interests too much access to the president. But the counsel of the NSC was largely dismissed. The situation was serious enough to prompt a congressional inquiry, during April of 1997, into the campaign financing of the Clinton administration. In hearings before the Senate Governmental Affairs Committee, no direct evidence proved that the Chinese government had succeeded in directing money to the DNC or that Democratic officials knew about the effort.

What was revealed, however, was as troubling as the events that provoked the hearing. An NSC staffer was apparently pressured by both the DNC and an official at the CIA to censor her negative findings on a Lebanese-American oil tycoon who had expressed an interest in donating as much as $600,000 in return for an audience with the president. The donor, Roger Tamraz, hoped to receive the administration's blessing on a controversial oil pipeline project in the Mediterranean. The hearings also revealed that a deputy assistant to the president for national security affairs had attended a political fundraising dinner, at which she was seated next to none other than John Huang. The appearance of a senior NSC aide at a political dinner raised further questions about whether politics and foreign policy were becoming entangled at the Clinton White House.

The hearings were a huge embarrassment for the president and the NSC, and prompted National Security Adviser Samuel Berger, Lake's successor, to institute new rules within his organization. Specifically, Berger worked to both limit the DNC's access to the NSC staff, and to more effectively screen foreign visitors from the White House. Since a number of NSC advisers had warned the White House well in advance of the controversial meetings with donors, it appeared that Berger was taking the blame for mistakes that were not the fault of NSC staff.

SUCCESSES AND FAILURES

Under administrations in which the roles of the national security adviser and the secretary of state were not clearly defined by the president, political infighting and differences in opinion over national security needs have resulted in tension between the two agencies, as well as confusion over the overall policies of the administration. In recent administrations, the president who most effectively balanced and defined the roles of these two key figures was President George Bush, who was a former CIA head and vice president under the Reagan administration. Bush's extensive experience in national security affairs allowed him to orchestrate a close, collegial working relationship between his national security adviser, Brent Scowcroft and Secretary of State James Baker. During the Bush administration, the NSC worked effectively in bringing about a number of foreign policy successes—establishing good relations both with the newly-formed states that resulted after the collapse of the Soviet Union and a newly reunified Germany; implementing Operation Just Cause, which sent U.S. troops into Panama in 1989; and Operation Desert Shield and Desert Storm, which brought the Persian Gulf War to a swift end.

FUTURE DIRECTIONS

Since the breakup of the Soviet Union, the United States's Cold War enemy for more than 50 years, U.S. national security policy has had to adjust to the nation's changing security needs, as well as to the economic opportunities provided in the newly independent states that had been part of the Soviet Union. In addition, the economic rise of several Asian states, especially China, has prompted a renewed interest in cooperation and friendly diplomatic relations in this region. The foreign policy of the United States must accommodate the changing global environment, and the NSC and other agencies concerned with national security are engaged in this ongoing process. Among the current goals of U.S. national security policy are the integration of Eastern and Western Europe without provoking tensions with Russia; the promotion of more open international trade; and the encouragement of a stable Asian-Pacific community by seeking cooperation with China while avoiding confrontation on Chinese human-rights issues.

AGENCY RESOURCES

The NSC maintains a Web site that contains information about the council's functions, history, membership, and publications. Information about the council may also be obtained by sending a request in writing to National Security Council, Old Executive Office

Bldg., Washington, DC 20506 or by phoning (202) 456–1414.

The NSC is only one of the many government agencies involved in forming and implementing national security policy. For further information about international relations, foreign policy, and U.S. diplomacy, contact the State Department at (202) 647-4000 or visit their Web site at http://www.state.gov. E-mail inquiries can be sent to secretary@state.gov. For further information about national defense policy and strategy, the Defense Department is perhaps the best source, and can be telephoned at (703) 545-6700. The department Web site is http://www.dtic.mil/defenselink.

Information about NSC's partner agency, the NEC, can be found at http://www.whitehouse.gov/WH/EOP/nec/html/index.html. The CIA at http://www.odci.gov/cia; phone (703) 482-1100, is the core agency of the United States intelligence effort.

AGENCY PUBLICATIONS

The NSC makes a number of its documents available to the public, including speeches delivered by assistants and deputy assistants to the president for national security affairs. Other important documents include statements of policy, such as the *Clinton Administration's Policy on Reforming Multilateral Peace Operations.* Since the NSC observed its 50th anniversary in 1997, there are also a number of brief speeches and messages by the president and national security adviser addressing the event. Many of these documents are available for viewing or downloading from the NSC's Web site at http://www.whitehouse.gov/WH/EOP/NSC/html/nschome.html. For further information about NSC publications, contact the council at (202) 456-1414.

BIBLIOGRAPHY

Andrianopoulos, Gerry A. *Kissinger and Brzezinski: The NSC and the Struggle for Control of the National Security Council.* New York: St. Martin's Press, 1991.

Campbell, David. *Writing Security: United States Foreign Policy and the Politics of Identity.* Minneapolis: University of Minnesota Press, 1992.

Gibbs, Nancy. "Cash and Carry Diplomacy." *Time*, 24 February 1997, pp. 22–27.

Mitchell, Alison. "New Measures to Separate Foreign Policy from Politics." *The New York Times*, 21 April 1997, p. A12(N); p. B9 (L).

Prados, John. *Keepers of the Keys: A History of the National Security Council from Truman to Bush.* New York: Morrow, 1991.

Sarkesian, Sam C. *U.S. National Security: Policymakers, Process, and Politics.* Boulder, Colo.: Lynne Rienner Publishers, 1994.

Stewart, Alva W. *The National Security Council: Its Role in the Making of Foreign Policy.* Monticello, Ill.: Vance Bibliographies, 1988.

Taylor, William J., and Amos A. Jordan. *American National Security: Policy & Process.* Ann Arbor, Mich.: Books on Demand, 1986.

Watson, Cynthia. *U.S. National Security Policy Groups: Institutional Profiles.* Westport, Conn.: Greenwood Publishing Group, 1990.

Weltman, John J., ed. *Challenges to American National Security in the 1990s.* New York: Plenum Publishing, 1991.

National Technical Information Service (NTIS)

PARENT ORGANIZATION: Department of Commerce
ESTABLISHED: 1945
EMPLOYEES: 370

Contact Information:

ADDRESS: 5285 Port Royal Rd.
Springfield, VA 22161
PHONE: (703) 605–6000
TOLL FREE: (800) 553–6847
TDD (HEARING IMPAIRED): (703) 487-4639
FAX: (703) 605-6900
E-MAIL: info@ntis.fedworld.gov
URL: http://www.ntis.gov
ACTING DIRECTOR: Donald Corrigan

WHAT IS ITS MISSION?

The mission of the National Technical Information Service (NTIS) is to collect and disseminate information produced by the U.S. government and worldwide sources in order to increase the competitiveness of the United States in the global economy. The NTIS collects scientific, engineering, and business-related information, and then organizes, maintains, and distributes that information in a variety of forms and formats for its customers, which include both the public and other government agencies. Besides collecting and disseminating information, the NTIS currently offers a number of support and production services to its clients.

HOW IS IT STRUCTURED?

The NTIS is one of three agencies—along with the National Institute of Standards and Technology (NIST) and the Office of Technology Policy (OTP)—within the Technology Administration of the Department of Commerce (DOC), a cabinet-level agency in the executive branch of the federal government. The director of the NTIS reports to the undersecretary for technology. Several offices help the director carry out the administrative duties of the NTIS: the FedWorld Office, which handles the NTIS's extensive on-line locator service, and the Office of Strategic Planning, which is responsible for the NTIS's Joint Venture Program.

The remaining programs of the NTIS are handled by various offices. The Office of Business Development functions primarily to acquire reports from U.S. federal agencies and international organizations, and is also responsible for new product management and marketing. The Office of Customer Services runs the NTIS's sales desk and handles orders and subscriptions; it also offers research help, information services, and data processing to individuals and groups. The Office of Production Services collects information requested by other federal agencies and produces it in the requested format, whether it be print, CD-ROM, audiovisual media, micrographics, or computer diskette.

Two other NTIS offices handle the inner workings of the service. The Office of Financial and Administrative Management is responsible for internal affairs matters such as budgeting and personnel management. The Office of Information Resources Management handles the service's internal database for orders, lists, and reports, which must be communicated efficiently from one office to another.

FAST FACTS

The NTIS collection numbers nearly 3 million titles; the NTIS adds new titles to its collection at a rate of about 100,000 a year.

(Source: National Technical Information Service. "NTIS in Brief," 1997.)

PRIMARY FUNCTIONS

The NTIS's most basic function is to serve as a central clearinghouse and government-wide information resource. The agency acquires material from other U.S. government agencies and their contractors and grantees, as well as from foreign government sources. The NTIS then makes that material available in various formats: printed reports, CD-ROMs, computer tapes and diskettes, audiocassettes and videocassettes, microfiche, and online computer access.

The NTIS also assists other federal agencies by providing a wide range of products and services, including FedWorld, an on-line service; database services such as the Federal Research in Progress (FEDRIP); audio and visual training materials; CD-ROM production and packaging; fax-on-demand services for Freedom of Information Act (FOIA) requests; financial brokerage; and collection and billing services. Many of these services are offered to the public as well.

In addition, the NTIS reaches out to the private business sector in several ways. Its Joint Venture Program seeks to form strategic alliances with businesses, creating new information products and opening new channels of sales and distribution. Through its *Directory of Federal Laboratory and Technology Resources*, the service also guides private citizens to hundreds of federal agencies, laboratories, and engineering centers willing to share expertise that will aid in research efforts.

PROGRAMS

NTIS programs are classified according to the services provided by the agency. For example, the Electronic Media Services (EMS) Program permits interested federal agencies to tap into a broad array of CD-ROM and multimedia services through an interagency agreement. EMS provides service personnel who work closely with customers and help define media needs.

The NTIS is one of a few government agencies that have been legislated the unique authority to enter into partnerships with members of the private business sector. Its Joint Venture Program reaches out to the American business community in an effort to form partnerships for designing, producing, and distributing information products and services. The NTIS releases quarterly advertisements that suggest possible future needs. Bids are then submitted from members of private industry. The NTIS screens these responses and selects partners based on their qualifications.

One of the newer NTIS enterprises is the National Audiovisual Center (NAC), which provides unique centralized access to government-developed training and education materials. The NAC has training materials in subject areas such as occupational safety and health, fire services, law enforcement, and foreign languages. It also offers information and educational materials on history, health, agriculture, and natural resources.

BUDGET INFORMATION

Under the provision of Title 15, U.S. Code 1151-1157, NTIS is required to be self-supporting and to recover its costs through the sale of items from its family of information products and services. Therefore, NTIS is run more like a business than a government agency, with none of its funding acquired from taxpayers through congressional appropriations. It is true, however, that NTIS's customer base is made up largely of other government agencies, which pay for NTIS services with funds derived from taxpayers. NTIS financial expenditures amount to about $80 million annually.

HISTORY

The NTIS began as a result of the government's attempts to deal with the release of thousands of war-related documents to U.S. industry following World War II (1939–45). During the war effort, many technical documents had been captured from Germany; these documents, as well as U.S. government materials, became available in such overwhelming numbers after the war that it became necessary to develop a means of handling their disclosure efficiently.

The situation led President Harry S Truman to sign Executive Order 9568 in 1945, which created a Publications Board to collect and declassify World War II technical information and release it to industry. A year later the board's functions were absorbed by a new agency within the DOC—the Office of Technical Services. The clearinghouse functions of the office were expanded in 1950, and in 1964 a newly expanded agency, the Clearinghouse for Federal Scientific and Technical Information (CFSTI) was created within the DOC.

The Information Explosion

The launching of the first-ever space satellite, Sputnik, by the Soviet Union in the 1960s provoked another rapid expansion of technical information as U.S. scientists moved to acquire and retain a technological edge over their Cold War enemies. The production of data increased along with U.S. research, and Congress moved quickly to stay on the pace.

In September of 1970 Congress created the NTIS to replace the CFSTI and assume full authority to establish and monitor a clearinghouse for scientific, technical, and engineering information and analyses. It was also charged with disseminating business and statistical information in order to stimulate U.S. productivity and innovation. By the 1980s the agency had become the primary source for approximately 1.5 million technical reports from the United States and around the world, along with federally generated machine-processable data files and software.

The American Technology Preeminence Act

The form of the NTIS was further refined in February 1992 with the passage of the American Technology Preeminence Act (Public Law 102-245). For the NTIS, the most significant element of the legislation was the requirement of each head of a federal executive department or agency to transfer "in a timely manner" to the NTIS all unclassified scientific, technical, and engineering information that results from federally funded research. The information would then be disseminated by the NTIS to private industry, academia, state and local governments, and other federal agencies. With its new wealth of information, the NTIS was able to expand its services.

The act also proposed an on-line access service to be added to the NTIS, establishing a rough framework for what would become FedWorld, the NTIS's on-line information network. Initial projections were that the network would have one thousand simultaneous connections, and would, after start-up costs, be supported entirely by user fees.

CURRENT POLITICAL ISSUES

The rapid rate at which information is received by the NTIS and subsequently made available to the public is a source of concern to those interested in protecting copyrights. A copyright is an exclusive legal right to print or publish certain materials. In most cases involving the NTIS, the materials are printed matter. Although by law the U.S. government cannot claim copyright in its works, not all the material submitted to the NTIS is in the public domain. Often documents contain some copyrighted material (usually in the form of charts or graphs used with the author's permission) that were prepared by private-sector individuals or organizations. In many cases, the copyright question is a simple matter—the NTIS determines who the authors are, permits them to claim copyright, and makes the necessary arrangements for payment. In other cases, the NTIS is able to secure a release from authors, thus allowing it to add the materials to its collection.

The matter of copyrights becomes more complicated, however, when the NTIS wants to make international materials available in its collections. The federal prohibition on copyrighting government materials only applies to works of the U.S. government. If the author is not a U.S. government entity, the publication is fully protected by copyright under U.S. law, as well as applicable foreign treaties. Many foreign governments and international bodies claim copyright protection in a number of countries, including the United States. This requires the NTIS to make special arrangements with these organizations before it can legally include such works in its collection.

Case Study: World New Connection

For example, a recent NTIS special collection, World New Connection, is an on-line service that serves as a comprehensive foreign news service. It accesses thousands of non-U.S. media sources, which are customized and delivered daily via E-mail to subscribers. Information is drawn from foreign political speeches, television programs, radio broadcasts, newspaper articles, magazines, and books, and is then translated directly into English. In order to gain permission for the use of these sources, the NTIS needed to come up with a way to compensate the authors. The solution was a royalty pool, compiled from user subscription fees, that was established to distribute funds. Since the service is on-line, the NTIS keeps track of how often specific items are accessed, and then divides up the royalty pool accordingly. So far, the system has run smoothly with few complaints. In 1998 NTIS Director Donald Johnson acknowledged that though this system appeared to be working well and within the confines of international law, the way the database is handled might some day need to change to stay current with changes in the global media environment.

SUCCESSES AND FAILURES

One of the NTIS services that has seen remarkable growth in recent years is FedWorld, the on-line service that assists agencies and the public to electronically locate federal government information. Begun in 1992 as a small dial-up system, FedWorld has expanded into an integrated network available through various computer on-line systems. Users can browse through the NTIS permanent collection of information, as well as make use of FedWorld's gateway facility.

The gateway facility allows users to browse a list of over one hundred other independent government on-line systems at other agencies. When a user selects from the FedWorld list, he or she is connected directly to the other system. When finished with the agency's system, the user is returned to FedWorld. The feature, which now accounts for 20 to 25 percent of FedWorld activity, allows users to explore hundreds of other agency offerings through just one call. Through FedWorld, Americans can browse the federal job announcements database to view available jobs, search the U.S. Customs traveler information site for travel advice, review and download tax forms at the Internal Revenue Service (IRS) site, and explore the U.S. business advisor site.

FUTURE DIRECTIONS

The NTIS's future growth will be closely tied to the growth of the Internet and World Wide Web services. As the NTIS collection increases in size, the agency will work to expand access to resources such as FedWorld, and to make more information available through electronic means.

AGENCY RESOURCES

General inquiries about the NTIS can be directed to the Public Affairs division of the Office of the Director, NTIS, 5285 Port Royal Rd., Suite 200F, Springfield, VA 22161, or by calling (703) 487-4778. To connect to FedWorld on the World Wide Web, go to http://www.fedworld.gov. To learn how to connect through direct dial-up connection, Telnet, or FTP, call the FedWorld help desk at (703) 487-4223.

For information about the NTIS's products and services, including catalogs, listing, and price quotes, call the NTIS sales desk at (703) 487-4650. To learn about the NTIS's audiovisual products, contact the manager of the NAC at (703) 487-4743.

AGENCY PUBLICATIONS

Because the purpose of the NTIS is to publish and disseminate information, its publications number in the millions. The service does publish a number of directories and catalogs to help people sort through this information. The primary source is the *NTIS Products and Services Catalog* (PR-827NEB). Others include *Government Reports Announcements and Index Journal, Directory of U.S. Government Software for Mainframes and Microcomputers*, and the *Media Resource Catalog*, a listing of government audiovisual materials. Other subject-specific listings of NTIS information are *Environmental Highlights*, *Business Highlights*, and *Health Care Highlights*. Most of these catalogs are free and can be obtained through the NTIS sales desk, (703) 487-4650.

The NTIS also releases a number of periodical updates to its products and services. *NTIS Alerts* are published twice each month and contain summaries of the latest government-sponsored projects and their findings, and are available in more than 30 broad subject areas. Another twice-monthly publication, *Foreign Technology Update*, tracks scientific and technological developments from around the world. Both publications can be ordered from the sales desk. Updates to on-line services and products are available through *NTIS NewsLine*, a newsletter that can be downloaded from the service's web site under "NTIS Services of Federal Agencies."

BIBLIOGRAPHY

Anthes, Gary H. "Board Offers Free Access to U.S. Data." *Computerworld*, 11 January 1993, p. 40.

Crawford, Mark. "NTIS: Up for Grabs Again?" *Science*, 11 March 1988, pp. 1236–37.

"Doing Business with the Feds." *PC Week*, 18 December 1995, p. N1.

Levin, Mark A. "Government for Sale: The Privatization of Federal Information Services." *Special Libraries*, 1988.

"New Commerce Department Service Offers Legal Texts from Central and East Europe." *Business America*, 11 March 1991, p. 18.

Schwarin, Rich. "Uncle Sam Is Wired." *PC/Computing*, February 1995, p. 327.

National Telecommunications and Information Administration (NTIA)

PARENT ORGANIZATION: Department of Commerce
ESTABLISHED: March 27, 1978
EMPLOYEES: 280

Contact Information:

ADDRESS: Herbert C. Hoover Bldg.
14th and Constitution Ave. NW
Washington, DC 20230
PHONE: (202) 482-7002
FAX: (202) 482-1635
URL: http://www.ntia.doc.gov
ASSISTANT SECRETARY: Larry Irving
DEPUTY ASSISTANT SECRETARY: Shirl G. Kinney

WHAT IS ITS MISSION?

The mission of the National Telecommunications and Information Administration (NTIA) is to promote the development of an advanced telecommunications and information infrastructure that efficiently serves the needs of all Americans, creates job opportunities for U.S. workers, and increases the competitiveness of U.S. industry in the global marketplace. As the president's principal voice on domestic and international domestic policy making, the NTIA works to encourage innovation and competition and to provide customers with better telecommunications and information services and products at lower prices.

HOW IS IT STRUCTURED?

The NTIA is a bureau of the Department of Commerce, and its administrator holds the title of assistant secretary for communications and information. The assistant secretary reports to the secretary of commerce, who is the United States's principal adviser on telecommunications policy. The Office of the Assistant Secretary is assisted by a variety of administrative offices, including the Office of Congressional Affairs, the Office of Public Affairs, and the Office of Chief Counsel, which provides legal review and oversight of the NTIA's policies and programs.

The main program work of the NTIA is carried out through five offices. The Office of Policy Analysis and Development (OPAD) is responsible for NTIA's domestic communications policy development and includes the

Minority Telecommunications Development Program. Representation of the United States in international telecommunications forums is the responsibility of the Office of International Affairs (OIA), which also provides policy analysis and technical guidance.

The Office of Spectrum Management (OSM) develops and implements policies and procedures for domestic issues concerning the use of the radio frequency spectrum, and it manages the use of the spectrum by federal agencies. The Office of Telecommunications and Information Applications (OTIA) is responsible for administering the NTIA's various federal grant programs. The principal research laboratory for telecommunications science and engineering is the Institute for Telecommunications Science (ITS), the NTIA's Boulder, Colorado, laboratory facility.

PRIMARY FUNCTIONS

As the principal executive branch adviser to the president on telecommunications and information policy, the NTIA develops and presents U.S. plans and policies at international communications conferences and related meetings. It also prescribes policies for federal use of the radio frequency spectrum and manages the government's use of the airwaves through the Interdepartment Radio Advisory Committee, which it chairs.

The NTIA is also the government's primary research and engineering institution for telecommunications, working through the ITS. The ITS conducts research for the NTIA and Department of Commerce as well as other government agencies.

The NTIA also provides and monitors grants for promoting development and widespread availability of advanced telecommunications technologies. NTIA program grants also help deliver public telecommunications services to U.S. citizens. The agency monitors grants through the National Endowment for Children's Educational Television to encourage the creation and production of educational television programming for children.

PROGRAMS

The NTIA's largest and best known program is the Telecommunications and Information Infrastructure Assistance Program (TIIAP), which provides seed money for innovative, practical technology projects throughout the United States. Projects supported by the TIIAP are designed to bring advanced telecommunications services to millions of Americans, most of them living in rural or underserved urban areas. The selection process for the TIIAP is highly competitive and only about 1 in 10 applications is funded.

Other NTIA programs include the Public Telecommunications Facilities Program (PTFP), which offers grants to public broadcasting stations to help purchase telecommunications equipment, and the Minority Telecommunications Development Program (MTDP), whose goal is to increase minority ownership of broadcast and telecommunications businesses. MTDP offers a wide variety of services, including broadcast management training and hands-on internships, to support the development of minority- and women-owned telecommunications businesses.

Nearly all of the NTIA's grant programs are "matching" programs; their activities are not backed solely by U.S. taxpayers but also by members of the private telecommunications industry who have an interest in the success of the programs. For most NTIA programs, private funds either match or exceed federal government expenditures—in 1994, the program's first year, $24.4 million in federal funds for the TIIAP was matched by $43 million from the private sector.

BUDGET INFORMATION

Including the funds appropriated for the NTIA's Information Infrastructure Grants, the agency spent approximately $70 million in 1997: $36 million on grants, and $34 million on direct program expenses. Grant funds and a little more than half of direct program expenses are budgeted through congressional appropriations, but about $16 million of the NTIA's program expenses in 1997 were financed through fees collected from NTIA services (primarily research) to other agencies and institutions.

Approximately 44 percent of the NTIA's program expenditures are in the formulation of domestic and international policy; spectrum management activities account for 40 percent of the program budget; and research accounts for about 6 percent.

HISTORY

Because the earliest telecommunications medium was radio, which originally was used primarily by ships, the agency with the first responsibility for implementing communications legislation was the Department of Navigation. By 1915 the Department of Commerce was beginning to receive funds for investigating the standardization of methods and instruments employed in radio communication.

Following the first appearance of commercial radio broadcasting, the Department of Commerce assumed another communications role in the 1920s when Secretary Herbert Hoover called a series of national radio conferences to discuss the need for regulation to control the

FAST FACTS

The Commerce Department's first major responsibilities for communications were a result of the Titanic disaster of 1912. After the Titanic sank, the department strengthened laws governing the use of radio equipment on ocean liners.

(Source: U.S. Department of Commerce. "From Lighthouses to Laser Beams.")

increasingly congested airwaves in the United States. Soon after, the Department of Commerce began its first studies of radio wave propagation.

In February of 1927, a Federal Radio Commission was created to issue broadcast licenses, allocate frequencies, and control power output. A Radio Division was created within the Department of Commerce and was later transferred to what is now the Federal Communications Commission (FCC). The FCC became the agency that regulates the private sector's use of the radio spectrum—the range of frequencies available for radio communication—and the Commerce Department retained its technical research and its management of government use of the spectrum.

New Technologies

After World War II, the communications industry experienced an explosion in the variety, complexity, and uses of telecommunications, and it became clear that the government's telecommunications structure would have to be reorganized. Following studies from the 1960s to the 1970s, the Office of Telecommunications Policy was created in the White House. The Office of Telecommunications was created within the Department of Commerce to continue research and fulfill new responsibilities.

The new office didn't last long, however; the Reorganization Plan of 1978 established the NTIA and authorized the secretary of commerce to serve as the president's principal adviser on telecommunications policies concerning the nation's economic and technological advancement, and to the regulation of the telecommunications industry. Some research and development functions of the Office of Telecommunications were transferred to the FCC. In 1992 the NTIA Organization Act codified the NTIA's authority in detail and legally defined its organizational structure.

CURRENT POLITICAL ISSUES

Because the NTIA's mission and function are not regulatory, most controversies regarding telecommunications and the growing information infrastructure involve the Federal Communications Commission (FCC), the independent agency which regulates telecommunications and is charged with implementing the Telecommunications Act of 1996.

One of the most difficult problems facing the NTIA and the public is the high cost of computers and other equipment necessary to stay abreast of rapid advances in information technology. As the world becomes more dependent on computers and media such as the Internet, low-income Americans seem to lose ground to those who can better afford to keep up with emerging telecommunications technologies.

Because of this economic barrier the White House defined its goal to have every school, library, hospital, and clinic wired to the National Information Infrastructure (NII) by the year 2000. Accordingly, the NTIA provides seed funding for projects that link communities and computer technology through its Telecommunications and Information Infrastructure Assistance Program (TIIAP). By focusing on disadvantaged, underserved communities, the TIIAP attempts to help close the gap between the technological haves and have-nots.

Politically few oppose the TIIAP—a program that selects from a competitive pool of innovative and resourceful applicants and rewards the winners with tools to help them become key players in the nation's economy.

Case Study: Plugged In

Plugged In, based in East Palo Alto, California—a predominantly low-income, minority-populated area—is an organization that has received assistance from the TIIAP. Founded in 1992, Plugged In provides computer and Internet access to 250 people a week.

Plugged In is also assisted by funds and equipment donated by companies such as Bay Networks, Intel Corp., and Global Village—big Silicon Valley corporations that are locally based. Donations from the business sector are an important part of programs such as Plugged In, which now has 30 computers with Internet access and continues to form partnerships with other community service agencies.

SUCCESSES AND FAILURES

The NTIA was recently responsible for formulating policy and legislation authorizing a new way to allocate portions of the radio spectrum to the private sector—the spectrum auction, in which unallocated bandwidths are auctioned off to the highest bidder. The methods designed by the NTIA provided the basis for those implemented by the Federal Communications Commission (FCC) after Congress passed legislation in 1993. To date, the FCC has received bids that will result in payments of about $19 billion to the U.S. Treasury.

FUTURE DIRECTIONS

One of the NTIA's most significant goals for the future is the development of a National Information Infrastructure (NII), often referred to as the Information Superhighway, that will be accessible to everyone. Such an infrastructure will provide the key to delivering new and innovative multimedia services in distance learning, health and safety, law enforcement, finance, and other areas. Developing telecommunications standards—a function of the NTIA—will be a primary means of achieving a unified infrastructure. The NTIA's primary goal is to support the intention of President Bill Clinton's administration to make the benefits of the NII available to all U.S. schools, libraries, and other public institutions by the year 2000.

As the FCC proceeds with adopting regulations required by the recent Telecommunications Act of 1996, the NTIA intends to participate in the process by drafting and submitting comments on behalf of the Department of Commerce and the Clinton administration. The legislation is designed to open up competition among telephone companies; connect public institutions to the NII; and give families control of the television programming that comes into their homes.

The NTIA is also working with other agencies to develop new technologies for the future. For example, the agency is providing key technical support to the Department of Transportation in its development of intelligent transportation systems, to the Federal Highway Administration in using the Global Positioning System (GPS) to provide more accurate navigation and positioning information, and to the National Communications System in enhancing communications survivability during national emergencies.

AGENCY RESOURCES

Inquiries about the work of the NTIA should be directed to the appropriate office or to the Office of Public Affairs, Department of Commerce/NTIA, HCHB 4898, 1401 Constitution Ave. NW, Washington, DC 20230; phone (202) 482-7002. At the NTIA's World Wide Web site, users can access the hypertext *Glossary of Telecommunications Terms* developed by the ITS, or the NTIA's *Table of Frequency Allocations.*

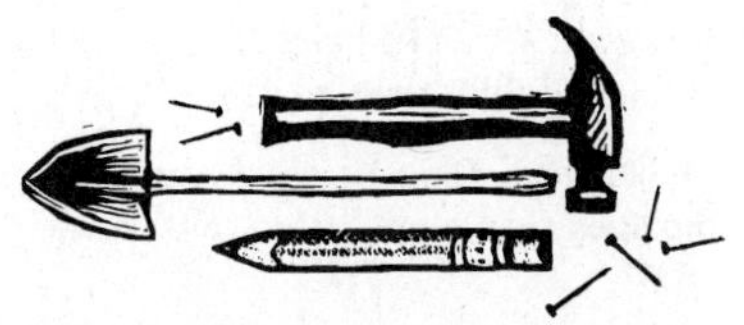

GET INVOLVED:

The NTIA's Telecommunications and Information Infrastructure Assistance Program (TIIAP) provides support to schools involved in a nationwide program called NetDay. NetDay is a grassroots volunteer effort to connect schools to the Internet. Labor and materials come from volunteers with support from private companies, parents, unions, teachers, students, and school employees. In 1997 President Clinton and Vice President Al Gore called on students, teachers, and businesspeople throughout the United States to hold NetDays in all 50 states to help local schools connect at least one classroom, media center, or library to the Internet. Interested participants should contact a neighborhood school or the national NetDay office at netday@netday.org.

AGENCY PUBLICATIONS

NTIA publications consist primarily of reports such as *Privacy and Self-Regulation in the Information Age*, *High Frequency Spectrum Planning Options*, and *Survey of Rural Information Infrastructure Technologies.* Nearly all of these reports are available on-line through the NTIA Web site and can be ordered in print from the Public Affairs Office.

BIBLIOGRAPHY

Echols, Elizabeth. "NTIA Promotes Opportunities for U.S. Companies through Telecom Reform in Southern Africa." *Business America*, January-February 1997, p. 28.

Golding, Peter. "World Wide Wedge: Division and Contradiction in the Global Information Infrastructure." *Monthly Review*, July–August 1996, pp. 70–75.

Gonzalez, Emilio. *Connecting the Nation: Classrooms, Libraries, and Health Care Organizations in the Information Age*. Washington, D.C.: U.S. Department of Commerce, 1995.

Guglielmi, David. "Developing a Framework for Global Electronic Commerce." *Business America*, March 1997, pp. 21–22.

Hernandez, Debra Garsh. "Telecommunications and the Clinton Administration." *Editor and Publisher*, 15 January 1994, pp. 11–12.

Kalil, Thomas. "Public Policy and the National Information Infrastructure." *Business Economics*, October 1995, pp. 15–20.

Katz, Harry, ed. *Telecommunications: Restructuring Work and Employment Worldwide*. Ithaca: Cornell University Press, 1997.

Kawasaki, Guy. "Potholes Along the Information Superhighway." *Macworld*, July 1994, p. 274.

Muhammad, Tariq K. "And Access for All? Underserved Communities Go Online." *Black Enterprise*, May 1996, p. 41.

"The National Information Infrastructure." *Public Management*, May 1995, p. 14.

Teinowitz, Ira. "Clinton Task Force Says 'Hands Off' the Internet." *Advertising Age*, 12 May 1997, p. 66.

National Transportation Safety Board (NTSB)

WHAT IS ITS MISSION?

The mission of the National Transportation Safety Board (NTSB), as mandated by Congress, is "investigating every civil aviation accident in the United States and significant accidents in other modes of transportation—railroad, highway, marine and pipeline—and issuing safety recommendations aimed at preventing future accidents."

The NTSB's investigative mission is determining the probable cause of accidents, that is, the particular mechanical failure or human error that was responsible for an accident so that future accidents of the same sort can be prevented. The NTSB's mission does not extend to establishing whether a crime has been committed or determining criminal culpability.

HOW IS IT STRUCTURED?

The NTSB is an independent agency; it can recommend action be taken by other bodies, but it can neither enact nor enforce regulation. The board is composed of five members. Each serves a five-year term. Members are appointed by the president and are confirmed by the Senate. The Aviation Insurance Program of 1982 requires that at least three Safety Board members possess expertise in accident reconstruction, safety engineering, human factors engineering, transportation safety, or transportation regulation.

In addition, two Safety Board members are appointed chairman and vice chairman by the president. Each serves a two-year term and can be appointed to

PARENT ORGANIZATION: Independent
ESTABLISHED: April 1, 1967
EMPLOYEES: 370

Contact Information:

ADDRESS: 490 L'Enfant Plaza SW
Washington, DC 20594
PHONE: (202) 314-6000
TDD (HEARING IMPAIRED): (800) 877-6799
FAX: (202) 314-6018
URL: http://www.ntsb.gov
CHAIRMAN: James E. Hall
VICE CHAIRMAN: Robert Francis, II

The NTSB's goal is the prevention of accidents like this crash of USAir Flight 427 near Pittsburgh, Pennsylvania, which killed 132 people. (Reuters/Corbis-Bettmann)

more than one term of office. The chairman's appointment must also be confirmed by the Senate.

The two most important divisions under the board are the Office of Aviation Safety and the Office of Surface Transportation Safety. The specialists who lead major accident investigations undertaken by the NTSB are drawn from these offices. The NTSB runs its own laboratory, the Office of Research and Engineering. The lab is one of the world's most advanced facilities for the analysis of flight and voice-recorder data. The laboratory is also equipped to run tests on materials as well as to carry out performance tests on aircraft, locomotives, automobiles, and watercraft.

Investigations of accidents that are not major are conducted by the NTSB's 13 regional offices: six for aviation accidents (plus three additional field offices), three for railroad accidents, and four for highway accidents.

PRIMARY FUNCTIONS

The law specifies two important functions the NTSB is to carry out in the course of its duties: the first is the investigation of transportation accidents to determine their probable cause; the second is to formulate safety recommendations that will make the occurrence of similar accidents less likely and that will, in general, further transportation safety in the United States.

Investigation

The NTSB investigates all accidents involving civil aviation in the United States and provides accredited representatives to foreign investigations involving aircraft of American ownership or manufacture. The majority of NTSB investigations involve aircraft accidents; however, when fatalities, substantial property damage, or problems of a recurring nature are involved, the board investigates highway, marine, railroad, and pipeline accidents.

The NTSB maintains 24-hour readiness with its Go-Team system. A Go-Team is composed of an investigator in chief, plus six or more specialists in various fields such as witness statements, aircraft systems and structures, air traffic control, and meteorology. Each Go-Team works a week-long shift during which members are on call 24 hours a day. When a major accident occurs, the Go-Team, led by the investigator in charge, responds immediately and is often on the scene within a couple of hours.

Its small staff and limited budget make it impossible for the NTSB to conduct investigations on its own. In response it has devised what it calls the "party system." Under this system, individuals, companies, and organizations with specialized expertise are asked by the NTSB to take part in the investigation with the NTSB. Parties to an investigation usually have some direct interest in an investigation. For example, parties to the investigation of the crash of USAir Flight 427 near Pittsburgh,

Pennsylvania, in 1994 included the affected airline, USAir, and Boeing, the plane's manufacturer. It seems a ready-made plan for conflict. But such parties contribute knowledge and expertise that would be unavailable elsewhere. Corporate viewpoints are balanced by the presence of other parties on the team: the manufacturers of major components and pilot, mechanic, flight attendant, and air traffic controller unions among others. The investigator in chief assigned by the NTSB always directs the investigation. Parties receive a place on the investigating team only when invited to participate by the Safety Board. No private group or individual is guaranteed a place in an investigation.

By law, only the federal agencies that regulate the various modes of transportation must be allowed to take part in investigations into accidents in their particular transportation area. These include the Federal Aviation Agency (FAA), the Federal Railroad Administration (FRA), Research and Special Programs Administration (RSPA), the Coast Guard, the National Highway Traffic Safety Administration (NHTSA), and the Federal Highway Administration (FHA). One reason the NTSB was constituted as an independent body to head accident inquiries was that it often must investigate the actions of various governmental bodies regarding accidents.

After the parties to an investigation have been designated, they assign representatives, and groups are formed by the investigator in charge to look into various aspects of the accident. The groups formed are determined by the nature of the accident. A typical aviation accident might be studied by experts on aircraft structures, systems, human performance, meteorology, fire and explosion, radar data, flight recorder data, and witness statements. Each group is headed by an NTSB investigator and eventually produces a report detailing the group's findings. After each member of a group attests to the accuracy of its report, the document is deposited in the docket at a public hearing, the second stage of an investigation.

The purpose of a public hearing is twofold: it is an opportunity for the NTSB to gather sworn expert testimony and it enables the public to observe the progress of an investigation. Hearings are normally held within six months of an accident, but they can be delayed by a complicated search and recovery operation and other circumstances. Sometimes, as in the case of the USAir crash near Pittsburgh in 1994, more than one round of hearings is held.

More tests and analyses are performed after the hearing. Eventually the NTSB staff prepares a report that contains a narrative account of the "facts, conditions, circumstances, analyses, conclusions and probable cause" of the accident. Such a report is produced for all major transportation accidents. The parties to the investigation do not participate in the analysis or the report-writing phases of the investigation. They are, however, invited to submit proposed findings and recommendations of their own, which the NTSB includes in the public docket.

FAST FACTS

In the search and recovery operation for TWA Flight 800, 375 divers made 4,344 dives, often in water where visibility was 10 feet or less.

(Source: Gary Stoller. "Flight 800: Anatomy of an Investigation." *Popular Science*, July 1997.)

Minor accidents are investigated in much the same way. They are handled by the regional offices, however, rather than by NTSB headquarters in Washington, D.C. Findings in these accidents are placed in a public docket, but no public hearing is held. Instead of a final report, regional offices issue a two-page computerized accident brief.

Recommendations

The NTSB calls the safety recommendation its "most important product," describing it as "the lever used to bring changes and improvements in safety to the nation's transportation system." Each recommendation specifies a particular action the NTSB deems necessary, the group or individual expected to take the action, and the safety need that justifies the action. A recommendation might suggest a change in law or regulation, in mechanical requirements, or in industry practice. It might be directed to Congress, state governments, a regulatory agency, an industry as a whole, or a particular corporation.

The NTSB can issue recommendations any time it has reason to believe a safety problem exists. It need not wait until an investigation has been concluded nor until evidence conclusively shows that a specific problem led to an accident. For example, after the Flight 800 crash in 1996 the NTSB issued recommendations about reducing the levels of volatile fumes in fuel tanks long before it was clear that such fumes had actually been responsible for the accident.

NTSB recommendations are not mandatory; they do not carry the force of a law or federal regulation. Nonetheless, Congress has stipulated that the Department of Transportation shall respond to all NTSB recommendations within 90 days of their issuance.

PROGRAMS

The "Most Wanted" program, adopted by the NTSB in 1990, lists those changes it deems to be the most urgently needed and with the greatest potential to avert future fatalities. Recommendations are added to the list when the board believes they will have a national impact on safety or if there is a large degree of public interest. So, for example, after improperly capped oxygen tanks caught fire and caused a ValuJet plane to crash in the Florida Everglades, the NTSB recommended reexamining the way hazardous cargoes are transported. Furthermore, recommendations on the Most Wanted list are those whose implementation the NTSB pursues most vigorously. The NTSB tries to use the list to promote public awareness of the nation's most pressing safety issues, a critical role considering the board's nonregulatory status.

In mid-1997, there were 21 items on the Most Wanted list, including recommendations for tightened control over vehicle operator licenses, for studies of human fatigue in transportation, for safer school buses, for fire and explosion risk reduction, and improved boating safety measures. As the recommended measures are implemented, the NTSB removes them from the Most Wanted list. The NTSB had long advocated mandatory seat belt laws, for example. By 1994 every state but two had enacted such laws and the recommendation was dropped from the Most Wanted list.

Another program was generated in the wake of two major airliner crashes in 1996. The Federal Family Assistance Plan was the result of legislation instructing the NTSB to coordinate the various services available to victims and families of victims of aviation accidents. These include the timely provision of information, victim identification, burial, and counseling services, when necessary. The program also entails coordinating services available from airlines; from governmental agencies at all levels, federal, state, and local; and from private welfare organizations. During 1997 President Bill Clinton sent a presidential memo to the NTSB requesting that it undertake the same activities for families and victims of accidents in other transportation modes.

BUDGET INFORMATION

The NTSB, an independent agency, receives its budget monies directly from the Congress. In 1997, the agency's total appropriation was $42.4 million, which was used for salaries and for the costs of investigations. In the Clinton administration's proposed 1998 budget, the Safety Board received $46 million. The additional 8.5 percent was intended to pay for additional staff, for contracting services from private corporations and for executing the presidential memorandum instructing the Safety Board to coordinate assistance to the families of accident victims. Any costs in 1998 associated with the ongoing investigation of the Flight 800 crash will not be paid out of NTSB's regular budget. They will be funded through a supplemental appropriation.

Since 1988 an additional $1 million has been appropriated to the Safety Board annually. This money forms an emergency fund meant to cover unexpected expenses. As the NTSB has no control over the frequency or costs of its investigations, this money is meant to provide a safety net so all investigations can be carried out without critical delays. The Clinton administration asked that this fund be doubled to $2 million in 1998.

HISTORY

The Department of Commerce was the first federal agency charged with investigating aviation accidents. The Aeronautics Branch was formed in 1926, and combined in embryo the authority today found in the Federal Aviation Administration (FAA) and the NTSB. In 1938 the Civil Aeronautics Administration (CAA) was formed as an independent agency to remove aviation regulation from the Commerce Department. Two years later the Civil Aeronautics Board (CAB) was separated from the CAA. Part of the CAB's responsibility was to investigate airplane crashes. Over the next 20 years, the CAB's Bureau of Safety, which conducted the investigations, became one of the most respected agencies in the federal government.

In 1966 President Lyndon Johnson proposed the creation of a new cabinet-level department that would bring the nation's disparate transportation bureaucracies under one administrative umbrella. Part of the plan for the new Department of Transportation (DOT) included removing the Bureau of Safety from the CAB and reestablishing it as the National Transportation Safety Board, an independent agency of the DOT.

Congress criticized the proposed NTSB on the grounds that it would no longer be an independent agency, as the Bureau of Safety had been under the CAB. Some senators warned that the transportation secretary could "pigeonhole" any reports, recommendations, or other findings of the NTSB that he or she did not care for. Aviation insiders criticized the parts of the bill that gave the NTSB responsibility for investigating all types of transportation accidents. No five-man board, they charged, could possibly possess the expertise to deal with such a broad range of accidents.

The Department of Transportation Act was passed with only minor changes. On April 1, 1967, the NTSB came into existence. Its first chairman was Joseph O'Connell, a tax attorney. By 1968 the NTSB had a 275-member staff; its budget was a mere $4.7 million.

When Congress passed the Independent Safety Board Act of 1975, all ties between the NTSB and the DOT were severed, and the NTSB became fully independent.

The NTSB suffered under the budget politics of the early years of President George Bush's administration. Deficit-reduction measures were instituted that cut the budgets of smaller agencies to increase those of larger ones. By mid-1989 the NTSB had lost nine investigators and could not afford to replace them. Most were aviation accident investigators, the loss of whom adversely affected the Safety Board's ability to conduct thorough investigations. NTSB insiders feared that if the trend continued the NTSB would be forced to let some airplane accidents go without being investigated. Under new chairman James L. Kolstad, however, the agency regained the leadership it had lacked as well as some financial equilibrium.

In late 1996, following the crash of TWA Flight 800, a major new element was added to the NTSB mission. Congress passed the Aviation Disaster Family Assistance Act of 1996, which makes the NTSB responsible for coordinating resources available to victims and the relatives of victims of aviation disasters. Resources included those available from state, local, and federal governments; from the airlines, and from private relief organizations. A presidential memorandum later instructed the NTSB to provide the same relief for accidents in other transportation modes.

CURRENT POLITICAL ISSUES

The NTSB faces a set of problems unique in the federal government. It is a watchdog that oversees government and private industry, yet it has no regulatory or enforcement powers. It works under intense public scrutiny, almost always in the wake of death and disaster. The public often puts a great deal of pressure on the NTSB to produce clear, persuasive answers to highly complex questions as quickly as possible with an overworked staff and an inadequate budget. No case so well illustrates the problems faced by the NTSB as does its investigation into the crash of TWA Flight 800.

Case Study: The Crash of Flight 800

On July 17, 1996, shortly after taking off from John F. Kennedy Airport in New York, TWA Flight 800 exploded and plunged into the Atlantic Ocean off Long Island. All 230 people on board were killed. The crash shocked the nation. Only 60 days earlier a ValuJet plane had crashed into the Florida Everglades, killing everyone on board. More disturbing was the apparently inexplicable nature of the TWA crash, which resembled that of a USAir jet that had crashed near Pittsburgh, Pennsylvania, in 1994.

The NTSB Go-Team responded immediately, but its investigation was hampered by some atypical elements. Unlike most crashes, Flight 800 had not gone down on land. The wrecked Boeing 747 jet lay submerged under 120 feet of water. It had to be found and recovered. In addition, a high priority was being given to finding the remains of as many victims as possible, second only to finding the flight data and cockpit voice recorders.

The search and recovery operation was the largest the NTSB had undertaken since the National Aeronautics and Space Administration (NASA) asked it to investigate the *Challenger* disaster in 1986. It was a cooperative effort in which several federal and local government agencies participated that included the U.S. Navy; the Navy Supervisor of Salvage; the Coast Guard; the National Guard, Oceaneering, Underwater Search and Survey; the National Oceanic and Atmospheric Administration (NOAA); and the New York City Police Department. In the end 95 percent of the aircraft (some 400,000 pounds of wreckage) and the remains of all 230 victims were recovered.

The investigation stretched the meager resources of the NTSB thin. It turned out to be the most expensive investigation in the Safety Board's history. More than 18 investigative groups were formed—far more than in other investigations—and often more than one NTSB investigator was assigned to each group. More NTSB personnel took part in this investigation than in any other in its history: about one-third of its total staff.

The aircraft was reassembled in a hangar on Long Island. Although a missile strike was high on the NTSB's list of probable causes, there did not appear to be any evidence of such an attack in the wreckage. What investigators established was that there had been an explosion in the central fuel tank, a tank that had been nearly empty when the plane took off. The investigative team speculated that fuel-air vapors had reached a dangerous concentration.

Although it had not been decisively shown that volatile vapor levels had been reached nor how the vapors could have been ignited, the NTSB immediately issued recommendations calling for the redesign of the Boeing 747's fuel system. However, neither the Federal Aviation Administration (FAA) nor Boeing, the plane's manufacturer, took any action at first. It was not until the investigative hearing, held one and one-half years after the crash, that Boeing finally admitted that the NTSB had demonstrated that "explosive conditions are far more common than many people had previously believed."

By the time of the hearings, the FAA had agreed that changes to the fuel system might be necessary, but it had only issued directives to airlines to check fuel systems. The agency had refused to require any changes. The FAA had agreed to consider requiring airlines to use a different fuel, which would lower the risk of explosions to one-twentieth of the current rate. The NTSB considered the FAA's willingness to consider the issue an important change in attitude.

The Flight 800 hearings were, like the investigation, unprecedented. Normally when hearings open, the NTSB knows the fundamental problem that led to an accident, and the hearings are used to explore the general ramifications of that problem. However, the board had not reached a point of certainty in the Flight 800 hearings because there was no exhaustive explanation for the accident. The Safety Board was disturbed that the public opinion at the time of the hearings was that the cause of the crash was unknown. The board maintained that the cause was known: an explosion in the central fuel tank. What it did not know was the cause of the explosion.

The action of the Federal Bureau of Investigation (FBI) was also unprecedented. In November 1997 it concluded that there was no evidence that a crime had been committed, but it refused to allow its agents to testify at the hearings. In meetings with the Safety Board, the FBI indicated that it wanted no public discussion or publication of witness interviews, no presentation of a video simulation of the crash created by the Central Intelligence Agency (CIA), and no discussion of the search for explosives among the wreckage. NTSB chairman James Hall reluctantly agreed. But the Safety Board was uncomfortable with the FBI's requests, because they impeded the "complete factual accounting" the hearings were meant to pursue. The requests also seemed to contradict the NTSB's mandate from Congress to conduct its investigations in as public a manner as possible.

Despite pressures from all sides to reach the "popular" decision, the NTSB worked through the investigation in its own time and reached conclusions that will further the cause of aviation safety in the United States and internationally.

SUCCESSES AND FAILURES

Since it was founded in 1967, the NTSB has issued approximately 10,000 safety recommendations, more than 80 percent of which have been implemented. As a result, possibly tens of thousands of accidents have been prevented. Safety measures first advocated by the NTSB are evident today in cars, buses, trains, planes, and on highways. Three important areas in which NTSB recommendations have had an impact are aircraft fire safety, the development of midair collision avoidance systems, and the implementation of new regulations regarding automobile brake lights.

The leading cause of death in aviation accidents is smoke inhalation and fire. The NTSB first recommended installing smoke detectors and automatic fire extinguishers in airliner lavatories after a fire forced a crash landing in Paris in July 1973. Ten years later, despite repeated recommendations and several in-flight fires, the FAA had not required the changes. Only after a fire on an Air Canada plane in which 23 people were overcome by smoke were the NTSB recommendations finally adopted. Today all American airliners are required to be equipped with smoke detectors and automatic fire extinguishers, and it is a federal crime to tamper with an onboard smoke detector. Other measures first advocated by the NTSB include floor-level lighting that leads to exits when visibility is reduced by smoke. Since 1990 all seat and cabin materials must be fire retardant.

In 1967 the NTSB advocated the development of an airborne collision-avoidance system, one that would be independent of air traffic control on the ground and would provide pilots with information on possible danger situations. Since 1993 some airliners have been equipped with the system, called traffic alert and collision avoidance system (TCAS). All aircraft are required to be equipped with transponders that transmit altitude to a central computer. The previous transponder systems made airborne TCAS feasible for all civil aviation.

In 1975 the NTSB recommended clearly separating stoplights from taillights on automobiles. The idea was to reduce confusion, to make it clear to drivers when a car ahead of them was stopping. They were also meant to let drivers see what other drivers more than one car length ahead were doing so as to increase reaction times. In September 1985 the National Highway Safety Administration adopted the recommendation to require center high-mounted stoplights. The Department of Transportation (DOT) estimates that once all cars are equipped with the new lights there will be some 126,000 fewer accidents, 80,000 fewer nonfatal injuries, and nearly $1 billion less in insurance claims every year.

FUTURE DIRECTIONS

The main challenge faced by the NTSB is to find ways to persuade the FAA and other regulatory agencies, as well as the airlines and other corporate bodies, to implement its recommendations. Among those the NTSB considers most urgent are: a collision-avoidance system for the nation's railroads; flight recorders for the nation's airlines that record a broader range of data; a study of human fatigue and its relation to transportation; data recorder systems, similar to those used in aviation, for the nation's railroads, ships, and highway system; and the prevention of explosive fuel-air mixtures in airplane fuel tanks.

A more interesting challenge will be to integrate a brand new set of duties—victim family services coordination—with accident investigation duties. Up to the end of 1997 the NTSB had not had a chance to try out its new role on a major accident. It will undoubtedly have to work through the aftermath of a number of accidents before the system begins to function efficiently and before the NTSB begins to feel comfortable with its new role of social welfare provider.

AGENCY RESOURCES

The NTSB Reading Room contains copies of all Safety Board documents including records, reports, and recommendations. They can be examined or photocopied at the Reading Room, in Room 5111 at the NTSB's Washington headquarters. It is open to the public every business day from 9 A.M. until 4 P.M. Requests to examine materials can be made in person at the Reading Room or by writing or telephoning the Public Inquiries Section, National Transportation Safety Board, 490 L'Enfant Plaza SW, Washington, DC 20594; (202) 314-6551.

AGENCY PUBLICATIONS

The NTSB's *Annual Report* is a fascinating breakdown of the major accidents investigated by the NTSB and the safety recommendations made during a calendar year. It can be obtained free of charge, while supplies last, by calling the NTSB Office of Public Inquiries at 1-800-877-6799 or (202) 314-6551.

Published accident reports, as well as the NTSB's *Annual Review of Aircraft Data*, are available to the public in limited quantities free of charge. For further information call the Office of Public Inquiries. When the free supplies have been exhausted, copies can be purchased from the National Technical Information Services, 5285 Port Royal Rd., Springfield, VA 22161; phone (703) 487-4650.

The *NTSB News Digest* contains regular summaries of the board's activities and a review of upcoming publications. Free subscriptions are available by calling the Office of Public Inquiries.

BIBLIOGRAPHY

Benenson, Tom. "What Is the NTSB and How Does It Investigate Wrecks?" *Flying*, August 1993.

Harr, Jonathon. "The Crash Detectives." *New Yorker,* 5 August 1996.

Moorman, Robert W. "Identity Crisis." *Air Transport World,* April 1997.

Nader, Ralph. *Collision Course: The Truth about Airline Safety.* Blue Ridge Summit, Pa.: TAB Books, 1994.

National Transportation Safety Board. *We Are All Safer*. Washington, D.C.: Government Printing Office, 1995.

"Planes, Trains, Automobiles." *Federal Times*, 9 January 1995.

Stoller, Gary. "Flight 800: Anatomy of an Investigation." *Popular Science*, July 1997.

Wald, Matthew L. "At Flight 800 Hearings, Don't Expect the Routine." *New York Times*, 7 December 1997.

———. "In Flight 800 Study, Consensus Favors Cutting Fuel Tank Risk." *New York Times*, 13 December 1997.

Nuclear Regulatory Commission (NRC)

PARENT ORGANIZATION: Independent
ESTABLISHED: January 19, 1975
EMPLOYEES: 3,000

Contact Information:

ADDRESS: One White Flint N
11555 Rockville Pike
Rockville, MD 20852
TDD (HEARING IMPAIRED): (301) 415-5575
FAX: (301) 415-5575
E-MAIL: opa@nrc.gov
URL: http://www.nrc.gov
CHAIRMAN: Shirley Ann Jackson
COMMISSIONER: Greta J. Dicus
COMMISSIONER: Nils J. Diaz
COMMISSIONER: Edward McGaffigan, Jr.
COMMISSIONER: Kenneth C. Rogers

WHAT IS ITS MISSION?

The stated mission of the Nuclear Regulatory Commission (NRC) is to ensure adequate protection of the environment, public health, and safety in the civilian use of nuclear materials in the United States. The NRC also seeks to promote the nation's common defense and security. The commission regulates by-product, source, and special nuclear materials used by civilians in all types of applications, from nuclear power reactors to nuclear medicine programs at hospitals. It also seeks to improve its regulatory function through the application of research findings.

HOW IS IT STRUCTURED?

The NRC is an independent agency, created by the Energy Reorganization Act of 1974, that works to fulfill regulatory mandates legislated over the last two decades. The commission is composed of five members appointed by the president of the United States and confirmed by the Senate. The commission is headed by a chairman who is designated by the president. The chairman is the principal executive officer of, and the official spokesperson for, the NRC. The chairman is responsible for conducting the organizational, administrative, planning, budgetary, and certain personnel functions of the agency.

The major program components of the NRC are the Office of Nuclear Material Safety and Safeguards, the Office of Nuclear Regulatory Research, and the Office of Nuclear Reactor Regulation. Most of the programs associated with the commission are carried out by these offices, and policy is formulated largely through their work and findings.

The Office of International Programs, a commission staff office, organizes and conducts the commission's international activities. In addition, the commissioners are aided in an advisory capacity by the Atomic Safety and Licensing Board, the Advisory Committee on Reactor Safeguards, and the Advisory Committee on Nuclear Waste. The committees and the board review the policy and operations of NRC programs and advise them on current and future courses of action. Several other staff offices assist in carrying out the administrative responsibilities involved in running the commission.

Some regulatory responsibilities of the commission are further divided among the Office of State Programs, the Office of Enforcement, and the Office of Investigation.

The NRC also has four regional offices, responsible for executing established NRC policies and assigned programs within regional boundaries. These offices are located in Philadelphia, Pennsylvania (Region I), Atlanta, Georgia (Region II), Chicago, Illinois (Region III), and Dallas, Texas (Region IV). Region IV, the largest, has an additional field office in Walnut Creek, California.

The NRC licenses and inspects nuclear facilities such as the Davis-Besse Nuclear Power Plant on Lake Erie in Oak Harbor, Ohio. *(Photograph by Robert J. Huffman. Field Mark Publications)*

PRIMARY FUNCTIONS

The commission's scope of responsibility includes the authority to license the following: construction and operation of nuclear reactors and other nuclear facilities; the possession, use, handling, and export of nuclear material; the siting, design, construction, and closure of low-level radioactive waste sites; and the operators of nuclear power and nonpower test and research reactors. It also inspects these licensed facilities and activities.

In addition to its licensing duties, the NRC develops and implements rules and regulations that govern licensed nuclear activities. It is responsible for enforcing these regulations and the conditions for its licenses. The enforcement tools at the commission's disposal can be very powerful; it can fine violators of its licenses or regulations up to $100,000 a day.

The commission collects, analyzes, and disseminates information about the operational safety of commercial nuclear power reactors and certain nonreactor activities, and it conducts public hearings on matters of nuclear and radiological safety. The NRC is also responsible for conducting the primary U.S. government research program on light-water reactor safety. It conducts a variety of other research activities to provide independent expertise and information for making good regulatory judgments and for anticipating problems that have the potential for creating safety risks.

PROGRAMS

Nearly all of the NRC's programs are mandated by the legislation the commission was charged to uphold and therefore are strictly related to its regulatory and research functions. Examples of such programs are the Fuel Cycle Facility Licensee Performance Review Program, which assesses overall licensee performance at each major fuel cycle facility; the Uranium Recovery Program, a cost-control system for supervising and tracking licensed work of uranium recovery licensees; and the Site Decommissioning Management Plan, which provides for streamlining the decommissioning responsibilities of the NRC when it comes time for a nuclear plant to end its operations.

The NRC also participates in a broad program of international cooperation related to nuclear safety and regulations. The NRC has 33 arrangements or letters of agreement with international regulatory relations to ensure prompt notification of safety problems that warrant action or investigation and to provide for bilateral cooperation on nuclear safety. Under the U.S. Comprehensive Threat Reduction Program, the NRC, and the Department of Energy assist the new independent states of the former Soviet Union that inherited the country's nuclear arsenal—Kazakhstan, Russia, and the Ukraine—

BUDGET:

Nuclear Regulatory Commission

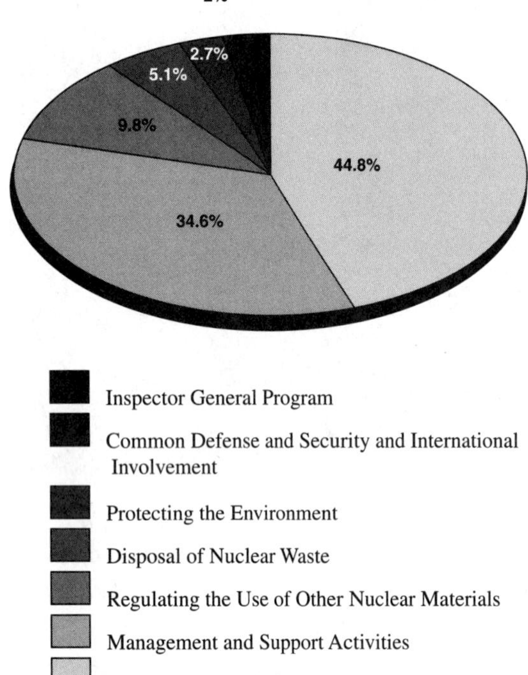

in the areas of nuclear material control, accounting, and physical protection. In addition, the NRC is involved in approximately 45 joint international safety projects.

BUDGET INFORMATION

Because the NRC is authorized to charge licensing and other fees, very little of its budget is provided through congressional appropriations; for example, of the commission's estimated 1998 budget of $472.8 million, $454.8 million was covered by offsetting fee receipts.

Just under half of the NRC budget (44.8 percent) is spent on nuclear reactor safety. These funds regulate and standardize nuclear reactors, which pose the greatest potential danger to the public. About 9.8 percent is spent regulating the use of other nuclear materials (fuel facilities and medical isotopes, for example) and 5.1 percent for the disposal of nuclear waste. The management and support activities of the Nuclear Regulatory Commission, including the formulation of policy and direction and the administration of the various offices, accounts for a sizable portion of the NRC budget—about 34.6 percent. The final 5.7 percent of the NRC budget is spent on protecting the environment (2.7 percent); the Common Defense and Security and International Involvement (2.0 percent); and the Inspector General Program (1.0 percent).

HISTORY

The history of the NRC dates from its predecessor, the Atomic Energy Commission (AEC), which was established in 1946 and was granted a government monopoly in the development and utilization of nuclear energy. In 1954 Congress passed a revised Atomic Energy Act that allowed private commercial participation in several areas of nuclear technology.

From the start, the AEC encountered difficulties that were created primarily by the unique nature of nuclear technology, which had just barely come to light upon the AEC's creation, and about which very little was known. The 1954 act charged the agency with promoting the potential of the new technology as an energy source but also recognized concerns in the areas of public health and safety, as well as in the area of national security. As a result the commission was charged with the somewhat contradictory tasks of promoting the new industry as well as regulating it, even before it had come into general use. Not surprisingly, these tasks proved to create much internal friction over time.

From 1955 to 1963 the AEC and representatives from private companies formed the Power Demonstration Reactor Program. Endorsed by the Power Demonstration Reactor Program, the light-water reactor (boiling-water and pressurized-water designs) became the favored power generator of the nuclear industry. Over time, however, serious doubts about the validity of the agency's regulatory process surfaced: how could the agency provide incentives and form developmental partnerships with private companies while regulating their activities?

A Division of Power

By 1963 the agency's regulatory functions were physically separated from the promotional offices and the operational and developmental programs. This action was taken none too soon—throughout the 1960s and early 1970s, the power levels of proposed plants increased by as much as ten times, posing difficult safety questions for the agency's regulatory office. In the mid-1960s the agency was able to define a minimal level of reactor standardization by adopting a set of general design criteria.

Controversy over the safety of nuclear power began grew markedly during the early 1970s, spurred on by the increasing concern for preserving the environment. Blind faith in the goodness of technological advances, so common in the 1950s, no longer seemed to be an element of

American popular culture. The twenty-year-old idea of completely severing the regulatory and promotional roles of the AEC resurfaced and this time resulted in the passage of the Energy Reorganization Act of 1974. The act abolished the AEC and created the Nuclear Regulatory Commission and the Energy Research and Development Administration.

The Safety Issue Escalates

Much of the NRC's early efforts were dedicated to organizing an adequate management and support structure for the complex responsibilities of the agency—to this day, administrative and support duties account for a third of the commission's budget—and it was not until after its first year that the new agency could devote itself to the additional urgent problems arising from the growing nuclear industry. The agency needed to identify new generic reactor safety questions, monitor the safety and environmental impact of the nuclear fuel cycle, safeguard nuclear materials, review state programs, assume an increased role in the export and import of nuclear materials, and participate in interagency efforts to limit international proliferation of nuclear weapons capabilities.

Two high-profile nuclear accidents soon presented the NRC with new challenges. The Three Mile Island incident of 1979 and the violent explosion at the Soviet Union's Chernobyl (Ukraine) nuclear power station in April 1986, which released massive amounts of radioactivity into the environment, added new sources of concern to existing controversies over the licensing of reactors in the United States. Over the next several years, the commission would dedicate itself to strengthening its own licensing and radiation standards.

CURRENT POLITICAL ISSUES

Ever since the NRC's creation in 1974, when it was constructed from the ruins of the AEC, the commission has been accused of harboring sympathies for the nuclear industry that contradict its regulatory mandate. The specialized, technical nature of nuclear energy makes it less likely that a person who does not have a scientific understanding of it could become involved in overseeing the process. For example, Chairman Shirley Jackson was a professor of nuclear physics before being appointed to the NRC, and many people have argued that a nuclear physicist is much more likely than a layperson to have an interest in the success of the nuclear industry. Along with these concerns, the nuclear industry's power to veto commission nominees it believes too hostile (one or two of the commission's seats remain vacant for long periods of time before a commissioner can be found that is acceptable to the industry) shakes the faith of many in the power of the NRC to regulate.

Critics of the NRC charge that it has neglected its regulatory duties in order to keep costs down for nuclear power plants. The NRC itself suggested as much in 1985, when it initiated a directive on "discretionary enforcement," which allowed the agency to set aside certain regulations for power plant operators who complain that the regulations are cost prohibitive. Utility companies with nuclear plants are at a relative disadvantage, because nuclear-generated electricity can cost twice as much as power generated from fossil fuels. No new nuclear plants have been ordered since 1978, in fact, and many have been shut down since. Critics of the NRC argue that despite the early growth of the nuclear power industry, it has proven to be an ineffective source of energy, and NRC officials have an incentive to protect their jobs, which would disappear in the absence of a widespread nuclear power industry.

Case Study: The Millstone Plant

In 1992 an engineer for Northeast Utilities, a company that operates five nuclear power plants in New England, became aware of what he considered to be serious safety hazards at the company's Millstone plant in Connecticut. Although further investigations later revealed about five thousand "areas of concern" at Northeast Utilities, the most serious and immediate problems found were as follows:

- During refueling operations, the Millstone plant habitually moved all of its "spent" radioactive fuel rods into an adjacent storage pool. The pool, licensed to handle a "full-core load" only in emergency situations, was overcrowded with thousands of spent fuel rods, and had in fact been taking the entire load for nearly twenty years.
- To speed up the refueling process (a plant loses money when fuel is not in the reactor), Millstone ignored the NRC mandate to cool down for 250 hours after shutdown. Sometimes the plant moved fuel after just 65 hours, so early that on one occasion a worker's protective boots melted off while opening the reactor.
- Perhaps most disturbing was the discovery that a Millstone safety report, in which Northeast Utilities was required to demonstrate to the NRC that its cooling systems would function even if the plant's primary system failed, did not contain the required information. It contained instead an evaluation of a far less critical system.

It was later revealed that at least two officials at the NRC had been aware of the problems at the Millstone plant but claimed not to know Millstone was in violation of NRC regulations. Chairman Shirley Jackson, in just the tenth month of her appointment, was embarrassed by the scandal and launched a series of policies designed to improve training, accountability, and vigilance among inspectors and the NRC staff. She ordered a review of the refueling processes of all 110 nuclear plants in the

United States. She publicly reaffirmed that the NRC's primary responsibility is to ensure public safety.

Many remained unconvinced; some government officials, including Democratic congressman Joseph Biden, have argued for disbanding the NRC to form another regulatory agency whose interests would lie outside of promoting and assisting the industry.

SUCCESSES AND FAILURES

The nature of the NRC's work tends to dictate that its successes receive little publicity. Typically only its failures are noted by the public.

On March 28, 1979, just four years after the formation of the NRC, the most serious nuclear accident in the country's history occurred at the Three Mile Island nuclear station near Harrisburg, Pennsylvania. Both mechanical failure and human error caused severe damage to uranium in a reactor's core. The immediate cause of the accident, a stuck pressure-relief valve, was compounded when reactor operators misread the signs of a loss-of-coolant accident and failed to take action for several hours. By the time the nature of the accident was recognized, the Unit 2 reactor had suffered irreparable damage.

Fortunately no one was injured in the accident, and little radioactivity was released into the environment. However, the credibility of the nuclear industry, and of the NRC, was roundly questioned by the public and the press. The commission's assumption had been that the most likely cause of a loss-of-coolant accident at Three Mile Island would be a break in a large pipe that fed coolant to the core. However, the destruction of the core had been caused not by a large pipe break but by a relatively minor mechanical failure that had been drastically compounded by operator errors.

The NRC responded to the Three Mile Island incident quickly. It reexamined the adequacy of its safety requirements and imposed new regulations to correct deficiencies. It placed a much greater emphasis on human factors in plant performance by developing new requirements for operator training, testing, and licensing, and for shift scheduling and overtime at nuclear plants. In addition the agency expanded its resident inspector program, stationing at least two inspectors at each plant site. The commission devoted more attention to the smaller "breaks and transients" that had received limited attention before. It also expanded research programs in areas that had been highlighted at Three Mile Island, including fuel damage, hydrogen generation and control, and fission-product release.

These and other initiatives taken after the Three Mile Island accident have resulted in fewer incidents since 1979.

FUTURE DIRECTIONS

The NRC's vision of the future involves redesigning many of its licensing and regulating processes in order to make them more expedient for those who operate nuclear facilities and use nuclear materials and for those seeking a license to do so. At the same time, the commission wants to maintain or improve public safety and to reduce risk to the environment.

A particular issue under consideration is the regulatory authority of the By-products Materials Program, which currently regulates about 6,400 specific and 35,000 general licenses for the possession and use of nuclear materials in medical, academic, and industrial applications. The NRC, whose members have no medical expertise, is considering whether to continue to regulate the medical uses of nuclear by-product materials such as x rays or radiopharmaceuticals. In consultation with the National Academy of Sciences and the Institute of Medicine, the NRC is considering several options: expanding its control; retaining but revising existing regulations; retaining authority but transferring the regulation of some uses of nuclear energy to other federal or state authorities; or eliminating the Nuclear By-products Materials Program, particularly those operations associated with medical uses.

AGENCY RESOURCES

Most information about the NRC is available through the Office of Public Affairs, U.S. Nuclear Regulatory Commission, Washington, DC 20555; telephone (301) 415-8200. For access to the commission's public document room, write the U.S. Nuclear Regulatory Commission, Public Document Room LL-6, Washington, DC 20555; or telephone 1-800-397-4209.

Information on how to do business with the NRC can be obtained by calling the director of the Division of Contracts at (301) 415-7305. Information on how to help small businesses meet NRC requirements is available from the Office of Small Business and Civil Rights at (301) 415-7380.

AGENCY PUBLICATIONS

The publications of the NRC are typically limited to reports on its operations and policies. Subscription items such as the quarterly *Regulatory and Technical Reports* and *Contractor and Vendor Status Report* are available, as are some scientific, technical, or administrative information publications. Regulatory guides in ten areas (power reactors, occupational health, etc.) are also published by the NRC. All of these publications can be purchased through the Government Printing Office, PO Box 37082, Washington, DC 20013; telephone (202) 512-1800.

Single copies of draft versions of some publications, such as *Draft Environmental Statements* and *Draft Regulatory Guides*, are available free of charge, based on supply, from the Distribution and Mail Section of the Nuclear Regulatory Commission, Washington, DC 20555. Some of the NRC's public documents are available on FedWorld, a government computer bulletin board system. FedWorld can be reached by telephone at (703) 487-4608.

BIBLIOGRAPHY

Anderson, Oscar E. and Richard G. Hewlett. *The New World: A History of the United States Atomic Energy Commission, 1939–1946* . Berkeley: University of California Press, 1990.

Feder, Barnaby J. "The Nuclear Power Puzzle." *New York Times*, 3 January 1997, p. C1.

Foreman, Harry, ed. *Nuclear Power & the Public*. Ann Arbor, MI.: Books on Demand, 1985.

"Industry Challenges U.S. Nuclear Waste Policy." *New York Times*, 2 February 1997, p. 25.

Kaku, Michio and Jennifer Trainer. *Nuclear Power: Both Sides*. New York: Norton, 1982.

Lau, Foo-Sun. *A Dictionary of Nuclear Power and Waste Management with Abbreviations & Acronyms*. New York: John Wiley and Sons, 1987.

Nuclear Nonproliferation: Information on Nuclear Exports Controlled by the U.S.-Euratom Agreement. Upland, Penn.: Diane Publishing Co., 1995.

Pooley, Eric. "Nuclear Warriors." *Time*, 4 March 1996, pp. 46–53.

Rhodes, Richard. *Nuclear Renewal*. New York: Whittle Books, 1993.

Sich, Alexander R. "The Shutdown Question." *Bulletin of the Atomic Scientists*, pp. 36–7.

Wald, Matthew L. "Why Safety is Not Always So Public." *New York Times*, 16 March 1997, p. E4.

Walker, J. Samuel. *Containing the Atom: Nuclear Regulation in a Changing Environment, 1963–1971*. Berkeley: University of California Press, 1992.

Occupational Safety and Health Administration (OSHA)

PARENT ORGANIZATION: Department of Labor
ESTABLISHED: 1970
EMPLOYEES: 2,200

Contact Information:

ADDRESS: 200 Constitution Ave. NW
Washington, DC 20210
PHONE: (202) 219-8151
FAX: (202) 219-4595
URL: http://www.osha.gov
ASSISTANT SECRETARY: Charles N. Jeffress

WHAT IS ITS MISSION?

The stated mission of OSHA is to "save lives, prevent injuries and protect the health of America's workers" by coming up with safety standards that apply to places of employment and then making sure that these standards are followed.

HOW IS IT STRUCTURED?

OSHA is an independent agency within the U.S. Department of Labor. It is headed by an assistant secretary who is appointed by the President. The assistant secretary's office has 10 main divisions: Office of Field Programs; Office of Statistics; Directorate of Administrative Programs; Directorate of Compliance Programs; Directorate of Construction; Directorate of Federal-State Operations; Directorate of Health Standards Programs; Directorate of Policy; Directorate of Safety Standards Programs; and Directorate of Technical Support. Within each of these divisions are various other offices that offer technical support to the agency's overall goals. For example, under the Directorate of Technical Support are the offices of Ergonomic Support; Occupational Medicine; Science and Technology Assessment; Variance Determination; the Technical Data Center; the OSHA Cincinnati Laboratory; and the OSHA Salt Lake City Technical Center. Altogether, OSHA has more than 200 offices throughout the country.

OSHA also provides a forum for businesses to dispute its safety and health inspections and enforcement actions. These cases are brought before the Occupational

Safety and Health Review Commission, an independent, quasi-judicial agency of administrative law judges also created by the OSHA Act of 1970. Employees and employers argue either the charges themselves or the penalties imposed. Any decisions made by the Commission can then be appealed in the U.S. courts of appeals, if the parties so desire.

FAST FACTS

Over 13 million people are injured on the job every year.

(Source: Sabra Chartrand. "The Troubling Numbers of Job-Related Injuries." *New York Times,* August 31, 1997.)

PRIMARY FUNCTIONS

OSHA is responsible for the safety and protection of more than 100 million workers and six and a half million employers in the United States. It must create standards that protect workers in a variety of situations and workplaces using research and analysis by trained professionals in a variety of fields. In addition, OSHA then must inspect workplaces to ensure that its standards are being applied correctly and fairly. OSHA also educates the public about its standards and the laws regarding workplace safety and answer questions and inquiries. It investigates complaints both from employees about where they work and from employers about its standards they are trying to apply and understand. OSHA must also perform ongoing studies and analysis of the continually changing workplace.

OSHA states that it employs "approximately 2100 inspectors, complaint discrimination investigators, engineers, physicians, educators, standards writers, and other technical and support personnel" to accomplish these tasks in field offices nationwide. OSHA regularly sends these inspectors and investigators out to businesses and workplaces to make sure that they are complying with the existing OSHA standards. It also performs surveys and studies to monitor its own performance and the effectiveness of the standards it is enforcing.

PROGRAMS

OSHA allows U.S. states and territories to create their own standards of workplace safety and health as long as these standards are at least as effective as OSHA's own standards. The Office of State Programs within the Directorate of Federal-State Operations monitors and approves these state plans and will fund up to 50 percent of the costs of running them. As of 1996, 23 states and territories had their own workplace safety and health plans.

OSHA also offers free consultation services for employers on how to improve their workplaces in order to comply with OSHA standards. Most of these consultations take place at the business site and most of the participants are small businesses.

When a business establishes a successful and exemplary record of safety in the workplace, OSHA will grant it certain privileges under the Voluntary Protection Program (VPP) and work with it to educate other businesses. For example, businesses in the VPP will be exempt from regular inspections and will be inspected once a year or once every three years, depending on the VPP for which they qualify.

OSHA also overseas the workplace safety of federal employees through the Office of Federal Agency Programs (OFAP). Its stated mission is "to ensure that each federal agency is provided with the guidance necessary to implement an effective occupational safety and health program within the agency and to inform the President on the progress being made through detailed evaluations, reports, and inspections of agencies' occupational safety and health programs." OSHA's Training Institute Outreach Education Centers, found in various universities and colleges throughout the country, offer information and training about workplace safety and health. They are available to the workers and employers in federal and state agencies as well as private sector businesses. Further training to government and public organizations is made available through the Office of Training and Education. Various courses are offered, such as Principles of Ergonomics, Electrical Standards, Hazardous Wastes, and Machinery and Machine Guarding Standards.

In conjunction with other laboratories in the private sector, OSHA operates the Nationally Recognized Testing Laboratory (NRTL) Program, under the Directorate of Technical Support, which tests equipment and chemicals used in the workplace to make sure they work correctly and do not pose any potential threat to workers. Under the NRTL program, OSHA inspects and approves the testing methods used by private sector laboratories throughout the country. These laboratories then do their own testing of equipment and chemicals, and OSHA examines the results to make sure the equipment and chemicals meet OSHA's minimum safety standards.

BUDGET:

Occupational Safety and Health Administration

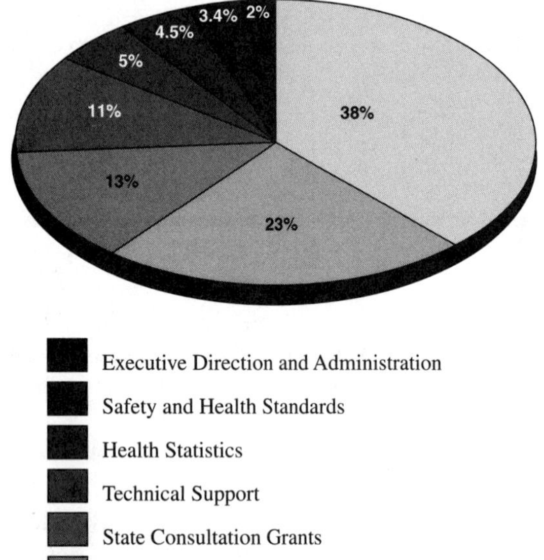

BUDGET INFORMATION

In 1999 the estimated amount of money appropriated by Congress from the overall budget of the United States for the operation of OSHA was $356 million. This was an increase from the estimated amount appropriated in 1998 of $337 million. In 1999, these amounts were to be divided among eight main areas of OSHA as follows: safety and health standards, $12 million; federal enforcement, $135 million; state programs, $81 million; technical support, $18 million; compliance assistance, $47 million; state consultation grants, $39 million; safety and health statistics, $16 million; and executive direction and administration, $7 million.

HISTORY

Men and women have always suffered injuries, illnesses, and death in the workplace. Before the creation of OSHA, there were few standards and little enforcement in U.S. industries. The history of OSHA begins in 1913 with the creation of the U. S. Department of Labor (DOL), which was created to protect workers' interests as well as deal with other pressing problems. The DOL states that it was created to "foster, promote and develop the welfare of working people, to improve their working conditions, and to enhance their opportunities for profitable employment." Significant laws have been passed and reforms made throughout the DOL's existence in the attempt to protect American workers. One of the DOL's first actions was to create the War Labor Administration (WLA), which set working conditions and wages for workers during World War I. In succeeding decades, legislative acts such as the Fair Labor Standards Act of 1938 provided unemployment insurance to American workers and set minimum wage, overtime and child labor standards, and then assured veterans jobs after returning to civilian life.

The DOL, however, did not actually gain a comprehensive and effective role in the enforcement of safety and health standards until the 1950s, when mining disasters increased throughout the country and popular sentiment in the country demanded better standards of safety in that industry. As a result, the 1952 Federal Coal Mine Safety Act was passed in order to set stricter regulations and then enforce them through inspections. Prior to that time, enforcement efforts were often lax and not very well supported by legislation. In the years that followed, however, mining disasters continued and public concern grew. At the same time, a new public interest in protecting the environment emerged. As a result of these two increasing public concerns the government passed the Occupational Safety and Health Act of 1970, which created OSHA and gave it the power not only to study the workplace in America and devise standards for what was expected, but also to enter the workplace with more expanded and in some cases new rights to inspect and therefore enforce these standards. The agency estimates that before its existence nearly 200,000 work-related deaths occurred every year. OSHA statistics show that now, after 25 years of operation, the agency has cut that number in half.

As a result, the success of OSHA has led to the creation of other agencies concerned with assuring worker safety, such as the Mining Safety and Health Administration (MSHA), which began with passage of the Federal Mine Safety and Health Act of 1977. The MSHA was created specifically to protect mine workers' rights, because their particular workplace was very large and complex and required a separate agency to meet their needs.

By the early 1990s OSHA had become a large agency with extensive power to regulate safety standards in businesses throughout the country. After 25 years of operation, there were complaints about its enforcement tactics and its cumbersome size. As a result, the Clinton administration proceeded to reform the agency with three sets of regulatory initiatives to make it less of a traditional enforcer of rules and more of a partner with businesses to achieve the desired standards; to review and rewrite out-of-date standards and eliminate confusing or overlapping rules; and to reduce the bureaucracy required to operate the agency and to focus more on results.

Today, nearly every worker in America is covered by the standards set by OSHA, and it is one of the federal government's primary mechanisms for identifying dangers in the American workplace and for protecting U.S. workers.

CURRENT POLITICAL ISSUES

The OSHA must study a large number of work hazards and determine how to prevent them, but workplace hazards can be difficult to define. Employers may think something is safe, but workers think it is not. Often scientific studies can determine specifically what is dangerous and what is not, as with certain chemicals or types of machinery.

Case Study: Repetitive Stress Injuries

Repetitive Stress Injuries (RSIs) are fast becoming one of the leading causes of injuries in the U.S. workplace. RSIs occur from doing the same motion over and over again all day long. The people who usually suffer from them are seamstresses, musicians, and factory workers, although most sufferers work on a computer keyboard. Insurance agencies have reported that claims are up as much as 770 percent since 1984. The OSHA estimates that 100 million people—nearly 40 percent of the workforce—have some type of RSI injury. The number of cases has increased 1,000 percent in the last 10 years, and the Bureau of Labor Statistics says that 700,000 new cases are reported every year.

With such overwhelming evidence, OSHA has repeatedly tried to define a clear set of safety standards for the prevention of RSIs, but their attempts have so far been unsuccessful and have met with opposition from members of Congress and from the private sector. RSIs are not well defined, and prevention methods are not clear. Digital Equipment Co., for example, has said that there is no definitive scientific proof that keyboards cause musculoskeletal disorders. Such opponents think there is no clear definition of what constitutes the workplace where these injuries occur–whether it is the computer, the chairs used, type of lighting, desks, or a combination. Other factors beyond the companies' or manufacturers' responsibility, such as the individual's prior health or medical record, may also cause the problems. At this point, OSHA's emphasis is on ergonomic solutions. Ergonomics is the study of how machinery and office furniture can be designed to most effectively and safely suit its users. Businesses protest that if such standards are passed, the expense of preventing such injuries would be too high, and they do not want to incur such costs.

Proponents and OSHA, however, claim that the injuries are occurring, they can be defined, and solutions can be found. They argue that the connection between the types of tasks performed and the number of cases is clear, in spite of the absence of a clear consensus about the physiology of the injuries. They cite cases of nerve and muscle damage to hands, wrists, and arms caused by bad positioning at desks, and poor design of keyboards and factory machinery. OSHA says that "adjusting the height of working surfaces, varying tasks for workers and encouraging short rest breaks can reduce risks. Reducing the size of items workers must lift or providing lifting equipment also may aid workers. Specially designed equipment, such as curved knives for poultry processors, may help." Solutions must be found because RSIs affect such an enormous portion of the workforce. According to the OSHA, each reported case costs an average of $43,000 to handle, and nearly 18 workdays per worker per year are lost due to RSIs.

Public Impact

As a result of this controversy, many lawsuits have been brought against the makers of computer equipment claiming that the manufacturers did not sufficiently warn consumers of the dangers of using their products. Many claims have been settled out of court, but in 1997 Digital Equipment Co. paid $6 million to three women who suffered from RSIs. Such a loss now presents a significant financial threat to businesses and manufacturers. The threat of large lawsuits for RSI-related injuries has, therefore, given the OSHA more persuasive power, and Congress and businesses are now taking the OSHA's point of view more seriously.

SUCCESSES AND FAILURES

OSHA describes its success as follows: "experience has . . . shown that OSHA inspections can have real, positive results: according to a recent study, in the 3 years following a [typical] OSHA inspection that results in penalties, injuries and illnesses drop on average by 22 percent. Overall injury and illness rates have declined in the industries where OSHA has concentrated its attention—yet have remained unchanged or have actually increased in the industries where OSHA has had less presence."

On the other hand, OSHA also admits that despite all its efforts, more than 6,000 Americans die every year from workplace injuries, another 50,000 die from illnesses caused by workplace chemical exposures, and nearly six million suffer from workplace injuries that are not fatal, costing the economy more than $110 billion a year.

FUTURE DIRECTIONS

OSHA schedules regular inspections of businesses to make sure they are complying with their standards. In some cases, when infractions keep occurring, inspections can become more vigorous and the company can begin to face stiffer and stiffer penalties. This is a costly and time-consuming process. As a result, OSHA tries to offer incentives for those organizations that voluntarily meet OSHA standards and even exceed them if possible. Some of these incentives include fewer inspections or making inspections only in response to complaints. As a result, there are fewer injuries on the job and these employers do not have to deal with the cost of fines. Because of this benefit, some states and individual companies have begun their own programs to enforce safety standards that at least meet with OSHA standards and in some cases exceed them. States and companies then sometimes go further and mandate more specific standards tailored for their particular area or industries. The state of Maine, for example, created its own system of standards that are more effective than OSHA's, the *Maine 200* program. OSHA, in turn, supports such efforts, encouraging businesses to become partners with the state to create higher standards of safety and avoid even stricter enforcement measures. This partnership has resulted in a higher number of new hazards being discovered and eliminated than under OSHA's methods. As a result, OSHA hopes to nationalize this approach, adapting the most successful elements of the Maine program, offering incentives and support to other states and businesses and encouraging voluntary compliance.

AGENCY RESOURCES

Information about OSHA in the form of news releases, fact sheets, and other types of notices can be obtained by calling (202) 219-4784 or by writing U.S. Department of Labor, c/o Occupational Safety and Health Administration, 200 Constitution Ave. NW, Washington D.C., 20210. Information can also be obtained from the OSHA Web site at http://www.osha.gov.

AGENCY PUBLICATIONS

OSHA publications and information on free publications and publications available for a nominal fee are available at (202) 219-4667. Others can be downloaded from http://www.osha.gov/oshpubs.

BIBLIOGRAPHY

Chartrand, Sabra. "Debate Over Repetitive Stress Injuries Heats Up." *New York Times,* 23 March 1997.

———. "Little Attention Given to Workplace Violence." *New York Times,* 7 September 1997.

———. "The Troubling Numbers of Job-Related Injuries." *New York Times,* 31 August 1997.

Freierman, Shelly. "Government Regulations, In Their Electronic Form." *New York Times,* 22 April 1996.

Furger, Roberta. "Time Is Running Out For Ergonomic Standards." *PC World,* March 1995.

Gordon, Sandra. "Derail Desk Distress." *Shape,* July 1997.

Liscio, John. "Time for a Little Reverse Bias." *U.S. News and World Report,* 6 April 1992.

Pascarelli, Emil F. *Repetitive Strain Injury: A Computer User's Guide.* New York: J. Wiley, 1994.

Seligman, Daniel. "Where Quotas Came From." *Fortune,* 30 May 1994.

Weise, Elizabeth. "Complex Regulatory Questions Answered on OSHA Web Site." *New York Times,* 4 June 1997.

Office of Government Ethics (OGE)

WHAT IS ITS MISSION?

According to the Office of Government Ethics' (OGE) Web site, the agency's mission is to exercise "leadership in the executive branch to prevent conflicts of interest on the part of government employees, and to resolve those conflicts of interest that do occur. In partnership with executive branch agencies and departments, OGE fosters high ethical standards for employees and strengthens the public's confidence that the government's business is conducted with impartiality and integrity."

HOW IS IT STRUCTURED?

OGE is a small agency under the jurisdiction of the executive branch of government established by the Ethics in Government Act of 1978 and reorganized by the Government Ethics Reauthorization Act of 1988. The chief officer is a director, who is appointed by the president to a five-year term. This appointment is approved by the Senate. The OGE's administration consists of five offices: the Office of the Director; the Office of General Counsel and Legal Policy (OGC & LP); the Office of Agency Programs (OAP); the Office of Administration (OA); and the Office of Information Resources Management (OIRM).

The Office of the Director concentrates on coordinating the overall efforts of the OGE and ensuring that all congressional and presidential mandates are fulfilled. The OGC & LP establishes and maintains a legal framework for the OGE. It develops legal policies, laws, and regulations, assists agencies in legal and policy implementation,

PARENT ORGANIZATION: Independent
ESTABLISHED: October 1, 1989
EMPLOYEES: 84

Contact Information:

ADDRESS: Ste. 500
1201 New York Ave. NW
Washington, DC 20005-3917
PHONE: (202) 208-8000
TDD (HEARING IMPAIRED): (202) 208-8025
FAX: (202) 208-8037
URL: http://www.usoge.gov
DIRECTOR: Stephen D. Potts

FAST FACTS

In government offices, gift giving, even among employees, is under scrutiny. For instance, only on an occasional basis are the following individual gifts permitted: gifts other than cash that are valued at no more than $10; food and refreshments shared in the office among employees; personal hospitality in the employee's home that is the same as that customarily provided to personal friends; and gifts given in connection with the receipt of personal hospitality that is customary to the occasion.

(Source: Office of Government Ethics. "Ethics Program Topics," 1998.)

and recommends changes that are caused by conflicts of interest. The OA provides essential support services to all OGE operating programs. The OIRM promotes and provides information technology within OGE. OIRM provides internal support in the areas of information technology, telecommunications, graphics, records management, produces the Ethics CD-ROM, and maintains the office's Web site. There are three divisions within the OGE that assist it in accomplishing its goals: the Education and Program Services Division, the Financial Disclosure Division, and the Program Review Division.

In addition to regular OGE staff, there is also staff supplied by each federal agency in the executive branch. The head of each agency appoints an employee as the agency's Designated Agency Ethics Official (DAEO). These individuals, along with their staffs, support an agency's ethics program (known as the executive branch "ethics community") that deals with OGE. The OGE communicates policy and regulatory changes to these officials who handle the distribution of these policies to their respective agencies.

PRIMARY FUNCTIONS

The OGE only handles ethics policies and procedures for the executive branch of government and its departments. The legislative and judicial branches operate their own ethics offices, the U.S. Special Counsel and the Department of Justice respectively.

The OGE primarily monitors agencies to see that they are in compliance with the ethics rules and regulations that it issues. On occasion, the OGE is asked by Congress to provide an opinion on the conduct of various executive branch agencies and employees regarding their ethical conduct. Its findings are reported to Congress which decides whether or not the issue needs to be pursued any further.

By presenting educational programs to federal employees, as well as answering ethical questions posed to the agency by other executive branch agencies, the OGE helps the employees of the executive branch follow ethics rules and laws. In addition the OGE sponsors conferences and public information forums. The OGE trains the DAEOs. These officials act as liaisons between the OGE and their respective agencies to help ensure that their agencies are acting in an ethical fashion.

The Financial Disclosure Division (FDD) manages the annual and termination public financial disclosure reporting system for approximately 1,000 presidential appointees confirmed by the Senate (PAS positions) and the 125 DAEOs. FDD collects, tracks, and reviews these reports to ensure they are complete and do not raise any unaddressed questions of potential financial conflicts of interest.

PROGRAMS

The OGE issues statements and other documents to inform all executive branch agencies regarding government ethics. The most effective ways of communicating to the different agencies are through the ORIM's Ethics CD-ROM and other software programs, such as the Ethics Training Games. The OAP offers a variety of ethics programs as well.

Ethics Training Workshops

A variety of ethics training workshops offered to agency ethics officials focus on how to apply the standards of ethical conduct and what constitutes a criminal conflict of interest. These workshops offer attendees the opportunity to work through case studies and problems that enhance their knowledge of the ethics rules. Many ethics officials use the knowledge and materials obtained through these workshops to train employees. These workshops are conducted in the Washington, D.C., area and other regions around the country.

Part of the ongoing ethics training available to both the government and the public is *Gameshow P.A.L.,®* an interactive question-and-answer ethics game that can be downloaded from the OGE Web site. OGE developed the game using Gameshow P.A.L.® (Player Assisted Learning), a software program for designing interactive computer games. The Gameshow P.A.L.® software was purchased through the Ethics Trainers' Partnership. The game consists of 25 ethics questions in a Jeopardy®-style. The game provides the answer; the player responds with a question. The format is intended to challenge players' thinking. Players can compete against themselves or other players at a computer workstation. The game is preset at 20 minutes for a single round and includes a bonus question and a final question. Gameshow P.A.L.® keeps a running tally of the score.

Annual Ethics Conference

Every year since 1990 the OGE has hosted a conference of government ethics officials to review the role that ethics plays in government and to renew their personal dedication to ensuring that their offices comply with OGE rules and regulations. The conference also provides participants with the opportunity to review any new policies, recognizes achievement in the form of distinguished service awards, and allows for study of a wide range of subject areas such as lobbying, outside activities, new types of conflicts of interest, and professional responsibility. There is a conference track for new ethics officers to learn the basics of the OGE's standards and forms.

BUDGET INFORMATION

In 1998 $8.3 million was appropriated to the OGE by Congress. The majority of this money was allocated to staff salaries; the remainder was divided between civilian personnel benefits and rental payments to the General Services Administration.

HISTORY

OGE was established by the Ethics in Government Act of 1978 originally as part of the Office of Personnel Management (OPM). The OGE became a separate agency on October 1, 1989, as part of the Office of Government Ethics Reauthorization Act of 1988. President Jimmy Carter, in the wake of the Watergate scandals that toppled the presidency of Richard Nixon, created the office to ensure that employees of the executive branch of government performed their public duties in an ethical manner. Overseeing the executive branch's ethics proved to be a difficult task over the succeeding years.

Ultimately the OGE's task is to ensure that the American people have trust in their government. The years prior to the establishment of the OGE were years filled with distrust and anger over the antics of various government officials. The war in Vietnam had bred an aura of mistrust and skepticism about the goals of the government and its honesty. On the heels of the war, the role of the executive branch of government was further tarnished by the break-in by a group of administration-backed burglars of the Democratic headquarters office at the Watergate complex. This fiasco led to the resignation of President Nixon to avoid impeachment proceedings.

From this era of mistrust and concealment came a new desire for a standard of ethical behavior for government officials. Under the presidencies of Jimmy Carter and Ronald Reagan, the OGE was part of the OPM. Under the reorganization of the government during the George Bush administration, the OGE became an independent agency. Since its beginning the OGE has issued numerous policies that range from how much money someone can receive as a gift or from speaking engagements while in office to assisting the president in the formation of executive orders that delineate ethical matters important to an administration. Under the administration of President Bill Clinton, the OGE drafted "Ethics Commitments by Executive Branch Appointees." The OGE was charged with monitoring and guiding the process. Throughout this process, the OGE has acted as a watchdog to ensure that the government officials maintained a high standard of ethical behavior.

CURRENT POLITICAL ISSUES

One of the most prevalent issues confronting the OGE is that rather than remaining an independent watchdog of executive branch ethics, it is pulled into political situations and forced to act on behalf of the administration it is charged to oversee ethically. These criticisms tend to tarnish the OGE's reputation as a free agent whose responsibility is to find and correct ethics violations and not be involved in bipartisan squabbles. The agency has been referred to pejoratively as "the Ethics Cops" by Daniel Seligman in *Fortune*. Seligman also charges that "the federal Office of Government Ethics (OGE), [is] an agency whose name verges perilously on the oxymoronic and whose handiwork has recently resulted in the phrase 'ethics, shmethics.'" He finds that its investigations into ethics issues are themselves questionable and biased in favor of the investigated.

Case Study: Whitewater

Sixteen years before he became president, Bill Clinton and his wife Hillary invested money into a failed savings and loan land deal that ended up costing taxpayers approximately $60 million to bail out. This failed development deal became an ongoing ethical and legal controversy for the president, which involved an independent counsel, millions of dollars in legal bills, and links to the suicide of a White House legal counsel.

In May of 1995 the Senate voted to establish the Special Committee to Investigate Whitewater Development Corporation and Related Matters to be administered by the Committee on Banking, Housing, and Urban Affairs. Its responsibility was to conduct an extensive investigation into and to hold public hearings on specified matters that related to President and Mrs. Clinton's investment in the Whitewater Development Corp., James and Susan McDougal, and Madison Guaranty Savings and Loan Association. The Whitewater case became extremely complicated, with almost 20 years of documents to trace and numerous conversations to follow.

In March of 1994 Secretary of the Treasury Lloyd Bentsen contacted the OGE about looking into the ethical propriety of communications that had gone on between the Department of the Treasury staff and the White House. It was alleged that these communications regarded the Whitewater investigation and therefore represented a possible violation of ethical statutes since the White House should not have been apprised of any confidential components of that investigation. The OGE agreed to review factual material and give its opinion to the public on whether or not it felt that any unethical actions had taken place.

What happened next was an issue of intense debate between Republican and Democratic Senate committees reporting on Whitewater. Republicans claim that the Treasury Department fed the OGE materials that had been edited by Treasury staff so that the materials claimed within did not reflect so poorly upon the Clintons. The OGE's report, therefore, was biased because it had insufficient information. Democrats, on the other hand, held that no such "editing" had taken place by the Department of the Treasury and thus the OGE's report was completely valid.

Regardless, White House officials often cited the OGE report in their defense, saying that it exonerated them of any wrongdoing. This fueled attacks by Republicans and other critics that the OGE did not act in an impartial manner regarding this issue and that it was protecting President Clinton's political position. OGE Director Stephen Potts insisted, however, that the OGE had fulfilled its duty without being influenced by one side or the other.

FUTURE DIRECTIONS

An immediate goal for the OGE is to implement the post-employment law. The OGE watches that certain high-level officials respect a so-called "one-year cooling off period." For a period of one year after leaving a "senior" position, officials may not make any appearance on behalf of any person (other than the United States) before his former agency with the intent to influence the agency on any matter in which that person seeks official action.

Maintaining an active outreach program in order to ensure public confidence in the integrity of the federal workforce is another goal of the OGE. It also plans to improve the services offered to the ethics community by upgrading its technology and improving Web site updates and access so that changes in ethics policies are immediately available to both ethics officials and the public at large.

AGENCY RESOURCES

OGE has developed a wide variety of ethics training materials for use by all executive branch departments and agencies so that they can meet the mandatory ethics training requirements. These materials include videotapes, pamphlets, booklets, and reference manuals. All of the printed materials are available for purchase. Contact the OGE at (202) 208-8000. One may also order many of the documents, a copy of the PAL program, and other ethics-related materials from the OGE Web site at http://www.usoge.gov, or from the OGE Information Center at Office of Government Ethics, Ste. 500, 1201 New York Ave. NW, Washington, DC, 20005-3917. The OGE also takes telephone orders. The numbers are (202) 208-8000; (202) 208-8025 (for TDD); or fax (202) 208-8037.

AGENCY PUBLICATIONS

The Office of Government Ethics annually updates its publication, *The Informal Advisory Letters and Memoranda and Formal Opinions of the United States Office of Government Ethics*, which is available from the Government Printing Office at (202) 512-1800. In addition, the office publishes a periodic newsletter on government ethics and makes available ethics publications, instructional videotapes, and a CD-ROM. Some of the other OGE publications include reference works, such as *OGE Form 450: A Review Guide, Public Financial Disclosure: A Reviewer's Reference,* and *Standards of Ethical Conduct* (English and Spanish versions). Among the OGE's booklets and pamphlets are the following: "Take the High Road," "Do It Right," "Conflicts of Interest and Government Employment," "Gifts of Travel and Other Benefits." These can be obtained by contacting the OGE by mail or phone or on-line at their Web site http://www.usoge.gov. The "Government Ethics Newsgram" is printed three times per year and provides an update on the most recent events and issues in the government ethics arena. "Newsgram" is circulated to about 4,000 interested parties including agency ethics officials, the Federal Executive Boards, and many private organizations. Both of these products are available on-line at http://www.usoge.gov/usoge006.html#publications.

BIBLIOGRAPHY

Bedard, Paul. "Clinton Finds Loophole, Creates New Legal Defense Fund." *Washington Times*, 15 February 1998, p. 7.

"John Conyers U.S. Representative (D-MI) Holds News Conference on Kenneth Starr's Investigation." Washington Transcript Service, 26 February 1998.

Norton, Robert. "Politics & Policy: Who Wants to Work in Washington?" *Fortune*, 14 August 1989, p. 77.

Seligman, Daniel. "Keeping Up: Sexism Among Plumbers, Ethicists and Their Conflicts, Why Perot Ran, and Other Matters." *Fortune* , 21 August 1995, pp. 120+.

Wilson, James C. "Whitewater and the White House Pattern of Deceit." *Washington Times*, 1 January 1996, p. 30.

———. "Did Taxpayers Underwrite Whitewater Cover-up?" *Washington Times,* 13 November 1995, p. 31.

Zwerdling, Daniel. "Federal Ethics Office Report Clears Officials." *NPR All Things Considered.* National Public Radio, 31 July 1994.

Office of Justice Programs (OJP)

PARENT ORGANIZATION: Department of Justice
ESTABLISHED: 1984
EMPLOYEES: 750

Contact Information:

ADDRESS: 810 Seventh St. NW
Washington, DC 20531
PHONE: (202) 307-0703
URL: http://www.ojp.usdoj.gov
ASSISTANT ATTORNEY GENERAL: Laurie Robinson

WHAT IS ITS MISSION?

The Office of Justice Programs's (OJP) stated mission is "to provide federal leadership, coordination, and assistance to make the nation's justice system more efficient and effective in preventing and controlling crime." The OJP's primary mission is to find ways to prevent crime and to assist victims of crimes once it has occurred. This is done primarily by initiating policies that are promoted on the state level through federal grants.

HOW IS IT STRUCTURED?

The OJP is an independent agency within the U.S. Department of Justice. It is headed by an assistant attorney general who is appointed by the president. The assistant attorney general is responsible for coordinating the wide range of OJP functions cohesively and for directing OJP policies. The priorities that the agency should focus on are recommended by the president and attorney general. Two deputy assistant attorney generals help the assistant attorney general to carry out the responsibilities of the OJP. Eleven bureaus and offices are responsible for operating the day-to-day functions of the OJP. There are five bureaus: the Bureau of Justice Assistance; the National Institute of Justice; the Office of Juvenile Justice and Delinquency Prevention; the Bureau of Justice Statistics; and the Office for Victims of Crime. In addition to these bureaus, the OJP has a policy office, the Violence Against Women Office; and five program offices: the Executive Office for Weed and Seed; the Violence Against Women Grants Office; the Corrections Program Office; the Drug Courts Program Office; and the American Indian and Alaskan Native Affairs Desk. Seven administrative offices within the OJP provide agency wide support: the Office of Congressional and Public Affairs; the Office of Administration; the Equal Employment Opportunity Office; the Office for Civil Rights; the Office of Budget and Management Services; the Office of the Comptroller; and the Office of General Counsel.

PRIMARY FUNCTIONS

The OJP's stated function is to "be responsible for collecting statistical data and conducting analyses; identifying emerging criminal justice issues; developing and testing promising approaches to address these issues; evaluating program results, and disseminating these findings and other information to state and local governments." The primary way that OJP accomplishes this is by awarding large grants to state agencies which, in turn, award smaller grants to local agencies within their area.

The agency states that "through the programs developed and funded by its bureaus and offices, OJP works to form partnerships among federal, state, and local government officials to control drug abuse and trafficking; reduce and prevent crime; rehabilitate neighborhoods; improve the administration of justice in America; meet the needs of crime victims; and address problems such as gang violence, prison crowding, juvenile crime, and white-collar crime." The agency's bureaus rely largely upon grant recipients as well as other federal agencies to supply data that is needed to create crime fighting initiatives and programs.

OJP describes its work system in the following manner: "the functions of each bureau or program office are interrelated. For example, the statistics generated by the Bureau of Justice Statistics may drive the research that is conducted through the National Institute of Justice and the Office of Juvenile Justice and Delinquency Prevention. Research results, in turn, generate new programs that receive support from the Bureau of Justice Assistance and the Office of Juvenile Justice and Delinquency Prevention. Although some research and technical assistance is provided directly by OJP's bureaus and offices, most of the work is accomplished through federal financial assistance to scholars, practitioners, experts, and state and local governments and agencies."

Each of the five bureaus has a different emphasis. The Bureau of Justice Assistance provides grants to states to support the development and functioning of their criminal justice systems. The most important grant given by this bureau is the Local Law Enforcement Block Grants, which provides money directly to local law enforcement agencies for the improvement of their operations.

The National Institute of Justice is the research agency within the OJP. Its function is to study whether programs now in operation are working; come up with new programs; create demonstration programs for new theories and methods; develop technology to aid in the fight against crime; and to make sure that all of this information is available to those who need it.

The function of the Office of Juvenile Justice and Delinquency Prevention is to develop an overall strategy on how to prevent juvenile crime, how to control it, and how to make the juvenile justice system work in the fairest and most efficient way possible.

The Bureau of Justice Statistics gathers, analyzes, and then makes available statistics about crime. It also does the same with information about the justice systems in all levels of the government, such as municipal governments, state governments, and the federal justice systems. To that effect, BJS makes public every year a series of publications. Some of the trends BJS tracks are: the types of crimes committed, the types of victims, and the locations of the crimes. The most comprehensive of these is the *Bureau of Justice Statistics Fiscal Year 1997: At a Glance*, which provides a summary of the findings of some of BJS's programs and the type of programs being funded at the state and local levels.

The function of the Office for Victims of Crime (OVC) is to oversee programs that are in operation to help the victims of crimes. These programs are intended to help victims cope with the aftermath of crime. Services offered include counseling, compensation, and legal help. There are also programs to ensure that the criminal justice system pays attention to victims' rights.

PROGRAMS

There are many types of programs funded by OJP grants. They address a wide variety of crime prevention programs. Their day-to-day operations are administered by individual state and local governments. These locally implemented programs arise from larger political mandates that originate with the president and Congress.

Two of the most important initiatives that the OJP administers nationwide are the Crime Act and the National Weed and Seed programs. With the passage of the 1984 Victims of Crime Act, the OVC was created within the OJP. This office oversees grants and training to organizations on both a state and federal level. The OVC's goal is to provide services for victims of crimes. It does this by providing the funding and guidelines for training professionals in the best, most up-to-date methods. Some of these services include: counseling for victims of child abuse; counseling for victims of violent crimes; emergency shelter; and emergency child care.

The National Weed and Seed program is operated by the Executive Office for Weed and Seed (EOWS). This program brings together a variety of law enforcement agencies and social services to work together to tar-

Advocates of stricter laws for juvenile criminals wish to see more of them tried as adults and incarcerated in prisons such as this one. *(Courtesy of the Library of Congress)*

get specific neighborhoods in the country that are being overrun by crime. Working together, these agencies go in and rid or "weed" the selected neighborhood of criminals and criminal activity, and then follow up this activity with economic and social service efforts to "seed" the area and make it a safe and viable neighborhood to live in. The program uses a four-pronged attack: 1) law enforcement; 2) community policing; 3) prevention, intervention, and treatment; and 4) neighborhood restoration. The OJP coordinates the different agencies and provides direction and guidelines and administrative support for their activities.

BUDGET INFORMATION

In 1997 Congress appropriated $174 million for the operation of the OJP. In 1998 the estimated amount appropriated rose to $254 million. In 1999, however, the total estimated amount is estimated to be $213 million. This money is spent on a wide variety of programs, such as those handling cases of missing children; the criminal justice statistics program; emergency assistance; a national sex offenders registry; and a regional information sharing system. By far the largest portion of the budget went to the category of research, evaluation, and demonstration programs, which required $31 million in 1997, an estimated $47 million in 1998, and an estimated $44 million in 1999. The cost of management and administration, which required $28 million in 1997, an estimated $41 million in 1998, and an estimated $40 million in 1999, requires the next largest portion of the budget.

HISTORY

In 1968, during Lyndon Johnson's administration when the nation's crime rate was soaring, the federal government took action by creating an agency called the Law Enforcement Assistance Administration (LEAA). Congress backed this new agency with a large amount of funding and the appropriate legislative acts to support it. LEAA's goal was to increase the efforts in the battle against crime in the country. Up until that time, law enforcement in the United States was primarily a responsibility of local and state governments. Although the federal government had jurisdiction through enforcement agencies such as the Federal Bureau of Investigation (FBI), Central Intelligence Agency (CIA), and the U.S. Marshals Service, it was hoped that the LEAA would increase its influence on local crime-fighting efforts. The primary role of the LEAA was to dispense federal aid to local law enforcement agencies and to direct their efforts, as much as possible, in fulfilling the presidential administration's agenda. The LEAA operated for 14 years and spent nearly $8 billion on a variety of sweeping initiatives, such as the improvement of the equipment used by local police departments and the building of shelters for homeless youth.

The grant that funded LEAA came to an end in 1982 though federal funding for programs continued and was administered through the Department of Labor. In 1984, after much political debate about how to fund and organize the program's efforts, the OJP was created with the passage of the Justice Assistance Act. Essentially, the OJP replaced the old LEAA, but it was backed by new funding and new political initiatives under the Reagan Administration.

In 1994, under the President Bill Clinton administration, the OJP was once again given a new breath of life with the passage of the 1994 Anti-Crime Bill. This bill appropriated approximately $30.2 billion to be put toward the fight against crime, much of it funding the programs and initiatives of the OJP. With this money came a new emphasis on specific methods of crime prevention. Some of these included: helping local communities hire nearly 100,000 new police officers over a six-year period; providing nearly $7.9 billion for the construction of prisons and boot camps; providing $6.9 billion for programs aimed at preventing crime; another $1.6 billion to support the Violence Against Women Act; and mandating life imprisonment for anyone convicted of a third violent felony, the "three strikes and you're out" philosophy.

As a political agency dealing with the volatile issue of crime prevention on a nationwide level, the OJP has always been subject to the rapidly changing political climate in the United States. Its goals have, nevertheless, remained essentially the same: to increase the federal government's influence on local and state governments' crime-fighting efforts and to find ways to prevent crimes from occurring.

CURRENT POLITICAL ISSUES

The types of programs the OJP creates and allocates funds toward depends largely on the types of crimes being committed and the public's perceptions of these crimes. At its inception in 1984, and again in 1994, the OJP's mission was fueled by a wave of popular political sentiment calling for an end to the rising crime rate. Polls indicated that the public in 1994 felt that crime was their number one concern. In addition, the type of crimes that concerned them most were those committed by teenagers. It was one area where the crime rates had risen sharply. As a result, Congress passed the Anti-Crime Bill in 1994, providing billions of dollars of renewed funding, and calling for specific attention to be given to teenage crime.

Case Study: Teenage Crime

In the OJP, under the Office of Juvenile Justice and Delinquency Prevention (OJJDP), there are many programs aimed at preventing crime by teenagers. With the passage of the 1994 Anti-Crime Bill, Congress allocated millions of dollars to be given to states that agreed to toughen the way they handle juveniles who commit serious felonies. Just how to go about this "toughening" is the subject of much controversy.

Some people believe that the punishment for committing crimes needs to be harsher, with longer sentences and fewer paroles, especially for repeat offenders. Senator Orrin Hatch (R-Utah) has been instrumental in spearheading efforts by the Senate Judiciary Committee to push through bills that cracked down on juvenile crime in 1994–97. Proponents of the tougher laws also want to see more teenagers tried as adults for their crimes. These advocates frequently suggest that teenagers should be imprisoned with adults, though not in the same cells. They claim that the number of crimes committed by juveniles has increased dramatically in the last ten years, rising 67 percent from 1985 to 1995, and that stricter methods are necessary in order to curtail this trend.

Some people, however, are opposed to making the judicial system harsher for teenagers. Senator Joseph Biden (R-Delaware) has introduced bills that emphasize crime prevention measures instead of punishment. Proponents of this perspective on juvenile violence claim that channeling teenagers into the adult system has no positive effect on the amount of crime that occurs. For example, when comparing Connecticut, which practices the highest "juvenile-to-adult transfer rate," to Colorado, which has the lowest, the number of crimes committed by youths is the same. Proponents say that due to some states' self-imposed tough laws for state offenses, there are already 8,000 teenagers imprisoned with adults and that these juveniles are at risk for abuse, rape, and violence. Proponents believe that when the teenage offenders are released, they are only more violent and more prone to crime than when they entered prison.

Public Impact

As a result of this new effort by the government to crack down on crime, the White House reported in 1997 that "for the first time in seven years, the rate of young people arrested for violent crime and murder has gone down." The government considers the "get tough on crime" approach successful and plans to continue the initiative. In addition, the government is also advocating a number of alternative, less controversial measures aimed at crime prevention. One such initiative is called the Anti-Gang and Youth Violence Strategy. Its goals are to encourage communities to enforce curfews for juveniles; encourage the use of school uniforms; and require drug testing for high school athletes. Though the controversy about how to best battle juvenile crime continues, the

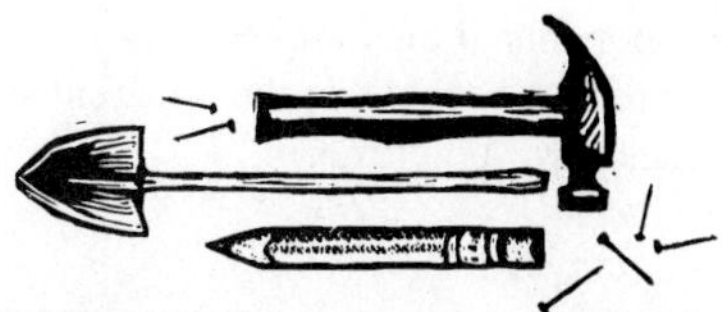

GET INVOLVED:

Internships are available at the OCPA for qualified applicants. These positions are unpaid and are meant to familiarize the intern with the government and provide work experience. The OCPA states that the duties an intern can expect to perform are as follows: reviewing incoming mail from the White House, the attorney general, and citizens, and drafting responses to these communications; performing research in order to respond to written or oral inquiries from the Congress, media, or the public and for material produced by OCPA; assisting in analyzing pending legislation affecting or of interest to OJP or the criminal justice community; assisting in preparing briefing books and special reports; monitoring and reporting on congressional hearings, conferences, or other events of interest to OJP; and assisting in congressional notification of grants or other routine administrative duties as needed. For further information, contact the Office of Congressional and Public Affairs, Office of Justice Programs, 810 Seventh St. NW, Washington, DC 20531 or telephone (202) 307-0703.

proponents of the tougher measures appear to be winning the debate because of the apparent success of the current crackdown on crime.

FUTURE DIRECTIONS

One problem area in the fight against crime is the great number of different agencies that are at work across the country. The OJP hopes to find ways to coordinate the information and the needs of these various law enforcement and social services agencies so that they can work together and reduce any overlapping functions. Therefore, the OJP Executive Council is developing a strategy to coordinate the funding of grants to a variety of state and local governments in order to help them obtain and use technologies that will streamline communication, such as computers, telecommunication equipment, and data banks.

AGENCY RESOURCES

For further information about the OVC's programs for aid to victims of crime, please access the OVC Web site at http://www.ojp.usdoj.gov/ovc. Anyone seeking information, statistics, or specific questions about issues concerning juvenile justice can contact the Juvenile Justice Clearinghouse at 1-800-638-8736.

For more information on developing and implementing a Weed and Seed strategy, write or call: The Executive Office for Weed and Seed, U.S. Department of Justice, Office of Justice Programs, 810 Seventh St. NW, 6th Fl., Washington, DC 20531; telephone (202) 616-1152 or fax (202) 616-1159. Inquiries can be directed to the main OJP headquarters by writing to 810 Seventh St. NW, Washington, DC 20531 or by calling (202) 307-0781.

AGENCY PUBLICATIONS

A list of the types of publications OJP offers, called *Publications and Reports* can be found at their Web site at http://www.ojp.usdoj.gov/reports.htm. Publications about the work being done by OJP can be found in *350 Tested Strategies To Prevent Crime: A Resource for Municipal Agencies and Community Groups.* Although it is published by the BJA and the National Crime Prevention Council (NCPC), this book offers a comprehensive view of the types of crime prevention strategies considered and applied by OJP. It can be obtained from the Government Printing Office by writing 732 N. Capital St., Washington, DC 20401 or calling (202) 512-2034.

BIBLIOGRAPHY

Allis, Sam, and Ratu Kamlani. "Now for the Bad News: Teenage Time Bomb." *Time*, 15 January 1996.

Aspis, Simone. "Screen Test for Anti-Crime Project: Crime Against People with Learning Difficulties." *Times Educational Supplement*, 21 October 1994.

Bradley, Bill. "America's Efforts to Curb Violence: The Anti-Crime Bill Is Not Enough." *USA Today*, November 1994, pp. 30–33.

Gessen, Masha. "Prime Suspect." *New Republic*, 8 April 1996, pp. 17–18.

Morganthau, Tom. "Too Many Guns? Or Too Few?" *Newsweek*, 15 August 1994, pp. 44–45.

Reibstein, Larry. "Back to the Chain Gang?" *Newsweek*, 17 October 1994.

Rosen, Jeffrey. "Crime Bill Follies." *New Republic*, 21 March 1994, pp. 22–25.

Shapiro, Bruce. "One Violent Crime." *Nation*, 3 April 1995, pp. 87–90.

Office of Management and Budget (OMB)

PARENT ORGANIZATION: Executive Office of the President
ESTABLISHED: July 1, 1939
EMPLOYEES: 520

Contact Information:

ADDRESS: New Executive Office Bldg.
725 17th St. NW
Washington, DC 20503
PHONE: (202) 395-3080
FAX: (202) 395-3504
URL: http://www.whitehouse.gov/WH/EOP/omb
DIRECTOR: Jacob J. Lew

WHAT IS ITS MISSION?

The primary mission of the Office of Management and Budget (OMB) is to help the president oversee the preparation of the federal budget and to supervise its administration in agencies of the executive branch. In this capacity, the OMB formulates, evaluates, and coordinates management procedures and program objectives within and among federal departments and agencies. In all its activities, the agency aims to ensure that OMB reports, rules, testimony, and proposed legislation are consistent with the budget and administration policies of the president.

HOW IS IT STRUCTURED?

As an agency that exists to support the Executive Office of the President, the OMB is headed by a director who is appointed by the president and confirmed by the Senate. The deputy director, who serves as the director's primary administrative assistant, is selected in the same way. The director's office is served by key staff offices, such as legislative affairs, economic policy, communications, and general counsel. In addition the director and the entire OMB are served by a support staff offering expertise in all areas of government. Although the scope of OMB operations is as broad as practically any other government agency, its basic structure rests on two main divisions: budget and management.

The offices that serve the budget staff are generally divided among program areas called "resources management offices": national security and international affairs,

general government and finance, human resources, and natural resources, energy, and science. Budget staff members prepare agency funding requests, supervise spending that has been authorized by Congress, and compose economic and financial analyses and forecasts. The work of budget analysts is compiled by the Budget Review Division, which places the programs in the context of overall government spending. The budget and review offices in the OMB report directly to the director and the deputy director.

The management and regulatory division is subdivided into important "statutory" offices: information and regulatory affairs, which oversees federal regulation and information requirements; federal procurement policy, which develops and monitors government purchasing policies; information policy and technology; and federal financial management, which develops financial management policies and systems. Management staff oversee government procurement and management, evaluate the efficiency of programs, and recommend methods for improving interagency coordination. In general, they report to the deputy director for management.

PRIMARY FUNCTIONS

The scope of the OMB's activities is broad, especially for a staff of fewer than 550. The agency's primary function is to assist the president in supervising the preparation of the federal budget and to oversee its administration in executive branch agencies, but it has expanded to fill other roles. The agency reviews the organization and management procedures of the executive branch; assists the president in considering, clearing, and preparing executive orders and proclamations; and develops information systems that will provide the president with program performance data. At all times the OMB is responsible for keeping the president informed of the progress of activities within all federal agencies. The office also coordinates advice from each department about proposed legislation and then makes recommendations affecting presidential action on legislation.

The OMB's influence goes beyond the executive branch, especially in the area of management. The office assists in developing coordinating mechanisms that will expand interagency cooperation within the federal system. It plans and promotes evaluation efforts that help the president to evaluate the performance of specific government programs, sets spending priorities based on its evaluations, and oversees the administration's financial management, procurement, and regulatory policies. In this capacity, the OMB also develops programs for paperwork reduction, especially when reporting and application procedures become burdensome to the public.

PROGRAMS

As a coordinator and evaluator of all the government's programs, the OMB has little time or resources to undertake initiatives of its own; usually, its activities are either required by law or ordered by the president. When special needs arise, however, the OMB is empowered to develop and undertake programs that will assist the president or solve government problems. An example is the OMB 2000 program, an effort coordinated by the OMB to solve a seemingly simple problem: the inability of computers in government information systems to recognize the coming year 2000.

When the year 2000 arrives, people will understand that "00" is a short way of denoting 2000. However, if the coding of many computers' system software is not changed or replaced before January 1, 2000, machines that have been coded in this familiar shorthand will automatically place a "19" in front of these zeros, interpreting the date as 1900. The computers will then reject legitimate data entries, compute incorrect results, or simply fail to run at all. Trivial as this problem sounds, it could shut down the entire government if not corrected. With a fixed deadline of January 1, 2000, the OMB and the chief information officers of all federal agencies are working to either rewrite or replace software code that will not recognize the year 2000. It is estimated that the effort will cost agencies a total of $2.3 billion.

BUDGET INFORMATION

While the scope of OMB's operations is broad, the agency carries out its activities with a relatively small staff, and a limited budget: about $59 million in 1998. Just over half of this budget, 52 percent, is spent by the resource offices that carry out the OMB's primary budgeting mission: $8 million by the Office of Natural Resources, Energy, and Science; $7 million by General Government and Finance; $6 million each by Health/Personnel and National Security and Affairs; and about $4 million by the Office of Human Resources.

Because of the OMB's scope of operations, it spends a sizable portion of its budget, about 30 percent, on the offices of its agency-wide support staff. The final 17 percent of the budget is consumed by OMB's management offices: $5 million by Information and Regulatory Affairs; $3 million by the Office of Federal Procurement Policy; and $2 million by the Office of Federal Financial Management.

HISTORY

Before 1921 there was no system within the executive branch for central consideration or control of the nation's economic policy; the secretary of the treasury simply compiled each department's budget estimate and then forwarded the batch to Congress for approval. In the early twentieth century the need for a more coordinated approach to the federal budget became apparent, and the OMB's predecessor agency, the Bureau of the Budget (BOB), was established in the Department of the Treasury by the Budget and Accounting Act of 1921. The agency's first director, Charles Dawes, saw the BOB as primarily responsible for ensuring economy and efficiency in government; under his leadership, it was to be an impartial and apolitical agency that had nothing to do with making economic policy.

Dawes's view of the new agency's role, then, excluded a key function that many members of American government saw as crucial: leadership in the overall management of government administration. To Dawes, the BOB's management function consisted of approving or denying items included in budget requests. His next three successors shared this view, and the office experienced little growth or influence for more than a decade.

Roosevelt's Reorganization and the First OMB

President Franklin D. Roosevelt expressed dissatisfaction with the way the budgeting process continued to work; he was often unpleasantly surprised to learn of departmental budget requests of which he had not yet heard. He wanted a budget office that would provide him and his executive office with assistance in overseeing the submission of the budget to Congress. In 1939, acting on the recommendations of his Committee on Administrative Management, Roosevelt issued the first governmental reorganization plan in American history. The Executive Office of the President was formed, and to it were transferred the BOB and a Department of the Interior agency, the National Resources Planning Board. The newly institutionalized presidency made President Roosevelt—not the secretary of the treasury—the official to whom the BOB was directly accountable.

Under the leadership of director Harold Smith, who served from 1939 to 1946, the BOB expanded its role in the federal system. Although it continued to act as the central budget review agency, the bureau increased its powers in the areas of legislative clearance of budget requests and administrative management of the departments. During Smith's tenure, the BOB was given oversight authority for all proposed legislation, executive orders, and recommendations for reorganization. Smith's successor, James Webb, further expanded the BOB's influence in program development, thereby securing the bureau's ability to stop wasteful spending and unreasonable budget requests before they were submitted by the departments and agencies.

Pressure for Reform

Throughout its next 30 years, the BOB generally enjoyed the reputation of being a fairly impartial and

BUDGET:

Office of Management and Budget

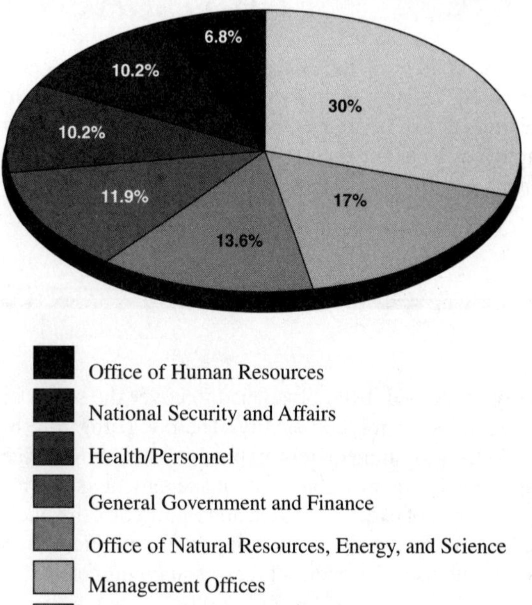

objective presidential staff agency. However, it did appear to suffer from certain problems and inefficiencies that changed with each presidential administration. Under President Dwight D. Eisenhower it was accused of serving almost exclusively as a means to secure presidential control of the budget. Under President John F. Kennedy the bureau took a more activist approach toward influencing policy making—and consequently neglected the management of its own day-to-day affairs. Under President Lyndon B. Johnson the BOB shifted its focus from budget overseer to coordinator of interagency activities. By 1965 officials at all levels of government agreed that a clear definition of the agency's role in the executive branch needed to be developed.

In 1970 President-elect Richard Nixon, undertaking his own reorganization plan, created two separate executive offices, the Office of Management and Budget (which would contain a newly formulated budget bureau) and the Domestic Council. According to Nixon, the plan called for the Domestic Council to be primarily concerned with "what we do; the Office of Management and Budget will be primarily concerned with how we do it, and how well we do it." Although many questioned the assumption that policy could be separated from administration, the management authority of the president had

FAST FACTS

The Bureau of the Budget's second director, General H. M. Lord, was so focused on trimming waste in government that he frequently checked to make sure that employees were not excessively using paper clips or stationery.

(Source: Larry Berman. *Government Agencies*, 1983.)

finally, it seemed, been broadened to cover the scope of the federal system's complexity. The budgeting role of the OMB was immediately expanded. The new office emphasized organization and management systems, development of executive talent and a more broadly qualified staff, better dissemination of information, and appropriate use of modern processes and equipment.

The OMB After Watergate

The prestige of Nixon's OMB, despite its early promise, was clearly damaged as Nixon became bogged down in the Watergate affair. With Nixon and many of his domestic council staff under investigation for criminal activity, the OMB was forced to move into the role of the Domestic Council. According to some journalists, the OMB was at times virtually running the government. Its interference into the internal management processes of departments and agencies earned it the nickname "the Office of Meddling and Bumbling", and by the end of Nixon's administration the OMB's reputation as an impartial agency was lost.

President Jimmy Carter, who took office in 1977, tried to restore some of this reputation by making it clear his Office of Management and Budget would act as the agency that could firmly say "no" to the president. President Ronald Reagan, however, in a frankly political move, appointed David Stockman, a two-term Republican congressman as his first OMB director. Stockman undertook leadership of the president's agenda to cut taxes and government spending. In 1981, by executive order, Reagan added the controversial Office of Information and Regulatory Affairs (OIRA) to the OMB. The OIRA was to oversee and review the actions of all major regulatory agencies to determine whether they met administrative guidelines for studying the costs and benefits of proposed and existing regulations. In effect, regulations on virtually everything—from environmental protection to commercial radio frequencies to food safety—now had to be cleared through the OMB and, by extension, the president.

Members of Congress and the public were quick to attack the OMB's new role as "regulatory czar." The ability to influence agency regulations, they argued, was an encroachment on Congress's legislative authority, as well as on agency independence and expertise. A federal district court in Washington, D.C., upheld this opinion, and the OIRA's role as a final arbiter of government regulation has been seriously curtailed since—although the "smaller government" political atmosphere of the 1990s reintroduced debate about the OMB's potential role in regulation.

The 1990s, dominated by a Republican-led Congress and a moderate Democratic president, Bill Clinton, was an era of increased emphasis on governmental accountability in both its programs and its spending. The Government Performance and Results Act (GPRA) of 1993 requires all federal agencies to submit periodic strategic plans, aimed at specific goals, to the OMB and to follow up with clear measures of performance. The OMB works with agency heads to decide fair and specific means of determining these measures. Another landmark piece of legislation, the Balanced Budget Act of 1997, requires the federal government to discontinue its pattern of "deficit spending," or spending more than it takes in every year in taxes and revenues. The legislation presented the OMB with a new challenge: to help trim all agency budgets to the point where there will be no budget deficit by 2002.

CURRENT POLITICAL ISSUES

Throughout its history, the president's budget office has assumed such a variety of functions and responsibilities, covering nearly all aspects of government, that criticism of at least some aspects of its work has been unavoidable—especially from those who feel short-changed by the budgeting process. The root of most criticism seems to rest with a contradiction inherent in the OMB's mandate: although it is the closest thing the president has to an impartial reviewer of executive branch programs, the OMB's effectiveness depends in part on its responsiveness to the needs of the president. Thus, OMB decisions and operations are frequently attacked, usually by members of Congress, as serving the president's political agenda rather than as conclusions or judgments reached through impartial analysis.

Case Study: The OIRA's Measure of Regulatory Burdens

The Republican-led Congress of the Clinton administration, emphasizing the need for a true accounting of the cost to society of government regulation, pressured the OMB's Office of Information and Regulatory Analysis (OIRA) throughout most of the 1990s to arrive at an estimate of how much regulatory programs cost in dollars. Skeptics within and outside the OMB questioned the attempt to put a price tag on the system of social, economic, and environmental safeguards installed by the government over the last 50 years. How could one quantify the value of cleaner air or improved medical care, for example?

Lawmakers, however, argued that it was necessary to have a bottom line in order to let taxpayers know how much regulatory programs were costing them. Upon congressional insistence, the OIRA released a draft report of its first annual estimate of the cost and benefit of government regulation during the summer of 1997. The estimate settled on a cost of about $300 billion, or about four percent of the nation's gross domestic product.

The estimate sparked much debate and brought accusations from Republicans that the OMB was doctoring its numbers to benefit the Democratic political agenda of the Clinton administration. The real figure, they claimed, was closer to $600 billion; the OMB, they said, had intentionally excluded important costs such as the costs of filling out government forms for income tax or veterans payments.

Defenders of the OIRA estimate claimed that Congress had charged the office with an impossible job and that the estimate was a good first step toward keeping track of the costs and benefits of government regulation. Still others, most notably agency administrators, made it clear they did not want the success of their programs to be measured by numerical outcomes. However, the 1998 political climate seemed to demand that some sort of cost accounting of government regulation be performed, even if it was not used to replace political or social judgments about regulatory programs.

SUCCESSES AND FAILURES

Any measurement of the OMB's success ultimately rests with an assessment of overall government effectiveness, and as a result, responsibility for individual success can never be wholly claimed by the OMB. Nor, given the partisan nature of American politics and government, can such successes be unqualified. For example, when the OMB and the Clinton administration announced in the winter of 1997–98 that they had succeeded in balancing the budget ahead of schedule, showing a small surplus in their 1999 budget estimate, their accounting methods were immediately attacked by some members of the Congressional Budget Office as inaccurate, misleading, and self-serving—there was no budget surplus they claimed, just a rearranging of numbers to reflect more favorably upon the administration's economic and budgetary policies.

FUTURE DIRECTIONS

In addition to being in charge of coordinating the OMB 2000 program, the OMB is a primary player in two of the most important laws enacted by Congress in the 1990s. The OMB's role in the Government Performance and Results Act (GPRA) is to help agencies decide upon the criteria by which their performance will be measured and to evaluate each agency's progress when these reports are submitted. In addition, virtually every activity the agency undertakes until 2002 must be intended in part to secure enactment of tax, appropriations, and mandatory spending program policies that are consistent with the Balanced Budget Act.

AGENCY RESOURCES

In addition to general information about its roles, structure, and publications, the OMB's Internet home page contains links to other important sites about the budgeting and management of the U.S. government. General inquiries about the OMB should be directed to the Administrative Office, (202) 395-3080.

The importance of the OMB's work is perhaps illustrated by the fact that an independent watchdog group, OMB Watch, monitors the progress of OMB-related issues. The group describes itself as "a nonprofit research, educational, and advocacy organization that focuses on budget issues, regulatory policy, nonprofit advocacy, access to government information, and activities at the Office of Management and Budget (OMB)." The most recent discussion of these issues from the OMB's viewpoint can be accessed at the group's Web site, http://www.ombwatch.org.

AGENCY PUBLICATIONS

The OMB's flagship publication is, of course, *The Budget of the United States Government* and its related documents, such as *The Budget System and Concepts* and *Catalog of Federal Domestic Assistance*. The OMB also makes available a variety of other publications, including press releases, regulations under OMB review, OMB circulars (instructions or information issued by the OMB to federal agencies), bulletins, and miscellaneous documents such as the *Report to Congress on the Costs and Benefits of Federal Regulations* and *Evaluating Information Technology Investments*.

OMB publications can be accessed in a number of ways. The easiest is probably to view, download, or print from the OMB's Internet home page http://www.whitehouse.gov/WH/EOP/omb, and the links provided there—virtually every page of the current budget and related documents can be searched and viewed from this site. Printed copies of larger documents such as the budget can be purchased from the Superintendent of Documents at the Government Printing Office, Washington, DC 20402, or from the Executive Office of the President's publications office, at the OMB New Executive Office Bldg., 725 17th St. NW, Washington, DC 20503; phone (202) 395-7332. The OMB also operates a 24-hour fax-on-demand service for publications such as OMB circulars, standard forms, and miscellaneous documents. The service can be reached at (202) 395-9068.

BIBLIOGRAPHY

Ball, Karen. "Middle Man: The Poker-Faced Pragmatism of Frank Raines." *New Republic*, 15 December 1997, pp. 20–3.

Barr, Stephen. "OMB Assailed for Allowing "Buyout" Offers After Deadline." *Washington Post*, 12 June 1996, p. A19.

———. "OMB Releases Budget Hit List." *Washington Post*, 14 March 1997, p. A25.

Berman, Larry. *Government Agencies.* Westport, Conn.: Greenwood Press, 1983.

Marshal, Eliot. "Universities Balk at OMB Funding Rules." *Science*, 7 November 1997, p. 1007.

Mosher, Frederick C. *Tale of Two Agencies: A Comparative Analysis of the General Accounting Office & the Office of Management and Budget.* Baton Rouge: Louisiana State University Press, 1986.

Office of Management and Budget. *The Budget of the United States Government.* Washington, D.C., 1998.

Office of Management and Budget: Changes Resulting from the OMB 2000 Reorganization. Upland, Penn.: Diane Publishing, 1996.

Skrzycki, Cindy. "What Price Rulemaking? And According to Whom?" *Washington Post*, 25 July 1997, p. G1.

Tomkin, Shelley L. *Inside OMB: Politics & Process in the President's Budget Office.* Armonk, N.Y.: M.E. Sharpe, 1998.

Office of National Drug Control Policy (ONDCP)

PARENT ORGANIZATION: Executive Office of the President
ESTABLISHED: January 29, 1989
EMPLOYEES: 124

Contact Information:

ADDRESS: Executive Office of the President
Washington, DC 20503
PHONE: (202) 395-6700
TOLL FREE: (800) 666-3332
FAX: (202) 396–6708
E-MAIL: ondcp@ncjrs.org
URL: http://www.whitehousedrugpolicy.gov
DIRECTOR: Barry R. McCaffrey

WHAT IS ITS MISSION?

The Office of National Drug Control Policy (ONDCP) provides information for citizens, strategies for governmental agencies, and technology for law enforcement. According to the agency, its principal purpose is "to establish policies, priorities, and objectives for the nation's drug control program, the goals of which are to reduce illicit drug use, manufacturing, and trafficking; drug-related crime and violence; and drug-related health consequences." The ONDCP is the principal link between the Executive Office of the President and all other departments and agencies of the federal government in matters of illegal drugs and drug abuse. The director of the ONDCP is the nation's spokesperson in these matters.

HOW IS IT STRUCTURED?

The ONDCP is a cabinet-level agency and is part of the executive branch of the federal government. Heading the ONDCP are a director, two deputy directors, and a chief of staff. The director of the ONDCP is a member of the presidential cabinet.

The director's office consists of the legal counsel, public affairs office, and strategic planning office. Two deputy directors assist the director: the deputy director for demand reduction and the deputy director for supply reduction. The deputy directors are assisted by the chief of staff, who takes responsibility for the administrative functions of the ONDCP. An associate director for National Drug Control Policy is appointed to head the ONDCP's Bureau of State and Local Affairs.

The ONDCP's intelligence office coordinates with the deputy director for supply reduction and with regional law enforcement in efforts to curtail the flow of illegal drugs. The deputy director of demand reduction manages programs related to prevention and treatment of drug abuse in efforts to curtail the demand for contraband (illegal substances).

The ONDCP works with federal agencies, such as the U.S. Customs Service, which has a prominent role in "the drug war." The contributions of other agencies, such as the Agricultural Research Service (ARS), are less publicized. The ONDCP, the ARS, the Department of State, and the United Nations work together to prevent the cultivation of illegal crops around the world. The ARS not only identifies and eliminates the crops but works with foreign countries to develop alternative agricultural programs and to rehabilitate economies that have become enmeshed in the illegal international drug trade.

The Counterdrug Technology Assessment Center (CTAC) is an independent research center that is funded in part through the ONDCP. The head of CTAC is the chief scientist. The chief scientist of CTAC serves as the chairperson of the Science and Technology subcommittee of the Research, Data, and Evaluation Advisory committee of the ONDCP.

PRIMARY FUNCTIONS

The ONDCP serves as a continual reminder of the dangers of illegal drugs and the many crimes associated with illegal drug abuse. Within this context, the director of the ONDCP symbolizes the unity of federal, state, and local governments in an ongoing commitment to eliminate drug abuse and illegal trafficking of drugs in the United States and around the world.

Perhaps the most crucial function of the ONDCP is to develop programs to discourage drug use and to eliminate drug abuse, particularly among young people. The ONDCP interacts with many departments of the federal government, including the Department of Justice and the Department of Health and Human Services, in an effort to encourage and coordinate drug treatment and prevention programs.

PROGRAMS

National Youth Anti-Drug Media Campaign

The National Youth Anti-Drug Media Campaign is a five-year, three-phase, media-based education program designed to prevent first-time drug use and abuse among youth, particularly to discourage experimentation with marijuana, inhalants, and other "starter drugs." The program initially involved a 12-city prototype campaign, conducted between December 1997 and April 1998. The campaign targeted schoolchildren and their parents. Initial data collected from the 12 cities in the test group were compared against a 12-city control group.

Information about the success of the prototype campaign was collected by various means: interviews with children, interaction with target groups, and direct phone calls to parents. Feedback from the target (test) cities was used to improve the campaign by increasing its effectiveness. Target cities included Atlanta, San Diego, Denver, Milwaukee, Boise, and Tucson. Statistical results derived from the National Youth Anti-Drug Media Campaign are available through the Drugs and Crime Clearinghouse by calling 1-800-666-3332.

Counterdrug Technology Assessment Center

Approximately one-half of the ONDCP budget supports the Counterdrug Technology Assessment Center (CTAC) to research, develop, and prescribe effective technology to stop drug traffickers and to combat drug abuse.

The CTAC is engaged in a number of diverse projects. The center develops methods to anticipate the size of crop yields of drug-related produce, plus tactical messaging systems and global positioning systems to assist law enforcement personnel in locating illegal crops. The CTAC develops high-tech, nonintrusive surveillance devices to monitor border activity and devises innovative methods to reduce drug addiction and abuse. The CTAC also makes recommendations to drug enforcement organizations at all levels of government and is involved in the research and development of treatment and rehabilitation techniques for addicts.

BUDGET INFORMATION

The ONDCP operating budget for 1998 was $35.8 million. ONDCP funds are allocated by Congress as part of the federal budget. The ONDCP is responsible for less than one-tenth of one percent of federal anti-drug allocations, a fact that can be explained in part by the limited function of the ONDCP.

Approximately one-half of the ONDCP budget was spent on payroll, other operating expenses, and programs that are run in conjunction with other law enforcement agencies and nonprofit organizations. Except for the $1 million that was allocated to policy research, the remainder of the ONDCP budget supported the CTAC.

HISTORY

The idea for the ONDCP originated in the House of Representatives during the administration of President Ronald Reagan. The office began official operations under President George Bush on January 29, 1989, under the provisions of the National Narcotics Leadership Act of 1988. According to some observers, the ONDCP was devised as a political ploy by a Democratic Congress during a Republican administration. The "war on drugs" became a battle cry, and the director of the ONDCP was quickly nicknamed "the drug czar." Gordon Witkin of *U.S. News and World Report* challenged the motive behind the ONDCP when he wrote, "The drug 'czar' is a joke. . . . The Office of National Drug Control Policy has been a political shuttlecock since the idea first arose. . . . The office had no real power."

William Bennett, the first director, was appointed by President George Bush. Although well liked, he accomplished little before he resigned in 1990. Bennett's successor, former Florida governor Bob Martinez, suffered harsh criticism for using his office as a vehicle for political payback. It was rumored that nearly one-half of the ONDCP staff members under Martinez were appointed in repayment of political favors.

When President Bill Clinton took office in 1993, he appointed John Walters as acting director and reduced the ONDCP staff from 146 to 25 employees. Walters eventually resigned. Clinton later elevated the directorship of the ONDCP to a presidential cabinet position, and he appointed former police chief Lee Brown to fill the position. In January 1996 Clinton seemingly reversed his policy, increasing the ONDCP budget and staff. He also appointed Barry McCaffrey to replace Brown.

Some critics maintained that the abrupt restoration of ONDCP was no more than a ruse to establish a "tough on drugs" image during an election year. Whatever the motives, the ONDCP is a cabinet office, and Clinton continued to speak out about the need to eliminate drugs even after he was reelected.

The Counterdrug Technology Assessment Center (CTAC) uses global positioning systems to locate illegal crops, such as this field of marijuana. CTAC then passes this information on to federal, state, and local law enforcement agencies responsible for its confiscation or destruction. (AP/Wide World Photos)

CURRENT POLITICAL ISSUES

The latter half of the twentieth century saw an upsurge in the use of illegal drugs in the United States and around the world. The growing prevalence of "recreational" drug use led some to question whether or not the laws prohibiting drug use were perhaps unjustifiable in a progressive society, and the idea that the use of certain drugs should be illegal has since been a subject of debate.

Perhaps the most frequently pursued and highly contested topic in these debates concerned the laws regarding the use of certain types of hemp, or marijuana, as an intoxicant. The illegal selling of marijuana, rumored to be the largest cash crop in the United States during the 1980s, became a topic of major controversy.

Case Study: Medical Use of Marijuana

Support for the legalization of marijuana came from many factions of society during the years from 1960 to 1995, although grassroots attempts to repeal the laws prohibiting the cultivation and use of marijuana were largely unsuccessful. Finally, during the 1996 presidential election, voters in Arizona and California passed what came

FAST FACTS

According to the 1997 ONDCP survey, *Monitoring the Future* (MTF), more than one-half (54.3 percent) of American students try an illicit drug by their senior year of high school. Over 25 percent of high school students further report that they regularly use at least one illicit substance.

(Source: Office of National Drug Control Policy, 1998.)

to be known as "medical marijuana" initiatives: legalization of marijuana use for medical purposes. The medical marijuana propositions were the result of an ongoing controversy surrounding the potential medical value of tetrahydrocannabinol (THC), the intoxicant in marijuana. The proposals stood in direct opposition to federal law, which classified marijuana as a Schedule I substance (i.e., one with no recognized medicinal value).

Proponents of the issue insisted that the THC derived from smoking marijuana was absorbed more quickly than the legal, synthetic form of THC that was already available in pill form. Supporters argued further that smoking marijuana had been proven to be highly effective in quelling seizures associated with multiple sclerosis and epilepsy and that smoking marijuana could reduce the extreme ocular pressure characteristic of glaucoma. Natural THC was further touted as an appetite stimulant, a drug that could ease the nausea associated with cancer chemotherapy, stimulate the appetites of anorexia nervosa patients, and relieve the "wasting syndrome" of acquired immunodeficiency syndrome (AIDS). It was argued that these benefits are most effectively derived only when absorbed by smoking the drug. Moreover, there are few verifiable side effects or drug interactions associated with marijuana.

Supporters of marijuana for medical use maintained that keeping the drug illegal was a violation of the physician's right to prescribe appropriate medication for a patient. Others insisted that no one could legally gather data regarding the therapeutic effectiveness of marijuana as long as possession of the plant remained illegal.

Opponents of the measures argued that in 1985 a synthetic form of THC, called Dronabinol, was approved for medicinal use and sold under the trademark of Marinol. According to this argument, the availability of the prescription Marinol eliminated any need for "medical marijuana." Opponents argued further that THC is associated with tachycardia and hypotension, even in the synthetic form. Marijuana impairs mood and coordination, and the side effects of inhaling smoke present further dangers, akin to the dangers of smoking tobacco opponents said.

Public Impact

Director of the ONDCP Barry McCaffrey acknowledged the growing support for medicinal marijuana. He was quoted by *U.S. News and World Report* when he said, "It is essential that we remain prepared to reschedule marijuana as a Schedule II drug if the medical evidence supports a conclusion that the drug does have effective therapeutic uses."

Despite tentative acknowledgment from McCaffrey, and voter approval of the medical marijuana resolutions in California and Arizona, much of the matter was left to the test of time. Additionally, the initiatives that passed left a question unanswered: if it is legal to smoke marijuana for medicinal purposes, is it legal to grow, harvest, and possess it?

Following the passage of the initiatives, some doctors in Arizona and California prescribed medical marijuana, but growers and sellers—although they were requiring proof of prescription—were arrested by federal forces shortly thereafter. Federal officials point out that, regardless of state laws on the subject, the cultivation, possession, or distribution of marijuana remain prohibited by federal law. Criticism of the government's actions soon mounted, with many physician groups calling for marijuana to be reclassified as a Schedule II drug, making it legal under federal law for physicians to prescribe it. The ONDCP insists that further research is necessary before such a move can be made, however, and that as long as marijuana remains a Schedule I drug, the government will take action against those who grow and sell it. Meanwhile, the California Supreme Court ruled in February 1997 that the 1996 ballot initiative accepted by the voters, while it legalized the use of marijuana for medicinal purposes, did not alter California's laws against its cultivation and sale.

SUCCESSES AND FAILURES

According to ONDCP statistics there has been a substantial decline in both drug use and drug trafficking since the 1980s. Federal agents reportedly seized more than $1 billion in assets and almost 70 tons of cocaine in 1989 alone, seriously crippling the flow of drugs from powerful drug cartels in Latin America. "We're on the road to victory," declared President George Bush in an interview with Elaine Shannon of *Time* magazine.

In 1995 ONDCP Director Lee Brown estimated that drug use had been slashed from 24 million users down to some 11 million users and that spending on illegal drugs was reduced from $64 billion in 1988 to $49 billion in 1993.

Despite these upbeat statistics, one physician in Detroit reported that the decline in the supply of illegal street drugs, caused by successful interception of drug shipments by law enforcement, had resulted in increased street violence as witnessed by emergency room statistics. Local law enforcement officials echoed the doctor's cynicism, claiming an upsurge in violent crimes, especially robberies, was caused by the new, higher street prices for drugs that resulted from the limited supply.

Conclusive results are not available, although one thing is clear—the problem is far from being resolved.

FUTURE DIRECTIONS

In its *National Drug Control Strategy* for 1998, the ONDCP outlines a 10-year plan for drug control, with the goal of reducing illegal drug use and availability by 50 percent by 2007. Implementing this strategy will require focused efforts in five areas: educating American youth to reject illegal drugs; reducing drug-related crime and violence; reducing the health and social costs to the public of illegal drug use; shielding U.S. borders from drug traffic; and breaking foreign and domestic sources of drug supply. The 1998 strategy emphasizes an expansion of existing programs, such as government-sponsored antidrug advertising campaigns, more funding for law enforcement agencies, and improved border security, as key to meeting its long-term goals.

The ONDCP continues to study the effects of marijuana on the mind and body in an attempt to determine if it has legitimate medical uses. A study by the National Academy of Science's Institute of Medicine was commissioned in 1997. The ONDCP refuses to alter its position on marijuana until the results of this study are known, maintaining that marijuana must be studied with the same scientific rigor required for any potentially harmful substance before any conclusions can be reached. This process of study, and with it, the controversy surrounding marijuana, is expected to last for some years.

AGENCY RESOURCES

Literature from the ONDCP can be obtained from the Drugs and Crime Clearinghouse, toll-free, at 1-800-666-3332 or through the fax number at (301) 251–5212. An assortment of pamphlets is available. Also call this number for specific drug-related data. Recent surveys include *Monitoring the Future* (MTF) and the *National Household Survey on Drug Abuse* (NHSDA). These provide current data on drug use among adolescents—customized bibliographic data is available.

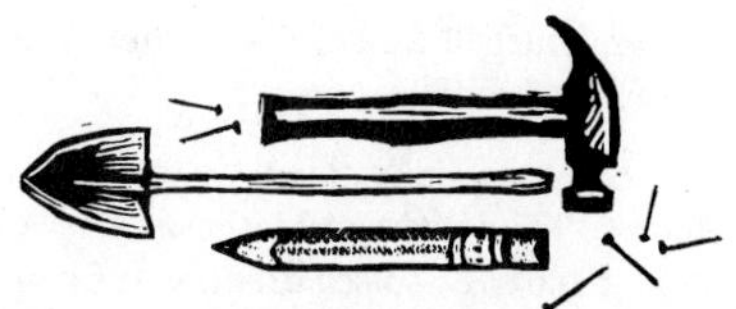

GET INVOLVED:

Community Anti-Drug Coalitions

In 1997 President Clinton signed the Drug-Free Communities Act of 1997 to encourage citizen participation in community-based programs. The Community Anti-Drug Coalitions (CADCA) was developed as part of the Drug-Free Communities Support Program to assist and encourage community members in coordinating and organizing their efforts. Memberships are available for individual professionals ($50), government agencies ($100), organizations ($100), coalitions between community groups ($100), state associations ($2,000), and national organizations ($3,000). Membership benefits include coalition newsletters, faxes, discounts on seminar registrations, and more. Enrollment information may be requested by writing to CADCA—Forum VIII, 901 N. Pitt St., Ste. 300, Alexandria, VA 22314; or fax the CADCA Membership Desk at (703) 706-0565; or call directly to the CADCA Membership Desk at (703) 706-0560, extension 226.

AGENCY PUBLICATIONS

CTAC "blueprint" reports are published periodically. These papers document the numerous projects undertaken by the CTAC since its inception in 1992. "Blueprints" are available from ONDCP's Drugs and Crime Clearinghouse, at 1-800-666-3332, or through the Internet at http://www.whitehousedrugpolicy.gov/policy/factsht.html.

BIBLIOGRAPHY

Capaldina, Lisa, Donald Tashkin, William Vilensky, and Lori D. Talarico. "Does Marijuana Have a Place in Medicine?" *Patient Care*, 30 January 1998, p. 41.

Crenshaw, Mary Ann. *End of the Rainbow*. New York: MacMillan, 1981.

Gall, Timothy L., and Daniel M. Lucas, eds. *Statistics on Alcohol, Drug & Tobacco Use*. Detroit: Gale Research, 1996.

O'Brien, Robert, Sidney Cohen, Glen Evans, and James Fine. *The Encyclopedia of Drug Abuse*. New York: Facts on File, 1992.

Ratner, Mitchell S., ed. *Crack Pipe as Pimp*. New York: Lexington Books, 1993.

"Report of the US National Commission of Marijuana and Drug Abuse, 1972: History of Marijuana Use: Medical and Intoxicant." http://206.61.184.43/schaffer/library/studies/nc/nc1a.htm.

Rosenthal, E., T. Mikuriya, and D. Gieringer. *Marijuana Medical Handbook: A Guide to Therapeutic Use*. Oakland, Calif: Quick American Archives, 1997.

Shannon, Elaine. "A Losing Battle: Despite Billions of Dollars and More than a Million Arrests the War on Drugs Has Barely Dented Addiction or Violent Crime." *Time*, 3 December 1990, p. 44.

Smith, Peter H. *Drug Policy in the Americas*. Boulder, Colo: Westview Press, 1992.

Watson, Joyce M. *Solvent Abuse: the Adolescent Epidemic*. Wolfeboro, NH: Croom Helm, 1986.

Voelker, Rebecca. "NIH Panel Says More Study is Needed to Assess Marijuana's Medicinal Use. *JAMA, The Journal of the American Medical Association*, 19 March 1997, p. 867.

Office of Science and Technology Policy (OSTP)

PARENT ORGANIZATION: Executive Office of the President
ESTABLISHED: May 11, 1976
EMPLOYEES: 39

Contact Information:

ADDRESS: 1600 Pennsylvania Ave. NW
Washington, DC 20502
PHONE: (202) 395-7347
E-MAIL: Information@ostp.eop.gov
FAX: (202) 456-6022
URL: http://www.whitehouse.gov/OSTP.html
DIRECTOR: Dr. Neal F. Lane

WHAT IS ITS MISSION?

The mission of the Office of Science and Technology Policy (OSTP), is to encourage world peace and global prosperity through the application of science and technology. The office fosters a diverse range of scientific research initiatives that include, among other goals, eliminating infectious disease, implementing population controls, and introducing modern food production methods. It also seeks to promote the status of the United States as a world leader in science and technology.

HOW IS IT STRUCTURED?

The director of the OSTP is appointed by the president of the United States, and sits at the hub of a complex advisory structure which involves a wide spectrum of government agencies and departments. The director reports to the president in several capacities: as assistant to the president for science and technology, director of OSTP, co-chair of the President's Committee of Advisors on Science and Technology Policy (PCAST), and manager of the National Science and Technology Council (NSTC).

The director's position requires a candidate who is extremely versatile. In addition to running OSTP, the director serves on outside committees and panels at the president's request. These administrative groups are convened at the discretion of either the president or the director of OSTP to respond to specific circumstances or issues. The purpose of such assignments may vary widely between the many scientific disciplines. Most

commissions are authorized by Congress only for a limited time period. If Congress does not reauthorize a commission before its charter expires, it ceases to exist. A typical example is the President's Committee of Advisors on Science and Technology Policy, which was set to expire on September 30, 1997. Its charter was later extended until 1999.

The core OSTP organization is divided into four separate offices. Each is headed by an associate director appointed by the president who serves directly under the director of OSTP.

By law a maximum of four associate directors assist the head of OSTP, and the number of associates and their respective titles may vary from one administration to the next. President Bill Clinton, for example, appointed four associate directors: associate director for environment, associate director for national security and international affairs, associate director for science, and associate director for technology.

The Federal Coordinating Council for Science, Engineering and Technology (FCCSET), chaired by the director of OSTP, was established under the same law that established OSTP. The FCCSET works closely with the presidential cabinet offices. It is not unusual for members of the president's cabinet to sit on FCCSET, or at least to send a close assistant as a representative. The FCCSET is an autonomous entity that is closely allied and associated with OSTP.

The FCCSET is subdivided into smaller groups such as the High Performance Computing and Communications and Information Technology Subcommittee. A comprehensive FCCSET roster includes diverse representation from several federal departments and agencies: the Departments of Energy and Commerce, the National Science Foundation, the National Security Agency, the Environmental Protection Agency, and perhaps a dozen or more additional groups including OSTP itself.

PRIMARY FUNCTIONS

The OSTP provides information and advice to the president on science and technology issues. The president and Congress then use this information to make informed decisions in developing programs and in defining policies which hinge on complex technological issues.

OSTP operates in a dynamic fashion, often interacting with federal committees and other government agencies whose existence might be temporary in nature. The various OSTP directorships serve as channels of advice and information between the public sector and the executive and legislative branches of the federal government.

FCCSET works closely with the Office of Management and Budget (OMB) to coordinate research and development (R & D) projects and to allocate funds for this purpose. Many such programs are contracted and funded through grants from the National Science Foundation (NSF) and the National Institutes of Health (NIH).

PCAST is cochaired by the head of OSTP and a representative from private industry. This commission considers input and feedback from the associate director of OSTP in combination with input and feedback from organizations in the private sector as a basis for presenting advice to the NSTC.

NSTC provides feedback directly to the president of the United States. NSTC assesses input from private industry through PCAST in conjunction with input both from the public and from relevant advisory committees and commissions.

OSTP assists OMB in the analysis and assessment of most research and development (R & D) expenditures within the federal government. Many of these policies originate within the context of specialized committees that are geared to respective scientific disciplines.

One such committee is the National Bioethics Advisory Commission. This commission works with the Director of OSTP and the Secretary of Health and Human Services to interact between the public sector, the Congress, and executive agencies. Recommendations from the commission are presented to the NSTC through the director of OSTP.

PROGRAMS

The OSTP takes particular interest in educational programs such as the Next Generation Internet Initiative (NGI) and the National Research and Education Network (NREN). NGI is a plan to upgrade significantly the speed and capacity of existing Internet technologies. NREN, a plan to develop an enhanced intranet (a private internet), between major educational computing facilities, would enhance educational resources nationwide and at all levels of study.

NREN is a long-range project originally budgeted for fiscal year 1994 and authorized by FCCSET's High Performance Computing and Communications (HPCC) subcommittee. NREN's goals and objectives were to encourage technological research and development and to stimulate the economy. Specifically, the program defines the creation of a state-of-the-art high-speed network for all levels of the U.S. academic community. NREN was conceived to spur research and development in specific areas of network technology and to stimulate the economy in the private sector, in particular among vendors and manufacturers of NREN supporting technologies. NREN technology will ultimately serve as a model for a high-speed communications infrastructure in the non-academic sector. Teachers, students, and other members of the educational community stand to gain technological proficiency in the NREN environment. NREN was originally scheduled to begin a prototype phase in 1996, but lack of equipment delayed its start.

Next Generation Internet Initiative (NGI)

The Next Generation Internet, like its predecessor the Internet, is a product of the Defense Advanced Research Projects Agency. NGI incorporates high-performance connectivity, ultrahigh-performance connectivity, and cryptographic (security code) technology to surpass the Internet technology of the late twentieth century.

The "NGI Draft Implementation Plan" was a joint endeavor by the Presidential Advisory Committee on High Performance Computing and Communications Information Technology and the Next Generation Internet, the Congress, a cross-industry working team, the academic community, and others. The plan received an enthusiastic recommendation from former OSTP head John H. Gibbons.

The scientific and ethical dilemmas posed by genetic engineering and cloning experiments like these transgenic cows gave rise to the National Bioethics Advisory Commission, a division of the OSTP devoted to researching and regulating government involvement in this new field. *(AP/Wide World Photos)*

BUDGET INFORMATION

Congress allocated approximately $4.9 million to the Office of Science and Technology Policy in 1998. The spending breakdown of those resources is fairly simple—OSTP pays salaries to a modest staff and the remainder of the money is allocated to expenses such as transportation, official reception costs, and incidentals.

HISTORY

The origins of OSTP can be traced to the Manhattan Project that developed the atomic bomb during World War II (1939–45). During the war, many American scientists were summoned by the federal government to develop sophisticated weaponry. They performed their duties under the auspices of the Office of Scientific Research and Development, headed by Dr. Vannevar Bush, which was responsible for many modern weapons technologies including hand-held rocket launchers, remote control detonators, and nuclear arms.

In 1958 a permanent presidential science advisory position was created, partly in response to the launch of *Sputnik* (the first man-made satellite) by the Russian government and partly in response to the increasing complexity of the technology-oriented postwar society. OSTP was eventually established by the Office of Science and Technology Policy Organization and Priorities Act of 1976, which mandates a presidentially appointed director to provide support and counsel to the president in matters of science and technology. The act provides for a maximum of four associates, also appointed by the president.

The first science advisers under Presidents Carter and Reagan maintained very low profiles. William Graham, Reagan's Science Adviser from 1986 to 1989, was described by Barbara J. Culliton of *Science* as ". . . nearly invisible."

When D. Allan Bromley was appointed to the post by President George Bush in 1989, the character of OSTP began to change. Bromley's title was upgraded from "adviser" to "assistant to the president," endowing him with quasi-cabinet status. Bromley restructured OSTP to include four associate divisions, each headed by an associate. The President's Council of Advisers on Science and Technology (PCAST) also was begun during Bromley's tenure.

When President Bill Clinton took office in 1992, he named John H. Gibbons director of OSTP and assigned Gibbons and his staff to work closely with the office of the vice president. Gibbons, as head of OSTP and assistant to the president for science and technology, continued to report directly to the president. President Clinton then merged the National Space Council and the Critical

FAST FACTS:

Citing productive relationships between government and industry, the OSTP estimates that the United States is saving $150 to $200 billion per year on energy due to technological innovations put in place since 1970.

(Source: Office of Science and Technology Policy. "Statement of the Honorable Kerri Ann Jones, Acting Director, Office of Science and Technology Policy before the Committee on Commerce, Science and Transportation, United States Senate," April 30, 1998.)

Materials Council into the OSTP, and it was he who conceived the NSTC.

CURRENT POLITICAL ISSUES

The director and associates of the OSTP exert powerful influence over the Office of Management and Budget. Research and development funds totalling $75 billion each year are distributed throughout the government hierarchy by OMB after careful consultation with OSTP. The nature of these spending allocations is a subject of constant controversy. Projects which receive huge amounts of R & D funding, such as the space program, are frequently subject to criticism. Others feel strongly that it is not the government's responsibility to provide R & D funding at all to the private sector, especially to corporations.

As technology expands its presence in the modern world, controversies multiply. Many people believe the government should not fund some kinds of scientific research, and many political disputes over funding are founded in differences over ethics or religion.

Case Study: Biotechnology and Genetic Research

Biotechnology is a field of modern science in which biological organisms are used to perform industrial processes. By the mid-1980s researchers in biotechnology developed methods of "genetic engineering," the discipline of artificially designing or altering the genetic makeup of living things. An urgent need for regulation of biotechnological research was realized in 1986 when Monsanto Company applied to the Environmental Protection Agency (EPA) for approval to test a bacterium that had been genetically altered to retard the spoilage of corn plants. Soon afterward the University of California at Berkeley requested permission to test a microbe that had been genetically engineered to protect plants from frost damage. Both of these requests to field-test genetically engineered matter for biotechnological applications were denied by the EPA, which believed that too many questions remained unanswered about how genetically altered organisms might affect the balance of nature. Environmental protection groups questioned the wisdom of releasing a substance whose side effects were unproven. For example, the frost microbe might just as easily prove harmful to other microorganisms or animals within the ecosystem.

The debate over biotechnology accelerated and was spurred by a series of experiments beginning in 1970, when a British scientist attempted to "clone" a frog. Cloning is the process of reproducing an animal from the genetic material of a single biological parent. In 1997 Ian Wilmut, a Scottish scientist, stunned the world by successfully cloning and gestating a mammal—a sheep named Dolly.

The revolutionary pursuits of biotechnology sparked a major public controversy. Some people feared that biomedical intervention into human reproduction might result in mutated life forms. Others objected to the science on moral grounds. Many other people, however, were excited at the prospect of new medical resources such as "organ farms." The ethical implications of this new form of biotechnology were highly provocative—inspirational to some, and frightening to others.

Public Impact

By the mid-1990s practical applications for biotechnology, including genetically altered substances, were increasingly commonplace. Doctors developed therapies in which altered genes were implanted in humans to combat otherwise incurable disease and genetic abnormalities. Research scientists justified experimentation into animal cloning to develop vaccines, to perpetuate endangered species, and to create superior species of animals, such as cows with better quality milk and sheep with better wool.

Political and moral questions posed by these scientific developments spawned reactionary organizations. One group, the Foundation of Economic Trends, opposed any type of genetic testing. Foundation member Jeremy Rifkin, quoted in *Science News*, stated: "No research institution or corporation in the United States has the financial reserves to cover the liability claims for one genetic engineering accident of . . . [a large] scale." Activists imagined nightmare scenarios, such as an infected herd of cattle completely wiped out by an adverse reaction to an experimental virus.

As early as 1985 the OSTP recognized the need to establish a federal regulatory commission or agency to oversee the issues associated with biotechnology and genetic engineering. Not until October 3, 1995, did President Bill Clinton issue Executive Order 12975 for the "Protection of Human Research Subjects and Creation of National Bioethics Advisory Commission (NBAC)," which prescribed voluntary and involuntary guidelines regarding genetic research and engineering. Government departments and agencies involved in genetic research, regulation, or funding of such activities were required to review and report their policies and procedures.

The guidelines specifically recommended against the process of cloning of human beings and called for international cooperation in such a ban. The executive order established the NBAC to oversee the genetic sciences and to enforce the guidelines. The NBAC filters input from the Congress and from public sources and passes recommendations on enforcement to the president through the Director of OSTP. The purpose of the guidelines was ". . . as . . . first priority, protection of the rights and welfare of human research subjects."

More than ten years passed between the initial response to the problem by OSTP and the establishment of NBAC. Outlines of proposals defining regulatory mechanisms were mired in the bureaucracy many times during the intervening years. Experimentation with genetically altered organisms persists, and so does the debate over what should and should not be allowed in this field.

FUTURE DIRECTIONS

The OSTP remains strongly committed to fostering research programs that improve and enrich a global society. OSTP will pursue an *Environmental Technology Export Strategy* to assist American industries in exporting technologies that benefit less-developed nations and spur the international economy.

OSTP will also work to develop more efficient automated systems for research management that will permit the federal government to monitor research activities at universities and elsewhere more closely. New research management initiatives, such as the Federal Demonstration Project to Increase Research Productivity, are being developed in conjunction with funded agencies such as the National Science Foundation and the National Institutes of Health.

AGENCY RESOURCES

OSTP maintains a site on the World Wide Web which is accessible through the White House home page at http://www.whitehouse.gov/WH/EOP/OSTP/. Contact the National Science and Technology Council at (202) 456-6100. PCAST information, calendars, and documents are available online at http://www.whitehouse.gov/WH/EOP/OSTP/NSTC/PCAST/pcast.html. Information about MS grants is posted on the World Wide Web at http://www.nsf.gov.

AGENCY PUBLICATIONS

OSTP publications abound. These are available at the OSTP site on the World Wide Web. The Publications Highlights page is located at http://www.whitehouse.gov/WH/EOP/OSTP/html/greatest.html. Each directorship also maintains a page on the Internet which includes links to specific documents.

BIBLIOGRAPHY

Culliton, Barbara J., "A Conversation with D. Allan Bromley." *Science,* 13 October 1989, p. 203.

David, B. D., *The Genetic Revolution.* Baltimore, Md.: John Hopkins University Press, 1991.

Fox, Michael W. "Genetic Engineering: Cornucopia or Pandora's Box?" *The Futurist,* January–February 1986, pp.12–16.

Lawler, Andrew, and Jeffrey Mervis "OSTP: a Mixed Midterm Report." *Science*, 14 April 1995, p. 192(3).

National Research Council. *Field Testing Genetically Modified Organisms: Framework for Decisions.* National Academy Press, 1989.

Piel, J. "Communications, Computers and Networks." *Scientific American*, September 1991.

Stiefel, Chana Freiman. "Cloning: Good Science or Baaaad Idea." *Science World,* 2 May 1997, p. 8.

Womack, J. B., et al. "The Machine That Changed The World," New York: Macmillan, 1990.

Office of Special Counsel (OSC)

PARENT ORGANIZATION: Independent
ESTABLISHED: January 1, 1979
EMPLOYEES: 95

Contact Information:

ADDRESS: 1730 M St. NW
Washington, DC 20036-4505
PHONE: (202) 606-1800
URL: http://www.access.gpo.gov/osc
SPECIAL COUNSEL: Kathleen Day Koch

WHAT IS ITS MISSION?

The mission of the U.S. Office of Special Council (OSC) is to protect federal employees, former federal employees, and applicants for federal employment from the violation of their rights as mandated by the Civil Service Reform Act of 1978 (CSRA). The OSC investigates and prosecutes such violations and brings its cases before the Merit Systems Protection Board (MSPB), a body of judges who review accusations of wrongdoing in regards to the rights and procedures involving federal employees.

HOW IS IT STRUCTURED?

The OSC is an independent federal investigative and prosecutorial agency within the executive branch of the U.S. government. The OSC is headed by the special counsel, who is appointed by the president. Under the special counsel is the deputy special counsel and the Office of Legislative and Public Affairs, and under them are four divisions: Investigation, which includes field offices; Planning and Advice; Management; and Prosecution, which also includes the Complaints Examining Unit and the Disclosure Unit. Headquarters for these divisions are in Washington, D.C.; Dallas, Texas; and the San Francisco Bay area.

PRIMARY FUNCTIONS

The goals of the OSC are guided primarily by the Civil Service Reform Act of 1978 (CSRA), the Hatch

Act of 1939, and the Whistleblower Protection Act of 1989. The OSC protects its members from specific "Prohibited Personnel Practices" (PPP) that occur when one federal employee uses his authority to violate the rights of another employee. The OSC states that these violations can be generally described as follows: (1) unlawful discrimination; (2) requesting unnecessary background information for political reasons, such as to exert political influence on the employee; (3) forcing someone to support a political cause or candidate; (4) using power to interfere with a company's right to compete for business (contracts must be awarded based on merit—not favors); (5) influencing withdrawal of applicants from competition; (6) unauthorized preferences, such as awarding positions based on political party membership; (7) nepotism; (8) reprisal for whistleblowing; (9) reprisal for the exercise of an appeal right, or for cooperation with the OSC or the Inspector General's office; (10) discrimination based on non-job-related conduct, such as lifestyle choices; and (11) violation of laws or regulations used in implementing the merit system.

Under the Hatch Act, federal employees are not permitted to take part in certain political activities, such as soliciting contributions at work for a political cause or running for certain elected offices. This prohibition is meant to prevent abuses of power. For example, a building inspector cannot solicit political contributions from the owners of the buildings he is inspecting because a building owner could feel coerced into giving the inspector money in order to have his building pass inspection. The OSC would investigate and prosecute such a violation.

Under the Whistleblower Protection Act of 1989, the OSC is mandated to protect civil servants from repercussions caused by an act of whistleblowing. This provision is meant to encourage employees to report illegal or abusive incidents in the workplace. The OSC provides methods, such as an anonymous hot line, for whistleblowers to come forward to volunteer information. It then investigates such claims and prosecutes if necessary.

Complaints are sent to the Complaints Examining Unit (CEU). If a complaint cannot be resolved there, it is sent to the Investigation Division for field investigation. For certain types of allegations, such as sexual or racial discrimination, the complaint is then referred back to the agency head that is involved, where a different and more appropriate set of laws and procedures outside the OSC's jurisdiction are followed. If the issue involves a whistleblowing complaint, the matter is referred to the OSC Disclosure Unit, which then handles it in the appropriate manner. Otherwise, the Investigation Division determines which regulation or law has been violated and what action to take. The OSC then tries to negotiate with the parties involved to reach a solution. If they cannot do so, then the matter is litigated before the Merit Systems Protection Board (MSPB), which then renders a final decision.

If it is determined that no violation occurred, the Prosecution Division sends a letter to the complainant explaining the OSC's finding and allowing the complainant to make a final comment before the matter is closed. If an investigation discovers that a violation occurred that is outside the OSC's jurisdiction, the complaint is referred back to the agency involved with recommendations for further action. If the investigation finds evidence that the violation is of a criminal nature and federal laws have been broken, then the complaint is referred to the Department of Justice for investigation.

PROGRAMS

OSC programs are intended to help civil service employees better understand their rights and provide assistance with reporting their grievances. In accordance with the Hatch Act, the OSC offers a service to advise individuals on what types of political activities they may or may not legally participate in. Individuals may submit requests for advice by phone or mail and may request a response either orally or in writing.

In a 1994 reauthorization act, the OSC was given greater leeway in providing educational services. Heads of government agencies are required to inform employees of their rights and to do so in compliance with the OSC's guidelines. To facilitate this process, the OSC has developed an informational program guide, "Outline Of Employee Rights And Remedies Under 5 U.S.C., Chapters 12 and 23."

The OSC also operates a Whistleblower Disclosure Hotline, which provides a confidential method for employees to report illegal or abusive activities. The OSC then informs the head of the specific agency involved about the complaint and requires the agency to investigate. At all times the employee's identity remains confidential. This service is available through the Disclosure Unit, U.S. Office of Special Counsel, 1730 M St. NW, Suite 300, Washington, DC 20036-4505; telephone: 1-800-572-2249 or 202-653-9125.

BUDGET INFORMATION

In 1997 the money appropriated by Congress from the overall budget of the United States for the operation of the OSC was $8.3 million. These funds were roughly divided into the following categories: $6 million in salaries for full-time and part-time personnel; $1 million for civilian personnel benefits; and $1 million in rental payments to the General Services Administration (GSA), which governs some federal office space.

FAST FACTS

In 1997, the OSC handled 551 allegations of discrimination based on race, color, sex, national origin, religion, age, or handicap.

(Source: Office of Special Counsel Annual Report, 1997.)

HISTORY

In 1883 Congress passed the Pendleton Act, which established the Civil Service Commission and an employment system for U.S. government employees that was based on merit. This legislation arose from a desire to reform the federal government and end the practice of awarding jobs as political favors. It was thought that a well-policed merit-based system would allow workers to succeed or fail on the basis of their skills rather than on their contacts or political loyalties.

Under the Civil Service Reform Act of 1978, Congress replaced the Civil Service Commission with three new independent agencies—the Office of Personnel Management (OPM), the Federal Labor Relations Authority (FLRA), and the Merit Systems Protection Board—that would better be able to handle the government's growing responsibilities. The MSPB's responsibilities were to handle employee complaints about violations of the rights guaranteed them under the CSRA. At the same time the CSRA created the OSC, whose responsibilities were focused specifically on the investigation and prosecution of Prohibited Personnel Practices (PPPs) and violations of the Hatch Act.

The OSC was originally meant to act as a part of the MSPB, but from the outset, it largely operated independently because of the nature of its investigative work. It needed independence in order to investigate claims without interference from the governmental agency it was investigating. Also, because its workload had increased so much, a separate body with its own authority was required in order to remain effective. In July of 1989 it became an independent executive branch agency under the Whistleblower Protection Act of 1989, an amendment to the CSRA that was meant to protect employees who reported wrongdoing in the workplace. In 1994 the OSC's role was expanded even further with the Uniformed Services Employment and Reemployment Rights Act of 1994, which brought veterans and reservists under the OSC's protection and granted them the same consideration as other civil servants.

The OSC today investigates alleged violations and then presents these cases to the MSPB in the same way a prosecutor presents a case before a jury. The MSPB and the OSC then determine whether discipline is required. If so, the OSC takes the necessary legal actions.

CURRENT POLITICAL ISSUES

One of the OSC's most important goals is to investigate and prosecute complaints made by whistleblowers against powerful and influential agencies within the government and protect the employee who is lodging the complaint. For many whistleblowers, although the OSC is able to protect them from legal repercussions, it cannot guarantee or secure their jobs after their complaints have been investigated and prosecuted. Many whistleblowers emerge from the experience with very uncertain career paths and regret having gone through the process.

Case Study: Frederic Whitehurst and the FBI

Frederic Whitehurst was an explosives expert in the FBI's crime laboratory. He and his lab performed tests on evidence used in federal criminal cases such as the World Trade Center and the Oklahoma bombings. Such evidence is crucial and is often the primary basis for a prosecutor's case. Whitehurst claimed he was often under pressure to falsify or obfuscate the results of his scientific tests in order to strengthen the government's case against a defendant. He also alleged that his bosses insisted that he rewrite his reports to bolster the prosecution's case.

For ten years, Whitehurst complained to various authorities and unsuccessfully tried to express his concerns. When an investigation was finally launched, Whitehurst's accusations were found to be true. It was concluded that the FBI lab was indeed substandard. One example Whitehurst cited was that open vents in the ceiling allowed contaminants to drop down onto evidence, creating incorrect conclusions about the explosives being tested. Whitehurst also proved that he was often pressured into altering his reports. As a result, hundreds of federal convictions began to be reexamined to make sure no one had been wrongfully prosecuted. Though protected from legal ramifications as a whistleblower and theoretically free from reprisals, Whitehurst was placed on leave from his duties. It is unlikely that he will ever be able to return to his job at the FBI, and he will almost certainly be unable to return to the same lab.

Public Impact

Though reforms were enacted and the FBI's procedures have apparently been made stricter in response to the public attention Whitehurst brought to its problems, he did so at great risk to himself and his family. Although some say the Whistleblower Act adequately protected Whitehurst and forced problems to be examined and fixed, others say that it is not effective enough and that its high personal cost could make other whistleblowers hesitate to come forward in the future.

SUCCESSES AND FAILURES

Revised case review procedures have been in effect since 1994 that require fewer reviews of cases and advice from the senior management, which allows more cases to be handled more quickly and efficiently. Also, more detailed explanations are now being offered to individuals about the OSC's final determination on their cases, reducing the need for further follow-up by senior management.

The OSC has begun using interdisciplinary teams consisting of an investigator and an attorney to pursue allegations. Such cooperation allows more focused attention and better investigative strategy for each case. The team approach has enabled the OSC to act on 40 percent more cases.

FUTURE DIRECTIONS

One of the OSC's challenges for the future is to continue to clarify and interpret the laws as defined by the Hatch Act and its 1993 revision. Under the Uniformed Services Employment and Reemployment Rights Act of 1994, the OSC can now investigate and prosecute cases that involve the rights of veterans and reservists who are trying to return to work in the federal system after active duty in the armed services. The OSC can now help these former military personnel by representing them before the MSPB to ensure that they receive equal treatment in the federal employment system.

As part of a 1994 reauthorization act, the OSC will also continue to support the education of federal employees about their rights under PPPs, the Whistleblower Protection Act, and the Hatch Act through the new Office of Special Counsel Outreach Program, which makes representatives available for educational programs and seminars on request.

In the future, the OSC hopes to put the agency online on the World Wide Web, and to offer more information about the service and its duties.

AGENCY RESOURCES

General information about the OSC is available through the U.S. Office of Special Counsel, 1730 M St. NW, Suite 300, Washington, DC 20036-4505; phone: (202) 653-7122 or (202) 653-6005; fax (202) 653-5161. Resources are also available on-line. The informational program guide, "Outline Of Employee Rights And Remedies Under 5 U.S.C., Chapters 12 and 23," is offered in both a short-form and a full-text version at http://www.access.gpo.gov/osc.

To file a complaint or for information on the rights of government employees, contact: Complaints Examining Unit, U.S. Office of Special Counsel, 1730 M St. NW, Suite 300, Washington, DC 20036-4505; phone 1-800-872-9855 or (202) 653-7188. To report illegal or abusive incidents in the workplace anonymously, call the Whistleblower Disclosure Hotline at either 1-800-572-2249 or (202) 653-9125, or write to Whistleblower Disclosure Hotline: Disclosure Unit, U.S. Office of Special Counsel, 1730 M St. NW, Suite 300, Washington, DC 20036-4505.

For more information on the Hatch Act contact: Hatch Act Unit, U.S. Office of Special Counsel, 1730 M St. NW, Suite 300, Washington, D.C. 20036-4505; phone or 1-800-854-2824 or (202) 653-7143. The E-mail address is hatchact@osc.gov.

AGENCY PUBLICATIONS

Publications offered to the public include *The Role of the Office of Special Counsel*, *Political Activity and the Federal Employee*, *Political Activity and the State and Local Employee*, and *Annual Reports to Congress from the U.S. Office of Special Counsel*. Individual copies of these publications or further information about the OSC is available by contacting the U.S. Office of Special Counsel, 1730 M St. NW, Suite 300, Washington, DC 20036-4505; phone (202) 653-7122 or (202) 653-6005; or fax (202) 653-5161. These publications may also be found on the World Wide Web at http://www.access.gpo.gov/su_docs/locate.html.

BIBLIOGRAPHY

Beha, Richard. "Don't Whistle While You Work." *Time*, 16 July 1990.

Clinton, Bill. "Remarks on Signing the Hatch Act Reform Amendments of 1993." *Weekly Compilation of Presidential Documents*, 11 October 1993, pp. 2012–14.

Crowe, Maire. "Whistleblowers, Unite!" *Audubon* , January 1995.

Holden, Constance. "Whistleblower Woes." *Science*, 5 January 1996.

Johnson, Jeffrey. "Hugh Kaufman: EPA Whistle-Blower." *Sierra*, November 1988, pp. 94–99.

Macilwain, Colin. "Whistleblowers Face Blast of Hostility." *Nature*, 20 February 1997.

Noah, Timothy. "Shielding the Whistle-Blowers." *Newsweek*, 27 March 1989.

Ponessa, Jeanne. "Senate Governmental Affairs OKs Hatch Act Rewrite." *Congressional Quarterly Weekly Report*, 15 May 1993, p. 1225.

Office of Surface Mining Reclamation and Enforcement (OSM)

PARENT ORGANIZATION: Department of the Interior
ESTABLISHED: August 3, 1977
EMPLOYEES: 674

Contact Information:

ADDRESS: 1951 Constitution Ave. NW
Washington, DC 20240
PHONE: (202) 208-2719
TDD (HEARING IMPAIRED): (202) 208-2737
FAX: (202) 501-0549
E-MAIL: getinfo@osmre.gov
URL: http://www.osmre.gov/osm.htm
DIRECTOR: Kathy Karpan

WHAT IS ITS MISSION?

It is the mission of the Office of Surface Mining Reclamation and Enforcement (OSM) to assist states in operating a nationwide federal regulatory and enforcement program that protects citizens from the adverse effects of surface coal mining, while ensuring that mining is accomplished in ways that avoid permanent damage to land and water resources.

HOW IS IT STRUCTURED?

The OSM falls within the framework of the Department of the Interior, a cabinet-level agency. The OSM's director is nominated by the president and confirmed by the Senate. Under the supervision of the Department of the Interior's assistant secretary of land and minerals management, the director formulates policy and administers OSM programs nationwide. Under the director are the deputy director and the Offices of Equal Employment, Communications, and Strategic Planning and Budget. Regional coordinating centers that report to the director are located in Pennsylvania, Illinois, and Colorado and provide technical support to the states as well as to 12 field offices and seven area offices. The field offices interact with state, tribal, and other federal agencies by assisting with their regulatory and reclamation programs. Regional coordinating centers review mine plans and permit applications on federal lands. The director is also supported by the Program Support Directorate and the Finance and Administration Directorate. The offices of regulatory support, reclamation support, and the Applicator/Violator System are responsible to the Program Support Directorate, whereas the offices of compliance management, financial management, information systems management, and administration answer to the Finance and Administration Directorate.

PRIMARY FUNCTIONS

The OSM was established to provide regulatory and enforcement activities as part of the Surface Mining Control and Reclamation Act of 1977 (SMCRA). The SMCRA gave federal oversight of coal mining activities throughout the nation to the OSM. The implementation of the SMCRA is intended to be managed primarily by the states and tribal governments, with the OSM guiding their efforts. Additionally the OSM oversees state coal mining regulation and land reclamation programs on a state-by-state basis as part of the SMCRA. Assistance is provided to states in meeting the objectives of coal mining law, as well as regulated coal mining and land reclamation on federal and American Indian lands when states do not assume the responsibility of managing these tasks themselves.

Environmental Restoration

The OSM is responsible for facilitating the environmental restoration of areas affected by mining projects begun before the SMCRA was passed. Primarily the OSM works with the 28 states and tribes that have set up local structures to manage surface mining reclamation and regulation. The OSM also provides support to states that have not set up their own programs as well as to tribal governments and programs for federal lands. States that wish to manage their own reclamation projects do so by getting approval from the OSM for Abandoned Mine Land (AML) program grants. Grant monies are primarily acquired through a fee on mine operators calculated by tonnage of material extracted. These funds are deposited into the Abandoned Mine Reclamation Fund. The OSM approves programs that are submitted for these funds provided they meet the guidelines for reclamation set by the SMCRA. For the states, tribal governments, and federal lands without established programs, the OSM organizes reclamation projects itself.

The OSM also coordinates the efforts of private citizens, students, and local, state, and government agencies to reduce acid mine damage through the Clean Streams Initiative. Old coal mines are a major source of polluting acids that destroy the land and water in surrounding areas. The OSM helps a wide range of organizations—from university groups to the Environmental Protection Agency (EPA)—consolidate their efforts to find funding and clean up the environmental destruction left behind by abandoned mines.

Environmental Protection

Whereas the function of environmental reclamation represents the OSM's efforts to repair the damage caused by old mines, the OSM also works to prevent any new damage from being caused by existing or new mining operations. This includes enforcing mining regulations established by the SMCRA that penalize violators with fines. The SMCRA requires that certain environmental maintenance activities be performed by any surface mining operation, both while the operation is in progress and once it has been completed. The OSM encourages additional efforts to be made beyond the guidelines set by SMCRA with its Excellence in Surface Coal Mining and Reclamation awards. When OSM standards are not met, the agency also accepts complaints and petitions, usually from environmental agencies but also from private citizens, seeking injunction (legal action) against mining operations. Injunctions to halt surface mining are issued against mining operators when the OSM agrees with the petitioner that a particular site or practice is unsuitable for mining operations.

Other Functions

The OSM conducts and sponsors a great deal of research to help understand the myriad of environmental problems involved in surface mining. Topics include topsoil erosion, acid drainage, and the effect of mining on native plants and animals. Additionally the OSM operates the Technology Information Processing System (TIPS), a nationwide computer system that helps states and tribal governments evaluate and analyze various aspects of surface mining operation and reclamation.

PROGRAMS

The OSM administers regulatory specifications as outlined in the SMCRA. The primary focus of the agency is its Abandoned Mine Reclamation Fund, which allocates monies to states to enforce SMCRA regulations and restore water and land resources where environmental damage has occurred from the impact of surface mining. These funds are collected largely in the form of fees and royalties paid on the volume of coal extracted by mining companies.

The OSM also administers the computerized Applicator/Violator System (AVS), a database of unresolved violations, that monitors the complex interrelationships of coal mine ownership and control links. The system allows the OSM to develop cases against companies that have been involved in mining indirectly through contract operations or other arrangements. When a coal mining company applies for a permit to mine a new site, the information is checked against the AVS to determine whether the company is eligible for a mining permit. If violations are discovered and successfully connected to offending companies, permits are withheld and fines levied until appropriate environmental reclamation is completed. This process usually includes the reconstruction of topsoil layers in areas where surface mining has

BUDGET:

Office of Surface Mining Reclamation and Enforcement

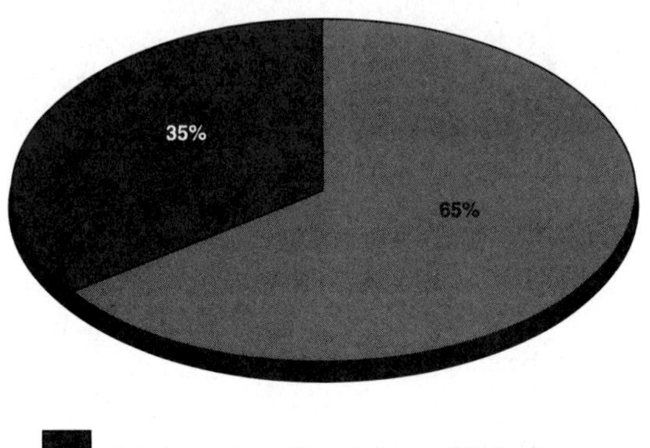

Administration of Regulation and Technology

Management of the Abandoned Mine Reclamation Fund

taken place, allowing vegetation and wildlife to return to normal states.

BUDGET INFORMATION

The approximate budget of the Office of Surface Mining, Reclamation and Enforcement for 1998 was $271.1 million. Administration of Regulation and Technology accounted for $93.7 million, or 35 percent, of the budget. Budget areas within this category include environmental restoration and protection, technology development and transfer, financial management, as well as executive direction and administration. Management of the Abandoned Mine Reclamation Fund accounted for $177.4, or 65 percent, of the agency's budget.

HISTORY

The OSM was established within the Department of the Interior by Congress as a requirement of the Surface Mining Control and Reclamation Act of 1977 (SMCRA). Before the passage of the SMCRA, 25 states regulated surface mining but not at the level required by the new law. The central reason for the law's passage was that not enough was being done about the environmental disasters caused by abandoned mines and existing mining operations. Abandoned mines posed a serious threat to human and environmental safety, with open mine shafts and polluted rivers dotting the landscapes of many states. New or existing mining operations had only minimal responsibility for the damage that their mining techniques caused.

Following a two-year period of public comment and committee review, the final draft of regulatory statutes was published in September of 1978. In 1979 the OSM began to develop the first abandoned mine land inventory system by collecting data on sites from the 25 coal-producing states and one Indian tribe. With the publication of federal regulations, coal-producing states began to submit proposals for their own regulatory programs. The first American Indian tribes to receive approval to regulate surface mining on reservation lands were the Navajo, the Crow, and the Hopi.

Four years after its creation, the OSM reorganized to reflect its changing role from that of provider of direct regulation. Following the approval of approximately 24 state-sponsored regulatory agencies, the OSM began to focus on its new role of providing federal oversight and technological assistance. During this period the OSM established technical centers in Pittsburgh, Pennsylvania and Denver, Colorado and created 13 field offices and six area offices to assist states in the application of federal regulations.

In 1982, following the appointment of Secretary of the Interior James Watt, a vocal critic of the SMCRA, a regulatory reform task force was established that led to changes to 91 percent of the surface mining regulations. Watt's involvement in regulatory reform instigated numerous legal cases against the Department of the Interior for its soft approach to the coal mining industry. Ultimately, the original requirements of the SMCRA were upheld by the courts, providing environmental agencies with a small victory in environmental regulatory enforcement.

After the antiregulatory period of the 1980s, the OSM gained momentum. It developed federal regulatory programs for states that either had not submitted proposals for their own programs or had not received approval for their programs. After finding program deficiencies in two states, the OSM set a precedent by taking over their inspection procedures of mining operations. In one case this led to the repeal of approval of the state program for issuing permits for mining and enforcing regulations.

In 1987 the OSM completed the development of the first Applicator/Violator System (AVS), which prevents mining operators who are known violators of federal regulations from receiving new mining permits. Utilizing this system the OSM developed a promising record of tracking the behavior of mine operators and enforcing the payment of fees and legally required reclamation efforts.

The OSM has developed strong regulatory programs that encourage environmentally sound methods of surface coal mining. Through its fee collection programs,

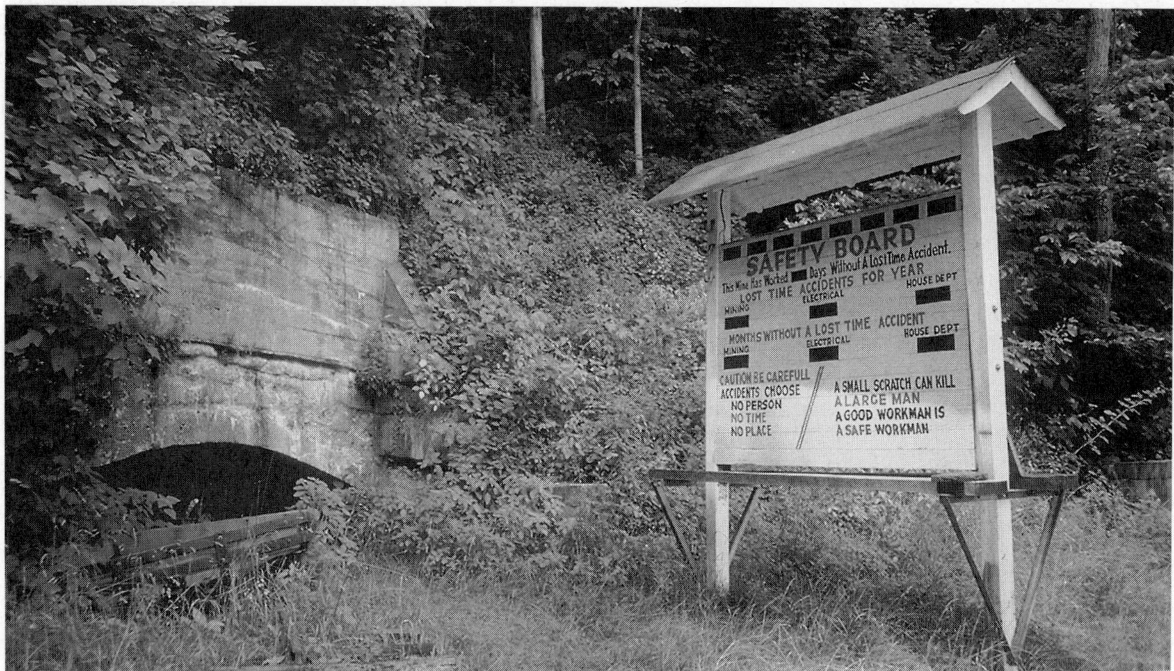

Under the Surface Mining Control and Reclamation Act of 1977, the OSM is responsible for closing abandoned mines, like this one in West Virginia, making the area much safer and eventually restoring much of the surrounding natural habitat. (Photograph by Susan D. Rock)

millions of dollars in reclamation funds are distributed to states where coal mining takes place. Additionally, the OSM began to sponsor forums on technology transfer, encouraging partnerships between scientists, mining representatives, and the OSM. These partnerships further enhance the efficiency and safety of coal production, thus ensuring energy production and environmental stability for future generations.

CURRENT POLITICAL ISSUES

During the 1980s environmental groups waged a legal battle against the OSM to change its mine operation permit process. Close inspection of mining permits and legal records revealed that common practices among mine operators included nonpayment of OSM fees and misinformation about coal output. Mine operators who were not correctly paying their fees were being given new permits regularly, seriously weakening the credibility of the agency and angering agencies that wished to see environmental reclamation projects more vigorously pursued.

Secretary of the Interior James Watt, an opponent of all federal environmental industry regulation where federal lands were concerned, ignored the problem. Watt openly sided with coal companies that did not feel obligated to abide by federal law and even went so far as to refuse to enforce the law. Much of Watt's time at the Interior Department was spent in court, where he tried to weaken regulations, specifically those within the SMCRA.

After nearly a decade of legal cases involving regulatory actions, the courts sided with the environmental agencies, and operators were forced to submit accurate information and settle outstanding payments to the OSM. By 1991 the Applicator/Violator System (AVS) was sufficiently strengthened so that nonpayment of fees makes operators ineligible for mining permits. The tightening of enforcement has led to a debate about fees and their costs to the industry. In response, some mining companies moved to countries where permit fees and environmental regulations do not cut into profits. This fuels the debate on the role of regulatory action and the overall ability of the mining industry to function profitably in the United States.

Case Study: AVS Brings Results

The National Wildlife Federation (NWF) was influential in the development of the computerized system that has become the AVS. The system allows researchers, through the permit process, to connect abandoned mines in violation of federal law back to the original company responsible for the mine. The process is complicated by

FAST FACTS

In the coal-producing states of West Virginia and Pennsylvania, approximately one million pounds of acid from unreclaimed mines flows into rivers and streams every year.

(Source: Michael Lipske. "Cracking Down on Mining Pollution." *National Wildlife*, June 16, 1995.)

the ability of mining companies to dodge responsibility for abandoned mines through complicated contracts and partnerships. Mining contractors who perform the actual mining are often funded by larger "parent" companies. These individual contractors sometimes go out of business, and parent companies claim no financial responsibility for the abandoned mine. This has been the case in heavy coal-producing states such as Kentucky, West Virginia, and Pennsylvania. The NWF successfully utilized the data from the AVS to petition the OSM against releasing additional mining permits to the parent companies. The enforcement presented a tremendous obstacle to mining companies and threatened the overall profitability of their operations. In reaction to the permit blocks, companies reclaimed previously mined sites in order to maintain coal production.

Public Impact

The AVS has given the federal government and environmental agencies a powerful enforcement tool. As a result, 75 percent of abandoned mines have been reclaimed. There has been a significant reduction in acid mine drainage. Revegetation of landscapes ravaged by the mining process has also occurred. Reclamation projects create jobs that help support economies dependent on energy-related work. Water resources in coal-producing states have been protected from acid contamination; in some cases improvements in water quality are directly linked to reclamation projects. This is particularly important to wildlife protection and the maintenance of clean water for industry and human consumption.

FUTURE DIRECTIONS

The OSM plans to expand computer technology in assessing the issues of surface mining reclamation and enforcement. Use of the Technology Information Processing System (TIPS) more than doubled from 1995 to 1998, and the OSM plans to augment its existing resources with new machines with higher capacities and greater efficiency.

AGENCY RESOURCES

The OSM Web site at http://www.osmre.gov, provides general information, such as the agency's functions and budget, as well as statistics associated with mining operations. The OSM also maintains a list of links to other sites at http://www.osmre.gov/links.htm. Many regional surface mining reclamation and regulation links are provided, as are those of environmental protection groups. Information may also be requested by mail at Office of Communications, Office of Surface Mining Reclamation and Enforcement, Department of the Interior, Washington, DC 20240 or by phone at (202) 208-2719.

AGENCY PUBLICATIONS

The OSM provides publications that describe federal management of mining and reclamation under the Surface Mining Law. Titles include *Surface Coal Mining Reclamation: 15 Years of Progress, 1977–1992* and the *Office of Surface Mining 1997 Annual Report.* Publications are available at no cost from the OSM's Office of Communications at (202) 208-2719.

BIBLIOGRAPHY

Hobbs, Erika. "On Shaky Ground: U.S. Mining Reform." *Engineering and Mining Journal*, 1 September 1996, p. 39.

Lipske, Michael. "Cracking down on Mining Pollution." *National Wildlife*, 16 June 1995, p. 20.

"Mining Budget Adds $1 Million for Appalachian Clean Streams." US Newswire, 6 February 1997.

"Office of Surface Mining and Pittson Coal Company Settle Contract Mine Ownership and Control Case." US Newswire, 23 July 1996.

"OSM Surveying Information Needs, Interests in Prime Farmland Reclamation." US Newswire, 4 December 1996.

Office of Technology Policy (OTP)

WHAT IS ITS MISSION?

The Office of Technology Policy (OTP) is the only federal office whose specific mission is to develop and promote national policies that use technology to build U.S. economic strength. As part of the Department of Commerce's (DOC) Technology Administration (TA), the office supports the TA's broader mission of maximizing technology's contribution to U.S. economic growth.

HOW IS IT STRUCTURED?

The OTP is one of three agencies within the TA, a bureau of the DOC, which in turn is one of the cabinet agencies that reports directly to the president of the United States. The OTP is directed by the DOC's undersecretary for technology. Its chief administrator holds the title of assistant secretary of commerce for technology policy and reports to the undersecretary. The assistant secretary supervises the OTP's staff of 55.

PRIMARY FUNCTIONS

The OTP works to promote the mission of the TA—technology development and commercialization—by participating in cooperative efforts to facilitate the application of new technologies. The OTP helps to identify barriers to the implementation of certain technologies and remove these barriers when possible. It also investigates the effectiveness of government-industry partnerships

PARENT ORGANIZATION: Department of Commerce
ESTABLISHED: 1988
EMPLOYEES: 55

Contact Information:

ADDRESS: 14th St. and Constitution Ave.
Washington, DC 20230
PHONE: (202) 482-8321
FAX: (202) 482-4817
E-MAIL: public_affairs@mail.ta.doc.gov
URL: http://www.ta.doc.gov/OTPolicy/default.htm
ASSISTANT SECRETARY: Graham Mitchell
DEPUTY ASSISTANT SECRETARY: Kelly S. Carnes

and incorporates the results of this research into federal policy recommendations and annual reports to Congress. The office also distributes a series of reports that attempt to determine what is required to remain competitive in industry.

Through its PACE program, the OTP hosts town hall meetings and roundtable discussions in which the public and private sectors can interact to reach agreements regarding the direction of U.S. technology policy. The OTP is active in international technology policy as well; through participation in organizations such as the Asian-Pacific Economic Cooperation (APEC), it pursues regional economic growth through technology and negotiates intellectual property rights in the U.S. government's science and technology agreements. The OTP also works to recognize and promote technological achievement in U.S. business.

PROGRAMS

Perhaps the OTP's most visible function is the administration of the National Medal of Technology, a presidential award program that recognizes excellence in technological innovation and commercialization. First awarded in 1985, the Medal of Technology is given annually to individuals, teams, or companies for accomplishments in the innovation, development, commercialization, and management of technology. Evidence for these accomplishments is provided through significantly improved products, processes, or services. The medal's primary purpose is to recognize technological innovators who have made lasting contributions to America's competitiveness and standard of living.

An example of the OTP's cooperative effort at improving and promoting U.S. technology is the Rapid Commercialization Initiative (RCI), a large-scale federal, state, and private collaboration to speed up the implementation of new environmental technologies. The program uses cooperative demonstration projects to identify and remove obstacles to the application of specific technologies; ten individual projects are under way which each demonstrate a different environmental technology.

The OTP is also involved in several international efforts. For example, it participates in APEC, an association of 18 Asian-Pacific nations seeking to share technology and open access to research and development among member countries. APEC also seeks to enhance the positive gains of international economic interdependence by encouraging the free flow of goods, services, capital, and technology among its members.

BUDGET INFORMATION

The OTP's budget authority is granted through congressional appropriations. For budgeting purposes, OTP program spending is lumped together with spending for the programs of the Office of the Under Secretary for Technology, to create the category of "US/OTP" within the Department of Commerce budget. Currently, the US/OTP budget is approximately $7 million.

HISTORY

The need for a central technology policy organization began in the late twentieth century, when U.S. competitiveness in an emerging global marketplace first became a concern. Among the most significant issues was the effectiveness of technology transfer, or the transfer of research findings from federal laboratories to the private industrial sector. Because the results of federal information were available to everyone, companies did not want to make investments in technology that they could not protect.

The first congressional legislation to address the technology transfer problem was the Stevenson-Wydler Technology Innovation Act of 1980, which gave federal laboratories the following mandates: to actively seek cooperative research partnerships with state and local governments, academia, nonprofit organizations, or private industry; to disseminate information related to the results of this research; to establish the Center for the Utilization of Technology at the National Technical Information Service (NTIS); and to establish and define the activities of the newly created Offices of Research and Technology Applications (ORTA) at each federal laboratory. The act also set aside a small part of each laboratory's budget to fund technology transfer activities and established the National Medal of Technology Program, which would later fall under the control of the OTP. The ORTA was a precursor to the OTP, but because there were separate offices for each laboratory, technology policy in the U.S. was still not centralized.

The Technology Innovation Act was amended in 1986 to reward the work of inventors and commercial developers of technologies. Inventors from federal laboratories were required to receive a minimum of 15 percent of any royalties generated through the patenting or licensing of technologies developed there; the act also allowed both current and former federal employees to participate in commercial development of these technologies if there was no conflict of interest.

A New Agency

The movement toward a centralized technology policy was further refined through a series of amendments and acts in the 1980s and reached its present form in 1988 with the passage of the National Institute of Standards and Technology Authorization Act. The act mandated an important structural change—the establishment of the TA as a single bureau within the DOC.

The OTP was created by this new Technology Administration with the mission of developing technology policies that would strengthen the U.S. economy. The new office was assigned responsibility for the National Medal of Technology Program together with other policy functions such as the protection of intellectual property through contractual agreements. In recent years, the OTP's policy concerns have expanded to include the international community.

CURRENT POLITICAL ISSUES

There is a growing concern that the pace of U.S. technological advancement is declining, with negative consequences for economic growth, productivity, and international competitiveness. Debate over the cause of this perceived weakening in technological advancement inevitably becomes a debate over technology policy in the United States. Rapid changes in technology make the concept of a single U.S. "technology policy" uniquely difficult to define in political circles, and recent administrations have struggled to articulate a position. Some officials and scientists want a more carefully constructed, centralized technology policy; some want federal technology policy to play a facilitating, rather than regulating, role in bringing about technological advances in U.S. private industry; and some want to get rid of the term "technology policy" altogether, claiming the government has no business being involved in any part of U.S. technological development.

A quick browse through the names of various government agencies that contain the word "technology" provides evidence that the U.S. government has no single, cohesive idea of its role in technological development. The OTP should not be confused with the Office of Science and Technology Policy (OSTP), an office that directly serves the president in making policy decisions. The National Aeronautics and Space Administration (NASA) and the Department of Defense (DOD) have their own programs for technological development. President Clinton's effort to coordinate science, space, and technology policies within the federal government, the 1993 establishment of the National Science and Technology Council (NSTC), may eventually serve to clarify the situation; on the other hand, it may provide more confusion by adding another agency with "technology" in its name. If the U.S. efforts at advancing technology were more unified, some argue, more progress would be made, U.S. companies would become more competitive, and the nation would experience stronger economic growth.

The current method of encouraging technological advancement in the United States, at least in the private sector, stresses government "partnerships" with industry in which the government receives bids on research and development (R & D) projects, selects the projects it considers to be most worthy of support, and then supplies resources—money, laboratories, and personnel—to back the effort. This system is criticized by some as a high-stakes horse race.

FAST FACTS

Past recipients of the OTP's National Medal of Technology include Stephanie Kwolek, a research chemist who developed Kevlar, (the material used in bulletproof vests); Steve Jobs and Stephen Wozniak, founders of Apple Computer, for their pioneering work in personal computers; and Johnson and Johnson for its continuous innovations in professional and home health care products.

(Source: Office of Technology Policy. "Press Release," April 30, 1997.)

Case Study: Sematech

Some critics of U.S. technology policy argue that government support has not proven to be particularly good at either choosing which areas of technology to support or in leading the R & D efforts of certain projects. Recent history provides examples of government ineptitude in driving technological growth; in the 1980s, when it became clear that the Japanese semiconductor (computer chip) industry was outselling its U.S. counterpart, the government subsidized an organization called Sematech, a unification of semiconductor manufacturing technologies among large U.S. chip makers. The U.S. government contributed about $100 million a year to finance the R & D efforts of these companies.

Sematech has been a relative failure, with few new advances to offer after government funding. The U.S. chip industry has since made a moderate comeback based on innovations in the industry that were not connected to Sematech. Examples of government failure in driving technology are not limited to the United States; Japan's efforts in developing high-definition television (HDTV) are also instructive. The Japanese government chose the technology that would be used for HDTV and financed its development, but the analog technology it chose later proved to be inferior to some alternatives. Without the benefit of similar government assistance, private industry in the United States developed promising alternatives to Japanese HDTV using digital technology of a higher quality.

The HDTV example, along with other stories of successes and failures, leads some members of U.S. science and industry to conclude that government involvement in the development of technology is doomed to failure; technological growth in the United States, they argue, should result from direct competition within the free market system. Despite the successes claimed by the OTP and various other technological agencies within the U.S. government, their involvement in private industry's R & D will always have its detractors.

SUCCESSES AND FAILURES

Two unique enterprises of the OTP are the Japanese Translation Center at the OTP offices in Washington, D.C., and the Techno Growth House in Tsukuba Science City, Tokyo, which are designed to help the U.S. business community learn more about Japan. The translation center provides free translations of Japanese reports and literature for U.S. businesses, researchers, and students, and the Techno Growth House is a low-cost facility that provides U.S. researchers in Tokyo with office space and technical and language support.

FUTURE DIRECTIONS

According to the DOC's 1997 Draft Strategic Plan the OTP's future goals involve furthering the international competitiveness of U.S. private industry, in part by observing successful practices of technologically successful economic rivals such as Japan and Germany. Specific goals are to monitor and evaluate how competitor nations support research and development and enhance industrial competitiveness; and to comparatively monitor and evaluate the strengths, weaknesses, and barriers faced by U.S. industrial sectors. The OTP intends to translate these studies into policy options with its partners in industry, academia, and the states.

AGENCY RESOURCES

General inquiries about OTP programs can be directed to the Public Affairs Office of the Office of Technology Policy; phone (202) 482-8321. For information about the National Medal of Technology, write to National Medal of Technology, Technology Administration, Rm. 4226, U.S. Department of Commerce, 14th Street and Constitution Ave. NW, Washington, DC 20230. The main office of the National Medal of Technology can be telephoned at (202) 482-5572.

Detailed policy statements or technical reports issued by the OTP are available through the Technology Administration's National Technical Information Service (NTIS) at http://www.fedworld.gov/ntis/ntishome.html.

AGENCY PUBLICATIONS

OTP publications include U.S. technology policy studies such as *Technology in the National Interest* or international technology policy studies such as *International Science and Technology—Emerging Trends in Government Policies and Procedures*. Some of these OTP reports can be downloaded from the OTP Internet site at http://www.ta.doc.gov. Others are available through the NTIS Internet site at http://www.fedworld.gov/ntis/ntishome.html. Paper copies of all reports may be obtained through the OTP's Publications Request Line at (202) 482-3037.

As part of its Meeting the Challenge Initiative, the OTP is publishing a series of industry sector reports examining the opportunities and obstacles faced by U.S. businesses today. Reports in the series "Meeting the Challenge: U.S. Industry Faces the 21st Century" can be accessed on-line at http://www.ta.doc.gov/reports.

The OTP's newsletter, *Pacesetter*, is a quarterly periodical offering current news from the OTP. The most recent issue of *Pacesetter* can be downloaded from the OTP Internet site at http://www.ta.doc.gov. Back issues can be requested from the publications request line at (202) 482-3037.

BIBLIOGRAPHY

Branscomb, Lewis M. *Empowering Technology: Implementing a U.S. Policy*. Cambridge: M.I.T. Press, 1993.

DeWilde, T., ed. *The Other Policy: The Influence of Policies on Technology Choice and Small Enterprise Development.* New York: Women Ink, 1990.

Mendelsohn, L. D. "Technology Transfer Policy: Its Role and a Scientific and Information Policy and its Impact on Technological Growth." *American Society for Information Science*, January 1992, pp. 80–88.

Meyers, C. E. "High Technology: The Glue Between Government and Industry." *Security Management*, September 1992, pp. 99–100.

Office of Economic Cooperation and Development. *Progress in Structural Reform: An Overview.* Washington, D.C.: OECD, 1992.

Sclove, Richard E. *Democracy and Technology*. New York: Guilford Press, 1995.

Steele, T. J., W. L. Schwendig, and G. A. Johnson. "The Technology Innovation Act of 1980, Ancillary Legislation, Public Policy, and Marketing: The Interfaces." *Journal of Public Policy and Marketing*, 1990, pp. 167–82.

United States General Accounting Office. *Technology Transfer: Constraints Perceived by Federal Laboratory and Agency Officials.* Washington, D.C.: U.S. General Accounting Office, 1988.

White, R. M. "A Catalyst for U.S. Competitiveness." *IEEE Spectrum*, March 1992, pp. 49–50.

Office of the United States Trade Representative (USTR)

PARENT ORGANIZATION: Executive Office of the President
ESTABLISHED: January 15, 1963
EMPLOYEES: 165

Contact Information:

ADDRESS: 600 17th St. NW
Washington, DC 20508
PHONE: (202) 395-3230
FAX: (202) 395-7226
URL: http://www.ustr.gov
UNITED STATES TRADE REPRESENTATIVE: Charlene Barshefsky
DEPUTY UNITED STATES TRADE REPRESENTATIVE: Richard W. Fisher
DEPUTY UNITED STATES TRADE REPRESENTATIVE: Rita D. Hayes

WHAT IS ITS MISSION?

The Office of the United States Trade Representative (USTR) is responsible for developing and coordinating U.S. international trade, commodity, and direct investment policy; the office also leads negotiations with other countries on such matters. Through an interagency structure, the USTR coordinates trade policy, resolves agency disagreements, and presents issues for presidential decision. USTR is an acronym referring to both the office and the head of the office, the U.S. trade representative.

HOW IS IT STRUCTURED?

The Office of the U.S. Trade Representative is a cabinet-level agency under the Executive Office of the President of the United States. The U.S. trade representative is thus a cabinet member who holds the additional title of ambassador. The trade representive acts as the principal adviser, negotiator, and spokesperson to the president on trade and related matters. Three deputy U.S. trade representatives also hold the rank of ambassador. Two are assigned to the Washington, D.C., office and one to the USTR's Geneva, Switzerland, office. The U.S. trade representative serves as a nonvoting member of the board of directors of the Export-Import Bank, as the vice chair of the Overseas Private Investment Corporation (OPIC), and also as a member of the National Advisory Council for International Monetary and Financial Policy.

The Washington, D.C., office of the USTR is structured along four organizational lines: general support,

bilateral negotiations, multilateral negotiations, and sectoral activities. General support includes offices such as Congressional Affairs, Policy Development and Coordination, Public/Media Affairs, Administrative Services, and General Counsel. Bilateral negotiations include treaties and negotiations with nations in the Western Hemisphere, Europe and the Mediterranean, Asia and the Pacific, and Africa.

Multilateral negotiations include participation in the affairs of the Asia-Pacific Economic Cooperation (APEC), the World Trade Organization (WTO)—formerly known as the General Agreement on Tariffs and Trade (GATT)—and the United Nations Conference on Trade and Development (UNCTAD). Sectoral offices form policies and strategies related to specific industry sectors, such as Textiles; Financial and Investment Policy, Services, Investment and Intellectual Property; Agricultural Affairs; Industrial Affairs; and Environment and Natural Resources.

The Geneva office is organized to cover general WTO affairs, nontariff agreements, agricultural policy, and commodity policy. Special attention is given to textiles, with one staff member designated as U.S. representative to the Textiles Surveillance Body. The Geneva deputy U.S. trade representative is the U.S. ambassador to the WTO and the UNCTAD on commodity matters.

The Interagency Trade Policy Mechanism

It is impossible to understand how the USTR functions without first understanding the three-tiered interagency structure in which it operates in order to formulate trade policy. The USTR coordinates the first two levels of this cooperation and input, the Trade Policy Staff Committee (TPSC) and the Trade Policy Review Group (TPRG). Both groups are administered and chaired by the USTR and involve 17 federal agencies and offices; they make up the subcabinet mechanism for developing and coordinating U.S. government positions on international trade and related issues.

The TPSC is the first-line operating group, supported by more than 60 subcommittees, each responsible for specialized areas, and several special task forces working on specific issues. If agreement cannot be reached in the TPSC, or if no particularly significant policy questions are being considered, then issues are taken up by the TPRG, a smaller group at a higher level in the government hierarchy (the deputy USTR/undersecretary level).

The final level of the interagency trade policy mechanism, and the most authoritative, is the National Economic Council (NEC), chaired by the president. The Deputies Committee of the NEC considers recommendations of the TPRG and particularly controversial or significant trade-related issues.

PRIMARY FUNCTIONS

The USTR's trade policy leadership and negotiating expertise involve the following areas of responsibility: all matters within the WTO, including implementation of the Uruguay Round Multilateral Trade Negotiation (MTN); export expansion policy; industrial and services trade policy; bilateral and multilateral trade and investment issues; import policy; international commodity agreements and policy; trade-related intellectual property protection issues; and commodity, trade, and direct investment matters handled by international institutions such as the Organization for Economic Cooperation and Development (OECD) and UNCTAD.

In formulating U.S. trade policy, the USTR administers and coordinates meetings of the policy-making bodies in which 17 federal agencies have a voice. In these meetings, agency representatives relate their concerns and preferences for international trade issues. Often the discussion centers on a particular issue of concern, such as export expansion or intellectual property issues. If agreement is not reached in meetings of the specialized groups making up the TPSC, then the matter is passed on to the TPRG, whose members have a higher level of authority within each participating agency (the deputy trade representative and undersecretaries). If an issue is still not resolved by this organization, then the matter is passed on to the National Economic Council, or NEC, which includes the president, the U.S. trade representative, secretaries of cabinet agencies, and other top officials. Once a trade policy matter is passed on to the NEC, the USTR surrenders its chairing authority to the president, although the U.S trade representative does play a significant role in the discussion of the issues at hand. Typically, an issue to be discussed by the NEC is framed and introduced by the trade representative for trade-related issues.

The USTR is also the leader in directing trade negotiations for the president. Although many trade agreements are negotiated by the president, the USTR nearly always acts as the principal adviser in these situations, and at times the trade representative directly negotiates agreements. Once a policy has been decided or an agreement reached, the trade representative serves as the primary spokesperson for the administration, articulating and explaining positions and agreements to the press and the public.

PROGRAMS

One of the most significant agreements and organizations in which the USTR has been involved is the North American Free Trade Agreement (NAFTA), the 1994 pact between the United States, Canada, and Mexico. NAFTA is an agreement that it is designed to gradually eliminate tariffs and other barriers to trade in goods. It is also intended to improve access for services trade and to create a consensus on rule making, dispute settlement, investment, and intellectual property rights.

The USTR was also instrumental in the most recent round of international trade talks, the 1986–94 Uruguay Round, in which the loosely organized General Agreement on Tariffs and Trade (GATT) was expanded to deal with international trade in services and intellectual property. Formerly, GATT had merely helped establish standards and tariff reductions for trade in goods, but it was not recognized as an international organization by law, and it had little power to enforce its recommendations. Immediately following the Uruguay Round, in 1995, the GATT became the World Trade Organization (WTO); *GATT* now refers to one of the agreements incorporated into the new WTO agreements. One of the more recent WTO agreements is the Information Technology Agreement, a tariff reduction measure involving a long list of electronic and technological components and devices.

Another important program in which the USTR is involved is Asia-Pacific Economic Cooperation (APEC), which was formed in 1989 in response to the growing interdependence among Asia-Pacific economies. APEC has become a regional vehicle for promoting open trade and practical economic cooperation between its 18 member economies, which represent one of the fastest-growing economic regions in the world.

BUDGET:

Office of the United States Trade Representative

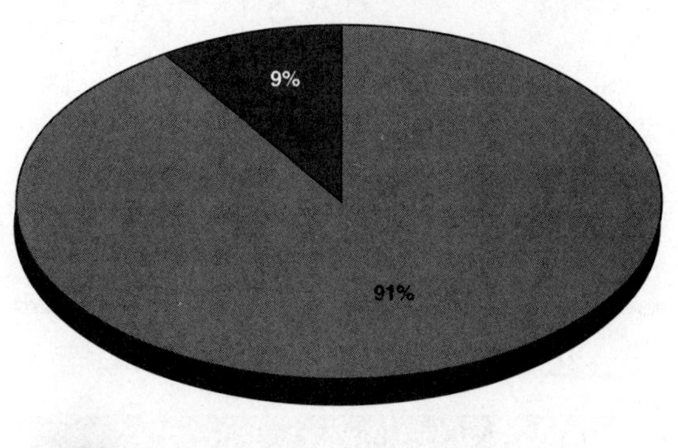

Geneva Office's Trade Negotiations
Washington-Based Trade Coordination and Negotiation

BUDGET INFORMATION

The budget authority of the USTR is granted entirely through congressional appropriations. In 1997 a budget of $22 million was authorized. About $20 million of the USTR budget is spent on Washington, DC-based trade coordination and negotiation, and the remaining $2 million is spent on the Geneva office's trade negotiations. USTR's 1997 budget appropriations bill stipulated that not more than $98,000 of the office's budget could be spent on official reception and representation expenses.

HISTORY

In 1962 the Office of the United States Trade Representative was created by Congress as part of the Trade Expansion Act; on January 15, 1963, President John F. Kennedy issued Executive Order 11075, effectively implementing the office's functions. The office was initially named the Office of the Special Trade Representative and was given responsibility and authority to negotiate all international trade agreements programs that had been authorized under the Tariff Act of 1930 and the Trade Expansion Act of 1962. The first special trade representative was Christian A. Herter, who held the post from 1962 to 1966.

In 1974, with the passage of a new Trade Act, Congress broadened and codified the trade representative's functions in the areas of policy making and negotiating. The Trade Act of 1974 established the special trade representative's office as a cabinet-level agency within the Executive Office of the President. It also established the tradition of close congressional relationships with the office—a relationship that required congressional consultation with, and advisement and oversight of, the special representative's office. This close relationship with Congress remains today as a fundamental element of the USTR's operational mechanism.

The Office of the Special Trade Representative was renamed the Office of the United States Trade Representative (USTR) in 1980 under President Jimmy Carter's Executive Order 12188, which designated the USTR as the nation's chief trade negotiator and the representative of the United States in the major international trade organizations. The order also authorized the USTR to set and administer overall trade policy.

In response to increasing global trade competition, the USTR was granted additional authority under the Omnibus Trade and Competitiveness Act of 1988. Perhaps the most significant power granted the USTR under this legislation was the authority to take action regarding section 301 complaints, or U.S. responses to foreign unfair trade practices under the terms of international trade agreements.

FAST FACTS

U.S. copyright industries contribute more than $350 billion a year to the U.S. economy, which accounts for more than 6 percent of the U.S. gross domestic product.

(Source: Charlene Barshefsky. "U.S.-China Relationship," June 17, 1997.)

CURRENT POLITICAL ISSUES

In recent history, the "globalization" of the world's economy has opened new international markets to U.S. businesses. Many of the nations in the Asia-Pacific region—China, Indonesia, Korea, Malaysia, the Philippines, Singapore, Taiwan, and Thailand—are particularly attractive export targets for U.S. businesses because their economies have seen annual growth rates of up to 10.2 percent, compared with 2 percent for the United States.

Doing business with these economies has had mixed results; a large number of U.S. industries targeted for export and investment opportunities in Asia rely on high technology to be competitive. In recent years product development costs have been higher than ever before, and many people, especially in fast-growing Asian economies, find it easy to simply copy many high-tech items for a fraction of the production costs. Products such as compact discs (CDs), computer software, and videodiscs have been "pirated" by the millions in these countries, which collectively have the world's worst record for copyright piracy and other types of intellectual property rights (IPR) violations.

The issue of IPR was first addressed by the U.S. Congress in the 1974 Trade Act, Section 301, which names IPR infringements as unfair trade practices. Under the legislation, industry complaints are investigated and then a "watch list" and "priority watch list" of the worst-offending countries are published each year. At least four Asia-Pacific economies have consistently appeared on this list in the last few years.

The U.S. law for protecting IPR has provided a domestic approach to unfair trade, but has resulted in little help in IPR protection from the governments of some other countries. The establishment of the World Trade Organization in 1995 provided an international organization with the authority to establish and enforce rules and policies concerning the violation of intellectual property rights. The implementation of IPR legislation throughout the Asia-Pacific region has been a huge step forward, but the question of how the agreement will be enforced remains.

Case Study: China

China is one of the United States's most important emerging partners in trade; in 1996 U.S. Trade Representative Charlene Barshefsky estimated that at least 160,000 Americans owed their jobs to U.S. exports to China. It is the fastest-growing major economy in the world—and one of the world's worst violators of intellectual property rights. In 1996 there were 26 CD and LASER disc factories in central and southern China manufacturing 50 million pirated CDs, CD-ROMs, and LASER discs annually for export to Southeast Asian countries and even to Canada. Pirated versions of Microsoft Corporation's Windows 95, a computer interface, were being sold in China before the product's release in the United States. By the summer of 1997, motion pictures were being pirated and made available on videodiscs before they were released in the United States. In Hong Kong and in countries to which China exported, it was possible to find $10,000 software packages for $5. Obviously, U.S. industry was losing billions of dollars of Chinese trade in stolen intellectual property.

The formation of the World Trade Organization in 1995 was immediately followed by the passage of the Intellectual Property Rights Enforcement Agreement, which was a first step in mending U.S.-China trade relations. The Chinese government did take a few well-publicized steps toward cracking down on "pirates," including making four thousand underground factory raids and destroying two million pirated CDs, but one year later the United States was not satisfied that China had undertaken satisfactory implementation of the IPR Enforcement Agreement. U.S. Trade Representative Charlene Barshefsky announced a trade retaliation proposal, targeted at $2 billion in Chinese imports to the United States, that would occur if China did not make serious progress toward implementation. The Chinese countered with the statement that such sanctions would result in "retaliation."

A trade war was averted, however, as cooler heads prevailed. China undertook improved customs enforcement to cut off shipments of pirated goods and strengthened protection for well-known trademarks. It was also substantiated that 15 factories engaged in piracy had been shut down; that there had been a remarkable increase in fines issued for piracy; and that improved regulations concerning the import of CD presses had been passed. Once these changes were verified by U.S. investigators, the threat of U.S. trade sanctions was withdrawn.

IPR enforcement has since become part of China's nationwide anticrime campaign, and trade relations between China and the United States have improved. Although the piracy of foreign sound recordings has dropped dramatically as a result of Chinese efforts, the piracy of computer software continues at an alarming rate. Many issues concerning the international markets for intellectual property remain to be resolved.

SUCCESSES AND FAILURES

In the 1990s the USTR and its associated agencies appeared to be on top of the rapid economic growth of Latin American nations in the Western Hemisphere; for the first half of the decade, exports to these nations increased at a greater rate than exports to anywhere else in the world, including Asia and the European Union. Since 1991 the United States has consistently run a trade surplus with every nation in Latin America and the Caribbean, excluding Mexico.

FUTURE DIRECTIONS

Policy advisers and other committee members are constantly in the process of anticipating economic trends around the world and formulating national responses to them. In 1994, at the Summit of the Americas held in Miami, Florida, the swift economic growth of the Latin American region was recognized by the 34 democratically elected leaders of the Western Hemisphere, and these leaders agreed to establish a Free Trade Area of the Americas (FTAA) by 2005. Since then the United States and these countries have been constructing the FTAA; the United States hosted an important meeting of trade ministers in Denver, Colorado, in 1995 and continues to work with the USTR and other agencies to establish its role in the FTAA.

In many ways, the economic region of primary future interest to the United States is the Asia-Pacific, which not only includes the most rapidly growing economies in the world but also includes two economic powerhouses with whom the United States continues trade squabbles: Japan and China. The Commission on United States-Pacific Trade and Investment Policy, in its 1997 report titled *Building American Prosperity in the 21st Century: U.S. Trade and Investment in the Asia Pacific Region,* made several recommendations to U.S. policymakers for securing and expanding access to these important markets, especially China and Japan.

The commission recommended that the United States use all means at its disposal to assist China's integration into the world economy and its accession to the WTO; redouble its efforts to gain greater access to the Japanese market for U.S. exporters; and to assign a greater priority and visibility within the U.S. government to trade and investment interests in the Asia-Pacific region. The commission also recommended that the United States work with Asia-Pacific nations and in multilateral conferences to promote human rights—but that it do so in a manner "balanced with commercial interests."

AGENCY RESOURCES

General inquiries about the work of the Office of the United States Trade Representative can be directed to the Office of Public/Media Affairs, USTR, 600 17th St. NW, Washington, DC 20508; phone (202) 395-3230. For an extensive listing of foreign trade information, researchers can visit the Foreign Trade Information System of the Organization of American States (OAS)—the principal forum in the Western Hemisphere for dialogue on political, economic, and social issues—on-line. The Foreign Trade Information System includes Trade Forums (articles and opinions about trade in the Western Hemisphere); progress reports on the formation of the Free Trade Area of the Americas (FTAA); the full text or summaries of all trade agreements or investment treaties involving OAS nations; quantitative trade data; copies of GATT panel reports; and links to several other official sources on trade information. The Foreign Trade Information System is found on the World Wide Web at http://www.sice.oas.org.

The World Wide Web is also a valuable resource for learning more about the World Trade Organization (http://www.wto.org) and Asia-Pacific Economic Cooperation (http://www. apecsec.org.sg).

AGENCY PUBLICATIONS

The USTR and the various committees involved in its operations release many reports and publications each year. Reports released periodically are *Trade Policy Agenda and Annual Report of the President of the United States on the Trade Agreements Program* and *National Trade Estimate Report on Foreign Trade Barriers* (NTE), among others. Recent releases include *Building American Prosperity in the 21st Century: Report of the Commission on United States-Pacific Trade and Investment Policy; Report to Congress on Section 301 Developments;* and *A Comprehensive Trade and Development Policy for the Countries of Africa.* A number of these USTR reports and publications can be downloaded from the office's Web site. For more complete listings, contact the Office of Public/Media Affairs, USTR, 600 17th St. NW, Washington, DC 20508; phone (202) 395–3230.

BIBLIOGRAPHY

Barshefsky, Charlene. "Barshefsky: What We've Accomplished in China." *Business Week*, 23 June 1997, p. 12.

The Basics of Foreign Trade and Exchange. New York: Gordon Press, 1994.

Bhagwati, Jagdish, and Hugh T. Patrick, eds. *Aggressive Unilateralism: America's 301 Trade Policy and the World Trading System*. Ann Arbor: University of Michigan Press, 1990.

Clasan, Thomas F. *Foreign Trade and Investment*. Charlottesville: Michie Butterworth, 1991.

Foreign Commerce and the Antitrust Laws. New York: Little, Brown, 1990.

"GATT and You." *Time*, December 1994, p. 21.

"A Guide to Intellectual Property Rights in Southeast Asia and China." *Business Horizons*, November-December 1996, pp. 43-51.

Hardie, Crista. "Info Tech Tariff Talks Made Headway in the Pacific Rim." *Electronic News*, 2 December 1996, p. 8.

Levinson, Marc. "Scorecard: Making the Grade on Trade." *Newsweek*, 30 May 1994, p. 52.

Sanger, David E. "U.S. Settles Trade Dispute, Averting Billions in Tariffs." *New York Times*, 29 June 1995, p. A1.

Stern, Paula. "Reorganizing Government for Economic Growth and Efficiency." *Issues in Science and Technology*, Summer 1996, pp. 67–73.

Walsh, Elsa. "The Negotiator." *New Yorker*, 18 March 1996, pp. 86–97.

Office of the Vice President (OVP)

WHAT IS ITS MISSION?

The Office of the Vice President (OVP) serves as the support staff for the vice president of the United States, and assists in the various (and numerous) activities that are contingent with the vice presidential office.

HOW IS IT STRUCTURED?

The structure of the OVP is subject to decisions by the vice present regarding what shape it should take. Vice President Al Gore is directly supported by his chief of staff and two deputy chiefs of staff. Under the deputy chiefs of staff are several department heads who focus on the areas that are important to the vice president: communications, policy, scheduling, legislative affairs, legal counsel, the National Security Council (NSC), the Council on Environmental Quality (CEQ), and the National Partnership for Reinventing Government (NPR).

PRIMARY FUNCTIONS

According to Vice President Gore's Office of Communications, the central functions of the OVP are to generate, develop, and communicate the ideas of the vice president. These ideas include those given to the vice president by the president as well as those that the vice president has a personal interest in fulfilling. Because functions vary depending on who is vice president, it is impossible to describe the functions of the OVP in concrete terms. Under Vice President Gore, the OVP has

PARENT ORGANIZATION: Executive Office of the President
ESTABLISHED: 1789
EMPLOYEES: Not Available

Contact Information:

ADDRESS: Old Executive Office Building
Washington, DC 20501
PHONE: (202) 456-2236
E-MAIL: vice.president@whitehouse.gov
URL: http://www.whitehouse.gov/WH/EOP/OVP/html/GORE_Home.html
ASSISTANT TO THE PRESIDENT; CHIEF OF STAFF; COUNSELOR TO THE VICE PRESIDENT: Ronald A. Klain
DEPUTY CHIEF OF STAFF: David M. Strauss

FAST FACTS

The many initiatives undertaken by Vice President Nelson Rockefeller (1974–1977) to enhance the status of the vice presidency included a better airplane for Air Force Two; an official residence (the Admiral's House at the Naval Observatory); and a new vice presidential seal (the older seal showed an eagle at rest, the new one an eagle with its wings spread, clutching a quiver of arrows, its head surrounded by a burst of stars).

(Source: *Guide to the Presidency*. Washington, D.C.: Congressional Quarterly, Inc., 1996.)

focused on issues such as protecting the environment, insuring equal access to technological opportunities, reinventing government efforts, and working on ways to strengthen family values.

PROGRAMS

Programs in the OVP are undertaken because the vice president has ordered them, and the extent to which they involve the vice president's staff varies dramatically. The largely advisory status of the vice president's staff usually means they are involved in information gathering and the design phase of these programs, but rarely participate in the actual operation of resulting initiatives.

For example, one of Vice President Gore's programs, the National Partnership for Reinventing Government (NPR), an interagency task force devoted to making the federal government smaller and more efficient, involves very few OVP staff; the program has been led by a vice presidential assistant, but staffed by personnel from other government agencies. Another domestic program unveiled by President Bill Clinton and Vice President Gore, the Empowerment Zone and Enterprise Community Program (EZ/EC Program), after being designed chiefly by the vice president and his domestic policy staff, was turned over to the Rural Development mission area of the Department of Agriculture. The vice president serves as chair of the program's Community Enterprise Board. The vice president and his staff have also drafted the agenda for the development of the National Information Infrastructure (NII)—the Clinton Administration's effort to connect U.S. classrooms, libraries, hospitals, and clinics to the electronic information network by the year 2000.

BUDGET INFORMATION

The unusual nature of the vice presidency has led to a complex and sometimes confusing budgeting arrangement. Because the vice president is officially the President of the Senate, and until 1961 had his office in the Capitol, the Senate still shares some responsibility for funding the vice presidential staff. The 1998 Senate budget included an appropriation of slightly more than $1.6 million for the salaries and expenses of certain vice presidential staff members and functions.

The growing alignment of the vice president with the executive branch, however, has necessitated a larger budgetary emphasis on functions assigned by the president, and as a result the staff necessary to fulfill these tasks. The funds set aside in the budget of the Executive Office of the President (EOP) for the "specially assigned" functions of the Office of the Vice President—including, for example, his role as a foreign policy adviser and member of the National Security Council—totaled nearly $3.4 million in the 1998 budget.

HISTORY

Throughout most of U.S. history, the role of vice president of the United States has not been well defined. And, on several occasions, the abolishment of the office was seriously considered. Under the original Constitution, the second-highest vote getter in presidential elections was named to the vice presidential slot until 1804. The two Constitutional mandates of the vice presidency were to preside over the Senate and to succeed to the presidency in time of emergency. Though officially president of the Senate, the vice president never really exercised much influence over Senate proceedings due to the rapid rise of party politics. Even today this role is largely ceremonial and requires very little of the vice president's time.

Selected as running mates by presidential candidates, candidates for the vice presidency were often considered to be "ticket balancers" who would take the presidential campaign appeal to the broadest possible electorate. Many of the nineteenth-century vice presidential candidates tended to be older men in bad health. During this period, six vice presidents died in office of natural causes. Because the post was an inherently weak position, and because the vice president was entrusted with very little responsibility, vice presidential staffs were virtually nonexistent for much of the nineteenth century, consisting mainly of clerical personnel and low-level aides. If other assistance was needed, members of the White House staff usually stepped in to provide it.

BIOGRAPHY:
Albert Gore Jr.

Vice President of the United States (b. 1948) When Albert Gore became vice president of the United States it represented more than merely a changing-of-the-guard at the executive level. Rather, it noted a shift of influence toward the first generation of Americans born after World War II (1939–45). Gore, 44 when he became vice president, embodied the baby boomers' rise to political power. Gore's running mate, Bill Clinton, was 45 when he was first elected president in 1992. For Gore, reaching the White House marked the culmination of many years of public service and professional achievement. His career includes four terms in the U.S. House of Representatives and two in the U.S. Senate. But despite Gore's immersion in political affairs, one of the defining moments in his life was highly personal. In 1989 Gore's son was seriously injured in a car accident and during the months of recovery Gore began to empathize more with the world around him. It was during this time that he wrote *Earth in the Balance,* an in-depth examination of how mismanagement of the environment leaves children with what Gore calls "a degraded earth and a diminished future." His strong opinions on preserving the environment, his experience with Congress, and his exposure to foreign affairs made Gore an excellent choice as Clinton's running mate. Since the elections in 1992 and 1996, Gore has worked on environmental issues as well as reducing government spending and bureaucracy. Gore is the Democratic Party's front-runner for the presidential race in 2000.

In the twentieth century, both Presidents Theodore Roosevelt and Franklin Roosevelt argued publicly for an expanded role for the vice president; Franklin Roosevelt argued specifically for the vice president to serve in four distinct roles: as cabinet member, presidential adviser, liaison to Congress, and policy maker in areas that did not directly involve any of the cabinet agencies.

Such roles were slow to develop until a period that lasted from the Great Depression to the end of World War II (1939–45). These events helped to broaden the power of the executive branch and increased the influence of the president over Congress and the political parties. As presidents developed legislative agendas, following the lead of Franklin Roosevelt's New Deal, vice presidents became active liaisons to Capitol Hill, and began to receive other presidential assignments as well. For the first time in history, the vice president was becoming firmly established in the executive branch of government. Presidents also began to appoint vice presidents to head executive commissions. In 1949 under the direction of President Harry S. Truman, the vice president was made a statutory member of the National Security Council.

The vice president's changing status became apparent when, in 1961, the vice presidential office was moved from the Capitol to the Executive Office Building, adjacent to the White House at the request of President John F. Kennedy's vice president, Lyndon Johnson. In 1969 during the administration of President Richard Nixon, Vice President Spiro Agnew argued for, and won, a line item in the executive budget specifically devoted to vice presidential staff. This meant that the vice president no longer had to rely on Congress for office space and operating funds and was a landmark event in the development of the OVP, becoming the groundwork for the office's further expansion.

Perhaps the single most important event in the development of the OVP was the Watergate scandal that arose during Nixon's presidency. When Vice President Agnew resigned from the vice presidency following his criminal indictment, President Nixon had to choose a new vice president as mandated by the terms of the Twenty-Fifth Amendment, which was passed in 1967. Before accepting the nomination, Gerald Ford, President Nixon's choice to replace Agnew, persuaded the president to dramatically increase the budget for hiring a vice presidential staff. The new personnel included support staff for press relations, scheduling, speech writing, and administration. Vice presidents previously had waited for White House staff to take time out from serving the president to perform such duties. Vice President Ford was even granted a political staff that would help him to protect his interests and further his political career.

Ford and his successor to the vice presidency, Nelson Rockefeller, reorganized and expanded the OVP to make it more closely resemble the White House staff, with its own press secretary, legal counsel, and national security adviser. Subsequent vice presidents were able to capitalize on the gains made during this period. In 1976 Vice President Walter Mondale participated in the first nationally televised debate between vice-presidential candidates; as vice president, he served President Jimmy Carter as a valued adviser on important matters of politics and public policy. In 1988 George Bush became the first incumbent vice president since 1836 to be elected to the presidency. After the election of President Bill Clinton in 1992, Vice President Al Gore heightened public awareness of the position by serving the president as a high-profile diplomatic envoy; advising the president on issues of domestic and foreign policy; and performing as a top administrator for a number of highly publicized executive programs, such as the NPR and the EZ/EC.

CURRENT POLITICAL ISSUES

Among the various qualities that a presidential candidate seeks in a running mate, loyalty is one of the most important: the vice president is expected to publicly support the administration's policies and activities. Usually, political controversies land squarely on the shoulders of the president, and it is the vice president's job to act as a defending spokesperson.

As the vice president's political importance has grown in the latter half of the twentieth century, one of the roles of his staff has been to protect him from politically harmful situations. The presidential election of 1996 created at least two situations in which Vice President Al Gore's staff committed errors that were serious enough to damage the political image of the vice president, who was considered by many members of the Democratic Party as a viable presidential candidate for the elections in the year 2000.

Case Study: The 1996 Presidential Campaign

As part of President Clinton's 1996 reelection campaign, the vice president was expected to help raise money. This was a typical role for a vice president involved in a reelection campaign, but the manner in which Al Gore conducted himself exposed him to stern criticism from political opponents and members of the media. In particular, it was revealed that throughout the campaign Gore made more than 40 telephone calls from his vice presidential office to political donors, soliciting contributions. This was a clear violation of federal election laws, which prohibit such calls from being made on government property. Gore denied that the calls were improper, but his claim seemed to be undermined when, as Republican leaders called for an investigation into the vice president's fund-raising activities, his executive assistant and her staff began discarding records of these calls. Under heavy pressure from Republican leaders, Attorney General Janet Reno began a 90-day investigation into Gore's telephone solicitations to determine if there was enough evidence to warrant appointing an independent counsel to conduct a full investigation.

Another controversy involved Gore's attendance, in April of 1996, of a luncheon at the Hsi Lai Buddhist Temple in California. This event turned out to be a fund-raiser and one that was illegal in the way its contributions were submitted. After the luncheon, a total of $140,000 was sent to the Democratic National Committee (DNC) by the temple—$58,000 came from nuns and devotees who were later reimbursed by temple leaders. Federal law prohibits financing contributions in another person's name and the DNC later acknowledged that it was inappropriate to collect cash in a religious building. Vice President Gore denied being aware that the event had been a fund-raiser. He characterized it as a community outreach event that was intended to thank Asian American supporters and to inspire further political and fund-raising efforts.

While the vice president may not have known the true nature of the luncheon, it became evident that his staff was aware that the event was a fund-raiser, and may have failed to communicate that fact to him. Gore knew he was to attend fund-raisers in the San Jose and Los Angeles areas from April 27 to 29, and had acknowledged that fact in memos and electronic messages to his staff. He even referred to "the fund raisers for Monday, April 29th"—the day he was to visit the temple. However, because his visit to the temple was one of several visits that day, it remained unclear whether he was aware of the status of the event.

The vice president's staff had been clearly informed about the nature of the luncheon. The event's organizer, Johnny Huang, had sent a memo to the vice president's director of scheduling that was titled "Fund-raising lunch for Vice President Gore." At least two other aides, in internal schedules and messages, also referred to the event as a fund-raiser. If the vice president had not been apprised of the fact that the luncheon was a fund-raiser, it appeared that his mid-level staff may have been responsible for not informing him of the situation. The U.S. attorney general has authorized an investigation into the allegedly illegal fund raising activities of the vice president.

FUTURE DIRECTIONS

According to Vice President Gore's Office of Communication, the future directions of the OVP are confidential. Any plans that the vice president might have must remain undisclosed until such time as he is ready to make them public.

AGENCY RESOURCES

Probably the most complete information source about the work of the vice president is available from Al

Gore's home page at the White House's Web site: http://www.whitehouse.gov/WH/EOP/OVP/html/GORE_Home.html. For further information about the internal organization and functions of the OVP, contact the vice president's Press Office at (202) 456-7035.

AGENCY PUBLICATIONS

The OVP does not produce many publications; primarily it distributes press releases, prepared remarks, and media advisories, all of which are issued by the vice president. These works are available by accessing the vice president's Web site at http://www.whitehouse.gov/WH/EOP/OVP/html/GORE_Home.html, by mailing a request to Old Executive Office Building, Washington, DC 20501, or by phoning (202) 456-2326.

BIBLIOGRAPHY

A Heartbeat Away: Report of the Twentieth Century Fund Task Force on the Vice Presidency. New York: Twentieth Century Fund Press, 1989.

Broder, David S. "Elevating the Office: Gore Changes Role of No. 2 Spot." *The Washington Post*, 26 August 1996, p. A1.

Calmes, Jackie. "The Gore Guys: At His Ear, Young Chief of Staff, an Older Media Strategist and Lots of Lobbyists." *Wall Street Journal*, 13 February 1998, p. A16.

Feinberg, Barbara. *Next in Line: The American Vice Presidency*. New York: Franklin Watts Inc., 1996.

Goldstein, Joel K. *The Modern American Vice Presidency: the Transformation of a Political Institution*. Princeton, NJ: Princeton University Press, 1982.

Guide to the Presidency. Washington, D.C: Congressional Quarterly, 1996.

MacCann, Richard. *A New Vice Presidency for a New Century*. Iowa City: Image and Idea, Inc., 1991.

Natoli, Marie D. *American Prince, American Pauper: the Contemporary Vice Presidency in Perspective*. Westport, Conn.: Greenwood Press, 1985.

Simons, John. "How a Vice President Fills a Cyber-Cabinet: with Gore-Techs." *The Wall Street Journal*, 13 March 1998, p. A1.

Walch, Timothy, ed. *At the President's Side: the Vice Presidency in the Twentieth Century*. Columbia, Mo: University of Missouri Press, 1997.

Witcover, Jules. *Crapshoot: Rolling the Dice on the Vice Presidency: from Adams and Jefferson to Truman and Quayle*. New York: Crown, 1992.

Patent and Trademark Office (PTO)

PARENT ORGANIZATION: Department of Commerce
ESTABLISHED: 1802
EMPLOYEES: 5,900

Contact Information:

ADDRESS: 2121 Crystal Dr.
Arlington, VA 22202
PHONE: (703) 308–4357
TOLL FREE: (800) 786-9199
TDD (HEARING IMPAIRED): (703) 305–7785
FAX: (703) 305-7786
URL: http://www.uspto.gov
COMMISSIONER OF PATENTS AND TRADEMARKS:
Bruce Lehman
DEPUTY COMMISSIONER OF PATENTS AND TRADEMARKS: Lawrence Goffney

WHAT IS ITS MISSION?

The mission of the U.S. Patent and Trademark Office (PTO) is derived from the U.S. Constitution, which states that "Congress shall have the power . . . to promote the progress of science and the useful arts by securing for limited times to . . . inventors the exclusive right to their . . . discoveries." The PTO seeks to promote industrial and technological progress in the United States, and to strengthen the national economy, through three general activities: administering the laws relating to patents and trademarks; advising the secretary of commerce, the president, and the administration on patent, trademark, and copyright protection; and advising them on trade-related aspects of intellectual property.

HOW IS IT STRUCTURED?

The Patent and Trademark Office is one of 14 bureaus within the Department of Commerce. The Commissioner of Patents and Trademarks, a presidential appointee, also holds the administrative title of Assistant Secretary of Commerce. The Office of the Deputy Commissioner is an administrative office which deals with the various consulting boards and committees that help the PTO carry out its work. These include the Board of Patent Appeals and Interferences, the Office of Trademark Quality Review, and the Administrator for Legislative/International Affairs.

The main program work of the PTO is carried out in three organizational areas: the Office of the Associate Commissioner and Chief Financial Officer; the Patent

Office; and the Trademark Office. Most of the internal administrative work of the PTO is conducted by the Office of the Associate Commissioner and Chief Financial Officer. Internal functions such as budgeting, human resources, and public affairs, as well as the complex information dissemination function of the PTO, are carried out by offices in this area. The Center for Patent and Trademark Information and the Office of Electronic Information Products are under the supervision of this associate commissioner. The Patent Office conducts patent examinations, issues patents, and administers essential related issues such as patent policy, publication, and classification groups. The Patent Office also takes responsibility for structuring patent information in order to make it easily accessible to the public. The Trademark Office conducts trademark examinations, issues trademarks, and coordinates trademark program control.

The PTO's Information Office is responsible for designing and maintaining internal information processes—computer systems and databases—necessary for workers to examine and research patent and trademark applications, including computerized searches of "prior arts" and existing patents and trademarks. The PTO also uses another organizational area, the Non-Patent and Trademark Office Organizations, whose primary agency, the World Intellectual Property Organization, works to establish international policy and settle disputes concerning the use or abuse of intellectual property in the international community.

PRIMARY FUNCTIONS

A patent for an invention is a grant of property right by the government for the inventor—a right "to exclude others from making, using, or selling" the invention. The term of a patent is typically 17 years from the date the patent is granted, subject to the payment of maintenance fees.

A trademark is any word, name, symbol, or device which is used in trade to indicate the source or origin of goods and to distinguish them from the goods of others. If granted, trademark rights may be used to prevent others from using a confusingly similar mark but not to prevent others from making the same goods or from selling them under another mark.

The PTO provides incentives to invent, invest in, and disclose new technology through the examination and issuance of patents. It assists businesses in protecting their investments, promoting goods and services, and guarding against marketplace deception through the registration of trademarks. By distributing patent and trademark information to the public, the PTO promotes an understanding of intellectual property protection and facilitates the sharing of new technologies worldwide. Throughout all of its activities, the agency's goal is to foster a domestic and international climate in which intellectual property can thrive.

PROGRAMS

In spite of the vast information network structure required to carry them out, PTO program operations are fairly simple and are limited to three basic functions: conducting patent and trademark examinations, issuing patents and trademarks, and distributing patent and trademark information to the public. Nearly all of the PTO's programs are subordinate to these functions, and very few have official titles or names. Exceptions are the Patent and Trademark Depository Library Program, a nationwide network of libraries designated by the PTO to receive and house copies of U.S. patents and patent and trademark materials; and the Disclosure Document Program.

The Disclosure Document Program is a service provided by the PTO for accepting and preserving "disclosure documents" as evidence of the date of an invention's conception. A disclosure document, which describes the nature of the invention and a detailed description, is not a substitute for a patent application, but it may provide an inventor some defense if the invention is later alleged to have been the work of another party. Disclosure documents are kept in confidence by the PTO for a period of two years.

BUDGET INFORMATION

The PTO is an almost entirely self-supporting government agency. For its total budget of about $656 million, the PTO supplies most of its budget authority through patent, trademark, and related fee collections of nearly $630 million. A small amount, about $27 million, comes from congressional appropriations.

The budget is broken down into four areas. By far most of the PTO's expenses—about 75 percent—involve the patent process and its related activities. The trademark process accounts for a much smaller portion, about 11 percent. Nearly 9 percent is spent designing, maintaining, and evaluating the PTO's information dissemination program, and 6 percent is spent on the expert and executive direction and consultation that the office requires to carry out its work.

HISTORY

The Patent and Trademark Office is one of the oldest government agencies and perhaps one of the most unusual in its function. Protection for inventors was part of the debate at the Constitutional Convention, where delegates had a generalized fear of "monopolies" of the kind granted by European kings and queens. Yet the Founding Fathers realized that the granting of a limited patent would be of greater benefit to society at large than to the individual inventor. Not long before passage of the Patent

BUDGET:

Patent and Trademark Office

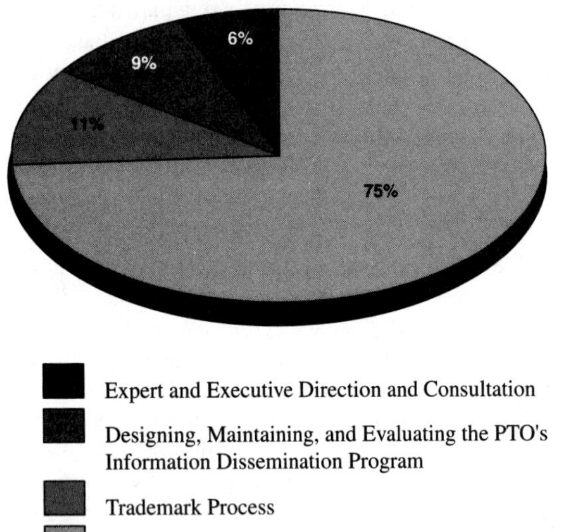

Expert and Executive Direction and Consultation

Designing, Maintaining, and Evaluating the PTO's Information Dissemination Program

Trademark Process

Patent Process and Related Activities

Act, President George Washington wrote Congress urging "encouragement to the exertion of skill and genius at home."

On April 10, 1790, President Washington signed the bill that laid the foundations of the modern U.S. patent system. Several weeks later, the first U.S. patent was granted to a Mr. Samuel Hopkins for an improvement in the "making of Pot ash and Pearl ash." The Patent Board at that time consisted of three cabinet members—Secretary of State Thomas Jefferson, Secretary of War Henry Knox, and Attorney General Edmund Randolph.

Establishing a Permanent Office

In 1802, a full-time Patent Office was created in the Department of State, and an 1836 reorganization of the office gave it a form and function that closely resembles the modern patent examination system. Inventors had to demonstrate three important criteria to expert patent examiners: the invention must be completely new; it must be useful; and it must be a genuine invention beyond what would have been obvious to an ordinary person with ordinary skill in the relevant technology. For a time, the Patent Office, already responsible for collecting and managing its patent documents, was charged with taking care of historic U.S. documents such as the Declaration of Independence.

In its first 80 years, the Patent Office issued more than 100,000 patents, but the years between 1870 and 1900 are considered perhaps the greatest period of invention in U.S. history. At the turn of the century, patent holders included Thomas Edison (light bulb, phonograph), Henry Ford (improved carburetors and motor cars), Alexander Graham Bell (telephone), Nikola Tesla (electric motor), and Rudolph Diesel (internal combustion engine). The Patent Office assumed official responsibility for recognizing trademarks in 1905.

Expanding Access

In the second half of the twentieth century, the Patent Office struggled to maintain control of its growing responsibilities. In order to provide access to patent information to those who could not search files at the Patent Office, patent depository libraries were established around the country. There were 78 such libraries in 1998. In 1925, the Patent Office was transferred to the Department of Commerce; and in 1930, a third category of patentable subjects was added to inventions and designs: hybrid or mutant plants.

In 1975, shortly after the one millionth trademark was registered in the United States, the name of the Patent Office was officially changed to the Patent and Trademark Office. The agency struggled under the pressure to handle and make available all of its records, especially after a 1980 congressional order to begin automating its search procedures to provide electronic access to the more than 27 million documents on record. This automation procedure is still being shaped and refined today.

The PTO made the announcement in 1987 that it would accept applications for patents on new types of animals produced by human intervention. The technologies of hybridization and genetic engineering used to produce these animals created significant nationwide debate, and the PTO's controversial decision was to set the tone for a still-to-be resolved question—whether the scientific discovery of human genetic material is, or should be, a patentable discovery.

As an agency that has literally been in existence since the establishment of the United States as an independent country, the PTO has grown from its original three cabinet officers to a staff of nearly 6,000 today. Its basic task—to reward the inventor of any new and useful process, machine, manufacture, or composition of matter through the grant of a patent—remains exactly the same.

CURRENT POLITICAL ISSUES

The U.S. patent system was designed as a trade-off between the stimulation of innovation and the obstacles that monopolies can create. Whether it has been effective has always been debated, especially in recent years when the United States has begun to bear very little resemblance to the country in which the patent system was established. Due to the technical nature of most contemporary advances in our society, most invention and innovation is accomplished by the well-funded research and development departments of defense industries, universities, and large corporations rather than by individual entrepreneurs. Independent inventors and small businesses often suffer a substantial disadvantage in using the patent system; in a legal battle over patent rights, they simply don't have the money to challenge the big corporations who are able to defeat them by outspending them in legal and attorney fees.

This imbalance of power in the patent system was shaken up in 1982. As a remedy for differing patent law interpretations in district courts around the country, a single U.S. Court of Appeals for the Federal Circuit was created. The new court was either a victory for the independent inventor or a further exertion of power by big companies. Opponents of the move claim that establishing a single court created a big-business environment in which large companies could simply shut down their competitors; but it is also true that the court has issued sizable awards to smaller companies. In 1996, a small Michigan office-furniture maker won $211.5 million in damages from industry giant Steelcase, Inc. over patents dating to the 1970s, and in 1997 a small manufacturer of magnetic resonance equipment, Fonar Corp., won $103 million in a suit against General Electric Co. As the PTO changes to keep pace with the development of new technologies, the conflict between these two traditional enemies—independent entrepreneurs and big business—is sure to continue.

Alexander Graham Bell on the telephone at the formal opening of telephone service between New York and Chicago in 1892. He received a patent for the telephone in 1876. *(U.S. National Aeronautics and Space Administration/NASA)*

Case Study: The 1997 Patents Bills

In 1997 two bills were making their way through Congress that would bring about profound changes in the way the Patent and Trademark Office does business. Backed by members of the industrial community, they proposed three major changes: to turn the PTO into a semi-independent government corporation still linked to the Commerce Department but freed from certain bureaucratic rules; to publish patent applications 18 months after they are filed; and to allow third parties to participate in reexaminations of patents. Each of these proposals was supported by sound reasoning, but each was also strongly opposed, for equally specific reasons, by independent inventors.

PTO Commissioner Bruce Lehman, a supporter of the bills, argued that in order to be able to adapt to an ever-changing business and technological environment, the PTO should be freed of some government rules that slow down changes such as layoffs, equipment acquisition, and organizational restructuring. Opponents argued that making the PTO into a government corporation and reducing government oversight would allow big companies to exercise an unfair influence over patent decisions.

At the time the bills were proposed, patent applications remained confidential until the patents were actually granted—a process that sometimes took years. Another provision of the 1997 bills would require that all applications be published 18 months after filing. The change was designed to help companies avoid investing in ideas for which there was already a patent pending; that year, a large biotechnology firm, Genentech, discovered it had wasted millions of dollars researching a project when a patent was granted to a competitor for a product similar to the one it was developing. The patent application had been on file for some time without Genentech's knowledge. Opponents to the 1997 bills argue that publishing patent applications early also exposes innovations to the public eye before a patent is granted and makes it easier for a large company to steal a patent or develop alternative technologies that would sidestep it.

A third provision of the bills was perhaps the one most obviously in favor of big business—to allow third parties to question a patent's validity. Under the provision, companies could ask patent officers to reexamine patents granted to others—and to participate in the review process to determine whether the patent should remain with the original patent holder. The provision constituted a cheap, effective way of weeding out bad patents, sup-

FAST FACTS

The PTO estimates that new patents are added to its records at a rate of 2,250 per week.

(Source: U.S. Patent and Trademark Office. "Mission and History," 1998.)

porters claimed, but critics charged that it was just one more way big business could squash small inventors.

Despite heavy opposition from independent inventors, the House of Representatives passed the patent bills in mid-1997. In the Senate, however, the bills faced continued delays. The Senate Judiciary Committee approved the bills, but the Senate itself took no action on them in 1997.

SUCCESSES AND FAILURES

The Patent and Trademark Office sets a high standard for customer service involving patent applications, trademark applications, and information requests. Numerous offices within the agency are assigned with improving customer satisfaction in different areas, and the PTO's efforts have been generally successful. With its extensive system of patent and trademark depository libraries, an increasingly automated electronic search structure, and a toll-free number available for inquiries, the PTO enjoys one of the highest rates of customer satisfaction among government agencies.

FUTURE DIRECTIONS

The PTO's 1997 Strategic Plan names five specific goals for the office as it approaches the twenty-first century: to reduce processing time to 12 months or less for all inventions; to more efficiently establish patent categories that reflect the complexity of developing technology; to receive applications and publish patents electronically; to exceed customers' quality expectations; and to charge fees that are fair with regard to resource utilization and customer efficiency.

The goal to receive applications and publish patents electronically involves the greatest degree of change within the PTO. Currently the office cannot electronically process patent applications, although it uses a vast computer information system to research them. Despite a limited budget, the PTO recognizes the need to stay current with developing technologies and the increasing demands placed on its processing system by customers. Once in place, an electronic application process will greatly reduce the number of personnel required to examine and issue patents.

AGENCY RESOURCES

General information and documents on the patent and trademark systems, products, services, facilities, and procedures of the Patent and Trademark Office are available to the public through the agency's General Information Services, which can be contacted by telephone at 1-800-786-9199.

The Center for Patent and Trademark Information provides and encourages public use of the PTO collections. Access and assistance are provided both at the PTO's Arlington, Virginia, facilities and through the nationwide network of patent and trademark depository libraries (PTDLs). The center provides expert reference assistance and computerized patent searching, including full-text databases of patents. The trademark database is available on CD-ROM, as are all PTO manuals, guides, and indexes. For more information, write the Center for Patent and Trademark Information, Crystal Park 3, Suite 461, U.S. Patent and Trademark Office, Washington, DC 20231.

AGENCY PUBLICATIONS

In addition to the manuals, guides, and indexes made available on its databases, the PTO publishes informational brochures such as "Basic Facts About Registering a Trademark" and "Basic Facts about Patents." Free copies of these brochures, along with the Patent and Trademark Office's newsletter, the *Official Gazette*, are available through General Information Services: 1-800-786-9199. Patent Office documents can also be found in government depository libraries. All law school libraries and most science libraries subscribe to patent materials.

BIBLIOGRAPHY

Barber, Hoyt L. *Copyrights, Patents & Trademarks*. New York: McGraw-Hill Corp., 1996.

Carey, John. "Rumble at the Patent Office." *Business Week*, 2 June 1997, pp. 142–43.

Chartrand, Sabra. "Self-Supporting Agency is Open for Business." *New York Times*, 20 November 1995, p. C2(N).

Dobyns, Kenneth W. *The Patent Office Pony: A History of the Early Patent Office*. Fredericksburg: Sergeant Kirkland's Museum and Historical Society, 1994.

From Lighthouses to Laserbeams: A History of the U.S. Department of Commerce. Washington, D.C.: U.S. Department of Commerce, Office of the Secretary, 1995.

Gruenwald, Juliana. "Bill to Revamp Patent System Dodges Foes in House." *Congressional Quarterly Weekly Report*, 19 April 1997, p. 911.

Marshall, Eliot. "Patent Office Faces 90-Year Backlog." *Science*, 3 May 1996, p. 643.

"Patent Leather: Is the U.S. Patent System Giving Small Business the Cold Shoulder?" *Entrepreneur*, April 1996, p. 18.

"Patents, Trademarks, Copyrights: Intellectual Property in a Global Economy." *Congressional Digest*, December 1996, p. 289.

Weber, Gustavus A. *The Patent Office: Its History, Activities, and Organization*. New York: AMS Press, Inc., 1980.

"What's Ahead in Patents and Trademarks? An Interview with Bruce Lehman." *Bulletin of the American Society for Information Science*, April/May 1995, pp. 26–29.

Peace Corps

PARENT ORGANIZATION: Independent
ESTABLISHED: March 1, 1961
EMPLOYEES: 700

Contact Information:

ADDRESS: 1990 K St. NW
Washington, DC 20526
PHONE: (202) 606-3886
TOLL FREE: (800) 424-8580
TDD (HEARING IMPAIRED): (202) 606-1313
FAX: (202) 606-3108
URL: http://www.peacecorps.gov
DIRECTOR: Mark Gearon

WHAT IS ITS MISSION?

The Peace Corps states that its mission is "to promote world peace and friendship by providing qualified volunteers to interested countries in need of trained manpower, by fostering a better understanding of Americans on the part of the people served and by fostering a better understanding of other people on the part of Americans." The Peace Corps promotes world peace and friendship by performing social and humanitarian services overseas and sharing experiences and cultures from other nations with Americans.

HOW IS IT STRUCTURED?

The Peace Corps is an independent agency within the executive branch of the federal government. The director of the Peace Corps is appointed by the president and confirmed by the Senate. The administrative offices of the Peace Corps include the Office of the Director, the Office of Communications, Human Resources, Volunteer Support, and Information Resource Management.

Program offices include the Private Sector Relations Office; the Domestic Programs Office; and the International Operations Office. Regional offices include Inter-America, Africa, Asia Pacific, and Europe, Central America, and Mediterranean. Peace Corps headquarters are in Washington, D.C. The Volunteer Recruitment and Selection Office has an administrative unit in Washington, D.C. and 12 field offices.

PRIMARY FUNCTIONS

The Peace Corps trains and furnishes volunteer personnel to aid developing countries on local projects at the request of host countries. Service areas include youth development, environment, education, economic development, health, water/sanitation, forestry, and business.

Volunteers participate in a rigorous selection process and complete a three- to four-month training period before being placed in a host country. Volunteers live in the community they serve and receive only living expenses and a small termination payment for their two years of service. After placement, volunteers determine projects based on local needs, in partnership with community residents and host-country officials. Members of the Peace Corps participate in an enormous range of beneficial activities. They help coordinate projects and, with the assistance of the home offices of the Peace Corps, garner the funds necessary to implement them. For example, in Bolivia, volunteers worked with the community of Chimeo to enhance the sanitary conditions of the town. Latrines, a garbage disposal collection system, and a burial project have all worked to substantially improve life in Chimeo.

The Peace Corps also aims to "bring the world back home" by coordinating domestic partner and education programs. Returning volunteers play a major role in sharing, publicizing, and continuing the Peace Corps experience throughout the United States. Many feel that participation was their greatest accomplishment and hope to share that feeling with others.

PROGRAMS

The Peace Corps International Program places more than 6,500 volunteers in 91 countries. Volunteers may teach English or agricultural methods, design and construct water purification and sanitation projects, organize health clinics, or coordinate reforestation projects.

The Peace Corps Fellows Program helps returning volunteers arrange for scholarships for master's degree programs while they teach or work in public health or community development.

World Wise Schools is a program that provides American teachers with materials to teach about other countries and cultures. American students may correspond with volunteers, and returned volunteers often visit schools. Books, slides, stories, and correspondence with people involved in Peace Corps projects are all part of the curriculum.

Through the Peace Corps Partnership Program, American individuals or groups are linked to a particular overseas project and raise funds to assist the project. The Gifts in Kind Program links specific Peace Corps project needs, such as books or computer equipment, with private-sector donations and contributions.

BUDGET:

Peace Corps

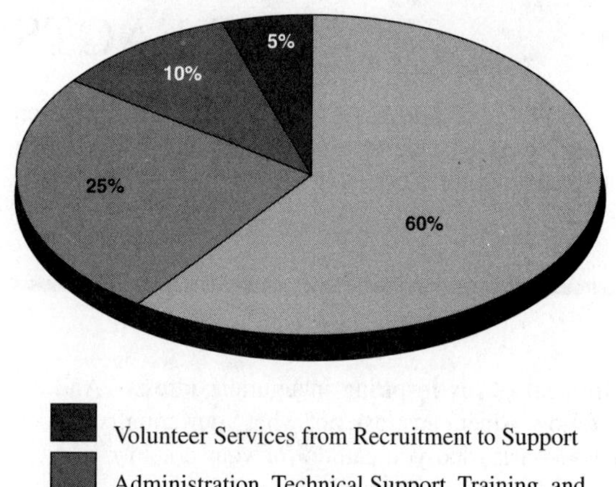

Volunteer Services from Recruitment to Support

Administration, Technical Support, Training, and Resources

Domestic Programs

International Programs, Field Offices, Pre- and In-Service Training, and Project and Volunteer Support

BUDGET INFORMATION

The budget for the Peace Corps is developed by the director of the Peace Corps and the president of the United States and is approved and allocated by Congress. The Peace Corps was budgeted $226 million in 1998. Approximately 60 percent of the Peace Corps budget funds the international programs, field offices, pre- and in-service training, and project and volunteer support. Domestic programs receive approximately 25 percent of total funds and volunteer services from recruitment to support, another 5 percent. The remaining funds are allocated to administration, technical support, training, and resources. Some limited funds and equipment for specific projects are contributed by the private sector.

HISTORY

On the evening of October 13, 1960, presidential hopeful John F. Kennedy gave a speech at the University of Michigan in Ann Arbor that first presented the Peace Corps to the public. It would be one of several concepts that the idealistic Kennedy would institute when he became president the following month. On March 1, 1961, the Peace Corps was established by President Kennedy in

FAST FACTS

In 1996, 133,000 Americans requested information on serving as a Peace Corps volunteer; of those, about 10,000 applied for 3,500 slots.

(Source: U.S. Newswire, February 28, 1997.)

fulfillment of his inspiring inaugural address: "And so, my fellow Americans: ask not what your country can do for you—ask what you can do for your country."

The initial years of the Peace Corps were a great success. Applicants to the program far outweighed those admitted. The first volunteers left for service in Ghana in August 1961, and by the end of 1961 Peace Corps programs were operating in 13 countries with 750 volunteers. The Peace Corps Partnership Program was started in 1964 to provide a link between U.S. contributors and requests for project assistance from the overseas communities in which Peace Corps volunteers serve. By 1966 membership had increased to 14,000 volunteers in 52 countries.

During the Vietnam War and the 1970s, however, both the public and Peace Corps volunteers grew disillusioned with U.S. foreign policy. Many of the volunteers expressed displeasure with standing as a symbol for the government when they disagreed with its involvement in Vietnam. Some countries hosting the Peace Corps volunteers saw them as representing the figure of an oppressive United States and created an unfriendly, hostile atmosphere toward the Peace Corps members stationed there.

From July 1971 through February 1982 the Peace Corps was part of ACTION, an independent umbrella agency within the executive branch of the government. In 1981 the Peace Corps was established as an independent agency. The difficulties that the Peace Corps faced continued when some host countries hostile to U.S. policies asked that volunteers be made to leave.

The Peace Corps Fellows program was created in 1985 to offer scholarships for graduate studies to returning volunteers in exchange for a two-year work commitment as teachers or in community service. World Wise Schools was launched in 1989 and over 550 schools participated in the unique education program by the end of the year.

The Peace Corps recovered from some of its woes of the 1970s and 1980s when President Bill Clinton took office in 1992. Clinton declared a recommitment to volunteer programs, and the Peace Corps benefited with an increased budget. Changing political climates in the 1990s made it possible for the Peace Corps to expand its frontiers to countries previously off-limit. For example, Peace Corps volunteers went to Hungary in 1989 to establish the first Peace Corps program in an Eastern European country. After the Soviet Union officially dissolved in 1991, programs were established in Lithuania, Estonia, and Latvia. In 1993 the first group of Peace Corps teachers left for China. In 1997 volunteers went for the first time to South Africa, formerly forbidden because of that country's stance on apartheid. President Clinton submitted a budget proposal to Congress to have the number of active volunteers in the Peace Corps reach 10,000 by 2000.

CURRENT POLITICAL ISSUES

Since the Peace Corps was conceived, its role in international relations has been the subject of partisan dispute. Some political administrations thought the Peace Corps was a vehicle to foster pro-American sentiment in host countries and strengthen political bonds with those countries. Others thought the Peace Corps was a form of American intervention or a way to exert political dominance and therefore should be abolished. Still others believed the corps to be a way to promote peace and understanding and struggled to maintain this role despite political pressure.

As the Peace Corps establishes programs in Eastern Europe and in countries created from the former Soviet Union, the debate over the Peace Corps is heating up again. The Peace Corps continues to provide its traditional agricultural and sanitation projects, but recent project requests focus on business and economic training. This new area of service has reopened the question of what is appropriate assistance and what is economic exploitation. Developing countries that wish to play a greater role in an increasingly global economy are anxious to learn how to establish and expand viable business systems. Yet many Peace Corps traditionalists believe that imitating American business practices may create hardships for average citizens by placing economic goals ahead of health and social needs. Local populations, whose support is the key to successful Peace Corps projects, are often resentful of volunteers and see them as fostering the business interests of a few individuals rather than addressing the needs of the community as a whole.

Case Study: Uzbekistan

When Communism collapsed, the Peace Corps moved quickly into the former Soviet empire. Uzbekistan was one of several former Soviet-bloc countries to receive members of the Peace Corps. However, from the outset of the agency's program there, things did not go very smoothly. Volunteers complained that they were stymied by a lack of books, office space, telephones, and computers. In Uzbekistan's male-dominated society, Peace Corps women were the targets of physical violence and lewd comments. Half of the volunteers sent to Uzbekistan left during the first year. Of the volunteers who remained, more than half were transferred from their original sites because of harassment by the local population.

The workers who did manage to weather the storm made an effort to improve their relationships with local citizens. To assist countries in meeting business needs for the global economy, volunteers helped develop business clubs and a chamber of commerce, created credit unions, and gave advice on marketing and bookkeeping. American and other foreign firms have established local affiliates, with the aid of Peace Corps volunteers, to provide personnel training, and advertising. Part of the strategy to improve the Peace Corps image and make its volunteers more acceptable in Uzbekistan was also to create more traditional projects. Volunteers taught in local schools and offered English classes. As part of the Peace Corps' new emphasis on services to women, sewing collectives and women's health clinics were established. Volunteers integrated themselves into the social and cultural activities of local communities, especially those outside the business world.

Public Impact

The events in Uzbekistan indicate the need for the Peace Corps to continue its traditional role while increasing services. Focusing on community needs while assisting specific sectors of the population is the balance that the Peace Corps must strike. Americans will continue to support the Peace Corps' mission as long as service is the goal as opposed to profit. Prospective volunteers must realize that a wide variety of skills will continue to be necessary in Peace Corps service.

Although a recent survey shows that 90 percent of Americans support the Peace Corps, there are many questions about its future role. Host countries have always requested Peace Corps volunteers for projects deemed important by local communities. Volunteers have brought their American education and skills to the countries they serve. Economics and the environment are growing global issues. How to bring together traditional service with modern needs through the Peace Corps will continue to be a topic for political debate.

SUCCESSES AND FAILURES

Thanks to the efforts of over 140,000 Peace Corps volunteers, 2.5 million acres of cropland are more productive and more than 14 million people worldwide have benefited from water, sanitation, and health programs. Five million people have learned English and tens of thousands of new small businesses have been launched.

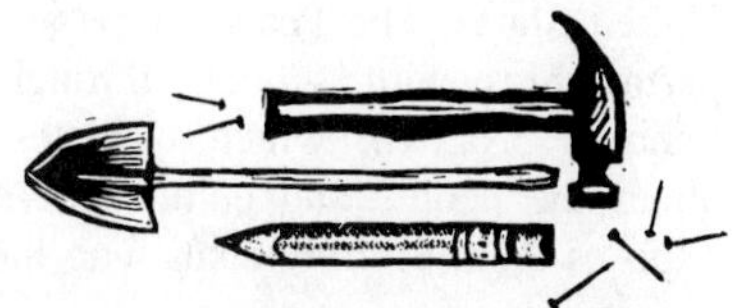

GET INVOLVED:

- The Peace Corps recruits young people from all over the United States to provide volunteer services in foreign countries. Most volunteers are college graduates, but some students with specialized skills are accepted without college degrees. Contact the Peace Corps at 1-800-424-8580 for information on volunteering and the recruitment office near you.
- Corcoran High School in New York annually designs, prints, and markets note cards in support of education related partnership programs operated by the Peace Corps. Contact the Peace Corps at 1-800-424-8580 for a list of current project requests. Develop a plan for your family, school, or church group to become part of the Peace Corps Partnership Program and raise funds for projects.
- World Wise Schools is a Peace Corps program designed to educate American students about cultures in other countries. Students may correspond with Peace Corps volunteers and the communities they serve in addition to classroom learning experiences. Contact the Peace Corps at 1-800-424-8580 for information on World Wise Schools and work with your teachers to bring the program to your school.

The Peace Corps continues to expand its sites and projects, establishing services for the first time in South Africa and Jordan. Previous Peace Corps hosts such as Chile and Ethiopia have reestablished relationships to address more advanced development issues.

In 1995 the Peace Corps branched out from its previous focus on long-term development projects and joined the International Rescue Committee in working with refugees and displaced persons. The Peace Corps concentrated on providing refugees with training in life-long skills such as farming techniques and environmental preservation. The Peace Corps has worked with refugees in Tanzania, Rwanda, and Burundi.

FUTURE DIRECTIONS

To prepare for the twenty-first century, the Peace Corps remains committed to youth development by recruiting and training young people throughout the

United States. The Peace Corps also plans to triple its partnerships with schools through the World Wise Schools program, which educates young Americans about the people and cultures of other countries and exposes them to individuals who have engaged in public service.

The Peace Corps will also expand its efforts to recruit experienced business people in response to growing requests for economic and financial expertise and guidance. The Gifts in Kind Program continues to try new avenues of approach to get private-sector businesses interested in contributing to various Peace Corps projects.

Programs that strengthen the role of women in the development of their countries will be funded through grants by the new Laret Miller Ruppe Fund for the Advancement of Women.

AGENCY RESOURCES

Information on volunteering, host countries, and domestic programs can be obtained by writing the Peace Corps in Washington, D.C., contacting the Peace Corps by calling 1-800-424-8580, or by accessing the Peace Corps' Internet site at http://www.peacecorps.gov.

AGENCY PUBLICATIONS

The Peace Corps publishes a variety of resource and technical materials, including profiles of nations the Peace Corps serves. Technical manuals available include: *Peace Corps Water/Sanitation Case Studies and Analyses*, *Freshwater Fisheries: Program Planning*, *Small Scale Beekeeping*, *Peace Corps Literacy Handbook*, and *Earning College Credit for your Peace Corps Service*. The primary source for Peace Corps publications is the Peace Corps Information Collection and Exchange (ICE), which can be accessed through the Internet at http://www.peacecorp/www/otaps/ice. ICE materials can also be obtained through the Educational Resources Information Clearinghouse (ERIC). Contact ERIC for a complete listing of materials and ordering information at 1-800-443-3742.

BIBLIOGRAPHY

Bron, Betsy. "The Handshake of Peace." *House Beautiful*, September 1995, p. 17.

Jarvis, Louise. "Two Managers Take Their Show on the Road." *Executive Female*, January-February 1996, p. 17.

Kent, Zachary. *The Story of the Peace Corps*. Chicago: Children's Press, 1990.

Perrin, Perry. "Cable From Kabul: Spartan Samaritan at Large." *Modern Maturity*, March-April 1997, p. 16.

Simon, Jon. "The Peace Corps: Travel, Adventure and Professional Opportunity." *Glamour*, January 1995, p. 78.

Watson, Bruce. "The New Peace Corps Steppes Out—In Kazakhstan." *Smithsonian*, August 1994, p. 26.

Weitsman, Madeline. *The Peace Corps*. New York: Chelsea House, 1989.

Zimmerman, Jonathan. "Beyond Double Consciousness: Black Peace Corps Volunteers in Africa, 1961-1971." *Journal of American History*, December 1995, p. 999.

Pension and Welfare Benefits Administration (PWBA)

PARENT ORGANIZATION: Department of Labor
ESTABLISHED: January 1986
EMPLOYEES: 667

Contact Information:

ADDRESS: 200 Constitution Ave. NW
Washington, DC 20210
PHONE: (202) 219-8776
FAX: (202) 219-5526
URL: http://www.dol.gov/dol/pwba
ASSISTANT SECRETARY: Berg Olena

WHAT IS ITS MISSION?

The mission of the Pension and Welfare Benefits Administration (PWBA) is to protect the large number of pension plans, health plans, and related employee benefit plans currently offered by businesses in the United States. More than 200 million people have money invested in privately funded pension plans, and these are governed by laws and statutes which the PWBA enforces.

HOW IS IT STRUCTURED?

The PWBA is a subcabinet agency in the executive branch. It falls under the Department of Labor (DOL) and is headed by an assistant secretary who is appointed by the president. Under the assistant secretary are two divisions, Policy and Program Operations. Within the Policy division is the Office of Policy and Research. In the Program Operations division, by far the larger division of the two, are the Offices of Chief Accountant (OCA), Enforcement (OE), Exemption Determinations (OED), Information Management, Program Planning Evaluation and Management, Program Services, and Regulations and Interpretations (ORI). In addition, a number of field offices throughout the country implement many of this division's programs.

PRIMARY FUNCTIONS

The PWBA educates the public on the laws governing pensions, which it also enforces. With so many

varying plans, the task of monitoring all PWBA programs and educating participants on pension laws and statutes is complex. The PWBA states that it "oversees approximately 700,000 pension plans with assets of more than $3 trillion and another 6 million plans involving other job benefits such as health and dental policies."

Three main pieces of legislation give the PWBA its mandate: the Employee Retirement Income Security Act of 1974 (ERISA), the Consolidated Omnibus Budget Reconciliation Act (COBRA), and the Health Insurance Portability and Accountability Act of 1996 (HIPAA). These laws are administered by a large national bureaucracy. For example, ERISA regulates pensions and other job benefit plans by private companies and unions, specifying what can and cannot be done in setting up and running a pension. To enforce this broad mandate, each office of the PWBA operates diverse programs to fulfill the diverse goals of ERISA. For example, the ORI develops the specific policies and regulations mandated by the general provisions of ERISA, and the OED helps pension providers determine if they are exempt from specific provisions of ERISA. The OCA uses outreach programs to help businesses prepare their yearly required annual reports. These programs deal primarily with the state societies of certified public accountants, which educate those who audit and provide accounting services for pension plans.

Together with other agencies such as the American Savings Education Council (ASEC), the PWBA educates the public about maintaining a stable personal financial plan through its publications and public awareness campaigns. Similarly, the OE investigates possible violations, such as mismanagement of pension plans, and publishes the *Enforcement Manual*, which details its investigation methods. The PWBA also publishes materials to inform the public of its rights under federal law and to assist individuals and businesses in understanding these laws.

The PWBA makes an effort to locate specific audiences that will benefit from its instruction, such as employers, unions, accountants, attorneys, and administrators. The PWBA also conducts research and provides analysis used for recommendations to Congress in developing future policy and legislation. Form 5500 annual reports, submitted by the businesses it polices, are a major tool in helping the PWBA track the many pension and benefit plans in operation.

PROGRAMS

The PWBA has two types of programs: those aimed at monitoring how current pension plans are run and those that seek to educate the public about the necessity of saving for retirement and the types of savings plans available. The PWBA states that it takes very seriously "the congressional finding in the introduction to ERISA 'that the continued well-being and security of millions of employees and their dependents are directly affected' by employee benefit plans and is committed to taking regulatory and enforcement actions that will be both protective of the interests of participants and beneficiaries and encourage the creation and growth of plan coverage."

One example of its commitment is a major nationwide program called the Retirement Savings Education Campaign, begun in July 1995, which addresses the PWBA's concern that not enough people are preparing adequately for their retirement. It was launched in conjunction with other public and private organizations as well as government agencies such as the Department of Treasury.

As part of this campaign, President Bill Clinton announced the Savings Are Vital to Everyone Retirement Act of 1997 (SAVER) to further promote education about the benefits of saving for retirement. The secretary of the DOL stated that the SAVER Act "will encourage employers to provide pension plans and help teach workers to plan and save adequately for retirement." The act incorporates public service announcements, public meetings, and other educational materials for publication and for the Internet. In addition, national summits have been and will be held to bring together participants and to discuss pension savings possibilities.

BUDGET INFORMATION

In 1996 the amount of money appropriated by Congress from the overall budget of the United States for the operation of the PWBA was $64 million. In 1997 the amount appropriated rose to $85.4 million. This money is spent in three main categories: enforcement and compliance; policy, regulations, and public services; and program oversight. Enforcement and compliance commands the largest portion of the budget, with $49 million in 1996 and an estimated $67 million in 1997. Policy, regulations, and public services is next with $11 million in 1996 and $14 million in 1997. Oversight of the programs required $4 million in 1996 and the same amount in 1997.

HISTORY

The history of the PWBA is that of legislation intended to prevent abuse and mismanagement of funds collected from employees in the private sector as part of pension and benefit plans, which were originally regulated by the Internal Revenue Service (IRS).

The Revenue Acts of 1921 and 1926 set some minimum standards. At that time employers were allowed to deduct pension contributions from corporate income and to accumulate profits in the pension funds tax-free. That money remained in those accounts and the contributing employees received no benefit or income until they retired. In order to qualify to run such a tax-free fund, which was clearly profitable to the company, employers had to meet two requirements: employees must receive at least a basic pension coverage from their contributions and employers must make sufficient contributions to the fund. The exact amount and minimum standards for employee coverage varied according to the company, plan, and work situation.

Most importantly, companies were not required to publicly disclose how these pension funds were being run. It was often kept secret, and as a result many incidents of abuse arose. Some employers mismanaged or stole from the accounts or invested them recklessly. Employees often did not discover that they had lost their retirement money until they retired. With the Revenue Act of 1942 the requirements for operating such funds were made stricter, and some initial steps were taken to require employers to disclose how they were operating their funds.

By 1959, with the passage of the Welfare and Pension Plans Disclosure Act (WPPDA), new standards were enacted, chiefly a new requirement that companies file full descriptions of their funds as well as yearly financial reports. This information was also required to be made available to the participating employees. As a result, the DOL was instructed to collect these financial reports, study them, and ensure that any cases of mismanagement or abuse were stopped. In 1962, the WPPDA was amended, and the DOL was given even broader jurisdiction to investigate any cases of fraud and then to take legal action in the courts against those at fault.

The PWBA as it is recognized today began with the enactment of the ERISA. The PWBA had been known as the Pension and Welfare Benefits Program within the DOL, but in January 1976, its name was changed to the PWBA, and the program was upgraded to an agency with appointed assistant secretary and deputy assistant secretary positions.

ERISA is the primary legislative mandate for the PWBA's actions today. Administration of the act is shared between the DOL, the IRS, and the Pension Benefit Guaranty Corporation (PBGC). In addition, new legislation has broadened even further the responsibilities of the PWBA. The Consolidated Omnibus Budget Reconciliation Act of 1985 (COBRA) and the Health Insurance Portability and Accountability Act of 1996 (HIPAA) incorporated specific health care benefits as part of ERISA and specified the minimum benefits that must be provided.

COBRA makes it possible for employees to keep their health insurance for a limited period of time after leaving a job. Sometimes employees cannot qualify for new insurance and would otherwise be left with no coverage at all. COBRA specifies how long these employees can keep their insurance and how much they must pay for it. The Newborns' and Mothers' Health Protection Act of 1996, prohibits group health plans from limiting the amount of time that newborn babies and their mothers can spend in the hospital and provides that they cannot be made to leave sooner than 48 hours after childbirth. Previously, some plans required women to leave the hospital before they were healthy enough to go in order to save money.

New legislation continues to be debated and passed in order to deal with constantly changing financial needs. However, in spite of political and economic fluctuations, the PWBA's primary goal remains the same: to protect privately funded pension plans in the United States.

BUDGET:

Pension and Welfare Benefits Administration

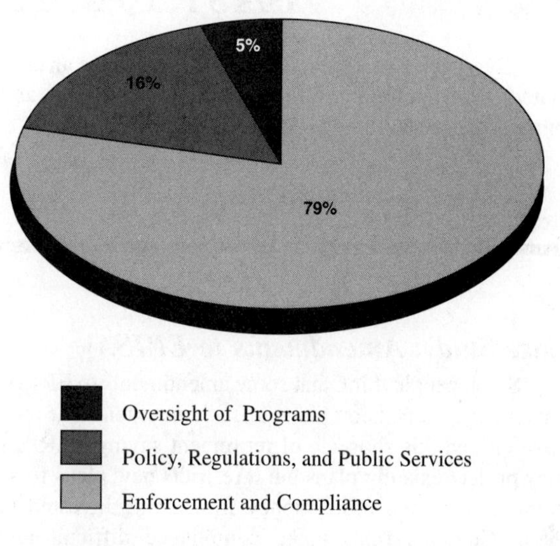

Oversight of Programs
Policy, Regulations, and Public Services
Enforcement and Compliance

CURRENT POLITICAL ISSUES

Most U.S. citizens are not saving enough money to support themselves when they retire. If social security expenditures continue at their 1990s rate, the system will either go bankrupt or simply not provide enough money to support future retirees. Although the PWBA was created to protect existing pension plans, such plans cannot support the upcoming surge of baby boomers who will reach retirement age in the twenty-first century. Ironically, ERISA may be partly to blame for this projected shortfall.

FAST FACTS

"Every payday, 18.5 million Americans have an estimated $747 million withheld from their wages and salaries and placed in 401(k) accounts."

(Source: John Greenwald. "Is Your 401(k) At Risk?" *Time,* December 11, 1995.)

Case Study: Amendments to ERISA

Some people think that some amendments to ERISA have restricted pension plans to such an extent that they have caused this shortage of retirement savings. ERISA may protect existing plans but it restricts new plans from being created and more money from being invested in them. Complex rules make compliance difficult and many plans could not operate successfully if they were to fully comply. For example, more than 600 pages of rules protect participants from discrimination that involve complex calculations for every person involved for every year, regardless of how large or small the plan. In addition, the Tax Equity and Fiscal Responsibility Act of 1982 reduced the maximum amount that can be contributed to certain plans and froze those maximum amounts despite continual cost of living increases.

Proponents, however, argue that the PWBA has done much to protect plans from being abused and mismanaged. Without the PWBA and ERISA, many people would have saved even less or perhaps lost their retirement money altogether through fraud and poor fund management. For example, ERISA has regulations to prevent pension plans from being too underfunded. Excess claims by employees in a given year for health or retirement benefits can deplete the fund, and the company must then reinvest the money or reallocate other funds to cover the plan. Severe underfunding could leave the company unable to pay employees their earned benefits. ERISA monitors plans and enforces regulations to protect against such underfunding.

Public Impact

The result of this controversy is that Congress is under pressure to enact further legislation to reduce the maze of regulations and to make it more profitable to save for retirement. The IRS will have to consider tax incentives and the social security system will need to be strengthened to handle the increased need. Unless remedies are found, lack of funds for retirement will put pressure on young workers to use their incomes to help support the nation's aging population as well as themselves. Continuing analysis is needed in order to keep up with the changing financial climate and the aging population.

FUTURE DIRECTIONS

The DOL hopes to develop a new, more efficient system for the processing of Form 5500, one of the PWBA's most important tools for keeping track of pension funds. Companies must submit a Form 5500 to the government each year explaining in detail the condition of the pension funds and benefit plans they operate, including their financial state, where and how assets are invested, and how the funds and plans are administered. With these reports, the PWBA can enforce the laws and prevent mismanagement. In 1997, the PWBA began searching for a contractor to help instigate and refine a new system. As of March 31, 1997, the PWBA also began addressing another major problem by cracking down on specific abuses of the 401(k) form. Some employers were found to have been illegally using pension plan contributions for their own benefit.

AGENCY RESOURCES

The PWBA can be found on the World Wide Web at http://www.dol.gov/dol/pwba/welcome.html. The national office can be reached by writing the U.S. Department of Labor, 200 Constitution Ave. NW, Washington, DC 20210 or by calling (202) 219-8771. Answers to technical questions can be obtained at (202) 219-8776. More information can also be obtained from the nearest regional office. For more information about the Retirement Savings Education Campaign or to obtain publications call 1-800-998-7542 or write to the U.S. Department of Labor, 200 Constitution Avenue NW, Room N-5656, Washington, DC 20210. To report abuses in the use of the 401(k), call 1-800-998-7542.

AGENCY PUBLICATIONS

The PWBA publishes a great many reports, brochures, booklets, and press releases which are available to the public. Some of the more popular titles are: "Top Ten Ways to Beat the Clock and Prepare for Retirement," "What You Should Know About Your Pension Rights," "Women and Pensions—What Women Need to Know and Do," "Protect Your Pension," and "Power to Choose." These and many other publications can be downloaded from the Web at http://www.dol.gov/dol/pwba/welcome.html, or can be obtained by calling the PWBA Brochure Request Line at 1-800-998-7542 or by contacting the nearest PWBA field office.

BIBLIOGRAPHY

"Are You Due A Pension?" *Consumer's Digest,* May 1997, pp. 18–9.

Barry, Brian. "Tick, Tock." *Economist,* 25 October 1997, pp. S10–S17.

Bierck, Richard. "Have You Misplaced a Fortune?" *McCall's,* August 1997.

Church, George J. "Robin Hood In Reverse." *Time,* 18 August 1997.

Donlan, Thomas G. "Editorial Commentary: Exposure Fear?" *Barron's,* 29 September 1997, p. 62.

"Four Steps Women Must Take To Retire Comfortably." *Money,* November 1997, p. 88.

Norton, Leslie P. "Worth the Trip?" *Barron's,* 6 October 1997, p. F8.

Rock, Andrea. "Protect Yourself From America's Flawed Pension Plans." *Money,* December 1997, pp. 150–64.

Scott, Sarah. "More Risk, Higher Rewards?" *Maclean's,* 29 September 1997, pp. 46–8.

Smalhout, James H. "Editorial Commentary: Pension Plans From Hell." *Barron's,* 18 August 1997, p. 46.

Pension Benefit Guaranty Corporation (PBGC)

PARENT ORGANIZATION: Independent
ESTABLISHED: 1974
EMPLOYEES: 750

Contact Information:

ADDRESS: 1200 K St. NW
Washington, DC 20005
PHONE: (202) 326-4000
TDD (HEARING IMPAIRED): (800) 877-8339
FAX: (202) 326-4042
URL: http://www.pbgc.gov
EXECUTIVE DIRECTOR: David M. Strauss

WHAT IS ITS MISSION?

The mission of the Pension Benefit Guaranty Corporation (PBGC) is to protect the pensions of Americans whose private sector (nongovernment) corporations are premium-paying members in defined benefit pension plans. A defined pension program is one in which the employer allocates funds for retirement based on years of service and a stated dollar amount or salary history. These programs differ from self-directed financial programs such as a 401(k) plan or IRA. The goal of this mission is to ensure that pension plans continue and are maintained, provide protection to existing plans, and make certain that if a plan fails, timely payments are made to the pensioners.

HOW IS IT STRUCTURED?

The PBGC is a self-financing independent corporation owned and operated by the U.S. government. Congress created the corporation under Title IV of the Employee Retirement Income Security Act (ERISA) of 1974. The PBGC is governed by a board of directors headed by the secretary of labor that includes the secretaries of commerce and treasury. A seven-member advisory committee appointed by the president, two labor leaders, two business representatives, and three members of the public, advises to the board on pension-related matters. The role of the advisory board is to ensure that labor, management, and the general public's interests are represented in all decisions made by the board. The PBGC works as an insurance company to make certain that its members' pension plans are strong and able to meet their obligations. When they fail, the PBGC makes certain that pension recipients still get some of the pensions owed them by their parent company. Employees of the PBGC review cases, make recommendations, examine plans for possible failures, act as advocates for pensioners to make sure that their pensions are paid, and administer two insurance programs.

PRIMARY FUNCTIONS

The PBGC insures most private-sector defined benefit pension plans that provide a pension benefit to employees based on age, years of service, and salary. The PBGC does not cover such plans as the 401(k), which are described as defined contribution pension plans and are part of a profit-sharing retirement plan. It provides uninterrupted pension income to participants whose companies have paid premiums if the company's pension plan or the company itself fails.

The PBGC also sells insurance to companies that have defined pension plans to ensure that the pensions that companies promise their employees are safe, up to certain legal limits, and will be paid, even if the company itself fails. In case of bankruptcy, the PBGC takes the plan over, administers it, and makes pension payments to recipients based on how much insurance the company bought from the PBGC. To take over a pension plan, the PBGC is notified by the employer that the plan is in trouble or that the employer is going bankrupt. It then steps in and insures the pension plan. By law, the PBGC can publish rules for the reporting of underfunded plans and other issues that are important to the well-being of the U.S. pension system. The PBGC conducts surveys, issues publications, opinion letters and rulings, closely monitors the performance of shaky plans, and educates employers on how to maintain their plans.

PROGRAMS

The PBGC separately administers two insurance programs covering single-employer and multi-employer plans.

Single Employer Program

Under the Single Employer Program (SEP), when a company closes its pension plan using either a standard termination or a distress termination procedure, the PBGC steps in to ensure that the pensions promised to retirees are paid. The single-employer program protects about 33 million participants in nearly 48,000 pension plans.

A standard termination occurs when a pension plan has enough money to pay all the benefits it has promised, both vested and nonvested, before the plan is allowed to end. The company purchases an annuity from an insurance company, or it offers a lump-sum payment to everyone who has participated in the plan. Once all the money has been paid, the PBGC's guarantee is ended.

A distress termination happens when the employer can prove through a series of stringent criteria that if the pension program continues, the resulting financial crisis to the company could cause severe financial crisis and distress (that is, the company could shut down if it had to continue its pension program). If the distressed company does not have enough funding to pay even the PBGC guaranteed benefits, then the PBGC uses its own funds to make certain that entitled employees and those persons already receiving benefits get at least the amount the corporation covers. Even when most of the employees' benefits are paid, however, the amount the covered individual expects and what the PBGC can pay, as dictated by law, may differ. Since companies are required by law to have enough funds to pay for their plans, the PBGC tries to recover any funds it pays out from these companies.

The PBGC may close a plan without the employer's consent to protect the interests of plan participants, the plan itself, or of the PBGC—such as when a plan cannot pay current benefits. The amount that the SEP pays to pensions is usually less than the original pension plan dictated, and its payments are limited by law. In 1997 that amount could not exceed $2,642.05 per month per person age 65 or older.

Multi-Employer Plans Program

Multi-Employer Plans (MEP) are maintained under collective bargaining agreements involving unrelated companies, generally in the same industry, that offer the same benefits to employees. These MEPs cover 8.5 million workers in about 2,000 plans. If a multi-employer plan insured by the PBGC is in trouble and cannot pay its guaranteed benefits, the PBGC bails the program out by providing financial assistance, usually in the form of a loan. In 1997 this loan rate meant that the PBGC paid recipients up to $16.25 a month per year of credited service—that is, the PBGC would pay a person who had worked for 30 years at a company covered by the MEP $487.50 per month.

BUDGET INFORMATION

The PBGC annual budget was $1.1 billion for 1998. This figure includes $982 million for benefit payments to participants in single-employer plans, $6 million for multi-employer financial assistance, and $148 million for operating expenses. The PBGC is not supported by any general tax revenues but is fully supported by the premiums paid each month by its insured companies, which are set by Congress. In 1997 premiums were $19 per employee each month for single-payer participants and $2.60 for multi-payer participants. According to the *1996*

FAST FACTS

According to a survey conducted by the PBGC, 13.7 percent of pension participants are being underpaid.

(Source: *Los Angeles Times,* June 15, 1997, sec. A p. 1.)

Annual Report, the single employer program had a year-end surplus of $869 million for the first time in its history, and the MEP had a surplus of $124 million.

HISTORY

Since 1974, when Congress enacted the Employee Retirement Income Security Act of 1974 (ERISA), the Pension Benefit Guaranty Corporation (PBGC) has been the government's primary means of ensuring pension benefit payments to private sector employees who are in a defined pension program. Before 1974 there was no real government guarantee of pension payment for private sector employees. An employer could arbitrarily end costly plans, and no one had any way of getting retirement benefits. From 1974 to 1996, according to testimony before Congress, the PBGC paid benefits to 480,000 individuals as a result of 2,410 pension plan failures. In addition, the PBGC protected the benefits of more than 42 million workers in 50,000 ongoing pension plans, and each month the PBGC paid over $65 million to retirees.

Pension plans may end because: (1) the employer is having financial problems and can no longer support the plan; (2) the plan has enough money to pay all promised benefits and the employer wants to end it; or (3) the plan's funds are inadequate to pay participants, and the PBGC decides to end it in order to protect the interests of participants or PBGC. Due to the number of bailouts it has provided over the years, the PBGC operates mainly in the red.

Throughout its history the PBGC has fought to establish secure financial solvency. Throughout the 1980s and early 1990s there were concerns in Congress that the PBGC would become a liability to the government on the order of the savings and loan debacle that ended up costing each taxpayer between $5,000 and $10,000. In 1992 the *New York Times* voiced these fears with the headline "U.S. Pension Agency is in Deep Trouble, Economists Warn—A Bail Out May Be Needed." In 1993 the agency was operating its single employer plan at a long-term deficit of $2.9 billion.

Through a combination of luck, solid financial management that corrected costly management mistakes, and good investments, by the middle of 1996 the PBGC was showing a significant surplus for the first time since its inception—$869 million from single-employer program members and $124 million from multi-employer program members. With these funds the PBGC began an aggressive campaign to enroll more companies and their pension plans into the insurance program.

CURRENT POLITICAL ISSUES

One of the main criticisms of the PBGC is the way it pays its benefits and attempts to recover what it considers overpayments. Critics believe that the program shortchanges recipients by paying only a fraction of the benefits they were originally owed. Since the PBGC guarantees a limited portion of an original pension, it may not pay all the other benefits promised by the company or even the amount that the employee expected or was actually receiving.

Case Study: Pan Am Flight 103

After Pan American World Airways (Pan Am) Flight 103 was destroyed by terrorists in Lockerbie, Scotland, in December 1988, the widow of slain flight engineer Jerry Avritt began receiving a $1,322 monthly pension benefit as his survivor. According to an October 19, 1997, *Newsday* article, this pension amount was paid from early 1989 until May 1997, when it was suddenly cut by $500 a month.

Judith Avritt's benefits had been suddenly halved because in 1991, Pan Am Airlines went bankrupt, throwing thousands of people out of work—8,000 in New York City alone—and revealing in the process that its pension plan was underfunded by $900 million. Pan Am's was the largest deficit that the PBGC ever had to administer. Generally the pension plan paid the same benefits to recipients at the rate that they were receiving while the company was still solvent. Some of the peripheral benefits, such as health care plans, were stopped at once, but the monthly checks remained the same until the PBGC adjusted the monthly payments six years later to rates they considered appropriate. Therefore, many pensions paid to retirees and survivors were adjusted downward to reflect compliance with the amount the PBGC could pay according to the legally established limits. The PBGC had also adjusted the monthly checks to recover overpayments to beneficiaries such as Mrs. Avritt. Retirees, legislators, and advocacy groups agitated for a congressional investigation of the PBGC and many called for it to be dissolved.

The problems with Pan Am reflect the difficulties that the PBGC faced in trying to equitably calculate pensions for employees of bankrupt companies. In 1992 the Government Accounting Office (GAO) found the PBGC a "high risk" agency with vast deficits and poor management. After the deficit problem was corrected by raising premiums paid to the agency, the claims of mismanagement and slow settlement of claims still abounded. Not only was Mrs. Avritt affected by the slow time it took for PBGC to settle the Pan Am affair, but other widows of flight engineers were hurt as well. A 66-year-old widow of another flight engineer, who was living on a fixed income and dependent on her pension check, was sent a bill for $7,600 that the PBGC claimed was overpaid to her husband before he died.

The PBGC claims that the reason Mrs. Avritt's pension was reduced was because she was in her forties when it began. Because she was the widow of a flight engineer scheduled to receive a higher pension amount than the legal limit the adjustment had to be made because the PBGC doesn't cover all the benefits promised to higher-level employees. Mrs. Avritt has sued the PBGC to reinstate the pension. She claims that she called to have the cuts explained to her and never received an answer. The PBGC stated that it had no record of her call.

Mrs. Avritt's problems with the PBGC reflect the overall difficulties the agency faces with Pan Am's former employees and retirees. In 1996 the Association of Former Pan Am Employees filed a class action suit against the agency demanding that it be removed as the pension trustee for the 46,000 persons who lost their jobs when Pan Am went bankrupt. The case charged that the corporation "inordinately delayed rendering final benefit determinations" and that the PBGC was granting smaller pensions than Pan Am would have given. "I don't think I should be penalized because the company went out of business" Bernard Meltzer told *Newsday* (November 23, 1997), reflecting the sentiments of many former employees whose benefits were halved. By November 1997, a federal judge had ruled that the association had every right to sue the PBGC to ensure that their future pensions were fairly paid.

FUTURE DIRECTIONS

Although intended as a benevolent safety net, the PBGC still suffers from lack of public trust. While many have benefited from its programs and received some of the money they anticipated upon retirement, many, including legislators, feel that the PBGC must reestablish itself in regard to underfunded pensions so that retirees and others contributing to a company can be assured a full and equitable pension upon retirement, even if the originating company no longer exists.

The PBGC plans to tighten controls and ensure that pension funds in the United States are fully funded by increasing its premiums; a national survey by the agency discovered that 13 percent of funds are underfunded. The stated goals of the agency are to protect existing defined benefit plans and their participants, and encourage new plans; provide high-quality services and accurate and timely payment of benefits to participants; strengthen financial programs and systems to keep the pension insurance system solvent; and improve internal management support operations.

AGENCY RESOURCES

Information about the Pension Benefit Guaranty Corporation can be obtained by contacting PBGC headquarters at (202) 326-4000, or by writing them at 1200 K St. NW, Washington D.C. 20005. PBGC also has a Web site at http://www.pbgc.gov that offers information about its programs, employee rights, employer rights and responsibilities, as well as a search engine for those who want to know if they are entitled to a pension.

AGENCY PUBLICATIONS

PBGC publications include *Your Guaranteed Pension, Your Pension, Things You Should Know About Your Pension Plan, Divorce Orders and PBGC*, and the *Pension Insurance Data Book 1996*. These books can be obtained by writing: 1200 K St. NW, Washington DC 20005 or viewed on-line at http://www.pbgc.gov.

BIBLIOGRAPHY

Carter, Craig C. "Politics and Policy: Patching the Holes in the Pension Safety Net." *Fortune*, 28 October 1985, p. 117.

"Federal Judge Ruling Allows Go Ahead for Pan Am Pension Suit." *Business Wire*, 2 December 1997.

Fresco, Robert. "The Vanishing Pension." *Newsday*, 19 October 1997, p. F08.

"Gap Growing for 50 Worst Underfunded Pension Plans." *Newsday*, 23 November 1995, p. 30.

"Grassley: PBGC Will Change its Policy on Permanently Reducing Pensions." *Capitol Hill Press Releases*, 3 November, 1997.

"Grey Area: American Pensions." *The Economist*, 3 June 1995, p. 71.

Hylton, Richard D. "Money and Markets: Don't Panic About Your Pension—Yet." *Fortune*, 18 April 1994, p. 121.

Reynolds, Larry. "White House Plan for Pension Reform Could Prove Costly for Employers." *HR News*, 1 August 1994, p. 1.

Rosenblatt, Robert A. "13% Underpaid on Pensions, U.S. Audit Finds." *Los Angeles Times*, 15 June 1997, p. A1.

Rowland, Mary. "A Threat to Defined-Benefit Plans." *Nation's Business*, 1 June 1995, p. 64.

Tumulty, Brian. "Nation's Underfunded Pensions Grew to $71 Billion in 1993." Gannett News Service, 5 December 1994.

Postal Rate Commission (PRC)

PARENT ORGANIZATION: Independent
ESTABLISHED: August 1, 1970
EMPLOYEES: 45

Contact Information:

ADDRESS: 1333 H St. NW, Ste. 300
Washington, DC 20268
PHONE: (202) 789-6800
FAX: (202) 789-6861
E-MAIL: prc-admin@prc.gov
URL: http://www.prc.gov
CHAIRMAN: Edward J. Gleiman

WHAT IS ITS MISSION?

The primary mission of the Postal Rate Commission (PRC) is to oversee the rate-making and classification activity of the U.S. Postal Service (USPS). As Edward J. Gleiman, the chairman of the PRC, testified before the House Subcommittee on the Postal Service Committee on Government Reform and Oversight on March 2, 1995, the Postal Rate Commission "was created to prevent the unfair exploitation afforded the Postal Service under the Private Express Statutes, a monopoly that applies to more than 80 percent of domestic mail volume." The PRC, through its Office of the Consumer Advocate, also has the mission to protect the interests of the general public in all hearings and to represent the public in complaints that Postal Service rates or services do not meet the requirements of the Postal Reorganization Act of 1970.

HOW IS IT STRUCTURED?

The Postal Rate Commission is an independent agency in the executive branch of the U.S. government. The commission consists of five members nominated by the president and confirmed by the Senate. No more than three commissioners may be members of one political party. The president names one of the five commissioners as chairman. The chairman is the chief executive and administrator of the PRC. Once a year the PRC meets and elects a vice chairman from among its members.

Under the chairman are four other PRC components: the Administrative Office; the Office of the General Counsel; the Office of Rates, Analysis, and Planning; and the Office of the Consumer Advocate. In addition to other duties, the consumer advocate represents the interests of the general public at all PRC hearings. The Office of Rates, Analysis, and Planning collects and analyzes relevant data to aid the commissioners in reaching decisions.

PRIMARY FUNCTIONS

The Postal Rate Commission's responsibilities fall into four broad areas. First and foremost, it investigates and makes recommendations to the USPS Board of Governors regarding postal rate and classification changes. Second, it investigates complaints that are national in scope regarding postal rates, fees, and mail service and classification and makes recommendations to the USPS governors based on its findings. Third, it reviews changes in available postal service, in particular complaints about USPS decisions to consolidate or close post offices. Finally, it issues advisory opinions to the USPS governors upon request and on occasion prepares reports on special issues when requested to do so by Congress.

The PRC's primary function is the setting of postal rates. Proceedings begin when the USPS governors formally request a rate change. Following the notice of hearings, which is published in the *Federal Register*, is a "discovery period" when the PRC collects written testimony, first from the Postal Service, and then from other intervenors—organizations and individuals who will be affected by the change in question. Typical intervenors are professional societies for publishers, mail order companies, direct marketing companies, financial institutions, shippers, and labor unions. Then a hearing or series of hearings are held so all intervenors can be questioned orally. After the hearings the PRC holds a "briefing period" during which it considers the evidence and testimony it has collected and prepares a detailed finding called the "recommended decision." The decision is then transmitted to the USPS Board of Governors.

The PRC is required by law to present a decision within 10 months of receiving a rate request from the USPS. In coming to a decision, it considers a number of different factors: whether the proposed change is "fair and equitable" to all parties; whether the mail affected will recover its own costs; how USPS operating costs are distributed over different types of mail; whether the Postal Service will be able to operate and "break even." The criteria are dictated by the law that created the PRC and the USPS, and there is a great deal of controversy over how they are to be applied.

The Board of Governors of the Postal Service can either accept or reject the PRC's recommended decision. If it accepts it, the change is implemented. If it rejects it, the question goes back to the PRC for reconsideration and the process essentially starts all over. The 11 governors of the Postal Service can modify the recommendation of some PRC decisions by unanimous vote. The PRC follows essentially these same procedures in considering other questions, such as classification changes, post office closures, and complaints.

PROGRAMS

Because of the highly specialized nature of the mission of the Postal Rate Commission—to offer qualified opinions on rate and classification changes proposed by the Postal Service—it does not administer public or interdepartmental programs in the way that many other government agencies do. The PRC area closest to a classical government program, however, is its ombudsman, the Office of the Consumer Advocate.

The Office of the Consumer Advocate (OCA) serves as a watchdog for the interests of the general public whenever the PRC considers an issue. The OCA participates in all PRC cases: rate changes, classification changes, and complaints. Complaints are heard when a group or individual believes a rate, classification, or service change that has been made does not conform to the requirements of the law. Post office closings or reductions in local service are often the subjects of complaint cases.

Before every hearing one member of the OCA staff is named officer of the commission and acts as recording secretary, making sure a complete and accurate record of the proceedings is kept. More important, the officer presents arguments on behalf of the general public that might not be voiced by the many special interest groups that normally make up the intervenors—groups like banks, magazine publishers, and mail order companies. The officer is entitled to question all witnesses, including Postal Service representatives, at hearings. In addition to appearing at hearings, the OCA helps individuals prepare presentations they wish to make before the PRC.

The OCA also makes its own proposals, independent of requests from the USPS. For example, the OCA formulated two proposals in 1990 that suggested making it possible for individuals to lower their postal rates by preparing their non-bulk mail so that it was compatible with the USPS automated sorting equipment. When the OCA develops such a proposal, it goes through nearly the same process before the PRC as a rate change request from the USPS would.

The OCA provides additional services to the public. Its Informal Assistance service aids members of the public interested in making presentations in PRC rate, classification, or complaint hearings. In addition to providing information on arranging such a presentation, the OCA will assist with its actual preparation. The OCA has established an electronic bulletin board that provides public access 24 hours a day to PRC decisions, notices, and opinions.

FAST FACTS

From 1900 to 1967 first-class postage rose only four cents—from two cents to six cents. From 1971 to 1998 postage rose 24 cents—from eight cents to 32 cents.

(Source: Postal Rate Commission. "Fact File," 1998.)

BUDGET INFORMATION

The PRC's total budget for 1998 was $6.5 million. This money is used to pay commissioners, whose positions are full-time, PRC staff salaries, and administrative costs. The money is appropriated annually as part of the United States Postal Service budget.

HISTORY

The PRC was created by the Postal Reorganization Act of 1970. The law defined the agency's primary responsibilities as reviewing postal rate and mail classification changes requested by the U.S. Postal Service, which was formed by the same statute. The PRC was to weigh the merits of the proposed changes and issue recommendations to the USPS. Postal rates had previously been set by Congress. The PRC was created based on the model provided by other regulatory commissions that establish rate structures for public utilities, like gas and electric companies. The model was considered appropriate because the Postal Service, like many utilities, had a statutory monopoly on certain services.

Under the terms of the Postal Reorganization Act, the PRC was required to deliver decisions within three months of its receipt of a request from the USPS governors. Its first rate case, in 1971, however, took 18 months to complete. The next two cases, a classification request and a rate request, had been under consideration for more than six months each—with no outcome in sight—in 1974, when hearings on postal organization were held in the U.S. House of Representatives. PRC officials described to the Committee on the Post Office and Civil Service their difficulties interpreting the parameters of the new law and implementing it. Delays were also ascribed in part to lack of continuity in leadership at the PRC: despite their six-year terms, not a single original commissioner remained after the agency's first three years. But, most critically, commissioners pointed to the time-consuming process of collecting data and testimony that was involved in every case. In 1976 the Postal Reorganization Act was amended to give the PRC 10 months to submit recommended decisions to the Postal Service.

The amended act also gave the PRC authority to review the closing of small-town and rural post offices when a formal complaint is made. In 1980 the PRC published a report entitled *At the Crossroads,* which described the important role post offices play in the life of small communities. Coming just a few years after a General Accounting Office report detailed the money that could be saved if the Postal Service phased out many unprofitable small post offices, *At the Crossroads* seemed to signal that the PRC would make it difficult for the Postal Service to carry out such closures. However, the PRC has supported most of the closures it has reviewed. In 1995 it also approved a rate increase on post office boxes that hit small-town post offices particularly hard.

In the 1980s and 1990s the relationship between the PRC and the USPS was often rocky. The Postal Service maintained that PRC practices sometimes interfered with the prerogatives of USPS management—for example, when the PRC changed rate requests or redistributed them across various classes of mail. The Postal Service also complained about the long rate-making process which, it said, made it difficult to adapt quickly in its competitive market. In 1994 Postmaster General Marvin Runyon asked Congress to pass legislation that would give the USPS much more freedom in setting postal rates and cut PRC power. He was unable or unwilling to present a concrete proposal, however, and the idea quickly died.

For its part, the PRC was often critical of USPS accounting procedures. The PRC has been publicly critical of Postal Service spending practices, which the PRC terms wasteful. In general, though, the PRC gives USPS the rate increases it asks for; they are sometimes less, sometimes more, and sometimes the PRC shifts increases from one type of mail to another. The Postal Service has rarely protested a recommendation of the Rate Commission.

CURRENT POLITICAL ISSUES

When the Postal Reorganization Act of 1970 created the USPS and the PRC, it created two agencies with very different perspectives on postal service in the United States. The Postal Service was set up as an independent "federal corporation" that, like any private corporation, was expected to support itself financially. The PRC, on the other hand, was set up as a watchdog to keep postal prices fair to the public and to business customers. Turning a profit became the prime motivation for the Postal Service, whereas the Rate Commission's goal was to make the Postal Service justify the prices it wanted to charge in strict cost-analysis terms. These very different interests have led to conflict and, at times, outright animosity between the two agencies.

Case Study: PRC vs. USPS

At its root, the disagreement between the Postal Service and the PRC revolves around how the Postal Service's operational costs should be distributed over different types of mail. The Postal Reorganization Act of 1970 stipulated certain criteria for postal rates: rates had to be fair and equitable; the postage charged for each type of mail had to cover all the costs related directly to that type of mail, plus a portion of other Postal Service costs; and the cost of postage had to reflect the value of the mail service to the sender and the recipient. Conflict arose when the Postal Service sent rate increase requests to the PRC based on market demand and the PRC changed or rejected them on the grounds that the proposed change increased the rate for one or another mail classification disproportionately. Court decisions in the late 1970s seemed to favor the PRC's interpretation.

Disagreement continued during the 1980s. In the early 1990s, a joint PRC-USPS commission on rate-making was formed. The body was unable to work out a compromise before USPS participation was shelved by Postmaster General Marvin Runyon, who was focusing efforts on reorganizing the USPS itself. Runyon continued to complain about the PRC's approach to postal rates. He maintained that many of the PRC's actions interfered in decisions that more properly belonged to USPS management. He claimed also that the lengthy rate-making process virtually handcuffed the Postal Service in its efforts to do business effectively in the increasingly competitive parcel delivery market. Other businesses could react in a day's time when prices changed in that market; the Postal Service was often forced to wait nearly a year.

The PRC, for its part, stated that the quality of information provided by the Postal Service in rate cases was often poor, and that this was in part responsible for the length of some cases. The USPS also tended to misinterpret data when calculating its rate increase proposals, according to the PRC. For example, when the USPS requested a 10 percent rate increase for Priority Mail, intervenors pointed out that there was no evidence in the Postal Service accounting that could justify the increase. It would have placed an unfair cost burden on the users of this mail class. The PRC looked at the data and agreed. It recommended a 5 percent increase.

By 1994 the battle was heating up between the two agencies. Runyon was demanding increased rate-making power for USPS if it was to survive in the era of faxes and E-mail. Rate commissioners were unsympathetic and publicly lambasted the Postal Service for being "extremely wasteful with the American people's money," as Vice Chairman William LeBlanc told the *Washington Post.*

It reached a head in 1995 when Postmaster General Runyon asked Congress to give the Postal Service greater control over rate-making. In April 1996, Senator Ted Stevens of Alaska announced he was going to introduce reform legislation, but lack of interest in postal matters coupled with outright hostility toward reform made him back off soon afterwards. Stevens's retreat was seen as a defeat for Runyon, but two months later, in June, Rep. John McHugh (R-N.Y.) announced he was going to present a postal reform bill to the House.

McHugh's bill gave broader rate-making authority to the Postal Service, but it would have reined the USPS in as well, creating a postal inspector general to oversee the agency's operations. Additionally, the bill would have eliminated, on a test basis, the USPS monopoly on letters by suspending the laws known as the Private Express Statutes, which give the USPS the sole right to deliver normal first-class letter mail (exceptions being mail that gets special handling, like overnight delivery by Federal Express). The repeal of the Private Express Statutes would give companies like United Parcel Service (UPS) and Federal Express (FedEx) the right to deliver all first-class mail, in particular things like bills and letters, all the mail that now has a base cost of a 32-cent stamp. It would have given much greater powers to the PRC as well. Although losing its right to control postal rates, the PRC would have been directed to conduct an annual audit of the Postal Service. It would have received subpoena powers as well.

The plan was received with interest by the commissioners of the PRC. Marvin Runyon was disappointed in it. The bill died in committee. Mailers, such as mail order houses, publishers, and banks, were opposed to giving the Postal Service control over rates, whereas the mail carriers' union opposed the revocation of the USPS monopoly on letter delivery.

Public Impact

The ongoing controversy over rate-making has proved that the postal organization created by the 1970 Postal Reorganization Act was able to safeguard, if imperfectly, the interests of the public and business in mail prices. The PRC was judicious, if not picky, about fairly distributing increases over the entire postal customer base. Occasionally it would reduce increases requested by the Postal Service. On other occasions, however, it increased rate requests to keep them fair. The Postal Service's ambiguous relation to the PRC cuts is illustrated in advertisements that often follow them, with slogans like "We're keeping mail prices down!"

Bodies like the General Accounting Office and the Institute of Public Administration have recommended that the USPS be given much broader rate-making power, in the interest of making it competitive. It is not clear how the public would react to "competitive" rates being enacted by the Postal Service. They would probably lead to parcel service prices in line with those charged by the major private shippers, UPS and FedEx; whether USPS service would change as well is more difficult to say. A rate structure determined exclusively by the Postal Service would undoubtedly entail much higher prices for first-class mail, which the Postal Service is required by law to deliver everywhere in the United States at a uniform rate. According to the Postal Service, this requirement causes much of its high overhead costs. But given the complex web of private interests that surround the issue, it seems unlikely that any major overhaul of the postal rate-making system will take place in the foreseeable future.

SUCCESSES AND FAILURES

In an age of cutbacks and drawdowns coupled with increasingly complex postal business, the Postal Rate Commission has not merely avoided growth and bureaucratic bloat, it has consolidated, focused, and decreased its staff. In 1993 the PRC conducted a study of its workforce. The findings showed that although there were many attorneys on the staff, the work they were doing was much more often technical, not legal. Consequently the PRC took moves to strengthen the technical side of its staff while reducing the number of lawyers. The number of agency staff on rate cases at that time dropped from 62 to 56. In all, between 1971 and 1998 the PRC staff fell from 70 to 45. When more help is needed, it hires private consultants.

FUTURE DIRECTIONS

The future of the Postal Rate Commission depends on the success or failure of the Postal Service. If the Postal Service is able to make itself a fully competitive player in the delivery services market, it is likely that legislators will choose to leave the PRC untouched. In recent years the USPS has reported billion dollar profits at year's end. On the other hand, a less competitive Postal Service could lead to legislative reforms that would significantly alter the PRC's mandate, perhaps as in John McHugh's 1996 bill that would have made the PRC the financial auditor of the Postal Service. The decision to completely privatize the USPS and revoke its monopoly on letters would leave the future purpose of the PRC in question.

AGENCY RESOURCES

Questions about the activities of the PRC, requests for information, and Freedom of Information Act inquiries should be addressed to the Postal Rate Commission Information Office, 1333 H St. NW, Ste. 300, Washington, DC 20268. It can be contacted by phone at (202) 789-6800, by fax at (202) 789-6861. The office can also provide information on PRC studies.

The PRC Web site contains recent docketed materials and decisions, descriptions of the agency's functions, hearing schedules, and biographies of the rate commissioners. It can be accessed at http://www.prc.gov.

The Office of the Consumer Advocate maintains an electronic bulletin board that contains all docketed materials, opinions, reports, and commissioner biographies. It can be accessed by modem 24 hours a day at (202) 789-6891.

The PRC Reading Room contains copies of all Rate Commission decisions, reports, and docketed materials. All materials can be photocopied there. The PRC Web site can be accessed in the Reading Room as well. It is located at the PRC headquarters at 1333 H St. NW, Ste. 300, Washington, DC 20268, and is open from 8 A.M. until 5 P.M., Monday through Friday. The Reading Room's telephone number is (202) 789-6877.

AGENCY PUBLICATIONS

A brief description of the PRC entitled "The Postal Rate Commission: An Introduction" is available upon request from the PRC Information Office, 1333 H St. NW, Ste. 300, Washington, DC 20268. It can be contacted by phone at (202) 789-6840.

BIBLIOGRAPHY

Congressional Research Service. "Functions at the Margins of Government: The Case of the Federal Corporation." Report 83-236 GOV. Washington, D.C., 1983.

———. "Mail Service in the United States: Exploring Options for Improvements." Washington, D.C., 1995.

General Accounting Office. *United States Postal Service: Pricing Postal Services in a Competitive Environment.* Washington, D.C.: Upland, 1998.

———. *Pricing Postal Services in a Competitive Environment.* Washington, D.C.: The General Accounting Office, 1992.

Greene, Angela, and Cheryl Dowdy. *Protecting Competition from Postal Monopoly.* Washington, D.C., 1996.

House Subcommittee on the Postal Services. "Operational Organization of the PRC." 1998.

McAllister, Bill. "Commission Delivers on Postal Rates." *Washington Post,* 1 December 1994.

———. "Making the Post Office an Outpost." *Washington Post,* 4 May 1997.

———. "Postal Reform Bill to Be Offered." *Washington Post,* 26 June 1996.

Postal Rate Commission. *At the Crossroads.* Washington, D.C., 1980.

Sidak, Gregory J. *Governing the Postal Service.* Washington, D.C., 1991.

Rural Utilities Service (RUS)

WHAT IS ITS MISSION?

The Rural Utilities Service (RUS) of the U.S. Department of Agriculture plays a key role in improving the quality of life in rural America; its means of doing this is through administering electrification, telecommunications, and water and waste programs in a manner that is forward looking, financially responsible, and oriented toward customer needs.

HOW IS IT STRUCTURED?

The RUS is one of three agencies (the other two are Rural Business-Cooperative Service and the Rural Housing Service) within the Rural Development Bureau of the U.S. Department of Agriculture (USDA). The administrators of these three agencies report to the undersecretary for rural development. The RUS administrator, who makes the primary policy and program decisions for the agency, is assisted by a borrower and program support staff that includes a financial services staff, an administrative liaison staff, and a program accounting services division. Because of the financial nature of the agency's work, the administrator and associated staff work closely with two other agencies that are not part of the USDA: the Federal Financing Bank (FFB) and the Rural Telephone Bank (RTB). These banks provide the funds for many of the loan programs administered by the RUS.

The program functions of the RUS are divided among three operating units—water and waste, electric, and telecommunications—each of which is led by an assistant administrator. The administrator and his support

PARENT ORGANIZATION: Department of Agriculture
ESTABLISHED: 1936
EMPLOYEES: 415

Contact Information:

ADDRESS: 1400 Independence Ave. SW, Rm. 4051-S
Washington, DC 20250
PHONE: (202) 720-1255
TDD (HEARING IMPAIRED): (202) 720-1127
FAX: (202) 205-9219
URL: http://www.usda.gov/rus
ADMINISTRATOR: Wally B. Beyer
DEPUTY ADMINISTRATOR: Adam M. Golodner
DEPUTY ADMINISTRATOR: John P. Romano

BUDGET:

Rural Utilities Service

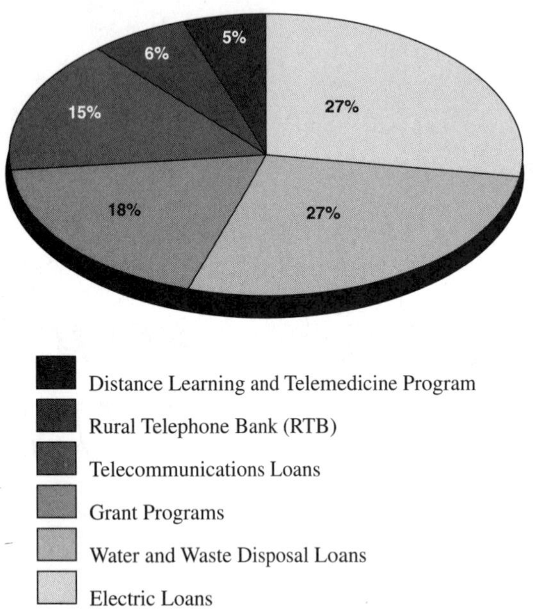

Distance Learning and Telemedicine Program

Rural Telephone Bank (RTB)

Telecommunications Loans

Grant Programs

Water and Waste Disposal Loans

Electric Loans

staff concentrate on the financial details of individual RUS projects, and these three operating units provide the engineering and technical personnel needed to plan and execute the projects.

PRIMARY FUNCTIONS

The RUS is a credit agency that helps rural electric and telephone utilities with financing needs and administers a nationwide water and waste loan and grant program to improve the quality of life and promote economic development in rural areas of the United States. Financial assistance from the RUS helps rural electric utilities to construct electric generating plants, transmission lines, and distribution lines for reliable electric service. The legislation authorizing RUS work, the Rural Electrification Act of 1936, requires that the agency give preference to nonprofit and cooperative associations and to public organizations.

Because of the way in which the telecommunications industry has developed, however, about 75 percent of telephone systems financed by the RUS are commercial companies, and only 25 percent are subscriber-owned cooperatives. The RUS supplies electric and telecommunications programs with either direct financing or guarantees of repayment of loans given by commercial creditors. Usually the RUS will guarantee up to 80 percent of a loan. When the RUS approves electric loans, it requires most borrowers to obtain 30 percent of their financing from a nonguaranteed, nonagency source.

Water and waste disposal programs involve more urgent, health-related community needs than electric or telephone service, and therefore are the only RUS programs that can be funded through grants. Water and waste loan and grant programs provide for the investment of funds in the most needy communities for critical water and waste facilities. In some cases, RUS grants are made for up to 75 percent of the cost of establishing a water supply or waste disposal system. If a community experiences a significant decline in quantity or quality of drinking water, the RUS is authorized to provide a grant of up to 100 percent of the cost. RUS programs also fund technical assistance and training by nonprofit organizations in these communities.

PROGRAMS

The three major program areas of the RUS—electric, telecommunications, and water and waste—are each broken down into a number of specific programs that are intended to fulfill specific needs. One water and waste program, for example, is the Rural Water Circuit Rider Technical Assistance Program, designed to provide technical assistance for the operation of rural water systems. Through contracting, the RUS assists rural water systems with day-to-day operational, financial, and management decision making. The program complements the RUS's loan-supervision responsibilities.

One of the RUS's most recent programs in the area of telecommunications is the Distance Learning and Telemedicine Program, authorized by the 1990 Farm Bill. The program provides grants and loans to rural schools and health care providers to invest in telecommunications facilities and equipment that will bring educational and medical resources that might otherwise be unavailable to these areas. Distance learning includes linking rural schools within regions to share limited teaching resources and using libraries or training centers as distance learning centers linked with on-line resources or regional institutions. Telemedicine links rural hospitals and clinics to major medical centers and provides clinical interactive video consultation and distance training of rural health care providers.

BUDGET INFORMATION

The RUS budget, a component of the USDA budget, is granted through congressional appropriations. Some financing for RUS programs comes from the Federal Financing Bank (FFB), which is budgeted within the Department of the Treasury. Of the total 1997 RUS budget of approximately $3 billion, electric loans and water and waste disposal loans each accounted for 27 percent. Grant programs within the RUS, most notably water and waste disposal grants, accounted for 18 percent of the budget. Another 15 percent of the budget was spent on telecommunications loans; 6 percent on operating the Rural Telephone Bank (RTB); and 5 percent on the Distance Learning and Telemedicine Program.

FAST FACTS

In the first 25 years of the rural electrification program, the number of farms with electricity in the United States increased from 10.9 percent to 96.8 percent.

(Source: *Government Agencies*. Greenwood Press, 1983.)

HISTORY

The Rural Utilities Service was known for 60 years as the Rural Electrification Administration (REA), until the secretary of agriculture's departmental reorganization in 1994. Like many agencies within the Department of Agriculture the REA was created in a time of dire economic need when Americans were suffering from the depths of the Great Depression. The distances that had to be covered by power transmission lines, the scarcity of potential consumers, and their low income combined to make most rural areas unprofitable ventures for private utilities.

In the $4 billion Emergency Relief Appropriation Act of 1935, Congress included rural electrification as one of eight funding categories. Initially, the REA was assumed to be an agency that would operate primarily to get people back to work and money into circulation. A later executive order removed work relief requirements, and in 1936, with the Rural Electrification Act, the REA was established as primarily a lending agency. Its operations were specifically confined to making loans to provide electricity to people in rural areas defined as, "any area of the United States not included in the boundaries of any city, village or borough having a population in excess of fifteen hundred inhabitants."

Originally an independent agency, the REA was transferred to the Department of Agriculture in 1939. Although it was originally designed to lend money to electrify farms not receiving central-station service, the REA gradually became an agency that tended to finance the development of integrated power systems that were organized and operated through cooperatives. The excitement of these early years, when power was first supplied to rural homes, is still felt by people who remember "the night the lights came on." Activities and luxuries that most Americans took for granted—listening to the radio, refrigerating food, heating water before it came out of the tap—were over time made available to the majority of American farm families.

The Rural Electrification Act was amended in 1949 to provide for a rural telephone program; further amendments in 1971 established the Rural Telephone Bank within the REA for financing these telephone system loans. In 1973, a Rural Electrification and Telephone Revolving Fund was established in the U.S. Treasury for REA loan funds. This fund replaced the direct-loan program. Although REA did make use of direct loans in the future, its emphasis for both telephone and electrification programs became loan guarantees. Its spending for large-scale generation and transmission projects far surpasses its spending for local electric distribution.

The RUS's water and waste disposal programs were never a function of the REA; they were administrated by another USDA agency, the Farmer's Home Administration (FmHA), until 1994, when the secretary undertook a dramatic reorganization of the entire department. The REA was abolished, its functions were assumed by the newly created Rural Utilities Service, and the water and waste programs of the FHA were transferred to the new agency as well. RUS's name was intended to more fully reflect the scope of its activities.

With the 1996 Telecommunications Act, the emphasis of RUS programs turned from simple telephone service to the connection of rural communities with the national information infrastructure. Computer literacy and connectivity became a new focus of RUS telecommunications programs.

CURRENT POLITICAL ISSUES

The USDA reorganization of 1994 was in part a response to a perennial threat for the RUS. The issue is, simply, whether the RUS, created solely to run power lines into needy communities during the dark days of the Great Depression, should continue to exist, at the expense of taxpayers. The RUS itself was proud to point out that by the 1950s about 97 percent of all rural homes had been wired by the agency. Why, then, members of Congress asked, did it continue to make government-subsidized loans to not-so-poverty-stricken communities? (In recent years, one of the groups to receive RUS support was the wealthy resort community of Hilton Head, South Carolina.)

Over the years members of Congress have attempted to do away with the REA and the RUS. The attempts have failed, however; one of the agency's strongest advocates is the National Rural Electrical Cooperative Association (NRECA), a powerful Washington lobbying group. With a $43 million budget and an accomplished lobbying staff, the NRECA richly rewards politicians who vote for rural development programs and RUS lending authority continues to increase.

The RUS is aware of its need to remain up-to-date. Some of its new goals—to build an on-ramp to the information superhighway or Internet for rural America and to fulfill the mandates of the Water 2000 initiative, for example—are expressly designed to make the agency seem indispensable to the future of the United States. Secretary of Agriculture Dan Glickman's 1994 combination of rural development programs into a new agency, the RUS, was in part an effort to consolidate and strengthen the standing of rural development programs and to ensure the survival of the RUS against its political opponents in Washington.

SUCCESSES AND FAILURES

The RUS considers each of its funded projects to be a success, but among the most prominent is the Alaska Village Electric Cooperative (AVEC), headquartered in Anchorage. AVEC, funded by loans from the RUS, is a major electric utility in Alaska; it provides electrical service to approximately 5,300 consumers located in 50 remote, isolated villages scattered throughout western Alaska. Only one of these villages is accessible by road—the rest are separated by hundreds of miles of wilderness terrain or large bodies of water. AVEC's service area is the largest of any electric cooperative in the world, measuring approximately eight hundred miles across at its longest point.

The introduction of dependable electricity has brought about many changes in this part of rural Alaska, which is populated largely (95 percent) by native Alaskans. The electric infrastructure has meant better health care; improved housing, schools, and water and sewer systems; improved communications; and new or improved businesses.

FUTURE DIRECTIONS

To a large degree, the future of the Rural Utilities Service has been decided by two key sources external to the agency. The Telecommunications Act of 1996 provided the RUS with a new mandate—ensuring rural online access to the information superhighway. To many, the law marked a new era for rural telecommunications and new opportunities for rural Americans. The 1996 legislation provided for the establishment of the Universal Services Fund to finance the effort. The Distance Learning and Telemedicine Program is the RUS's flagship program in this initiative.

Another significant directive for the RUS is Water 2000, President Bill Clinton's initiative to improve the quality of drinking water in rural areas, launched in 1994. The president's goal for the program was to improve the quality of life, protect public health and safety, and promote economic development in regions without a safe, reliable drinking water supply. The initiative earmarked more than $70 million for 54 Water 2000 projects in 35 states. Currently the RUS faces a backlog of nearly one thousand additional applications for assistance, and its funding is drastically short—the Water 2000 project requests alone amount to approximately $2.7 billion. The USDA and the RUS are working to leverage additional funds from other sources, including other agencies, state programs, bond banks, and local organizations.

AGENCY RESOURCES

General inquiries about the work of the RUS should be directed to the Legislative and Public Affairs Staff, RUS, USDA, 1400 Independence Ave. SW, Washington, DC 20250; phone (202) 720-1255. Specific questions about electric and telecommunications programs can be directed to the deputy administrator for program operations at (202) 720-9542. Questions about the water and waste program or the Water 2000 initiative can be directed to the deputy administrator at (202) 720-0962.

AGENCY PUBLICATIONS

The publications of the RUS are primarily regulations and bulletins, some of which ("A Short Description of the Rural Utilities Service," "Rural Development") are likely to be of interest to the general public. Other publications ("Preparation and Use of the RUS Form 254, Construction Inventory," "Rural Telephone Bank Loan Policies") are intended to be technical or policy guides for those who are interested in making use of RUS programs. Most of these publications are available for downloading at the RUS Web site, http://www.usda.gov/rus. For further information about RUS publications, contact the legislative and public affairs staff.

BIBLIOGRAPHY

Berilla, Ray. "Utilities Wrestle Over Poor, Rural Subsidies." *Business First-Columbus*, 2 October 1995, pp. 31–32.

Brown, D. Clayton. *Electricity for Rural America: The Fight for the REA*. Westport, Conn.: Greenwood Publishing, 1980.

"Cross-Country Co-Operation." *The Economist*, 3 May 1997, p. 22.

Government Agencies. Westport, Conn.: Greenwood Press, 1983.

Ingersoll, Bruce. "U.S. Is Giving Electric Co-ops Relief on Loans." *Wall Street Journal*, 3 October 1996, p. A3.

Lane, Joe. "The Board's Job in a Competitive Utility Environment." *Management Quarterly*, Winter 1995, pp. 8–15.

Norton, Rob. "Why Federal Programs Won't Die." *Fortune*, 21 August 1995, p. 35.

Tobey, Ronald C. *Technology as Freedom: The New Deal and the Electrical Modernization of the American Home*. Berkeley: University of California Press, 1996.

Securities and Exchange Commission (SEC)

PARENT ORGANIZATION: Independent
ESTABLISHED: July 2, 1934
EMPLOYEES: 2,800

Contact Information:

ADDRESS: 450 Fifth St. NW
Washington, DC 20549
PHONE: (202) 942-0020
TOLL FREE: (800) 732-0330
TDD (HEARING IMPAIRED): (202) 942-8092
FAX: (202) 942-9654
E-MAIL: chairmanoffice@sec.gov
URL: http://www.sec.gov

CHAIRMAN: Arthur Levitt
COMMISSIONER: Isaac Hunt, Jr.
COMMISSIONER: Norman S. Johnson
COMMISSIONER: Steven M. H. Wallman

WHAT IS ITS MISSION?

The Securities and Exchange Commission (SEC) administers federal securities laws that are designed to provide protection for American investors in securities (stocks and bonds) and seeks to ensure that securities markets are fair and honest. Although the commission considers its work remedial, not punitive, it also attempts to provide the means necessary to enforce securities laws through civil action or other sanctions.

HOW IS IT STRUCTURED?

Five commissioners sit on the SEC. Each is appointed by the president and serves staggered five-year terms; from the five commissioners, one is appointed chairman. To insure a balanced commission, not more than three members may be of the same political party. The commission meets several times each month to decide on regulatory issues; these meetings are generally open to the press and the public.

The staff of the commission is organized into divisions and offices responsible for administering various segments of the federal securities laws. To ensure that disclosure requirements are met by publicly held companies registered with the commission, the Division of Corporate Finance reviews registration statements for publicly traded securities and other documents. The Division of Market Regulation is responsible for overseeing the securities markets and regulating trading and sales policies. The Division of Investment Management works to ensure compliance with regulations regarding the registration, financial responsibility, sales practices, and advertising of investment companies and advisers. For enforcing the regulations of the commission, the Division of Enforcement investigates possible violations of securities law and recommends appropriate remedies for the commission's consideration.

One of the SEC's principal offices is the Office of Compliance, Inspections, and Examinations, which conducts all compliance inspection programs of brokers, dealers, self-regulatory organizations, investment companies and advisers, transfer agents, and clearing agencies to determine whether they are in compliance with federal securities laws.

Several offices serve the commission in an advisory capacity, keeping the commission up to date on the legal, economic, and political environment in which it is working. These offices include the Office of International Affairs, the Office of Administrative Law Judges, and the Office of Economic Analysis.

Many offices exist to carry out certain administrative functions for the commission. They include the offices of Executive Director, Filings and Information Services, Information Technology, Policy Evaluation and Research, and Comptroller.

PRIMARY FUNCTIONS

The primary activities of the commission are to ensure investor protection through full disclosure of material information and to ensure that the securities markets are fair and honest in compliance with federal securities laws and rules. The commission's counseling, interpretations, and rulemaking are all aimed at ensuring compliance, and most of the commission's time is spent discussing, reviewing, and attempting to improve existing rules.

The SEC does, however, have the civil authority to enforce federal securities laws when it has reason to believe they have been violated. The commission works closely with criminal authorities in matters of investigation which are usually conducted in private. If facts show possible fraud or other violations, the commission may pursue civil action, in which civil monetary penalties may be ordered through a U.S. court, or an administrative remedy. As a result of an administrative remedy, members may be expelled from stock exchanges or dealers' associations; broker-dealers' registrations may be denied, suspended, or revoked; or individuals may be temporarily or permanently censured or barred from any association with the securities industry.

PROGRAMS

The SEC's programs are not typically discretionary in nature, nor do they have their own official titles. They are simply the operations the SEC carries out to meet the demands of the law that it is charged to uphold. The Full Disclosure Program, for example, is the commission's effort to uphold the disclosure rules put forth in the Securities Act of 1933, which requires that investors be provided with material information about the companies in which they are considering investing.

BUDGET:

Securities and Exchange Commission

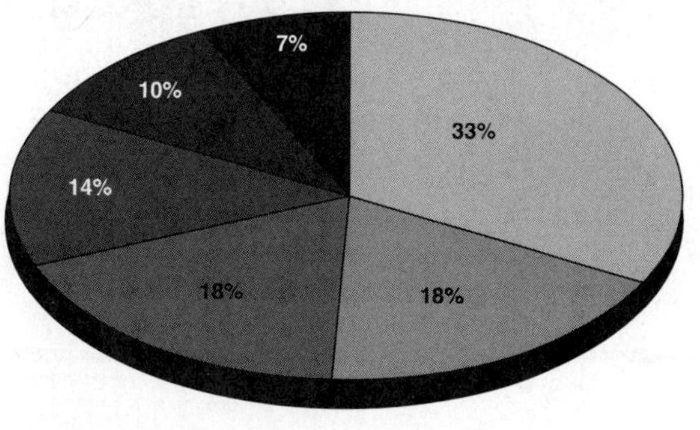

Legal and Economic Services
Program Direction
Supervision and Regulation of Securities Markets
Full Disclosure Program
Regulation of Investment Management
Prevention and Suppression of Securities Fraud

BUDGET INFORMATION

As a government agency, the SEC is fairly self-sufficient: about 97 percent of the money it spends on its operations and administration comes from receipts the commission receives through its registration and collection activities; the other 3 percent comes from congressional appropriations.

The estimated budget for the SEC in 1998 was almost $320 million. The largest portion of the SEC's spending, about 33 percent of its budget, is devoted to the prevention and suppression of securities fraud. The regulation of investment management and the full disclosure program each account for 18 percent of the budget, and the supervision and regulation of securities mar-

FAST FACTS

The SEC is one of the government's few profitable agencies: in 1997, it deposited $795 million in fee revenues into the accounts of the U.S. Treasury—260 percent of the agency's budget.

(Source: Budget of the United States Government, 1998.)

kets accounts for 14 percent. The remainder of the budget is spent on program direction (10 percent) and legal and economic services (7 percent).

HISTORY

The United States has historically lagged behind other nations in designing measures that would curb fraudulent stock and investor practices. Great Britain's Companies Acts were passed nearly one hundred years before the need to establish minimal standards of financial honesty in securities trading became apparent in the United States. During the earliest years of the twentieth century, several states passed securities laws to protect the unguarded investor and regulate the sale of securities.

The need for regulation extending beyond a single state's borders became shockingly evident during the 1920s—the Roaring Twenties—when many Americans prospered from the stock market. Fraudulent practices seemed to be the rule rather than the exception in the sale of securities, and the most powerful corporate interests were able to take advantage of less experienced traders by using short-selling strategies such as the "bear raid" (the practice of selling a large quantity of a stock to force its price down, and then rebuying it at the lower price) and by organizing secret pools rigged by stock exchange members. Stocks and bonds were frequently offered to investors without any substantial basis for investment.

These practices came to light after the stock market crash of 1929, the greatest loss to the investing public in history. The focal point of this debacle was the New York Stock Exchange, which handled 90 percent of all U.S. securities transactions. Its president, Richard Whitney, insisted that the exchange was a completely impersonal operation governed only by the free market, but it was obvious to Congress and the public that in its fraudulent practices it was more like a private club which permitted the bilking of the public as long as it did no harm to a fellow member. The post-crash investigation eventually resulted in a prison sentence for Whitney.

The SEC

The Securities Act of 1933 and the Securities Exchange Act of 1934, which officially established the SEC, took the first steps toward exerting congressional control over securities and stock exchanges. Over the next several years the scope of the commission's responsibilities was broadened by a series of legislative enactments, including the Public Utility Holding Act of 1935 and the Investment Adviser Act of 1940. The SEC now supervised the accounting practices in securities trading, set forth complete corporate accountability for any stock sold to the public, established financial requirements for brokers, and set rigid standards for dealers and investment advisers—in short, it exercised some control over almost all aspects of the sale of securities.

In its formative years, the commission exercised the philosophy of President Franklin D. Roosevelt's New Deal program: its mission was primarily to save U.S. capitalism from its own excesses regardless of criticism from those who insisted that it was destroying business and business confidence. Its first three chairmen were high-profile, politically powerful men (its first chairman was Joseph P. Kennedy, father of future President John F. Kennedy) who were convinced that uncontrolled economic individualism was a danger to the financial community and the capitalist structure. They were relatively successful in convincing Wall Street that there was more to gain from public confidence in the stock market than from the loose, overindulgent activities of the past.

The SEC was served by a small staff of competent and passionate individuals, and soon developed the reputation it enjoys to this day of being one of the most capable government regulatory agencies with one of the smallest staffs. By the end of World War II (1939–45), the agency had matured; most of the post-war years were stable and prosperous, and the securities markets profited from strong public confidence.

Growing Pains

The growing complexity and the sheer volume of investment in the securities industry soon made adaptations necessary for the SEC. By 1960 the average daily number of shares traded had doubled since 1950 and the number of brokers, advisers, and salespeople had tripled. Investment in new "glamor" stocks was on the rise, and inevitably several startling fraudulent schemes were perpetrated on the growing investment public. Armed with the support of the Wall Street community, the SEC and Congress launched an investigation which resulted in the expulsion of several brokerage firms from their exchanges. The investigations produced the 1964 Amendments to the Exchange Act, which extended dis-

BIOGRAPHY:
Joseph P. Kennedy

Businessman and Statesman (1888–1969) Joseph Kennedy was considered a consummate businessman, but is probably best known as the patriarch of one of America's great political dynasties. Throughout his life, Kennedy controlled a variety of immensely successful business enterprises, amassing a fortune estimated at $200 million. By World War I he had become the youngest bank president in U.S. history, and in the 1920s he moved into the fledgling motion picture business while at the same time speculating with great success on Wall Street. In return for Kennedy's political and financial support, President Franklin Roosevelt appointed him as the first chairman of the Securities Exchange Commission (1934), chairman of the Maritime Commission (1937), and ambassador to Great Britain (1938). Representing U.S. interests in England during a crucial period in Anglo-American relations, Kennedy stirred a bitter controversy in the United States over his staunchly isolationist and, some thought, anti-Semitic views. In 1940 he resigned as ambassador and used his considerable political and financial influence to help his son, John Kennedy, win election to the U.S. House of Representatives (1946) and later the U.S. Senate (1952). When John Kennedy was elected president in 1960, Joseph Kennedy emerged from a seclusion that he had maintained since 1952. President Kennedy often consulted with his father on matters related to U.S. business. Joseph Kennedy also provided encouragement, advice, and inspiration to other members of his family including U.S. Senator Robert Kennedy, U.S. Senator Ted Kennedy, Eunice Kennedy Shriver, who founded the Special Olympics, and Jean Smith, ambassador to Ireland.

closure requirements for corporations and further tightened other restrictions.

In the 1980s high-powered investors were accused of questionable practices including insider trading (profiting from privileged information about a corporation that has not been made public) and the unbridled sale of high-risk "junk bonds" to uneducated investors. The violations did not result in much new legislation because, for the most part, the rules already existed. The prosecutions and punishments of these individuals were highly publicized, and by the 1990s the securities market was again enjoying the prosperity that results from public confidence.

CURRENT POLITICAL ISSUES

The SEC's partnership with state legislatures and with state commissions for regulating and investigating securities trading is a necessary element of its efforts. However, there are inevitable differences in the way state securities legislation is enacted and enforced—each new state law tends to favor, to varying degrees, either the corporation or the investor. As a result, whenever a new law is proposed on a state ballot, it becomes a topic for nationwide discussion. The nation watches as advocates for investors and corporations debate their positions and trends in securities legislation develop—especially in influential states such as New York and California.

Case Study: California's Proposition 211

The ballot measures for the November 1996 general election in California included Proposition 211, a measure that would make it easier for California shareholders to prevail in lawsuits in state courts alleging securities fraud by corporate directors. Proponents of the initiative, the most vocal of whom was San Diego securities attorney William Lerach, claimed that the measure was designed to provide additional protection to the elderly from securities fraud. In short, the wording of the measure made it easier for shareholders to file lawsuits against companies when their stock prices went down, not only because of a company's withholding information but also because of its failure to predict the bad news that would lead to a decrease.

Business interests in California, home to some of the largest high-technology companies in the world, opposed the legislation. Apple Computer, Sun Microsystems, Hewlett Packard, and other high-tech companies' stocks are notoriously volatile—their stock prices fluctuate widely—in response to rapidly changing technologies.

Proposition 211, these companies argued, would increase their exposure to lawsuits and result in the loss of thousands of jobs as companies fled California in search of a less litigious place to do business. The companies that stayed stood to lose millions of dollars fighting off lawsuits, dollars they claimed could be spent on research and development, employee salaries, or expanding business. They argued that Proposition 211 would undermine the risk-taking entrepreneurial pursuit of rewards that had traditionally been the backbone of new business growth in the United States. Most state government officials agreed, and federal officials, including President Bill Clinton, were quick to join the opposition. Proposition 211, they argued, would do much more harm than good to an economy involving so many high-tech companies.

The more the measure was discussed in public, the more it began to be perceived as the brainchild of California attorneys. A significant feature of the initiative was the prohibition of any new restrictions on attorney's fees, and most of the money for promoting the ballot measure came from securities law firms around the country.

California voters, suspicious of the true intentions of the measure's proponents, soundly defeated the measure by three to one. However, Proposition 211 raised important questions that were destined to be further debated by other state legislatures and securities commissions around the country: specifically, to what degree are companies responsible to shareholders for the failures of their business enterprise or for failing to anticipate a fall in their stock prices?

SUCCESSES AND FAILURES

In the 1970s, realizing that investor complaints were often the first indicators of wrongdoing on the securities market, the SEC established the Office of Investor Education and Assistance (OIEA). Aware that an educated investor provides the best defense against securities fraud, the office attempted to teach investors how to identify securities fraud and to report suspicious activity to securities regulators. The office has created several brochures, handbooks, and fact sheets on important investment topics and distributes them free of charge to the public.

In the 1990s, the remarkable growth of the mutual fund industry, together with the increasing number of middle-class Americans who invested in the stock market, made the work of the OIEA more important than ever. The office's staff analyzes and responds to nearly 40,000 complaints and inquiries annually from the public, which appears to be better informed than in the past.

FUTURE DIRECTIONS

In the 1990s individual investments surged, resulting in the widespread growth of investment products such as mutual funds as well as services such as financial advice. The SEC and Congress saw this growth as a sign of a strong economy but also recognized that similar periods of growth—the 1920s, 1960s, and 1980s—were all marked by coexisting flurries of fraudulent activity.

The SEC's and Congress's desire to carefully supervise this new growth in investment activity soon became evident. In 1996, Congress passed the National Securities Markets Improvement Act, which further regulated the conduct of money managers, financial advisers, and other investment advisers. The new law distributes some of this regulatory responsibility over market professionals to the states. Realizing that the securities market and the professionals associated with it have grown beyond its immediate control, the SEC is likely to form similar partnerships with state agencies.

AGENCY RESOURCES

General inquiries about the work of the SEC can be directed to the Office of Public Affairs at (202) 942-0020. Inquiries about more specific matters should be directed to the appropriate office. For information about consumer activities, including assistance to potential investors, contact the Office of Investor Assistance's toll-free consumer information line at 1-800-732-0330. For information about securities laws that apply to small businesses, call (202) 942-2950. The commission also maintains a public reference room and library where additional information may be obtained; call (202) 942-7090.

AGENCY PUBLICATIONS

The SEC's publications include its *Official Summary,* a monthly summary of securities transactions and holdings; "The Work of the SEC," an informational booklet, and a number of free pamphlets for individual investors, including "What Every Investor Should Know," "Invest Wisely—An Introduction to Mutual Funds," and "Arbitration Procedures." Many of the SEC's publications can be downloaded from http://www.sec.gov/consumer/online.htm, but they can also be ordered from the automated toll-free information service, 1-800-732-0330. To purchase other SEC publications, contact the Superintendent of Documents, Government Printing Office,. (202) 512-1800.

BIBLIOGRAPHY

Bench, Nachman. *Questions and Answers about Today's Securities Market.* Englewood Cliffs, N.J.: Prentice Hall, 1987.

Benjamin, Jeff. "Discount Dilemma." *Wall Street Journal,* 4 April 1997, p. C19.

Eaton, Leslie. "Stock Trades: A Better Deal for Investors Isn't Simple." *New York Times,* 25 April 1997, p. C1.

Gasparino, Charles. "SEC Wants Mutual Funds to Personalize Their Data." *Wall Street Journal,* 7 April 1997, p. C1.

Hill, Patrice. "Dancing the D.C. Wall Street Two-Step." *Insight on the News,* 18 July 1994, pp. 12–4.

Koslow, Philip. *The Securities and Exchange Commission.* New York: Chelsea House Publishers, 1990.

Laing, Jonathan R. "Up & Down Wall Street." *Barron's,* 22 January 1990, pp.1–3.

Loss, Louis. *Fundamentals of Securities Regulation.* New York: Little, Brown and Co., 1987.

"Stop the Plague of Insider Trading." *Business Week,* 28 April 1997, p. 128.

Selective Service System (SSS)

PARENT ORGANIZATION: Independent
ESTABLISHED: 1940
EMPLOYEES: 88

Contact Information:

ADDRESS: 1515 Wilson Blvd.
Arlington, VA 22209-2425
PHONE: (703) 605-4000
FAX: (703) 605-4106
URL: http://www.sss.gov
DIRECTOR: Gil Coronado
EXECUTIVE DIRECTOR: Willie L. Blanding, Jr.

WHAT IS ITS MISSION?

For more than 50 years, the Selective Service System (SSS) has furnished a backup system for providing the U.S. armed forces with personnel. The mission of the Selective Service System is simple and limited to two functions: providing manpower to the armed forces in an emergency, and conducting an alternative service program for men classified as conscientious objectors during a draft.

The act of drafting or conscripting men into military service occurs when the government compels young men, under penalty of a fine or imprisonment, to join the nation's military forces. Typically this takes place in times of war. The military draft in the United States was suspended in 1973 and has not been reactivated since.

HOW IS IT STRUCTURED?

The Selective Service System is an independent agency within the executive branch of the U.S. government. In the case that a military draft is ever deemed necessary by the president and the U.S. military, the SSS would in certain respects fall under the control of the Department of Defense. The agency's main center of administration is its national headquarters in Arlington, Virginia, which is headed by a director appointed by the president, subject to Senate approval. Most of the administrative work for the agency is conducted in Arlington through these offices: Public and Congressional Affairs, which maintains public and legislative relations; Financial Management; Resource Management, which handles human resources, publications, and records; and Information Management, which maintains and supports the agency's computer information systems.

Another central facility of the SSS is the agency's Data Management Center, located in Palatine, Illinois. Employees at the center process the registration cards sent in by young men who register, and thereby assemble the registration database. Most of the agency's operations, however, take place within a vast field structure of military reservists and civilian volunteer board members. For administrative purposes, these field operations are divided into three regions, headquartered in North Chicago; Marietta, Georgia; and Denver. Each state within these regions, the District of Columbia, and U.S. territories also have a state director. The reservists, board members, and state directors are considered standby components, serving part time for the agency and remaining trained and ready to be called into service in the event of a military draft.

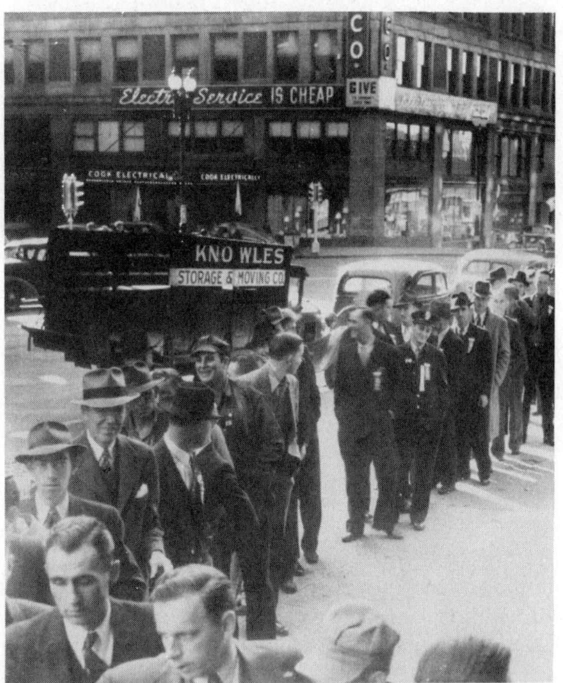

The first peacetime draft was instituted in late 1940, shortly before the United States entered World War II. Men from registration lines such as this one would soon join a total of 10 million others that were conscripted for the war. *(Corbis-Bettmann)*

PRIMARY FUNCTIONS

In times of peace, the activities of the SSS are limited to collecting and maintaining the names and addresses of all registered 18- to 25-year-old men in the United States. In the event of a national emergency, Selective Service would provide manpower to the military by conducting a draft using these records; which branch of service a man is drafted into—the army, navy, or air force—would depend on the service requirements determined by the Department of Defense. Once the men have been drafted, the training and transport of the new inductees would become the responsibility of the military branch into which they have been drafted. In addition, Selective Service's Alternative Service Program would provide public service work assignments in American communities in lieu of military service for men who are classified as conscientious objectors to all military service.

Although no draft is currently in effect, men are required to register with Selective Service within 30 days of their 18th birthday. Because Selective Service law applies only to men, women are not required to register. Men may register at any U.S. post office, embassy, or consular office. Failing to register or otherwise comply with the Military Selective Service Act (the current draft registration law) is a felony, punishable by a fine of up to $250,000, imprisonment for up to five years, or both.

PROGRAMS

Other than draft registration, the only program that Selective Service is responsible for is the Alternative Service Program, established in 1971 for conscientious objectors—those inductees who have a firm moral or religious opposition to serving in the military. To be classified as a conscientious objector, an inductee must be interviewed to determine that his reasons for not wanting to serve are in fact true personal convictions against war or the military, rather than simply political motivations or fear of entering into an unknown environment in which he might be called upon to serve in combat. Once classified, conscientious objectors are still compelled to serve their country, but in a capacity that does not require military service.

In 1998 the Selective Service System joined an interagency initiative known as Service to America. The program uses the Selective Service's registration acknowledgment card to convey the importance of public service and extend the opportunity for peacetime military or civilian service to all registered young men. In this way, Selective Service becomes a means by which other government agencies can encourage America's youth to serve the nation during peacetime.

BUDGET INFORMATION

The SSS is funded entirely through congressional appropriations. The SSS was appropriated about $23

FAST FACTS

As of 1998, the number of men ages 18 to 25 whose names are on file with the Selective Service System is about 13 million; this represents about a 90.1 percent registration rate.

(Source: Selective Service System. "Quick Facts and Figures," 1998.)

million in 1998; over half of this total, approximately $13 million, was spent on the salaries of full-time workers, for part-time wages, and for compensation to those who provide the SSS with special services. The remaining $10 million of the budget was spent on benefits for civilian personnel, printing and reproduction of forms and materials, utilities, rental payments, and other services.

HISTORY

Military conscription has never really been accepted in the United States as a permanent institution, but its history dates back to the colonial days. Colonies (and later states) drafted men for militia service regularly, and because most colonists were passionately for the cause of independence during the Revolutionary War (1775–83), the practice did not meet much resistance.

It was not until the American Civil War (1860–65), when conscription was enacted on a national scale, that the military draft encountered notable political resistance. Both the Union and the Confederacy passed draft laws during the war, but both laws turned out to be poorly constructed. The draft was centrally administered by both governments, and registration was accomplished by house-to-house canvasses. The laws also allowed a number of exemptions from service, mostly among upper- or middle-class professionals; in the North, it was actually possible under the law to simply buy one's way out of service by paying an exemption fee. Many poor whites in both the North and the South considered the Civil War a rich man's war and a poor man's fight.

By the time these Civil War conscription laws were passed, in 1862 and 1863, many Americans were already strongly opposed to the war, which ended up costing over 600,000 lives. The unpopularity of the war, along with the unfairness of the draft laws, left many Americans strongly against the draft, and some rose up in violent opposition. The tragic experience of the Civil War draft was a powerful influence on later conscription policies.

Early Reforms

Brigadier General James Oakes, in an 1866 report, strongly criticized the Civil War draft and recommended specific changes in the process. Among the general's recommendations were local administration by civilians, voluntary registration at central locations, and the imposition of a personal, nontransferable obligation to serve (no more buying one's way out of service). These recommendations were implemented in the next round of draft legislation that took place in 1917 during World War I (1914–18). Later legislation, instituting the first national peacetime draft in 1940, and later wartime and postwar extensions, retained the principal spirit of these reforms.

Neither the World War I, or the World War II (1939–45) drafts encountered much resistance; each war had broad, if not unanimous, support in America, and the sheer number of draftees inducted to serve in World War II (about 10 million) ensured that there would be little room or time for discrimination. All classes were represented in America's World War II fighting force.

The Vietnam Era and Beyond

The draft was much less popular in the postwar period. Both the Korean (1950–53) and Vietnam (1959–75) conflicts, both undeclared and unpopular wars in which many thousands of soldiers lost their lives, incited fiery public criticism of the draft. The selection process, with its exemptions or deferments based on occupation, dependency, or student status, was still considered by many to be unfair to those Americans from the lower classes. The burden of fighting the Korean and Vietnam Wars did in fact fall almost exclusively upon the poor and disproportionately upon ethnic minorities.

It was also during this period, especially during the Vietnam War, that the issue of conscientious objection arose. What right, protesters wanted to know, did a government have to force citizens to fight in a war that they considered unjust or immoral? The debate led to the Selective Service's Alternative Service Program, which allows men opposed to war or military service on religious, moral, or ethical grounds to serve the United States as a civilian rather than as a soldier.

The unpopularity of the draft led to its termination in 1973, and in 1975 the requirement for registration itself was suspended. Although there has been no draft at all since then, registration was reinstated in 1980 by President Jimmy Carter in response to the Soviet invasion of Afghanistan. President Carter advocated that both men and women of draft age be registered, but Congress decisively rejected female registration in its final drafting of the legislation.

A federal district court ruled in 1980 that the exclusion of women from the draft was unconstitutional, a position that was endorsed by the National Organization for Women, an advocacy group for women's rights. In 1981, the Supreme Court, in *Rostker v. Goldberg*, reversed the decision of the district court and upheld the validity of male-only registration. Although many feminists still see this policy as discriminatory, the ability of women to volunteer and serve with distinction in all branches of the U.S. armed forces has kept this debate from becoming a topic of major concern for American women.

Talk of a draft resurfaced during the United States's most recent war, the Persian Gulf War in 1991, but the opinion in both public and military circles was overwhelmingly against conscription; military leaders instead hoped to rely on their reserve forces. The swift and decisive end to the war ensured that the draft did not become an issue.

FAST FACTS

The 1862 draft of the Confederate States of America exempted preachers, pharmacists, newspaper editors, teachers, and all men who owned 20 or more slaves.

(Source: David R. Kiernan. "Caught in the Draft: Looking Back at the Selective Service System." *USA Today*, 1991.)

CURRENT POLITICAL ISSUES

Other than the issue of requiring women to register for the draft, the most substantial political question involving the Selective Service is the justification for a government requiring its members to register for the draft. This debate has existed ever since the first federal conscription laws were passed in the United States during the American Civil War. The arguments against the draft have always centered on two issues: the draft selection process is often unfair, and it forces citizens who are often unwilling into military service. In the 1990s, however, a surge in antidraft sentiment arose that objects to the process of registration itself. The current debate concerning the Selective Service stems from unlikely sources, and it presents some new, surprising arguments.

The federal government spends about $23 million each year running the Selective Service System. In terms of federal spending, this is a very small amount, but for 25 years it has been spent registering men for a draft that has become decreasingly likely to occur. Throughout the Persian Gulf War, a relatively large-scale deployment of American armed forces, the real possibility of a draft was never raised. Congressional conservatives, anxious to cut the federal budget any way they can, see the Selective Service as an annual waste of millions of dollars. It is a throwback to another era, they argue, and should be eliminated entirely.

In 1994 President Clinton defended the Selective Service System as a relatively low-cost insurance policy against the maximum level of threat we expect our armed forces to face. But critics of the system point out that wars are no longer fought in the same way as before; because of advances in war-fighting machinery and technology, members of the military require greater training than ever. According to the Congressional Research Service, which has investigated the issue, any requirement for a sudden increase in combat forces could be met more quickly and efficiently by mobilizing reserve forces who are already trained. Turning to the general population by instituting a draft would not provide the trained officers and noncommissioned officers needed to staff effective units—it would instead turn out a large volume of freshly trained junior recruits.

Politicians became increasingly vocal about this issue in the 1990s, but perhaps the most credible participant in the debate is the Defense Department itself, which has acknowledged little interest in resurrecting the draft. Most officials at the Pentagon believe that a draft would be of little value in future wars and might even create considerable disadvantages: increased personnel turnover as draftees enter and leave the armed forces; a huge component concerned mostly with getting out of, rather than staying in, the military; and uncertain social conditions that might become a problem upon the injection of large numbers of raw recruits into the military. Despite these concerns, however, no action has yet been taken to eliminate or modify selective service.

SUCCESSES AND FAILURES

The blatant unfairness of the earliest military drafts in the United States continued in some form up to the Vietnam conflict; wealthy or politically connected young men in the United States have always appeared to be able to escape the draft if they wanted. The Selective Service has been careful to institute three reforms that would make the draft more equitable: the draft lottery, in which inductees are selected by birth date rather than name; the abolition of widespread deferments; and the establishment of a single year of prime vulnerability to the draft (a young man's 20th year). Although some exemptions from the draft still exist, and Selective Service's reforms have not been tested by an actual draft, the agency makes it clear that it intends to enforce the draft registration laws fairly, regardless of socioeconomic status or race.

FUTURE DIRECTIONS

At present, the Selective Service sends messages about volunteering in the military when it acknowledges those men who register. The agency has made plans to provide additional information on how to receive student loans and grants, the negative aspects of drug use, and AIDS prevention.

Additionally, the Selective Service plans to upgrade its Web site to be even more helpful to men required to register. Currently the registration process can be initiated by accessing the Selective Service home page at http://www2.sss.gov/forms/registra.htm. After beginning the process, however, a registrant must still sign a card that is mailed to him after he completes the on-line forms. The complete process will soon be handled on-line with immediate confirmation that the user has indeed registered. Men who wish to verify their registration will also be able to do so on-line.

AGENCY RESOURCES

For more information about the Selective Service or its publications, write the Office of Public and Congressional Affairs, Selective Service System, Arlington, VA 22209-2425 or phone (703) 605-4100. Information about the Selective Service can also be accessed on-line at http://www.sss.gov.

AGENCY PUBLICATIONS

Selective Service publications are limited to the agency's annual report to Congress and brief information pamphlets such as "The Selective Service Primer," "A Teacher's Guide to the Selective Service," and "Time to Register: the Selective Service and You." Some of these can be ordered, free of charge, from the agency Web site at http://www.sss.gov; the *Teacher's Guide* can be viewed and downloaded. Publications may also be obtained by writing to the Office of Public and Congressional Affairs, Selective Service System, Arlington, VA 22209-2425 or by calling (703) 605-4100.

BIBLIOGRAPHY

Katz, Jeffrey L. "Military Draft System May Just Fade Away." *Congressional Quarterly Weekly Report*, 19 June 1993, p. 1579.

Kiernan, David R. "Caught in the Draft: Looking Back at the Selective Service System." *USA Today*, March 1991, pp. 66–68.

Kohn, H., and B. Cronin. "How Bush Dodged the Draft, for Now." *Rolling Stone*, 7 March 1991, p. 62.

Rosenbaum, David E. "The Republicans are Threatening to Bury the Ghost of the Military Draft." *New York Times*, 16 July 1995, p. 16.

Royall, Kenneth C. "Selective Service 1948." *Military Review*, January/February 1997, pp. 7–10.

Smith, Bob, and Peter DeFazio. "Should Congress Keep the Selective Service System?" *American Legion*, February 1997, p. 11.

Senate

PARENT ORGANIZATION: Congress
ESTABLISHED: September 17, 1787
EMPLOYEES: 100 senators plus support staff

Contact Information:

ADDRESS: The Capitol
Washington, DC 20510
PHONE: (202) 224-3121
URL: http://www.senate.gov
PRESIDENT OF THE SENATE: Al Gore
PRESIDENT PRO TEMPORE: Strom Thurmond
MAJORITY LEADER: Trent Lott
MAJORITY WHIP: Don Nickles
MINORITY LEADER: Thomas Daschle
MINORITY WHIP: Wendell Ford

WHAT IS ITS MISSION?

The Senate and the House of Representatives form the U.S. Congress which is responsible, under the terms of the Constitution, for making and passing laws, raising taxes, declaring war, raising an armed force, and proposing constitutional amendments. The Senate is the "upper" house of the bicameral (two-chambered) U.S. Congress. While the House of Representatives, the Senate's legislative counterpart in Congress, was designed to be large and responsive to local interests, the Senate was intended by the framers of the Constitution to be a smaller, more deliberative body, with a less volatile membership (senators serve six-year terms) that would focus on long-term national issues. While the House is generally thought to be the federal government's nearest association with the general public, the Senate is thought to be more closely affiliated with the president and the executive branch.

HOW IS IT STRUCTURED?

The Senate is composed of 100 members—two members for each of the United States, regardless of population. Senators are elected by popular vote from the citizens of their respective states, and serve six-year terms. A senator's six-year term runs the duration of three consecutive congressional terms. In general Congress meets for two annual sessions during each congressional term, unless the president orders a special session of Congress, which is an executive power granted by the Constitution. There is no limit on the number of terms that a U.S. senator may serve. In order to qualify for a seat in the Senate, a candidate must be at least 30 years

of age, and must have been a U.S. citizen for a minimum of nine years.

Important differences between the House and the Senate are revealed by the frequency and manner of their elections: representatives in the House are re-elected at the end of every congressional term, so theoretically it is possible for the voters to elect an entirely new membership to the House of Representatives every two years. Senators are elected somewhat differently; only about one-third of Senate seats comes up for election every two years. This method of balloting helps to keep the Senate a more stable legislative body that is less sensitive to sudden shifts in public opinion.

Senate Leadership

The vice president of the United States is the president of the Senate. While he or she is the presiding officer, the president is only allowed to vote on measures in the event that a vote is needed to break a straight tie. Over time it has become customary for the vice president to enter the Senate chamber only on ceremonial occasions, or when a close vote on an issue is expected. The Constitution provides that the Senate choose a *president pro tempore* (temporary president) to serve when the vice president is absent. This position is usually a matter of form and granted to the senator of the majority party with the longest continuous service—and he or she rarely presides over floor debate. Other senators take turns presiding over the chamber in an honorary and routine way.

The leaders of the Senate named by the Constitution, then, are not significant in the Senate. Real power resides in the leaders of the Senate's Democratic and Republican parties. The most powerful leader in the senate is one chosen by a conference, or caucus, of all the senators of the majority party. The minority leader is likewise chosen by the opposing party caucus. It is customary to choose the party leader for a two-year term when each session of Congress opens.

Majority and Minority Leaders. Majority and minority leaders are the elected spokespersons on the floor for their respective political parties; they have in effect been granted the authority to act on behalf of the entire party in order to carry out legislative programs or opposition. The majority leader, in consultation with the minority leader, determines the Senate's agenda. The relationship between party leaders and other party members in the Senate is one of compromise and patience. Individual senators often consult the party leader about such matters as the party stance on certain pieces of legislation; where the party is positioned in terms of presidential appointments or nominations; and committee assignments.

On the floor, the respective party leaders are charged with managing all procedural questions in consultation with the parties' policy-making bodies. In turn, they are expected to advise the party membership on proposed action on pending measures. The majority leader, in particular, remains constantly in touch with the various standing committees of the Senate to keep informed on the progress of legislation, and often posts the entire Senate on the results of these briefings.

The majority leader, or someone named by him, remains continuously on the Senate floor each day to ensure that the party's program is carried out. Likewise, the minority leader or an appointee is always present to protect the rights of the loyal opposition. If an unexpected and relatively noncontroversial action arises in the Senate, the majority leader or his appointee is generally authorized (subject to the approval of other key Senators) to alter the planned legislative program and act on the business at hand.

Party Whips. Like the House of Representatives, the Senate makes use of party whips, Senate members elected by party caucus who function as assistant floor leaders to the party leaders. In the larger and more elaborate House, whips serve as important messengers and mediators between the individual representatives and party leadership. In the much smaller Senate, however, party leaders tend to communicate directly with other senators. Senate whips commonly serve the party leaders in the capacity of general assistants.

In the Senate, each party's legislative agenda and strategy is formulated within the Democratic Policy Committee or the Republican Policy Committee. Each of these generally includes three subcommittees: one for determining general party policy, one for determining party representation on the various Senate committees, and one for helping orchestrate and strengthen upcoming electoral campaigns. Policy committees are sometimes chaired by the party leaders, especially in the minority party.

The Committee System

Most of the work performed by the Senate is done in committees. Though not mentioned in the Constitution, the committee system in both houses of Congress is an important mechanism for helping the legislature deal with the enormous growth in its responsibilities. Like the House, the Senate relies on standing committees—those authorized permanently by public laws or Senate resolutions—to process most of the important legislation that flows through the Senate. Typically over 10,000 bills are introduced in Congress every year that result in several hundred public laws enacted annually.

There are currently sixteen standing committees in the Senate, most of which have several subcommittees that work in specialized areas. The areas of standing committee legislation are generally structured to correspond to the types of bills under consideration, and also to the structure of the executive branch departments. For example, there is the Committee on Commerce, Science, and Transportation; the Committee on Labor and Human Resources; and the Committee on Agriculture, Nutrition, and Forestry. Other committees (Appropriations, Budget, and Finance) handle laws associated with the national budget, economy and taxation, while some are concerned with oversight of the federal government (Judiciary, Armed Services, and Governmental Affairs). The Committee on Rules and Administration is generally nonlegislative in nature, and sticks to matters relating to the internal workings and administration of the Senate itself.

Select or special committees in the Senate are established periodically to study special problems or concerns. One of these would be the Committee on Indian Affairs. Typically the work of these committees is investigative in nature, rather than legislative, and the life spans of these committees are determined by the Senate resolutions that create them. Most last only for one or two terms; nevertheless, there are some that have become permanent in everything but name. Currently the Select Committee on Intelligence and the Select Committee on Aging are examples of "special" committees that have been operating continuously since their creation.

Joint or conference committees consist of members from both the House and Senate. Conference committees are generally short-lived and exist only for the time it takes to resolve differences in bills that have passed through both houses. Joint committees are generally investigative, and are formed to deal with issues that concern both houses, such as economics or the environment.

Nearly all of the committees in the Senate are organized into subcommittees, which handle the bulk of the committee work. Members of the majority party generally chair committees and subcommittees. They are chosen to chair a committee by the party caucus and then elected by the entire Senate. Seniority is usually the primary criteria in the selection process, but other factors, such as service and party loyalty, are also considered. The composition of committees by party membership is generally negotiated among Democratic and Republican party leaders, and it is usually—but not always—agreed that the number of committee members from both parties be proportionate to the parties' overall representation in the Senate.

Other Important Senate Officers

To carry out its deliberative functions, the Senate makes use of several important officers who are elected by the entire Senate. Perhaps the most important of these is the sergeant at arms, who heads the largest single staff office within the Senate. The sergeant at arms, as the chief law enforcement officer and protocol officer of the Senate, carries out many duties, which include the management of most of the Senate's support services. Protocol duties include escorting the president and other official guests of the Senate into the chamber, arranging funeral services for senators who die in office, organizing the swearing-in and orientation of new senators, and leading the Senate wherever it may go (such as into the House chamber or to the presidential inaugural platform) as a united body. The sergeant at arms, as the Senate's executive officer, has custody of the Senate gavel.

As chief law enforcement officer in the Senate, the sergeant at arms is charged with maintaining security in the Capitol and all Senate buildings, and with enforcing all Senate rules. The support services managed by the sergeant at arms include the Senate Post Office, Computer Center, News Media Galleries, and even Hair Care Services and the Parking Office.

Many of the legislative and administrative elements of the Senate's day-to-day operations are overseen by the secretary of the Senate, who supervises the daily recordkeeping of Senate proceedings (performed by the journal clerk); the disbursement of staff payrolls; the acquisition of supplies; and the maintenance of public records. When the Senate is in session, the secretary is typically seated beside the presiding officer, and he or she examines and signs every act passed by the Senate. Important Senate floor staff who report to the secretary are the parliamentarian (the main interpreter of Senate rules and the person who refers introduced bills to the appropriate committees); the legislative clerk (who prepares the legislative calendars and supervises all recorded votes); and the bill clerk (who receives and titles newly introduced bills and enters them into the Senate' computer data system, LEGIS).

Due to the volume of work handed over to the Senate from the House of Representatives, and the specialized knowledge sometimes required to review and analyze it, the Senate employs a sizable professional and clerical staff. Senate staff, who serve both individual senators and committees, help the Senate to shape legislation and to communicate with the public, the House of Representatives, and the executive branch. In 1998 the size of the Senate staff was estimated to consist of over 3,000 personnel.

PRIMARY FUNCTIONS

The Senate's primary task is the consideration of legislation. After a senator introduces a bill to the Senate, it is sent to a committee for study. The committee may either release the bill back to the chamber with a recommendation either to pass or to reject it, or the committee may set it aside, thereby preventing the Senate from voting on it. Once a bill has been released by a committee, it is placed on a list for consideration by the full Senate, and it is generally the majority leader who decides when bills on the list will be considered—if at all.

Under normal Senate rules, members may speak for as long as they wish, on any topic, while discussing legislation. Some senators use this privilege to deliver long speeches, or filibusters, which prevent the Senate from voting on a bill. Filibusters are sometimes used by small

BUDGET:

Senate

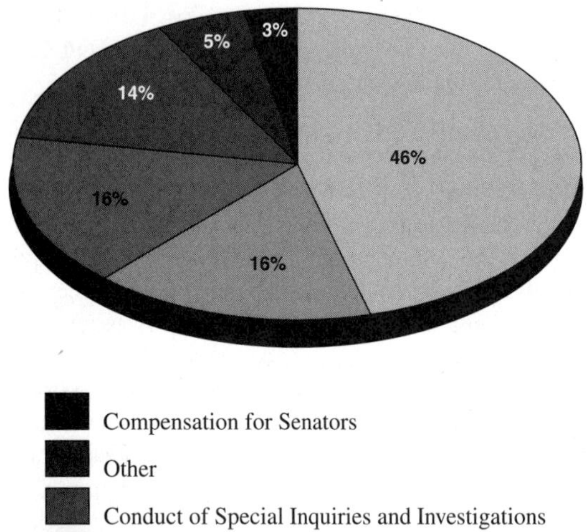

Compensation for Senators

Other

Conduct of Special Inquiries and Investigations

Staff and Functions of the Office of the Sergeant at Arms

Salaries of Officers and Employees

Official Personnel and Office Expense Accounts of Individual Senators

groups of senators to force a change in or withdrawal of proposed legislation. To end a filibuster, the Senate can vote cloture, meaning that debate is brought to an end. A cloture vote requires a majority vote of at least three-fifths of all the members present. For a bill to pass, a simple majority—more than half the senators present—is required. For a bill to become law, identical versions of the bill must be passed by both the House and the Senate, and then signed by the president. If the president vetoes a bill, it may still become law if at least two-thirds of the members present in both houses vote to override the veto.

The Senate also conducts special investigations or inquiries when the need arises. These investigations are typically led by an elected committee that ceases to exist once it has completed and reported on its investigation. A recent example has been the Senate "Whitewater" Committee, which was responsible for looking into allegations of corrupt real estate deals made by President Bill Clinton and his wife, Hillary Rodham Clinton, when Clinton was governor of Arkansas.

The Senate is charged with "advice and consent" when it comes to government appointments and treaties negotiated by the president. Over the years, the element of consent has become an important and politically charged political function, while the function of serving as presidential adviser has never really materialized. Especially when the Senate majority is of a different party from that of the president, the president does not generally seek the advice of senators about treaties and appointments. In order to read the political winds, however, the president does confer with the Senate leader (if a member of his party) or other senators in his party that are from a state in which he plans to make a federal appointment. If the senators from the state are opposed, and the president proceeds with the appointment, then the Senate will show courtesy to its member by not approving the appointment. This is known as senatorial courtesy.

The Senate votes on thousands of appointments yearly, and approves most of them without debate. However, the president's appointments to cabinet positions and the Supreme Court are closely scrutinized and are sometimes blocked by Senate members who are opposed to the appointments. Approval or denial of presidential appointments (cabinet members, supreme court justices, and federal judges, for example) is decided by a simple majority vote. Treaties must be approved by a two-thirds vote.

In addition to these functions the Senate shares with the House of Representatives the right to propose amendments to the Constitution, whenever two-thirds of both houses consider it necessary. If two-thirds of the state legislatures demand changes to the Constitution, it is Congress's duty to call a constitutional convention. Proposed amendments may only be ratified if three-fourths of the state legislatures agree.

Less often exercised, but equally significant, is the Senate's responsibility to select a vice president if the electoral college (the group of representatives chosen by the voters in presidential elections), fails to give any candidate a majority. Finally the Senate serves as the court where impeachment cases are tried. Impeachment is a charge leveled by the House of Representatives against a federal official, accusing him or her of misconduct in office.

BUDGET INFORMATION

The Senate's annual budget in fiscal year 1998 was $498 million. Nearly half (46 percent) of this amount was spent on the official personnel and office expense accounts of individual senators. This allowance is used to pay the salaries of staff, stationed at offices in Washington, DC and in the senator's home state. The size of staff allowances, based on the population of the senator's state, range from about $1 million to over $2 million. An additional 16 percent of the Senate's budget is spent on the salaries of "officers and employees," including those who work for committees rather than individual senators. The staff and functions of the large Office of the Sergeant

This joint session of Congress illustrates the enormity of the combined Senate and House of Representatives. When the Senate and House of Representatives meet in a joint session, they convene in the House chambers. Senators are led into the chambers by the Senate's sergeant at arms. *(Photograph by L. Mark. UPI/Corbis-Bettmann)*

at Arms also accounts for about 16 percent of the Senate budget, while 14 percent is spent on the Senate's conduct of special inquiries and investigations.

A relatively small portion (about 3 percent) of the Senate's budget is spent compensating the Senators themselves: the 1998 base salary was $136,673. Senators in leadership positions, including majority and minority leaders and whips, earn about $151,800 annually.

HISTORY

Early in the Constitutional Convention of 1787, the idea of a two-tiered legislature was agreed upon by the framers of the Constitution. The final form of each of the resulting houses—especially the Senate—was an issue that was debated openly, and which was finally resolved by what became known as the Great Compromise of the Constitutional Convention. While the House of Representatives was intended to be a large, politically sensitive body, the Senate was designed to be a moderating influence that would check the powers of the House. It would be a protector of states' rights, rather than serving local interests, and it would serve to advise both the president and the House of Representatives.

The Senate's intended role was reflected in the unanimous decision at the Constitutional Convention to have senators selected by the state legislatures rather than by popular election, and by the six-year terms of officers. The Senate would be a "continuing body," protected from the passions of the electorate, with only one-third of its number up for reelection at a time.

The Early Senate

In the first decade of its existence, from 1789 to 1809, the Senate had little to do with legislation (nearly 80 percent of the laws proposed during this period originated in the House), and instead concentrated on questions concerning its own roles, structure, and responsibilities. Perhaps even more so than the House of Representatives, the Senate began to alter itself in important ways from the body that had been conceived by the framers of the Constitution. The concept of the Senate as an advisory council to the president, for example, was almost immediately rejected. President George Washington set the precedent of looking to his cabinet advisers, not the Senate, for formal advice in policy making.

Likewise, the vice president's role as the presiding officer of the Senate was all but abandoned after the precedent set by John Adams, Washington's vice president. Adams, realizing that the vice president was not

SENATE COMMITTEES

Standing Committees

- Agriculture, Nutrition, and Forestry
- Appropriations
- Armed Services
- Banking, Housing, and Urban Affairs
- Budget
- Commerce, Science, and Transportation
- Energy and Natural Resources
- Environment and Public Works
- Finance
- Foreign Relations
- Governmental Affairs
- Judiciary
- Labor and Human Resources
- Rules and Administration
- Small Business
- Veterans' Affairs

Select Committees

- Committee on Indian Affairs
- Select Committee on Ethics
- Select Committee on Intelligence
- Special Committee on Aging
- Special Committee on the Year 2000 Technology Problem

Joint Committees of Congress

- Joint Economic Committee
- Joint Committee on the Library
- Joint Committee on Printing
- Joint Committee on Taxation

elected by the Senate but imposed upon it from outside, made little attempt to guide Senate action. The *president pro tempore*, because of the random and temporary nature of his term, was not much of a leader either. It soon evolved that legislative leadership was granted to individual senators who showed strength and authority. It was in this atmosphere that the beginnings of the party system within the Senate began to develop. The Senate's role in American government remained to be tested.

From "Executive Supremacy" to Reconstruction

The Senate briefly began a rise to power after President James Madison came to office in 1809. Its membership included powerful figures such as Henry Clay, Daniel Webster, and John Calhoun, each of whom contributed to the prestige of the upper house. But party alignments were undergoing a rapid change. As the right to vote was extended to the more rural areas of the United States and its territories, the democratic masses began to resent the elitism of government—and especially of the Senate, which often met in closed sessions and was chosen by state governments rather than by the people.

When Andrew Jackson, the frontier's choice for president, came to office in 1829, he was able to dominate the House of Representatives, but the Senate, led by members of the new Whig party, gave him trouble. The Whigs did everything they could to discredit Jackson's theory of "executive supremacy" in American government, blocking his appointments and even boldly initiating a movement for impeachment—a power specifically granted to the House of Representatives by the Constitution.

The partisan bickering between the Democratic Jackson and the Senate Whigs foreshadowed a term of bitterness in the Senate over the issues of slavery and states rights. Speeches in the chamber were harsh and antagonistic; the pre-Civil War Senate seemed to serve as the forum for the nation's own anguish during this period. The first significant filibusters were practiced during this time, and the frustration over obstruction and delays in Senate action led to occasional violence—most notably in 1856, during the debate over Kansas statehood. As Massachusetts senator Charles Sumner sat at his desk in the Senate chamber, a House member from South Carolina attacked him with a walking stick, beating him so severely that he could not resume his seat for three years.

During this period of hostile partisanship, the committee system in the Senate changed significantly. Standing committees, a relatively recent addition to the Senate, had previously been selected by Senate ballot; in 1846, in order to ensure majority party control of these committees, the responsibility for selecting committee members was transferred to the party organizations in the chamber. Party influence in the Senate was greatly increased by this move.

During the Civil War and Reconstruction periods, the new Republican party controlled the presidency, the House, and the Senate until 1875. As the Democrats disappeared from the government, a power struggle developed between Congress and the president. Radical Republicans in Congress pushed for control of the Reconstruction process, which was carefully held and guarded by President Abraham Lincoln. After Lincoln's assassi-

BIOGRAPHY:

Henry Clay

Politician (1777–1852) A renowned statesman of the antebellum period, few American political leaders have received greater praise or sharper denunciation than Henry Clay. His exhaustive career in public service included terms as a U.S. representative, a U.S. senator, the U.S. secretary of state, and three unsuccessful bids for the presidency. Clay was a brilliant speaker who won supporters and infuriated just as many. He was so adept at striking a balance between opposing factions that he became widely known as "the great compromiser." Clay served on the commission that negotiated the Treaty of Ghent, which ended the War of 1812, and he played a major role in helping the United States expand its territory by negotiating the Missouri Compromise (1820) and the Compromise of 1850. Clay's reputation suffered, however, as a result of one less-celebrated deal. Having finished fourth in the presidential election of 1824, Clay was out of the running. And since no other candidate held a majority within the electoral college, the House of Representatives had to choose a president from among the three leading candidates. While his home state of Kentucky supported Andrew Jackson, who had in fact won the most popular and electoral votes, Clay backed John Quincy Adams. Clay's supporters followed, and Adams became president. Clay's actions should have been above reproach since his political views more closely paralleled those of Adams, however Jackson supporters were positive the two were in collusion after Adams appointed Clay secretary of state.

nation, Congress was able to weaken his successor, Andrew Johnson, by a vote of impeachment in the House. Although the charges were politically motivated, Johnson came within one vote of being convicted in the Senate and was unable to exercise much control or influence over the government after that.

In the post-Civil War era, the character of the Senate underwent a significant change. The great pre-war orators, such as Daniel Webster, were replaced by party bosses who had mastered the politics of the state legislatures. These were career politicians who generally served longer than previous senators. As state politics became more centralized, business lobbies became more involved in the process of selecting senators. Also party discipline in the Senate itself became more significant—access to positions of influence depended more and more on the favor and support of party leaders. This development, along with a boom in the use of the filibuster as a partisan tactic to block legislation, led to a widespread decline in public confidence concerning the work of the Senate.

The Reform Era

The turn of the nineteenth century marked a rise in Progressive politics, which reflected a movement to gain more democratic control over government processes. The issues of the day were the right of women to vote, the way the legislature conducted its business, and the way in which politicians were elected to office. In particular, the popular demand for senators to be directly elected had reached a peak—it was common to attribute legislative disappointments to the dealings of special interest groups operating behind closed doors. Though this movement was understandably blocked by senators who were reluctant to change the political system that had brought them to office, popular sentiment finally prevailed in 1913, with the ratification of the Seventeenth Amendment to the Constitution. Senators were no longer to be chosen by state governments, but were to be elected in direct polling of state voters.

Another public complaint against the Senate concerned the use of the filibuster. While the Senate did—and still does—cherish its long tradition of unlimited debate, it was obvious that the intent of many senators was to frustrate and delay action, rather than produce results. Dramatic filibusters in 1908 and 1917, in which important bills were literally talked to death, spurred President Woodrow Wilson to call the Senate into special session. He demanded that it amend its rules so that it could take action on the important issue of the U.S. entry into World War I (1914–18). The resulting rule—Rule 22—was the first significant cloture rule adopted by the Senate. It provided for restricting further debate on any pending measure once a debate-limiting resolution was approved by two-thirds of the senators present and voting. At the end of World War I, the seemingly endless debates over ratification of the Wilson-inspired Treaty of Versailles provided the first opportunity for the cloture motion to be invoked; debate was ended after fifty-four days, and the treaty was brought to a vote. The outcome was that Wilson's desire to enter into a new

FAST FACTS

Of the 100 senators that served in the 105th Congress (1996–1998), nine were women.

(Source: Congressional Research Service, 1998.)

defense compact with certain European countries, a treaty organization that was to be called the League of Nations, was rejected by the Senate.

Party leadership was increasingly formalized in the Senate during this period; the first majority and minority leaders emerged in 1911. Party whips were added in 1913 and 1915, and from this period forward, majority and minority leaders were the acknowledged spokespersons for their parties in the Senate. The party organizations within the Senate appeared to go overboard, however, in awarding committee positions to the faithful—several committees were actually created merely for their chairmanships, and by 1921 the committee system was in need of serious pruning. On the eve of World War I, the number of standing committees in the Senate had reached an all-time high of 74. After the reorganization the number of standing committees was reduced to 34, and a number of long-outdated organizations were abolished outright. In part, this reorganization resulted in the creation of more centralized congressional oversight of the spending of executive departments. A General Accounting Office was established by the Budget and Accounting Act of 1921 as a congressional agency charged with overseeing all aspects of government spending.

The effect of Rule 22 on Senate debate appeared to be limited in the first years of its existence, and it seemed that the delaying tactics of certain senators were due in part to the structuring of congressional sessions. Under the Constitution and existing law, a new Congress elected in November did not take office until the following March. The old Congress regularly met in December following the election of its successors, and remained in session until the March hand over. This short session of Congress had become known as the lame duck session, whereby the business of Congress appeared to be purely political, meant to block action until the new Congress could be installed. To the public, this was an inexcusably inefficient waste of government time, and another reform was eventually undertaken in the form of the Nineteenth Amendment—the Lame Duck Amendment—which set the beginning of Congressional terms in January.

The Roosevelt Years and the Post-War Decline of the Senate

When President Franklin D. Roosevelt took office in 1933, the United States was in the depths of the Great Depression of 1929. Called into special session in March of 1933, Congress undertook an emergency legislative course that was practically dictated by the president and his New Deal program to save the economy. On the first day of the session, it took the House and the Senate about three hours to pass an emergency banking bill. For a great while, due to the president's popularity and the condition of the economy, congressional opposition to Roosevelt's programs was not tolerated.

In Roosevelt's second term a conservative coalition emerged in Congress which succeeded in blocking many New Deal spending programs. Most significantly, they influenced Congress to block Roosevelt's plan to enlarge the Supreme Court, which had invalidated several important pieces New Deal legislation. Roosevelt sent to the Senate a proposal to enlarge the Court by providing for the appointment of additional justices, who would, of course, approve of his New Deal programs. The Senate ultimately rejected the court plan.

With the onset of World War II (1939–45), opposition to Roosevelt was silenced, but as the war progressed, it became clearer that the Senate was filled with members who were strongly opposed to the president's domestic policies, and parliamentary obstruction of those policies continued to be a problem. By the mid-1930s, the filibuster had come to be associated with attempts to frustrate proposed civil rights legislation. While several changes to Rule 22 were proposed, few were undertaken, and those that were implemented proved ineffective. The demand for passage of civil rights legislation increased in the 1950s and 1960s, but those hoping for substantial changes to Rule 22 would have to wait until 1975.

Under Roosevelt the federal government had expanded greatly in its size and authority, and at the end of World War II, Congress was forced to assess its size and propose new ways to deal with bigger government. The Reorganization Act of 1946, the legislature's first major reorganization, created a considerably expanded congressional staff, which was intended to help Congress and its committees undertake the increasingly complex review of the federal budget.

To many Americans, the Senate did not present a favorable image in the post-war era. It often seemed unable, because of its outdated procedures, to do the work expected of it by the public, and the integrity of its members was often publicly challenged. In particular, the public was shocked by investigations that took place between 1950 and 1954 under the auspices of Senator Joseph McCarthy, who encouraged a nationwide "Red Scare" (fear of communism) by making broad accusations of communist infiltration into the highest levels of U.S. government. The phenomenon of "McCarthyism" (unsubstantiated, highly publicized, and personal attacks on those who are thought to be subversive) produced an atmosphere of fear in which opponents generally avoided attacking the senator, for fear of being labeled a communist. Eventually, McCarthy's ardent attacks—many of them baseless—led to his censure by the entire Senate chamber.

The treatment of witnesses by McCarthy's Government Operations Committee, along with a pair of major financial scandals (one in 1963 involving the Senate minority's secretary, Robert Baker; and another in 1966 involving Connecticut senator Thomas J. Dodd), led to the adoption of the Senate's first official code of conduct, which addressed such matters as the employment of Senators outside of their office, campaign contributions, and financial disclosure.

A More Open Senate

In the 1960s, a democratic surge in national politics led to a more open and egalitarian Senate that was in tune with the Great Society programs of Democratic president Lyndon B. Johnson. In 1970 a major institutional reform, a second Legislative Reorganization Act, was adopted that enabled less senior members to gain power based on merit, rather than reliance on the party system. With the larger staff and greater freedoms granted by this legislation, individual senators were able to maintain their independence from party leaders and more easily pursue their own goals and interests.

Many reformers in the Senate felt that the greatest obstacle to a more democratic and responsible Senate was the continued use of the filibuster by the minority to frustrate the will of the majority. After decades of trying, reformers eventually succeeded in 1975 in making it easier to ratify a cloture motion—instead of two-thirds of all the senators present and voting, cloture could be achieved by a vote of three-fifths of the full Senate. While this did result in more cloture motions passing, the filibuster is still an important tool used in the conduct of Senate business.

The Senate's inquiry into the Watergate scandal associated with the administration of President Richard Nixon began in 1973, and the televised proceedings of the Senate Select Committee on Presidential Campaign Activities were watched closely by the American public. Increased public interest eventually led to the creation of a permanent television broadcast system, operated by congressional employees, that would provide full coverage of House and Senate proceedings. The resulting network, the Cable Satellite Public Affairs Network (C-SPAN) has broadcast the daily House and Senate deliberations to the public ever since.

The Watergate scandal also led to an increased demand for congressional supervision of the federal government, and, during the 1970s, Senate investigations into the activities of the Federal Aviation Administration (FAA), the Central Intelligence Agency (CIA), and the Federal Bureau of Investigation (FBI) earned it a reputation as a tough overseer of executive agencies.

FAST FACTS

The gavel used by the president of the Senate was presented to the Senate by the government of India in 1954. It is intricately carved from ivory and is uniquely shaped, without a handle. It is kept in a wooden box and brought to the Senate chamber before each day's session.

(Source: Senate Art and Historical Collections, 1998.)

Beginning with the election of President Ronald Reagan in 1980, and continuing into the administration of President Bill Clinton, many Senate observers have noted the adverse effects of greater individualism in the chamber. The continued use of obstructionist tactics, the decline of the tradition of professional courtesy, and the ineffectiveness of many party leaders led some to conclude that the Senate was no longer a closely knit body intent on carrying out the will of the public; it is a loose collection of individuals who were more concerned with defending their views than with making laws. The 1990s saw the resignations of several respected Senators who, frustrated by partisan bickering and the increasing burdens of Senate election campaigns, no longer believed that the Senate was the place to create meaningful change.

CURRENT POLITICAL ISSUES

In its efforts to carve out a clearly defined role in the governmental structure of the United States, the Senate has always struggled with the boundary between its own powers and the powers of the U.S. president. In the past, these boundaries have been defined as much by the personalities of individual senators or presidents, and their attending strengths and weaknesses, as by contemporary issues.

The framers of the Constitution were very careful to supply the executive and the legislature with checks on each others powers. However, the interchange between the president and the legislature in the United States has become so complex that the pace of change is often frustratingly slow, even for the most routine appropriations bills. An attempt to solve this problem is the line item veto, which Congress granted to the president in 1996. The line item veto gave the president the power to veto specific items in spending bills that are sent to him by Congress, rather than sending the entire bill back to Congress. Although applauded by the president and many members of Congress as the answer to the slow and often antagonistic budgeting process, the line item veto did not prove its worth as a time- and money-saving tool. Recently it was declared unconstitutional by a federal district court judge, who saw it as disruptive to the balance of powers between the three branches of government. On June 25, 1998, the Supreme Court upheld the lower court's decision that the line item veto was unconstitutional and thus the president is no longer allowed to utilize it.

Case Study: Fast-Track Trade Negotiation and NAFTA

The line item veto was by no means the only evidence of Americans caution regarding shifts in the balance of power between branches of government. Since 1994 the Senate's authority to approve or reject presidential treaties with foreign nations has also been a subject of intense debate.

For over two decades, since its inception during the administration of Richard Nixon to the first two years of Bill Clinton's presidency, the president of the United States enjoyed fast-track negotiating authority with foreign nations. Designed primarily as a way to encourage free trade among countries, fast-track was intended to accelerate the passage of trade agreements and avoid lengthy negotiations, thus placing the United States in a better bargaining position. With the adoption of fast-track, Congress agreed to vote on trade agreements within a specified time period, and agreed to refrain from amending the agreements which could render them unacceptable to trading partners. Congress did not, however, surrender its power to oversee trade negotiations or to vote on any agreement that requires a change in U.S. law.

Congressional renewal of fast-track authority, which expired in 1994, would probably have been a routine matter if it hadn't been for the ratification of a sweeping trade agreement, the North American Free Trade Agreement (NAFTA), in January of that year. NAFTA was an agreement between the United States, Canada, and Mexico to gradually eliminate tariffs and other barriers to trade in goods, and to improve access for the international members of the services trades.

NAFTA has produced mixed reaction in the United States, and has proven to be extremely unpopular with a large political constituency: the working-class and agricultural classes, many of whom are represented by the powerful lobbying group, the American Federation of Labor-Congress of Industrial Organizations (AFL-CIO). Members of the labor movement contend that NAFTA has opened access to the cheaper labor markets of Mexico, where corporations can pay workers a fraction of what workers earn in the United States. The result, they maintain, has been a loss of over 400,000 jobs in the United States.

Proponents of fast-track authority claim that as the global marketplace expands, the inability to negotiate trade agreements is a handicap to the United States. Most countries—including the United States—are reluctant to begin negotiating with a country that does not have a fast-track apparatus in place. Without fast-track, agreements can be held up by endless squabbling between executives and legislatures over details. While some jobs may be lost in the short term because of NAFTA, proponents of fast-track argue that in the long run such agreements will help to build and strengthen the U.S. economy, that can then support more jobs.

The complexities of the interaction among the president, the House, and the Senate is nowhere more apparent than in the status of fast-track. The Senate is the legislative body more concerned with the long-term national benefits of a treaty such as NAFTA, and it is the assembly which ultimately has the power to approve or reject the president's trade agreements. However, it is the House that is more sensitive to the short-term political demands of its districts. If members want to keep their seats, they must be responsive to their local interests. While fast-track is an issue that concerns mostly the Senate and the president, it is a power which requires the consent of the House as well. As a result, fast-track authority has not yet been renewed by Congress, largely because of the influence of local interests on members of the House.

FUTURE DIRECTIONS

An important issue facing the Senate is the current public outcry for campaign finance reform. Financial demands on candidates seeking office in the Senate have grown steadily in recent years, and the impact of money on election outcomes has increased. According to a study by the Center for Responsive Politics, during the 1996 election cycle, the Senate candidate who raised the most money won 88 percent of the time. Given such a direct correlation between campaign spending and electoral success, it is not surprising that illegal fund-raising scandals have plagued both parties. A majority of U.S. voters now believe that major changes should be made in the way election campaigns are financed. The biggest obstacle in bringing about reform is obstruction by senators who have benefited from the current campaign system. They must be persuaded to make the process more open to less well-funded challengers. Legislation that would ban certain types of political contributions and would make all campaign advertisers play by the same rules has been introduced by senators John McCain (R-Arizona) and Russ Feingold (D-Wisconsin). Senate debate on this legislation has begun.

AGENCY RESOURCES

Perhaps the simplest way to get in touch with any Senate office is to phone the U.S. Capitol switchboard at (202) 224-3121. A switchboard operator will connect you directly with the Senate office you wish to speak with.

The *Weekly Report* of Congressional Quarterly, a private, nonpartisan research organization, is an important resource for both houses of Congress and provides updates about members and legislation.

The Library of Congress Information Service (LOCIS) also offers a number of resources at its Web site at http://www.loc.gov. To many researchers, the most helpful of these is probably the THOMAS site, named for Thomas Jefferson. THOMAS is an on-line public access system of legislative and congressional information, which offers the full text of laws and the *Congressional Record*, summaries and status reports on bills, E-mail addresses for members and committees of both the House and the Senate, and the Constitution of the United States. The THOMAS site can be reached directly at http://www.thomas.loc.gov.

Since the 1980s, gavel-to-gavel television coverage of Senate proceedings has been available on C-SPAN, (the Cable Satellite Public Affairs Network). Broadcasts also include speeches, interviews, and public appearances by senators. If your television is wired for C-SPAN, daily listings are posted on its Web site at http://www.c-span.org.

Information about the history of the Senate is available from the Senate Historical Office, U.S. Senate, Washington, DC 20510.

AGENCY PUBLICATIONS

The *Standing Rules of the Senate* is available for viewing on the Senate's Web site, along with several publications offered by the Senate Historical Office. A significant congressional publication is the *Congressional Directory*. Edited by the Joint Committee on Printing, it lists biographies of senators, committee assignments, and seniority rankings. Also available is the *Congressional Record*, the daily word-for-word account of congressional proceedings. The second section of the *Congressional Record* is always devoted to the proceedings of the Senate. Printed copies of the *Congressional Record*, the Senate's *Rules* , and the *Congressional Directory* can be obtained from the Superintendent of Documents, Government Printing Office, Washington, DC 20402.

The Office of the Senate Curator offers several informational brochures to the public free of charge. Titles include "The Senate Chamber, 1810-1859," "The Senate Seal," and "Between the Eyes: Thomas Nast and the U.S. Senate." The address of the curator's office is S-411, U.S. Capitol Building, Washington, DC 20510. The Senate Historical Office address is 201 Hart Office Building, U.S. Capitol, Washington, DC 20510. It has its own set of free brochures in print, which include "The Senate Caucus Room" and "Official Reporters of Debates of the United States Senate." Other publications, including books written by senators, are available from the Government Printing Office.

BIBLIOGRAPHY

Abramson, Jill. "1996 Campaign Left Finance Laws in Shreds." *New York Times*, 2 November 1997, p. 1.

Binder, Sarah A., and Steven S. Smith. *Politics or Principle?: Filibustering in the United States Senate.* Washington, D.C.: Brookings Institution Press, 1997.

Cassata, Donna. "Relatively Calm, Collected Senate Willingly Takes the Driver's Seat." *Congressional Quarterly*, 11 January 1997, pp. 114–15.

"A Challenge to Senate Secrecy." *New York Times*, 4 July 1998, p. A22(N); p. A10(L).

Davidson, Roger H., and Richard A. Baker. *First Among Equals: Senate Leaders of the 20th Century*, Washington, D.C.: Congressional Quarterly, 1991.

Doherty, Carroll J. "As Majority Leader, Trent Lott Discovers his Pragmatic Side." *Congressional Quarterly Weekly Report*, 11 April 1998, pp. 931–35.

Duvall, Jill. *Congressional Committees.* New York: Franklin Watts, 1997.

Greenberg, Ellen. *The House and Senate Explained.* New York: W. W. Norton, 1996.

Guide to Congress. Washington, D.C.: Congressional Quarterly, 1993.

Harris, Fred R. *Deadlock or Decision: The United States Senate and the Rise of National Politics.* New York: Oxford University Press, Inc., 1993.

Hickey, Jennifer G. "Senate Feminists Have Big Troubles." *Insight on the News*, 29 June 1998, pp. 16–8.

How Congress Works. Washington, D.C.: Congressional Quarterly, 1991.

"Is the Senate Serious?" *The Economist*, 28 March 1998, pp. 24–7.

Kubiak, Greg D. *The Gilded Dome: The U.S. Senate and Campaign Finance Reform.* Norman: University of Oklahoma Press, 1994.

Ornstein, Norman J. "Prima Donna Senate." *New York Times*, 4 September 1997, p. A17(N); p. A25(L).

"A Senate for a Video Age." *Time*, 8 September 1997, p. 24.

Smith, Steven S. *Call to Order: Floor Politics in the House & Senate.* Washington, D.C.: The Brookings Institution, 1989.

Small Business Administration (SBA)

PARENT ORGANIZATION: Independent
ESTABLISHED: 1953
EMPLOYEES: 4,400

Contact Information:

ADDRESS: 409 3rd St. SW
Washington, DC 20416
PHONE: (202) 205-6600
TOLL FREE: (800) 827-5722
TDD (HEARING IMPAIRED): (704) 344-6640
FAX: (202) 205-7064
E-MAIL: feedback@www.sbaonline.sba.gov
URL: http://www.sba.gov
ADMINISTRATOR: Aida Alvarez

WHAT IS ITS MISSION?

According to the agency, the mission of the Small Business Administration (SBA) is "to maintain and strengthen the Nation's economy by aiding, counseling, assisting, and protecting the interests of small businesses and by helping businesses and families recover from economic and other disasters."

HOW IS IT STRUCTURED?

The SBA is an independent agency that operates under the authority of the Small Business Act of 1953. The secretary of commerce delegates small business responsibilities to the SBA. The organization and management of the SBA consists of an administrator and deputy administrator, who are appointed by the president and approved by Congress; field office directors; and administrators for the various program areas. The SBA also has associate administrators for the following offices: Disaster Assistance; Field Operations; Public Communications, Marketing, and Customer Service; Congressional and Legislative Affairs; Equal Employment Opportunity and Civil Rights Compliance; Hearings and Appeals; and Management and Administration.

There are also associate administrators for Investment; Small Business Development Centers; Surety Guarantees; regular Government Contracting; and Minority Enterprise Development. Assistant administrators handle International Trade; Native American Affairs; Veterans Affairs; Women's Business Ownership; and Size Standards, and Technology. There is an associate deputy administrator for Government Contracting and Minority Enterprise Development. These offices are then the backup and resource for over 68 field offices that administer the programs and monitor loans. The Inspector General Office audits and maintains the integrity of the loans and the SBA programs.

PRIMARY FUNCTIONS

The SBA aids, counsels, assists, and protects small business. It provides personnel to work with prospective business owners and offers assistance in completing applications for loans offered by the agency. Seminars are offered by the SBA concerning small business development. The SBA works to ensure that small business receives a fair share of government contracts and is able to purchase government property at the same level as big business. There is loan assistance available through the SBA to small business owners who are victims of disasters, such as floods, earthquakes, or certain types of economic injury. The SBA also guarantees loans to small business made through lending institutions. up to 70 to 80 percent.

PROGRAMS

The SBA operates a number of programs and administrates them through its Washington, D.C., headquarters and its district field offices. In addition to its vast loan programs for business development, the SBA operates specialized programs that focus on the needs of specific groups. Such programs include: the Office of Women's Business Ownership (OWBO), Minority Enterprise Development (MED), and Small Business Development Centers (SBDC).

Women's Business Ownership Program

Through a network of local SBA offices, the OWBO provides assistance to and advocates for female business owners. OWBO offers training, education, and resources to new, as well as established businesswomen. There are 56 centers with more than 900 service locations and more are planned for the future. One of the services offered is the Women's Network for Entrepreneurial Training (WNET), a mentoring program that links established professionals with women just starting their own businesses. WNET helps women avoid the common mistakes of new business owners by offering training, mentoring, and a year-long series of seminars to enhance their business skills. The SBA also offers the Women's Prequalification Loan Program, in which SBA officers assist women applying for SBA loan guaranties to prequalify.

Small Business Development Centers

The SBDC counsels and trains prospective and existing small business owners in all aspects of business ownership and business regulations. The Office of SBDC sets national policies and goals to improve the operations of existing centers and sets standards for their performance. There are more than 900 SBDC offices throughout the United States and its territories. Each center partners with the state government in which it is located to develop and coordinate efforts to ensure small business success. The offices offer technical assistance to small business, give seminars on matters pertinent to business, and are a primary source of information about regulations and other government matters that affect the operation of small business.

Minority Enterprise Development

The MED Program was designed and implemented to promote business ownership among socially and economically disadvantaged people. The SBA provides training, economic assistance, management, and technical assistance to small business owners who qualify under the SBA's definition of socially and economically disadvantaged. At the local level, assistance is provided in the areas of bookkeeping, accounting, technical advice on production, market analysis and strategies, and specialized management training. There are often disputes as to who should qualify as a disadvantaged minority; however, the MED tries to develop programs and assistance for all groups including Asian Americans, Hispanic Americans, American Indians, and African Americans.

Along with other miscellaneous programs, the SBA also administers the SBA Disaster Loan Program, which provides physical disaster relief. This is the SBA's largest loan program and is available to homeowners, renters, nonprofit organizations, and nonfarm businesses of all sizes. These loans are not grants and must be repaid. Since this program began in 1953, it has provided over $25 billion for 1.3 million disaster loans.

BUDGET INFORMATION

In 1998 $716.1 million was appropriated by Congress for the SBA. These funds were divided among its regional and district offices, disaster assistance for small businesses, entrepreneurial development, management and administration, capital access, and government contracting and minority enterprise development. The SBA also enacted nearly $36 billion in loan guarantees.

HISTORY

Congress authorized the SBA in 1953 for a trial period of two years. Over the past 40 years the SBA has become a vast bureaucracy with thousands of employees and volunteers, nevertheless, it still has to prove its worth before Congress where critics abound. Although it was

FAST FACTS

Aida Alvarez was appointed SBA administrator in 1997. She was the first Hispanic woman and the first person of Puerto Rican heritage to hold a position in the president's cabinet.

(Source: SBA On-line. http://www.sba.gov 1998.)

plagued with mismanagement throughout the 1970s and 1980s, accusations of discrimination, and the hostility of many government officials, the SBA still distributed and guaranteed billions of dollars in loans to small business.

After a promising beginning in the 1950s and 1960s, when there was a great demand for small business loans in the post-World War II (1939–45) economy, the SBA became bogged down in red tape and inefficient management. The loan application had become more than five hundred pages long and the application process was so cumbersome that many applicants became discouraged and deals perished before the loans even came through. Many small business owners avoided dealing with the SBA if they possibly could.

One matter of concern for critics has been the SBA's inability to consistently track billion of dollars it has loaned to small businesses. One example of an irresponsible loan, cited in *Newsday,* occurred in the 1970s when the agency loaned $200,000 to a "contractor" who invested the money in a racehorse that later caught cold and died. During the 1970s the SBA admitted that it lost track of possibly $50 million throughout the United States, although it was not certain if that was all the money that was unaccounted for.

In the 1980s the situation remained grim. President Ronald Reagan's budget director was in favor of eliminating the agency altogether. Although Congress did not abolish the SBA, because many small business lobbyists pleaded for its continued existence, it did cut its budget and staffing levels drastically. The Government Accounting Office (GAO) appeared before Congress and recommended that the SBA tighten its risk management and lending procedures. Ultimatums for getting the agency on track were given and new computers and software were installed to track the $36 billion in loan guarantees.

The 1990s brought about the greatest change to the agency since its inception. After 40 years of "big government" style operations, with huge tracts of policies and guidelines, the SBA was redesigned to be more manageable and cost effective. Although the agency was awarded a number of Vice President Al Gore's "Hammer Awards" (recognizing achievement in reinventing government) for simplifying its regulations and application processes, Congress remained skeptical of the SBA's abilities to manage its appropriations. During the twenty six-month tenure of Administrator Philip Lader (1995–97), Congress called upon him to appear at hearings a record 66 times. Lader responded to congressional efforts to "kill" the SBA entirely by reducing expenses by $1.2 billion over five years, offering buyouts to employees to save on salaries, and closing twenty field offices.

Lader's successor, Aida Alvarez, continued efforts to streamline the SBA and instituted new programs to address small business needs in the late 1990s. On-line Internet services for the SBA, the women's on-line center, and other innovations reduced criticism and allowed the SBA to continue its operations into the twenty-first century.

CURRENT POLITICAL ISSUES

Despite the fact that the SBA funded and assisted many businesses that eventually became major corporations, such as Federal Express and Intel, there were numerous critics of the agency. For years Congress debated the necessity of the SBA altogether. Many organizations, according to the *Los Angeles Times,* "want the agency to concentrate on loan programs and avoid 'social agendas.'" Examples of social agendas, according to critics, would be the minority and women's loan programs. Other interest groups felt the SBA discriminates against African Americans by favoring other minority groups, such as Asian Americans.

Case Study: Exporting the SBA Way

An area that typifies the SBA's commitment to streamlining the bureaucracy and encouraging innovation in business is the Export Working Capital Program (EWCP). To encourage small business growth in the export industry, the EWCP was redesigned in 1994 to be a more user-friendly program which helps exporters purchase materials, manufacture, or market exports. For instance the EWCP introduced the Export Express, a fast-track program that guarantees $250,000 for an expedited approval on single export transactions. The SBA, through a one-page application, fast turnaround, and preliminary commitment to lenders took much of the risk and fear out of the export sector. Lenders were assured that the program managed their risk by focusing on single transactions that required financing for only six months or less. The process is initiated by the lender receiving the name and address of the small business's buyer and a description of what the transaction involves (letter of credit, the name of the bank, etc.). The lender then inputs the data into the program located at the SBA's Web site. The data is then analyzed by computer to assess the level of risk of the transaction. Within moments the lender is advised regarding the acceptability of the loan.

In the past lenders based loans only on anticipated domestic sales, not taking into account sales from exports. With SBA backing Royce Instruments was able to secure a $350,000 loan to expand into the international market. Jim Dartez, president of Royce Instruments, told *Business America* "[we] turned to the SBA's Export Working Capital Program to meet [our] finance needs. The loan helped us dramatically. We showed a 40 percent increase in European sales by the end of 1996." The export sales of Royce grew from 9 percent in 1987 to 45 percent in 1996 and garnered for Royce Instruments Corp. the SBA's 1997 National Small Business Exporter of the Year award.

Public Impact

Although not every one of the 22 million small businesses in the United States have had direct contact with the SBA, the agency's policies and regulations have impacted their operations. The SBDC, the minority and women's programs, and the advocacy office, have all had an impact on how small business is perceived in the United States. The SBA has forced government to recognize that smaller enterprises account for 39 percent of new jobs and has given smaller enterprises a voice in the way government regulates business.

FUTURE DIRECTIONS

In its "Strategic Plan 1997–2003" the SBA assessed its strengths and weaknesses. New program innovations detailed the direction the agency would have to take in order to remain viable and effective in future years. According to the plan, the first goal of the agency is to increase opportunities for small business by offering access to capital and credit, expanding small business procurement opportunities, and enhancing entrepreneurial development assistance. Another goal is to transform the SBA into a twenty-first century leading-edge financial institution by maintaining strong internal control, identifying and managing risk, implementing effective oversight, managing with high quality information, and delivering excellent customer service. Other goals of the agency are to help businesses and families recover from disasters, to lead small business participation in welfare-to-work initiatives through SBA programs, and to serve as the voice for U.S. small business in government.

AGENCY RESOURCES

More information about the SBA can be obtained on-line at http://www.sba.gov, by calling 1-800-827-5722, or by visiting a local SBA field office or SBDC.

AGENCY PUBLICATIONS

The SBA publishes the "Catalog of Small Business Research," "The Facts About the Women's Prequalification Loan Program," "The Facts About SCORE Counselors to America's Small Business," and other brochures and pamphlets relating to small business. Some are available on-line at http://www.sba.gov or from the Office of Advocacy, Small Business Administration, 409 3rd Street SW, Washington, DC 20416. Brochures and pamphlets can also be requested by calling (202) 205-6531 or by contacting the local SBA office or SBDC in your area.

BIBLIOGRAPHY

Alford, Harry C. "Small Business Loans Programs." *Congressional Testimony,* 22 October 1997.

Broome, J. Tol. "SBA Gives Women a Foot in the Door." *Nation's Business,* 1 December 1997 p. 44(2).

Cassidy, Eileen. "SBA's New Trends in Trade Finance." *Business America,* 1 October 1997 p. 29(3).

Czerwinski, Stanley J. "SBA Performance." *Congressional Testimony,* 29 October 1997.

"Gore, SBA Launch Internet Site for Women Business Owners." *US Newswire,* 5 January 1998.

Masson-Draffen, Carrie. "More With Less: Demand for SBA Loans Surges" *Newsday,* 12 June 1995, p. C1.

"SBA Implements Weekly Limit on Loan Approvals." *Los Angeles Sentinel,* 11 June 1997.

"SBA's FY 1998 Budget Provides for Modest Program Increases" *U.S. Newswire,* 26 November 1997.

"Small Business Administration—Better Planning and Controls Needed for Information Systems." *Government Accounting Office Report,* 27 June 1997.

Torres, Vicki. "The Big Hurdles of Small Business" *Los Angeles Times,* 28 February 1997, p. D1.

Smithsonian Institution (SI)

PARENT ORGANIZATION: Independent
ESTABLISHED: August 10, 1846
EMPLOYEES: 6,300

Contact Information:

ADDRESS: 1000 Jefferson Dr. SW
Washington, DC 20560
PHONE: (202) 357-1300
TDD (HEARING IMPAIRED): (202) 357-1729
E-MAIL: viarc.info@ic.si.edu
URL: http://www.si.edu
SECRETARY: I. Michael Heyman

WHAT IS ITS MISSION?

The stated mission of the Smithsonian Institution (SI) is to "foster the increase and diffusion of knowledge," taken from the will of Englishman James Smithson, who bequeathed his estate to the United States to found the SI in 1829. Over the years the core mission has remained the same, but the SI has expanded its vision. It has grown from its original single museum to a system of numerous museums, educational and research programs, traveling exhibitions, and historical preservation projects. A longtime leader in the research that increases knowledge, the SI continues to focus on the diffusion of knowledge through technologies such as the World Wide Web and through its publications, recordings, and widespread exhibitions.

HOW IS IT STRUCTURED?

The Smithsonian is an independent trust instrumentality of the United States. Control of the SI rests with the Board of Regents which is composed of the chief justice and the vice president of the United States, three members each from the Senate and the House of Representatives, and nine private citizens. The board elects the secretary who is the administrative head of the SI. Nine administrative offices oversee the legal, communication, and financial affairs of the SI as well as its publishing operations.

The SI is composed of sixteen museums and galleries, the National Zoo, and several research facilities. The nine Smithsonian museums located on the National

Mall in Washington, D.C. between the Washington Monument and the Capitol are the National Air and Space Museum, the National Museum of Natural History, the National Museum of American History, the Freer Gallery of Art (Asian and nineteenth- and early twentieth-century art), the Arthur M. Sackler Gallery (Asian art), the National Museum of African Art, the Arts and Industries Building, the Hirshhorn Museum and Sculpture Garden (modern art), and the National Gallery of Art. The original Smithsonian Institution Building, known as the "Castle," is also located on the Mall and now serves as the information center.

Located elsewhere in Washington are the National Museum of American Art, the Renwick Gallery (American crafts), the National Portrait Gallery, the National Postal Museum, and the Anacostia Museum (African American history and culture).

The Cooper-Hewitt National Design Museum and the George Gustav Heye Center of the National Museum of the American Indian are located in New York, New York.

The John F. Kennedy Center for the Performing Arts and the Woodrow Wilson International Center for Scholars are independent bureaus of the SI, and are administered by separate boards of trustees.

Smithsonian research facilities include the Conservation Analytical Laboratory, the Archives of American Art, the Center for Folklife Programs and Cultural Studies, the Smithsonian Astrophysical Observatory, the Smithsonian Environmental Research Center, and the Smithsonian Tropical Research Institute. These research facilities as well as education services and regional offices of several facilities are located throughout the country and the world.

FAST FACTS

Only one percent of the entire Smithsonian Institution's holdings can be displayed at its facilities at any given time.

(Source: "Smithsonian Year 1996: Annual Report for the Smithsonian Institution." Washington, D.C.: Smithsonian Institution Press, 1997.)

PRIMARY FUNCTIONS

The SI is the world's largest complex of museums and art galleries with a collection of more than 140 million objects, scientific specimens, and works of art. Examples range from a 3.5 billion-year-old fossil to the Apollo lunar landing module; from Muhammad Ali's boxing gloves to the gowns of the First Ladies; and from a collection of ancient Chinese bronzes to specimens of almost every kind of butterfly. Rotating exhibits of the Smithsonian's collection are displayed throughout SI museums for the public to experience free of charge.

The vast majority of the SI's holdings are used by scientists and scholars for research purposes as they work to expand our knowledge of science, art, and history. Expeditions to all parts of the world are sponsored by the SI to gather new facts and specimens.

In addition, the SI is deeply committed to and involved in public education programs and the performing arts. Traveling exhibitions, research information, concerts, theater and dance programs, and lectures are made available for students from elementary to post-graduate levels. Each museum and research facility within the SI system offers a variety of educational and entertainment opportunities to the general public, and a large publications program spreads information and ideas throughout the country.

Many Smithsonian projects and programs are carried out in cooperation with universities, government agencies, and other museums. The SI provides information and technical assistance to government projects and other museums; this might entail lending artifacts, reporting on volcanic eruptions, or identifying evidence in FBI murder investigations.

PROGRAMS

The SI presents hundreds of exhibits, programs, educational experiences and research opportunities each year. Some programs are presented by the SI itself with member museums and galleries contributing to a common theme or event; many other programs are offered by the member museums and facilities.

The Smithsonian's Festival of American Folklife is an annual program presented by the entire institution. The festival includes programs of music, song, dance, crafts and cooking demonstrations, storytelling, illustrations and examples of workers' culture, and opportunities to discuss cultural issues. It is designed to celebrate the traditions of a particular state, region, ethnic community, or occupation. To date more than 53 nations, every region of the United States, more than 100 American Indian groups, and more than 40 occupations have been the focus of the festival.

The festival is held on the Mall in Washington and, in attempts to recreate physical settings for the traditions presented, it has included a horserace track, an Indian village with 40-foot-high bamboo and paper statues, a Japanese rice paddy, and a New Mexican adobe plaza.

BUDGET:
Smithsonian Institution

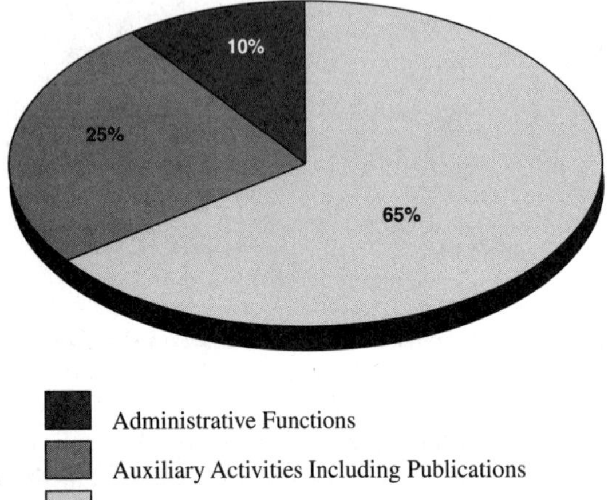

Administrative Functions
Auxiliary Activities Including Publications
Facilities and Activities of the Museums, Galleries, Research Facilities, and Educational Services

Books, films, recordings, and artifacts from the festival enable people worldwide to experience the cultures celebrated each year. The festival encourages regional and local communities to research, preserve, and celebrate cultural resources and serves as a model for cultural presentations.

The Smithsonian Institution Traveling Exhibition Service (SITES) circulates exhibitions to more than 200 American towns and cities each year. From 1997 to 2002, in collaboration with the National Geographic Society, SITES is offering the "Earth 2U, Exploring Geography" program, a hands-on exhibition that teaches geography. More than 300,000 curriculum guides are being printed for teachers whose students will experience the exhibit, and interactive computer programs will present "Earth 2U" to thousands of other students.

In 1996 the National Zoo began its "Think Tank" program. It is the only zoo or museum exhibit in the nation that examines thinking in animals. The program challenges visitors to explore the relationship between complex animal behaviors and thinking by watching, discussing, and sometimes participating in on-site research. An innovative aspect of the program, the Orangutan Language Project, attempts to teach apes language skills through the use of interactive computers, in full view of visitors who can ask questions of the working scientists.

BUDGET INFORMATION

The Smithsonian Institution operated on a budget of approximately $705 million in 1997. The federal government supplies approximately 70 percent of the Smithsonian Institution funding and the other 30 percent of funding comes from trust fund revenues, grants and contracts, donations, and revenues derived from membership dues, *Smithsonian Magazine,* museum shop, restaurant, and catalogue sales.

Approximately 65 percent of funds go toward the facilities and activities of the museums, galleries, research facilities, and educational services. Another 25 percent of funds support auxiliary activities such as *Smithsonian Press*, *Smithsonian Productions* and the Smithsonian magazines. The remaining 10 percent of funds cover administrative functions or are reinvested in the general-endowment trust fund.

HISTORY

In 1829 an English scientist and inventor named James Smithson died and left a will bequeathing his estate to his nephew. The will stipulated that if Smithson's nephew left no heirs, his entire estate of $500,000 should go to the United States of America to found an establishment in Washington known as the Smithsonian Institution for the "increase and diffusion" of knowledge. No one knows why Smithson chose to bestow his extraordinary gift on the United States. He had never traveled there, nor did he correspond with American scientists or read much about the United States. Yet some historians speculate that Smithson's gift was prompted by a belief that the United States, a new nation, would be the country to boldly pursue the newly emerging sciences without being held to past traditions.

When Smithson's nephew died childless in 1835, President Andrew Jackson was notified of this unprecedented gift. President Jackson, known as a defender of the common man, was not enthusiastic about the gift from a wealthy Englishman and claimed he had no authority to accept it. Fortunately, John Quincy Adams, the former president and then a representative from Massachusetts, advocated accepting the gift on behalf of the American people and took the issue to the House of Representatives.

Despite Adams's unwavering support, the debate over the SI went on for a decade. Representatives opposed accepting the bequest for a number of reasons: they feared it was a foreign attempt to dominate Americans, they questioned continued funding, and they felt it would encourage a rash of ridiculous bequests from people wanting memorials. Even after it was decided to accept the gift, controversy continued over exactly what the SI should be. Scientific study was a newly emerging field and difficult to define. Several individuals wanted Smithson's gift to be turned over to their own organizations or existing educational institutions.

Finally Congress passed a bill largely based on Adams's committee recommendation that the Smithsonian Institution should be created to include a national museum for government collections, a laboratory, an art gallery, and a library. On August 10, 1846, President James Polk signed a bill setting out the rules for governing the SI by a board of regents that would allow it to grow without rigid congressional oversight. It also provided for ongoing support by establishing a general trust fund and a pledge of continued government support.

In 1848 the SI published its first book, *Smithsonian Contributions to Knowledge*, and in 1849 it initiated the International Exchange Service to trade publications between the United States and other nations. In 1855 the Smithsonian Building (the "Castle") was completed. The SI was then designated in 1858 the National Museum of the United States .

Over the next 150 years, the SI grew into the world's largest museum complex and a leader in scientific and historical research. Donations from individuals and foundations enabled the SI to expand its collections and research as well as create museums for specific purposes and collections, such as the Sackler, Freer, and Hirshhorn galleries. Botanists, geologists, historians, paleontologists, entomologists, musicians, craftspeople, and many others donated their collections, research, and writings to the SI. With the continued support of the federal government and the American people, the SI has opened a new museum nearly every twenty years, welcomed millions of visitors, and expanded research facilities to meet new challenges.

FAST FACTS

The Hope Diamond, the largest blue diamond in the world at 45.5 carats, is on display in the Hall of Gems at the National Museum of Natural History.

(Source: Edwards Park. *Treasures of the Smithsonian Institution.* New York: Smithsonian Books, 1983.)

CURRENT POLITICAL ISSUES

Despite its growth and accomplishments over the past 150 years, the SI has one problem in common with most nonprofit organizations: continuing to grow and provide excellent services in an era of reduced and limited funding. Although the federal government supports the Smithsonian, it has not increased funding at a rate which will keep pace with the SI's renovation and growth plans. Donations from individuals and foundations are greatly appreciated, but they are declining and are rarely enough to cover major exhibitions or expansion projects. Faced with shrinking or limited public and private funds, the SI began in the 1990s to turn toward a long rejected source of support: corporate sponsorship.

Purists with a personal and a professional interest in the Smithsonian oppose using corporate money because they feel accepting such funds jeopardizes the integrity of the institution. Opponents feel that funds from industry are not freely given but carry an expectation of returns through advertising, publicity, or endorsement. There is also a concern that corporations could dictate the content or nature of programs and exhibits they sponsor according to their own values or tastes.

Individuals and groups who support the cultivation and acceptance of corporate sponsorship do not deny that these concerns are valid. Given the reality of limited funds, however, they view these concerns as issues to be resolved, not reasons to reject corporate funding. Supporters feel that the continuing growth and vitality of the Smithsonian depends on corporate partnerships that accommodate the needs of the institution and the industry without damaging either.

With this goal in mind, the Smithsonian revised its policy in 1991 banning the display of corporate logos. The SI's position was that displaying a contributor's logo simply allows corporations full public recognition and appreciation for funding important exhibits and programs, thus encouraging such funding. The SI also began a corporate membership program to allow corporations to get to know the SI and identify possible projects that would be acceptable to the company as well as the Smithsonian prior to any specific funding request.

In 1996 Secretary I. Michael Heyman gave a speech declaring that it was not only the Smithsonian's responsibility but also its obligation to continue providing the American people with an institution of the highest quality and with increased access to its programs and services through growth. Heyman also stated that it was the SI's responsibility to juggle funds and needs so that its integrity would not be compromised, sponsors would take pride in supporting it, and its collections and expertise would be easily available. Heyman strongly advocated that each case of corporate sponsorship should be approached as an opportunity to further the mission of the SI by working out problems through partnerships.

Case Study: The Insect Zoo

One of Secretary Heyman's prime examples of a successful corporate partnership is the Smithsonian's Insect Zoo.

The Insect Zoo is one of the SI's most popular and educational offerings with thousands of specimens and opportunities for visitors to participate in research and

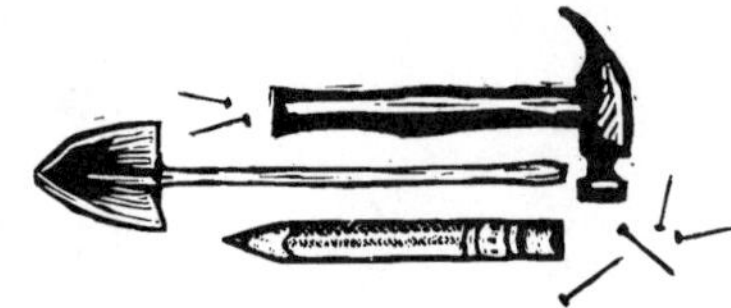

GET INVOLVED:

- The SI operates a Student Educational Employment Program for college and high school students. Long- and short-term volunteer and paid positions are available at the Smithsonian museums and research facilities and with traveling Smithsonian exhibitions. Positions are available throughout the year. Interested students should call the SI at (202) 357-1568 or inquire on-line at http://www.si.edu.
- The Smithsonian Environmental Research Center (SERC) investigates relationships among atmospheric, terrestrial, and aquatic environments and studies ecological processes. SERC offers a wide variety of educational programs including teacher and study guides, workbooks, puzzles, experiment ideas, visual aids, and workshops. Contact SERC at http://www.serc.si.edu for information on these materials.

hands-on activities. By 1989 the zoo needed to be replenished and its storage and cataloging systems upgraded and updated. Plans to meet repeated requests for traveling exhibits were also being made. Existing operating funds could not cover the cost of such a large project and repeated attempts to raise enough donated funds had been unsuccessful. Finally, one corporation volunteered to finance the entire undertaking, but the offer created two problems: the corporation expected its logo to be displayed during the restoration phase—the SI had never permitted such recognition except for an individual—and the corporation was Orkin Pest Control.

Faced with certainty that the Insect Zoo would not survive without the necessary funds, the SI Board of Regents agreed to display the name of the company's founder, O. Orkin, and the company agreed. Public outcry was loud and angry. Opponents of the decision felt that naming the Insect Zoo after the founder of a company whose sole purpose is to exterminate insects was like naming a cancer clinic after a tobacco company. The SI countered that if the survival of an important facility is at stake and corporate support does not interfere with content, then everything must be done to preserve and continue the facility.

As a result, the Insect Zoo was restored and the company enabled the SI to disseminate information about insects. Other plans for corporate sponsorship have not worked out as well, but the SI assesses each instance of corporate funding individually.

SUCCESSES AND FAILURES

In 1996 the SI launched the largest traveling exhibition ever organized by a museum called America's Smithsonian. More than 300 specimens from the SI collection—including presidential artifacts, works of art, priceless gems, a 4.5 million-year-old fossil shark jaw, and the ruby slippers from the *Wizard of Oz*—are being presented in cities throughout the country. Millions of Americans will have the opportunity to visit the Smithsonian treasures in their own regions during the exhibit's five-year tour. This is the first Smithsonian exhibition to represent every aspect of the institution, including each museum and every research organization as well as public programs such as the Festival of American Folklife.

Other successful efforts by the SI to increase accessibility to its resources include the development of interactive education materials and the creation of a Smithsonian home page on the World Wide Web in 1996. With the Web site's launching, millions of people throughout the world can visit the world's largest museum organization, view its treasures, watch films, listen to audio recordings, and conduct and gather research.

By mid-1997 the Smithsonian home page was receiving more than five million visitors each month. Such use of new technology has allowed the SI to greatly extend its historic mission.

FUTURE DIRECTIONS

In an effort to represent major American cultures more fully, the SI will continue to expand the role and collections of the Center for African American History and Culture. Also included in this effort is a long-term initiative to represent the Latino cultures of the United States more fully in its collections, programs, and staffing.

A National Museum of the American Indian is planned for the site east of the National Air and Space Museum in Washington. Scheduled to open in 2002 it will illustrate the historic traditions as well as the contemporary cultures of the many and varied American Indian nations. The collection currently housed at the Heye Center in New York will also expand.

AGENCY RESOURCES

The Smithsonian Institution Libraries (SIL) support the research, exhibitions, education programs, publishing, and administration of the Smithsonian as well as serve scholars and the general public. SIL contains more than 1.2 million books, 7,000 current journals, 40,000 rare books, and 1,800 manuscript groups as well as access to national databases and information networks. Each museum and research facility houses a library branch, and interlibrary loans and on-line access are available. SIL can be contacted by calling (202) 357-2240 or TTY (202) 357-2328, by E-mail at libmail@sil.si.edu, or through its home page at http://www.sil.si.edu.

The SI Web site also provides resource information; program updates; volunteer, intern, and employment opportunities; and access to Smithsonian collections online at http://www.si.edu.

The Smithsonian Institution Traveling Exhibition Service (SITES) program provides information on traveling Smithsonian exhibitions and local programming and educational opportunities across the country. SITES can be accessed on-line at http://www.si.edu/organiza/offices/sites.

AGENCY PUBLICATIONS

The SI publishes innumerable books, study guides, pamphlets, sound recordings, posters, and research reports through its publishing offices, individual museums, and research facilities.

Two of the SI's most popular publications are *Smithsonian* magazine which features articles on activities and collections throughout the Smithsonian system, and *Air and Space*, which highlights the programs and research of the National Air and Space Museum. Subscriptions to both magazines can be ordered on-line at http://www.si.edu or by calling the SI at (202) 357-1300.

Books include *Revolutionary Posters from Central and Eastern Europe*, *Fragile Ecologies*, *People of the Tropical Rainforest*, *Women and Flight*, and *Mexico: A Landscape Revisited*. These titles as well as catalogues of other books and materials available thorough the SI can be ordered on-line at http://www.si.edu/organiza/offices/sites/pub or by contacting the SI at (202) 357-1300.

The SI Office of Education promotes learning through the museums and their objects. Sample materials include *Resource Guide for Teachers: Education Materials Available through the Smithsonian*, and curriculum booklets such as "Protest and Patriotism: A History of Dissent and Reform," and "Image and Identity: Clothing and Adolescence." These materials and many others can be ordered on-line at http://educate.si.edu/about or by contacting the SI at (202) 357-1300.

BIBLIOGRAPHY

"America's Attic." *USA Today*, July 1996.

Heyman, I. Michael. "Smithsonian Institution's Corporate Partnership Program." *Smithsonian*, February 1997.

———. "Smithsonian Institution's Gardens and Plantings." *Smithsonian*, April 1997.

———. "Smithsonian Perspectives: In its Early Days, the Smithsonian Faced the Civil War, a Disastrous Fire and a Vastly Uncertain Future." *Smithsonian*, June 1996.

———. "Traveling Exhibition and Voices of Discovery Program." *Smithsonian*, March 1997.

Leech, Michael. "150 Years of Lucky Dip." *History Today*, July 1996.

Official Guide to the Smithsonian. Washington, D.C.: Smithsonian Institution Press, 1986.

Park, Edwards. *Treasures of the Smithsonian Institution*. New York: Smithsonian Books, 1983.

Smithsonian Year 1996: Annual Report for the Smithsonian Institution. Washington, D.C.: Smithsonian Institution Press, 1997.

Wiley, John P., Jr. "Phenomena, Comment and Notes: Looking at the Smithsonian from the Inside, a 'Random Sample' of Anthropologists, Biologists and Geologists Explain Why They Consider it an Inimitable Place to Work." *Smithsonian*, June 1996.

Social Security Administration (SSA)

PARENT ORGANIZATION: Independent
ESTABLISHED: August 14, 1935
EMPLOYEES: 64,085

Contact Information:

ADDRESS: Office of Public Inquiries
6401 Security Blvd.
Baltimore, MD 21235
PHONE: (410) 965-7700
TOLL FREE: (800) 772-1213
TDD (HEARING IMPAIRED): (800) 325-0778
URL: http://www.ssa.gov
COMMISSIONER: Kenneth S. Apfel

WHAT IS ITS MISSION?

The Social Security Administration (SSA) states that its mission is "to administer national Social Security programs as prescribed by legislation, in an equitable, effective, efficient, and caring manner." It is dedicated to administering the nation's "social insurance" program for the elderly and the disabled and to proposing solutions to the problems of poverty and financial insecurity through other SSA programs.

HOW IS IT STRUCTURED?

The SSA is an independent agency in the executive branch of the federal government. At the head of the SSA is a commissioner appointed by the president, with the advice and consent of the Senate. The commissioner is assisted by a chief actuary, a general counsel, an inspector general, and a chief of staff. Deputy commissioners head the Offices of Communications, Finance, Assessment and Management, Human Resources, Legislation and Congressional Affairs, Operations, Programs and Policy, and Systems. The SSA is headquartered in Baltimore, Maryland, with 1,292 district and branch offices, 38 tele-service centers, and six program service centers in 10 regions. These field offices inform the public about Social Security programs and assist beneficiaries with claims, referrals, and appeals.

PRIMARY FUNCTIONS

The SSA administers the social insurance programs of the federal government. Social insurance, which originated in nineteenth-century Europe, is the insuring of citizens by their government against loss of the ability to earn an income through uncontrollable or unavoidable circumstances. In general, social insurance is funded through government collection of tax money, which is then used to supplement the income of those in need. The Social Security programs of the United States are its primary means of ensuring a continuance of income for families and individuals when earnings from employment stop or decrease because of retirement, death, or disability. Employees, employers, and the self-employed contribute to Social Security through payroll deductions and taxes that go into a general fund from which the SSA distributes monthly payments to beneficiaries.

PROGRAMS

The SSA administers four major programs and provides support to several others. The Old Age and Survivors Insurance and the Disability Insurance (OASDI) programs are commonly referred to as Social Security. The monthly benefit amount to which an individual (or spouse and children) may become entitled under the OASDI program is based on the individual's taxable income, therefore, on how much the individual paid into the SSA over the course of his or her employment.

Supplemental Security Income (SSI) provides or supplements the income of elderly, blind, or disabled individuals. Children and adults may receive SSI payments because of disability or blindness. SSI benefits are financed from general tax revenues and are often supplemented by state benefits.

The SSA also administers the Black Lung Program which pays monthly cash benefits to coal mine workers who are victims of black lung disease and their dependents and survivors. The SSA covers only those claims filed by miners before July 1973 and survivor claims filed before January 1974 or within six months of the death of the miner or widow on the SSA rolls, whichever is later. Any claims filed after these dates are the responsibility of the Department of Labor.

The SSA also provides service-delivery support to the Medicare, Medicaid, and Food Stamp programs by providing public information, referrals, and assistance with applications. Medicare is the nation's program to aid the elderly and the severely disabled in paying for medical care; Medicaid provides a similar service for the financially disadvantaged.

BUDGET INFORMATION

The projected 1999 budget for the SSA is $433.72 billion, approximately 25 percent of federal expenditures. OASDI benefits account for 91 percent of SSA's expenditures. All other benefits total 7 percent of expenditures. The administrative costs of the SSA, paid for through the Limitation on Administrative Expenses Account, make up the remaining 2 percent of the budget.

BUDGET: *Social Security Administration*

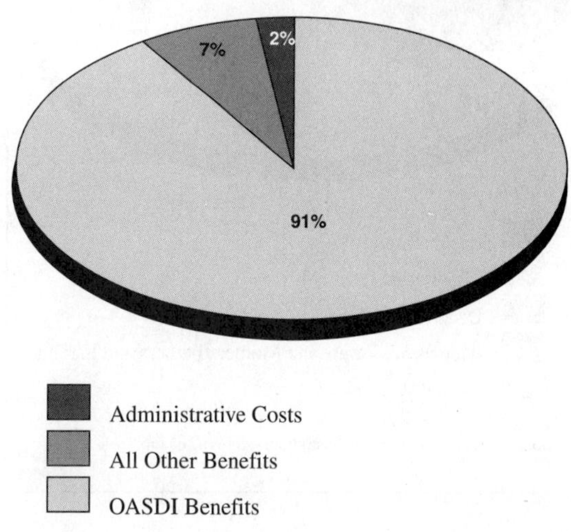

HISTORY

The SSA originated as the Social Security Board (SSB) in 1935 to oversee the new social insurance programs that were developed to respond to the economic crises of the Great Depression. Social Security became a family-based economic security program in 1939 when amendments to the original act added two new categories of benefits. Income assistance was made available to the spouse and children of a retired worker (so-called dependent benefits), and survivors benefits were to be paid to the family in the event of the premature death of a covered worker.

In 1939 the Federal Security Agency (FSA) was created, encompassing the SSB, the Public Health Service, the Office of Education, the Civilian Conservation Corps, and the U.S. Employment Service. The SSB was renamed the Social Security Administration in 1946.

When President Dwight D. Eisenhower abolished the FSA and created the Department of Health, Education and Welfare (HEW) in 1953, the SSA was made a part of the new cabinet agency. HEW was replaced by the Department of Health and Human Services in 1980.

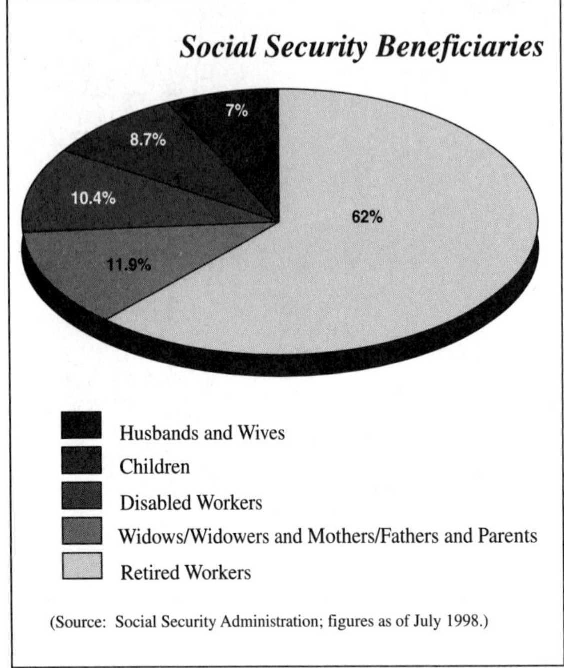

(Source: Social Security Administration; figures as of July 1998.)

Legislation signed by President Bill Clinton in 1994 returned the SSA to its original status as an independent agency, effective March 31, 1995.

CURRENT POLITICAL ISSUES

When Social Security was established in 1935 there were 13 workers paying into the fund for every worker receiving benefits, and the average American lived to be 62 years old. In 1997 there were only three workers for every beneficiary, and life expectancy had increased to 76 years. These demographics, along with expanded programs, have caused a long-term funding crisis for the SSA. According to reports by the Social Security Trustees, by 2013 Social Security will begin to pay out more each year than it collects in taxes.

Every week's collection of Social Security payroll taxes first goes to pay benefits to retirees, then the surplus is used to finance other federal spending. The Social Security "trust fund" is the equivalent of a series of government bonds that can be repaid only by raising the money through a combination of spending cuts, tax increases, and further borrowing. Thus, relying on the trust fund to cover future shortages is futile.

Efforts to confront Social Security's problems have been hampered by political considerations. Americans over age 60 represent 50 percent of the voting population, and they have made it clear through their votes and their lobbying organization, the American Association of Retired Persons (AARP), that they will not support candidates who endorse cutting Social Security benefits or increasing taxes on benefits. In 1996, 68 percent of Americans surveyed expressed a desire to see all social insurance programs continue but said they believed that special interests would stand in the way of necessary reforms.

Case Study: Social Security Reforms

In January 1997 the government's advisory council on Social Security proposed three reform options to resolve the Social Security funding crisis. Instead of cutting benefits, the options centered on investing existing funds in the stock market to make the assets work harder. Five of the 13 council members favored the option to direct 40 percent of payroll taxes into new personal-security accounts, similar to Individual Retirement Accounts (IRAs), and to allow individuals to choose where to invest their money. A second option, backed by two other council members, would impose an additional 1.6 percent payroll tax. Monies collected would be put into individual accounts to be managed by the government, with individuals choosing from limited investment options. Six members of the advisory council backed a third option, which would allow the government to invest up to 40 percent of Social Security assets in the stock market. This option would also increase payroll taxes.

Although 50 percent of Americans favored investing Social Security funds in the stock market, critics charged that the investment proposal would work only if the stock market continued to rise indefinitely. Opponents also voiced concern that individuals who were knowledgeable enough to invest their deductions for high profits might want to reap those profits rather than have them redistributed to all recipients. Further, they countered that such possessiveness of profits could endanger benefits to the working poor and the disabled.

Some critics of the investment proposal supported the recommendations of yet another commission. In 1996 it had been discovered that the Consumer Price Index (CPI), which measures changes in wages and costs of consumer goods, had overestimated the cost-of-living increase by 1.1 percent. Because Social Security check amounts are increased according to the CPI's projected cost-of-living increases, recipients were receiving benefits that exaggerated the inflation rate. The commission found that by simply reducing the CPI by that 1.1 percent per year, the government could save $1 trillion by 2015. Benefit amounts would continue to rise with the true cost of living, and the Social Security reserves would be solvent until the middle of the twenty-first century.

Politicians, like many Americans, were reluctant to reduce Social Security benefits in any way. Critics of the 1.1 percent plan charged that it still would not pay for Medicaid, Medicare, and Social Security benefits at their present rates of growth. Instead, many Congressmen, including Senators Daniel Moynihan (D-NY) and Bob Kerry (D-Nebr), continued to propose privatizing the system, to some degree or another, by having people invest some of the money currently going toward their payroll taxes into the stock market. Such plans continue to attract critics who question if it is safe for Americans to rely on the unstable stock market for their retirement benefits. Even those who support the various plans admit that the proposed funding options will not totally solve a very serious long-term problem. In truth, it is almost impossible to predict how the U.S. economy will fare over an extended period, especially since Social Security is itself a substantial part of the economy. This fundamental uncertainty about the economy will surely spark debate and criticism as the various reform packages are considered.

FUTURE DIRECTIONS

Top priority for the SSA in the twenty-first century is to find a long-term solution to its funding problems. Legislation passed in 1996 requires the SSA to also develop long-term procedures for reviewing disability claims for children and adults more frequently to determine whether they qualify for continued benefits.

AGENCY RESOURCES

Answers to questions about Social Security, SSI, and disability benefits, as well as information on applying for benefits, can be obtained on-line at http://www.ssa.gov or by calling the SSA at 1-800-772-1213. For this or other information about the SSA, write the Office of Public Inquiries, Social Security Administration, 6401 Security Blvd., Baltimore MD 21235.

To report Social Security fraud, call the SSA Fraud Hot Line at 1-800-269-0271 or write SSA Fraud Hot Line, PO Box 17768, Baltimore MD 21235.

AGENCY PUBLICATIONS

SSA pamphlets and fact sheets include *The Social Security Handbook, Social Security: How You Earn Credits, Welfare Reform and SSI Childhood Disability, Social Security: What Every Woman Should Know,* and *Social Security: Numbers for Newborns.* These and other publications are available on-line at http://www.ssa.gov or by contacting the SSA at 1-800-772-1213. The SSA also produces the *Social Security Bulletin* and its *Annual Statistical Supplement.* Contact the publications staff at the Office of Research, Evaluation, and Statistics, 500 E St. SW, Washington, DC 20254 for further information on SSA publications.

FAST FACTS

The first three digits of Social Security numbers are assigned by the geographical region in which the person applying for a number resides. Generally numbers are assigned beginning in the Northeast and moving westward, so people on the East Coast have the lowest numbers and people on the West Coast have the highest numbers.

(Source: Social Security Administration, 1997.)

BIBLIOGRAPHY

Berkowitz, Edward D. *Social Security: The Life of Wilbur J. Cohen.* Lawrence, Kansas: University of Kansas Press, 1995.

Coll, Blanche D. *Safety Net: Welfare and Social Security 1929–1979.* Lanham, Maryland: University Press, 1995.

Goodgame, Dan. "Many Happy Returns." *Time,* 20 January 1997.

Kingson, Eric, and James Schulz. *Social Security in the Twenty-first Century.* New York: Oxford University Press, 1997.

Leuchtenburg, William. *The Supreme Court Reborn: The Constitutional Revolution in the Age of Roosevelt."* New York: Oxford University Press, 1995.

Lynch. Michael W. "Retirement Plans: Genuine Social Security Reforms Appear Surprisingly Likely." *Reason,* August–September 1998, p. 56(3).

Thomas, Evan. "Social Insecurity." *Newsweek,* 20 January 1997.

Substance Abuse and Mental Health Services Administration (SAMHSA)

PARENT ORGANIZATION: Department of Health and Human Services
ESTABLISHED: October 1, 1992
EMPLOYEES: 574

Contact Information:

ADDRESS: 5600 Fishers Lane
Rockville, MD 20857
PHONE: (301) 443-8956
FAX: (301) 443-9050
URL: http://www.samhsa.gov
ADMINISTRATOR: Nelba Chavez, Ph.D.

WHAT IS ITS MISSION?

The Substance Abuse and Mental Health Services Administration (SAMHSA) is the agency of the federal government that helps Americans with the physical and psychological problems associated with substance abuse and mental illness. According to the agency, "SAMHSA's mission within the Nation's health system is to improve the quality and availability of prevention, early intervention, treatment, and rehabilitation services for substance abuse and mental illnesses, including co-occurring disorders, in order to improve health and reduce illness, death, disability, and cost to society." In particular, SAMHSA provides the infrastructure for community prevention and treatment programs to help those in need. The agency also expresses the desire to "focus national attention and resources on improving service delivery and setting standards of care."

HOW IS IT STRUCTURED?

SAMHSA is an operating division of the Department of Health and Human Services. The different branches of SAMHSA forge partnerships with states, counties, communities, employers, consumers, families, health care professionals, and other federal agencies in order to service the public. For example, SAMHSA is working with the Health Care Financing Administration to develop state health care reforms. In addition, the organization has joined other federal agencies within the Department of Health and Human Services (DHHS) in the fight against teenage smoking. The agency is led by an administrator who is appointed by the president to serve an open-ended term.

SAMHSA consists of four main administrative offices as well as several special-focus offices. The Office of Applied Studies (OAS) is responsible for collecting, analyzing, and disseminating substance abuse data. Two of the most important studies this office oversees are the *National Household Survey on Drug Abuse* and *The Drug Abuse Warning Network.* The Office of Program Services manages the information resources, human resources, finances, as well as grants and contracts for the entire agency. The Office of Extramural Activities Review oversees the many programs that SAMHSA funds and assists, but which are administered mainly outside the agency itself. Finally, the Office of the Administrator is responsible for policy development, communications, and public affairs. It also consists of special-focus offices that concentrate on specific topics such as managed health care, women's services, alcohol policy, acquired immunodeficiency syndrome (AIDS), and minority concerns.

In addition to these offices, SAMHSA has three major program centers. The Center for Mental Health Services (CMHS) provides services to facilitate the treatment of mental illness and educates the public and policymakers about the disease. A key focus of this center is knowledge exchange, especially scientific information. CMHS sponsors many service-related programs, including consumer and family self-help programs.

The Center for Substance Abuse Prevention (CSAP) focuses on preventing alcohol, tobacco, and illicit drug problems. It emphasizes education and services at both the individual and community levels. The center pays special attention to groups at high risk for addictions.

The Center for Substance Abuse Treatment (CSAT) develops and supports programs that specialize in treatment services for people who are addicted to alcohol and drugs. It emphasizes community-based, comprehensive services. Because no one treatment program is effective for everyone, CSAT supports a wide range of services to offer assistance to all those in need.

PRIMARY FUNCTIONS

To achieve its goal of improving substance abuse and mental health prevention and treatment, SAMHSA sponsors a wide range of services. In particular, SAMHSA develops knowledge about substance abuse prevention, addiction treatment, and mental health services. It supports high-quality research in these areas and ensures that the information gathered is made easily available to policymakers, health professionals, and the public. To accomplish this, SAMHSA has created electronic databases, toll-free hot lines, and numerous publications. The agency also develops, implements, and sponsors national education campaigns to promote general awareness about substance abuse and mental illness and to address specific problem areas or populations, such as teen smoking and AIDS. It also works with states, communities, health professionals, and consumers to provide the necessary services and programs to those in need.

SAMHSA conducts most of its work through grants and contracts with state and local governments and private organizations that provide substance abuse and mental health services. However, SAMHSA is more than a funding agency. It establishes national goals, priorities, and strategies to create a national perspective about how to deal with substance abuse and mental health issues that spans across states and organizations.

PROGRAMS

Each center of SAMHSA sponsors a variety of programs for its particular interest area. The Center for Mental Health Services (CMHS) is responsible for the mental health programs of SAMHSA. The largest program of this center is the National Mental Health Services Knowledge Exchange Network (KEN). This is a database of resources on mental health services at the federal, state, and local levels, including mental health organizations, professional associations, and consumer and family advocacy. The information can be accessed online at http://www.mentalhealth.org or via a toll-free information line at 1-800-789-2647.

CMHS also sponsors Community Mental Health Services Block Grants. These are federal partnerships with states to develop mental health services. CMHS offers financial support, training programs, and program planning to state mental health organizations. In addition, the center organizes programs around particular issues (such as mental health statistics) and populations in need (such as children, the homeless, and those with AIDS).

The Center for Substance Abuse Prevention (CSAP) develops funding and education programs and works with states, businesses, labor, and international organizations to encourage intervention and prevention. The CSAP grant programs fund a wide range of activities, providing support for high-risk youth, pregnant women and infants, and community partnerships.

Knowledge dissemination programs are a key part of CSAP. Public education campaigns include "Be Smart Don't Start," "By Our Own Hands," "Reality Check," and "Girl Power." In addition, CSAP sponsors the National Clearinghouse for Alcohol and Other Drug Information, which offers numerous publications on alcohol and other substance abuse through the Internet at http://www.health.org/pubs.htm or through a toll-free number, 1-800-729-6686. It also sponsors PREVLine (Prevention Online), which is an electronic database on alcohol and drug information available at http://www.health.org.

BUDGET:

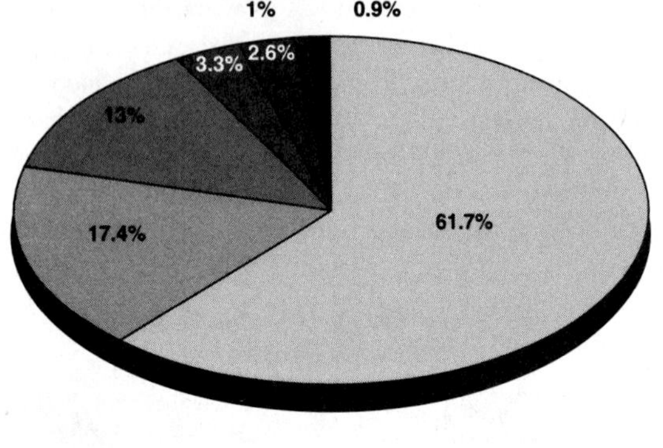

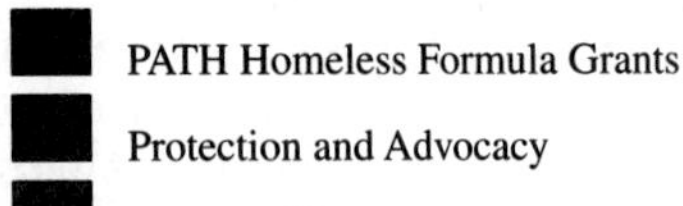

Like the other centers of SAMHSA, the Center for Substance Abuse Treatment (CSAT) works closely with states and communities to develop needed programs, in this case focusing on treatment. For example, CSAT offers a Substance Abuse Prevention and Treatment Block Grant, which provides funding to states to design effective treatment programs for their citizens.

CSAT also supports the National Drug and Alcohol Treatment Routing Service. This is a toll-free number, 1-800-662-HELP, offering referrals and other information for people seeking alcohol and drug treatment. In addition, the center sponsors demonstration programs that focus on particular problem areas, including criminal justice programs to help substance abusers in the criminal justice system. There are also programs for women, their infants and children, and outreach programs for people with AIDS.

BUDGET INFORMATION

In 1997 the total budget for SAMHSA was $2.1 million. The largest portion of this budget, 61.7 percent, went to the Substance Abuse Block Grant. The next-largest amount, 17.4 percent, was spent on knowledge development and application. Of this 17.4 percent, 7.3 percent was spent on substance abuse prevention, the same amount on substance abuse treatment, and the remaining 2.7 percent on mental health. The remaining 20.9 percent of the total 1997 budget was allocated as follows: 13 percent for Mental Health Block Grant, 3.3 percent for children's mental health services, 2.6 percent for program management, 1.0 percent for protection and advocacy, and 0.9 percent for PATH Homeless Formula Grants.

In 1998, the SAMHSA budget appropriation was slightly larger than in 1997 at $2.1 million. The extra money was allocated for two new activities, $6,000 for High Risk Youth and $18,000 for National Data Collection. The estimated 1999 budget was $2.3 million.

HISTORY

The first mental hospitals in the United States were established in the late 1700s. The federal government became involved with issues involving mental health in the mid 1850s, when it opened the first Government Hospital for the Insane. In 1930 the government founded the Narcotics Division of the Public Health Service, which later became the Division of Mental Hygiene. This was the first time that substance abuse and mental illness were treated as part of an overall mental health movement.

On July 3, 1946, President Truman signed the National Mental Health Act into law and solidified the government's commitment to treating mental illness. This act created the National Institute of Mental Health (NIMH) to facilitate mental health research. By the mid-1960s alcohol and drug abuse had gained public attention as serious health problems. The federal government responded to this problem by creating the National Institute on Alcohol Abuse and Alcoholism (NIAAA). In 1974 mental health and substance abuse programs were joined together under the Alcohol, Drug Abuse, and Mental Health Administration (ADAMHA). This agency was responsible for both the federal research and service activities in the areas of substance abuse and mental health. ADAMHA was composed of the NIMH, the NIAAA, and the newly created National Institute of Drug Abuse (NIDA).

In 1992 Congress proposed a bill to reorganize ADAMHA and separate the research and services programs. The bill was passed on October 1, 1992, as Public Law 102-321. Under this legislation, the three research institutes of ADAMHA were transferred to the National Institutes of Health. What remained of ADAMHA became SAMHSA, a services administration. The Offices of Substance Abuse Prevention and Substance Abuse Treatment under ADAMHA became two centers of SAMHSA. In addition, the 1992 law created the Center for Mental Health Services. The first administrator of SAMHSA, Dr. Nelba Chavez, was appointed by the president in 1992.

CURRENT POLITICAL ISSUES

Since its creation in 1992, SAMHSA has been a very active agency. It has worked to create partnerships with other federal agencies, with other levels of government, with private organizations, and with consumers to attain its goals of substance abuse and mental health prevention and treatment. It has also invested a great deal of energy and resources in public services, particularly those that give Americans direct access to the agency, such as toll-free numbers and a Web site.

However, social, political, and financial changes have a serious impact on the government, and agencies such as SAMHSA need to be able to respond to new challenges. These new challenges may arise from new products that pose civil rights issues, like the home drug-testing kit, patented by Psychemedics, approved by the Food and Drug Administration, and supported by the U.S. Department of Health and Human Services. New research findings can also pose a challenge to the agency. For example, the Parents' Resource Institute for Drug Education published results from its 1997 study of drug use among youth that contradicted some of the findings of the *National Household Survey on Drug Abuse*, which claimed that the number of teenagers using drugs was decreasing. In addition, budget restraints and health care reform initiatives, such as managed health care, have challenged SAMHSA to develop ways to provide quality services at lower costs.

Case Study: Managed Mental Health Care

One of the hottest political issues of the 1990s, and a cornerstone of the Clinton administration, was health care reform. The skyrocketing costs of health care and the growing number of Americans without health insurance have created the demand for health care reform. One response to this demand has been managed health care, a system whereby the type and amount of health care for each individual is determined by managed health care companies, rather than by physicians. The system is designed to eliminate unnecessary treatments, thereby reducing costs yet still providing adequate health care.

Managed health care has become the norm for mental health care. According to a *Newsweek* report called "How More Mental-Health Insurance Can Lead to Even Less Care" (1996), approximately 125 million Americans have managed mental health care benefits. Although this money-saving plan looks good on paper, many mental health care professionals and patients are questioning the quality of care under this new system.

Under the managed care system, a patient seeking mental health care must first call the company's toll-free number and explain the problem to an anonymous caseworker. The caseworker then gives the patient a list of approved therapists, from which the patient can choose a doctor for one consultation. After the initial consultation, if more sessions are needed, the therapist must appeal to the managed care company for approval.

Critics of this system argue that the quality of mental health care is being compromised to save money. For example, the caseworker who handles the toll-free calls and who makes the first important decision about the type of care may not be qualified to deal with the wide range of calls that are received. In addition, managed care companies favor drug treatment over psychotherapy because it is more cost-effective. However, some companies will not allow prescriptions for the newest drugs because they are more expensive. Instead, these companies recommend older, cheaper drugs, even though they may not be as safe or effective.

Another drawback to the managed care system is its breach of patient confidentiality. For a therapist to request more therapy for a patient, detailed reports of the patient, sometimes even including the therapist's notes, must be given to the managed care company to make a case for more treatment. This means that intimate details about a patient could end up in computer data banks with little security over who can access this information.

Mental health groups and politicians have been publicly challenging the quality of managed health care. Congress passed a parity law in 1997 to ensure that health plans applied the same dollar limits to mental and physical conditions. Action to protect patient confidentiality has been more complicated. By the Health Insurance Portability and Accountability Act of 1996, however, Congress must enact medical privacy legislation by August 1999, or the DHHS can and must impose confidentiality measures of its own devising.

SAMHSA has actively responded to the changes under managed mental health care. In November 1995 the agency created the Office of Managed Care to address the issues of consumers, payers, and providers. In addition, each of SAMHSA's three centers also has an Office of Managed Care to deal with matters specific to those centers.

SAMHSA is also working with other state and federal agencies to improve the quality of managed care. For example, the Health Care Financing Administration (HCFA) created the Quality Improvement System for Managed Care (QISMC) to oversee Medicare and Medicaid managed care plans. The program sets standards, provides technical assistance, and rewards good performances in order to improve the quality of care. SAMHSA formed an interagency agreement with HCFA to fund the QISMC project to include mental health and substance abuse services.

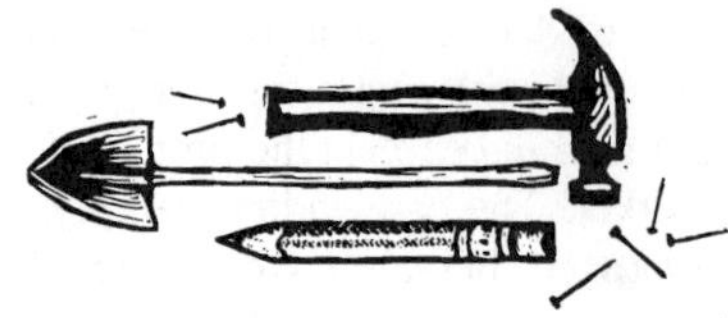

GET INVOLVED:

- September is "Treatment Works! Month." To celebrate, the Center for Substance Abuse Treatment, along with the National Association of Alcoholism and Drug Abuse Counselors, has designed a free information kit for individuals to organize a "Treatment Works! Month" promotion in their communities. The kit includes fact sheets on substance abuse and a "how to" guide to promote substance abuse treatment. More information is available on-line at http://www.health.org/cstat/txtfiles/index.htm or by calling CSAT at (301) 443-5700.
- In 1996 the Department of Health and Human Services launched the "Girl Power!" campaign. "Girl Power!" is a nationwide education initiative aimed at nine- to fourteen-year-old girls. It is within this age group that girls lose self-confidence, perform less well in school, and are more susceptible to negative influences such as drugs and alcohol. It is the hope of "Girl Power!" that girls will gain a sense of empowerment. Information and campaign materials can be obtained through the National Clearinghouse for Alcohol and Drug Information at 1-800-729-6686, TDD 1-800-487-4889, or by sending E-mail to gpower@health.org. Information is also available on-line at http://www.health.org/gpower/campaign.
- The Center for Substance Abuse Prevention sponsors a Teleconferencing Initiative to promote substance abuse prevention. It has scheduled monthly broadcasts on satellite and cable television on informative drug-related topics. It encourages the public to not only watch these programs but also use them at community meetings or in the classroom. For more information, call CSAP at (301) 443-0365, or E-mail nnadal@samhsa.gov, or go to the teleconferencing Web site at http://www.health.org/promos/youth.html.

SAMHSA is working to improve managed mental health and substance abuse care in four key areas. First, it aims to consolidate managed care information and collect reliable data on managed care systems. Second, it seeks to identify the types of technical assistance states, counties, and local providers will need to work within managed care systems. Third, SAMHSA provides technical assistance and training in managed behavioral health care. And finally, SAMHSA is evaluating the quality and effectiveness of managed health care, especially for high-risk groups.

FUTURE DIRECTIONS

SAMHSA seeks to improve its services through many new activities. For example, the 1998 fiscal year budget was increased in order to meet the needs of two particular areas: high-risk youth and national data collection. The Center for Substance Abuse Prevention plans to dedicate more resources to identifying high-risk youth and implementing programs to prevent substance abuse among these groups. Two groups that will receive special attention from this initiative are children of substance abusing parents and teen parents. In addition, SAMHSA plans to improve the quantity and quality of national data collection on substance abuse. Until 1998, the National Survey on Drug Abuse had been used to calculate national estimates of substance abuse. Beginning in 1999 SAMHSA will expand this survey to collect more detailed state and local data so that state comparisons can be made. This will increase the usefulness of the data being collected.

AGENCY RESOURCES

As part of the National Archive and Analytic Center for Alcohol, Drug Abuse, and Mental Health Data, SAMHSA created the Substance Abuse and Mental Health Data Archive (SAMHDA) at the University of Michigan to house research data on substance abuse and mental health and to encourage researchers to share this data. SAMHDA provides a description of all the data it archives, as well as an on-line analysis system, at http://www.icpsr.umich.edu/SAMHDA. Questions about the archives and its data can be directed to the toll-free number 1-888-741-7242.

The most comprehensive mental health resource is the National Mental Health Services Knowledge Exchange Network (KEN), which is a database of mental health resources at the federal, state, and local levels. KEN can be accessed at 1-800-789-2647, TDD (301) 443-9006, or fax (301) 984-8796. Its services are available on the Internet at http://www.mentalhealth.org. Information is also available at PO Box 42490, Washington, DC 20015. In addition, KEN operates a bulletin board that can be reached by calling 1-800-790-2647.

In addition to KEN, other mental health information resources include the Mental Health Services Database, which includes two thousand organizations that provide mental health services and information. There is also a Mental Health Directory, which lists 18,000 organizations that directly provide mental health services. The Center for Mental Health Services organizes a consumer/survivor database, which is a directory of consumers and survivors who are interested in CMHS activities. In addition there is the Mental Health Services Publications Database, with more than two thousand abstracts and a complete bibliography of published materials on the subject of mental health. Information about these services can be found at the Web site address http://www.mentalhealth.org/mhorgsdb, and other mental health resources can be found at http://www.mentalhealth.org/Resource/resource.html. In addition, more information about these and other resources can be obtained by calling the Center for Mental Health Services at (301) 443-0001.

General substance abuse information can be found at the National Clearinghouse for Alcohol and Other Drug Information by calling 1-800-729-6686, TDD 1-800-487-4899, or fax (301) 468-6433. This information is available in both English and Spanish. The Web address for this service is http://www.health.org/pubs.htm. In addition substance abuse treatment information is available through the National Drug and Alcohol Treatment Routing Service at 1-800-662-HELP. This service provides alcohol and drug abuse information and also gives referrals for people seeking treatment or other assistance.

Two important prevention resources are PREVLine and CSAP's Workplace Hotline. PREVLine (Prevention Online) is an on-line electronic database of alcohol and drug information located at http://www.health.org. CSAP's Workplace Hotline is a toll-free number, 1-800-967-5752, that provides information on substance abuse prevention and intervention strategies for the workplace. CSAP also offers a number of on-line databases, such as the Prevention Materials Database, Information About Drugs and Alcohol database, a smoking database, and the National Substance Abuse Web Index. These and other databases are available at www.health.org/dbases.htm.

AGENCY PUBLICATIONS

Information about all of SAMHSA's activities can be found in the *Substance Abuse and Mental Health Sourcebook*. This publication is available on-line at http://www.samhsa.gov/oasoasftp.htm, or by calling SAMHSA's Office of Communications at (301) 443-8956, or via E-mail at padams@samhsa.gov.

A list of publications from the Center for Mental Health Services can be found in the Mental Health Services Publications Database at http://cdmgroup.com/Ken-ef/HHRes.ctm or by calling CMHS at (301) 443-0001. In addition, there are a variety of publications produced by the National Health Services Knowledge Exchange Network (KEN). Two important KEN brochures are *Mental Illness Is Not a Full-Time Job* (1996) and *Before You Label People, Look at Their Contents* (1996). A complete list of KEN publications and videos is available on the Internet at http://www.mentalhealth.org/resource/orderfrm.htm or by calling KEN at 1-800-789-2647.

The National Clearinghouse for Alcohol and Drug Information also has a wide variety of publications, videos, and posters available to the public. These include important fact sheets about different types of drugs and tips for teens. In addition, the Treatment Improvement Protocols (TIPS), published by the Center for Substance Abuse Treatment, are available through the clearinghouse. A complete list of publications can be found on-line at http://www.health.org/pubs.htm. Consumers can also call 1-800-729-6686 or write to PO Box 2345, Rockville, MD 20847-2345 to request a list of publications.

BIBLIOGRAPHY

Beck, Melinda, et al. "Follow the Money: How More Mental Health Insurance Can Lead to Even Less Care." *Newsweek*, 20 May 1996.

Brink, Susan. "I'll Say I'm Suicidal," *U.S. News and World Report*, 19 January 1998, p. 63.

Brown, Barry S. *50 Strategies for Substance Abuse Treatment*. Rockville, MD: U.S. Department of Health and Human Services, Substance Abuse and Mental Health Services Administration, Center for Substance Abuse Treatment, 1997.

Chavez, Nelba. "A Renewed Mission: Where Should We Be Going in the 21st Century?" Rockville, MD: U.S. Department of Health and Human Services, Substance Abuse and Mental Health Services Administration, 1996.

Findlay, Steven. "Mental Health Groups Challenge Managed Care." *USA Today*, 21 February 1997, p. 1A.

Johnston, Lloyd, Patrick O'Malley, and Jerald G. Bachman. *National Survey Results on Drug Use From Monitoring the Future Study, 1975–1995*. Rockville, MD: U.S. Department of Health and Human Services, National Institute on Drug Abuse, 1996.

Schwartz, John. "Kit for Home Drug Testing Is Approved." *Washington Post*, 22 January 1997, p. A01.

Spragins, Ellyn. "Shortchanging the Psyche: Will Your HMO Be There If You Need Therapy?" *Newsweek*, 25 August 1997.

Supreme Court of the United States

ESTABLISHED: February 2, 1790
EMPLOYEES: 9

Contact Information:

ADDRESS: United States Supreme Court Bldg.
1 First St. NE
Washington, DC 20543
PHONE: (202) 479-3000
FAX: (202) 479-3388
URL: http://www.uscourts.gov
CHIEF JUSTICE: William H. Rehnquist

WHAT IS ITS MISSION?

The Supreme Court is the highest court in the United States, with ultimate jurisdiction over all cases arising under the Constitution, laws, and treaties of the United States. As the institution in which all of the nation's judicial power is vested, the Supreme Court has original jurisdiction in all cases involving ambassadors, public ministers, and counsels, and those arising from disputes between states. Original jurisdiction simply means that such cases are first argued in front of the Supreme Court. The Court's appellate jurisdiction (the right to review decisions of lower courts) is determined by Congress, under the legislature's constitutional authority.

HOW IS IT STRUCTURED?

The Supreme Court resides at the top of a federal court system that includes 14 courts of appeals, 94 district courts, and a few special courts. The pyramidal hierarchy of the U.S. court system makes two important assurances: the courts of appeals can correct errors made in trial courts, and the Supreme Court can make judgments uniform by reviewing cases in which Constitutional issues have been decided or in which two or more lower courts have reached different results. Traditionally, the judicial officers of the Supreme Court are called justices, while those in all other courts are called judges.

Supreme Court justices and federal judges are appointed by the president, with the advice and consent of the Senate. The Constitution states no qualifications for serving on the Supreme Court, or in any federal court;

BIOGRAPHY:

John Jay

Jurist and Statesman (1745–1829) John Jay played an important part in the early years of America's history. A highly-respected moderate who supported the Patriot cause, Jay represented New York at the First and the Second Continental Congress. As such, Jay was instrumental in the drafting and passage of the U.S. Constitution. In addition, he collaborated with Alexander Hamilton and James Madison in writing the *Federalist*, a series of papers that explained the U.S. Constitution. Jay also played a major role in drafting New York's first constitution. Although considered an elitist, Jay believed that people are the source of government authority, and he was fearful of corruption and nepotism in the federal bureaucracy. In a move rare for the time, Jay attempted to insert a clause in the New York constitution forbidding slavery. The motion, however, did not pass. Serving as chief justice of New York until 1779, Jay interpreted the state constitution he had helped compose. In 1790 President George Washington offered Jay the position of chief justice of the U.S. Supreme Court. Jay established two precedents as chief justice: states were deemed subordinate to the national government, and national treaties were established as supreme over state laws. His term as chief justice ended in 1795. In the same year Jay was elected governor of New York. He served two terms but declined the bid for reelection in 1801. He also refused renomination as chief justice; after 28 years of public service Jay longed to retire.

there is no age requirement, no citizenship requirement, nor even a requirement that an appointee have a background in law. Of course, clearly unsuitable candidates would not be confirmed by the Senate, and every Supreme Court nominee has been a skilled and accomplished legal professional. There is no mandatory age for retirement for justices or judges, and they can only be removed from office after being impeached, tried, and convicted by Congress for misconduct. To date, no Supreme Court justices have been removed in this way, although a few have been threatened with impeachment.

The Justices

The position of chief justice has developed steadily over the past two centuries into one of the most prestigious offices in the U.S. government. The chief justice, appointed by the president, is the chief administrative officer of the Court. While he or she holds no more judicial power than the associate justices, the chief justice administers the oath of office to the president, presides when the Court is in public session, and often assigns the writing of opinions. The chief justice is also the first to speak when the Court is in conference.

In addition to Court duties, the office of chief justice has acquired a number of responsibilities as head of the federal judicial system. The chief justice is chairman of the Judicial Conference of the United States, which is, in effect, the board of directors for the entire judiciary. He or she is chairman of the board of the Federal Judicial Center, a research, training, and planning organization for the judiciary. In these roles, a chief justice often spends as much as a third of his time on administrative duties that do not involve the associate justices. The chief justice has a personal administrative assistant to help coordinate and perform these tasks, and since 1939 has received additional assistance from the Administrative Office of the U.S. Courts, which draws up the budget and legal agenda for the judiciary, provides administrative assistance to judges and court staff, and audits and disburses funds for the operation of the courts.

The eight associate justices of the Supreme Court share equal judicial power with the chief justice. The only differences between the justices arise out of seniority; justices who have served longer on the Court are typically allowed to speak first during conference, and the junior justice traditionally serves as doorkeeper and messenger during these secret meetings. Although there are no laws prohibiting justices from serving other roles in government, most are careful to avoid the perceived conflict of interest. While a few justices have served diplomatic or advisory functions for certain presidents, nearly all have faced criticism for doing so.

Supporting Personnel

Clerk of the Court. The clerk is the Court's judicial business manager, and ensures that the Court can carry out its business in an orderly manner. The clerk's office has a wide range of important responsibilities, including the administration of dockets and argument calendars; the recording of all motions, petitions, briefs, and other documents filed with the Court; the preparation of the Court's formal judgments and mandates; the preparation and maintenance of the orders list; and the supervision

FAST FACTS

In 1998 the salary of the chief justice was $175,400; the salary of each of the eight associate justices was $167,900

(Source: U. S. Supreme Court Public Information Office, 1998.)

of the admission of attorneys to the Supreme Court bar. The clerk's office is also a constant source of procedural advice to those attorneys and litigants who need assistance with the Court's rules and procedures.

Marshal of the Court. As the overseer of the Supreme Court building's operations, the marshal is the Court's paymaster, general manager, and chief security officer. The marshal's wide range of responsibilities require the supervision of more than 200 employees, who help the marshal supervise federal property used by the Court, pay the justices and other Court employees, order supplies, and pay bills. In addition, the marshal oversees the armed Supreme Court Police Force, which polices the grounds, buildings, and streets adjacent to Supreme Court property.

The marshal also has a few important roles relating specifically to the daily business of the Court. The marshal and his aides receive visiting dignitaries, and escort the justices to formal functions outside the Court. During public sessions of the Court, the marshal announces the beginning of the proceedings, and during oral arguments, he or an assistant flashes the white and red lights that warn attorneys when a time limit for argument is about to expire.

Reporter of Decisions. After the opinions of justices have been delivered, the reporter of decisions, aided by a small staff, check all citations, correct typographical and other errors, and otherwise prepare the opinions for publication. It is the reporter who is ultimately responsible for both editing the opinions and supervising their printing and publication in the official *United States Reports.*

Public Information Officer. The Court's public information officer is responsible for answering questions from the public, facilitating accurate coverage of Court proceedings and decisions by the news media, and distributing information about the Court and the justices. On all matters other than the interpretation of opinions and orders, the public information officer is the Court's spokesperson.

Librarian. The Supreme Court Library contains about 300,000 volumes, and its access is generally restricted to Court personnel, members of the Supreme Court bar, members of Congress, their legal staffs, and government lawyers. However, the library will usually grant access to members of the public or press who specify a research interest.

Curator. The curator serves a historical function for the Court, tending the Court's papers and possessions, developing Court-related exhibits, and developing and offering educational programs about the Court's history and its collections of historical documents and artifacts. The curator also records events at the Court for future researchers.

Legal Office and Law Clerks. Supreme Court justices are permitted to hire as many as four law clerks for personal assistance in dealing with the heavy workload required of them. Clerks are hired personally by each justice, usually from the nation's top law schools, and consistently serve two primary functions. First, they read and analyze the thousands of cases that reach the Court each year, and often prepare summaries or memoranda for the justices' consideration. They also help, in whatever way a justice feels is appropriate, with the preparation of an opinion to be delivered. Depending on the justice for whom he or she works, a clerk may assume other responsibilities as well.

Supreme Court Lawyers

Although they are not employed by the Court, the attorneys who argue cases before it are an indispensable element of the Court's work. These lawyers counsel clients who bring cases before the Court, file petitions, file briefs, and argue cases before the Court. In order to appear before the Court, a lawyer must first pass the Supreme Court bar. The requirements for attorneys who hope to pass the bar are set by the clerk of the Court, who screens applicants and notifies them of their acceptance or rejection. New members may be welcomed formally by the chief justice, and are always sworn in by the clerk of the Court.

The Supreme Court bar is not a formal organization, but its unspoken leader is the solicitor general of the United States, who is appointed by the president to represent the U.S. government before the Court. Because the U.S. government is involved in so many of the cases that are argued before the Court, the solicitor general and staff appear more often than any other legal representatives.

PRIMARY FUNCTIONS

The Supreme Court is the only federal court that is mandated by the Constitution, and as such is the essence of the judicial branch of government. As the "court of last resort" in the U.S. justice system, it has two important powers: the authority to declare laws or actions of government officials (typically the president) unconstitutional, and the power to determine the constitutionality of state laws. These authorities are often referred to as the Court's power of judicial review.

Under the Constitution, both the executive and legislative branches are equipped with the means to check the power of the Supreme Court. If a president is unhappy with the rulings of justices, he can appoint new justices when vacancies occur. Presidents may also, in certain cases, refuse to enforce the ruling of the Court, though this is a rare occurrence that puts a president at risk of losing public support—even President Richard M. Nixon complied with the Court's rulings when it ordered him to turn over the incriminating Watergate tapes. Congress's checks on the Court are broader: it can overturn the Court's rulings by adopting constitutional amendments or new laws; it can limit the appellate jurisdiction of the Court; and it can impeach and remove justices from the Court.

Though the Supreme Court is assigned the first hearing of all cases involving interstate disputes, ambassadors, ministers, and counsels, very few cases like this surface in a given year. Most of the cases the Court hears are appeals of decisions of lower courts involving federal questions, or of the final decisions of the highest court in a given state where constitutional issues are involved. The Court chooses which cases it will hear, and limits its review to cases involving national issues. Appellants, or those who want to bring a case in front of the Court, usually petition the Court through a legal instrument known as a *writ of certiorari*. If the Court accepts the writ, the case is placed on the schedule, or docket, for argument. If the writ is rejected, the decision of the lower court is considered to be affirmed. Each year the Court receives thousands of writs—as many as 7,000—of which only a few hundred, at most, are accepted.

Operations of the Court

The Court's business is conducted in an annual session that begins on the first Monday in October and runs until its review of the cases on the docket are complete, usually some time in early summer. During the annual session, certain times are set aside for formal argument, for conferences, for the writing of opinions, and for the announcement of decisions. The Court may also hold a special term when necessary. Special terms are for urgent matters that cannot be postponed until the next session; an example is the 1958 *Cooper v. Aaron* case, in which the Court upheld a lower court order enforcing a desegregation plan for Little Rock High School.

Granting or Denying Review. When a case comes before the Supreme Court, it must first be accepted by the justices for discussion. The decision to accept or deny review of cases are made in conferences, where cases on the "discuss list" are first brought up. Only about one-fourth of appeals to the Court ever make it to the discuss list; the others are rejected without further consideration. Any justice can have a case placed on the discuss list through a simple request.

FAST FACTS

Of the 108 Americans who have served as Supreme Court justices, 104 have been white males. There have been only two African American justices and two women justices.

(Source: Joan Biskupic and Elder Witt, ed. *Guide to the U.S. Supreme Court.* Washington, D.C.: Congressional Quarterly, 1997.)

Conferences are held in strict secrecy—no staff or legal assistants are present. After each case on the list is discussed, the Court decides which will proceed to the oral argument stage. Traditionally, it takes the approval of at least four justices to have a case scheduled for oral argument, though this is not a formal rule. Cases approved for further review are placed on an "orders list," and then the Clerk of the Court arranges the schedule for oral arguments.

Oral Arguments. Cases are generally argued in the same order in which they are granted review, but the order is often changed due to changing circumstances. Before any are made, lawyers from each side supply the justices with written briefs and records. The attention these briefs receive before the arguments varies widely among the justices —some merely scan them, while others study them thoroughly.

Under the most recent rules of the Court, each side of a case is to be argued by one lawyer only unless special permission is granted, and lawyers are allowed only 30 minutes each to argue their side. During oral arguments, the justices may interrupt with questions or remarks as often as they please. Because the time limit for argument includes these questions and their answers, Supreme Court attorneys are required to be quick on their feet as well as thoroughly prepared. Questions typically consume about a third of a counsel's 30 minute time limit.

Conferences. Cases on which oral arguments have been heard are discussed and decided in conference; these conference sessions are also used to consider new motions, appeals, and petitions. Like the discuss list conferences, these are conducted in absolute secrecy; no other staff or messengers are allowed into the room for any reason. The strong tradition of conference secrecy has made the Supreme Court among the most leakproof of government institutions.

FAST FACTS

William O. Douglas was the longest serving Supreme Court justice. He retired in 1975 after serving 36 years and seven months

(Source: *World Almanac of U.S. Politics*, 1995.)

After the chief justice has introduced the case to be discussed, he speaks until his point is made, and then the associate justices speak in the order of their seniority. Theoretically, justices in conference may speak as long as they like, but time constraints have often led the chief justice to suggest that associate justices limit their commentary. The justice whose turn it is to speak is also, ideally, never to be interrupted, though stories of rare, quarrelsome conferences throughout history suggest that this informal rule is occasionally broken. Generally, however, discussions are polite and orderly.

It takes a simple majority vote of the justices participating in a conference to decide a case—five votes, if all nine justices are participating. At least six justices (a quorum) must participate in a conference to make a Supreme Court ruling.

Writing Opinions. In the Supreme Court, an opinion is a reasoned argument which explains the legal issues in a case and the precedents on which the opinion is based. Once the justices have voted on a case, the work of writing the majority opinion is assigned. In the cases in which the chief justice was in the majority, he assigns the task; if he is in the minority, the work is assigned by the most senior associate justice in the majority. The assigning justice considers a variety of factors before making a choice: the workload of the justices; the need to avoid extreme opinions; points made by certain justices during conference; and expertise in the particular area of law involved in a case. Often, an opinion has to be revised more than once to please each member of the majority.

Any justice may decide to write a separate opinion. If a justice agrees with the Court's decision but disagrees with some of the reasoning in the majority opinion, he or she may write a concurring opinion based on a different line of reasoning. If a justice disagrees with the majority, he may write a dissenting opinion or simply go on record as a dissenter without opinion. More than one justice may sign a concurring or dissenting opinion.

Issuing the Decision. After the drafts of all opinions concerning a case have been written, circulated, discussed, and revised, the final versions are printed. As the decision is announced in Court, copies are distributed among journalists and others in the Court's Public Information Office. Another copy is sent to the U.S. Government Printing Office (GPO), which reproduces it and distributes copies among federal and state courts and agencies. The Supreme Court itself receives 400 of these copies, and makes them available to the public free of charge for as long as the supply lasts. The GPO also prints the opinion for inclusion in the *United States Reports*, the official record of Supreme Court opinions.

BUDGET INFORMATION

The increased workload of the Supreme Court has forced a remarkable expansion in the support staff required by the nine justices; the full-time total personnel included in the 1998 budget numbered over 360. About two-thirds of the Court's 1998 $29 million budget was devoted to the salaries of these personnel, while the remainder was spent on items such as benefits, supplies, materials, and equipment. The Court's budgetary authority is acquired through the congressional appropriations process.

HISTORY

The Supreme Court took several years to establish itself in the federal system. The framers of the Constitution expected it to be the weakest branch of the government—while Congress would pass laws and appropriate money, and the president would execute the laws, the judiciary would apply the Constitution and laws to decide cases. They would not have any means to enforce these decisions once they were made, and they would use only the law—not their own values or beliefs—to decide cases. For this reason, according to constitutional framer Alexander Hamilton, the judiciary would be the "least dangerous branch."

In the government's early years, this prediction seemed to be true. The Constitution provided only for one Supreme Court, and it was Congress's responsibility to add other federal courts and determine their jurisdictions. This was done promptly after the ratification of the Constitution, in the Judiciary Act of 1789. But the newly created Court was not highly regarded, and many nominees refused to accept their appointments. Each of the first two chief justices resigned their appointments to take other positions in government, and one associate justice resigned (to take a state judgeship) in 1791 without ever attending a full formal session of the Court. Though the Court was given the authority by the Judiciary Act to review the rulings of state courts, there was very little business to conduct at the outset, except staffing the

Court and admitting attorneys to practice before it. Most of the new government's earliest tasks turned out to be executive and legislative, rather than judicial.

Origin and Development of the Court's Power

The status of the Court changed remarkably after the appointment of the third chief justice, John Marshall, in 1801. While his first term began slowly, there were significant events occurring outside the Court's chamber that would have a dramatic effect on the future of the entire government.

President John Adams was defeated in his reelection bid by Thomas Jefferson in 1800, the same year that the Supreme Court's chief justice, Oliver Ellsworth, resigned. Although Adams was a "lame duck" president, he took advantage of the opportunity to appoint his secretary of state, John Marshall, to the position of chief justice. A few days before Jefferson's victory, Congress, still controlled by Adams's party, passed two laws that would provide a new staff of circuit judges in the lower courts as well as new local judgeships in the District of Columbia.

This legislation would allow Adams to pack the courts with judges sympathetic to his party, just before Jefferson's inauguration. When the commissions were made out and signed for these new judgeships, it was the responsibility of Chief Justice Marshall to deliver them. He delivered some, but not all of them, before Jefferson took office, apparently assuming that Jefferson would merely confirm their appointments. Jefferson did follow through on some of the commissions, but he rejected many others. One of the rejected appointees was William Marbury who, along with three others, applied to the Supreme Court for a *writ of mandamus* (a document ordering government officials to do as they have been ordered) to Jefferson's Secretary of State, James Madison.

Marshall's Court appeared stuck—if it issued the writ, it was likely that Jefferson would instruct Madison to disobey it, and the Court would be powerless to enforce it. If it did not issue the writ, the Court would appear to be giving in to the power of the executive. Either way, the Court would appear weak and the commissions would not be delivered. Interpreting the law literally and speaking for a unanimous Court, Marshall insisted that Marbury was entitled to the commission, but the Court could not order it because its power to do so, though granted by the Judiciary Act of 1789, was not granted in the Constitution. Therefore, the Court ruled, the law itself was unconstitutional and the *writ of mandamus* could not be enforced.

This clever bit of logic established the case of *Marbury v. Madison*, in the eyes of many historians, as the most important in Supreme Court history because it set the precedent for the Supreme Court's power of judicial review. Marshall sacrificed the commissions to establish the Court as a powerful player in the federal government. In a single ruling, the Court at once claimed, applied, and defended its power to review and nullify congressional legislation that conflicted with the Constitution. This power was not explicitly granted by the Constitution, but it would be accepted as part of the Court's function from that point onward.

It was more than fifty years later before the Court overturned a congressional law for the second time, and it turned out to be a decision that both damaged the Court's reputation and threatened its newfound effectiveness. Under Roger Taney, the new chief justice under President Andrew Jackson, the Court struck down the Missouri Compromise of 1820, which regulated slavery in the territories. The ruling was angrily denounced by justices in the minority and by abolitionists throughout the country; it meant that Congress was essentially unable to control the spread of slavery. This case, the *Dred Scott* case, was to many Americans a clear over-extension of the Court's power, and the Court's reputation suffered. It was considered presumptuous for Taney and his majority to think that the courts could decide the issue of slavery, and by extension resolve the conflicts between federal and state governments.

After the Civil War

Industrialization proceeded at a rapid pace after the war. This development brought many economic benefits, but also some significant social problems. The businesses involved in this new commercial growth often exploited workers—employing young children, often in dangerous settings such as coal mines; forcing laborers to work brutally long hours; and paying them the lowest wages possible.

Court rulings throughout this period generally found in favor of business, due in part because the Court was dominated by justices who had been lawyers for large corporations. Beginning in the 1870s and intensifying into the 1900s, the Court struck down state laws that would regulate child labor, establish a minimum wage, establish the maximum number of hours in a work day, and allow employees to form and join labor unions. The rationale behind these Court decisions was often based on a person's right to conduct his own business, on his own property, as he pleased, in accordance with the Constitution. The Court even limited the provisions of many congressional antitrust laws, designed to break up monopolies within certain areas of business.

During this period, the Court's social views were as conservative as their economic viewpoint. The case that serves as the clearest example is *Plessy v. Ferguson*, an 1896 case involving a Louisiana state law requiring railroads operating in the state to provide separate rail cars for white and black passengers. The Court upheld the law, stating that it did not violate the equal protection provision of the Fourteenth Amendment because it was merely an exercise of police power to protect the peace. Justice John M. Harlan, the sole dissenter, argued that the ruling was inconsistent with the personal liberty of citizens, and contrary to the spirit and the letter of the Constitution. The decision, he warned, would prove to be "as pernicious as the decision made by this tribunal in the *Dred Scott* case." It would take several decades for Harlan to be proven right.

The New Deal Court

Supreme Court justices remained persistently conservative during the early years of President Franklin Roosevelt's administration. Roosevelt, elected to pull the nation out of the Great Depression, had launched a number of government programs that were designed to progressively repair the economy. Together, the programs were known as the New Deal, but the legislation required to enact them was struck down repeatedly by the Supreme Court—twelve New Deal laws were overturned from 1935 to 1936.

The Court's rulings sparked a serious crisis. Roosevelt, overwhelmingly re-elected in 1936, believed the voters were mandating that he take action to resolve the nation's economic problems. Frustrated, he began to look for ways to change the Court's views. He devised a judicial reform plan, explaining to Congress that the Court was handicapped by the advanced age of it members. His plan, which asked Congress to allow him to appoint an additional justice for each justice over the age of 70, was quickly labeled a "court-packing" plan, meant to install a majority of justices sympathetic to the New Deal. Since six justices were older than 70, the plan would have created a Court of 15 members.

While most members of Congress, and the American public, wanted to see the New Deal enacted, most disapproved of Roosevelt's attempt to tamper with the Supreme Court. Debate over the plan, however, appeared to convince at least two justices of the public's overwhelming support for the New Deal, and the majority's opinions began to reflect the popularity of the president and his agenda. It was the clearest evidence to date that the Court could be swayed by public opinion, and it began to shift its rulings to support the regulation of business.

Civil Rights

More recently the Court has turned its attention to the relationship between government and the individual in cases involving civil liberties and rights. The issue began to gather steam in the 1950s, when President Dwight Eisenhower appointed Earl Warren to be chief justice. Over the next two decades, the Warren Court began to overhaul government doctrine in three important areas: the rights of criminal defendants, racial segregation, and the reapportionment of congressional districts. It declared many laws unconstitutional during this period. In one of the most noteworthy civil rights cases, *Brown v. Board of Education* (1954), the Court ruled against racial segregation in schools, rejecting the idea of "separate but equal" institutions for citizens of different races.

The Court's stance on more unpopular civil rights issues involving criminal defendants or those accused of subversion, led to an eventual backlash against liberal Court rulings. President Richard M. Nixon, hoping to push the Court in a different direction, appointed the conservative Warren Burger to be chief justice in 1969; however, the Burger Court was generally reluctant to revise or overturn the Warren Court's doctrine. In addition, it appeared to take additional liberal stances on such issues as sexual discrimination and abortion. Republican President Ronald Reagan continued efforts to reshape the Court, appointing three conservative justices, including Chief Justice William Rehnquist, in his 1980–88 administration. Though the Rehnquist Court eventually contained seven conservatives during the Reagan years, divisions between these conservatives, and a reluctance to overturn judicial precedents, did little to alter the civil rights doctrine of the Warren Court.

Most expected the administration of Democratic President Bill Clinton, elected to a first term in 1992, to take the Supreme Court in a more liberal direction, but Clinton's two appointments generally reflected the moderate political opinions of the American public. The Court—though often by the narrowest of margins—ruled in favor of individual rights in cases involving such issues as gay rights and abortion, but also made several rulings that appeared to take a more conservative stance—including a ruling that race could not be the sole factor used to determine the shape of congressional districts. Opposed by a Republican-dominated Congress, the Clinton administration has had difficulty appointing judges to the federal courts, and in 1998 an overworked judicial system found itself threatened not only by a lack of qualified judges, but also by proposed legislation that would reshape the Court in a way that reflected Republican values.

CURRENT POLITICAL ISSUES

At the time the Constitution was drafted, some of the nation's founders opposed the structure of the new government because they feared it might allow the judicial branch to change laws through the process of interpretation. The Constitution is noticeably vague on the extent and limits of judicial power; the founders probably expected that the Supreme Court would exercise judicial restraint—that in the absence of clear constitutional provisions, existing state or federal laws, or legal precedents, the Court would simply uphold the ruling of lower courts and refrain from making policy. The idea is that the Court will attempt to apply a law as it was understood when it was enacted, rather than rule according to personal convictions or the apparent will of a political majority.

The ideal of judicial restraint has been difficult for the Supreme Court and the federal judiciary to uphold, however, and as a result some Court decisions have broken new ground and established legal doctrine. When

Court decisions do this, as in rulings such as *Brown v. Board of Education*, the Court involves itself in policy-making, and practices judicial activism. Depending on the political climate in which such rulings are made, judicial activism can be branded as either conservative or liberal. The generally pro-business rulings of the early twentieth-century Supreme Court were considered by many to be conservative activism, while later decisions such as *Roe v. Wade*, which established abortion rights for many U.S. women, were examples of liberal activism.

In recent years, several high-profile cases of judicial activism have prompted debate about the role of the Supreme Court and the judiciary in our federal system. Judicial activism is always unpopular with the party that opposes a ruling, especially in Congress where legislators do not appreciate encroachment on their power to make laws. But more forward-thinking critics of judicial activism oppose it on the grounds that when rulings are made not on the basis of constitutional principle or existing laws, but on the basis of politics or personal beliefs, the reputation of the federal judiciary as being judicious and objective is threatened. As a result, they claim, American citizens are deprived of the one national forum in which they have usually been assured of an impartial legal hearing.

The issue of judicial activism is one of the most complex problems in American government for two important reasons. First, the term "activism" has become relatively meaningless, applied as a derogatory term by those who disagree with Court rulings. Whether a ruling is truly ground-breaking or not, it is often denounced as activist by political opponents. In 1996, for example, a federal judge in California blocked the enforcement of a voter referendum that would repeal affirmative action programs in the state. Many conservative legislators branded the decision as activist for overturning the will of the state's voters. In 1994, however, when a federal judge in Oregon invalidated a referendum that approved physician-assisted suicide, these same conservatives were silent.

The second factor that makes the issue of activism so complicated is this: if the Constitution, existing state laws, and legal precedents pointed clearly and absolutely to how a case should be decided, the case would never reach the Supreme Court in the first place. The Court appears in some ways to always be breaking new ground, applying the law to difficult, particular situations that have not previously been debated to any great extent. During the Clinton administration, for example, the issues of congressional term limits, gay rights, and single-sex education were each at the core of prominent cases brought before the Supreme Court. The Constitution does not directly address these issues, and there were few precedents at the time the cases were brought before the Court.

Regarding these cases, opponents of judicial activism would ask the following: Does the Constitution address the issues of gay rights, term limits, or single-sex education? If not, why should the Supreme Court involve itself in these questions? Supporters of more activist rulings would respond with an example such as *Brown v. Board of Education*, which ended a long period of racial injustice in the United States. If not for the Court, how would the right to an equal education have been assured?

To strict advocates of judicial restraint, the answer would be that racial justice was the will of the people, and the people eventually would have elected representatives and officials who would have passed new laws prohibiting racial segregation. It might have taken longer, but it would have happened in accordance with the principles on which the U.S. government was designed to operate.

Case Study: The Judicial Reform Bill of 1998

After the mid-term elections of 1994, the administration of Democratic President Bill Clinton met with strong Republican opposition in both houses of Congress. As a result, the president experienced some trouble gaining confirmation for his appointments to federal judgeships (his two Supreme Court nominees, Ruth Bader Ginsburg and Stephen Breyer, were moderates who had been confirmed fairly easily). The rulings of federal judges who had already been approved, meanwhile, proved unpopular with many congressional Republicans who believed federal judges were overwhelmingly liberal, soft on criminals, and generally practiced a form of judicial activism that carried them beyond the mandates of their appointments.

The perceived liberal activism of Clinton-era judges was particularly frustrating for Republicans in the House of Representatives, who are constitutionally excluded from the process of confirming judges and justices. In 1997, House Republicans drafted a bill that became known as the Judicial Activism Bill, designed to reign in federal judges. As originally drafted, the bill would have required appeals of public referendums (such as California's Proposition 185 and Oregon's assisted-suicide measure) to be heard by three-judge panels rather than a single federal judge. A more controversial measure was to give litigants in civil cases the right to reject the first judge assigned to their case, for any reason.

Democratic legislators, predictably, opposed the bill, arguing that it was nothing more than an attempt to bully judges into making rulings more in line with Republicans' conservative policy goals. The bill, Democrats argued, would damage the independence of the judiciary without really stopping judges or justices from making unpopular decisions. However, some criticism of the bill came from within the ranks of Republicans in Congress—most notably, from Representative Henry Hyde (R-Illinois), the chairman of the House Judiciary Committee.

In the end, the bill was watered down with amendments to a point where few provisions of any consequence remained—the idea of a three-judge panel for hearing appeals to referendums was the only important measure preserved—and the Republican majority passed the bill in early 1998. The bill was largely a symbolic measure, however, that served primarily to mark conservative dissatisfaction with the judiciary; the Senate, which already exerts control over the federal bench through the confirmation of judges, had little interest in considering such legislation. Still, the attempt of the legislature to exert control over the judicial branch was troubling to many in all branches of government who saw the bill as a direct challenge to the independence of the judiciary.

FUTURE DIRECTIONS

In its *Long Range Plan for the Federal Courts*, published in 1995, the Judicial Conference of the United States claims that since 1904, while the population of the United States has increased by 200 percent, the number of appeals brought before the federal courts has increased more than a stunning 3,800 percent. A recent annual report by Chief Justice William Rehnquist refers to the federal judiciary's increasing workload as the most crucial issue facing the courts today. The challenge for the judiciary will be to preserve its core values while attempting adjustments in the courts' jurisdiction, function, structure, and governance.

Possible solutions to the overloaded and overworked courts include restructuring the way in which appeals are reviewed; limiting the rights of litigants to appeal the decisions of lower courts; diverting civil cases to other courts; limiting the jurisdiction of certain federal courts; maintaining a more efficient means of administrating the courts; and speeding and improving the process by which federal judges are appointed to fill vacant seats. Though no specific recommendations have been ordered, many alternative means to reaching these goals are put forth in the Judicial Conference's *Long Range Plan*. Implementation of these goals, of course, can only be brought about by congressional legislation that would enact such changes in the judiciary system.

AGENCY RESOURCES

Other than publications from outside sources, the best information resource on the Supreme Court is the Internet World Wide Web site of the Federal Judiciary at http://www.uscourts.gov. The site contains brief explanations of the organization and work of the federal court system, as well as links to other sites related to the Federal Judiciary. Tapes or transcripts of oral arguments can be accessed through the National Archives and Records Administration, 8601 Adelphi Rd., College Park, MD 20740.

For further information about the Supreme Court, contact the Public Information Office, United States Supreme Court Building, 1 First St. NE, Washington, D.C. 20543; phone (202) 479-3211.

AGENCY PUBLICATIONS

Federal court publications of interest to the general public include the annual report of the chief justice, short pamphlets such as "Understanding the Federal Courts," and the newsletter of the federal courts, titled *The Third Branch*. Many of these publications are available for viewing or downloading from the Federal Judiciary's Web site.

The decisions of the Court are edited and published annually by the Reporter of Decisions in the official *United States Reports*. Orders and opinions are available through the Government Printing Office's Superintendent of Documents, Washington, D.C., 20402; phone (888) 293-6498 or E-mail gpoaccess@gpo.gov.

BIBLIOGRAPHY

Baum, Lawrence. *The Supreme Court*. Washington, D.C.: Congressional Quarterly Press, 1998.

Biskupic, Joan. *The Supreme Court at Work*. Washington, D.C.: Congressional Quarterly, 1997.

Cheney, Timothy D. *Who Makes the Law: The Supreme Court, Congress, the States, and Society*. Upper Saddle River, N.J. : Prentice Hall, 1998.

Epstein, Lee, ed. *The Supreme Court Compendium: Data, Decisions, and Developments*. Washington, D.C.: Congressional Quarterly, 1996.

Greenberg, Ellen. *The Supreme Court Explained*. New York: W.W. Norton, 1997.

Hall, Kermit L., et al. *The Oxford Companion to the Supreme Court of the United States*. New York: Oxford University Press, 1992.

Heath, David. *The Supreme Court of the United States*. Mankato: Capstone Press, 1999.

Langran, Robert. *The United States Supreme Court: An Historical & Political Analysis*. Needham Heights: Ginn Press, 1992.

Leahy, James E. *Freedom Fighters of the United States Supreme Court: Nine Who Championed Individual Liberty*. Jefferson, N.C.: McFarland & Co., 1996.

Paddock, Lisa. *Facts About the Supreme Court of the United States*. New York: H.W. Wilson, 1996.

The Supreme Court of the United States: Its Beginnings & Its Justices, 1790–1991. Washington, D.C.: Commission on the Bicentennial of the U.S. Constitution, 1992.

Wagman, Robert J. *The Supreme Court: A Citizen's Guide*. New York: Pharos Books, 1993.

Walker, Thomas G. *The Supreme Court of the United States: An Introduction*. New York: St. Martin's Press, 1993.

Warren, Charles. *The Supreme Court in United States History*. Littleton: Fred B. Rothan & Co., 1987.

Witt, Elder, ed. *Congressional Quarterly's Guide to the U.S. Supreme Court*. Washington, D.C. : Congressional Quarterly, 1990.

———. *The Supreme Court A to Z: A Ready Reference Encyclopedia*. Washington, D.C.: Congressional Quarterly, 1993.

Tennessee Valley Authority (TVA)

WHAT IS ITS MISSION?

According to its *1997 Annual Report*, the mission of the Tennessee Valley Authority (TVA) is "to develop and operate the Tennessee River system to minimize flood damage and improve navigation and to provide energy and related products and services safely, reliably and at the lowest feasible cost to residents and businesses in the multi-state Tennessee Valley region. TVA's integrated management of the entire Tennessee River watershed optimizes the benefits of the water resource."

PARENT ORGANIZATION: Independent
ESTABLISHED: May 18, 1933
EMPLOYEES: 14,793

Contact Information:

ADDRESS: 400 W. Summit Hill Dr.
Knoxville, TN 37902
PHONE: (423) 632-2101
E-MAIL: jhhayes@tva.gov
URL: http://www.tva.gov
CHAIRMAN: Craven Crowell
DIRECTOR: Johnny H. Hayes
DIRECTOR: William H. Kennoy

HOW IS IT STRUCTURED?

The TVA is a federal corporation that falls under the executive branch. It is headed by a three-member board of directors: a chairman and two directors who oversee the TVA's operations. Directors lead the effort to ensure that TVA enhances its role as an economic driver for the region's economy. Directly beneath the board of directors is the executive committee, consisting of the following officers: senior vice president and general counsel, executive vice-president (VP) of the Fossil and Hydro Group, executive VP of the resource group, executive VP of the Customer Services and Marketing Group, executive VP of the Transmission & Power Supply Group, chief nuclear officer, chief financial officer, chief operating officer, and chief administrative officer. These officers work to manage their individual departments within the TVA.

The Kingston steam plant in Knoxville, Tennessee, is one of many such plants that contribute to making the TVA the largest supplier of electric power in the United States. (UPI/Corbis-Bettmann)

PRIMARY FUNCTIONS

As the nation's largest electric power producer, regional economic development agency, and national center for environmental research, the TVA functions in a variety of capacities to fulfill its mission. The five major functions of the corporation are: generating electricity, selling and transmitting electricity, governing the Tennessee Valley, encouraging economic development, and acting as steward for the TVA's interests through research and development.

The TVA operates 11 coal-fired plants, 29 hydroelectric dams, a pumped storage plant and three nuclear plants. Through its various power plants, the TVA produces more than 140 billion kilowatt-hours of electricity each year. This makes the TVA the nation's largest power corporation. The TVA serves seven states in the southeastern United States.

The TVA's electrical power travels across 17,000 miles of transmission lines. These lines carry power to customers in parts of seven states. TVA electricity is among the lowest priced in the nation. The TVA sells its electricity to 160 distributors who, in turn, resell the power to their customers. In addition to the electric lines, the TVA owns and maintains an extensive telecommunications network to enable automated control of its electricity transmission. These lines provide for voice and data flow, like basic telephone services and connection to the Internet. These communications networks are very helpful among rural communities in bringing schools and business access to the Internet.

One of the first mandates given to the TVA was to guard the natural environment in the area it serves. From the earliest days, the TVA recognized that while it had to provide electricity for its clients, it also had to preserve the natural resources. The 29 dams of the Tennessee River provide hydroelectric power, but also maintain flood control on the Tennessee River, protecting the residents who live along its banks from devastating floods that destroyed homes and crops before the inception of the TVA. The TVA also continues to improve water quality and conditions for aquatic life on the Tennessee River. The TVA works with other federal agencies, private citizens, and organizations to preserve and protect natural resources.

The TVA has also been working to spur economic development throughout the seven-state region that it serves. From its beginning, the TVA has created jobs, provided the flood control and soil erosion solutions that spurred agriculture to expand, and provided reasonably priced electricity to encourage industry to settle in the area. The TVA has played a major role in the area's economic growth. It encourages companies to pursue new avenues of development and works diligently to ensure that future economic growth and its power needs are met. The TVA also offers job training and industrial site studies to help local companies participate more fully in the global economy.

The TVA's Environmental Research Center located in Muscle Shoals, Alabama, is committed to solving critical environmental problems. Together, scientists and engineers study and work toward finding solutions to problems involving air quality, waste treatment, and watershed protection. The TVA sponsors research and development of alternative power sources in an effort to reduce the use of fossil fuels whose consumption has a negative impact on the environment.

PROGRAMS

Among the many environmental initiatives developed and managed by the TVA is the Land Between the Lakes (LBL), a 170,000-acre National Recreation Area (a federally designated area similar to a National Park but more developed) located on a peninsula sandwiched between the Tennessee River's Kentucky Lake and the Cumberland River's Lake Barkley. Visitors are welcome to camp at any of over 1,000 sites; other activities, such as biking, hiking, fishing, and water sports, are also available. TVA's Land Between the Lakes is an example of successful land management that partners outdoor recreation with environmental education.

The LBL is part of TVA's effort to preserve and protect the 250,000 acres along 11,000 miles of shoreline in its care. While some of the land is used to maintain the TVA dams, lakes, and flood control projects, the TVA also provides areas such as the LBL as places where people can enjoy natural resources. The LBL National Recreation Area attracts more than 2.2 million visits a year and is the centerpiece of a $580 million regional tourism industry.

BUDGET INFORMATION

The TVA's power sales are financially self-supporting, bringing in approximately $5.5 billion in 1998. Congress provides a small part of TVA's funding for regional development (about $120 million per year). A majority of the TVA budget was directed toward its power program, with the rest divided among environmental restoration and economic development of the Tennessee Valley and the Land Between the Lakes program.

HISTORY

Originally established to provide flood control, navigation, and electric power to the people in the Tennessee Valley area, the TVA has grown since its inception in 1933 to become the United States's largest electric power producing company. The Great Depression of the 1930s moved President Franklin D. Roosevelt's administration to create the New Deal, a set of initiatives designed to find new and innovative answers to the nation's deep economic woes. One of these solutions was the development of the TVA: a "corporation clothed with the power of government but possessed of the flexibility and initiative of a private enterprise." (TVA Website).

FAST FACTS

The TVA has repaid the U.S. government more than $3 billion in principal and interest since the federal government's original 1959 investment of $1.4 billion in the TVA.

(Source: *TVA Annual Report 1997.*)

The newly formed TVA began its renovation of the depressed Tennessee Valley—a place that even in those difficult times was worse than most. The timber was gone, the soil was hard, and the crops were barren in what had once been a fertile valley. The TVA built dams, which helped to control the flooding of the valley and improved the navigation of the rivers. The TVA taught the residents of the area how to generate more crops. It also produced new fertilizers, replanted deforested lands, and controlled fires. The most significant aspect of the TVA's work, however, was producing and bringing electricity to the area.

By 1945 the TVA was the largest producer of power with a 650-mile navigable river to feed its dams. Despite this the TVA's hydroelectric dams were not enough to meet the energy needs during the economic booms of the 1940s and 1950s. Prevented from requesting federal appropriations that would have been used for supplementary coal-fired plants, the TVA's power production fell behind the area's need for electricity. The solution to this problem was to allow the TVA to issue bonds to pay for its expansion. In 1959 Congress allowed the TVA to generate income and become self-sufficient.

Once the TVA was able to regulate itself and become self-sustaining, it experienced tremendous growth in the 1960s. Power rates to customers were cheap and the TVA was able to keep costs down by bringing larger and more efficient generators on-line. They even began the construction of nuclear plants to meet the region's growing energy needs. The replanted trees and wildlife in the area were abundant and economic development and growth seemed assured for years to come.

This development and growth was brought to an abrupt end in the 1970s. The international oil embargo in

1973 caused a ripple effect and energy conservation became a watchword. The oil embargo resulted when the members of Organization of Petroleum Exporting Countries (OPEC) decided that they were not being paid enough per barrel of crude oil. They decided to forego the sale of oil until their prices were met. The TVA was affected by the accelerating fuel costs and was forced to raise its prices fivefold in that decade. With the expenses of energy production skyrocketing, the TVA turned its attention to promoting energy conservation. The TVA canceled a number of its nuclear plants and concentrated its efforts on improving efficiency and cost cutting. By the end of the 1980s, however, the costs of power had stabilized.

The 1990s brought concern that electric utility companies were moving toward price deregulation and the TVA began preparing for this possibility. By cutting $800 million from its annual operating costs, reducing its staff by half, increasing the power generated from its existing plants, and abandoning nuclear power plant construction, the streamlined power giant developed a plan that it believed could meet the growing energy needs of the Tennessee Valley. Despite the cost-cutting measures, the budget-conscious Congress of the mid and late 1990s forced the TVA to evaluate and consider the possibility of the corporation becoming privatized.

CURRENT POLITICAL ISSUES

One of the main issues facing the TVA is funding. Although the power-generating arm of the TVA is self-sustaining, each year it needs an infusion of federal dollars to assist in economic development, environmental management, and recreational areas. For this and other reasons the TVA faces stiff criticism in Congress and there have been times that the authority has been in danger of having its funds cut and being dismantled.

Case Study: Why Pay for the TVA?

The TVA's ability to generate power and pay for that generation is not a point of contention. It is the other side of the TVA's duties that comes under federal fire each time the budget is debated in Congress. Some lawmakers, such as Representative Jim Ramstad (R-Minnesota), refer to the TVA as "pork-barrel politics in its purest form" and say TVA has outlived its usefulness and should be sold, or at least cut loose from the federal government. This would mean setting up the TVA as an independent company with no government ties. Each year Congress appropriates anywhere between $100 million to $140 million for the TVA to operate all of its nonpower-generating programs.

A General Accounting Office (GAO) Report issued in 1995 indicated that the TVA's $26 million debt for building nuclear power plants must be pared down in order for the TVA to avoid a government bailout. The GAO suggested that the TVA could not compete with other utilities if allowed to expand beyond the seven-state area. The report fueled measures by a number of congressmen, such as Representative Sherwood Boehlert (R-New York), to propose dismantling the TVA. The Republican Senators Fred Thompson and William Frist, both representing Tennessee, wanted to allay lawmakers's concerns about the TVA and squash the bill in its infancy.

In 1997 Chairman Craven Crowell recommended that Congress not appropriate federal funds to the TVA. Crowell felt that separating the TVA from federal funding would be the surest way of preserving the agency. Instead his recommendations further sparked ideas of selling the TVA or freeing it from federal control in both the House and the Senate. The chairman then feared that the agency would undergo a restructuring that would eliminate much of its nonpower-related activities. Crowell told Gannet News Service, "I don't appropriate the money. I can make proposals, I can make suggestions, but it's up to Congress to determine whether we continue them or not."

The issue of budget cuts and privatization of the TVA constantly arises due to the disparity between the price of electricity in the Tennessee River Valley and other parts of the country. In the Northeast and Midwest, electrical rates are double what TVA customers pay. This fact has caused some to resent that the government subsidizes the TVA. According to Representative Boehlert, "In 1933, when TVA was created, we cheered it on. We helped provide the funding for it because that was a region of the country that was in difficult economic straits. Now that region of the country is doing quite well. It's stealing our jobs and one of the reasons they are stealing our jobs is because they can offer much lower utility rates." As the debate continues the TVA must modify its programs and its positions or risk not surviving congressional cuts. At the end of hearings over the TVA Boehlert was adamant when he said, "There is a very strong federal interest in flood control and navigation that we cannot abandon; TVA must change to reflect the reality of the coming century."

In November of 1997 a privatization task force commissioned by Congress submitted its report and determined that the TVA should remain unchanged. It went on to report that "the Tennessee Valley Authority is better suited than other government agencies to oversee recreation areas such as Land Between the Lakes, flood control, [and] land and water management programs" according to Gannett News Service (11-04-97). These findings reported that 97 percent of 600 people surveyed found that the TVA was doing a good job and should be kept intact. Chairman Crowell pleaded his case to Congress in 1998 and, at least, temporarily achieved a victory for the TVA as Congress was swayed by its task force's report. According to the *Rocky Mountain News*, the TVA subsequently offered to give up its federal money in 1999. The TVA decided that by shedding its nonpower programs and concentrating its resources on its core industry, it might be able to end the speculation by the TVA's opponents that the TVA should be sold to the highest bidder.

Public Impact

Privatization of the TVA would likely mean that customers, whose utility rates have remained stable for over ten years, would see substantial increases. The predicted double-digit fee raise might discourage new development and keep new businesses from moving into the region. Senators Thompson and Frist along with the senators and congressional representatives from the other states served by the TVA have banded together to lobby their colleagues to delay any actions that would affect the TVA and its affiliates. On one hand, the privatization of the TVA and the dismantling of its nonpower components might help to streamline its operations and cut some unnecessary costs. On the other hand, the lack of government-subsidized power and the inability of smaller companies to provide adequate service could potentially cost the American taxpayer more money.

SUCCESSES AND FAILURES

One of the TVA's successful ventures has been the reclamation and replanting of the Tennessee River Valley. Because of the TVA efforts, the area has undergone change from a barren treeless land where crops often failed and soil eroded, to a region with tree-lined rivers and arable land. Thousands of tourists come each year to the Land Between the Lakes National Recreation Area.

FUTURE DIRECTIONS

Because one of the TVA's main goals is to maintain or even improve the environment throughout the valley in which it operates, it is constantly looking for ways to reduce its power stations' output of pollutants. The TVA announced in June 1998 that it would be installing a new method of nitrogen oxide reduction for its coal-fired plants by the year 2003. Nitrogen oxide emissions, a key contributor to smog, would decrease by 168,000 tons once the TVA's new technologies are put in place. The authority will install selective catalytic reduction systems (SCRs) devices, which are among the newest and most efficient devices for eliminating nitrogen oxides. These SCRs will cost between $500 and $600 million but will conform to new guidelines that the Environmental Protection Agency (EPA) proposed in 1997.

AGENCY RESOURCES

For information on the TVA as well as investment resources, access the TVA's Web site at http://www.tva.gov; send a written request to TVA Communications, 400 W. Summit Hill Dr., Knoxville, TN 37902-1499; or phone (423) 632-1201.

The TVA has established a Web site at http://lakeinfo.tva.gov that provides current and predicted lake levels and stream flow information to the public. The Web site contains the same information that has been available for many years through a voice-activated telephone system, which receives about one million inquiries a year. It provides daily rainfall data for more than 250 stations in and near the Tennessee Valley. Investor information is also available on-line at http://www.tva.gov/finance/home.htm. This site indicates the price per share for persons interested in buying TVA stock.

In addition to the TVA's Web site and written information, there is a related Web site that gives insight into the early days of the TVA, with pictures and written accounts. The site, called the New Deal Network, has extensive information about the history of the TVA. The address is http://newdeal.feri.org.

AGENCY PUBLICATIONS

The TVA publishes the *Economic Edge* available from its Web site at http://www.tva.gov and in hard copy from the Tennessee Valley Authority, Hill Dr., 400 W. Summit, Knoxville TN 37902. The TVA also publishes material such as annual reports, investor prospectuses, maps, and schedules. Information is also available by calling (423) 632-2101.

BIBLIOGRAPHY

Anthan, George. "Using Industrial Waste to Manufacture Fertilizer Causing Concern." Gannett News Service, 19 April 1998, pp. ARC.

"Beleaguered TVA Faces One Funding Battle After Another." Gannett News Service, 2 August 1995.

Bender, Penny. "Clinton Budget Would Add to TVA Funding." Gannett News Service, 19 March 1996.

Harmon, John. "Mistakes Aside, TVA Ranks High in Its Field." *Atlanta Journal and Constitution*, 17 May 1998, p. A15.

Margulies, Ellen. "Task Force Recommends Leaving TVA Alone." Gannett News Service, 4 November 1997.

"McConnell Introduces Bill That Would Change Way TVA Does Business." Gannett News Service, 29 April 1998, pp. ARC.

"TVA Debt Must Be Cut To Avert Bailout." Gannett News Service, 17 August 1995.

"TVA Officials Meet with Caucus to Soothe Members' Anger." Gannett News Service, 25 February 1997.

Trade and Development Agency (TDA)

PARENT ORGANIZATION: Independent
ESTABLISHED: July 1, 1980
EMPLOYEES: 38

Contact Information:

ADDRESS: 1621 N. Kent St., Ste. 300
Arlington, VA 22209
PHONE: (703) 875-4357
FAX: (703) 875-4009
E-MAIL: info@tda.gov
URL: http://www.tda.gov
DIRECTOR: J. Joseph Grandmaison
DEPUTY DIRECTOR: Nancy D. Frame

WHAT IS ITS MISSION?

The mission of the U.S. Trade and Development Agency (TDA) is to promote economic development in certain developing and middle-income nations in the world for the purpose of exporting U.S. goods and services to these countries. The most important motive for the export mission is a desire to assist in the creation of American jobs by helping U.S. companies pursue overseas business opportunities. Through its varied activities, the TDA provides American firms with market entry, exposure, and information, helping them to establish a position in markets that are otherwise difficult to penetrate.

HOW IS IT STRUCTURED?

The TDA is an independent agency within the executive branch of the U.S. government. Out of necessity, it does occasionally work in collaboration with the larger trade-related agencies, but in general the TDA is operationally self-sufficient. One of the smallest federal agencies, the TDA uses its 38 employees to leverage large-scale commercial activities between private U.S. companies and foreign governments.

The agency is led by the Office of the Director, which is ultimately responsible for the administration and leadership of the agency, although its operations are subject to overall U.S. trade policy. Several officers—including a financial manager, a contracting officer, and an economist/evaluation officer—assist the director in administrative tasks. The director's office is assisted in its major operational functions by a legislative liaison who serves as a go-between for the TDA and Congress; an export promotion director, who leads the agency's efforts to increase U.S. exports; an office of general counsel, which serves as the agency's primary legal adviser; and a special assistant for policy and public affairs.

Beyond its U.S. headquarters and the director's office, the TDA exists as a network of offices in key developing world regions: Africa/Middle East, Asia/Pacific, Central and Eastern Europe, Latin America and the Caribbean, and the New Independent (former Soviet) States. Within each of these regions, markets are targeted, individual studies and projects are hatched, and the work of the TDA takes shape.

PRIMARY FUNCTIONS

The TDA, with its small administrative staff, serves as a funding agency rather than an operational organization. It funds feasibility studies, orientation visits, specialized training grants, business workshops, and various forms of technical assistance. The ultimate aim in these undertakings is to enable American businesses to compete in middle-income and developing countries. Because of its export-promotion mission, the TDA considers only projects that have the potential to mature into long-term, significant business opportunities for U.S. companies. The TDA learns of possible public- and private-sector projects from the U.S. business community and from other government agencies, such as the Commerce Department's U.S. & Foreign Commercial Service (US&FCS). Official requests for assistance must be made directly to the TDA by the sponsoring organization or government of the host country, and a description of the proposed project should accompany the official letter of request.

The next step in the project development process is the feasibility study, the agency's most common and important funding activity. Feasibility studies evaluate the technical, legal, economic, and financial implications of the proposed development project. The studies are ultimately used to determine whether the resources exist to take the project into the development stage; they are also used to advise project sponsors about the availability of specific U.S. equipment and services for use in the project. As an example, the TDA cites a recent feasibility study on a South American wastewater treatment plant, that resulted in the sponsor's purchase of millions of dollars of U.S. pollution control equipment that had been specified in the feasibility study. Costs associated with feasibility studies in private investor projects are shared between the TDA and the U.S. company.

The TDA also funds other activities, including definitional missions (DMs) (teams of technical specialists contracted to gather additional information to analyze whether a feasibility study should proceed) and desk studies, which are performed by a technical specialist to review the proposed project without leaving the United States. The agency sponsors events (technical symposia, orientation visits, business briefings) that will familiarize foreign decision makers with U.S. goods and services and provide them with an opportunity to meet U.S. suppliers. In certain regions the TDA also funds training that will enable host country project personnel to receive necessary managerial training where a U.S. firm is selected for a project. In situations when the required technical expertise is unavailable in the host country, the TDA may also fund technical assistance for a given project.

In 1996 the TDA took on responsibility for another funding activity as part of its South Balkan Development Initiative (SBDI): procurement assistance. This program provides funding for the direct purchase of American goods and related services in support of specific initiatives.

PROGRAMS

TDA acts as a facilitator; its activities are limited to the processes of conducting feasibility studies and providing training or technical assistance in a host country. Actual "programs" or projects are carried out by the U.S. companies involved in a project and the host organization. Each region has its own continuously changing projects: for example, a recent TDA foray into South Africa resulted in the arrangement of 45 projects that have the potential for more than $8.2 billion in U.S. exports. The projects profiled in the TDA's report include projects in the areas of transportation, environment, telecommunications, power, industry, and tourism.

BUDGET INFORMATION

Because of the constantly changing needs within the scope of TDA activity, the agency's budget tends to fluctuate from year to year depending on the costs of studies and activities. The 1998 TDA budget was $56 million.

The budget breakdown also varies from year to year. The greatest part of the agency budget, however, is always consumed by feasibility studies. About 89 percent of the agency's budget was spent in this area in 1998, the remaining 11 percent paid for the agency's operating expenses. Programs under the heading of feasibility studies include: Technical assistance, which typically accounts for about 7 to 15 percent of the agency budget; procurement assistance at about 11 percent; trade-related training at about 3 to 5 percent of the agency's total budget; orientation visits at about 4 percent; conferences 3 to 4 percent; and 2 to 3 percent of the overall budget is spent on definitional missions and desk studies.

BUDGET:

Trade and Development Agency

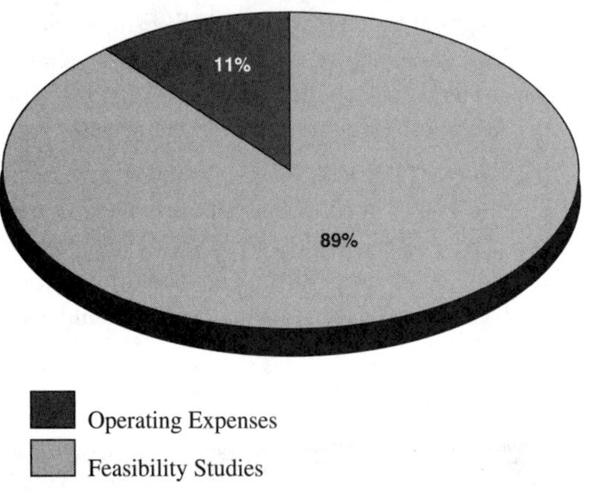

Operating Expenses
Feasibility Studies

HISTORY

U.S. economic aid as a structured national program dates back to President Harry Truman's Marshall Plan, initiated in 1949 to assist war-torn Europe's economic recovery. The success of the Marshall Plan helped spark a dramatic European recovery and strengthened U.S. influence around the world. Since the Marshall Plan, every president, both Democratic and Republican, has been a strong advocate of foreign aid.

As a distinct government agency, however, the Trade and Development Agency traces its origins back to the Trade and Development Program, an operating unit within the U.S. Agency for International Development (USAID), established by President John F. Kennedy in 1961. USAID's focus grew over time to encompass five principal areas crucial to achieving U.S. foreign policy objectives: promoting economic growth; promoting democracy; delivering humanitarian assistance to victims of famine and other natural and man-made disasters; protecting public health and supporting family planning; and protecting the environment.

The Trade and Development Program was initially designed to meet the first of these objectives, the promotion of economic growth in developing countries. As the TDA's current practices make clear, however, that objective has changed over time. In the early years of the administration of President Ronald Reagan, an increasing emphasis began to be placed on the use of American businesses in foreign assistance roles. As the administration, led by a conservative president intent on cutting expenditures, began to scale back its funds for foreign assistance, programs were established to involve U.S. companies in development projects abroad. The goal, of course, was to help develop the infrastructure of developing countries while broadening the market for U.S. firms.

At the same time as this foreign policy trend was beginning, a change was occurring in trade-related business. As the "globalization" of the world economy took shape, companies all over the world began to seek overseas markets. The competition for these markets soon became intense, and foreign governments, especially in the European community, began to subsidize businesses' efforts to expand into these markets. The foreign policies of many governments, including that of the United States, began to focus on the problem of how to keep the economies and governments of developing countries stable so that they could increasingly import products from abroad. To keep up with the competition, the Trade and Development Program focused its efforts on opening doors for U.S. companies in these emerging foreign markets.

Because its programs were no longer really "aid" in the traditional sense, the Trade and Development Program separated from USAID in 1981 to reflect the agency's new commercial focus. Eleven years later, in 1992, the agency changed its name to the Trade and Development Agency. In the 1990s dramatic changes took place in the world economy: the breakdown of the Soviet Union and the establishment of the Newly Independent States; the growing integration of western European economies; and the rise of the Asia-Pacific nations. All of these presented the TDA with new challenges and opportunities for expanding the market access of U.S. companies.

CURRENT POLITICAL ISSUES

The 1990s was a decade of uncertainty for the Trade and Development Agency. The TDA was nearly eliminated entirely in 1995 by an unlikely alliance of liberals and conservative budget cutters who branded TDA assistance a form of "corporate welfare" that could not be justified at a time when the administration was preparing to cut assistance programs to America's poor under the terms of pending welfare reform legislation.

The "corporate welfare" debate soon appeared to be one of the simpler issues facing the TDA, however. The agency is just one of many trade-related agencies in the U.S. government, and because many of these agencies were authorized by Congress individually, at different times, their duties tend to overlap or even conflict with one another. In 1996 a conservative House of Representatives refused to reauthorize the charters of several trade-related agencies, including the TDA, until this problem could be resolved. The Senate refused to go along with the House, however, and the agency survived.

Case Study: Trade Agency Mergers

The issue of streamlining the government's trade-related agencies remained, however. In 1996 the White

House's Office of Management and Budget (OMB) recommended merging three government agencies: the Export-Import Bank, which provides financing for American exporters; the Overseas Private Investment Corporation (OPIC), which provides risk insurance for companies who trade or invest overseas; and the Trade and Development Agency. A more radical idea was proposed by other sources, primarily intellectuals and scientists in the private sector: an entirely new government agency, called the Department of Economics, Industry and Trade, should be formed out of the many existing trade-related agencies. The existing agencies—the Office of the U.S. Trade Representative, the wide-ranging economic and trade functions of the Commerce Department, the Export-Import Bank, OPIC, the TDA, and the export-assistance program of the Small Business Administration—would be incorporated in this new department.

Although they clearly made some sense, these ideas ultimately proved to be too wild and too politically risky for the administration of President Bill Clinton. In January 1997 the administration announced that although the OMB study demonstrated that the current system was fragmented and awkward at times, the costs and risks associated with reorganization were too high. The idea of forming a Department of Economics, Industry and Trade was not discussed in the White House announcement. In its present form, the TDA has so far survived, but it is still under fire from liberals and conservatives alike, who do not believe that the creation of jobs through exports should be a government-subsidized activity.

FAST FACTS

Since the agency's creation, the TDA has been associated with approximately $11.5 billion in exports; this constitutes a leveraging of nearly $30 in exports for every dollar invested in TDA activities.

(Source: Trade and Development Agency. "TDA at a Glance," 1998.)

SUCCESSES AND FAILURES

Any TDA venture that leads to increased exports is considered a success. As a result of a $1.1 million study financed by the TDA, AT&T has recently won a contract linking Colombia and several other Latin American nations by fiber optic cable. In addition to helping such large corporations, however, the TDA believes its increased focus on America's small-business sector will produce remarkable future success. Already the agency's efforts to increase small-business community involvement in its activities show promising returns. For example, the TDA recently provided a $115,000 grant to Energy Conversion Devices, a small Michigan-based firm, to conduct a study of a joint venture with a company in India that manufactures photo cells. Through this grant, the TDA has helped generate $10 million in U.S. exports.

FUTURE DIRECTIONS

Under pressure from both the public and private sectors to cut costs and provide greater access to small businesses, the TDA has already begun to change the way it conducts its affairs. Although it funds many feasibility studies on a cost-sharing basis, it plans to rely increasingly on matching funds from participating companies. The agency is still waiting to experience the benefits of its "success fee" program, begun in 1995, which requires a contribution from companies that participate in programs that achieve significant exports. The TDA's plans for the future also include more U.S. studies on projects in big emerging markets around the world, as well as increasing the number of small businesses involved in TDA activities.

AGENCY RESOURCES

The general information resource for the TDA is its public affairs staff, which can be reached at (703) 875-4357. Information on definitional missions can be obtained by calling the TDA's "DM Hotline" at (703) 875-7447. Much TDA information—a catalog of TDA library holdings, agency news, information on TDA-sponsored studies, a calendar of events, and more—is available on the agency's World Wide Web site at http://www.tda.gov.

AGENCY PUBLICATIONS

The TDA releases two regular publications: the "TDA Pipeline," which provides U.S. suppliers and manufacturers with timely information on agency-supported projects, and the *TDA Update*, a quarterly publication that contains current items of interest on many program activities. These publications are subscription items, but recent issues may be viewed via the agency's Web site at http://www.tda.gov. Requests for Proposals (RFPs) to conduct feasibility studies funded by TDA are listed in the *Commerce Business Daily*, another government publication. For on-line information about the CBD, call (202) 482-0632; for subscription information, call (202) 783-3238.

TDA's library maintains final reports on all TDA activities; these reports are available for public review during regular library hours. Copies of completed feasibility studies may be purchased through the National Technical Information Service (NTIS) at (703) 487-4650. NTIS order numbers for these studies are available in the "TDA Pipeline" section of the TDA's Web site at http://www.tda.gov.

BIBLIOGRAPHY

Corbo, Vittorio, Anne O. Krueger, and Fernando Ossa, eds. *Export-Oriented Development Strategies: The Success of Five Newly Industrializing Countries*. Boulder, Colo.: Westview Press, 1985.

"Deals on Wheels." *Industry Week,* 15 July 1996, p. 48.

Doherty, Carroll J. "House Refuses to Reauthorize Trade Promotion Agencies." *Congressional Quarterly Weekly Report*, 14 September 1996, p. 2584.

Fessler, Pamela. "Looking to the Private Sector." *Congressional Quarterly Weekly Report*, 13 March 1993, p. 615.

Lachica, Eduardo. "Congress's 'Corporate-Welfare' Cutters Target Trade and Development Agency." *Wall Street Journal*, 14 July 1995, pp. B5B(W), A7B(E).

Sanger, David E. "Administration Won't Merge Export Programs." *New York Times*, 24 January 1997, pp. A10(N), A18(N).

Stern, Paula. "Reorganizing Government for Economic Growth and Efficiency." *Issues in Science and Technology*, Summer 1996, pp. 67–71.

United States Air Force Academy (USAFA)

PARENT ORGANIZATION: Department of the Air Force
ESTABLISHED: 1954
EMPLOYEES: 14,430

Contact Information:

ADDRESS: 2304 Cadet Dr.
U.S. Air Force Academy, CO 80840
PHONE: (703) 333-7593
FAX: (703) 333-4094
URL: http://www.usafa.af.mil
SUPERINTENDENT: Maj. Gen. Tad J. Oelstrom
COMMANDANT OF THE CADETS: Brig. Gen. Stephen R. Lorenz
DEAN OF THE FACULTY: Brig. Gen. Ruben A. Cubero

WHAT IS ITS MISSION?

The mission of the U.S. Air Force Academy belongs to the staff and faculty, who are charged with developing and inspiring prospective air and space leaders with a vision for the future. At the Air Force Academy, this individual development focuses on four types of growth: intellectual, professional, physical, and character, which includes spiritual, moral, and ethical growth.

HOW IS IT STRUCTURED?

The Air Force Academy reports directly to the chief of staff of the Department of the Air Force. The academy is led by the superintendent who is a general officer, usually a lieutenant general, and whose position is comparable to that of a university president. The superintendent is the senior military officer of the academy and, through the academy staff, directs the administration, personnel, logistics, and other functions that would be found in any other major Air Force command.

The unique nature of the Air Force Academy's education program is reflected in the three areas of responsibility directly related to cadet activities: academics, military training, and athletics. The academic program at the academy is led by the dean of the faculty who is responsible for courses, curriculum, majors, and other activities in the academic arena. The dean, who is also a permanent professor, is usually a brigadier general and directs a faculty consisting of approximately five hundred pro-

U.S. Air Force Academy cadets perform at the Pentagon in 1997 at an event that kicked off the Air Force's nationwide fiftieth anniversary celebrations. (Courtesy of United States Air Force)

fessors and instructors. Career air force officers provide most of the instruction. About 45 percent of the faculty hold doctorates, and more than 25 percent are rated pilots and navigators.

The student body at the Air Force Academy is known as the cadet wing and is commanded by the commandant of the cadets. The commandant is a brigadier general with the operational, administrative, and logistical responsibility for the entire cadet wing; he or she organizes and supervises all cadet military training programs. The leadership of the commandant's staff is a major component in developing cadet responsibility and judgment.

For many cadets, daily life is also influenced by the Department of Athletics. Each cadet is required to take physical education courses as well as intramural or varsity sports throughout the four-year program. Nearly all of the coaches who direct and administer the athletics program are career air force officers; their primary mission is the physical development of cadets.

The academy also houses and administers two other significant organizations: the U.S. Air Force Academy Preparatory School, a secondary school with the mission of preparing and evaluating cadet candidates for academy appointments; and the military installation of the 10th Air Base Wing, the support wing for the Air Force Academy.

PRIMARY FUNCTIONS

The core curriculum of the Air Force Academy provides the common body of knowledge that prepares all cadets for the air force profession. The core consists of about 48 semester hours in engineering and basic sciences and about 46 semester hours in humanities and social sciences. This core constitutes about 65 percent of a cadet's total academic load. The academy offers 26 academic majors, but about half of the cadets major in science and engineering; an academy cadet typically graduates with a bachelor of science degree.

Professionally, a cadet graduates from the academy as a second lieutenant in the air force. The professional development program is a key component of the academy experience and distinguishes it from other institutions of higher learning. Four primary areas of professional development are stressed in the academy programs: professional military studies, theoretical and applied leadership experiences, aviation science and airmanship programs, and military training.

In addition to the administration of its core curriculum, professional and athletic training, the Air Force Preparatory School, and the 10th Air Base Wing, the academy hosts numerous conferences designed to foster improved communication between cadets and students from other universities and service academies. The Academy Assembly, for example, is an annual gathering of students from colleges and universities throughout the United States and Canada for the debate of public policy issues.

PROGRAMS

The Air Force Academy operates numerous programs within its core curriculum and training plan. An important academic program is the Cadet Summer Research Program, during which selected cadets spend six weeks at various air force or other Department of Defense installations around the world. Participants in the program apply knowledge from the classroom to air force research topics such as computer modeling of airframe structures or enhancing the low-resolution pictorial displays of fighter cockpits.

The military programs of the academy include the Commandant's Leadership Series, a guest speaker program designed to increase cadet exposure to active duty officers and other distinguished persons in the military community. More concrete military training is provided by activities such as the Survival, Evasion, Resistance, and Escape (SERE) Training Program. The SERE program is designed to train personnel at high risk of capture—those vulnerable to a greater than average exploitation by an enemy captor during combat or peacetime detention and hostage situations—how to survive, evade, resist, and escape.

BUDGET:

United States Air Force Academy

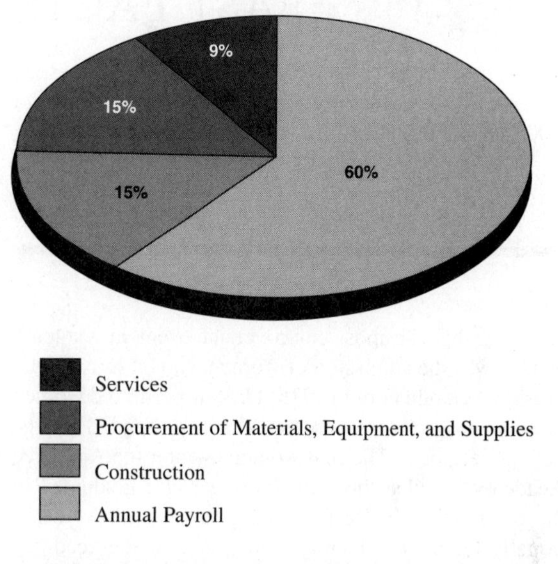

BUDGET INFORMATION

The USAFA's budget is a component of the annual Department of the Air Force budget. The sophisticated technical nature of some USAFA programs make a cadet's education expensive for taxpayers (about $250,000 to put one cadet through the four-year program). The 1998 operating costs totaled about $357 million. A little more than 60 percent of this budget was spent on the academy's annual payroll of military and civilian employees, while 39 percent was spent on the academy's other operating expenditures: construction ($55 million), services ($33 million), and procurement of materials, equipment, and supplies ($52 million).

HISTORY

The establishment of the Air Force Academy was an outgrowth of the air force's decades-long struggle for leadership independent of the U.S. army command structure was finally achieved in 1947. It was quickly understood that full air force independence could not be realized as long as much of the senior air force leadership was still being drawn from graduates of the army's Military Academy at West Point, New York, and from the Naval Academy at Annapolis, Maryland. In 1948 the air force appointed a board of leading civilian and military educators to plan the curriculum for an air force academy.

The board made little progress until a separate board was formed in 1949 to recommend a general system of education for the army, navy, and air force. This board was led by Dwight D. Eisenhower, then president of Columbia University, and Robert L. Stearns, president of the University of Colorado. Within a year, the board found that the needs of the air force could not be met by simply expanding the programs of the older service academies, and it recommended that an air force academy be established without delay.

The creation of the U.S. Air Force Academy was legislated by Congress and signed into law by President Eisenhower in 1954. Secretary of the Air Force Harold Talbott appointed a commission to assist him in selecting the academy's permanent site. After considering 580 proposed sites in 45 states, the commission recommended three locations to Secretary Talbott, who decided upon the site near Colorado Springs. Construction of the site was sufficiently complete for the cadet wing to move into its permanent home in the summer of 1958. The academy was expanded in 1964 when more than one thousand cadets matriculated. The cadet wing had nearly doubled in size since the academy's creation.

FAST FACTS

Approximately nine thousand men and women seek entrance to the academy each year; only about 1,500 to 2,000 gain acceptance.

(Source: United States Air Force Academy. "Leaders of Tomorrow," 1998.)

Probably the most controversial event in academy history was the admission of women, signed into law by President Gerald Ford in 1975. The law permitted women to enter any military academy that was funded by the U.S. government. The first women to enter the Air Force Academy enrolled the following year and graduated in the class of 1980. Despite initial resistance, the traditionally male staff, faculty, and cadets at the academy have grown over the years to generally accept and encourage their female colleagues. However, academy life at times seems to present the same difficulties for women—ranging from simple lack of concern or awareness to outright harassment—as the rest of the U.S. military establishment.

CURRENT POLITICAL ISSUES

Like its counterparts in the other branches of the military service, the Air Force Academy has struggled with the overwhelming political and sexual issues brought on by the admission of women cadets. These issues were brought to a head in 1993, when a female freshman complained to the campus authorities that she had been sexually assaulted outside the cadet gymnasium by several young men. Immediately following this charge other female cadets at the Air Force Academy began to step up, complaining of harassment, fondling, and in extreme cases, date rape by male cadets. The navy's disastrous Tailhook scandal in 1991, in which female officers were crudely harassed by male colleagues and the navy administration's subsequent involvement in an embarrassing cover-up, served as a lesson to all military institutions in how now to mishandle such a crisis. The Air Force Academy wanted its response to be honest, forthright, and above all to eradicate the problem of sexual harassment before it could go any further.

The response was implemented quickly with very little debate. The complaints were investigated, and a twenty-four hour confidential telephone number to report sexual assaults was installed. The investigations resulted in the court-marshaling and jailing of an instructor and a cadet on charges of sexual misconduct; three other cadets resigned, and three more were disciplined by the administration. Through further discussions with female cadets, the superintendent learned that the problem at the academy was far worse than he had imagined, and that simply responding to complaints would not be an effective solution.

In many ways, the resulting program has served as a model for similar institutions: counselors and investigators were added to the academy staff, and the entire cadet wing—all four thousand of them—were divided into groups of eight to twelve men and women to discuss sexual harassment and leadership ethics. A center for character development was established to unify the fragmented ethics, honor code, and human relations training programs.

However, some male cadets who found these initial discussion sessions eye-opening, later began to tire of the focus on gender issues and human relations. Male cadets have also complained that at times these symposiums and discussions serve to put barriers between men and women on campus, rather than focusing on more universal issues. Since the program's implementation, however, very few incidents of harassment or assault have occurred at the academy.

SUCCESSES AND FAILURES

The Air Force Academy takes pride in its status as one of the nation's outstanding academic institutions. Thirty-one cadets have been selected as Rhodes scholars; 92 have received Guggenheim Fellowships; 57 have accepted scholarships to attend Harvard University's John F. Kennedy School of Government; and 30 have been selected as Fulbright-Hays scholars. In addition, three cadets have received Marshall scholarships; 30 cadets have been selected as Hertz Fellows; and 484 have gone on to attend medical school.

AGENCY RESOURCES

General information about the Air Force Academy is available in the form of numerous fact sheets and biographies accessible via the academy's Web site at http://www.usafa.af.mil. For further information, contact the USAF Academy Public Affairs Office at (719) 333-7460. For information on admissions, contact USAF Academy Admissions, 2304 Cadet Dr., USAF Academy, CO 80840.

AGENCY PUBLICATIONS

The Air Force Academy publishes a weekly newspaper, the *Academy Spirit,* along with a number of informational publications in areas such as flying, operations support, the medical command, history, and command policy. A comprehensive electronic library of these publications is available from the academy Web site. For further information, contact the Office of Public Affairs at (719) 333-7460.

BIBLIOGRAPHY

"Air Force Academy Drops Resistance Training." *New York Times*, 30 April 1995, pp. 20 (N), 32 (L).

Fagan, George V. *The Air Force Academy: An Illustrated History*. Boulder, Colo.: Johnson Books, 1988.

Gender & Racial Disparities at the Air Force Academy. Lancaster, Penn.: BPI Information Services, 1993.

Liu, Elizabeth G., et al. *Spirit & Flight: A Photographic Salute to the United States Air Force Academy*. Air Force Academy, 1996.

Schmitt, Eric. "Air Force Academy Zooms in on Sex Cases." *New York Times*, 1 May 1994, p. 1.

———. "Study Says Sexual Harassment Persists at Military Academies." *New York Times*, 5 April 1995, pp. A13 (N), B8 (L).

Thompson, Mark. "Academies Out of Line." *Time*, 18 April 1994, pp. 37–8.

Whelchel, Sandy. *A Guide to the U.S. Air Force Academy*. Parker, Colo.: Parker Distributing, 1990.

United States Arms Control and Disarmament Agency (ACDA)

PARENT ORGANIZATION: Department of State
ESTABLISHED: 1961
EMPLOYEES: 250

Contact Information:

ADDRESS: 320 21st St. NW
Washington, DC 20451
PHONE: (202) 647-2034
TOLL FREE: (800) 581-2232
FAX: (202) 647-6928
URL: http://www.acda.gov
DIRECTOR: John D. Holum

WHAT IS ITS MISSION?

According to the *U.S. Government Manual* "the United States Arms Control and Disarmament Agency (ACDA) formulates and implements arms control nonproliferation and disarmament policies that promote the national security of the United States and its relations with other countries."

HOW IS IT STRUCTURED?

The ACDA is a tool of the executive branch of government that studies and negotiates weapons and arms control. The director, appointed by the president and approved by Congress, serves as the principal adviser to the president, the National Security Council (NSC), the secretary of state, and other senior government officials on arms control, nonproliferation (stopping the growth and spread of arms), and disarmament matters. The ACDA is composed of a number of bureaus, each with a different focus. While the staff of 250 is supplemented by visiting scholars and military personnel expert in the arms control area, the thrust of the operations falls upon the regular experts within the agency. The bureaus, each with its own specialty, include the following: the Multilateral Affairs Bureau (MA); the Intelligence, Verification, and Information Management Bureau (IVI); the Nonproliferation and Regional Arms Control Bureau (NP); and the Strategic and Eurasian Affairs Bureau (SEA). There are a number of offices that comprise the administrative staff of the ACDA as well, which include: the Office of the Director, the Office of the Deputy Director, the Office of Administration, the Office of Congres-

ACDA achieved major victories in the 1980s with the Strategic Arms Reduction Treaties (START I and II). President George Bush (seated, left) *and Russian President Boris Yeltsin* (seated, right) *are shown signing START II at the Kremlin on July 31, 1991.*

(Photograph by Gennady Galperin. Reuters/Corbis-Bettmann)

sional Affairs, the Office of the General Counsel, and the Office of Public Affairs. ACDA headquarters are located in Washington, D.C.

PRIMARY FUNCTIONS

The function of the ACDA is to prepare reports, conduct studies, and participate in discussions and negotiations with other countries on issues related to strategic arms limitations, conventional force reductions, prevention of the spread of nuclear weapons, chemical weapons bans, and international arms trading. The ACDA advises the president, the National Security Agency (NSA), and the Department of State (DOS) about the status of negotiations on particular treaties. It evaluates the balances of power among the nations involved in discussions and how each treaty would contribute to the overall goal of arms reduction.

Each bureau focuses its efforts on a particular aspect of nuclear and conventional disarmament or control and provides reports, treaty recommendations, speeches, and other documentary evidence to support its positions to the president and the president's advisers.

The IVI coordinates intelligence computer databases, conducts research, and analyzes data for the ACDA bureaus. It establishes, manages, and maintains all information systems within the agency.

The MA provides policy guides and instructions to U.S. delegations participating in multilateral arms control conferences and meetings. It also advises on nuclear test ban treaties, outer space arms control, transparency in armaments and the United Nations (UN) Register of Conventional Arms, negative security assurances, and negotiations for a missile material cutoff convention. This division also provides delegates and support for the Conference on Disarmament, the UN Disarmament Commission, the UN General Assembly First Committee, other UN-related disarmament forces, and the North Atlantic Treaty Organization (NATO) Disarmament Experts' Group.

The NP provides advice, assessments, and policy recommendations on a wide range of areas that include: international relations aspects of nuclear nonproliferation; national negotiations on conventional arms transfers, missile and chemical/biological weapons nonproliferation, dual use export controls, and commercial space usage. It also offers technical advice and policy recommendations on nuclear proliferation issues including nuclear safeguards, nuclear fuel cycle, and the technological aspects of nuclear nonproliferation, including the safe disposition of fissile material.

FAST FACTS

The Comprehensive Test Ban Treaty bans any nuclear weapon test explosion or any other nuclear explosion. While 146 nations have already signed the treaty, any country can accede to the treaty at any time.

(Source: "CTBT/ACDA Fact Sheet," February 24, 1998.)

The SEA is involved in nuclear arms control and disarmament negotiations with the nations of the former Soviet Union and with China. It negotiates and monitors the various disarmament treaties, creates policy statements for the government's stance on nuclear and arms issues in Asia, and provides analysis and support to the ACDA director on all issues concerning ballistic missile defenses and the Anti-Ballistic Missile (ABM) Treaty. It develops, for presidential approval, options for arms control policy, strategy, tactics, and instructions for the ongoing negotiations of ABM and other treaties, especially in regard to Asia and the former Soviet Union states.

PROGRAMS

Among the several fellowship programs sponsored by the ACDA is the William C. Foster Fellows Visiting Scholars Program. This initiative was established by Congress in 1983 to honor the ACDA's first director, William C. Foster. The ACDA offers visiting scholars who are specialists in the physical sciences and other disciplines relevant to ACDA's activities, an opportunity for active participation in arms control, nonproliferation, and disarmament activities for one year. The specialists undergo intense scrutiny and background investigations before they are assigned to one of the bureaus. Once cleared, the fellow is given top security clearance. Foster fellows must be citizens of the United States, on the faculty of a recognized institution of higher learning, and either be tenured or on a tenure-track (or its equivalent) for at least ninety days before selection for the program. Since 1984, approximately 40 fellows have served at ACDA. The ACDA also sponsors the *Hubert H. Humphrey Doctoral Fellowship in Arms Control and Disarmament,* which assists doctoral students completing their dissertations. This fellowship is awarded only when funding is available.

BUDGET INFORMATION

Approximately $41.7 million was appropriated by Congress to ACDA in 1998. These funds were allocated to the agency's activities in areas such as the Comprehensive Test Ban Treaty (CTBT), the Chemical Weapons Convention (CWC), the Nuclear Nonproliferation Treaty (NPT); and the AC Data Repository.

HISTORY

At the height of the Cold War in the late 1950s, Senators Hubert H. Humphrey and John F. Kennedy called for the establishment of a new organization to deal with arms control and the threat of nuclear proliferation. The goal of the legislation was to form an agency that was independent from the executive branch and the DOS, but that advised the president on arms control issues. President Eisenhower was a proponent of a test ban on nuclear weapons and wanted the formation of an agency dedicated to this purpose to be his last gift to the American people. He stated this intent in his final State of the Union address in 1960. The ACDA was subsequently established in 1961.

Since its inception the ACDA has acted as an independent voice urging the reduction of the world's nuclear arsenals and advocating limits on conventional weapons. The history of the ACDA is the history of disarmament agreements. SALT I (Strategic Arms Limitation Talks, series 1) discussions extended from November 1969 to May 1972. During that period the United States and the Soviet Union negotiated the first agreements to place limits and restraints on some of their central and most important armaments. The resulting Treaty on the Limitation of ABMs in 1972 moved to end an emerging competition between the two superpowers in defensive systems. In an Interim Agreement on Certain Measures With Respect to the Limitation of Strategic Offensive Arms, the two nations took the first steps to check the rivalry in their most powerful land- and submarine-based offensive nuclear weapons. The ACDA provided the data that helped U.S. negotiators successfully conclude these treaties. Other negotiations and treaties followed, targeting such issues as biological weapons, nuclear disarmament, chemical weapons, use of space, and commercial arms proliferation.

During the 1980s President Ronald Reagan launched a massive build-up of nuclear and conventional weapons. He ignored the SALT process and by 1983 he even advocated the idea of "Star Wars," which would place heavily armed satellites in space to intercept nuclear missiles fired at the United States. Although this concept was not ratified by Congress, the idea of this type of defense program still remained a viable possibility because it had its supporters in Congress. By the end of his administration Reagan softened his harsh stance against arms control and signed a treaty to eliminate intermediate nuclear weapons.

During the late 1980s and early 1990s President George Bush worked closely with the ACDA to negotiate and implement the Strategic Arms Reduction Treaties (START I and II), the Chemical Weapons Convention, and the Treaty on Conventional Forces in Europe. These treaties were the first major steps in reducing the number of weapons of mass destruction around the world. Although the treaties had presidential backing and support, many members of a conservative Congress saw them as a sign that U.S. defense had weakened, and launched attacks against the ACDA and its role in negotiating arms control. By the end of the 1990s the agency was slated for merger with the DOS. This occurred after years of congressional efforts to eliminate the agency altogether. Even as part of the DOS, the role of the ACDA would continue to focus on international disarmament and arms control and act as the chief adviser to the nation on these volatile issues.

CURRENT POLITICAL ISSUES

One issue underlies many of the ACDA's concerns. Although the United States was once the principal possessor of many types of weapons, including the nuclear bomb, other nations have slowly been catching up. Through research and development efforts, espionage, and purchases, countries around the world have stepped up their capabilities. The United States no longer holds the unmatched global leveraging power it once did. Such proliferation makes the control and reduction of arm an effort that must be undertaken by multiple countries. Cooperation, however, is not always easily enforced.

Case Study: Limiting Nuclear Testing

Worldwide agreement that nuclear testing should be banned became evident in 1996, when the United Nations General Assembly voted to adopt a nuclear test ban treaty. President Bill Clinton was the first of 146 world leaders to sign the Comprehensive Test Ban Treaty (CTBT), saying "it will help to prevent the nuclear powers from developing more advanced and more dangerous weapons. It will limit the possibilities for other states to acquire such devices."

The CTBT, which needs ratification by 44 countries to enter into force, would prevent the testing of nuclear weapons by nations who currently possess or are developing them. According to a September 23, 1997, *Washington Post* article, "Two prominent holdouts from the signatories are India, which has said it does not envision signing soon, and Pakistan, which has said it cannot sign as long as India abstains. Both nations are among the 44 actual or potential nuclear powers that, under the treaty's rules, can block it from taking effect."

There was further cause for alarm after India surprised the world, especially neighboring Pakistan, by testing five nuclear weapons on May 11, 1998. Pakistan was especially concerned because it had already fought three full-scale wars with India. Such a bold move by India was widely condemned around the world. India justified the need for testing because of security issues; citing particularly its fear of neighboring Pakistan. Pakistan responded with its own nuclear tests only days later. Months of speeches, talks, and public pressure followed.

Prominent U.S. figures were among the most outspoken forces pleading for India and Pakistan to halt testing and sign the CTBT. Yet the United States was hardly a nation that could lay claim to leading nuclear test ban efforts. Clinton had brought the treaty to the U.S. Senate on September 22, 1997, for advice and consent (ratification). He held it for a year while trying to build up the support of at least two-thirds of the Senate, the required majority needed to ratify a treaty. The administration also used the time to carefully analyze the specifics of the treaty. However, the treaty stalled.

National Security Council arms control director Robert Bell tried to assure members of Congress that banning nuclear tests would not lead to a security threat. He referred to reports from the Department of Energy, the Joint Chiefs of Staff, and weapons labs that supported the assertion that the U.S. nuclear arsenal can be safely and effectively maintained without detonating test blasts. Spurgeon Keeny, president of the Arms Control Association and a former deputy director of the ACDA, noted that there was also support from the U.S. military and nuclear weapons testing labs.

More than a year after presenting the treaty to Congress, no move had been made to begin hearings on ratification. Meanwhile, France and the United Kingdom became the first nuclear weapon states to ratify the treaty. Many other countries followed suit after India and Pakistan tested their weapons. Ratification by the United States was still of major importance, however, as the treaty could not enter into force without having been ratified by the remaining three nuclear weapon states—China, Russia, and the United States. Supporters claimed U.S. passage was needed to push remaining nuclear powers to ratify.

The ACDA tried to garner public support through press releases claiming "the cessation of all nuclear weapon test explosions and all other nuclear explosions, by constraining the development and qualitative improvement of nuclear weapons, constitutes an effective measure of nuclear disarmament and nonproliferation. It will thus contribute effectively to the prevention of nuclear proliferation and the process of nuclear disarmament and strengthen international security and peace." After continued public pressure by high-profile figures like Secretary of State Madeline Albright, Secretary of Energy Federico Pena, and scores of others, Clinton announced in a September 25, 1998, speech that the Senate remained unwilling to hold hearings on ratification. According to the ACDA, early Senate votes show that the two-thirds Senate majority needed to ratify the CTBT is lacking. Yet ACDA Director John Holum continues to urge the Senate to hold the hearings. Meanwhile India and Pakistan made a pledge to sign the CTBT.

SUCCESSES AND FAILURES

The list of successes achieved by the ACDA began with the SALT I and II treaties, which brought the United States and the former Soviet Union closer to agreement on arms limitations. The START I and II treaties actually provided a schedule and framework for reducing the nuclear arsenals in both nations. ACDA expertise has provided valuable insights into the negotiating process on the proliferation of nuclear, biological, chemical, and other weapons systems. It has also alerted the United States to the procurement and development of armament systems by developing nations and has provided analyses on the dangers these new weapon systems have on the stability of world peace.

FUTURE DIRECTIONS

As the ACDA merges with the DOS, a new role will emerge. The verification of arms control treaties will continue, as will independent arms control advocacy including the ability to submit policy recommendations to the president. Under this integration plan, all of the arms control and nonproliferation functions of both the ACDA and the DOS will be combined under a new undersecretary for arms control and international security affairs. The undersecretary will also serve as the senior adviser to the president and the secretary of state for arms control, nonproliferation, and disarmament.

AGENCY RESOURCES

The ACDA director and other senior officials participate frequently in seminars, conferences, and press briefings. The ACDA welcomes all requests for speakers, and accommodates as many as resources and schedules permit. Call 1-800-581-2232 to request a speaker.

AGENCY PUBLICATIONS

ACDA publications are available on the Internet at http://www.acda.gov. You may also obtain ACDA publications by calling 1-800-581-2232, or fax-on-demand at (202) 647-1322. Available publications include press releases, arms control texts, fact sheets, ACDA readers, ACDA annual reports, and a brief "who's who" in the ACDA.

BIBLIOGRAPHY

Boldrick, Michael R. "Mutual Assured Obstruction." *Reason,* 1 July 1995, p. 54(2).

Burns, John F. "India Sets 3 Nuclear Blasts, Defying a Worldwide Ban." *New York Times,* 12 May 1998.

Cornwell, Susan. "Arms Control Chief Attacks Foreign Policy Bill." Reuters, 6 June 1995.

Crossette, Barbara. "Pakistan Pledges A-Bomb Test Ban if Sanctions End." *New York Times,* 24 September 1998.

Deen, Thalif. "U.N. Members Refuse to Reveal Military Budgets." Inter Press Service English News Wire, 2 August 1996.

Gertz, Bill. "China Said to Have Biological Arsenal." *Washington Times,* 24 July 1995, p. 17.

———. "Holum Seeks Ratification of Chemical Arms Pact." *Washington Times,* 2 March 1997, p. 17.

Haniffa, Aziz. "S. Asia Said to Lead Military Spending Growth." *India Abroad,* 21 July 1995, p. PG.

———. "U.S. Says China Gave Pakistan Nuclear Help," *India Abroad,* 28 July 1995, p. PG.

Isaacs, John. "Right Says Arms Control Wrong." *Bulletin of the Atomic Scientists,* 19 September 1995, p. 18(2).

Maynes, Charles William. "The Big Chill at State as Helms Battles the White House." *Los Angeles Times,* 1 October 1995, p. M-2.

Mitchell, Allison. "Clinton Makes Final Push on Chemical Arms Treaty." *New York Times*23 April 1997, p. A10.

Myers, Steven Lee. "State Department Set for Reshaping, Pleasing Helms." *New York Times,* 18 April 1997, p. A1.

"White House Fact Sheet on Reorganizing State, ACDA, USIA, AID." US Newswire, 18 April 1997.

Worsnip, Patrick. "U.S. Sees Delay in Russian START Ratification." Reuters, 14 November 1995.

United States Army Corps of Engineers (USACE; CE)

PARENT ORGANIZATION: Department of Defense
ESTABLISHED: 1779
EMPLOYEES: 39,600

Contact Information:

ADDRESS: 20 Massachusetts Ave. NW
Washington, DC 20314
PHONE: (202) 761-1803
FAX: (202) 761-1803
URL: http://www.usace.army.mil
CHIEF OF ENGINEERS AND COMMANDER: Lt. Gen. Joe N. Ballard
DEPUTY CHIEF OF ENGINEERS AND DEPUTY COMMANDER: Maj. Gen. Albert J. Genetti, Jr.

WHAT IS ITS MISSION?

The U.S. Army Corps of Engineers (USACE or CE) is a major army command with a broad range of missions and capabilities. Its primary mission is to provide high-quality, responsive engineering service to the nation. This mission is divided into two primary areas—civil works and the military program. The civil works mission of the corps includes the maintenance and improvement of navigable waterways; the reduction of flood damage; the generation of hydroelectric power; the storage of water supplies; and the management of man-made lakes and reservoirs for recreation and wildlife conservation. The military program mission is to design and construct military facilities for the army and the air force and other Department of Defense agencies and to provide real estate service for lands where army and air force installations are located. The corps also serves as a disaster response team in its role as an engineering agency.

HOW IS IT STRUCTURED?

The CE is a unique command within the U.S. Army. At the top of the chain of command is the Office of the Chief of Engineers, which formulates policy decisions, engineering regulations, and project reviews; it is also the office that reports directly to the president and Congress. The field structure of the corps consists of eight division offices, each led by a division engineer, and 41 district offices. Programs are administered and carried out in a decentralized manner through these field offices.

Working with the Environmental Protection Agency, the Corps of Engineers endeavors to resolve long-standing environmental problems such as this clean up of a hazardous waste site once owned by a chemical plant in Massachusetts. (AP/Wide World Photos)

The Office of the Chief Engineer is assisted in its function by numerous other units in the corps. These include the Office of the Chief Counsel, the corps' primary legal adviser; the Small Business Office, responsible for recruiting small, local businesses for corps project contracts; and the Office of Public Affairs. The more complex corps functions are divided among eight directorates. The main program work of the corps is carried out through the Directorate of Civil Works and the Directorate of Military Programs. The Directorate of Real Estate also has a significant and complex role, carrying out all of the activities (requirements, programming, acquisition, and disposal) involved in the corps' role as the army's real-property manager. The Directorate of Resource Management serves to operate and maintain many of these real properties.

The Directorate of Research and Development conducts the corps' research program at four laboratory installations: the Cold Regions Research and Engineering Laboratory (CRREL), the Construction Engineering Research Laboratories (CERL), the Engineer Waterways Experiment Station (WES), and the Topographic Engineering Center. Because the corps employs so many civilians in so many different places, another directorate, the Directorate of Human Resources, exists to serve the corps' personnel recruitment, training, and development duties. The Directorate of Logistics is responsible for analyzing the security and logistical concerns associated with corps projects; the Directorate of Information Management handles the complex information infrastructure of the agency.

PRIMARY FUNCTIONS

The Corps of Engineers helps to defend America's security on three levels—military, economic, and environmental. Its military activities include the design, construction, and management of living, working, and training areas for the army and air force. In this function, the corps serves as the nation's largest real-property manager, with holdings in military installations and civil projects approximately equal to the size of Kentucky.

The corps' civil works programs serve to protect the nation's waterways and wetlands. The agency plans, designs, builds, and often operates and maintains projects that provide river and harbor navigation, flood control, water supply, hydroelectric power, environmental restoration, wildlife protection, and recreation. The corps also uses its engineering expertise in times of crisis to undertake disaster relief and recovery work. Both the military and civil works programs are supported by the research and development programs of the corps, carried out at the agency's four laboratories.

The corps also puts its skills and resources to work for other government agencies on projects ranging from toxic cleanup (for the Environmental Protection Agency) to the construction of space facilities (for the National Aeronautics and Space Administration).

PROGRAMS

As an agency, the Corps of Engineers is involved in numerous programs. This involvement is divided at the division and district levels; literally hundreds of programs, in areas such as construction, design, research, and planning, are carried out by employees of the corps. Among the most far-reaching and significant of corps projects is its involvement in the Federal Response Plan. The plan, developed through the efforts of 27 federal departments and agencies, describes the basic procedure by which the U.S. government will mobilize resources and conduct activities to assist states in handling the consequences of serious disasters. Under the terms of the plan, the Corps of Engineers is the primary agency for planning, preparedness, and response for public works and engineering. Some of the activities within the corps' scope of responsibility include emergency clearance of debris, temporary construction of emergency access routes, and emergency restoration of critical public services and utilities.

Another important function of the corps is its regulatory program. Under Section 404 of the 1972 Clean Water Act, the discharging of dredged or fill material into U.S. waters without a permit from the corps is illegal. The corps is responsible for deciding whether to grant these permits, weighing the need to protect aquatic resources against the benefits of proposed development.

Of course, most of the programs of the Corps of Engineers are smaller in scope. A current program of the Directorate of Information Management, the Information Technology Initiative, is a set of related programs designed to upgrade the hardware involved in the CE's information infrastructure and to train corps employees in handling this new hardware and technology.

BUDGET INFORMATION

The spending authority granted to the Corps of Engineers comes from a complex combination of funding through federal, regional, and local appropriations of tax revenues, as well as financing through trust funds and private sources. Of the CE's total expenditures in 1998 of a little over $10.6 billion, about $3.5 billion were funded through federal appropriations. By far the largest portion of the agency's budget, 57 percent, is spent on the various activities included in the military program; while 34 percent is spent on civil works. The remaining 9 percent of the budget is spent financing projects that the CE performs for other government agencies. Most of the costs of this work are reimbursed through the budgets of these agencies.

BUDGET:

United States Army Corps of Engineers

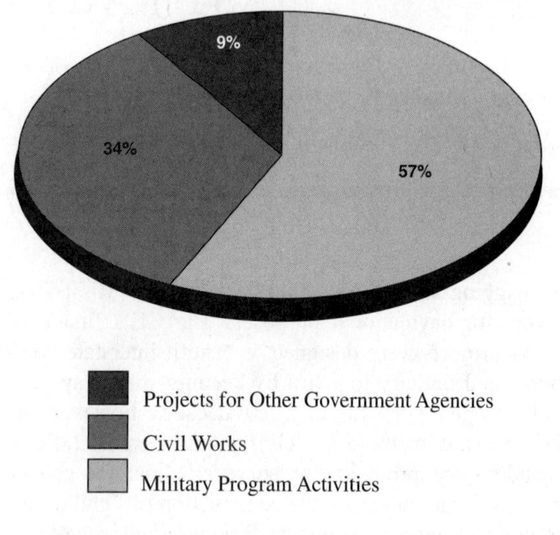

Projects for Other Government Agencies

Civil Works

Military Program Activities

HISTORY

On June 16, 1775, General George Washington appointed Colonel Richard Gridley as chief engineer of the Continental Army. The new chief engineer was to lead the organization in its traditional and most fundamental mission—to support the nation's military forces in times of war and peace. The Army Corps of Engineers was officially established by Congress in 1779, and thus began the corps' long history of planning and constructing many of Washington, D.C.'s most famous monuments and public buildings. The corps was disbanded near the end of the American Revolution (1775–83), however. The unit officially named the Corps of Engineers was later established in 1802, the same year as the United States Military Academy—the first engineering school in the United States and the primary training ground for army engineers—was founded.

The Corps of Engineers received its civil works mission from Congress in 1824 with the passage of the General Survey Act, which committed the CE to surveying and planning internal improvements of national importance. In the same year, the corps was assigned the task

FAST FACTS

The Corps of Engineers provides one-fourth of the nation's hydroelectric power.

(Source: Corps of Engineers. "CorpsFacts," 1997.)

of snagging and clearing the Ohio and the Mississippi Rivers for navigational purposes. The CE's first civil works projects were designed to benefit interstate commerce and military logistics by keeping waterways and harbors open. Over the next few decades, however, the CE received many other civil works responsibilities, including the provision of surveys; plans for canals, roads, and railroads; and the construction of lighthouses, public buildings, monuments, bridges, and aqueducts. Before long the CE was the nation's principal water resource development and management agency and the largest engineering agency in the world.

The civil works mission of the Corps of Engineers underwent dramatic changes in the early twentieth century. Before 1900 its principal responsibilities were navigation and harbor improvements. As early as 1879 the corps had received some responsibility for flood control, but these projects were justified only as efforts to improve navigation. The conservation movement of the early twentieth century shifted the focus of these programs to multiple-purpose planning for the nation's water resources. The CE gradually became more involved in the planning and development of water resources, and in 1909 Congress directed the corps to consider the potential for hydroelectric power generation in all of its surveys for navigational projects.

A series of Flood Control Acts passed in 1917, 1924, 1936, and 1944 laid the groundwork for the corps' expansion as the agency responsible for a nationwide program to protect against flooding. Navigation is no longer the only criterion used to judge the worth of CE projects; the corps must also consider water supply, flood control, hydroelectric power production, irrigation, recreation, and fish and wildlife conservation. By the 1960s the improvement of water quality had become another important mission for the Corps of Engineers.

The water quality improvement mission came about in part through the expansion of the corps' regulatory authority, which dated back to 1893 when the agency was assigned the task of regulating the dumping of waste from hydraulic mining operations into California's navigable streams. In 1970 the courts reinterpreted the regulatory authority of the corps to consider aesthetics, pollution, and conservation in its regulatory actions. The agency thus undertook a nationwide program of regulating the discharge of pollutants into navigable waters—a function that was later transferred to the Environmental Protection Agency. The corps did retain some regulatory authority for dredge-and-fill operations, and its jurisdiction was broadened to include wetlands, tributaries, and headwaters.

The rapid expansion of the CE's civil works mission throughout the twentieth century led it to rely increasingly on civilian personnel for engineering and management expertise. By 1996 the corps was made up of about 185 army officers in leadership positions, along with a staff of about 28,500 civilian employees.

CURRENT POLITICAL ISSUES

The flood control policy of the Corps of Engineers has long been an obvious feature of the American landscape—the corps seeks to contain the nation's rivers with an enormous network of dams and levees, "channelizing" rivers into small, confined routes that will stay clear of settled floodplains when the water rises. The courses of rivers are compressed and elevated during times of low flow. As a command of the U.S. Army, the CE apparently views the nation's rivers as an enemy to be fought; one of the agency's early training films speaks of the corps' "battle" with its adversary, Mother Nature. After much of the levee system was in place on the Mississippi River, the Corps of Engineers declared victory: "We harnessed it, straightened it, regularized it, shackled it."

Case Study: The Flooding of the Mississippi

The policy of flood control on the Mississippi River was caustically ridiculed more than one hundred years ago when Mark Twain wrote that the corps "cannot bar [the river's] path with an obstruction which it will not tear down, dance over, and laugh at." And the corps' flood control had long been criticized by environmentalists for aesthetic and conservation reasons; by channeling America's rivers into straight concrete gutters, by cutting the rivers off from access to their natural floodplains, the corps was creating an eyesore and an environmental disaster. Since Twain's commentary, the army dams, channelization projects, and levees on the Missouri River have eliminated 100,000 acres of sloughs, backwaters, and wetlands. From northern Nebraska to St. Louis, bottomland forests were reduced by 96 percent. On the entire Mississippi system above St. Louis, 19 million acres of wetlands—considered by many to be the only reliable means of flood control—were destroyed.

Many army engineers were sympathetic to these concerns, but nothing of substance was done until the results of the corps' flood control policies were put in more obvious terms. The flooding of the Mississippi, the Missouri, and their tributary rivers during the summer of 1993 was one of the worst and most costly natural disasters in U.S. history. The Mississippi blasted through its levees, shearing some off at ground level, and flooded the settled areas beyond that had once been its natural floodplain. The floods killed 50 people, displaced 62,000 families, and caused a stunning $12 billion worth of property loss. Before long, conservatives who were appalled at the costs of flood recovery had lined up alongside the environmentalists, calling for the Corps of Engineers to reevaluate its "victory" over the Mississippi. The movement gained momentum after disastrous floods in California's similarly engineered Central Valley in 1997, in which 16,000 homes were destroyed and $1.6 billion in property was lost.

The traditional corps policy of pouring concrete, building reservoirs, and channeling rivers to control floods was now firmly called into question, and the questioning was led on many fronts by army engineers. A consensus was reached that rivers needed more room to behave naturally—to expand and fill their floodplains, to meander, and to be contained by natural wetlands during flooding. The Corps of Engineers, for years responsible for channeling rivers into small spaces, undertook the process of restoring streams and rivers and constructing wetlands to slow down, retain, and spread out floodwaters. Levees were moved back along the fringes of the floodplains to give rivers room to meander, to develop pools and vegetation, and to store water on floodplains, which would reduce upstream and downstream flooding. The federal government has become committed to the long, complex, and controversial process of purchasing floodway lands from farmers and residents. Although expensive, the purchase price for the Mississippi floodway—estimated at about $232 million—was still a very small fraction of the $12 billion in damage caused by the 1993 floods.

SUCCESSES AND FAILURES

The Corps of Engineers has achieved remarkable success in implementing the standards outlined by Vice President Al Gore's National Performance Review (NPR), an initiative designed to streamline the federal government, reduce wasteful spending, and return the focus of government work to the customer. In 1996 the Corps of Engineers received the NPR's Hammer Award for improving government operations. The corps' efforts in this area were conducted by a team of engineers responsible for streamlining the corps' processes and regulations for the operation and maintenance of corps reservoirs, dams, and recreation areas. The streamlining reduced the number of regulations for operation and maintenance of corps facilities and processes from 89 to seven and reduced the total number of pages of regulation from 1,596 to 212.

FUTURE DIRECTIONS

In addition to its efforts at reevaluating its flood control program, the Corps of Engineers underwent a restructuring operation mandated by the 1997 Energy and Water Development Appropriations Act, which required the corps to reduce the number of its divisions. The agency has not yet entirely sorted out the ramifications that this initiative will have at the district level. In the future, the number of total corps districts, as well as the reporting responsibilities of each district, will be sorted out by the Corps of Engineers.

AGENCY RESOURCES

General inquiries about the Corps of Engineers can be directed to the Public Affairs Office at (202) 761-0011. The corps also maintains an on-line library designed primarily for corps employees but some of which is accessible to the public. The library can be accessed at http:/libweb.wes.army.mil.usace.html. For information about the history of Corps of Engineers projects, contact the Office of History, HQ U.S. Army Corps of Engineers, Humphreys Engineer Center, ATTN: CEHO-ZA, 7701 Telegraph Rd., Alexandria, VA 22315; phone (703) 428-6554.

AGENCY PUBLICATIONS

Corps of Engineers publications include numerous regulations, circulars, manuals, and brochures. For nonengineers, most of these make for fairly dry reading, but some corps publications are designed for the public, including two periodicals: *Engineer Update*, an unofficial monthly newspaper with news and features on corps people and activities, and *Information Management News*, which offers current news about the corps' information technology programs and activities. The Public Affairs Office also publishes *CorpsFacts*, a series of fact sheets on corps programs and missions, as well as informational brochures. Many of these publications can be viewed or downloaded from the CE's World Wide Web site at http://www.usace.army.mil. For further information, contact the Corps of Engineers Public Affairs Department at (202) 761-0011.

BIBLIOGRAPHY

Beck, Alfred M. *U.S. Army in World War II, Technical Services, the Corps of Engineers: The War Against Germany*. Washington, D.C.: Government Printing Office, 1985.

Christenson, Jon. "California Floods Change Thinking on Need to Tame Rivers." *New York Times*, 4 February 1997, p. C4.

Cushman, John H., Jr. "Rule on Wetlands Tightened by U.S. to Limit Draining." *New York Times*, 11 December 1996, p. A1.

Horgan, Arthur E. *Dams & Other Disasters: A Century of the Army Corps of Engineers in Civil Works*. Boston: Porter Sargent, 1971.

Kirkpatrick, David D. "Beachfront Property . . . Going . . . Going." *Wall Street Journal*, 9 August 1996, p. B8.

"On Quitting, Scientists Say Beach Repair is Foolhardy." *New York Times*, 9 August 1997, p. 28.

Shallat, Todd, and William H. Goetzmann. *Structures in the Stream: Water, Science, & the Rise of the U.S. Army Corps of Engineers*. Austin: University of Texas Press, 1994.

Vongs, Paul. "The Corps of Engineers Gives a Damn." *Audubon*, January–February 1994, pp. 96–97.

Williams, Ted. "The River Always Wins." *Audubon*, July–August 1994, pp. 78–115.

———. "The Wetlands Protection Farce." *Audubon*, March–April 1995, pp. 30–35.

United States Coast Guard (USCG)

PARENT ORGANIZATION: Department of Transportation
ESTABLISHED: April 28, 1915
EMPLOYEES: 45,099 (1997)

Contact Information:

ADDRESS: 2100 Second St. SE
Washington, DC 20593-2229
PHONE: (202) 267-2229
URL: http://www.uscg.mil
COMMANDANT: Adm. Robert E. Kramek
VICE COMMANDANT: Vice Adm. Richard D. Herr

WHAT IS ITS MISSION?

The United States Coast Guard (USCG) has multiple missions, including law enforcement, maritime safety, marine environmental protection, and national security. Its complex of ships, aircraft, boats, and shore stations is organized to enable Coast Guard personnel to respond flexibly in various mission areas. A single Coast Guard vessel is responsible for carrying out different mission roles, sometimes executing different roles simultaneously in the course of a single operation. This "multimission approach" enables the Coast Guard to respond quickly to changing public needs.

HOW IS IT STRUCTURED?

The Coast Guard is part of the nation's armed forces, although it normally falls under the administrative jurisdiction of the Department of Transportation. In times of war or at the discretion of the president it becomes part of the Department of the Navy. The service is headed by a commandant who is selected by the president from a list of names submitted by the secretary of transportation and confirmed by the Senate. The Coast Guard hierarchy and order of rank mirrors that of the navy.

The Coast Guard has two main administrative area offices, the Atlantic and the Pacific, which are divided into 17 district offices along U.S. coastal waters. The Marine Safety Council, which approves all Coast Guard regulations, is chaired by the Coast Guard's chief counsel; other members are the heads of the four Coast Guard directorates: Information and Technical Systems, Law

The refusal of the Coast Guard to accept Haitian refugees was a source of embarrassment for the agency. Before and after the 1994 decision to accept Haitians who could prove political refugee status, the Coast Guard was seen as a merciless enforcer. (AP/Wide World Photos)

Enforcement and Defense Operations, Marine Safety and Environmental Protection, and Navigation Safety and Waterway Services. The Coast Guard maintains its own academy for the education of officers.

PRIMARY FUNCTIONS

The Coast Guard is the primary maritime law enforcement agency of the federal government. It is the federal agency most responsible for enforcing regulations and laws that protect the marine environment, especially the Federal Water Pollution Control Act. In carrying out this function it works closely with the Environmental Protection Agency. The Coast Guard is one of the federal agencies charged with enforcing laws relating to smuggling, drug trafficking, and illegal immigration. In theory the Coast Guard is meant to cooperate with other federal bodies, like the United States Customs Service, in executing these duties; in practice jurisdictional conflict has occasionally arisen. It enforces or assists other agencies in enforcing international laws and treaties to which the United States is party, for example, treaties governing fishing.

The Coast Guard is responsible for establishing and enforcing a variety of maritime regulations. It sets standards for the design, construction, and maintenance of all commercial vessels flying the American flag and can board such vessels anywhere in the world to ensure that standards are met. The Coast Guard is also responsible for establishing standards for offshore structures, like oil rigs, and for bridges over navigable waters in the United States. It oversees licensing of U.S. Merchant Marine personnel. Regulations for the equipment and operation of recreational boats are an important and visible area of Coast Guard responsibility. The Marine Safety Council deliberates regulations relating to ships, bridges, boating, and harbors.

The Coast Guard provides search and rescue (SAR) services to boats and commercial vessels on the high seas and navigable waters in the United States. SAR is provided to vessels that are lost, mechanically or structurally disabled, or faced with life-threatening maritime conditions. Related functions include flood relief, removing hazards to navigation, and investigating accidents.

In keeping with its motto, *Semper Paratus* (Always Prepared), the Coast Guard maintains a constant state of military readiness. The Coast Guard Reserve trains individuals and maintains units for active duty to back up the regular service in time of war. The Coast Guard Auxiliary is composed of private citizens who own boats, aircraft, or radio equipment. It aids the Coast Guard in its SAR missions and in providing public boating education.

PROGRAMS

The U.S. Coast Guard administers many programs in a wide range of responsibilities, including the environment, law enforcement, navigation, icebreaking, and recreational boating.

The Coast Guard's marine environmental response program enforces laws protecting the U.S. marine environment. For example, it checks that all American and foreign vessels using U.S. waters are insured and that cleanup costs for any pollution they cause will be paid. If a serious incident of pollution occurs in U.S. coastal waters—an oil spill for example—the Coast Guard serves as the onsite coordinator of the investigation and cleanup work. The Coast Guard mans the National Response Center and is part of the National Response Team, a group of 16 government agencies, including 10 cabinet departments, together with the Environmental Protection Agency, the National Oceanic and Atmospheric Administration, the Nuclear Regulatory Commission, the Federal Emergency Management Agency, and the General Services Administration. The National Response Center is "the sole national point of contact for reporting all oil, chemical, radiological and biological discharges." It was established to receive reports of hazardous material spills, initiate civil penalties, monitor cleanups, and, when necessary, coordinate various federally funded spill response programs. The National Strike Force assists federal on-scene coordinators in responding to pollution incidents.

The Coast Guard is also active in protecting endangered marine species. It tracks whale, manatee, and sea turtle populations. The Sea Partners Campaign works with communities to heighten awareness of the effects of garbage dumping and toxic spills on marine life. Sea Partners also encourages environmentally friendly care and maintenance of pleasure craft.

A vital Coast Guard program, and one of its oldest, is the Navigation Center, which installs, operates, and maintains a system of navigational aids in U.S. waters. These include lighthouses, lights, buoys, beacons, fog signals, radio beacons, radar beacons, and long-range navigational aids. New York harbor, with its relatively shallow waters traversed by deeper channels, would be practically unnavigable by large oceangoing vessels without the Coast Guard buoys and beacons signaling deep water. The Navigation Center broadcasts regular reports on maritime conditions for vessels of all types. It publishes "Local Notice to Mariners" and "Light Lists" for navigators.

The Coast Guard's national boating safety program establishes safety standards for recreational boats and related equipment and provides funding to safe-boating programs at the state level. The aim of the program, which provides courses for both adults and children, is to prevent deaths, personal injuries, and property damage involving recreational boats. It works closely with the Coast Guard Auxiliary to promote public awareness and provide public education.

BUDGET:

United States Coast Guard

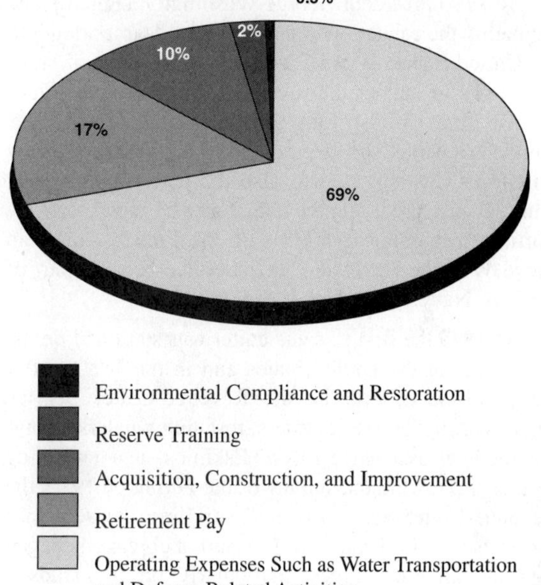

Environmental Compliance and Restoration

Reserve Training

Acquisition, Construction, and Improvement

Retirement Pay

Operating Expenses Such as Water Transportation and Defense Related Activities

BUDGET INFORMATION

The estimated congressional appropriations for the Coast Guard's budget in 1998 was $3.9 billion. About 69 percent of the Coast Guard's annual budget went toward operating expenses such as water transportation and defense-related activities. These include search-and-rescue programs, ice-breaking, and law enforcement activities, together with military preparedness. The second largest budget item in 1998 was retirement pay, accounting for approximately 17 percent of the budget. Other Coast Guard expenditures included acquisition, construction, and improvement (10 percent); reserve training (2 percent); and environmental compliance and restoration (0.5 percent).

A plan instituted by the Office of Budget and Management calls for a spending freeze in the Coast Guard budget between 1998 and 2002. The freeze, which would not be adjusted for inflation, would be the equivalent of a $90 million per year cut.

HISTORY

Several government services with relatively isolated functions—the Revenue-Cutter Service, the Life-Saving

Service, the Steamboat Inspection Service, the Bureau of Navigation, and the Lighthouse Service—were united over the course of America's history to ultimately become the complex, multifunctional organization that is today's Coast Guard.

In 1790 President George Washington signed a law regulating the collection of duties on goods imported into the United States. It provided for a small fleet of ships and crews to collect the revenue. This Revenue-Cutter Service, the earliest form of the Coast Guard, was founded as part of the Department of the Treasury's new Bureau of Customs. It was also the nation's first maritime service, predating the U.S. Navy by eight years. In wartime, beginning in 1798 with the Franco-American Naval War, the Revenue-Cutter Service became part of the U.S. Navy.

In 1849 the first revenue cutter was stationed on the west coast of the United States and in the 1880s, after the purchase of Alaska, the Revenue-Cutter Service began sailing the Arctic waters, rescuing whalers, bringing medical assistance to the Eskimos, and enforcing treaties. Following the sinking of the *Titanic* in 1912, the Revenue-Cutter Service began patrolling the sea-lanes for icebergs; in 1936 Coast Guard icebreakers began clearing shipping routes, particularly on the Hudson River and on the Great Lakes. Three Coast Guard cutters broke a path through the ice north of Canada from the Pacific to the Atlantic in 1957.

In 1848 Congress began funding a shore-based lifesaving organization; in 1878 it became a civilian agency within the Treasury Department, the U.S. Life-Saving Service. It was based up and down the coasts of the United States, with buildings located right on the beaches and full-time, trained personnel to help those in distress.

Plagued by wasteful spending, the Life-Saving Service and the Revenue-Cutter Service were nearly abolished in 1912 by the Commission on Economy and Efficiency. Under the commission's recommendation, the U.S. Navy would have taken over the functions of the Revenue-Cutter Service, and the Life-Saving Service would have been merged with the U.S. Lighthouse Service in the Department of Commerce and Labor. The Revenue-Cutter Service fought back, though, claiming it could perform its duties more efficiently than the navy could. The compromise reached by President Woodrow Wilson, Congress, and the Treasury Department resulted in the merging of the two services into the Coast Guard on January 28, 1915. As defined by the new law, the Coast Guard became part of the military forces under the administration of the Department of the Treasury. In World Wars I and II and in the Vietnam War the Coast Guard was taken over by the navy. In the 1920s the Coast Guard's most important responsibility was enforcing the temperance laws introduced by Prohibition, an activity that parallels its frequent drug interdiction work in the 1980s and 1990s.

When it took over the Bureau of Navigation and Steamboat Inspection from the Commerce Department during World War II, the Coast Guard assumed two new duties: the regulation and oversight of the Merchant Marine and the establishment of safety standards for steam-powered vessels. The original Steamboat Inspection Service dated back to 1838. It was the result of congressional action after three serious steamboat explosions. At first the Steamboat Service was only responsible for inspections. But after a series of new ship disasters it was empowered to set standards for ship and steam engine construction. Originally part of the Treasury Department, it was transferred to the Department of Commerce and Labor in 1903 and merged with the Bureau of Navigation by the Hoover administration.

The last organization taken over by the Coast Guard was the U.S. Lighthouse Service. A small system of lighthouses, beacons, and buoys was the nation's very first public works project, funded by the First Congress in 1789. The Lighthouse Service was founded in 1912 and in 1939 President Franklin Roosevelt signed a law that merged it with the Coast Guard.

In the 1980s two Coast Guard responsibilities took on unprecedented importance. The mass exodus of Cubans to the United States that began in 1980 signaled the start of large-scale involvement with refugees, often known as boat people, in the Caribbean. Sometimes, as in the case of the Cubans, the service helped thousands flee their homeland and gain asylum in the United States; other times, as was often the case with fleeing Haitian boat people, they were stopped and returned to an uncertain fate in their native country. The Coast Guard came under criticism for the latter actions, although it was only executing the policies of the administrations of Presidents George Bush and Bill Clinton.

Drug interdiction also became a major focus of Coast Guard activity during the administration of President Ronald Reagan. The Coast Guard was given the order to stop the flow of drugs, in particular marijuana and cocaine, from Latin America into the United States. However, jurisdictional conflict with the U.S. Customs Service, which also had a fleet of boats it used to patrol coastal waters, finally reached such a point that the Reagan administration had to intervene. The Coast Guard was given jurisdiction for interdiction at sea, the Customs Service for interdiction at U.S. borders.

In all, presidential drug interdiction policies have been a mixed blessing for the Coast Guard. It credited the new focus with a rise in recruits in the early 1990s, and major budget increases in the decade have been for drug control programs. But the policeman image of the Coast Guard has not set well with everyday Americans, especially in programs like Zero Tolerance. A program of the Reagan administration, Zero Tolerance gave the Coast Guard the right to seize and put up for auction any vessel flying an American flag for *any* amount of drugs found on board. The program was quickly modified after two million-dollar yachts were seized within two weeks for having a fraction of an ounce of marijuana on board.

CURRENT POLITICAL ISSUES

In the latter half of the 1990s, the Coast Guard was told by Congress to streamline its services in order to reduce expenditures. A plan from the Office of Management and Budget to freeze the Coast Guard budget appropriation for the five years between 1998 and 2002 made it obvious that drastic cuts would have to be made. To manage in the new financial climate, the Coast Guard planned the closure of a number of facilities throughout the country, in particular boat stations, search and rescue bases, and lighthouses. Communities often have very different feelings about these facilities, however.

Case Study: The Great Lakes Lighthouses

In fall 1997 the Coast Guard announced its intention to close eight lighthouses along the Great Lakes coast. Hearing the news, citizens reacted with protest. The lighthouses were still needed, they argued. Many recreational and fishing boats still used their waters and needed the security the lighthouses offered. Community residents were also loathe to give up structures they had grown up with, that had often come to symbolize their communities.

Public outcry was so great in Fort Gratiot, Michigan, that the Coast Guard initially relented and agreed to continue to operate its facility. The service has offered, as well, to seek private sponsors to take over the other seven. Under its provisional plan, the Coast Guard would retain ownership of the property and continue to maintain the equipment while private bodies take over operation of the lighthouses. The $1,000 or more per year per lighthouse that the Coast Guard would not have to spend on electricity amounted to an important savings.

The communities were not satisfied with the proposal. Some did not want to see the Coast Guard relinquish *any* control of the lighthouses. The harbormaster in Port Sanilac, Michigan, said that if his town were given the local lighthouse it would, most likely, refuse to operate it—townspeople were concerned that as operators of the safety facility they could be held liable if a ship went down in the area. A Coast Guard spokesperson countered that the lights were never meant to be hazard warnings; they are merely points of orientation for navigation, and as such their operation is an injudicious use of scarce resources. Indeed, despite the protests of lighthouse aficionados, the Coast Guard eventually decided to relinquish control of all 123 lighthouses in the state of Michigan by 2005 as a cost-cutting measure. The Great Lakes Lighthouse Association hopes to be able to maintain those that are located on the mainland, but few of the lighthouses located offshore are likely to be preserved.

Public Impact

The lighthouse dispute emphasizes how local attitudes toward the Coast Guard differ from Washington's. That is one reason citizens are so vocal when Washington tampers with the service on a local level by closing facilities like the lighthouses. Another incident occurred in summer 1997 when budget cuts were about to force the Coast Guard to close its search and rescue base in Brooklyn. It would have had to rely on stations on Cape Cod and in Atlantic City for emergency helicopter service to Long Island, an area with thousands of pleasure boats. An editorialist for *Newsday* summed up the local attitude: "The lawmakers have been cutting back military spending but the Coast Guard budgets can't be cut as much as those of the other services. The end of the cold war did not reduce boating accidents or calls for emergency helicopter service." So far it has been the lawmakers that have had the final say. Air Station Brooklyn was consolidated into the Coast Guard's Atlantic City base in 1998.

SUCCESSES AND FAILURES

In 1996 the Coast Guard produced a series of public service announcements that reduced the number of hoax distress calls from boaters off Long Island by 45 percent from the previous year. It was the first significant drop in such calls in six years. Most hoax callers, the Coast Guard believed, were not criminally motivated; they were simply misinformed. The commercials were designed to show boaters that "Mayday! Mayday!" was to be used only in genuine emergency situations. The Coast Guard also recruited students of Boston University to put together two commercials featuring Coast Guard vessels and personnel.

After the announcements were broadcast along the East coast, the number of hoax calls dropped from 121 to 66 on Long Island, and from 416 to 294 in the entire Northeast, a drop of 29 percent. The rate of decline is significant because perpetrators of hoaxes are rarely apprehended. Even the stiff penalties—up to six years in prison, a $250,000 fine, and possible restitution to the Coast Guard—had little effect on the rate of hoax distress calls. It is doubly significant because it is the Coast Guard's policy to respond to every call it receives. That policy was adopted in 1990 after two men drowned in the Atlantic after their legitimate distress call was mistaken for a hoax.

Less successful was the Coast Guard's involvement with waves of Haitian refugees. The policy of using the Coast Guard to intercept refugees—mostly Haitian—attempting to sail to the United States and return them to their homelands was begun in 1981 under the Reagan administration and was continued by President Bush, especially after the coup that overthrew Jean-Bertrand Aristide in September 1991. The sight of Coast Guard cutters rounding up frail boats filled with refugees became commonplace on the evening news. While campaigning, President Bill Clinton had criticized the policy of forcing Haitians to return to an uncertain fate under

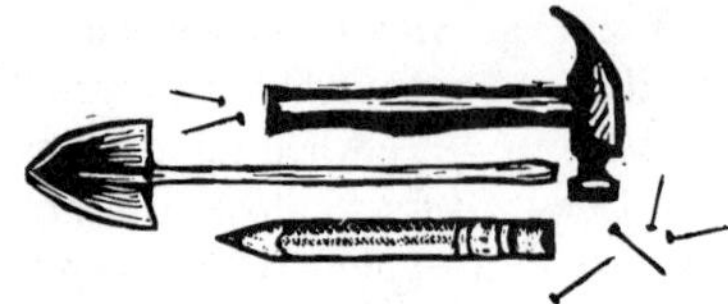

GET INVOLVED:

U.S. citizens over age 17 can become one of the 35,000 volunteer members of the Coast Guard Auxiliary. Members receive specialized training in boating and lifesaving skills. The auxiliary helps all boaters by participating in Coast Guard search and rescue missions and boating safety classes for the public. You can find a membership application form at the USCG Web site. Information is also available at the Coast Guard Infoline, 1-800-368-5647; (202) 267-0780 in Washington, D.C. TDD numbers are 1-800-689-0816; (202) 267-6707 in Washington, D.C.

the military junta. He did not modify it until May 1994, however, when he finally announced that refugees would be admitted to the United States if they could show they were legitimate political refugees.

The decision opened the floodgates. In the two months after the policy change, 10,000 Haitian boat people were intercepted by the Coast Guard. Nearly a thousand drowned trying to escape the island; the rest were taken to crowded, unsanitary refugee camps for processing. The Coast Guard's reputation suffered doubly: it was the agent of the Clinton administration's indecisive Haiti policy, perceived by many as heartless and opportunistic, and after more than 10 years of high-profile activity patrolling the Caribbean for drug smugglers, the image of the Coast Guard herding refugees into the naval base at Guantanamo Bay seemed to confirm its new image as ruthless police force.

FUTURE DIRECTIONS

In the future the Coast Guard will likely be concerned with fulfilling all of its duties under increasingly tight budget constrictions. Congress demands that the USCG remain involved in drug enforcement and other areas that are politically popular at a given moment, but at the same time it refuses to appropriate funds to buy ships and equipment to carry out those jobs. If the climate does not change, the Coast Guard will most likely be forced to continue closing its smaller centers, pare back larger ones, and trim its community-based safety programs. It is a trend that could end up affecting the USCG services most important to the average American.

Automation is going to play a greater role in the future of the Coast Guard. It is developing a fleet of "smart ships"—vessels whose operations are fully computerized—as a way of reducing crew sizes and expenses. The new technology is expected to necessitate a transformation of shipboard procedures, indeed, of seagoing culture. Crew members must learn to trust the new technology as well as know how to work it. As younger more computer literate persons join the service, "smart ships" will be more acceptable and will accelerate training times.

AGENCY RESOURCES

The Coast Guard Historian's Office is a good source of information on maritime disasters and other events, Coast Guard aviation, and aids to navigation. Letter and phone inquiries are handled as quickly as possible by the office's small staff. The office also publishes several short booklets every year, which are available upon request. It can be contacted at United States Coast Guard, Historian's Office, 2100 2nd St. SW, Washington, DC 20593. The phone number is (202) 267-0948.

The Coast Guard Law Library contains resources related to maritime law and standards. It is open from 9 A.M. until 4 P.M. Monday through Friday. Its address is United States Coast Guard Law Library, Transportation Administrative Services Center, Room B726, 2100 2nd St. SW, Washington, DC 20593. Its phone number is (202) 267-2536; its fax number is (202) 267-4204.

Information on boating regulation and conditions can be obtained by calling the toll-free Boating Hotline at 1-800-368-5647. For information on the Coast Guard Auxiliary and boating safety classes, call toll-free 1-800-BOAT; in Virginia, call 1-800-245-BOAT. Coast Guard patches and other souvenirs are available to the general public from the U.S. Coast Guard Exchange, U.S. Support Center, 4000 Coast Guard Blvd., Portsmouth, VA 23703-2199. The telephone number is (757) 483-8618; and the fax number is (757) 483-8621. The exchange can be contacted by E-mail at cges@norfolk.infi.net.

Freedom of Information requests should be submitted in writing—E-mail requests will not be honored—to Commandant, G-SII-2, U.S. Coast Guard, 2100 2nd St. SW, Washington, DC 20593-0001.

AGENCY PUBLICATIONS

Most Coast Guard publications, including the "Proceedings of the Marine Safety Council," "The Marine Safety Newsletter," "The Marine Safety Manual," and many specialized works on navigation and regulations can be obtained on-line at the Coast Guard Web site at http://www.uscg.mil/hq/g-m/nmc/genpub.htm. They can also be ordered from the National Technical Information Service at NTIS, 5285 Port Royal Rd., Springfield, VA 22161. The NTIS sales desk takes orders by phone Monday through Friday between 8 A.M. and 8 P.M., Eastern time. The sales desk telephone number is 1-800-553-NTIS; TDD (hearing impaired only) is (703) 487-4639—available between 8:30 A.M. and 5:00 P.M., Eastern time, Monday–Friday; fax is (703) 321-8547.

Individuals who register with the Coast Guard's boating safety Web site at http://www.uscgboating.org/ will be sent boating safety updates periodically. A full list of Coast Guard publications on boating safety is available at http://www.uscgboating.org/pubs.html. The publications are available for downloading as well. Publications may also be ordered through the Boating Hotline at 1-800-368-5647.

BIBLIOGRAPHY

Barnes, Edward. "Incident at Baie du Mesle." *Time*, 11 July 1994.

Benson, Matthew. "Less than Zero." *Motor Boating and Sailing*, August 1988.

Bleyer, Bill. "On the Water: Ad Leads to Drop in Hoax Calls." *Newsday*, 3 March 1997.

Gibbs, Tony. "Semper Paratus." *New Yorker*, 7 August 1989.

Johnson, Robert Erwin. *Guardians of the Sea: History of the United States Coast Guard*. Annapolis, Md.: Naval Institute Press, 1987.

Katz-Stone, Adam. "17 Lighthouses Up for Adoption." *Navy Times*, 24 March 1997.

Metz, Andrew. "A Coast Guard Deal Proposed at Gabreski." *Newsday*, 11 July 1997.

Schreiner, Samuel Agnew. *Mayday! Mayday!*. New York: D.I. Fine, 1990.

United States Commission on Civil Rights (USCCR)

PARENT ORGANIZATION: Independent
ESTABLISHED: 1957
EMPLOYEES: 90

Contact Information:

ADDRESS: 624 Ninth St. NW
Washington, DC 20425
PHONE: (202) 376-7700
FAX: (202) 376-8315
URL: http://www.usccr.gov
CHAIRMAN: Mary F. Berry
VICE CHAIRMAN: Cruz Reynoso
STAFF DIRECTOR: Ruby G. Moy

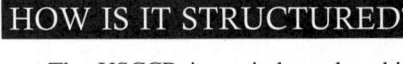

WHAT IS ITS MISSION?

The mission of the United States Commission on Civil Rights (USCCR) is to assess the effectiveness of civil rights laws and policies, study complaints about inequities in all aspects of civil rights matters, make public service announcements on civil rights issues, and issue reports and studies concerning the state of discrimination or the denial of rights to the president and Congress.

HOW IS IT STRUCTURED?

The USCCR is an independent bipartisan agency that consists of eight part-time commissioners, four appointed by the president and four appointed by Congress, each of whom serves a six-year term. The president then selects the chair and vice chair from among the appointed commission members. The commission meets monthly (except in August) and also convenes hearings, conferences, consultations, and briefings. The commission employs a staff director who is appointed and serves at the will of the president to oversee day-to-day operations. Remaining personnel are all appointed in accordance with federal civil service guidelines. The commission operates six regional district offices as well as a Washington, D.C. headquarters, which houses the Robert S. Rankin Civil Rights Memorial Library. There are 51 advisory committees (one for each state and the District of Columbia) consisting of citizens who serve without compensation and assist the commission in fact-finding and investigations. These citizens serve for two years and are recommended by the regional director for their area.

PRIMARY FUNCTIONS

The USCCR investigates complaints of civil rights violations against citizens because of race, color, religion, sex, age, disability, or national origin. To facilitate its fact-finding initiatives, the USCCR holds hearings and can issue subpoenas for documents and witnesses. The USCCR also studies and collects information related to discrimination or the denial of equal protection under the law. The commission serves as a national repository for information about discrimination.

A major function of the USCCR is to create and submit reports and recommendations about discrimination and equal protection issues to the president and Congress. Another important initiative is the issuing of public service announcements concerning discrimination violations that impact the nation, such as the church burnings in the South in the middle 1990s.

The USCCR works closely with a number of federal agencies. For example, the commission conducts massive studies on issues critical to ensuring the civil rights of all students in U.S. schools. Such an analysis was the 1997 six-part study of educational equal opportunity conducted "to assist the Department of Education in its efforts to strengthen its partnership with all of these groups—school administrators, teachers, students, parents, and the community at large—and thereby enhance the Department's civil rights enforcement program" (Mary Berry).

The Department of Labor requests inquiry into workplace-related discrimination; the Department of the Interior requires studies on American Indian issues; and the Department of Housing and Urban Development researches fair-housing practices. The commission also monitors, appraises, and reports on how well the federal agencies themselves maintain and enforce civil rights laws.

BUDGET INFORMATION

The USCCR was allocated approximately $9 million by Congress in 1998. About 78 percent of this money went toward personnel compensation and civilian personnel benefits. Another 11 percent was spent on rental fees to the General Services Administration (GSA) which leases some buildings to federal agencies. The remaining 11 percent was spent on other services required by the USCCR. The 1999 budget called for an increase to $11 million with the additional funding allocated to raise staffing levels.

HISTORY

The Civil Rights Act of 1964 was enacted as a bipartisan effort to redress centuries of bias against minorities, especially African Americans, and give them true equality under federal law. When President Lyndon B. Johnson signed this historic document, he recognized that the U.S. history of discrimination " . . . cannot continue. Our Constitution, the foundation of our Republic, forbids it. The principles of our freedom forbid it. Morality forbids it. And the law I will sign tonight forbids it." He was determined that as a part of his "Great Society" all Americans regardless of race, color, or national origin would be protected under the law. Johnson spent months with civil rights leaders such as Dr. Martin Luther King, Andrew Young, and members of the Southern Christian Leadership Conference lobbying powerful members of Congress, especially those from southern states, to get the act passed into law.

As part of sweeping reforms enabled by the act, the U.S. Commission on Civil Rights (USCCR), originally founded in 1957, was revitalized as an investigative and reporting agency. Its mission was to report to the president and Congress about all forms of discrimination throughout the United States. A major early concern was the redress of discrimination to African Americans, but other minorities also benefited from the studies of racism, stereotyping, and other forms of victimization. Programs such as affirmative action and the reports and recommendations of the USCCR were part of an attempt to bring those who had experienced discrimination into the mainstream of society.

Since 1964 the USCCR has studied racism, education, gender issues, stereotyping, bigotry, violence, handicapped rights, housing discrimination, and affirmative action. Its conclusions often influenced legislators to enact laws to correct the injustices that were reported. The Civil Rights Act of 1964, the Voting Rights Act of 1965, and the Fair Housing Act of 1968 are among the many laws passed to ensure equal treatment under the law for minorities.

The years 1981 to 1992 brought about a change in the government's position on civil rights. Presidents Ronald Reagan and George Bush opposed affirmative action programs and lacked previous administrations' commitment to the USCCR. Although the USCCR was reviewed through congressional hearings and reestablished through the Civil Rights Act of 1983 to continue its mandate of finding the causes of discrimination and making recommendations, the commission's focus became blurred as the nature and commitment of the commissioners changed to reflect the attitudes of the administration. During this time, whenever Congress renewed its annual budget, the voices of civil rights advocates both within and outside Congress criticized the commission for failing to fulfill its reporting and fact-finding obligations. A rival group of former USCCR commissioners who were intent on advancing the fact-finding and reporting that were neglected by the official USCCR, the Citizen's Commission on Civil Rights was formed during this time. This commission was deeply disturbed by what it perceived as damages to civil rights

BIOGRAPHY:

Mary Frances Berry

Professor and Social Activist (b. 1938) Dr. Mary Frances Berry's achievements are most notable in the arenas of education, law, and civil rights. Born into poverty, the African American woman overcame racial and gender prejudice at Fisk University, Howard University, and the University of Michigan, where she received her Ph.D. in 1965. She earned a law degree in 1970, and in 1974 Berry became the highest-ranking black woman on the University of Maryland's College Park Campus. There, she was named provost of the Division of Behavioral and Social Sciences. In 1976 Berry accepted chancellorship of the University of Colorado at Boulder, becoming the first black woman to head a major research university. At the invitation of President Jimmy Carter she served in the Department of Health, Education, and Welfare. As the assistant secretary for education from 1977 to 1980, Berry again broke new ground as the first African American woman to serve as chief educational officer of the United States. In 1980 Carter appointed Berry to the U.S. Commission on Civil Rights, a bipartisan agency that monitors the enforcement of civil rights laws. Throughout the 1980s Berry increased her involvement in social activism. She also became active in efforts to raise awareness of apartheid in South Africa. She returned to domestic issues including women's rights and child care issues in the 1990s. Dr. Berry continues to be active in social and political issues and is a professor at the University of Pennsylvania.

during these years. Congress even considered disbanding the USCCR in 1989, and its continued existence was accompanied by hearings and reprimands for its perceived inefficiencies.

When Bill Clinton became president in 1993, a second revitalization of the USCCR began. After 12 years of setbacks and lack of focus, the USCCR was once again on track in studying and recommending ways to eliminate discrimination in the United States. In addition to holding briefings on discrimination against Asian Americans, the commission also issued a report about the inordinate number of minority students in special education programs and suggested that the USCCR and the Department of Special Education work together to enforce civil rights in schools and regional offices. The USCCR was once again at the forefront of the fight against discrimination and protecting equal rights under the law.

CURRENT POLITICAL ISSUES

The argument over whether or not the United States Commission on Civil Rights should continue created a great deal of turmoil during the 1990s. Accusations that Republicans hounded one director out of office and ominous trends such as a 58 percent budget cut and a reduction in staff from 250 in 1983 to 90 in 1997 all affected the performance of the USCCR. Such hurdles, however, did not stop the commission from tackling some of the most incendiary and controversial issues of the 1990s. The commission examined the role of minorities in Hollywood both in front of and behind the camera, studied equal educational opportunities in U.S. schools, civil rights problems facing Asian Americans, and continued its ongoing investigation into African American issues.

Case Study: Church Burnings

One of the most USCCR's challenging investigations was a 1996 tour of Alabama, Louisiana, Mississippi, Tennessee, and North and South Carolina to examine a rash of suspicious fires in predominantly African American churches. Although only 20 percent of the 250 church burnings in the South were racially motivated, and there was no apparent conspiracy in the setting of these fires, more than 100 of these churches had largely African American congregations. Some of the fires seemed to be the result of malicious pranks or financial scams. Seventy-four predominantly white churches were also burned during the same period, but those fires were also not racially motivated.

The USCCR found that at least 24 churches were targeted by arsonists due to their racial composition. More importantly, the commission's inquiry uncovered a disturbing rise of racism and resegregation in the South. "It was like turning over a rock and seeing what's beneath it," USCCR chairman Mary Frances Berry said.

For example, the commission discovered that churches, banks, and schools in Greene County, Alabama, remained racially segregated. The division was most acute in the school system, where student enrollment at private academies in the county was 100 percent white and in the public schools was 99 percent black. In a hearing held in Mississippi, racial animosity was so prevalent that black residents refused to attend forums at a predominantly white college. According to Mary Frances Berry, "Racial tensions are a major problem in the states in which the (church) burnings took place. Out of national sight and mind, racial segregation exists in schools and other public facilities reminiscent of Jim Crow days before segregation was outlawed."

The results of the investigations prompted the USCCR to meet with leaders both within and outside of government to initiate a grassroots movement against racial inequities and racism. Commission officials sent letters to governors and legislators in all six states requesting meetings to discuss race relations and to develop strategic plans involving state agencies. An official of the USCCR's central region, where most of the fires occurred, remarked that "over the years, the nation has grown comfortable with the appearance of racial harmony. These recent events have drawn us back into reality."

In a 1996 report the USCCR concluded that lingering racism and the refusal of some whites to open the doors of society to African Americans provided the impetus for a string of church burnings across the South. Although many whites assisted in the church rebuilding efforts, they came from out of state and not from the affected areas. Further, the USCCR commented that racism was not confined to the overt actions observed in the South but also existed in other more subtle forms throughout the rest of the country.

Public Impact

The USCCR's report intensified a dialogue about race and its existence in U.S. society. Even though physical, monetary, and spiritual assistance was generously provided to rebuild the destroyed churches, the problems that prompted the 24 cases of racially motivated arson still existed. The USCCR's role in revealing these problems brought to light not only the problems that African Americans encounter in cases of overt racism but also the more subtle forms of discrimination that exist in employment, housing, or education.

SUCCESSES AND FAILURES

In July 1997 Representative Mazine Waters, in an address to the House of Representatives Committee on the Judiciary, informed the committee chairman that her "patience with Chairman Canady's unrelenting and mean-spirited attempts to dismantle civil rights protections is wearing thin . . . . Our struggle for civil rights is far from over. More than ever, we need a strong, viable U.S. Commission on Civil Rights." Government officials acknowledge the need for the USCCR, but the commission's effectiveness and daily operations are often called into question.

The Government Accounting Office (GAO) 1996 annual report concluded that the "commission appears to be an agency in disarray" and "the lack of attention to basic requirements applying to all federal agencies, such as up-to-date descriptions of operations and internal guidance for employees, reflects poorly on the overall management of the commission." This report prompted a response from all commissioners that they would make certain the recommendations would be followed. Other commission members, including the chair and vice chair, also felt that the report was a "great injustice," although it was acknowledged that many reports often took too long to complete because of constant turnover and changing focus.

The USCCR will never be without detractors because of the nature of its investigations. Its reports are not always popular, and the bipartisan commission has been accused of being too liberal in interpreting its mandate. The messages the USCCR sends the nation are often uncomfortable and sometimes shocking, but its studies and hearings bring to light issues of race, gender, and other discrimination. It has opened and will continue to stimulate dialogue among different racial, ethnic, and cultural groups in the United States. Even though it has no enforcement powers, the USCCR has given voice to new initiatives by the president and Congress to rectify inequities caused by years of institutional discrimination. Public service announcements regarding racism, sexism, and other forms of discrimination have become important weapons in the USSCR's mandated war against discrimination.

FUTURE DIRECTIONS

With the growing number of laws curtailing such initiatives as affirmative action or education for illegal aliens, the USCCR's task is to find alternative recommendations to ensure that insidious discrimination is contained and eventually eliminated. Such alternate methods include taking an active role in forming task forces to formulate strategic plans for dealing with racism at all levels of society. In addition, the USCCR plans to report its findings more quickly so that recommendations may be applied to timely issues. A closer working relationship among federal, state, and local civil rights organizations to reveal problems earlier and suggest solutions are also inherent in the future plans of the USCCR.

AGENCY RESOURCES

The USCCR operates the Robert S. Rankin Civil Rights Memorial Library from its headquarters in Washington D.C. The library houses 50,000 reference works on civil rights, including journals, periodicals, microfilm, microfiche, reports, textbooks, and other sources. It is open to the public Monday through Friday from 10:00 A.M. to 4:00 P.M.

AGENCY PUBLICATIONS

As a reporting agency, the USCCR has provided 70 statutory reports to the president and Congress and issued more than 160 reports and studies on civil rights matters. The state advisory committees have also produced more than 240 reports on local and regional civil rights matters. These reports are on file in most government depository libraries.

Some titles and reports include: *Federal Title VI Enforcement to Ensure Nondiscrimination in Federally Assisted Programs, Racial and Ethnic Tensions in American Communities: Poverty, Inequality, and Discrimination. Vol. III: The Chicago Report, The Fair Housing Amendments Act of 1988: The Enforcement Report, Civil Rights Issues Facing Asian Americans in the 1990s,* and *Who Is Guarding the Guardians? A Report on Police Practices.*

A catalogue of USCCR publications can be found at its Web site at http://www.usccr.gov; by mailing a request to the United States Commission on Civil Rights, 624 Ninth St. NW, Washington, DC 20425; or calling (202) 376-8128. All publications are free.

BIBLIOGRAPHY

"Civil Rights Commission says Racial Tensions High in States with Church Burnings." *Jet*, 28 October 1994.

Drinan, Robert F. "Civil Rights in the First 100 Days. *America*, 13 March 1993.

Harris, Christy. "Storm Surrounds Civil Rights Commission." *Federal Times*, 4 August 1997.

Masci, David. "Senate OKs 3-Year Compromise for Civil Rights Commission." *Congressional Quarterly Weekly Report*, 2 November 1991.

———. "With Time Running Short, Panel OKs Four Bills." *Congressional Quarterly Weekly Report*, 1 October 1994.

Seligman, Daniel. "Up from Inscrutable." *Fortune*, 6 April 1992.

Waters, Maxine. "Opening Statement of Rep. Maxine Waters Committee on the Judiciary Oversight Hearings on the United States Commission on Civil Rights." *Capitol Hill Press Release*, 17 July 1997.

United States Customs Service

PARENT ORGANIZATION: Department of the Treasury
ESTABLISHED: July 31, 1789
EMPLOYEES: 17,143

Contact Information:

ADDRESS: 1301 Constitution Ave. NW
Washington, DC 20229
PHONE: (202) 927-6724
URL: http://www.customs.treas.gov
COMMISSIONER: George J. Weiss

WHAT IS ITS MISSION?

The stated mission of the U.S. Customs Service is to "ensure that all goods entering the United States are in compliance with United States laws and regulations." To this end the Customs Service is responsible for the "collection of duties, taxes, and fees; intercepting contraband; and enforcement of laws and regulations in partnership with other federal government agencies." The agency is also responsible for the enforcement of the Tariff Act of 1930 and other customs laws.

HOW IS IT STRUCTURED?

The Customs Service is a bureau within the Department of Treasury, a cabinet-level agency, and falls within the executive branch of government. The agency is administered by a commissioner who is appointed by the president and confirmed by the Senate. The commissioner establishes policy and supervises all activities from the agency's headquarters in Washington, D.C.

The fifty states, plus the Virgin Islands and Puerto Rico, are divided into 20 Customs Management Center areas, which are responsible for monitoring activity at approximately three hundred ports of entry. Each center is headed by a director who supervises Customs Service personnel. Twenty-two foreign field offices of the Customs Service are located throughout the world. A Customs Service official represents the agency in the U.S. Mission to the European Communities in Brussels. The Customs Service also operates a Canine Enforcement Training Center at Front Royal, Virginia.

PRIMARY FUNCTIONS

The Customs Service is responsible for assessing and collecting fees associated with import and export of goods at official customs facilities including; sea ports, border facilities, and airports. Customs duties, excise taxes, and penalties due on imported merchandise are charged based on the volume of goods moved across the nation's borders. These revenues are provided to the federal government to be used in the provision of federal government services. As the agency in control of entry and exit to and from the United States, the Customs Service is in charge of processing persons, carriers, cargo and mail, and administering certain navigation laws. The Customs Service supports commerce regulations by detecting and apprehending persons engaged in fraudulent practices designed to circumvent customs and related laws, provisions, quotas and marking requirements for imported merchandise. The Customs Service is specifically charged with seizing all contraband, including narcotics and illegal drugs, and preventing the entry of these goods into the U.S. marketplace.

As the principal border enforcement agency the Customs Service helps to administer and enforce some four hundred provisions of law on behalf of more than forty government agencies. Such agencies include the Drug Enforcement Administration (DEA) and the Immigration and Naturalization Service (INS).

The Customs Service cooperates with other federal agencies and foreign governments in suppressing the traffic of illegal narcotics and pornography, enforcing export control laws by interception of illegal high-technology and weapons exports, enforcing reporting requirements of the Bank Secrecy Act, and collecting international trade statistics.

The Customs Service is also charged with the enforcement of a wide range of requirements to protect the public, such as: auto safety and emission control material standards; counterfeit monetary instruments; flammable fabric restrictions; animal and plant quarantine requirements; and food, drug, and hazardous substance prohibitions.

The Customs Service is extensively involved with outside commercial and policy organizations, trade associations, international organizations, and foreign customs services. Customs is a member of the multinational World Customs Organization, the Cabinet Committee to Combat Terrorism, and the International Narcotics Control Program.

Finally, the Customs Service participates in and supports the activities and programs of various international organizations and agreements including the World Trade Organization (WTO), the International Civil Aviation Organization, and the Organization of American States (OAS).

PROGRAMS

Each day Customs Service officials are engaged in monitoring the traffic of people and goods at border crossings, airports, and ports-of-entry around the United States. Specific programs include Operation Hard Line, which is focused on the prevention of illegal import of narcotics into the United States. Initiated in 1995, the program was designed to address the threat of drug smuggling along the U.S.-Mexico border. As part of the program Customs Service inspectors perform extensive examinations of all incoming commercial vehicles, private passenger cars, and pedestrians. In addition Operation Hard Line utilizes special agents who are responsible for investigations into the organized smuggling of drugs across U.S. borders. Customs inspectors, enforcement officers, and special agents are responsible for seizure of thousands of pounds of illegal narcotics each year.

The Customs Service operates the Canine Enforcement Training Center, which trains dogs to locate narcotics as they are smuggled across U.S. borders. As early as 1969, the Customs Service was carrying out studies to determine the feasibility of using dogs in the detection of drugs. After reviewing these studies the agency began to work with branches of the military in the training of animals. Dogs were initially used in the detection of marijuana and hashish. After dogs were successfully trained to detect these substances, they were trained in the detection of heroin and cocaine as well. In light of these proven results Congress approved funding for a facility improvement program in 1991 and firmly placed the canine within the ranks of the Customs Service. Today the facility has a staff of 32, consisting of instructors, animal caretakers, storage specialists, and administrative personnel. The center has an average population of 100 to 150 dogs and successfully trains 120 per year. Canine enforcement teams are assigned to border patrol duty and special assignments around the United States.

BUDGET INFORMATION

The Customs Service's projected budget for 1999 was approximately $2.107 billion. The Customs Service budget is divided into two categories: Commercial, and Drug and Other Enforcement. Commercial, which covers all activities not directly related to enforcement, such as passenger processing, trade compliance, and intelligence gathering and analysis on potential enforcement targets, receives 64 percent of the budget. Drug and Other Enforcement, which covers the actual investigation of violations and also interdiction activities, takes up the remaining 36 percent of the budget.

HISTORY

The U.S. Customs Service is one of the oldest federal agencies in the country. It was established by the fifth act of the first U.S. Congress, which directed customs districts and officials to collect various duties that had been imposed just 27 days before on July 4, 1789. The primary responsibilities of the officers in those early days were to collect the taxes on imported and exported goods, to document data relating to cargo and passenger ships, and to fine people or companies that defied the newly instituted laws. For the next 125 years the money that the customs districts collected through fees and fines would be the primary source of income for the U.S. government.

The functions of the customs officers rapidly expanded as the country passed into and through the nineteenth century. In 1790 ten cutters (small but armed ships) were built for use by the customs districts in securing the revenue collected from duties. This responsibility would later become the task of the U.S. Coast Guard. During the War of 1812 (1812–14) the customs districts were responsible for assessing steep penalties to those companies that wished to do overseas business with England. Customs officers were assigned an additional duty in 1819 when the districts became responsible for maintaining immigration statistics. The names and nationalities of all those entering the country were collected and given to the State Department. This task was assigned to the Immigration and Naturalization Service in 1882. During the Civil War, customs officers were responsible for keeping track of any property that Union armies seized from the Confederacy.

During World War I (1914–18), customs officers carried out similar responsibilities. The officers were instrumental in upholding neutrality laws and preventing illegal shipments of arms. Because large amounts of U.S. currency was prohibited from leaving the country during this time, customs officials searched passengers and their luggage. In the brief respite between global wars the customs districts, which had been administered by the Secretary of the Treasury or the Division of Customs, reorganized so that their duties could be performed more efficiently. The Bureau of Customs was established as a distinct and separate federal agency under the Department of the Treasury in 1927. When World War II engulfed the United States in the mid-to-late 1940s, the new Bureau of Customs set about its familiar wartime duties of restricting exports and imports as well as the flow of excessive amounts of money. Additionally, the bureau worked to prevent illegal aliens from the Axis countries from entering the United States.

The years following World War II (1939–45) were another period of rapid change. In 1973, the Bureau of Customs was again reorganized and redesignated the United States Customs Service. More important, as illegal narcotics smuggling into the United States increased, the scope of the agency's focus broadened to include curtailing this activity. Many drug smugglers were transporting their contraband by air and it was necessary for the Bureau of Customs to respond to this threat. The late 1960s saw a vast increase in air support for the functions of the bureau. Detector dogs, dogs that could sniff out hidden stashes of drugs, came into wide use at various ports of entry at the end of 1970. New technology, such as radar nets, night vision goggles, and different forms of undetectable surveillance, came into use to further decrease the likelihood that illegal substances would find their way into the United States.

The U.S. Customs Service reorganized itself again in the 1990s. During this time the agency stepped up airport security and did more to prohibit fruits, vegetables, and meat from other countries from entering the United States. In 1995 the Customs Service underwent a complete overhaul to enhance its administrative effectiveness and provide better service to U.S. commerce and industry.

BUDGET:

United States Customs Service

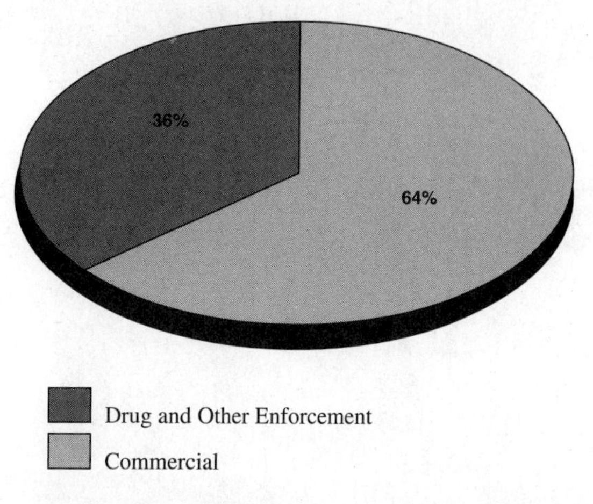

Drug and Other Enforcement

Commercial

CURRENT POLITICAL ISSUES

As a law enforcement agency, the Customs Service works to stop the flow of smuggled drugs from entering the United States. Customs Service officials accomplish this through investigation and search of suspicious transport or individuals. With millions of dollars in drug profits at stake, drug smugglers take every opportunity to guarantee their smuggling schemes, including offering bribes to customs officials. Corruption is a sensitive issue, especially for an agency like Customs which prides

One of the central duties of the Customs Service is to stop the passage of illegal goods into the United States. Several Customs agents uncover a large quantity of cocaine. (Photograph by Larry Rubenstein. UPI/Corbis-Bettmann)

itself on the honesty and integrity of its employees. But because of the amount of money involved, corruption is a concern taken seriously by federal government officials within the Treasury and legislative offices.

Case Study: Investigations of Corruption in the Pacific Region

The U.S. Customs Service uses informants to penetrate drug smuggling operations. When it is suspected that smuggling activity is aided by a customs official, often the only way to catch the offending officer is through a paid informant. In 1992, Mexican national Eloy Fernandez-Fernandez, a 10-year veteran informant, described to his contacts within the Customs Service the alleged acceptance of a bribe by the Pacific Regional Customs commissioner and a second Customs official. News of the allegation spread to the Treasury which assigned the inspector general to investigate. The allegations of corruption were revealed publicly during a series of articles which publicized possible corruption within border patrol agencies. Customs officials spoke with journalists about the internal affairs investigation, which only served to heighten tensions within the agency.

As a result of the Treasury's inspector general's investigation, informant Fernandez-Fernandez was arrested for making false statements to the U.S. government. The Customs Officials were cleared of the charges after Fernandez-Fernandez failed a polygraph test. Not long after, while still in custody, Fernandez-Fernandez was said to have confessed to lying about the allegations. Customs officials who worked closely with Fernandez-Fernandez were disturbed that such a long-time ally of the Customs Service would risk so much by making false allegations against a high-ranking customs officer. Others explained that he was facing money and immigration problems and had hoped the bribery story would help him and his family gain entrance into the United States. However, some journalists believed Fernandez-Fernandez had been paid off in return for an admission of guilt.

Throughout the internal investigation, Customs employees who spoke with journalists shared their suspicions about corruption within the agency. Those discussions led to a series of articles on border corruption that proved to be embarrassing to the commissioner and the agency. The response of Commissioner George Weise was to question suspected Customs employees in an effort to end rumor and speculation. The media believed that the questioning of Customs employees was intended to intimidate and discourage employees from cooperating with the media. A representative of the National Treasury's Employee Union described the internal affairs search for whistleblowers within the agency as part of a strategy to keep Customs employees from cooperating with House and Senate investigators.

As a result of this investigation and similar investigations against Customs officials along the West Coast, the FBI Border Corruption Task Force conducted a probe that concluded there was no evidence of graft or misconduct by the Pacific Regional commissioner. At the close of the inquiry Commissioner George Weise gave the Customs Service a clean bill of health in regard to allegations of corruption. However, the media reported details of the investigations from a more critical standpoint and found inconsistencies in the train of events. Journalists reported that the timing of the 1992 presidential election may have played a role in the quick resolution of the investigation.

Public Impact

While the arrest of Fernandez-Fernandez ended that particular investigation, the media continued to investigate and describe possible motives and activities within the Customs Service. Congressional and Senate inquiries into border patrol corruption were scheduled to follow. The Clinton administration has downplayed the possibility of corruption within the Customs Service. Barry McCaffery, director of the Office of National Drug Control Policy, contradicted the administration's comment and stated that a law enforcement corruption problem does exist. Justice Department officials have made similar statements.

FAST FACTS

Over 100 million vehicles, 55 million commercial airline travelers, and 40 million pedestrians pass through U.S. border crossings and ports-of-entry every year.

(Source: U.S. Customs Service. "Press Release," 1998.)

FUTURE DIRECTIONS

In 1995 the Customs Service began a five-year program focused on developing a new computer network designed to keep the United States competitive in the transportation of goods to international markets. The program, Automated Export System (AES), is a computerized network that helps the Customs Service speed the exportation of goods from U.S. manufacturers, as well as maintain a more accurate account of these goods. The information recorded is typically used in Commerce Department statistics on American businesses.

At the start of the program, the first two industries automated were ocean transportation and air transportation. In time the Customs Service will mandate participation in the program as they develop systems to handle specific industries. Industry support for the program is widespread even at a time when the role of the federal government in private sector business is being criticized or eliminated. This support stems from the fact that U.S. exporters depend on the efficiency and speed of the Customs Service. Without automation, the United States could fall behind other developed countries in the ability to bring manufactured goods to the international marketplace quickly and efficiently. The development of the system has software manufacturers, port authorities, and transport companies all cooperatively involved in the development of AES. Implementation of the new system should keep U.S. goods competitive in the global marketplace.

AGENCY RESOURCES

The U.S. Customs Service operates an easy-to-use Web site at http://www.customs.treas.gov with informa-

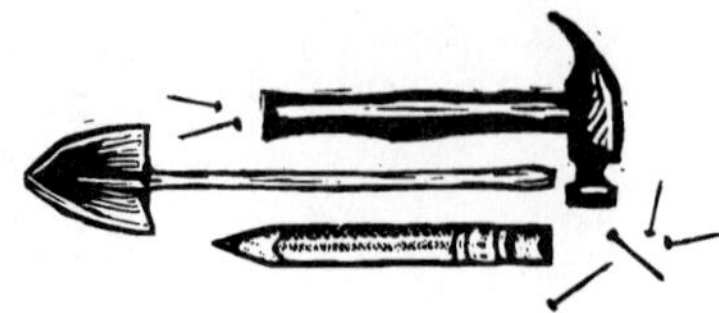

GET INVOLVED:

The Customs Service administers the Explorer Program for youth. This program is a division of the Boy Scouts of America (BSA). BSA, in partnership with the Customs Service offers young people the opportunity to develop leadership skills through participation in activities such as law operation, first aid, firearms safety, and self-defense. To learn more about the program, call (202) 927-2294.

tion on all aspects of fees and duties, travel regulations, and importing and exporting goods. Additional information may be obtained by contacting the U.S. Customs Service, Department of the Treasury, 1301 Constitution Ave. NW, Washington, DC 20229 or by phoning (202) 927-6724.

AGENCY PUBLICATIONS

The U.S. Customs Service provides free copies of many of its publications such as *Customs in Brief, Guide for Private Flyers, Know Before You Go, Pets & Wildlife,* and *Tips for Visitors*. Publications may be requested via the Customs Service's Web site at http://www.customs.treas.gov or by calling the National Distribution Center at (317) 290-3046.

BIBLIOGRAPHY

Bonner, Raymond. "Altering Labels, Not Clothes (China Sidesteps Limits)." *New York Times*, 1 April 1997, p. A1.

Dettmer, Jaime. "Battle for the Border: Is the U.S. Customs Going After the Messenger Instead of Dealing with the Message of Corruption?" *Insight on the New*, 3 December 1996, p. 13.

———. "Exposed Border Bosses Embarrass U.S. Customs." *Insight on the News*, 24 March 1997, p. 7.

Kaminer, Ariel. "The Shipment (Customs Officials Impound AIDS Drugs Shipped from Mexico)." *New York Times*, 29 July 1996, p. 10.

Williams, Alex. "Chanel's Priciest Bag." *New York Times*, 6 November 1995, p. 18.

Zuckerman, Amy. "Exporters Should Gear Up for On-Line Customs System." *Electronic News*, 8 January 1996, p. 30.

United States Fish and Wildlife Service (FWS)

PARENT ORGANIZATION: Department of the Interior
ESTABLISHED: 1940
EMPLOYEES: 8,045

Contact Information:

ADDRESS: 1849 C St. NW
Washington, DC 20240
PHONE: (202) 208-5634
URL: http://www.fws.gov
DIRECTOR: Jamie Rappaport Clark

WHAT IS ITS MISSION?

The published mission of the U.S. Fish and Wildlife Service (FWS) is to work " with others to conserve, protect, and enhance fish and wildlife and their habitats for the continued benefit of the American people." Among the agency's major concerns are migratory birds, endangered species, certain marine mammals, freshwater and anadromous fish, such as salmon, that swim upriver to breed, the National Wildlife Refuge System (NWRS), wetlands, habitat conservation, and scientific research on environmental contaminants.

HOW IS IT STRUCTURED?

The FWS is administered by a director who is nominated by the president and confirmed by the Senate. The assistant secretary of Fish, Wildlife, and Parks, at the Department of the Interior (DOI), oversees the activities of the director. The Office of the Director, as well as the Offices of Information Services, Human Resources and Policy, Management and Budget, and other administrative offices are headquartered in Washington, D.C.

The FWS has established seven U.S. regions. Each region is administered by a regional director and a deputy regional director. Regions implement DOI and FWS policy and develop programs that are specific to the region, for example, programs related to the needs of specific wildlife and ecological systems.

The FWS also administers numerous field stations, including 500 national wildlife refuges, 166 waterfowl production areas, 78 national fish hatcheries, fish health

FAST FACTS

Five hundred national wildlife refuges have been established from the Arctic Ocean to the South Pacific and from Maine to the Caribbean. They encompass more than 92 million acres and support 22 percent of all threatened and endangered species.

(Source: U.S. Fish and Wildlife Service. "History and Activities," 1997.)

centers, fishery/wildlife assistance offices, and ecological services offices. Law enforcement agents are deployed nationwide from the FWS Division of Law Enforcement. Each site is staffed by FWS personnel responsible for site maintenance, resource management, research activities, and supervision of recreational and private use of lands under FWS supervision.

PRIMARY FUNCTIONS

Regional offices implement programs nationwide to further the agency's goals of protection and conservation of migratory birds, endangered species, certain marine mammals, and inland sport fisheries. To this end, the FWS works to foster the ethic of environmental stewardship based on ecological principles and scientific knowledge of wildlife. For example, the FWS works with individual states to improve conservation and management practices of the nation's fish and wildlife resources and administers a national program providing opportunities to the American public to understand, appreciate, and wisely use these resources.

The FWS also implements resource management techniques for the protection and improvement of land and water ecosystems—also called habitat preservation—which directly benefits wildlife. Resource management techniques range from fire management to water management to restocking fish in streams and rivers. These techniques are based on scientific research and observation of healthy wildlife habitat throughout the refuge system and FWS sites.

FWS personnel monitor the quality and overall composition of natural resources under its control through surveillance of pesticides and other contaminants, studies of fish and wildlife populations, and ecological studies. The service also provides the federal government with environmental impact assessments of existing or new projects such as hydroelectric dams, nuclear power sites, stream channelization, dredge-and-fill permits, and environmental impact statement reviews.

In addition, the FWS helps fulfill the public demand for recreational fishing while maintaining the nation's fisheries to ensure their continued survival.

PROGRAMS

As the agency responsible for the implementation of the Endangered Species Act, the FWS provides national and international leadership in identifying, protecting, and restoring endangered species of fish, wildlife, and plants. This includes development of the federal list of endangered and threatened species. In addition, the FWS conducts wildlife status surveys, prepares recovery plans, and coordinates efforts nationally and internationally to promote the protection and conservation of wildlife in this category. To this end the FWS operates national wildlife refuges, which provide critical habitat for wildlife.

The service also enforces laws regarding the sale and foreign importation of wildlife appearing on the endangered and threatened species list. Because wildlife is not aware of national borders, the FWS also consults with foreign governments and organizations on the protection of specific species and on law enforcement issues across borders.

The protection of migratory birds is a long-standing priority for the FWS. Wildlife refuges and waterfowl production areas are managed to provide these animals with flight corridors for their annual north-to-south migrations. FWS hunting and law enforcement programs supervise the taking of game birds, bird populations, and harvest surveys. Programs are also implemented to manage mammals and nonmigratory birds living in refuges to better understand the behavior and needs of waterfowl.

National fish hatcheries are another program area of the FWS and involve the production and stocking of coastal anadromous fish to promote stable populations. Additionally, hatcheries produce lake trout and are involved in fishery management in the Great Lakes region. This work is done in cooperation with Canada, participating states, and other inland fisheries. Fish hatcheries also work with American Indian tribes to keep rivers and streams located on tribal lands stocked with fish.

The FWS provides public information programs, leaflets, and brochures. The service also operates environmental study tours on FWS lands for school groups. Other programs for public recreation and education are visitor centers, self-guided nature trails, observation towers, and display ponds. The FWS works to provide a safe environment for public enjoyment of recreational activities such as hunting, fishing, and wildlife photography.

The FWS also manages federal programs that generate funds through excise taxes on sporting equipment and firearms. These funds are disbursed to the states and territories for projects designed to conserve and enhance the U.S. fish and wildlife resources.

Each FWS field site, specifically those of the NWRS, administers multiple programs aimed at the conservation and appreciation of wildlife as well as the use of resources on federal lands. Roads are built, lands are surveyed and studied, and, when properly legislated by Congress, resources are taken from these lands for use by public and private institutions. Funds from the contract sale of resources such as timber and water or the use of grazing land is used in part to support the FWS's mission of conservation throughout the system.

One of the FWS's most successful programs is the Federal Duck Stamp Program. Duck stamps bearing illustrations of North American waterfowl are sold through the U.S. Postal Service and are carried by those hunting waterfowl. Revenue from the sale of duck stamps totals approximately $350 million, providing for the purchase and preservation of more than four million acres of wetland refuges for North American waterfowl.

BUDGET:

United States Fish and Wildlife Service

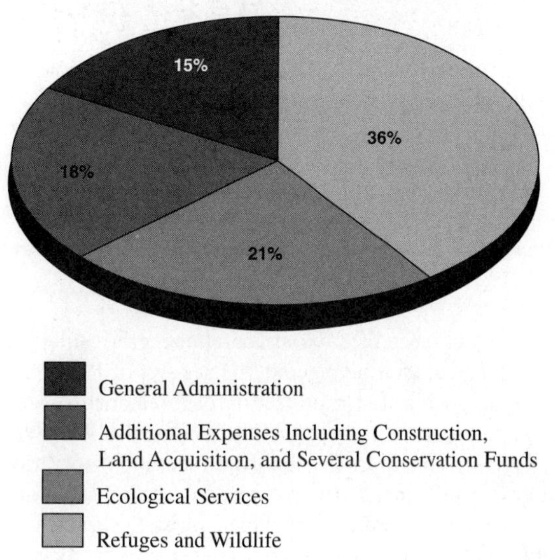

General Administration
Additional Expenses Including Construction, Land Acquisition, and Several Conservation Funds
Ecological Services
Refuges and Wildlife

BUDGET INFORMATION

The approximate 1998 budget for the Fish and Wildlife Service was $687.9 million. The agency divided its funding into four major funding areas. Refuges and Wildlife accounted for $245 million, or 36 percent, of the budget. Ecological Services accounted for $144.8 million, or 21 percent of the budget. General administration accounted for $102.5 million, or 15 percent, of the budget. Additional expenses included construction, land acquisition, and several conservation funds that accounted for $125 million, or 18 percent of the budget.

HISTORY

As early as 1871 Congress established the U.S Fish Commission to study fish populations used for food, which were reported to be declining. In 1885 Congress created the Office of Economic Ornithology to study the patterns of migratory birds, especially those with an impact on agriculture. This office underwent several name changes as its responsibilities grew to include the study of abundance, distribution, and habits of birds and mammals. In 1905 the agency was renamed the Bureau of Biological Survey, and it began to manage the nation's first wildlife refuges.

President Theodore Roosevelt, known for his avid enthusiasm for outdoor recreation—especially hunting—designated the first national wildlife refuge in 1903. He chose Florida's Pelican Island to initiate protection of egrets and herons, which were being overhunted. In 1929 Congress passed the Migratory Bird Conservation Act, authorizing a system of wetlands refuges serving as protected corridors for birds during their annual migrations.

In 1934 President Franklin D. Roosevelt showed his support for wildlife when he appointed a committee on wildlife restoration; it was composed of three notable conservationists, who wasted no time allocating $50 million in federal funds for the acquisition and conservation of lands for wildlife. The conservationists of that era were often hunters who experienced firsthand the importance of preserving habitats for wildlife. Sportsmen translated their concern into the passage of the Duck Stamp Act, which requires each hunter to purchase a $1 stamp to be carried while hunting. With proceeds from the act, national wildlife refuge sites increased sevenfold in the following years and still play an important role in recreation and wildlife preservation. In 1939 the Bureau of Fisheries and the Biological Survey were transferred to the DOI. One year later they were combined to create a new agency, the FWS.

During the 1950s and 1960s U.S. economic growth spurred interest in the valuable resources under refuge protection. In 1966 Congress passed the National Wildlife Refuge System Administration Act to develop revised guidelines for refuge management. Legislators passed the law to strike a balance between "economic necessity" and wildlife conservation strategy.

FAST FACTS

As of September 9, 1998, there were 675 species of plants and 469 species of animals listed as either endangered or threatened in the United States.

(Source: U.S. Fish and Wildlife Service. "Box Score, Endangered Species," 1998.)

A resurgence of environmental concern resulted in the passage of the Endangered Species Act of 1973, providing a legal basis for protection of threatened species of plants, fish, birds, reptiles, and mammals. The FWS was chosen to administer this first federal conservation program, and amends the list based on its research and that of other government agencies, or as the result of a public petition. All species must meet certain requirements to be placed on the list, and proposed additions or removals are subject to review by the public and the judiciary.

The FWS has developed into a conservation agency of international scope. Its activities now extend to international treaties and cooperative efforts in the preservation of wildlife whose migratory patterns cross national boundaries. Additionally, the service enforces laws affecting the importation of the remains of endangered species. From its beginning as a collection of federal agencies researching particular fish and bird species, the agency has grown to reflect the complexities of international environmental issues.

CURRENT POLITICAL ISSUES

Observers have noted that congressional representatives critical of environmental regulation seem to use the federal budget deficit to weaken regulations for economic reasons. Some members of Congress have sought to change legislation prohibiting the use of revenue from parks and refuges to reduce the federal budget. Legislation of this kind could provide a way for the government to generate revenue from federally owned lands by opening them up to industrial use, allowing the government to meet the goal of total deficit reduction by 2002. Advocates of these measures say the new legislation would continue to preserve the "crown jewels" of federal lands, such as the major parks but would provide revenue from privatizing more marginal lands.

Efforts to allow generation of revenues from federal lands is an ongoing process. Riders to legislation have been used for decades to allow many different uses of federal lands supposedly protected for use and appreciation by future generations. Grazing, farming, logging, drilling, and motor vehicle recreation are activities that have been legalized within the NWRS. Pollution from these and other sources also exists on protected lands, fueling a continuing debate concerning the future integrity of these lands. President Bill Clinton's administration and its leading conservationist, Secretary of the Interior Bruce Babbitt, favor long-term protection of these resources and argue that generation of revenue from the NWRS is a short-term solution to the federal government's broader economic problems. President Clinton pledged to defend these natural resources through presidential veto.

Case Study: The Future of the Arctic National Wildlife Refuge

Congressional budget resolutions could force the opening of parts of Alaska's Arctic National Wildlife Refuge (ANWR) to oil well drilling. Opponents of the proposals say drilling on the ANWR would ruin the fragile coastal plain area that is home to polar bears and caribou. Advocates of the plan remind them that the ANWR could hold the nation's last major untapped onshore oil reserve.

Although Congress has not yet acted on a bill to completely legalize oil development in the ANWR, House and Senate bills count on more than $1 billion in federal revenues from this source through 2002. This means the committees with jurisdiction, both chaired by Alaskans eager to develop the wildlife refuge's coastal plain, would have to either approve bills allowing the drilling or cut other programs under their jurisdiction to find offsetting money. "Opening up ANWR through the budget process is the only way to get away with plundering an irreplaceable long-term asset in pursuit of short-term gains," Babbitt said.

The House bill, however, stated that allowing oil development in the refuge "could provide enormous revenues to the Treasury, jobs to the U.S. economy and a valuable domestic energy resource to offset the current transfer of U.S. wealth to other nations."

Babbitt added that drilling in the refuge may not be as valuable as once thought because world oil prices were "far below" levels expected when earlier projections were made. The U.S. Geological Survey sharply lowered its estimate of how much oil might be found in the coastal plain, further fueling the debate on the value of ANWR oil reserves.

Public Impact

Proponents of the plan to allow oil and gas development on the ANWR see the creation of more than 750,000 jobs nationwide as a result and approximately $1 billion in federal revenues. These figures are contested by opponents of the plan, who say that jobs in the energy sector have always been volatile and dependent on multiple factors, including the actual amount of oil that is pumped and fluctuating world oil prices. However, the governor and pro-drilling politicians of Alaska continue to aggressively lobby to allow drilling on the refuge largely because of its dramatic impact on the Alaskan economy, which is heavily reliant upon energy development.

SUCCESSES AND FAILURES

The North American Waterfowl Management Plan has shown significant impact on increasing the amount of wetlands available for migrating waterfowl. Ninety-two million waterfowl were observed making their annual migratory flights in 1996. The plan owes its success in part to the Partners for Wildlife program, which works to establish relationships between the FWS and landowners nationwide in order to restore wetland and upland habitats on private property. The FWS has focused on the development of habitat conservation plans, which support economic development while working to ensure long-term conservation of species listed as endangered or threatened.

The FWS has made strides in the areas of law enforcement and international cooperation. For example, environmental groups in Argentina began to report the die-off of large numbers of Swainson's hawks. This raptor migrates thousands of miles annually from North America to its wintering grounds in South America. Investigations proved that the deaths were the result of pesticide contamination. The FWS worked with Argentinean government representatives, private landowners, and environmental groups to uncover the cause of the deaths. Known contaminants were replaced with equally effective, yet less deadly, pesticides, and the Swainson's hawk has shown a remarkable comeback.

The FWS has also been successful in the area of law enforcement, both nationally and internationally. Law enforcement officials are responsible for monitoring the importation of wildlife at specific ports around the nation. Importation of endangered and threatened species is against the law. For example, Operation Renegade successfully supported the conviction of 38 parrot smugglers attempting to bring the birds into the United States for sale. Law enforcement and educational campaigns have been successful in reducing the value of animals captured in the wild and sold in the United States.

FUTURE DIRECTIONS

The FWS is focused on the development of sound partnerships with other governmental agencies and on forming new partnerships with private business and landowners. It is mobilizing its workforce to deal with tight budgets and decreasing resources while focusing its ability to provide information and planning to continue conservation of critical habitat for wildlife.

Under the leadership of Jamie Rappaport Clark, a career biologist appointed director of the FWS in August 1997, there has been a renewed commitment to bringing an ecosystem approach to the management of FWS sites across the country. Clark has also placed an emphasis on training at the FWS's newly completed National Conservation Training Center near Shepherdstown, West Virginia, which provides state-of-the-art training opportunities for FWS personnel.

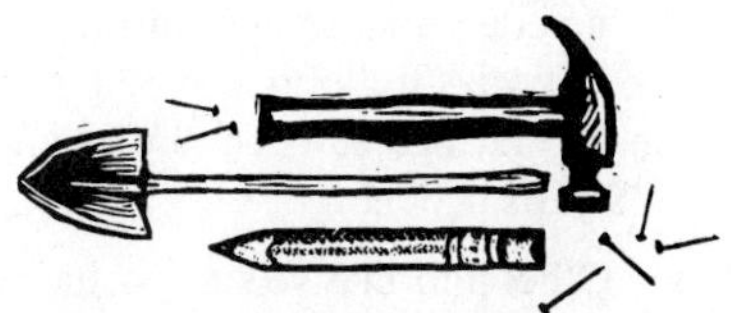

GET INVOLVED:

- The FWS has a variety of volunteer opportunities available to the public. For example, volunteers can band birds at a national wildlife refuge, work at a national fish hatchery, or do research in a laboratory. Although there are no age requirements, anyone under eighteen years old must have written parental approval. The FWS encourages groups of young people under sixteen years old to volunteer in supervised groups, such as a Boy Scout troop, Girl Scout troop, or 4–H club. Contact the FWS at (202) 208-5634 for information on regional programs.
- Young men and women ages fifteen through eighteen, who are interested in conservation work on public lands, can contact the U.S. Youth Conservation Corps at (202) 343-5514. The Youth Conservation Corps is a summer employment program managed in partnership with the Forest Service of the U.S. Department of Agriculture. Projects include constructing trails, building campground facilities, planting trees, collecting litter, clearing streams, improving wildlife habitats, and working in offices.

AGENCY RESOURCES

The FWS Web site, located at http://www.fws.gov, offers a wide variety of information about the agency, from bird migration and endangered species to press releases regarding legislative action. Highlights of the site include visual images of the NWRS and the Endangered Species Bulletin, providing state-by-state information on endangered species of plants and animals under FWS jurisdiction.

Other informative sites include the Fish and Wildlife Reference Service (FWRS), which receives, indexes, stores, and distributes copies of reports produced by state fish and wildlife agencies from research studies supported by Federal Aid in Sport Fisheries Restoration Act and Federal Aid in Wildlife Restoration Act funding. More than 25,000 documents are referenced using an on-line database that responds to keywords. Requested documents are available for a fee. For more information about the FWS call 1-800-582-3421.

AGENCY PUBLICATIONS

The FWS has a variety of publications, including wildlife and ecosystem reports, booklets, brochures, and posters. From descriptions of the American alligator to the whooping crane, FWS publications are available to provide data on habitats, populations, and threats to specific wildlife species. Other publication subjects include descriptions of the FWS itself, federal wildlife laws, endangered species, international cooperation efforts, and career opportunities within the service. A list of free FWS publications can be found at http://www.fws.gov/r9nctc/PUBS.HTML. To order, call (304) 876-7203 or fax (304) 876-7689.

BIBLIOGRAPHY

Allen, Vicki. "Senate Panel Passes Bill to Sell U.S. Reserve Oil." Reuters, 21 September 1995.

Gerstenzang, James. "Wildlife Refuges: Compromise Helps but Environmental Debate Goes On." *Los Angeles Times,* 19 May 1997, p. A12.

Richardson, Anna M., and Jeff Pickett. "AFN Board Votes for Arctic Refuge Oil Drilling." *Tundra Times,* 21 June 1995.

Roberts, Paul. "A Green Coup? (The GOP and Environmental Protection)." *New Republic,* 20 November 1995, p. 25.

Spiegelman, Arthur. "Babbitt Calls for Veto on Arctic Refuge Drilling." Reuters, 2 August 1995.

"U.S. FWS: Millions of Americans Enjoy Wildlife-Related Recreation." M2 PressWIRE, 10 July 1997.

Williams, Ted. "Defense of the Realm: Is the Endangered Species Act Really Working?" *Sierra,* 11 January 1996, p. 34.

——— "Natural Allies: If Only Hunters, Anglers, and Environmentalists Would Stop Taking Potshots at Each Other, They'd Be an Invincible Force for Wildlands Protection." *Sierra,* 19 September 1996, p. 46.

United States Geological Survey (USGS)

PARENT ORGANIZATION: Department of the Interior
ESTABLISHED: March 3, 1879
EMPLOYEES: 10,097

Contact Information:

ADDRESS: 12201 Sunrise Valley Dr.
Reston, VA 20192
PHONE: (703) 648-4000
TOLL FREE: (800) 872-6277
FAX: (703) 648–4888
URL: http://www.usgs.gov
DIRECTOR: Charles G. Groat

WHAT IS ITS MISSION?

According to the United States Geological Survey (USGS), its mission is to provide "reliable, impartial information to describe and understand the Earth. This information is used to minimize loss of life and property from natural disasters; manage water, biological, energy, and mineral resources; enhance and protect the quality of life; and contribute to wise economic and physical development."

HOW IS IT STRUCTURED?

The USGS, headquartered in Reston, Virginia, is an agency within the Department of the Interior (DOI), a cabinet-level agency within the executive branch of the federal government. The agency is headed by a director who is appointed by the president and confirmed by the Senate. The USGS is composed of four major earth science divisions: water resources, geologic resources, national mapping, and biological resources. The director, assisted by two associate directors, oversees these divisions and implements agency policy. Division chiefs are highly trained scientists and administrators. Associate division chiefs assist in the management of division programs and personnel. Overall the USGS is staffed by approximately 10,000 scientists, engineers, administrators, and support personnel who work to provide objective scientific data to the people of the United States.

The USGS relies significantly on partnerships through its cooperative research programs, encompassing 54 research units and study units. These studies are

FAST FACTS

The USGS has identified approximately 1,500 active volcanoes around the globe that could put the lives of 500 million people at risk.

(Source: Jeffrey Kluger, et. al. "Science: Volcanoes with an Attitude." *Time,* February, 24, 1997.)

done in cooperation with more than one thousand state agencies, municipalities, utilities, and private industries.

Additional principal regional USGS offices are located in Reston, Virginia; Denver, Colorado; Menlo Park, California; Leetown, Washington; and Seattle, Washington. Special earth science facilities are located throughout the United States.

PRIMARY FUNCTIONS

The USGS provides earth science data to the federal government, as well as to the general public, in areas as diverse as the geospatial location of the boundaries of the United States and the chemical composition of geological structures on the moon.

As the primary scientific agency within the Department of the Interior (DOI), the USGS conducts and sponsors basic research in geology, hydrology, mapping, and related sciences. The USGS publishes and disseminates thousands of reports and topographic, geologic, and other thematic maps each year. In addition, the agency produces and updates geographic, cartographic, and remotely sensed information in graphic and digital forms. The USGS establishes and maintains earth science databases and disseminates earth science information for use by government, educational, and private-sector institutions.

PROGRAMS

USGS programs are divided into four major divisions: water resources, geologic mapping, national mapping, and biological resources.

In 1984 the Water Resources Division published the first *National Water Summary.* Water-related issues are described in depth, in a state-by-state overview, with particular focus on groundwater contamination and acid rain. In cooperation with the Interagency Task Force on Acid Precipitation, the USGS also conducts an ongoing study of the effects of acid deposition on lakes, streams, and aquifers. Data is used to assist in the restoration and protection of the nation's water resources.

The Geological Division of the USGS conducts programs such as coastal and marine surveys, mineral resource surveys, energy resource surveys, and volcanic and geothermal investigations. This division supports the National Earthquake Information Center, which developed the Earthquake Notification System, intended to provide the public with immediate information on earthquakes in the United States.

The National Mapping Division is involved in the development and application of advanced cartographic techniques and systems. It has established the National Cartographic Data Base using newly developed standards of digital cartography for the advancement of U.S. cartography. In addition, the National Mapping Division is responsible for all functions relating to domestic geographic names. This information is compiled and published in the *National Gazetteer of the United States of America.*

The Biological Resources Division is responsible for researching and monitoring wildlife species and providing access to the resulting data for use in conservation or restoration programs. For example, the Biological Resources Division works with the U.S. Fish and Wildlife Service (FWS) in the management of the endangered and threatened species list. Other federal and state agencies use this data to assist in the management and development of natural resources.

BUDGET INFORMATION

The 1998 budget for the USGS was approximately $745.4 million. The National Mapping program accounted for $130.9 million, or 17.5 percent, of the budget. Geologic Hazards, Resources and Processes accounted for $227.7 million, or 30.5 percent of the budget. Water Resources Investigations accounted for $194.4 million, or 26 percent of the budget. The newly developed Biological Resources Division accounted for $145 million, or 19.4 percent, of the budget. General administration and facilities accounted for $47.3 million, or 6 percent of the budget. As the offices and programs of the USGS are spread throughout the U.S., they are able to achieve program goals using additional funds from state and local governments to support research and facilities.

HISTORY

The earliest land surveys were completed to support agriculture, which was the principal occupation of most

Americans. Since little federal money was available for this activity, surveying was largely privately funded. However, some government appropriations were made to the Army Corps of Engineers to prepare estimates for roads and canals for military use.

A turning point in the attitudes of government officials toward surveying came with the discovery of gold in California in 1848. With the discovery of gold and the promotion of U.S. rights to land acquisition, classification and development of these vast western lands represented an opportunity for putting money into the Treasury. In 1853 Congress appropriated $150,000 for land surveys to establish the most economical route for coast-to-coast railroad transportation. During this period the industrial output of the nation grew. Gold and silver were discovered in other western states, and the nation's first oil well was successfully drilled in western Pennsylvania. Also during this period, universities, such as Harvard and Yale, began to develop geology programs; a few years later some of the first American geologists graduated, eager to exercise their skills in the study of natural and mineral resources.

In 1879 Congress established the USGS, charging it with a combination of responsibilities, including "classification of the public lands, and examination of geological structure, mineral resources, and products of the national domain." As an agency within the DOI, the USGS took on tasks that had previously been scattered throughout the federal and state governments. Clarence King became the first director of the USGS and made the exploration of the fortieth parallel his first priority.

During the USGS's first twenty five years the United States became an industrial world power with a rapidly increasing population. The value of U.S. mineral products increased fourfold to $1 billion in 1904. With the U.S. energy needs increasing so quickly, the USGS was assigned to study coal and petroleum resources.

World War's I (1914–18) and II (1939–45) made a significant impact on the USGS as use of energy resources underwent a radical wartime shift. Worldwide demands for petroleum led to the creation of many new oil companies—so many that the USGS had problems keeping its offices staffed with trained scientists. Within the USGS the focus was shifted from the classification of public lands to the study of the geological structure of oil-and gas-producing fields. In 1921, because of energy production concerns, Congress authorized a comprehensive study of electric power distribution and generation for the region between Massachusetts and Washington, D.C. This study, completed under the direction of the USGS, anticipated the large electric power network existing on the East Coast today.

Both world wars interrupted the completion of topographic data needed for industrial development, land reclamation, power generation, and highway construction. At the conclusion of World War I, federal officials observed that nearly 60 percent of the nation was still unmapped. During this period, however, a group of skillful USGS administrators were able to accomplish multiple energy and mapping goals for the nation despite scarce government funding and loss of scientists to private-sector companies.

BUDGET:

United States Geological Survey

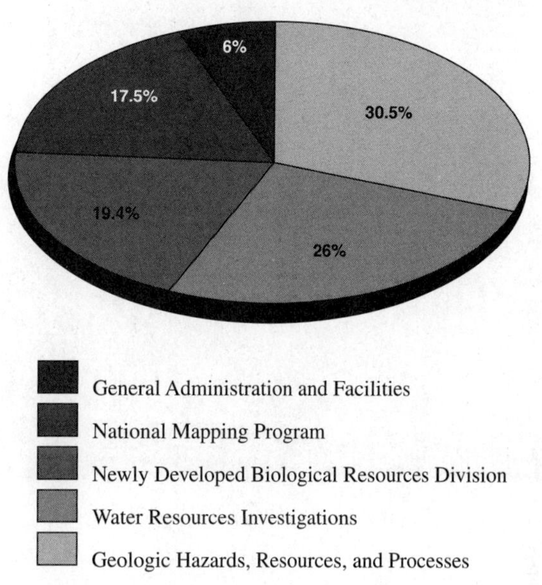

- General Administration and Facilities
- National Mapping Program
- Newly Developed Biological Resources Division
- Water Resources Investigations
- Geologic Hazards, Resources, and Processes

The post-war years brought tremendous scientific advancements to the USGS in the areas of nuclear and space research. The successful launching of *Explorer* and *Vanguard* brought about new partnerships for the USGS with agencies such as the American Association for the Advancement of Science (AAAS) and the National Aeronautics and Space Administration (NASA). For the first time in history, the practical study of the geology of the moon was considered. By the 1960s, under Presidents John F. Kennedy and Lyndon B. Johnson, appropriations to the USGS doubled, for the first time exceeding $100 million. Scientific studies by the agency began to include undersea geology, the effects of underground nuclear explosions, and the study of earthquakes and volcanoes. By July 1969 the USGS had trained two astronauts in geological principles for their proposed walk on the moon, during which they would collect samples of lunar soils and rock for study on earth. By 1976 USGS scientists had prepared more than one hundred maps of Mars, Mercury, Venus, and the moon in support of space exploration. Advances in space exploration led to the development of satellites, which ushered in a new era in the study of geology, hydrology, geography, and cartography.

The USGS commissions research vessels such as the Samuel P. Lee *to perform oceanographic research in areas around the world.* *(U.S. Geological Survey Photographic Library Denver, Colo.)*

CURRENT POLITICAL ISSUES

The USGS is distinctive among federal agencies in that it exacts no regulatory action and enforces no laws. However, in striving to provide objective scientific data free from political interpretation, the USGS sometimes finds itself in the midst of debate. This is because the USGS studies the impact of human activity on the environment—an activity that is often profitable.

In the early 1990s the USGS was called to research a situation in Summitville, Colorado, where the Summitville Consolidated Mining Company had started open pit mining in 1984 at an elevation of 11,500 feet. The company had used a chemical process to leach, or extract, gold from the rock. Not long afterward, environmental contaminants began to appear downstream from the site.

Case Study: Downstream from Summitville

When the Summitville Consolidated Mining Company started open pit mining for gold in Summitville in 1984, it was not the first company to do so. Gold had been mined in the area as early as 1870, and mining had continued throughout the 1950s until the gold began to run out. As new mining technologies were developed, however, traces of gold remaining in the rock at the Summitville mine became available.

To extract the gold, the ore was crushed and piled, then a cyanide solution that dissolves gold was sprinkled over the rock, pulling dissolved gold with it to the bottom of the pile, where it was collected. This process was conducted over a protective liner, but the solvent was still escaping into an underground drainage system that also contained acid groundwater from a nearby waste dump. The cyanide solution leaked out of its pipes, sometimes draining directly into the Wightman Fork of the Alamosa River.

By 1993 the mining company had declared bankruptcy and had begun environmental remediation, which is the government-mandated process of restoring mined areas to their previous state or at minimum to a usable form. However, because the cleanup was too massive an effort for the bankrupt company to undertake, the federal government stepped in, and the U.S. Environmental Protection Agency (EPA) eventually added the project to its Superfund program.

The USGS, which had studied the area when open pit mining began, provided geologic maps of the pit, characterization of the site's geology and geochemistry, studies of cyanide degradation, and geophysical resistivity surveys. Ultimately, the USGS found that the geology and geochemistry of the site, before open pit mining began, was actually one of the factors that fueled the problem because of the geological and chemical reactions it facilitated. The open pit mining process had uncovered unoxidized sulfides, and it was the reaction between these sulfides and oxygenated groundwater that produced the acidic, metal-rich drainage waters.

The USGS tested water samples from different locations along the Alamosa River and soil, sediment, crops, and natural growth in the downstream San Luis Valley. Researchers concluded that "increased acid and metal loadings from Summitville are suspected to have caused the 1990 disappearance of stocked fish from Terrace Reservoir and farm holding ponds downstream on the Alamosa River. However, significant natural contamination also enters the Alamosa from unmined or minimally mined mineralized areas," (USGS report, *The Summitville Mine and Its Downstream Effects*).

Public Impact

The Summitville site became a concern because the Alamosa River is extensively used downstream. Wildlife and livestock drink from it and farmers depend on it to grow crops like alfalfa, which is used for livestock feed, barley, wheat, and potatoes. People worried about the potential adverse effects the acid and metal could have on crops and wetlands where aquatic life, migratory waterfowl such as ducks, and the endangered whooping crane live. For the most part, however, the USGS found that the Summitville site had not had an extreme adverse effect on the area and that mining was only partially responsible for the acids and metals found in the region.

The USGS studies can be used to prevent environmental problems in the future. According to the USGS Summitville report, "Results of Summitville research to date underscore the crucial need for geoscientific information in predicting, assessing, and remediating the environmental effects of mining." The report emphasized that "Summitville's effects on aquatic life, agriculture, and wetlands ecosystems can best be understood only when examined in an integrated geologic, geochemical, and biological context." The Summitville incident sparked national debate about mining's environmental consequences and whether revision of the 1872 Mining Law is necessary.

SUCCESSES AND FAILURES

Although the findings of the USGS affect humans and wildlife worldwide, its work often goes unnoticed by the general public. Conversely, in 1980 residents of the state of Washington directly benefited from USGS efforts.

On March 20, the USGS and University of Washington scientists monitoring geothermal potential within the Cascade Range detected an earthquake northwest of Mount Saint Helens, which was immediately followed by earthquakes below the volcano. The Geological and Water Resources divisions of the USGS immediately began collecting data and determined that the possibility of an eruption was serious enough to issue an official hazard warning. One week later the warning was issued, and on the same day Mount Saint Helens began to issue steam and ash from its peak. Following the initial warning, the hazard watch was updated to indicate the potential threat posed by the volcano, prompting the governor to declare two hazard zones around the mountain. On May 18, 1980, Mount Saint Helens erupted, spewing the top 1,300 feet of the mountain's peak and causing a massive avalanche of debris that destroyed everything in its 17-mile path. The hazard watch initiated by the USGS is credited with minimizing loss of human life on that day. The successful use of USGS data provided a practical understanding of geological studies and their potential for minimizing the impact of natural disasters.

FUTURE DIRECTIONS

The USGS has been involved with U.S. space flight agencies since the first moon walks took place with the assistance of USGS scientists. The USGS continues to be involved in the mapping of planets in Earth's solar system and the collection of interplanetary data, including data from the 1997 landing on Mars. The USGS has prepared surface maps used by NASA and other space agencies in the planning and execution of space missions. In addition, the USGS has developed satellite systems for collecting a wide variety of technologically advanced data useful to climatologists and geologists studying global conditions. With its scientific understanding of advanced technologies, the USGS will continue to be involved in space exploration as that endeavor matures.

AGENCY RESOURCES

USGS staff at earth science information centers (ESICs) around the nation respond to the public and assist in the selection and ordering of USGS publications and products. For more information, the Washington, D.C., ESIC can be contacted at (202) 208-4047 or via the USGS Web site (www.usgs.gov), which lists phone numbers and addresses for all local ESICs. The USGS also operates reading rooms open to the public at its national center in Reston, Virginia; the Denver Federal Center in Colorado; and at the nine ESICs.

The USGS also utilizes a fax-on-demand system called EARTH FAX, enabling anyone with a touchtone phone and access to a fax machine to quickly retrieve the latest information on earthquake activity around the world, order USGS maps, or request other information.

FAST FACTS

The USGS reports that 90 percent of the damage related to natural disasters, excluding droughts, is caused by floods and has cost the nation an average of $3.1 billion annually from 1985 to 1994.

(Source: U.S. Geological Survey and the National Weather Service, 1997.

The EARTH FAX number is (703) 648-4888 or 1-800-872-6277.

The National Geospatial Data Clearinghouse Node serves as a primary on-line source for extensive geospatial data, and the Global Land Information System is an interactive computer system developed by the USGS for scientists seeking sources of information about the Earth's land surfaces. The Geographic Names Information System (GNIS), also developed by the USGS, contains information about almost two million physical and cultural geographic features in the United States; it is the United States's official U.S. repository of domestic geographic names information. The National Geologic Map Database can locate maps and related data pertaining to geology, hazards, earth resources, geophysics, geochemistry, geochronology, paleontology, and marine geology.

The USGS Learning Web is directed at K–12 students and can be found at http://www.usgs.gov/education/othered.html. The site features selected topics aimed at showing how biology, geology, hydrology, and geography apply to everyday life. The Ask-A-Geologist service is accessible from this site as well.

AGENCY PUBLICATIONS

The USGS makes available thousands of publications relating to its work; use the appropriate locator at http://www.usgs.gov/pubprod to find a particular item. Specific locators may be used to find formal publications such as bulletins, circulars, professional papers, and thematic maps; geospatial data and aerial photography; USGS Map Dealers; and the USGS National Spatial Data Clearinghouse Node, which provides a pathway to find information about geospatial data available from the USGS. Also available are books, fact sheets, reports, yearbooks, periodicals, Biological Resources Division publications, CD-ROM products, geologic products, geospatial data and information, mapping publications and software, mineral resources publications and data products, the national water conditions information, National Water-Quality Assessment (NAWQA) publications and digital map products, the national water summary on wetland resources, water resources abstracts and applications software, and USGS water-use data. The Government Information Locator Service (GILS) and a catalog of new publications of the USGS, which lists new publications by month, can also be found at this site.

BIBLIOGRAPHY

"Dams and Rivers: Scientists Take a New Look Downstream." US Newswire, 13 December 1995.

Dye, Lee. "Science Watch: Talk of Killing U.S. Quake Agency Rattles Geologists." *Los Angeles Times,* 13 September 1995, p. D-5.

Howe, Steve. "The Last Mountains." *Backpacker,* 1 June 1995, p. 56.

Kluger, Jeffrey, Dan Cray, and Dick Thompson. "Science: Volcanoes with an Attitude." *Time,* 24 February 1997, p. 56.

"NASA: New Technology to Help Measurement and Study of Earthquakes." M2 PressWIRE, 1 October 1996.

"USGS: Fish Hormones Affected by Contaminants in Streams Nationwide." US Newswire, 28 April 1997.

United States Holocaust Memorial Museum (USHMM)

PARENT ORGANIZATION: Independent
ESTABLISHED: October 1980
EMPLOYEES: 246 (1999)

Contact Information:

ADDRESS: 100 Raoul Wallenberg Pl. SW
Washington, DC 20024-2150
PHONE: (202) 488-0400
TDD (HEARING IMPAIRED): (202) 488-0406
URL: http://www.ushmm.org/index.html
COUNCIL CHAIR: Miles Lerman

WHAT IS ITS MISSION?

The United States Holocaust Memorial Museum (USHMM) is dedicated to the memory of the victims of the Nazi regime under Adolf Hitler in German-occupied Europe between 1933 and 1945. The museum is charged with disseminating information about the events that took place during the years of persecution known as the Holocaust. It is the mission of the museum to ensure that the citizens of the United States, and the entire world, will never forget the tragedy. Another part of the USHMM's mission is to encourage individuals to grapple with moral and spiritual issues that are the responsibility of each citizen within a democracy, in order to prevent such persecution in the future.

Background

The word *holocaust* is derived from the Greek adjective *olokanston* which means "totally consumed by fire" and refers to burnt sacrificial offerings. After World War II (1939–45), *holocaust* was commonly used to describe the systematic annihilation practices employed by Nazi Germany in its effort to exterminate so-called undesirables in an attempt to perpetuate a light-skinned master race. The Nazi persecutions were targeted toward Jews, homosexuals, and handicapped persons in particular, but others were included in the slaughter. Only fair-skinned, blue-eyed people of Teutonic descent would be ultimately spared, according to the Nazi agenda.

By 1945, when Allied armies liberated Europe from the Nazi terror, millions of innocent victims had been sterilized, tortured, or put to death. Some were shot to death. Many others were executed in gas chambers disguised as shower facilities. The bodies of victims were

loaded by the thousands into crematoriums. Thus the term *holocaust* quite literally describes the horror of those times.

HOW IS IT STRUCTURED?

The director of the USHMM holds his or her position with the approval of the U.S. Holocaust Memorial Council, which functions as the board of directors of the museum. This 68-member council is composed predominantly of 55 private citizens appointed by the president of the United States. Additionally, 10 members of the U.S. Congress (five senators and five members of the House of Representatives) are included on the panel. The three remaining positions are filled by one representative from each of the following departments: Department of State, Department of the Interior, and Department of Education.

PRIMARY FUNCTIONS

A central function of the USHMM is the maintenance of its Permanent Exhibition of artifacts and documents pertaining to the Holocaust. The museum also supports a variety of research and learning facilities, including archives, a library, and a computer-assisted learning center. The museum develops educational and outreach programs in an ongoing effort to provide a dynamic, "living" memorial to the victims of the Holocaust. Cultural events such as film screenings are organized by museum staff. Finally, the museum hosts public ceremonies and special events to perpetuate the memory of the victims of the Holocaust.

Representatives of the USHMM travel the world to the scenes of the Holocaust, often negotiating with foreign governments in a far-reaching effort to preserve the sites and relics of the Holocaust. Documents from the archives of eastern European countries are examined, and pertinent information is reproduced on microfilm for transmittal to the museum library and archives. Some artifacts are procured for permanent display at the museum.

Through its International Relations Committee, the USHMM has established itself as a persuasive force for preserving human rights throughout the world. It is the commitment of the committee to intercede wherever and whenever genocide or other atrocities prevail.

PROGRAMS

The main structure of the museum facility houses the majestic and sometimes overwhelming Permanent Exhibition, which features countless provocative memorabilia from the Holocaust. Among the more poignant highlights is the display of museum ID cards, which contains pictures and stories of countless victims of the Holocaust. Every visitor touring the museum is asked to carry an ID card along the journey to personalize the experience. The museum's oral history archives (containing recorded accounts from Holocaust survivors) are equally powerful. In addition, the museum houses an extensive collection of artifacts, photographs, maps, and videotapes.

Daniel's Story

The tales of the Holocaust depicted by the exhibits at the USHMM are extremely disturbing. Children under age 11 are discouraged from viewing the Permanent Exhibition because the experience might be too overwhelming. Instead, a special exhibit called "Remember the Children: Daniel's Story" is provided for younger museum visitors.

Six-year-old Daniel is a fictitious character. In this children's exhibit visitors revisit Daniel's home where he lived with his family until things began to change. The story is revealed through the pages of Daniel's diary, which he received as a birthday present from his father. His story begins in Frankfurt, Germany, in 1933 with the words, "Have you ever been punished for something you didn't do?"

As visitors tour the exhibit, the mood becomes somber. Daniel's family is forcibly uprooted and deported to Lodz Ghetto in Poland. The sound effects and scenery of the exhibit become chaotic and unnerving as the story unfolds. Eventually the family is taken away to a concentration camp, where Daniel's mother and his sister Erika die. At the end of the exhibit visitors are invited to reflect on the experience and to express their thoughts in pencil or crayon in memory of the children of the Holocaust.

Community Programs and Outreach

In addition to the artifacts and other displays contained in the Permanent Exhibition, which serves as the core of the USHMM program, the museum proclaims its mission through a variety of supplemental programs. It sponsors a series of special traveling exhibits that circulate throughout the United States, carrying the memory of the Holocaust to neighborhoods across the country. The museum's Gonda Education Center offers enhanced learning experiences in the form of film screenings, cultural events, and educational and outreach programs (details are available by calling (202) 488-0427). Selected displays from the traveling exhibits can be viewed on the Internet at http://www.ushmm.org.

Registry of Jewish Holocaust Survivors

The Benjamin and Vladka Meed Registry of Jewish Holocaust Survivors was established by the American

Gathering of Jewish Holocaust Survivors in 1981 for those who were "displaced, persecuted, and/or discriminated against by . . . the Nazis and their Allies." The purpose of the registry is to assist survivors in tracing and contacting relatives missing since the Holocaust. For this reason all survivors are urged to register.

The registry database is located on the fifth floor of the USHMM Holocaust Research Institute. To obtain a registration form call (202) 488-6130. Information seekers should contact their local Red Cross International Tracing Service or write to the Registry of Holocaust Survivors, United States Holocaust Memorial Museum, 100 Raoul Wallenberg Pl. SW, Washington, DC 20024-2150. For help in locating survivors who are believed to be in Israel, contact the Jewish Agency Search Bureau for Missing Relatives at POB 92, Jerusalem 91920, Israel.

BUDGET:

United States Holocaust Memorial Museum

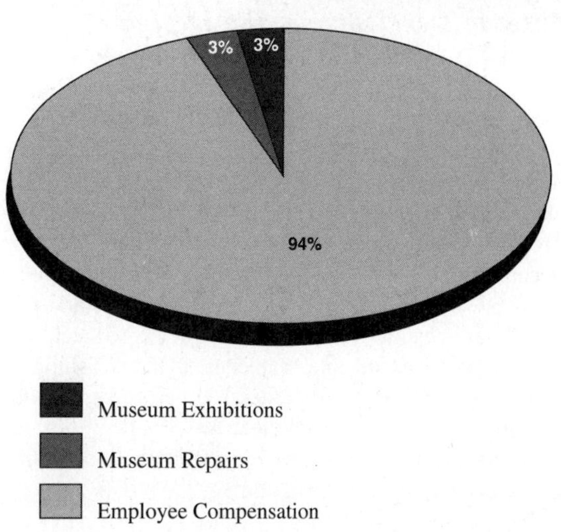

Museum Exhibitions
Museum Repairs
Employee Compensation

BUDGET INFORMATION

USHMM is funded as a public-private partnership, as are many federal cultural institutions such as the Presidential Libraries of the National Archives and Records Administration. In keeping with this scheme, USHMM was constructed completely from private donations, while the management and upkeep of the museum is funded in part through congressional allocations to the Holocaust Memorial Council. The annual museum budget is approximately $49 million including $19 million from private sources. In 1999 the council received $31.7 million in funding from federal tax dollars, of which $1.6 million was designated for museum repairs and $1.3 million was designated to finance museum exhibitions. Funds allocated to the museum for upkeep and exhibitions remain permanently available until expended. The majority of the remaining federal funds to the memorial council are reserved for employee compensation. (Museum employees are federal employees under OPM.) The total sum of private donations to the museum approached $200 million by the 1998. The number of benefactors to the museum at that time had reportedly surpassed 300,000, from every facet of society including private individuals, corporations, and foundations.

HISTORY

On November 1, 1978, President Jimmy Carter signed Executive Order 12093 to create an "advisory committee on the establishment of a memorial to the victims of the Holocaust." The committee, known as the President's Commission on the Holocaust, was charged with the task of orchestrating a suitable commemoration for the observation of the Days of Remembrance of Victims of the Holocaust. The Days of Remembrance, mandated by Congress, were scheduled to occur on April 28 and 29, 1979. The commission later amended that mandate and prescribed that the Days of Remembrance should be observed annually. The history of that preliminary commission and its evolution into the Holocaust Memorial Council and the history of USHMM are essentially one and the same. The presidential commission, headed by Elie Wiesel, renowned Jewish writer and teacher, officially commenced its operation on January 15, 1979, and presented a report to the president on September 27, 1979.

In the process of preparing their recommendations, some members of the presidential commission (at their own expense) took a 14-day work-study trip to eastern Europe, Denmark, and Israel. The trip included a visit to the infamous concentration camp at Auschwitz in Poland. While in Israel they visited the Museum of the Diaspora, which commemorates the Jewish migration to Israel during and after World War II in search of refuge from the Holocaust. The commissioners examined the museum archives to learn more about the Holocaust and those who fled.

In the completed report to the president the commission proposed a "living memorial" to the Holocaust and defined a three-point plan for the memorial. The plan included the establishment of a memorial museum, an educational foundation, and a "committee on conscience." The memorial museum was proposed as a federal institution to be supported financially through a public-private partnership. In response to the report of the commission, the United States Holocaust Memorial Council was established in October 1980 by a unanimous vote of Congress (Public Law 96-388) to fulfill the recommendations of the commission.

Museum Development and Design

The architectural structures of the USHMM were designed by James I. Freed of New York City, according to a mandate from the Holocaust Memorial Council. The council specified that the museum complex should combine symbolism in art to appropriately reflect the solemnity of the memory of the Holocaust. In preparation for the task, Freed visited the sites of the European concentration camps and incorporated the atmosphere into his designs through the pervasive use of stark, disjointed, and chaotic frameworks of cold, bare steel. The land for the museum site, adjacent to the Washington Mall, was provided by the federal government, and the $194 million construction project was financed through donations, including the proceeds from national fundraising efforts.

The focal point of the museum architecture is the majestic Hall of Remembrance. The hall, with its 60-foot-high ceiling and skylight, serves as a rest area for tourists when they exit the Permanent Exhibition. There, like in a place of worship, they stop and reflect on what they have seen. The hall also serves as a gathering area for ceremonies and other events. The six-sided perimeter of the hall symbolizes the six-pointed star of David. (During the Holocaust years the Nazi regime forced every Jew to purchase or make a six-pointed gold star the size of a human hand and emblazoned with the word "JEW"—and to wear the star prominently and at all times when out in public.)

A central foyer, the Hall of Witness, serves as the main gateway for visitors to enter the museum facility. Like the Hall of Remembrance, the Hall of Witness is expansive and skylit, to inspire awe and to preserve the solemnity of the memorial. A large landscaped plaza connects the museum proper with the administrative facilities.

International Relations Committee

When the museum facility was under planning and construction, the memorial council organized the International Relations Committee to intercede with foreign governments and to procure artifacts, documents, and other memorabilia for the museum. Thousands of items were acquired from the Polish government in August 1989, including shoes and suitcases belonging to victims. A month later, in September, the government of what was then East Germany added more documents and relics to the U.S. collection. Among the objects in the East German concession was a "Hollerith machine," a primitive computer used by the Nazis to maintain detailed counts and demographics of intended victims. Three months later the East German prime minister presented the museum with the keystone of a historical Berlin synagogue that was destroyed by Nazis in 1938. Hungary and Czechoslovakia also contributed artifacts, documents, and photographs.

On April 22, 1993, President Bill Clinton presided over the official dedication of the museum facilities. During the first two years of operation, the museum welcomed three and one-half million visitors, and on April 7, 1988, the museum hosted its 10 millionth patron.

CURRENT POLITICAL ISSUES

The International Relations Committee of the Holocaust Memorial Council underwrites crucial lobbying efforts to protect human rights. In 1991 the council pleaded for the Iraqi government to stop its senseless slaughter of Iraq's Kurdish people. In 1992 the council issued a public condemnation of atrocities promulgated by the Serbian government against its own people. (A rally was later organized at the USHMM to further protest that situation.) In the mid-1990s the directors of the USHMM spearheaded an investigation into the rights of those who survived the Holocaust and families of Holocaust victims.

Case Study: Nazi Gold

A series of reports surfaced in 1996 concerning the existence of "Nazi gold." The breaking story erupted into an international debacle as hoards of gold, stored in numerous locations around the world, were uncovered. The treasures were originally acquired by the Nazi regime when it ravaged Europe, confiscating everything of value—including jewelry and even gold fillings from the teeth of Holocaust victims. After the war, the United States, France, and Great Britain divided the confiscated gold and other valuables according to the terms of a pact called the Tripartite Gold Commission (TGC).

Under the TGC agreement more than 90 percent of the wealth was redistributed to the liberated nations of Europe because it was presumed to have been looted from the coffers of those countries. The remaining gold was divided among the TGC member countries, where it remained undetected for 50 years. A huge vault in a secret location in New York City was believed to contain five thousand pounds of the Nazi gold.

The U.S. government conducted an investigation in response to the reports. The under secretary of commerce, assisted by the Justice Department Office of Special Investigations and State Department archivists, compiled a report about the incident, in collaboration with eight federal agencies. The report cited the existence of hundreds of millions of dollars worth of looted gold that remained unaccounted for since World War II.

Caches of Nazi gold were reported to exist in the United States, France, Great Britain, Switzerland, and many other countries. An estimated $4.2 billion in gold was reportedly being held in banks in the United States and Great Britain.

The story unraveled over the course of several months. Substantial amounts of confiscated assets were uncovered in Swiss bank accounts. The Swiss banks reluctantly admitted that the deposits in the accounts were received almost exclusively from Jews who were taken prisoner during the Nazi aggression. It was ultimately revealed that virtually all of the gold and other wealth belonged to Jewish Holocaust victims. According to the findings of investigators, the TGC was never aware that a substantial portion of the Nazi treasure was originally taken from Holocaust victims; it assumed instead that the money belonged to the governments of eastern Europe.

Late in 1996 an international conference was held in London to attempt to determine the magnitude of the dilemma and to discuss possible solutions. The United States proposed that an international fund for restitution be established and that all of the countries involved in the incident contribute to the money pool. Great Britain agreed to pay a few million dollars, but France refused to acknowledge any liability for the situation.

In mid-1997, the Swiss government bowed to international pressure, and announced a plan to finance a $4.7 billion fund to compensate Holocaust victims. Enacting the plan would require a constitutional amendment, and was expected to take several years. Meanwhile, Swiss investigators began to publish the names of account holders on dormant accounts from the war years. This would enable depositors or their descendants to recover money that has been held in Swiss banks and kept secret by Switzerland's strict banking privacy laws for decades. In June 1998, three of Switzerland's largest banks offered to pay Holocaust survivors $600 million, in compensation for the assets they were unable to recover from the banks after World War II.

Public Impact

The full implication of these discoveries might not be known for years to come, especially since it seems impossible to accurately determine the monetary value of the uncovered wealth. Erratic accounts place the value at anywhere between $55 million and $115 billion. The U.S. Holocaust Memorial Council is actively involved in this ongoing project. Its goal is to assist Holocaust survivors and families of Holocaust victims recover what rightfully belongs to them. The USHMM makes available the original government study concerning the study of the "Nazi Gold," along with all subsequent documents and briefings that have been issued. Listings have been compiled and are continually updated with information about both international and private relief programs to assist in the asset recovery for all involved. Persons seeking information, as well as persons with further information, should contact Dr. Wesley A. Fisher, United States Holocaust Memorial Museum, 100 Raoul Wallenberg Pl. SW, Washington, DC 20024-2150, USA; phone (202) 479-9732; fax (202) 488-2693; or E-mail wfisher@ushm.org.

FUTURE DIRECTIONS

The Wexner Learning Center, located inside the USHMM, is a computer-driven educational guide to learning more about the Holocaust through articles, film footage, and excerpts of testimony. While already an excellent resource, the USHMM will use recent technological innovations to enhance the center by late 1998. New features will include animated map sequences, digital images of artifacts drawn from the Museum's collection, and greater access to the biographies in the Museum's Permanent Exhibition. The USHMM also has plans to make the materials in the Wexner Learning Center available to other places of Holocaust study around the world.

AGENCY RESOURCES

In keeping with its mandate to disseminate knowledge and to further education about the Holocaust, the USHMM maintains a variety of facilities. Visitors to the Wexner Learning Center may access videotapes, maps, and textual data in a self-directed, computer-assisted learning experience.

The museum archives and library are available to researchers at the Holocaust Research Institute. Specific archives include the photographic archives, transcripts of museum lectures and programs, and *Haftlingspersonalbogen* (prisoner registration forms from Auschwitz). Information regarding the museum archives is available from the U.S. Holocaust Memorial Museum, 100 Raoul Wallenberg Pl. SW, Washington, DC 20024-2150. The telephone number of the photo archives is (202) 488-6111.

The USHMM Information Access System, a searchable database of museum archives, is available on the Internet at http://www.ushmm.org/misc-bin/add_goback/queryinfo_archives.html. Actual documents and photographs are not available on-line. E-mail the archives at archive@ushmm.org. Inquiries regarding museum research facilities can be addressed to library@ushmm.org or research@ushmm.org.

The Gonda Education Center offers enhanced learning in the form of film screenings, cultural events, and educational and outreach programs. The number for information on community programs is: (202) 488-0427.

GET INVOLVED:

The USHMM is open daily except for Yom Kippur and Christmas. Visitors to the museum must acquire tickets in advance. A limited number of tickets are distributed daily from the Pass Desk. Admission is free. Groups of 10 or more who are interested in touring the museum's Permanent Exhibition are urged to contact the museum before the planned visit. Requests for a group reservation should be submitted to Group Scheduling Office, United States Holocaust Memorial Museum, 100 Raoul Wallenberg Pl. SW, Washington, DC 20024-2150; E-mail group_visit@ushmm.org.

National Art and Writing Contest

Every year in May the Holocaust Memorial Museum sponsors the May Family National Art and Writing Contest. The purpose of the contest is to foster awareness of the Holocaust by encouraging students to document the implications of the Holocaust in a contemporary context. Contest entries may be developed in written or artistic media. Entries, not to exceed 2,000 words, must be typewritten or printed in English. Artwork, not to exceed 24" by 24", must be flat (two-dimensional) and framed or matted. Entries must be accompanied by an official entry form. The contest is open to students in grades seven through 12. Entries are judged on creativity and historical accuracy. For further info contact the United States Holocaust Memorial Museum in Washington D.C., Attention Art & Writing Contest. Entries are due on a specified date each year in May. Winners are announced in mid-June.

AGENCY PUBLICATIONS

The Holocaust Memorial Museum Resource Center for Educators provides a variety of educational materials to schools and to students for school projects. The center prepares and distributes an annotated bibliography, *Teaching About the Holocaust: A Resource Book for Educators*. This publication is available at no charge by calling (202) 488-2661 (or E-mail education@ushmm.org). The resource center also publishes a videography of documentaries with source information.

USHMM publishes a journal, *Holocaust and Genocide Studies*, in conjunction with Oxford University Press. The journal is available from the Center for Advanced Holocaust Studies, United States Holocaust Memorial Museum, 100 Raoul Wallenberg Pl. SW, Washington, DC 20024-2150. The Center for Advanced Holocaust Studies also accepts scholarly manuscripts for consideration for publication. Inquiries regarding available publications and/or manuscript submission should be sent to Director of Academic Publications, United States Holocaust Memorial Museum, 100 Raoul Wallenberg Pl. SW, Washington, DC 20024-2150.

BIBLIOGRAPHY

Ayer, Eleanor H. *The United States Holocaust Memorial Museum: America Keeps the Memory Alive*. New York: Dillon Press, 1994.

Bachrach, Susan D. *Tell Them We Remember: The Story of the Holocaust With Images*. Boston: Little, Brown, 1994.

Bower, Tom. *Nazi Gold: The Full Story of the Fifty-Year Swiss-Nazi Conspiracy to Steal Billions*. New York: HarperCollins, 1997.

Gurdus, Luba K. *The Death Train*. New York: Holocaust Publications, 1987.

Josephs, Jeremy. *Swastika over Paris: The Fate of the Jews in France*. New York: Arcade Publishing, 1989.

Patterson, Charles. *Anti-Semitism: The Road to the Holocaust and Beyond*. New York: Walker and Company, 1988.

Tec, Nechama. *Dry Tears: The Story of a Lost Childhood*. New York: Oxford University Press, 1984.

"Traumatic Material for Staff." *American Journal of Orthopsychiatry* 10 January 1995, p. 66.

U.S. Holocaust Memorial Memorial Museum. "Building Design Fact Sheet," 1998.

———. *The World Must Know: The History of the Holocaust*. Boston: Little, Brown, 1993.

Wiesel, Elie. "Report to the President." Washington, D.C.: President's Commission on the Holocaust, 27 September 1979.

United States Information Agency (USIA)

PARENT ORGANIZATION: Independent; merger with Department of State slated for 1998
ESTABLISHED: August 1, 1953
EMPLOYEES: 7,008

Contact Information:

ADDRESS: 301 4th St. SW
Washington, DC 20547
PHONE: (202) 619-4700
FAX: (202) 619-6988
URL: http://www.usia.gov
DIRECTOR: Joseph D. Duffey

WHAT IS ITS MISSION?

The mission of the United States Information Agency (USIA) is "to understand, inform and influence foreign publics in promotion of the national interest, and to broaden the dialogue between Americans and U.S. institutions and their counterparts abroad."

The goals of this mission are to increase understanding and acceptance of U.S. policies and U.S. society by foreign audiences; broaden dialogue between Americans and U.S. institutions and their counterparts overseas; and increase U.S. government knowledge and understanding of foreign attitudes and their implications for U.S. foreign policy.

HOW IS IT STRUCTURED?

The leadership of the USIA is appointed by the president and confirmed by the Senate. These positions include the director, deputy director and three associate directors of education and cultural affairs, information, and management. A nine-member Broadcasting Board of Governors (BBG) is also appointed and confirmed. In turn, the BBG appoints the director of the International Broadcasting Bureau. The director and deputy directors advise the president on foreign attitudes, customs, and the conduct of public diplomacy.

Outside the United States, the USIA is known as the United States Information Service (USIS). There are more than 200 USIS posts in 143 countries. Foreign service officers are assigned to USIS in almost all U.S. embassies and missions abroad. In the United States, the

USIA, through its Washington, D.C., office provides a 24-hour clearinghouse for policy guidance and support for overseas posts. It maintains contact with private sector groups through publications and cultural, educational, and informational programs.

The four main bureaus of the USIA are the International Broadcasting Bureau, the Bureau of Information, the Bureau of Education and Cultural Affairs, and the Bureau of Management. The bureaus operate the programs that make up the USIA and USIS services. For instance, the USIA is the only agency that monitors and reports about foreign media reactions to American initiatives. This function, under the Bureau of Information, is housed in the Research and Information Office. The Research and Information Office advises U.S. officials regarding foreign public opinion on U.S. policies.

The International Broadcasting Bureau is responsible for broadcasting *Voice of America*, *Radio Free Europe*, and other broadcast initiatives that give persons in other countries a distinctly American view of the world. The Bureau of Educational and Cultural Affairs promotes understanding of U.S. culture by sponsoring citizen exchanges, study in the United States by foreign nationals, and educational and training programs to promote the history, culture, and philosophy of the United States. The Bureau of Management oversees the operations of the main office and all the posts.

The counselor is the highest ranking overseas office. Senior foreign service officers serve as directors of six geographic offices managing the USIA's overseas presence. Other personnel important to the structure of the USIS are: the public affairs officer (PAO), whose tasks include managing the embassy's information and cultural activities and advising the ambassador on public affairs policies; the information officer (IO), who works with host countries and international media, serving as the embassy spokesperson; and the cultural affairs officer (CAO), who administers educational and cultural programs including lectures, speakers, seminars, and events. The USIS also employs foreign service nationals (FSN), who are citizens of the host country and who provide support and continuity at overseas posts.

PRIMARY FUNCTIONS

The USIA's overseas operations are mainly carried out by the foreign service officers who are assigned to U.S. missions abroad. With guidance, support, and material from Washington headquarters, they manage cultural and information programs in support of American foreign policy objectives and greater mutual understanding between the United States and foreign societies. The Research and Information Office is the only office in the U.S. government responsible for advising the president, secretary of state, and other foreign affairs policymakers of foreign public opinion about the U.S. policies and their impact on U.S. public diplomacy programs. The research staff commissions public opinion surveys in nearly every country of the world. It also provides twice-daily reports on foreign media commentary around the world on various issues that are provided to officials throughout the government.

The USIA also reports to the Senate Foreign Relations Committee, the House International Relations Committees, and the Senate and House Appropriations Committees as needed on foreign policy matters and programs. The USIA operates a number of advisory committees, such as the U.S. Advisory on Public Diplomacy, a bipartisan board to oversee U.S. government public diplomacy, the Broadcast Board of Governors, the J. William Fulbright Foreign Scholarship Board, the Cultural Property Advisory Committee, and the Advisory Board for Cuba Broadcasting.

PROGRAMS

The USIA supports many programs dedicated to U.S.-international exchange. These include: academic exchanges with Russia and the new independent states, special academic exchanges and services under the Hubert H. Humphrey Fellowship program, study of the United States at foreign universities and secondary schools, teaching English overseas, presenting U.S. performing and visual arts to international audiences, developing programs for building democratic institutions, operating foreign press centers, and maintaining a speaker's bureau.

The Fulbright Exchange Program, which operates in over 125 countries, is probably the best-known program operated by the USIA. Established in 1946 under legislation introduced by Senator J. William Fulbright (D-AK), it is a major component of the USIA's academic exchange and training services and provides the agency with a popular program to enhance U.S. public diplomacy. Fulbright grants are awarded to American and foreign scholars to study, teach, lecture, or conduct research either abroad or in the United States. A presidentially appointed Fulbright Scholarship Board, the USIA's Office of Academic Programs, and binational Fulbright commissions coordinate with host countries on the scope and operation of each year's selections. Approximately 5,000 American and foreign citizens receive grants based on academic or professional qualifications and their willingness to share ideas and experiences with people of diverse cultures.

International Broadcasting Bureau

The International Broadcasting Bureau (IBB) is another USIA program that has a significant role in shaping U.S. policy and disseminating information to the world. The International Broadcasting Act of 1994 established a Broadcasting Board of Governors to oversee

USIA's *Voice of America, Radio and TV Marti,* and *WORLDNET Television,* as well as two surrogate international broadcast services, *Radio Free Europe/Radio Liberty* and the Asia Pacific Network. The IBB allows the USIA to reach a global community in a highly effective and timely manner. The programs operated under the IBB provide outlets for international news, commentaries, discussions, and programs about the Untied States, its policies, and its people.

The *Radio Free Europe/Radio Liberty* and Asia Pacific Network are private corporations of the USIS that broadcast local and regional news and information in a country's native language. Both cover international events as well and are without commercial constrictions. *Voice of America* broadcasts more than 900 hours of programming weekly in 47 languages, including English, to an international audience. *Radio Marti,* established in 1985, broadcasts in Spanish 24 hours a day to Cuba. *TV Marti* telecasts four and one-half hours daily. Programming consists of news, information, and entertainment from a variety of sources. WORLDNET, USIA's satellite television network, transmits news and educational or cultural programming 24 hours a day to millions of foreign viewers through American embassies, USIS posts, and foreign television and cable networks.

BUDGET:

United States Information Agency

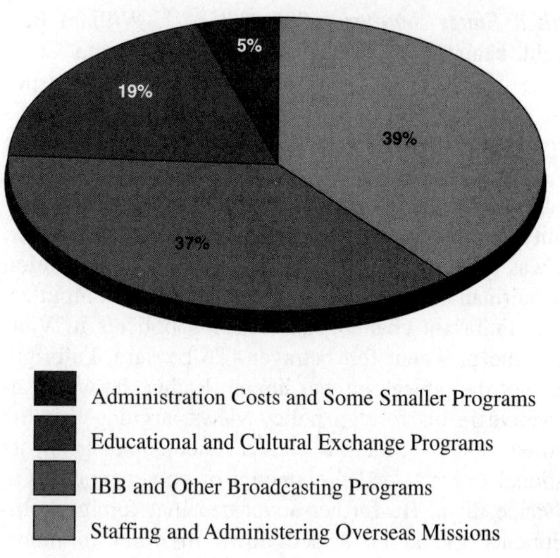

BUDGET INFORMATION

Congress appropriated $1.14 billion for the USIA in 1998. Of these funds, $463 million, approximately 39 percent of the total budget, was devoted to staffing and administering the USIA's overseas missions. Another 19 percent of the budget, $213 million, went to Educational and Cultural Exchange programs, including the Fulbright Scholarship program. The USIA spent $418 million, 37 percent of its budget, on the IBB and other broadcasting programs, and on the acquisition and maintenance of broadcast facilities. The remaining 5 percent of the budget covered administration costs and a number of smaller programs.

HISTORY

After World War I (1914–18) efforts of the government to disseminate information to foreign countries was minimal until 1938. Then, on the brink of World War II (1939–45), Congress formed the Inter-departmental Committee for Scientific Cooperation, as a challenge to Germany and Italy's communications efforts, especially in Latin America. This led to the appointment of Nelson Rockefeller as coordinator of commercial and cultural relations between all American republics in 1940. Rockefeller developed programs that created libraries, culture and people exchanges, and binational centers. In 1942 *Voice of America* was started to counter the Axis powers's programs and allow the U.S. voice to be broadcast abroad. Later that year, the Office of War Information was established to assist the *Voice of America* broadcasts.

The years after World War II saw a growth in U.S. efforts to spread its information to Europe. Europe was embroiled in conflicting ideologies, such as communism, capitalism, socialism, and totalitarianism. The United States's role was to offer a view of world affairs, as seen from the U.S. perspective. As such, Congress enacted the Fulbright Act of 1946 that mandated a "peacetime international exchange program" of scholars and the 1948 Smith-Mundt Act which "served as a charter for a peacetime overseas information program." The 1949 Hoover Commission further stipulated that these various initiatives should become separate from the State Department and established as a consolidated agency.

On August 1, 1953, President Dwight D. Eisenhower officially created the United States Information Agency. The purpose of the agency was to centralize all the United States's overseas information and cultural programs into a single identifiable agency. The USIA was the culmination of a long line of attempts made since World War I to sponsor and host information activities that were favorable to U.S. interests abroad.

The various components of the new agency included the *Voice of America,* which moved its headquarters from New York to Washington, D.C. The Department of State, for the time being, kept the educational programs under its auspices.

BIOGRAPHY:
J. William Fulbright

United States Senator (1905–1995) J. William Fulbright, chairman of the Senate Foreign Relations Committee from 1959 to 1974, was one of the most outspoken and powerful critics of the Vietnam War. His opposition to the war culminated in 1967 when he broke away from President Lyndon B. Johnson, a turning point that gave the antiwar movement a boost in political credibility. In 1959 when Johnson was Senate majority leader, he was instrumental in securing Fulbright's installation as chairman of the Senate Foreign Relations Committee. After Fulbright challenged Johnson's policies in Vietnam, the president felt betrayed. To be sure, Fulbright was not the typical antiwar liberal. Rather, he was conservative in his foreign policy views, arguing that the United States needed a clearer understanding of its national interests and the amount of power required to advance them. He further advocated that foreign commitments should be scaled down in order to more-effectively defend areas vital to national security. Vietnam, he maintained, fell outside that definition and commitment of half a million troops was risking U.S. power and prestige internationally. Fulbright was also conservative in his views on domestic issues. Such conservative positions are believed to have weakened his political support, and Fulbright lost his bid for reelection in 1974. Fulbright is perhaps best known for his lasting legacy—the Fulbright Scholarship Program. Named for its sponsor and established by Congress in 1946, the program provides grants to teachers and students for international educational exchange.

In 1961 more changes in the design of the USIA were enacted by Congress when it passed the Mutual Education and Cultural Exchange Act. The act consolidated U.S. educational and cultural programs that existed in different departments under the control of the USIA and established government operation of cultural and education centers abroad. It also expanded other programs, such as athletics, book translating, and international fair representation.

The next sweeping change occurred in 1977 when President Jimmy Carter combined the State Department's Bureau of Educational and Cultural Affairs with the USIA and changed the agency's name to the United States International Communication Agency (USICA). The name change and the president's mandate to Congress in support of this agency consolidation added a new dimension to the mission of the agency. The newly devised mission stated that the main function of the USICA was "to reduce the degree to which misperceptions and misunderstandings complicate relations between the United States and other nations. It is also in our interest—and in the interest of other nations—that Americans have the opportunity to understand the histories, cultures, and problems of others, so that we can come to understand their hopes, perceptions and aspirations."

Without altering the mission or purpose of the USICA, President Ronald Reagan changed the name of the agency back to USIA in 1982. No other major changes occurred in the history of the agency until 1997 when the administration of President Bill Clinton, in its ongoing attempts to streamline government, declared that the USIA, along with two other agencies concerned with foreign affairs, would be consolidated under the Department of State, commencing in October 1998.

CURRENT POLITICAL ISSUES

While the USIA is for the most part involved in cultural exchanges, selecting Fulbright scholars, and disseminating information, it is also the agency responsible for "people exchanges." These programs include the exchange of scholars and teachers, or business professionals. However, one of the agency's programs, the Au Pair (babysitter) Program, has come under attack by critics who claim that the government should not be involved in the "nanny business."

Case Study: The Au Pair Tragedy

In 1997 a nineteen-year-old British au pair named Louise Woodward was found guilty of manslaughter in the death of an eight-month-old baby named Matthew Eappen. The baby died as a result of Woodward allegedly shaking him violently to quiet him. The judge in the case freed Woodward allowing her 279 days in jail during the trial to act as time served for the crime. The only legal recourse the Eappens have is to sue the au pair agency that sent them Woodward, or the USIA, which passed along her qualifications to the agency.

In 1986 Congress, led by the foreign affairs committees of both the House and the Senate, authorized the Au Pair Program and placed it under the control of the USIA. Congress reasoned that the program reflected a "cultural exchange," which meant that this type of program was clearly the responsibility of the USIA. The USIA complained at the time, and has continued to complain, that the Au Pair Program should be a part of the Department of Labor. Nonetheless, the program has grown and remained under the auspices of the USIA. In 1995 Congress expanded the program to include au pairs from the rest of the world, not only Europe.

The role of the USIA is to contract with reputable agencies and set the guidelines for the 11,000 au pairs (ages 18 to 26) who enter the United States every year. In the wake of the Eappen tragedy, the USIA issued more stringent rules for qualifications for au pairs and higher standards for checking these qualifications. Psychological profiles, child development courses, age requirements for those who are involved in infant care, stress management, and shaken-baby syndrome lessons have all been included in the new rules. Although the USIA was reluctant to become the permanent host of the program, it nevertheless tried to compensate for the problems that the program was undergoing. It proposed a higher pay scale for the au pairs in an effort to attract a higher level of applicant. However, when that plan was announced, Congress was bombarded with thousands of angry letters from parents who did not want the pay increase and the issue was dropped.

SUCCESSES AND FAILURES

One of the USIA's most noteworthy endeavors is the Fulbright Scholarship Program, which celebrated its fiftieth anniversary in 1996. For a total cost of $1.9 billion over 50 years, thousands of Americans have studied and taught in countries around the globe, and thousands of foreign students and teachers have come to the United States. These scholars have gone on to great success in many different fields. Notable Americans who have participated in the Fulbright Program include Maya Angelou, poet; Aaron Copeland, composer; Daniel Patrick Moynihan, U.S. Senator; Emilio Segre, Nobel Prize in Physics; Richard Thomas, CEO of First National Bank of Chicago; Roslyn Yallow, Nobel Prize in Medicine; and John Updike, author. The participants from outside the United States are equally accomplished, and include Boutros Boutros-Ghali, UN Secretary-General; Ingvar Carlsson, Prime Minister of Sweden; Umberto Eco, writer; Khalid Omari, Minister of Education for Jordan; Toru Hashimoto, Chairman of Fuji Bank, Japan; Jorge Martinez, pianist; and Sir Wallace Rowling, Prime Minister of New Zealand. Established to encourage international understanding and cooperation through study in foreign countries, the program is regarded by many as a major success for U.S. diplomacy and world peace.

FAST FACTS

The USIA issues over 300,000 visas each year to foreign visitors to the United States.

(Source: *New Republic*, November 24, 1997.)

FUTURE DIRECTIONS

The future of the USIA as an independent agency is limited. President Clinton, in his efforts to streamline government, is returning the USIA under the auspices of the Department of State. The reasoning is that since the USIA is involved in overseas programs and cultural events, the natural place for these activities is within the authority of the secretary of state. This means *Voice of America*, the IBB, all the PAOs, and culture officers will be part of the diplomatic missions within each embassy.

AGENCY RESOURCES

The USIA operates a number of information services that are available to the public. These include the Electronic and Printed Materials, an information service in five languages that provides both time-sensitive and in-depth information. The Speaker and Specialist Program enables hundreds of Americans to share their expertise with audiences abroad and at home. Over 100 Information Resource Centers are electronically equipped for rapid delivery of information relevant to U.S. interests abroad, and to foreign leaders in government, media, and academia. Foreign Press Centers that the USIA operates in Washington, D.C., New York, and Los Angeles assist resident and visiting foreign journalists. The centers work cooperatively with privately sponsored international press centers in Chicago, Houston, Atlanta, Miami, and Seattle. You can retrieve information concerning the USIA from its Web site at http://www.usia.gov or by writing to USIA, 301 4th St. SW, Washington, DC 20547.

AGENCY PUBLICATIONS

The USIA publishes many different brochures, policy statements, international events calendar, press conference transcripts, articles, and wireless forum. The broad range of booklets, pamphlets, and brochures in multiple language editions, about American society, values, history, and culture are available overseas at postal, embassy, and cultural centers operated by the USIS. The focus of these documents is to educate foreign nationals about the United States. The USIA also produces and distributes CD-ROMs that depict the complexity and variety of American life to prospective students. A more complete list of publications is available from the USIA, 301 4th St. SW, Washington, DC 20547 or E-mail the agency at inquiry@usia.gov.

BIBLIOGRAPHY

Clary, Mike. "Radio Marti's Move to Miami" *Los Angeles Times*, 20 August 1996, p. A-5.

Cohen, Warren. "Congress' Role in the Au Pair Tragedy." *New Republic*, 24 November 1997.

McAllester, Matthew. "Life in Cyberspace/Suit Seeks Access." *Newsday*, 14 July 1996, p. A61.

Powers, Evelyn Tan. "USA Widens Global Information Links." *USA Today*, 15 May 1996, p. 7A.

"USIA May Nix Budapest Funding." *Editor & Publisher*, 4 March 1995, p. 5.

"White House Fact Sheet on Reorganizing." U.S. Newswire, 18 April 1997.

United States Institute of Peace (USIP)

WHAT IS ITS MISSION?

As stated on its Web site, "the mission of the United States Institute of Peace is to strengthen the nation's capabilities to promote the peaceful resolution of international conflicts."

HOW IS IT STRUCTURED?

The United States Institute of Peace (USIP) is an independent nonpartisan federal institution governed by a bipartisan board of directors, all of whom are appointed by the president and confirmed by the Senate. The board includes a chairman, vice chairman, the president of USIP, four federal officers, and a varying number of other members who are drawn from outside of the government. These other members of the board are most often high-ranking public policy or political science professors from various universities or special-interest groups in Washington, D.C. The four federal officials serve *ex officio* (by virtue of being in a particular office): the deputy director of the U.S. Arms Control and Disarmament Policy, the assistant secretary of state for intelligence and research, president of the national defense university, and the under secretary of defense for policy. The president of USIP serves the board in a nonvoting capacity.

There are 12 officials that operate USIP: a president (in addition to his role on the board), an executive vice president, a vice president, and eight directors that head various aspects of USIP's functions: education and training; research and studies; grants programming; administration; the Jennings Randolph Fellowship Program for

PARENT ORGANIZATION: Independent
ESTABLISHED: 1984
EMPLOYEES: 55 (1997)

Contact Information:

ADDRESS: 1550 M St. NW, Ste. 700
Washington, DC 20005-1708
PHONE: (202) 457-1700
FAX: (202) 429-6063
E-MAIL: usip_requests@usip.org
URL: http://www.usip.org
PRESIDENT: Richard H. Solomon
CHAIRMAN: Chester A. Crocker

Since the November 21, 1995, signing of the Dayton Peace Accord, USIP has devoted extensive research efforts to maintaining the fragile peace between the countries. Pictured are Serbian President Slobodan Milosevic (seated, far left)*, Bosnia-Herzegovinan President Alija Izetbegovic* (seated, second left)*, and Croatian President Franjo Tudjman* (seated, third left). *(Photograph by Paul J. Richards. Agence France Presse/Corbis-Bettmann)*

International Peace; the Jeannette Rankin Library Program; the Office of Communications; and the Rule of Law Initiative. The final official is a senior scholar for religion, ethics, and human rights. Additionally, USIP has various Working Groups that concentrate on peaceful resolution of conflicts in particularly troubling spots throughout the world. The number and focus of these teams varies from year to year based on situational requirements.

PRIMARY FUNCTIONS

The central function of USIP is to encourage peaceful rather than violent resolutions to conflicts. The institute has several ways of fulfilling this responsibility.

USIP awards grants, usually from $25,000 to $40,000 over one or two years, to a number of different institutions, organizations, and people that wish to explore ways of fulfilling USIP's mission of peace. USIP offers grants to research the causes of war and how it might be prevented as well as what the conditions are in various countries regarding peace. Also, monies are granted to educators wishing to form student curricula on studies of war and peace; this involves the development of lesson plans, syllabi, and other educational material that help students gain a better understanding of conflict resolution. Implementing training or conducting seminars for policy makers and the public that will enhance peacemaking skills is also considered for USIP grants. People who wish to create public information efforts, such as commercials, pamphlets, community forums, and speakers' programs to increase public awareness about the need for peaceful solutions to problems are also granted USIP money. Finally, grants are given to increase the volume of material about the prevention of war and peace through the expansion of library or bibliographic resources as well as efforts directed toward resource-sharing mechanisms such as the Internet. In addition to the grants USIP awards, it also sponsors a fellowship program, the Jennings Randolph Program, that is directed toward achieving further research into aspects of peaceful conflict resolution. The institute supports two fellowships: a Senior Fellowship, which involves paid research at the institute; and Dissertation Fellowships, which involves funding of a doctoral dissertation.

USIP also maintains a database of specialists who are experts on international regions of conflict. These specialists often are former professors from prestigious universities throughout the world; their assignment is to answer questions regarding their area or areas of expertise and offer opinions on the best way to resolve conflicts in these regions in a peaceful manner. Their services are available to anyone who needs information about international affairs, from policymakers in Congress to print and television journalists. These specialists also report to USIP regarding international situations and USIP occasionally publishes these reports through their own press. Additionally, the specialists and USIP staff members can be called on by Congress to give their thoughts on situations around the world. While these specialists do not necessarily represent the opinions of USIP, the agency does sponsor them and their efforts by providing them with offices in the institute and money for research.

USIP hosts conferences and seminars in and around Washington, D.C., concerning subjects of importance to its mission of peaceful conflict resolution. USIP's staff and scholars present their thoughts on the latest situations and problems to an audience made up of policymakers and the general public. Topics have included "Counterterrorism Strategy: Lessons after Nairobi, Dar es-Salaam and Omagh" in the wake of 1998 bombings in East Africa and Ireland as well as a 1997 conference on "Virtual Diplomacy."

FAST FACTS

Over the past 3,500 years, approximately 8,000 peace treaties have been signed throughout the world. The average treaty is estimated to have brought peace for about two years.

(Source: *Business Daily*, February 17, 1998.)

PROGRAMS

One area where USIP concentrates its attention is the Research and Studies Program (R & S). The R & S executes, directs, devises, and oversees research and study on the topic of international peace. The main objective of the R & S is to close the gap between the academic world and government positions by organizing and holding meetings that consist of academics and government policymakers to discuss topics related to the quest for international peace.

The R & S forms highly focused small working groups that meet to discuss key issues in reference to their areas of expertise. The groups convened for 1998 expanded the initial Working Groups that were focused primarily on North and South Korea. The Korean Peninsula Working Group expanded its attention to focus on the Asian economic crisis and other factors that would destabilize the Asia-Pacific Rim area after years of peace and prosperity. The Central Asia Working Group focuses its concerns on what is occurring in the continuing war in Tajikistan, the tensions in the Ferghana Valley (occupied by Uzbekistan, Tajikistan, and Kyrgyzstan), and the issues between Russians and Central Asians in these newly independent states. The Middle East Working Group concentrates its efforts on Afghanistan, and has held a series of high-level meetings between Turkish and U.S. officials and experts to deal with each country's policy issues concerning Iraq (especially the Kurds in Northern Iraq) and relations with Iran, Syria, and Iraq. The aim of the meetings is to build greater understanding between the two countries on volatile and potentially divisive matters. Other Working Groups tackle problems concerning Europe and its hot spots, convene conferences regarding Bosnia, Russian stability, and other foreign policy objectives. R & S works closely with USIP's Grants and Fellowship programs to find the most qualified participants for these Working Groups.

BUDGET INFORMATION

USIP was appropriated a 1998 budget of approximately $11 million by Congress. The majority of USIP's budget is fairly evenly divided between grants, subsidies, and contributions and staff salaries. The remainder of the budget is allocated to civilian personnel benefits.

HISTORY

The idea of a government organization devoted to finding ways to resolve conflicts peacefully has long been present in the collective minds of U.S. legislatures. From 1935 to 1976, over 140 bills were introduced to establish peace-related departments, agencies, bureaus, and committees of Congress. In 1981 a congressionally chartered commission recommended the creation of a national peace academy. In 1984 after countless bills and debates over the concept of a peace institute, President Ronald Reagan signed the legislation that created the United States Institute of Peace (USIP). USIP's first president, Richard Solomon, described the new agency as "a complement to the military academies, which train for war fighting. We were set up to wrestle with ways to manage conflict with peaceful means" (*Rocky Mountain News*).

USIP spent its first four years focusing on international trouble spots in Afghanistan and Latin America. However, the institute was soon faced with a by-product of the changing geography of Eastern Europe. When the United Soviet Socialist Republic (USSR) collapsed in 1991, it created new scenarios for study by USIP experts: which states would emerge from the former USSR, how would these borders be drawn, and how could disputes among the forming nations be handled peacefully.

The early 1990s brought a new crisis to the attention of USI: a brutal civil war in the former state of Yugoslavian. When the Dayton Accords were signed, ending the conflict there in November 1995, USIP devoted research to how the peace that was established could be made to last. Since that time, the institute has crafted and actively implemented peace-building programs in Bosnia-Herzegovina, and helped to shape policy discussions in Washington on how to approach the troubled area. USIP worked with regional leaders to encourage democratization and find ways to ensure the region's stability and peacefulness.

Despite the threat of a nuclear war between the United States and Russia being greatly lessened by the end of the Cold War, the issue of nuclear weapons capability came into much sharper focus in the late 1990s. India and Pakistan both illustrated their status as a nuclear power by detonating test bombs in early 1998. Other countries, such as North Korea and those in the former Soviet Bloc, were also thought to have nuclear weapons. The institute studied these issues in an attempt to determine the best ways to stop a return to the days of global nuclear buildup.

CURRENT POLITICAL ISSUES

USIP holds a number of different conferences every year, often related to the most recent concerns in the areas of diplomacy and the politics of peaceful resolutions. These may focus on particularly problematic regions of the world or on certain issues that affect the way that diplomacy is done. Examining the global explosion of the Internet and other forms of electronic communications, USIP thought that a broad-based conference addressing the issues presented by this new information technology was necessary.

Case Study: Virtual Diplomacy

The impetus for USIP's wish to hold a conference on diplomacy and new communications technology began in 1993 and 1994. The institute held a number of conferences that began to show how much the community of organizations devoted to conflict resolution were changing with the advent of this technology. These realizations led to another conference, *Managing Communications: Lessons from Interventions in Africa*, that showed how information technology impacted relief efforts in war-torn Somalia. USIP decided the issue of technology was so pervasive that a conference based solely on the subject was necessary.

USIP sponsored its *Virtual Diplomacy* conference in April 1997 to explore what ramifications the Internet and global communications had on international affairs. By bringing together diplomats, foreign policy experts, and technology experts, USIP began a dialog that discussed how technology would impact diplomacy, negotiations, and even international government policy. "Communications technologies are reshaping international relations," said Richard H. Solomon, president of the U.S. Institute of Peace to *Reuters*. "With close to 70 million people in over 100 countries connected to the Internet, these technologies are paving the way for on-line international coalitions who are influencing international politics and policies, humanitarian missions, and globalizing economic growth," Solomon said.

For two days, over 2,000 policymakers, technology experts, business representatives, scholars, students, and journalists from across the country and abroad sought a common ground of understanding about the promises of information technologies in foreign affairs. The *Virtual Diplomacy* conference included a number of speeches and small focus groups intent on trying to come to grips with the way that diplomatic procedures had changed and could be enhanced with communications technology. Additionally the conference worked to develop ways in which organizations and groups could coordinate and share resources using the Internet. Participants also discussed ways of helping those that lacked the necessary technology frameworks to obtain resources that could involve them in the global changes taking place.

The USIP began a number of projects based on what occurred at the conference, including an initiative by the Jeannette Rankin Library Program to create a digital collection of peace agreements from around the world, and a study by USIP staff on the role of the media and media technologies in achieving the political will needed to bring international conflicts to a peaceful conclusion. In addition, USIP distributed several grants to support the ideas of virtual diplomacy, including grants to the University of Malta for the development of teaching materials designed to advance the knowledge of conflict resolution and the Nansen Environmental and Remote Sensing Center of Norway to enhance the utility of high-resolution satellite images used in capturing pictures of humanitarian efforts around the globe.

FUTURE DIRECTIONS

USIP plans to focus on trouble spots around the world. To help with this goal, USIP intends to increase the number of its Working Groups. In his 1998 testimony before Congress, President Solomon defined the necessity of the institute. "We are approaching a new millennium, at the end of what has been the most violent era in human history. Estimates are that more than one hundred and fifty million people have died in the 20th century as a result of wars, revolution and civic violence. . . . Our own national interests, ethos and values demand that we not ignore the outrages and gross injustices that persist in many corners of the globe. Traditional diplomacy and the foreign affairs institutions which served us well during the Cold War are frequently ill-suited to meet contemporary challenges to security and human justice. To meet these challenges, the Institute has been working to develop new approaches and instruments for managing the political turmoil and human suffering that result from failing nation states, ethno-religious conflict, and the ambitions of local tyrants."

AGENCY RESOURCES

The USIP operates the Jeannette Rankin Library, an in-house collection that houses more than 8,000 core books, monographs, periodicals, journals, and related materials on topics such as conflict management and resolution, negotiations, diplomacy, mediation, peacekeeping, peace theory, war, the United Nations (UN), and arms control. Library staff members are available Monday through Friday, from 9:00 A.M. until 5:00 P.M. Please call the Information Services Librarian at (202) 429-3851 to set up an appointment to use the library resources on site; fax information requests to (202) 429-6063; send requests via E-mail to library@usip.org; or mail requests to the Jeannette Rankin Library Program, United States Institute of Peace, 1550 M St. NW, Ste. 700, Washington, D.C. 20005–1708.

AGENCY PUBLICATIONS

The institute develops, produces, and markets books, periodicals, and other publications that are available through print and on-line forms. These materials are the results of USIP's research, workshops, and related events. The U.S. Institute of Peace Press publishes many books on vital issues, including such titles as *Revolutionary Movements in Latin America: El Salvador's FMLN and Peru's Shining Path* and *Russian Negotiating Behavior: Continuity and Transition*. The bimonthly newsletter *Peace Watch* is published both in print and on-line at http://www.usip.org/pubs.html. USIP also publishes special reports on various international situations, such as *Between Impediment and Advantage: Saddam's Iraq* and *Kosovo Dialogue: Too Little, Too Late*, and reports on different peace initiatives in other places in the world. To obtain these and a list of other publications, write USIP, 1550 M St. NW, Ste. 700, Washington D.C., 20005-1708; access the USIP's Web site at http://www.usip.org/pubs.html; or call (202) 457-1700.

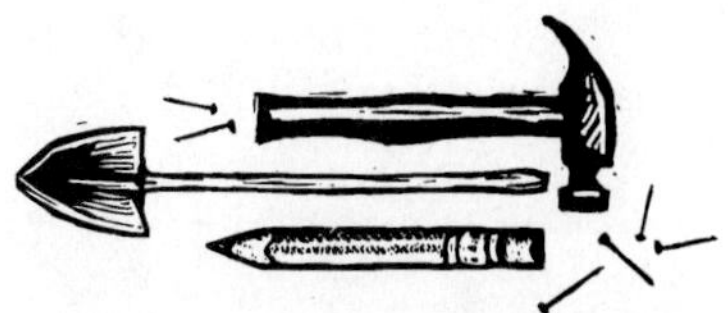

GET INVOLVED:

USIP runs a state and national essay contest for students who wish to learn and write about the U.S. role in international peace. All high school students living in the United States are invited to participate. USIP chooses a different topic each year and awards first-place winners of the national contest a $5,000 college scholarship as well as an all-expenses paid trip to the institute for the awards ceremony. For information on how to become involved in this contest, access the USIP Web site at http://www.usip.org/et/NPEC98/npec.html or write to National Peace Essay Contest, United States Institute of Peace, 1550 M St. NW, Ste. 700, Washington, D.C. 20005-1708.

BIBLIOGRAPHY

"Conference Explores 'Virtual Diplomacy' To Manage International Conflicts." *US Newswire*, 1 April 1997.

Davant, Charles. "U.S. Institute of Peace Well Worth the Money." *Rocky Mountain News*, 7 September 1997, p. 57A.

Giacomo, Carol. "U.S. Officials Urge Democracy After Abacha's Death." *Reuters*, 8 June 1998.

Grimes, Charolotte. "Power & Purpose: U.S. Seeking a New Role in Post-Cold War World." *St. Louis Post-Dispatch*, 17 October 1993, p. 1B.

Miller, Rhonda. *Institutionalizing Peace: The Conception of the United States Institute for Peace and its Role in American Political Thought*. Jefferson, N.C.: McFarland and Co., 1994.

Sawyer, Jon. "Managing Chaos: 'We Know Where The Crises Are Going To Be. The Problem Is There Is Never Enough Human And Political Will To Do Anything About Them.'" *St. Louis Post-Dispatch*, 4 December 1994, p. 1B.

Wicker, Christine. "Reconciliation's Army: Agents of Peace Quietly Tend to Old Wounds Around Globe." *Dallas Morning News*, 30 November 1997, p. 1A.

Worsnip, Patrick. "Mideast Issues Complicate Iraq Strike Decision." *Reuters*, 15 February 1998.

United States International Trade Commission (ITC)

PARENT ORGANIZATION: Independent
ESTABLISHED: September 8, 1916
EMPLOYEES: 380

Contact Information:

ADDRESS: 500 E St. SW
Washington, DC 20436
PHONE: (202) 205-2000
TDD (HEARING IMPAIRED): (202) 205-1810
FAX: (202) 205-2798
URL: http://www.usitc.gov
CHAIRMAN: Lynn M. Bragg
VICE CHAIRMAN: Marcia E. Miller

WHAT IS ITS MISSION?

The United States International Trade Commission (ITC) seeks to define, in a fundamental sense, the trade relationships of the United States. It does this in an almost purely advisory capacity, furnishing the president, Congress, and government agencies with studies, reports, and recommendations involving international trade and tariffs. To reach its conclusions, the ITC conducts investigations and public hearings relative to the international trade policies of the United States. The ITC does not make trade policy or negotiate trade agreements, and it does not have the power of a court of law.

HOW IS IT STRUCTURED?

The ITC prides itself on its objectivity and its independence from political parties and government agencies. The commission is composed of six commissioners, each of whom is appointed to a nine-year term by the president with the advice and consent of the Senate. The chairman and vice chairman of the commission are designated by the president for two-year terms; succeeding chairmen may not be of the same political party. The chairman is responsible for the administration of the commission. Not more than three commissioners may be members of the same political party, making the ITC one of the only federal government agency that does not permit a partisan majority.

The chairman and the commission are assisted in their administrative and policy work by several offices. Legally, the commission is assisted by the Offices of

General Counsel and Administrative Law Judges, which advise and interpret the legal status of commission findings and recommendations. Administrative offices include the Office of Finance and Budget, the Office of Management Services, and the Office of Personnel.

The mandates of the ITC are carried out through five operations offices. The Office of Investigations is responsible for looking into accusations of countervailing duty cases (involving goods sold with the benefit of a hidden illegal subsidy) and antidumping cases (involving goods sold in the United States at less than their fair market value). The Office of Unfair Import Investigations is responsible for exploring accusations of international patent infringements and other intellectual property issues. The Office of Tariff Affairs and Trade Agreements tracks articles imported into and exported out of the United States, and it reports to the president and government agencies in regard to duties and tariffs.

Two operational offices serve in a primarily advisory capacity. The Office of Economics advises the commission on developments in world economics and how they might affect the policies of the commission. The Office of Industries offers analysis and advice concerning the global competitiveness of certain industries, the United States in general, and the resulting implications for trade and policy developments. A sixth operations office, the Office of Information Services, is responsible for maintaining the internal computer systems and databases through which ITC personnel interact.

The ITC closely scrutinizes the type and amount of imports entering the United States through ports such as the Dundalk Marine Terminal in Baltimore, Maryland, one of the most heavily-trafficked ports for Japanese automobiles. (UPI/Corbis-Bettmann)

PRIMARY FUNCTIONS

The ITC's investigations usually focus on determining whether one of four conditions is created by the import of certain goods: whether a U.S. industry is being materially injured or threatened by reason of imports that are subsidized or are being sold at less than fair value; whether increased fair imports are a substantial cause of serious injury to an industry; whether there are unfair import practices in import trade; or whether imports of agricultural products are materially interfering with certain programs of the U.S. Department of Agriculture.

As a result of these investigations, the commission recommends to the president the action that would address such injuries and facilitate positive adjustment. The president alone has the discretion to take action on the ITC's recommendations; these actions could be in the form of an increase in duties, negotiation of marketing agreements, or provision of adjustment assistance to groups of workers, companies, or communities. In some cases, the president is prevented from taking such actions against countries, for example those that belong to the World Trade Organization.

The commission advises the president as to the likely economic effects of duties and other trade barriers that may be considered in proposed trade agreements. It prepares trade studies, research projects, and summaries of trade and tariff information subject to the request of the president, the Senate Finance Committee, and the House Ways and Means Committee. In cooperation with the secretary of the Treasury and the secretary of commerce, the ITC establishes for statistical purposes a listing of articles imported into and exported out of the United States.

PROGRAMS

Nearly all the initiatives undertaken by the ITC are part of its legislative mandate. For example, through its Office of Tariff Affairs and Trade Agreements, the ITC is responsible for publishing the Harmonized Tariff Schedule of the United States, which provides the tariff rates and statistical categories for all merchandise imported into the United States and is based on the international Harmonized System, the global classification system that is used to describe most world trade in goods.

The Omnibus Trade and Competitiveness Act of 1988 required the commission to conduct several industry competitiveness investigations, which it does through its Office of Industries. Reports of this work appear in the *Industry, Trade, and Technology Review*. Another example of a specific ITC program is its North American Free Trade Agreement (NAFTA) investigations. Subject to U.S. legislation concerning NAFTA, the commission conducts specific bilateral safeguard investigations to determine whether a Canadian or Mexican article is being imported in such increased numbers or under such conditions that the imports constitute an injury or threat to U.S. producers of the same.

BUDGET INFORMATION

The budget of the ITC is granted entirely through congressional appropriations of tax revenues. Pursuant to Section 175 of the Trade Act of 1974, the ITC's budget request is submitted directly to Congress for approval, without revision by the president. This provision is intended to insure the commission's political independence. In 1998 ITC was budgeted $42 million for conduct of research, investigations, and reports.

HISTORY

Early attempts to establish independent, nonpartisan tariff boards in the United States proved unsuccessful until the early twentieth century, when a wave of political reform sentiment overtook U.S. politics. A major goal of the Progressive Party was to take decisions about tariffs and trade out of the hands of uninformed politicians and assign them to panels of experts. With the support of divergent groups such as the American Federation of Labor and the U.S. Chamber of Commerce, Congress fulfilled President Woodrow Wilson's request for the establishment of a tariff commission. The 1916 legislation created the United States Tariff Commission, the ITC's predecessor agency, which was charged with the primary duty of providing Congress with trade information and statistics that would help members of Congress make rational decisions regarding tariff revisions.

Because of World War I (1914–18), which began one week after the Tariff Commission began operations, the commission got off to a slow start. In its early years, it confined its activities to gathering data and had no direct input on tariff decisions. However, the data gathered was important. Since the very beginning of the two-party political system, two opposing philosophies had battled over international trade. Conservatives generally adopted a protectionist policy involving high tariffs and even barring some imports. Progressives (liberals) argued for a more open, free trade policy involving fewer restrictions on imports. Before the Tariff Commission had been created, arguments had been based on little factual evidence. Now, the data was there for the two parties to debate.

In 1923 a Tariff Commission conflict with President Calvin Coolidge exposed a glaring weakness in the commission's authority to conduct investigations. The commission had begun investigating the sugar industry, and one of its commissioners, Henry Glassie, was married to a woman whose entire family grew and processed sugar. Congress expected Glassie to withdraw from the commission's investigation. When he refused, Coolidge, a staunch conservative, fiercely defended Glassie's decision. Congress was eventually able to overrule Coolidge and force Glassie's withdrawal from the investigation, but when the commission gave its final recommendation—to lower the sugar tariff by forty percent—Coolidge ignored it for a year before finally rejecting it outright. He then went about carefully selecting new commissioners who shared his ultraconservative philosophy.

Most members of Congress, excluding the very conservative ones, were furious. Some took the conflict as proof that the Tariff Commission was utterly worthless and should be abolished outright. But the commission had its defenders, and the result of this controversy was the Smoot-Hawley Tariff Act of 1930, which revised the commission's investigative duties, canceled the terms of all sitting commissioners, and cut the term of future commissioners in half.

After the Depression

The controversies surrounding the Tariff Commission quieted somewhat when the U.S. economy collapsed in the early 1930s, making the consideration of tariff rates nearly irrelevant. In an effort to create an entirely new trade structure, Congress granted the president authority to conduct specific bilateral trade agreements aimed at reducing trade barriers. The expertise of the Tariff Commission proved to be extremely useful in these negotiations, and the reputation of the agency began to rebound.

At the end of World War II (1939–45), statesmen around the world considered the development of a common trade policy for all the members of the United Nations. The Tariff Commission participated in the comprehensive round of discussions that resulted in the General Agreement on Tariffs and Trade (GATT) in 1947. In 1948 the commission's role was dramatically altered by a Congress that was suspicious of the intentions of President Harry Truman. Since 1934 commissioners and staff had commonly served as members of trade negotiation teams, but Congress, again concerned about the political influence of the president on the commission, now specifically outlawed this practice. The legislation also ordered the commission to review all concessions that the president's negotiators might propose and indicate the points at which the concessions might endanger domestic producers.

Greater Independence

Later, in the early 1970s, serious ideological differences developed between the executive and legislative branches of government. Republican President Richard Nixon had assigned the authority for conducting trade negotiations to his office's special trade representative, and a Democratic Congress wanted to make it clear that the Tariff Commission's activities would be sharply distinguished from the activities of the president's office. The Trade Act of 1974 was an effort to reinforce the commission's political independence. It legislated that seniority alone, rather than the president, would determine the chairman; that the commission would have an independent budget authorization that bypassed presidential approval; and that no member of the commission was to ever participate directly in any trade negotiations. The agency's new name, the International Trade Commission, symbolized a thorough restructuring that would grant the commission the truly independent status it had always been meant to have.

In the years since the 1974 Trade Act, political pressures from the White House, from Congress, and from the business community, intensified by unfavorable trade balances and increased import competition from growing economies around the world, have kept the ITC from thriving. Its decisions remain controversial, its investigations tend to be drawn out, and emotional and political appeals have often interfered with its performance. At the heart of these difficulties is the age-old partisan argument between protectionists and free traders.

CURRENT POLITICAL ISSUES

Traditionally trade issues in the United States have involved a two-way split between protectionists (those who wanted to protect American businesses from foreign competition by implementing heavy tariffs and other trade barriers) and free traders (those who believed in the right of all people to trade freely across international borders). In the late twentieth century, these issues became much more complicated. Trade sanctions now are often argued for moral reasons by both liberals and conservatives alike, over issues such as human rights violations or environmental destruction by foreign governments. Though the ITC is not a policy-making body and cannot negotiate trade agreements, it is a powerful resource of ideas and facts concerning issues of international trade. Frequently, however, the objective findings of the ITC are disregarded when trade matters become a political issue.

Few people disagree that there are certain situations in which a protectionist stance is appropriate—against goods produced by slave labor, for example, or in the case of trade that aids an enemy who directly threatens the nation's security. However, the argument that trade sanctions can help force a foreign government become more civil and democratized has been criticized by people of all political persuasions. The arguments against trade sanctions are that they further isolate societies and therefore strengthen the government's control and that the denial of trade to foreign manufacturers and businessmen is in itself a violation of a natural human right.

Critics of trade sanctions and other protectionist practices point to two examples for support. The 1991 fall of the Soviet Union and the democratization of the newly independent states, they argue, would not have happened without U.S. engagement with the Soviet economy, or without the network of U.S.-manufactured computers, copiers, and fax machines that helped circumvent the government's control over the flow of information. These countries became democratized because they were exposed to, and desired, the freedoms they saw in the Western world.

After much discussion about possible trade sanctions against the harsh dictatorial government of China, a society similarly isolated from the world and one where political dissidents are often imprisoned for long periods, the administration of President Clinton decided in 1994 to sever the connection between China's trade status and its record on human rights. The president was careful to explain that the reason for this was not because Americans did not care about human rights, but because the administration believed the best way to secure the long-term opening of the Chinese government was to allow the economy and civilized society to lead the way through an active free-market exchange. More contact with the outside world, the president argued, was the way in which China would become a more democratically governed country.

Case Study: The Helms-Burton Act

In 1995 conservative congressmen Jesse Helms (R-N.C.) and Dan Burton (R-Ind.) introduced a bill that would formalize U.S. trade sanctions against Cuba, a country that had long suffered under a U.S. trade embargo against the Communist regime of Fidel Castro. The bill's provisions included the right to deny U.S. visas to executives or shareholders of businesses investing in property that had belonged to U.S. companies before the Communist takeover of Cuba. It also proposed to grant Cuban Americans exiled from Cuba the right to sue, in U.S. federal courts, foreign companies doing business on land once owned by these exiles.

Supporters of the bill claimed that those investing in Cuba were helping to prop up a corrupt and abusive regime while exploiting poor Cuban workers. They also pointed out that the bill did not propose to stop investment in Cuba; it merely stopped those investors from doing business in the United States. The unspoken idea behind the bill was to undermine Cuba's financial recovery, resulting in the collapse of the Castro regime and the introduction of freedom and democracy to an oppressed people.

Opponents, however, argued that the bill's actual consequences would be much different; the bill would further impoverish Cuban workers, who would resent the United States for it, not Castro; it would isolate Cuba and play into the hands of Castro by allowing him greater control of Cuban society; and it would not allow the U.S. government or economic communities to position themselves to influence the future democratic development of Cuba. If Congress had asked, the ITC could have performed studies that would have revealed as much—but, critics said, the bill was a transparent attempt to bypass the normal procedures for researching and forming U.S. trade policy. Furthermore, they charged, the bill's supporters were aware of these probable results and had strategically introduced the bill just prior to the 1996 elections, in order to enhance the Republican reputation for being tough on Communism.

But perhaps the most vocal criticism came from foreign countries that were traditional U.S. allies—countries such as Mexico, France, Canada, and Great Britain, who were angered at the sudden possibility of having their industries sued by Cuban Americans. They complained that they had not been consulted about the contents of the bill and that it effectively made foreign and domestic policy decisions for the entire world. Most of these countries argued, also, that engagement, not isolating sanctions, was the best way to reform the Cuban government.

FUTURE DIRECTIONS

One of the most significant recent events in U.S. trade has been the 1995 formation of the World Trade Organization (WTO) at the Uruguay Round of GATT discussions. The discussions of the Uruguay Round produced 22,500 pages listing international commitments to lowering tariffs and a number of agreements concerning the import of goods, services, and intellectual property. The ITC recognizes that the agreements reached at the Uruguay Round will significantly increase the workload of the ITC staff. Faced with budget restrictions, the commission intends to reassess its investigative processes thoroughly and revise those procedures frequently to increase the efficiency of responses to Uruguay Round agreements.

Specifically, the ITC intends to establish "critical success indicators" for its investigative practices, which will target their cost-effectiveness for the agency and the public. As part of these reforms, the agency plans to identify the maximum time allowable for commissioners to make decisions on studies and to periodically decide whether functions in the investigative process should be retained, streamlined, or eliminated altogether.

AGENCY RESOURCES

Inquiries about the commission should be directed to the appropriate bureau or to the Secretary, ITC, 500 E St. SW, Washington, DC 20436; phone (202) 205-2000. The commission also conducts a fax-on-demand service for copies of *Federal Register* notices, news releases, meeting agendas, monthly calendars, general information "fact sheets," and schedules of pending investigations. The number for the service is (202) 205-2023. News releases, the commission's annual report, and general information about the ITC are also available through the public affairs officer at (202) 205-1819.

The ITC's site on the World Wide Web at http://www.usitc.gov is an excellent resource for those seeking information about the commission's activities. The site contains an index and description of major commission and record systems—with instructions for accessing them on-line—as well as links to other sites related to international trade.

AGENCY PUBLICATIONS

The commission publishes reports on the results of its investigations, some of which are available for downloading from the ITC Web site at http://www.usitc.gov. Other publications include *Industry and Trade Summaries*, an annual report to Congress on the conduct of the trade agreements program. Specific information about these publications can be obtained from the Office of the Secretary, ITC, 500 E St. SW, Washington, DC 20436; phone (202) 205-2000.

Two of the commission's operational bureaus publish their own periodicals. The *International Economic Review* is a monthly staff publication of the Office of Economics intended to keep the commission informed about significant developments in international economics and trade, as well as to provide technical information and advice on international trade matters to U.S. policymakers. The Office of Industries publishes a quarterly staff publication, the *Industry, Trade, and Technology Review*, analyzing important issues and providing insight into the global position of U.S. industries and the technological competitiveness of the United States. Some issues of these publications are available for downloading at the ITC Web site; for more specific information, contact the publishing office.

BIBLIOGRAPHY

Analytical and Negotiating Issues in the Global Trading System. Ann Arbor: University of Michigan Press, 1994.

Bernhardt, Joshua. *The Tariff Commission: Its History, Activities and Organization*. New York: AMS Press, 1981.

Bovard, James. *The Fair Trade Fraud*. New York: St. Martin's Press, 1991.

Butler, David Alan. *Does "Independent" Mean "Free from Influence?": Escape Clause Decision Making at the United States International Trade Commission*. New York: Garland Publishing, 1995.

Economic Effects of Antidumping and Countervailing Duty Orders and Suspension Agreements. Upland, Pennsylvania: DIANE Publishing Company, 1995.

The GATT, the WTO and the Uruguay Round Agreements Act: Understanding the Fundamental Changes. New York: Practising Law Institute, 1994.

Gould, David M. "Will Fair Trade Diminish Free Trade?" *Business Economics*, April 1997, pp. 7–15.

Lorentzen, Ronald K. "Subsidies and Countervailing Measures." *Business America*, January 1994, pp. 13–14.

Mueller, David. "Antidumping." *Business America*, January 1994, pp. 15–16.

"A Political Football Called Trade." *Business Week*, 14 April 1997, p. 118.

"Retreating on the Trade Pact." *New York Times*, 27 July 1994, p. A18.

"The Uruguay Round of Trade Negotiations." *Congressional Digest*, November 1994, pp. 264–66.

Wolf, Julie. "EU Panel Moves Against U.S. Rules on Textile Imports." *Wall Street Journal*, 29 November 1996, p. B3A.

United States Marine Corps (USMC)

PARENT ORGANIZATION: Department of the Navy
ESTABLISHED: November 10, 1775
EMPLOYEES: 216,000 including reserve personnel

Contact Information:

ADDRESS: 2 Navy Annex
Washington, DC 20380
PHONE: (703) 614-2334
FAX: (703) 614-2182
URL: http://www.usmc.mil
COMMANDANT: Gen. Charles C. Krulak
ASSISTANT COMMANDANT: Gen. Richard I. Neal

WHAT IS ITS MISSION?

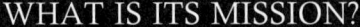

The United States Marine Corps (USMC), as a service within the Department of the Navy, shares the navy's primary mission: to protect the United States by the effective prosecution of war at sea. The Marine Corps has a specific function within the navy. It serves to coordinate and carry out the navy's seizure or defense of advance naval bases and to conduct any land operations necessary to the execution of a naval campaign.

HOW IS IT STRUCTURED?

The Marine Corps, along with the Operating Forces of the Navy, is a service force within the Department of the Navy. Although the Marine Corps is considerably smaller in size than the navy's Operating Forces, its important function in naval operations places its chief administrator, the commandant of the Marine Corps, in a position equal in stature to that of the chief of naval operations. Both are members of the Joint Chiefs of Staff and in the defense chain of command report to the secretary of defense. At Marine Corps headquarters, the Office of the Commandant is assisted in its administrative functions by five important divisions: Public Affairs (PA); Manpower and Reserve Affairs (M & RA); Installations and Logistics (I & L); Safety (SD); and Command, Control, Communication, Computer, and Intelligence (C4I).

The corps is further composed of the Operating Forces and the Supporting Establishment. The Operating Forces consist of the Fleet Marine Force Pacific, the Fleet Marine Force Atlantic, the Marine Corps Reserve,

Marine Security Forces, and Marine Detachments Afloat. The units the corps deploys for combat are known as marine air ground task forces (MAGTFs). There are four types of MAGTFs, each with a command element, a ground combat element, an aviation combat element, and a combat service support element. The size and specific organization of an MAGTF is determined by the task to be accomplished. The smallest and most common type of MAGTF is the marine expeditionary unit (MEU). An MEU has a total strength of about 2,200 personnel and is employed to fulfill routine forward deployments with fleets in the Mediterranean, the Pacific, and occasionally the Atlantic and Indian Oceans.

The Supporting Establishment of the Marine Corps includes recruiting activities, training installations, reserve support activities, ground and aviation installations, and logistics bases. The facilities at which these functions are carried out are spread across the country and in certain other parts of the world, but much of recruitment and training activity is centered at Parris Island, South Carolina, home of the Marine Corps Recruit Depot.

FAST FACTS

The motto of the Marine Corps is Semper Fidelis, which is Latin for "always faithful." Prior to its adoption in 1883, the marines had three mottoes: Fortitudine, By Land and Sea, and To the Shores of Tripoli.

(Source: U.S. Marine Corps. "Did You Know?" Marine Corps News Release, 1997.)

PRIMARY FUNCTIONS

The Marine Corps is organized, trained, and equipped to provide Fleet Marine Forces and their supporting air components for service with the navy in seizure or defense of advance naval bases and for the conduct of land operations essential to a naval campaign. In addition to this fundamental mission, the corps provides detachments for service on armed vessels of the navy and provides security detachments for the protection of property at naval stations and bases.

In coordination with the army and the air force, the corps plans and develops amphibious operations that pertain to the activity and equipment of landing forces. It is responsible, in accordance with the integrated joint mobilization plans, for the expansion of peacetime marine components to meet the needs of war.

The corps has a unique status among branches of the military—to be used "in such cases as the President may direct." This standing ensures that in most cases when an international emergency arises in a foreign country, and in which U.S. forces are deemed necessary to resolve it, it is the marines who are sent in first—and sometimes the only forces employed. In the 1990s alone, marines have been sent to resolve crises in several African countries, including Somalia and Rwanda; Bosnia; Caribbean nations such as Cuba and Haiti; and areas in and around the Persian Gulf.

PROGRAMS

Marine Corps programs vary in scope from the very numerous and specific developments of weapons, aircraft, watercraft, equipment, and systems to initiatives such as the recent Marine Corps Continuous Process Improvement Program (MCCPIP). Implemented by the commandant after a 1995 analysis of marine administrative processes such as resource allocation, human resource development, infrastructure management, and operational planning (in Marine Corps terminology, "the business enterprise") the MCCPIP revealed some upsetting facts: more than one functional organization often claimed responsibility for overseeing some processes, and none claimed ultimate responsibility for the important function of information management. The MCCPIP is a comprehensive overhaul of the Marine Corps business enterprise, designed to clearly apportion responsibility in order to avoid duplicating efforts and inefficiency, while integrating resources to streamline and simplify processes.

Most Marine Corps programs, however, are not as far-reaching. The Combat Identification Program, for example, has one simple and concrete goal: to identify armor units as "friend or foe" in order to prevent fratricide or "friendly fire." The system consists basically of a precise narrow-beam antenna that gives gunners or commanders a visual or audio signal identifying potential targets under all climatic conditions. A program of the C4I, the Reserve Cryptologic Program trains and provides marine reserves highly skilled in cryptology (code breaking) to respond to marine and national intelligence requirements in war and peacetime.

BUDGET INFORMATION

Because it is directly included in the budget for the entire U.S. Navy, many components of the Marine Corps budget, such as family housing or base realignment, are entirely integrated with Navy expenditures, and are impossible to isolate as strictly "Marine Corps" expenses.

The most significant parts of the Marine Corps budget are clear, however; each year, the Marine Corps spends a little over $6.5 billion annually organizing, training, and outfitting its Corps and Reserve personnel. Operating and maintaining the Corps and Reserves costs about $2.4 billion. Procurement of items such as weapons, aircraft, ships, and other systems account for about $374 million of the Marine Corps budget.

HISTORY

The Marine Corps traces its origins to November 10, 1775, when two battalions of "marines" were authorized by the Continental Congress to serve in the American Revolution (1775–83) against Great Britain. Later, the ratified Constitution allowed for the buildup of an army and navy, and with this navy came the first organization officially named the Marine Corps, in July 11, 1798.

In its earliest years, the Marine Corps existed to police the ship on which its members served, in order to keep order among crews who often spoke several different languages. In battle, marines took to the "fighting tops" (ship's masts) with their muskets, providing fire to harass enemy cannoneers. The marines' training also qualified them to serve in an expeditionary fashion in ships' landing parties. Early conflicts in which the marines served in this capacity were the French conflict of 1799 to 1800, the Tripolitan War (1801–1805), and the War of 1812.

A Changing Role

Both the North and South employed marines during the American Civil War (1860–65) , serving primarily in the ships of their respective navies. The marines mostly performed guard duties, but some did take part in action ashore. Toward the end of the nineteenth century, however, the introduction of steam propulsion and modern gunnery caused some to question the need for marine detachments. One of the marines' initial functions was to serve as sharpshooters in the masts of the ships. Such close-quarters sea battles were obsolete now, and the navy, now an established, disciplined force in its own right, resented the idea that its ships needed to be policed. This controversy has extended to this day, with many people arguing that the marines should be taken off navy ships and based ashore to serve as a readily transportable expeditionary force. Others believe that the marines should disappear altogether to be absorbed into the army, whose missions the marines at times appear to duplicate.

Marine detachments, nevertheless, continued to prove valuable to the navy. In 1894 Congress assigned the corps one of the duties it still bears today—to provide fleet infantry, or ground expeditionary forces, to establish and defend advance bases for the navy. Throughout the early twentieth century, the marines provided this service in a number of "police actions" throughout Latin America and the Caribbean.

During World War I (1914–18), a quickly mobilized marine brigade, deployed overseas for service in France, distinguished itself in combat and earned the respect of its German enemies. The German soldiers called the marines "Teufel Hunden," or "devil dogs." After Armistice Day, the marines took part in the occupation of Germany.

A Growing Corps

Schools and training programs established in the wake of World War I permitted the corps to concentrate almost solely on developing amphibious assault techniques and fortifying advanced bases. Marines were on duty from the Philippines to Pearl Harbor when the Japanese began their attacks on American, British, and Dutch outposts in the Pacific. Although beaten at Guam and Wake in 1941 and at Corregidor in 1942, the marines took part in the epic defense of Midway and achieved the first major assault landing of the Pacific campaign at Guadalcanal in the summer of 1942. Through a succession of landings, ending with the conquests of Iwo Jima and Okinawa in 1945, the marines figured prominently in the Pacific theater. By the end of World War II (1939–45), the Marine Corps had grown to a peak strength of more than 485,000.

Part of this numerical strength was found in the Women's Reserve, which had been formed in July 1942. As the first women ever to be enlisted in the marines, members of the reserve served at shore establishments to free men for combat duty. When it became clear that the Pacific theater would involve many long, drawn-out battles, the Marine Corps Women's Reserve grew substantially. About 20,000 women joined the marines during the war. On June 12, 1948, Congress passed legislation that gave women regular military status in each of the armed forces.

Although many critics claimed after World War II that amphibious landings were a thing of the past, the marines disproved this at the onset of the Korean War (1950–53) with a daring landing at Inchon, North Korea. Korea was also the proving ground for a new concept—"vertical envelopment." The use of helicopters in the Korean War for purposes such as reconnaissance, supply, transport, communication, and evacuation functions was a sign of things to come.

In 1965 the first marine brigade was sent to South Vietnam, the beginning of a large-scale marine involvement in the Vietnam War (1959–75). Marines were used throughout the conflict as mobile forces capable of striking from land, sea, or air (supported by Marine helicopters and other forces), until the withdrawal of American ground forces in 1970 and 1971. Marines were involved in several international police actions throughout the 1970s but found their presence resented in many places; in 1984, 241 American service personnel—220 of them marines—were killed in the bombing of the 24th

Marine Amphibious Unit Headquarters in Beirut, Lebanon.

In 1990 the marines also took part in Operation Just Cause, a joint operation to overthrow the regime of Panama's dictator, Manual Noriega, and restore democracy. In their largest conflict of the 1990s, the Persian Gulf War (1991), the marines participated in Operation Desert Storm, a joint operation to retake the independent nation of Kuwait from its conqueror, Iraq. The ground maneuvers of Operation Desert Storm lasted only four days, but 22 marines lost their lives.

CURRENT POLITICAL ISSUES

The marines are sometimes called "America's 911 force" because they are the nation's forward-deployed response team, ever ready to respond to crisis situations. As a result, many marines are stationed overseas in defense complexes that exist by treaty, most notably in Europe and Japan, according to security treaties signed after World War II.

Defense bases and U.S. military personnel are not always welcome by native populations overseas for a number of reasons. Most bases involve aircraft maneuvers and are therefore noisy installations that take much land out of the hands of the local people. Many people simply resent the oversight of a foreign nation and the intrusion of foreign nationals into their territory and culture.

Case Study: Okinawa

U.S. occupation of the Japanese island of Okinawa was made official by security treaty in 1951 but had begun immediately following World War II. From the beginning there were problems with the behavior of U.S. soldiers; in a six-month period in 1948, U.S. soldiers committed 29 murders, 18 rapes, 16 robberies, and 33 assaults. Many of these crimes were committed against the host population of Okinawa. Between 1953 and 1956 the marines, using armed troops, removed Okinawan farmers from their homes and then bulldozed the land to make runways for B-52 bombers—the planes used for countless bombing missions during the Vietnam War. The treaties signed by the United States and its conquered enemy, Japan, virtually gave the island of Okinawa to the United States.

In 1960, as the security treaty was being revised by President Dwight D. Eisenhower, serious anti-American rioting took place in Japan and the president was forced to cancel a trip to Okinawa. In 1972 the United States returned Okinawa to Japan—but the military bases, which now covered much of the island, remained. Over 75 percent of all U.S. bases in Japan were crammed onto the island. Most Okinawans had always been opposed to this occupation, but the island was populated largely by poor, rural people with little political power. In 1990, when Okinawans elected Masahide Ota as governor on his platform of getting all Okinawan bases back from the United States by 2015, not much attention was paid by either the Japanese leadership or the American military, who had heard anti-American slogans in such campaigns before.

Three marines dramatically changed all of that on September 4, 1995, when they abducted and raped a 12-year-old Okinawa schoolgirl. The largest Japanese protest against U.S. bases since the 1960s soon followed, and Governor Ota increased pressure on the Japanese government. Within a year, the United States had agreed to hand back more than one-fifth of the land it was leasing on Okinawa, closing 11 bases—among them the Futenma Marine Air Station, which was home to the marines charged with rape.

It was not long, however, before the old patterns in Japanese-U.S. relations began to reemerge. In April 1996, the United States asserted its intention to maintain forward bases in Japan and neighboring South Korea; it considered them "the cornerstone for achieving common security objectives." Critics of this strategy have charged that the real reason the United States is determined to retain a military presence in Asia is because it wants to keep an eye on Japan and its neighbors; at least one of the Okinawa bases housed a listening station for the National Security Agency, a U.S. military spy agency.

In Tokyo, some unspoken truths about the U.S.-Japanese relationship became obvious. While Japan continued to spend very little on its defense budget, it continued to drive up huge trade surpluses with the United States, which was largely bankrolling its defense. Even the Okinawans, many of whom lost jobs during the 1996 closings, began to recognize their dependence on the U.S. bases. Although 90 percent of all Okinawans wanted all the bases closed in the wake of the rape, only 14 to 23 percent insisted on this a year later.

SUCCESSES AND FAILURES

In 1997 the Marine Corps Reserve marked the 50th anniversary of one of its best-known programs: Toys for Tots. The marines' premier community action program began in 1947 when Marine Corps Reserve Major Bill Hendricks could not find a charitable organization in his home city of Los Angeles that would deliver his gift donations to needy children. With the permission of his commanding officer, Hendricks and a few fellow marine reservists launched the first Toys for Tots campaign, collecting nearly five thousand donated toys and distributing them among children of the Los Angeles area. The success of their first campaign brought much public attention, and the next year the program was expanded into a national campaign. Since 1947, more than 112 million children across America have received donated gifts through the program, carried out by Marine Corps reservists and community volunteers.

FUTURE DIRECTIONS

In the summer of 1995 Commandant Charles C. Krulak composed and released a comprehensive memorandum, "Commandant's Planning Guidance," to be distributed to all Marine Corps personnel. The Commandant's Planning Guidance, or CPG, is the commandant's outline for the strategic direction for the Marine Corps. The CPG notes several issues that will affect the corps in the future: a changing global economy, changes in weapons and weapons accessibility, increasing urbanization, reduced access to land bases overseas, and increasing cultural and religious conflict, among others. The commandant stressed the need to adapt to these changes and outlined a number of adjustments to be made by the Marine Corps. The corps of the future will have to become the world's premier crisis response force, ready to project the power and influence of the United States from the sea to any foreign shore.

Many of the specifics of the CPG have not yet been implemented, but one of the first changes to be made has been in the recruitment and training of new marines, and it reflects the commandant's belief that societal changes have made the transformation of recruits into marines more difficult. Beginning in 1996 all marine recruits were required to face additional instruction. Known as "the Crucible," the added 54 hours of training are designed to promote teamwork and confidence, better prepare recruits to overcome physical and mental challenges, and make them good followers as well as promising potential leaders. The commandant warned that the added training would be very difficult and would probably become the defining moment in a marine's life.

AGENCY RESOURCES

For general inquiries about the Marine Corps, contact the Division of Public Affairs at (703) 614-1492. Other information about the U.S. Navy and the Marine Corps is available from the Navy Department Library, located at the Naval Historical Center, Washington Navy Yard Bldg. 44, 901 M St. SE, Washington, DC 20374; phone (202) 433-4132. The library's collection includes historic documents and manuscripts, and information on shipbuilding, navigation, and naval customs and traditions; stations, yards, and bases. The Navy Department Library has a searchable Web site at http://navy.library.net.

Another valuable on-line source of information is NavyOnLine, the "technical gateway" to the navy's other on-line resources, some of which are related to the Marine Corps. NavyOnLine is on the World Wide Web at http://www.ncts.navy.mil/nol.

AGENCY PUBLICATIONS

Other than *Marines* magazine, the official periodical of the Marine Corps, and a few brief informational publications available through recruitment centers, most of the Marine Corps' publications consist of handbooks and technical manuals that are intended for personnel. The Marine Corps Association publishes two magazines, the *Marine Corps Gazette* and *Leatherneck,* which provide a forum (mostly for marines and ex-marines) for the discussion of issues and the relating of marine experiences. For further information about Marine Corps publications, contact the Division of Public Affairs at (703) 614-1492.

BIBLIOGRAPHY

Gerson, Joseph. "Go-Banken-Sama, Go Home." *Bulletin of the Atomic Scientists*, July/August 1996, pp. 22–9.

Gleick, Elizabeth. "Marine Blood Sports." *Time*, 10 February 1997, p. 30.

Hackworth, David. H. "How to Make a Real Warrior." *Newsweek*, 4 September 1995, p. 28.

Janofsky, Michael. "Women in the Marines Join the Firing Line." *New York Times*, 1 April 1997, p. A8.

Krulak, Victor H. *First to Fight: An Inside View of the U. S. Marine Corps.* Annapolis, Md.: Naval Institute Press, 1984.

The Marine Corps: A Handbook. New York: Gordon Press, 1991.

Marutollo, Frank. *Organizational Behavior in the Marine Corps: Three Interpretations.* Westport, Conn.: Greenwood Publishing Group, 1990.

Millett, Allan Reed. *Semper Fidelis: The History of the United States Marine Corps.* New York: Macmillan, 1980.

Newman, Richard J. "The Few, the Proud, the Smart, the Moral." *U.S. News and World Report*, 16 December 1996, pp. 33–4.

Smith, Patrick. "Japan Debased." *The Nation*, 19 May 1997, pp. 5–6.

Thompson, Mark. "Boot Camp Goes Soft." *Time*, 4 August 1997, pp. 20–3.

Verhovek, Sam Howe. "In Marine's Killing of Teen-ager, Town Mourns and Wonders Why." *New York Times*, 29 June 1997, p. 1.

United States Marshals Service (USMS)

PARENT ORGANIZATION: Department of Justice
ESTABLISHED: 1789
EMPLOYEES: 4,408

Contact Information:

ADDRESS: 600 Army-Navy Dr.
Arlington, VA 22202
PHONE: (703) 307-9065
FAX: (202) 307-9177
URL: http://www.usdoj.gov/marshals
DIRECTOR: Eduardo Gonzalez

WHAT IS ITS MISSION?

The stated mission of the United States Marshals Service (USMS) "is to protect the federal courts and ensure the effective operation of the judicial system." The USMS does this in communities throughout the country by enforcing federal laws and carrying out the orders of judges, the Congress, and the president.

HOW IS IT STRUCTURED?

The USMS falls within the Department of Justice. It is headed by a director who is appointed by the president and is made up of seven main divisions: Business Services, Executive Services, Human Resources, Investigative Services, Judicial Security, Management and Budget, and Prisoner Services. Under these divisions are 95 district offices and 154 nationwide suboffices. One marshal is assigned to each district who in turn hires deputy marshals to assist him. The majority of USMS employees—approximately 4,000—work in the field, while the remainder are located in the main headquarters in Arlington, Virginia. In addition to their law enforcement responsibilities, many marshals and deputy marshals perform administrative and office duties. They are involved in such tasks as running the bureaucracy of the agency, handling budgets, hiring and firing personnel, and more. As in any other large government agency, employees come from varied educational backgrounds.

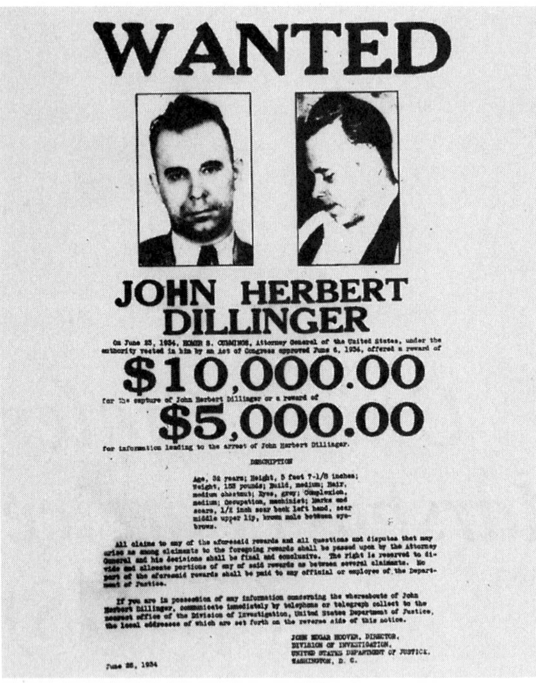

John Herbert Dillinger was one of many elusive gangsters of the early 1930s. The USMS works with other federal law enforcement agencies to track down the criminals on the Justice Department's "Most Wanted" lists. (Corbis-Bettmann)

PRIMARY FUNCTIONS

The marshals of the USMS and their deputies perform a variety of functions specifically for the federal courts, located for the most part within local judicial districts throughout the United States. The USMS serves "subpoenas, summonses, writs, warrants, and other processes issued by the courts"; makes arrests and handles prisoners; and handles the money to pay "the fees and expenses of the court clerks, U.S. attorneys, jurors, and witnesses."

The USMS has seven major programs:

1. *Prisoner Transport.* Under a program called the National Prisoner Transportation System (NPTS), the USMS handles the movement of prisoners throughout the country as is demanded by the needs of the federal court system.
2. *Prisoner Custody.* The USMS takes custody of any individuals arrested by federal agencies who must be directed through the system prior to being sentenced or found guilty. This workload is approximately 20,000 unsentenced prisoners per day in more than 1,000 federal, state, and local jails nationwide.
3. *Investigation and Apprehension of Federal Fugitives.* The USMS conducts investigations involving escaped prisoners who are usually awaiting trial or in the process of trial. USMS investigations usually concern parole issues, probation, or defaulting on bond.
4. *Court Security.* U.S. marshals protect members of the court system such as judges, witnesses, jurors, and officers of the court. This duty sometimes includes protection outside the courts when necessary. There are more than 2,000 federal court officers as well as more than 700 court locations nationwide.
5. *Asset Forfeiture.* Under current federal law, marshals are permitted to seize property and goods bought with the proceeds from illegal drug trafficking and organized crime activities. The USMS then manages these assets and sells them to the public. Profits from these transactions are then used to finance their expenses and are shared with other law enforcement agencies to help finance their activities as well.
6. *Witness Security.* The USMS protects witnesses who are endangered by their testimony in criminal cases. Since 1971 more than 6,000 witnesses and their families have been relocated and given new identities with which to continue their lives under the Witness Security Program (WITSEC).
7. *Special Operations and Programs.* The Special Operations Group (SOG) is an emergency response team trained in special weapons and tactics in order to handle unusual situations. The marshals in this area of expertise are highly trained in specific skills and are on-call 24 hours a day.

The duties of the USMS have expanded with the growing complexity of federal laws since the USMS began in the 1700s. Many crimes or investigations of crimes overlap with the jurisdictions of other law enforcement agencies such as the Federal Bureau of Investigation (FBI) or local police forces and the USMS has an unusually broad jurisdiction in an array of situations. The USMS also has the specific responsibility to carry out orders from the president or Congress. Because of its broad mandate and jurisdiction, the USMS is regularly called upon to perform unusual tasks and to be involved in many special operations. Some of these unique situations have included the sealing of borders against armed invasion; the capturing of runaway slaves in the 1800s; investigating incidents of terrorism and hostage-taking; and the exchange of spies with the former Soviet Union.

PROGRAMS

The USMS operates a number of programs, from the worldwide pursuit of the most dangerous fugitives to protecting nuclear missiles while they are being transported. The USMS must apprehend fugitives, bring them into the court system, and provide them with transportation, housing, and food. Within the court system the USMS must protect federal judges, officials, witnesses, and jurors against any threats, and they must maintain order within courtrooms and courthouses. In addition, they must carry out any special orders or operations assigned to them by Congress, the courts, or the president, and they must inform the public about their mission by providing education and training.

One public awareness program is the "Top 15 Most Wanted Fugitives" list. This list identifies the fugitives the USMS is seeking and is displayed in post offices, on television, and on the Internet. In addition, the agency operates "Operation Gunsmoke," a periodic 10-week program which is an intensive worldwide manhunt for the nation's most dangerous fugitives. The USMS coordinates many agencies in this program to seek out and apprehend the most wanted fugitives throughout the world.

The Witness Security Program (WITSEC) protects any witnesses that are in danger because of their testimony in a criminal case. The USMS has protected more than 6,000 witnesses since 1971, sometimes by relocating and even inventing entirely new identities for the witnesses and their families.

The Missile Escort Program helps the Department of State and the U.S. Air Force transport Minuteman and cruise missiles from one military facility to another using the marshals' extensive prisoner transport system already in place.

BUDGET:

United States Marshals Service

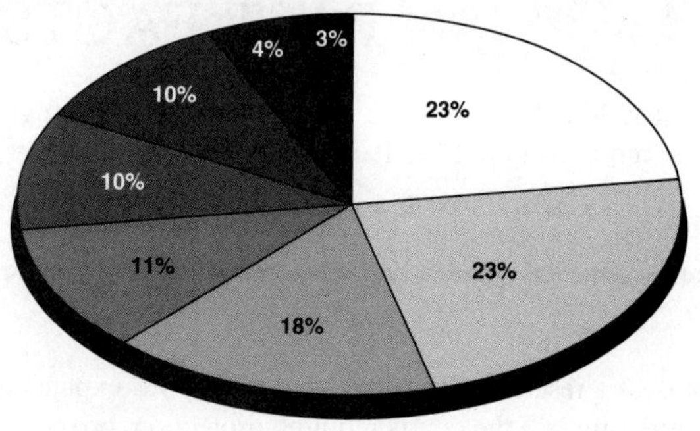

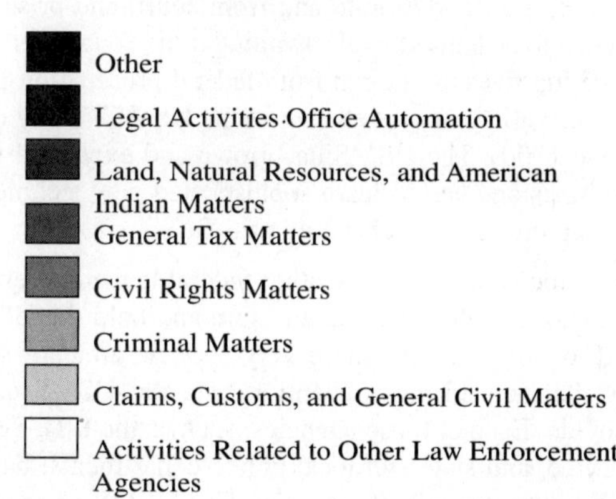

BUDGET INFORMATION

In 1998 the USMS budget was approximately $595 million. Since many of the duties of the USMS overlap with and aid other law enforcement agencies; of this total, $138 million (23 percent) was contributed from the budgets of many other agencies. These included the INS and Bureau of Prisons for the transportation of illegal immigrants and prisoners and the U.S. Air Force for the role the USMS plays in the transportation of weapons in the Intercontinental Ballistic Missile Program.

Of the estimated $457 million appropriated by Congress directly to the USMS in 1998, most of it was allocated to claims, customs, and general civil matters (23 percent of the total USMS budget). The rest of the USMS funds were allocated to criminal matters (16 percent); civil rights matters (11 percent); general tax matters (10 percent); land, natural resources, and American Indian matters (10 percent); and legal activities office automation (4 percent). The remaining 3 percent of the USMS budget was distributed among Interpol, conduct of Supreme Court proceedings, and review of appellate, and legal opinions.

HISTORY

The United States Marshals Service is the nation's oldest law enforcement agency. It was created by the first Congress in the Judiciary Act of 1789. At that time, George Washington and the members of the first Congress discovered a problem with the government as established by the Constitution: the federal government was located in one place and it had no way to administer and enforce the laws it created in distant areas. An organization was needed to enforce federal laws and administer and maintain the federal courts in distant states. The USMS was thus created to be the federal government's representatives among the civilian population of the frontier and outlying states.

At first federal laws were few and simple and the states made and enforced their own laws. Most of the marshals' duties in the 1800s involved accounting for funds used to operate the courts. They would also deliver arrest warrants, and subpoenas requiring people to show up at a trial in order to be a witness. Until 1870 marshals were usually paid by the task.

Eventually, however, as the country grew and became more complicated, the federal government created more laws that needed to be enforced, and federal courts could be found throughout the country in every

FAST FACTS

The Marshals arrest 55 percent of all federal fugitives, more than all other federal agencies combined.

(Source: United States Marshals Service, 1998.)

state. As a result the jurisdiction of the USMS expanded accordingly. All the courts required protection, prisoners required transportation to and from court, and prisoners needed to be housed while awaiting trial. Today there are more fugitives on the run from federal prosecution for a greater variety of crimes than in the USMS's early days in the 1700s. The USMS has grown and expanded with the times and had to learn sophisticated new techniques for finding and apprehending criminals.

Since the early days, other federal law enforcement agencies have been created to join and help the USMS and to further police other very specific areas of society that needed more attention than the USMS could provide. Each of these agencies, such as the FBI, Secret Service, and state and local police departments, has its own particular area of expertise. The USMS often combines forces and works with these other law enforcement agencies.

The USMS continues to be the enforcement liaison between the federal government and the people and to be charged specifically with supporting the daily duties of the federal courts: issuing warrants, handling the funds to maintain the courts, protecting jurors, transporting prisoners, and protecting witnesses.

CURRENT POLITICAL ISSUES

One of the main obstacles to stopping illegal drug trafficking is the enormous cost of operating law enforcement programs. The government needs the latest technologies and an adequate number of law enforcement officers in order to fight the battle against drug traffickers but it must compete with the criminals who are making huge profits from their illegal activities and can afford whatever they need. As a result many cities and states, especially throughout the 1980s, have not been able to afford to enforce the laws. Drug traffickers have had the advantage and law enforcement officials across the nation have been accused of losing the war on drugs.

Case Study: Asset Seizure and Forfeiture Program

In the effort to meet this challenge the USMS began the Asset Seizure and Forfeiture Program in 1984 under a congressional program that specifically targeted drug trafficking. The program gave the USMS and other law enforcement agencies the power to seize all property and money involved in suspected illegal drug activity. These assets are then sold to the public and the USMS uses the money to pay part of its operating expenses. Some of the money is also shared with other federal law enforcement agencies and with state and local law enforcement. Since 1986 more than $1 billion has been given to state and local agencies.

Proponents of the program have claimed that this large amount of revenue is proof of the program's success and produces funds for fighting crime. They claim that criminals are driven out of business if they have no money with which to operate. They further claim that this financial punishment is even more of a deterrent than jail time. For example, in Greer, South Carolina, the Greenville County sheriff's department seized a large tract of wooded land from a local heroin dealer, convicted him and transformed his seized assets and land into a law enforcement training center for local, state, and federal officers, that included amenities such as a shooting range and a training course for high-speed driving.

Opponents have agreed that this extra funding is beneficial, but they argue that the program is badly flawed. Often innocent individuals are harmed when law enforcement officials act on anonymous tips to confiscate property on the basis of little solid evidence or information. Marshals commonly seize boats, cars, homes, and entire businesses, and the owners must then prove to the government that they are innocent—the opposite of the normal judicial process, which maintains that we are innocent until proven guilty. This proof of innocence can be so time consuming and expensive that the average citizen cannot afford to go through the legal process needed to reclaim seized property.

In 1989 a Connecticut couple, the Cwiklas, suddenly had their home seized because federal agents claimed their garage had once been used for a short time to store the drugs of a known marijuana trafficker. The couple, however, insisted they were innocent, and that they knew nothing about it. No drugs were ever found, and the Cwiklas were not charged with drug trafficking, but because of the tip agents had received, their property was still subject to seizure. For years the Cwiklas spent all their money and time trying to get back their possessions, and the government finally agreed to settle if they would admit guilt and pay a $25,000 fine. The Cwiklas refused, and the effort to ultimately prove their innocence left them nearly destitute. Though proponents admit that such cases have occurred, they claim they are rare and highly exaggerated.

The result of this controversy is that some members of Congress have taken up the cause of citizens who have lost everything due to mistaken asset seizures. Representatives argue for amendments to the program, but there is little support for abolishing it altogether. In 1997 the USMS was managing more than $1.6 billion in assets seized under this program.

FUTURE DIRECTIONS

The USMS is seeking congressional passage of the Marshals Service Improvement Act, which would reorganize how the USMS is administered and how marshals are selected. Currently each district selects its own marshal, usually based on political allegiances. The USMS wishes to reorganize so that through a "comprehensive and highly competitive assessment process" the centralized federal headquarters will select the marshals for each district, eliminating local political influences. The new selection process will identify federal officers who are more in agreement with and are more easily controlled by overall USMS policy.

AGENCY RESOURCES

The USMS operates a Web site at http://www.usdoj.gov/marshals. Further information about the agency may be obtained by writing USMS, 600 Army-Navy Dr., Arlington, VA 22202, or by calling (202) 307-9000. Those interested in careers in the USMS can find further information at the local district offices or at the USMS Web site at http://www.usdoj.gov/marshals/contacts.html.

AGENCY PUBLICATIONS

Publications about the USMS can be obtained from the Office of Public Affairs, 600 Army-Navy Dr., Arlington, VA 22202, or by calling (202) 307-9065. The agency also publishes a list of the 15 most wanted fugitives. This list can be obtained by calling the Office of Public Affairs or at http://www.usdoj.gov/marshals/wanted/wanted.html. The agency also publishes a regularly updated list of assets available for purchase by the public. This list can be obtained free by calling 1-800-688-9889, or by fax from (202) 307-9777.

BIBLIOGRAPHY

Calhoun, Fredrick S. *The Lawmen: United States Marshals and Their Deputies 1789–1989.* Washington, D.C.: Smithsonian Institution Press, 1989.

Dillin, John. "Citizens Caught in the Cross-Fire." *The Christian Science Monitor*, 1 October 1993.

———. "The Law Enforcement Center That Seized Assets Built." *The Christian Science Monitor*, 30 September 1993.

Pascucci, John. *The Manhunter: The Astounding True Story of the U.S. Marshals Service*. New York: Pocket Books, 1996.

Sabbag, Robert. "Rudy's Cop." *New York*, 3 June 1996, pp. 22–9.

———. *Too Tough To Die*. New York: Simon and Schuster, 1992.

Sinanoglu, Elif. "Sailboats for $16,000, Gucci Watches for $400: It All Goes Under the Gavel at Government Auctions." *Money*, July 1996, pp. 146–7.

Steinberg, Eve P. *Special Agent: Deputy U.S. Marshal*. New York: Macmillan, 1996.

Stroud, Carsten. *Deadly Force: In the Streets With the U.S. Marshals*. New York: Bantam Books, 1996.

Tefertiller, Casey. *Wyatt Earp: The Life Behind the Legend*. New York: J. Wiley, 1997.

United States Military Academy (USMA; West Point)

PARENT ORGANIZATION: Department of the Army
ESTABLISHED: 1802
EMPLOYEES: 8,300

Contact Information:

ADDRESS: West Point, NY 10996
PHONE: (914) 938-4261
FAX: (914) 446-5820
URL: http://www.usma.edu
SUPERINTENDENT: Lt. Gen. Daniel W. Christman
DEAN OF THE ACADEMIC BOARD: Brig. Gen. Fletcher M. Lamkin
COMMANDANT OF CADETS: Brig. Gen. John P. Abizaid

WHAT IS ITS MISSION?

The mission of the U.S. Military Academy (USMA) is to develop leaders of character for the U.S. Army who are inspired to serve careers as commissioned officers in lifetime service to the United States. The academy seeks to educate and train its corps of cadets so that each graduate will have the qualities necessary for professional growth throughout his or her career as an officer of the army.

HOW IS IT STRUCTURED?

The USMA is the army's four-year academic institution, housed at the U.S. Army Garrison at West Point, New York—the oldest active garrison in the U.S. Army. First established in 1778 as an American Revolutionary War (1775–83) fortress, the garrison became home to the USMA in 1802. It has since become a national historic landmark. The commander of the garrison, which exists primarily to support the mission of the academy, directs daily command and operational control of West Point, its attendant training complex of close to 17,000 acres, and local military holdings. This supervision also includes the providing of all cadet services of care, clothing, funding, equipping, and pay.

The academy itself is directed by the superintendent, the chief administrative official at the institution. Through the academy's chief of staff, the superintendent directs activities in the areas of personnel, operations, plans, security, and public affairs. Other than the superintendent, the most important administrative position at the academy is that of the dean of the academic board, who oversees the activity of each of the academy's thirteen academic departments. The Office of the Dean is served by two vice deans: one for education, who handles academic affairs, library services, and information and educational technology; and one for administration, who oversees the registrar's office, the academic research division, and planning, programming, and budgeting functions.

The commandant of the corps of cadets is the military officer in charge of the professional development of West Point cadets. The primary department serving the Office of the Commandant is the Department of Military Instruction, which plans, organizes, and conducts military instruction for the entire corps of cadets. The department is further divided into its theoretical and practical elements: military science and military training. The Directorate of Intercollegiate Athletics at West Point oversees the varsity sports programs of the academy.

Cadets at the academy are considered to be members of the army and receive about half of the base pay of a second lieutenant. Cadets must pay for their own uniforms, textbooks, computers, and supplies. Quarters, rations, and medical care are provided by the army.

Andrea Hollen was the first woman to graduate from West Point. She graduated in 1980. (United States Military Academy at West Point)

PRIMARY FUNCTIONS

The purpose of the academy at West Point, in its simplest terms, is to supply the army with qualified commissioned officers. A West Point cadet receives a fully funded four-year college education. Tuition, room, board, and medical and dental care are provided by the army, and as members of the armed forces, cadets also receive an annual salary of more than $6,500. This pay covers the cost of uniforms, books, a personal computer, and living incidentals. By law, graduates of West Point are appointed to active duty as commissioned officers and serve in the army for a minimum of five years.

PROGRAMS

The USMA's academic and professional programs include a variety of activities and initiatives to develop cadets. The military program, administered primarily in the summer months, is generally uniform for all cadets during the first two summers—for the first summer, intensive basic training; for the second summer, enhancement of specific military skills such as hand-to-hand combat and air mobile operations. During the third summer of training, a cadet may elect to train in either airborne operations, jungle warfare, or northern (extreme cold) warfare. During the fourth year, a cadet may be assigned as a leader in cadet basic training or as an instructor at Camp Buckner, where the military programs generally take place.

The USMA's academic curriculum consists of a core program of 31 courses designed to give cadets a fundamental knowledge of the arts and sciences. The academy's elective program allows cadets to explore any one of the 26 fields of study or majors offered. A typical cadet day unfolds as follows: breakfast at 6:30 A.M.; classes from 7:15 A.M. to 11:35 A.M.; lunch from 11:45 A.M. to 12:30 P.M.; a dean's or commandant's lecture hour from 12:30 P.M. to 1:25 P.M.; classes from 1:35 P.M. to 3:40 P.M.; and organized athletics, parade practice, or drills from 3:40 P.M. to 6:00 P.M.

The military sciences instruction of cadets takes place during special military "intercession" periods and in a series of academic electives that may culminate in a degree in the military arts and sciences. Cadet military training takes place during the summer months, in Cadet Basic Training, Cadet Field Training, the Drill Cadet Program, and the Cadet Troop Leader Training Program. Generally cadets graduate from the USMA with a bachelor of science degree and a commission as second lieutenant in the army.

Some of the academic programs at the academy are provided by the Dean's Office, which employs two units to help both cadets and teachers: the Center for Enhanced Performance (CEP) and the Center for Teaching Excellence (CTE). The Reading and Study Skills Program, provided by the CEP, provides instruction in academic sup-

FAST FACTS

In 1997 it was estimated that the cost to taxpayers of sending a single cadet through the USMA's four-year program was about $299,000.

(Source: Amy Argetsinger. "Academies Stir Some Doubts, Some Salutes." *Washington Post*, August 12, 1997.)

port skills designed to help cadets succeed in the classroom. The CEP also offers the Peak Performance Program, an unusual, comprehensive disciplinary training that uses sports psychology, biofeedback, stress management, and attention control and imagery. The CTE hosts numerous workshops, discussions, conferences, seminars, and individual consultations to improve instruction at the academy.

BUDGET INFORMATION

The U.S. Military Academy does not compile a single budget document, and its expenditures are commonly interwoven with the costs of operating and maintaining the Army garrison at West Point. By the academy's own estimate, however, the annual cost of operating the U.S. Military Academy is about $164 million.

HISTORY

The USMA was founded in 1802, during President Thomas Jefferson's first administration, primarily as a training facility for military engineers. The need for such a facility had been obvious to American leaders since the American Revolution (1775–83), when the lack of available military engineering and technical skills had forced the revolutionary forces to rely on hired foreign officers. After the war the domestic unrest of the confederation period and the continuing need to mount a military force along the western frontier supported those who argued for a better-trained armed force. The new academy was founded at an existing army fortress—West Point, New York—and until after the Civil War (1860–65), the academy was under the control of the Corps of Engineers.

The first superintendent of the academy, Jonathan Williams, established a curriculum with heavy emphasis on math and science. Because he knew the education provided at the academy would not produce professional artillerymen and engineers of the caliber found in Europe, he hoped to encourage cadets to continue their studies after graduation.

In 1812 the corps of cadets was expanded and organized into companies and a standardized military training program was put into place. In addition admissions standards were set that required all prospective candidates for cadetship to be competent in reading, writing, and arithmetic.

The curriculum and educational philosophy of the academy were dramatically altered throughout the leadership of Sylvanus Thayer, who assumed the superintendent's position in 1817. The general outline of the Thayer system still remains as the foundation of the educational philosophy at the academy: small classroom sections to facilitate individual instruction, a prescribed curriculum, the encouragement of competition, and a rounded educational experience that includes philosophy and the study of languages. Throughout following administrations Thayer's contributions to the West Point educational system—as well as to American higher education in other parts of the country—endured.

Growing Tensions; Later Reforms

Troubles at West Point began to reflect national troubles in the early nineteenth century. Southerners felt that the academy was too far north to be devoted to the national (rather than the North's sectional) interest. Others thought West Point was encouraging an undesirable elitist tradition in the army; some even argued that the academy should be abolished and the funds made available for improving the state militia system. When sectional issues heated up in 1860 with the election of Abraham Lincoln as president, many Southern cadets resigned to return to their seceding home states. As a national institution, the military academy at West Point had failed to replace sectional loyalty with loyalty to the American nation.

The academy that had flourished under the reforms of Sylvanus Thayer appeared to stall out after the Civil War, in spite of (or perhaps because of) its transfer to the control of the War Department. It took many years of gradual changes to bring the quality of a West Point education back to the respectable status it enjoys today.

Continuing Academic and Social Changes

Because the academy's administrators believed that young officers should all have the same education and believed that all cadets should be treated alike, the curriculum at the academy remained prescribed until the 1950s, when the first elective courses were permitted. Once this was allowed, academic reforms were inevitable; by the 1970s cadets were able to concentrate their studies in particular areas; by the 1980s the prescribed curriculum was shrunk to a core curriculum and an academic majors program was in place that resembled that of other four-year universities.

West Point has tended to respond slowly to the social currents of the United States. The first black cadets were admitted at the academy immediately following the Civil War but were often subject to prejudice and discrimination. The number of black cadets graduating from West Point did not become proportional to the percentage of the black population as a whole until the 1970s.

The first female cadets were admitted to the academy in 1976, and having women at the school has required some attitude adjustment among the old guard at West Point. Although women at West Point generally have complained less of harassment and discrimination than women at other U.S. military academies, their introduction into the traditionally male warrior culture at the USMA has created some growing pains within the academy establishment.

Another significant change for the academy, which happened gradually, throughout the 1980s and 1990s, came from within military society: West Point, like the other two military academies, became a less important source of officers for the U.S. military. In fact all of the academies gained some critics during this period for being elitist and expensive. Other training grounds, such as the Reserve Officers' Training Corps (ROTC) and Officer Candidate School (OCS), were producing officers of equal ability at a fraction of the cost. Although the academies still remained a prestigious component of their respective military branches, they were declining in influence; in 1997 the academies accounted for only about 15 percent of all officers in the military.

CURRENT POLITICAL ISSUES

Like other service academies, the USMA struggled throughout the latter half of the twentieth century with several issues, including the integration of women into the corps of cadets and the resulting problems of sexual politics and discrimination. The academy has also become a source of heated debate over how such a four-year institution should be managed—as a military academy with a firm command structure or as a college where issues are debated and questioned openly by faculty and students. Although the transformation of the academy curriculum has made its academic program more like that of other four-year undergraduate universities—and has attracted more academic instructors—the academy has also struggled to maintain the edge and discipline of an army installation, where top administrators expect to be obeyed rather than questioned. Recently, however, the academy has suffered from a problem that is unique to West Point.

Case Study: The Highland Falls—Fort Montgomery School District

The academy, and the federal government that runs it, have angered residents of the neighboring communities—the villages of Highland Falls (population 4,000) and Fort Montgomery (population 2,000). About 93 percent of the communities' land is owned by the West Point garrison and academy along with a few other government agencies, and all of them are exempt from paying state and local taxes. This is a huge problem for the municipalities of Highland Falls and Fort Montgomery, which, like other communities, need an ample tax base to fund their school district.

Beginning in 1950, the federal government, recognizing that it was robbing communities of their tax base, began a program to reduce the financial impact on school districts that include tax-free federal property. In 1986 the Highland Falls—Fort Montgomery district received about $31.1 million from the federal government, which helped to cover the district's obligations.

By the middle of the Reagan administration, however, budget-cutting in Congress began attacking such aid as an unfair distribution of federal funds. Program funding began to drop steadily. The budget-cutting climate continued throughout the George Bush and Bill Clinton presidential administrations, and in 1996 the Highland Falls—Fort Montgomery funding was down to $16.1 million, with President Clinton and the House of Representatives both proposing to eliminate this funding entirely. By this time, the school district had increased its class sizes; closed an elementary school; cut music, art, and technical programs; and laid off 23 of its 100 teachers. As the budget proposals were being debated in Washington, the school district was considering whether to close down entirely, because it did not have enough money to finish out the academic year. The situation left many local residents angry at the government for breaking a promise it had made to the community years ago—while still continuing to increase its defense budget.

To make matters worse, the USMA, which has also suffered from losses in federal aid, has recently begun an attempt to compensate for those losses by expanding its own retail businesses. Because the academy is housed within a walled fortress, to which the 4,000 cadets are often restricted either literally or because of time constraints, and because federally owned retailers do not charge sales tax, the retailers of Highland Falls and Fort Montgomery see this as an unfair competitive advantage. In 1996, when the academy opened Ike's Express, a hamburger and pizza delivery establishment, business at the Highland Falls West Point Pizza, a restaurant on the village's Main Street, fell by $200 a day, an amount that accounts for several employees' salaries.

Of even more concern for the area is West Point's plans to construct a strip mall that would expand the academy's commissary services and add a gas station and a minimart. The plan has the town of Highland Falls in an uproar. Because it already needed to raise property taxes by 25 percent to cover its losses in aid to the school district, it would have no money to help retailers promote business in the community. The towns of Highland Falls and Fort Montgomery see themselves today as shrinking communities that may some day disappear entirely as the USMA robs them entirely of their income.

FUTURE DIRECTIONS

West Point is undergoing major change as military budgets follow the trend of other government agencies—they are generally either decreasing or increasing at a much slower rate. It does, however, hope to carry out a $400 million infrastructure improvement program, updating older buildings as well as expanding the electronic communications network that links all cadets to campus information systems. To help meet these costs the academy intends to streamline its workforce while improving the quality of services administered to cadets. In the near future, it hopes to civilianize 25 percent of its faculty, to both round out its academic programs and trim some of its budget.

AGENCY RESOURCES

The Web site of the USMA at http://www.usma.edu is an excellent source of information about the admissions process, eligibility requirements, upcoming events and activities, and sporting events. General inquiries about the USMA can be directed to the Public Affairs Office, West Point, NY 10996; phone (914) 938-4261. For further information about the academy's admission criteria and policies, contact the Office of the Registrar at (914) 938-2050.

AGENCY PUBLICATIONS

The Public Affairs Office at West Point publishes a weekly newspaper, *The Point Review*, which contains articles and features of general interest to the public, and also publishes various brochures and fact sheets. Most of these publications can be obtained for no charge from the Public Affairs office. The annual Academic Catalog, a listing of courses available to cadets, is available from the Admissions office, (914) 938-4041.

BIBLIOGRAPHY

Ambrose, Stephen E. *Duty, Honor, Country: A History of West Point.* Baltimore: Johns Hopkins University Press, 1966.

Argetsinger, Amy. "Academies Stir Some Doubts, Some Salutes." *Washington Post*, 12 August 1997, p. A1.

Atkinson, Rick. "The West Point Story." *U.S. News and World Report,* 9 October 1989, pp. 44–54.

Donnithorne, Larry. *West Point Way of Leadership* . New York: Doubleday, 1994.

Ellis, Joseph J. *School for Soldiers: West Point and the Profession of Arms.* New York: Oxford University Press, 1974.

Glaberson, William. "Tax Revolt Over West Point." *New York Times*, 6 March 1996, p. A14 (N).

Hughes, Libby. *West Point.* Parsippany, N.J.: Silver Burdett Press, 1997.

Moses, Edward M. *West Point, the Making of Leaders: An Historical Sketchbook.* Alexandria, Va.: Edward M. Moses & Robert A. Getz, 1996.

Pahl, David. *West Point.* New York: Simon & Schuster, 1987.

Salter, James. "You Must." *Esquire* , December 1992, pp. 145–56.

Stewart, Robert. *The Corps of Cadets: A Year at West Point.* Annapolis, Md.: Naval Institute Press, 1996.

United States Mint (USM; The Mint)

PARENT ORGANIZATION: Department of the Treasury
ESTABLISHED: April 2, 1792
EMPLOYEES: 2,250

Contact Information:

ADDRESS: 633 Third St. NW
Washington, DC 20220
PHONE: (202) 874-6000
TOLL FREE: (800) 646-8872
E-MAIL: 50states@usmint.treas.gov
URL: http://www.usmint.gov
DIRECTOR: Phillip N. Diehl

WHAT IS ITS MISSION?

According to the agency, the mission of the United States Mint (USM) is "to produce an adequate volume of circulating coinage for the Nation to conduct its trade and commerce." To this end, the USM produces 14 billion to 20 billion coins each year and releases them for use while also taking in mutilated or severely damaged, coins to be processed. The USM also makes proof and uncirculated coins, commemorative coins, and medals, all of which are available for purchase by the general public.

HOW IS IT STRUCTURED?

The USM, a cabinet-level agency under the Department of the Treasury, is headed by a director, who is appointed by the president and confirmed by the Senate. The director, a deputy director, and three associate directors work out of USM headquarters in Washington, D.C. Together their offices administer the three major areas of administrative duties: policy and management, operations, and marketing. Responsibilities that fall under these areas include: policy formulation; program development, implementation, and management; research and development; marketing and customer service; order processing; and operation of the Union Station sales center. Additional facilities are located in Philadelphia, Pennsylvania; Denver, Colorado; San Francisco, California; West Point, New York; and Fort Knox, Kentucky.

The unpopular Susan B. Anthony dollar, which resembles a quarter in size and shape, was discontinued after only a few years of production. Congress and the U.S. Mint hope that a new dollar coin, gold in color rather than silver, will be more successful. (EPD Photos)

PRIMARY FUNCTIONS

The USM primarily produces coins, making it the world's largest manufacturer of coins, medals, and coin-based consumer products, according to the agency. The amount of circulating coins produced is based on demand, which is determined by the Federal Reserve Bank. The agency also takes care of mutilated (badly damaged) coins and makes the dies, or molds, used to make medals and coins themselves. The Philadelphia and Denver facilities operate tours so that the public can see the process of turning raw metals into shaped, decorated coins.

Consumer products produced by the USM include coin-theme jewelry, commemorative coins, medals, proofs, and other noncirculating coins. "Unlike ordinary coins in circulation, proof coins display brilliant, mirror-like background surfaces, with frosted, sculpted foregrounds—a special effect created by the exacting proofing process and individual care given by Mint craftsmen," says the USM's consumer catalog. Many items are incorporated into sets that revolve around a theme. For example, the Young Collector's Edition of the Black Patriots Commemorative Coin includes an uncirculated silver dollar, which is packaged and intended for display. The coin bears art and text that highlights African American patriot Crispus Attucks and the Revolutionary War. The USM sells consumer items at the Denver and Philadelphia sites and also at Union Station in Washington, D.C.

The USM also protects the nation's gold and silver bullion (bars), coins, and coinage metals, some of which it sells. The majority of the nation's gold is stored and guarded at the U.S. Bullion Depository in Fort Knox, Kentucky.

PROGRAMS

USM programs revolve around the conception, design, and collecting of circulating and noncirculating coins. One of the more extensive programs was initiated by the the 50 State Quarters Program Act that was passed in 1997. This program provides for the release of 50 newly designed quarters, one to commemorate each state, to be rolled out over 10 years. The first one, honoring Delaware, is slated to be in circulation by January 1999. The order of release will follow the order in which the states ratified the Constitution or joined the Union.

As part of the "celebration of the 50 States," five new quarters will appear each year from 1999 to 2008. The act places special emphasis on "the diffusion of knowledge among the youth of the United States about the individual states, their history and geography, and the rich diversity of the national heritage."

The quarter was chosen for this program because it allows room for creative designs. However, the designs for the program may not include any portrait of a living person; any head-and-shoulder portrait or bust of any person, living or dead; state flags or seals; controversial subjects or symbols; inscriptions; or logos or depictions of specific commercial, private, educational, civic, religious, sports, or other organizations whose membership or ownership is not universal. Rather, consumers can expect to see features such as state landmarks, landscapes, historical buildings, symbols of state resources or industries, official state flora and fauna, state icons, and outlines of states. Selection of a design is decided by the governor, the USM, the Citizens Commemorative Coin Advisory Committee, the Fine Arts Commission, and the secretary of the Treasury.

No tax dollars will be put toward this program, and the USM expects to generate $2.6 to $5.1 billion in profits over 10 years. Profits will go into the general fund of the U.S. Treasury.

BUDGET INFORMATION

The USM is operated by the United States Mint Public Enterprise Fund. The fund is outside of the appropriations process due to its importance to the financial soundness of U.S. banks, institutions, and economy. In 1997 the USM generated revenues of $1 billion through its commemorative and bullion coin programs. Much of this revenue went back to the foundations and other institutions that sponsored the coins.

HISTORY

As a colony of England, the fledgling United States was not permitted to coin its own money. The currencies in use at that time were primarily from Great Britain, Portugal, France, and Germany. And, of course, the ancient barter system was used too. This assortment was not only confusing, but it also stunted economic growth. Commerce was difficult because each merchant dealt in a different currency.

One of the first proponents of a standardized currency and a domestic mint was Alexander Hamilton, the secretary of the Treasury during the Washington administration. Hamilton argued that these initiatives would allow for increased commercial dealings and trade. Hamilton authored the Mint Act of 1792, which established the Mint, authorized its construction in Philadelphia, and placed it under the authority of the then Secretary of State Thomas Jefferson. The act also determined the materials, denominations, and inscriptions to be used in making U.S. coins.

The First Coins

The first coins, made of gold, silver, and copper, were struck at the Mint in Philadelphia in 1793. The methods used were labor intensive. Mint workers heated the metals in an open furnace, then sent them through rollers to produce flat metal sheets. They punched blank coins out of the sheets, then hand fed them into a stamp. Horses were needed to provide power for some of the machinery. A day's work yielded only a few coins.

Growth

The Mint became an independent agency in 1799. Westward expansion and the discovery of gold fueled coin production. In 1801 the Mint started producing peace medals, which were given to American Indian leaders and chiefs as a seal of promise and a symbol of goodwill in treaties and agreement.

Three new minting facilities had opened by 1838. The gold $20 piece appeared in 1850, reflecting the nation's excitement over gold discoveries in the West, and new minting facilities opened in San Francisco (1854) and Denver (1863). Additional assay, or appraisal, offices opened in larger cities such as St. Louis and Salt Lake City. In 1873 the Mint was repositioned under the Treasury Department and its headquarters was moved to Washington, D.C.

FAST FACTS

The USM is responsible for the protection of U.S. gold and silver reserves valued at $100 billion.

(Source: United States Mint. "Director's Message," 1998.)

In 1892 the Mint started producing special commemorative coins, and after the Spanish-American War (1898), the Mint started making money for foreign nations including Mexico, Panama, and Peru. President George Washington first appeared on a coin in 1899, contrary to the desire he reportedly expressed during his lifetime not to be on a coin because it would be too monarch-like. The Lincoln penny appeared in 1909 to commemorate the late president's 100th birthday. Washington appeared again on the quarter in 1932; Thomas Jefferson was put on the nickel in 1938, and in 1946 Franklin Roosevelt was stamped on the dime to symbolize his close connections to the March of Dimes. John F. Kennedy was honored with a half-dollar bearing his resemblance in 1964.

The Mint stopped making coins composed of gold in 1933 when the economic hardship of the Great Depression did not make it financially feasible. A silver crisis in 1965 forced the Mint to discontinue making coins of silver, except for half-dollars, which continued to be minted of 40 percent silver for five more years. Quarters, dimes, and half-dollars are now made of copper and covered with a copper-nickel alloy that gives them their silver color. The nickel is made totally of the same alloy, and the penny is made of copper-plated zinc. In 1984 the Mint's name was officially changed to the United States Mint.

Legislation passed in 1997 allowed, for the first time, minor alterations of some of the provisions of the Mint Act. This was done to facilitate the 50 States Commemorative Coin Program. More room was made for new tails-side designs by allowing for some of the mandatory elements that were otherwise to be on the back to be put on the front, such as *E Pluribus Unum* (out of many one). Additionally, new technologies have improved the processes involved in making coins, enabling the USM to produce more than 15 billion general circulation coins each year.

FAST FACTS

The production cost of the penny is 60 percent of its face value, making it the most expensive coin to produce.

(Source: United States Mint. "Specifications of Circulating Coins," 1998.)

CURRENT POLITICAL ISSUES

Because the production of coins is commissioned and controlled by Congress, the appearance of coins produced by the USM can become an issue. For example, many oppose the engraving of "in God we trust" on each U.S. coin. A lawsuit over this failed in the U.S. Supreme Court in 1962 (*Engel v. Vitale*), and since then the courts have basically refused to hear similar cases. While *Engel v. Vitale* was more specifically a lawsuit over prayer in school, it attempted to address a broader issue found in the First Amendment which prohibits enactment of any law "respecting an establishment of religion." And within its comprehensive decision on the case, the Court effectively sanctioned the engraving of the phrase on coins.

Another battle over coin design arose in the late 1990s when Congress passed S.1228, which includes the 50 States Commemorative Coin Program Act as well as the United States Dollar Coin Act of 1997, which commissioned the design of a new coin worth one dollar. Although the act prescribes some features the new coin is to have, like its gold color, it left the choice of design up to the secretary of the Treasury.

Case Study: Sacajawea v. the Statue of Liberty

One of the first drafts of the United States Dollar Coin Act of 1997 mandated that the Statue of Liberty would appear on the new dollar coin, a provision strongly supported by U.S. Representative Michael Castle (R-DE) who had sponsored the bill. A preliminary roll-call vote in the House showed support, with a vote of 416 to seven in favor of the Statue of Liberty.

Upon review the Senate Banking Committee decided a real, instead of an allegorical, or symbolic, woman would be a more appropriate image to put on the dollar coin and the bill was sent back to the House for revision. At this stage, in order to ensure passage of the legislation within the year, Castle agreed to remove from the act the provision requiring the image on the coin to be that of the Statue of Liberty. President Clinton signed the bill into law on December 1, 1997, with the provision that "the Secretary of the Treasury, in consultation with the Congress, shall select appropriate designs for the obverse and reverse sides of the dollar coin."

Foreseeing a debate, Secretary of the Treasury Robert E. Rubin established a Dollar Coin Design Advisory Committee. Among the nine members on the committee were chairman of the USM Philip Diehl, Representative Castle, and representatives from the Smithsonian Institution, the President's Committee on the Arts and the Humanities, the American Numismatic Society, and Business and Professional Women, U.S.A. The committee's purpose was to consider public testimony, the specific provisions of the act, and guidelines from Rubin, who had determined the design should be a representation of one or more nonliving women, and use this input to recommend a design. Among women considered to be on the coin were: leading suffragette Susan B. Anthony; American Red Cross co-founder Clara Barton; Congressional Black Caucus leader Shirley Chisholm; poet Emma Lazarus; civil rights activist Rosa Parks; first Congresswoman Jeannette Rankin; First Lady Eleanor Roosevelt; abolitionist and Underground Railroad founder Harriet Tubman; the Statue of Liberty; Sacajawea, Lewis and Clark's American Indian guide.

After reviewing historical coin designs and developing decision factors, the committee recommended a design of "Liberty represented by a Native American woman, inspired by Sacajawea." The awkwardness of their recommendation was due to the fact that a true likeness of Sacajawea would not be possible to create as none exists to draw from.

Rubin accepted the committee's recommendation, but Congressman Castle continued his campaign for an image of the Statue of Liberty saying in a July 29, 1998, press release that "the success or failure of the new gold-colored dollar coin will rest on whether Americans will be willing to use them. The Statue of Liberty is the greatest and most recognizable symbol of freedom worldwide, and it has never been placed on a circulating coin. Under the law Congress passed last year, the Secretary was authorized to select the design 'in consultation with Congress.' There has not been consultation on this recommendation. Congress can pass legislation to direct him to choose another design. I intend to pursue that option if necessary."

Castle proposed H.R. 4329 in the House in late July 1998. This one-page piece of legislation sought to secure the Statue of Liberty as the image to appear on the new dollar coin. However, the USM moved confidently ahead by publicly announcing that the new coin will bear the image of a American Indian woman, inspired by Sacajewea.

Diehl, who was chairman and a nonvoting member of the Dollar Coin Design Advisory Committee, wrote an editorial saying "never before in this century had the U.S. Congress directly delegated to the Secretary of Treasury the discretion to chose a design for a new circulating coin of the Nation. Never before has the public played such a unique role in the process of selecting a design concept for the Nation's circulating coinage." His comments seem to imply that such public involvement may become a lasting tradition in designing coins. However, whether or not the public or the secretary of the Treasury will be given the same degree of power in the future will largely depend on the success of the new dollar coin.

FUTURE DIRECTIONS

In the nineteenth and early twentieth centuries the penny was a valuable purchasing tool. Items could be purchased with one or several of them fairly easily. However, as time progressed the U.S. economy has grown to the point that the penny has very little purchasing power; it is possible that the penny has outlived its usefulness. General Accounting Office (GAO) reports in 1990 and 1994 were inconclusive as to whether or not the public felt that the penny should be made. Some felt that the penny should be kept, others felt that rounding to the nearest five cents (in the absence of the penny) was a good idea. The GAO maintains that the federal government loses money in penny production, although not such a substantial amount that the penny must no longer be produced for that reason alone. The Mint will gauge the public's feelings about the penny after the new dollar coin is introduced to determine if it still has a place in today's United States. Pennies make more than 65 percent of the total number of coins that the Mint stamps each year, so to halt production would cause a major change in Mint operations.

AGENCY RESOURCES

The USM Web site, located at http://www.usmint.gov offers information on a wide range of coins, medals, and sets for sale. For information on current coin offerings, please write: United States Mint, Customer Service Center, 10003 Derekwood Lane, Lanham, MD 20706, or telephone 202-283-2646. The Mint will place interested individuals on its customer mailing list. In addition to general information about the agency itself, its Web site offers a "reading room" where USM annual reports, strategic plans, press releases, a freedom of information handbook, press photos, and legislation affecting the USM can be found.

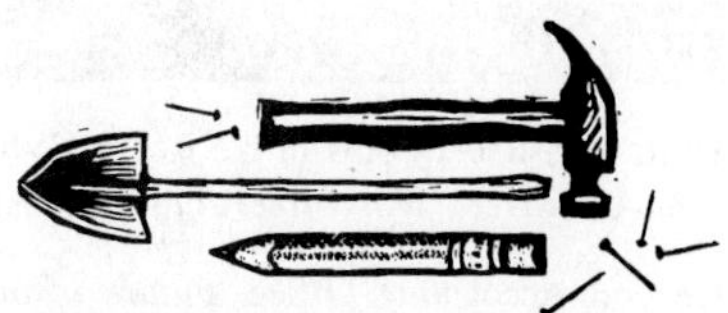

GET INVOLVED:

The Mint and the Treasury Department encourage the general public to suggest designs for the new quarters to be issued as part of the 50 State Quarters Program. Under the guidelines established by the Treasury Department and the 50 States Commemorative Coin Program Act of 1997, the secretary of the Treasury will select each state's quarter design out of a group of designs submitted by that state's governor.

Each year, quarters for 5 states will be issued in the order that the states ratified the Constitution or joined the Union. The first 5 quarters, those for Delaware, Pennsylvania, New Jersey, Georgia, and Connecticut, will be issued in 1999. Their designs have already been chosen. The coin for Delaware features American patriot Caesar Rodney on horseback, riding to Philadelphia to vote in favor of the Declaration of Independence. The coin for Georgia features a peach, enclosed within an outline of the state, and a banner bearing the state motto: Wisdom, Justice, Moderation. These coins, along with the three other winning designs, can be viewed on-line at http://www.usmint.gov/50states/5winners.cfm.

The Mint provides a blank quarter template, as well as the official design content guidelines, on its Web site at http://www.usmint.gov/50states/design.cfm#blanktemplate. Guidelines for submission are established by individual state's governors; contact your governor's office for more information. The selection process begins approximately 18 months before a state's quarter is scheduled to be issued. Consult the Mint's on-line schedule at http://www.usmint.gov/50states/schedule.cfm.

AGENCY PUBLICATIONS

The USM produces few publications available to the general public. Its annual reports and strategic plans are available on-line at http://www.usmint.gov/reading_room/reading.html. A newsletter containing current information on coin offerings is available by writing or calling the United States Mint, Customer Service Center, 10003 Derekwood Lane, Lanham, MD 20706; phone (202) 283-2646.

BIBLIOGRAPHY

Duff, Christine. "Coins of the Realm: What Will You Pay for a Eunice Shriver." *Wall Street Journal*, 8 April 1998, p. A1.

General Accounting Office. *Future of the Penny: Options for Congressional Consideration*, 1994.

"Keeping God's Name in Mint Condition."*Time*, 9 December 1991, p. 66.

"Liberty in Mint Condition." *World*, October 1986, p. 14.

Samuel, Peter. "Uncle, Can You Spare a Coin?" *Forbes*, 8 November 1993, pp. 92–93.

Schmitt, Eric. "Desperately Seeking the Next Susan B." *New York Times*, 9 November 1997, p. 4.

Schwarz, Ted. *A History of United States Coinage*. London: Tantivy Press, 1980.

White, Peter T. "The Power of Money." *National Geographic Magazine*, January 1993, p. 80.

Wilcox, Melynda Dovel. "Prospects for a Dollar Coin: A Tossup." *Kiplinger's Personal Finance Magazine*, August 1995, p. 45.

United States Naval Academy (USNA)

PARENT ORGANIZATION: Department of the Navy
ESTABLISHED: October 10, 1845
EMPLOYEES: 2,316 employees; 3,991 midshipmen

Contact Information:

ADDRESS: U.S. Naval Academy
Annapolis, MD 21402
PHONE: (410) 293-1000
TOLL FREE: (800) 638-9156
FAX: (410) 293-3133
E-MAIL: pao@nadn.navy.mil
URL: http://www.nadn.navy.mil
SUPERINTENDENT: Vice Admiral John R. Ryan
ACADEMIC DEAN AND PROVOST: Dr. William C. Miller

WHAT IS ITS MISSION?

The mission of the United States Naval Academy is to direct the moral, mental, and physical development of its students (midshipmen) to provide the U.S. Navy with graduates who are dedicated to a career of naval service and have potential for future advancement. The ultimate goal of the Naval Academy is to produce candidates for assuming the navy's highest responsibilities of command, citizenship, and government.

HOW IS IT STRUCTURED?

The U.S. Naval Academy is the undergraduate college of the naval service. It is led by the superintendent, who usually carries the rank of admiral and whose position is comparable to that of a university president. The superintendent is the senior military officer of the academy; the staff of the superintendent's office directs the general administration of the academy, including areas such as personnel and budgeting. The admissions and academic affairs of the academy are directed by the academic dean and provost, who oversees the admissions and registration processes for all midshipmen, the academy's academic programs, and the information technology services that support these functions.

The academic dean is responsible for five divisions within the academy structure. Three of these divisions are academic departments: the Division of Humanities and Social Sciences, which includes departments such as English, history, and political science; the Division of Mathematics and Science, which includes all math and science departments; and the Division of Engineering and

Midshipmen at the U.S. Naval Academy march in formation with the color guard. (Courtesy of the U.S. Navy)

Technology, which includes some departments unique to military training, such as aerospace engineering and weapons and systems engineering.

The other divisions under the academic dean and provost are the Division of Character Development, a division established in 1994 to shape the moral and ethical character of midshipmen, and the Division of Information Technology Services, which designs, maintains, and keeps secure the campus wide computer information networks. The academic program at the academy is taught and carried out by a faculty of six hundred, which is made up of about half military officers and half civilian professors.

Another significant leadership position at the academy is that of the commandant of midshipmen. Roughly equivalent to the dean of students at a civilian college, the commandant is responsible for directing and assisting the professional development and everyday activities of all the midshipmen. The commandant is always a naval officer. Subject to the direct authority of the superintendent and the supervisory authority of the academic dean and provost, the commandant oversees another division in the academy structure, the Division of Professional Development, which includes the Departments of Seamanship and Navigation; Leadership, Law, and Ethics; and Professional Programs. The student body, officially called the Brigade of Midshipmen at the Naval Academy, consists of about four thousand students.

Other than the academy's physical education requirements, midshipmen are obligated to participate in a competitive sport at the intercollegiate or intramural level every season. The many varsity sports programs at the academy are administered under the direct authority of the superintendent.

PRIMARY FUNCTIONS

The sole function of the U.S. Naval Academy is to prepare its midshipmen for service as officers in the navy or marines. To accomplish this goal, midshipmen complete a four-year academic program, including military and physical training. Midshipmen are also encouraged to become active in one or more of the 73 extracurricular activities offered at the academy, including choirs, a drum and bugle corps, publications, drama, a flying club, and many other areas. Midshipmen graduate with a bachelor of science degree and receive a commission as either a navy ensign or a marine second lieutenant.

PROGRAMS

The Naval Academy conducts numerous programs in four areas: academic, professional, character development, and athletics. The academic program of the Naval Academy offers 18 academic majors in engineering, science, mathematics, social sciences, and the humanities. A midshipman must also complete about 45 semester hours of military-professional courses, such as seamanship, navigation, naval engineering, electrical engineering, weapons, and leadership. Professional training also consists of drills and practical training conducted during the summer at shore bases and at sea. Through physical education courses, midshipmen meet minimum requirements in applied strength tests, including running, swimming, and gymnastics.

The character development program is intended to instill the virtues of honor, integrity, and personal respect in midshipmen. The academy's character development program has been the platform for several new initiatives. An example is the Human Education Resources Officer (HERO) program. A peer education and peer resource network, the program places specially trained midshipmen as advisers for each class. The program is designed to provide support to the chain of command in all human relations areas, resolve peer issues among midshipmen, and provide education and information that will assist midshipmen in making responsible decisions.

BUDGET INFORMATION

The Naval Academy's budget is an expenditure from the Department of the Navy. This amount was approximately $127 million in 1997. The largest portion of the academy's budget, about 60 percent, is consumed by labor costs. Supplies and purchased services each account for about 17 percent of the budget; the academy's utilities account for 4 percent, and 1 percent is spent on communications equipment and services.

HISTORY

For the first 50 years of its existence, the U.S. Navy followed the British practice of relying on at-sea apprenticeships for midshipmen. During the War of 1812 Congress authorized the employment of schoolmasters to give instruction on the navy's larger ships. For about 30 years after the war, many advocates for a naval academy spoke out—including President John Quincy Adams in 1825—but opponents argued against it out of three basic fears: that an academy would produce an elitist aristocracy within the navy, that it would be an unacceptable drain of tax revenues, and that naval officers could not be trained on land.

The Somers *and the Birth of the Naval Academy*

In September 1842 an American school ship, the *Somers,* set sail on a training mission for naval apprentice volunteers. Discipline aboard the *Somers* eventually deteriorated. A court of inquiry determined that Midshipman Philip Spencer, along with two confederates, was guilty of an attempt to commit a mutiny. The three were hanged.

FAST FACTS

Since 1845 more than 60,000 men and women have successfully completed work at the Naval Academy.

(Source: U.S. Naval Academy, 1997.)

The *Somers* incident shocked the nation and cast doubt on the wisdom of sending midshipmen directly aboard ship where they were expected to learn by doing. After additional setbacks, Secretary of the Navy George Bancroft decided to leave Congress out of the picture; he established the Naval School—without congressional funding—at a 10-acre army post, Fort Severn, in Annapolis, Maryland. In 1950 the school became the U.S. Naval Academy. A curriculum was devised that required midshipmen to study at the academy for four years and to train aboard ships each summer; this format was the basis for the more advanced and sophisticated curriculum at the Naval Academy today.

Civil War Troubles

Like most of the nation, the Naval Academy was devastated by the onset of the American Civil War (1861–65). Because of strong Southern sentiment in the state of Maryland, the academy was moved to a temporary headquarters at Newport, Rhode Island. After the upper classes were graduated early for wartime service, moral and academic standards at the academy declined considerably. The academy enjoyed a remarkable rebirth once it returned to Annapolis under new leadership, and in 1878 it was awarded a gold medal at the Paris Universal Exposition for the best system of education in the United States.

The academy expanded along with the navy into the next century but suffered the same type of wartime setbacks during and after World Wars I (1914–18) and II (1939–45): classes were graduated early, the strength of the midshipman regiment was expanded without sufficient supervision, and problems continued into the postwar period. Once again, most of these problems were overcome by new leadership, in this case the direction of Rear Admiral J. L. Holloway, who served as superintendent from 1947 to 1950.

The Academic Revolution and Social Changes

For the most part, the Naval Academy had always offered a fixed curriculum, but this tradition was changed

FAST FACTS

In 1991 Juliane Gallina became the first woman to be named brigade commander at the U.S. Naval Academy. In this capacity, Gallina acted as the leader of the brigade of midshipmen at Annapolis, presiding at ceremonies and acting as a liaison between midshipmen and officers.

(Source: *Women's Firsts.* Gale Research, 1997.)

in the 1960s by a series of reforms that came to be known as the Academic Revolution. Elective courses were introduced to midshipmen who wanted to specialize in certain areas, and a minors program of 15 percent elective courses was inaugurated in 1964. Five years later, an accredited majors program was introduced, making the Naval Academy more closely resemble a four-year university. An independent study program, the Trident Scholarship, was also introduced in 1964. During the same decade steps were taken to give the civilian faculty—a feature unique among the service academies—a role in the administration of the faculty. The post of academic dean was created, and departmental chairs were opened to civilians.

The academy also underwent important and, in the opinion of many, long-overdue social changes. Only six African Americans had been appointed to the academy when Wesley Brown became the first to graduate in 1949, and minority appointments remained low for many years until an aggressive minority recruitment program was launched in 1965. The imbalance was soon corrected. The first women instructors joined the academy staff in the early 1970s, and the first 81 female midshipmen entered the academy in the summer of 1976. Such rapid social changes proved to be associated with some of the problems that arose in the 1980s and 1990s, but, as it turned out, they had little to do with the decline in morale and discipline that plagued the academy throughout this period.

CURRENT POLITICAL ISSUES

Throughout the post-World War II period, each of the nation's service academies occasionally suffered from some sort of scandal—typically involving academic cheating or sexual harassment—but in the 1990s, the frequency and seriousness of problems surfacing at the Naval Academy led some outside critics, and even the Pentagon itself, to question the way the academy was operated.

Scandals at the Academy

The most notorious of Naval Academy scandals occurred in 1992, when more than one hundred midshipmen were implicated in a widespread effort to secure copies of a difficult electrical engineering exam that had been procured for $1,000 by one midshipman. After word reached the faculty, 81 of the midshipmen admitted to cheating, but only 24 were expelled. This raised questions about the academy's consistency in upholding its honor code, which specifically condemns cheating and lying.

The cheating scandal was not the only instance of serious student misconduct at the academy. Midshipmen had periodically been found guilty of sexual harassment, including a 1989 incident in which a female student was chained to a urinal by a group of male midshipmen. In 1994 Admiral Charles Larson was hired as superintendent of the academy with the understanding that these blemishes on the academy's record should be remedied and the reputation of the academy restored.

But soon the Naval Academy's students were engaged in additional forms of criminal misconduct. A sting operation conducted by naval officials in October 1995 resulted in the expulsion and imprisonment of five midshipmen for drug distribution. The resulting investigations led to the expulsion of 15 more students, making this the worst drug scandal in the academy's history. A total of 26 students were suspected of being involved in a conspiracy to buy and distribute the drug LSD. Additionally, within a single month in early 1996, a midshipman and four former students were charged with taking part in a car-theft ring; a top student officer was accused of rape and sexual harassment; a midshipman was accused of child molestation; and two midshipmen were arrested for alcohol-related misconduct.

Efforts to Restore Honor

During April 1996, as the extent of the 1995 drug scandal was becoming clear, Admiral Larson ordered an unprecedented stand-down at the academy, designed to tighten discipline among the midshipmen. Upperclassmen were required to wear their uniforms off the academy grounds, and the weeknight curfew was changed from midnight to 10 P.M. The stand-down was a period of reflection during which students discussed the academy's problems and devised ways to restore its honor.

But many critics of the academy—midshipmen and alumni alike—complained that the problem lay in a failure to create an environment in which principles of honor and integrity were meaningful. According to these critics, the trouble had two distinct sources. First, the midshipmen were intentionally overworked, forced to bear heavy academic loads while marching, training, and performing chores such as memorizing obscure facts about the academy. Although the intention was to build character, the midshipmen were often so exhausted and discouraged that they did simply enough to get by. Second, the written honor code at the Naval Academy appeared to differ from the unwritten code, which seemed to value loyalty among the midshipmen more than truth. This disparity was evident in the 1992 cheating scandal, in which many midshipmen lied to protect one another.

The academy's problems proved serious enough to warrant a Pentagon investigation during the summer of 1997. In addition to a generalized inquiry into the methods by which the academy taught and enforced ethical behavior, the Defense Department specifically questioned whether the administration of Admiral Larson had interfered with outside investigations into recent scandals in order to limit damage to the academy's reputation. In July 1998 a report was issued from the inspector general's office of the Pentagon. It exonerated Larson but did implicate one of his former legal aides in wrongdoing.

SUCCESSES AND FAILURES

The Naval Academy directs attention to the success of its graduates as a measure of its success as an institution of education and leadership training. Graduates of the U.S. Naval Academy include former president of the United States Jimmy Carter, more than 25 Rhodes Scholars, and 34 National Aeronautics and Space Administration (NASA) astronauts and mission specialists.

FUTURE DIRECTIONS

The academy is in the process of implementing several changes that were adopted in the mid-1990s and will be a focus for the academy into the twenty-first century. The leadership curriculum at the Naval Academy has been restructured to bring the emphasis back to practical basics that have proved successful in the past. Specifically, the administration wants to draw less from academic theory and more from real-life case studies presented by officers who have experienced the kinds of leadership situations being studied by midshipmen. Through these interactions, it is hoped that midshipmen will learn how to command, how to interact with troops, and how to become successful leaders.

Partly as a result of scandals in the mid–1990s, the academy introduced a formal, required ethics course for all third-class midshipmen (sophomores). Its purpose is to strengthen the midshipmen's foundations in moral and ethical thought so they will be better prepared to make moral decisions as they progress through the academy.

AGENCY RESOURCES

For further information about the U.S. Naval Academy, contact the Public Affairs Office, 121 Blake Rd., Annapolis, MD 21402; phone (410) 293-2293. Information about appointment to the Naval Academy, admissions, and registration are available from the Office of the Academic Dean and Provost at 1-800-638-9156.

AGENCY PUBLICATIONS

The students of the Naval Academy publish a biweekly newspaper, the *Trident*, which includes articles on current events and items of interest to midshipmen. Most other academy publications are admissions related; two examples are the yearly *Academic Catalog* and the *Navy Guide to Annapolis*, an overview for midshipman candidates. The faculty of the Naval Academy has its own list of field-related publications, and the Public Affairs Office makes available numerous fact sheets and historical information. For more information about the Naval Academy's publications, call the publications division of the Public Affairs Office at (410) 293-2291 or write Public Affairs Office, 121 Blake Rd., Annapolis, MD 21402.

BIBLIOGRAPHY

Bowman, Tom. "Report Faults Navy Lawyer." *Baltimore Sun*, 7 July 1998, p. 1B.

Brock, Pope. "The Extremes of Honor." *Esquire*, October 1994, pp. 114–20.

Burke, Carol. "Annapolis: Capital and Port." *American History*, December 1995, p. 58.

———. "Dames at Sea." *New Republic*, 17 August 1992, pp. 16–8.

Donnelly, Elaine. "Prenatal Blues Test Academy's Honor Code." *Insight on the News*, 20 November 1995, pp. 23–4.

Janofsky, Michael. "Adrift at the Naval Academy." *New York Times*, 11 August 1996, p. E2.

Pahl, David. *Annapolis: The United States Naval Academy*. New York: Exeter Books, 1987.

"Report: Probe Clears Academy Officials." *Journal Newspapers of Virginia and Maryland Online.* June 1998.

Stand-down Ordered at Naval Academy. *Facts on File*, 25 April 1996, p. 283.

Thomas, Evan, and Gregory L. Vistica. "A School for Scandal." *Newsweek*, April 1996, pp. 24–5.

Weiner, Tim. "Pentagon Investigates Naval Academy Over Scandals." *New York Times*, 20 June 1997, pp. A12 (N), A11(L).

Women's Firsts. Detroit: Gale Research, 1997.

United States Postal Service (USPS)

PARENT ORGANIZATION: Independent
ESTABLISHED: August 12, 1970
EMPLOYEES: 753,000 (1997)

Contact Information:

ADDRESS: 475 L'Enfant Plaza SW
Washington, DC 20260
PHONE: (202) 268-2000
URL: http://www.usps.gov
POSTMASTER GENERAL: William J. Henderson
CHAIRMAN: Sam Winters

WHAT IS ITS MISSION?

The stated mission of the United States Postal Service (USPS) is "to provide every household and business across the United States with the ability to communicate and conduct business with each other and the world through prompt, reliable, secure, and economic services for the collection, transportation, and delivery of messages and merchandise." An essential element of the Postal Service's mission—as mandated by law—is to provide postal delivery to the entire nation at a uniform cost.

The USPS has also adopted a vision statement committing itself to becoming the most effective and productive provider of twenty-first century postal communications. To achieve this end, the Postal Service plans to equip itself with leading-edge technologies for letter and parcel delivery, to become active in electronic mail, and to modify its operations to reflect retail practice at the end of the twentieth century.

HOW IS IT STRUCTURED?

The U.S. Postal Service is an independent agency within the executive branch of the federal government that does not have cabinet-level status. It has the distinction of being a private corporation wholly owned by the U.S. government. It is administered by an 11–member board of governors. Nine board members are appointed by the president and confirmed by the Senate. These governors serve nine-year terms, staggered so that one term expires on December 8 every year. No more than five governors may be members of one political party.

The nine board members appoint a postmaster general who serves as the chief executive officer of the Postal Service and as the tenth member of the board. The office of postmaster general is not limited to a fixed term. The ten members then appoint an eleventh who serves as the deputy postmaster general.

The United States is divided into ten postal administrative areas: Allegheny, Great Lakes, Mid-Atlantic, Mid-West, New York, Northeast, Pacific, Southeast, Southwest, and West. There are approximately 39,430 post offices, branches, stations, and contract post offices throughout the United States.

One of the most important departments of the USPS is the Postal Inspection Service, one of the largest federal law enforcement agencies. The Postal Inspection Service is responsible for enforcing laws relating to the integrity and security of the mails. At its head is the inspector general who reports directly to the postmaster general. The Postal Inspection Service has five operations support groups and five forensic labs located throughout the country.

The Labor Relations Department plays a significant role in the USPS hierarchy, because the Postal Service is the only federal agency whose employees enjoy the rights to collective bargaining defined by the National Labor Relations Act. The Consumer Advocate acts as an ombudsman for postal customers.

FAST FACTS

As of December 21, 1996, the Japanese paid 70 cents and the Germans 64 cents for a piece of first class mail. The U.S. rate of 32 cents for first class mail is among the lowest rates in the industrialized world.

(Source: United States Postal Service. "Postal Facts," 1998.)

PRIMARY FUNCTIONS

The USPS oversees the U.S. mail in all its aspects. Federal statute gives the USPS the exclusive right to deliver letters in the United States—the one exception being express mail. Along with that monopoly, however, the statute requires the Postal Service to provide delivery service that is uniform in scope and cost for the nation.

In addition to delivering the mail and selling postage, the USPS is responsible for establishing various standards, including the size of packages and envelopes, the conditions for bulk mailing, the construction and installation of mailboxes in apartment buildings, and the production and use of postage meters. It provides information to customers on postal rates and classifications. Postal rates are set by the Postal Rate Commission (PRC) (an independent agency), not by the Postal Service. However, the USPS Board of Governors can request rate changes or make other recommendations to the PRC, and they can, by unanimous written decision, modify recommended decisions of the PRC on postal rate and mail classification changes.

To meet the challenges of rapidly evolving communications technology, the Postal Service created the Technology Applications Department. The department's most important responsibility is to identify key technologies that will enable the Postal Service to carry out its core business most efficiently and to become a leader in the communications field as it makes its transition from paper to electronic mail. The department has introduced state-of-the-art address and bar code scanning to mail sorting and is developing programs to help the Postal Service overcome its slow start in the area of E-mail.

The USPS, through its arm, the Postal Inspection Service, enforces more than two hundred federal laws related to crimes against the mail, the USPS, and its employees. These include statutes on mail fraud, mail bombs, child pornography, illegal drugs, mail theft, attacks on postal workers, burglary of postal facilities, and other crimes. The Postal Inspection Service acts as the financial auditor of the USPS as well: it checks all contracts entered by the Postal Service, audits its financial records and transactions, and oversees financial aspects of the Postal Service's major programs and projects.

PROGRAMS

The most visible Postal Service program is its commemorative stamp initiative. Recommendations for subjects of stamps are made by the Citizens' Stamp Advisory Committee. The committee, which was founded in 1957, is made up of twelve to fifteen members appointed by the postmaster general. Every year the committee selects 25 to 40 subjects from the thousands of suggestions it receives and presents them to the postmaster general, who decides which themes will be adopted. Important considerations for selecting a theme for commemorative stamps are public sentiment, its significance to the nation as a whole, and its potential interest to collectors.

Since the 1930s commemorative stamps have also been issued in conjunction with special programs in which the Postal Service takes part. For example, in June 1996, as part of a four-month program with the YWCA, the American Cancer Society, and LIFETIME television,

BUDGET:

United States Postal Service

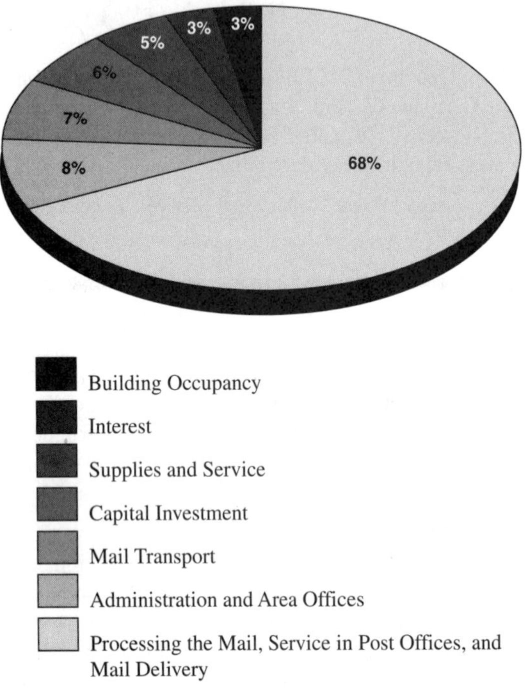

the Postal Service issued a stamp intended to raise public awareness of breast cancer. As part of the same program, the Postal Service published a breast cancer awareness brochure that related the stories of four people who had been touched by the disease. Special interest postage stamps on topics like AIDS, drug abuse, and environmental protection have been issued.

In addition to its long-standing philatelic and commemorative stamp programs, in 1993 the USPS drafted its Strategic Environmental Plan aimed at making its everyday activities more environmentally sound. It launched programs for dealing with the enormous volume of undeliverable mail that accumulates every year and paper that customers discard in post offices. Methods for producing compost as well as pencils from old mail have been put into practice. The Postal Service also maintains a large fleet of alternate fuel vehicles. In 1996 recycling earned the Postal Service more than $5 million; it saved nearly as much by simply eliminating the need to dispose of waste materials.

The USPS passed up the opportunity to get involved in E-mail on the ground floor when the Internet was being set up in the late 1970s. Its Electronic Postmark program is the Postal Service's attempt to win back a segment of this market. For 22 cents customers will be able to route an E-mail through the Postal Service computers and the Postal Service will verify that the communication was sent, tell when it was sent, and guarantee that it has not been tampered with. Target customers are financial institutions, law firms, government agencies, and hospitals, which require greater accountability in the transmission of electronic documents. The Postal Service aims to become the third party with whom these organizations will entrust their important documents.

BUDGET INFORMATION

The Postal Service, as created by the Postal Reorganization Act of 1970, is fully self-sufficient and independent; its operations are meant to be covered entirely by the revenues it earns from its operations. Nonetheless it is eligible for three types of federal appropriation. The public service appropriation is a government payment for the provision of uniform nationwide mail service. By law, the USPS is entitled to around $460 million for this each year. It did not request these funds in 1998 or in any of the previous fifteen years.

A special type of appropriation is the "transitional cost appropriation," which is targeted for postal workers who began collecting workers compensation benefits from the old Post Office Department. Since the department was privatized, the Postal Service has continued to administer the payments, but monies come from the federal governments. The Postal Service is also eligible to receive an annual "revenue foregone" appropriation. These monies are a reimbursement for free mail rates for the blind and for mailing absentee ballots overseas.

In 1998 the Postal Service's operating budget totaled $62.6 billion. Nearly 68 percent of that money, or $42.5 billion, went toward processing the mail and service in post offices and mail delivery. Much of the rest was spent on administration and area offices ($4.9 billion or 8 percent of the total USPS budget), mail transport ($4.4 billion or 7 percent), capital investment ($3.5 billion or 6 percent), supplies and service ($3.3 billion or 5 percent), interest ($1.8 billion or 3 percent), and building occupancy ($1.8 billion or 3 percent).

HISTORY

For many years, mail in the American colonies was carried by private riders who charged a small fee for their service. The first official postal service in the American colonies was established by Thomas Neale, who was granted a 21–year license by King William and Queen Mary in 1692. The service was hampered by the scarcity of decent roads and the long distances mail often had to travel. Before his postal patent had expired, Neale went bankrupt.

By 1711 the population of the thirteen colonies had reached 295,000. The quality of postal delivery had changed little since 1650, however: post roads were virtually nonexistent, and an official letter between Virginia and New York could take six weeks to arrive in good weather, and twelve weeks in bad.

In 1753 Benjamin Franklin and William Hunter were appointed co-postmasters general for the colonies. Franklin set out to overhaul the American postal service. He lobbied state legislatures to provide funding to build post roads. He instituted night service between Philadelphia and New York; in good weather a letter sent one day would arrive the next. By the time Franklin and Hunter had finished their reforms, one could send a letter from New York to Boston and receive a reply within three weeks. Franklin's post office, after only four years, returned a profit to the British crown, the first such profit ever received. After heading a committee to establish a new postal system, on July 26, 1775, the Second Continental Congress appointed Franklin the nation's first postmaster general.

The new postal system thrived and soon it drove the royal post out of business. One of Franklin's successors, Ebenezer Hazard, proposed a postal reform law that established centralized governmental control of the post office and a federal government monopoly on all mail delivery. The law remained in effect until after the ratification of the U.S. Constitution.

The Constitution reaffirmed the postal authority of the federal government. Article 1, Section 8 gave Congress the power to establish post offices and post roads. President George Washington called for the establishment of an efficient postal infrastructure to connect the states and far-flung pioneer settlements saying, "Let us bind them with a chain that can never be broken." Washington was the first president to appoint a postmaster general, but it was not until President Andrew Jackson's administration that the Post Office Department became part of the cabinet.

As the country grew, so did the Post Office. Post roads including land and eventually water routes were added to its network annually. The Post Office was an early supporter of railroads as a means of mail delivery. It began experimenting with air mail delivery as early as 1911, although the first commercial airmail flight in the United States did not occur until February 15, 1926.

Rural Free Delivery, instituted in 1896, marked a significant turning point in the nation. Previously, hundreds of thousands of Americans who lived on farms or in other areas far from cities, had to travel to a post office in the next town to pick up their mail, a trip that could consume an entire day. Rural delivery spurred the construction of new roads and, with the institution of Parcel Post in 1912, the growth of big mail order houses like Montgomery Ward and Sears, Roebuck.

By the 1960s the mail volume in the United States had grown enormously. By and large, though, it was still being handled as it had been one hundred years before—shipped by train and sorted by hand. In order to more efficiently deal with the huge volume of mail, in 1963 the Post Office Department introduced the Zone Improvement Plan or ZIP codes, five-digit numbers that pinpoint the location of addresses. In 1984 ZIP+4 was instituted to make mail delivery even more exact by narrowing addresses down to a specific entrance or floor of a building.

FAST FACTS

The Supai route, along which mail and other goods are brought to the Havasupai Indian Reservation deep below the south rim of the Grand Canyon, is the last mule-train delivery in the United States. Undeliverable by helicopter or air drop, mail is carried eight miles, some of it along treacherous switchbacks on the canyon walls.

(Source: "History of the United States Postal Service, 1775–1993.")

The Post Office was in trouble, both administratively and financially, in the 1960s. It had deficits of around $1 billion, its facilities were deteriorating, and its workforce—whose wages had not kept pace with other American workers—was shrinking. The situation came to a head in October 1966. In the wake of an unexpected 15 percent increase in mail volume and tight restrictions on overtime, mail delivery in the Midwest ground to a halt. Chicago alone had around one million pounds of backlogged mail. (One despairing postal administrator suggested *burning* mail to get it down to manageable levels, a recommendation that was rejected.) Only a $30 million emergency appropriation by the Bureau of the Budget to pay overtime to post office workers got the mail moving again.

President Lyndon Johnson's postmaster general, Lawrence O'Brien, recommended transforming the Post Office into a private corporation, owned and administered by the federal government but self-supporting, like the Tennessee Valley Authority (TVA) or the Federal Deposit Insurance Corporation (FDIC).

The idea of a private post office had been discussed since the beginning of the republic. Thomas Jefferson, for one, had expressed concern over the power inherent in controlling the mails. In 1859 the House Committee on the Post Office considered a bill that would have privatized the Post Office but rejected it at the time as ill-advised.

President Johnson appointed a blue ribbon commission to study the issue, and in June 1968 it released its report endorsing O'Brien's "public corporation" approach. The Postal Reform Act met with some opposition, primarily from the mailmen's union, the National Association of Letter Carriers.

In an unprecedented meeting, President Richard Nixon and the head of the union hammered out an agreement. In order to win the union's support Nixon promised them collective bargaining rights and a sizable pay raise. The act was signed into law on August 12, 1970. The United States Postal Service, created by the act, began official operations on July 1, 1971.

This was the beginning of the U.S. Postal Service as it is known today. The department lost its cabinet-level status, and the postmaster general was no longer appointed by the president but by a board of governors. The new USPS was expected to function on revenues generated by stamp and delivery charges, like a private company. The Postal Service would no longer receive money for operations from the federal government, but it was granted tax-exempt status. The act also created the Postal Rate Commission to recommend changes in postal rates and classification. The act extended collective bargaining rights to employees as spelled out by the National Labor Relations Act. Postal Service employees are the only federal workers to enjoy this right. Like other federal employees, however, they are banned from striking.

The 1980s were growth years for the Postal Service. In the 1990s, however, the USPS experienced the most serious decline in mail volume since the Great Depression, due in part to the rise in use of fax machines, E-mail, and other electronic communication technologies. At the same time the Postal Service faced growing competition from companies like United Parcel Service (UPS) and Federal Express (Fed Ex).

In response, the USPS was streamlined from within. Five regions and 73 field divisions were replaced by 10 areas with their own managers for customer service and processing and distribution. Recognizing that it was, in essence, engaged in retailing, the Postal Service began taking steps to make post offices more like stores by offering a wider range of products and more customer-oriented services. Finally, the USPS began integrating new technologies, such as bar coding and scanning into its delivery process.

CURRENT POLITICAL ISSUES

Competition in the open market has proved to be politically complicated for the Postal Service, falling as it does into the gray area between the public and private sectors. Although the USPS no longer receives funding from the federal government, it is required to provide uniform service at a uniform cost to the entire nation. But its competitors claim the Postal Service is an extension of the government, with many unfair advantages in the marketplace.

Case Study: USPS vs. UPS

Public outcry from the United Parcel Service (UPS) and other parcel delivery companies emerged when the Postal Service launched its advertising campaign for Priority Mail: "FedEx at $12 is a good deal, UPS at $6 is a better deal, Priority Mail at $3 is the best deal." UPS spokesperson Gina Ellrich, speaking to the *Los Angeles Times,* called the ads "misleading" and added, "We want them to focus on their mandate of delivering the mail. Or if they want to compete, just give up their tax-free and monopoly status."

Pressure from UPS on the Postal Service heated up in the summer of 1997. The USPS had been testing Global Package Link, a program that enabled shippers of large volumes to move their international shipments through foreign customs quickly. UPS opposed the new service as government interference in the private sector. Ellrich told the *Atlanta Journal and Constitution,* "It is not the Postal Service's role to be competing with the private sector where the public is already being well-served."

UPS took its complaints to the U.S. Capitol where it had a great deal of influence (it contributed more to congressional campaigns between 1993 and 1995 than any other company in the United States, and Federal Express was number three on the list). By July 1997 the USPS had completed test runs of Global Package Link in Japan, Canada, and the United Kingdom and planned to expand the program to China, Germany, France, Chile, and Brazil. Late in the month, the House Appropriations Committee passed a bill with an amendment that would stop expansion of the program while the General Accounting Office determined how it would affect market competition. (The amendment was sponsored by U.S. Representative Anne M. Northrup of Kentucky, where UPS has its main air hub.) The next day the bill was passed by the full House of Representatives—but not before the head of the Postal Service oversight subcommittee managed to get the anti-Postal Service language dropped from the bill.

Just days later UPS went on strike and the USPS, for all its alleged advantages, was unable to capitalize. So many customers were going to post offices that the Postal System's relatively primitive parcel-sorting system—the work is still done by hand—was quickly overwhelmed. In response, the USPS limited walk-in customers to four parcels at a time. Customers wanting to ship more than four had to make an appointment, sometimes days later. The move drew accusations of USPS ineptitude from the public.

Public Impact

The Postal Service is the government agency that Americans have the most contact with on a daily basis.

For decades it has had a reputation as an inefficient bureaucracy. The UPS strike demonstrated that the government connections that supposedly gave the Postal Service an advantage was possibly a liability because it limited the ability of the USPS to adapt quickly to meet its customers needs.

SUCCESSES AND FAILURES

One of the Postal Service's most significant recent successes was the $1 billion in profits it recorded three years in a row. Profits totaled $1.8 billion and $1.6 billion in 1995 and 1996, respectively. It was well on its way to another billion-dollar plus performance in 1997 following the rise in business occasioned by the UPS strike. As a result of the strong performances, the USPS debt was reduced from $6 billion to $2.7 billion by the end of fiscal year 1996.

A failure of the Postal System as a whole is a lack of the flexibility needed to adapt to changing business conditions. An example is the federal government's contract for overnight delivery with Federal Express. Although the Postal Service is owned by the U.S. government, it could not match or undercut FedEx's bid, because rates, once set, can only be changed after deliberation of the Postal Rate Commission. The bureaucracy imposed by the Postal Reorganization Act limits the Postal Service's ability to respond to quickly changing market conditions.

FUTURE DIRECTIONS

Two areas in which the Postal Service is concentrating future efforts are the modernization of its retail operations and the automation of its mail handling. In September 1996 it opened a prototype store, Postmark America, in Bloomington, Minnesota's, Mall of America. In addition to traditional post office merchandise, the store sells a new line of Postal Service merchandise: Pony Express jackets, historical postal uniforms, and a variety of other related goods, many of them bearing the Postal Service logo.

Postmark America is part of a broader USPS project to replace post offices as they have been known for decades with postal stores that incorporate expanded inventory, trained and specialized staff, self-service, extended hours of operation, and standardized appearance and signage. In fall 1997 the USPS opened its 500th postal store; it plans, wherever feasible, to incorporate key postal store elements into all of its existing post offices.

In keeping with its vision statement, the USPS has undertaken an enormous automation project to enable it to better compete with high-tech delivery service providers like UPS and Federal Express, to meet customer expectations and to more efficiently sort and track the vast number of letters and parcels that pass through its doors every year. During 1996 the Postal Service Board of Governors approved more than $700 million in expenditures for automation equipment, such as bar code generators, bar code readers, and address scanners. More than 40 percent of the Postal Service's automation equipment was deployed in fiscal year 1996. The Board of Governors plans to spend another $5.3 billion on automation by 1998. The Postal Service has purchased 300,000 handheld scanners that postal drivers will use when delivering Express Mail, Priority Mail, parcels, international shipments, and registered and certified mail. The USPS is working with companies like Microsoft Corp. to develop a system that will enable customers to buy stamps on-line and print them as bar code stickers with their laser printers.

AGENCY RESOURCES

Consumers wanting general postal information, for instance postal rates, classifications, ZIP codes, or postal products can write to USPS Consumer Affairs, 475 L'Enfant Plaza SW, Washington, DC 20260; call (202) 268-2281 or TDD (202) 268-2310); or fax (202) 268-2304. The Postal Service Web site http://www.usps.gov has a rate calculator, a ZIP code finder, and a parcel tracker. Individuals with complaints about the Postal Service can call the Complaint Hotline at 1-800-268-2284. Postal customers can report suspected violations of postal laws to the Fraud and Abuse Hotline, 1-800-654-8896. Information on stamp collecting is provided by Stamp Services at (202) 268-2562. To purchase stamps for a collection, contact the Philatelic Fulfillment Service Center, Kansas City, MO 64179-1009; phone 1-800-782-6724.

The Postal Service maintains its own library (open from 9 A.M. until 4 P.M. Monday through Friday) at 475 L'Enfant Plaza, Rm. 8650, Washington, DC 20260; phone (202) 268-2900. Dockets and Regulatory Matters, Rm. 8650 of the Postal Service Building, can be contacted for information about databases maintained by the Postal Service, which include information on consumer complaints, delivery analyses, prohibited mailings, and controlled circulation publications.

The Corporate Information unit of the office of Postal Service Historian maintains a collection of various postal histories and other material related to the history of mail in the United States. Individuals interested in obtaining information on post offices, postmasters, or other aspects of American postal history should write Historian, Corporate Information Service, U.S. Postal Service, 465 L'Enfant Plaza SW, Washington, DC 20260-0012.

Every year the Postal Service receives thousands of letters and parcels that are undeliverable. Objects found

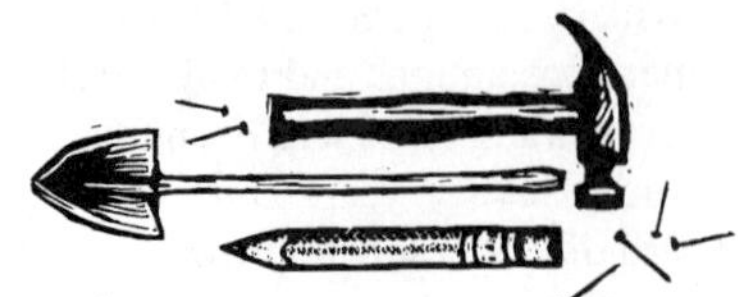

GET INVOLVED:

The Citizens' Stamp Advisory Committee recommends topics to the postmaster for use on upcoming stamps. The general public is invited to make recommendations to the committee. Motifs are selected three years before they are actually released in order to provide adequate time for the selection of artwork and the production of the stamp. Ideas should be sent to the Citizens' Stamp Advisory Committee, c/o Stamp Management, U.S. Postal Service, 475 L'Enfant Plaza SW, Rm. 4474EB, Washington, DC 20260-6756. Only ideas for subjects will be considered; the board does not accept suggestions for artwork to be used on stamps, and it does not accept unsolicited artwork.

in such packages are sold at postal auctions. They include jewelry, books, TVs, compact discs, VCRs, and clothes. Auctions are held about every two months in San Francisco, phone: (415) 536-6425; St. Paul, phone (612) 293-3335; and Atlanta, phone (404) 344-1625. Call to be put on a free mailing list. Information is also available at http://www.usps.gov/consumer/auctions.htm. *The Guide to Federal Government Sales*, published by the General Services Administration, contains detailed information on auctions by all government agencies.

AGENCY PUBLICATIONS

"The Consumer's Directory to Postal Services and Products" (Pub 201) and "A Consumer's Guide to Crime Prevention" (Pub 300), as well as numerous other pamphlets, can be obtained at all main post offices. *Directives and Forms Catalog*, a list of all USPS publications, can be requested by writing New Jersey Material Distribution Center, U.S. Postal Service, 2 Brick Plant Rd., South River, NJ 08877-9998; phone (908) 613-2375; fax (908) 613-2330. *The National ZIP Code and Post Office Directory* (Pub 65) may be purchased for $18 at government bookstores or ordered directly from the Government Printing Office, 732 N. Capitol St. NW, Washington, DC 20401, phone (202) 512-1800; fax (202) 512-2250. It can also be ordered at the GPO Web site http://www.gpo.gov.

The USPS annual report, *Comprehensive Statement on Postal Operations*, can be obtained from USPS Legislative Affairs (202) 268-2505 or from the USPS Library (202) 268-2905. It can also be downloaded from the USPS Web site, http://www.usps.gov.

The Postal Service publishes a number of brochures on environmental programs. Titles include "You Can Make a Ton of Difference," and "Mail that Mother Earth Can Love," which deal with recycling and waste reduction, "Alternative Fuel Vehicles For a Cleaner Environment," and "United States Postal Service Environmental Facts." The brochures can be requested from Environmental Management Policy, U.S. Postal Service Headquarters, Rm. 2140, 475 L'Enfant Plaza SW, Washington, DC 20260-2180 or fax at (202) 268-6016.

BIBLIOGRAPHY

Bates, S. "Post Office Tackles Competition." *Nation's Business*, April 1997.

Bowyer, Matthew J. *They Carried the Mail: A Survey of Postal History and Hobbies*. New York: Robert B. Luce, 1972.

Bridger, Chet. "Congress Again to Weigh Reforms," *Federal Times*, 20 January 1997.

Cullinan, Gerald. *The U.S. Postal Service*. New York: F. A. Praeger, 1973.

Darlin, D. "Data-Mining the Mail." *Forbes*, 24 February 1997.

"Follow up: The Postal Service and E-Mail," *Barron's*, 3 June 1996.

Girard, Kim. "Postal Service Plans to Deploy Mobile Scanners." *Computerworld*, 8 September 1997.

Goldstein, Michael A. "Can the U.S. Postal Market Itself to Success?" *Los Angeles Times Magazine*, 22 December 1996.

"Repackaging the Postal Service," *Business Week*, 8 January 1996.

Rubin, Rita. "The Change of Address Two Step," *US News and World Report*, 22 April 1996.

Rush, Tonda S. "USPS Misses UPS Strike Opportunity," *Editor and Publisher*, 6 September 1997.

"The U.S. Postal Service is likely to Show another Billion-Dollar Annual Profit," *Wall Street Journal*, 8 October 1997.

United States Secret Service (USSS)

PARENT ORGANIZATION: Department of the Treasury
ESTABLISHED: July 5, 1865
EMPLOYEES: 4,200

Contact Information:

ADDRESS: 1800 G St. NW
Washington, DC 20223
URL: http://www.treas.gov/usss
DIRECTOR: Lewis C. Merletti

WHAT IS ITS MISSION?

The mission of the United States Secret Service (USSS), defined by U.S. Code, is expressed in the USSS vision statement: "Built on a tradition of excellence and meeting the challenges of the future, the United States Secret Service moves as one to protect our Nation's leaders, visiting world leaders, and the integrity of the Nation's financial systems."

HOW IS IT STRUCTURED?

The Secret Service is a bureau within the U.S. Treasury Department, headed by a director who is directly accountable to the secretary of the Treasury through the undersecretary of the Treasury. The director of the Secret Service is appointed by the secretary of the Treasury contingent upon the approval of the Civil Service Commission. The director is supported by a deputy director, seven assistant directors, and a chief counsel.

Functional Operations

In addition to the administrative offices, internal audit and inspection departments, legal counsel, and training divisions, the USSS is organized into three functional operations: the Office of Protective Operations, the Office of Protective Research, and the Office of Investigations.

The Office of Protective Operations is a dynamic one. It may be organized into six or more divisions at any time. Protective Operations divisions include the presidential protective division, the vice presidential protective division,

Secret Service agents tend to James Brady, (ground, right)*, press secretary to President Ronald Reagan, and a policeman,* (ground, left). *Both were shot during an attempt on President Reagan's life on March 30, 1981. The assailant, John Hinckley Jr., is being held by police and agents in the background* (right). *(Photograph by Don Rypka. UPI/Corbis-Bettmann)*

the dignitary protective division, and the candidate nominee protective division. The presidential protective division is intricately organized into three units: support/logistics, operations, and training and special programs. The operations unit is further divided into presidential protection, first family protection, and transportation. Former presidents, who receive protection for at least ten years unless they decline it, are also protected under this division.

Together, the White House Uniformed Police Force and the Treasury Security Force comprise the USSS uniformed division which falls under Protective Operations, but uniformed division officers are not classified as Secret Service agents.

The Office of Protective Research and the Office of Investigations are subdivided into six smaller divisions. For instance the Intelligence Division falls under the Office of Protective Research, while USSS field offices (approximately 125 world wide) belong to the Office of Investigations.

PRIMARY FUNCTIONS

The USSS works toward a three-fold mission. First, as guardians of the integrity of U.S. currency, the USSS combats counterfeiting operations. Second, as investigators of federal crimes of fraud and forgery, the USSS attempts to ensure the reliability of government stocks, bonds, and checks and guarantee the integrity of electronic data and financial transactions. Third, the USSS protects the president and the vice president, their families, and other designated individuals.

White House Detail and Foreign Dignitaries

Protecting the president entails long work shifts that collectively maintain a 24-hour vigil around the chief executive and the first family. The agents who do this are known as the White House detail. Although these agents do not live in the White House, they virtually live with the president in every other sense of the word. Although the President may be alone in a room, an agent is just outside the door, and when the president travels the White House Detail accompanies the president wherever he goes in the White House.

When the president travels the USSS makes countless arrangements beforehand. A team of agents goes in to scour the environment, especially the building in which the president will stay. Agents inspect the building, entries, exits, and adjacent and nearby buildings that provide roof access or hiding places. Hotel workers are thoroughly screened, and the rooms adjoining the presidential suite are reserved for the Secret Service and the presidential entourage. Secret Service agents inspect the kitchen where the president's food will be prepared, and an agent is present during preparation to safeguard against poisoning.

When the president travels by train or car, the route ahead is inspected by agents, and a "pilot" car of Secret Service agents immediately precedes the presidential vehicle to ensure the route is safe. A Secret Service agent always drives the presidential car. When the president rides in a motorcade, Secret Service agents accompany—in the car, on the sideboards, and walking along beside the car. The agents continually watch the crowd for anything suspicious, like a large package or suitcase which might contain a concealed weapon.

The Secret Service occasionally solicits backup from the U.S. military. And the agency coordinates with the Department of State to protect the foreign heads of state and other dignitaries who visit the president.

Protective Research

The Protective Research Section handles threatening letters sent to the president, each of which constitutes a federal crime. This section analyzes handwriting samples and fingerprints and studies the ink, typewriter, printer, or other device used to convey a threat. Investigators work with the United States Postal Service in trying to pinpoint the origin of threatening correspondence, and every attempt is made to identify and apprehend the individual responsible for the threat.

The Uniformed Division

The Uniformed Division consists of the White House Uniformed Police Force and the Treasury Guard Force. The White House Uniformed Police Force is a special detail whose members traditionally are selected from the ranks of the Washington, D.C., municipal police force. These officers are highly trained and renowned for their marksmanship in particular. The White House Police Force patrols the grounds of the White House and guards foreign dignitaries while they are in Washington, D.C. The uniformed police are not Secret Service agents, but they operate under the command of the director of the Secret Service. The Treasury Guard Force protects the billions of dollars in the U.S. Treasury.

Counterfeit Control

The primary purpose for which the Secret Service was created was to control counterfeit currency, coins, and government bonds. When the Secret Service is alerted to counterfeiting, undercover "operatives" investigate the situation. Once agents trace the source of counterfeited documents or coins, undercover agents infiltrate the illegal operation to gather evidence, and after obtaining it, they arrest the perpetrators.

In the late twentieth century, counterfeit-control operations expanded to include a new breed of crime—cybercrime—that is carried out by criminal "hackers" who penetrate computer systems and steal or damage the stored data. Cybercrimes often involve the theft of money from banking computers.

Special Assignments

On occasion the federal government assigns the Secret Service to special assignments that require exceptional bravery or cunning. One of the more interesting of these happened during World War II (1939–45) when the Secret Service was entrusted with hiding priceless documents of U.S. history. The original copies of the Declaration of Independence, the Constitution and other precious artifacts like the Gutenberg Bible, were secreted to an unknown location where they remained safe until the war ended and the documents could return to their displays in Washington, D.C.

PROGRAMS

For the most part the USSS does not operate programs. Each detail is essentially a security program in itself. For example, the Financial Crimes Division of the Secret Service targets specific types of crime including credit card fraud, money laundering, telecommunications fraud, and other financial and computer-related crimes.

The Financial Crimes Division does run an international training program in which participants learn about investigative techniques, international fraud, and weaknesses in a financial system that can lead to fraud. More than 2,000 foreign law enforcement and banking officials, from nations such as Russia, Australia, Peru, Korea, France, and Aruba have trained in this program.

BUDGET INFORMATION

Congressional allocations to the USSS for the 1999 fiscal year totaled $625 million. USSS funds are designated for a wide variety of purposes: rental of buildings and other property for protective purposes, employee compensation and expenses including per diem and overtime, maintenance of the Secret Service Training Center, uniforms, technical support, and more. An additional $6 million was appropriated and designated for structure maintenance and repair. Annuity benefit contributions totaling $72 million were allocated to reimburse the District of Columbia for benefit payments made to the Uniformed Division and to other employees of the Secret Service from local revenues. The agency received an additional $11 million from the Violent Crime Reduction Trust Fund.

HISTORY

The USSS is one of the oldest federal law enforcement agencies in the United Sates. The Secret Service Division of the Treasury Department dates back to July 5, 1865, when Treasury Secretary William P. McCulloch named William P. Wood the first director of the Secret Service. At his swearing-in ceremony Wood was charged, not with protecting President Andrew Johnson, but with identifying and confiscating counterfeit U.S. currency and arresting the manufacturers and distributors of the counterfeit items. This was a monumental task because by the end of the Civil War (1860–65) about one-third of U.S. currency in circulation was believed to be counterfeit.

By 1869 Wood and his small group of agents had apprehended hundreds of counterfeiters. Secret Service operations were slowly expanded to encompass the detection of forgery, piracy and smuggling, land fraud, mail robbery, and peonage (the practice of selling laborers). Eleven Secret Service field offices were operational by 1870, and later, during the Spanish-American War (1898) Secret Service agents gathered military intelligence and carried out counter-espionage assignments.

Herman C. Whitley assumed the directorship of the Secret Service in 1869. He was credited with centralizing and organizing the fledgling agency. By 1874, when Whitley stepped down, the number of Secret Service agents had doubled from the original ten, to twenty. However, the Secret Service fell into political disfavor during the ensuing 15 years. The agency's budget was cut nearly in half, and the number of agents reverted to ten. This was largely a response to criticism for the agency's use of aggression and questionable tactics.

Presidential Protection

In 1898 the agency came under attack again. This time the Secret Service was accused of misusing funds to provide protection at the vacation home of President William McKinley. After McKinley was killed by an assassin's bullet, in 1901, protective services were extended to McKinley's successor, President Theodore Roosevelt, even in the absence of legislation allowing it. In 1906 the Secret Service was finally authorized to protect the president.

After the election of 1908 the Secret Service extended protection to the president-elect, and in 1917 the White House Detail was expanded to include protection of the immediate family of the incumbent president. By 1950 the Secret Service had aborted assassination attempts on presidents Franklin D. Roosevelt and Harry Truman.

In 1962 the agency had 450 agents, and Secret Service protective functions were expanded to include full protection for the vice president. The following year, after the assassination of President John F. Kennedy, protection was extended to his widow and children, and eventually to all former presidents and their families in 1965.

Less than five years later, in 1968, the Kennedy tragedy was virtually repeated when Robert F. Kennedy, brother of the late president, was shot and killed while running for president. Legislation that followed the second Kennedy assassination provided for the protection of viable presidential candidates. That legislation was soon justified. Four years later, during the next presidential campaign, Governor George Wallace of Alabama was shot four times despite elaborate Secret Service precautions. Although Wallace survived the ordeal he was critically wounded and permanently paralyzed. The assailant thus ended the Wallace candidacy, as he intended.

The Secret Service halted many more assassination attempts during the years that followed. President Gerald Ford was assaulted twice in California in 1975, and President Ronald Reagan was shot in the lung while exiting a hotel in Washington, D.C., in 1981.

In response to the growing incidence of computer crimes, the Secret Service was given the authority in 1984 to investigate credit card and computer fraud; and in 1990 the Secret Service was assigned to assist the Department of Justice in investigating crimes involving federally-insured financial institutions.

The mid-1990s saw slight revisions in several aspects of the Secret Service's responsibilities. A 1994 crime bill permitted the Secret Service to prosecute those who counterfeit U.S. currency overseas as if the counterfeiting had occurred in the United States. This offers greater ability to stop counterfeiters who attempt to elude prosecution by performing illegal actions outside the United States. Additionally, the length of time a president and his family remain under Secret Service protection was limited to 10 years in 1997. This was due to the agency's desire to cut its budget in accordance with a government-wide effort to reduce expenditures.

Throughout the history of the agency two Secret Service agents were killed in the line of duty. Agent Joseph A. Walker died in 1906 during an investigation. In 1950 Officer Leslie Coffelt of the White House Police was killed during an assassination attempt on President Truman, which ended in a historic shoot-out outside Washington's Blair House, just across the street from the White House.

Uniformed Police

The Washington, D.C., metropolitan police force assumed responsibility for providing special protection to the White House grounds in 1864, during the Civil War (1860–65). That arrangement continued until 1922 when President Warren Harding requested creation of a select police force to protect the White House. For the next eight years the White House Police Force, under the supervision of the president, handled White House grounds security. In 1930 the White House Uniformed Police Force officially came under the Secret Service, though White House officers are not Secret Service agents.

In 1970 the White House Police Force became the Executive Protective Service. At that time the uniformed police force was charged with protecting foreign diplomats visiting Washington, D.C. In 1977 the Executive Protective Service was again renamed, to become the U.S. Secret Service Uniformed Division. The uniformed division merged with the Treasury Police Force in 1986.

CURRENT POLITICAL ISSUES

The U.S. justice system protects a special kind of trust between certain individuals. For example, attorney-client privilege protects attorneys from being forced to divulge the content of communications with clients. Not even a subpoena can force such testimony. Similar privileges are extended to physicians and members of the clergy, nor can spouses be subpoenaed to testify unwillingly against one another. These tenets have consistently been upheld by the U.S. Supreme Court, cementing the understanding that such relationships are based on a special confidence. If that confidence is jeopardized the relationship is impaired. Likewise, protecting the president requires that Secret Service agents be willing to sacrifice their own lives to shield the president from harm. Therefore the relationship between the president and the agents is also founded in a mutual trust.

Case Study: Testimony of Secret Service Agents

This unique relationship was put to the test in 1998 when President Bill Clinton was under investigation by Kenneth Starr, an independent counsel for the federal government. Starr accused Clinton of instructing a White House staffer to lie when giving a deposition, which is done under oath. Starr further charged that in doing so Clinton was guilty of obstructing justice, which may be grounds for impeachment when committed by the president.

To substantiate his accusations Starr had to first establish that the White House staffer had indeed lied under oath. The subject matter of the employee's testimony, however, related to a personal matter between the employee and the president, so no witnesses could refute or corroborate the sworn deposition except Secret Service agents who protected Clinton. When Starr attempted to subpoena White House Secret Service agents, a judicial battle ensued. The president and the agents maintained that it would be unethical to require agents to reveal information learned while guarding the president. To force such testimony, they argued, would jeopardize the bond of trust between the chief executive and the agents. The Secretary of the Treasury maintained that it may be reasonable for uniformed security agents to testify, but not the plainclothes agents who are constantly at the president's side. To force testimony could drive the president to avoid security measures in a quest for privacy.

Critics pointed out that Secret Service agents have cooperated with subpoenas in other matters, especially with regard to assassination attempts, but no agent on active duty ever testified specifically against the president. It is important to distinguish this issue from executive privilege, the right of the president to refuse to disclose information that could jeopardize national security. Some suggested that in refusing to testify, Secret Service agents were essentially a secret police force abetting a cover-up. The directors of the Secret Service and the Justice Department, however, ignored public pressure and refused to force agents to testify.

Eventually, however, pressure from Starr forced the issue to be resolved in court. In a ruling that was upheld by a federal court of appeals and Chief Justice William Rehnquist, Judge Norma Holloway Johnson ruled that there was no legal basis for the precedent of privilege that the Secret Service had attempted to create by refusing Starr's subpoenas. In July and August of 1998 seven Secret Service agents, including the agent assigned to lead the detail for presidential protection, testified.

SUCCESSES AND FAILURES

Statistics show that in 1997 the Secret Service worked on and completed (closed the files on) more than 32,000 cases relating to counterfeit, fraud, and forgery. More than 13,000 arrests were reported by Secret Service field offices during that year, with $101,516,212 in counterfeit notes seized. Statistical projections for 1998 predict that the dollar amount of notes seized may double.

FUTURE DIRECTIONS

In light of the growing number of incidents of terrorism worldwide, the USSS will increasingly shift its focus toward minimizing the potential for terrorist attacks against the chief executive. The newly organized counterterrorist assault team (CAT) is a special unit of the USSS White House Detail. Agents assigned to the CAT unit are specially trained in combatting terrorism. And, because of limited financial resources, the agency works in tandem with the Central Intelligence Agency (CIA) to acquire sophisticated devices and weapons to provide optimum surveillance and protection to USSS protectees.

AGENCY RESOURCES

For extensive information about the USSS, visit the agency's Web site at http://www.treas.gov/usss. The

Web site contains facts about the agency's function and history as well as photographs of agents in action. Alternatively, information can be obtained by sending a request in writing to U.S. Secret Service, Government Liaison and Public Affairs, 1800 G St. NW, Rm. 805, Washington, DC 20223 or by phoning (202) 435-5708.

AGENCY PUBLICATIONS

The USSS provides a pamphlet to merchants, banks, and others who handle money frequently; "Know Your Money" offers information about identifying counterfeit currency, coins, and other U.S. obligations and securities. Information on how to obtain a copy is available from most Secret Service field offices. The information can be downloaded from the Internet at http://www.treas.gov/usss/money. The USSS also distributes an assortment of informational pamphlets about its work and employees. These are available free of charge from U.S. Secret Service, Government Liaison and Public Affairs, 1800 G St. NW, Rm. 805, Washington, DC 20223. Pamphlets include: "The Secret Service Story," "United States Secret Service Uniformed Division," "Secret Service Protection," "Special Agent," and "Counterfeiting and Forgery." Also available is a 52-page souvenir booklet, *Moments in History 1965–1990.*

BIBLIOGRAPHY

Baughman, U. E., with Leonard Wallace Robinson *Secret Service Chief.* New York: Harper and Brothers Publishers, 1962.

Bowen, Walter Scott. *The United States Secret Service.* Philadelphia: Chilton Company, 1960.

Dorman, Michael. *The Secret Service Story.* New York: Delacorte Press, 1967.

Hersh, Seymour. *The Dark Side of Camelot.* Boston: Little, Brown, 1997.

Hyde, Wayne. *What Does a Secret Service Agent Do?* New York: Dodd, Mead, & Company, 1962.

McCarthy, Dennis. *Protecting the President.* New York: Morrow, 1985.

Melanson, Philip H. *The Politics of Protection: The U.S. Secret Service in the Terrorist Age.* New York: Praeger Publishers, 1984.

Smith, Elbert B. "Shoot-out on Pennsylvania Avenue," *American History*, July–August 1997, p. 16(9).

United States Sentencing Commission (USSC)

ESTABLISHED: October 1985
EMPLOYEES: Approximately 110

Contact Information:

ADDRESS: One Columbus Circle NE
Washington, DC 20002
PHONE: (202) 273-4510
FAX: (202) 273-4529
E-MAIL: OLPA@ussc.gov
URL: http://www.ussc.gov
CHAIRMAN: Richard P. Conaboy

WHAT IS ITS MISSION?

The primary purpose of the U.S. Sentencing Commission (USSC) is to make policy concerning sentencing for federal crimes, primarily by determining the appropriate length and severity of punishment for specific crimes. The commission also studies sentencing practices and their effects and serves as an information resource for Congress for these issues.

HOW IS IT STRUCTURED?

The United States Sentencing Commission is an independent agency in the judicial branch made up of seven voting members who are appointed by the president and confirmed by the Senate. The attorney general of the United States and the chairman of the U.S. Parole Commission are also included on the commission because of their positions and responsibilities. The commission is headed by a chairman.

Under the commission are five staff offices, which have a total of 100 employees. The director of each of these offices reports directly to the commission's staff director. The five offices are: General Counsel; Monitoring; Training and Technical Assistance; Policy Analysis; and Administration.

PRIMARY FUNCTIONS

The commission monitors current sentencing practices of federal and state courts, studies them, and then

FAST FACTS

In 1980, 9 percent of New York's felons were serving time for drug crimes. In 1997, 34 percent were in prison for drug crimes.

(Source: Alexandra Marks. "Cost Concerns Drive States To Ease Tough Sentences For Some Drug Offenders." *Christian Science Monitor*, May 5, 1997.)

proposes further guidelines to Congress. It combines current information on court practices with research on the most effective types of sentencing, which is gathered through the commission's own studies and from other professionals in the field, such as academics or other government agencies involved in law enforcement. With this information, the commission comes up with policy amendments to current sentencing rules and sends them to Congress. If Congress does not enact a law to counteract these amendments, they then go into effect automatically within 180 days.

In addition, the commission also provides training on the sentencing guidelines currently in use for judges, probation officers, prosecutors, defense attorneys, and others who work in the judicial field. The commission also provides information from its research to other groups, such as professors, students, and congressional offices.

PROGRAMS

The commission's programs primarily involve the collection and analysis of information. Frequently it is directed by Congress to study specific issues. For example, under the Violent Crime Control and Law Enforcement Act of 1994, it was directed to research and submit the following reports to Congress: Adequacy of Penalties for the Intentional Exposure of Others, through Sexual Activity, to Human Immunodeficiency Virus; Analysis of Penalties for Federal Rape Cases; Sex Crimes Against Children; and Cocaine and Federal Sentencing Policy.

Each of the commission's five offices also operates programs specific to its responsibilities. For example, the Office of Monitoring maintains a database of sentencing guideline information which is available to the public through the Inter-University Consortium for Political and Social Research at the University of Michigan. In the Office of Training and Technical Assistance, the sentencing guidelines are taught to judges and attorneys and others involved in the justice system. This office also offers a hot line to answer questions from professionals of the court system. According to the commission, 32 percent of staff resources is spent on monitoring sentence guidelines currently in effect, 13 percent on research and analysis, 10 percent on technical training, 16 percent on legal activities, and 29 percent on administrative support.

BUDGET INFORMATION

For the fiscal year 1996, Congress appropriated $8.5 million from the overall budget of the United States for the operation of the Commission. Of this total, the following were the most significant expenditures: $5.5 million for salaries and wages; $1.1 million for benefit packages for the employees; $325,000 for travel and transportation; $157,000 for communications, utilities, and other rent (for equipment and office space); $187,000 for printing and copying costs; $343,000 for supplies and equipment. In 1997, the estimated budget rose to $9.2 million.

HISTORY

Before the commission was created, sentencing was left largely to the discretion of individual federal judges. Judges had a great deal of latitude in determining how defined types of sentences would be applied. As a result, many sectors of society began to protest that sentences being handed down were inconsistent and ineffective. Opponents complained that some segments of society, such as minorities, were more vulnerable than others and were being given harsher sentences. They also complained that the same offense could bring widely varying punishments resulting in miscarriages of justice. Others wanted to force judges to impose harsher sentences. As a result of this ongoing controversy, Congress created the commission under the Sentencing Reform Act provisions of the Comprehensive Crime Control Act of 1984 as a permanent independent agency for formulating national sentencing guidelines that strictly defined judges' actions.

The commission was first organized in October 1985. Public hearings were held, more than 1,000 position papers were collected, and feedback was solicited for two years before the first guidelines and policies were submitted to Congress on April 13, 1987.

Once these guidelines were in effect, however, the constitutionality of the Sentencing Reform Act was immediately questioned, and opponents claimed the legislature did not have the power to make such guidelines. The Supreme Court eventually heard the case, and in *Mistretta v. United States*, it upheld the constitutionality of the act in January 1989. The commission has been in operation ever since.

CURRENT POLITICAL ISSUES

The debate that engendered the USSC has continued well after its initial guidelines were put into effect. The commission's mission to define and restrict the discretion federal judges have in sentencing has been put into practice and challenged in many different cases. The commission, nevertheless, continues to look for further guidelines that will streamline and make consistent the meting out of justice. With the great number and complexity of cases heard each year, problems have inevitably begun to arise.

Case Study: Mandatory Drug Sentencing

Included in the new federal sentencing guidelines that came into effect in 1984 were mandatory sentences for certain drug offenses that were not negotiable nor open to plea bargaining. In one case in Illinois a woman, coerced by her husband and fearing for the safety of her children, received cocaine on behalf of her husband from a policeman posing as a drug dealer. Because of mandatory drug sentencing laws, she was sentenced to six years in prison while her husband was sentenced to eight years. As the couple was tried in a federal court, the judge had no choice but to give the wife the mandatory federal sentence, even though the facts in the case may have suggested leniency.

Proponents of mandatory sentencing agree that some cases are mishandled but they insist that these are rare. They assert that mandatory sentencing discourages people from committing crimes and claim that society must find the money to build more prisons, because harsher laws mean fewer criminals on the streets.

Opponents claim that the result of such sentencing guidelines is often unjustly harsh. Additionally prisons are overflowing with drug offenders who are there for life with no parole. The states and the federal government cannot afford to build enough prisons or to keep them running efficiently. More than 90 percent of mandatory sentences handed down are for drug-related crimes.

Mandatory sentences cause other problems, opponents claim. Incarceration deprives children of their parents, and according to the Justice Department, 80 percent of the women in prisons are mothers. In addition, when given the choice of either pleading guilty and receiving the mandatory sentence or going to trial, defendants almost always choose trial, no matter how long the odds are against an acquittal. In the past, judges and prosecutors could plea bargain with defendants who faced a trial they most likely would lose, which allowed the courts to avoid the expense and time of a trial and moved clear-cut cases through the system quickly. Proponents of mandatory sentencing say that the judiciary must grow to meet these needs. Some proponents believe that a measure of discretion should be restored to the system, but they do not want a return to the pre-commission level of sentencing flexibility.

Public Impact

Congress and the commission continue to study and debate mandatory sentencing. Meanwhile, the courts are overloaded, the prisons full to capacity, and costs are escalating. New prisons are being built, although not quickly enough to meet immediate needs. At the same time, the overall murder rate in the nation's largest cities has dropped. In some areas, such as New York City, the overall crime rate is down. The country as a whole continues to adopt a "tough on crime" stance.

FUTURE DIRECTIONS

The commission's main goal is to simplify sentencing guidelines. Another agency goal is to provide a comprehensive review of all guidelines. Staff members will continue to research and analyze the guidelines' effectiveness and present reports of their findings.

AGENCY RESOURCES

Inquiries may be made by both surface and electronic mail. E-mail inquiries can be sent to OLPA@ussc.gov; surface mail can be sent to the Office of Legislative and Public Affairs, U.S. Sentencing Commission, One Columbus Circle NE, Washington, DC 20002-8002. The commission's Web site may be accessed at http://www.ussc.gov.

AGENCY PUBLICATIONS

Many publications are available at the commission's Web site under Guideline Training and Education at http://www.ussc.gov/training.htm. Topics at this site include educational materials, court decisions, and training opportunities. Available also at http://www.ussc.gov/research.htm is the *Commission's 1997 Guide to Publications and Resources*, as are various reports on the commission's latest studies. The commission also publishes a *Guidelines Manual*, as well as a companion *Video Reference Guide to the 1997 Amendments to the Federal Sentencing Guidelines.* These and many other publications may be obtained directly from the commission at the Office of Legislative and Public Affairs, U.S. Sentencing Commission, One Columbus Circle NE, Washington, DC 20002-8002.

BIBLIOGRAPHY

"Drug Policy: The Enemy Within." *Economist*, 15 May 1993.

"Drugs and Sentencing." *Christian Science Monitor*, 28 July 1997.

Fannon, Gary. "I Am Free." *Rolling Stone*, 19 September 1996.

Forer, Lois G. "Justice by Numbers." *Washington Monthly*, April 1992.

Hoffman, Jan. "Youths Held in Central Park Killing to Be Tried as Adults." *New York Times*, 28 May 1997.

Kamisar, Yale. "This Judge Was Not for Hanging." *New York Times Book Review*, 17 July 1994.

Marks, Alexandra. "Cost Concerns Drive States to Ease Tough Sentences for Some Drug Offenders." *Christian Science Monitor*, 5 May 1997.

Smolowe, Jill. "A High Price to Pay." *Time*, 19 December 1994.

Steinberg, Neil. "The Law Of Unintended Consequences." *Rolling Stone*, 5 May 1994.

Strauss, Neil. "The Acid Test." *Rolling Stone*, 14 July 1994.

"Three Strikes, You're Hoodwinked." *Economist*, 5 February 1994.

Tyson, James L. "Mandatory Sentences Lead to Surge of Women in Prison." *Christian Science Monitor*, 11 November 1993.

Wise, Daniel. "Prosecutors End-Run Guidelines." *National Law Journal*, 21 June 1993.

White House Office

WHAT IS ITS MISSION?

The White House Office assists the president in performing the many complex activities that are carried out under the president's authority. Because the president's most trusted and intimate advisers serve on the White House staff, the agency's primary loyalty is to the president himself. In general, the staff's mission is to promote and advance the president's programs and agenda, while deflecting or confronting the political criticisms and hazards that might harm the president's credibility.

PARENT ORGANIZATION: Executive Office of the President
ESTABLISHED: September 8, 1939
EMPLOYEES: 400

Contact Information:

ADDRESS: 1600 Pennsylvania Ave.
Washington, DC 20500
PHONE: (202) 456-1414
FAX: (202) 456-2461
E-MAIL: president@whitehouse.gov
URL: http://www.whitehouse.gov
CHIEF OF STAFF: Erskine B. Bowles
ASSISTANT TO THE PRESIDENT: John D. Podesta

HOW IS IT STRUCTURED?

Once elected, a president and his advisers have three months to organize a new White House. Two general structures have developed since the creation of the White House staff. The pyramid structure is a firm hierarchy with a strong chief of staff and clearly defined rules of access to the president. While this structure uses the staff's and president's time efficiently, it can also restrict his access to a range of opinions. The "spoked wheel" structure is more open, with the president at the center and accessible to many aides. This style presents the president with many different opinions, but it may also force aides to compete for the president's attention, exhausting the staff and preventing focus in the administration.

Unlike other agencies within the Executive Office of the President, the White House Office is not institutionalized, and it changes in size and form with each new administration. Staff members are appointed by the president and are not subject to congressional confirmation,

BIOGRAPHY:

William Jefferson Clinton

42nd President of the United States (b. 1946) When Arkansas elected Bill Clinton governor in 1978, the 32-year-old was the youngest governor in the United States since 1938. Although his enactment of higher gas taxes and license fees cost him his bid for reelection in 1980, Clinton returned as governor in 1982 to serve five consecutive terms. Clinton's bid for the presidency and, indeed, both terms in office were rocked by personal and political scandal. After announcing his candidacy for president in 1991, Clinton's character was called into question when he was accused of sexual harassment and evading military service during the Vietnam War. This did not damage his campaign enough, and his economic and domestic policies led to his election in 1992, making him the forty-first president. President Clinton initially met with frustration as Congress disapproved many of his appointees and failed to enact the national health care system on which he campaigned. However as his term progressed, he did succeed in convincing Congress to approve massive deficit-reduction legislation; the Brady Bill, which strengthened gun control; the Family and Medical Leave Act; and an increase of the minimum wage. Despite allegations of misconduct by Clinton and his wife, Hillary, in a real estate deal in the 1980s (dubbed "Whitewater"), Clinton was reelected in 1996. In 1998 Clinton was again embroiled in controversy after admitting to what he called an "inappropriate" relationship with a 21-year-old White House intern. Throughout it all he continued to maintain high public approval ratings, which most attribute to a booming U.S. economy.

so they have no official government status and can be hired or dismissed at any time for any reason. Presidents may create, abolish, or reorganize offices within the White House as they choose and in fact are free to eliminate the entire staff if they so desire. Functions assigned to one office tend to vary from one administration to another, and job titles do not always give an accurate picture of a staff member's responsibilities. Nevertheless, some White House positions have become somewhat standardized over the years.

The chief of staff has become the most important White House post because that person is responsible for the smooth operation of the entire staff. The chief often acts as the "gatekeeper" to the president, determining who actually needs to see and discuss things with the president and which requests or personnel can be funneled to other offices.

Every president's White House staff is also served by a special counsel, which most likely is a team of legal professionals rather than a single individual and acts as the president's private legal staff. Traditionally, presidents have placed valuable aides with jobs not formally described in the White House staff structure in this office, such as Theodore Sorensen, President John F. Kennedy's domestic policy adviser and speechwriter; and Lloyd Cutler, President Jimmy Carter's adviser on foreign and domestic policy.

The president is also served by a number of national security and domestic advisers, including the national security adviser—the president's primary adviser on foreign policy. Because of the wide array of executive departments, each acting as a separate source of policy advice, domestic advisers have less control than do security advisers.

Many offices in the White House are liaisons to the world outside. They include: (1) The office of the press secretary. This office manages the adminstration's relationship with the news media. In some administrations, a separate Communications Office has been set up to take a more activist approach in "managing the news" or serving as a kind of public relations office for the president; (2) The congressional liaison office. Most administrations have some form of congressional liaison office which controls the interactions between the president and Congress and serves as a channel through which individual members of Congress can communicate with the president; and (3) The public liaison office. Most administrations have also employed some sort of public liaison office, established to build public support for the administration's policies. Presidential speechwriters are sometimes associated with these staffs, but in recent administrations they have tended to occupy distinct and increasingly specialized positions. In many administrations, speechwriters have played an important role in policy formation.

All presidential staffs maintain a central personnel office, that is responsible for recruiting and interviewing potential officeholders.

PRIMARY FUNCTIONS

The various staff offices and positions within the White House Office provide the president with the advice, information, and administrative assistance necessary for making executive decisions.

The chief of staff maintains the swift and accurate flow of business inside the White House by managing personnel, information, materials, and workload. The chief of staff is also responsible for assuring that the proper offices have viewed proposed presidential documents in order to give commentary and clearance. Most chiefs of staff have denied serving as policy-making assistants to the president, but in reality many chiefs do serve the president as a policy adviser. Informal but important parts of the chief's job description are carrying out unpleasant personnel decisions (dismissals and transfers) made by the president and also shielding the president from certain mistakes or failures. For example, a loyal chief will take the blame for furnishing incorrect information or for making a misstatement in order to deflect criticism from the president. The most effective chiefs have been willing when necessary to serve as a presidential scapegoat.

The special counsel provides legal advice on a number of topics and reviews proposed legislation before it is sent to Congress. The counsel also advises the president about the legality of certain executive actions and often reviews proposed treaties for potential legal problems. Since the Watergate scandal of President Richard M. Nixon's administration, the office of special counsel has also been responsible for ensuring proper behavior by the presidential staff.

Foreign and domestic policy advisers help the president make effective policy decisions. The national security adviser position was formerly an administrative post responsible for coordinating elements of the foreign policy establishment, such as the National Security Council, the State and Defense Departments, and the Central Intelligence Agency. This position's duties have evolved, however, to include offering foreign policy recommendations to the president. Domestic policy advisers generally collect, rather than offer, advice. They settle disputes between domestic agencies and use input from them to formulate legislative proposals.

The liaison offices facilitate communication between the president and the world outside the Executive Office. Members of the congressional liaison office present the president's positions to Congress, nurture good relationships with congressional supporters, and provide these allies with information and support in order to help persuade others in Congress and defend their positions in their home states. Public liaison staff contact constituency groups and try to educate them about the administration's goals and successes. The Communications Office or press secretary actively promotes presidential achievements, issues news summaries and daily briefings to the press, and undertakes "damage control" in time of crisis.

FAST FACTS

The first presidential "staff" member was the nephew of President George Washington, who was hired to assist the first president in 1792. Washington paid his nephew $300 a year—money that came out of Washington's own pocket.

(Source: *Cabinets and Counselors*, Congressional Quarterly, Inc., 1997.)

The personnel office recruits and interviews candidates. It also works with the special counsel's office to conduct background checks on candidates and presents the nominee to the president and the Senate (if necessary) for approval. Once a White House staffer is recommended, the personnel office is responsible for briefing the appointee on questions he or she might face from a Senate confirmation panel.

BUDGET INFORMATION

Arriving at an accurate figure for the White House budget is a complex task that depends on a number of variables. For instance, many presidents "detail" personnel from the executive departments, or essentially use department employees as staffers who are paid out of the department's budget. The practices of contracting out short-term tasks or of hiring temporary staff out of discretionary funds also make an accurate estimate of staff and budget difficult. The 1998 federal budget documents provide a budget for the White House that lists 400 White House personnel and includes the president's compensation (a salary of $200,000 and a $50,000 expense account). According to the 1998 budget, by far the greatest portion, about 45 percent, of the White House's $53 million budget goes to the compensation of full-time salaried employees. The rest is spent on expenses associated with benefits, supplies, and services such as utilities, travel, printing and reproduction, and communications.

HISTORY

Large presidential staffs are a relatively recent development, a response to the growing complexity of the executive's job. Staff positions for early presidents involved merely clerical tasks such as paperwork or scheduling appointments. Congress did not specifically appropriate funds for a presidential staff until 1857, when it provided an allowance for a single presidential secretary. Presidents who wanted more help were expected to pay for it themselves.

Presidents' personal financial limitations, along with the small size of the federal government, kept the White House staff fairly small throughout the entire nineteenth century, although many presidents surmounted financial obstacles by borrowing employees from the cabinet agencies. By the early twentieth century, however, the growing demands of the president's job and the expansion of the federal government created a need for more in-house advisers who were not burdened by other jobs. During this time the presidential secretary evolved from that of an office assistant to one of a presidential aide skilled in political and personnel matters.

The Beginning of the Staff System under Roosevelt

The modern White House staff system was created under the administration of Franklin Roosevelt, who served as president from 1933 to 1945. Like the presidents before him, Roosevelt requisitioned aides from the executive departments. Faced with the daunting task of rebuilding the U.S. economy during the Great Depression, however, he quickly found this arrangement hopelessly inadequate. Dealing with the nation's problems, he believed, required a larger permanent staff who would work only for him.

In 1937 Roosevelt's beliefs were supported by a report from the Committee on Administrative Management, more commonly known as the Brownlow Commission, which was directed to study the staffing needs of the presidency. The commission concluded that the president needed help in dealing with the "managerial agencies and departments of the government" and recommended the creation of additional staff to assist him. The committee also proposed that this new staff would "remain in the background, issue no orders, make no decisions, [and] emit no public statements." Its job was solely to support decisions and policies made by the president himself.

Within two years, Congress agreed to implement the committee's findings. The president was authorized to hire six new administrative assistants and to reorganize the executive branch. In 1939 Roosevelt created the Executive Office of the President (EOP), which was designed to be a more permanent and professional support staff than that of the White House. The White House was then considered a small contingent of personal assistants to the president, while the new EOP would be the institutionalized foundation of the presidency. His staff remained rather small and unstructured, however, and he worked with each member individually, assigning all tasks himself.

A Growing Staff

Roosevelt's staff grew considerably during World War II, and his successor, Harry S. Truman, began his administration distrustful of such a large staff, fearing it would impair his interaction with the cabinet agencies. He initially planned to reduce the staff, but economic and political demands at the end of the war resulted in a staff that was even larger than Roosevelt's. By 1947 Truman employed over 200 White House staffers.

Under Truman, the staff not only grew but became more structured. In 1946 he created the position of assistant to the president, a direct forerunner of the modern chief of staff. The assistant's responsibilities included controlling staff access to the president and helping to solve problems that arose in the cabinet agencies.

Perhaps the most significant development of the Truman White House was the emergence of staffers as policy advocates. The Brownlow Commission had envisioned White House aides as neutral facilitators of presidential policy, leaving policy advice to the cabinet; but special counsel Clark Clifford became a key figure in advocating liberal positions to the president. His role represented one of the most potentially significant changes in the balance of power within the executive branch, but its impact would not be realized until later.

The Consolidation of White House Power

When President John F. Kennedy took office in 1961, he was determined to return the White House staff structure to the openness that existed under Franklin Roosevelt. He had no formal chief of staff, preferring to control the paper flow through the White House himself. As the public began to look increasingly toward the president rather than the legislature to solve the nation's problems, the Kennedy White House expanded in influence as well as size. Kennedy's senior advisers were far more powerful than any previous White House officers and became involved to an unprecedented degree in policy decisions. Under Kennedy the top-level staff became advisers and advocates more than aides, especially in foreign policy, and the White House became a kind of "shadow government" as influential as the other elements of the bureaucracy. Kennedy's successor, Lyndon Johnson, further concentrated power within his White House, and the staff that he passed on to President Richard Nixon in 1969 was both the largest and the most influential in history.

When President Richard Nixon took office, the White House soon took on the most elaborate structure ever, a complex hierarchy staffed by increasingly specialized advisers, aides, liaisons, and speechwriters. It was a small bureaucracy in its own right, parallel to that of the rest of the federal government. In 1970 the number of White House staffers exceeded 600.

During this period the unintended consequence of the president's autonomy became clear: the White House's virtual self-rule had interfered with its ability to distinguish between the public's interest and its own. The staff's power, its passion for serving Nixon, and the lack of any outside supervisory agency led to the criminal excesses known collectively as Watergate, which would eventually drive many staffers as well as Nixon himself from office. The Watergate scandals severely damaged the public's faith in the presidency and slowed the steady trend toward a larger and more powerful White House staff.

Later Trends

White House staffs since Watergate have been carefully structured to avoid the same kinds of abuses of power that can result in public humiliation and criticism. Virtually every president since Nixon has declared a desire to return to an executive branch whose policies and decisions are driven by the cabinet agencies, only to turn to the White House staff, however, after becoming frustrated with the slow pace of the bureaucracy. Gerald Ford and Jimmy Carter, Nixon's immediate successors, tried seriously to curtail the power of the chief of staff and return to a more informal structure, abandoning the Nixon hierarchy altogether. As a result, the presidents spent too much time settling internal disputes and debates themselves, and neither president was able to reduce the staff's influence as much as he had wanted. By 1980 the White House staff had again grown so large that staff reductions were difficult. Staff operations did not appear to be possible without a chief of staff and clear lines of authority.

President Ronald Reagan's staff was designed specifically to keep unnecessary details away from the president. Policy specifics were worked out at lower levels, and only the most important questions and issues were taken to the president. Despite Reagan's initial desire to return to cabinet government, his White House staff remained a large, structured, and influential force.

The White House staff has become increasingly concerned with the president's public image, especially during the terms of President Bill Clinton. Beset by an unusual number of intense political attacks from opponents, along with a few serious public-relations blunders by the president himself, the Clinton White House was seen by many to be unusually occupied with promoting and, at times, repairing the president's public image. Following Clinton's 1996 reelection, it was revealed that many staffers had conducted campaign promotion and fundraising activities to a degree with which many members of Congress and the public were not comfortable. Many felt that the White House's ultimate duty of public service had once again been forgotten in its quest to consolidate presidential power.

CURRENT POLITICAL ISSUES

The dramatic and rapid growth of the White House Office over the last half-century has been seriously criticized by a number of scholars and political scientists: they argue that the staff has grown too large to be sufficiently supervised and managed; the possibility for the distortion or loss of information on its way to the president is too great; and too many special interests vie for the president's attention. The Nixon White House has served as a lesson and a warning to all later presidential staffs that politics and ambition can corrupt the presidency.

All post-Watergate presidents have installed a prominently independent force of lawyers in the Office of Counsel to the President in order to keep corruption and questionable legal practices out of the White House and away from the president. These lawyers are typically led by a Washington veteran and are meant to sound the alarm when politics or special interests threaten the president's integrity. The Office of Counsel also drafts legal guidelines in order to protect the president and his subordinates from questionable practices and associations.

The Clinton White House

The Office of Counsel has also traditionally served as a kind of "catch-all" office for staffers with no official job titles (speechwriters, for example) who reported not to the chief counsel but to designated staffers in charge of their areas of responsibility. In the Clinton administration, the president's method of staffing his Office of Counsel added fuel to the controversies surrounding the 1996 campaign.

Federal laws make it a crime to receive political contributions from foreign nationals, to accept campaign contributions in the name of another, to provide a governmental favor in return for a political contribution, and for any person to request or receive political contributions in public buildings. Many government officials and members of the media believed that the Clinton White House had violated each of these rules to some degree during the 1996 presidential election. The president himself acknowledged that "mistakes were made" by his staff, although he denied that any laws had been broken.

Some of the faultfinding was aimed at the particulars of White House activities. For example, "coffees" and "sleepovers" that took place in the White House and were explicitly referred to in staff memos as "fundraisers." Others were most concerned by the state of the Office of Counsel. Instead of a cadre of independent lawyers headed by a steadfast Washington veteran, the Clinton administration's Office of Counsel had five chief counsels by 1997, and the office was consistently staffed by previous acquaintances of the president or his aides.

One attorney hired as a special council to the president, Jane Sherburne, reported directly to Harold Ickes, head of the president's re-election drives, instead of to the White House counsel's office.

SUCCESSES AND FAILURES

In the White House staff's brief history, one of its greatest successes has also been one of its most consistently criticized features: the office's commanding role in the formation of policy. The White House's political dominance has arisen naturally as a consequence of the president's desire to control the policy-making functions of government. Whereas the Brownlow Commission envisioned a staff of aides who would provide the president with only objective information and options, it became obvious during the Kennedy administration, which employed a group of powerful political figures, that this ideal of neutrality had been lost. While staffs since Watergate have not dominated the cabinet departments—the true intended makers of policy—as much as the Nixon White House, they still tend to be primary actors in the policy-making process.

A White House policy-making mechanism, critics charge, necessarily lacks long-term focus, concentrating instead on policies that will prove advantageous in the election cycle. An additional criticism is that there is something disturbing in a constitutional government about having major policy decisions made by unelected staff members who are accountable only to the president.

FUTURE DIRECTIONS

The future of any White House staff extends only as far as the administration it serves. Early in 1998, White House Chief of Staff Erskine Bowles expressed his hopes that with no federal deficit concerns, the White House could pursue an activist program of spending in areas such as day care and health care, education and the environment, and public works.

AGENCY RESOURCES

Further information about the White House can be obtained by calling the White House Office directly at (212) 456-1414. Another resource is *CQ's Guide to the Presidency*, published by Congressional Quarterly, Inc., a private, nonpartisan organization. It is regularly updated and contains a great deal of information about the history, structure, and functions of the White House staff.

Another information resource is the White House Help Desk at http://www.whitehouse.gov/WH/html.helpdsk.html, a search engine at the White House's Internet site that provides information about the staff and answers to frequently asked questions.

AGENCY PUBLICATIONS

The White House staff prints and publishes literally hundreds of press releases each year, as well as transcripts of all the president's executive orders, speeches, and radio addresses since the start of the administration. Nearly all of these documents may be viewed or downloaded from the White House Virtual Library at http://www.whitehouse.gov/WH/html/library.html, a component of the White House's Internet site. The Virtual Library also offers subscriptions to daily releases of presidential speeches or White House briefings at http://www.pub.whitehouse.gov/WH/Publications/html/Publications.html. White House publications may also be ordered from the Superintendent of Documents, Government Printing Office, Washington, DC 20402; phone (202) 512-1800.

BIBLIOGRAPHY

Broder, John M. "Bowles Tells Cheering Staff He's Staying." *New York Times*, 14 January 1998, p. A12(N), A14(L).

Cabinets and Counselors. 2d ed. Washington, D.C.: Congressional Quarterly, 1997.

Congressional Quarterly's Guide to the Presidency. Washington, D.C.: Congressional Quarterly, 1989.

Freidel, Frank, et al. *The White House: The First Two Hundred Years.* Boston: Northeastern University Press, 1993.

Garrett, Wendell, ed. *Our Changing White House.* Boston: Northeastern University Press, 1995.

Kessler, Ron. *Inside the White House.* New York: Pocket Books, 1996.

Nelson, Michael, ed. *Congressional Quarterly's Guide to the Presidency.* Washington: Congressional Quarterly, Inc., 1996.

Olson, Theodore B. "Why Isn't the White House Counsel's Office Doing Its Job?" *Wall Street Journal*, 5 March 1997, p. A19.

Peterson, Jonathan, and Ralph Frammolino. "Papers Reveal More White House Fund-Raising Practices." *Los Angeles Times*, 3 April 1997, p. A14.

Seale, William. *The White House: The History of an American Idea.* Washington: American Institute of Architects Press, 1992.

The White House: An Historic Guide. Washington: National Geographic Society, 1987.

White House Office for Women's Initiatives and Outreach (OWIO)

PARENT ORGANIZATION: Executive Office of the President
ESTABLISHED: June 5, 1995
EMPLOYEES: 2

Contact Information:

ADDRESS: Rm. 15, Old Executive Office Bldg.
Washington, DC 20502
PHONE: (202) 456-7300
FAX: (202) 456-7311
URL: http://www.whitehouse.gov/WH/EOP/Women/OWIO
ACTING DIRECTOR: Maureen Tayse Shea

WHAT IS ITS MISSION?

The mission of the White House Office for Women's Initiatives and Outreach (OWIO) is to create a network for the national women's community and to keep its leaders apprised of new policies and issues associated with women that are being considered by the White House. OWIO serves as a contact point and an advocacy office within the White House for women's organizations and their concerns.

HOW IS IT STRUCTURED?

OWIO is an office within the White House Office of Public Liaison, a part of the Executive Office of the President. OWIO differs from many other units of the federal government in that it is not an agency, bureau, or department but serves as a deputy assistant to the president with the director being appointed at the president's discretion. Although the permanent OWIO staff only consists of the director and one assistant, it is extremely dynamic. OWIO regularly hosts representatives from an assortment of government agencies as well as White House interns.

The director of OWIO also serves as a member of the President's Interagency Council on Women, founded in 1995 as an executive response to the United Nations Fourth World Conference on Women in Beijing, China. The council's purpose is to implement the *Platform for Action* defined at the China conference and consists of representatives from agencies within the executive branch, including the Departments of Labor, Education, Justice, Agriculture, and State.

PRIMARY FUNCTIONS

OWIO conducts political outreach by funneling information from the administration to a national constituency of established women's groups and other organizations. OWIO is not a lobbying office; rather, it presents issues and provides feedback directly to the president to help him better understand the public's needs and concerns. OWIO also collaborates with other federal agencies on projects that specifically relate to women's issues using interagency representatives who are temporarily assigned as assistants to the OWIO director.

OWIO maintains regular communication with a variety of women's organizations and distributes a timely fact sheet to groups such as the Business and Professional Women of the USA, the Women's Law Center, the Young Women's Christian Association (YWCA) of the U.S.A., and the National Organization for Women (NOW). OWIO also provides reprints of speeches and shares information with a number of health organizations, civic groups, and others about the status of relevant legislation and other items of special interest.

The director of OWIO is also a resource to the vice president and to the spouses of the president and vice president, furnishing information and feedback for their roles as goodwill ambassadors of the administration.

PROGRAMS

The director of OWIO arranges a series of "At the Table" roundtable conferences throughout the nation, each of which is hosted by a presidential appointee from within the administration (not necessarily a member of OWIO). Group members discuss a wide range of issues including welfare reform, health care, education, childcare, and equal opportunity. Following every "At the Table" affair, the appointee submits a follow-up report to OWIO, which in turn compiles monthly reports for the White House.

Roundtables can be held anywhere, and agendas vary depending on the host, sponsors, and specific interest groups involved. Anyone can initiate an "At the Table" function by serving as a contact or by providing organizational assistance.

Girl Power!

"Girl Power!" was initiated by the Department of Health and Human Services but endorsed by the entire White House, including OWIO. Geared to young women, "Girl Power!" focuses on health promotion and drug abuse prevention and is supported by a variety of public and private organizations including Girls Incorporated, the Young Women's Christian Association (YWCA), and the American Association of University Women. It typifies the networking and support that the OWIO was created to help establish.

BUDGET INFORMATION

OWIO expenses are included in the budget of the Office of Public Liaison, under the President's White House budget authority, which is itemized as the Executive Office of the President. OWIO expenses are not detailed specifically in the federal budget, and unlike agencies and other types of departments, OWIO does not receive a yearly allocation with predefined purposes. Instead, the director of OWIO submits expenditures to the administrative office of the White House. The administrative office then handles the finances.

HISTORY

President Clinton started the White House Office for Women's Initiatives and Outreach in 1995 to serve as a liaison between the White House and women's groups around the country, and to ensure that the concerns of women would be heard by the administration. Betsy Myers was appointed the first director of OWIO.

The members of OWIO immediately focused their energies and attention on promoting "At the Table" roundtable discussion groups to encourage the discussion of women's issues in an open environment. More than 1,000 women participated in scores of roundtables across the country during the program's first six months of operation. Discussions were hosted by representatives from several federal agencies including the Office of Management and Budget, the Department of Energy, and the Department of Commerce. Among the attendees were representatives from the Asian Business Women's Group of San Francisco, professional women from Chicago, Russian women visitors, and influential women leaders from Delaware.

In 1996 a group met to discuss women's reproductive rights. Taxation issues were also on the agenda of that roundtable, which was hosted by U.S. Treasurer Mary Ellen Withrow. Another 1996 project, hosted by Lydia Bickford of the Department of the Interior, was organized through E-mail resources on the Internet in an effort to reach thousands of women simultaneously. Another program in that same year incorporated 12 separate and concurrent roundtable gatherings, highlighted by a panel discussion with First Lady Hillary Rodham Clinton. On July 23, 1996, President Clinton hosted an "At the Table" discussion in Denver, Colorado. The presidential roundtable of sixteen women was organized by *Family Circle* and discussed children, education, and crime. OWIO has sponsored other media events since its inception, including the President's and First Lady's Suffrage celebration in Wyoming in 1995.

CURRENT POLITICAL ISSUES

OWIO is involved in issues that range from guaranteeing better educational opportunities and equal pay for women to domestic violence, sexual abuse, and sexual harassment in the workplace. Sexual harassment in the workplace came to public attention following the passage of the Civil Rights Act (Title VII) of 1964. Because norms of sexual harassment differ between regions of the country as well as among different professions it was never clearly defined by the courts. For lack of definition, some factions argued that sexual harassment in the workplace constitutes sexual discrimination under the Civil Rights Act. Most agree that the psychological effects of sexual harassment can be devastating and that victims should be encouraged to come forward.

Case Study: Paula Corbin Jones vs. President Bill Clinton

A highly publicized case of sexual harassment in the workplace was brought against President Bill Clinton in 1994 by a former Arkansas state employee, Paula Corbin Jones. Jones alleged that Clinton used his position as governor of Arkansas in 1991 to lure her to a hotel room, where he made unwanted sexual advances toward her.

Her lawsuit was delayed by a long series of motions filed by lawyers for both parties. At the peak of the controversy, White House reporters predicted that the president might resign or even be impeached. OWIO was in a difficult position. It was an office created to voice women's concerns by a president who was now being attacked by many women's organizations. When confronted directly, OWIO remained supportive of the president. The director at that time, Director Haynes, admitted that the issue deserved scrutiny, but she also maintained that opinions varied and discouraged a "rush to judgment."

Haynes's moderate attitude prompted outrage and accusations of political hypocrisy when she and other prominent OWIO members did not condemn Clinton. Observers compared the Paula Jones harassment case to the 1991 incident between Anita Hill and Clarence Thomas, when Hill publicly accused Thomas, a nominee for the Supreme Court, of sexual harassment. Few could understand why Paula Jones received little support from the women's rights coalition.

A *Time/CNN* poll early in 1997 revealed public ambivalence in the matter—37 percent of respondents believed Bill Clinton, 29 percent believed Paula Jones, and 34 percent were not sure. *Time* also published the results of a separate public opinion poll in June 1997 showing that the majority of people surveyed (62 percent) believed that Paula Jones's sexual history should be considered relevant evidence in the case, a stance traditionally rejected by women's support groups. John Leo of *U.S. News and World Report* claimed "[I]t's a sad thing to see the presidency brought so low that it may be dragged into a long [civil] trial. [The people of the United States are] desperate for stable and honest leaders who are what they appear to be. The search isn't going well."

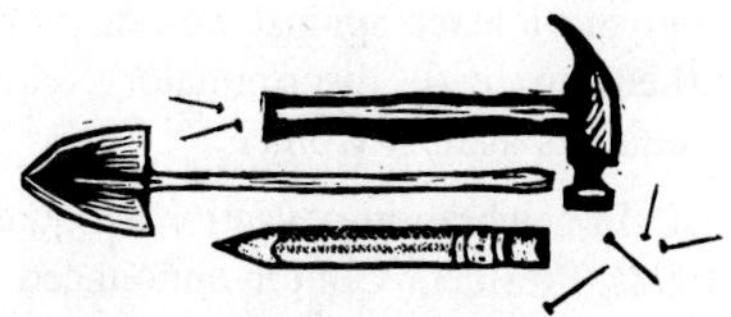

GET INVOLVED:

Although "At the Table" discussions must be hosted by presidential appointees, anyone can initiate a discussion group by calling the OWIO office at (202) 456-7300 or by sending a fax to (202) 456–7311. The office furnishes "At the Table" kits with information on how to organize and stage a roundtable and provides connections with host/hostess volunteers and other support as needed.

Paula Jones's lawsuit left the country confused and at odds, even when the case was dismissed in 1998 for lack of evidence.

In June 1998, the Supreme Court handed down two precedent-setting decisions about the definition of sexual harassment. One decision upheld an employer's ultimate liability for incidents of harassment, regardless of whether or not the employee complained. In the second decision, the Court ruled that the crime of harassment may exist even in the absence of a detriment to the employee's career. That is, the plaintiff does not have to prove damages, such as failure to receive a promotion as a result of having refused unwelcome sexual advances.

The new Supreme Court decisions reflected favorably on the Clinton administration and OWIO, and for a time their stance on the Paula Corbin Jones lawsuit appeared to be vindicated. Ironically, it was later discovered that President Clinton had lied or been misleading in his answers in a deposition taken for the Jones case. The resulting revelations about a voluntary relationship Clinton engaged in with Monica Lewinsky, a White House intern, gave Paula Jones's charges new credibility, and provided her with powerful ammunition for her appeal. OWIO was once again opened to charges of hypocrisy as a representative of women's concerns.

FUTURE DIRECTIONS

Because the director of OWIO is an assistant to the president, the office's accomplishments and future success of OWIO are measured in light of the policies and actions of the administration which it serves. On International Women's Day (March 6, 1998), President Clinton urged ratification of the "Convention on the Elimination of All Forms of Discrimination Against Women," an international treaty among 162 nations that would combat violence against women worldwide. It also proposed to end discriminatory laws and economic inequities against women.

In celebration of National Equal Pay Day (April 3, 1998), President Clinton announced a proposed funding package of $43 million to assist the Equal Employment Opportunity Commission and the Department of Labor in enforcing laws against workplace discrimination and expediting the resolution of complaints in this area.

AGENCY RESOURCES

The President's Interagency Council on Women was formed to carry out the mission and platform established at the United Nations Fourth World Conference on Women in Beijing, China (August 1995). Information about the council is available from President's Interagency Council on Women, U.S. Department of State, Room 2906, 2201 C St. NW, Washington, D.C. 20520; phone: (202) 647-6227 or fax: (202) 647-5337. For background, archives, and council news, see the World Wide Web at http://secretary.state.gov/www/iacw/index.html.

BIBLIOGRAPHY

Aburdene, Patricia, and John Naisbit. *Megatrends for Women.* New York: Villard Books, 1992.

Becker, Susan D. *The Origins of the Equal Rights Amendment.* Westport, Ct.: Greenwood Press, 1981.

Beinart, Peter. "Hypocritics: The Right's Newfound Feminism." *New Republic*, 30 March 1998, p. 9(2).

Bernikow, Louise. *The American Women's Almanac.* New York: Berkley Books, 1997.

Ireland, Patricia. *What Women Want.* New York: Plume Books, 1997.

Lawrence, Candida. *Reeling & Writhing.* Aspen, Colo.: MacMurray and Beck, 1994.

President's Interagency Council on Women. *America's Commitment: Federal Programs Benefitting Women and New Initiatives as Follow-Up to the U.N. Fourth World Conference on Women.* Washington, D.C., 1997.

Swisher, Karin L., ed. *What Is Sexual Harassment?* San Diego: Greenhaven Press, Inc., 1995.

Wall, Edmund, ed. *Sexual Harassment: Confrontations and Decisions.* Buffalo, N.Y.: Prometheus Books, 1992.

Appendixes, Glossary, & Subject Index

The United States Government

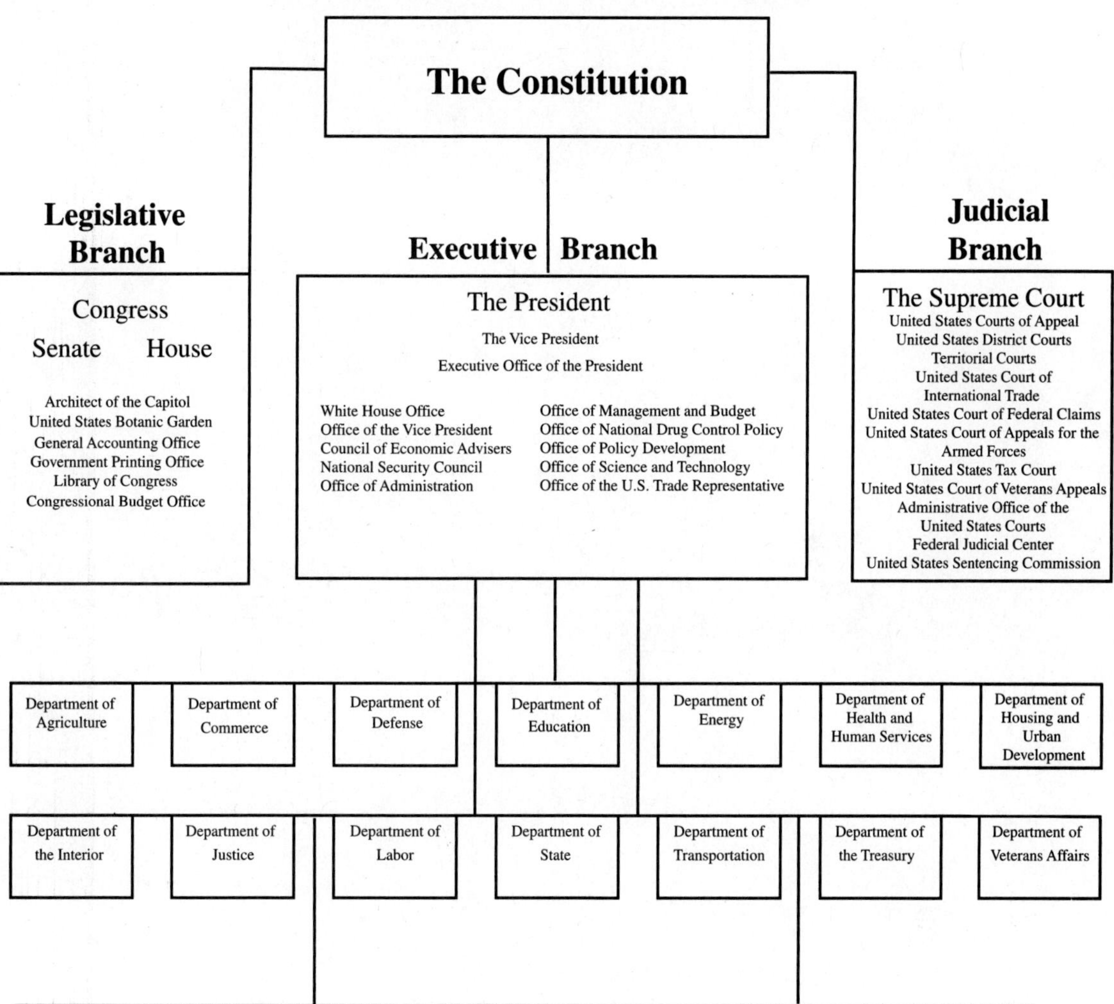

Government Corporations and Independent Establishments

African Development Foundation
Central Intelligence Agency
Commodity Futures Trading Commission
Consumer Product Safety Commission
Corporation for National and Community Service
Defense Nuclear Facilities Safety Board
Environmental Protection Agency
Equal Employment Opportunity Commission
Export-Import Bank of the United States
Farm Credit Administration
Federal Communications Commission
Federal Deposit Insurance Corporation
Federal Election Commission
Federal Emergency Management Agency
Federal Labor Relations Authority
Federal Maritime Commission
Federal Mediation and Conciliation Service
Federal Reserve System
Federal Trade Commission
General Services Administration
Inter-American Foundation
Legal Services Corporation
National Academy of Sciences
National Aeronautics and Space Administration
National Archives and Records Administration
National Council on Disability
National Credit Union Administration
National Endowment for the Arts
National Endowment for the Humanities
National Labor Relations Board
National Mediation Board
National Railroad Passenger Corporation (Amtrak)
National Science Foundation
National Transportation Safety Board
Nuclear Regulatory Commission
Office of Government Ethics
Office of Special Counsel
Peace Corps
Pension Benefit Guaranty Corporation
Postal Rate Commission
Securities and Exchange Commission
Selective Service System
Small Business Administration
Smithsonian Institution
Social Security Administration
Tennessee Valley Authority
Trade and Development Agency
United States Arms Control and Disarmament Agency
United States Commission on Civil Rights
United States Holocaust Memorial Museum
United States Information Agency
United States Institute of Peace
United States International Trade Commission
United States Postal Service

Federal Government System of Checks and Balances

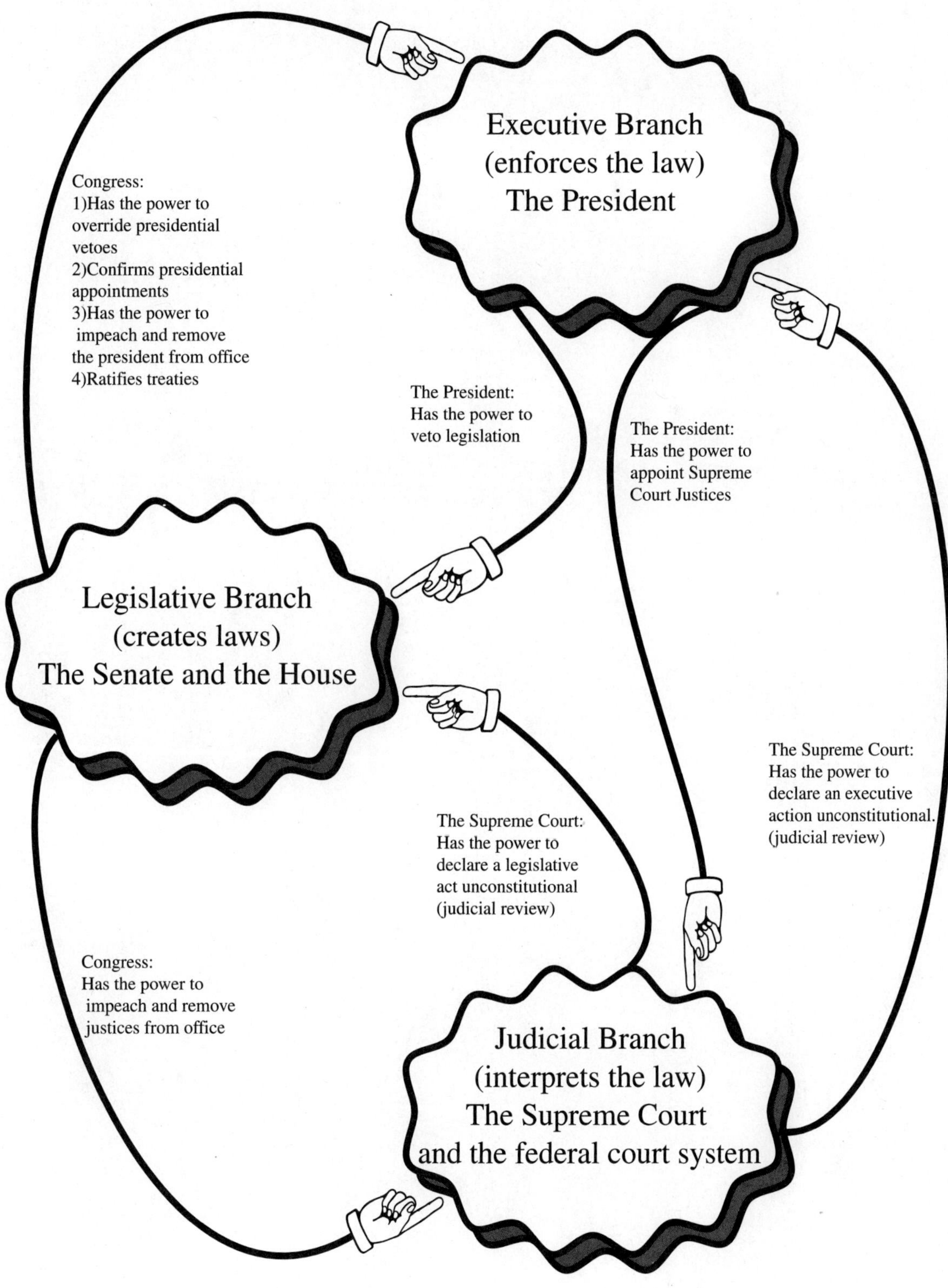
Executive Branch
(enforces the law)
The President
Congress:
1)Has the power to override presidential vetoes
2)Confirms presidential appointments
3)Has the power to impeach and remove the president from office
4)Ratifies treaties
The President:
Has the power to veto legislation
The President:
Has the power to appoint Supreme Court Justices
Legislative Branch
(creates laws)
The Senate and the House
The Supreme Court:
Has the power to declare an executive action unconstitutional.
(judicial review)
The Supreme Court:
Has the power to declare a legislative act unconstitutional
(judicial review)
Congress:
Has the power to impeach and remove justices from office
Judicial Branch
(interprets the law)
The Supreme Court
and the federal court system

Breakdown of Federal Government Expeditures

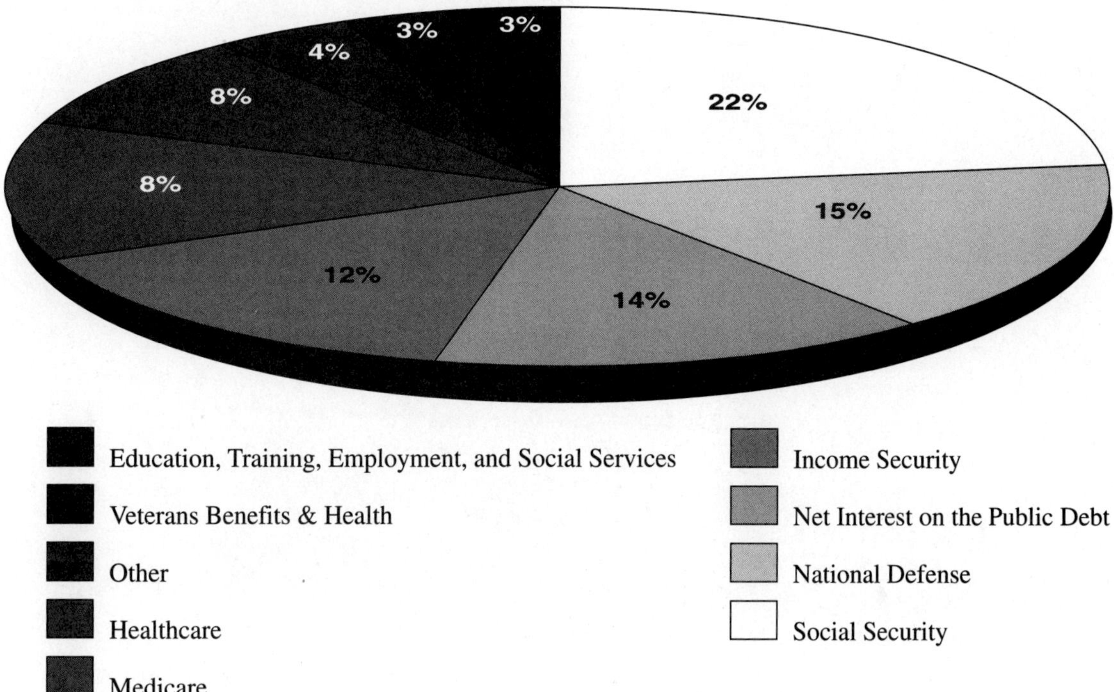

Breakdown of Federal Government Revenues

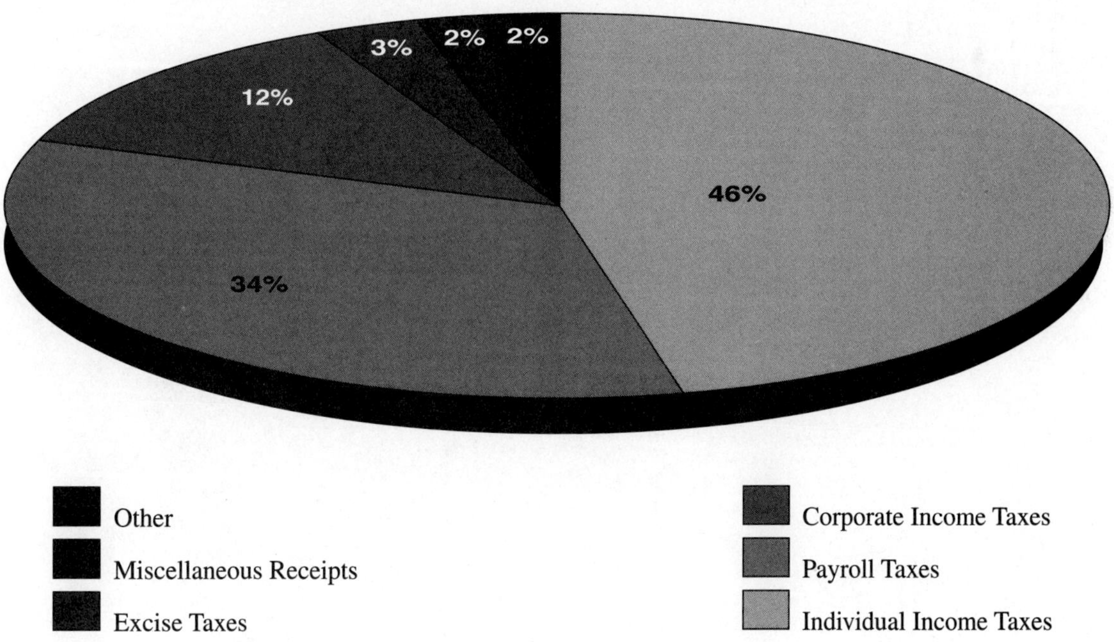

Source: A Citizen's Guide to the Federal Budget: Budget of the United States Government Fiscal Year 1999.

How a Bill Becomes a Law

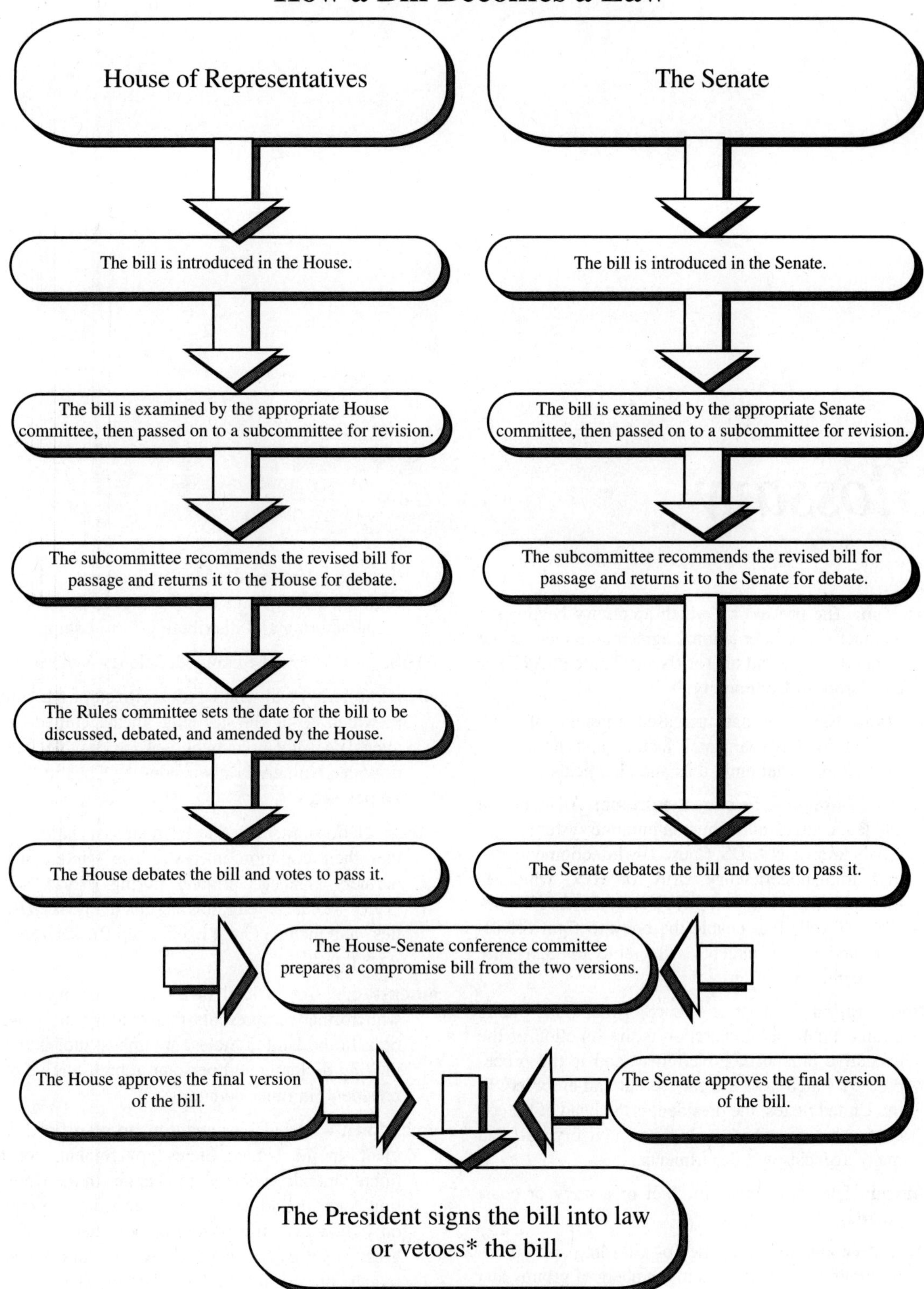

House of Representatives
The Senate
The bill is introduced in the House.
The bill is introduced in the Senate.
The bill is examined by the appropriate House committee, then passed on to a subcommittee for revision.
The bill is examined by the appropriate Senate committee, then passed on to a subcommittee for revision.
The subcommittee recommends the revised bill for passage and returns it to the House for debate.
The subcommittee recommends the revised bill for passage and returns it to the Senate for debate.
The Rules committee sets the date for the bill to be discussed, debated, and amended by the House.
The House debates the bill and votes to pass it.
The Senate debates the bill and votes to pass it.
The House-Senate conference committee prepares a compromise bill from the two versions.
The House approves the final version of the bill.
The Senate approves the final version of the bill.
The President signs the bill into law or vetoes* the bill.

*If the bill is vetoed by the President, it can become law if two-thirds of both houses vote to override.

Glossary

A

accession: The process by which a country becomes a member of an international agreement, such as the General Agreement on Tariffs and Trade (GATT) or the European Community.

acid rain: Rain that has increased amounts of acid. Caused by environmental factors and pollutants, such as industrial emissions and chemicals.

Acquired Immunodeficiency Syndrome: An incurable and lethal attack of the human immune system, commonly known as AIDS. Caused by infection with human immunodeficiency virus, or HIV, which is transmitted by humans through body fluids. HIV destroys T cells that enable the body to fight off illness and leaves patients vulnerable to many life threatening conditions.

administration: The art or science of managing public affairs. Public administration is the function of the executive branch of government and is the procedure by which laws are carried out and enforced. In the United States, the president is the head of the executive branch, which includes an advisory staff and many agencies and departments.

admiral: The commander in chief of a navy or coast guard.

affirmative action: The policy of affording special opportunities or advantages to members of groups that have been the historic victims of discrimination; taking positive steps to remedy past acts of discrimination.

agency: Term used to define any governmental body.

agribusiness: An industry involved in farming operations on a large scale. May include producing, processing, storing, and distributing crops as well as manufacturing and distributing farm equipment.

AIDS: *See* Acquired Immunodeficiency Syndrome

alien: An individual who is not a citizen of the country in which he or she is living. In the United States, aliens may not hold public office or vote, but are provided with civil rights under the Constitution and do pay taxes.

Allies: Nations or states that form an association to further their common interests. The United States's partners against Germany during World War II (1939–45) are often known collectively as "The Allies" and include Great Britain and Russia. (*See also* Axis powers)

ambassador: An official of a country or organization who formally represents that country or organization. In the United States, an ambassador is the top ranking diplomat and personal representative of the president, in other countries.

amendment: Changes or additions to an official document. In the United States government, constitutional amendments refer to changes in the Constitution. Such amendments are rare and may be proposed only by a two- thirds vote of both houses of Congress or by a convention called by Congress at the request of two-thirds of the state legislators.

amnesty: An act of government by which pardons are granted to individuals or groups who have violated a law. Generally, amnesty is a power exercised by the president when a federal law is violated, but Congress may also grant amnesties.

antidumping: A system of laws to remedy dumping, which is the sale of a commodity in a foreign market at less than fair value. (*See also* dumping)

antitrust (laws): Laws designed to prevent a company from completely dominating portions of the economy by the elimination of competitors through unethical business practices. Antitrust laws are designed to maintain competition in a market economy.

appellate jurisdiction: The authority of a court to review the decisions of a lower court. In the federal court system the court of appeals and the Supreme Court have the power to review and reverse the decisions of district courts.

apportionment: The process by which a state's number of seats in the House of Representatives is determined. Each state is allotted one representative, then a formula based on population is used to determine how many additional seats a state is entitled to.

appropriations: Funds for specific government and public purposes as determined by legislation.

armistice: An agreement or truce that ends military conflict in anticipation of a peace treaty.

arms control: Reducing, eliminating, or otherwise restricting the production, use, or sale of weapons of war. During the Cold War the United States and the former Soviet Union developed numerous treaties to control such weapons as nuclear, biological, chemical, and space-based arms.

Articles of Confederation: The compact made among the thirteen original colonies to form the basis of their government. Prepared in 1776, the Articles were adopted by all states in 1781 and replaced by the United States Constitution in 1789.

atomic (weapons): Weapons of mass destruction with violent explosive power that results from the splitting of the nuclei of atoms (usually uranium or plutonium) by neutrons in a rapid chain reaction.

attaché: A representative of a government typically stationed at an embassy who serves the diplomatic staff in a support position.

attorney general: The chief legal officer of a state or nation. In the government of the United States, the attorney general is the legal adviser to the president and to all agencies of the executive branch and is the highest law enforcement officer in the country. The attorney general is also head of the Department of Justice and a member of the president's cabinet. (*See also* cabinet)

Axis powers: The countries aligned against the Allied nations in World War II (1939–45). The term originally applied to Nazi Germany and Fascist Italy (Rome-Berlin Axis), and later extended to include Japan. (*See also* Allies)

B

ballot: Instrument used for casting a secret vote. It may be a paper or electronic system.

bicameral: A legislative body consisting of two chambers; an example is the U.S. Congress, which consists of the House of Representatives and the Senate.

bilateral negotiations: Discussions between, and problem solving efforts of, two parties or nations.

bill: A proposed law. In the United States bills may be drawn up by anyone, including the president or citizen groups, but they must be introduced in Congress by a senator or representative.

Bill of Rights: The first ten amendments to the Constitution of the United States that list the rights a person is entitled to that cannot be interfered with by the government, including freedom of speech and religion, and the due process of law.

biological warfare: Warfare that uses living organisms, such as diseases, germs, and their toxic products, as weapons.

bipartisan: Cooperation between the two major political parties; for example, Republican and Democratic. (*See also* partisan)

bond: A type of loan, such as savings bonds, issued by the government to finance public needs that cost more than existing funds can pay for. The government agrees to pay lenders back the initial cost of the bond, plus interest.

budget deficit: Occurs when money spent by the government or other organization is more than money coming in.

bureau: A working unit of a department or agency with specific functions.

bureaucracy: An administrative system, especially of government agencies, that handles day-to-day business and carries out policies. Workers within a bureaucracy create and process forms, implement procedures, exist in chains of command, and establish routines that must be followed in order to get work accomplished.

C

cabinet: A group of advisers. In the federal government the cabinet is made up of advisers who offer assistance to the president. Each president determines the make up and role of their cabinets, although most include the heads of major departments such as State, Treasury, and Justice, and the vice president.

campaign: The organized activities of candidates seeking office to convince voters to vote for them, rather than their opponents. Campaigns raise money to pay for print and media messages to convince voters to support a particular candidate or cause.

capitalism: An economic system based on private ownership of industries, and supply and demand, where suppliers sell products for profit and buyers determine which products they will purchase at what cost.

cartel: An organization of independent producers formed to regulate or fix the production, pricing, or marketing practices of its members in order to limit competition and maximize their market power.

caucus: The meeting of a political or other organized group in order to decide upon issues and policies or to choose a political candidate; also refers to the group itself.

censure: A measure by which legislative bodies can discipline their own members with punishments ranging from withdrawal of privileges to expulsion.

census: An official counting of the inhabitants of a state or country; compiled data usually includes such details as gender, age, family size, and occupation.

Certiorari, writ of: The primary method by which cases reach the Supreme Court of the United States. The writ is discretionary and allows the Court to pick and choose which lower court cases it deems appropriate for a full hearing and possible decision.

checks and balances: A system, particularly in government, where equal branches must cooperate with each other, oversee each other, and enforce and support each others' decisions according to established rules. (*See also* separation of powers)

chief administrator: Person in charge of a particular agency or organization, and charged with ensuring that the agency's responsibilities are carried out. In the federal government the chief administrator is the president.

chief executive: The head of a nation or state. In the United States the president is the chief executive who heads the government and formulates policies.

chief of state: The ceremonial head of government. In the United States the president is the chief of state whose duties include greeting foreign dignitaries, hosting state dinners, and many more symbolic events.

citizen: An individual who is a native or naturalized member of a nation or state and is entitled to all the protections and privileges of its laws.

civilian: An individual who is not on active duty in the military.

civil disobedience: Refusal to obey the law on the grounds that the law is morally wrong. Civil disobedience may also encompass actions to change such laws.

civil law: The code that governs interactions between private persons as opposed to the code known as criminal law that governs individual conduct. Civil law provides a forum to settle disputes involving contracts, business dealings, and accidents. (*See also* criminal justice system)

civil liberties: Those recognized principles of American law that limit the powers of government and also guarantee the privileges of citizenship, such as voting and equality of treatment. (*See also* citizen)

civil rights: The privileges of all individuals to be treated as equals under the laws of their country; specifically, the rights given by certain amendments to the U.S. Constitution.

civil service: A term describing the system employing people in non-military government jobs. The system is based on merit classifications.

class action: A lawsuit in which one or more persons sue or are sued as representatives of a larger group such as a company or group of people with similar illnesses or grievances.

classified: Information or documents withheld from the public because their circulation could threaten national security. (*See also* declassify; secured document)

cloture: A parliamentary procedure used by a decision making body, such as Congress, to end discussion on a matter and move to a vote.

coalition: An alliance between political or special interest groups forged to pursue shared interests and agendas.

cold war: Conflict over ideological differences that is carried on by words and diplomatic actions, not by military action. The term is usually used to refer to the tension that existed between the United States and the United Soviet Socialist Republic from the 1950s until its breakup in 1991.

collective bargaining: The negotiations between workers who are members of a union and their employer for the purpose of deciding upon such issues as fair wages and work-day hours.

commander in chief: The officer who is in command of a major armed force; the role of the president as the supreme commander of the nation's military forces and the national guard when it is called into federal service.

committee: A group of individuals charged by a higher authority with a specific purpose such as investigation, review, reporting, or determining action.

commonwealth: A free association of sovereign independent states that has no charter, treaty, or constitution. The association promotes cooperation, consultation, and mutual assistance among members.

communism; communist: A political, economic, and social theory that promotes common ownership of property for the use of all citizens. All profits are to be equally distributed and prices on goods and services are usually set by the state. Communism also refers directly to the official doctrine of the former United Soviet Socialist Republic.

Communist bloc: Refers to a group of countries in Eastern Europe with Communist governments that supported and were influenced by the former Soviet Union. In the 1990s, many of these countries, such as Poland and Czechoslovakia overthrew Communist regimes and established democratic systems of government.

comptroller: An official who oversees spending to determine whether funds have or have not been spent on purchases they were intended for. The federal title is Comptroller General and the responsibility is to oversee funds to be spent according to legislative approval.

confederation: A unified group of independent states or nations where a central body makes decisions about matters of common concern but units make decisions affecting individuals.

confirmation: The process by which the Senate approves of presidential appointees to offices.

conflict of interest: When an individual's actions in a business or political situation are affected or motivated by their personal interest. Examples include politicians who vote on particular issues to gain financial support from like minded groups, or a federal official in charge of regulating an industry owning businesses in that industry.

conflict resolution: The process by which two or more opposing groups or individuals work out their differences non-violently through discussion, compromise, and mediation.

Congress: The term used to describe the combined Senate and House of Representatives.

congressional appropriation: Money that Congress approves for a specific purpose. (*See also* appropriations)

congressional district: The geographic area that a member of the House of Representatives is elected from and represents in Congress. Congressional districts are drawn up to include a nearly equal number of voters.

conscientious objector: A person who refuses to serve in the military because of personal beliefs. In the United States a person cannot refuse to serve, but Congress has allowed conscientious objectors to participate in non-combat duty or complete an exemption process on religious grounds. This exemption does not include objection for political, sociological, philosophical, or personal reasons, although the Supreme Court has upheld some requests for exemption based on these grounds if they are held with the fervor of religious beliefs.

conscription: The mandatory enlistment of citizens to serve in the military. (*See also* draft)

consensus: Agreement that is supported by all parties involved.

conservative: In the United States, a political philosophy that generally favors state over federal action, and opposes regulation of the economy, extensive civil rights legislation, and federally funded social programs.

consortium: A group of business organizations that join together to achieve things they did not have the resources to accomplish individually.

constant-dollar: The dollar value after adjusting the inflation rate to a base value.

constituent; constituency: The registered voters in a governmental district; a group of people who support a position or a candidate.

constitution: Fundamental laws that establish government organization, determine the roles and duties of segment of government, and clarify the relationship between the people and their government. The United States Constitution, was created in 1787 and ratified in 1788.

consul: Officials sent to other countries to assist and provide support to citizens of the country the official represents. (*See also* consulate)

consulate: The official residence and place of business of a consul in a foreign country. (*See also* consul)

Consumer Price Index (CPI): The change in the cost of certain current goods and services used by the average consumer compared to the cost for the same goods and services in a chosen base year. Legislators use the CPI when considering wage and subsidy increases as well as other legislation affected by economic factors.

containment: Generally, the process of limiting or restraining something. Specifically, a policy adopted during President Harry Truman's administration (1945–53) to build up areas of U.S. military strength around the world to isolate and intimidate communist nations. The belief behind the policy was that communism would eventually collapse on its own if it was not allowed to spread and expand its power.

copyright: The exclusive right to own or use written documents or visual images. Copyrights are generally granted to the author or creator of a work by the Copyright Office of the Library of Congress for 28 years, with the option of renewing the copyright for another 28 years.

corporate welfare: An ironic phrase used to describe tax breaks and favorable laws the government creates for industry. The implication is that such supports are "charity" for big business. (*See also* welfare)

counterfeit: A copy or imitation of something valuable especially money, that is made with the intention of convincing people it is real.

counterinsurgency: Military force directed at a revolutionary group that tries to overthrow an established government.

CPI: *See* Consumer Price Index

criminal justice system: The United States court system that deals with criminal violations and punishment. Criminal law differs from civil law in that it regulates individual actions and not conduct between parties. (*See also* civil law)

customs: The fees imposed by a country on items imported and exported. In the United States, Customs can also apply to the agency that collects these fees.

D

declassify; declassification: The process of making previously secret information available to the public by removing or reducing its security classification. (*See also* classified)

decommission: When something is removed from active military service. Usually refers to military vessels such as ships and submarines.

deficit: The amount by which spending exceeds income over a given period.

demobilize: To disband or discharge military troops.

democracy: A form of government in which the power lies in the hands of the people, who can govern directly, or indirectly by electing representatives.

Democratic Party: One of the two major political parties in the United States that evolved from the Democratic-Republican group that supported Thomas Jefferson. In the twentieth century, the Democratic Party has generally stood for freer trade, more international commitments, greater government regulations, and social programs. Traditionally considered more liberal than the Republican Party.

demographic(s): Statistics about human populations including such categories as age, density, income, and distribution.

department: An administrative unit with responsibility for a broad area of an organization's operations. Federal departments include Labor, Interior, Health and Human Services, and Defense.

deposit insurance: Government-regulated protection for interest-bearing deposits, such as savings accounts, to protect the depositor from failure of the banking institution.

deregulation: The process of removing government restrictions and regulations.

diplomacy: The process by which nations carry out political relations with each other. In the United States, diplomacy is the primary responsibility of the Department of State.

diplomatic envoy: A person sent to represent their nation in dealings with another nation.

directorate: May refer to the office of a director, a board of directors, or the executive staff that works with a director.

discretionary program: A program or service that is not mandated by law or regulation. Federal discretionary programs are provided by the government only if Congress approves.

domestic policy: Policies that focus on issues internal to the United States. (*See also* foreign policy).

draft: The general term for the federal selective service system that allow a government to enlist individuals for service in the armed forces. (*See also* conscription)

due process: Protects the rights of individuals to life, liberty, and property by guaranteeing a fair system of justice. While due process of law is not specifically defined in government documents, it is understood that it limits the power of government over individuals through a series of laws that affect privacy and treatment of individuals suspected of crime.

dumping: The sale of a commodity in a foreign market at less than fair value. Dumping is generally recognized as unfair because the practice can disrupt markets and injure producers of competitive products in an importing country. (*See also* antidumping)

E

economic forecast: Predictions about a country's economic future including projected revenues, employment statistics, and interest rates.

electoral college: The group of qualified voters chosen to represent their individual states, who ultimately elect the president and vice president of the United States. Their votes are based on the popular vote of their states and the number of voters is equal to the number of each state's congressional representatives.

electorate: The individuals who are qualified to vote in an election.

embargo: A legal restriction on commercial ships from entering a country's ports; any legal restriction of trade.

embassy: The office or residence of the ambassador of a foreign country; also collectively refers to an ambassador and his staff.

ethics: The principles and morals that govern an individual or group and clarify right behavior and wrong behavior.

excise tax: A tax or duty on the sale of specific commodities or groups of commodities; for instance, tobacco or liquor.

executive branch: In the United States, the branch of government charged with administering the laws and policies of the nation or state. In contrast, the legislative and judicial branches of government have the respective powers of creating and interpreting the laws.

executive order: A rule or regulation issued by the president or a governor that has the effect of law. Executive orders are limited to those that implement provisions of the Constitution, treaties, and regulations governing administrative agencies.

executive privilege: The right of executive officials to keep information from or refuse to appear in front of a court or legislative body. In the United States only the president and officials designated by the president enjoy executive privilege.

export: Goods sold to foreign buyers; the act of selling goods to foreign buyers. (*See also* import)

extramural: Activities that take place outside of organized and recognized institutions. (*See also* intramural)

F

faction: Segment or group within an organization or government that is identified by its tendency to create dissension and disagree with the majority opinions.

fair housing laws: Group of laws that make discrimination in renting, purchasing, or selling housing, illegal.

fair labor practices: Group of laws that guarantee fair treatment of employees by employers including the right to unionize and the right to pursue grievances according to established personnel policies.

feasibility study: Process used by legislators (and others) to determine if proposed policies and programs are economically sound and capable of achieving desired results.

federal aid: Funds collected by the federal government (generally through taxes) and distributed to states for a variety of reasons including education and disaster relief.

federal budget: The annual financial plan of the United States government including all sources and amounts of income and items and amounts of expenditure. The federal budget must be approved by Congress and the president.

federal deposit libraries: Selected libraries throughout the United States where government publications are available.

federal government; federalism: The national system of government in the United States including the executive, legislative, and judicial branches.

federalist: A member of the Federalist political party, the first in America. The party developed during the later part of George Washington's (1789–96) administration that created national financial and economic programs.

federal poverty guidelines: Federal guidelines that define the maximum amount of income that families can earn to be considered living in poverty.

Federal Reserve notes: Currency issued by the Federal Reserve banks that is backed by government bonds and gold certificates.

felony: A serious criminal offense, usually punishable by a year in prison or more.

filibuster: A tactic used in the Senate to defeat a bill by refusing to end discussion on an issue. The true purpose of a filibuster is to defeat proposed legislation by forcing the Senate to move on to other business, leaving the disputed measure unresolved.

fiscal: Relating to financial matters.

floor leader: Representatives and Senators who are selected by their party to carry out party decisions during legislative battles by influencing and working with undecided members.

FOI: *See* Freedom of Information Act

foreign aid: Funds provided by the United States government to assist other countries.

foreign policy: The plans and course of actions that the United States develops regarding other nations. (*See also* domestic policy)

foreign trade barrier: Government regulations and controls that limit or prevent free trade with other nations.

Freedom of Information Act (FOIA): A law established in 1966 that requires federal agencies to provide citizens with any public records they request. Some exceptions are national security materials, confidential personnel and financial data, and law enforcement files.

free enterprise system: The system of economics in which private business may be conducted with minimum interference by the government.

free market economy: An economic system that relies on the market, as opposed to government planners, to set the prices for wages and products.

free trade(rs): Trade between two entities, particularly the United States and another country, that is not limited by regulations and other restrictions.

friendly fire: When a military unit mistakenly fires or launches weapons at their own forces.

G

GDP: *See* Gross Domestic Product

gender bias: Discrimination against or favoritism toward someone because of his or her sex.

general: A high ranking official in the army, marine corps, or air force.

gerrymandering: Apportionment of voters in such a way as to give unfair advantage to a political party or racial group.

glasnost: Policy of openness and freedom of expression. Embraced by Mikhail Gorbachev in the late 1980s as part of his attempt to reform the Soviet Communist system.

globalization: Expanding a policy or activity to apply worldwide.

global market(place): The buying and selling of products throughout the world, rather than limiting sales within a country or region.

Global Positioning System (GPS): A navigation network consisting of 24 satellites developed by the U.S. military. These satellites send signals that can be used for many purposes including time and date definition, and position locating.

global warming: Also called the greenhouse effect. The supposed gradual warming of the earth's climate as a result of various environmental factors including the burning of fossil fuels, the use of man-made chemicals, and deforestation.

GNP: *See* Gross National Product

government: The political and administrative system of a nation or state including legislative, executive, and judicial functions.

government securities: Certificates issued by the government as guarantees to repay loans.

GPS: *See* Global Positioning System

grand jury: A group of 12 to 23 people who hear evidence presented by a prosecuting attorney against someone accused of a serious crime and decide whether the person should be indicted, or charged with the crime.

grant: Money provided by a government or organization to an individual or group for a specific purpose. For example, the federal government makes education grants to students for college expenses and to states to improve schools.

grassroots: Political organizing at the most fundamental level of society—among the people.

Great Depression: Period in U.S. history from 1929 until the early 1940s when the economy was so poor that many banks and businesses failed and millions of people lost their jobs and their homes. The terrible business problems were combined with a severe drought that ruined many farms and contributed to the economic disaster.

Great Society: Term used by Lyndon Johnson during his presidential administration (1963–69) to describe his vision of the United States as a land without prejudice or poverty, that would be possible by implementing his series of social programs.

Gross Domestic Product (GDP): A measure of the market value of all goods and services produced within the boundaries of a nation, regardless of asset ownership. Unlike gross national product, GDP excludes receipts from that nation's business operations in foreign countries, as well as the share of reinvested earnings in foreign affiliates of domestic corporations.

Gross National Product (GNP): A measure of the market value of goods and services produced by the labor and property of a nation. Includes receipts from that nation's business operation in foreign countries, as well as the share of reinvested earnings in foreign affiliates of domestic corporations.

Gross State Product: The total value of goods and services produced within an individual state.

H

House of Representatives: One of the two bodies with specific functions that make up the legislative branch of the United States government. Each state is allocated representatives based on population. (*See also* Congress; Senate)

humanitarian: A person who works for social reform and is concerned about the welfare of people.

I

ICBM: *See* intercontinental ballistic missile

illegal immigrant: A person who comes from another country to live in the United States without applying for entrance or completing the appropriate documents.

immigration: The process of leaving one's native country to live in another country.

impeach(ment): To charge someone with an offense that may lead to removal from the office they hold. In the United States, the House of Representatives has the power to bring charges and the Senate tries impeachment cases to determine the outcome.

implied powers: Authority granted to the federal government that is not specifically granted by the Constitution, but can be deduced from what is written in the Constitution.

import: Goods purchased from foreign suppliers; the act of purchasing goods from foreign suppliers. (*See also* export)

income tax: A tax levied on personal or corporate income, whether that income is in the form of wages or income from investments or property.

independent: A voter who does not belong to any political party and votes for individual candidates regardless of their party affiliation.

independent agency: A federal agency that is not part of a cabinet department. Such agencies include independent regulatory commissions, government corporations, or independent executive agencies.

inflation: An economic situation that occurs when prices increase to such a degree that the purchasing power of an average person decreases.

infrastructure: A basic system of public works such as roads, sewers, and power sources, and the people and resources needed to conduct activity.

intelligence: Gathering information on another country's military capabilities and political plans. In the United States, these operations are conducted by the Central Intelligence Agency, the National Security Agency, and military intelligence units.

intercontinental ballistic missile (ICBM): Missiles that are capable of traveling from one continent to another.

interest rate: A percentage of money borrowed that must be paid back in addition to the sum of the original loan for the privilege of being able to borrow.

intermodal (transportation): Using more than one kind of transportation during one journey.

interstate (commerce): Interstate commerce is business that is conducted between two or more states.

interstate highway system: The system of major highways built by the federal government that crisscross the country.

intramural: An activity conducted within the boundaries of, and limited to, the members of a particular institution. (*See also* extramural)

isolationism: A policy whereby one country refuses to become involved politically or economically with other countries.

J

joint committee: A committee composed of members from both the House of Representatives and the Senate to address an issue of mutual concern.

joint resolution: A measure that must be approved by the House of Representatives and the Senate and signed by the president to become law. However, if a joint resolution proposes an amendment to the Constitution, the president does not have to sign for the measure to become law.

judicial branch: The segment of government that protects citizens against excessive use of power by the executive or legislature and provides an impartial setting for the settlement of civil and criminal cases. In the United States, the judiciary system is divided into state and federal courts with further divisions at those levels. State and federal courts are independent except that the Supreme Court of the United States may review state court decisions when a federal issue is involved. (*See also* executive branch; legislative branch)

jurisdiction: The right and authority of a court to hear and decide a case.

L

labor market: The people available for employment.

labor union: A group of organized workers who negotiate with management to secure or improve their rights, benefits, and working conditions as employees.

lame duck: An elected official who is not re-elected, serving out the portion of their term until the newly elected person is seated.

League of Nations: The forerunner of the United Nations, envisioned by its originator, Woodrow Wilson, as a forum where countries could resolve their differences without resorting to war. Formed in 1919, the League also promoted economic and social cooperation. Congress did not support President Wilson's plan and the United States did not join the League which contributed to its collapse in the late 1930s.

legislation: Measures that are intended to become law after approval by legislative bodies.

legislative branch: The branch of government that makes or enacts laws. (*See also* executive branch; judicial branch)

liberal: A political philosophy that generally favors political, economic, or social change to benefit individuals. Liberals traditionally support federal action in the areas of civil rights, employment, and social programs.

line-item veto: The power of the president to disapprove a particular expense in the federal budget while approving the budget as a whole.

lobby, lobbies: A group of people who conduct activities designed to influence legislators to vote the way the lobby wants them to, or to convince legislators to introduce bills that are favorable to lobby interests.

lobbyist: Someone who is paid to promote the interests of a particular group or industry in an attempt to influence the actions of legislators. (*See also* lobby)

M

macroeconomics: The study of the economy as a whole terms of income, employment, output, price levels, and rates of growth. (*See also* microeconomics)

major party: A political party that has many supporters and a great deal of power and influence.

mandate: Popular support for a political program or politician. Candidates espousing particular political plans are considered to be given a mandate by the people if they are elected, meaning that people agree with the candidates plans and want them to be implemented.

Mandus, writ of: A court order demanding an action. The court has the right to order an individual to perform an act that someone else has a legal right to expect, such as the fulfillment of a business contract.

Marshall Plan: Formally known as the European Recovery Program, a joint project between the United States and most Western European nations under which $12.5 billion in U.S. loans and grants was expended to aid European recovery after World War II (1939–45). Expenditures under the program, named for U.S. Secretary of State George C. Marshall, were made from fiscal years 1949 through 1952.

McCarthy Era: Period in American history from the late 1940s to the 1950s when Senator Joseph McCarthy of Wisconsin headed a committee investigating communist influence in the United States. Begun as a legitimate investigation, the committee began questioning individuals about their activities with little or no evidence that they had been involved in communist activities. The excesses of the committee and McCarthy created widespread suspicion and hysteria concerning national security. McCarthy was censured by the Senate in 1954 and the committee's activities were severely restricted.

mediation: The intervention of an unbiased party to settle the differences between two other disputing parties; any attempt to act as a go-between in order to reconcile a problem.

merchant marine: The ships of a nation, whether privately or publicly owned, that are involved in commercial business. The term may also refer to someone who works on such ships.

metropolitan area: A large important city and the outlying suburbs that are connected to it geographically and economically.

microeconomics: The study of the economy of a particular unit such as a business, or of a specific activity such as pricing. (*See also* macroeconomics)

military intervention: When a government sends its armed forces into a situation to restore order or halt a conflict without a formal declaration of war.

military junta: The small military group in power of a country, especially after a coup.

military regime: Government conducted by a military force.

minimum wage: The wage established by law as the lowest amount to be paid to workers in particular jobs.

minor party: A small political party with little influence that is very often created around a single issue.

monopoly, monopolies The exclusive control of goods and services in a particular market, often leading to complete control over prices of those commodities.

moratorium: An emergency legislation allowing a delay in the payment of a debt; also an official delay or stoppage of some activity.

mortgage: A document held by a lender allowing them to take property if a borrower does not repay a loan.

most-favored-nation: A trading system in which all participants receive the same tax benefits. Although the term implies special treatment for one nation, it actually guarantees fair treatment of all trade participants.

multilateral negotiation: Discussions and meetings to resolve conflicts in which many countries participate.

multiparty system: Political system in which many political parties representing different viewpoints are participants. (*See also* two-party system)

N

NAFTA: *See* North American Free Trade Agreement

nation: A large group of people united by bonds of geography, language, customs, and shared collective experiences. Some nations that have developed governmental systems are also referred to as states. (*See also* state)

National Income and Product Accounts (NIPA): Tracking system for a variety of statistics that give information about income and productivity.

national security: Ensuring that a country is protected from internal and external attacks.

national security adviser: A member of the National Security Council who consults with the president on matters of national security.

NATO: *See* North Atlantic Treaty Organization

naturalization: The legal process by which an alien becomes a citizen. An individual who is at least 18 may become a U.S. citizen after meeting certain qualifications including: residing in the United States for five years; reading, writing, and speaking English; and taking an oath of allegiance to the United States. (*See also* alien; citizen)

nepotism: Showing favoritism toward someone because they are related to you. For example, granting a family member a job only because he or she is a family member.

New Deal: The name given to Franklin Roosevelt's plan to save the nation from the devastating effects of the Great Depression. His programs included direct aid to citizens and a variety of employment and public works opportunities sponsored by the federal government.

NIPA: *See* National Income and Product Accounts

nonpartisan: An action free from political party influence or undertaken by members of all political parties involved.

nonproliferation: Stopping the increase in the number and spread of nuclear weapons.

North American Free Trade Agreement (NAFTA): An agreement between the United States, Canada, and Mexico that removes all trade barriers between the three countries. For purposes of trade, all boundaries disappear and the nations conduct business as if one country, rather than as foreign nations.

North Atlantic Treaty Organization (NATO): An organization formed in 1949 by countries bordering and near the north Atlantic Ocean. The purpose of NATO is to provide security to member nations that agree to come to each others defense if any member is attacked.

nuclear: Relating to radioactive materials that may be used for weapons, energy, or medicine.

nuclear waste: The toxic by-products created by the manufacture or use of radioactive materials.

O

ombudsmen: An appointed official who investigates private complaints against an organized group, such as a government.

omnibus: A term describing something that includes or involves many items. Used in government to describe bills that contain a variety of proposals.

P

paramilitary: An organization created along military lines that is not part of any official military unit.

parliamentary: Related to a supreme legislative body made up of many representatives and similar to the British system of government.

partisan: An action or person that adheres to a political party's platform or opinion. (*See also* bipartisan)

patent: An official document granted by the federal government to an inventor of a product that gives the inventor the exclusive right to make, use, or sell the product. A patent also enables an inventor to pursue legal action against anyone who interferes with their exclusive rights.

peacekeeping: Describes military troops sent into conflict situations to keep the peace and restore order until a permanent resolution can be reached.

pension(s): Money given to an employee when they retire from a company. Pensions can be funded by the government, an employer, or through employee contributions.

per capita: Literally, per person; for each person counted.

pocket veto: A special veto wherein any bill passed by Congress but unsigned by the president when Congress adjourns, dies. Unlike an ordinary presidential veto, which can be overridden, the pocket veto is absolute.

political action committee: A group that raises money to support the election of politicians that the group feels will support their interests.

political party: A group of individuals who organize for the purpose of nominating candidates for office, winning elections, operating government, and determining public policies.

political science: The academic study of political systems and theories.

politician: A person experienced in government as an appointed official or officeholder or someone involved in party politics. (*See also* politics)

politics: Relating to government or the conduct of government especially the making of government policies and organization.

popular vote: The actual vote of the population. (*See also* electoral college)

pork barrel: Funds appropriated by Congress for local projects that are not critically needed. Members of Congress generally do not question other members' pork barrel legislation for fear their own local projects could be defeated.

press secretary: Assistant to the president who interacts regularly with the media on the president's behalf through press conferences and briefings. The press secretary provides information on the president's activities and plans.

price support: A program in which the federal government helps stabilize agricultural prices by buying up surplus products and granting loans.

primary: Election where voters choose one candidate to represent a political party in a race for an elected office.

private sector: The division of an economy in which production of goods and services is privately owned.

privatization: To change from public to private control or ownership.

pro bono: Providing professional services, particularly legal, to the people who could not afford them. Literally, "for the public good."

progressive tax: Any tax in which the tax rate increases as the amount to be taxed increases. For example, a progressive income tax might have a tax rate of 10% on the first $10,000 of income, a tax rate of 15% on the second $10,000, and a 20% tax rate on all income above $20,000.

Prohibition: The sale, manufacture, or transportation of alcoholic beverages was made illegal by constitutional provision between 1920 and 1933. The rapid repeal of this provision showed the unpopularity of this ban.

proliferation: The growth or expansion of something. Often refers to the increase in the number or spread of nuclear weapons. (*See also* nonproliferation)

proportional tax: Any tax wherein the tax rate remains the same no matter how much the amount to be taxed increases.

protectionist: Someone who supports restrictive government regulations on foreign products and companies to protect domestic producers.

pro tempore: Literally means "for the time being." The vice president is technically the head of the Senate, but a president pro tempore presides on a daily basis.

public corporation: Industries or businesses that are owned by the public through stock purchases or investments.

public debt: The entire debt of a government or nation.

public domain: Land owned by the federal government including national parks, forests, and grazing lands.

public interest: On behalf of the people, or for the good of the people.

public opinion: The combined opinions, attitudes, or beliefs of a large portion of a community that influences public policy and legislation.

public sector: The people of a country or community. Differs from the private sector which is made up of industries and organizations controlled by a few individuals, not the public as a whole.

public works: Facilities that are built or improved using government funds and benefit the general public. Parks, roads, hospitals, and harbors paid for by the government are all examples of public works.

Q

quorum: The minimum number of members that must be present for a decision making body to conduct business. The constitution states that "a majority of each (house) shall constitute a quorum to do business." This means 218 members must be present in the House of Representatives, and 51 in the Senate, to transact business.

R

ratification, ratified: The process by which constitutional amendments or treaties are formally approved. Amendments to the United States Constitution must be ratified by three-fourths of the states to become official. Treaties are approved in the Senate and by the president who officially ratifies a treaty in a signing ceremony with representatives of the treaty's other parties.

rearmament: To become armed again with new and better weapons.

recession: An economic slowdown of relatively short duration. During a recession, unemployment rises and purchasing power drops temporarily.

reconnaissance: A maneuver to gain information or explore territory. Often describes a military operation, when troops investigate enemy positions and plans.

Reconstruction: The period following the Civil War (1860–65), when the economy and infrastructure of the war-ravaged southern United States was rebuilt with the aid of the federal government.

regressive tax: Any tax in which the burden to pay falls relatively more heavily upon lower income groups than upon more wealthy taxpayers. Sales tax is an example of regressive tax because a larger portion of low income families wages are spent on necessary purchases, than that of higher earning families.

regulatory agency: A government office that makes rules for or concerning a particular product or service. For example, the Food and Drug Administration (FDA) determines which new foods and drugs will be made available to the public, and what quality standards these products must meet to be sold in the United States.

regulatory reform: Attempts to streamline the processes of regulatory agencies because they are creating too many rules, rules that are too restrictive, or taking too long to make decisions.

remediation: The process of pursuing legal action to prevent or reverse a wrong done to an individual.

representative: An elected member of the United States House of Representatives.

Republican Party: One of the two major political parties in the United States. The Republican Party emerged in the 1850s as an antislavery party. In the twentieth century, the Republican Party represents conservative fiscal and social policies and advocates a more limited role for federal government.

revenue: The total income collected by state or federal governments.

rider: A provision, unlikely to pass on its own merits, that is added to a bill so it will "ride" into passage. What may be considered an unrelated rider by one legislator, may be regarded as a legitimate amendment to a bill.

S

secretary: In the federal government, secretary is the title of the head of an executive department.

secured document: An official document that is protected from general viewing due to high level security classification. (*See also* classified)

securities: Documents that prove debt or ownership such as a stock certificate or bond.

selective service: The program that determines which men will be selected for mandatory military service, also known as the draft.

Senate: One of the two bodies with specific functions that make up the legislative branch of the United States government. Each state is allocated two Senators. (*See also* Congress; House of Representatives)

Senator: An elected member of the United States Senate.

senatorial courtesy: An informal understanding among senators that the president will confer with senators of his party from a particular state before filling federal positions within that state. If there are no senators from the president's party in a state with openings, the president may consult state party leaders.

separation of powers: The cornerstone of U.S. government wherein power is divided among three branches of government—the executive, legislative, and judicial. Officials of each branch are selected differently, have different responsibilities, and serve different terms. The separation of power is not absolute, however, due to the system of checks and balances. (*See also* checks and balances)

social insurance: Benefits or subsidies provided to citizens fully or partially to prevent economic or health problems. Unemployment insurance and worker's compensation are examples.

socialized medicine: Medical and hospital services that are provided by state or federal agencies and paid for by taxes or donations.

Social Security: A public program that provides economic aid and social welfare for individuals and their families through social insurance or assistance. In the United States, Social Security was passed into law in 1935, as a life and disability insurance and old-age pension for workers. It is paid for by employers, employees, and the government.

sovereignty: The rule of a supreme political power, such as a king or queen; the complete independent authority of a governmental unit; also, freedom from external control.

special interest group: A group that organizes to influence legislation and government policies to further their specific interests. Special interest groups include the National Rifle Association, which advocates the right to own guns responsibly, and the Sierra Club, which promotes protecting the environment.

staggered term: System wherein only a portion of the Senate or House of Representatives is up for re-election at a time. This ensures that there are always experienced members at each session to guide new members through the legislative process.

state: A body of people, occupying a specific geographic location, that organize into a political unit. State can also refer to the smaller geographic and political units that make up a larger state.

statutory: Laws enacted by Congress or a state legislature. Statutes are public and private laws that are consecutively numbered during each session of Congress.

steering committee: Committees formed to direct the flow of work and the operations of a body. In legislative bodies, the steering committee determines in what order work will be addressed.

stewardship: The act of carefully managing and safeguarding something. In the United States government, the president not only has the right to administer the country, but the duty to protect the nation and its people.

stock market: A market where shares of stock, or certificates of ownership in a company, are bought and sold.

subsidy, subsidies, subsidized: Money granted by one state to another or from a government to an individual or company for an activity that benefits the public.

suffrage: The right to vote.

Superfund: Special federal pool of money created to clean up and restore areas affected by toxic waste.

T

tariff(s): Tax imposed on foreign products brought into the United States to protect domestic businesses from excessive competition.

tax: A charge, in the form of money, imposed on people or property by an authority and used for public purposes.

terrorism: Systematic acts of violence designed to frighten or intimidate.

third-world: A term used to describe less developed countries; as of the mid-1990s, it is being replaced by the United Nations designation less developed countries, or LDCs.

trade: The business of buying and selling goods and services.

trademark: A name or mark used by a manufacturer to identify a particular product or service the public. Trademarks are officially registered at and granted by the Patent Office.

trade sanction: A trade restriction imposed on another country by the United States to convince that country to reverse or amend a course of action that is unacceptable.

trade surplus: The extent by which a country's exports exceed its imports.

treaty: An agreement entered into by two or more nations that creates or limits mutual rights and responsibilities. In the United States all treaties are negotiated by the president and approved by the Senate.

two-party system: A political system dominated by two major political parties; for instance, the Democratic and Republican parties in the United States. (*See also* multiparty system)

U

unconstitutional: Acts or laws that violate the written or implied principles of a constitution.

unemployment insurance: Money paid into a fund by employers and paid out to employees for a limited time when the worker is laid off work.

United Nations: Assembly organized in 1945 to find peaceful resolutions to international disputes and encourage cooperation in dealing with worldwide social and economic issues. Nations from all over the world are represented at the United Nations.

V

veteran: A person with long term experience in a skill or occupation. Veteran often refers to a former member of the armed services.

veto: When someone refuses to approve a measure or action. Particularly the power of the president to disapprove legislation.

voter referendum: A process by which voters in a state can disapprove a bill passed by state legislators. In states providing for referendums, a bill passed by the legislature does not take effect for a certain time period. During this period a bill may be suspended if the required number of voters sign a petition to do so. A suspended bill is then voted on by the public to determine whether or not it will go into effect.

W

watchdog (agency): A government agency that is responsible for ensuring that laws and regulations are followed. Such agencies often focus on specific activities such as trade and commerce.

welfare: Aid, in the form of money or services, to people who are economically disadvantaged.

welfare reform: The process of dismantling the longstanding system of nearly unconditional, unlimited aid to the economically disadvantaged. Welfare reform establishes a system of aid that is conditional and aims to move recipients to self sufficiency as quickly as possibly.

white-collar crime: Non-violent crime involving violations of law that often take place in a business setting.

workers' compensation: An insurance program that provides money to workers injured in the workplace from a fund created by employer payments.

writ(s): A written order of a court commanding an individual or group to perform or cease a particular activity.

Z

zoning: The process of designating sections of a geographic area for specific purposes such as business or residential.

Subject Index

A

B

Subject Index

D

G

Subject Index

H

I

J

K

L

M

O

Subject Index

P

Subject Index

S

Subject Index

T

U

Subject Index

V

X

Y

Z